Hazardous Waste Management
Compliance Handbook

Hazardous Waste Management Compliance Handbook

Brian Karnofsky, Editor

Environmental Resource Center

VNR VAN NOSTRAND REINHOLD
New York

Library of Congress Catalog Card Number 92-1331
ISBN 0-442-01106-7

Printed in the United States of America.

Van Nostrand Reinhold
115 Fifth Avenue
New York, New York 10003

Chapman and Hall
2-6 Boundary Row
London, SE1 8HN, England

Thomas Nelson Australia
102 Dodds Street
South Melbourne 3205
Victoria, Australia

Nelson Canada
1120 Birchmount Road
Scarborough, Ontario, MIK 5G4, Canada

16 15 14 13 12 11 10 9 8 7 6 5 4 3 2 1

Library of Congress Cataloging-in-Publication Data

Hazardous waste management compliance handbook/Brian Karnofsky,
    editor.
        p.   cm.
    ISBN 0-442-01106-7
    1. Hazardous wastes — United States — Management — Handbooks,
manuals, etc. 2. Hazardous wastes — Law and legislation — United
States — Handbooks, manuals, etc. 3. United States. Resource
Conservation and Recovery Act of 1976. I. Karnofsky, Brian.
TD1040.H373 1992
363.72'876'0973 — dc20   92-1331
                                                  CIP

Contents

Figures

Tables

Acronyms

ACGIH   American Conference of Governmental Industrial Hygienists
BTU   British Thermal Unit
CERCLA   Comprehensive Environmental Response, Compensation, and Liability Act
CFR   Code of Federal Regulations
CHRIS   Chemical Hazard Response Information System
coliwasa   composite liquid waste sampler
DOT   Department of Transportation
EP   extraction procedure
U.S. EPA   United States Environmental Protection Agency
FEP   fluorinated ethylene propylene
FFCA   Federal Facility Compliance Agreement
HMIS   Hazardous Materials Information System
HSWA   Hazardous and Solid Waste Amendments
MSDS   material safety data sheet
NA   North America
NFPA   National Fire Protection Association
NON   notice of noncompliance
n.o.s.   not otherwise specified
NPDES   National Pollutant Discharge Elimination System
NRC   nonreusable container
OMB   Office of Management and Budget
ORM   other regulated materials
PCB   polychlorinated biphenyl
pH   potential of hydrogen (unit of acidity or alkalinity)
POTW   publicly owned treatment works
PPE   personal protective equipment
ppm   parts per million
RCRA   Resource Conservation and Recovery Act
RQ   reportable quantity
SARA   Superfund Amendments and Reauthorization Act
SCBA   self-contained breathing apparatus
SPCC   spill prevention, control, and countermeasures
STC   single-trip container
TC   toxicity characteristic
TCLP   toxicity characteristic leaching procedure
TSCA   Toxic Substances Control Act
TSD   hazardous waste treatment, storage, and disposal facilities
UIC   underground injection control
UN   United Nations
USCG   U.S. Coast Guard

Preface

This handbook is intended to assist the reader in understanding hazardous waste management requirements. This guide is not intended to act as a replacement for current U.S. Environmental Protection Agency (EPA) or Department of Transportation (DOT) regulations. It does, however, present detailed procedures for compliance with the regulations that were in force at the time of publication.

SCOPE OF THIS HANDBOOK

To facilitate the training program, this book closely follows the topics covered in the Environmental Resource Center hazardous waste management training seminar. Extensive background and guidance materials are provided to ensure that the student is aware of the regulatory requirements for virtually all aspects of hazardous waste management under the Resource Conservation and Recovery Act (RCRA) as well as amendments to that act. The following is a brief abstract of the contents of each chapter of the guide.

Chapter 1 is an overview of the federal laws and regulations that govern the management of hazardous waste. This chapter explains the hazardous waste management statutes and shows the relationship between the law and the regulations which enforce the law. This chapter sets the stage for the remainder of the handbook, which presents the federal regulatory requirements applicable to the management of hazardous waste.

Chapter 2 presents the federal definition of hazardous waste and solid waste, and also identifies those materials which are exempted from the definitions of hazardous waste and solid waste. In this chapter, the relationship between hazardous waste and solid waste is elucidated. Terms that must be understood by anyone who manages hazardous waste, such as: characteristic waste, listed waste, specific source waste, nonspecific source waste, commercial chemical products, waste mixtures, and treatment residues are clearly explained. Chapter 11 presents sampling and analytical methods that should be followed during the hazardous waste determination process.

Chapter 3 presents the federal requirements for hazardous waste generators, including how to accumulate waste in containers or tanks at accumulation points and satellite accumulation points, container selection, inspection, and recordkeeping requirements. Also included are requirements for emergency preparedness, and small quantity generators.

Chapters 4 and 5 cover procedures for the shipment of hazardous waste off-site. Chapter 4 describes the hazardous waste manifest, including when the manifest must be used, selecting the appropriate manifest, and instructions for completing the manifest. Chapter 4 also includes guidance for compliance with the land disposal ban, instructions for completing exception reports, and what to do if a manifest discrepancy is discovered. Chapter 5 presents instructions for the selection of a transporter for hazardous waste

shipments and includes guidance for properly preparing a shipment of hazardous waste for transportation off-site.

Chapter 6 presents an overview of the requirements for operation of hazardous treatment, storage, and disposal facilities, including the general requirements applicable to all permitted or interim status facilities and the specific requirements for hazardous waste storage facilities. Chapter 8 covers the regulations for the closure of these facilities.

Chapter 7 presents information on RCRA training requirements, including who must be trained, the scope and frequency of the training required, and the topics which must be covered during training.

Chapter 9 presents emergency response procedures required by the regulations for responding to spills, fires, explosions or other releases involving hazardous waste. This chapter also identifies which facilities must have a contingency plan, what should be included in the plan, and when to implement the plan.

Chapter 10 identifies the enforcement actions federal or state government agencies may take in the event that a facility fails to comply with hazardous waste management regulatory requirements. It also details what will happen if an enforcement action is commenced. Chapter 11 focuses on Sampling and Analytical Methods.

Many states have applied for and received authorization from U.S. EPA to operate and enforce their own hazardous waste management regulations. State programs must be consistent with the federal program but may also be more stringent. Consequently, your facility may be subject to hazardous waste regulations promulgated by both U.S. EPA and your state environmental agency. *State Hazardous Waste Regulations Differing from Federal Requirements,* available from Environmental Resource Center, identifies state environmental agencies and more stringent state requirements concerning identification, accumulation, transportation, and on-site treatment of hazardous waste.

As will be described later in this document, not all wastes that are *hazardous* are *hazardous wastes*. EPA has issued regulations that define hazardous wastes as those wastes that meet certain characteristics or wastes which are included on one of several lists of wastes. Because this definition is quite narrow, there are wastes that have hazardous properties which may not currently be considered hazardous wastes as defined by the federal regulations.

However, just because a waste is not considered a hazardous waste by EPA, does not mean that it can be wantonly managed. For example, pesticide and polychlorinated biphenyl (PCB) wastes are regulated by EPA under the Federal Insecticide, Fungicide and Rodenticide Act and the Toxic Substances Control Act. Contamination due to non-hazardous solid wastes managed in any location within a facility that operates a hazardous waste management facility may be regulated under certain portions of the RCRA cleanup and closure regulations.

I
Overview of Hazardous Waste Management Laws and Regulations

THE RESOURCE CONSERVATION AND RECOVERY ACT

The goal of the Resource Conservation and Recovery Act, (RCRA), is to promote the protection of health and the environment and to conserve valuable material and energy resources. RCRA has kept in stride with current waste management issues and problems by way of congressional amendments, the most notable of which occurred in 1984 with the passage of the Hazardous and Solid Waste Act Amendments. RCRA is currently up before Congress for reauthorization, and at that time Congress may enact additional requirements which impact the management of hazardous waste. We should therefore anticipate additional and/or modified requirements that may be added when RCRA is reauthorized.

In its current form, RCRA has ten subtitles, each of which addresses some aspect of resource conservation and waste management. Figure 1.1 lists the Subtitles of RCRA as well as what each Subtitle covers. Subtitle C is the primary portion of RCRA that deals with the management of hazardous waste. The sections of Subtitle C and their scope of coverage are identified in Figure 1.2.

The goal of Subtitle C of RCRA is to identify what a hazardous waste is and to establish standards for the accumulation, transportation, storage, treatment, and disposal of hazardous waste. Consequently, the provisions of Subtitle C apply to a waste the moment it becomes "hazardous" until it is no longer a hazardous waste. This is commonly referred to as the "cradle to grave" regulation of hazardous waste.

REGULATIONS THAT IMPLEMENT THE ACT

Federal Regulations

RCRA requires the Environmental Protection Agency (EPA) to promulgate and enforce regulations regarding the management of hazardous waste. These regulations set out the mandatory procedures and requirements for compliance with RCRA and must be followed by facilities that accumulate, transport, treat, store, or dispose of hazardous waste.

Hazardous waste management regulations are issued by EPA and are published in the *Federal Register*, which is published daily, except for official holidays, by the Office of the Federal Register of the National Archives and Records Administration. The *Federal Register* provides a uniform system for making available to the public regulations and legal notices issued by Federal agencies. It is available by mail through the U.S. Government Printing Office in Washington, DC. Because of the broad scope of RCRA and regulatory timetables imposed on EPA by Congress, it is likely that you will see new or revised hazardous waste regulations published in the *Federal Register* several days per week.

EPA regulations are compiled annually into Title 40 of the Code of Federal Regulations (40 CFR). The CFR is divided into Parts, with Parts 124, 260 through 268, 270 and 271 devoted to hazardous waste management. The parts of the CFR and their corresponding applicability are listed in Figure 1.3. Figure 1.4 indicates where the regulations implementing RCRA appear in the CFR.

Subtitle of RCRA	Coverage
Subtitle A	General provisions
Subtitle B	Office of Solid Waste, Authorities of the EPA Administrator
Subtitle C	Hazardous waste management
Subtitle D	State or regional solid waste plans
Subtitle E	Duties of the Secretary of Commerce in resource recovery
Subtitle F	Federal responsibilities
Subtitle G	Miscellaneous provisions
Subtitle H	Research, development demonstration, and information
Subtitle I	Underground storage tanks
Subtitle J	Demonstration Medical Waste Tracking Program

FIGURE 1.1
RCRA Subtitles

Summary of the Regulations

Part 124 contains EPA procedures for issuing, modifying, revoking, and reissuing or terminating all RCRA (as well as other other environmental-related) permits. Part 124 is organized into six subparts: Subpart A contains general procedural requirements applicable to all permit programs covered by the regulations, while Subparts B through F supplement the general provisions with requirements that apply to certain permit programs.

Part 260 of the regulations provides definitions of terms, general standards, and overview information applicable to Parts 260 through 265 and Part 268. It includes the rules that EPA uses in making information it receives available to the public; sets forth the requirements that must be followed to assert claims of business confidentiality with respect to information that is submitted to EPA; and establishes procedures for petitioning EPA to:

- amend, modify, or revoke parts of the regulations,
- approve testing methods that are equivalent to EPA-approved methods, and
- exclude a particular hazardous waste from regulation.

Part 261 identifies the wastes that are subject to regulation as hazardous waste. It defines the terms "solid waste" and "hazardous waste," identifies those wastes that are excluded from regulation, and establishes special management requirements for hazardous waste produced by conditionally exempt small-quantity generators and for hazardous waste that is recycled. Part 261 identifies characteristics and contains the list of hazardous wastes.

Part 262 contains the rules with which generators of hazardous waste must comply. This part of the regulations requires you to evaluate all wastes generated on-site to determine if they meet the definition of hazardous waste. It also explains the conditions under which a hazardous waste manifest must be used, describes a generator's pretransportation requirements (including the amount of time a hazardous waste can remain on-site), details the recordkeeping and reporting requirements, and presents the rules for exporting hazardous waste.

Section of RCRA	Coverage
3001	Identification and listing of hazardous waste
3002	Generators of hazardous waste
3003	Transporters of hazardous waste
3004	Treatment, storage, and disposal facilities
3005	Permits for treatment, storage, and disposal
3006	Guidelines for state programs
3007	Inspections
3008	Enforcement and penalties
3009	Retention of state authority
3010	Notification of hazardous waste activity
3011	Financial assistance to states
3012	Hazardous waste site inventory
3013	Monitoring, analysis, and testing
3014	Restrictions on recycled oil
3015	Expansion during interim status
3016	Inventory of federal agency facilities
3017	Export of hazardous waste
3018	Domestic sewage
3019	Exposure information and health assessments
3020	Interim control of hazardous waste injection

FIGURE 1.2
Sections of RCRA Subtitle C: Hazardous Waste Management

40 CFR Part	Coverage of the Regulations
124	Public participation
260	General requirements, definitions, petitions
261	Identification and listing of hazardous waste
262	Generators of hazardous waste
263	Transporters of hazardous waste
264	Permitted hazardous waste facilities
265	Interim status hazardous waste facilities
266	Certain specific hazardous wastes and facilities
267	New interim status land disposal facilities
268	Land disposal restrictions
270	EPA administered permits
271	State hazardous waste program requirements

FIGURE 1.3
Federal Regulations Implementing the Hazardous Waste Management Requirements of RCRA

Part 263 establishes standards that apply to persons transporting hazardous wastes within the United States. In promulgating the regulations, EPA has expressly adopted certain regulations of the Department of Transportation (DOT) governing the transportation of hazardous materials.

These regulations pertain to such activities as container labeling, marking, placarding, using proper containers, and reporting discharges of hazardous waste. The regulations apply to both interstate and intrastate transportation of hazardous waste, but do not apply to on-site transportation of hazardous waste.

Part 264 presents requirements that apply to owners and operators of all facilities that treat, store, or dispose of hazardous waste. Part 264 contains general standards by which all hazardous waste treatment, storage, and disposal facilities must be operated, as well as specific requirements for surface impoundments, waste piles, landfills, incinerators, land treatment facilities, and facilities with containers and tank systems used for storing or processing hazardous waste.

Part 265 establishes minimum standards that apply to owners and operators of facilities that treat, store, or dispose of hazardous waste and that have interim status. The regulations in this part are very similar to the regulations in Part 264, except that the Part 265 regulations apply to owners and operators of facilities that were operating before the RCRA regulations were finalized and have not yet received a final permit to operate their facility or have closed but are under EPA orders to correct some problem on-site. This part also contains the requirements for training, preparedness, and prevention, and contingency planning that are referenced in the generator standards.

Part 266 contains standards for the management of specific hazardous wastes and specific types of hazardous waste management facilities. This part includes regulations that apply to recyclable materials, hazardous waste and used oil burned for energy recovery, recyclable materials utilized for precious metal recovery, and spent lead-acid batteries being reclaimed.

Section of RCRA	Coverage	Final Regulation (40 CFR Part)
1004	Definitions	260
3001	Identification and listing of hazardous waste	261
3002	Generators of hazardous waste	262
3003	Transporters of hazardous waste	263
3004	Treatment, storage, and disposal facilities	264, 265, 266, 267
3005	Permits for treatment, storage, and disposal	270 and 124
3006	Guidelines for state programs	271
3007	Inspections: Public availability of information	260
3014	Regulation of used oil	266
3017	Export of hazardous waste	262
3020	Hazardous waste injection	267

FIGURE 1.4
Correlation between RCRA Section and CFR Parts

Part 267 establishes standards for owners and operators of new hazardous waste land disposal facilities. The regulations in this part apply specifically to owners and operators of new hazardous waste landfills, surface impoundments, land treatment facilities, and Class I underground injection wells. The regulations include design and operating requirements, closure and postclosure requirements, and groundwater monitoring procedures.

Part 268 identifies hazardous wastes that are restricted from land disposal and defines those limited circumstances under which a restricted waste may continue to be land disposed. The requirements of this part apply to persons who generate or transport hazardous waste and owners and operators of hazardous waste treatment, storage, and disposal facilities.

Part 270 contains regulations that cover basic EPA permitting requirements for hazardous waste management facilities, such as the general information required to be included in a Part A and Part B Permit application, monitoring and reporting requirements, and the conditions under which permits can be transferred or modified.

Part 271 specifies the minimum requirements with which a state must comply to receive authorization to administer and enforce its own hazardous waste management program in lieu of the federal program. This part also describes the procedures that EPA will follow in approving, revising, and withdrawing approval of a state's hazardous waste management program.

With each amendment of RCRA, a state must apply for authorization with respect to the amendments. In other words, a particular state may have been granted the authority to implement a RCRA program, but may not yet have the authority to administer and enforce the requirements that resulted from the Hazardous and Solid Waste Amendments (HSWA) of 1984. Consequently, your facility may be subject to inspection from both EPA and your state environmental agency.

State Regulations

Section 3006 of RCRA provides a means for each state, at their option, to operate and enforce their own hazardous waste management regulations after they have received authorization from EPA. In order to receive authorization, a state must submit a description of the program it proposes to administer for EPA to review. To obtain approval, a state program must be consistent with the federal program and must not be:

- unreasonably restrictive, or impede, or ban the free movement of hazardous waste across the state border;
- unreasonably protective of human health and the environment (such that the prohibitions of the program have no basis); and
- less stringent than the federal requirements.

Because of the ongoing evolution of federal hazardous waste management regulations for specific waste types and facilities, there is usually a lag between the promulgation of new federal regulations and their adoption by the states

with authorization to enforce RCRA. Therefore, each state may have its own particular level of authorization. One state, for example, may be authorized to administer the program covering hazardous waste generators and storage facilities, while another state may have authorization to administer the program for hazardous waste generators, storage facilities, and certain treatment facilities. As a consequence, your facility may be subject to inspection from both EPA and your state environmental agency.

APPLICABILITY OF RCRA REGULATIONS

Many facilities are either directly or indirectly involved in several aspects of hazardous waste management. For example, when materials such as solvents, cleaning agents, and ordnances no longer meet their specifications and are declared waste, many become hazardous waste (refer to the definition of "hazardous waste" in Chapter 2). This is a hazardous waste generation activity. For a brief period of time, the waste may be kept in some type of tank or container until it is carried away for subsequent treatment, disposal, or long-term storage. This *temporary storage* constitutes hazardous waste accumulation.

Hazardous waste carried off-site is regulated by both EPA and DOT as a transportation activity (on-site transportation has no specific requirements associated with it). So, for example, when off-specification chemicals falling into the definition of hazardous waste must be carried off-site for disposal, the generator is involved in hazardous waste transportation.

Some generators have received authorization from EPA to store hazardous waste on-site indefinitely in a permitted hazardous waste storage facility. These facilities may maintain a building or area dedicated to long-term hazardous waste storage.

The treatment of hazardous waste takes many forms and encompasses many levels of sophistication. The reclamation of dirty solvents using a solvent distillation unit constitutes hazardous waste treatment (albeit a form of treatment currently unregulated).

Subtitle F of the law addresses the federal responsibilities towards RCRA and details the application of federal, state, and local law to federal facilities. According to Section 6001, each department of the federal government engaged in a hazardous waste management activity is subject to all federal RCRA requirements as well as applicable state and local hazardous waste management laws. Therefore, no federal installation is immune or exempt from the requirements of RCRA. The President may exempt an installation if it is "in paramount interest" of the United States, but exemptions are only granted on a year-to-year basis.

Therefore, both public and private facilities are involved in many facets of hazardous waste management. And regardless of the type of activity, all applicable RCRA regulations must be complied with. The remainder of this book is devoted to helping you determine if a waste item is a hazardous waste and providing you insight into the requirements of RCRA that impact your facility.

OTHER HAZARDOUS WASTE MANAGEMENT LAWS

In 1980, Congress enacted the Comprehensive Environmental Response, Compensation and Liability Act (CERCLA), better known as the Superfund Act, to clean up hazardous waste sites that posed a potential danger to the public. The Act gives U.S. EPA broad authority to take action to clean up hazardous waste sites. According to the law, EPA can require those deemed responsible to clean up a site, or it can clean up the site itself using Superfund money or funds from suits against the responsible parties. Cleanup costs may be sought from:

- the current owner or operator of a facility or site from which a release or threatened release of a hazardous substance emanates,
- past owners or operators of a facility or site,
- any person or corporation who contracted or arranged for the disposal or treatment of a hazardous substance, and
- any person or corporation who accepted hazardous substances for transport to disposal or treatment facilities.

Currently there are approximately 1200 Superfund sites nationwide, and EPA has published numerous regulations dictating how these sites are investigated, ranked on the National Priorities List of sites, and ultimately remediated. EPA has also published in 40 CFR Part 302.4 a list of CERCLA Hazardous Substances that can trigger the Superfund process as well as reporting requirements for when the substances are released to the environment. This list has also been adopted by DOT as the List of Hazardous Substances and Reportable Quantities and is reproduced in Appendix D of this handbook. Both characteristic and listed hazardous wastes identified pursuant to RCRA are included on the list of CERCLA Hazardous Substances.

In 1986, CERCLA was amended with the passage of the the Superfund Amendments and Reauthorization Act (SARA). SARA Titles I and II strengthened CERCLA giving EPA even broader authority to mandate the clean up of hazardous waste sites. SARA Title I also mandated the establishment of health and safety standards and training requirements during cleanup of uncontrolled hazardous waste sites and RCRA corrective action sites, during operations conducted at hazardous waste treatment, storage or disposal facilities, and during emergency response operations for releases or threatened releases of hazardous substances. The Occupational Safety and Health Administration (OSHA) has been given authority under SARA for setting and enforcing job safety and health standards which apply to these operations and has promulgated the Hazardous Waste Operations and Emergency Response rule in 29 CFR 1910.120. EPA has also adopted this rule as one of its own regulations in order to protect public sector employees working in about 25 states where OSHA has no jurisdiction.

2

What Is Hazardous Waste?

This chapter will provide you with guidance regarding how to determine which of the wastes generated at your facility are regulated by RCRA as hazardous wastes. The first step is to determine if the waste in question is considered a *solid waste*. You must make this determination first, because if the waste is not a solid waste, it is not subject to regulation under RCRA Subtitle C. It may, however be subject to regulation under Subtitle D or other regulatory requirements which are beyond the scope of this handbook.

Keep in mind that all solid wastes are not hazardous wastes. After you have determined that the waste is a solid waste, you must determine if it is a hazardous waste as defined in 40 CFR 261.3. Also keep in mind that there are exemptions to both the definition of solid waste and hazardous waste, which are described below and detailed in the regulations.

SOLID WASTE

A solid waste is any *discarded material* that is not excluded by 40 CFR 261.4(a) or that is not excluded by variance granted under 40 CFR 260.30 or 260.32. A discarded material is any material that is *abandoned, recycled, or considered inherently waste-like* as defined below:

Abandoned — Wastes are classified as abandoned if they are disposed of, burned or incinerated, or accumulated, stored or treated (but not recycled) before or in lieu of being abandoned by being disposed of burned, or incinerated.

Recycled — Wastes that are recycled or accumulated, stored, treated before recycling if they are:

* *Used in a manner constituting disposal.* Materials with a ■ in column 1 of Table 2.1 are solid wastes when they

are either applied to or placed on the land in a manner that constitutes disposal or used to produce products that are applied to the land or are otherwise contained in products that are applied to or placed on the land (however, commercial chemical products listed in 40 CFR 261.33 are not solid wastes if they are applied to the land and that is their ordinary manner of use); or

* *Burned for energy recovery.* Materials with a ■ in column 2 of Table 2.1 are solid wastes when they are burned for energy recovery, used to produce a fuel or are otherwise contained in fuels (however, commercial chemical products listed in 40 CFR 261.33 are not solid wastes if they are themselves fuels); or

* *Reclaimed.* Materials with a ■ in column 3 of Table 2.1 are solid wastes when reclaimed; or

* *Accumulated speculatively.* Materials noted with a ■ in column 4 of Table 2.1 are solid wastes when accumulated speculatively.

Inherently waste-like — Materials with hazardous waste numbers F020, F021 (unless used to make a product at the site of generation), F023, F026, and F028 are classified as inherently waste-like by EPA. In addition, secondary materials fed to a halogen acid furnace that have a hazardous waste characteristic or are listed as a hazardous waste are inherently waste-like. Other materials may be added to the list of inherently waste-like materials by EPA depending on their usual disposition, constituents and hazard to human health and the environment when recycled.

TABLE 2.1
Materials That Are Solid Wastes If They are Recycled

	Use Constituting Disposal	Energy Recovery Fuel	Reclamation	Speculative Accumulation
Spent materials	■	■	■	■
Sludges (listed in 40 CFR 261.31 or 261.32)	■	■	■	■
Sludges exhibiting hazardous waste characteristic	■	■		■
By-products (listed in 40 CFR 261.31 or 262.32)	■	■	■	■
By-products exhibiting hazardous waste characteristic	■	■		■
Commercial chemical products listed in 40 CFR 261.33	■	■		
Scrap metal	■	■	■	■

Solid Waste Exemptions

The following materials are not solid wastes if they are recycled:

Materials used or reused as ingredients in an industrial process to make a product, provided the materials are not being reclaimed; or

Materials used or reused as effective substitutes for commercial chemical products; or

Materials returned to the original process from which the materials are generated, without first being reclaimed. The material must be returned as a substitute for raw material feedstock, and the process must use raw materials as principal feedstocks.

The following materials *are* solid wastes, even if the recycling involves use, reuse, or return to the original process as described above:

Materials used in a manner constituting disposal or used to produce products that are applied to the land; or

Materials burned for energy recovery, used to produce a fuel, or contained in fuels; or

Materials accumulated speculatively; or

Materials with hazardous waste numbers F020, F021 (unless used to make a product at the site of generation), F023, F026, and F028.

Other materials exempted from classification as solid wastes are:

Domestic sewage and any mixture of domestic sewage and other wastes that passes through a sewer system to a publicly-operated treatment works for treatment. *Domestic sewage* means untreated sanitary wastes that pass through a sewer system.

Industrial wastewater discharges that are point source discharges subject to regulation under Section 402 of the Clean Water Act. This exclusion applies only to the actual point source of discharge. It does not exclude industrial wastewaters while they are being collected, stored, or treated before discharge, nor does it exclude sludges that are generated by industrial wastewater treatment.

Note: On July 24, 1990, EPA published a rule in the *Federal Register* to enhance control of toxic pollutant and hazardous waste discharges to Publicly Owned Treatment Works (POTWs). According to the rule, industrial users of POTWs must notify the POTW, EPA Regional Waste Management Division Director, and state hazardous waste authorities in writing of any discharge into a POTW of a substance, which otherwise disposed of, would be hazardous waste under 40 CFR Part 261. Industrial users who discharge less than 15 kilograms of nonacute hazardous waste per month are exempt from the notification requirements. The notification, which need be submitted only once for each hazardous waste being discharged, must include the name of the waste, the EPA hazardous waste number, and the type of discharge. If the industrial user discharges more than 100 kg/month of hazardous waste, the identity of the hazardous constituents contained in the waste, an estimate of the mass and concentration of such constituents discharged during the month, and an estimate of the mass and concentration of such constituents expected to be discharged during the following 12 months must also be submitted. All notifiers must certify that they have a program in place to reduce the volume or toxicity of hazardous wastes generated to the degree it has been determined to be economically practical.

For industrial users discharging hazardous waste on August 23, 1990, the notifications should have been submitted by February 19, 1991. Facilities that commence hazardous waste discharges after August 23, 1990 must submit notifications within 180 days of starting the discharge.

- Source, special nuclear, or byproduct material as defined by the Atomic Energy Act of 1954, as amended
- Materials subject to in situ mining techniques that are not removed from the ground as part of the extraction process
- Pulping liquors that are reclaimed in a pulping liquor recovery furnace and then reused in the pulping process, unless it is accumulated speculatively
- Spent sulfuric acid used to produce virgin sulfuric acid, unless it is accumulated speculatively
- Secondary materials that are reclaimed and returned to the original process or processes in which they were generated where they are reused in the production process, provided:

  Only tank storage is involved and the entire process through completion of reclamation is closed by being entirely connected with pipes or other comparable enclosed means of conveyance.

  Reclamation does not involve controlled flame combustion.

  The reclaimed material is not used to produce a fuel, or used to produce products that are used in a manner that constitutes disposal.

- Spent wood preserving solutions that have been used and are reclaimed and reused for their original intended purpose, and wastewaters from the wood preserving process that have been reclaimed and are reused to treat wood
- Coke and coal tar from the iron and steel industry used as a fuel that contains or is produced from decanter tank tar sludge (EPA hazardous waste number K087)

HAZARDOUS WASTE

A solid waste, as defined above, is classified as a hazardous waste if it is not excluded from regulation (either excluded because it is not a solid waste, as defined above, or excluded as described in Hazardous Waste Exemptions, beginning on page 11), and it meets any of the descriptions of items a, b, c, or d below:

a. Solid waste that exhibits one or more of the hazardous waste characteristics (ignitability, corrosivity, reactivity, or toxicity), and other characteristics as added by EPA or state regulation. Wastes in this group are classified as *characteristic* hazardous waste. Characteristic hazardous wastes are identified in 40 CFR 261 Subpart C.

b. Solid waste that is identified on any of the hazardous waste lists:
   - non-specific source wastes (F list)
   - specific source wastes (K list)
   - commercial chemical products (P and U lists)
   Wastes in this group are classified as *listed* hazardous waste. The lists of hazardous waste are located in 40 CFR 261 Subpart D.

c. Solid waste that is a mixture of a solid waste and one or more listed hazardous wastes (unless it is an exempt mixture, as described in Hazardous Waste Exemptions, beginning on page 11). Wastes in this group are classified as hazardous waste mixtures.

d. It is a mixture of solid waste and one or more characteristic hazardous wastes (unless it is an exempt mixture, as described in Hazardous Waste Exemptions, beginning on page 11). Wastes in this group are classified as characteristic haz- ardous wastes.

Characteristic Hazardous Waste

Ignitability

A solid waste that is not excluded from regulation (see Solid Waste Exemptions beginning on page 8, and Hazardous Waste Exemptions beginning on page 11) that has any of the following properties, displays the characteristic of ignitability and has the EPA Hazardous Waste Number D001.

1. It is a liquid, other than an aqueous solution containing less than 24% alcohol by volume, and has a flashpoint less than 60°C (140°F), as determined by EPA specified test methods; or
2. It is not a liquid and is capable under standard temperature and pressure, of causing fire through friction, absorption of moisture or spontaneous chemical changes, and when ignited burns so vigorously and persistently that it creates a hazard; or
3. It is an ignitable compressed gas as defined in 49 CFR 173.300; or
4. It is an oxidizer as defined in 49 CFR 173.151.

Corrosivity

A solid waste that is not excluded from regulation (see Solid Waste Exemptions beginning on page 8, and Hazardous Waste Exemptions beginning on page 11) that has any of the following properties, displays the characteristic of corrosivity and has the EPA hazardous waste number D002.

1. It is aqueous and has a pH less than or equal to 2 or greater than or equal to 12.5, as determined by an EPA specified or approved test method; or
2. It is a liquid and corrodes steel (SAE 1020) at a rate greater than 6.35 mm (0.25 inch) per year at a test temperature of 55°C (130°F) as determined by an EPA specified or approved test method.

Reactivity

A solid waste that is not excluded from regulation (see Solid Waste Exemptions beginning on page 8, and Hazardous Waste Exemptions beginning on page 11) that has any of the following properties, displays the characteristic of reactivity and has the EPA Hazardous Waste Number D003.

1. It is normally unstable and readily undergoes violent change without detonating.
2. It reacts violently with water.
3. It forms potentially explosive mixtures with water.
4. When mixed with water, it generates toxic gases, vapors, or fumes in a quantity sufficient to present a danger to human health or the environment.
5. It is a cyanide or sulfide bearing waste that when exposed to pH conditions between 2 and 12.5, can generate toxic gases, vapors, or fumes in a quantity sufficient to present a danger to human health or the environment.
6. It is capable of detonation or explosive reaction if it is subjected to a strong initiating source or if heated under confinement.
7. It is readily capable of detonation or explosive decomposition or reaction at standard temperature and pressure.
8. It is a forbidden explosive as defined in 49 CFR 173.51, a Class A explosive (49 CFR 173.53), or a Class B explosive (49 CFR 173.88).

Toxicity Characteristic (TC)

A solid waste that is not excluded from regulation (see Solid Waste Exemptions beginning on page 8 and Hazardous Waste Exemptions, beginning on page 11) that fails the Toxicity Characteristic Leaching Procedure (TCLP) for one or more of the contaminants listed in Table 2.2, displays the characteristic of toxicity and has the EPA Hazardous Waste Number(s) listed in Table 2.2.

If the extract from a representative sample of the waste contains any of the contaminants listed in Table 2.2 at a concentration equal to or greater than the respective value listed in the table, then the waste is hazardous. If the waste itself contains less than 0.5% filterable solids, the waste itself, after filtering, is considered to be the extract for determining toxicity. The TCLP is designed to determine the mobility of both organic and inorganic contaminants present in solid, liquid, and multiphasic wastes.

The toxicity characteristic became effective for generators on September 25, 1990, and for small-quantity generators on March 29, 1991. As of these dates, generators of solid waste were required to determine if their wastes exhibits the toxicity characteristic by either using their knowledge of the waste generating process, or by testing the wastes in accordance with the TCLP. Waste determinations based only on extraction procedure (EP) toxicity test results are not valid as of these dates.

Listed Waste

A solid waste is classified as a listed hazardous waste if it is not excluded from regulation (see Solid Waste Exemptions, beginning on page 8 and Hazardous Waste Exemptions beginning on page 11) and it is identified on any of the lists in 40 CFR 261, Subpart D. Currently these lists include:

- hazardous waste from nonspecific sources (F list),
- hazardous waste from specific sources (K list),
- discarded commercial chemical products, off-specification species, container residues, and spill residues thereof (P list and U list).

TABLE 2.2
Maximum Concentration of Contaminants for the Toxicity Characteristic

EPA HW Number	Contaminant	Regulatory Level (mg/l)
D004	Arsenic	5.0
D005	Barium	100.0
D018	Benzene	0.5
D006	Cadmium	1.0
D019	Carbon tetrachloride	0.5
D020	Chlordane	0.03
D021	Chlorobenzene	100.0
D022	Chloroform	6.0
D007	Chromium	5.0
D023	o-Cresol	200.0[2]
D024	m-Cresol	200.0[2]
D025	p-Cresol	200.0[2]
D026	Cresol	200.0
D016	2,4-D	10.0
D027	1,4-Dichlorobenzene	7.5
D028	1,2-Dichloroethane	0.5
D029	1,1-Dichloroethylene	0.7
D030	2,4-Dinitrotoluene	0.13[1]
D012	Endrin	0.02
D031	Heptachlor (and its epoxide)	0.008
D032	Hexachlorobenzene	0.13[1]
D033	Hexachlorobutadiene	0.5
D034	Hexachloroethane	3.0
D008	Lead	5.0
D013	Lindane	0.4
D009	Mercury	0.2
D014	Methoxychlor	10.0
D035	Methyl ethyl ketone	200.0
D036	Nitrobenzene	2.0
D037	Pentachlorophenol	100.0
D038	Pyridine	5.0[1]
D010	Selenium	1.0
D011	Silver	5.0
D039	Tetrachloroethylene	0.7
D015	Toxaphene	0.5
D040	Trichloroethylene	0.5
D041	2,4,5-Trichlorophenol	400.0
D042	2,4,6-Trichlorophenol	2.0
D017	2,4,5-TP (silvex)	1.0
D043	Vinyl chloride	0.2

[1] Quantitation limit is greater than regulatory level. The quantitation limit therefore becomes the regulatory level.

[2] If the o-, m-, and p-Cresol concentrations cannot be differentiated, the total cresol (D026) concentration is used. The regulatory level of total cresol is 200 mg/l.

Hazardous Waste from Nonspecific Sources

Wastes in this category include those which are listed on the F list (see Appendix E). In general, these wastes are those that EPA has determined to be hazardous but are not generated by a particular industry or manufacturing process. Wastes on the F list currently include certain solvent wastes, plating wastes, metal treating wastes, wood preserving wastes, petroleum refinery oil/water/solids separation sludge, leachate from treatment, storage or disposal facilities, wastes from the manufacture of certain chlorinated compounds, and treatment residue from the incineration or thermal treatment of soil contaminated with certain chlorinated compounds.

Hazardous Wastes from Specific Sources

Wastes in this category include those which are listed on the K list (see Appendix E). These wastes include certain wastes from particular industries which EPA has determined to be hazardous. Wastes on the K list currently include certain wastes generated by the wood preservation industry, inorganic pigments, organic chemicals, inorganic chemicals, pesticides, explosives, petroleum refining, iron and steel, primary copper, primary lead, primary zinc, primary aluminum, ferroalloys, secondary lead, veterinary pharmaceutical, ink formulation, and coking industries.

Mixtures

If a hazardous waste (as defined above) is mixed with a solid waste (as defined above) the resulting mixture is generally classified as a hazardous waste. In other words, one cannot dilute a hazardous waste in an effort to make the waste no longer subject to regulation as a hazardous waste. This requirement, known as the mixture rule, is published in 40 CFR 261.3(b) and (d). According to the mixture rule:

- A mixture of a solid waste and one or more listed hazardous wastes (except for exempt mixtures, as described in Hazardous Waste Exemptions below) are classified as hazardous waste, and bear the same EPA hazardous waste number as the hazardous waste number for the listed waste in the mixture.
- A mixture of solid waste and one or more characteristic hazardous wastes is classified as hazardous waste unless the mixture does not exhibit any of the hazardous waste characteristics.

Treatment, Storage, Disposal, and Spill Residues

Solid wastes generated from the treatment, storage, or disposal of hazardous waste, including sludge, spill residue, ash, emission control dust, or leachate (but not including precipitation runoff) is classified as hazardous waste. EPA has established a hazardous waste code of F039 for leachate resulting from the treatment, storage, or disposal of listed hazardous wastes, or from a mixture of listed and characteristic hazardous wastes. Leachate resulting from the management of one or more of the following wastes and no other hazardous wastes retains its hazardous waste code(s): F020, F021, F022, F023, F026, F027, and/or F028.

Hazardous Waste Exemptions

The following materials are not classified as hazardous waste:

- Materials that are exempt from classification as solid waste (see Solid Waste Exemptions on page 8)
- Materials that are not classified as solid waste
- Mixtures of wastewater subject to either Section 307(b) or Section 402 of the Clean Water Act and any of the following hazardous wastes:

One or more of the following spent solvents listed in 261.31 (F list): carbon tetrachloride, tetrachloroethylene, trichloroethylene, provided that the maximum total weekly usage of these solvents (other than those not to be discharged to wastewater) divided by the average weekly flow of wastewater into the facility's wastewater treatment or pretreatment system does not exceed 1 ppm, or

One or more of the following spent solvents listed in 261.31 (F-list): methylene chloride, 1,1,1-trichloroethane, chlorobenzene, o-dichlorobenzene, cresols, cresylic acid, nitrobenzene, toluene, methyl ethyl ketone, carbon disulfide, isobutanol, pyridine, and spent chlorofluorocarbon solvents provided that the maximum total weekly usage of these solvents (other than those not to be discharged to wastewater) divided by the average weekly flow of wastewater into the facility's wastewater treatment or pretreatment system does not exceed 25 ppm, or

K050 waste, or

Discarded commercial chemical products or chemical intermediates listed in 261.33 (P and U lists) arising from de minimus losses of these materials from manufacturing operations in which these materials are used as raw materials or are produced in the manufacturing process. De minimus losses include losses from normal material handling operations such as spills from unloading or transfer of materials from containers, leaks from pipes, valves, or other devices used to transfer materials, minor leaks of process equipment, storage tanks or containers, discharges from safety showers and cleaning of personal protective equipment (PPE), and rinsate from empty containers or from containers that are rendered empty by rinsing, or

Wastewater resulting from laboratory operations containing toxic wastes listed in Subpart D, provided that the annualized average flow of laboratory wastewater does not exceed one percent of total wastewater into the headworks of the the facility's wastewater treatment or pretreatment system, or provided the waste's combined annualized average concentration does not exceed 1 ppm in the headworks of the facility's wastewater treatment or pretreatment facility.

This exemption includes wastewater at facilities which have eliminated the discharge of wastewater.

- The following wastes generated from the treatment, storage, or disposal of hazardous waste, unless they exhibit one or more of the characteristics of hazardous waste:

  Waste pickle liquor sludge generated by lime stabilization of spent pickle liquor from the iron and steel industry

  Wastes from burning any of the following recyclable materials: fuels produced from the refining of oil-bearing hazardous wastes; oil reclaimed from hazardous waste resulting from certain normal petroleum refining operations, hazardous waste fuel and oil produced or reclaimed from oilbearing hazardous wastes from certain petroleum refining, production or transportation operations where the hazardous wastes are reintroduced into a process that produces a fuel meeting the used oil specifications in 266.40(e); and certain petroleum coke produced from petroleum refinery hazardous wastes containing oil at the same facility at which such wastes were generated.

- Household waste, including household waste that has been collected, transported, stored, treated, disposed, recovered, or reused. *Household waste* is defined as any material derived from households. Households are defined to include single and multiple residences, hotels, motels, bunkhouses, ranger stations, crew quarters, campgrounds, picnic grounds, and day-use recreation areas.
- Waste generated by resource recovery facilities managing municipal solid waste, provided that the facility burns only household waste, nonhazardous solid waste, and does not accept hazardous waste.
- Solid wastes from any of the following sources which are returned to the soil as fertilizers:

  Wastes from the growing and harvesting of agricultural crops
  Wastes from the raising of animals, including animal manures

- Mining overburden returned to the mine site
- Fly ash waste, bottom ash waste, slag waste, and flue gas emission control waste, generated primarily from the combustion of coal or other fossil fuels. (Note regulations on facilities that burn or process hazardous waste in 40 CFR 266.112)
- Drilling fluids, produced waters, and other wastes associated with the exploration, development, or production of crude oil, natural gas, or geothermal energy.
- Wastes that fail the test for the TC because chromium is present or are listed in Subpart D due to the presence of chromium, which do not fail the test for the TC for any other constituent or are not listed due to the presence of any other constituent, and do not fail the test for any other characteristic, if all of the following can be demonstrated:

  The chromium in the waste is exclusively or nearly exclusively trivalent chromium.
  The waste is generated from an industrial process which uses exclusively or nearly exclusively trivalent chromium.
  The waste is typically and frequently managed in non-oxidizing environments.

- Solid waste from the extraction, beneficiation, and processing of ores and minerals including coal, phosphate rock, and overburden from the mining of uranium ore. This exception does not include facilities that burn or process hazardous waste. Beneficiation of ores and minerals is restricted to the following activities: crushing, grinding, washing dissolution, crystallization, filtration, sorting, sizing, drying, sintering, pelletizing, briquetting, or calcining to remove water and/or carbon dioxide, roasting, autoclaving, and/or chlorination in preparation for leaching (except where the roasting [and/or autoclaving and/or chlorination]/leaching sequence produces a final or intermediate product that does not undergo further beneficiation or processing), gravity concentration, magnetic separation, electrostatic separation, flotation, ion exchange, solvent extraction, electrowinning, precipitation, amalgamation, and heap dump, vat, tank, and in situ leaching. See 40 CFR 261.4(b)(7) for materials in this category that are conditionally retained by this exclusion.
- Cement kiln dust waste except as regulated for facilities that burn or process hazardous waste
- Solid waste that consists of discarded wood or wood that fails the TC for arsenic and that is not a hazardous waste for any other reason if the waste is generated by persons who utilize the arsenical-treated wood and wood products for these materials' intended end use.
- Petroleum-contaminated media and debris that fail the test for the TC (Hazardous Waste Codes D018 through D0443 only) and are subject to corrective action regulations under 40 CFR part 280 for owners and operators of underground storage tanks.
- Injected groundwater that exhibits the TC (Codes D018 through D043 only) that is reinjected through an underground injection well pursuant to free phase hydrocarbon recovery operations undertaken at petroleum refineries, marketing terminals, bulk plants, pipelines, and transportation spill sites until January 25, 1993. Consult 40 CFR 261. 4(b)(11) for the conditions of this exclusion.
- Used chlorofluorocarbon refrigerants from totally enclosed heat transfer equipment, including mobile air conditioning systems, mobile refrigeration, and commercial and industrial air conditioning and refrigeration systems that use chlorofluorocarbons as the heat transfer fluid in the refrigeration cycle, provided the refrigerant is reclaimed for further use.

Figure 2.1 presents four flow charts that can assist you in the hazardous waste determination process.

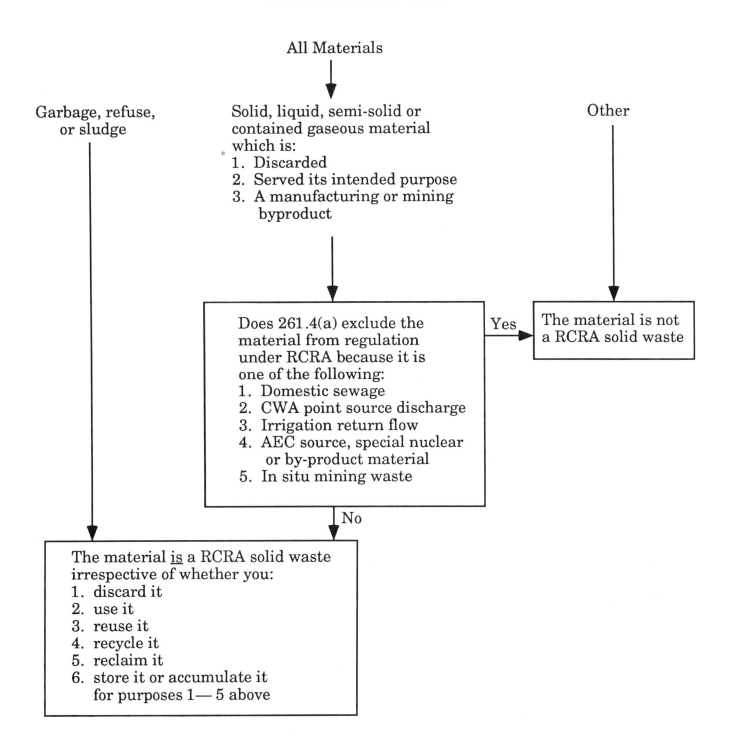

Chart 1
Definition of Solid Waste

All Materials

Garbage, refuse, or sludge

Solid, liquid, semi-solid or contained gaseous material which is:
1. Discarded
2. Served its intended purpose
3. A manufacturing or mining byproduct

Other

Does 261.4(a) exclude the material from regulation under RCRA because it is one of the following:
1. Domestic sewage
2. CWA point source discharge
3. Irrigation return flow
4. AEC source, special nuclear or by-product material
5. In situ mining waste

Yes

The material is not a RCRA solid waste

No

The material is a RCRA solid waste irrespective of whether you:
1. discard it
2. use it
3. reuse it
4. recycle it
5. reclaim it
6. store it or accumulate it for purposes 1— 5 above

FIGURE 2.1
Solid and Hazardous Waste Determination Flow Charts

Chart 2
Definition of a Hazardous Waste

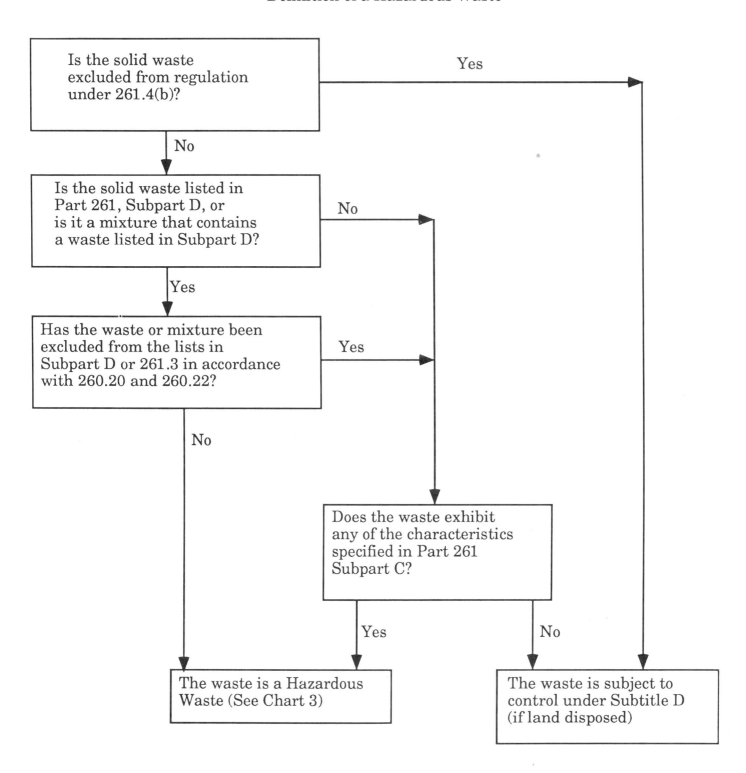

FIGURE 2.1
Solid and Hazardous Waste Determination Flow Charts (continued)

14

Chart 3

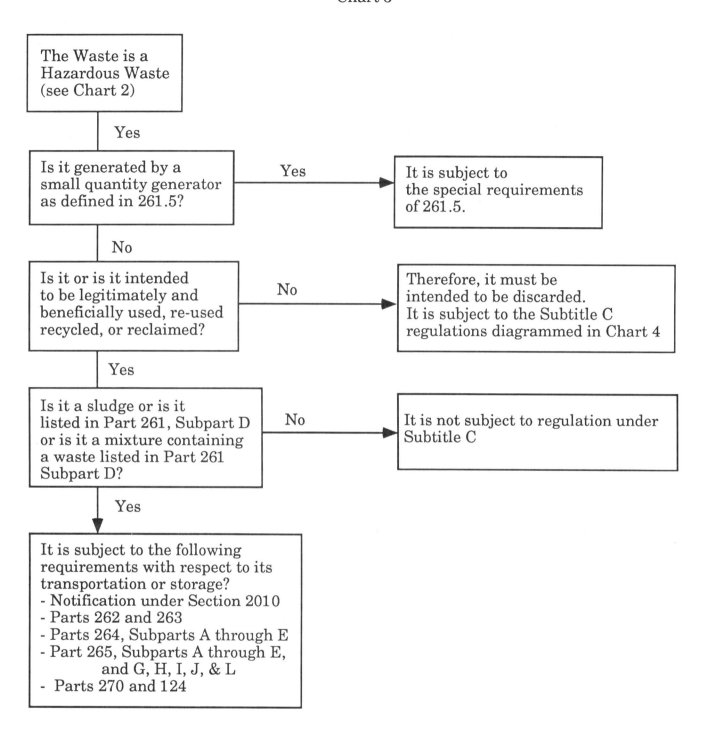

FIGURE 2.1
Solid and Hazardous Waste Determination Flow Charts (continued)

Chart 4
Regulations for Hazardous Waste
Not Covered in Chart 3

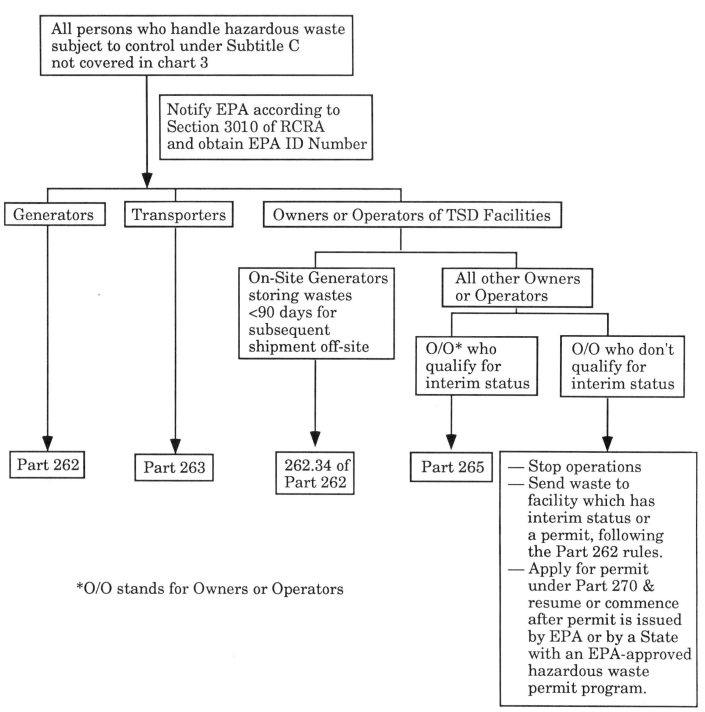

*O/O stands for Owners or Operators

FIGURE 2.1
Solid and Hazardous Waste Determination Flow Charts (continued)

- Hazardous wastes that are generated in any of the units listed in Table 2.3 are not subject to the regulations for hazardous waste generators (40 CFR 262), transporters (40 CFR 263), TSD facilities (40 CFR 265 & 265), land disposal restrictions (40 CFR 268), facility permits (40 CFR 270), or state-operated programs (40 CFR 271) or the RCRA notification of hazardous waste activity requirements (RCRA section 3010) until the waste exits the unit in which it was generated, unless the unit is a surface impoundment, or unless the hazardous waste remains in the unit more than 90 days after the unit ceases to be operated for manufacturing, or for storage or transportation of product or raw materials.

All persons who generate solid waste must determine if that waste is hazardous waste by testing the waste or by applying knowledge of the hazard characteristics of the waste in light of the materials or processes used. The results of the waste determination process must be documented, and the generator must keep records of any test results, waste analyses, or other determinations for at least 3 years from the date that the waste was last sent for treatment, storage or disposal. Figure 2.2 presents a waste stream data sheet that can be used to document the waste determination process.

TYPICAL HAZARDOUS WASTES PRODUCED BY GENERATORS

The following are examples of some wastes that are typically generated in each of the hazardous waste classifications. This list is not exhaustive and should not be used alone for the determination or classification of hazardous waste.

Nonspecific Source Wastes

Solvent Wastes

The spent solvents listed below are classified as hazardous waste if they are solid wastes (as defined above), and any of the following:

- one of the spent solvents listed below in F001 through F005
- a waste generated from a solvent mixture or blend that contained before use a total of 10% or more (by volume) of any of the solvents listed below in F001, F003, F004, or F005
- a waste generated from a solvent mixture or blend which contained before use a total of 10% or more (by volume) of any of the solvents listed below in F003
- still bottoms from the recovery of the spent solvents listed below and mixtures as described above

F001 Spent solvents used for degreasing: tetrachloroethylene, trichloroethylene, methylene chloride, 1,1,1-trichloroethane, carbon tetrachloride, chlorinated fluorocarbons

F002 Solvents: tetrachloroethylene, methylene chloride, trichloroethylene, 1,1,1-trichloroethane, chlorobenzene, 1,1,2-trichloro-1,2,2-trifluoroethane, orthodichlorobenzene, trichlorofluoromethane, and 1,1,2-trichloroethane

F003 Ignitable solvents: xylene, acetone, ethyl acetate, ethyl benzene, ethyl ether, methyl isobutyl ketone, n-butyl alcohol, cyclo-hexanone, and methanol

F004 Solvents: cresols, cresylic acid, and nitrobenzene

F005 Solvents: toluene, methyl ethyl ketone, carbon disulfide, isobutanol, pyridine, benzene, 2-ethoxy-ethanol and 2-nitro-propane

Examples of F list wastes include spent solvents generated from cleaning, degreasing, surface preparation, fingerprint removal, and painting operations.

Electroplating Wastes

Wastes from the following electroplating operations are classified as hazardous waste:

F006 Wastewater treatment sludges from electroplating operations except from the following processes: sulfuric acid anodizing of aluminum, plating on carbon steel using any of the following metals: tin, zinc, aluminum, or zinc-aluminum; cleaning/stripping associated with tin, zinc, and aluminum plating on carbon steel; and chemical etching and milling of aluminum

F007 Spent cyanide plating bath solutions from electroplating operations

F008 Plating sludges from the bottom of plating baths from electroplating operations where cyanides are used in the process

F009 Spent stripping and cleaning bath solutions from electroplating operations where cyanides are used in the process

TABLE 2.3
Waste Units Exempted from Certain RCRA Regulations

Product tanks
Raw material storage tanks
Product or raw material transport storage vehicles or vessels
Product or raw material pipelines
Manufacturing process units or associated nonwastewater treatment manufacturing units

WASTE STREAM DATA SHEET

Department _____ Waste Coordinator _____

Waste Name _____

Process Generating the Waste _____

_____

Waste Generation Rate (Gallons or Pounds per Month) _____

Current Disposal Procedure _____

_____ One-time Disposal? ❑

How Have You Classified The Waste?

Hazardous ❑_____ (If So List the EPA Waste Codes)   Non Hazardous ❑

How Have You Made This Determination?

Testing ❑ (If so attach results)   Process Knowledge: ❑

Waste Composition	Percent
1. _____	_____
2. _____	_____
3. _____	_____
4. _____	_____
5. _____	_____
6. _____	_____
7. _____	_____
8. _____	_____
9. _____	_____

General Parameters: Flashpoint _____ °F pH _____ Specific Gravity _____

Physical State at 70°F: Solid ❑ Liquid ❑ Semisolid ❑ Gas ❑

Identify Waste Packaging Type and Size_____

Waste Coordinator Signature _____ Date _____

FIGURE 2.2
Waste Stream Data Sheet

Metal Treating Wastes

Wastes from the following metal treating operations are classified as hazardous waste:

F010 Quenching bath residues from oil baths from metal heat treating operations where cyanides are used in the process

F011 Spent cyanide solutions from salt bath pot cleaning from metal heat treating operations

F012 Quenching wastewater treatment sludges from metal heat treating operations where cyanides are used in the process

F019 Wastewater treatment sludges from the chemical conversion coating of aluminum except from zirconium phosphating in aluminum can washing when such phosphating is an exclusive conversion coating process

Wood Preserving Wastes

Wastes from the following wood preserving operations are classified as hazardous wastes:

F032 Wastewaters, process residues, preservative drippage, and spent formulations from wood preserving processes generated at plants that currently use or have previously used chlorophenolic formulations (see 40 CFR 261.35 for exemptions)

F034 Wastewaters, process residues, preservative drippage, and spent formulations from wood preserving processes generated at plants that use creosote formulations

F035 Wastewaters, process residues, preservative drippage, and spent formulations from wood preserving processes generated at plants that use inorganic preservatives containing arsenic or chromium

Wastes from the following petroleum refining operations are classified as hazardous waste:

F037 Petroleum refinery primary oil/water/solids separation sludge

F038 Petroleum refinery secondary (emulsified) oil/water/solids separation sludge

In addition, process wastes, discarded unused formulations, and incineration residues from the production of certain chlorinated aliphatic hydrocarbons, trichlorophenol, tetrachlorophenol, pentachlorophenol, and tetra-, penta-, or hexachlorobenzenes are included on the list of nonspecific source wastes as well as leachate resulting from treatment, storage, or disposal of wastes classified by more than one waste code (see Appendix E).

Specific Source Wastes

Specific source wastes include wastes generated by specific industries or manufacturing processes listed in 40 CFR 261.32 (see Appendix E). Specific source wastes currently in this category include wastes generated by the following industries:

Wood preservation
Organic chemical production
Inorganic chemical production
Pesticide production
Explosives manufacturing and production
Petroleum refining
Iron and steel production
Primary copper production
Primary lead production
Primary zinc production
Ink formulation
Coking operations

Region	Waste Exchange	Contact
California	California Waste Exchange	(916) 324-1807
Indiana	Indiana Waste Exchange	(317) 634-2142
Illinois	Illinois Industrial Material Exchange Service	(217) 782-0450
Midwest	Industrial Waste Exchange	(314) 231-5555
Midwest	Great Lakes Regional Waste Exchange	(616) 363-7367
MidAtlantic	Industrial Waste Information Exchange	(201) 623-7070
Montana	Montana Industrial Waste Exchange	(406) 442-2405
Northeast	Northeast Industrial Waste Exchange	(315) 422-6572
West	Pacific Materials Exchange	(509) 623-4244
Southern	Southern Waste Information	(800) 441-SWIX
Southeast	Southeast Waste Exchange	(704) 547-2307
Southwest	Renew	(512) 463-7773

FIGURE 2.3
Regional Waste Exchanges

Discarded Commercial Products, Off-specification Species, Container Residues, and Spill Residues

This classification of hazardous waste includes certain commercial chemical products having the generic names listed on the P and U lists located at 40 CFR 261.33 (see Appendix E), if and when they are discarded or intended to be discarded. This classification does *not* include materials that are manufacturing process wastes. EPA has indicated that if a manufacturing process waste containing materials on the P or U lists is hazardous, the agency will list the material on either the F list (40 CFR 262.31), the K list (40 CFR 262.32), or it will be identified as a characteristic hazardous waste (40 CFR 261 Subpart C). The following materials on the P list or the U list are classified as hazardous wastes if they are intended for disposal:

- The material itself, including commercially pure grades and technical grades of the material that are produced or marked for commercial or manufacturing use, if the material is intended for disposal
- A formulated product in which the chemical is the sole active ingredient
- Off-specification commercial chemical products or manufacturing intermediates that, if specifications were met, would have the generic name listed
- Residues remaining in a container or in a container liner that has held any of the materials on the P or U list, unless the container is empty (see the definition of empty containers in Chapter 4)
- P or U listed materials that are mixed with oil or other materials and applied to the land for dust suppression or road treatment in lieu of their original intended purpose
- P or U listed materials contained in products that are applied to the land in lieu of their original intended purpose
- P or U listed materials that are produced for use as (or as a component of) a fuel, distributed for use as a fuel, or burned as a fuel
- Spill residues of P and U listed materials, including contaminated soil, contaminated water, and other debris resulting from the cleanup of a spill of any of the items listed above

Examples of commercial chemical product hazardous wastes include products with the generic names listed on the P and U lists from hospitals (e.g., expiration dated drugs, unused reagents), research laboratories (expiration dated or unused reagents intended for disposal), photography laboratories, and analytical laboratories. These items become hazardous waste when a decision has been made that they must be discarded or disposed of. For example, when the expiration date of the commercial products have been reached or when they are no longer needed, it becomes hazardous waste.

However, the expiration date on a product is not necessarily indicative of the end of its useful life. The expiration date for some products may be extended by testing or other means. Some products can be tested in order to determine if their expiration date can be extended. If there is another beneficial use for the material either on-site or off-site (excluding the fuel or land application uses described above), the material can be stored or used for this purpose without being classified as a hazardous waste.

Materials on the P list are classified as acute hazardous waste and materials on the U list are classified as hazardous waste. The designation of acute hazardous waste indicates that the material is acutely toxic. As described in Chapter 3, acutely toxic hazardous waste management regulations regarding satellite accumulation points and small quantity generator status are more stringent than those for hazardous waste.

Characteristic Hazardous Wastes

Examples of characteristic (D list) hazardous wastes include:

Ignitable Hazardous Wastes (D001)
Wastes generated from the following processes are examples of ignitable hazardous wastes (if they meet the definition of D001 waste, as described in Hazardous Waste, beginning on page 9):

Solvents used for parts cleaning or degreasing
Paint thinners and paint removing compounds
Carbon remover and fingerprint remover solutions
Organic solvent based wheel strippers

Corrosive Hazardous Waste (D002)
Wastes generated from the following processes are examples of corrosive hazardous wastes (if they meet the definition of D002 waste, as described in Hazardous Waste, beginning on page 9):

Parts-cleaning operations using highly alkaline cleaning
    solutions
Alkaline strippers used to strip the paint
Acidic wastes generated from electroless metal plating lines
Battery acid and other waste acids
Phenol wastes

Reactive Hazardous Waste (D003)
Wastes generated from the following processes are examples of reactive hazardous wastes (if they meet the definition of D003 waste, as described in Hazardous Waste, beginning on page 9):

- Cyanide-bearing electroplating solutions (unless they are listed in 40 CFR 261.31, F list)
- Ordnances and explosives listed by DOT as Class A or Class B explosive, or forbidden explosive.

Toxicity Characteristic Hazardous Waste:

The following wastes are examples of common TC wastes:

- paint waste containing metals such as lead, chromium, silver, or cadmium
- metal strip baths used to remove paint and chrome plating
- mercury waste from analytical instruments, dental amalgam, and batteries
- wastewater and sludge from fabric finishing containing tetrachloroethylene
- oily wastes and sludge from the petroleum marketing industry containing benzene
- oil filters, oily rags, and oily absorbents containing lead, benzene, or other toxicity characteristic constituents

WASTE EXCHANGE

Certain materials are not solid wastes, and therefore not hazardous wastes, when they are used or reused (see Solid Waste Exemptions on page 8). Regional waste exchanges have been organized to identify waste materials that could potentially be reused by other facilities, and to facilitate the exchange of waste between generators and users. The waste exchanges publish catalogs that organize waste generators and users in such categories as acids, alkalis, inorganic chemicals, solvents, other organic chemicals, oils and waxes, plastics and rubber, textiles and leather, wood and paper, metals and metal sludges, and miscellaneous. Figure 2.3 identifies contacts at twelve major regional waste exchanges.

3

Hazardous Waste Accumulation Requirements

Hazardous waste may be temporarily accumulated on-site at accumulation points and satellite accumulation points. It may be accumulated in tanks or containers prior to transport to a permitted treatment, storage, or disposal facility. This chapter examines EPA requirements for the temporary on-site accumulation of hazardous waste at accumulation points and satellite accumulation points and provides information on how to manage hazardous waste during accumulation.

GENERAL REQUIREMENTS FOR ALL GENERATORS

The hazardous waste generator is the first link in the cradle-to-grave management of hazardous waste. A hazardous waste generator is the facility (or person) that first creates a hazardous waste, or a facility (or person) that first makes a waste subject to RCRA regulation, such as by initiating a shipment or mixing wastes. The EPA regulations applicable to generators are located in 40 CFR 262 (see Appendix E).

Any person who imports hazardous waste into the United States and any TSD facilities that generate hazardous wastes are also subject to generator requirements. When shipping hazardous waste off-site, TSD facilities must also comply with applicable generator pretransportation requirements concerning manifesting, labeling, marking, and placarding.

Treatment, Storage, and Disposal of Hazardous Waste

With few exceptions, a hazardous waste generator who treats, stores, or disposes of hazardous waste on-site must obtain a permit and must comply with the applicable standards and permit requirements set forth in 40 CFR 264, 265, 266, and 270. Treatment and disposal facilities are the final links in the cradle-to-grave management of hazardous waste.

Treatment is defined as any method, technique, or process, including neutralization, designed to change the physical, chemical, or biological character or composition of any hazardous waste. Treatment includes neutralizing wastes, recovering energy or material resources from the wastes, and rendering wastes nonhazardous or less hazardous and safer to transport, store, or dispose of. Treatment also includes making wastes fit for recovery or storage, and reducing the volume of wastes. *Disposal* means the discharge, injection, dumping, spilling, leaking, or placing of any solid waste or hazardous waste into or on any land or water so that such solid waste or hazardous waste or any constituent thereof may enter the environment or be emitted into the air or discharged into any waters including ground water.

Certain types of treatment and disposal are exempt from permitting requirements and may be conducted on-site without a RCRA permit including:

- Treatment in a container or tank at an accumulation point, as long as you only treat wastes generated onsite, comply with 40 CFR 265 Subparts I and J, have a waste analysis plan in which you determine how your treatment residues meet the land disposal restrictions, and hazardous incompatible chemical reactions are prevented during treatment.
- Certain on-site recycling activities such as the recovery of solvents in a still. The next section of this chapter defines recyclable materials and provides guidance for specific management requirements applicable to these materials.
- Operation of a totally enclosed treatment facility. A totally enclosed treatment facility is a facility for the treatment of hazardous waste which is directly connected to an industrial production process and which is constructed and operated in a manner that prevents the release of any hazardous waste or any hazardous waste constituent into the environment during treatment. An example is a pipe in which waste acid is neutralized.
- A farmer disposing of waste pesticide from his own use provided he triple-rinses each emptied pesticide container and disposes of the pesticide residues on his own farm in a manner consistent with the disposal instructions on the pesticide label.
- Operation of an elementary neutralization unit, a device used for neutralizing wastes that are hazardous only because they exhibit the corrosivity characteristic or they are listed only because of corrosivity. The unit must also meet the definition of a tank, tank system, container, transport vehicle, or vessel.
- Operation of a wastewater treatment unit, a device that is permitted and regulated under the Clean Water Act.
- Treatment or containment activities during immediate response to a discharge of hazardous waste, an imminent and substantial threat of discharge of hazardous waste, or a discharge of material that, when discharged, becomes a hazardous waste.
- The addition of absorbent material to waste in a container or the addition of waste to absorbent material in a container, provided that these actions occur at the time waste is first placed in the container and precautions are taken to prevent hazardous chemical reactions.

Note: Generators and small-quantity generators who treat a land-disposal-prohibited waste in tanks or containers in order to meet applicable treatment standards must develop and follow a written waste analysis plan which describes the procedures the generators will carry out to comply with the treatment standards. The plan must be based on a detailed chemical and physical analysis of a representative sample of the waste, must contain all information necessary to treat the waste in accordance with the treatment standard, and must be submitted to EPA or the authorized state 30 days prior to the treatment activity with delivery verified.

Chapter 6 describes treatment activities, requirements, and exemptions in greater detail.

Many states have their own permitting requirements and may not exempt the activities listed above from the RCRA permit requirements. *State Hazardous Waste Regulations Differing from Federal Requirements,* available from Environmental Resource Center, identifies more stringent state requirements concerning on-site treatment of hazardous waste.

Management of Recyclable Materials

Hazardous wastes that are recycled are known as *recyclable materials*. A material is recycled if it is used, reused, or reclaimed. Spent solvents and used oil are often reclaimed and reused or they are burned for energy recovery. If this occurs, the solvents and oil are recyclable materials.

Facilities that generate certain recyclable materials are not subject to most hazardous waste management regulations when generating, transporting and disposing of those materials. Generators are not required to notify EPA or the state about their activities concerning those materials. These "unregulated" recyclable materials are:

- Industrial ethyl alcohol that is reclaimed in the United States. A material is reclaimed if it is processed to recover a useable product, or if it is regenerated.
- Used batteries or used battery cells returned to a battery manufacturer for regeneration.
- Used oil that exhibits one or more of the characteristics of hazardous waste but is recycled in some other manner than being burned for energy recovery. The used oil may be rerefined or processed to produce a usable product.
- Scrap metal, meaning bits and pieces of metal parts, bars, turnings, rods, sheets, wire, or metal pieces that may be combined together with bolts or soldering which when worn or superfluous can be recycled.
- Hazardous waste fuel and oil reclaimed or produced from oil-bearing hazardous waste produced during petroleum refining, production, and transportation so long as the material meets the used-oil fuel specification.
- Petroleum coke produced from petroleum refinery hazardous wastes containing oil at the same facility which such wastes were generated, unless the coke exhibits a hazardous waste characteristic.

Other recyclable materials are subject to more strict management practices found in 40 CFR 266, Subparts C, E, F, G, and H. These more strictly regulated recyclable materials include:

- Recyclable material used in a manner constituting disposal. A manner constituting disposal meaning they are applied to the land or used to produce products that are applied to the land.
- Hazardous wastes burned for energy recovery in boilers and industrial furnaces which are not subject to EPA's incinerator regulations.

- Used oil that exhibits one or more of the characteristics of hazardous waste and is burned for energy recovery in boilers and industrial furnaces which are not subject to EPA's incinerator regulations.
- Recyclable materials from which precious metals are reclaimed.
- Spent lead-acid batteries that are being reclaimed.

The special requirements for these hazardous recyclable materials are presented below. All other recyclable materials must be managed in accordance with all applicable hazardous waste regulations from the point of generation though transportation to storage prior to recycling.

Hazardous Waste Used in a Manner that Constitutes Disposal

Any hazardous waste that a facility generates which is recycled by being placed on or applied to the land with or without mixing with any other substance(s) is used in a manner constituting disposal. This waste must be managed on-site in accordance with all generator requirements and transported off-site via a regulated transporter with a hazardous waste manifest. Storage of these materials prior to recycling is also fully regulated.

The products produced from these recyclable materials are not regulated if the recyclable materials have undergone a chemical reaction in the course of producing the products so as to become inseparable by physical means and such products meet the applicable land ban treatment standards or prohibition levels.

Using waste or used oil contaminated with dioxin or any other hazardous waste for dust suppression or road treatment is considered hazardous waste disposal and, unless a permit was obtained for this activity, is illegal.

Used Oil Burned for Energy Recovery

The 1984 amendments to RCRA instructed EPA to determine whether used oil should be regulated as a hazardous waste. In partial response, EPA issued final used oil burning and blending rules in November 1985 which prohibit the burning of used oil that contains contaminants in greater amounts than specified in certain nonindustrial burners (refer to Table 3.1).

The rule also requires industrial burner owners to notify EPA whenever they burn used oil that does not meet specifications. In essence, two classifications of used oil were created: on-specification used oil which could be burned almost anywhere and off-specification oil which was restricted to industrial furnaces and boilers.

Used oil that is mixed with hazardous waste or contains more than 1000 ppm total halogens is presumed to be hazardous waste and is subject to the hazardous waste fuel requirements presented earlier when it is burned for energy recovery. All used oil burned for energy recovery is also presumed to be off-specification and subject to regulation unless its is analyzed and shown to meet the specifications presented in Table 3.1.

A facility that generates off-specification used oil which will be burned for energy recovery may only offer that oil to marketers who have notified EPA of their used oil management activities and have an EPA identification number. They may also offer the used oil directly to burners who have an EPA identification number, have notified EPA of their burning activities, and who burn the oil in an industrial furnace or an industrial or utility boiler.

Facilities may burn off-specification used oil in a used oil-fired space heater as long as the heater only burns the facility's waste oil (i.e., used oil cannot be accepted from off-site), the heater is designed to have a maximum capacity of not more than 0.5 million British thermal units (BTUs) per hour, and combustion gases are vented to the ambient air. The generator must keep records of any analytical results from testing the used oil fuel for at least 3 years. Generators should review state regulations to determine if an air permit is required to burn used oil fuel in a space heater.

If a facility markets its off-specification used oil fuel directly to a burner or industrial furnace, it must notify EPA that it is a used oil fuel marketer using the EPA notification form described in Appendix A. The facility must also obtain a one-time written notice from the burner certifying that the burner has notified EPA of its used oil burning activities and will burn your oil only in an industrial furnace or boiler meeting EPA definitions. All analytical records, certifications, and notices must be kept for at least 3 years.

Recyclable Materials Utilized for Precious Metal Recovery

Facilities that generate wastes containing gold, silver, platinum, paladium, irridium, osmium, rhodium, ruthenium, or any combination of these metals should consider reclamation as an alternative to disposal. Reclamation offers an economic incentive depending on the selling price of the different precious metals and an environmental incentive to reduce the volume of hazardous waste that is disposed of.

Facilities that generate recyclable material used for precious metals recovery are required to use a hazardous waste manifest for transporting the waste. However they are exempt from other accumulation point requirements regarding the management of the waste on-site. If a facility stores recyclable material used for precious metal recovery, the facility must keep the following records to show that it is not accumulating the material speculatively:

- records showing the volume of these materials stored at the beginning of the calendar year
- the amount of these materials generated or received during the calendar year
- the amount of these materials remaining at the end of the calendar year

If these recyclable materials are accumulated speculatively, they are subject to all applicable hazardous waste management regulations.

TABLE 3.1
RCRA Specifications for Used Oil Burned for Energy Recovery

Constituent/Property	Allowable Level
Arsenic	5 ppm maximum
Cadmium	2 ppm maximum
Chromium	10 ppm maximum
Lead	100 ppm maximum
Total Halogens	4000 ppm maximum
Flash Point	100°F minimum

Spent Lead Acid Batteries Being Reclaimed

Facilities that generate, collect, transport, or store spent lead-acid batteries prior to shipping them off-site for reclamation are not required to manage the batteries in accordance with any hazardous waste management regulations. If batteries are stored prior to reclamation on-site, the storage facility must comply with all applicable provisions of 40 CFR 264 except for the waste analysis and manifesting requirements.

Hazardous Waste Fuel Burned In Boilers and Industrial Furnaces

Hazardous waste burned or processed in a boiler or industrial furnace must be managed in accordance with all generator requirements. When transported off-site, the generator must use a regulated transporter and a hazardous waste manifest.

Facilities that store these wastes are subject regulations in 40 CFR 264 and 265. Facilities that burn hazardous waste in boilers and industrial furnaces must control emissions of toxic organic compounds, toxic metals, hydrogen chloride, chlorine gas, and particulate matter. In addition, the rules subject these facilities to the general facility standards applicable to hazardous waste treatment, storage and disposal facilities as well as permitting requirements that may include trial burns, emission monitoring, and dispersion monitoring.

Exempt Wastes and Small-Quantity Exemptions

These requirements do not apply to burning of used oil that exhibits a hazardous waste characteristic, burning of gas from hazardous waste landfills, burning of hazardous waste exempt under 40 CFR 216.4 and 261.6(a)(3)(v through viii), and coke ovens burning K087 wastes. In addition, owners and operators of smelting, melting, and refining furnaces that process hazardous wastes for metals recovery are conditionally exempt if they provide a written notice to EPA and comply with sampling, analysis, and recordkeeping requirements.

The facility standards described above do not apply to boilers or industrial furnaces that burn only hazardous waste from conditionally exempt small-quantity generators.

Facilities that only burn small quantities of hazardous waste are also exempt from the facility standards. To be exempt,

- the hazardous waste must not exceed 1% of the total fuel requirements,
- F020, F021, F022, F023, F026, and F027 wastes, which may contain dioxins, can not be burned,
- the hazardous waste must have a minimum heating value of 5000 BTUs per pound,
- the hazardous waste must be generated and burned on the same site, and
- monthly, hazardous waste burning quantity limits published in 40 CFR 266.108 (a)(1) must be observed.

EPA Identification Number

All facilities generating hazardous waste at a rate greater than 100 kg a month (approximately 220 pounds or 25 gallons) must have an EPA identification number and are subject to generator standards. All facilities that generate acute hazardous waste at a rate greater than 1 kg per month (approximately 2.2 pounds) must also obtain an EPA identification number and comply with generator standards.

An EPA identification number is a unique nine-digit number, preceded by a state-specific three-letter code, which identifies the facility as a generator of hazardous waste. All transporters and TSD facilities must also have EPA identification numbers. It is illegal to offer hazardous waste to a transporter or to a TSD facility that does not have an EPA identification number.

If a facility generates hazardous waste and does not have an EPA identification number, it must obtain a number either from its state, if the host state has authorization to manage its own hazardous waste program, or from EPA. To obtain a number, either the host state or EPA must be notified using prescribed forms. Some states require detailed notification information on the chemical characteristics and proposed management methods for each hazardous waste which is generated.

EPA requires the use of EPA Form 8700-12 for notification of hazardous waste activity. A copy of Form 8700-12 along with instructions for completing the form is included in Appendix A.

ACCUMULATION OF HAZARDOUS WASTE ON-SITE

A hazardous waste *accumulation point* is an area on-site at which hazardous waste can be accumulated for up to 90 days without a permit. At an accumulation point, any amount of hazardous waste can be collected and stored providing no container remains in the accumulation point storage over 90 days. If hazardous waste is added to a container at the accumulation point, the 90-day limit for the container begins as soon as the waste is first added to the container.

A *satellite accumulation point* is an area at or near the point of generation that is under the control of the operator of the process generating the waste. No more than 55 gallons of hazardous waste or 1 quart of acute hazardous waste can be accumulated at a satellite accumulation point.

The differences between a satellite accumulation point and an accumulation point are the volume and the length of time wastes may be accumulated. At a satellite accumulation point, up to 55 gallons of hazardous waste may be accumulated for an unlimited amount of time. At an accumulation point, an unlimited volume of waste may be accumulated in tanks or containers for up to 90 days.

An accumulation point manager and an alternate accumulation point manager should be assigned to each accumulation point and satellite accumulation point. These two points of contact are responsible for ensuring that all regulatory requirements for the point are met. These individuals are among those who would be required to attend hazardous waste management training.

MANAGEMENT OF HAZARDOUS WASTE AT SATELLITE ACCUMULATION POINTS

Satellite accumulation points are typically used to increase the efficiency of waste collection and to reduce the costs of waste disposal. Wastes collected at satellite accumulation points are collected right at the point where the wastes are generated so it is not necessary to immediately transfer wastes to a central collection area or accumulation point. In addition, wastes may be collected at that point indefinitely until 55 gallons of hazardous waste is accumulated. There is no need to ship partially full drums of waste off-site at full cost due to accumulation time restrictions.

All waste at satellite accumulation points must be under the control of the operator of the process generating the waste. For example, the container at a satellite accumulation point must be placed right next to or near the process which generates the hazardous waste and the person who operates that process or area must control the hazardous waste placed in that container.

EPA has set the following management standards for wastes collected at satellite accumulation points:

- Hazardous waste at satellite accumulation points must be collected in containers.
- No more than 55 gallons of hazardous waste or 1 quart of acutely hazardous waste (i.e., the P list wastes) may be accumulated.
- If the 55-gallon limit is exceeded at a satellite accumulation point, you must mark the container holding the excess waste with the date the excess began accumulating. You have 3 days to transfer the excess waste to either an accumulation point or to a permitted treatment, storage or disposal facility.
- Containers must be marked either with the words "Hazardous Waste" or with other words that identify the contents of the container.
- The waste being placed in the container must be compatible with the container.
- A container holding hazardous waste must always be kept closed during accumulation except when it is necessary to add or remove waste.

MANAGEMENT OF WASTE AT ACCUMULATION POINTS

Wastes may be accumulated at accumulation points in tanks, containers, or on drip pads. A *container* is defined as any portable device in which a material is stored, transported, treated, disposed of, or otherwise handled. The most common container is a 55-gallon drum, but many other types of containers, ranging from sample bottles to tote tanks, are containers and may be used for hazardous waste accumulation. A *tank* is defined as a stationary device designed to contain an accumulation of hazardous waste and is constructed primarily of nonearthen materials (e.g. wood, concrete, steel, plastic) that provide structural support. If drip pads are used for waste accumulation, the generator must comply with subpart W of 40 CFR part 265 concerning drip pads and must maintain records of 90-day waste removal procedures and documentation of the waste removed from the drip pads.

The following requirements apply to waste accumulated in both containers and tanks at accumulation points.

Marking

The date upon which each period of accumulation begins must be clearly marked on each container and must be visible for inspection. Additionally, while being accumulated on-site each container and tank must be clearly marked with the words "Hazardous Waste." This mark must be visible for inspection.

Emergency Preparedness and Prevention

Accumulation points must be maintained and operated to minimize the possibility of a fire, explosion, or a release of hazardous waste that could threaten human health or the environment. Unless none of the hazards posed by the waste handled at the accumulation point could require a particular type of equipment, the following emergency equipment must be available:

- an internal communications or alarm system capable of providing immediate emergency instructions to facility personnel
- a device, such as a telephone, immediately available at the scene of operations or a handheld two-way radio capable of summoning emergency assistance from local police departments, fire departments, or state or local emergency response teams
- portable fire extinguishers
- fire control equipment
- spill control equipment
- decontamination equipment
- water at adequate volume and pressure to supply water hose streams, or foam producing equipment, or automatic sprinklers, or water spray systems

All emergency response equipment must be tested if necessary and maintained to ensure its proper operation in time of emergency.

Adequate aisle space must be maintained at accumulation points to allow for the unobstructed movement of personnel, fire protection equipment, spill control equipment, and decontamination equipment. Communications, fire, and spill control equipment must be kept readily accessible so it can be used quickly and safely in the event of an emergency.

Arrangements must be made to familiarize the police department, fire department, emergency response teams, and the local hospital with the facility layout and the properties of the hazardous waste handled at the accumulation point. These emergency arrangements are described further in Chapter 9.

Accumulation points must have a written contingency plan designed to minimize hazards due to fires, explosions, or the release of hazardous waste. Contingency plan requirements are described in Chapter 9.

Training

Personnel who handle or are occupationally exposed to hazardous waste are required to be trained annually in the proper methods for the management of hazardous waste and the implementation of the facility's contingency plan. The training program must be directed by a person trained in hazardous waste management. Personnel who are assigned to a position related to hazardous waste management must complete training within 6 months of their assignment. These personnel must not work in unsupervised positions until they have completed training. Refer to Chapter 7 for details regarding who must be trained and the scope of the required training.

Biennial Reports and Additional Reporting

Generators who ship hazardous waste off-site to TSD facilities or treat hazardous waste on-site must submit biennial reports to EPA by March 1 of each even-numbered year, or to the state if it has authorization to manage its own hazardous waste program. Biennial reports must be on an EPA or state approved form and must cover generator activities over the previous calendar year. Each biennial report must contain at least the following information:

- Generator's EPA identification number, name and address;
- The calendar year covered by the report;
- The EPA identification number, name, and address for each off-site TSD facility in the United States to which the waste was shipped during the year;
- The name and EPA identification number of each transporter used during the reporting year for shipments to a TSD facility within the United States;
- A description, EPA hazardous waste number, DOT hazard class, and quantity of each hazardous waste shipped off-site to a TSD within the United States (this information must be listed by identification number of each off-site facility);

- A description of the efforts undertaken during the year to reduce the volume and toxicity of waste generated (see Waste Minimization and Segregation beginning on page 42);
- A description of the changes in volume and toxicity of waste actually achieved during the year in comparison to previous years to the extent such information is available for years prior to 1984; and
- A certification signed by the generator.

Generators must keep a copy of each biennial report for at least 3 years from the due date of the report.

EPA, as it deems necessary, may require additional reports concerning the quantities and dispositions of hazardous wastes which are generated. Furthermore, many states require annual reports rather than biennial reports and may also require additional information.

Closure of Accumulation Points

When closing an accumulation point, the need for any further maintenance at the accumulation point must be reduced or eliminated. In addition, the generator must control, minimize, or eliminate to the extent necessary to protect human health and the environment, the post-closure escape of hazardous waste, hazardous constituents, leachate, contaminated runoff, or hazardous waste decomposition products to the ground, surface water, or to the atmosphere. During closure all contaminated equipment, structures, and soil must be properly disposed of or decontaminated. Chapter 8 provides details on the closure of hazardous waste accumulation and TSD facilities.

SELECTING AN AREA FOR HAZARDOUS WASTE ACCUMULATION

When you select an area for the accumulation of hazardous waste, you should select one that will minimize the threat to human health or the environment in the event of a release of hazardous waste and keep four factors in mind:

- EPA requirements for the location and design of accumulation points
- state requirements for the location and design of accumulation points
- local requirements such as those adopted by your local fire department for the location and design of accumulation points
- liability for cleanup if hazardous waste is released from the accumulation point during a spill, fire, or explosion

EPA has few standards governing the location or design of accumulation points for containers, but RCRA requires the minimization of threats to the environment that would be caused by the release of hazardous waste. Containers placed at accumulation points which hold ignitable or reactive wastes must be located at least 15 meters (50 feet) from the facility's property line.

Although EPA does not require an impermeable base or containment system at an accumulation point, many states have more stringent regulations and may require impermeable bases, containment systems, roofs over accumulation points located outside and a security system such as a fence. To comply with the RCRA regulations, the site and design should minimize threats to human health or the environment in the event of an accidental release. The use of the following design features and operational practices will help minimize threats to the environment.

- Place containers on an impervious concrete surface free from cracks and gaps. Avoid placing containers on dirt, sand, gravel, or grass surfaces.
- Containers must not be located near any floor drains that lead to sanitary or storm water sewers.
- Install a containment system designed to contain the volume of the largest container or 10% of the volume of all containers, whichever is greater, in the event of a spill or leak.
- Slope the base of the containment system so liquids resulting from leaks, spills, or precipitation are drained and removed, or place all containers on pallets.
- Design the containment system to prevent runon into the container area or with enough excess capacity (beyond that needed for the waste) so any runon will be contained.
- Remove spilled or leaked waste and accumulated precipitation from the system as soon as it is identified to prevent container corrosion or mixing with wastes. Check to ensure accumulated precipitation does not contain hazardous waste or hazardous waste constituents prior to discharge.
- Erect a fence with a means to control entry around the accumulation point to prevent the unknowing or unauthorized entry of personnel.
- Cover containers accumulated outdoors with a roof or tarpaulin to protect volatile materials from direct light.
- Ventilate any area used for the accumulation of hazardous wastes. Highly volatile organics in particular can present a serious health hazard when in storage. Also, in the event of a spill or leak, effective ventilation should be installed to safely direct toxic or flammable vapors and fumes out of the work area. Care must be taken to prevent exhausted air from reentering work areas through doors, windows, and air intakes on buildings.

MANAGEMENT OF WASTES AT ACCUMULATION POINTS IN CONTAINERS

Only DOT-specification containers may be used for the transportation of hazardous waste. In order to avoid repackaging hazardous waste prior to shipment and to avoid compatibility problems between the waste and the container, it is wise to use DOT-specification containers for hazardous waste accumulation as well. DOT has recognized that not all wastes are compatible with every type of container. Acids will destroy metal drums and some

organic solvents will dissolve the materials in certain plastic containers. In addition, containers must be designed and constructed to hold hazardous materials and wastes during the stresses that occur during container handling and transportation. No one container has been designed which is appropriate for the transportation of all hazardous waste. Consequently, DOT has specified which containers are best suited for particular materials and wastes.

Container Selection

To select the proper container for transportation off-site, you must use the DOT hazardous materials table found in 49 CFR 172.101 The DOT hazardous materials table is reprinted in Appendix D, and 49 CFR may be purchased from the U.S. Government Printing Office which is located in Washington, DC. The hazardous materials table identifies the regulatory requirements for hazardous material containers. A *hazardous material* is defined by DOT as a substance or material in a quantity and form that may pose an unreasonable risk to health and safety and property when transported in commerce. All hazardous wastes are DOT hazardous materials when transported in commerce.

DOT Hazardous Material Table

DOT hazardous materials are listed in alphabetical order on the DOT hazardous material table. The DOT hazardous materials table also includes specific information on each hazardous material's hazard class, DOT identification number, label requirements, packaging requirements, and shipping requirements during transportation via aircraft, railcar, and water.

The DOT hazardous material table is divided into seven columns which present most of the information a generator needs to know in order to properly package, mark, label, and document a shipment of hazardous waste. Each column of the hazardous materials table contains a different type of information or tells you how to find further information. The information presented in each column is described below.

Column 1   This column contains one or more of three symbols:

+   When the (+) sign appears, the proper shipping name and the hazard class of the material must be shown on the manifest and the package whether or not the material or its mixtures or solutions meet the definition of the class.

A   When the letter A appears, the material is subject to DOT regulations only when transported by air, unless the material is a hazardous substance or a hazardous waste.

W   When the letter W appears, the material is subject to DOT regulations only when transported by water, unless the material is hazardous substance or a hazardous waste.
If neither A or W appear, the substance is regulated for all modes of transportation.

Column 2   This column lists the proper shipping name for all hazardous materials. You are required to use proper shipping names on hazardous waste manifests and on packages containing hazardous waste. The names in italic type that sometimes appear next to the proper shipping name may be included but are not required. Only names in roman type are proper shipping names. Any of the series of names in roman type separated by the word "or" may be used as proper shipping names. When an entry in Column 2 includes the word "see" in italics, and both names are printed in Roman types, either name may be used as the proper shipping name. The abbreviation "n.o.s." means that the material is "not otherwise specified."

Column 3   This column shows the hazard class to which a material belongs. In some instances column 3 will contain the word "forbidden," which means the material may not be offered or accepted for transportation.

Column 3a   This column shows the DOT identification number assigned to the hazardous material. These numbers must be included on manifests and on packages of hazardous wastes. These numbers prefixed by "UN" are recognized internationally and in the United States by emergency personnel. Those numbers prefixed by "NA" are only recognized in North America.

Column 4   Column 4 shows the labels that must be applied to the outside of the package of hazardous waste. There are additional labeling requirements not specified in Column 4 that must be complied with. Additional details are provided in Chapter 5.

Column 5   This column is a two-part column which shows you which section of the regulations contains packaging requirements for the hazardous waste you are shipping. Column 5(a) either indicates that there are no exceptions to the packaging requirements in Column 5(b) using the word "none," or indicates which section of the regulations contains exceptions. Exceptions to specific packaging requirements are typically for very small or "limited quantities" of hazardous waste and materials. Column 5(b) lists the specific section of 49 CFR that describes the packaging requirements for the hazardous waste or material.

Column 6   This is a two-part column which provides the restrictions on the transportation of hazardous material by air and rail. Column 6(a) shows the maximum amount of material that may be shipped in one package by passenger aircraft or passenger railcar. Column 6(b) shows the maximum amount of material that may be shipped in one package by cargo-only aircraft.

Column 7   Column 7 provides requirements for water shipments for cargo-only vessels 7(a) and passenger vessels 7(b). The number that appears in the columns refer to methods for stowing hazardous materials and wastes on the vessel:

1. Material should be stored on-deck (if both numbers 1 and 2 appear, number 2 is the preferred method).
2. Material should be stowed under the deck.
3. Material should be stowed under the deck, away from heat, in ventilated containers.
4. Material may be transported only in limited quantities (see column 5) and is subject to specific stowage requirements.
5. Transportation of the material is forbidden.
6. Material must be transported in a magazine subject to specific requirements.

Column 7(c) contains additional requirements for water shipments such as "Keep Dry" or "Keep Cool."

The following procedure may be used to select the proper container for waste accumulation.

1. Select a proper shipping name for the hazardous waste. For example, if the waste generated is spent acetone, look up the word "acetone" in column 2. If the hazardous waste is a mixture containing more than one chemical compound or element, use the most descriptive proper shipping name. (A procedure for determining the proper shipping names for mixtures is presented in How to Determine U.S. DOT Description for Item 11 of the Manifest, on page 58.)
2. In column 5, find the packaging specifications corresponding to the proper shipping name you have selected. Column 5(a) refers to packaging specifications for very small or limited quantities of hazardous materials. Column 5(b) is often used to determine which regulations specify the containers that can be used for accumulation and transportation of hazardous waste.
3. Identify the specific packaging requirements and packaging codes for the material in the referenced section of 49 CFR 173. (See Figure 3.1 for example.)
4. Obtain containers marked with one of the specification codes identified in the referenced section of 49 CFR.

If a container is a DOT specification package, somewhere on the container (e.g., top or bottom) will be a mark with the DOT specification number. This mark indicates the container manufacturer has followed DOT requirements when manufacturing and testing the container.

Note: U.S. DOT hazardous material regulations were amended on December 21, 1990 to align the regulations with United Nations recommendations and International Civil Aviation Organization Technical Instructions in the areas of classification, packaging, and hazard communication during the transport of hazardous materials. International performance-oriented packaging standards will replace the current DOT-specification system used for container selection and must be used for non-bulk, domestic shipments by October 1, 1996. New packaging requirements for materials that are poisonous by inhalation become mandatory on October 1, 1993. Under the new system, packaging requirements for a hazardous material are based on the material's packing group and vapor pressure, and the chemical compatibility between the packaging and the hazardous material.

The new regulations designate hazard classes by their international numbers, change the definitions of certain hazard classes such as flammable liquids, adopt international units of measure, amend and consolidate the hazardous material tables (49 CFR 172.101, and 172.102 have been consolidated into one table), change labeling, marking and placarding requirements, amend the hazard communication requirements, and change the requirements on the reuse of plastic and metal drums. Use of the new hazardous materials table and associated classification, labeling, marking, and packaging requirements became mandatory as of October 1, 1991 for new explosives and most infectious substances. By October 1, 1992, hazard communication requirements are effective for all materials which are poisonous by inhalation. October 1, 1993 is the date after which most other provisions of this final rule become effective (certain performance-oriented packaging requirements become effective in 1994 and 1996 as noted above).

Single-Trip Containers

A container may be marked "NRC" meaning nonreusable container or "STC" meaning single-trip container. The implications are the same for containers marked with either acronym. These containers may be reused for the shipment of hazardous waste only if the following conditions are met: the waste must be packaged and offered for transportation in accordance with DOT regulations, transportation is by highway only, the container may not be offered for transportation less than 24 hours after it is finally closed for transportation, the container must be inspected for leakage immediately before being offered for transportation, each container must be loaded by the shipper and unloaded by the consignee, unless the motor carrier is a private or contract carrier, and unless the container has been reconditioned or altered and retested according to prescribed methods, the container may be reused only once for the transportation of hazardous waste.

Container Condition Requirements

Both EPA and DOT regulate the condition of containers used to accumulate and ship hazardous waste. During waste accumulation, 40 CFR 265.171 requires that hazardous waste in containers at both accumulation points and at satellite accumulation points must be in good condition. *Good condition* means that drums should have no severe rusting, no sharp-edged creases or dents, no bulging heads caused by overpressuring a container, and no severe structural defects. If a container is not in good condition or begins to leak, the hazardous waste must be immediately transferred to another container or must be overpacked in a salvage drum. Containers with pools of hazardous waste on the top are not in good condition and must be decontaminated or overpacked prior to transportation off-site.

All waste placed in containers must be compatible with the container. By following the container selection process outlined above, you will ensure that your hazardous waste is compatible with the container you have selected.

Container Management Procedures

A container holding hazardous waste must always be kept closed during accumulation except when it is necessary to add or remove waste from the container. Open head drums are considered to be closed when the lid is placed on the drum, the lid is secured to the drum with a retaining ring or other DOT-specification closure device, and the ring is bolted closed.

At accumulation points, containers must not be stored or handled in a manner that may cause them to rupture or leak. The following precautions should be taken at both accumulation points and satellite accumulation points to prevent container ruptures and leaks:

- Do not overfill container. For example, only fill a 55-gallon drum to 50 gallons. Liquids expand in containers as the temperature increases. A steel drum painted a dark color can easily rise to temperatures above 100°F and the pressure created by the expansion of the liquid causes bulging heads and damages the integrity of the container. Bulging containers also create a safety hazard for personnel expected to add waste to or handle the containers.
- Protect containers from freezing. Many materials go through a freeze/thaw cycle during changing weather conditions. This freeze/thaw cycle causes metal stress and can result in leaking containers.
- Ground ignitable hazardous waste to prevent a spark generated by static electricity to ignite flammable vapors which may be present. Use a bonding wire and a ground wire when transferring flammable liquids into containers to prevent sparks caused by the buildup of static electricity during pouring operations.
- Handle drums and other containers with equipment designed for the task. Drum grappler attachments may be purchased for tow motors to securely grab and move containers. Secure containers to pallets before moving pallets. Use drum carts designed for the types of containers used by your facility to reduce the likelihood of dropping a container during handling. Never balance drums on the forks of a forklift or tow motor.

§173.119 Flammable liquids not specifically provided for.

(a) *Flammable liquids with flash points of 20°F, or below.* Flammable liquids with flash points of 20°F or below and having vapor pressure (Reid [1] test) not over 16 pounds per square inch, absolute, at 100°F, other than those for which special requirements are prescribed in this Part, must be offered for transportation in DOT specification packagings constructed of materials that will not react dangerously with or be decomposed by the chemical packed therein as required in the following paragraphs (see paragraphs (c) to (i) of this section for high pressure liquids, paragraphs (j) to (l) of this section for viscous liquids, and paragraph (m) of this section for flammable liquids which are also oxidizers, radioactive materials, corrosive liquids, poison B liquids, or organic peroxides and §173.134 for flammable liquids that are also pyrophoric liquids):

(1) Spec. 1A, 1D, or 1M (§§178.1, 178.4, 178.17 of this subchapter). Glass carboys in boxes or expanded polystyrene packagings. Rated capacity may not exceed 5 gallons for Spec. 1A. Not authorized for transportation by aircraft.

(2) Spec. 5, 5A, 5B, 5C or 5M (§§178.80, 178.81, 178.82, 178.83, or 178.90 of this subchapter). Metal barrels or drums, with openings not exceeding 2.3 inches in diameter.

(3) Spec. 17E (§178.116 of this subchapter). Metal drums (single-trip) with openings not over 2.3 inches in diameter. Drums with a marked capacity of more than 5 gallons but not more than 30 gallons must be constructed of 19-gauge body and head sheets. Drums with a marked capacity in excess of 30 gallons must be constructed of 18-gauge body and head sheets. Drums with a marked capacity of more than 5 gallons are not authorized for transportation by air.

(4) Spec. 17C (§178.115 of this subchapter). Metal drums (single-trip), with openings not exceeding 2.3 inches in diameter.

(5) [Reserved]

(6) [Reserved]

(7) Spec. 12B (§178.205 of this subchapter). Fiberboard boxes with inside containers which must be glass or earthenware, not over 1 quart each; metal cans, not over 1 gallon each.

NOTE[1]: Spec. 12B fiberboard boxes (§178.206-28(a) of this subchapter), with one inside rectangular metal cans, Spec. 2F (§178.25 of this subchapter) not to exceed 5 gallons capacity, are authorized for gasoline only. Gross weight of completed package not over 65 pounds.

(8) Spec. 15A, 15B, 15C, 16A, 19A or 19B (§§178.168, 178.169, 178.170, 178.185, 178.190, 178.191 of this subchapter). Wooden boxes with inside containers which must be metal pails, kits, or cans, not over 10 gallons each or inside glass or earthenware containers not over 1 gallon each, except that glass or earthenware containers up to 3 gallons each are authorized when only one inside container is packed in each outside container.

(9) Spec. 21C, 22A, or 22B (§§178.224, 178.196, or 178.197 of this subchapter). Fiber drums and plywood drums with a single inside glass, earthenware, or metal container of not over

---

[1] ATSM Test D323.

---

one gallon capacity in each drum. Inside container must be so cushioned at top, sides, and bottom, as to prevent breakage or leakage in transit.

(10) Spec. 42B (§178.107 of this subchapter). Aluminum drums.

(11) Cylinders as prescribed for any compressed gas, except acetylene.

(12) Specification 103[1], 103W, 103ALW, 103DW, 104[1], 104W, 105A100[1], 105A100ALW, 105A100W, 106A500X, 106A800XNC, 106A800NCI[1], 109A100ALW, 109A300W, 110A500W 111A60ALW1, 111A60F1, 111A600W1, 111A100W3, 111A100W4, 111A100W6, 112A200W, 112A400F, 114A340W, 115A60W1, 115A60ALW, or 115A60W6, (§§179.100, 179.101, 179.200, 179.201, 179.220, 179.300, 179.301 of this subchapter) tank cars. For cars equipped with expansion domes, manway closures must be so designed that pressure will be released automatically by starting the operation of removing the manway cover. Openings in tank heads to facilitate application of lining are authorized on tank cars constructed before January 1, 1975. These openings must be closed in an approved manner (§179.3 of this subchapter).

(13) The use of Spec. 103AL special riveted aluminum tank cars is authorized for the transportation of gasoline, ethyl acetate, acetone, methanol, or butyraldehyde as provided in special orders of November 5, 1937 and February 1, 1939.

(14) Spec. 15X (§178.181 of this subchapter). Wooden boxes with inside metal containers. For shipment by common carriers by water to noncontiguous territories or possessions of the United States and foreign countries; shipments from inland points in the United States which are consigned to such destinations are authorized to be transported to ship side by rail freight in carload lots only and by motor vehicle in truck load lots only.

(15) [Reserved]

(16) [Reserved]

(17) Specification MC 300, MC 301, MC 302, MC 303, MC 304, MC 305, MC 306, MC 307, MC 310, MC 311, MC 312, DOT 406, DOT 407, DOT 412, MC 330, or MC 331 (§§178.345, 178.346, 178.347, 178.348, 178.337 of this subchapter) cargo tank motor vehicle, subject to the following conditions:

(i) Each cargo tank is equipped with a pressure relief system meeting the requirements in §178.346-10 or 178.347-10 of this subchapter, except that pressure relief devices on Specification MC 330 and MC 331 cargo tanks must meet the requirements in §178.337-9 of this subchapter.

(ii) Bottom outlets of the cargo tank are equipped with internal self-closing stop-valves meeting the requirements in §178.345-11 of this subchapter, except that bottom outlets on Specification MC 330 and MC 331 cargo tanks must be equipped with internal self-closing stop-valves meeting the requirements in §178.337-11(a) of this subchapter. (See §173.33(b)(3) for limitations on the use of air pressure unloading.)

(iii) MC 300, MC 301, MC 302, MC 303, MC 305, MC 306, and DOT 406 cargo tanks equipped with a 1 psig normal vent used to transport gasoline are subject to the following requirements. Based on the volatility class determined by using ASTM D439 and the Reid vapor pressure (RVP) of the particular gasoline, the maximum lading pressure and maximum ambient temperature permitted during the loading of gasoline may not exceed that listed in Table 1.

(18) [Reserved]

(19) Spec. 5L (§178.89 of this subchapter). Metal barrels or drums for gasoline shipments offered by or consigned to the Departments of the Army, Navy, and Air Force of the United States Government or Allies. Use of this container will be permitted because of the present emergency and until further order of the Department.

TABLE 1.—MAXIMUM AMBIENT TEMPERATURE—GASOLINE

ATSM D439 volatility class	Maximum lading and ambient temperature (see note 1)
A (RVP < = 9.0 psia)	131 •F
B (RVP < = 10.0 psia)	124 •F
C (RVP < = 11.5 psia)	116 •F
D (RVP < = 13.5 psia)	107 • F
E (RVP < = 15.0 psia)	100 • F

NOTE 1: Based on maximum lading pressure of 1 psig at top of cargo tank.

---

[1] The use of existing tank cars authorized but new construction not authorized.

FIGURE 3.1
49 CFR 173.119

Special Requirements for Incompatible, Ignitable, and Reactive Wastes

Special procedures must be followed whenever ignitable, reactive, and incompatible wastes are accumulated at accumulation points. Containers accumulating ignitable or reactive waste must be located at least 50 feet away from the facility's property boundary. These containers must also be kept away from sparks, open flames, extreme heat, or other sources of ignition.

Prevent hazardous chemical reactions such as heat, fire, explosion, pressure, and the evolution of toxic or flammable decomposition products by not mixing incompatible chemicals in the same container or tank. If you are unsure of whether a waste to be disposed of is incompatible with the waste in a container or the container itself, contact a chemist. Incompatible wastes, or incompatible wastes and materials, must not be placed in the same container. In addition, hazardous waste must not be placed in an unwashed container that previously held an incompatible waste or material.

At accumulation points and satellite accumulation points, wastes should not be located near anything with which they are incompatible. For example, a container of waste acid should not be located near any aluminum structures or surfaces because contact between acid and aluminum may produce flammable hydrogen gas and could lead to a fire or explosion. Containers holding hazardous waste which is incompatible with any other wastes or materials present should be physically separated from the other materials by means of a dike, berm, or wall.

Waste Minimization and Segretation, beginning on page 42, provides details on procedures to follow to ensure proper waste segregation and avoid incompatible chemical reactions when accumulating different hazardous wastes.

Container Inspection Requirements

To ensure that accumulation points are maintained in good condition, RCRA regulations require that accumulation points be inspected weekly. Areas where containers are stored must be inspected for leaks and deterioration caused by corrosion or other factors. Inspection records must be maintained on-site for at least 3 years from the date of the inspection. Figure 3.2 provides a sample accumulation point inspection log.

Management of Empty Containers

It is very important to responsibly manage all *empty* containers of chemicals to comply with EPA regulations and to prevent contamination of the environment from residues left in *empty* containers.

Used drums may be handled in several different ways. They may be reconditioned and reused as shipping containers, they may be processed for steel scrap recycling, they may be crushed and buried at a permitted TSD facility, and they may, under certain circumstances, be sent to a solid waste disposal facility. Reconditioning or recycling are usually preferred methods for handling empties due to the cost involved in disposal of empties at a TSD facility, and the long term environmental liability associated with land disposal at a solid waste facility.

Under EPA regulations, and most state environmental rules, certain *empty* containers (and the residues therein) are not subject to hazardous waste regulations. A container or an inner liner removed from a container that held hazardous waste is empty and is not regulated as a hazardous waste if:

* all waste has been removed that can be removed by using common practices such as pouring, pumping, and aspirating, and
* No more than 1 inch of residue remains on the bottom of the container or inner liner, or
* No more than 3% by weight of the total capacity of the container remains in the container or inner liner if the container is less than or equal to 110 gallon in size, or no more than 0.3% remains if the container is larger than 110 gallons in size.

If the container held an acute hazardous waste, to be considered *empty*, one of the following must occur:

* The container or inner liner must be triple-rinsed using a solvent capable of removing the commercial chemical product or manufacturing chemical intermediate;
* the container or inner liner has been cleaned by another method that has been shown in the scientific literature, or by tests conducted by the generator, to achieve equivalent removal; or
* in case of the container, the inner liner that prevented contact of the commercial chemical product or manufacturing chemical intermediate with the container, has been removed.

A container that has held a hazardous waste that is a compressed gas is empty when the pressure in the container reaches atmospheric pressure.

If containers that held hazardous waste have not been emptied in accordance with this definition, the containers must be managed as hazardous waste.

DOT Requirements for Empty Packages

DOT regulates the shipment of containers that previously held hazardous materials. 49 CFR 173.29 states that a container having a capacity of 110 gallons or less that previously contained a hazardous material may not be offered for transportation unless offered in the same manner as required when it previously contained the hazardous material. This requirement does not apply to a container that has been cleaned and purged of all residues or that has been filled with a material that is not hazardous. Consequently, containers that contain less than 1 inch of residue may be empty per EPA regulations, but are still regulated by DOT during transportation.

Containers with hazardous material residues must be properly marked and labeled in accordance with DOT requirements for the material which was previously in the container. (DOT marking and labeling requirements are discussed in more detail in Chapter 5). Shipment of these packages by common carrier must be accompanied by shipping papers, such as bills of lading, that contain a proper shipping description for the hazardous material. Shipping papers are not required if the empty packages are collected and transported by a contract or private carrier for reconditioning or reuse. Placards are required on vehicles transporting containers, if the residues in the containers meet the definitions of the hazard classes listed in Table 1 of the Placard Key in Chapter 5. Each empty container with residues of a hazardous material must be free from leaks, and each opening must be closed.

An empty container may not be marked and labeled as a hazardous material unless the it contains some of the hazardous material that previously required display of the label or marking. However, marks and labels may be left on cleaned, empty containers if they are loaded on-site and the containers are placed into a closed vehicle so the containers are not visible during transportation.

Location: _____ Organization: _____

Inspected By: _____ Date: _____ No. of Containers: _____

Signature: _____ Accumulation Point #/Location: _____

Date of Reinspection: _____ Inspector: _____

Hazardous Waste Containers			
		Yes	No
Container Condition	Are any open?		
	Are any severely rusted?		
	Are any container heads bulging?		
	Are any leaking?		
If any of these questions were marked YES, comment:_____			
Describe actions taken to correct situation:_____			
		Complete	
Container Marking	Begin Accumulation Date marked on container(s)		
	Hazardous waste warning marked on container(s)		
	Contents marked on container(s)		

Figure 3.2
Accumulation Point Inspection Log

Accumulation Point	Yes	No
Is the accumulation point free of structural deterioration?		
Is adequate aisle space present between drums to allow unobstructed movement for emergency response?		
If either of these questions were marked NO, comment:_____ _____		
Describe actions taken to correct situation:_____ _____		

Emergency Response Equipment	Yes	No
Telephone — Is it easily accessible in case of emergency?		
Is it in working order?		
Spill Control — Is an empty salvage drum near by?		
Is unused absorbent material nearby?		
Is all personal protective equipment nearby? ☐ Gloves ☐ Boots ☐ Apron ☐ Goggles ☐ Respirator		
Fire Protection — Is a fire extinguisher readily accessible?		
Is the fire extinguisher fully charged?		
Is the fire extinguisher seal intact?		
If any of these questions were marked NO, comment:_____ _____		
Describe actions taken to correct situation:_____ _____		

Figure 3.2
Accumulation Point Inspection Log (continued)

MANAGEMENT OF WASTES AT ACCUMULATION POINTS IN TANKS

Special management requirements must be complied with when accumulating hazardous waste in tanks due to the large volume of hazardous waste which could be released during an incident. EPA regulations governing the accumulation of hazardous waste in tanks are published in 40 CFR 265, Subpart J.

Generators who accumulate hazardous waste in tanks must employ secondary containment systems and must be able to detect releases of hazardous waste unless the hazardous waste contains no free liquids, and the tank is situated inside a building with an impermeable floor. Secondary containment for tanks includes a liner external to the tank, a vault, a double-walled tank, or an equivalent device approved by EPA. Tanks, including sumps, that serve as part of a secondary containment system to collect or contain releases of hazardous wastes are exempt from having additional containment and leak detection systems.

Assessment of Existing Tank System's Integrity

If a tank does not have secondary containment, the generator must determine that the tank is not leaking or is unfit for use. In order to have made this determination, by January 12, 1988, the generator should have obtained and must keep on file a written assessment of the tank system's integrity, which has been reviewed and certified by an independent, qualified engineer attesting to the tank system's integrity. At a minimum, the assessment must have considered the following:

- Design standards, if available, according to which the tank and ancillary equipment were constructed.
- Hazardous characteristics of the wastes that have been or will be handled.
- Existing corrosion protection measures.
- Documented age of the tank system, if available (otherwise estimate the age of the tank).
- Results of a leak test, internal inspection, or other tank integrity examination, such that the effects of temperature variations, tank end deflection, vapor pockets, and high water table effects are taken into account (for nonenterable underground tanks), or cracks, leaks, corrosion, and erosion are taken into account (for other than non-enterable underground tanks and for ancillary equipment). This assessment must be either a leak test or an internal inspection and/or other tank integrity examination certified by an independent, qualified, registered professional engineer.

If a material in a tank system became hazardous waste after July 14, 1986, the assessment must be conducted within 12 months after the date that the waste becomes a hazardous waste. If the assessment turns up a leak or unfit tank, generator must comply with the requirements outlined below.

Design and Installation of New Tank Systems or Components

To prevent tank rupture or failure, facilities which install new tank systems must take the following precautions:

- Ensure that the foundation, structural support, seams, connections, and pressure controls (if applicable) are adequately designed.
- Ensure that the tank system has sufficient structural strength, compatibility with the wastes to be stored or treated, and corrosion protection.
- Obtain a written assessment reviewed and certified by an independent, qualified, registered professional engineer attesting that the system has sufficient structural integrity and is acceptable for the storing and treating of hazardous waste, with the following information:

    Design standards that will be followed during tank or ancillary equipment construction,

    Hazardous characteristics of the wastes to be handled,

    For tank systems where the tank or any external components of the system will be in contact with soil or water, factors affecting the potential for tank corrosion must be documented, including soil moisture content, soil pH, soil sulfides content, soil resistivity, structure to soil potential, influence of nearby underground metal structures, stray electric currents, and existing corrosion protection measures such as coatings and cathodic protection,

    For tank systems where the tank or any external components of the system will be in contact with soil or water, the type and degree of external corrosion protection that is needed, including the use of corrosion-resistant materials such as special alloys or fiberglass-reinforced plastic, the use of corrosion-resistant coatings with cathodic protection, and/or the use of electrical isolation devices such as insulating joints and flanges,

    For underground tank system components that could be affected by vehicular traffic, design or operational measures that will protect the system from damage,

    Design considerations to ensure that the tank foundations will support the fully loaded tank, tank systems must be anchored to prevent flotation or dislodgement, and tank systems must withstand the effect of frost heave.

- Tank systems must be installed properly to prevent damage to the system during installation. Prior to covering, enclosing, or casing a new tank, a qualified inspector or professional engineer must inspect the system for weld breaks, punctures, scrapes of protective coatings, cracks, corrosion, and other structure damage. Any problems must be corrected before the tank is installed.
- Backfill used to cover underground tank systems and piping must be noncorrosive, porous, and homogeneous and must be placed completely around the systems and compacted to ensure uniform support.

- All new tanks and ancillary equipment must be tested for tightness prior to installation. If a tank system is not tight, the system must be repaired prior to installation.
- Ancillary equipment must be supported and protected against physical damage and excessive stress due to settlement, vibration, expansion, or contraction.
- The installation of a field-fabricated corrosion protection system must be supervised by an independent corrosion expert to ensure proper installation.
- All written assessments, statements, and certifications that attest to the proper design and installation of the tank system must be kept on file (indefinitely) at the facility installing a new tank.

Containment and Detection of Releases

Secondary containment is required for all new tank systems or components prior to being put in service. Secondary containment was also required by January 12, 1989 for all existing tank systems used to store or treat F020, F021, F022, F023, F026, and F028 hazardous wastes; by January 12, 1989 or when the tank was 15 years old (whichever came later) for all tanks of known and documented age; and by January 12, 1995, for existing tanks whose age cannot be documented. If the facility is more than 7 years old, secondary containment was required by January 12, 1989 or when the facility was 15 years old (whichever came later). Figure 3.3 is a decision aid for determining when secondary containment must be installed for existing tanks.

Secondary containment systems must be designed, installed, and operated to prevent — when the tank is in use — migration of hazardous waste to soil, ground water, or surface water, and capable of detecting and collecting releases and accumulated liquids until the liquid is removed. To meet these design, installation and operational requirements, containment systems must:

- be constructed of or lined with materials compatible with the waste
- have sufficient strength and thickness to prevent failure due to pressure gradients, physical contact with the waste, climatic conditions, and the stress of daily operation (including vehicular traffic)
- be placed on a foundation or base capable of providing support to the secondary containment system, resisting pressure gradients above and below the system, and preventing failure due to settlement, compression, or uplift
- have a leak detection system capable of detecting failure of the tank or containment system failure or release of liquids within 24 hours (or as soon as possible in the absence of such technology)
- be sloped or designed or operated to drain and remove liquids resulting from leaks, spills, or precipitation within 24 hours.

Secondary containment systems must also satisfy the following requirements:

- External liner systems must contain at least 100% of the capacity of the largest tank in the containment area. The containment system must have a collection system with enough excess capacity to contain precipitation from a 25-year, 24-hour rainfall event, or must not allow run-on or infiltration of precipitation. (A 25-year, 24-hour rainfall event measures the greatest amount of rainfall received in one 24-hour period over the last 25 years.) Liner systems must also be free of cracks or gaps and must surround the tank completely to retain any release.
- Vault systems must contain 100% of the capacity of the largest tank in the containment area. The containment system must have a collection system with excess capacity (enough to contain precipitation from a 25-year, 24-hour rainfall event) or must not allow run-on or infiltration of precipitation; and must be constructed with chemical resistant water stops in place at all joints (if any); and must have an impermeable interior coating/lining compatible with the wastes stored that will prevent migration of waste into concrete; and for ignitable or reactive wastes, must be provided with a means to protect against the formation and ignition of vapors within the vault; and if the vault is subject to hydraulic pressure, must be provided with an exterior moisture barrier to prevent migration of moisture into the vault.
- Double-walled tanks must be designed so that any release from the inner tank is contained by the outer shell (i.e., an integral structure); and if constructed of metal, must be protected from corrosion on interior and exterior of tank; and must be provided with a built-in continuous leak detection system capable of detecting releases within 24 hours (or as soon as possible in the absence of such technology).

All ancillary equipment must also be provided with secondary containment meeting the requirements listed above except for the following equipment, if it is inspected on a daily basis:

- above-ground piping (except flanges, joints, valves, and other connections)
- flanges, joints, and other connections, if they are welded
- sealless or magnetic coupling pumps
- pressurized above-ground piping systems with automatic shutoff devices (e.g., excess flow check valves, flow metering shutdown devices, loss of pressure-actuated shut-off devices)

EPA may grant a variance from secondary containment requirements if the generator can demonstrate to EPA that alternative design and operating procedures along with location characteristics will prevent the migration of hazardous waste and hazardous waste constituents into the ground water or surface water at least as effectively as secondary containment during the life of the tank system. EPA will also grant a variance if the generator can demonstrate that in the event of a release that does migrate to ground water or surface water, no substantial present or potential hazard will be posed to human health or the environment. New underground tank systems may not be exempted from secondary containment requirements.

37

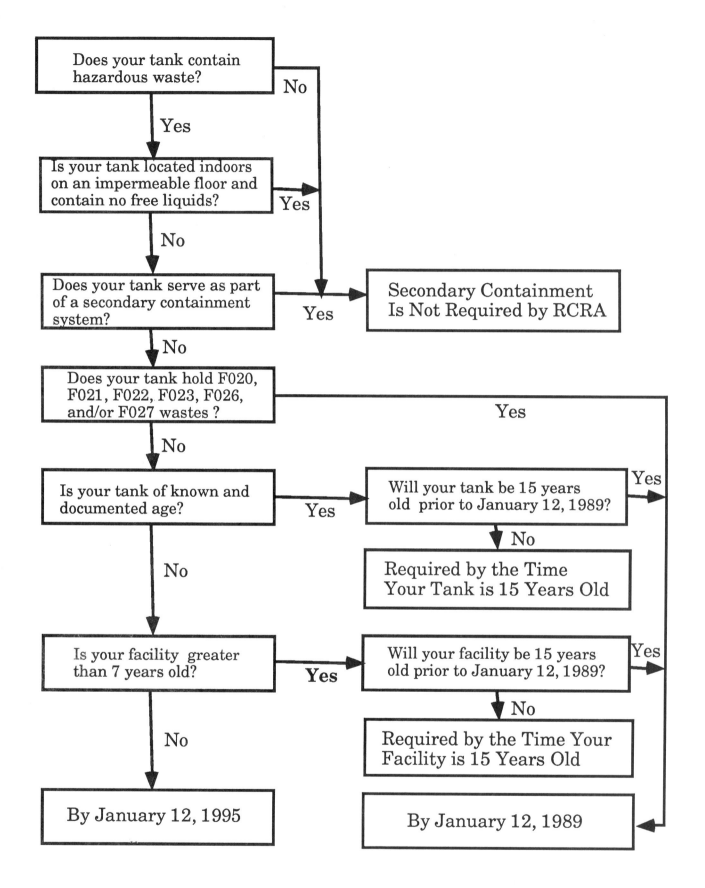

FIGURE 3.3
Secondary Containment Installation Deadlines for Existing Tanks

EPA has established procedures to be followed if a variance is requested. EPA must be notified in writing that a demonstration will be submitted at least 24 months before the date secondary containment must be provided for existing tanks and at least 30 days prior to entering into a contract for a new tank system. A timetable for completing the demonstration must also be submitted. The demonstration must be submitted within 180 days after notifying EPA of the intent to conduct the demonstration. EPA will notify the public and there could be a public hearing. EPA will approve or disprove the request for the variance within 90 days of receipt of a complete demonstration.

Until secondary containment is provided, all tanks must be leak tested annually. Tanks that are enterable and other ancillary equipment may be leak tested or there must be an internal inspection or other tank integrity examination by an independent, qualified, and registered professional engineer that address cracks, leaks, corrosion, and erosion.

General Tank Operating Requirements

Never place anything in a tank that could cause the system to rupture, leak, corrode, or fail. Controls and practices must be implemented to prevent spills and overflows. These practices include spill prevention controls such as check valves and dry disconnect couplings, and overfill prevention controls such as level sensing devices, high-level alarms, automatic feed cutoff systems, and mechanisms to bypass flow to a standby tank. Sufficient freeboard must be maintained in uncovered tanks to prevent overtopping by wave or wind action or by precipitation.

Tank Inspections
The following equipment and systems (when present) must be inspected at least once per operating day:

- overfill and spill control equipment such as waste feed cutoff systems, bypass systems, and drainage systems to ensure that it is in good working order;
- above-ground portions of the tank system, to detect corrosion or releases;
- data gathered from monitoring and leak detection equipment, to ensure that the tank system is being operated according to its design; and
- the construction materials and the area immediately surrounding the externally accessible portions of the tank system, to detect erosion or signs of releases such as wet spots or dead vegetation.

Cathodic protection systems must also be inspected within 6 months after installation, and annually thereafter, to confirm the proper operation of the system. All sources of impressed current must be inspected at least every other month. All inspections must be documented.

Response to Leaks or Spills
A tank system or secondary containment system from which there has been a leak or spill, or that is unfit for use, must be removed from service immediately. In addition, the tank must cease to be used and waste must be prevented from being added to the tank. Hazardous waste must then be removed from the tank or secondary containment system within 24 hours after detection of the release, or at the earliest possible time if it is not possible to remove the waste within 24 hours.

A visual inspection of the release and the area surrounding the tank system must be conducted. The further migration of the released material onto the soil or into water must be prevented and any visibly contaminated soil or water must be removed and properly disposed of (determine if the collected material is hazardous waste according to the procedures outlined in Solid Waste, beginning on page 7).

Unless the release is less than or equal to 1 pound and is immediately contained and cleaned up, your regional EPA office (refer to Table 5.1 for a list of phone numbers for EPA's regional hazardous waste offices) must be notified within 24 hours of detection of the release. A written follow-up report must be submitted to your regional EPA office within 30 days after the detection of a release that contains the following information:

- likely route of migration of the release;
- characteristics of the surrounding soil (soil composition, geology, hydrogeology, climate);
- results of any monitoring or sampling conducted in connection with the release (if available). If sampling or monitoring data relating to the release are not available within 30 days, these data must be submitted as soon as they become available;
- proximity to downgradient drinking water, surface water, and population areas; and
- description of response actions taken or planned.

Tank Closure
Upon closure, all waste residues, contaminated containment system components, contaminated soils, and structures and equipment contaminated with waste must be decontaminated or removed and managed as hazardous waste (unless not considered a hazardous waste). Chapter 8 presents details concerning closure and post-closure care of tanks and tank systems.

Special Requirements for Ignitable, Reactive, and Incompatible Wastes

Do not place ignitable or reactive waste in a tank system unless: the waste no longer meets the definition of ignitable or reactive either before or immediately after it is placed into the tank; the waste is stored or treated in such a way that it is protected from any material or condition that may cause the waste to ignite or react; or the tank is used solely for emergencies. Additionally, precautions must be taken to prevent reactions that:

- generate extreme heat or pressure, fire or explosions, or violent reactions
- produce uncontrolled toxic mists, fumes, dusts, or gases in sufficient quantities to threaten human health or the environment
- produce uncontrolled flammable fumes or gases in sufficient quantities to pose a risk of fire or explosions

- damage the structural integrity of the tank system or facility
- through other like means threaten human health or the environment.

Never place hazardous waste in a tank system that previously held an incompatible waste or material that has not been decontaminated. Never place incompatible wastes or incompatible waste or materials in the same tank unless the incompatible chemical reactions described earlier in this section are prevented.

The 1977 or 1981 edition of the National Fire Protection Association (NFPA) *Flammable and Combustible Liquids Code* (Tables 2-1 through 2-6), must be reviewed to ensure protective distances are maintained between tanks and any public ways, public streets, public alleys, and any adjoining property lines that can be built upon. The distances specified in this publication range from 5 feet to 1400 feet and depend on the type of tank, the size of the tank, whether fire control equipment is available, the stability of the liquids in the tank, and the flashpoint of the liquids in the tank.

SMALL-QUANTITY AND CONDITIONALLY EXEMPT SMALL-QUANTITY GENERATOR REQUIREMENTS

Facilities that generate 100 kilograms or less of all hazardous waste, 1 kilogram or less of acute hazardous waste, and 100 kilograms or less of acute hazardous waste spill cleanup debris per calendar month are exempt from most hazardous waste management requirements. These facilities are only required to determine which wastes are hazardous, and treat or dispose of wastes on-site or deliver wastes to an off-site treatment, storage, or disposal facility which meets one of the following criteria:

- Permitted under 40 CFR Part 270
- In interim status under Parts 270 and 265
- Authorized to manage hazardous waste by an authorized state
- Permitted, licensed, or registered by a state to manage municipal or industrial solid waste
- Facilities that beneficially use or reuse, or legitimately recycle or reclaim waste or treat waste prior to use, reuse, recycling, or reclamation.

Conditionally exempt small-quantity generators may accumulate hazardous waste on-site, but if at any time more than 1000 kilograms of hazardous waste, 1 kilogram of acute hazardous waste, or 100 kilograms of acute hazardous waste spill cleanup debris is accumulated, all of the wastes become subject to full regulation

Small-Quantity Generator Requirements

Facilities that generate greater than 100 kilograms (approximately 25 gallons, or 220 pounds) but less than 1000 kilograms (approximately 300 gallons, or 2200 pounds) per calendar month, or less than 1 kilogram of acute hazardous waste per month, are called small-quantity generators. *Small-quantity generators* are subject to many, but not all of the requirements previously discussed in this chapter.

One advantage to being a small-quantity generator is that hazardous waste may be accumulated on-site up to 180 days at an accumulation point. This accumulation time is extended to 270 days if the waste must be transported a distance of 200 miles or more to a TSD facility. However, at no time can the quantity accumulated on-site exceed 6000 kilograms.

Small quantity generators must determine which wastes are hazardous wastes, obtain EPA identification numbers, manifest shipments of hazardous waste, ship hazardous waste via transporters who have EPA identification numbers, and offer waste only to a permitted TSD facilities. Small-quantity generators must also comply with all pretransportation requirements concerning the packaging, labeling, marking, placarding, and documentation of hazardous waste shipments prior to shipment off-site.

Container Management

Containers used by small-quantity generators must be managed properly in accordance with the following requirements:

- On each container, the date upon which each period of accumulation begins must be clearly marked and visible for inspection. Each container must also be marked with the words "Hazardous Waste."
- Containers used to accumulate waste must be in good condition (e.g., no severe rusting or apparent structural defects). A container that begins to leak must immediately have its contents either transferred to another container or the leaking container must be overpacked in a salvage drum.
- The waste being placed in the container must be compatible with the container.
- A container holding hazardous waste must always be closed during storage, except when it is necessary to add or remove waste. Containers must not be stored or handled in a manner that may cause them to rupture or leak.
- Areas where containers are stored must be inspected at least weekly looking for leaks and for deterioration caused by corrosion or other factors. A container not in good condition must have its contents transferred to a container that is in good condition or the container must be overpacked in a salvage drum.
- Incompatible wastes, or incompatible wastes and materials, must not be placed in the same container if the placement could lead to a hazardous chemical reaction. Hazardous waste must not be placed in a unwashed container that previously held an incompatible waste or material.
- Storage containers holding a hazardous waste that is incompatible with any waste or other materials stored nearby must be separated from the other materials or protected by means of a dike, berm, or wall.

Tank Management

Small-quantity generators may accumulate hazardous waste on-site in tanks if the procedures and precautions described below are followed:

Precautions must be taken to prevent reactions within tanks that:

- Generate extreme heat or pressure, fire or explosions, or violent reactions.
- Produce uncontrolled toxic mists, fumes, dusts, or gases in sufficient quantities to threaten human health or the environment.
- Produce uncontrolled flammable fumes or gases in sufficient quantities to pose a risk of fire or explosions.
- Damage the structural integrity of the tank system or facility.
- Through other like means threaten human health or the environment.

Hazardous wastes or treatment reagents must not be placed in a tank if they could cause the tank or its inner liner to rupture, leak, corrode, or fail. All uncovered tanks must maintain at least two feet of freeboard unless the generator has installed a containment structure such as a dike or trench, or a diversion structure such as a backup tank with sufficient capacity to contain at least the volume of the top two feet of waste in the holding tank.

If hazardous waste is continuously fed into a tank, the tank must be equipped with some type of device that may be used to stop the flow. Examples of these devices include waste feed cutoff systems and bypass systems which divert flow to backup tanks.

Tank Inspection

Small-quantity generators who accumulate hazardous waste in tanks must also inspect those tanks regularly. Discharge control equipment such as waste feed cut-off systems, by-pass systems, and drainage systems must be inspected at least once per operating day. Any data which is gathered from monitoring equipment such as pressure and temperature gauges must also be inspected daily to ensure the tank is being operated in accordance with its design. The level of waste in the tank must be checked daily to ensure two feet of freeboard is maintained within the tank.

Small quantity generators must also conduct weekly inspections of tank construction materials, dikes and containment system construction materials, and the area immediately surrounding the tank. The purpose of these inspections is to detect corrosion, leaking fixtures or seams, erosion, and any obvious signs of leakage such as wet spots or dead vegetation.

Tank Closure

If a small-quantity generator's tank or facility is closed, all hazardous waste within the tank, discharge control equipment, and discharge confinement structure must be removed and disposed of properly.

Special Requirements for Ignitable, Reactive, and Incompatible Wastes

Do not place ignitable or reactive waste in a tank system unless the resulting substance going into the tank no longer meets the definition of ignitable or reactive either before or immediately after it is placed into the tank, the waste is stored or treated in such a way that it is protected from any material or condition that may cause the waste to ignite or react, or the tank is used solely for emergencies. Additionally, precautions must be taken to prevent incompatible chemical reactions such as those identified earlier in this section.

Never place hazardous waste in a tank system that has not been decontaminated and that previously held an incompatible waste or material. Never place incompatible wastes or incompatible waste or materials in the same tank unless incompatible chemical reactions are prevented.

The appropriate parts of the NFPA's 1977 or 1981 edition of *Flammable and Combustible Liquids Code* (Tables 2-1 through 2-6) must be reviewed to ensure protective distances are maintained between tanks and any public ways, public streets, public alleys, and any adjoining property lines that can be built upon. The distances specified in this publication range from 5 to 1400 feet and depend on the type of tank, the size of the tank, whether fire control equipment is available, the stability of the liquids in the tank, and the flashpoint of the liquids in the tank.

Emergency Preparedness and Prevention

The following safety and emergency equipment must be available to small-quantity generators unless it can be demonstrated to EPA that none of the hazards posed by the waste requires a particular kind of equipment. The equipment must be tested and maintained as necessary to assure its proper operation in time of emergency.

- An internal communications or alarm system capable of providing immediate emergency instruction (either voice or signal) to facility personnel. Whenever hazardous waste is being handled, all personnel involved in the operation must have immediate access to an internal alarm or emergency communication device, either directly or through visual or voice contact with another employee.
- A device, such as a telephone (immediately available at the accumulation point) or a hand-held two-way radio, capable of summoning emergency assistance from local police departments, fire departments, or state or local emergency response teams.
- Portable fire extinguishers, fire control equipment (including special extinguishing equipment, such as that using foam, inert gas, or dry chemicals), spill control equipment, and decontamination equipment.
- Water at adequate volume and pressure to supply water hose streams, or foam producing equipment, or automatic sprinklers, or water spray systems.

The following arrangements must be attempted to be made with local authorities (as appropriate for the type of waste handled and the potential need for the services of these organizations). Where the authorities decline to enter into such agreements, such refusals must be documented.

- Arrangements to familiarize local police, fire departments, and emergency response teams with the layout of the facility, properties of hazardous waste handled at the facility and associated hazards, places where facility personnel would normally be working, entrances to and roads inside the facility, and possible evacuation routes. Where more than one police or fire department might respond to an emergency, agreements must be made designating primary emergency authority to a specific police and a specific fire department, and agreements should be made with any others to provide support to the primary emergency authority.
- Agreements with state emergency response teams, emergency response contractors, and equipment suppliers.
- Arrangements to familiarize local hospitals with the properties of hazardous waste handled at the facility and the types of injuries or illnesses that could result from fires, explosions, or releases at the facility.

At all times there must be at least one employee either on the premises or on call with the responsibility for coordinating all emergency response measures. This is the emergency coordinator. The emergency coordinator or his designee must respond to any emergencies that arise. The applicable responses are as follows:

- In the event of a fire, call the fire department or attempt to extinguish the fire using a fire extinguisher.
- In the event of a spill, contain the flow of hazardous waste to the extent possible, and as soon as is practicable, clean up the hazardous waste and any contaminated materials or soil.
- In the event of a fire, explosion, or other release that could threaten human health outside the facility or when it is known that a spill has reached surface water, the emergency coordinator must immediately notify the National Response Center (800-424-8802). The report must include the following information:
    The generator's name, address, and U.S. EPA Identification Number;
    Date, time, and type of incident (spill or fire, for example);
    The quantity and type of hazardous waste involved in the incident;
    The extent of injuries, if any; and
    The estimated quantity and disposition of recovered materials, if any.
- Next to the telephones near where hazardous waste is accumulated, the following information must be posted:
    Name and telephone number of the emergency coordinator
    Location of fire extinguishers, spill control equipment, and fire alarms
    Telephone number of the nearest fire department

Recordkeeping Requirements

Small-quantity generators must keep copies of waste analyses, inspection reports, manifests, and exception reports for a period of at least 3 years or longer if needed to comply with state or local requirements. Small quantity generators are exempt from the requirement to submit biennial reports to EPA.

WASTE MINIMIZATION AND SEGREGATION

Waste Minimization

The 1984 Solid and Hazardous Waste Act (HSWA) amendments to RCRA dictate that, whenever feasible, the generation of hazardous waste is to be reduced or eliminated as expeditiously as possible.

EPA defines *waste minimization* as the reduction, to the extent feasible, of hazardous waste that is subsequently treated, stored, and disposed of. Waste minimization includes any source reduction or recycling activity undertaken by a generator that results in either the reduction of the total volume or quantity of hazardous waste, or the reduction of toxicity of hazardous waste, or both, so long as the reduction is consistent with the goal of minimizing the present and future threat to human health and the environment.

EPA has not, thus far, issued mandatory standards for waste minimization. Rather, EPA allows the waste generator to determine the most practical method of waste minimization according to the generator's unique circumstances. Nevertheless, each generator must certify on the manifest that a program is in place on-site to reduce the volume and toxicity of waste generated to the degree that the generator has been determined to be economically practicable, and the generator has selected the practicable method of treatment, storage, or disposal currently available that minimizes the present and future threat to human health and the environment.

A generator must describe in his biennial report the efforts undertaken during the year to reduce the volume and the toxicity of waste generated. Small-quantity generators certify on the manifest that they have made a good faith effort to minimize the generation of hazardous waste and have selected the best waste management method that is available and that they can afford.

EPA issued a proposed pollution prevention policy statement in January 1989 which has broad emphasis on source reduction and recycling of all pollutants, including hazardous waste. The proposed policy encourages organizations, facilities, and individuals to fully utilize source reduction techniques in order to reduce risks to public health, safety, welfare, and the environment, and as a second preference, to use environmentally sound recycling to achieve these same goals. Source reduction of pollutants and hazardous waste can be achieved through input or material substitution, product reformation, process modification, improved housekeeping, and on-site, closed-loop recycling.

EPA has also issued a *Draft Guidance to Hazardous Waste Generators on the Elements of a Waste Minimization Program* which is provided in Figure 3.4. EPA believes an effective waste minimization program should contain the following elements:

- top management support
- characterization of waste generation
- periodic waste minimization assessments
- a cost allocation system
- encouragement of technology transfer
- program evaluation

The main ideas behind waste minimization are toxicity and volume reduction and material substitution. *Toxicity reduction* means reducing the degree of hazard associated with the raw material which consequently reduces the degree of hazard of the waste. *Material substitution* means the use of lesser or even nontoxic materials.

Toxicity Reduction

The following example is an illustration of toxicity reduction. Certain solvents are typically used for degreasing various metal parts. Methylene chloride, a commonly used degreasing solvent, is considered to be a carcinogen. By substituting a noncarcinogenic degreasing solvent such as mineral spirits, which is less toxic than methylene chloride, the raw material as well as the waste may be less hazardous.

Hazardous waste minimization can also be accomplished by substituting water-based, heavy metal-free paints for solvent-based paints containing metals such as lead or chromium. Paints that do not contain heavy metals are generally less toxic than those with heavy metals. Water-based, heavy metal-free paint may not be considered hazardous waste by RCRA because the waste paint would not be considered toxic due to the absence of heavy metals, and the waste paint would not be considered ignitable due to the absence of flammable solvents.

Volume Reduction

Volume reduction is another approach to waste minimization. Reduction of the volume of hazardous waste generated begins at the point where the raw material is first used. By taking and using no more than is absolutely necessary, the amount of waste generated will be kept to a minimum.

One way to reduce the volume of hazardous waste generated is to avoid mixing hazardous and nonhazardous waste. As discussed in Hazardous Waste, beginning on page 9, when hazardous and nonhazardous wastes are combined, the resulting mixture is classified as hazardous waste. Thus, by taking measures to ensure that only hazardous wastes are accumulated in a dedicated container, the generation of excessive amounts of waste is precluded.

An alternative to chemically stripping parts is dry paint stripping with plastic media, that is, bead blasting. Bead blasting is a dry, mildly abrasive substitute for paint-removing solvents. Because most of the plastic media is recycled, this method only produces small amounts of spent media and paint solids. This is one of a number of technologies that can substantially reduce the volume of hazardous waste generated.

A common method used to reduce the volume of hazardous waste that must be sent off-site for treatment, storage or disposal is solvent reclamation through recycling on-site. Recycling of solvents typically involves the operation of a distillation machine that produces "clean" solvent and a hazardous waste residue. Not only is the residue substantially reduced in volume because the reusable solvent has been removed from it, but also the residue is often a solid or semisolid material which is much safer to transport for further treatment, storage, and disposal. Recycling is practical for a variety of materials such as paint thinner, fingerprint remover, and other solvents.

Waste Segregation

Mixing dissimilar wastes may make a waste stream more difficult or impossible to recycle. Therefore, by segregating waste, you may make each segregated waste stream more amenable to recycling or recovery. The proper segregation of hazardous wastes also affects the costs associated with treatment or disposal. Treatment and disposal cost are generally lowest when similar wastes are segregated depending on how they will be treated, stored, or disposed of after the containers have been filled. For example, wastes banned from land disposal should not be mixed with wastes that may be land disposed because the entire mixture would then be subject to the land disposal restrictions.

Even though they may be chemically compatible, flammable and halogenated solvents should not be mixed together. Flammable solvents, if the heat value or BTU rating is high enough, are often burned in cement kilns as hazardous waste fuel. Costs for this type of disposal are relatively low. Halogenated solvents such as 1,1,1-trichloroethane or Freon® may be recovered in a distillation unit and then reused, so disposal costs are lowered since a lower volume of waste is actually disposed of. However, if the chlorinated solvents are mixed with the flammable solvent, the resulting mixture may not be able to be burned for its fuel value due to the presence of halogens (which will be released as hydrochloric or hydrofluoric acid), and it becomes more difficult and expensive to recover the halogenated solvents in such a mixture through distillation.

Proper hazardous waste segregation is also very important from a safety point of view. Many hazardous wastes, when mixed with other wastes or materials, can produce effects which can affect human health and the environment. These effects include the generation of heat or pressure; the generation of toxic dusts, fumes, mists, or gases; and violent reactions, fires, and explosions.

Waste segregation is also one means of waste minimization. If hazardous waste is mixed with a non-hazardous waste, the resulting mixture is classified as hazardous (refer to Hazardous Waste, beginning on page 9). Thus, by segregating wastes, you can help diminish the generation of excess hazardous waste.

ENVIRONMENTAL PROTECTION AGENCY

(OSWER-FR-3421-1)

Draft Guidance to Hazardous Waste Generators on the Elements of a Waste Minimization Program

AGENCY: Environmental Protection Agency (EPA).
ACTION: Draft guidance and request for comment.

SUMMARY: Comments are being solicited on the following document, entitled *Draft Guidance to Hazardous Waste Generators on the Elements of a Waste Minimization Program.* This guidance was developed to assist hazardous waste generators in complying with the certification requirements of sections 3002(b) and 3005(h) of the Solid Waste Disposal Act, as amended by the Resource Conservation and Recovery Act (RCRA) and the Hazardous and Solid Waste Amendments of 1984 (HSWA), which became effective on September 1, 1985.

An effective waste minimization program as viewed by the Agency should have the following basic elements: (1) Top Management Support; (2) Characterization of Waste Generation; (3) Periodic Waste Minimization Assessments; (4) A Cost Allocation System; (5) Encouragement of Technology Transfer, and (6) Program Evaluation. While these elements provide guidance to generators on how a minimization program for hazardous waste may be structured, the Agency believes that they are equally valid for the design of a multi-media source reduction and recycling program. This guidance is consistent with EPA's belief that facilities should have broad pollution prevention programs with the goal of preventing or reducing wastes, substances, discharges, and/or emissions to all environmental media—air, land, surface water, and ground water.

Related Action: EPA published in the **Federal Register**, on January 26, 1989 (54 FR 3845), a proposed policy statement on source reduction and recycling. This policy commits the Agency to a preventive strategy to reduce or eliminate the generation of environmentally-harmful pollutants which may be released to the air, land, surface water or ground water. It further proposes to incorporate this preventive strategy into EPA's overall mission to protect human health and the environment by making source reduction a priority for every aspect of Agency decision-making and planning, with environmentally-sound recycling

as a second priority over treatment and disposal. Today's draft guidance is an example of the application of this policy in the RCRA program for hazardous waste.

DATES: EPA urges interested parties to comment on this draft notice in writing. The deadline for submitting written comments is September 11, 1989.

ADDRESSES: All comments must be submitted (original and two copies) to: EPA RCRA Docket (room SE-201) (mail code OS—305), 401 "M" Street, SW., Washington, DC 20460. Place the docket number #F-88-WMPP-FFFFF, on your comments.

FOR FURTHER INFORMATION CONTACT:
James Lounsbury, Office of Solid Waste, (202) 382-4807 or RCRA Hotline (800-424-9346).

Draft Guidance to Hazardous Waste Generators on the Elements of a Waste Minimization Program

I. Purpose
The purpose of today's notice is to provide non-binding guidance to generators of regulated hazardous wastes on what constitutes a "program in place" to comply with the certification requirements of sections 3002(b) and 3005(h) of the Solid Waste Disposal Act, as amended by the Resource Conservation and Recovery Act (RCRA) and the Hazardous and Solid Waste Amendments of 1984 (HSWA). Such certifications require generators to implement programs to reduce the volume and toxicity of hazardous wastes generated to the extent economically practicable. This guidance is intended to fulfill a commitment made by EPA in its 1986 report to Congress entitled, *Minimization of Hazardous Waste.*[1]

II. Background
With the passage of the HSWA, Congress established a national policy declaring the importance of reducing or eliminating the generation of hazardous waste. Specifically, section 1003(b) states:

The Congress hereby declares it to be a national policy of the United States that, wherever feasible, the generation of hazardous waste is to be reduced or eliminated as expeditiously as possible. Waste that is nevertheless generated should be treated, stored, or disposed of so as to minimize present and future threat to human health and the environment.

In this declaration, Congress established a clear priority for reducing or eliminating the generation of hazard-

ous wastes (a concept referred to as waste minimization) over managing wastes that were "nevertheless" generated.

EPA believes that hazardous waste minimization means the reduction, to the extent feasible, of hazardous waste that is generated prior to treatment, storage or disposal of the waste. It is defined as any source reduction or recycling activity that results in either: (1) Reduction of total volume of hazardous waste; (2) reduction of toxicity of hazardous waste; or (3) both, as long as that reduction is consistent with the general goal of minimizing present and future threats to human health and the environment.[2]

Waste minimization can result in significant benefits for industry. EPA believes an effective waste minimization program will contribute to:

(1) Minimizing quantities of regulated hazardous waste generated, thereby reducing waste management and compliance costs;
(2) Improving product yields;
(3) Reducing or eliminating inventories and releases of "hazardous chemicals" reportable under Title III of the Superfund Amendments and Reauthorization Act; and/or
(4) Lowering Superfund, corrective action and toxic tort liabilities.

Besides establishing the national policy, Congress also enacted several provisions in HSWA for implementing hazardous waste minimization. These included a generator certification on hazardous waste manifests and permits for treatment, storage, or disposal of hazardous waste. RCRA 3002(b). These certifications (effective September 1, 1985) require generators certify two conditions: That (1) the generator of the hazardous waste has a program in place to reduce the volume or quantity and toxicity of such waste to the degree determined by the generator to be economically practicable; and (2) the proposed method of treatment, storage or disposal is that practicable method currently available to the generator which minimizes the present and future threat to human health and the environment.

---

[1] FR 44683 (12/11/86), Notices of Availability of the Report in Congress.

[2] Hazardous waste minimization involves volume or toxicity reduction through either a source reduction or recycling technique and results in the reduction of risks to human health and the environment. The transfer of hazardous consitituents from one environmental medium to another does not constitute waste minimization. Neither would concentration conducted solely for reducing volume unless, for example, concentration of the waste allowed for recovery of useful constituents prior to treatment and disposal. Likewise, dilution as a means of toxicity reduction would not be considered waste minimization, unless later recycling steps were involved.

FIGURE 3.4
Draft Guidance to Hazardous Waste Generators of the Elements of a Waste Minimization Program

In addition, Congress also added a new provision in 1984 that requires hazardous waste generators to identify in their biennial reports to EPA (or the State): (1) The efforts undertaken during the year to reduce the volume and toxicity of waste generated; and (2) the changes in volume and toxicity actually achieved in comparison with previous years, to the extent such information is available prior to 1984 (RCRA 3002 (a)(6)).

Today's notice provides non-binding guidance to hazardous waste generators in response to the certification requirements in HSWA. Specifically, it addresses the first of the certification conditions that states that, "the generator of the hazardous waste has a program in place to reduce the volume or quantity and toxicity of such waste to the degree determined to be economically practicable."

EPA is not, however, providing guidance on the determination of the phrase "economically practicable". As congress indicated in its accompanying report to HSWA[3] the term "economically practicable" is to be defined and determined by the generator and is not subject to subsequent reevaluation by EPA. The generator of the hazardous waste, for purposes of this certification, has the flexibility to determine what is economically practicable for the generator's circumstances. Whether this determination is made for all of its operations or on a site-specific basis is for the generator to decide.

EPA has received numerous inquiries on what constitutes a waste minimization program. In today's notice EPA is providing draft guidance to hazardous waste generators on what the Agency believes are the basic elements of a waste minimization program.

EPA believes that today's guidance may provide direction to large quantity and small quantity generators in fulfilling their manifest certification requirement. Small quantity generators, while not subject to the same "program in place" certification requirement as large quantity generators, have to certify that they have "made a good faith effort to minimize" their waste generation.

The elements discussed here reflect the results of agency analyses conducted over the last several years and extensive interaction with private and public

sector waste minimization program managers. EPA believes that an effective waste minimization program should include each of the general elements discussed below, although EPA realizes that some of these elements may be implemented in different ways depending on the preferences of individual firms.

A. *Top Management Support.* Top management support should ensure that waste minimization is a company-wide effort. There are many ways to accomplish this goal. Some of the methods described below may be suitable for some firms and not others. However, some combination of these techniques should be used by every firm to demonstrate top management support.

—Make waste minimization a company policy. Put this policy in writing and distribute it to all departments. Make it each person's responsibility to identify opportunities for minimizing waste. Reinforce the policy in day-to-day operations, at meetings and other company functions.

—Set specific goals for reducing the volume or toxicity of waste streams.

—Commit to implementing recommendations identified through assessments, evaluations or other means.

—Designate a waste minimization coordinator at each facility to ensure effective implementation of the program.

—Publicize success stories. It will trigger additional ideas.

—Reward employees that identify cost-effective waste minimization opportunities.

—Train employees on aspects of waste minimization that relate to their job. Include all departments, such as those in product design, capital planning, production operations, and maintenance.

B. *Characterization of Waste Generation.* Maintain a waste accounting system to track the types, amounts and hazardous constituents of wastes and the dates they are generated.

C. *Periodic Waste Minimization Assessments.* Track materials that eventually wind up as waste, from the loading dock to the point at which they become a waste.

—Identify opportunities at all points in a process where materials can be prevented from becoming a waste (for ex-

ample, by using less material, recycling materials in the process, finding substitutes, or making equipment changes). Individual processes or facilities should be reviewed periodically. Larger companies may find it useful to establish a team of independent experts.

—Determine the true costs of the waste. Calculate the costs of the materials found in the waste stream based on the purchase price of those materials. Calculate the cost of managing the wastes that are generated, including costs for personnel, recordkeeping, transportation, liability insurance, pollution control equipment, treatment and disposal and others.

D. *A cost allocation system.* Departments and managers should be charged "fully loaded" waste management costs for the wastes they generate, factoring in liability, compliance and oversight costs.

E. *Encourage Technology Transfer.* Seek or exchange technical information on waste minimization from other parts of your company, from other firms, trade associations, State and university technical assistance programs or professional consultants. Many techniques have been evaluated and documented that may be useful in your facility.

F. *Program Evaluation.* Conduct a periodic review of program effectiveness. Use these reviews to provide feedback and identify potential areas for improvement.

Although waste minimization practices have demonstrated their usefulness and benefits to those generators that have implemented such programs, many others still have not practiced waste minimization. Today's guidance on effective waste minimization practices may help encourage regulated entities to investigate waste minimization alternatives, implement new programs, or upgrade existing programs. Although the approaches described above are directed toward minimizing hazardous solid waste, they are equally valid for design of multi-media source reduction and recycling programs.

EPA requests comments on all aspects of this guidance.

Date: June 2, 1989.
William K. Reilly
Administrator
(FR Doc. 89-13845 Filed 6-9-89: 8:45 am)
BILLING CODE 6560-50-M

---

[3]U.S. Rep No. 98-284, 98th Cong., 1st Sess. (1983)

FIGURE 3.4
Draft Guidance to Hazardous Waste Generators of the Elements of a Waste Minimization Program (continued)

EPA Compatibility Table

EPA has published a list of potentially incompatible wastes, waste components and materials along with the harmful consequences of mixing those materials together (refer to Table 3.2). This list does not include every possible hazardous chemical reaction, but should be used as a guide in packaging and storing these materials. The list indicates the potential consequences of the mixing of a Group A material with a Group B material.

For example, mixing any Group 2-A waste, which include reactive metals and metal hydrides, with a Group 2-B waste, which include the Group 1-A alkaline and the Group 1-B acidic wastes, may produce a fire and explosion and the generation of flammable hydrogen gas. Mixing a Group 3-A waste, which include alcohols and water, with a Group 3-B waste, which encompass Groups 1-A, 1-B, and Group 3-B chemicals, may produce a fire, explosion, or the generation of flammable or toxic gases.

These compatibility listings and packaging guides should not be the only information used when packaging or accumulating waste chemicals. RCRA regulations require that wastes should be adequately analyzed by TSD facilities so uncontrolled substances or reactions do not occur. Pay close attention to any waste characterization data you receive on material reactivity and compatibility. There are also other sources of data that may help determine waste compatibility. Material Safety Data Sheets (MSDSs) contain a section devoted to chemical reactivity and incompatibility. The NFPA publishes a manual of hazardous chemical reactions which contains over 3500 documented dangerous chemical reactions.

SAFE PROCEDURES AND SAFETY EQUIPMENT FOR ALL GENERATORS

All personnel who handle, are occupationally exposed to, or manage hazardous waste should understand:

- where to go to obtain information about the hazards of the materials and wastes in their work environment,
- key terms to understand when assessing the degree of hazard, and
- what precautions to take to protect themselves from the hazards associated with hazardous materials and hazardous waste.

Worker health and safety at hazardous waste cleanup sites (Superfund, RCRA corrective action, and voluntary cleanup sites), at hazardous waste treatment, storage and disposal facilities, and during emergency response operations is regulated by the Occupational Safety and Health Administration (OSHA) in accordance with the Hazardous Waste Operations and Emergency Response rule promulgated in 29 CFR 1910.120. This rule requires employers to train emergency response and TSD facility personnel about the nature of the hazards associated with the wastes and how to protect themselves from those hazards.

Safety Information Sources

In order to protect themselves, personnel involved in hazardous waste management must first understand what hazards are posed by the materials and wastes in their work environment. There are a number of sources from which to obtain this information, beginning with the virgin material itself.

All OSHA hazardous chemicals must be labeled with an identity as used on the material safety data sheet and the physical and health hazards associated with the chemical. Although there is no standard format, that is, the information is not marked in the same place from container to container, each container of hazardous material must be marked with certain information, the most important of which is any physical or health hazards associated with a hazardous chemical.

The OSHA hazard communication standard also requires employers to maintain MSDSs for each hazardous chemical on-site. MSDSs are fact sheets for a particular material and contain such information as the hazardous components of a mixture, physical hazards associated with the material, the most typical ways an individual could be exposed to that material, and first-aid procedures to follow if an individual is overexposed. It is important to note that the hazards of a waste may be greater or less than the hazards of the raw material(s) from which it was generated due to the presence of contaminated and potential synergistic effects. Although MSDSs are not required for hazardous wastes (which are exempt from the OSHA hazard communication standard), they are required for hazardous chemicals before they become hazardous wastes.

In addition to these sources, many reference materials are available that provide additional health and safety information on a wide variety of hazardous materials. Appendix B presents a list of common reference materials that present such information.

Personal Protective Equipment

Each generator should evaluate the hazards posed by the materials and wastes with which hazardous waste handlers work and prescribe the personal protective equipment (PPE) that best guards them against the hazards. However, it is the handler's responsibility to wear the prescribed PPE.

Hazardous waste handlers should always wear appropriate PPE, since contact with hazardous waste can lead to a variety of health disorders. When there is possible exposure to hazardous waste, the degree of hazard will be considered and the PPE appropriate to safeguard against the hazard posed by the waste should be prescribed.

Protective clothing provides varying degrees of partial and/or total body protection from chemical exposure, fire, minor blasts, or explosions. Such clothing ranges from gloves, aprons, leggings, and sleeve protectors to fully-encapsulating suits. Each type of protective clothing has a specific purpose, as well as limitations. Individual components of clothing and respiratory equipment must be assembled into an ensemble to provide the appropriate level of protection.

TABLE 3.2
EPA Compatibility Table

Group 1-A	Group 1-B	Group 2-A	Group 2-B
Acetylene sludge	Acid sludge	Aluminum	Any waste in Group
Alkaline caustic liquids	Acid and water	Beryllium	1-A or 1-B
Alkaline cleaner	Battery acid	Calcium	
Alkaline corrosive liquids	Chemical cleaners	Lithium	
Alkaline corrosive battery fluid	Electrolyte, acid	Magnesium	
Caustic wastewater	Etching acid liquid or solvent	Potassium	
Lime sludge and other corrosive	Pickling liquor and other corrosive	Sodium	
alkalies	acids	Zinc powder	
Lime wastewater	Spent acid	Other reactive metals and metal hydrides	
Lime and water	Spent mixed acid		
Spent caustic	Spent sulfuric acid		

Potential consequences: heat generation; violent reaction

Potential consequences: fire or explosion; generation of flammable hydrogen gas

Group 3-A	Group 3-B	Group 4-A	Group 4-B
Alcohols	Any concentrated waste in	Alcohols	Concentrated Group 1-A
Water	Group 1-A or 1-B	Aldehydes	or 1-B wastes
	Calcium	Halogenated hydrocarbons	Group 2-A wastes
	Lithium	Nitrated hydrocarbons	
	Metal hydrides,	Unsaturated hydrocarbons	
	Potassium	Other reactive organic	
	Other water-reactive waste	compounds and solvents	
	SO_2Cl_2, $SOCl_2$, PCl_2,		
	CH_3SiCl_3		

Potential consequences: fire, explosion, or heat generation; generation of flammable or toxic gases

Potential consequences: fire, explosion, or violent reaction

Group 5-A	Group 5-B	Group 6-A	Group 6-B
Spent cyanide and sulfide solutions	Group 1-B waste	Chlorates	Acetic acid and other
		Chlorine	organic acids
		Chlorites	Concentrated mineral
		Chromic acid	acids
		Hypochlorites	Group 2-A wastes
		Nitrates	Group 4-A wastes
		Nitric acid, fuming	Other flammable and
		Perchlorates	combustible wastes
		Permanganates	
		Peroxides	
		Other strong oxidizers	

Potential consequences: generation of toxic hydrogen cyanide or hydrogen sulfide gas

Potential consequences: fire, explosion, or violent reaction

Source: 40 CFR 264, Appendix V—Examples of Potentially Incompatible Waste

Gloves are not only meant to protect the hands but the forearms as well. No one type of glove can offer protection from all hazardous materials and wastes. For example, a butyl glove will withstand chemical attack from acetone — a common cleaning solvent — for days but will decompose in less than an hour when exposed to paint thinner. Eventually, after repeated exposure to hazardous materials and wastes, a glove will degrade to the point that it no longer has the ability to offer protection to your hands and forearms.

Like gloves, no one type of boot can provide unlimited protection. If hazardous waste handlers work around solvents, acids, or bases; in a wet or slippery environment; or in an extremely cold environment and standard operating procedures do not call for special protective boots, handlers should discuss the situation with their shop supervisors or safety director.

OSHA standards require that workers be provided with suitable eye protection. To be effective, the eyewear must be of the appropriate type for the hazard encountered and must be properly fitted. Eye protection should be reasonably comfortable, fit snugly, and not hinder normal movement.

Over half of the injuries to workers wearing eye protection result from objects or chemicals going around or under the protector. Face masks preclude this consequence by protecting the entire face.

Respirators are designed to remove specific contaminants from the air before you inhale them. Filtration is accomplished by filters, cartridges, or canisters that remove airborne contamination. For each type of respirator, there are a variety of air-purifying filters, cartridges, or canisters designed to protect you against specific contaminants. Keep in mind that some contaminants cannot be removed by air-purifying respirators.

In situations where contaminants cannot be removed by an air-purifying respirator, a self-contained breathing apparatus (SCBA) must be used. SCBAs offer protection against most types and levels of airborne contaminants by providing clean air to a face piece from an air cylinder carried on your back. SCBAs must be used in situations:

- that are immediately dangerous to life and health
- where there is a high concentration of vapors or
- where there is poor ventilation or an oxygen deficiency, such as when performing maintenance operations in jet fuel storage tanks.

In general, waste paints and solvents necessitate face and hand protection to guard against the dermatitis that could result from contact with the waste. Waste acids and bases can pose a greater threat with just minimal contact. Therefore, in addition to wearing face and hand protection, eye goggles, a splash apron, and safety boots should be worn to guard against the corrosive effects of these types of wastes.

PPE is only effective when used properly. Hazardous waste handlers who are required to wear PPE should practice putting on and removing all ensembles at least annually. Additionally, all waste handlers must be trained in the operation and use of their PPE, including maintenance, decontamination, emergency procedures, and self-rescue in the event of equipment failure.

TABLE 3.3
Recordkeeping Requirements

Type	Retention Period	Regulatory Citation
Generators		
Manifest*	3 years	262.40(a)
Biennial report*	3 years	262.40(b)
Exception report*	3 years	262.40(b)
Test results, waste analysis data	3 years	262.40(c)
Hazardous waste determinations	3 years	262.40(c)
Land disposal notices, certifications, demonstrations, and waste analysis data	5 years	268.7(a)(7)
Transporters		
Manifest	3 years	263.22(a)
Shipping papers for rail, water shipments	3 years	263.22(b)
Manifest for shipment out of U.S.	3 years	263.22(c)
Off-Site Treatment, Storage, and Disposal Facilities		
Manifest	3 years	265.71(a)
Shipping papers for rail, water shipment	3 years	265.71(b)
Operating record	Until closure of facility, except as noted in regulations	265.73
On-Site Treatment, Storage, and Disposal Facilities		
Operating record	Until closure of facility, except as noted in regulations	265.73

*—Off-site shipments only

Safe Work and Emergency Procedures

All personnel handling hazardous waste should understand how to conduct their work safely both under normal conditions and in an emergency. Personnel must be trained in how to protect themselves and everyone around them from hazardous situations that could lead to fires or explosions.

There are three essential components to causing and sustaining a fire: fuel, oxygen, and heat. Keeping these items separate can prevent fire from starting and if one element is taken away, a fire cannot continue and will die out. Recently, reactive materials were added to this triad as a fourth component. A fire can be caused and/or sustained by substituting something that is reactive with any of the components in this triangle.

Whenever someone encounters a fire on-site, that person should immediately report the incident and obtain help. In the event of an explosion, everyone must act quickly. Since an explosion can lead to other explosions or fires, personnel must immediately respond by:

- warning those who may be threatened by subsequent fires or explosions, and
- contacting appropriate personnel for emergency assistance.

Everyone working at accumulation points must become familiar with the facility's contingency/emergency response plan so they can respond effectively to fires and explosions at the facility. Chapter 9 of this handbook presents details on how to respond to fires, explosions, and hazardous waste releases.

TABLE 3.4
Report Requirements

Generators		
Type	Due	Regulatory Citation
Biennial report*	March 1 of even-numbered years	262.41(a)
Exception report*	45 Days following initiation of manifest	262.40(b)
Exporting hazardous waste	At least 4 weeks prior to first shipment of calendar year	262.50(b)
Waste analysis plan	30 days prior to on-site treatment	268.7(a)(4)
Additional Reporting	As determined by EPA Administrator	262.43
Transporters		
Spill incident report	Within 15 Days following incident	40 CFR 263.30(c)(2) 49 CFR 171.16
Off-Site Treatment, Storage, and Disposal Facilities		
Biennial report	March 1 of even-numbered years	265.75
Sig. manifest discrepancies	Within 15 days of receiving waste	265.72
Unmanifested waste report	Within 15 days of receiving waste	265.76
Additional reports (releases, fires, explosions, ground-water contamination and monitoring data, closure)	As noted in regulations	265.77
On-Site Treatment, Storage, and Disposal Facilities		
Annual report	March 1 for preceding calendar year	265.75
Additional reports (releases, fires, explosions, ground-water contamination and monitoring data, closure)	As noted in regulations	265.77

*—Off-site shipments only

Chapter 4
Hazardous Waste Manifests

This chapter provides instructions for compliance with EPA and DOT requirements for manifesting hazardous waste. This chapter includes information on the manifest system, selection of the appropriate manifest, how to complete a hazardous waste manifest, land disposal notifications that must accompany the manifest, and records and reports associated with the manifest.

The hazardous waste manifest serves three purposes. First, the manifest is used as a tracking device to trace shipments of hazardous waste. The manifest identifies who generated the waste, who transported the waste, and who treated, stored, or disposed of the waste. Consequently the manifest identifies who is responsible for the waste from point of generation through ultimate disposal.

Second, the manifest provides information during transport emergencies. Drivers are required to keep the manifest with them in the cab of their vehicles either in their immediate reach, or in a holder mounted on the inside of the door on the driver's side of the vehicle.

In the event of an accident or an inspection, information on the manifest may be used to identify the hazardous waste loaded on the vehicle and emergency procedures to follow to control a fire, spill, or explosion involving the hazardous wastes.

Finally, the manifest is used as a basis for recordkeeping and reporting. Information needed for a biennial report may be obtained from the manifest. Additionally, a copy of a manifest must be submitted to EPA in case a shipment of hazardous wastes is not received by the designated TSD facility, or if there are significant discrepancies between what was shipped and what was received by the TSD facility.

THE MANIFEST SYSTEM

No person may transport or offer for transport hazardous waste without the proper hazardous waste manifest unless:

- the waste is generated by a generator of 100 kilograms (approximately one-half 55-gallon drum) or less of hazardous waste per calendar month or 1 kilogram (approximately 1 quart) or less of acutely hazardous waste per month (i.e., a conditionally exempt small-quantity generator), or
- the waste is produced by a generator of greater than 100 kilograms but less than 1000 kilograms of hazardous waste per month (i.e., a small-quantity generator) and the waste is reclaimed under a contractual reclamation agreement.

A manifest is the shipping document that identifies the hazardous waste generator, transporter, and TSD facility. It also describes the contents of the waste shipment.

When a waste shipment leaves your facility, the entire manifest to the signature of the transporter (blocks 1-18) must be completed. One copy of this "open" manifest must be kept on file at the facility that generated the waste and the remaining copies must be provided to the transporter. The open manifest accompanies the transporter to the designated TSD facility. The transporter may also deliver the hazardous waste to additional transporters who will move the waste to the designated TSD facility. The owner or operator of the TSD facility then signs the manifest signifying receipt of the shipment. A copy of this signed "closed" manifest is then returned to the waste generator to complete the paper trail. If the transporter is unable to deliver the hazardous waste to the designated TSD facility or to an alternate facility designated on the manifest, the generator must designate another permitted facility or in-struct the transporter to return the waste.

Enough duplicate copies of the manifest should be completed by the hazardous waste generator in order to provide the generator, each transporter, and the designated facility with one copy for their records, plus an additional copy to be returned to the generator. Each closed manifest must be retained on-site for at least 3 years from the date the waste was accepted by the initial transporter.

Many states have adopted their own versions of the manifest, and require generators to submit manifest copies to the state. States may also require additional information on the manifest. The publication *State Hazardous Waste Regulations Differing from Federal Requirements*, available through Environmental Resource Center, provides information on state manifesting requirements.

Rail and Water Shipments

When hazardous wastes are shipped in bulk solely by water, the generator must send three copies of the signed and dated manifest directly to the designated TSD facility. If the hazardous waste is exported solely by water, three copies must be sent to the last water transporter who will handle the waste in the United States.

When hazardous wastes are shipped via rail from the generator to the TSD facility, three copies of the signed and dated manifest are to be sent to:

the next nonrail transporter, if any, and
the designated facility if transported solely by rail, or
if the waste is exported, the last rail transporter to handle
    the waste in the United States.

Hazardous Waste Imports and Exports

In order to export hazardous waste, the generator must notify EPA of the intent to export in writing at least 60 days before the initial shipment. The notification of intent to export hazardous waste must include detailed information on the type, amount, disposition, and handling of the hazardous waste. EPA then notifies the receiving country and any transit countries. The receiving country *must* agree to accept the waste. If the country agrees, EPA will send the generator a copy of the EPA Acknowledgment of Consent form. The generator must attach a copy of this form to the hazardous waste manifest. In addition, the hazardous waste shipment must conform to the terms of the receiving country's written consent as reflected in the acknowledgment of consent form.

A generator that exports hazardous waste must include on the manifest the point of hazardous waste departure from the United States and must certify the shipment conforms to the terms in the acknowledgment of consent form. After exporting the waste, a generator will receive and must maintain on-site each written confirmation of delivery, which signifies that the waste has been received by the con-signee. A generator must also maintain a copy of the manifest signed by the transporter indicating date and place of departure from the United States.

Generators who export hazardous waste must submit annual reports to EPA's Office of International Activities no later than March 1. The report must include the following information:

- EPA identification number, name, and mailing and site address of the exporter (i.e., the generator exporting the waste)
- Calendar year covered by the report
- Name and site address of each consignee
- By consignee, for each hazardous waste exported:

    EPA hazardous waste number (from 40 CFR 261, Subpart C or D),
    DOT hazard class,
    Name and U.S. EPA ID number (where applicable) for each transporter used,
    Total amount of waste shipped, and
    Number of shipments pursuant to each notification.

- Except for hazardous waste produced by exporters of greater than 100 kilograms but less than 1000 kilograms in a calendar month (unless provided in a biennial report), in even numbered years:

    A description of the efforts undertaken during the year to reduce the volume and toxicity of waste generated, and
    A description of the changes in volume and toxicity of waste actually achieved during the year in comparison to previous years to the extent the information is available for years prior to 1984.

- A certification signed by the primary exporter which states:

    I certify under penalty of law that I have personally examined and am familiar with the information submitted in this and all attached documents, and that based on my inquiry of those individuals immediately responsible for obtaining the information, I believe that the submitted informations is true, accurate, and complete. I am aware that there are significant penalties for submitting false information, including the possibility of fine and imprisonment.

Copies of all export-related paperwork must be maintained on-site for at least 3 years from the date the hazardous waste was accepted by the initial transporter.

Importers of hazardous waste must prepare a manifest when the waste enters the customs territory of the United States. The manifest must be signed by the U.S. importer or his agent. In addition, the foreign generator's name and address and the importer's name, address, and EPA identification number are placed on the manifest in place of the generator's name, address, and EPA identification number.

MANIFEST SELECTION

Because different states may use different manifest forms, the RCRA regulations explain how to determine which state's manifest should be used. You must first determine whether or not the state to which the hazardous waste is being sent requires the use of its particular manifest. If the state to which the shipment is being manifested, that is, the consignment state, requires the use of its own manifest, the consignment state manifest must be used.

If the consignment state does not require a state manifest, but the state in which the waste was generated, that is, the generator state, requires its own manifest, the generator's state manifest must be used. The basic form and content of a state manifest is based on EPA's uniform hazardous waste manifest.

If neither the consignment state nor the generator's state requires the use of its own state manifest, then the uniform hazardous waste manifest may be used.

OMB Notice

In 1988, EPA renewed without change and extended the expiration date of the uniform manifest form to September 30, 1991. The new form includes a new expiration date and an Office of Management and Budget (OMB) burden statement. After June 30, 1989, all generators were required to use the new manifest form or overprint the new expiration date "9/30/91" over the old expiration date "9/30/88" and attach the burden disclosure statement. The following burden disclosure statement must be included with each uniform hazardous waste manifest, either on the form, in the instructions to the form, or accompanying the form:

Public reporting burden for this collection of information is estimated to average 37 minutes for generators, 15 minutes for transporters, and 10 minutes for treatment, storage, and disposal facilities. This includes time for reviewing instructions, gathering data, and completing and reviewing the form. Send comments regarding the burden estimate, including suggestions for reducing the burden to: Chief, Information Policy Branch, PM-223, U.S. Environmental Protection Agency, 401 M Street SW, Washington, DC 20460; and to the Office of Information and Regulatory Affairs, Office of Management and the Budget, Washington, DC 20503.

As of September 13, 1991, OMB was reviewing the manifest form once again and was expected to approve the existing form, with a new expiration date, for 3 more years without changes.

COMPLETION OF THE MANIFEST

There are three parts to a hazardous waste manifest. The top portion identifies the organizations that will be handling the waste; the middle portion identifies the shipment; and the bottom portion contains the signatures of the individuals who handled the waste. A copy of the current version of the uniform hazardous waste manifest is presented in Figure 4.1.

Instructions for Completion of the Manifest

Item 1. Generator's U.S. EPA ID Number and Manifest Document Number
Enter your facility's unique U.S. EPA identification number. Appendix A of this manual lists procedures for obtaining an EPA identification number.

Also enter your own unique five-digit number which you assign to this manifest. Many generators simply number each shipment consecutively. For example, 00001 would represent the first hazardous waste shipment from a generator for the year. Others use a Julian date which corresponds to the shipment date. For example, 90001 would represent a shipment on January 1, 1990. All five digits must be entered in this box.

Item 2. Page 1 of___.
Enter the total number of pages used to complete this manifest. If only the first page is used, enter "1." Continuation sheets must be used if more than four waste types are being shipped to the same TSD facility on the same shipment.

Item 3. Generator's Name and Mailing Address
Enter the name and mailing address of your facility. The address should be the mailing address for the location that will manage the returned manifest forms.

Item 4. Generator's Phone Number
Enter the phone number of an authorized person on-site who can be reached in the event of an emergency.

Item 5. Transporter 1 Company Name
Enter the company name of the first transporter who will transport the waste off-site.

Item 6. U.S. EPA ID Number
Enter the U.S. EPA identification number of the first transporter identified in Item 5.

Item 7. Transporter 2 Company Name
If a second transporter will be used to transport the waste to the designated TSD facility, enter the name of the second transporter. If more than two transporters are used, the additional transporters must be listed on the continuation sheet. Every transporter used between the generator and the designated facility must be listed.

Item 8. U.S. EPA ID Number
If a second transporter will be used, enter the second transporter's U.S. EPA identification number.

Item 9. Designated Facility Name and Site Address
Enter the company name and the site address of the facility you have designated to receive the hazardous waste listed on the manifest. The address must be the site address and cannot be a post office box or rural route number.

Please print or type *(Form designed for use on elite (12-pitch) typewriter)* *Form Approved OMB NO. 2050-0039 Expires 9-30-92*

GENERATOR

UNIFORM HAZARDOUS WASTE MANIFEST	1. Generator's US EPA ID No.	Manifest Document No.	2. Page 1 of	Information in the shaded areas is not required by Federal law.

3. Generator's Name and Mailing Address	A. State Manifest Document Number
	B. State Generator's ID
4. Generator's Phone ( )	
5. Transporter 1 Company Name / 6. US EPA ID Number	C. State Transporter's ID
	D. Transporter's Phone
7. Transporter 2 Company Name / 8. US EPA ID Number	E. State Transporter's ID
	F. Transporter's Phone
9. Designated Facility Name and Site Address / 10. US EPA ID Number	G. State Facility's ID
	H. Facility's Phone

11. US DOT Description *(Including Proper Shipping Name, Hazard Class, and ID Number)*	12. Containers No.	Type	13. Total Quantity	14. Unit Wt/Vol	Waste No.
a.					
b.					
c.					
d.					

J. Additional Descriptions for Materials Listed Above	K. Handling Codes for Wastes Listed Above

15. Special Handling Instructions and Additional Information

16. GENERATOR'S CERTIFICATION: I hereby declare that the contents of this consignment are fully and accurately described above by proper shipping name and are classified, packed, marked, and labeled, and are in all respects in proper condition for transport by highway according to applicable international and national government regulations

If I am a large quantity generator, I certify that I have a program in place to reduce the volume and toxicity of waste generated to the degree I have determined to be economically practicable and that I have selected the practicable method of treatment, storage, or disposal currently available to me which minimizes the present and future threat to human health and the environment; OR, if I am a small quantity generator, I have made a good faith effort to minimize my waste generation and select the best waste management method that is available to me and that I can afford.

Printed/Typed Name	Signature	*Month* *Day* *Year*

TRANSPORTER

17. Transporter 1 Acknowledgement of Receipt of Materials

Printed/Typed Name	Signature	*Month* *Day* *Year*

18. Transporter 2 Acknowledgement of Receipt of Materials

Printed/Typed Name	Signature	*Month* *Day* *Year*

FACILITY

19. Discrepancy Indication Space

20. Facility Owner or Operator: Certification of receipt of hazardous materials covered by this manifest except as noted in Item 19.

Printed/Typed Name	Signature	*Month* *Day* *Year*

EPA Form 8700-22 (Rev. 9-88) Previous editions are obsolete.

Figure 4.1
Uniform Hazardous Waste Manifest

TABLE 4.1
Type of Containers

Abbreviation	Type of Container
DM	Metal drums, barrels, kegs
DW	Wooden drums, barrels, kegs
DF	Fiberboard or plastic drums, barrels, kegs
TP	Portable tanks
TT	Cargo tanks (tank trucks)
TC	Tank cars
DT	Dump trucks
CY	Cylinders
CM	Metal boxes, cartons, cases (including roll-offs)
CW	Wooden boxes, cartons, cases
CF	Fiber or plastic boxes, cartons, cases
BA	Burlap, cloth, paper, or plastic bags

Item 10. U.S. EPA Identification Number
Enter the U.S. EPA identification number of the designated facility identified in Item 9.

Item 11. U.S. DOT Proper Shipping Name, Hazard Class, and DOT ID Number
Enter the best and most descriptive DOT proper shipping name, hazard class, and UN or NA DOT identification number. The Hazardous Materials Table and the appendix to the Hazardous Materials Table in 49 CFR 172 provides the information necessary to complete this item. The section titled How to Determine U.S. DOT description for Item 11 of the Manifest, beginning on page 58, identifies a procedure to follow to determine the proper shipping description for your waste. Use the continuation sheet if you need space for additional waste descriptions.

Item 12. Number and Type of Containers
Enter the number of containers for each waste. Also enter the type of containers by using the appropriate abbreviation from Table 4.1.

Item 13. Total Quantity
Enter the total quantity of waste described on each line.

Item 14. Unit of Measure
Enter the appropriate unit of measure for each waste listed in Item 13. Use Table 4.2 to identify the units of measure. Note that your waste must be measured either by weight or by volume.

Item 15. Special Handling Instructions
You may, but are not required, to use this space to indicate special transportation, treatment, storage, or disposal information or bill of lading information. For example, you may place the waste characterization or profile number assigned to your waste by your TSD facility in this space. If you are exporting the hazardous waste, you must enter the city and state where your wastes will depart from the United States in this space.

Item 16. Generator's Certification
The generator must read, sign by hand, and date the certification statement.

When the manifest is signed, the person signing it is legally certifying that:

- the shipment is fully and accurately described on the manifest,
- the containers are in proper condition for transport,
- a waste minimization program is in place at the facility, and
- the method of treatment, storage, or disposal is the best available to the generator.

If a mode of transportation different than highway is being used, cross out the word "highway" and insert the appropriate mode of transportations such as rail, water, or air. If rail, water, or air transportation of your waste will occur in addition to highway transportation, add the words "and rail," or "and water," or "and air" after the word "highway" in the certification.

If you are exporting the hazardous waste, add at the end of the first sentence of the certification the following words:

"and conforms to the terms of the EPA acknowledgment of consent to this shipment."

Item 17. Transporter 1 Acknowledgment of Receipt of Materials
(Completed by Transporter 1)
The first transporter must print or type the name of the person accepting the waste, sign, and date the manifest to acknowledge receipt of your shipment. You must obtain the handwritten signature of the first transporter before the waste is shipped off-site and retain this copy of the open manifest.

Transporters must then deliver the waste to the next designated transporter (if indicated in Item 7), the designated facility (as indicated in Item 9), an alternate facility designated by the generator, or a designated place outside the United States if you are exporting the hazardous waste.

TABLE 4.2
Units of Measure

Abbreviation	Units of Measure
G	Gallons (liquids only)
P	Pounds
T	Tons (2000 pounds)
Y	Cubic Yards
L	Liters (liquids only)
K	Kilograms
M	Metric tons (1000 kilograms)
N	Cubic meters

Item 18. Transporter 2 Acknowledgement of Receipt of Materials
(Completed by Transporter 2)
If more than one transporter is used, the second transporter must print or type the name of the person accepting the waste, sign, and date the manifest to acknowledge receipt of your shipment from the first transporter.

Item 19. Discrepancy Indication Space
(Completed by the Designated TSD Facility)
The designated TSD facility or alternate designated facility must note in this space any significant discrepancies between the quantity or type of waste described on the manifest and the quantity or type of waste actually received at the facility. Significant discrepancies in quantity are, for bulk wastes, variations greater than 10% percent by weight. A variation in piece count is considered to be a significant discrepancy for waste delivered in containers. For example, one missing or extra drum in a truckload is a significant discrepancy. Significant discrepancies pertaining to the type of waste would be obvious differences, discovered by the TSD facility, between the type of waste described on the manifest and the type of waste actually received. For example, waste solvent substituted for waste acid, or toxic constituents not reported on the manifest, are significant discrepancies.

Item 20. Facility Owner or Operator Certification of Receipt of Hazardous Materials Covered by this Manifest Except as Noted in Item 19
(Completed by the TSD facility)
The owner, operator, or authorized representative of the TSD facility must print or type their name, sign their name (by hand), and enter the date. By signing the manifest, the TSD facility acknowledges that the waste has been received and accepted, except for any discrepancies noted in Item 19. The TSD facility must retain a copy of the manifest and, within 30 days of delivery, send a copy of the closed manifest to the generator.

Items A through K
Items A through K are not required by the Federal regulations. However, many states may require the waste generator or the TSD facility to complete some or all of this information. For example, most states require generators to enter EPA or state hazardous waste numbers in Item I.

DOT regulations effective December 31, 1990 and published in 49 CFR Part 172, Subpart G, require hazardous waste and material shippers to provide a 24-hour emergency response telephone number on a shipping paper such as a manifest or hazardous material bill of lading for use in the event of an emergency involving the hazardous material. The telephone number must be the number of the person who is knowledgable concerning the hazards and characteristics of the material being shipped and has comprehensive emergency response information and accident mitigation information for that material, or has immediate access to a person who possesses such knowledge and information. The telephone number must be monitored at all times the material is in transportation or storage incidental to transportation. A generator could use an organization's telephone number, as long as the organization is capable of, and responsible for, providing detailed information concerning the hazardous material. The shipper must also ensure that the organization has received current information on the material.

Emergency response telephone numbers must be entered on a manifest either immediately following descriptions in block 11, or once in a clearly visible location if the number is for all wastes listed on the manifest and the manifest indicates that the number is for emergency response information. For example, the notation "EMERGENCY CONTACT: (919) 822-1172" is an appropriate way to identify the emergency response telephone number on a manifest.

TABLE 4.3
Continuation Sheet Information Requirements

Item Number	Corresponding Manifest Information	Item Number
21	Generator's U.S. EPA ID number and manifest document number	1
22	Page ___ of ___	2
23	Generator's name	3
24, 26	Transporter(s) company name(s) and order (enter the order of that transporter after the word "transporter")	5, 7
25, 27	Transporter(s) U.S. EPA ID number(s)	6, 8
28	U.S. DOT shipping description	11
29	Number and type of containers	12
30	Total quantity	13
31	Unit of measure	14
32	Special handling instructions	15
33, 34	Transporter(s) acknowledgment of receipt of materials	17, 18
35	Discrepancy indication space	19
L-T	Not required by EPA (check state requirements)	

UNIFORM HAZARDOUS WASTE MANIFEST (Continuation Sheet)	21. Generator's US EPA ID No.	Manifest Document No.	22. Page	Information in the shaded areas is not required by Federal law.

23. Generator's Name

L. State Manifest Document Number

M. State Generator's ID

24. Transporter ___ Company Name	25. US EPA ID Number	N. State Transporter's ID
		O. Transporter's Phone
26. Transporter ___ Company Name	27. US EPA ID Number	P. State Transporter's ID
		Q. Transporter's Phone

28. US DOT Description (Including Proper Shipping Name, Hazard Class, and ID Number)	29. Containers No.	Type	30. Total Quantity	31. Unit Wt/Vol	R. Waste No.
a.					
b.					
c.					
d.					
e.					
f.					
g.					
h.					
i.					

S. Additional Descriptions for Materials Listed Above	T. Handling Codes for Wastes Listed Above

32. Special Handling Instructions and Additional Information

33. Transporter ___ Acknowledgement of Receipt of Materials		
Printed/Typed Name	Signature	Month Day Year

34. Transporter ___ Acknowledgement of Receipt of Materials		
Printed/Typed Name	Signature	Month Day Year

35. Discrepancy Indication Space

EPA Form 8700-22A (Rev. 9-88) Previous editions are obsolete.

Figure 4.2
Continuation Sheet

DOT regulations also require emergency response information to be included on the manifest or attached to the manifest. Generators must also maintain this information near where the material is handled prior to shipment for use in the event of an incident and transporters must keep the information easily accessible during transportation. Chapter 5 provides details on the type of emergency response information that is required.

Continuation Sheets

Continuation sheets must be used if:

- More than two transporters are used to transport the waste, and/or
- More space is needed for additional U.S. DOT descriptions and related information because more than four different wastes are being shipped.

A continuation sheet is an official EPA form (see Figure 4.2) and should be obtained from the same sources as presented in Manifest Selection, beginning on page 53, for obtaining hazardous waste manifests. Most of the same information required on the manifest is also required on the continuation sheet to the manifest. Table 4.3 identifies the information you must enter on the continuation sheet.

HOW TO DETERMINE U.S. DOT DESCRIPTION FOR ITEM 11 OF THE MANIFEST

To properly complete the manifest you must enter the best and most descriptive DOT proper shipping description. The proper shipping description consists of at least the proper shipping name, hazard class, and DOT identification number in that order. For example:

Waste acetone, flammable liquid, UN 1090.

In order to determine the best shipping description, you must be familiar with the DOT Hazardous Materials Table and the Appendix to the Hazardous Materials Table in 49 CFR 172.101. These tables are provided in Appendix D of this handbook. You should also know detailed information about your waste including:

- Process that generated the waste
- Chemical constituents present
- Concentration or percent of each chemical constituent present
- Physical state (e.g., solid, liquid, gas)
- Specific gravity or density of the waste
- Hazard characteristics (e.g., oxidizer, flammable solid, flammable gas, etc.)
- Flashpoint
- pH
- Shipment method (e.g., bulk or container)

- Whether waste is reactive or contains cyanides or sulfides
- Concentration of any Toxicity Characteristic constituents which are present
- Amount of waste per container

You may obtain this information by reviewing the process generating the waste to determine the likely chemical constituents, by reviewing MSDSs and documents that provide chemical hazard information, and by analyzing wastes for hazard characteristics and chemical constituents. Once you have obtained this information, you can use the following key to determine the best US DOT description for your hazardous waste mixture.

Note: The DOT Hazardous Materials Table (49 CFR 172.101) was amended on December 21, 1990 in the *Federal Register* in order for the United States to adopt international hazardous material classification, hazard communication, labeling, placarding, marking, and packaging requirements. The following key is based on the preexisting version of the Hazardous Materials Table (reproduced in Appendix D of this handbook). This key and Appendix D may be used to determine proper shipping descriptions for domestic shipments of hazardous waste until October 1, 1993, unless the waste is considered to be poisonous by inhalation, a new explosive, or an infectious substance (see page 60 and Table 4.6 of the key). The U.N. hazard communication requirements must be followed as of October 1, 1991 for new explosives and most infectious substances, and by October 1, 1992 for materials that are poisonous by inhalation. Obtain a copy of the DOT Hazardous Materials Table published in the rule entitled HM-181 (published in the Federal Register on December 21, 1990) to determine the proper shipping descriptions, as well as marking and labeling requirements, for these materials.

Key to Determining the U.S. DOT Description for Mixtures

1. Does the waste contain more than one chemical compound or element?

   Yes: Go to question 2.
   No: The waste is not a mixture. Use Table 172.101 to find the proper shipping name that most accurately describes the material.

2. Is there a name on the hazardous materials table that describes the mixture? See, for example, chlorate and magnesium chloride mixture, carbon dioxide-oxygen mixture, boron trifluoride-acetic acid complex, arsenical mixture, etc.

   Yes: Use the proper shipping name listed in Table 172.101, column 2; add the word "waste" before the US DOT hazardous material description. Go to question 9.
   No: Go to question 3.

3. Is there a name listed in the table that defines the waste by its former use? See for example, compound cleaning liquid, compound polishing liquid, paint related material, etc.

Yes: Use the proper shipping name listed in Table 172.101, column 2; add the word "waste" before the US DOT hazardous material description. Go to question 9.
No: Go to question 4.

4. Is the waste a mixture of one material listed in table 172.101, column 2 and one or more other materials that *are not* listed in 172.101, column 2 and are not DOT hazardous materials?

Yes: Go to question 8.
No: Go to question 5.

5. Is the waste a mixture of at least two materials that *are* listed by name or hazard class in 172.101?

Yes: Go to question 6.
No: Go to question 7.

6. Does the material meet the description and the definition of more than one hazard class? For example, is the mixture both a flammable liquid and a corrosive material?

Yes: Select a proper shipping name from Table 4.5 that includes both hazard classes preceded by the word "waste." Add the hazard class from Table 172.101 to the shipping name you selected. If both hazard classes are not represented by one shipping name, use the hazard precedence list in Table 4.4 to select a hazard class for the material. Use the hazard class determined from the precedence list for the mixture as the proper shipping name preceded by the word "waste" and followed by the letters "n.o.s." Check the hazardous material table for proper wording and punctuation. Go to question 10.
No: Use the hazard class for the mixture as the proper shipping name preceded by the word "waste" and followed by the letters "n.o.s." Check the hazardous materials table for proper wording of the shipping name. If the hazard class is ORM-E, use the shipping description: Hazardous Waste, Liquid or Solid, n.o.s., ORM-E, NA 9189. Go to question 10.

Note: If there is a plus (+) in column 1 of the hazardous materials table for one or more of the components of the waste, then the hazard class of this material cannot be modified.

7. Is the waste a mixture of materials that *are not* listed by name or hazard class in 172.101, column 2 of the hazardous materials table?

Yes: Use your knowledge of the waste material's characteristics to determine an appropriate hazard class. (DOT hazard classes are defined in Chapter 5). Use the hazard class you select as the proper shipping name preceded by the word "waste" and followed by

the letters "n.o.s." Check the hazardous material table for proper wording and punctuation. If the waste does not meet the definition of any hazard class, except the class "ORM-E," use one of the following shipping descriptions and go to question 10.

• Hazardous waste, liquid, n.o.s., ORM-E, NA 9189, or
• Hazardous waste, solid, n.o.s., ORM-E, NA 9189

No: Error, return to question 1.

8. Is the mixture a homogeneous liquid consisting of two or more chemical compounds or elements that will not undergo any segregation under conditions normal to transportation?

Yes: The waste is a solution, according to DOT definitions. Refer to the hazardous materials table and select the name listed for the hazardous component of the waste. Add the word "waste" prior to the shipping name and the qualifying word "solution" after the name (e.g., waste acetone solution). Go to question 9.
No: The waste is a mixture, according to DOT definitions. The qualifying word "mixture" should be inserted after any shipping name you select (e.g., waste sodium hydroxide mixture). Go to question 9.

9. Does the waste meet the definition of the hazard class associated with the proper shipping name you selected? (DOT hazard classes are defined in Chapter 5.)

Yes: Use the shipping name you selected followed by the hazard class listed next to that shipping name in column 3 of table 172.101. Add the DOT identification number after the hazard class. Go to question 10.
No: Discard the shipping name you previously selected. If the waste has more than one hazard class, select a proper shipping name from Table 4.5 that includes both hazard classes preceded by the word "waste." Add the hazard class from table 172.101 to the shipping name you selected. If both hazard classes are not represented by one shipping name, use the hazard precedence list in Table 4.4 to select a hazard class for the material. Use the hazard class determined from the precedence list for the mixture as the proper shipping name preceded by the word "waste" and followed by the letters "n.o.s." Check the hazardous material table for proper wording and punctuation. If the waste does not meet the definition of any hazard class in the precedence list except the class "ORM-E," use one of the following shipping descriptions and go to question 10.

• Hazardous waste, liquid, n.o.s., ORM-E, NA 9189, or
• Hazardous waste, solid, n.o.s., ORM-E, NA 9189,

Note: If there is a plus (+) in column 1 of the hazardous materials table for one or more of the components of the waste, then the hazard class of this material cannot be modified. For example, if column 3 of the hazardous materials table calls the material a corrosive material, you may not change the hazard class to flammable, or any other hazard class even

59

though a different hazard class may more adequately describe the waste mixture.

10. Are the constituents of the waste and their respective concentrations (percentages) known?

    Yes: Go to question 12.
    No: Go to question 11.

11. Does the waste have a list D, F, or K hazardous waste code?

    Yes: Look up the waste stream listing and RQ in the Appendix to 172.101. Go to question 13.
    No: Error. You must know the waste constituents to determine that a waste has a P or U hazardous waste code. Return to question 1.

12. Is any component of the mixture on the Appendix to 172.101?

    Yes: Go to question 13.
    No: Go to question 11.

13. Is the material a hazardous substance? (Refer to the definition of hazardous substance in Table 4.4.)

    Yes: Add the letters "RQ" either before or after the proper shipping name. Use the hazardous materials table and, after the hazard class, add the DOT ID n umber that corresponds to the proper shipping name unless it was entered previously.
    After the U.S. DOT description, add in parentheses the name or the EPA hazardous waste number of the constituent(s) that caused the material to be a hazardous substance. Check the notes provided below.
    No: Go to 14.

14. Have you selected a proper shipping name listed in Table 4.5?

    Yes: After the US DOT description, add in parentheses the technical name of the hazardous material most predominantly contributing to the hazard. If the waste is a mixture of two or more hazardous materials, the technical names of at least two components most predominantly contributing to the hazards of the mixture or solution must be entered. Add the DOT ID number that corresponds to the proper shipping name unless it was entered previously. For example, "waste flammable liquid, corrosive, n.o.s. (contains methanol, potassium hydroxide), UN 2924." Check the notes provided below.
    No: Your proper shipping description is complete. Check the notes provided below.

    Notes: If the name of a compound that causes a mixture to meet the DOT definition of "poison" is not included in the proper shipping name for the mixture, the technical name of the compound must be incorporated into the description of the material. In addition, if a liquid or solid material meets the definition of a poison and the fact that it is a poison is not disclosed in the shipping name or hazard class entry, the word "poison" must be entered in association with the shipping description.

    The words "poison inhalation hazard" or "inhalation hazard" must be added to the basic shipping description for materials that are poisonous by inhalation. "Poison inhalation hazard" is defined on page 61, and Table 4.6 contains a list of proper shipping names from HM-181 for materials designated as poison inhalation hazards.

TABLE 4.4
Hazard Precedence List (40 CFR 173.2)

Term	Definitions
Hazardous material	A material that is listed on the DOT hazardous materials table, the appendix to the table, or a material that meets any of the hazard classifications identified in 49 CFR 173
Hazardous substance	A material, including its mixtures and solutions, that meets all of the following three criteria:

1. It (or any of its ingredients) is listed in the DOT reportable quantities table (Appendix to 172.101),
2. It is in a quantity, in one package, that equals or exceeds the reportable quantity (RQ) listed in the table, and
3. When the material is in a mixture or solution, it is in a concentration by weight that equals or exceeds the concentration corresponding to the RQ of the material, as shown by the following table:

RQ (lbs)	%	ppm
5000	10	100,000
1000	2	20,000
100	0.2	2,000
10	0.02	200
1	0.002	20

TABLE 4.4
Hazard Precedence List (40 CFR 173.2) (continued)

Term	Definitions
Infectious substance	A viable microorganism, or its toxin, that causes or may cause disease in humans or animals, and includes those agents listed in 42 CFR 72.3 of the regulations of the Department of Health and Human Services or any other agent that has a potential to cause severe, disabling, or fatal disease. The terms "infectious substance" and "etiologic agent" are synonymous. Cultures of infectious substances of 50 ml or less total quantity in one package are not subject to HM-181 hazard communication requirements until October 1, 1992.
Mixture	A material composed of more than one chemical compound or element
New explosive	An explosive produced by a person who has not previously produced that explosive or has previously produced that explosive but has made a change in the formulation, design, or process so as to alter the properties of the explosive
Poison inhalation hazards	"Division 2.3 Poisonous Gas" which means a material that is a gas at 20°C or less and a pressure of 101.3 kPA and which is known to be so toxic to humans as to pose a health hazard during transportation, or in the absence of adequate data on human toxicity, is presumed to be toxic to humans because when tested on laboratory animals it has an LC_{50} value not more than 5000 ppm. An LC_{50} value equals the lethal dose or concentration required to kill 50% of the test animal population given the dose measured in milligrams of the substance to kilograms of body weight or liters of air inhaled. "Division 6.1, Poisonous Material" which means a material, other than a gas, which is known to be so toxic to humans as to afford a hazard to health during transportation, or which, in the absence of adequate data on human toxicity, is presumed to be toxic to humans because when tested on laboratory animals: (1) it is dust or mist with an LC_{50} for acute toxicity on inhalation of not more than 10 mg/l or, (2) it is a material with a saturated vapor concentration at 20°C (68°F) of more than one-fifth of the LC_{50} for acute toxicity on inhalation of vapors of not more than 5000 ml/m^3, or (3) it is an irritating material, with properties similar to tear gas, that causes extreme irritation, especially in confined spaces.
Solution	Any homogeneous liquid mixture of two or more chemical compounds or elements that will not undergo any segregation under conditions normal to transportation
Technical name	A recognized chemical name currently used in scientific and technical handbooks, journals, and texts. Generic descriptions are authorized for use as technical names provided they readily identify the general chemical group. Examples of acceptable generic descriptions are organic phosphate compound, petroleum aliphatic hydrocarbons, and tertiary amines. Except for names that appear in Subchapter B of Part 172, trade names may not be used as technical names.

A hazardous material having more than one hazard must be classed according to the following order of hazards:

1. Radioactive material (except a limited quantity)
2. Poison A
3. Flammable gas
4. Nonflammable gas
5. Flammable liquid
6. Oxidizer
7. Flammable solid
8. Corrosive material (liquid)
9. Poison B
10. Corrosive material (solid)
11. Irritating materials
12. Combustible liquid (in containers having capacities exceeding 110 gallons)
13. ORM-B
14. ORM-A
15. Combustible liquid (in containers having capacities of 110 gallons or less)
16. ORM-E

This precedence list does not apply to the following materials:

- a material specifically identified in 49 CFR 172.101
- an explosive required to be classed and approved under 49 CFR 173.86, or a blasting agent required to be classed and approved under 49 CFR 173.114a
- an etiologic agent
- an organic peroxide
- a limited-quantity radioactive material that also meets the definition of another hazard class

TABLE 4.5
Proper Shipping Names Requiring Technical Names as Part of the Shipping Description

Acid, n.o.s.	Irritating agent, n.o.s.
Alcohol, n.o.s.	Nonflammable gas, n.o.s.
Alkaline liquid, n.o.s.	Organic peroxide, solid, n.o.s.
Cement, adhesive, n.o.s.	Organic peroxide, liquid or solution, n.o.s.
Combustible liquid, n.o.s.	ORM-A, n.o.s.
Compressed gas, n.o.s.	ORM-B, n.o.s.
Corrosive liquid, n.o.s.	ORM-E, n.o.s.
Corrosive liquid, poisonous, n.o.s.	Oxidizer, corrosive liquid, n.o.s.
Corrosive solid, n.o.s.	Oxidizer, corrosive solid, n.o.s.
Dispersant gas, n.o.s.	Oxidizer, n.o.s.
Etching acid, liquid, n.o.s.	Oxidizer, poisonous, liquid, n.o.s.
Etiologic agent, n.o.s.	Oxidizer, poisonous, solid, n.o.s.
Flammable gas, n.o.s.	Poisonous liquid or gas, flammable, n.o.s.
Flammable liquid, corrosive, n.o.s.	Poisonous liquid or gas, n.o.s.
Flammable liquid, n.o.s.	Poisonous liquid, n.o.s.
Flammable liquid, poisonous, n.o.s.	Poison B, liquid, n.o.s.
Flammable solid, corrosive, n.o.s.	Poisonous solid, corrosive, n.o.s.
Flammable solid, n.o.s.	Poisonous solid, n.o.s.
Flammable solid, poisonous, n.o.s.	Poison B, solid, n.o.s.
Hazardous substance, liquid or solid, n.o.s.	Pyrophoric liquid, n.o.s.
Hazardous waste, liquid or solid, n.o.s.	Pyroforic liquid, n.o.s.
Infectious substance, human, n.o.s.	Refrigerant gas, n.o.s.
Insecticide, dry, n.o.s.	Water reactive solid, n.o.s.
Insecticide, liquid, n.o.s.	

Note: Technical names are not required for n.o.s. descriptions of hazardous waste packaged in accordance with 49 CFR 173.12 (i.e., lab-packs), or for hazardous waste provided the chemical constituents are unknown and the EPA hazardous waste number is included in association with the basic description.

ADDITIONAL NOTIFICATIONS REQUIRED BY THE LAND DISPOSAL BAN

Under HSWA, Congress directed EPA to prohibit all hazardous wastes from land disposal by May 8, 1990 unless the wastes are treated to specific treatment standards. The purpose of the ban is to prevent threats to human health or the environment caused by leaking land disposal facilities. EPA was directed to follow a specific schedule in restricting wastes from land disposal and has, as of May 8, restricted the land disposal of most listed and characteristic hazardous wastes.

EPA has established treatment standards for almost all hazardous wastes only excluding wastes that exhibit the new toxicity characteristic but are not EP toxic, and five newly listed wastes. The agency granted a 3-month national capacity variance until August 8, 1990 for most wastes affected by the final rule published on June 1, 1990 in the *Federal Register*. Until August 8,1990 these wastes could still be land disposed even if they did not meet the treatment standard as long as the disposal facilities meet the minimum technical requirements (e.g., double liners, leachate collection systems) and the recordkeeping and notifica-tion/certification requirements are complied with.

Some treatment standards, such as those for mixed radioactive wastes, soil, and debris from third-third waste that have an incineration treatment standard, and certain surface disposed and deep well-injected hazardous wastes, have been delayed for 2 years under national capacity variances.

In general, dilution is prohibited as a form of treatment. However, EPA will continue to allow dilution of wastes that are hazardous only because they exhibit a characteristic in a treatment system that discharges wastewater subject to a National Pollutant Discharge Elimination System (NPDES) permit or an indirect discharge permit unless a treatment method has been specified as the treatment standard for the waste in 268.42 (e.g., deactivation for ignitable liquids).

The regulations applicable to land disposal restrictions are published in 40 CFR 268 which is reprinted in Appendix C of this handbook. These regulations identify which wastes are restricted from land disposal, procedures for obtaining extensions to and exemptions from land disposal restrictions, EPA's schedule for prohibiting specific waste codes from land disposal and establishing treatment standards for wastes, waste specific prohibitions, waste treatment standards, and prohibitions on the storage of restricted wastes.

TABLE 4.6
HM-181 Proper Shipping Names for Materials that are Poison Inhalation Hazards

Acetone cyanohydrin, stabilized
Acrolein, inhibited
Aerosols, poison, n.o.s.
Allyl alcohol
Allylamine
Allychloroformate
Allyl isothiocyanate, stabilized
Ammonia, anhydrous, liquified
Arsenic trichloride
Arsine
Boron tribromide
Boron trichloride
Boron trifluoride
Bromide chloride
Bromine
Bromine pentafluoride
Bromine solutions
Bromine trifluoride
Bromoacetone
n-Butylchloroformate
sec-Butylchloroformate
n-Butylisocyanate
tert-Butylisocyanate
Carbon dioxide and ethylene oxide
    mixtures
Carbon monoxide
Carbonyl fluoride
Carbonyl sulfide
Chlorine
Chlorine pentafluoride
Chlorine trifluoride
Chloroacetaldehyde
Chloroacetone, stabilized
Chloroacetonitrile
Chloroactyl chloride
Chloroformates, n.o.s.
Chloropicrin
Chloropicrin and methyl bromide
    mixtures
Chloropicrin and methyl chloride
    mixtures
Chloropicrin mixture, n.o.s.
Chloroplvailoyl chloride
Chlorosulfonic acid
Coal gas
Compressed gases, flammable, toxic,
    n.o.s.
Compressed gases, toxic, n.o.s.
Crotonaldehyde, stabilized
Cyanogen bromide
Cyanogen chloride, inhibited
Cyanogen, liquified
Cyclohexyl isocyanate
Diborane
Diborane mixtures
Dichlorodifluoromethane and ethylene
    oxide mixture
3,5-Dichloro-2,4,6-trifluoropyridine

Diktene, inhibited
Dimethyl hydrazine, symmetrical
Dimethyl hydrazine, unsymmetrical
Dimethyl sulfate
Dimethyl thiophospharyl chloride
Dinitrogen tetroxide, liquefied
    (nitrogen dioxide)
Ethylchloroformate
Ethyl chlorothioformate
Ethyl dichloroarsine
Ethylene chlorohydrin
Ethylene dibromide
Ethyleneimine, inhibited
Ethylene oxide
Ethyl isocyanate
Ethyl phosphonothioic dichloride,
    anhydrous
Ethyl phosponous dichloride, anhydrous
Ethyl phosphorodichloridate
Fluorine, compressed
Gas identification set
Germane
Hexachlorocyclopentadiene
Hexaethyl tetraphosphate and
    compressed gas mixtures
Hexafluoroacetone
Hydrocyanic acid, aqueous solutions
Hydrogen bromide, anhydrous
Hydrogen chloride, anhydrous
Hydrogen chloride, refrigerated liquid
Hydrogen cyanide, anhydrous, stabilized
Hydrogen selenide, anhydrous
Hydrogen sulfide, liquified
Insecticide gases, toxic, n.o.s.
Iron pentacarbonyl
Isobutyl chloroformate
Isobutyl isocyanate
Isocyanates, n.o.s.
Isophoronediisocyanate
Isopropyl chloroformate
Isopropyl isocyanate
Methoxymethyl isocyanate
Mesitylene*
Methylamine, anhydrous
Methyl bromide
Methyl bromide and ethylene dibromide
    mixtures
Methyl chloroformate
Methylchloromethyl ether
Methylchlorosilane
Methyldichloroarsine
Methylhydrazine
Methyl iodide
Methyl isocyanate
Methyl isothiocyanate
Methyl mercaptan
Methyl orthosilicate
Methyl phosphonic dichloride

Monochloroacetic acid, liquid*
Nickel carbonyl
Nitric acid, red fuming
Nitric oxide
Nitric oxide and nitrogen dioxide
    mixtures
Nitrogen dioxide, liquified
Nitrogen trifluoride
Nitrogen trioxide
Organic phosphate compound; mixed
    with compressed gas
Oxygen difluoride
Parathion and compressed gas mixture
Pentaborane
Perchloromethylmercaptan
Perchloryl fluoride
Phenylcarbylamine chloride
Phenyl isocyanate
Phenyl mercaptan
Phosgene
Phosphine
Phosphorus oxychloride
Phosphorous pentafluoride
Phosphorus trichloride
Poisonous liquids, corrosive, n.o.s.
    inhalation hazard
Poisonous liquids, flammable, n.o.s.
    inhalation hazard
Poisonous liquids, n.o.s. *inhalation*
    hazard
Poisonous liquids, oxidizing, n.o.s.
    inhalation hazard
n-Propyl chloroformate
n-Propyl isocyanate
Selenium hexafluoride
Silicon tetrafluoride
Stibene
Sulfur chlorides
Sulfur dioxide, liquified
Sulfuric acid, fuming
Sulfur tetrafluoride
Sulfur trioxide, inhibited
Sulfur trioxide, uninhibited
Sulfuryl fluoride
Tellurium hexafluoride
Tetraethyl dithiopyrophosphate and
    gases in solution (and gas mixtures)
Tetraethyl pyrophosphate and
    compressed gas mixtures
Tetramethoxysilane*
Tetranitromethane
Thio-4-pentanal
Thionyl chloride
Thiophosgene
Titanium tetrachloride
Trichloroacetyl chloride
Trimethoxy silane
Trimethylacetyl chloride
Tungsten hexafluoride

* Denotes chemicals which are not listed in the DOT Hazardous Materials Table

Land Disposal Notification

Generators that ship land disposal restricted hazardous waste off-site for treatment, storage, and disposal must notify the TSD facility in writing of the land disposal restrictions associated with the waste and any appropriate treatment standards. This notification must accompany every shipment of the restricted waste. The purpose of the notification is to ensure that the facility understands it is receiving a restricted waste and that the waste may or may not require further treatment prior to land disposal.

Generators and treatment facilities that treat characteristically hazardous waste to meet treatment standards must now submit notifications and certifications to the EPA Regional Administrator (or the the HSWA authorized state) when they ship the treated waste to RCRA Subtitle D land disposal facilities. Small-quantity gener-ators who ship waste out under a tolling arrangement are now permitted to make a one-time notification of applicable land disposal restrictions.

Land disposal notifications must reference EPA hazardous waste code(s), the applicable waste subcategories, treatability group(s), and the CFR section(s) where the treatment standards appear. Codes for treatment technologies, where applicable, must also be identified. This does not apply to F001-F005 spent solvents, multisource leachate, or California list wastes since these categories include many waste constituents. Different certifications have been promulgated for labpacks which now have alternate treatment standards of incineration for organics and incineration and stabilization of ash for EP toxic metals and organometallics. A certification has also been established for wastes which may have treatment standards for organics below practical quantification limits.

The Key to Land Disposal Notification Requirements presented in Appendix C identifies which wastes are subject to land disposal restrictions, illustrates exceptions to those restrictions, and provides forms that may be used to notify TSD facilities of the restrictions pertaining to a generator's waste shipment. In order to use the key, you must know the EPA hazardous waste number(s) for each of the wastes in a shipment. Hazardous wastes that are both listed and characteristically hazardous must be designated with all applicable hazardous waste codes. You may also have to test your waste in accordance with the Toxicity Characteristics leachate procedure in Appendix I to Part 268 of the regulations to determine if your waste meets a treatment standard.

After completing the key, complete the applicable notification forms and attach them to the manifest. TSD facilities may require the use of their own land disposal notification forms. TSD facility forms may be used instead of the forms in this key. These forms are acceptable if the the necessary notifications and certifications are present. Maintain copies of all notifications, certifications, and waste analysis data for at least 5 years from the date the waste subject to these requirements was last sent to treatment, storage, or disposal.

EXCEPTION REPORTS

If a generator does not receive a copy of the manifest with the signature of the owner, operator, or authorized representative of the designated facility within 35 days of the date the waste was shipped off-site, the status of the waste must be determined. The transporter and the TSD facility must be contacted to confirm that the waste shipment was in fact delivered and accepted, and to obtain a copy of the manifest.

If the waste was not delivered or accepted, the location of the waste must be determined. Remember that a generator continues to be liable for his hazardous waste until that waste is no longer hazardous.

If the generator does not receive a copy of the closed manifest within 45 days of the date the waste was accepted by the initial transporter, the generator must submit an exception report to the state environmental agency or the EPA regional administrator.

The exception report must include:

- a legible copy of the manifest for which you do not have a confirmation of delivery, and
- a cover letter describing the efforts taken to locate the hazardous waste and the results of those efforts.

For small-quantity generators, that is, facilities generating between 100 and 1000 kilograms of hazardous waste per calendar month, an exception report must be submitted if the closed manifest is not received within 60 days of the date the waste was accepted by the transporter. In this case, a legible copy of the manifest must be submitted with some indication that confirmation of delivery has not been received.

A generator exporting hazardous waste must submit an exception report to EPA if a copy of the closed manifest has not been received on-site within 45 days after the waste was accepted for shipment by the initial transporter. Alternatively, an exception report must be filed if a written confirmation of delivery has not been received from the consignee within 90 days, or if the waste is returned to the United States.

TRANSPORTER REPORTS

A transporter who releases hazardous waste at or above the DOT reportable quantity during transportation must:

- notify the National Response Center at (800) 424-8802 or in Washington DC, (202) 426-2675, and
- submit an incident report to DOT.

A written report of a hazardous material incident is required by all carriers when any quantity of a hazardous waste has been discharged during transportation (including loading, unloading, and temporary storage) The report must be filed on DOT Form 5800.1 within 30 days of the incident and submitted to the DOT. In most cases the state emergency response or environmental agency must also be notified. The transporter must also take appropriate immediate action to protect human health and the environment. Appropriate actions include adsorbing a spilled waste or diking the area around a spilled liquid to preclude it from spreading. Response actions toward releases of hazardous waste are discussed in more detail in Chapter 9.

DISCREPANCY REPORTS

Significant manifest discrepancies between the quantity or type of waste designated by the generator on the manifest and received by the TSD facility should be resolved as soon as possible. Significant discrepancies in quantity are, for bulk waste, variations greater than 10% in weight, and for batch waste, any variation in piece count such as a discrepancy of one drum in a truckload. Significant discrepancies pertaining to the type of waste would be obvious differences, discovered by the TSD facility, between the type of waste described on the manifest and the type of waste actually received, as well as differences discovered by inspection or waste analysis.

Upon discovering a significant discrepancy, the TSD facility must try to reconcile the discrepancy with the transporter and the generator. All parties should work together to determine the true quantity and type of waste. Hazardous waste generators should document discrepancy related telephone conversations and keep copies of all correspondence and waste analyses concerning the discrepancy.

If the discrepancy is not resolved within 15 days of receiving the waste, the TSD facility must immediately submit a discrepancy report to EPA or the authorized state. The discrepancy report must include:

- a letter describing the discrepancy and attempts made to reconcile the discrepancy, and
- a copy of the manifest or shipping paper at issue.

Chapter 5
Off-Site Management of Hazardous Waste

TRANSPORTER AND TSD FACILITY SELECTION

Unless a generator has a permit to treat or dispose of hazardous waste on-site, the hazardous waste generated and/or stored at a facility will eventually have to be transported off-site for treatment, storage, or disposal. The following guidelines have been developed to assist in the evaluation and selection of a hazardous waste transporter and TSD facility.

The task of selecting a reputable and reliable transporter and TSD facility must be taken seriously, for there are severe consequences for the mismanagement of hazardous waste. According to RCRA Section 7003, a generator will ultimately be held responsible for a hazardous waste (even after it leaves a facility) if it is ever determined to endanger human health or the environment. Thus, when a hazardous waste leaves the facility, legal liability for the waste—that is, "ownership" of the waste—is not transferred to the waste transporter or the treatment, storage, or disposal facility.

Transporters

Regulations applicable to transporters of hazardous waste are found in 40 CFR 263. A quick scan of these regulations will reveal that EPA has placed few restrictions on transporters; the regulatory requirements principally deal with the manifest system and discharge response and clean-up requirements. Although EPA has minimal checks and balances for transporters, the DOT enforces comprehensive hazardous material transportation requirements (codified in 49 CFR). Consequently, there is much information that you can collect to help make the best decision in selecting

the best company that can carry hazardous waste from your facility.

How to Identify Hazardous Waste Transporters

If you are completely unaware of what companies offer hazardous waste transportation services, a good source to contact to begin learning about available services is the state environmental agency. *State Hazardous Waste Management Regulations Differing from Federal Requirements*, available from Environmental Resource Center, contains information on each state's lead environmental agency. For states that have not obtained EPA authorization to administer their own RCRA program, the regional EPA office should be contacted. Phone numbers for each EPA region are listed in Table 5.1. On file with the agency is a list of companies registered to transport hazardous waste.

Such a list exists with each state agency because no transporter may carry hazardous waste along a public roadway without first having obtained an EPA identification number. A transporter receives an identification number by applying to either the state or regional EPA. Therefore, if a company offering hazardous waste transportation services is based in your state, it will have notified your state environmental agency. Keep in mind that in receiving an EPA identification number, the agency issuing the number is not attesting to the competency or capability of the transporter, it is only acknowledging that the company is registered to transport hazardous waste.

There are also many reference books commercially available that list hazardous waste transporters. For example, *Industrial and Hazardous Waste Management Firms* is a resource book with state-by-state listings. Additionally, *Hazardous Waste Services Directory* lists transporters from

Region	Phone Number	Division or Branch
1	617-565-3698	Waste Management Division
2	212-264-9881	Permits Administration Branch
3	215-597-8131	Hazardous Waste Management Branch
4	404-347-3931	Waste Management Division/RCRA Branch
5	312-353-3337	Waste Management Division
6	214-655-6745	Hazardous Waste Program Branch
7	913-236-2850	Hazardous Waste Division
8	303-294-1720	Hazardous Waste Division
9	415-974-7473	Waste Programs Branch
10	206-442-1906	Hazardous Waste Division

each state. Refer to Appendix B for additional details regarding these publications.

If you are familiar with a transporter who transports hazardous waste, you should ensure that the company has an EPA Identification Number. To do this, ask the transporter what their identification number is, and then call the state environmental agency to validate the number and confirm that the number has not been revoked, terminated, or suspended. Alternatively, you could directly inquire of the state environmental agency if the company under consideration has a current EPA Identification Number.

After a list of potential hazardous waste transporters is developed, you should work with your purchasing organization to establish a contract. Keep in mind when selecting a transporter and establishing a contract that you must ultimately assess whether:

- the transporter has the capability to carry the hazardous waste off-site,
- the transporter will responsibly carry the hazardous waste to the TSD facility,
- the service fits into your budget constraints.

In order to do this, there are a number of considerations to factor into the decision of which transporter should contract for this service, namely:

- Does the transporter have the proper vehicle and/or equipment to carry the hazardous waste?
- Has the transporter been cited for any violations by EPA or DOT?
- Does the transporter have the necessary permits to carry the waste interstate or intrastate?
- Does the transporter have at least the required amount of insurance?
- Would current or past customers recommend the transporter?
- What kind of and how much experience does the transporter have?
- How much lead time is required before a shipment can be carried off-site?
- How much does the service cost?

Proper Vehicle and Equipment

There are several shapes and sizes of motor vehicles available to transport hazardous waste as well as types of equipment that is used to load a shipment. As part of the evaluation, it should be determined whether the transporter operates vehicles that are capable of carrying the hazardous waste to be shipped.

Quite simply, a shipment of drums typically requires a type of flatbed truck (such as a closed trailer); therefore, a transporter with a fleet of tank trucks may not have the capability to carry the waste from your facility. By the same token, if your facility requires hazardous waste to be removed from a tank, a transporter providing only flatbed trucks may be of no value to you.

The equipment carried by a transporter to facilitate the loading of the shipment and to respond to spills should be factored into the equation to determine the best hazardous waste transporter. A transporter with a flatbed truck carrying pallet jacks, dollies, open head drums with fresh adsorbent and (sparkproof) shovels, whose truck has a hydraulic lift (if no loading dock is available) is better prepared and quite likely more capable of transporting your waste than a transporter with no loading or spill response equipment. A transporter with a tank truck who carries a vacuum pump and flexible hosing for evacuating a storage tank is more preferred than one without such equipment.

Violations

One avenue to pursue to help select a responsible transporter is to identify violations for which a motor carrier has been cited: the greater the number and severity of violations, the less the credence to have in a transporter. Since EPA, DOT, and the state regulate the transportation of hazardous waste, each can be contacted to identify transporter violations.

EPA regulates transporters primarily in the areas of manifest documentation and hazardous waste discharges. Therefore, by contacting the environmental protection agency in the state in which the transporter operates (or the regional EPA if the state does not have RCRA authorization), manifest-related and spill discharge violations can be identified.

If a transporter only carries hazardous waste within state boundaries (i.e., intrastate transportation), it is regulated by the state DOT in which the transporter operates. The enforcement branch of each state DOT primarily conducts and documents roadside inspections. By contacting the state DOT, you can determine if a hazardous waste carrier has been found in violation of requirements relating to safety equipment and motor vehicle safety. In addition, you can also determine if the transporter has been granted operating authority by the state, and if the insurance carrier for the transporter has provided certification of any state-required motor vehicle insurance.

A transporter who also crosses state lines (i.e., interstate transportation) is subject to inspection by federal DOT as well. When the U.S. DOT inspects a transporter, an on-site inspection is conducted, during which driver logbooks, vehicle maintenance files, accident report files, incident (spill) report files, driver qualification files, and the transporter's driver training program are examined. Copies of the inspection reports and subsequent violations can be obtained by contacting DOT at the following address:

U.S. Department of Transportation
Attn: Freedom of Information Officer
400 Seventh and D Street, SW
Washington, DC 20590

While all requests for information must be in writing, the Freedom of Information Officer can be contacted at (202) 366-0534 with specific questions about information requests.

Permits

While EPA does not require a permit for a transporter to carry hazardous waste (EPA only requires the submission of a notification form for a transporter to obtain an EPA identification number), most states do have permit requirements. Permit requirements for transporters range from the submission of annual permit fees to the licensing of vehicle operators, registering of motor vehicles, and identifying all TSD facilities to which hazardous waste may be carried. Additionally, while most states require a transporter to register in the state in which the transporter is based, many also require a permit for a vehicle to transport hazardous waste through their state. To establish that the transporter is permitted to operate (referred to above as "operating authority") in the state in which it is based by contacting the state DOT. Once the appropriate TSD facility is selected, determine the route that the transporter will follow to the TSD facility. If the route takes the transporter outside of the state in which it is based, contact each state DOT to determine if a permit is required for a vehicle to haul hazardous waste through the state. Finally, ask the transporter in which states it is permitted to operate. This will help determine both if a transporter has the authority to carry hazardous waste interstate, and if it is aware of state-specific permitting requirements.

Note: The Hazardous Materials Transportation Act of 1990 required shippers and carriers of certain highly danger-ous hazardous materials (HAZMAT) to register with DOT by March 31, 1992 and will eventually require HAZMAT employees to undergo training and be certified in the safe loading, unloading, handling, storing, and transportation of hazardous materials and emergency response to hazardous material transportation incidents.

Insurance

If a transporter is solely involved in intrastate transportation of small quantities of hazardous waste (i.e., less than 3500 gallons), it is only subject to state-specific requirements for insurance. While it may not be possible to determine exactly how much insurance a transporter carries, it is possible to determine whether or not the transporter has minimum state coverage by contacting the DOT for the state in which the transporter is based. Alternatively, this information may be obtained by requesting the transporter to furnish you with a copy of their certificate of insurance. This certificate is provided by an insurance company to a transporter; conse-quently, if there is any question regarding the validity of an insurance certification, the company issuing the certificate (and hence the policy) may be contacted.

When a transporter is involved in interstate transportation of hazardous waste, it is required to maintain a minimum of $1 million insurance. A transporter involved in carrying large amounts of hazardous waste (i.e., ≥ 3500 gallons per vehicle) must maintain at least $5 million insurance, regardless of whether the transporter is involved in intrastate or interstate commerce.

A transporter can either contract with an insurance carrier or, under certain conditions, it can self-insure. Federal transportation regulations require that proof of financial responsibility must be maintained on-site with the transporter. Therefore, you can verify that a transporter has adequate insurance by requesting a copy of the transporter's MCS 90 form (if insured through an insurance company) or their MCS 82 form (if self-insured).

Customer Recommendations

While the state and federal DOT can provide access to inspection results, describe the nature of violations and verify permits, the best way to gauge the dependability, reliability, and competence of a transporter prior to contracting their service is to contact past and present customers for their evaluation. Most transporters will gladly supply a list of customers, although that list may be biased toward favored customers.

A better route to pursue to obtain the names and addresses of a transporter's clients would be to obtain the manifest file for the transporter. This may be done if you conduct an on-site audit of the transporter or by contacting the state environmental agency in the state from which the transporter is based and requesting a copy of the manifest file for the transporter.

Note: Although there is no federal requirement under RCRA to file manifests with the appropriate state agency, many states have enacted hazardous waste management regulations that require the filing of manifests with the state. A determination of whether your state requires the filing of a state manifest may be found in *State Hazardous Waste Regulations Differing From Federal Requirements*, which is available through Environmental Resource Center.

Experience

The recommendations of past and present customers can provide information on a transporter's experience, other services that a transporter offers, and the length of time a transporter has been in business. For example, a transportation firm that also provides emergency remediation services in the event of a release is an indication that the transporter can efficiently and effectively handle its own spills.

Lead Time and Reliability

As discussed in Chapter 3, hazardous waste generators have up to 90 days to remove hazardous waste from an accumulation point; small-quantity generators have up to 270 days under certain circumstances. Neither the state nor the federal EPA will routinely make allowances for waste that remains on-site past the accumulation time (although your state may grant a 30-day extension on a case-by-case basis). Therefore, the amount of time required for a transporter to arrive at the facility once they have been notified that a shipment is ready is critical.

While short lead times are good, working with a transporter who reliably comes on the date that you have specified is better. Substantial penalties have been imposed on hazardous waste generators because their transporter arrived days after the date the shipment of hazardous waste was to be carried off-site. If the amount of waste generated by the site is fairly constant, knowing that a transporter is reliable and will arrive on time after having been notified is more valuable than working with a transporter who promises to come in a couple of days but typically arrives late.

Cost
Cost is sometimes viewed as the most significant factor in selecting a hazardous waste transporter, yet its significance should be weighed in the light of all other factors discussed above. While hazardous waste transportation is a competitive industry, a relatively low price may translate into delaying of vehicle maintenance, reduction of the amount of emergency response equipment carried on-board, and the employment of marginally qualified drivers and technical assistance personnel — all of which decreases the factor of safety with which all transporters must operate.

Therefore, the lowest cost should not necessarily translate into the most preferred transporter. When evaluating bids for hazardous waste transportation services, bids that are excessively low by comparison should be questioned and evaluated cautiously.

TSD Facilities

When a generator signs the hazardous waste manifest, he is certifying that the selection of the treatment, storage, or disposal facility represents the most practicable method available that minimizes the present and future threat of the hazardous waste to human health and the environment. A small-quantity generator must select the best waste management method that is available, but he is allowed to factor in cost as a consideration. It is mandatory, therefore, that you select a safe treatment, storage, or disposal facility for your waste.

How To Select A TSD Facility
As with the selection of a transporter, a good source to contact to begin learning about available services is your state (or regional) environmental agency. Because each TSD facility must submit a permit application to the state environmental agency in which it operates (or regional EPA if the state does not have RCRA authorization), each state environmental agency is aware of all facilities offering hazardous waste treatment, storage, or disposal services.

Furthermore, the reference materials discussed above for the selection of a transporter can be reviewed to determine which facilities offer TSD services. In addition, during the first quarter of every year, a directory of commercial hazardous waste management facilities is included in *The Hazardous Waste Consultant* (see Appendix B for additional details regarding this publication).

Determining the appropriate TSD facility to which to ship hazardous waste begins first by knowing the EPA Hazardous Waste Number for the waste (this determination is discussed in detail in Chapter II). Next, since TSD facilities are only permitted to accept wastes with certain hazardous waste numbers, you must learn which are permitted to accept hazardous waste generated by your facility. This determination is quite simply made by calling a TSD facility and inquiring if the facility is permitted to receive waste with the particular hazardous waste numbers which you must dispose of. Alternatively, by contacting the state environmental agency of the state in which the facility is located, you can obtain a list of hazardous wastes that a facility is permitted to accept.

Do not neglect to confirm that the facility has an EPA identification number. If you contact the facility about the types of waste it accepts, also ask what their EPA identification number is. This number should be verified with the state or regional EPA.

Selecting a TSD Facility: The Best Waste Management Option
When a hazardous waste manifest is signed, the generator is certifying that the methods used by the TSD facility to treat or dispose of the waste are the best available for minimizing the present and future threat of the hazardous waste to human health and the environment. Thus, of the possible TSD facilities that are permitted to accept your hazardous waste, you should determine the best treatment or disposal method for the waste. If the waste is land disposal restricted, then treatment must also be capable of meeting the treatment standards in 40 CFR Part 268 (see Appendix C).

While some wastes can be rendered nonhazardous by only a single method, there are a variety of treatment methods available for the majority of hazardous wastes. Evaluating each and determining your most practicable method may turn into a technically challenging as well as labor-intensive task.

Therefore, you should first consider recycling the waste or sending it to a TSD facility that can recycle or reclaim the hazardous waste. If none are available, you may want to consider a facility that offers one of the technologies presented the EPA publication *Treatment Technology Briefs: Alternatives to Hazardous Waste Landfills* (see Appendix B for details).

While the list in the referenced EPA publication is not comprehensive and the technologies presented are not mandatory for the treatment of the waste, the information provides a starting point to help you to determine the best treatment method and consequently a facility to treat your hazardous waste. If recycling or reclamation is not feasible, your main objective is to select a method that you consider practical and available which achieves environmentally beneficial reductions of waste toxicity and/or mobility.

Other Important Considerations in Selecting a TSD Facility

Even though a hazardous waste is consigned to a TSD facility, the waste generator retains legal responsibility for the waste. If the waste is mismanaged by the TSD facility, EPA or the state can ultimately bring suit against the generator to remedy the problem (e.g., a generator can be sued to finance a cleanup action). Consequently, three other factors pertaining to the TSD facility to which your waste is sent should be carefully evaluated: history of violations, condition of facility and cost for services. Always confirm that the facility can accept your facility's hazardous waste as packaged (i.e., determine if it can accept 55-gallon drums, bulk liquids, lab packs, etc. for treatment, storage, or disposal).

History of Violations

According to Section 3007 of RCRA, every TSD facility must be inspected by EPA or representatives of the state environmental agency at least once every 2 years; federal and state owned or operated TSD facilities must be inspected at least annually. As a result, there is a written record with respect to compliance with RCRA. Based on the inspections, TSD facilities may be cited for violations of the regulations. The inspection report records are publicly available and should be reviewed prior to selecting a TSD facility (as well as periodically while using the facility's services).

The records can be obtained by submitting a written Freedom of Information request to the Freedom of Information Officer at the state or regional EPA. A sample request is presented in Figure 5.1 on page 72. The address of regional EPA offices is presented in Table 5.2 on page 73. A fee may be charged for photocopying inspection reports.

When reviewing inspection reports and subsequent violations, keep in mind that because of the enormity of hazardous waste management regulations with which a facility must comply, some paperwork violations that occur on an infrequent basis may be inevitable. And though an excessive number of paperwork violations may signal a problem, more serious violations should be examined and evaluated carefully; serious violations may indicate serious problems with the facility.

Besides inspection files, there are a variety of other publicly available files that could be used to help establish reliability and compliance status of a TSD facility. Depending on the agency, there may be a file dedicated to enforcement actions, legal suits brought against the facility, correspondence to and from agency officials, as well as the facility permit application itself.

In addition to the hazardous waste requirements of RCRA, a TSD facility will also be required to comply with the requirements of the Clean Air Act if it there are any air emissions from the facility, the Clean Water Act if it discharges wastewater, and OSHA's Hazardous Waste Operations and Emergency Response rule (29 CFR 1910.120) and general industry standards. A comprehensive history of compliance can be developed by contacting each state agency that administers the law (e.g., the state air quality division, state water quality division, and the state OSHA).

Condition of the Facility

Another important consideration that should be factored into the TSD facility selection process is the condition of a facility. This is best evaluated by conducting an on-site visit. Typically, TSD facilities are happy to exhibit their storage facilities and structures, analytical instrumentation, disposal units, and treatment and processing equipment to present and potential customers. Such visits must often be scheduled in advance in order to arrange for a technically competent employee to be available to answer your questions.

When conducting a site visit, take note of the general housekeeping practices and appearance in the areas where the waste is off-loaded, stored, processed, treated, and disposed of. Poor housekeeping and appearance may be an indication of poor or weak management practices.

Also look for potential safety hazards, condition of facilities and equipment, availability and use of safety equipment, and be aware of detectable odors. Your decision to select a TSD facility can be strongly influenced by the degree of order and concern for safety at the facility. Although it could be a challenging task, you may find by reading the standards for TSD facilities in 40 CFR 264 or 265 that your site visit will be more focused because of a heightened awareness for what is required of the facility you are investigating.

Cost

As when selecting a transporter, the cost of treatment, storage, or disposal services must be heavily weighed, but it should not be the only criterion upon which a TSD facility is selected. Yet, the cost for a particular method of treatment or type of disposal will vary from facility to facility (and it may even vary from shipment to shipment for a given facility) and budget constraints will play a large part in selecting a facility. When the final selection is made, however, you should make an attempt to factor in all considerations presented above.

Also keep the perspective that, while you are certifying when the manifest is signed that the methods used by the TSD facility to treat or dispose of the waste are the best available for minimizing the present and future threat of the hazardous waste to human health and the environment, it is not the goal of EPA to force you to exhaustively search throughout the country and pay an unreasonable sum of money for any method of waste treatment, storage or disposal. EPA allows all generators the flexibility to reasonably, yet defensibly, select the most practicable method.

Generic Generators
123 Main St.
Hampton, TN 37990

5 April 1990

U.S. EPA, Region 4
Freedom of Information Officer
345 Courtland Street, N.E.
Atlanta, Georgia 30308

Dear Sir:

Pursuant to the Freedom of Information Act, please send me all RCRA inspection reports on file for the Waste Treatment Corporation, a TSD facility located in Savannah, Georgia. Please include copies of all other files that would indicate the facility's status with respect to compliance with RCRA, such as those relating to violations and enforcement actions.

Please contact me prior to commencing this request if there will be a charge for copying the information. When the request has been completed, please send it to the following address:

Douglas Adams
Generic Generators
123 Main St.
Hampton, TN 37990

Sincerely,

Douglas Adams
Environmental Engineer

FIGURE 5.1
Sample Letter for Freedom of Information Request

PRETRANSPORT REQUIREMENTS

Both DOT and EPA regulate shipments of hazardous waste off-site. When you sign the hazardous waste manifest prior to transportation off-site, you certify that the contents of the consignment are properly classified, packed, marked and labeled, and are in all respects in proper condition for transport by highway according to applicable national and international government regulations. To abide by the certification, your shipment must be properly packed, marked, and labeled, the truck must be properly placarded, and the shipment must be in proper condition for transportation in accordance with DOT and EPA regulations. Before offering hazardous waste to a transporter, you must:

- Ensure that all containers are properly labeled. The label is the diamond-shaped sticker applied to the drum indicating the hazard associated with the drum contents.

- Ensure that each container is marked with the hazardous waste warning statement, the proper shipping name of the waste, and corresponding DOT identification number. Apply any additional DOT-required marks to the container.
- Placard or offer the transporter the appropriate placard(s). The placard is the diamond-shaped sign that is placed on the truck.
- Complete and sign a hazardous waste manifest as "Generator" for the shipment.
- Complete a land disposal notice and certification if you are shipping a land disposal restricted waste, regardless of whether or not you are land disposing of your waste. Procedures for selecting and preparing manifests and disposal notices and certifications are presented in Chapter 4 and Appendix C.

TABLE 5.2
EPA Regional Contacts for Information Requests

U.S. EPA, Region 1
Office of Public Affairs
Mail Code RPA
Attn: Evelyn Sullivan
Kennedy Bldg.
Boston, MA 02203

U.S. EPA, Region 2
FOI Office
Attn: Wanda Vasquez
26 Federal Plaza
New York, NY 10278

U.S. EPA, Region 3
Office of Public Affairs
Mail Code 3PA00
841 Chestnut Street
Philadelphia, PA 19107

U.S. EPA, Region 4
Attn: FOI Officer
345 Courtland St., N.E.
Atlanta, GA 30365

U.S. EPA, Region 5
Office of Public Affairs
Mail Code 5PA
Attn: Robert Hartian
230 South Dearborn St.
Chicago, IL 60604

U.S. EPA, Region 6
Information Center
Mail Code 6M-II
Attn: Nita House
1445 Ross Avenue
Dallas, TX 75202

U.S. EPA, Region 7
FOI Office
Attn: Rowena Michaels
726 Minnesota Avenue
Kansas City, KS 66101

U.S. EPA, Region 8
Mail Code 80E-A
Attn: Louise Wiley
Denver Place
999 18th Street, Suite 500
Denver, CO 80202

U.S. EPA, Region 9
Mail Code E-2
Attn: Ida Tolliver
215 Fremont Street
San Francisco, CA 94105

U.S. EPA, Region 10
Mail Code MD103
Attn: Mary Nelson
1200 6th Avenue
Seattle, WA 98101

Before leaving the facility, all waste must also be packaged according to DOT regulations. This includes using DOT specification containers which are in good condition. Containers or tank trucks must be properly sealed and checked for leaks or other damage before transporting the waste. Chapter 3 includes procedures for selecting the proper DOT specified containers for accumulating and shipping hazardous wastes. Container condition requirements are also presented in Chapter 3.

DOT regulations published in 49 CFR 172, Subpart G and effective December 31, 1990, require the maintenance of certain types of emergency response information during transportation of hazardous materials and wastes. The following information must be available during transportation and handling and storage incident to transportation:

- the basic description and technical name of the hazardous material as required by DOT or other applicable regulations regulations
- immediate hazards to health
- risks of fire or explosion

- immediate precautions to be taken in the event of an accident or incident
- immediate methods for handling fires
- initial methods for handling spills or leaks in the absence of fire
- preliminary first aid measures

This information must be in English and available for use away from the hazardous material package. The information may be included on or attached to the manifest and may take the form of material safety data sheets for single component waste streams, or some kind of emergency response guidance manual such as the DOT *Emergency Response Guidebook*. However, if the *Guidebook* is used for emergency response information, the corresponding page of the manual must be clearly referenced on the manifest for each waste stream. This information must be maintained by the generator near where the waste is prepared for shipment, and must be maintained by the transporter at all times during transportation so it is available during an emergency. The emergency response information must also be maintained by hazardous waste

Name of Inspector: _____ Date: _____

Item	Conditions Reviewed	Status	
		Complete	Incomplete
Container Marking	Container Contents (Proper Shipping Name)		
	DOT ID Number		
	Begin Accumulation Date		
	U.S. EPA ID Number		
	Organization Name and Address		
	Manifest Document Number		
	Date Leaving Facility		
	Warning Mark: "Hazardous Waste – Federal Law Prohibits Improper Disposal. If found, contact nearest police or public safety authority of the U.S. Environmental Protection Agency."		
Container Label	Appropriate DOT Label(s) on Each Container		
Manifest	Current Manifest (Expires 9-30-91)		
	Signed by Generator Time Signed: _____		
Placard	Appropriate DOT Label(s) on Each Container		

Condition of Containers: ❑ Good ❑ Poor ❑ Leaking
Comments:

Does emergency response information accompany the shipment?   _____ Yes _____ No

Have special marks been applied to appropriate containers (RQ, Bung Label, ORM designation, Poison-Inhalation designation, Poison-Inhalation Hazard)?   _____ Yes _____ No

Is the waste restricted from land disposal?   _____ Yes _____ No

If "Yes" above, has the Appropriate Land Disposal Notice or Certification been attached to the manifest?   _____ Yes _____ No

FIGURE 5.2
Hazardous Waste Pretransportation Checklist

transfer, storage, and handling facilities so it is immediately accessible to facility personnel during an emergency.

Hazardous waste shipments should be thoroughly checked and inspected immediately before leaving the facility for treatment, storage or disposal to confirm compliance with these requirements. The Hazardous Waste Pretransportation Checklist presented in Figure 5.2 may be used to facilitate inspections of hazardous waste shipments.

Note: US DOT hazardous material regulations were amended on December 21, 1990 to align the regulations with UN recommendations and International Civil Aviation Organization Technical Instructions in the areas of classification, packaging, and hazard communication during the transport of hazardous materials. The new regulations designate hazard classes by their international numbers, change the definitions of certain hazard classes such as flammable liquids, adopt international units of measure, amend and consolidate the hazardous material tables (49 CFR 172.101 and 172.102 have been consolidated into one table), change labeling, marking and placarding requirements, amend the hazard communication requirements, and change the requirements on the reuse of plastic and metal drums. Use of the new hazardous material table and associated labeling, marking and hazard communication requirements is mandatory as of October 1, 1991 for new explosives and most infectious substances, and by October 1, 1992 for materials that are poisonous by inhalation. (see page 61 for a definition of poison inhalation hazard). October 1, 1993 is the date after which most other provisions of this final rule become effective (certain performance-oriented packaging requirements become effective in 1994 and 1996). Placards that conform to the DOT specifications in effect on September 30, 1991 may be used in place of the international placards until October 1, 1994. During the transition period from the preexisting DOT requirements to the new requirements, DOT recommends that hazard communication requirements be consistent where practical, that is, marking, labeling, placarding, and shipping paper descriptions should conform to either the old or the new requirements without intermixing of communication elements. The remainder of this chapter examines in detail marking, labeling, placarding, vehicle loading, and stowage requirements for domestic shipments of hazardous wastes not yet subject to these new requirements.

Container Marking Requirements

The DOT defines marking as applying the descriptive name, instructions, cautions, weight, or specification marks upon the outside of containers of hazardous materials. Marking does not require the use of a prescribed label. All marks required by the Department of Transportations must be:

- durable, in English, and printed on or affixed to the surface of a package or on a label, tag or sign
- displayed on a background of sharply contrasting color
- unobscured by labels or other attachments

- located away from any other marking, such as advertising, that might substantially reduce its visibility or effectiveness

The proper shipping name and the corresponding DOT identification number must be marked on each package of hazardous waste. The proper shipping name is obtained from column 2 and the DOT identification number is obtained from column 3A of the DOT hazardous materials table found in 49 CFR 172.101 and in Appendix D of this handbook. Chapter 4 provides a method for determining the proper shipping name and DOT identification number for mixtures of hazardous waste.

Packages containing hazardous substances, a term which is defined in Chapter 4, must be marked with the letters "RQ" in association with the proper shipping name. If the proper shipping name does not identify the hazardous substance by name, the package must also be marked with:

- the name of the hazardous substance as shown in the Appendix to the hazardous materials table, or
- the EPA hazardous waste number (for waste streams), or
- for characteristic hazardous wastes, the word "ignitability," "corrosivity," "reactivity," "toxicity," or the corresponding EPA hazardous waste identification number.

If a material is described on the manifest with one of the generic proper shipping names listed in Table 4.5, the technical names of the hazardous material must also be marked on the container in association with the basic description. If the material is a mixture or solution of two or more hazardous materials, the technical names of at least two components most predominantly contributing to the hazard of the mixture or solution must be marked on the container in association with the basic description. For example "Flammable Liquid, Corrosive, n.o.s. (contains methanol, potassium hydroxide), UN 2924." This marking requirement does not apply to a hazardous waste which is also hazardous substance that has been marked with the identity of the hazardous substance as described above.

Materials that pose a health hazard through inhalation must also be marked with the words "Inhalation Hazard." These include packages of each material containing a Division 2.3 poisonous gas or a poisonous liquid subject to the "poison inhalation hazard" shipping paper description requirement which is described on page 60 of the handbook.

When shipping overpacks or other packages with inside packaging containing liquid hazardous wastes, mark the outside package:

"THIS SIDE UP" or "THIS END UP" to indicate the upward position of the inside packaging, or an arrow symbol indicating "This Way Up." Also include a statement that the inner packagings comply with DOT specifications.

For packagings containing material classed as "other regulated materials" (ORM), mark the appropriate ORM mark on the container. The ORM mark is required on at least one side or end and must be placed immediately following or below the proper shipping name of the waste inside the package. ORM designations must be placed inside a rectangle which is at least 1/4 inch larger than the lettering on all sides. Figure 5.3 provides an example of a proper ORM mark.

ORM-C

FIGURE 5.3
Sample Mark for Other Regulated Materials

In addition to the DOT requirements, the EPA hazard warning must also be marked on each container of 110 gallons or less. The EPA hazard warning contains the following wording:

HAZARDOUS WASTE — Federal Law Prohibits Improper Disposal. If found, contact the nearest police or public safety authority or the U.S. Environmental Protection Agency.

Generator's Name and Address:
Manifest Document Number:

Some states have adopted slightly different wording for the hazardous waste warning which identifies local environmental and safety agencies to contact if hazardous waste is found.

Labeling Requirements

DOT hazard labels are different from marks in that their size, shape, design, and color are prescribed by the regulations. All labels must be durable and weather resistant. In addition, each diamond label must be a minimum of 4 inches on each side with each side having a black solid line border 1/4 inch from the edge. Specifications for color are prescribed in the Appendix to 49 CFR, Part 172. The labels must appear exactly as prescribed by the regulations except:

- labels may contain identification information such as the name of the maker as long as the information is outside the solid line inner border in 10 point type or less, and
- labels may contain UN and International Maritime Organization hazard class numbers and inscriptions required by the country of origin.

DOT hazardous materials warning labels which represent the hazard of the material being shipped must be affixed to containers before being offered for transportation. It is the responsibility of the shipper to determine whether or not labels are required, any multiple labeling requirements, and the location of the labels on the package.

These steps should be followed to determine the proper DOT label for hazardous waste shipments in containers, packages, overpacks, or freight containers:

- Locate the hazardous material description as listed in column 2 of the hazardous materials table in 49 CFR 172.101 or Appendix D of this handbook
- Locate the hazard class (or classes) for the material corresponding to the hazardous materials description in column 3 of the table
- Locate the hazard label required for each package, as listed in column 4 of the table

Hazard labels must be placed next to the proper shipping name marked on each container.

Some hazardous material descriptions have more than one hazard class listed in the hazardous material table. A waste may exhibit one or more of these hazard classes. If the container being shipped contains waste exhibiting only one of the hazard classes listed in the table, the appropriate label should be affixed to the container. If the container contains waste meeting the definition of more than one hazard class, multiple labels are required. Multiple labels must be located next to one another.

DOT Hazard Classes
DOT hazard classes are defined below to aid in determining the proper hazard class.

Radioactive material	Any material having a specific activity greater than 0.002 microcuries per gram
Explosive	Any chemical compound, mixture or device, the primary or common purpose of which is to function by explosion or with substantially instantaneous release of gas and heat (unless such compound, mixture, or device is otherwise specifically classified). Explosives are further classified as Group A, B, and C
Poison A	A poisonous gas or liquid of such nature that a very small amount of the gas or vapor of the liquid, mixed with air, is dangerous to life
Poison B	A liquid, solid, or semisolid substance which is known to be so toxic to man as to afford a hazard to health during transportation, or is presumed to be toxic to man because laboratory animal tests indicate an oral rat LD_{50} of 50 mg/kg or less, an inhalation rat LC_{50} of 200 mg/l or less, or an skin absorption rabbit LD_{50} of 2 mg/kg or less. An LD_{50} or LC_{50} is the lethal dose or concentration required to kill 50% of the test animal population

given the dose measured in milligrams of the substance to kilograms of body weight or liters of air inhaled

Flammable gas   A compressed gas that forms a flammable mixture with air at 13% or less by volume, has a flammability range in air exceeding 12%, or can have significant flame projection beyond the ignition source

Nonflammable gas   Any other compressed gas such as nitrogen or carbon monoxide that has an absolute pressure exceeding 40 psi at 70°F

Flammable liquid   Any liquid having a flashpoint below 100°F

Combustible liquid   Any liquid that does not meet the definitions of other classifications and has a flashpoint at or above 100°F and below 200°F

Flammable solid   Any solid that under conditions normally incident to transportation is liable to cause fires through friction, retained heat from manufacturing, or processing, or which can be ignited readily and when ignited burns so vigorously and persistently as to create a serious transportation hazard. Spontaneously combustible and water reactive materials are included in this hazard class

Oxidizer   A substance that yields oxygen which readily stimulates the combustion of organic material. Oxidizers include chemicals such as chlorates, permanganates, inorganic peroxides, and nitrates

Organic peroxide   An organic compound containing the bivalent [-O-O-] structure and that may be considered a derivative of hydrogen peroxide where one or more of the hydrogen atoms have been replaced by organic radicals. Organic peroxides are often temperature sensitive and unstable

Corrosive material   A liquid or solid that causes visible destruction or irreversible alterations in human skin tissue at the site of contact, or in the case of leakage, a liquid that has a severe corrosion rate on steel

Irritating material   A liquid or solid substance that upon contact with fire or exposure to air gives off dangerous or intensely irritating fumes. Examples include tear gas and brombenzylcyanide but not any poisonous materials

Etiologic agent   Any viable microorganism or its toxin that causes or may cause human disease. Etiologic agents are listed in 42 CFR 72.25 by the Department of Health and Human Services

ORMs   Other regulated materials that may pose an unreasonable risk to health and safety or property when transported in commerce and do not meet the definitions of other hazard classes. Specific materials have been classified as ORMs for transportation purposes

ORM-A   Material that has an anesthetic, irritating, noxious, toxic, or other similar property and that can cause extreme annoyance or discomfort to passengers or crew in the event of leakage

ORM-B   Material (including a wet solid) capable of causing significant damage to a transport vehicle from leakage during transportation

ORM-C   Material that has other inherent characteristics not described by an ORM-A or ORM-B, but that make it unsuitable for shipment, unless properly identified and prepared for transportation

ORM-D   Materials such as consumer commodities that present limited hazard during transportation due to their form, quantity, and packaging

ORM-E   Other materials not included in any other hazard classes but subject to regulation. Examples are hazardous substances and hazardous wastes

Additional Labeling Requirements

In addition to the hazard labels specified by the DOT hazardous material table, other labels are required under the circumstances described below:

- A material meeting the definition of an etiologic agent as defined in 42 CFR 72.25(c) must be labeled with the "Etiologic Agent" label.
- Empty radioactive materials packagings that have been emptied as far as practical must have previously applied labels removed and the "Empty" label applied.
- Wastes and materials that are a poison inhalation hazard as described in the Container Marking Requirements section of this chapter, must be labeled "Poison" in addition to any other labels which are required.
- "Cargo Aircraft Only" labels must be applied when shipping hazardous waste via air in quantities not permitted on a passenger-carrying aircraft.
- A bung label must be applied to metal barrel or drums containing a flammable liquid having a vapor pressure between 16 and 40 pounds psia at 100°F. The following warning is required on a bung label:

CAUTION Unscrew This Bung SLOWLY. Do not unscrew entirely until all interior pressure has escaped through the loosened threads. REMOVE BUNG IN OPEN AIR. Keep all open flame lights and fires away. Enclosed electric lights are safe.

Exceptions from Labeling Requirements

Labels are not always needed on every package containing a hazardous waste or material. For example, a freight container having a volume of 640 cubic feet or more should not be labeled, but should be placarded. The same is true for portable tanks which are properly placarded. Combustible liquids in packages do not require labels. Other Regulated Materials or ORMs are not labeled if they do not contain any other material classed as a hazardous material. These materials are identified by the ORM mark.

Multiple Labeling Requirements

The following DOT rules apply for containers bearing more than one hazard class or for those bearing special hazards:

- When two or more labels are required on a package (as specified in 49 CFR 172.101).
- When compatible hazardous materials of different hazard classes are in the same package, overpack, or container, the label for each class must be shown on the container.
- A material classed as an explosive A, poison A, or radioactive material that also meets the definition of another hazard class, must be labeled for each class.
- A poison B material that also meets the definition of a flammable liquid, flammable solid, corrosive mateiral, or oxidizing material must be labeled "Poison" in addition to the appropriate label for the other class.
- A flammable solid that also meets the definition of a water reactive material must be labeled "Flammable Solid" and "Dangerous When Wet."
- A flammable solid that also meets the definition of a corrosive material must be labeled "Flammable Solid" and "Corrosive."
- An oxidizer that meets the definition of a corrosive material must be labeled "Oxidizer" and "Corrosive."
- A flammable liquid that also meets the definition of a corrosive must be labeled "Flammable Liquid" and "Corrosive."

Preparation of Lab Packs

One of the areas where the threat of compatibility problems is most severe is when preparing packed laboratory chemicals or lab packs for transportation and disposal. "Lab Pack" is the term used when two or more waste materials in the same hazard class are packaged in the same outside packaging, provided the waste materials are chemically compatible. A chemist should inspect, classify, and segregate the individual bottles without opening them according to the hazards of the wastes. The purpose is to ensure safe segregation of the lab pack contents. Bottles should be packed in DOT specification-approved outside containers with enough cushioning and absorbent material to prevent movement of the bottles and absorb all free liquids in case of breakage.

DOT forbids the packaging of a hazardous material in the same container, freight container, or overpack with another hazardous material when the mixing of the two could cause a dangerous evolution of heat or gas or could produce corrosive materials. Although exceptions exist for hazardous materials, all hazardous wastes must be segregated so that each lab pack contains only one class of hazardous material and the materials must be chemically compatible.

EPA has established different treatment standards for organic wastes and organometallic wastes in lab packs. Consult Appendices IV and V of 40 CFR 268 for a list of EPA hazardous waste codes for materials that may be included in an organic and organometallic lab pack. Table 5.3 on page 79 is an example of a lab pack segregation scheme to ensure that incompatible materials are separated into different packages.

Please note that these classifications are different from DOT hazardous material classifications and some of the chemicals that are segregated for compatibility reasons may not be hazardous wastes. Wastes with different DOT hazard classes should not be placed in the same lab pack.

When packaging hazardous wastes for delivery to a specific treatment, storage, or disposal facility, a generator must also comply with that particular facility's packaging and material separation requirements. Often these facilities have operating permits that specify exactly how wastes must be packaged and segregated to prevent hazardous chemical reactions. Generators must be especially careful when packaging lab packs for disposal facilities to follow all DOT, EPA, and facility packaging and material segregation requirements. Certain highly reactive and explosive materials such as dry picric acid and potassium carbonyl may be forbidden both for transportation and disposal at most disposal facilities. Lab packs generally require a review of the package packing list and specific approval by the disposal facility prior to acceptance. This process ensures that all regulatory and permit requirements are met prior to shipping the waste.

Vehicle Placarding

Placards alert persons to the potential dangers associated with hazardous materials contained within motor vehicles, rail cars, freight containers, cargo tanks, and portable tanks. Placards also guide emergency personnel who respond to incidents involving hazardous wastes and materials.

Except under very limited circumstances, each highway transport vehicle containing any quantity of a hazardous waste must be placarded on each end and on each side with the placards specified by the DOT. It is the the generator's responsibility to provide the proper placard(s) to the transporter. Each generator must have a supply of appropriate placards on-hand which can be offered to transporters hauling hazardous waste. It is the transporter's responsibility to replace any placards which become dislodged from the vehicle enroute to the TSD facility.

TABLE 5.3
Example of a Lab Pack Content Classification System for Disposal

Classification	Examples
Inorganic acids	Hydrochloric Sulfuric
Inorganic bases	Sodium hydroxide Potassium hydroxide
Strong oxidizing agents	Ammonium nitrate Sodium peroxide Sodium chlorate
Strong reducing agents	Sodium thiosulfate Oxalic acid Sodium sulfite
Anhydrous organics and organometallics	Tetraethyl lead Phenylmercuric chloride
Anhydrous inorganics and metal hydrides	Potassium hydride Sodium hydride Potassium and sodium metal
Toxic organics	PCBs Insecticides
Flammable organics	Hexane Toluene Acetone
Inorganics	Sodium carbonate Potassium chloride
Inorganic cyanides	Potassium cyanide Copper cyanide
Organic cyanides	Cyanoacetamide
Toxic metals	Arsenic Cadmium

In general, freight containers of 640 cubic feet or more capacity must be placarded on all sides. Freight containers with a capacity less than 640 cubic feet must be labeled instead of placarded. Cargo tanks and portable tanks containing hazardous waste must also display placards on all four sides. However, if a portable tank has a rated capacity less than 1000 gallons, it may be placarded on two sides or it must be labeled. Cargo tanks and portable tanks that are required to be placarded must remain placarded when emptied until one or both of the following conditions exist:

• the tank is reloaded with a material that is not subject to hazardous material placarding regulations, or
• the tank has been sufficiently cleaned or purged of vapors to remove any potential hazards.

Placards may also display the four-digit DOT identification number. These numbers are generally required on portable tanks, cargo tanks, railroad tank cars, and bulk packages. Proper shipping names must also be marked on portable tanks, cargo tanks, and railroad tank cars.

The color, size, and design of placards have been specified by the DOT in 49 CFR, 172 Subpart F. The hazard class division number as prescribed by the United Nations may be printed in the lower corner of the diamond-shaped placard. All placards must be durable and able to withstand exposure to weather.

Placement of Placards
Placards must be visible from the directions in which they face. Placards must be placed on each side and each end of the motor vehicle. Placards may be placed on the front of the tractor of a tractor trailer instead of placarding the front of the trailer, or you may place placards on both units. Place each placard at least 3 inches away from any ladders, pipes, or other appurtenances that might reduce the effectiveness of the placard. In addition, place placards so dirt or water from the wheels of the vehicle will not be sprayed onto the placard. Securely fix each placard on the sides and ends of the vehicle or use a placard holder.

Selecting the Proper Placard
It is the generator's responsibility to select and offer the correct placard(s) to the transporter. In order to determine which placards are required, you must review placarding rules and tables established by the DOT. The key in Figure 5.4 incorporates these rules and tables into a procedure that may be followed to determine the correct placards for highway transportation vehicles carrying hazardous waste shipments. Figure 5.5 presents the DOT placard tables 1 and 2.

Special Placarding Requirements
There are three special placards that are not included in the DOT Placarding Tables which must be used under certain conditions. These are the *residue* placard, square background placard, and *fumigation* placard.

The *residue* placard is placed on each empty tank car in combination with the appropriate placard for the material that had been in the tank car. This placard remains in place until the tank car is reloaded with a nonhazardous material or sufficiently cleaned of residue and purged of vapors to remove any potential hazard.

The *square background* placard is simply a square box background. Required placards are then placed on top of this background. The square background placard is only used on rail cars transporting poison gas, poison gas residue, or Explosive A materials, and on motor vehicles transporting radioactive materials.

The *fumigation* placard is used for rail transport of motor vehicle, rail car, or freight container fumigated with a poisonous liquid, solid, or gas.

Loading and Stowage

Once hazardous wastes have been identified, classified, segregated, and packed, they may be loaded on a vehicle for transportation to a TSD facility. To prevent hazardous chemical reactions during the transportation of hazardous

This key will assist you in determining what placard(s) you must offer your transporter.

In order to use this key, you must know:

- the DOT hazard class for each waste being shipped (refer to 49 CFR 172.101, column 3), and
- the total quantity (in pounds) for each hazard class being shipped.

This key also utilizes placarding tables 1 and 2, which are included at the end of this key.

1. Does your shipment contain more than one hazard class?

   Y: Go to question 5.
   N: Go to question 2.

2. Is the hazard class for your shipment listed in the left column of Table 1?

   Y: Read across Table 1 to the right column and offer that placard to your transporter. Pay attention to the notes at the bottom of Table 1. Go to question 8.
   N: Go to question 3.

3. Is the hazard class for your shipment listed in the left column of Table 2?

   Y: Go to question 4.
   N: You are shipping an Other Regulated Material or "ORM." No placard is required unless the material meets the definition of a different hazard class.

4. Is the gross weight of your shipment less than 1000 pounds?

   Y: You are not required to offer placards for this shipment unless a poison inhalation hazard is present. However, shipment via tank car, air, or water must always be placarded. Go to question 8.
   N: Read across Table 2 to the right column and offer that placard to your transporter. You may offer the transporter the "DANGEROUS" placard if less than 5000 pounds of material from any one hazard class listed in Table 2 is offered for transportation. Pay attention to the notes at the bottom of Table 2. Go to question 8.

5. Are the hazard classes for your shipment all listed in the left column of Table 1?

   Y: Read across Table 1 to the right column and offer your transporter the placard corresponding to each hazard class. Pay attention to the notes at the bottom of Table 1. Go to question 8.
   N: Go to question 6.

6. Are the hazard classes for your shipment all listed in the left column of Table 2?

   Y: Read across Table 2 to the right column and offer your transporter the placard corresponding to each Hazard Class unless you are offering less than 1000 pounds of material from Table 2. If less than 1000 pounds of material from Table 2 is offered, no placard is required. Pay attention to the notes at the bottom of Table 2. Go to question 8.
          Offer your transporter the "DANGEROUS" placard. However, when 5000 pounds or more of one hazard class is to be loaded onto a vehicle (at one facility), the placard specified in the right column of Table 2 for that hazard class must be offered to your transporter in addition to the "DANGEROUS" placard. Pay attention to the notes at the bottom of Table 2. Go to question 8.
   N: Go to question 7.

7. Are the hazard classes for your shipment listed in the left column of both Table 1 and Table 2?

   Y: Read across Table 1 to the right column and offer your transporter the placard corresponding to each Hazard Class.
          You must also read across Table 2 to the right column and offer your transporter the placard corresponding to each hazard class, or you may offer the "DANGEROUS" placard for those items in Table 2. If less than 1000 pounds of hazardous material from Table 2 is offered, no placard is required for the Table 2 materials. However, if 5000 pounds or more of one Hazard Class listed in Table 2 is to be loaded onto a vehicle (at one facility), the placard corresponding to that Hazard Class must also be offered to your transporter. Pay attention to the notes at the bottom of Tables 1 and 2. Go to question 8.
   N: An error has been made. Determine the hazard class for your shipment using the hazard materials table (49 CFR 172.101) and return to question 1.

8. Does your shipment (or any constituent in it) cause a health hazard through inhalation†?

   Y: In addition to any other placard(s), the "POISON" placard must also be offered to the transporter and displayed on the transport vehicle.
   N: No additional placard is required.

†   A material is a health hazard through inhalation if it meets the DOT definition for an inhalation hazard.

FIGURE 5.4
Key for Determining How to Placard a Highway Transportation Vehicle Carrying Hazardous Waste Shipments

materials, DOT has issued regulations requiring the segregation and separation of those materials when loading vehicles. Although the carrier is responsible for the hazardous materials or wastes when they are enroute to their destination, you should check to ensure hazardous wastes are loaded properly prior to leaving your facility.

General Loading Safety Precautions

All hazardous wastes that are also DOT flammable liquids, compressed gases, corrosive materials, or poisonous materials must be secured against movement within the vehicle during transportation. Brace these containers by using load bars or other devices that will prevent movement. Be careful to avoid damaging valves and fitting on containers during loading and stowage.

Never load hazardous wastes or hazardous materials into pole trailers.

Never smoke while loading explosive, flammable, and oxidizing materials. Post signs or take other precaution to keep fire away and prevent anyone in the vicinity from smoking.

Make sure the hand brake of the vehicle is set before loading or unloading all hazardous wastes and materials. The engine must be stopped whenever explosive or flammable materials are loaded unless the engine is needed to operate a pump on a cargo tank.

Use tools designed for the containers which are loaded into the vehicle. Never use tools or equipment that could damage the containers or the closures on the containers. For example, a fork lift used to lift and move an open-head 55-gallon drum by the ring on the drum could damage the ring and result in a spill of hazardous waste during transportation.

Cargo heaters are always prohibited in vehicles hauling explosives. Cargo heaters used in hauling flammable liquids must be catalytic and must meet the design and operational requirements specified in 49 CFR 177.

Cargo tanks must be attended by a qualified person at all times during loading. "Attended" means throughout the process the person is awake, has an unobstructed view of the tank, and is within 25 feet of the tank or the delivery hose to the tank. A person is "qualified" if he is aware of the nature of the hazardous waste which is loaded, has been instructed on the procedures to follow in an emergency, and is authorized to move the tank and is able to do so.

Follow bonding and grounding procedures when loading flammable liquids into cargo tanks through open filling holes. Bonding and grounding is not required by DOT when when a cargo tank is loaded through a vapor tight top or bottom connection so that there is no release of vapor at a point where a spark could occur.

Load flammable solids and oxidizing materials only into trailers that have an enclosed body. Take precautions to prevent these materials from getting wet during loading and during transportation.

Never load poisons into a motor vehicle that also contains foodstuffs, feed, or any edible material meant for human or animal consumption. Hazardous waste should never be shipped with food and animal feed or in tank trucks used for shipping foodstuffs. Hazardous waste should not be transported in the cab of the vehicle.

Segregation and Separation of Hazardous Materials

DOT prohibits the loading of certain combinations of hazardous materials on the same motor vehicle in order to prevent fires, explosions, and spills caused by incompatible chemical reactions. When shipping hazardous materials, the following material segregation requirements must be followed:

- Charged electric storage batteries must not be loaded in the same vehicle with Class A explosives.
- Cyanides or cyanide mixtures must not be loaded or stored with acids or acidic materials. The reaction of cyanides with acids releases deadly hydrogen cyanide gas.
- Gas identification sets may not be loaded or stored with wet initiating or priming explosives.
- Nitric acid in carboys must be separated in a motor vehicle from other acids in carboys by a wooden dike nailed into the floor and filled with an incombustible absorbent material.

All other hazardous materials may be loaded or stored together only if the combination is not prohibited by the DOT segregation and separation chart. This chart is reproduced in Figure 5.6.

To read the chart you must know the hazard class for the material being shipped. Review the left slanted columns of the chart to determine whether any of the hazard classes listed are present in your shipment. If you are shipping a hazardous material with a hazard class that is listed, follow the row on the chart associated with that hazard class and specific material. If there is an "X" in the row, yourhazardous material is incompatible with another hazardous material listed on the chart. The letter "X" at an intersection means that these materials must not be loaded or stored together. If there is a number next to the "X" special exceptions may apply to the loading and stowage prohibition. Review the appropriate footnote at the top of the chart to determine special requirements and exceptions.

Much of the chart is devoted to the segregation of various types and classes of explosives since these materials have the greatest potential for explosive decomposition if they react with incompatible materials. Class A Explosives may not be loaded or stored with other hazardous materials such as flammables, nonflammable gases, oxidizers, corrosives, poisons, or radioactives. Corrosive liquids must not be loaded above or adjacent to flammable solids, oxidizers, organic peroxides, and certain Class B explosives, unless you have obtained approval from the DOT and you know that the mixture of those materials will not cause a dangerous evolution of heat or gas. Poisonous gases and liquids in tanks, cylinders, projectiles, or bombs may only be loaded with certain Class C explosives, nonflammable gases, and radioactive materials. All other combinations of hazardous materials that do not have an X at the intersection on the chart may be loaded or stored together.

Department of Transportation Placard Table 1

If the Hazard Class Is	Offer this Placard
Class A explosives	EXPLOSIVES A[1]
Class B explosives	EXPLOSIVES B[2]
Poison A	POISON GAS[1]
Flammable solid (DANGEROUS WHEN WET label only)	FLAMMABLE SOLID W[3]
Radioactive material	RADIOACTIVE[4,5]
Radioactive material (UF_6, fissile)†	RADIOACTIVE[4] and CORROSIVE[6]
Radioactive material (UF_6, low specific activity)‡	RADIOACTIVE[4,5] and CORROSIVE[6]

[1]See 49 CFR 172.510(a).

[2]EXPLOSIVES B placard is not required if the transport vehicle contains class A explosives and is placarded EXPLOSIVES A as required.

[3]FLAMMABLE SOLID W placard is required only when the DANGEROUS WHEN WET label is specified in the hazardous materials table for a material classed as a flammable solid.

[4]Applies only to any quantity of packages bearing the RADIOACTIVE Yellow-III label (refer to 49 CFR 172.403).

[5]For exclusive use shipments (as defined in 49 CFR 173.403) of low-specific-activity radioactive materials transported in accordance with 49 CFR 173.425(b) or (c).

[6]CORROSIVE placard is not required to be displayed on transport vehicles for shipments of less than 1000 pounds gross weight.

† Uranium hexafluoride, fissile (with $> 0.1\%$ U^{235}).

‡ Uranium hexafluoride, low specific activity (with $\leq 0.1\%$ U^{235}).

Department of Transportation Placard Table 2

If the Hazard Class Is	Offer this Placard
Class C explosives	DANGEROUS[1]
Blasting agents	BLASTING AGENT[9,10]
Nonflammable gas	NONFLAMMABLE GAS[8]
Nonflammable gas (Chlorine)	CHLORINE[7]
Nonflammable gas (Fluorine)	POISON
Nonflammable gas (Oxygen, cryogenic liquid)	OXYGEN
Flammable gas	FLAMMABLE GAS[8]
Combustible liquid	COMBUSTIBLE[3,4]
Flammable liquid	FLAMMABLE
Flammable solid	FLAMMABLE SOLID[5]
Oxidizer	OXIDIZER[9,10]
Organic peroxide	ORGANIC PEROXIDE
Poison B	POISON
Corrosive material	CORROSIVE[6]
Irritating material	DANGEROUS

[1]Applies only to a Class C explosive required to be labeled with an EXPLOSIVE C label.

[2][RESERVED].

[3]A COMBUSTIBLE placard is required only when a material classed as combustible liquid is transported in a package having a rated capacity of more than 110 gallons, a cargo tank, or a tank car.

[4]A FLAMMABLE placard may be used on a cargo tank or portable tank during transportation by highway, rail or water, and on a compartmented tank car containing materials classed as flammable liquid and combustible liquid.

[5]Except when offered for transportation by water, a FLAMMABLE placard may be displayed in place of a FLAMMABLE SOLID placard except when a DANGEROUS WHEN WET label is specified for the material on the hazardous materials table.

[6]Refer to 49 CFR 173.245(b) for authorized exceptions.

[7]A CHLORINE placard is required only for a packages having a rated capacity of more than 110 gallons; a NONFLAMMABLE GAS placard is to be displayed for packages having a rated capacity of 110 gallons or less.

[8]A NONFLAMMABLE GAS placard is not required on a motor vehicle displaying a FLAMMABLE GAS placard or an OXYGEN placard.

[9]BLASTING AGENTS, OXIDIZER, and DANGEROUS placards need not be displayed if a transport vehicle or freight container also contains Class A or Class B explosives and is placarded EXPLOSIVES A or EXPLOSIVES B as required.

[10]Except for shipments by water, OXIDIZER placards need not be displayed if a freight container, motor vehicle, or rail car also contains blasting agents and is placarded BLASTING AGENT as required.

FIGURE 5.5
Department of Transportation Placard Tables 1 and 2

Segregation and Separation Chart of Hazardous Materials

Instructions

The letter X at an intersection shows that these materials must not be loaded or stored together. Example: Detonating fuzes, class A, with or without radioactive components, (g), must not be loaded or stored with high explosives or propellant explosives (b).

Class	Row	Material	a	b	c	d	e	f	g	1	2	3	4	5	6	7	7a	8	8a	9	10	11	12	13	14	15
CLASS A EXPLOSIVES	a	Low explosive or black powder																								
CLASS A EXPLOSIVES	b	High explosives, propellant explosives or detonating card																								
CLASS A EXPLOSIVES	c	Initiating or priming explosives, wet; Diazodinitrophenol; fulminate of mercury, guanyl nitrosamino guanylidene hydrazine; lead azide; lead styphnate; nitro mannite; nitrosoguanidine; pentaerythrite tetranitrate; tetrazene; lead mononitroresorcinate	X	X																						
CLASS A EXPLOSIVES	d	Detonators, detonating primers		[1]X	[1]X																					
CLASS A EXPLOSIVES	e	Ammunition for cannon with explosive projectiles, gas projectiles, smoke projectiles, incendiary projectiles, illuminating projectiles; ammunition for small-arms with explosive projectiles, incendiary projectiles; rocket ammunition with explosive projectiles, gas projectiles, smoke projectiles, incendiary projectiles, illuminating projectiles, boosters (explosive), bursters (explosive), and supplementary charges (explosive) without detonators, 3/, 4/			X	[1]X																				
CLASS A EXPLOSIVES	f	Explosive projectiles, bombs, torpedos, mines, rifle or hand grenades (explosive), jet thrust units (jato), igniters, jet thrust rocket motors, igniters rocket motor, 3/			X	X																				
CLASS A EXPLOSIVES	g	Detonating fuses, class A, with or without radioactive components		X	X		X	X																		
CLASS B EXPLOSIVES	1	Ammunition for cannon with empty, inert-loaded or solid projectiles or without projectiles; or rocket ammunition with empty projectile, inert-loaded or solid projectiles or without projectile.			X																					
CLASS B EXPLOSIVES	2	Propellant explosives, jet thrust units (jato) igniters, jet thrust rocket motors, rocket engines (liquid), igniters, rocket motor, starter cartridges			X																					
CLASS B EXPLOSIVES	3	Fireworks, special or railway torpedeos	X	X	X	[1]X	X	X	X																	
CLASS C EXPLOSIVES	4	Small arms ammunition, or cartridges, practice ammunition			X																					
CLASS C EXPLOSIVES	5	Primers for cannon or small arms, empty cartridges—black powder igniters, empty cartridge cases, primed, empty grenades, primed, combination primers or percussion caps, toy caps, explosive cable cutters, explosive rivets			X																					
CLASS C EXPLOSIVES	6	Percussion fuzes, tracer fuzes, or tracers			X																					
CLASS C EXPLOSIVES	7	Time, combination or detonating fuzes.			X																					
CLASS C EXPLOSIVES	7a	Detonators, detonating primers		[1]X	[1]X		[1]X	[1]X				[1]X														
CLASS C EXPLOSIVES	8	Safety squibs, fuse lighters, fuse igniters, delay electric igniters, electric squibs, instanteneous fuse or igniter cord			X																					
CLASS C EXPLOSIVES	8a	Detonating cord			X	[1]X			X			X					[1]X									
CLASS C EXPLOSIVES	9	Fireworks, common	X	X	X	X	X	X	X																	
OTHER HAZARDOUS MATERIALS	10	Blasting agent, n.o.s., or ammonium nitrate fuel oil mixture; blasting agent label			X	[1]X						X					[1]X									
OTHER HAZARDOUS MATERIALS	11	Flammable liquids or flammable gases, flammable liquid or flammable gas label	X	X	X	X	X	X	X																	
OTHER HAZARDOUS MATERIALS	12	Flammable solids, flammable solid label; Oxidizer, oxidizer label; Organic peroxide, organic peroxide label	X	[5]X	X	[5]X	X	X	X																	
OTHER HAZARDOUS MATERIALS	13	Corrosive liquids, corrosive label	X	X	X	X	X	X	X	[2]X	[2]X												[2]X			
OTHER HAZARDOUS MATERIALS	14	Nonflammable gases, N.F.G. label	X	X	X	X	X	X	X																	
OTHER HAZARDOUS MATERIALS	15	Poisonous gases or liquids in tank car tanks, cylinders, projectiles or bombs, poison gas labels	X	X	X	X	X	X	X	X	X	X					X			X		X	X	X		
OTHER HAZARDOUS MATERIALS	16	Radioactive materials, radioactive labels	[5]X	[5]X	[5]X	[5]X	[5]X	[5]X	[5]X																	

Footnotes

1. Except as prescribed in §178.81(c) or 177.835(g) loading and transportation of detonators or detonating primers with materials named in rows b, c, e, f, 3, 8a or 10 is prohibited.

2. Corrosive liquids must not be loaded above or adjacent to flammable solids, oxidizing materials, ammunition for cannon with or without projectiles, or propellant explosives, except that shippers loading truckload shipments of corrosive liquids and flammable solids or oxidizing materials packages and who have obtained prior approval from the Department may load such materials together when it is known that the mixture of contents would not cause a dangerous evolution of heat or gas.

3. Explosives, class A, and explosives, class B must not be loaded or stored with chemical ammunition containing incendiary charges or white phosphorus either with or without bursting charges.

4. Bursters (explosive), boosters (explosive), or supplementary charges (explosive) without detonators when shipped by, to, or for the Departments of the Army, Navy, and Air Force of the United States Government may be loaded with any of the articles named except those in columns c, d, 3, 9, 11, 12, 13, 14, 15, and 16.

5. Does not include ammonium nitrate, fertilizer grade, which may be loaded, transported, or stored with high explosives, or with detonators containing not more than 1 gram of explosive each, excluding ignition and delay charges.

6. Normal uranium, depleted uranium, and thorium metal in solid form may also be loaded and transported with articles named in columns a, b, c, d, e, f, and g.

FIGURE 5.6
Segregation and Separation Chart of Hazardous Materials

Chapter 6

Treatment, Storage, and Disposal Facility Management

This chapter presents an overview of the requirements for hazardous waste TSD facilities. The EPA regulations for TSD facilities are found in 40 CFR 264 and 40 CFR 265. The Part 264 regulations present the minimum standards for the management of hazardous waste at facilities with RCRA permits and Part 265 of the regulations provides standards for facilities operating under interim status.

Interim status facilities are those existing facilities (facilities in operation or for which construction commenced on or before November 19, 1980) that have not yet received their RCRA permit from EPA or a state with authorization. As shown in Table 6.1, the scope of the interim status (Part 264) and the permitted status (Part 265) facility standards is similar.

TABLE 6.1
Scope of the Treatment, Storage, and Disposal Facility Regulations

		Part 265	Part 264
Subpart A	General	■	■
Subpart B	General facility standards	■	■
Subpart C	Preparedness and prevention	■	■
Subpart D	Contingency plan and emergency procedures	■	■
Subpart E	Manifest system, recordkeeping, reporting	■	■
Subpart F	Groundwater monitoring	■	■
Subpart G	Closure and post closure	■	■
Subpart H	Financial requirements	■	■
Subpart I	Use and management of containers	■	■
Subpart J	Tank systems	■	■
Subpart K	Surface impoundments	■	■
Subpart L	Waste piles	■	■
Subpart M	Land treatment	■	■
Subpart N	Landfills	■	■
Subpart O	Incinerators	■	■
Subpart P	Thermal treatment	■	
Subpart Q	Chemical, physical, and biological treatment	■	
Subpart R	Underground injection	■	
Subpart W	Drip pads	■	■
Subpart X	Miscellaneous units		■
Subpart AA	Air emission standards for process vents	■	■
Subpart BB	Air emission standards for equipment leaks	■	■

It is the intent of this chapter to provide only the basic framework of the current requirements for TSD facilities. Therefore, the following discussion focuses on the requirements that apply to all (or most) facility types in Subparts A, B, C, D, E, G, I, and J of the regulations. For details regarding the requirements for specific facility types, the reader should refer to the appropriate portions of the regulations in Parts 264 and 265.

WHEN PERMITS ARE NEEDED

RCRA requires a permit, known as a Part B permit (or perhaps by another name in states authorized to implement RCRA), for the treatment, storage, and disposal of any hazardous waste. The terms treatment, storage, and disposal are defined in 40 CFR 270.2 as follows:

Treatment   Any method, technique, or process, including neutralization, designed to change the physical, chemical, or biological character or composition of any hazardous waste so as to neutralize such wastes, or so as to recover energy or material resources from the waste, or so as to render such waste non-hazardous, or less hazardous; safer to transport, store, or dispose of; or amenable for recovery, amen-able for storage, or reduced in volume

Storage   The holding of hazardous waste for a temporary period, at the end of which the hazardous waste is treated, disposed, or stored elsewhere

Disposal   The discharge, deposit, injection, dumping, spilling, leaking, or placing of any hazardous waste into or on any land or water so that such hazardous waste or any constituent thereof may enter the environment or be emitted into the air or discharged into any waters, including ground water

All hazardous waste management facilities must have permits during the active life of the facility including the facility's closure period. Surface impoundments, landfills, land treatment units, and waste piles that received wastes after July 26, 1982 or that certified closure after January 26, 1983 are required to have postclosure permits unless they can demonstrate closure by removal or decontamination.

The information in this chapter is based on the interim status facility standards in Part 265. With few exceptions, the interim status standards are similar to the permitted facility standards in Part 264. In addition to the requirements presented below, all facilities should comply with any additional requirements that may be imposed by state regulations and permitted facilities must comply with the specific conditions of their permits.

FACILITIES FOR WHICH PERMITS OR PERMIT APPLICATIONS ARE NOT REQUIRED

1. Publicly owned treatment works receiving hazardous waste are not required to apply for permits because they are deemed issued a "permit by rule" if they possess a NPDES permit and comply with the following regulations:

   - Obtain an identification number (40 CFR 264.11)
   - Use of hazardous waste manifests (40 CFR 264.71)
   - Manifest discrepancies (40 CFR 264.72)
   - Maintain operating record (40 CFR 264.73 (a) and (b)(1))
   - Submit biennial reports (40 CFR 264.75)
   - Unmanifested waste reports (40 CFR 264.76)
   - Corrective action for solid waste management units (40 CFR 264.101, for NPDES permits issued after 8 November 84)
   - Hazardous wastes received must meet all federal, state, and local pretreatment requirements that would apply to the waste if it were being discharged into the publicly owned treatment works (POTW) through a sewer, pipe, or similar conveyance.

2. Ocean disposal barges or vessels are deemed issued a "permit by rule" if they possess a permit for ocean dumping issued under 40 CFR 220, and comply with the conditions of that permit. They also must comply with the following regulations:

   - Obtain an identification number (40 CFR 264.11)
   - Use of hazardous waste manifests (40 CFR 264.71)
   - Manifest discrepancies (40 CFR 264.72)
   - Maintain operating record (40 CFR 264.73 (a) and (b)(1))
   - Submit biennial reports (40 CFR 264.75) Submit unmanifested waste reports (40 CFR 264.76)

3. Injection wells are deemed issued a "permit by rule" if they meet the following requirements:

   - Possess a permit for underground injection issued under 40 CFR 144 or 145 (UIC permit) and comply with the conditions of the permit
   - If the UIC permit was issued after November 8, 1984, the facility must comply with the corrective action for solid waste management units (40 CFR 264.101).
   - If the UIC permit was issued after November 8, 1984 and the underground injection well is the only unit at the facility requiring a RCRA permit, the facility must submit the solid waste management unit information requirements for Part B permits to EPA or state with authorization (40 CFR 270.14 (d)).

4. Generators who accumulate hazardous waste on-site for not greater than the time periods allowed in 40 CFR 262.34. These maximum storage times allowable for hazardous waste generators without storage permits are presented in Chapter 3.
5. Farmers who dispose of hazardous waste pesticides generated from their own use
6. Facilities that only treat, store, or dispose of waste excluded from regulation in 40 CFR 261.4 (see solid and hazardous waste exemptions in Chapter 2 for a list of wastes excluded from regulation).
7. Facilities that only treat, store, or dispose of waste generated by conditionally exempt small-quantity generators.
8. Totally enclosed treatment facilities
9. Elementary neutralization units and wastewater treatment units
10. Transporters storing manifested shipments of hazardous waste in containers at a transfer facility for a period of 10 days or less
11. Persons adding absorbent material to waste in a container and persons adding waste to absorbent material in a container at the time the waste is first placed in the container
12. Cleanup and containment activities taken during a discharge of hazardous waste, an imminent and substantial threat of a discharge of hazardous waste, or a discharge of a material that when discharged becomes a hazardous waste
13. Facilities managing certain recyclable materials as defined in 40 CFR 261.6(a)(2) and (3), except to the extent that these facilities must meet the requirements identified in the referenced regulations
14. Hazardous waste generators and small-quantity hazardous waste generators who treat their own wastes on-site, provided they:

   • treat waste in accumulation tanks or containers which are in compliance with Subparts I and J of 40 CFR 265,
   • treat within the accumulation time constraints prescribed in the regulations (90 days for generators, 180-270 days for small quantity generators), and
   • comply with all other requirements for hazardous waste accumulations identified or referenced in 40 CFR 262.34 (see Chapter 3 for the details of the 40 CFR 262.34 requirements).

GENERAL REQUIREMENTS FOR TSDFS

Hazardous waste TSD facilities are subject to a permitting system that strives to ensure safe operation and protection of the environment. Under this permitting system, facilities must meet general standards for proper waste management and requirements specific to the individual facility.

This section presents an overview of the general standards for the operation of permitted and interim status facilities. This discussion applies only to the regulated portions of the facility, that is, the portions of the facility that either have a Part B permit, or are operating under interim status and are not exempt from regulation, as described in the sections above.

Notification of Hazardous Waste Activity

Each facility required to have a permit, as described in the section entitled When Permits Are Needed above, is required to obtain an EPA identification number. The identification number is obtained through the submission to EPA (or state with authorization) of EPA Form 8700-12 entitled Notification of Hazardous Waste Activity. This is a one-time notification and it need not be resubmitted unless any of the information included on the notification changes. A copy of the completed Form 8700-12 should be maintained in the facility's operating record.

Required Notices

Waste Received from Outside the United States
Facilities that receive hazardous waste from a foreign source are required to notify the EPA Administrator in writing at least 4 weeks in advance of the date that the waste is expected to arrive at the facility. A copy of this notice must be retained in the facility's operating record.

Transfer of Ownership
Before transferring ownership or operational control of a permitted or interim status facility during the facility's operating life, during closure, or during the postclosure care period, the facility owner or operator must notify the new owner of the requirements in 40 CFR Part 264 (for permitted facilities), Part 265 (for interim status facilities), and Part 270. A copy of this notice should be retained in the facility's operating record.

Waste Analysis

Permitted and interim status facilities are required to develop and follow a waste analysis plan which describes the procedures conducted to ensure that sufficient information is known about each waste stream to properly treat, store, or dispose of the waste and comply with regulatory requirements. The waste analysis plan must be approved (by EPA or state with authorization) as part of the Part B permit application process for permitted facilities. For interim status facilities, the waste analysis plan must be made available for inspection upon request by authorized EPA or state inspection and enforcement personnel.

Waste analysis plans must include the following information:

The parameters for which each hazardous waste will be analyzed and the rationale for the selection of these parameters, including:

• Test methods that are used to test for these parameters
• Sampling methods that will be used to obtain a representative sample of each waste to be analyzed

- The frequency with which the initial analysis of the waste will be reviewed or repeated to ensure that the analysis is accurate
- For facilities that accept waste from off-site, the plan must identify any analyses that hazardous waste generators from off-site have agreed to supply.
- Methods that will be used to meet any of the applicable requirements of 40 CFR 265.193 (analysis of releases to containment areas); 265.225 (trial treatment tests for surface impoundments); 265.252 (analyses required for waste piles); 265.273 (analyses required for land treatment); 265.314 (free-liquid determination for landfills); 265.341 (analyses required for landfills); 265.375 (analyses required for thermal treatment); 265.402 (analyses required for chemical, physical, and biological treatment facilities); 265.1034(d) and 265.1063(d) (analyses required for process vents and equipment leaks); and 268.7 (land disposal restrictions)
- Analysis procedures for materials in surface impoundments exempt from land disposal restrictions, if applicable
- For facilities that receive waste from off-site, procedures to ensure that the waste matches the identity of the waste designated on the accompanying manifest and to ensure that each movement of such waste on-site matches this identity

Analytical methods and sampling procedures identified in the waste analysis plan and used for hazardous waste determinations should be the same (or approved equivalent methods) as those identified in the current version of *Test Methods for Evaluating Solid Waste* (EPA publication SW-846).

Once the waste analysis plan is written, it is important to ensure that the methods and procedures outlined in the plan are followed. If changes in waste analysis procedures are needed, the waste analysis plan should be revised. For permitted facilities, a change in the waste analysis plan may constitute a permit modification which is subject to EPA or state approval.

For additional guidance regarding the required contents and implementation of a Waste Analysis Plan, refer to the document *Waste Analysis Plans: A Guidance Manual*, EPA/530-SW-84-012 and the current regulations at 40 CFR 265.13.

Security

Security must be maintained to prevent the unknowing entry and to minimize the possibility for the unauthorized entry of persons or livestock onto the facility. Security is required unless contact with the waste or waste management equipment will not injure unauthorized persons and disturbance of the waste or equipment will not cause a violation of the regulatory requirements for TSD facilities.

Security must include 24-hour surveillance which:

- continuously monitors and controls entry onto the active portion of the facility *or* an artificial (or natural) barrier such as a fence, which completely surrounds the active portion of the facility, and
- has a means to control entry, at all times, through the gates or other entrances to the active portion of the facility, such as a guard, television monitors, locked entrance, or controlled roadway access to the facility.

Signs with the warning "Danger—Unauthorized Personnel Keep Out" must be posted at each entrance to the active portion of the facility, and at other locations in sufficient numbers to be seen from any approach to the active portion of the facility. This warning must be written in English and in any other language predominant in the area surrounding the facility.

Inspections

Facility inspections must be periodically conducted to identify problems that may lead to the release of hazardous waste constituents to the environment or which may lead to a threat to human health. Any equipment or structures that can potentially cause these problems must be inspected frequently in order to identify problems in time to correct them before they harm human health or the environment.

A written inspection schedule must be followed for inspecting all monitoring equipment, safety and emergency equipment, security devices, and operating and structural equipment. The schedule must be maintained at the facility and it must identify the types of problems that are to be looked for during the inspection, the date and time of each inspection, the name of the inspector, a notation of the observations made, and the date and nature of any repairs or other remedial actions.

Inspection frequency may vary for the items on the schedule, however, each frequency must be based on the rate of possible deterioration of the equipment and the probability of an environmental or human health incident if

TABLE 6.2
Minimum Inspection Frequencies

Item	Minimum Inspection Frequency
Loading and unloading areas	Daily
Container storage areas	Weekly
Tank systems	Daily
Surface impoundments	Weekly
Incinerators	Daily
Thermal treatment units	Daily
Chemical, physical, and biological treatment units	Weekly
Closed vent systems and control devices	Daily
Pumps in light liquid service	Weekly
Compressor sensors	Daily

the deterioration, malfunction, or operator error goes undetected between inspections. Inspection frequencies for certain equipment specified in the regulations are listed in Table 6.2. Inspection records must be maintained on-site for at least 3 years from the date of the inspection. Because each facility is unique, it is recommended that each facility develops its own inspection logs which identify the specific items to be inspected and their frequency of inspection.

Training

Training is required for facility personnel involved in the management of hazardous waste. Chapter 7 identifies who must receive training, the required training frequency, and the scope of the mandatory training requirements.

- The job title for each position at the facility related to hazardous waste management *and* the name of the employee filling each job.
- A written job description for each position related to hazardous waste management. For the purposes of RCRA training records, the job description need only describe the job as it relates to the management of hazardous waste and must include the requisite skills, education, or other qualifications, and the duties of facility personnel assigned to each position.
- A written description of the type and amount of both introductory and continuing training that will be given to each person filling a position related to management of hazardous waste.
- Records that document that the training or job experience required to meet the training requirements have been given to and completed by facility personnel. These records must be kept for current employees as long as they work at the facility, and for an additional 3 years after the date they leave the facility (or stop working at a position related to hazardous waste management). Training records may accompany personnel transferred to another facility.

General Requirements for Ignitable, Reactive, or Incompatible Wastes

Precautions must be taken to prevent accidental ignition or reaction of ignitable or reactive waste. These wastes must be separated and protected from sources of ignition or reaction including (but not limited to) open flames, smoking, cutting, welding, hot surfaces, frictional heat, sparks (static, electrical, or mechanical), spontaneous ignition (such as that produced from heat producing reactions), and radiant heat.

When ignitable or reactive waste is being handled, smoking and open flames must be restricted to specially designated locations that are a safe distance from (or otherwise protected from) locations where ignitable or reactive waste are present. No Smoking signs must be conspicuously placed wherever there is a hazard from ignitable or reactive waste.

Precautions must be taken to prevent reactions which:

- generate extreme heat, pressure, fire, explosions, or violent reactions
- produce uncontrolled toxic mists, fumes, dusts, or gases in quantities sufficient to threaten human health or the environment
- produce uncontrolled flammable fumes or gases in sufficient quantities to pose a risk of fire or explosions
- damage the structural integrity of the device or facility
- through other like means threaten human health or the environment

The facility must document the precautions used to meet the requirements described above. This documentation may be based on references to published scientific or engineering literature, data from trial tests, or the results of similar wastes by similar treatment processes and under similar operating conditions.

Preparedness and Prevention

TSD facilities must be maintained and operated to minimize the possibility of a fire, explosion, or any unplanned sudden or nonsudden release of hazardous waste or hazardous waste constituents to air, soil, or surface water. In order to meet this requirement, TSD facilities must maintain certain emergency equipment, communication equipment, and aisle space necessary to respond to emergencies involving hazardous waste.

Unless it can be demonstrated that none of the hazards posed by waste handled at the facility could require a particular type of equipment, all facilities must be equipped with the following:

- An internal communications or alarm system capable of providing immediate emergency instructions to facility personnel
- A device, such as a telephone or a two-way radio, that is immediately available at the scene of waste operations, capable of summoning emergency assistance from the fire department, police department, or state and local emergency response personnel
- Portable fire extinguishers, fire control equipment, spill control equipment, and decontamination equipment
- Water at adequate volume and pressure to supply fire suppression equipment

Facility communications or alarm systems, fire protection equipment, spill control equipment, and decontamination equipment that may be used in the event of an incident involving hazardous waste must be tested and maintained as necessary to ensure its proper operation in time of emergency.

Wherever hazardous waste is being handled, all personnel involved must have immediate access to an internal alarm or communication device. If there is ever just one employee on the premises of the active portion of the facility, that person must have immediate access to a device such as a telephone or two-way radio capable of summoning emergency assistance.

Aisle space must be maintained to allow for the unobstructed movement of personnel, fire protection equipment, spill control equipment, and decontamination equipment to any area of the active portion of the facility.

Arrangements must be made (or attempted to be made) to familiarize appropriate fire departments, emergency response teams, and police with the layout of the active portion of the facility, properties of hazardous waste handled and their associated hazards, places where facility personnel would normally be working, entrances to and roads inside the facility, and possible evacuation routes.

In the event of a fire, where more than one fire or police department might respond to a fire, agreements designating primary emergency authority to a specific authority must be made.

Agreements must also be made, as appropriate, with state emergency response teams, emergency response contractors, and suppliers of equipment that may be used in an emergency incident involving hazardous waste. Arrangements must be made to familiarize local hospital personnel with the properties of hazardous wastes handled and the types of injuries or illness that could result from fires, explosions, or releases involving hazardous waste.

If state or local authorities decline to enter into the agreements described above, the facility must document the refusal in the facility operating record.

Contingency Plan and Emergency Response Procedures

Each hazardous waste TSD facility is required to have a contingency plan which details the actions that will be taken in the event of a fire, explosion, or any unplanned release of hazardous waste or hazardous waste constituents to the environment. The plan must be followed in the event that any such event may threaten human health or the environment. If the facility has previously prepared a spill prevention, control, and countermeasures (SPCC) plan or an other emergency response plan, the existing plan need only be amended to incorporate the procedures and operations described below.

The contingency plan must include the following information:

- Descriptions of the actions facility personnel must take in response to fires, explosions, or to any unplanned sudden or nonsudden release of hazardous waste constituents to air, soil, or surface water at the facility.
- Arrangements agreed to by local police and fire departments, hospitals, contractors, and state and local emergency response teams must be described in the plan.
- An up-to-date list of the names, addresses, and phone numbers (office and home) of all persons who are qualified to act as emergency coordinator. If more than one person is listed, a single person must be named as primary emergency coordinator and others must be listed in the order in which they will assume responsibility as alternates.

- An up-to-date list of all emergency equipment at the facility (such as fire control equipment, spill control equipment, communication and alarm systems, and decontamination equipment). This list must include the location and physical description of the equipment and a brief summary of its capabilities.
- If there is a possibility that evacuation could be necessary, the plan must include an evacuation plan for facility personnel. The evacuation plan must describe signals to be used to begin evacuation, primary evacuation routes, and alternate evacuation routes to be used in the event that the primary evacuation routes are blocked.

A copy of the contingency plan, including any revisions, must be maintained at the facility and copies must also be submitted to all local police departments, fire departments, hospitals, and State and local emergency response teams that may be called upon to provide emergency services.

The contingency plan must immediately be reviewed and amended whenever any of the following occur:

- The facility Part B permit is revised.
- The plan fails in an emergency.
- There is a change in the design, construction, operation, or maintenance in the facility that materially increases the potential for fires, explosions or releases of hazardous waste or hazardous waste constituents, or changes the response necessary in an emergency.
- There are changes in the list of emergency coordinators.

An emergency coordinator (or alternate) must be either on the facility premises or on call with the responsibility for coordinating all emergency response measures. The emergency coordinator must be thoroughly familiar with all aspects of the facility's contingency plan, all operations and activities at the facility, the location and characteristics of waste handled, the location of all records (that may relate to hazardous waste or emergency response) within the facility, and the facility layout.

OSHA regulations published in 29 CFR 1910.120(p) also require TSD facilities to develop emergency response plans to be incorporated into the written safety and health program required by OSHA for employees involved in hazardous waste operations. The emergency response plan need not duplicate any of the subjects fully addressed in the contingency plan, but must address the following areas: preemergency planning, coordination with outside parties, personnel roles, lines of authority, communications, emergency recognition and prevention, safe distances and places of refuge, site security and control, evacuation routes and procedures, decontamination procedures, emergency medical treatment and first aid, emergency alerting and response procedures, critique of response and follow-up procedures, PPE, and emergency equipment.

Chapter 9 presents detailed guidance for contingency planning, duties of the emergency coordinator in the event of an emergency, and specific emergency response procedures required by the RCRA regulations in the event of an emergency involving hazardous waste.

Hazardous Waste Manifests

The hazardous waste manifest system described in Chapter 4 applies to all hazardous waste transported from off-site hazardous waste generators (or TSD facilities) that are received at a permitted or interim status TSD facility, except for wastes received from conditionally exempt small-quantity generators (a conditionally exempt small-quantity generator is a facility that generates less than 100 kg hazardous waste and less than 1 kg acute hazardous waste per calendar month).

After receipt of hazardous waste accompanied by a hazardous waste manifest, the TSD facility must sign and date each copy of the manifest to certify that the hazardous waste covered by the manifest was received, immediately give the transporter at least one copy of the signed manifest, send a copy of the manifest to the waste generator within 30 days after the delivery, retain at the facility a copy of each manifest for at least 3 years from the date of delivery, and note any significant discrepancies on the manifest of each copy of the manifest.

A significant discrepancy is defined as any variation in weight greater than 10%. For batch waste, such as drums, any variation in the piece count would be a significant discrepancy. Other significant discrepancies include variations in the waste type, or hazardous constituents. If a significant discrepancy is discovered, the facility must attempt to reconcile the discrepancy with the waste generator. If the discrepancy is not resolved within 15 days after receiving the waste, the TSD facility must immediately submit to the EPA regional administrator (or state with authorization) a letter describing the discrepancy and attempts to reconcile it, and a copy of the manifest or shipping paper at issue.

Operating Record

Each TSD facility must maintain an operating record which describes all wastes accepted at the facility, the location of these wastes during storage, and the date which the wastes were run through the production process. The operating record must contain the following information:

- A description by its common name and EPA hazardous waste number(s) from Part 261 that apply to the waste received. The waste description must also include the waste's physical form (e.g., liquid, sludge, solid, or containerized gas). If the waste is not listed in Part 261, Subpart D, the description must also include the process that produced it.
- The estimated or manifest-reported weight, or volume and density, where applicable, in one of the units of measure specified in Appendix I, Table 1, of Part 264
- The method(s) (by handling code(s)) as specified in Appendix I, Table 2, of Part 264) and date(s) of treatment, storage, or disposal
- The location of each hazardous waste within the TSD facility and the quantity at each location. This information must include cross-references to specific manifest

document numbers, if the waste was accompanied by a manifest.

- Records and results of waste analyses performed as specified in Parts 264.13, 264.17, 268.4(a), and 268.7
- Summary reports and details of all incidents that require implementing the contingency plan as specified in Part 264.56(j)
- Records and results of inspections as required by Part 264.15(d)
- Monitoring, testing or analytical data, and corrective action where required by Subpart F and Parts 264.226, 264.253, 264.254, 264.276, 264.278, 264.280, 264.303, 264.309, 264.347, and 264.602, as appropriate
- Notices to generators as specified in Part 264.12(b)
- All closure cost estimates under Part 264.142
- A certification which is updated annually, that the TSD facility has a program in place to reduce the volume and toxicity of hazardous waste that it generates to the degree it has determined to be economically practicable, and the proposed method of treatment, storage, or disposal is that practicable method currently available to the facility that minimizes the present and future threat to human health and the environment
- Copies of the notices, certifications required by the land disposal restrictions in Part 268.7 or 268.8
- Equipment and procedures used to ensure that ignitable and reactive wastes are not involved in accidental reactions or cause fires, explosions, or other uncontrolled releases which may endanger human health or the environment

Unmanifested Waste Reports

TSD facilities may accept unmanifested waste from conditionally small-quantity generators. If such waste is to be accepted the TSD facility must obtain certification that the wastes from these generators qualify for a manifest exclusion according to 40 CFR 261.5. If such certification cannot be obtained, the TSD facility must file an unmanifested waste report to the EPA within 15 days of receiving the wastes.

The report must include:

- facility name, address and EPA ID number
- the date the wastes were received
- the name, address, and EPA ID number of the generator and transporter (if available)
- a description of the wastes received and quantities,
- method of treatment or storage for each hazardous waste
- certification signed by the operator of the TSD facility (or his authorized representative) and
- a brief explanation as to why the wastes were unmanifested (to the extent known).

Annual and Biennial Reports

A facility hazardous waste report must be submitted to EPA or state with authorization on a periodic basis. Federal regulations require that this report be submitted biennially, on March 1 of each even-numbered year. Many states require that this report be submitted to the state environmental agency on an annual basis and some require reporting on a more frequent basis. The report must cover activities during the previous calendar year (or two-years, as appropriate) and include the following:

- facility EPA identification number, name, and address
- the calendar year covered by the report
- the EPA identification number of each hazardous waste generator from which hazardous waste was received during the reporting year, and data on imported shipments (if any)
- a description and quantity of each hazardous waste received during the calendar year (listed by generator EPA identification number)
- the method for treatment or storage of each hazardous waste
- the most recent closure cost estimate
- a certification, signed by the operator of the facility (or his authorized representative)

For wastes generated at the facility, the annual report should include:

- facility EPA identification number, name, and address
- the calendar year(s) covered by the report
- the EPA identification number, name, and address of each off-site treatment, storage, and disposal company in the United States to which hazardous waste was shipped during the reporting year
- the name and EPA identification number of each transporter used during the reporting year
- a description, EPA hazardous waste number, DOT hazard class, and quantity of each hazardous waste shipped off-site to a TSD facility (listed by TSD facility EPA identification number)
- a description of the efforts undertaken during the reporting year to reduce the volume and toxicity of waste generated
- a description of the changes in volume and toxicity of waste actually achieved during the reporting in comparison to previous years
- a certification signed by the facility's authorized representative

Incident Report

In the event that the contingency plan is implemented, an incident report must be submitted within 15 days after the incident to the EPA Regional Administrator (or the state with authorization) as described in Chapter 9.

Additional Reporting Requirements

Within 60 days of the completion of final closure, the facility must submit to the EPA regional administrator, by registered mail, a certification that the facility has been closed in accordance with the specifications of the approved closure plan. The certification will be signed by the facility operator and an independent registered professional engineer.

If requested by EPA or otherwise required by regulatory requirements, the facility must submit reports pursuant to 40 CFR 264 (or 265, as appropriate) Subparts F and K through N.

REQUIREMENTS FOR PERMITTED AND INTERIM STATUS STORAGE FACILITIES

Facilities that store hazardous waste, except for hazardous waste generators that accumulate hazardous waste in accordance with the requirements presented in Chapter 3, must obtain a Part B permit for their storage activities.

Storage may occur in either tanks or containers. There is no maximum time limit for storage at permitted facilities. However, wastes subject to the land disposal restrictions may not be stored for over 1 year.

Container Storage

Container Condition
Each container used to store hazardous waste must be in good condition. Containers in good condition are free from severe rusting and structural defects. If a container begins to leak, the hazardous waste in the leaking container must be immediately transferred to a container (or tank) which is in good condition. If the container is to be used for the off-installation transportation of hazardous waste, the container must also meet DOT container condition requirements.

Compatibility of the Container with the Hazardous Waste Stored
Containers used to store hazardous waste must be made of or lined with materials which will not react with and are otherwise compatible with the hazardous waste to be stored. The DOT hazardous materials table identifies regulatory requirements for containers used to hold hazardous materials. If a DOT specification container is used for the specific waste type being stored, it can be assumed that the container is compatible with the waste. Keep in mind that hazardous wastes are frequently mixtures of several constituents, therefore it is important to ensure that all of the constituents are compatible with the container materials of construction (or liner).

Management of Containers
Containers used to store hazardous waste must be kept closed at all times, except for when waste is actually being added to or removed from the container. The federal regulations do not clearly define the word "closed," which may lead to some confusion. In general, a container is closed if its original closures, such as bung caps or drum heads, are secured to the container. Therefore, a closed-head 55-gallon drum should have its original (or equivalent replacement) bung caps screwed tightly into the bung openings. During storage, an open-head 55-gallon drum should have its drum head in place with the retaining ring properly secured with the appropriate nut and bolt. Any other types of containers used to store hazardous waste should be kept closed in a similar manner.

Containers used to store hazardous waste must not be opened, handled, or stored in any manner which may rupture the container or cause it to leak. This is a broad requirement that must be carefully considered because if container leakage does occur, the clean-up activities and costs could far outweigh the efforts taken to safely open, handle and store the containers.

Opening Containers

At a storage facility, there are only a few instances in which containers are to be opened:

- when adding waste to a container
- when collecting a waste sample for analysis
- when removing waste from a container, perhaps to transfer the waste to a container in good condition

To open a closed-head 55-gallon drum, a bung wrench should be used. If the material in the drum is combustible or flammable, a sparkproof (made of bronze or aluminum) bung wrench should be used to prevent accidental ignition of the waste due to sparks. Closed head drums should be opened by loosening the nut on the retaining ring, removing the retaining ring, and then removing the drum head. If the material in the drum is combustible or flammable, a spark-proof (made of bronze or aluminum) wrench should be used to prevent accidental ignition of the waste due to sparks.

If a drum cannot be open as described above because the bung cap has been corroded in place, do not attempt to open the drum by piercing the drum or adding a "cheater bar" to the bung wrench. Use of either of these devices may result in the release of hazardous waste when the drum is opened. Drums that cannot be opened by normal means should be overpacked and properly transported to a facility that has the appropriate equipment to safely open them.

Container Handling Recommendations

It is important to handle containers in a manner that will avoid ruptures or releases. Ruptures or releases may occur during waste accumulation, on-site transportation, and management at the storage facility. Precautions that should be followed to prevent releases during container handling are listed below:

- Fill containers with liquid waste to not more than 90% of their capacity. In warm weather, some liquids may expand or volatilize which may produce enough pressure to pop the head off of the container. In cold weather, liquids may freeze, and in doing so may pop the head of the container.
- Use a funnel in the bung to fill closed head containers. This will ensure that all waste is poured into the container and does not spill on the top of the container. After filling the funnel should be removed and the container closed. If the funnel has any hazardous waste residues remaining, the residues should be rinsed into the container, or the funnel should be placed in a suitable closed hazardous waste accumulation container.

- Do not transport drums by rolling, dragging, or pushing. The safest way to move a single drum is to use a drum caddy, dolly, hand truck, or forklift with a drum grappler attached (the drum should be tied down to the transport device). When moving several drums, the drums should be placed on pallets and moved with a forklift.
- Do not stack drums more than two high. Drums containing flammable liquids should not be stacked at all.
- Do not allow the movement of vehicles such as trucks, forklifts, private vehicles etc. in or near the container storage area.
- If containers must be stored outdoors, store in an area protected from precipitation.

Inspection Requirements

Areas where containers bearing hazardous waste are stored must be inspected at least weekly for deterioration of containers and deterioration of the containment system by corrosion or other factors.

Containment

For hazardous wastes containing free liquids or hazardous wastes with EPA hazardous waste numbers F020, F021, F022, F023, F026, or F027, a containment system is required for storage facilities to ensure that hazardous waste constituents are not released to the environment. The containment system must be designed and operated as follows:

- A base that is free of cracks or gaps and is sufficiently impervious to contain leaks, spills, and precipitation must underlie the containers.
- The containers must be stored in a manner that will protect them from contact with accumulated precipitation or spilled liquids, this may be accomplished by any of the following: base can be sloped in a manner which will drain and remove liquids resulting from leaks, spills or precipitation; the containment system can be designed or operated to drain and remove liquids resulting from leaks, spills, or precipitation; or, the containers may be elevated from the containment floor (such as on pallets).
- The containment system must have sufficient capacity to contain 10% of the total volume of containers stored or the volume of the largest container in storage, whichever is greater. Containers that do not contain free liquids need not be considered in this determination.
- Runon into the containment system must be prevented unless the collection system has sufficient excess capacity (in addition to that described in the requirement immediately above) to contain any runon which might enter the system.
- Spilled or leaked waste and accumulated precipitation must be removed from the sump or collection area in as timely a manner as is necessary to prevent overflow of the collection system. If the material collected in this manner is classified as hazardous waste (see Chapter 2 for guidance on classification of hazardous waste), it

must be managed as hazardous waste in accordance with all applicable regulatory requirements for waste accumulation, transportation, treatment, storage, and disposal. If the collected material is discharged through a point source to waters of the United States, it is subject to the requirements of Section 402 of the Clean Water Act.

Hazardous wastes that do not contain free liquids must be stored in an area that is sloped or is otherwise designed and operated to drain and remove liquid resulting from precipitation or the containers must be elevated or otherwise protected from contact with accumulated liquid.

Ignitable or Reactive Wastes in Containers
Containers holding ignitable or reactive waste must be located at least 50 feet from (inside) the facility property line.

Compatibility of Waste to Waste and Waste to Other Materials
To prevent fires, explosions, gaseous emissions, leaching or other discharge of hazardous waste constituents, wastes that are incompatible with each other must not be placed into the same container. Hazardous waste must also not be placed in a container that previously contained an incompatible waste or material unless the container has been decontaminated. When incompatible wastes are stored at a storage facility (in separate containers), the incompatible waste containers must be separated from each other by means of a dike, berm, wall, or other device. If there are other incompatible materials near the storage area, such as in open tanks or surface impoundments, the waste containers must be protected from these materials in a like manner.

Closure Requirements for Storage Facilities
At closure, all hazardous waste and hazardous waste residues must be removed from the container storage area containment system. Remaining containers, liners, bases, and soil containing or contaminated with hazardous waste or hazardous waste residues must be decontaminated or removed. Any hazardous waste removed from the storage area or containment system, such as residues removed from containment pads or sumps, must be managed in accordance with all the applicable requirements for waste accumulation, transportation, treatment, storage, and disposal of hazardous waste.

Management of Tank Systems

Existing Tanks
Existing tanks used to store hazardous waste must have secondary containment (as described below) or the tanks must be assessed by a independent, qualified registered professional engineer attesting to the tanks integrity. This assessment must have been accomplished by January 12, 1988 and must have considered at least the following parameters:

- design standards to which the tank system was constructed
- hazard characteristics of the wastes that have been and will be stored

- existing corrosion protection measures
- age of the tank system
- results of a leak test, internal inspection, or other examination

If the assessment shows that the tank system is leaking or unfit for use, the installation must repair, retrofit, or replace the tank in accordance with 40 CFR 265.196.

Up until existing tanks are provided with secondary containment, the tanks and ancillary equipment must be inspected annually for leaks. A record of the inspections must be maintained on file at the facility.

New Tanks
New tank systems or components must be certified by an independent, qualified registered professional engineer for structural integrity and compliance with applicable design standards. All components which contact soil or water must be evaluated by a corrosion expert. Factors to be evaluated during these certifications are identified in 40 CFR 264.192. A written certification obtained from the professional engineer and the corrosion expert attesting to the integrity of the tank system must be maintained on file at the facility.

Containment and Detection of Releases
Secondary containment is required for the following categories of tank systems:

- New tank systems or components, prior to being put into service.
- Existing tank systems used to store or treat wastes with EPA hazardous waste numbers F020, F021, F022, F023, F026, and F029.
- Existing tanks of known and documented age that are 15 years old or within two years of January 12, 1987, whichever is later.
- If the age of a tank system is unknown, secondary containment is required within 8 years of January 12, 1987, but if the age of the installation is greater than 7 years, secondary containment must be provided by the time the installation reaches 15 years of age, or within 2 years of January 12, 1987, whichever is later.
- For tank systems that store or treat materials that become hazardous waste after January 12, 1987, secondary containment is required as specified for new and existing tanks as described above, except that the date that a material becomes a hazardous waste must be used in place of January 12, 1987.

Secondary containment systems must be designed, installed, and operated to prevent migration of wastes or liquids to the environment and must be capable of detecting and collecting any releases and accumulated liquids until the collected material is removed. To ensure this requirement is met, the secondary containment system must be:

- constructed of or lined with materials that are compatible with the wastes to be stored and have sufficient strength and thickness to prevent tank failure
- placed on a foundation or base capable of providing support to the secondary containment system

- provided with a leak detection system that can detect failure of the tank
- a liner, vault, double-walled tank, or other device approved by the EPA regional administrator or the Administrator of the state with authorization
- designed or operated to contain 100% of the capacity of the largest tank within its boundary
- designed or operated to prevent prevent accumulation of precipitation and runon or have sufficient excess capacity to accommodate precipitation from a 25-year, 24-hour rainfall event
- free of cracks or gaps
- comply with other requirements identified in 40 CFR 264.193

General Operating Requirements

Tanks used to store hazardous waste must be operated in a manner that will prevent the release of hazardous constituents to the environment. To meet this requirement, the regulations require that nothing be put into the tank that may cause the tank or its ancillary equipment to fail and that each tank be provided with spill and overflow prevention equipment. Spill prevention controls should prevent the release of material during tank loading and unloading. Overfill controls may include devices such as level sensing devices, high-level alarms, automatic feed cutoff, or bypass to a standby tank. In uncovered tanks, sufficient freeboard must be maintained to prevent overtopping by wave or wind action or by precipitation.

Inspections

The following components of the tank system and its components must be inspected at least daily:

- overfill control equipment—to detect possible system failure
- above ground portions of the tank system—to detect corrosion or waste releases
- data from monitoring and leak detection systems—to ensure the tank is operated according to its design
- construction materials and areas surrounding externally accessible portions of the tank system—to detect erosion and signs of releases of hazardous waste (for example wet spots or dead vegetation).

Cathodic protection systems (if present) must be inspected to ensure that they are functioning properly. The proper operation of a cathodic protection system must be confirmed within six months after initial installation and annually thereafter. All sources of impressed current employed in a cathodic protection system must be inspected or tested at least every other month.

Response to Leaks and Spills

In the event of a spill, leak, or other imminent release from a tank system or if a tank system is unfit for use, the system must be immediately removed from service and the following actions must be taken:

- The flow of hazardous waste to the tank system and secondary containment must be stopped and the cause of the release determined.
- Waste must be removed from the tank system within 24 hours. If complete removal of waste from the system is not possible, as much waste must be removed as is necessary to allow for inspection and repair of the system.
- If materials are released to a secondary containment system, all released material must be removed within 24 hours or in as timely a manner as is possible to prevent harm to human health and the environment.
- A visual inspection of the tank area must be conducted and based on the inspection actions must be taken to prevent further migration of the leak or spill to soils or surface water; visual contamination of soils or surface water must be removed and properly disposed of.
- Any release from a tank to the environment (except for releases ≤ 1 pound and which are immediately contained and cleaned up) must be reported to the EPA regional administrator (or state with authorization) within 24 hours of its detection. If a report is made to the National Response Center in accordance with 40 CFR 302 (because of a release of a reportable quantity of a hazardous substance), that report will satisfy this requirement.
- Within 30 days of detection of a release to the environment, a written report must be submitted to the EPA regional administrator (or state with authorization) which provides the following information: likely route of migration of the release; characteristics of the surrounding soil (soil composition, geology, hydrogeology, climate); results of any monitoring or sampling conducted in connection with the release; proximity to downgradient drinking water, surface water, and populated areas; description of response actions taken or planned.

Based on the information submitted or other data obtained regarding the release, EPA or the state with authorization may issue a corrective action order or take other response actions deemed necessary to protect human health or the environment.

After a spill or release or a determination that a tank is unfit for use, the tank system may not be returned to use until certain requirements have been met. If the cause of the spill is not related to the system's structural integrity, the system may be returned to service as soon as necessary repairs have been made and any necessary operating modifications have been implemented to prevent a spill recurrence. If the system has secondary containment, it may be returned to service as soon as the primary containment system has been repaired and operating procedures have been modified to prevent a recurrence of the leak.

If a leak occurs from a tank system that does not have secondary containment, the system may not be returned to service until the leaking components have been repaired and provided with secondary containment. If the source of the leak is an above-ground component that can be visually inspected, the component must be repaired and may be returned to service, without the addition of secondary containment, provided that the repairs are certified by an independent, qualified, registered professional engineer. If the source of the leak cannot be inspected visually, the entire component must be provided with secondary containment before operations resume.

If extensive repairs such as installation of an internal liner or repair of a ruptured primary or secondary containment vessel are required, the repairs must be certified by an independent, qualified, registered, professional engineer.

Tank System Closure

A closure plan is required for tanks that store hazardous waste. The plan must specify how hazardous waste residues, contaminated containment system components, contaminated soils, and structures will be removed or decontaminated. The closure plan is required to be submitted along with the Part B permit application and a closure plan will become part of the permit, when granted.

If closure is required in response to a leak, spill, or determination that a tank system is unfit for use before the closure plan is approved, a closure plan must be submitted to EPA or the state with authorization as soon as a decision has been made to close the system. If a tank leaks and it can be demonstrated that all contaminated soils cannot be practicably removed or decontaminated, the tank system must be closed as a landfill and the requirements for landfill closure and postclosure must be complied with.

The closure plan for tank systems without secondary containment must describe the closure activities to be taken to remove waste residues and contaminated soils and equipment. The plan for these systems must also include contingent closure procedures to be taken in the event removal or decontaminated of all contaminated cannot be accomplished (which would require closure as a landfill).

TREATMENT AND DISPOSAL FACILITIES

Facilities that treat or dispose of hazardous waste generally require a RCRA permit or interim status. Some treatment facilities and operations however, as described on page 86, do not need permits (or are granted a permit by rule). To obtain a permit or to operate under interim status, hazardous waste treatment facilities must comply with the detailed regulations in 40 CFR Parts 264 (permitted facilities) and 265 (interim status facilities). These regulations present specific procedures that must be must be followed for particular types of treatment facilities. It is beyond the scope of this training guide to present the detailed requirements for each type of hazardous waste treatment facility; however, the reader may find the current requirements in 40 CFR 264 and 265, Subparts K through X.

Chapter 7
RCRA Training Requirements

WHO MUST BE TRAINED AND HOW OFTEN

The regulatory framework that identifies who must be trained may be circuitous, but must be complied with nevertheless. 40 CFR 265.16 and 40 CFR 264.16 require training for personnel at interim status and permitted hazardous waste management treatment, storage, and disposal (TSD) facilities. Hazardous waste generators are instructed in 40 CFR 262.34(a)(4) to comply with the requirements of 40 CFR 265.16 which is reprinted in Appendix E of this handbook. Therefore, hazardous waste management training is required for personnel who work at facilities that fit into any of the following categories:

Permitted hazardous waste TSD facilities
Interim status hazardous waste TSD facilities
Large quantity generators (see the definition in Chapter 3)

Persons who must be trained include those who are involved with or are occupationally exposed to hazardous waste. At a facility that generates, treats, stores, or disposes of hazardous waste, this may include (but is not limited to) persons who perform any of the following tasks:

- decide which wastes are hazardous waste
- add hazardous waste into accumulation containers or tanks at accumulation points
- remove hazardous waste from accumulation tanks or containers
- transport hazardous waste to or from accumulation points

- transport hazardous waste to or from storage and treatment units
- respond to spills, fires, or explosions involving hazardous waste
- complete hazardous waste manifests, annual reports, or exception reports
- inspect hazardous waste accumulation points, storage, treatment, or disposal facilities
- operate or work at accumulation points
- work at permitted or interim status TSD facilities
- conduct any tasks involving occupational exposure to or which require management of hazardous waste.

The required training must be successfully completed by all of the personnel described above. For new personnel, training must be successfully completed within 6 months after assignment to the facility or to a new position at the facility, whichever is later. Until that time, untrained personnel must not perform any tasks involving hazardous waste management unless they are supervised by trained personnel. Facility personnel must take part in an annual review of the entire training program.

The federal regulations do not specifically require small quantity generators to train their employees; however, employees at these facilities must be "thoroughly familiar with proper waste handling and emergency procedures, relevant to their responsibilities during normal facility operations and emergencies." There is no EPA requirement for transporters to train their employees regarding EPA regulations; however, DOT requires training for hazardous materials transporters. If a transporter imports hazardous waste into the United States or mixes hazardous waste of differing DOT shipping descriptions, the transporter must comply with the generator regulations and hence the training requirements.

SCOPE OF MANDATORY TRAINING

There are two general components to the training requirement in 40 CFR 265.16; personnel must be trained: 1. how to perform their duties in a way that ensures the facility's compliance with the regulations; and 2. how to respond to emergencies involving hazardous waste. EPA regulations published in 40 CFR 265.16 regarding personnel training are presented in Appendix E of this handbook.

To fully comply with the regulations, the training should be customized to meet your facility's specific requirements. If your facility has unique procedures for waste determination, accumulation, transportation, and turn-in, they should be incorporated into the program. Moreover, you will need to include your facility's specific emergency response procedures. The next sections provide guidance for customizing the training program.

Fitting the Course Scope to Course Attendees

At large facilities, it may not be feasible to present a single training program to the entire population of personnel who generate or manage hazardous waste on-site. Therefore, it is recommended that the training program be presented in a manner that allows the trainer to fit the course scope to the course attendees. You can best do this by arranging specific training for similar activities at the same time. For example, you can present one training program for activities that generate hazardous waste as a result of painting operations; a separate training program might be presented for activities that generate hazardous waste as a result of cleaning and degreasing operations; and another program for operators of the facility's hazardous waste storage facility.

Some personnel become involved in hazardous waste management from an administrative perspective. For example, laboratory technicians may collect samples for analytical analysis; the public relations department may field requests for information from the public or local media regarding wastes generated on-site; the plant manager may sign hazardous waste manifests; and the regulatory affairs department may become involved in permit applications. Each requires training so that they will be able to conduct their responsibilities in a manner which complies with the regulations. Each need not, however, receive the same depth of training as that required for accumulation point managers, or each other. For example, the laboratory technician needs to know regulatory definitions of solid waste and hazardous waste, and how to collect and preserve samples in accordance with SW-846 (a document detailing EPA-required sampling and analysis techniques), which analytical methods to specify when submitting samples for analysis, and safety procedures to be followed during sample collection. The public relations department need not receive training regarding sample collection and analysis, but should learn the definition of hazardous waste and when the public should be notified in the event of an emergency.

Some personnel may only become involved in hazardous waste management when they respond to emergencies. These personnel may include members of the your fire brigade or hazardous materials response team. These personnel need in-depth knowledge and experience in the implementation of the contingency plan.

Training Required by Other Laws

Both this handbook and the accompanying training course are designed to meet RCRA training requirements for hazardous waste. Other laws and regulations require training for many of the same personnel who must receive RCRA training. For example, persons who work at permitted TSD facilities as well as hazardous substance emergency response personnel are required to be trained in accordance with OSHA regulations published in 29 CFR 1910.120. Personnel who work in areas in which hazardous chemicals are present may be required to be trained in accordance with OSHA regulations published in 29 CFR 1910.1200 or in accordance with substance specific standards in 29 CFR 1910.1000. Personnel who prepare hazardous materials and wastes for shipment must be instructed as to applicable DOT hazardous material regulations in accordance with 49 CFR 173.1(b). To ensure that facility personnel meet all of the training requirements specified by environmental laws, you should review the regulations cited above and determine if training beyond the scope of this course is required.

Chapter 8

Closure of Hazardous Waste Accumulation and TSD Facilities

EPA regulations in 40 CFR 264, Subpart G, contain procedures for closing permitted TSD facilities. Regulations in 40 CFR 265, Subpart G, contain procedures for closing hazardous waste accumulation points and TSD facilities that have interim status.

"Closure" is the period after which hazardous wastes are no longer accepted at a facility or accumulation point, and during which time the generator ships the waste off-site or the operator of the TSD completes treatment, storage, or disposal operations. "Postclosure" is the period (usually 30 years) after closure when owners and operators of disposal facilities are subject to various monitoring and maintenance requirements. Storage facilities are not typically required to perform postclosure care if storage units are dismantled and removed or decontaminated and other contaminated materials and soil are removed or decontaminated. However, if hazardous waste or contamination remains on-site after closure, postclosure care may be required.

An entire facility does not have to be shut down in order to initiate closure. Closure refers to the shutdown of active hazardous waste accumulation, treatment, storage, or disposal portions of a facility. The "active portion" refers to that part of the facility where treatment, storage or disposal operations are conducted or have been conducted since RCRA hazardous waste regulations became effective.

CLOSURE OF ACCUMULATION POINTS

When closing an accumulation point, the need for any further maintenance at the accumulation point must be re-duced. In addition, the generator must control, minimize, or eliminate the postclosure escape of hazardous waste, hazardous constituents, leachate, contaminated runoff, or hazardous waste decomposition products to the ground, surface water, or to the atmosphere. During closure, all contaminated equipment, structures, and soil must be properly disposed of in accordance with hazardous waste management regulations or decontaminated.

A detailed closure plan is not required for accumulation points. However, you should be prepared to properly dispose of or decontaminate all equipment, structures, and soil that has been in contact with hazardous waste so further monitoring or maintenance of the accumulation point is unnecessary.

Closure of Tanks at Accumulation Points

Tanks that are used for the accumulation of hazardous waste must be closed in accordance with the RCRA regulations which require that all waste residues, contaminated containment system components such as liners, and contaminated soils, structures, and equipment must be decontaminated or removed and managed as hazardous waste.

If the soil surrounding the tank has become contaminated by hazardous waste and you determine that the contaminated soil cannot be practically removed or decontaminated, then the tank must be closed with the soil in place and you must manage that site as a closed landfill. You must also perform post-closure care of the site for 30 years.

CLOSURE OF TREATMENT, STORAGE, AND DISPOSAL FACILITIES

TSD facilities must close in a manner that minimizes the need for further maintenance of the facility and eliminates hazardous waste releases and runoff from the facility after closure. There are specific closure requirements for each type of hazardous waste management unit and facility. In general, closure and postclosure care requirements are more stringent and costly for disposal operations than they are for storage operations. When closure is completed, all hazardous waste residues and contaminated soil, structures, and equipment must be decontaminated or removed and disposed of properly. EPA requires specific management requirements for the closure of tanks, surface impoundments, waste piles, land treatment units, and landfills.

Closure Plans

Both permitted and interim status TSD facilities must have written closure plans. A *closure plan* is a document that identifies the steps that will be followed to completely or partially close the facility at any point during the facility's intended life, and to completely close the facility at the end of its operating life. In general, a closure plan must include the following information:

- a description of how each hazardous waste management unit at the facility will be closed
- a description of the maximum extent of unclosed operations during the active life of the facility
- an estimate of the largest inventory of hazardous waste ever on-site during the facility's life and a description of the methods that will be used to remove, transport, treat, store, or dispose of that amount of waste
- a detailed description of how hazardous waste residues and contaminated containment systems, equipment, structures, and soil will be decontaminated or removed. This description must include procedures for cleaning equipment, removing contaminated soil, sampling and testing surrounding soil, and determining the extent of decontamination
- a detailed description of other activities that may be necessary during closure including ground water monitoring, leachate collection, runon control, and runoff control
- a schedule specifying the time required to close each hazardous waste management unit and to close all units within the facility
- an estimate of the expected year of closure

If a TSD facility has a tank system that does not have a secondary containment as described in Chapter 3, and is not exempt from the secondary containment requirement, then a contingent closure plan and contingent postclosure plan are required in addition to the closure plan. The contingent closure plan must identify procedures the facility will follow if contaminated soil cannot be practicably removed or decontaminated. A tank system without containment is considered to be a landfill when preparing closure and postclosure plans.

Permitted facilities are required to submit closure plans to EPA or to the authorized state with their Part B permit application, and the closure plan becomes part of the permit. Facilities that have interim status and manage waste in tanks or containers must submit closure plans upon request and at least 45 days before the final volume of waste will be managed at the facility.

Closure plans must be amended within 60 days of the date of any changes in waste management activities that affect the terms of the plan. If the TSD facility has a Part B permit, changes to the closure plan are considered to be modifications to the permit, and the permittee must go through the permit modification process. If an unexpected event occurs during closure which affects the plan, the facility must submit a request for a permit modification within 30 days of the unexpected event. EPA also has the authority to ask a facility to modify its closure plan and permit during closure.

Closure Schedule and Certification

Permitted TSD facilities must notify EPA or the state in writing at least 60 days before the date the facility expects to begin closure of a surface impoundment, waste pile, land treatment unit, or landfill unit. The notification is required 45 days before closure is expected of treatment or storage tanks, container storage, or incinerator units. In general, the date the facility expects to begin closure must be 30 days after the date on which the hazardous waste management unit will receive the final volume of hazardous waste. The expected date of closure may be extended up to 1 year from the date the facility received the most recent volume of hazardous waste if there is a reasonable possibility the unit will receive additional hazardous wastes.

Within 90 days of receiving the final volume of hazardous waste, the facility must treat, remove from the unit, or dispose of (on-site) all hazardous waste in accordance with the closure plan. EPA or the state may approve longer periods if necessary. TSD facilities must complete all closure activities within 180 days after the final volume of waste is received at the closing unit. EPA or the authorized state may extend this time limit if the facility demonstrates that closure will take longer to complete or if a new owner begins operations at the facility.

Within 60 days of completion of closure activities of a hazardous waste surface impoundment, waste pile, land treatment unit, and landfill unit, the owner or operator of the facility and an independent registered professional engineer must certify to EPA or the authorized state that the facility has been closed in accordance with the specifications in the approved closure plan.

POSTCLOSURE CARE

Postclosure planning and care requirements apply to hazardous waste disposal facilities such as landfills and land treatment units, and to waste piles and surface impoundments from which the facility plans to remove the wastes at closure. Postclosure care also applies to tank systems that do not have secondary containment and are not exempt from requirements stipulating secondary containment systems.

Land disposal units are subject to groundwater monitoring, facility security, and general maintenance requirements where wastes remain on-site subsequent to closure. Monitoring and maintenance activities must continue for 30 years after closure. EPA or the authorized state can reduce or extend the postclosure period if groundwater or leachate monitoring results show that a different postclosure period will protect human health and the environment. Security is also required for the closed facility if hazardous waste remains exposed after closure or if access by the public or domestic livestock may pose a hazard.

Any postclosure use of the property that will disturb the integrity of the final cover, liner(s), or any other component of the waste containment systems or monitoring systems is prohibited. EPA may waive this prohibition if the proposed use of the property will not increase the hazard to human health or the environment, or the activity is necessary to reduce the threat to human health or the environment.

Postclosure Plans

Land disposal facilities must have a written postclosure plan. Postclosure plans must also be prepared for surface impoundments or waste piles from which the facility plans to remove the wastes at closure. A postclosure plan describes activities that will be carried out after closure and the frequency of those activities. A postclosure plan must include the following information:

- a description of the groundwater monitoring program and the frequency of monitoring
- a description of the planned maintenance of the landfill cap, final cover, other containment systems, and monitoring equipment and the frequency of those activities
- the name, address, and phone number of the person or office to contact about the disposal unit during postclosure care

Permitted facilities must submit postclosure plans as part of the Part B permit application. Facilities that have interim status must submit postclosure plans to EPA or the authorized state at least 180 day prior to closure. Postclosure plans must also be furnished to EPA or the authorized state at any time upon request.

A postclosure plan must be amended within 60 days of any changes in the operating plan or facility design or any other events during the active life of the facility that affect the plan. During the post-closure care period, the plan must be amended anytime there are changes in monitoring or maintenance plans or if there are events which affect the plan. To change the plan, the owner or operator of the facility must petition EPA or the authorized state to permit changes to the plan. EPA or the state may also require changes to the plan in response to a citizen's petition.

Postclosure Notices

Survey Plat

By the time the certification of closure of a hazardous waste disposal unit is submitted, the owner or operator of a closed disposal unit must also submit to the local zoning authority (or to the authority with jurisdiction over local land use) and to EPA or the state a survey plat. The survey plat must be prepared and certified by a professional land surveyor, must indicate the location and dimensions of landfill cells or other disposal units, and must contain a note that states the requirement not to disturb the hazardous waste disposal unit.

Postclosure Notices

Within 60 days of closure of a hazardous waste disposal unit, the owner or operator must submit to the local zoning authority and to EPA or the state a record of the type, location and quantity of hazardous waste disposed of in each landfill cell or other disposal unit. The owner or operator must record on the deed to the property a notation that will inform any potential purchaser that the land has been used to manage hazardous waste, that use is restricted in accordance with closure requirements, and the survey plat and the hazardous waste disposal record has been submitted to the local zoning authority and to EPA or the state.

The owner or operator must also certify to EPA or the state that the deed notification has been recorded and submit a copy of the deed.

Certification of Completion of Postclosure Care

Within 60 days of completion of postclosure activities at a hazardous waste disposal unit, the owner or operator of the facility and an independent, registered, professional engineer must certify to EPA or the authorized state that postclosure care was performed in accordance with the specifications in the approved postclosure plan. Documentation of maintenance and monitoring activities which occurred during postclosure and that support the certification must also be submitted.

Chapter 9
Spills, Fires, Explosions, and Other Releases

NATIONAL CONTINGENCY PLAN

Design of the National Contingency Plan

Until the early 1970s, there were few means for establishing responsibility of cleaning up a release (such as a spill) of a substance that was hazardous to human health or had contaminated the environment. Congress first addressed this issue in 1972 when it called for the National Contingency Plan in the amendments to the Federal Water Pollution Control Act. The National Contingency Plan assigned immediate responsibility for cleanup actions in the event of a discharge of petroleum products into U.S. waters to the individual(s) with stewardship over the materials at the time of the release. By the end of the 1970s, the coverage of the Plan included a wide range of chemical substances.

By the end of the 1970s, Congress also recognized that the environment was being contaminated and human health was being threatened through land and airborne releases of hazardous substances. In response, Congress revised the the National Contingency Plan (as well as changing the title to the National Oil and Hazardous Substances Pollution Contingency Plan) when it created the Comprehensive Environmental Response, Compensation and Liability Act (CERCLA). The reason for revising the Plan was to clearly delineate the responsibilities of federal, state, and local governments in response activities.

While the applicability of the plan was substantially broadened by CERCLA, its goal remained unchanged: to provide efficient, coordinated, and effective response to discharges of oil and releases of hazardous substances, pollutants, and contaminants. The National Contingency Plan applies to:

- discharges or substantial threats of discharges of oil into U.S. waters, and
- releases or substantial threats of releases of hazardous substances into the environment, and releases or substantial threats of releases of pollutants or contaminants that may present an imminent and substantial danger to public health or welfare.

The regulations that apply to the National Contingency Plan are published in 40 CFR 300. The contingency planning requirements of RCRA were inspired by and are a direct outgrowth of the National Contingency Plan.

On-Scene Coordinator

In order to plan for and respond to oil discharges and hazardous substance releases, a National Response Team has been established. The chairman of the National Response Team is a representative of the EPA, and the vice chairman is a representative of the U.S. Coast Guard (USCG). If a discharge or release cannot be remediated on a local, state, or regional level, it is the responsibility of the EPA and USCG to designate an on-scene coordinator to coordinate and direct response and removal efforts.

PREPAREDNESS AND PREVENTION

Applicability and Scope of Requirements

RCRA regulations published in 40 CFR 265.31 require facilities that generate hazardous waste to be maintained and operated in a way that is protective of human health and that minimizes the possibility of a fire, explosion, or release of hazardous waste into the environment. To meet this requirement, generators must maintain equipment on-site to facilitate remediation efforts and to protect human health. Additionally, arrangements must be made with local organizations and authorities who might be called upon to provide emergency assistance.

Required Equipment

Unless none of the hazards posed by your hazardous waste could require a particular type of equipment, your facility must be equipped with the emergency equipment listed below (see 40 CFR 265.32). When deciding on a location for the equipment, keep in mind that it should be near enough to the hazardous waste area to make it convenient and easy to get to in the event of an emergency, but not so close that it cannot be approached or could be damaged in the event of a spill or fire. Required equipment consists of:

- a device capable of summoning emergency assistance from emergency responders. Examples of a suitable device would be a telephone available in the area where hazardous wastes are handled or a hand-held two-way radio
- water at adequate volume and pressure to supply water hose streams, or foam producing equipment, or automatic sprinklers, or water spray systems
- an internal communications or alarm system capable of providing immediate emergency instruction to facility personnel who can be affected by the emergency incident

  The determination of what type of system to install near an area at which hazardous waste is handled is location specific. Consequently, the decision of whether to use a system that can provide voice instruction (such as a public address system) or one that sounds a signal (such as a bell or horn) is left up to you.

  Whenever hazardous waste is being handled, the person involved in the hazardous waste handling operation must have immediate access to the communications or alarm system. If more than one person is in the area when the waste is being handled, all personnel must have either direct access to the system or access through visual or voice contact with another person.

- portable fire extinguishers, fire control equipment, spill control equipment, and decontamination equipment

  Fire extinguishers are coded A, B, C, and/or D, depending on the types of fires they are most suited to extinguish (refer to Emergency Response Actions beginning on page 112). Ensure that the fire extinguisher selected for a hazardous waste handling area is suited

to the type of fire to which the waste could act as fuel. Also, ensure that the size of the fire extinguisher is commensurate with the amount of hazardous waste that may catch fire. (Contact your local fire department for assistance.)

Fire control equipment refers to all other types of equipment used to suppress the spread of a fire other than fire extinguishers. This includes stationary extinguishing equipment that dispense foam, inert gas, or dry chemicals.

The type and amount of spill control equipment placed near a hazardous waste handling area depends on the type and amount of hazardous waste in the area as well as its location. Solid, granular absorbent such as clay or vermiculite or commercially available absorbent pads or pillows could act as a suitable sorbent for liquid hazardous waste. If the liquid is corrosive, a neutralizing absorbent would be necessary.

If the waste handling area is near a stream, or a spill could potentially enter a stream or body of water, it would be beneficial to have a boom ready to set in place to prevent or restrict the spread of hazardous waste across the surface of the water. Hazardous waste handled in areas with floor drains necessitate a drain covering or plug to be on hand to prevent the waste from running into the drain.

The type of decontamination equipment required to be available near a hazardous waste handling area depends on the type of waste in the area and the types of equipment that may need to be decontaminated after responding to an emergency. In instances where personal protective equipment such as gloves, boots, and aprons, and spill response equipment such as brooms, shovels, and dustpans require decontamination, a hose that delivers a steady stream of water may accomplish adequate decontamination. Where waste residues prove more difficult to remove, such as contaminated soil hardened in the bucket of a backhoe, a scrub brush, and an appropriate cleaning solution or steam generating equipment may be necessary for effective decontamination.

Testing and Maintenance of Equipment

The RCRA regulations do not specify a schedule for inspecting the condition of emergency response equipment. However, all facility communications or alarm systems, fire protection equipment, spill control equipment, and decontamination equipment that has been determined to be necessary at a hazardous waste handling area must be tested and maintained as frequently as is necessary to assure its proper operation in the event of an emergency. Consequently, it is recommended that a periodic inspection schedule be established and inspections documented (refer to Facility Contingency Plan beginning on page 105 and Figure 9.2).

Arrangements with Local Authorities

If it is foreseeable that off-site agencies or organizations may be called upon to provide emergency support, the arrangements described below must be attempted to be made (see 40 CFR 265.37). All arrangements made are to be documented (e.g., a signed letter from the local fire chief stating the date he will visit your facility and that his fire department will provide assistance). In the case where state or local authorities decline to enter into an agreement, the refusal must also be documented.

- Arrangements to familiarize police, fire departments, and emergency response teams with:

  the layout of your facility,
  properties of hazardous waste handled at your facility and associated hazards,
  places where facility personnel would normally be working,
  entrances to roads inside the facility, and
  possible evacuation routes.

  This can be done by providing each agency or organization with a copy of your contingency plan and a copy of the material safety data sheets for all virgin materials from which hazardous wastes are derived. Alternatively, you can invite outside emergency response personnel to your site to familiarize them with your facility and wastes.

  To demonstrate compliance with this requirement, it is recommended that you document your efforts. This may be achieved by retaining a copy of the cover letter you submitted with your contingency plan, or having each visitor sign an attendance log that is attached to the day's agenda.
- Where more than one police or fire department might respond to an emergency, agreements designating primary emergency authority to a specific police and a specific fire department, and agreements with any others to provide support to the primary responding department.
- Agreements with state emergency response teams, emergency response contractors, and equipment suppliers.
- Arrangements to familiarize local hospitals with the properties of hazardous waste handled at the facility and the types of injuries or illnesses that could result from fires, explosions, or releases from your facility.

  Hospital personnel can be made familiar with the properties of the hazardous wastes generated at your facility by familiarizing them with the properties of the virgin materials from which they were derived.

References

Besides material safety data sheets, many reference materials are available that provide additional health and safety information on a wide variety of hazardous materials. These reference materials include:

a. *Dangerous Properties of Industrial Materials*, by N. Irving Sax, contains a compilation of data on thousands of materials, and covers all areas of hazards. The most recent edition of this book was published in New York in 1989.
b. *ACGIH Threshold Limit Values* is a compilation of worker exposure limits to airborne concentrations of

hazardous materials as determined by the American Conference of Governmental Industrial Hygienists. This publication is available as both a book and as microfiche. It is published annually every August by ACGIH in Cincinnati, Ohio
c. *The Registry of Toxic Effects of Chemical Substances* (RTECS) is a compendium of health and safety information put together by the National Institutes of Health. This is also published as both a book and as microfiche. RTECS is updated quarterly in January, April, July, and October by NIOSH in Cincinatti, OH.
d. *Fire Protection Guide on Hazardous Materials*, published by the National Fire Protection Association (Quincy, MA, 1991), identifies the hazardous properties of the most common chemicals in use today.

FACILITY CONTINGENCY PLAN

EPA requires generators, treaters, storers, and disposers of hazardous waste to develop procedures to respond to emergencies. Large quantity generators who have at least one accumulation point on-site, and TSD facilities must incorporate the emergency response procedures into a contingency plan. Other generators must develop emergency response procedures. However, RCRA does not require the procedures to be detailed in a written document. The requirements for developing a contingency plan are presented in Subpart D of 40 CFR 265 and in Appendix E of this handbook.

The contingency plan must be designed to minimize hazards to human health or the environment from fires, explosions, or any unplanned sudden or non-sudden release of hazardous waste into the air, soil, and water. The procedures that will be followed to respond to emergencies must be detailed in the contingency plan. Specific requirements which must be incorporated into the plan are described below.

A copy of the current contingency plan must be maintained on-site. In addition, a copy of the plan and all revisions to the plan must be submitted to all local police departments, fire departments, hospitals, and state and local emergency response teams that may be called upon to provide emergency services. It is also recommended that departments on-site that may provide emergency services (such as the security, the plant nurse, or the plant fire brigade) be provided with a copy of the plan and revisions.

Content of the Contingency Plan

Contingency plans must include the following information:

Emergency Coordinator

At all times, there must be at least one individual on-site or on call (and able to reach the facility in a short period of time) who has the responsibility of coordinating all emergency response procedures. This is the emergency coordinator. The contingency plan must contain a current list of names, addresses, and office and home phone numbers of all persons who have the authority to act as the emergency coordinator. If there is more than one name listed, one person must be named as primary emergency coordinator and others must be listed in the order in which they will assume responsibility as alternates.

Emergency Assistance Agreements

The contingency plan must describe arrangements agreed to by organizations that may provide assistance in the event of an emergency. Organizations that may be called upon may be the local police or fire departments, local hospitals, contractors, and State and local emergency response teams.

The plan should document the capabilities of each organization as well as present some evidence (such as a signed letter) that the organization has agreed to assist. For example, in the event of a spill, the police department may be asked to secure the area surrounding a spill, evacuate people nearby who may be affected by vapors from the spill, and transport injured people to the hospital. The local ambulance service may be called upon to transport injured people to the local hospital.

The local hospital may be asked to treat individuals injured or overexposed to the spilled waste. The local fire department may be asked to mitigate the potential for fires as well as control any fires that may develop as a result of the spill.

If outside organizations may ever be requested to come onto your site to assist with an emergency situation, you must make arrangements to familiarize the organizations with your facility and the types of hazardous waste generated on site. This requirement is explained in more detail in Preparedness and Prevention beginning on page 104.

Emergency Procedures

The most important part (and therefore the most descriptive) of the contingency plan is a description of the emergency procedures that will be followed for each type of hazardous waste-related emergency situation that may arise on-site. The plan should detail response actions in the event of a release, fire, or explosion in each area with hazardous waste. Emergency procedures must be directed by the emergency coordinator.

Emergency Equipment

Each location at which hazardous waste is generated, accumulated, stored, treated, or disposed of must be evaluated to determine what kinds of emergency equipment may be necessary to abate emergencies that may be reasonably anticipated to occur at that location. Emergency equipment includes (but is not limited to) fire extinguishing systems, spill control equipment, internal and external communications and alarm systems, and decontamination equipment (refer to Preparedness and Prevention beginning on page 104).

For example, situated near an accumulation point for drums of ignitable waste, your contingency plan may specify a fire extinguisher, overpack drums, sparkproof shovels, bags of granular absorbent, a telephone, and an alarm. An aboveground tank used for the accumulation of an aqueous extraction procedure (EP) toxic liquid may require recovery drums, shovels, bags of absorbent, a pump and hose, and a telephone.

Once emergency equipment has been determined, a list of all equipment must be incorporated into the contingency plan. The list must be kept up to date and must include the location of each piece of equipment, a physical description of each item, and a brief description of its capabilities. An example list is presented in Figure 9.1.

All emergency abatement equipment that has been determined to be necessary at a hazardous waste handling area must be tested and maintained as frequently as is necessary to assure its proper operation in the event of an emergency. It is recommended that periodic inspections of the equipment be conducted and documented in some manner. An example inspection checklist is presented in Figure 9.2.

Evacuation Plan

If there exists the possibility that evacuation from a building or facility may be necessary, the contingency plan must include an evacuation plan for facility personnel. The evacuation plan must describe signals to be used to begin evacuation and evacuation routes. Alternate routes must be described for the event where the primary route could be blocked by the release of hazardous waste or fire.

An evacuation plan should present a description of evacuation signals and assign responsibility to specific personnel to sound the signals. Additionally, it should present a diagram of each building in which hazardous waste is located with arrows from the location of hazardous waste showing escape routes to exits. Where more than one exit can be used, the path traced by each arrow should be designated as the primary or an alternate route.

OSHA Hazardous Waste Operations and Emergency Response Regulations

OSHA regulations published in 29 CFR 1910.120(p) and (q) also require generators who have emergency response teams, or "HAZMAT teams," and all TSD facilities to develop emergency response plans. A "HAZMAT team" is an organized group of employees, designated by the employer, who are expected to perform work to handle and control actual or potential leaks or spills of hazardous substances requiring possible close approach to the substance. The team members perform responses to releases or potential releases of hazardous substances for the purpose of control or stabilization of the incident.

The emergency response plan need not duplicate any of the subjects fully addressed in the contingency plan, but must address the following areas: preemergency planning, coordination with outside parties, personnel roles, lines of authority, communications, emergency recognition and prevention, safe distances and places of refuge, site security and control, evacuation routes and procedures, decontamination procedures, emergency medical treatment and first aid, emergency alerting and response procedures, critique of response and follow-up procedures, personal protective equipment, and emergency equipment.

```
┌─────────────────────────────────────────────────────────────────────────┐
│              Emergency Response Equipment Stored in Emergency Response    │
│                 Locker at Paint Shop for Accumulation Point No. 1         │
│                                                                           │
│   Item                          Use and Capabilities                      │
│                                                                           │
│     Salvage drum                Deposit spill residue and overpack leaking containers,
│                                 DOT-specification 85-gallon open head (2)  │
│                                                                           │
│     Gloves                      Protect hands from chemical exposure, chemical resistant (3 pair)
│                                                                           │
│     Self-contained              Protect workers from inhalation of toxic vapors and oxygen defficiency
│     breathing apparatus         during emergencies (2)                    │
│                                                                           │
│     Absorbent                   Absorb and prevent the spread of non-corrosive liquid spills
│                                 (two 50-pound bags)                        │
│                                                                           │
│     Push broom                  Sweep up spent absorbent (2)               │
│                                                                           │
│     Shovel                      Sweep up spent absorbent and solid spill residues, spark-proof blade (2)
│                                                                           │
│     Fire extinguisher*          10-pound dry chemical (ammonium phosphate) at 195 pounds pressure,
│                                 4-A:60-B:C (2)                             │
│                                                                           │
│     Apron                       Cover torso and partially cover legs to protect from exposure to hazardous
│                                 waste splashes, chemical resistant (3)     │
│                                                                           │
│     Goggles                     Protect eyes from exposure to hazardous waste splashes (3 pair)
│                                                                           │
│     Face shield                 Protect face from exposure to hazardous waste splashes, chemical resistant (3)
│                                                                           │
│     Boots                       Protect feet from chemical exposure, chemical resistant (3 pair)
│                                                                           │
│     Coveralls                   Chemically resistant pants and jacket combination to protect body and legs
│                                 from spills (3 pair)                       │
│                                                                           │
│   * Mounted on wall beside emergency response locker                      │
└─────────────────────────────────────────────────────────────────────────┘
```

FIGURE 9.1
A Sample List of Emergency Response Equipment, Location, and Capabilities

EMERGENCY PROCEDURES

Responsibilities of the Emergency Coordinator

Unless the national contingency plan is invoked for an emergency situation at your facility, it is the responsibility of the facility emergency coordinator (or his designee) to oversee all response actions and ensure the proper notifications are made to outside agencies. Whenever there is an imminent or actual emergency situation, the Emergency Coordinator must:

- immediately alert facility personnel who may be adversely affected by the situation. This may be accomplished by activating alarms or communication systems.
- immediately notify those emergency response organizations with designated response roles. This notification is to be made to appropriate organizations on-site as well as state or local agencies, if necessary.

- take all reasonable measures necessary to ensure that fires, explosions, and releases do not recur or spread to other hazardous waste on-site. If applicable at your facility, these measures must include:

collecting and containing released waste,
removing or isolating containers, and
stopping precesses and operations.

If operations are ceased for a fire, explosion, or release, the emergency coordinator must (if appropriate at your facility with respect to a certain situation) monitor for ruptures in valves, pipes, or other equipment; leaks; pressure buildup; or gas generation.

- immediately identify the character, exact source, amount of material released, and a determination of how far the release has spread. This may be done by direct observation of the situation, a review of facility records, and chemical analysis.

```
Name of Inspector: _____  Date: _____

Location: _____


Item                    Condition                               Comments

Salvage drum            2 DOT-specification 85-gallon
                        open head in place, empty               _____

Gloves                  3 pair of chemical-resistant gloves
                        in place, medium size, clean            _____

Self-contained          2 SCBAs, fully charged, disinfected,
breathing app.          in good condition                       _____

Absorbent               2 50-pound bags in place, full, dry     _____

Push broom              2 brooms in place, clean                _____

Shovel                  2 shovels in place, clean               _____

Fire extinguisher       2 mounted on wall beside emergency
                        response locker, 4-A:60-B:C, fully charged  _____

Apron                   3 aprons in place, clean                _____

Goggles                 3 pair with straps, provides unobstructed
                        view, clean                             _____

Face shield             3 face shields, visor in good condition, clean  _____

Boots                   3 pair, clean; free from tears, cracks,
                        punctures, etc.                         _____

Coveralls               3 pair, clean; free from tears, cracks,
                        punctures, etc.                         _____
```

FIGURE 9.2
A Sample Emergency Equipment Inspection Checklist

In characterizing the situation, the emergency coordinator must assess possible hazards to human health and the environment that may result from the release, fire, or explosion. This assessment must consider both direct and indirect effects of the situation. For example, the assessment must consider such questions as:

What are the effects of any toxic, irritating, or asphyxiating gases that may be generated?

Will contaminated water run off the site, and if so, will it harm human health or the environment?

How will chemical agents used to control fire or heat-induced explosions affect the environment surrounding the site?

If the emergency coordinator determines that evacuation of local areas off-site may be necessary, he must immediately notify appropriate local authorities and be available to help local authorities decide whether local areas should be evacuated.

Additionally, if the emergency coordinator determines that a release, fire, or explosion could threaten human health or the environment off-site, the on-scene coordinator (for that geographical area) must be notified and provided with the following information:

name and telephone number of the individual making the report;

name and address of the facility;

time and type of situation (e.g., release, fire, explosion);

name and quantity of material(s) involved, to the extent known;

name and quantity of the material(s) involved, to the extent known; and

possible hazards to human health and environment off site.

During the response, the emergency coordinator must ensure that no waste that may be incompatible with the released material is treated, stored, or disposed of in the area affected by the emergency situation until cleanup procedures are completed. After remediation efforts have been completed, the emergency coordinator must ensure that all emergency equipment listed in the contingency plan is cleaned and fit for its intended used before operations are resumed. Before operations can begin again in the areas of your facility that were affected by the situation, the facility owner or operator (or his designee) must report to the EPA regional administrator (or your state environmental agency if your state has RCRA authorization) on how the emergency coordinator met the requirements described in this paragraph.

Responsibilities of the Facility Owner or Operator

In addition to reporting to the regional EPA administrator as described above, the facility owner or operator (or his designee) must record the time, date, and details of any incident that requires implementing the contingency plan. Within 15 days after the emergency situation, he must submit a written report to the Regional Administrator (or state environmental agency) describing the situation. The report must include:

- name, address, and telephone number of the owner or operator (or his designee);
- name, address, and main phone number of the facility;
- date, time, and type of emergency situation (e.g., spill, fire, explosion);
- name and quantity of material(s) involved;
- the extent of injuries, if any;
- an assessment of actual or potential hazards to human health or the environment, where this is applicable; and
- estimated quantity and disposition of recovered material that resulted from the incident.

IMPLEMENTATION AND REVISION OF THE CONTINGENCY PLAN

The contingency plan must be implemented whenever there is a hazardous waste spill, fire, explosion or release of hazardous waste constituent that could threaten human health or the environment.

The plan must be kept current, meaning it must reflect changes at your facility. A contingency plan that, for example, has an old list of emergency coordinators and alternates or that does not show the locations of new hazardous waste accumulation points is in violation of the requirements of RCRA. Additionally, the plan must be reviewed and, if necessary, amended immediately if:

- any applicable regulations pertaining to contingency plans are revised
- the plan fails in the event of an emergency
- the facility changes in a way that increases the potential for fires, explosions, or releases of hazardous waste or

hazardous waste constituents (the plan may also have to be amended if the actions necessary to respond to an emergency change)
- the list of emergency coordinators changes
- the list of equipment necessary to respond to emergencies changes

DETERMINING IF AN INCIDENT MUST BE REPORTED TO OUTSIDE AGENCIES

The RCRA regulations require reporting to an outside agency (i.e., the on-scene coordinator with jurisdiction over your facility or the national response center) if there is a release, fire, or explosion that could threaten human health or the environment outside the facility. CERCLA Section 101(14) and Superfund Amendments and Reauthorization Act (SARA) Title III Section 304 also require immediate reporting of releases of reportable quantities of CERCLA hazardous substances and extremely hazardous substances to the national response center, state emergency response commission, and local emergency planning committee. Also, many states have more stringent release reporting requirements for hazardous wastes and substances. In the event of such an incident, decisions must be made rapidly in order to mitigate the effects of the incident, preserve the environment, and protect human life.

Background Work

The decision as to whether or not to report begins long before an incident ever takes place. In order to make the best decision at the time of an incident, you should start by identifying hazards at your facility.

The identification of hazards begins by determining the areas at your facility in which hazardous waste is generated and/or accumulated, as well as the roadways over which it is transported. You should also identify areas in which other materials that possess a physical or health hazard are used or stored and over which they are transported. Physical and health hazards can be assessed with assistance from your safety department and the reference materials described in Preparedness and Prevention, beginning on page 104.

For each hazardous waste and other hazardous materials present in an area, you should assess:

- The average amount of each material stored and/or used in that area. This quantity can vary from day to day, so you should estimate the amount that is typically on hand on any given day. This information is necessary to assess the potential impact should an incident involving this material ever occur.
- The maximum quantity of each material in that area. While the maximum amount may rarely be in a particular area, hazards associated with the maximum quantity may be much different than the hazards associated with the average amount, and these differences need to be considered when determining vulnerable zones and the extent of environmental and health impacts.

- The type of storage for each material in that area, including the maximum potential quantity in a single storage vessel. Record whether a material is present in a particular area in a 55-gallon metal drum, 35-gallon fiberboard container, 50-pound bag, 300-gallon steel tank, etc. The maximum potential quantity in a single vessel must be known to estimate the impact of an incident.

- The conditions under which a material is stored or used, including:

    temperature: some materials may be kept at temperatures other than ambient depending on their use;
    pressure: some materials are stored or used under pressure; and
    other features employed to store or use a material in that area, such as if a waste is accumulated on an impervious surface (if so, what are the dimensions) or in a room with a concrete floor, roof, and walls.

- The result a release, fire, or explosion may have on a material. For example, if a material catches fire, what hazardous decomposition products might result? If a material is released and comes in contact with water, will it react violently and give off harmful gases?

A useful way to compile and store this information would be to obtain a map of your facility. Mark all areas iden-tified in the hazards analysis with a letter or number code. For each coded area, develop a hazards profile on a sheet of paper in a notebook or binder listing the hazardous wastes and materials present, physical and health hazards, maximum amount, average daily amount, type and conditions of storage, and products that might result in the event of an incident.

Considerations at the Time of an Incident

At the time of an incident, you will need to establish vulnerable zones. A *vulnerable zone* is an estimated geographical area that, if exposed to a particular material as a result of a release, fire, or explosion, may be subject to a level that could cause:

- irreversible acute health effects or death to human populations, or
- immediate or delayed deterioration or destruction of the environment.

The size of an estimated vulnerable zone depends on a number of factors, including the rate of release, quantity, meteorological conditions, surrounding topography, and surrounding geography. The vulnerable zone for each area using or storing hazardous waste or materials (as well as facility transportation routes) should be determined for each incident scenario: spill, leak, fire, and explosion.

Rate of Release
The rate of release affects the size of the vulnerable zone depending on the type of release (e.g., a spill into a steadily

moving stream as opposed to a dry creek, or a swiftly spreading fire), size of the containing vessel, and the physical state of the material. The faster a material enters the environment, the faster it can cause damage to both the environment and human health, and consequently the larger the vulnerable zone. Keep in mind also that a slow release of a material over a long period of time could have the same effect as a large, instantaneous release of the same substance.

Quantity and Concentration
The amount of material in an area has a direct bearing on the size of a vulnerable zone. The more concentrated the material, the greater the impact of the release and the larger the vulnerable zone.

Meteorological Conditions
Meteorological factors to consider include wind speed, wind direction, and atmospheric instability. These factors have the greatest effect on the size of a vulnerable zone. Increased wind speed will result in greater airborne dispersion (and dilution) of a released material, potentially reducing the size of the vulnerable zone. Atmospheric instability such as rain will cause a spilled or leaked material to reach groundwater at a faster rate, but tends to dilute the effect of a released liquid into a stream.

Surrounding Topography
The principal topographic factors affecting the size of the vulnerable zone are natural obstructions such as hills and mountains, and manmade structures such as high-rise buildings. While natural formations and surface conditions produce site-specific effects and appropriate technical support should be solicited from local, state, or EPA regional experts, in general the rougher the terrain (uneven and mountainous), the smaller a vulnerable zone tends to be due to an increased dispersion (i.e., mixing and diluting of the chemical in the air). By the same token, the more urbanized the area (containing high buildings and other manmade structures) the smaller a vulnerable zone tends to be.

Surrounding Geography
The geographic features surrounding your facility could have a substantial impact on the size of a vulnerable zone, depending on the type of incident. For example, a vulnerable zone will increase in size in the event of a spill if a stream is nearby; the vulnerable zone in the event of a fire will enlarge if the area surrounding the fire is heavily forested.

Once the hazards have been identified and vulnerable zones are established, you have the information to help you determine whether the incident could threaten human health or the environment off-site, and subsequently whether to immediately notify the on-scene coordinator and report the incident.

Figure 9.3 is list of national emergency response agencies and telephone numbers as well as telephone numbers for obtaining further information regarding federal environmental regulations.

Organization	Telephone Number
National Response Center, U.S. Coast Guard, Washington DC	(800) 424-8802 (24-hour) or (202) 267-2675 (24-hour)
U.S. EPA, Region I, Boston, MA	(617) 223-7265 (24-hour) (617) 565-3715 (general info.)
U.S. EPA, Region II, New York, NY	(201) 321-6635 (24-hour) (212) 264-2525 (general info.)
U.S. EPA, Region III, Philadelphia, PA	(215) 597-9898 (24-hour) (215) 597-9800 (general info.)
U.S. EPA, Region IV, Atlanta, GA	(404) 347-4062 (24-hour) (404) 347-4727
U.S. EPA, Region V, Chicago, IL	(312) 353-2318 (24-hour) (312) 353-2000 (general info.)
U.S. EPA, Region VI, Dallas, TX	(214) 655-2222 (24-hour) (214) 655-2100 (general info.)
U.S. EPA, Region VII, Kansas City, KS	(913) 236-3778 (24-hour) (913) 236-2800 (general info.)
U.S. EPA, Region VIII, Denver, CO	(303) 293-7142 (24-hour) (303) 293-1603 (general info.)
U.S. EPA, Region IX, San Francisco, CA	(415) 974-8131 (24 hour) (415) 974-8071 (general info.)
U.S. EPA, Region X, Seattle, WA	(206) 442-1263 (24-hour) (206) 442-5810 (general info.)
CHEMTREC (Chemical Manufacturer's Emergency Response Network)	(800) 424-9300 (24-hour)
SARA Title III Hotline, Washington, DC	(800) 535-0202
RCRA and Superfund Hotline, Washington, DC	(800) 424-9346
Toxic Substances Control Act Assist. Office, Washington, DC	(202) 554-1404
National Pesticides Telecommunications Network	(800) 858-7378

FIGURE 9.3
Environmental Emergency Response and General Information Telephone Numbers

EMERGENCY RESPONSE ACTIONS

Initial Response Actions

In the event of a spill, fire, explosion or other type of release, the first action that should be taken by the person discovering the incident is to alert the facility command post or organization at your facility designated to receive emergency reports. Based on the type of incident, appropriately trained personnel will be dispatched in response.

While waiting for assistance to arrive, there are general measures you should ensure are taken to minimize the danger to those near the incident. First, approach the area cautiously; resist the urge to rush onto the scene in hopes of being able to size up the situation rapidly. Next, identify the hazards. The procedures to assess hazards, described in Determining If an Incident Must Be Reported to Outside Agencies beginning on page 109, should be used along with signs, placards, and container labels in the area.

Secure the scene. Without entering the immediate hazard area, do what you can to isolate the area and assure the safety of people and the environment in the vicinity of the incident. Keep people away from the scene and the perimeter. Allow room enough to move and remove equipment that may be necessary to respond to the emergency.

Decide on site entry. Any efforts you make to rescue persons, protect property or the environment must be weighed against the possibility that you could become part of the problem. Never allow anyone to enter a hazard area alone and always ensure that response workers wear appropriate personal protective equipment.

Responsibilities of the Emergency Coordinator

According to the RCRA regulations, the individual on-site acting as emergency coordinator has certain responsibilities that must be carried out whenever there is an imminent or actual emergency situation. These responsibilities, which are described in more detail in Emergency Procedures beginning on page 107, include activating alarms, notifying outside agencies, and characterizing the situation.

Response to Spills

Four steps should be taken by those responding to a spill. The first involves identifying the source of the spill. To do this you must determine where the spill is coming from and the identity of the spilled material. If a liquid is emanating from a group of containers, determine which one is leaking. If spilled material is detected in a waterway, trace the waterway back to determine where the material is entering the water. If a waterway leads you to an underground pipe, trace its path by examining facility diagrams. Be aware that approaching a liquid to determine its source may require you to don PPE so you will not be harmed or overcome by the material.

Next, stop the spill at its source. This may require turning a drum in such a way that the hole or rupture is above the surface of the liquid or closing a valve. The released liquid should then be confined to further prevent it from entering into the environment. Confining a liquid might involve pouring absorbent over the area of the spill, placing a boom in a stream, or shoveling dirt or gravel into a riverbed to stop a liquid from flowing further downstream.

Finally, all spill residues must be collected and packaged and spill response equipment must be decontaminated. Spill residues include absorbent, soil, and all other materials that came into contact with the released liquid and will not be decontaminated. The residues should be placed in DOT specification containers (refer to Chapter 3 to determine how to select the proper container).

Decontamination involves cleaning all equipment, clothing, and structures that have come into contact with the released liquid. The level of decontamination necessary to eliminate the hazardous properties of a waste depends on the amount of time an article was in contact with the waste, the affinity of the waste for the article, and the hazards of the waste. Decontamination can range from a soapy water washdown of shovels and rubber boots to a kerosene rinse followed by steam cleaning. Use care to contain all rinsate from decontamination activities because it must also be disposed of. OSHA regulations published in 29 CFR 1910.120 identify additional requirements for responding to incidents involving the release of hazardous waste and hazardous substances.

Response to Fires and Explosions

In the event of a fire or explosion, the safest response action is to warn others nearby, get away from the area as quickly as possible, and alert the local fire department. If you are ever in a situation in which you must contain a small fire until the fire department arrives, be aware that fire extinguishers are rated either A, B, C, or D (or any combination of those letters) depending on what type of fire they are best suited for.

A Class A fire involves combustible materials such as wood, paper, rubbish, and grass. This type of fire can be extinguished using water. A Class B fire involves volatile flammables such as oil, gasoline, grease, and paint. Class B fires can be extinguished using carbon dioxide, Halon™, foam, or a dry chemical extinguisher.

A Class C fire involves the burning of electrical equipment. Electrical fires can be extinguished with a carbon dioxide, Halon™ or dry chemical extinguisher. A Class D fire involves combustible metals such as magnesium and potassium. A Class D fire should be fought with a dry powder fire extinguisher. Since fire extinguishers are typically rated (by applying a mark or label to the extinguisher casing), the proper fire extinguisher can be determined by understanding what is fueling a fire and selecting the extinguisher with the corresponding rating.

Chapter 10
Enforcement

If hazardous waste is not managed in accordance with the regulatory requirements, the state and EPA have several options available to enforce compliance. These include administrative actions, civil actions, and criminal actions.

ADMINISTRATIVE ACTIONS AND CIVIL ACTIONS

EPA has the enforcement authority under several different sections of RCRA. Under Section 3013 of RCRA, EPA can order the owner or operator of a facility where hazardous waste is or has been treated, stored, or disposed of to perform the monitoring, testing, or analysis necessary to determine the potential hazard to human health and the environment at the site. A spill of hazardous waste into the environment is considered to be disposal and a generator could be subject to an administrative or judicial monitoring and analysis order. Failure to comply with the order can lead to the assessment of fines, or to EPA's performing monitoring activities and seeking reimbursement for the cost.

Section 3008(h) of RCRA authorizes EPA to issue administrative orders seeking corrective actions from facilities where a hazardous waste release has occurred. EPA may also assess a penalty of up to $25,000 per day for noncompliance with corrective action orders.

Under Section 7003 of RCRA EPA may file suit or issue an administrative order regarding sites that may present an imminent and substantial endangerment to human health or the environment. EPA can also suspend or revoke a TSD facility's operating permit.

EPA has established a RCRA Civil Penalty Policy for assessing administrative penalties and for providing guidance when setting fines in judicial cases. The gravity of the violation and, consequently, the amount of the penalty is assessed based two factors:

- the potential harm posed by the violation
- extent of deviation from the applicable law or regulation

The greater the potential for harm and the greater the deviation from compliance, the greater the penalty. EPA may adjust the penalty upward or downward based on several other factors including:

- the economic benefit of the violation to the violator
- presence or lack of presence of good faith efforts to comply
- degree of willfulness or negligence exhibited by the violation
- the history of noncompliance at the site
- the owner or operator's ability to pay
- other unique circumstances

In the event of a violation of the regulations, the state or the EPA can take both administrative and civil actions to compel your facility to comply with the regulations. A compliance order is one type of administrative action under which EPA or the state can require immediate compliance or cleanup and assess a penalty of up to $25,000 per day for each day of noncompliance. If an administrative order is issued, the alleged violator can contest the order within 30 days. Typical grounds for contesting a compliance order are that the violation did not occur as alleged or the penalties assessed appear excessive.

In a civil action, EPA or the state can take your facility to Federal District Court to force it to comply with the RCRA regulations or to clean up environmental contamination. EPA usually chooses administrative rather than judicial actions to enforce compliance, but both options are available to the agency.

CRIMINAL VIOLATIONS

Serious violations of the law can lead to criminal penalties and fines. Criminal penalties are available for "knowing" or "willful" violations. There are seven acts identified in the law that carry criminal penalties ranging from a fine of up to $50,000 per day and a prison sentence of up to 15 years. These violations and their associated maximum penalties are provided in Table 10.1.

EPA and authorized states may take actions against individual employees of facilities for criminal violations of environmental statues.

STATE ENFORCEMENT AUTHORITY

RCRA enables the states to take over the responsibility for implementing many of the regulatory requirements of the act. Today, most states have the authority to implement and enforce nearly all of the RCRA regulations. This means that most states have developed their own hazardous waste

management statutes and regulations and have received authority from EPA to enforce the RCRA program.

RCRA requires that state programs contain adequate authority to enforce the hazardous waste management regulatory program. Each state with authorization has inspection, enforcement, remedy, and penalty programs in place.

If hazardous waste is not managed in accordance with state regulatory requirements, the authorized state has several options available to enforce compliance. These include administrative actions, civil actions, and criminal actions.

In the event of a violation of the regulations, the authorized state can take an administrative action to compel a facility to comply with the regulations. This administrative action will sometimes be preceded by a notice of violation. An administrative compliance order is one type of administrative action under which the state can specify the nature of the violation and give a reasonable time for compliance. The order, if violated, can lead to civil penalties for each day of noncompliance and/or criminal penalties.

Authorized states may also issue an administrative complaint for civil penalties. Parties named in such a complaint must be given notice and an opportunity for a hearing on the alleged violations before a penalty can be assessed by EPA. In a civil action, the state can take a facility to court to force it to comply with the RCRA regulations or to clean up environmental contamination.

States generally may go directly to court seeking injunctive relief or a civil penalty without using administrative procedures. States also may obtain an emergency restraining order halting activity alleged to cause an "imminent hazard" to the health of persons.

TABLE 10.1
Criminal Provisions of the Resource Conservation and Recovery Act

Criminal Violation	Maximum Penalties
Knowingly transporting waste to a nonpermitted facility	$50,000 and 5 years imprisonment
Knowingly treating, storing, or disposing of waste without a permit or in violation of a permit	$50,000 and 5 years imprisonment
Knowingly falsifying manifests, labels, or other documents required by RCRA	$50,000 and 2 years imprisonment
Concealing or destroying any documents required to be retained or filed under RCRA	$50,000 and 2 years imprisonment
Knowingly transporting waste without a manifest	$50,000 and 2 years imprisonment
Knowingly exporting waste without the consent of the receiving country	$50,000 and 2 years imprisonment
Knowingly committing any of the above violations *and* knowingly placing other persons in imminent danger of death or serious bodily injury.	$250,000 ($1,000,000 for organizations) and 15 years imprisonment

EPA ENFORCEMENT OF ENVIRONMENTAL LAWS AT FEDERAL FACILITIES

Federal facilities must comply with RCRA in the same manner and degree as nonfederal entities, and EPA will utilize the full range of its available enforcement mechanisms to ensure compliance by federal facilities. However, EPA also recognizes that there are certain limitations and differences in the types of enforcement actions that EPA will take at a federal facility. EPA will pursue "timely and appropriate" enforcement responses to address violations at federal facilities in a manner similar to actions taken to address violations at nonfederal facilities. EPA's policy states that if a violation is not or will not be corrected within the time frame for violations of that class, an enforcement action will be taken.

RCRA regulations apply to all branches and agencies of the federal government. Section 6001 of RCRA waives federal facility sovereign immunity claims but requires federal facilities to be subject to and comply with all hazardous waste requirements in the same manner as any person subject to such requirements. Furthermore, federal facilities are not immune or exempt from any process or sanction of any state or federal court with respect to enforcement.

EPA's enforcement response under RCRA for Executive Branch agencies is somewhat different from its enforcement against nonfederal parties in that it is purely administrative, and does not provide for assessment of civil penalties. In general, EPA will negotiate compliance agreement or consent orders with federal installations to address violations at those installations.

This approach does not apply to enforcement actions taken by states as authorized nor to EPA actions directed to nonfederal operators of federal facilities. EPA will pursue the full range of its enforcement responses against private operators of federal facilities in appropriate circumstances. In addition, sanctions may be brought against individual employees of federal agencies for criminal violations of environmental statutes.

Chapter 11
Sampling and Analytical Methods

SAMPLING AND ANALYTICAL REQUIREMENTS

Waste sampling and analysis may be required during the waste determination process to determine which wastes generated at your facility are classified as hazardous waste. Generators, including small quantity generators, must determine if their waste is a hazardous waste by either testing the waste in accordance with methods specified by EPA in the appendices to 40 CFR 261, or by applying knowledge of the hazardous characteristics of the waste in light of materials or processes used. In general, a waste analysis may be required if the constituents of the waste stream are unknown, if hazardous waste characteristics are unknown, or if the waste is subject to the land disposal ban.

Before a TSD facility treats, stores, or disposes of hazardous waste, the facility must obtain a detailed chemical and physical analysis of a representative sample of the waste. At a minimum, the information must contain all of the information needed to treat, store, or dispose of the waste in accordance with EPA regulations for TSD facilities, and the land disposal ban. TSD facilities often require generators to supply this information before accepting the waste. The TSD may also require periodic analysis or additional analysis whenever the process or operation generating the hazardous waste has changed. If the generator does not supply a detailed physical and chemical analysis of a representative sample of the waste, and the TSD facility chooses to accept the waste, the TSD facility must then obtain the required information in accordance with its waste analysis plan.

TSD facilities must also inspect and, if necessary, analyze each hazardous waste shipment received at the facility to determine whether it matches the identity of the waste specified on the accompanying manifest.

EPA recommends the use of the waste sampling and analytical methods found in *Test Methods for Evaluating Solid Waste, Physical/Chemical Methods,* (EPA publication SW-846, Washington, D.C., March 18, 1991). The methods listed in 40 CFR 261 and SW-846 must be followed unless EPA specifically approves alternate procedures. EPA published a proposal in January 1989 requiring the use of quality control procedures found in Sections 1.2 and 1.3 of SW-846 when using any SW-846 method whether that method is mandatory or not. Consequently, generators should follow recommended procedures in SW-846 to assure reliable analytical data which is defensible if questions are raised about the data used to complete hazardous waste determinations.

SW-846 testing methods must be employed under the following circumstances:

- submission of data in support of waste delisting petitions at a particular facility
- evaluation of wastes for the corrosivity characteristic
- evaluation of waste to determine if free liquids are present as a component of the waste
- analysis of wastes prior to conducting a trial burn to support an incinerator permit application

40 CFR 261, Appendix III lists all of the test methods found in SW-846 (40 CFR 261 is updated annually every July in Washington, D.C.). Appendix III is divided into

three tables. Table 1 lists the appropriate analytical methods to follow for organic chemicals. Table II lists the appropriate analytical methods for inorganic chemicals. Table III summarizes the contents of SW-846 and supplies specific method and section numbers for sampling and analysis methods.

DEVELOPMENT OF A SAMPLING PLAN

After you have determined there is a need for sampling, those personnel directing the sampling effort should define the program's objectives. A sample plan is usually a written document that describes primary and specific sampling objectives, lists the individual tasks, and identifies how those tasks will be performed. To ensure that the sampling plan is designed properly, it is wise to have all aspects of the effort represented. The personnel involved in preparing the plan should include the end user of the data, an experienced member of the field team who will actually collect the samples, an analytical chemist, an engineer if a complex manufacturing process is involved, a statistician to review the sampling approach, a health and safety specialist, and a quality assurance specialist.

To develop a sampling plan:

* research background information about the waste
* determine which containers should be sampled
* select the appropriate sampling devices and containers
* identify the number, volume, and locations of samples to be taken
* develop standard procedures for opening drums, sampling, packaging samples, and shipping samples
* have a trained health and safety expert determine the appropriate personal protection to be used during sampling, decontamination, and sample packaging.

The more detailed the sampling plan, the less the opportunity for oversight or misunderstanding during sampling, analysis, and data treatment.

Statistical methods must be followed when developing a sample plan to judge the level of sample accuracy and precision. The following section addresses methods for achieving sample accuracy and precision. Besides statistics, other factors must be considered when developing and implementing a sampling plan. One of the most important factors is the waste itself and its properties.

The physical state of the waste affects most sampling aspects. The sampling equipment to be used will vary whether the waste is solid, liquid, gaseous, or multiphased. It will also vary if the liquid is viscous or free-flowing or if the solid is hard or soft. Sampling equipment deployment will also be affected by the physical state of the waste. For example a lagoon filled with a viscous sludge may have to be sampled from a boat while a lagoon filled with soil can be sampled on foot.

The volume of the waste has an effect upon the choice of sampling equipment and strategies. Sampling a large lagoon requires different equipment and a different approach than sampling a 55-gallon drum.

The hazardous characteristics of the waste will change safety and health precautions and the methods of sampling and sample shipping.

The composition of the waste also affects sampling strategy. The waste could be homogeneous, randomly heterogeneous, or stratified, and different sampling methods are better suited to different waste compositions.

Site-specific factors must be considered when developing a sampling plan. At least one person involved in the planning and implementation should be familiar with the site. The following site-specific factors should be considered:

Accessibility Accessibility can vary tremendously. Some waste samples may be obtained by turning a valve while other wastes must be excavated with heavy equipment in order to obtain a representative sample.

Waste generation and handling The waste generation and handling process must be understood to ensure that collected samples are representative of the waste. You must know if the waste is generated in batches, if there was a change in the raw materials used in the manufacturing process, or if waste composition has varied with temperature, pressure, or storage time.

Transitory events Startup, shutdown, slowdown, and maintenance periods can result in the generation of a waste that is not representative of the normal waste stream.

Climate The sampling plan should specify any clothing needed to accommodate extreme heat or cold. Dehydration and extensive exposure to sun, insects, or poisonous snakes must be considered.

Hazards Each accumulation area has its own hazards, and a thorough sampling plan will include the health and safety procedures to protect team members from both the physical and health hazards on site.

Sample Accuracy and Precision

When developing a sampling plan, your primary objective is to obtain samples that will allow measurements of the chemical properties of the waste that are sufficiently *accurate* and *precise* to be reliable. *Sampling accuracy* is the nearness of a sample value or the mean of a set of measurements to the true value. Sample accuracy is assessed in the laboratory by analyzing reference samples. *Sampling precision* is the agreement between a set of replicate measurement without assumption or knowledge of the true value. Sampling precision is assessed by analyzing duplicate and replicate samples. *Duplicate samples* consist of two separate samples taken from the same source in separate containers and analyzed independently. *Replicate samples* are two aliquots taken from the same sample container and analyzed independently.

Both sample accuracy and sample precision can be determined mathematically through statistics and must be considered when developing a sampling plan. Section 9.1 of SW-846 provides calculations and detailed examples of methods that can be used to quantify sample accuracy and sample precision.

When planning, you must judge the degree of sampling accuracy and precision that is required to estimate reliably the chemical characteristics of a solid waste for the purpose of comparing those characteristics with the regulatory requirements. Generally, high accuracy and high precision are required if one or more chemical constituents in a waste are present at a concentration close to the regulatory limit. However, if chemical constituents are present far below the regulatory limits, low accuracy and precision can be tolerated. You save money in sampling by lowering the number of samples taken or, in other words, by lowering the sample precision. Few cost savings are realized by lowering sample accuracy, so the wise sampling strategy is to maximize sampling accuracy and minimize sampling precision. At least two samples of a material are required for any estimate of sampling precision.

Statistical techniques for obtaining accurate and precise samples are relatively simple and easy to implement. Sampling accuracy is usually achieved by some form of random sampling. The word "random" does not mean haphazard, but that every part of the waste has a theoretically equal chance of being sampled. To obtain a random sample and therefore an accurate sample, you should divide the waste to be sampled into an imaginary grid, assign a series of consecutive numbers to the units of the grid, and select the numbers or units to be sampled from a random numbers table which can be found in any textbook on basic statistics. To obtain precise sampling results, you must increase the number of samples taken from the waste material or increase the volume or weight of the samples. Increasing the volume or weight minimizes sample-to-sample variation. Four types of sampling strategies may be used in waste material sampling. These are:

Simple Random Sampling
All units in the population (or essentially all locations or points in all batches of the waste) are identified, and a suitable number of samples is randomly selected from the population. This type of sampling is recommended if you know nothing about the distribution of chemical contaminants in a waste or if the waste is known to be homogeneous.

Stratified Random Sampling
The population is first stratified to divide the known differences in chemical characteristics, and then each stratum is randomly sampled. This method is useful for heterogeneous wastes where differences are known to exist from batch to batch or from location to location.

Systematic Random Sampling
The first sampling point or unit in the population is randomly selected and all subsequent units are taken at fixed locations or fixed time intervals in relation to the first unit. This method makes sample identification and collection easier since all sampling points after the first are systematically identified and collected at fixed intervals. For example, a homogeneous waste lagoon would be sampled at points located at each 3-foot interval along a line fixed by the first random sample.

Authoritative Sampling
An individual who is well acquainted with the solid waste to be sampled selects a sample without regard to randomization. The validity of the data gathered in this manner is totally dependent on the knowledge of the sampler and, although valid data can sometimes be obtained, authoritative sampling is not recommended for identifying the chemical characteristics of most wastes.

The appropriate number of samples is the lowest number required to generate a reasonably precise estimate of the true mean or average concentration of a chemical contaminant of a waste. This number can be calculated using statistical equations by considering the estimated probable error rate, variance of the sample, and difference between the expected mean result and the regulatory threshold. Much of this information is estimated prior to sampling so it is always prudent to gather a greater number of samples than is indicated by the preliminary estimate.

In order to lower sampling and analytical costs, composite samples are often used. A *composite sample* is obtained by collecting a number of random samples from a waste, combining the individual samples into a single sample, and analyzing the single sample for the chemical contaminants of concern. Sample compositing saves on analytical costs, but a disadvantage is the loss of concentration variance data. It is usually more expedient and more cost effective to collect component samples in the field and to composite parts of each sample later in the laboratory. Then if, after reviewing the data, any questions arise, the samples may be composited in different combinations or each sample could be analyzed separately to improve the reliability of the data.

Sampling Equipment

The choice of sampling equipment and sample containers depends on the previously described waste and site characteristics along with several other factors which will affect the performance and results obtained from the equipment. An analytical chemist should be consulted when selecting equipment and containers since a chemist should be aware of potential incompatibility problems, can specify decontamination procedures for equipment, and knows handling procedures for specific waste constituents.

When selecting sampling equipment, consider several factors including the potential for:

Negative contamination Negative contamination is the potential for the measured analyte concentration to be artificially low due to losses from volatilization or absorption.

Positive contamination Positive contamination is the potential for the measured analyte to be artificially high because of leaching from the sample container or from the introduction of foreign matter into the sample by air contaminants.

Cross contamination *Cross contamination* is positive contamination caused by the introduction of part of one sample with another during sampling, shipping, or storage.

Also select equipment based on the required sample volume for physical and chemical analysis, ease of use of the sampling equipment and containers on site, the degree of hazard associated with the use of one sampling device versus another, and the cost of the sampling device and of the labor for its deployment.

Sampling Equipment Selection

A variety of sampling equipment is available for obtaining waste samples. Table 11.1 contains examples of sampling equipment and potential applications. It should be noted that these suggested sampling devices may not apply to a user's situation due to waste or site-specific factors.

A *composite liquid waste sampler* or *coliwasa* is a device used to sample free-flowing liquids and slurries contained in drums, shallow tanks, and pits. It is especially useful for sampling wastes that have several liquid phases or layers. The coliwasa consists of a glass, plastic, or metal tube equipped with an end closure that can be opened and closed while the tube is submerged in the waste.

A *weighted bottle* consists of a glass or plastic bottle, sinker, stopper, and a line that is used to lower, open, and raise the bottle. The weighted bottle is used to sample liquids and free-flowing slurries at various depths in tanks or lagoons.

A *dipper* consists of a glass or plastic beaker clamped to the end of a two-or three-piece telescoping pole. A dipper samples liquids, free-flowing slurries., and other materials in pipes.

A *thief* consists of two slotted concentric tubes, usually made of stainless steel or brass. The outer tube has a pointed tip that allows the sampler to penetrate the material being sampled. The inner tube is rotated to open and close the sampler. A thief is used to sample dry granules or powdered wastes that will fit through the slots.

A *trier* consists of a tube cut in half lengthwise with a sharpened tip that allows the sampler to cut into sticky solids and to loosen soil. A trier samples moist or sticky solids with a particle diameter less than one-half the diameter of the trier.

An *auger* consists of sharpened spiral blades attached to a hard metal central shaft. An auger samples hard or packed solid wastes or soil.

Scoops and shovels are used to sample granular or powdered materials in bins or shallow containers.

Well water can be sampled using a variety of equipment ranging from a simple bailer to suction pumps and positive displacement pumps.

TABLE 11.1
Examples of Sampling Equipment for Particular Waste Types

	Waste Location or Container								
Waste Type	Drum	Sacks and Bags	Open-bed Truck	Closed-bed Truck	Storage Tanks or Bins	Waste Piles	Ponds, Lagoons, and Pits	Conveyor Belt	Pipe
Free-flowing liquids and slurries	Coliwasa	N/A[1]	N/A[1]	Coliwasa	Weighted bottle	N/A[1]	Dipper	N/A[1]	Dipper
Sludges	Trier	N/A	Trier	Trier	Trier	—[a]	—[a]		
Moist powders or granules	Trier	Trier	Trier	Trier	Trier	Trier	Trier	Shovel	Dipper
Dry powders or granules	Thief	Thief	Thief	Thief	Thief	Thief	Thief	Shovel	Dipper
Sand or packed powders and granules	Auger	Auger	Auger	Auger	—[a]	—[a]	—[a]	Dipper	Dipper
Large-grained solids	Large Trier	Large Trier	Large Trier	Large Trier	Large Trier	Large Trier	Large Trier	Trier	Dipper

—[a] This type of sampling situation can present significant logistical sampling problems, therefore sampling equipment must be specifically selected or designed based on site and waste conditions. No general statement about appropriate sampling equipment can be made.
—[1] NA, not applicable

120

Container Sampling Techniques

Take safety precautions including the use of appropriate personal protective equipment during all sampling operations. When sampling drums and other small containers, follow these additional sampling techniques.

- Keep sampling personnel at a safe distance while drums are being opened. Sample only after opening operations are complete
- Do not lean over other drums to reach the drum being sampled, unless absolutely necessary
- Cover drum tops with plastic sheeting or other suitable noncontaminated materials to avoid excessive contact with the drum tops
- Never stand on drums. (This is extremely dangerous.) Use mobile steps or other platforms to achieve the height necessary to safely sample from the drums.
- Do not use contaminated equipment or rags to sample. The contaminants may contaminate the sample and may not be compatible with the waste in the drum.

Obtaining Samples from Containers

If the waste is contained in several containers, every container should be sampled. However, if there are a large number of containers, a subset of containers to be sampled should be chosen randomly using a random number table. Ideally several samples should be taken from locations dispersed both horizontally and vertically through the waste. With an unknown waste, the sample collected must pick up any vertical stratification which is typical due to solids settling and differences in the waste itself.

If access to a container is unlimited, such as with an open-head drum, a useful strategy for obtaining a set of representative samples is a three-dimensional simple random sampling approach. The container is divided by using an imaginary three-dimensional grid as is pictured in Figure 11.1. Each section and level is assigned a number and specific sampling locations are selected by using a random number table. By using a drum thief or coliwasa, you can sample the entire vertical length of the container and minimize the number of individual samples required.

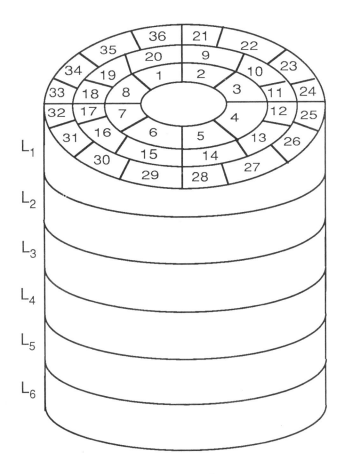

FIGURE 11.1
Container Divided into Imaginary Three-Dimensional Grid

121

TABLE 11.2
Sample Containers, Preservatives, and Sample Holding Times

Name	Container[1]	Preservation	Maximum holding time
Bacterial Tests:			
Coliform, fecal, and total	P, G	Cool, 4°C, 0.008% $Na_2S_2O_3$	6 hours
Fecal streptococci	P, G	Cool, 4°C, 0.008% $Na_2S_2O_3$	6 hours
Inorganic Tests:			
Acidity	P, G	Cool, 4°C	14 days
Alkalinity	P, G	Cool, 4°C	14 days
Ammonia	P, G	Cool, 4°C, H_2SO_4 to pH<2	28 days
Biochemical oxygen demand	P, G	Cool, 4°C	48 hours
Bromide	P, G	None required	28 days
Biochemical oxygen demand cabonaceous	P, G	Cool, 4°C	48 hours
Chemical oxygen demand	P, G	Cool, 4°C, H_2SO_4 to pH<2	28 days
Chloride	P, G	None required	28 days
Chlorine, total residual	P, G	None required	Analyze immediately
Color	P, G	Cool, 4°C	48 hours
Cyanide, total and amenable to chlorination	P, G	Cool, 4°C, NaOH to pH>12, 0.6 g ascorbic acid	14 days
Fluoride	P	None required	28 days
Hardness	P, G	HNO_3 to pH< 2, H_2SO_4 to pH< 2	6 months
Hydrogen ion (pH)	P, G	None required	Analyze immediately
Kjeldahl and organic nitrogen	P, G	Cool, 4°C, H_2SO_4 to pH<2	28 days
Metals:			
Chromium VI	P, G	Cool, 4°C	24 hours
Mercury	P, G	HNO_3 to pH<2	28 days
Metals, except chromium VI and mercury	P, G	HNO_3 to pH<2	6 months
Nitrate	P, G	Cool, 4°C	48 hours
Nitrate-nitrite	P, G	Cool, 4°C, H_2SO_4, to pH<2	28 days
Nitrite	P, G	Cool, 4°C	48 hours
Oil and grease	G	Cool, 4°C, H_2SO_4 to pH<2	28 days
Organic carbon	P, G	Cool, 4°C, HCl or H_2SO_4 to pH<2	28 days
Orthophosphate	P, G	Filter immediately, cool, 4°C	48 hours
Oxygen, dissolved probe	G bottle and top	None required	Analyze immediately
Winkler	Deionized water	Fix on site and store in dark	8 hours
Phenols	G only	Cool, 4°C, H_2SO_4 to pH<2	28 days
Phosphorus (elemental)	G	Cool, 4°C	48 hours
Phosphorus, total	P, G	Cool, 4°C, H_2SO_4 to pH<2	28 days
Residue, total	P, G	Cool, 4°C	7 days
Residue, filterable	P, G	Cool, 4°C	7 days
Residue, nonfilterable (TSS)	P, G	Cool, 4°C	7 days
Residue, settleable	P, G	Cool, 4°C	48 hours
Residue, volatile	P, G	Cool, 4°C	7 days
Silica	P	Cool, 4°C	28 days
Specific conductance	P, G	Cool, 4°C	28 days
Sulfate	P, G	Cool, 4°C	28 days
Sulfide	P, G	Cool, 4°C, add zinc acetate plus sodium hydroxide to pH>9	7 days
Sulfite	P, G	None required	Analyze immediately
Surfactants	P, G	Cool, 4°C	48 hours
Temperature	P, G	None required	Analyze immediately
Turbidity	P, G	Cool, 4°C	48 hours
Organic Tests:			
Purgeable halocarbons	G, Teflon-lined septum	Cool, 4°C, 0.008% $Na_2S_2O_3$	14 days
Purgeable aromatic hydrocarbons	G, Teflon-lined septum	Cool, 4°C, 0.008% $Na_2S_2O_3$, HCl to pH 2	14 days
Acrolein and Acrylonitrile	G, Teflon lined septum	Cool, 4°C, 0.008% $Na_2S_2O_3$, adjust pH to 4-5	14 days
Phenols	G, Teflon-lined cap	Cool, 4°C, 0.008% $Na_2S_2O_3$	7 days until extraction 40 days after extraction
Benzidines	G, Teflon-lined cap	Cool, 4°C, 0.008% $Na_2S_2O_3$	7 days until extraction
Phthalate esters	G, Teflon-lined cap	Cool, 4°C	7 days until extraction 40 days after extraction

TABLE 11.2
Sample Containers, Preservatives, and Sample Holding Times (continued)

Name	Container[1]	Preservation	Maximum holding time
Nitrosamines	G, Teflon-lined cap	Cool, 4°C, store in dark, 0.008% $Na_2S_2O_3$	40 days after extraction
PCBs, acrylonitrile	G, Teflon-lined cap	Cool, 4°C	40 days after extraction
Nitroaromatics and isophorone	G, Teflon-lined cap	Cool, 4°C, 0.008% $Na_2S_2O_3$, store in dark	40 days after extraction
Polynuclear aromatic hydrocarbons	G, Teflon-lined cap	Cool, 4°C, 0.008% $Na_2S_2O_3$, store in dark	40 days after extraction
Haloethers	G, Teflon-lined cap	Cool, 4°C, 0.008% $Na_2S_2O_3$,	40 days after extraction
Chlorinated hydrocarbons	G, Teflon-lined cap	Cool, 4°C	40 days after extraction
TCDD	G, Teflon-lined cap	Cool, 4°C, 0.008% $Na2S2O3$	40 days after extraction
Total organic halogens	G, Teflon-lined cap	Cool, 4°C, H_2SO_4 to pH<2	7 days
Pesticides Tests:			
Pesticides	G, Teflon-lined cap	Cool, 4°C, pH 5-9	40 days after extraction
Radiological Tests:			
Alpha, beta, and radium	P, G	HNO_3 to pH<2	6 months

[1]Polyethylene (P) or glass (G)

Some containers, such as drums with bungs, limit access to the contained waste and restrict sampling to what can be reached through the bung. Samples taken of one vertical plane can be considered representative of the entire container if the waste is homogeneous and if no horizontal stratification has occurred.

Tank and Waste Pile Sampling Techniques

Tanks are basically large containers that can be sampled in the same way as smaller containers. As with containers, the goal is to obtain enough samples from different locations within the tank to provide data which is representative of the entire tank. In general, subsurface samplers are used for sampling shallow tanks, and weighted bottles are used for tanks deeper than 5 feet.

Sampling methods for tanks often depend on the accessibility of the contents. If the tank is open, the tank is divided into horizontal and vertical sections just like containers, and the sections to be sampled are randomly selected. If you know the vertical distribution of wastes in the tank, dividing only the top surface and taking vertical compositing samples with a coliwasa will be sufficient. Another alternative is to use the stratified random sampling approach.

If the access to the tank is limited to inspection ports or because you can only reach the perimeter areas of an open tank, you must, at a minimum, take vertical samples. These samples will be representative only of the sampled area unless the tank contents are homogeneous. An alternative in this situation is to take a series of samples as the tank contents are drained. Estimate the time required to drain the tank and randomly select times when samples will be taken.

In waste piles, waste accessibility is the key factor in the design of sampling strategy. Thieves, triers, and shovels are used for sampling small piles and excavation equipment such as back hoes is useful for sampling larger piles.

Ideally, piles containing unknown wastes should be sampled using a three-dimensional random sampling strategy. If you can sample only certain portions of the pile, the samples will only be representative of those portions unless the entire pile is homogeneous. One alternative is to schedule sampling with pile removal. Estimate the number of truckloads which will be removed and randomly select the truckloads which will be sampled.

Sample Containers, Preservation Techniques, and Holding Times

The most important factors to consider when choosing containers for hazardous waste samples are compatibility with the waste, cost, resistance to breakage, and volume. Sample containers must not distort, rupture, or leak as a result of chemical reactions with constituents or waste samples. Containers with wide mouths are usually more suited to field operations, and all containers must have tight screw-type lids. Containers must also be large enough to accommodate the amount of material required for analysis.

Containers for collecting and storing hazardous waste samples are usually made of plastic or glass. Linear polyethylene containers usually offer the best combination of chemical resistance for inorganics and low cost. Teflon fluorinated ethylene propylene (FEP) containers are almost universally usable due to their chemical inertness and resistance to breakage. Glass containers may be used to collect and store almost all hazardous waste samples except strong alkalines and hydrofluoric acid. However, these containers are heavier than plastic and more susceptible to breakage. All containers must have adequate wall thickness to withstand handling during collection and transportation to the laboratory.

Glass or Teflon FEP containers must be used for waste samples which will be analyzed for organic compounds. If samples will be analyzed for volatile compounds, the

123

TABLE 11.3
Sample Containers, Preservatives and Sample Holding Times for Volatile and Semi-Volatile Organics

Parameter	Container	Preservation	Holding Time
Volatile Organics			
Concentrated Waste Samples	8-oz widemouth glass with Teflon liner	None	14 days
Liquid samples			
No residual chlorine present	2 40-mL vials with Teflon-lined septum caps	4 drops conc. HCl, cool 4°C	14 days
Residual chlorine present	2 40-mL vials with Teflon-lined septum caps	Collect sample in a 4-oz soil VOA container which has been pre-preserved with 4 drops of 10% sodium thiosulfate. Gently mix sample and transfer to a 40-mL VOA vial that has been pre-preserved with 4 drops conc. HCl, cool to 4°C	14 days
Acrolein and Acrylonitrile	2 40-mL vials with Teflon-lined septum caps	Adjust to pH 4-5, cool, 4°C	14 days
Soil/sediments and sludges	4-oz (120-mL) widemouth glass with Teflon liner	Cool, 4°C	14 days
Semivolatile Organics/Organchlorine Pesticides/PCBs			
Concentrated waste samples	8-oz widemouth glass with Teflon-liner	None	Samples must be extracted within 14 days and extract analyzed within 40 days following extraction.
Water Samples			
No residual chlorine present	1-gal. or 2 1/2-gal. amber glass with Teflon-liner	Cool, 4°C	Samples must be extracted within 14 days and extract analyzed within 40 days following extraction.
Residual chlorine present	1-gal. or 2 1/2-gal. amber glass Teflon-liner	Add 3 mL 10% sodium thiosulfate per gallon, cool, 4°C	Samples must be extracted within 7 days and extracts analyzed within 40 days following extraction.
Soil/sediments and sludges	8-oz. widemouth glass with Teflon-liner	Cool, 4°C	Samples must be extracted within 14 days and extracts analyzed within 40 days following extraction.

samples must be sealed in airtight containers. Table 11.2 lists EPA-recommended containers for different types of samples, preservation techniques, and holding times.

Both sampling equipment and sample bottles must be clean in order to prevent positive, negative, and cross contamination of the sample. Sample bottles used for holding samples that will be analyzed for metallics should be cleaned with detergent, rinsed with tap waster, rinsed with 1:1 nitric acid, rinsed with tap water, rinsed with 1:1 hydrochloric acid, rinsed with tap water, and finally rinsed with type II deionized water. Sample bottles used for holding samples which will be analyzed for organic compounds should be washed with detergent, rinsed with tap water, rinsed with distilled, deionized water, and dried at 105°C for approximately 1 hour.

It is important to keep air out of samples that will be analyzed for volatile organic components. When collecting samples of volatile organics, introduce the materials to the sample vials gently to reduce agitation that might drive off volatile compounds. Liquid samples should be poured into the vial without introducing any air bubbles within the vial as it is being filled. Should bubbling occur as a result of violent pouring, the sample must be poured out and the vial refilled. Each vial should be filled until there is a meniscus over the lip of the vial. The screw top lid with the septum should then be tightened onto the vial. After tightening the lid, the vial should be inverted and tapped to check for air bubbles. If there are any air bubbles present, the sample must be retaken. Two vials should be filled for each sample location.

Many waste samples must also be preserved to maintain the integrity of the sample before analysis. Preservation may involve the immediate placement of samples into an ice chest to cool samples to 4°C (approximately 40°F). Certain test procedures require the use of chemical preservatives such as nitric acid. EPA has also set maximum holding times for hazardous waste samples to help ensure sample integrity. Table 11.2 lists preservation methods and maximum holding times for different types of samples. Table 11.3 lists containers, preservatives, and holding times for volatile and semi-volatile organic samples.

Quality Assurance and Quality Control Procedures

Field Quality Control

Quality control procedures must be followed in both the field and in the laboratory to ensure reliable data are obtained from waste samples. SW-846 states that the following quality control procedures must be incorporated into field sample collection activities:

- the development of a sampling plan that incorporates or references accepted sampling techniques
- procedures for documenting and justifying any field actions that are contrary to the accepted sampling techniques documented in the sampling plan
- documentation of all prefield activities such as equipment checkout, calibrations, and container storage and preparation
- documentation of field measurement quality control data
- documentation of field activities
- documentation of postfield activities including sample shipment and receipt, field team debriefing, and equipment check-in
- generation of quality control samples including field duplicate samples, field blanks, equipment blanks, and trip blanks
- use of quality control samples to evaluate the significance of test data

Quality assurance is the process for ensuring that all data and the decisions based on these data are technically sound, statistically valid, and properly documented. Quality control procedures are the tools used to measure whether these quality assurance measures have been met.

Blanks

Blanks are often used to determine the degree of quality control during sampling operations. A variety of different types of blanks are employed including the following.

Trip blanks Trip blanks are unopened organic or aqueous solutions that accompany sample containers to and from the field. These samples can be used to detect any contamination or cross-contamination that could occur during handling and transportation. One trip blank should be analyzed with each analytical batch or every 20 samples, whichever is greater.

Field blanks Field blanks are solutions that are transferred from one vessel to another at the sampling site and are preserved with the appropriate reagents prior to shipment and analysis. Field blanks are checked to detect any environmental or reagent contamination. One field blank should be analyzed with each analytical batch or every 20 samples, whichever is greater.

Equipment blanks Equipment blanks are solutions which are transported to the site, opened in the field, poured over or through the sample collection device, collected in a sample container, and returned to the laboratory. Equipment blanks provide a check on sampling device cleanliness. One equipment blank should be analyzed with each analytical batch or every 20 samples, whichever is greater.

Duplicate samples Duplicate samples are two separate samples taken from the same source and analyzed independently. Duplicate samples are are used to document precision and variance.

Collector_____

Sample Number_____

Place of Collection_____

Date Sampled_____

Time Sampled_____

Field Information_____

FIGURE 11.2
Sample Label

```
┌─────────────────────────────────────────────────────────────────────┐
│              NAME AND ADDRESS OF ORGANIZATION COLLECTING SAMPLES      │
│                                                                       │
│   Person Collecting Sample_____Sample No._____  │
│   (signature)                                                         │
│                                                                       │
│   Date Collected_____Time Collected _____    │
│                                                                       │
│   Place Collected_____    │
│                                                                       │
└─────────────────────────────────────────────────────────────────────┘
```

FIGURE 11.3
Sample Seal

Field spikes Field spikes are used to determine the loss of parameters of interest during sampling and shipment. Since samples are spiked in the field where there is plenty of room for error, field spikes are not commonly used.

In addition to the above quality control samples, a complete quality assurance program will cover standard operating procedures for container and equipment preparation, sample preservation, packaging and shipping, design of sampling plans, definition of objectives, maintenance, calibration and cleaning of field equipment, health and safety protocols, and chain-of-custody procedures.

Sample Documentation

An essential part of any sampling and analytical process is ensuring the integrity of the sample from collection to data reporting. The possession and handling of samples should be traceable from collection through analysis and final disposition. The documentation of the sample history is called *chain of custody*.

Chain of custody is needed if there is any possibility that analytical data or conclusions based on the data will be used in litigation. The parts of the chain of custody process include the use of sample labels that are placed on containers prior to sampling and filled out at sample collection. Necessary information includes sample number, name of collector, date and time of collection, and place of collection. Figure 11.2 is an example of a sample label.

Sample seals are used to detect unauthorized tampering with samples. The seal is attached so it is necessary to break the seal to open the sample container. Necessary sample seal information includes sample number, name of collector, date and time of sampling, and place of collection. Figure 11.3 presents an example of a sample seal.

All information pertinent to the field survey and sampling must be recorded in a field logbook. The information that should be recorded includes:

- location of the sampling point
- name and address of the facility and activity that generated the waste
- type of process producing the waste
- physical form of waste such as sludge, liquid, solid, etc.
- suspected waste composition
- number and volume of sample taken
- purpose of sampling
- description of sampling point and sampling methodology
- date and time of collection
- collector's sample identification number
- laboratory that will analyze the sample and method of shipment
- references such as maps and photographs of the sampling site
- field observations
- any field measurements made such as pH or flammability
- signature of personnel responsible for logbook entries

A chain of custody record should also be filled out and accompany every sample. This record should contain the sample number, signature of collector, date and time of collection, place and address of collection, waste type, signature of persons involved in the chain of custody, and inclusive dates of possession. Figure 11.4 presents an example of a chain-of-custody form.

A sample analysis request sheet should accompany the sample to the laboratory. The field portion of the form is completed by the person collecting the sample and should include pertinent information noted in the logbook. The laboratory portion of the form is then completed by laboratory personnel and includes the name of the person receiving the sample, laboratory sample number, date and time of sample receipt, sample allocation, and analysis to be performed.

126

Proj. No.	Project Name					No. of Containers							Remarks
Samplers (*Signature*)													
Sta. No.	Date	Time	Comp.	Grab	Station Location								

Relinquished by: (*Signature*)	Date Time	Received by: (*Signature*)	Relinquished by: (Signature)	Date Time	Received by: (Signature)
Relinquished by: (*Signature*)	Date Time	Received by: (*Signature*)	Relinquished by: (Signature)	Date Time	Received by: (Signature)
Relinquished by: (*Signature*)	Date Time	Received for Laboratory by: (*Signature*)		Remarks	

FIGURE 11.4
Chain-of-Custody Form

Sample Shipping and Management Procedures

Hazard Determination Samples

A sample of solid waste or a sample of soil, air, or water that is collected for the sole purpose of testing to determine its characteristics and composition need not be managed as hazardous waste while the sample is shipped to a laboratory, temporarily stored by a laboratory, or returned to the generator.

This exception applies to any sample that is:

- temporarily stored by the sample collector at the facility before transport to a laboratory for testing
- transported to a laboratory for testing
- temporarily stored by the laboratory prior to testing
- temporarily stored by the laboratory after testing, or until the conclusion of a court case or enforcement action where further testing of the sample may be necessary, or
- transported to the facility after testing.

However, if the laboratory determines that a sample is a hazardous waste, the facility must manage that sample as hazardous waste once it is returned from the laboratory. If the laboratory has no further use for the sample and does not return the sample to the generator, the laboratory must manage the sample as a hazardous waste.

The generator and laboratory must comply with all applicable DOT classification, description, packaging, marking, labeling, and other transportation requirements for hazardous materials. Chapter 5 describes DOT requirements for shipping hazardous materials and hazardous wastes.

If you do not know the DOT hazard classification of the material until after analysis, and you know the material is not a radioactive material, poison A, flammable gas, or nonflammable gas, you should assume the material is a flammable liquid or a flammable solid. Collect the sample in a 16-ounce or smaller glass or polyethylene container, seal the sample, put the sample in a 4-mL thick polyethylene bag, place the sealed bag in a metal can with noncombustible absorbent cushioning material, and seal the can.

Mark the can "Flammable Liquid, n.o.s., UN 1993 or Flammable solid, n.o.s., UN 1325," depending on the physical state of the sample. Place one or more of the metal containers in a strong outside container such as a picnic cooler or fiberboard box, and mark the box with the same proper shipping name and UN number, the limited quantity notation, the net weight or volume of the samples, and an identification of the materials as laboratory samples. Mark the outside container "This End Up" or "This Side Up" to indicate the proper orientation of the container. If shipping via air, a Cargo Aircraft Only label is required.

Document the shipment with a hazardous chemical bill of lading which includes the proper shipping description for the sample. If the hazardous characteristics are unknown, describe the samples on the bill of lading with the words: "Flammable liquid, n.o.s., UN 1993" or "Flammable solid, n.o.s., UN 1325"; "Limited Quantity" or "Ltd. Qty."; "Laboratory Samples"; "Net Weight ___" or "Net Volume." Sign the shipper's certification to indicate the sample is properly classified, described, packaged, marked, and labeled, and is in proper condition for transportation according to the applicable regulations of the DOT.

Finally, ensure your sample is properly documented with a sample label, sample seal, sample analysis request form, and a chain of custody form. EPA requires that the following information accompany every sample shipment that is not covered by DOT regulations:

- sample collector's name, mailing address, and telephone number
- laboratory's name, mailing address, and telephone number
- quantity of the sample
- date of the shipment
- description of the sample

Treatability Study Samples

When evaluating new treatment technologies for your facility's hazardous waste, the TSD facility may request samples of your waste to conduct treatability studies. A *treatability study* means a study in which hazardous waste is subjected to a treatment process to determine whether the waste is amenable to the treatment process, what pretreatment, if any, is required, the optimal process conditions needed to achieve the desired treatment, the efficiency of a treatment process for a specific waste or wastes, or the characteristics and volumes of residuals from a particular treatment process. Treatability studies are also used to conduct liner compatibility, corrosion, and other material compatibility studies and toxicological and health effect studies. A treatability study may never be used as an excuse to commercially treat or dispose of hazardous waste from your facility without following appropriate regulations.

Treatability study samples are not subject to hazardous waste management regulations while being collected, accumulated, prepared for transportation, or transported to the laboratory or testing facility. However, you must abide by the following requirements applicable to treatability study samples:

1. Do not send more than 1000 kilograms of hazardous waste, 1 kilogram of acute hazardous waste, or 250 kilograms of soils, water, or debris contaminated with acute hazardous waste for each process being evaluated for each waste stream. The mass of each sample shipment must also be within these limits.

2. Transport samples in accordance with DOT, U.S. Postal Service, and other applicable shipping requirements. If shipping regulations do not apply to your waste, include with the shipment your name, address, and telephone number, the name, address, and telephone number of the facility that will perform the study, the quantity of the sample, the date of shipment, and a description of the sample including its EPA hazardous waste number.

3. Ship treatability study samples only to permitted or interim status TSD facilities or to facilities that have notified EPA or the state that they are conducting treatability studies and have an EPA identification number.

4. Keep the following records for at least 3 years after the completion of the study: copies of the shipping documents such as the hazardous material bill of lading; a copy of the contract with the facility conducting the treatability study; documentation showing the amount of wastes shipped, the name, address, and EPA identification number of the facility that received the waste, the date of shipment; and whether or not unused samples and treatment residues were returned to the generator.

5. Report the information from your records on any treatability studies in your biennial report.

If the facility conducting the study asks you to provide more of the sample than you are permitted to supply, you may apply to EPA or your state for additional quantity allowances. Be prepared to show why additional material is needed and to supply documentation describing the study and accounting for all previous waste which has been shipped.

Any samples or treatment residues returned to the generator that are hazardous waste must be managed as hazardous waste.

Facilities conducting treatability studies must notify EPA or the state 45 days before beginning such studies, must have an EPA identification number, and must keep records for 3 years on each treatability study that has been completed. These facilities are also limited in the amount of hazardous waste they may receive, store, and treat per day, and limited in the amount of time they may store treatability study samples. Facilities must submit annual reports to EPA or the state on studies conducted over the previous year and on the number of studies and amount of waste expected during the current year. The facility must also notify EPA or the state when it is no longer planning to conduct any treatability studies.

Appendix A
RCRA Forms and Instructions

Form Approved. OMB No. 2050-0028. Expires 10-31-91
GSA No. 0246-EPA-OT

Please refer to the *Instructions for Filing Notification* before completing this form. The information requested here is required by law *(Section 3010 of the Resource Conservation and Recovery Act).*

Notification of Regulated Waste Activity

United States Environmental Protection Agency

Date Received (For Official Use Only)

I. Installation's EPA ID Number *(Mark 'X' in the appropriate box)*

[ ] **A. First Notification**   [ ] **B. Subsequent Notification** *(complete item C)*   **C. Installation's EPA ID Number**

II. Name of Installation *(Include company and specific site name)*

III. Location of Installation *(Physical address not P.O. Box or Route Number)*

Street

Street (continued)

City or Town   **State**   **ZIP Code**

County Code   **County Name**

IV. Installation Mailing Address *(See Instructions)*

Street or P.O. Box

City or Town   **State**   **ZIP Code**

V. Installation Contact *(Person to be contacted regarding waste activities at site)*

Name *(last)*   *(first)*

Job Title   **Phone Number** *(area code and number)*

VI. Installation Contact Address *(See Instructions)*

A. Contact Address   **B. Street or P.O. Box**
Location   Mailing

City or Town   **State**   **ZIP Code**

VII. Ownership *(See Instructions)*

A. Name of Installation's Legal Owner

Street, P.O. Box, or Route Number

City or Town   **State**   **ZIP Code**

Phone Number *(area code and number)*   **B. Land Type**   **C. Owner Type**   **D. Change of Owner Indicator**   **(Date Changed)**
Yes   No   Month   Day   Year

Please print or type with ELITE type (12 characters per inch) in the unshaded areas only

Form Approved. OMB No. 2050-0028. Expires 10-31-91
GSA No. 0246-EPA-OT

ID – For Official Use Only

VIII. Type of Regulated Waste Activity *(Mark 'X' in the appropriate boxes. Refer to instructions.)*

A. Hazardous Waste Activity

1. Generator (See Instructions)
   - ☐ a. Greater than 1000kg/mo (2,200 lbs.)
   - ☐ b. 100 to 1000 kg/mo (220 – 2,200 lbs.)
   - ☐ c. Less than 100 kg/mo (220 lbs.)
2. Transporter (Indicate Mode in boxes 1–5 below)
   - ☐ a. For own waste only
   - ☐ b. For commercial purposes

   Mode of Transportation
   - ☐ 1. Air
   - ☐ 2. Rail
   - ☐ 3. Highway
   - ☐ 4. Water
   - ☐ 5. Other – specify

☐ 3. Treater, Storer, Disposer (at installation)
   Note: A permit is required for this activity; see instructions.
4. Hazardous Waste Fuel
   - ☐ a. Generator Marketing to Burner
   - ☐ b. Other Marketers
   - ☐ c. Burner – indicate device(s) – Type of Combustion Device
     - ☐ 1. Utility Boiler
     - ☐ 2. Industrial Boiler
     - ☐ 3. Industrial Furnace
☐ 5. Underground Injection Control

B. Used Oil Fuel Activities

1. Off-Specification Used Oil Fuel
   - ☐ a. Generator Marketing to Burner
   - ☐ b. Other Markerer
   - ☐ c. Burner – indicate device(s) – Type of Combustion Device
     - ☐ 1. Utility Boiler
     - ☐ 2. Industrial Boiler
     - ☐ 3. Industrial Furnace
☐ 2. Specification Used Oil Fuel Marketer (or On-site Burner) Who First Claims the Oil Meets the Specification

IX. Description of Regulated Wastes *(Use additional sheets if necessary)*

A. Characteristics of Nonlisted Hazardous Wastes. Mark 'X' in the boxes corresponding to the characteristics of nonlisted hazardous wastes your installation handles. *(See 40 CFR Parts 261.20 – 261.24)*

1. Ignitable *(D001)* 2. Corrosive *(D002)* 3. Reactive *(D003)* 4. Toxicity Characteristic *(D000)*

(List specific EPA hazardous waste number(s) for the Toxicity Characteristic contaminant(s))

B. Listed Hazardous Wastes. (See 40 CFR 261.31 – 33. See instructions if you need to list more than 12 waste codes.)

1	2	3	4	5	6
7	8	9	10	11	12

C. Other Wastes. (State or other wastes requiring an I.D. number. See instructions.)

1	2	3	4	5	6

X. Certification

I certify under penalty of law that I have personally examined and am familiar with the information submitted in this and all attached documents, and that based on my inquiry of those individuals immediately responsible for obtaining the information, I believe that the submitted information is true, accurate, and complete. I am aware that there are significant penalties for submitting false information, including the possibility of fines and imprisonment.

Signature	Name and Official Title *(type or print)*	Date Signed

XI. Comments

Note: Mail completed form to the appropriate EPA Regional or State Office. (See Section III of the booklet for addresses.)

Form Approved. OMB No. 2050-0028. Expires 10-31-91
GSA No. 0246-EPA-OT

ID – For Official Use Only

IX. Description of Regulated Wastes Continued *(Additional sheet)*

B. **Listed Hazardous Wastes.** (See 40 CFR 261.31 – 33. Use this page only if you need to list more than 12 waste codes.)

13	14	15	16	17	18
19	20	21	22	23	24
25	26	27	28	29	30
31	32	33	34	35	36
37	38	39	40	41	42
43	44	45	46	47	48
49	50	51	52	53	54
55	56	57	58	59	60
61	62	63	64	65	66
67	68	69	70	71	72
73	74	75	76	77	78
79	80	81	82	83	84
85	86	87	88	89	90
91	92	93	94	95	96
97	98	99	100	101	102
103	104	105	106	107	108
109	110	111	112	113	114
115	116	117	118	119	120

132

LINE-BY-LINE INSTRUCTIONS FOR COMPLETING EPA FORM 8700-12

Type or print in black ink all items except Item X, "Signature", leaving a blank box between words. The boxes are spaced at 1/4" intervals which accommodate elite type (12 characters per inch.) When typing, hit the space bar twice between characters. If you print, place each character in a box. Abbreviate if necessary to stay within the number of boxes allowed for each Item. If you must use additional sheets, indicate clearly the number of the Item on the form to which the information on the separate sheet applies.

Note: When submitting a subsequent notification form, notifiers must complete in their entirety Items I, II, III, VI, VIII and X. Other sections that are being added to (i.e., newly regulated activities) or altered (i.e., installation contact) must also be completed. All other sections may be left blank.

Item I — Installation's EPA ID Number

Place an "X" in the appropriate box to indicate whether this is your first or a subsequent notification for this site. If you have filed a previous notification, enter the EPA Identification Number assigned to this site in the boxes provided; Leave EPA ID Number blank if this is your first notification for this site.

Note: When the owner of a facility changes, the new owner must notify U.S. EPA of the change, even if the previous owner already received a U.S. EPA Identification Number. Because the U.S. EPA ID Number is "site-specific," the new owner will keep the existing ID number. If the facility moves to another location, the owner/operator must notify EPA of this change. In this instance, a new U.S. EPA Identification Number will be assigned, since the facility has changed locations.

Items II and III — Name and Location of Installation

Complete Items II and III. Please note that the address you give for Item III, "Location of Installation," must be a physical address, not a post office box or route number.

County Name and Code

Give the county code, if known. If you do not know the county code, enter the county name, from which the EPA can automatically generate the county code. If the county name is unknown contact the local Post Office. To obtain a list of county codes, contact the National Technical Information Service, U.S. Department of Commerce, Springfield, Virginia, 22161 or at (703) 487-4650. The list of codes is contained in the Federal Information Processing Standards Publication (FIPS PUB) number 6-3.

Item IV — Installation Mailing Address

Please enter the Installation Mailing Address. If the Mailing Address and the Location of Installation (Item III) are the same, you can print "Same" in the box for Item IV.

Item V — Installation Contact

Enter the name, title, and business telephone number of the person who should be contacted regarding information submitted on this form.

Item VI — Installation Contact Address:

A. Code: If the contact address is the same as the location of the installation address listed in Item III or the installation mailing address listed in Item IV, place an "X" in the appropriate box to indicate where the contact may be reached. If the location of installation address, the installation mailing address, and the installation contact address are all the same, mark the "Location" box. If an "X" is entered in either the location or mailing box, Item IV.B. should be left blank.

B. Address: Enter the contact address only if the contact address is different from either the location of installation address (Item III) or the installation mailing address (Item IV), and IV.A. was left blank.

Item VII — Ownership

A. Name: Enter the name of the legal owner(s) of the installation, including the proper owner. Also enter the address and phone number where this individual can be reached. Use the comment section in XI or additional sheets if necessary to list more than one owner.

B. Land Type: Using the codes listed below, indicate in VII.B. the code which *best describes* the current legal status of the land on which the facility is located:

F = Federal	C = County
S = State	M = Municipal*
I = Indian	D = District
P = Private	O = Other

Note: If the Land Type is *best described* as Indian, County, or District, please use those codes. Otherwise, use Municipal.

C. Owner Type: Using the codes listed below, indicate in VII.C. the code which best describes the legal status of the current owner of the facility:

F = Federal	C = County
S = State	M = Municipal*
I = Indian	D = District
P = Private	O = Other

Note: If the Owner Type is *best described* as Indian, County, or District, please use those codes. Otherwise, use Municipal.

D. Change of Owner Indicator: (If this is your installation's first notification, leave Item VII.D. blank and skip to Item VIII. If this is a subsequent notification, complete Item VII.D. as directed below.)

 If the owner of this facility has changed since the facility's original notification, place an "X" in the box marked "Yes" and enter the date the owner changed.

 If the owner of this facility has not changed since the facility's original notification, place an "X" in the box marked "No" and skip to Item VIII.

 If an additional owner(s) has been added/replaced since the facility's original notification, place an "X" in the box marked "Yes." Use the comment section in XI to list any additional owner(s), the dates they became owners, and which owner(s) (if any) they replaced. If necessary, attach a separate sheet of paper.

Item VIII — Type of Regulated Waste Activity

A. Hazardous Waste Activity: If you generate a hazardous waste that is identified by characteristic or listed in 40 CFR Part 261, mark an "X" in the appropriate box to show which hazardous waste activities are going on at this installation.

1. Generator: If you generate a hazardous waste that is identified by characteristic or listed in 40 CFR Part 261, mark an "X" in the appropriate box for the quantity of non-acute hazardous waste that is generated per calendar month. If you generate acute hazardous waste please refer to 40 CFR Part 263.

2. Transporter: If you transport hazardous waste, indicate if it is your own waste, for commercial purposes, or mark both boxes if both classifications apply. Mark an "X" in each appropriate box to indicate the method(s) of transportation you use. Transporters do not have to complete Item IX of this form, but must sign the certification in Item X. The Federal regulations for hazardous waste transporters are found in 40 CFR Part 263.

3. Treater/Storer/Disposer: If you treat, store or dispose of regulated hazardous waste, then mark an "X" in this box. You are reminded to contact the appropriate address for the lead agency in your State to request Part A of the RCRA Permit Application. The Federal regulations for hazardous waste facility owners/operators are found in 40 CFR Part 264 and 265.

4. Hazardous Waste Fuel: If you market hazardous waste fuel, place an "X" in the appropriate box(es). If you burn hazardous waste fuel on-site, place an "X" in the appropriate box and indicate the type(s) of combustion devices in which hazardous waste fuel is burned.

Note: Generators are required to notify for waste-as-fuel activities only if they market directly to the burner. "Other Market" is defined as any person, other than a generator marketing hazardous waste, who markets hazardous waste fuel.

5. Underground Injection Control: If you generate and/or treat, store, or dispose of hazardous waste, place an "X" in the box if an injection well is located at your installations. "Underground Injection" means the subsurface emplacement of fluids through a bored, drilled, or driven well: Or through a dug well, where the depth of the dug well is greater than the largest surface dimension.

B. Used Oil Fuel Activities: Mark an "X" in the appropriate box(es) to indicate which used oil fuel activities are taking place at this installation.

1. Off-Specification Used Oil Fuel: If you market off-specification used oil, place an "X" in the appropriate box(es). If you burn used oil fuel place an "X" in the box(es) below to indicate type(s) of combustion devices in which off-specification used oil is burned.

Note: Used oil generators are required to notify only if marketing directly to the burner.

"Other Marketer" is defined as any person , other than a generator marketing his or her used oil, who markets used oil fuel.

2. Specification Used Oil Fuel: If you are the first to claim the used oil meets the specification established in 40 CFR 266.40(e) and is exempt from further regulation, mark an "X" in this box.

Item IX — Description of Regulated Wastes

(Only persons involved in a hazardous waste activity (Item VIII A.) need to complete this item. Transporters requesting a U.S. EPA Identification Number do not need to complete this item, but must sign the "Certification" in Item X.

You will need to refer to 40 CFR Part 261 in order to complete this section. Part 261 identifies those wastes that EPA defines as hazardous.

A. Characteristics of Nonlisted Hazardous Wastes: If you handle hazardous wastes which are not listed in 40 CFR Part 261, Subpart D but do exhibit a characteristic of hazardous waste as defined in 40 CFR Part 261, Subpart C, you should describe these wastes by the EPA hazardous waste number for the characteristic. Place an "X" in the box next to the characteristic of the wastes that you handle. If you mark "4. Toxicity Characteristic," please list the specific EPA hazardous waste number for the specific contaminant(s) in the box(es) provided.

B. Listed Hazardous Wastes: If you handle hazardous wastes, please continue listing the waste codes on an additional sheet. If it is used, attach the additional page to the rest of the form before mailing it to the appropriate EPA Regional or State Office.

Note: If you must handle more than 12 listed hazardous wastes, please continue listing the waste codes on an additional sheet. If it is used, attach the additional page to the rest of the form before mailing it to the appropriate EPA Regional or State Office.

C. Other Wastes: If you handle other wastes or State regulated wastes that have a waste code, enter the appropriate code number in the boxes provided.

Item X — Certification

This certification must be signed by the owner, operator, or an "authorized representative" of your installation. An "authorized representative" is a person responsible for the overall operation of the facility (i.e., a plant manager or superintendent, or a person of equal responsibility). All notifications must include this certification to be complete.

Item XI — Comments

Use this space for any additional comments.

Appendix B
References

American Conference of Governmental Industrial Hygienists (ACGIH), *Threshold Limit Values and Biological Exposure Indices for 1988—1989*, Cincinnati, OH: ACGIH, 1988

Environmental Information Ltd., *Industrial and Hazardous Waste Management Firms*, 7400 Metro Boulevard, Suite 400, Minneapolis, Minnesota 55435

J.J. Keller and Associates, *Hazardous Waste Services Directory*, P.O. Box 368, Neenah, WI 54957

McCoy, Lark H., Ed., *The Hazardous Waste Consultant*, McCoy and Associates, Lakewood, CO.

National Fire Protection Association, *Flammable and Combustible Liquids Code*, NFPA, 1981

National Institute for Occupational Safety and Health (NIOSH), *Registry of Toxic Effects of Chemical Substances*, NIOSH Publication No. 80-102

Office of the Federal Register, *Code of Federal Regulations, Title 40, Parts 190 through 399*, U.S. Government Printing Office, Washington, DC, 20401

Sax, N. Irving, *Dangerous Properties of Industrial Materials*, New York: Van Nostrand Reinhold, 1989

U.S. Coast Guard, *Chemical Hazard Response Information System (CHRIS)*, U.S. Coast Guard (Call 202-267-1577 for additional information), 1992

U.S. EPA, *Federal Facilities Compliance Strategy*, Office of Federal Activities, Washington, D.C.: U.S. Government Printing Office, 1988

U.S. EPA, *Test Methods for Evaluating Solid Waste (SW-846), 3rd Edition*, Office of Solid Waste and Emergency Response, Washington, D.C.: U.S. Government Printing Office, 1986

U.S. EPA, *Treatment Technology Briefs: Alternatives to Hazardous Waste Landfills*, Hazardous Waste Engineering Research Laboratory, EPA/600/8-86/017, Washington, D.C.: U.S. Government Printing Office, 1986

U.S. EPA, *Waste Analysis Plans: A Guidance Manual*, Office of Solid Waste, EPA/530-SW-84-012, Washington, D.C.: U.S. Government Printing Office, 1984

Appendix C
Land Disposal Regulations and Notification Key

EPA REGULATIONS ON LAND DISPOSAL RESTRICTIONS

40 CFR 268

TITLE 40 -- PROTECTION OF ENVIRONMENT
CHAPTER 1 -- ENVIRONMENTAL PROTECTION AGENCY
PART 268 -- LAND DISPOSAL RESTRICTIONS

AUTHORITY: 42 U.S.C. 6905, 6912(a), 6921, and 6924.

Subpart A -- General

§ 268.1 Purpose, scope and applicability.

(a) This part identifies hazardous wastes that are restricted from land disposal and defines those limited circumstances under which an otherwise prohibited waste may continue to be land disposed.

(b) Except as specifically provided otherwise in this part or Part 261 of this chapter, the requirements of this part apply to persons who generate or transport hazardous waste and owners and operators of hazardous waste treatment, storage, and disposal facilities.

(c) Restricted wastes may continue to be land disposed as follows:

(1) Where persons have been granted an extension to the effective date of a prohibition under Subpart C of this part or pursuant to §268.5, with respect to those wastes covered by the extension;

(2) Where persons have been granted an exemption from a prohibition pursuant to a petition under §268.6, with respect to those wastes and units covered by the petition;

(3) Wastes that are hazardous only because they exhibit a hazardous characteristic, and which are otherwise prohibited from land disposal under this part, are not prohibited from land disposal if the wastes:

(i) Are disposed into a nonhazardous or hazardous injection well as defined in 40 CFR 144.6(a); and

(ii) Do not exhibit any prohibited characteristic of hazardous waste at the point of injection.

(4) [Removed]

(5) [Removed]

(d) The requirements of this part shall not affect the availability of a waiver under section 121(d)(4) of the Comprehensive Environmental Response, Compensation, and Liability Act of 1980 (CERCLA).

(e) The following hazardous wastes are not subject to any provision of part 268:

(1) Waste generated by small quantity generators of less than 100 kilograms of non-acute hazardous waste or less than 1 kilogram of acute hazardous waste per month, as defined in §261.5 of this chapter;

(2) Waste pesticides that a farmer disposes of pursuant to §262.70;

(3) Wastes identified or listed as hazardous after November 8, 1984 for which EPA has not promulgated land disposal prohibitions or treatment standards.

§ 268.2 Definitions applicable in this part.

When used in this part the following terms have the meanings given below:

(a) *Halogenated organic compounds or HOCs* means those compounds having a carbon-halogen bond which are listed under appendix III to this part.

(b) *Hazardous constituent or constituents* means those constituents listed in appendix VIII to part 261 of this chapter.

(c) *Land disposal* means placement in or on the land and includes, but is not limited to, placement in a landfill, surface impoundment, waste pile, injection well, land treatment facility, salt dome formation, salt bed formation, underground mine or cave, or placement in a concrete vault or bunker intended for disposal purposes.

(d) *Nonwastewaters* are wastes that do not meet the criteria for wastewaters in paragraph (f) of this section.

(e) *Polychlorinated biphenyls or PCBs* are halogenated organic compounds defined in accordance with 40 CFR 761.3.

(f) *Wastewaters* are wastes that contain less than 1% by weight total organic carbon (TOC) and less than 1% by weight total suspended solids (TSS), with the following exceptions:

(1) *F001, F002, F003, F004, F005 wastewaters* are solvent-water mixtures that contain less than 1% by weight TOC or less than 1% by weight total F001, F002, F003, F004, F005 solvent constituents listed in §268.41, Table CCWE.

(2) *K011, K013, K014 wastewaters* contain less than 5% by weight TOC and less than 1% by weight TSS, as generated.

(3) *K103 and K104 wastewaters* contain less than 4% by weight TOC and less than 1% by weight TSS.

(g) *Inorganic Solid Debris* means nonfriable inorganic solids contaminated with D004-D011 hazardous wastes that are incapable of passing through a 9.5 mm standard sieve; and that require cutting, or crushing and grinding in mechanical sizing equipment prior to stabilization; and, are limited to the following inorganic or metal materials:

(1) Metal slags (either dross or scoria);

(2) Glassified slag;

(3) Glass;

(4) Concrete (excluding cementitious or pozzolanic stabilized hazardous wastes);

(5) Masonry and refractory bricks;

(6) Metal cans, containers, drums, or tanks;

(7) Metal nuts, bolts, pipes, pumps, valves, appliances, or industrial equipment;

(8) Scrap metal as defined in 40 CFR 261.1(c)(6);

§ 268.3 Dilution prohibited as a substitute for treatment.

(a) Except as provided in paragraph (b) of this section, no generator, transporter, handler, or owner or operator of a treatment, storage, or disposal facility shall in any way dilute a restricted waste or the residual from treatment of a restricted waste as a substitute for adequate treatment to achieve compliance with subpart D of this part, to circumvent the effective date of a prohibition in subpart C of this part, to otherwise avoid a prohibition in subpart C of this part, or to circumvent a land disposal prohibition imposed by RCRA section 3004.

(b) Dilution of wastes that are hazardous only because they exhibit a characteristic in a treatment system which treats wastes subsequently discharged to a water of the United States pursuant to a permit issued under section 402 of the Clean Water Act (CWA) or which treats wastes for purposes of pretreatment requirements under section 307 of the CWA is not impermissible dilution for purposes of this section unless a method has been specified as the treatment standard in §268.42.

§ 266.4 Treatment surface impoundment exemption.

(a) Wastes which are otherwise prohibited from land disposal under this part may be treated in a surface impoundment or series of impoundments provided that:

(1) Treatment of such wastes occurs in the impoundments;

(2) The following conditions are met:

(i) *Sampling and testing.* For wastes with treatment standards in Subpart D of this part and/or prohibition levels in Subpart C of this part or RCRA section 3004(d), the residues from treatment are analyzed, as specified in §§268.7 or 268.32, to determine if they meet the applicable treatment standards or where no treat-

ment standards have been established for the waste, the applicable prohibition levels. The sampling method, specified in the waste analysis plan under §§264.13 or 265.13, must be designed such that representative samples of the sludge and the supernatant are tested separately rather than mixed to form homogeneous samples.

(ii) *Removal.* The following treatment residues (including any liquid waste) must be removed at least annually: residues which do not meet the treatment standards promulgated under Subpart D of this part; residues which do not meet the prohibition levels established under Subpart C of this part or imposed by statute (where no treatment standards have been established); residues which are from the treatment of wastes prohibited from land disposal under Subpart C of this part (where no treatment standards have been established and no prohibition levels apply); or residues from managing listed wastes which are not delisted under §260.22 of this chapter. However, residues which are the subject of a valid certification under §268.8 made no later than a year after placement of the wastes in an impoundment are not required to be removed annually. If the volume of liquid flowing through the impoundment or series of impoundments annually is greater than the volume of the impoundment or impoundments, this flow-through constitutes removal of the supernatant for the purpose of this requirement.

(iii) *Subsequent management.* Treatment residues may not be placed in any other surface impoundment for subsequent management unless the residues are the subject of a valid certification under §268.8 which allows disposal in surface impoundments meeting the requirements of section §268.8(a).

(iv) *Recordkeeping.* The procedures and schedule for the sampling of impoundment contents, the analysis of test data, and the annual removal of residues which do not meet the treatment standards, or prohibition levels (where no treatment standards have been established), or which are from the treatment of wastes prohibited from land disposal under Subpart C (where no treatment standards have

been established and no prohibition levels apply), must be specified in the facility's waste analysis plan as required under §§264.13 or 265.13 of this chapter.

(3) The impoundment meets the design requirements of §§264.221(c) or 265.221(a) of this chapter, regardless that the unit may not be new, expanded, or a replacement, and be in compliance with applicable ground water monitoring requirements of Subpart F of Part 264 or Part 264 of this chapter unless:

(i) Exempted pursuant to §264.221(d) or (e) of this chapter, or to §265.221(c) or (d) of this chapter; or,

(ii) Upon application by the owner or operator, the Administrator, after notice and an opportunity to comment, has granted a waiver of the requirements on the basis that the surface impoundment:

(A) Has at least one liner, for which there is no evidence that such liner is leaking;

(B) Is located more than one-quarter mile from an underground source of drinking water; and

(C) Is in compliance with generally applicable ground water monitoring requirements for facilities with permits; or,

(iii) Upon application by the owner or operator, the Administrator, after notice and an opportunity to comment, has granted a modification to the requirements on the basis of a demonstration that the surface impoundment is located, designed, and operated so as to assure that there will be no migration of any hazardous constituent into ground water or surface water at any future time.

(4) The owner or operator submits to the Regional Administrator a written certification that the requirements of §268.4(a)(3) have been met and submits a copy of the waste analysis plan required under §268.4(a)(2). The following certification is required:

I certify under penalty of law that the requirements of 40 CFR 268.4(a)(3) have been met for all surface impoundments being used to treat restricted wastes. I believe that the submitted information is true, accurate, and complete. I am aware that there are significant penalties for submitting false information, including the possibility of fine and imprisonment.

(b) Evaporation of hazardous constituents as the principal means of treatment is not considered to be treatment for purposes of an exemption under this section.

§ 268.5 Procedures for case-by-case extensions to an effective date.

(a) Any person who generates, treats, stores, or disposes of a hazardous waste may submit an application to the Administrator for an extension to the effective date of any applicable restriction established under Subpart C of this part. The applicant must demonstrate the following:

(1) He has made a good-faith effort to locate and contract with treatment, recovery, or disposal facilities nationwide to manage his waste in accordance with the effective date of the applicable restriction established under Subpart C of this Part;

(2) He has entered into a binding contractual commitment to construct or otherwise provide alternative treatment, recovery (e.g., recycling), or disposal capacity that meets the treatment standards specified in Subpart D or, where treatment standards have not been specified, such treatment, recovery, or disposal capacity is protective of human health and the environment.

(3) Due to circumstances beyond the applicant's control, such alternative capacity cannot reasonably be made available by the applicable effective date. This demonstration may include a showing that the technical and practical difficulties associated with providing the alternative capacity will result in the capacity not being available by the applicable effective date;

(4) The capacity being constructed or otherwise provided by the applicant will be sufficient to manage the entire quantity of waste that is the subject of the application;

(5) He provides a detailed schedule for obtaining required operating and construction permits or an outline of how and when alternative capacity will be available;

(6) He has arranged for adequate capacity to manage his waste during an extension and has documented in the application the location of all sites at which the waste will be managed; and

(7) Any waste managed in a surface impoundment or landfill during the extension period will meet the requirements of paragraph (h)(2) of this section.

(b) An authorized representative signing an application described under paragraph (a) of this section shall make the following certification:

I certify under penalty of law that I have personally examined and am familiar with the information submitted in this document and all attachments and that, based on my inquiry of those individuals immediately responsible for obtaining the information, I believe that the information is true, accurate, and complete. I am aware that there are significant penalties for submitting false information, including the possibility of fine and imprisonment.

(c) After receiving an application for an extension, the Administrator may request any additional information which he deems as necessary to evaluate the application.

(d) An extension will apply only to the waste generated at the individual facility covered by the application and will not apply to restricted waste from any other facility.

(e) On the basis of the information referred to in paragraph (a) of this section, after notice and opportunity for comment, and after consultation with appropriate State agencies in all affected States, the Administrator may grant an extension of up to 1 year from the effective date. The Administrator may renew this extension for up to 1 additional year upon the request of the applicant if the demonstration required in paragraph (a) of this section can still be made. In no event will an extension extend beyond 24 months from the applicable effective date specified in Subpart C of Part 268. The length of any extension authorized will be determined by the Administrator based on the time required to construct or obtain the type of capacity needed by the applicant as described in the completion schedule discussed in paragraph(a)(5) of this section. The Administrator will give public notice of the intent to approve or deny a petition and provide

an opportunity for public comment. The final decision on a petition will be published in the FEDERAL REGISTER .

(f) Any person granted an extension under this section must immediately notify the Administrator as soon as he has knowledge of any change in the conditions certified to in the application.

(g) Any person granted an extension under this section shall submit written progress reports at intervals designated by the Administrator. Such reports must describe the overall progress made toward constructing or otherwise providing alternative treatment, recovery or disposal capacity; must identify any event which may cause or has caused a delay in the development of the capacity; and must summarize the steps taken to mitigate the delay. The Administrator can revoke the extension at any time if the applicant does not demonstrate a good-faith effort to meet the schedule for completion, if the Agency denies or revokes any required permit, if conditions certified in the application change, or for any violation of this chapter.

(h) Whenever the Administrator establishes an extension to an effective date under this section, during the period for which such extension is in effect:

(1) The storage restrictions under §268.50(a) do not apply; and

(2) Such hazardous waste may be disposed in a landfill or surface impoundment only if such unit is in compliance with the technical requirements of the following provisions regardless of whether such unit is existing, new, or a replacement or lateral expansion.

(i) The landfill, if in interim status, is in compliance with the requirements of Subpart F of Part 265 and §265.301(a), (c), and (d) of this chapter; or,

(ii) The landfill, if permitted, is in compliance with the requirements of Subpart F of Part 264 and §264.301(c), (d) and (e) of this chapter;

(iii) The surface impoundment, if in interim status, is in compliance with the requirements of Subpart F of Part 265, 265.221(a), (c), and (d) of this chapter, and RCRA section 3005(j)(1); or

(iv) The surface impoundment, if permitted, is in compliance with the requirements of Subpart F of Part 264 and §264.221(c), (d) and (e) of this chapter.

(v) The landfill, if disposing of containerized liquid hazardous wastes containing PCBs at concentrations greater than or equal to 50 ppm but less than 500 ppm, is also in compliance with the requirements of 40 CFR 761.75 and Parts 264 and 265.

(i) Pending a decision on the application the applicant is required to comply with all restrictions on land disposal under this part once the effective date for the waste has been reached.

(Approved by the Office of Management and Budget under control number 2050-0062)

§ 268.6 Petitions to allow land disposal of a waste prohibited under Subpart C of Part 268.

(a) Any person seeking an exemption from a prohibition under Subpart C of this part for the disposal of a restricted hazardous waste in a particular unit or units must submit a petition to the Administrator demonstrating, to a reasonable degree of certainty, that there will be no migration of hazardous constituents from the disposal unit or injection zone for as long as the wastes remain hazardous.

The demonstration must include the following components:

(1) An identification of the specific waste and the specific unit for which the demonstration will be made;

(2) A waste analysis to describe fully the chemical and physical characteristics of the subject waste;

(3) A comprehensive characterization of the disposal unit site including an analysis of background air, soil, and water quality.

(4) A monitoring plan that detects migration at the earliest practicable time;

(5) Sufficient information to assure the Administrator that the owner or operator of a land disposal unit receiving restricted waste(s) will comply with other applicable Federal, State, and local laws.

(b) The demonstration referred to in paragraph (a) of this section must meet the following criteria:

(1) All waste and environmental sampling, test, and analysis data must be accurate and reproducible to the extent that state-of-the-art techniques allow;

(2) All sampling, testing, and estimation techniques for chemical and physical properties of the waste and all environmental parameters must have been approved by the Administrator;

(3) Simulation models must be calibrated for the specific waste and site conditions, and verified for accuracy by comparison with actual measurements;

(4) A quality assurance and quality control plan that addresses all aspects of the demonstration must be approved by the Administrator; and,

(5) An analysis must be performed to identify and quantify any aspects of the demonstration that contribute significantly to uncertainty. This analysis must include an evaluation of the consequences of predictable future events, including, but not limited to, earthquakes, floods, severe storm events, droughts, or other natural phenomena.

(c) Each petition referred to in paragraph (a) of this section must include the following:

(1) A monitoring plan that describes the monitoring program installed at and/or around the unit to verify continued compliance with the conditions of the variance. This monitoring plan must provide information on the monitoring of the unit and/or the environment around the unit. The following specific information must be included in the plan:

(i) The media monitored in the cases where monitoring of the environment around the unit is required;

(ii) The type of monitoring conducted at the unit, in the cases where monitoring of the unit is required;

(iii) The location of the monitoring stations;

(iv) The monitoring interval (frequency of monitoring at each station);

(v) The specific hazardous constituents to be monitored;

(vi) The implementation schedule for the monitoring program;

(vii) The equipment used at the monitoring stations;

(viii) The sampling and analytical techniques employed; and

(ix) The data recording/reporting procedures.

(2) Where applicable, the monitoring program described in paragraph (c)(1) of this section must be in place for a period of time specified by the Administrator, as part of his approval of the petition, prior to receipt of prohibited waste at the unit.

(3) The monitoring data collected according to the monitoring plan specified under paragraph (c)(1) of this section must be sent to the Administrator according to a format and schedule specified and approved in the monitoring plan, and

(4) A copy of the monitoring data collected under the monitoring plan specified under paragraph (c)(1) of this section must be kept on-site at the facility in the operating record.

(5) The monitoring program specified under paragraph (c)(1) of this section meet the following criteria:

(i) All sampling, testing, and analytical data must be approved by the Administrator and must provide data that is accurate and reproducible.

(ii) All estimation and monitoring techniques must be approved by the Administrator.

(iii) A quality assurance and quality control plan addressing all aspects of the monitoring program must be provided to and approved by the Administrator.

(d) Each petition must be submitted to the Administrator.

(e) After a petition has been approved, the owner or operator must report any changes in conditions at the unit and/or the environment around the unit that significantly depart from the conditions described in the variance and affect the potential for migration of hazardous constituents from the units as follows:

(1) If the owner or operator plans to make changes to the unit design, construction, or operation, such a change must be proposed, in writing, and the owner or operator must submit a demonstration to the Administrator at least 30 days prior to making the change. The Administrator will determine whether the proposed change invalidates the terms of the petition and will determine the appropriate response. Any change must be approved by the Administrator prior to being made.

(2) If the owner or operator discovers that a condition at the site which was modeled or predicted in the petition does not occur as predicted, this change must be reported, in writing, to the Administrator within 10 days of discovering the change. The Administrator will determine whether the reported change from the terms of the petition requires further action, which may include termination of waste acceptance and revocation of the petition, petition modifications, or other responses.

(f) If the owner or operator determines that there is migration of hazardous constituent(s) from the unit, the owner or operator must :

(1) Immediately suspend receipt of prohibited waste at the unit, and

(2) Notify the Administrator, in writing, within 10 days of the determination that a release has occurred.

(3) Following receipt of the notification the Administrator will determine, within 60 days of receiving notification, whether the owner or operator can continue to receive prohibited waste in the unit and whether the variance is to be revoked. The Administrator shall also determine whether further examination of any migration is warranted under applicable provisions of Part 264 or Part 265.

(g) Each petition must include the following statement signed by the petitioner or an authorized representative:

I certify under penalty of law that I have personally examined and am familiar with the information submitted in this petition and all attached documents, and that, based on my inquiry of those individuals immediately responsible for obtaining the information, I believe that submitted information is true, accurate, and complete. I am aware that there are significant penalties for submitting false information, including the possibility of fine and imprisonment.

(h) After receiving a petition, the Administrator may request any additional information that reasonably may be required to evaluate the demonstration.

(i) If approved, the petition will apply to land disposal of the specific restricted waste at the individual disposal unit described in the demon-stration and will not apply to any other restricted waste at that disposal unit, or to that specific restricted waste at any other disposal unit.

(j) The Administrator will give public notice in the Federal Register of the intent to approve or deny a petition and provide an opportunity for public comment. The final decision on a petition will be published in the Federal Register.

(k) The term of a petition granted under this section shall be no longer than the term of the RCRA permit if the disposal unit is operating under a RCRA permit, or up to a maximum of 10 years from the date of approval provided under paragraph (g) of this section if the unit is operating under interim status. In either case, the term of the granted petition shall expire upon the termination or denial of a RCRA permit, or upon the termination of interim status or when the volume limit of waste to be land disposed during the term of petition is reached.

(l) Prior to the Administrator's decision, the applicant is required to comply with all restrictions on land disposal under this part once the effective date for the waste has been reached.

(m) The petition granted by the Administrator does not relieve the petitioner of his responsibilities in the management of hazardous waste under 40 CFR Part 260 through Part 271.

(n) Liquid hazardous wastes containing polychlorinated biphenyls at concentrations greater than or equal to 500 ppm are not eligible for an exemption under this section.

(Approved by the Office of Management and Budget under control number 2050-0062)

§ 268.7 Waste analysis and recordkeeping.

(a) Except as specified in §268.32 of this part, if a generator's waste is listed in 40 CFR part 261, subpart D, the generator must test his waste, or test an extract using the test method described in part 261, appendix II, or use knowledge of the waste, to determine if the waste is restricted from land disposal under this part. Except as specified in §268.32 of this part, if a generator's waste exhibits one or more of the characteristics set out at 40 CFR part 261, subpart C, the generator must test an extract using the test method described in appendix IX of this part, or use knowledge of the waste, to determine if the waste is restricted from land disposal under this Part.

(1) If a generator determines that he is managing a restricted waste under this part and the waste does not meet the applicable treatment standards set forth in Subpart D of this part or exceeds the applicable prohibition levels set forth in §268.32 or RCRA 3004(d), with each shipment of waste the generator must notify the treatment or storage facility in writing of the appropriate treatment standards set forth in Subpart D of this part and any applicable prohibition levels set forth in §268.32 or RCRA 3004(d). The notice must include the following information:

(i) EPA Hazardous Waste Number;

(ii) The corresponding treatment standards for wastes F001-F005, F039, and wastes prohibited pursuant to §268.32 or RCRA section 3004(d). Treatment standards for all other restricted wastes must either be included, or be referenced by including on the notification the applicable wastewater (as defined in §268.2(f)) or nonwastewater (as defined in §268.2(d)) category, the applicable subdivisions made within a waste code based on waste-specific criteria (such as D003 reactive cyanides), and the CFR section(s) and paragraph(s) where the applicable treatment standard appears. Where the applicable treatment standards are expressed as specified technologies in §268.42, the applicable five-letter treatment code found in Table 1 of §268.42 (e.g., INCIN, WETOX) also must be listed on the notification.

(iii) The manifest number associated with the shipment of waste; and

(iv) Waste analysis data, where available.

(2) If a generator determines that he is managing a restricted waste under this part, and determines that the waste can be land disposed without further treatment, with each shipment of waste he must submit, to the treatment, storage, or land disposal facility, a notice and a certification stating that the waste meets the applicable treatment standards set forth in Subpart D of this part and the applicable prohibition levels set forth in §268.32 or RCRA §3004(d).

(i) The notice must include the following information:

(A) EPA Hazardous Waste Number;

(B) The corresponding treatment standards for waste F001-F005, F039, and wastes prohibited pursuant to §268.32 or RCRA section 3004(d). Treatment standards for all other restricted wastes must either be included, or be referenced by including on the notification the applicable wastewater (as defined in §268.2(f)) or nonwastewater (as defined in §268.2(d)) category, the applicable subdivisions made within a waste code based on waste-specific criteria (such as D003 reactive cyanides), and the CFR section(s) and paragraph(s) where the applicable treatment standard appears. Where the applicable treatment standards are expressed as specified technologies in §268.42, the applicable five-letter treatment code found in Table 1 of §268.42 (e.g., INCIN, WETOX) also must be listed on the notification.

(C) The manifest number associated with the shipment of waste;

(D) Waste analysis data, where available.

(ii) The certification must be signed by an authorized representative and must state the following:

I certify under penalty of law that I personally have examined and am familiar with the waste through analysis and testing or through knowledge of the waste to support this certification that the waste complies with the treatment standards specified in 40 CFR Part 268 Subpart D and all applicable prohibitions set forth in 40 CFR 268.32 or RCRA section 3004(d). I be-

lieve that the information I submitted is true, accurate and complete. I am aware that there are significant penalties for submitting a false certification, including the possiblity of a fine and imprisonment.

(3) If a generator's waste is subject to an exemption from a prohibition on the type of land disposal method utilized for the waste (such as, but not limited to, a case-by-case extension under §268.5, an exemption under §268.6, or a nationwide capacity variance under subpart C), with each shipment of waste he must submit a notice to the facility receiving his waste stating that the waste is not prohibited from land disposal. The notice must include the following information:

(i) EPA Hazardous Waste Number;

(ii) The corresponding treatment standards for wastes F001-F005, F039, and wastes prohibited pursuant to §268.32 or RCRA section 3004(d). Treatment standards for all other restricted wastes must either be included, or be referenced by including on the notification the applicable wastewater (as defined in §268.2(f)) or nonwastewater (as defined in §268.2(d)) category, the applicable subdivisions made within a waste code based on waste-specific criteria (such as D003 reactive cyanides), and the CFR section(s) and paragraph(s) where the applicable treatment standard appears. Where the applicable treatment standards are expressed as specified technologies in §268.42, the applicable five-letter treatment code found in Table 1 of §268.42 (e.g., INCIN, WETOX) also must be listed on the notification.

(iii) The manifest number associated with the shipment of waste;

(iv) Waste analysis data, where available; and

(v) The date the waste is subject to the prohibitions.

(4) If a generator is managing a prohibited waste in tanks or containers regulated under 40 CFR 262.34, and is treating such waste in such tanks or containers to meet applicable treatment standards under Subpart D of this part, the

generator must develop and follow a written waste analysis plan which describes the procedures the generator will carry out tocomply with the treatment standards. The plan must be kept on-site in the generator's records, and the following requirements must be met:

(i) The waste analysis plan must be based on a detailed chemical and physical analysis of a representative sample of the prohibited waste(s) being treated, and contain all information necessary to treat the waste(s) in accordance with the requirements of this Part, including the selected testing frequency.

(ii) Such plan must be filed with the EPA Regional Administrator (or his designated representative) or State authorized to implement Part 268 requirements a minimum of 30 days prior to the treatment activity, with delivery verified.

(iii) Wastes shipped off-site pursuant to this paragraph must comply with the notification requirements of §268.7(a)(2).

(5) If a generator determines whether the waste is restricted based solely on his knowledge of the waste, all supporting data used to make this determination must be retained on-site in the generator's files. If a generator determines whether the waste is restricted based on testing this waste or an extract developed using the test method described in Appendix I of this part, all waste analysis data must be retained on-site in the generator's files.

(6) If a generator determines that he is managing a restricted waste that is excluded from the definition of hazardous or solid waste or exempt from Subtitle C regulation, under 40 CFR 261.2 - 261.6 subsequent to the point of generation, he must place a one-time notice stating such generation, subsequent exclusion from the definition of hazardous or solid waste or exemption from Subtitle C regulation, and the disposition of the waste, in the facility's file.

(7) Generators must retain on-site a copy of all notices, certifications, demonstrations, waste analysis data, and other documentation produced

pursuant to this section for at least five years from the date that the waste that is the subject of such documentation was last sent to on-site or off-site treatment, storage, or disposal. The five year record retention period is automatically extended during the course of any unresolved enforcement action regarding the regulated activity or as requested by the Administrator. The requirements of this paragraph apply to solid wastes even when the hazardous characteristic is removed prior to disposal, or when the waste is excluded from the definition of hazardous or solid waste under 40 CFR 261.2 - 261.6, or exempted from Subtitle C regulation, subsequent to the point of generation.

(8) If a generator is managing a lab pack that contains organic wastes specified in Appendix V of this Part and wishes to use the alternate treatment standards under §268.42, with each shipment of waste the generator must submit a notice to the treatment facility in accordance with paragraph (a)(1) of this section. The generator also must comply with the requirements in paragraphs (a)(5) and (a)(6) of this section, and must submit the following certification which must be signed by an authorized representative:

I certify under penalty of law that I personally have examined and am familiar with the waste through analysis and testing or through knowledge of the waste and that the lab pack contains only organic waste specified in Appendix V to Part 268 or solid wastes not subject to regulation under 40 CFR Part 261. I am aware that there are significant penalties for submitting a false certification, including the possibility of fine or imprisonment.

(9) If a generator is managing a lab pack that contains organic wastes specified in Appendix V of this part and wishes to use the alternate treatment standards under §268.42, with each shipment of waste the generator must submit a notice to the treatment facility in accordance with paragraph (a)(1) of this section. The generator must comply with the requirements in paragraphs (a)(5) and (a)(6) of this section, and must submit the following certification which must be signed by an authorized representative:

I certify under penalty of law that I personally have examined and am familiar with the waste and that the lab pack contains only the wastes specified in appendix IV to part 268 or solid wastes not subject to regulation under 40 CFR part 261. I am aware that there are significant penalties for submitting a false certification, including the possibility of fine or imprisonment.

(10) Small quantity generators with tolling agreements pursuant to 40 CFR 262.20(e) must comply with the applicable notification and certification requirements of paragraph (a) of this section for the initial shipment of the waste subject to the agreement. Such generators must retain on-site a copy of the notification and certification, together with the tolling agreement, for at least three years after termination or expiration of the agreement. The three-year record retention period is automatically extended during the course of any unresolved enforcement action regarding the regulated activity or as requested by the Administrator.

(b) Treatment facilities must test their wastes according to the frequency specified in their waste analysis plans as required by §§264.13 or 265.13. Such testing must be performed as provided in paragraphs (b)(1), (b)(2) and (b)(3) of this section.

(1) For wastes with treatment standards expressed as concentrations in the waste extract (§268.41), the owner or operator of the treatment facility must test the treatment residues, or an extract of such residues developed using the test method described in Appendix I of this part, to assure that the treatment residues or extract meet the applicable treatment standards.

(2) For wastes that are prohibited under §268.32 of this part or RCRA section 3004(d) but not subject to any treatment standards under Subpart D of this part, the owner or operator of the treatment facility must test the treatment residues according to the generator testing requirements specified in §268.32 to assure that the treatment residues comply with the applicable prohibitions.

(3) For wastes with treatment standards expressed as concentrations in the waste (§268.43), the owner or operator of the treatment facility must test the treatment residues (not an extract of such residues) to assure that the treatment residues meet the applicable treatment standards.

(4) A notice must be sent with each waste shipment to the land disposal facility which includes the following information:

(i) EPA Hazardous Waste Number;

(ii) The corresponding treatment standards for wastes F001-F005, F039, and wastes prohibited pursuant to §268.32 or RCRA section 3004(d). Treatment standards for all other restricted wastes must either be included, or be referenced by including on the notification the applicable wastewater (as defined in §268.2(f)) or nonwastewater (as defined in §268.2(d)) category, the applicable subdivisions made within a waste code based on waste-specific criteria (such as D003 reactive cyanides), and the CFR section(s) and paragraph(s) where the applicable treatment standard appears. Where the applicable treatment standards are expressed as specified technologies in §268.42, the applicable five-letter treatment code found in Table 1 of §268.42 (e.g., INCIN, WETOX) also must be included on the notification.

(iii) The manifest number associated with the shipment of waste; and

(iv) Waste analysis data, where available.

(5) The treatment facility must submit a certification with each shipment of waste or treatment residue of a restricted waste to the land disposal facility stating that the waste or treatment residue has been treated in compliance with the applicable performance standards specified in Subpart D of this part and the applicable prohibitions set forth in §268.32 or RCRA section 3004(d).

(i) For wastes with treatment standards expressed as concentrations in the waste extract or in the waste (§§268.41 or 268.43), or for wastes prohibited under §268.32 of this part or RCRA section 3004(d) which are not subject to any treatment standards under Subpart D of this part, the certification must be signed by an authorized representative and must state the following:

I certify under penalty of law that I have personally examined and am familiar with the treatment technology and operation of the treatment process used to support this certification and that, based on my inquiry of those individuals immediately responsible for obtaining this information. I believe that the treatment process has been operated and maintained properly so as to comply with the performance levels specified in 40 CFR part 268, subpart D, and all applicable prohibitions set forth in 40 CFR 268.32 or RCRA section 3004 (d) without impermissible dilution of the prohibited waste. I am aware that there are significant penalties for submitting a false certification, including the possibility of fine and imprisonment.

(ii) For wastes with treatment standards expressed as technologies (§268.42), the certification must be signed by an authorized representative and must state the following:

I certify under penalty of law that the waste has been treated in accordance with the requirements of 40 CFR 268.42. I am aware that there are significant penalties for submitting a false certification, including the possibility of fine and imprisonment.

(iii) For wastes with treatment standards expressed as concentrations in the waste pursuant to §268.43, if compliance with the treatment standards in subpart D of this part is based in part or in whole on the analytical detection limit alternative specified in §268.43(c), the certification also must state the following:

I certify under penalty of law that I have personally examined and am familiar with the treatment technology and operation of the treatment process used to support this certification and that, based on my inquiry of those individuals immediately responsible for obtaining this information, I believe that the nonwastewater organic constituents have been treated by incineration in units operated in ac-

cordance with 40 CFR part 264, subpart O) or 40 CFR part 265, subpart O, or by combustion in fuel substitution units operating in accordance with applicable technical requirements, and I have been unable to detect then on wastewater organic constituents despite having used best good faith efforts to analyze for such constituents. I am aware that there are significant penalties for submitting a false certification, including the possibility of fine and imprisonment.

(6) If the waste or treatment residue will be further managed at a different treatment or storage facility, the treatment, storage or disposal facility sending the waste or treatment residue off-site must comply with the notice and certification requirements applicable to generators under this section.

(7) Where the wastes are recyclable materials used in a manner constituting disposal subject to the provisions of §266.20(b) regarding treatment standards and prohibition levels, the owner or operator of a treatment facility (i.e., the recycler) is not required to notify the receiving facility, pursuant to paragraph (b)(4) of this section. With each shipment of such wastes the owner or operator of the recycling facility must submit a certification described in paragraph (b)(5) of this section, and a notice which includes the information listed in paragraph (b)(4) of this section (except the manifest number) to the Regional Administrator, or his delegated representative. The recycling facility also must keep records of the name and location of each entity receiving the hazardous waste-derived product.

(c) Except where the owner or operator is disposing of any waste that is a recyclable material used in a manner constituting disposal pursuant to 40 CFR 266.20(b), the owner or operator of any land disposal facility disposing any waste subject to restrictions under this part must:

(1) Have copies of the notice and certifications specified in paragraph (a) or (b) of this section, and the certification specified in §268.8 if applicable.

(2) Test the waste, or an extract of the waste or treatment residue developed using the test method described in Appendix I of this part or

using any methods required by generators under §268.32 of this part, to assure that the wastes or treatment residues are in compliance with the applicable treatment standards set forth in Subpart D of this part and all applicable prohibitions set forth in §268.32 of this part or in RCRA section 3004(d). Such testing must be performed according to the frequency specified in the facility's waste analysis plan as required by §§264.13 or 265.13.

(Approved by the Office of Management and Budget under control number 2050-0062 and 2040-0042)

§ 268.8 Landfill and surface impoundment disposal restrictions.

(a) Prior to May 8,1990, wastes which are otherwise prohibited from land disposal under §268.33(f) of this part may be disposed in a landfill or surface impoundment which is in compliance with the requirements of §268.5(h)(2) provided that the requirements of this section are met. As of May 8, 1990, this section is no longer in effect.

(1) Prior to such disposal, the generator has made a good faith effort to locate and contract with treatment and recovery facilities practically available which provide the greatest environmental benefit.

(2) If a generator determines that there is no practically available treatment for his waste, he must fulfill the following specific requirements:

(i) Prior to the initial shipment of waste, the generator must submit a demonstration to the Regional Administrator that includes: a list of facilities and facility officials contacted, addresses, telephone numbers, and contact dates, as well as a written discussion of why he was not able to obtain treatment or recovery for that waste. The generator must also provide to the Regional Administrator the following certification:

I certify under penalty of law that the requirements of 40 CFR 268.8 (a)(1) have been met and that disposal in a landfill or surface impoundment is the only practical alternative to treatment currently available. I believe that the information submitted is true, accurate, and complete. I am aware that there are significant penalties for submitting false information, including the possibility of fine and imprisonment.

The generator does not need to wait for Regional Administrator approval of the demonstration/certification before shipment of the waste. However, if the Regional Administrator invalidates the demonstration/certification for the reasons outlined in §268.8(b)(2), the generator must immediately cease further shipments of the waste, and immediately inform all facilities that received the waste of such invalidation, and keep records of such communications on-site in his files.

(ii) With the initial shipment of waste, the generator must submit a copy of the demonstration and the certification discussed above in §268.8(a)(2)(i) to the receiving facility. With each subsequent waste shipment, only the certification is required to be submitted provided that the conditions being certified remain unchanged. Such a generator must retain on-site a copy of the demonstration (if applicable) and certification required for each waste shipment for at least five years from the date that the waste that is the subject of such documentation was last sent to on-site or off-site disposal. The five-year record retention requirement is automatically extended during the course of any unresolved enforcement action regarding the regulated activity or as requested by the Administrator.

(3) If a generator determines that there are practically available treatments for his waste, he must contract to use the practically available technology that yields the greatest environmental benefit. He must also fulfill the following specific requirements:

(i) The generator must submit to the Regional Administrator, prior to the initial shipment of waste, a demonstration that includes: a list of facilities and facility officials contacted, addresses, telephone numbers, and contact dates, as well as a written discussion explaining why the treatment or recovery technology chosen provides the greatest environmental benefit. The generator must also provide to the Regional Administrator the following certification:

I certify under penalty of law that the requirements of 40 CFR 268.8 (a)(1) have been met and that I have contracted to treat my waste (or otherwise provide treatment) by the practically available technology which

yields the greatest environmental benefit, as indicated in my demonstration. I believe that the information submitted is true, accurate, and complete. I am aware that there are significant penalties for submitting false information, including the possibility of fine and imprisonment.

The generator does not need to wait for Regional Administrator approval of the demonstration/certification before shipment of the waste.

(ii) With the initial shipment of waste, the generator must submit to the receiving facility a copy of the demonstration and the certification discussed above in §268.8(a)(3)(i). With each subsequent waste shipment, only the certification is required to be submitted provided that the conditions being certified remain unchanged. Such a generator must retain on-site a copy of the demonstration (if applicable) and certification required for each waste shipment for at least five years from the date that the waste that is the subject of such documentation was last sent to on-site or off-site disposal. The five-year record retention requirement is automatically extended during the course of any unresolved enforcement action regarding the regulated activity or as requested by the Administrator.

(4) Where the generator has determined that there is practically available treatment for his waste prior to disposal, with the initial shipment of waste, such generator must submit a copy of the demonstration and the certification required in paragraph (a)(2)(B) of this section to the receiving facility. With each subsequent waste shipment, only the certification is required to be submitted provided that the conditions being certified remain unchanged. Such a generator must retain on-site a copy of the demonstration (if applicable) and certification required for each waste shipment for at least five years from the date that the waste that is the subject of such documentation was last sent to on-site or off-site disposal. The five-year record retention requirement is automatically extended during the course of any unresolved enforcement action regarding the regulated activity or as requested by the Administrator.

(b) After receiving the demonstration and certification, the Regional Administrator may request any additional information which he deems necessary to evaluate the certification, and submit a new demonstration and certifica-

tion as provided in §268.8(a) to the receiving facility.

(1) A generator who has submitted a certification under this section must immediately notify the Regional Administrator when he has knowledge of any change in the conditions which formed the basis of his certification.

(2) If, after review of the certification, the Regional Administrator determines that practically available treatment exists where the generator has certified otherwise, or that there exists some other method of practically available treatment yielding greater environmental benefit than that which the generator has certified, the Regional Administrator may invalidate the certification.

(3) If the Regional Administrator invalidates a certification, the generator must immediately cease further shipments of the waste, and inform all facilities that received the waste of such invalidation and keep records of such communication on-site in his files.

(c) A treatment, recovery or storage facility receiving wastes subject to a valid certification must keep copies of the generator's demonstration (if applicable) and certification in his operating record.

(1) The owner or operator of a treatment or recovery facility must certify that he has treated the waste in accordance with the generator's demonstration. The following certification is required:

I certify under penalty of law that I have personally examined and am familiar with the treatment technology and operation of the treatment process used to support this certification and that, based on my inquiry of those individuals immediately responsible for obtaining this information, I believe that the treatment process has been operated and maintained properly so as to comply with treatment as specified in the generator's demonstration. I am aware that there are significant penalties for submitting false information, including the possibility of fine and imprisonment.

(2) The owner or operator of a treatment, recovery or storage facility must, for each initial shipment of waste, send a copy of the generator's demonstration (if applicable) and certification under §§268.8(a)(2)(i) or

268.8(a)(3)(i) and certification under §268.8(c)(1) (if applicable) to the facility receiving the waste or treatment residues. With each subsequent waste shipment, only the certification is required to be submitted provided that the conditions being certified remain unchanged.

(d) The owner or operator of a disposal facility must ensure that those wastes prohibited under §268.33(f) are subject to a certification according to the requirements of this section prior to disposal in a landfill or surface impoundment, and that the units receiving such wastes must meet the minimum technological requirements of §268.5(h)(2).

(e) Once the certification is received by the Regional Administrator, and provided that the wastes have been treated by the treatment (if any), determined by the generator to yield the greatest environmental benefit practically available, the wastes or treatment residuals may be disposed in a landfill or surface impoundment unit meeting the requirements of §268.5(h)(2), unless otherwise prohibited by the Regional Administrator.

(Approved by the Office of Management and Budget under control number 2050-0085)

§ 268.9 Special rules regarding wastes that exhibit a characteristic.

(a) The initial generator of a solid waste must determine each EPA Hazardous Waste Number (waste code) applicable to the waste in order to determine the applicable treatment standards under subpart D of this part. For purposes of part 268, the waste will carry the waste code for any applicable listing under 40 CFR part 261, subpart D. In addition, the waste will carry one or more of the waste codes under 40 CFR part 261, subpart C, where the waste exhibits a characteristic, except in the case when the treatment standard for the waste code listed in 40 CFR part 261, subpart D operates in lieu of the standard for the waste code under 40 CFR part 261, subpart C, as specified in paragraph (b) of this section.

(b) Where a prohibited waste is both listed under 40 CFR part 261, subpart D and exhibits a characteristic under 40 CFR part 261, subpart C, the treatment standard for the waste code listed in 40 CFR part 261, subpart D will operate in lieu of the standard for the waste code

under 40 CFR part 261, subpart C, provided that the treatment standard for the listed waste includes a treatment standard for the constituent that causes the waste to exhibit the characteristic. Otherwise, the waste must meet the treatment standards for all applicable listed and characteristic waste codes.

(c) In addition to any applicable standards determined from the initial point of generation, no prohibited waste which exhibits a characteristic under 40 CFR part 261, subpart C may be land disposed unless the waste complies with the treatment standards under subpart D of this part.

(d) Wastes that exhibit a characteristic are also subject to §268.7 requirements, except that once the waste is no longer hazardous, for each shipment of such wastes to a subtitle D facility the initial generator or the treatment facility need not send a §268.7 notification to such facility. In such circumstances, a notification and certification must be sent to the appropriate EPA Regional Administrator (or his delegated representative) or State authorized to implement part 268 requirements.

(1) The notification must include the following information:

(i) The name and address of the subtitle D facility receiving the waste shipment;

(ii) A description of the waste as initially generated, including the applicable EPA Hazardous Waste Number(s), the applicable wastewater (as defined in §268.2(f)) or nonwastewater (as defined in §268.2(d)) category, and the subdivisions made within a waste code based on waste-specific criteria (such as D003 reactive cyanides).

(iii) The treatment standards applicable to the waste at the initial point of generation.

(2) The certification must be signed by an authorized representative and must state the language found in §268.7(b)(5)(i).

Subpart B -- Schedule for Land Disposal Prohibition and Establishment of Treatment Standards

§ 268.10 Identification of wastes to be evaluated by August 8, 1988.

EPA will take action under sections 3004(g)(5) and 3004(m), of the Resource Conservation and

Recovery Act, by August 8, 1988, for the following wastes (for ease of understanding the wastes have been listed by the section of 40 CFR Part 261 under which they were listed):

§261.31 Wastes
F006 -- Wastewater treatment sludges from electroplating operations except from the following processes: (1) Sulfuric acid anodizing of aluminum; (2) tinplating on carbon steel; (3) zinc plating (segregated basis) on carbon steel; (4) aluminum or zinc-aluminum plating on carbon steel; (5) cleaning/stripping associated with tin, zinc and aluminum plating on carbon steel; and (6) chemical etching and milling of aluminum.

F007 -- Spent cyanide plating bath solutions from electroplating operations.

F008 -- Plating bath sludges from the bottom of plating baths from electroplating operations where cyanides are used in the process.

F009 -- Spent stripping and cleaning bath solutions from electroplating operations where cyanides are used in the process.

F019 -- Wastewater treatment sludges from the chemical conversion coating of aluminum.

§261.32 Wastes
K001 -- Bottom sediment sludge from the treatment of wastewaters from wood preserving processes that use creosote and/or pentachlorophenol.

K004 -- Wastewater treatment sludge from the production of zinc yellow pigments.

K008 -- Over residue from the production of chrome oxide green pigments.

K011 -- Bottom stream from the wastewater stripper in the production of acrylonitrile.

K013 -- Bottom stream from the acetonitrile column in the production of acrylonitrile.

K014 -- Bottoms from the acetonitrile purification column in the production of acrylonitrile.

K015 -- Still bottoms from the distillation of benzyl chloride.

K016 -- Heavy ends or distillation residues from the production of carbon tetrachloride.

K017 -- Heavy ends (still bottoms) from the purification column in the production of epichlorohydrin.

K018 -- Heavy ends from the fractionation column in ethyl chloride production.

K020 -- Heavy ends from the distillation of vinyl chloride in vinyl chloride monomer production.

K021 -- Aqueous spent antimony catalyst waste from fluoromethanes production.

K022 -- Distillation bottom tars from the production of phenol/acetone from cumane.

K024 -- Distillation bottoms from the production of phthalic anhydride from naphthalene.

K030 -- Column bottom or heavy ends from the combined production of trichloroethylene and perchloroethylene.

K031 -- By-products salts generated in the production of MSMA and cacodylic acid.

K035 -- Wastewater treatment sludges generated in the production of creosote.

K036 -- Still bottoms from toluene reclamation distillation in the production of disulfoton.

K037 -- Wastewater treatment sludge from the production of disulfoton.

K044 -- Wastewater treatment sludges from the manufacturing and processing of explosives.

K045 -- Spent carbon from the treatment of wastewater containing explosives.

K046 -- Wastewater treatment sludges from the manufacturing, formulation and loading of lead-based initiating compounds.

K047 -- Pink/red water from TNT operations.

K060 -- Ammonia still lime sludge from coking operations.

K061 -- Emission control dust/sludge from the primary production of steel in electric furnaces.

K062 -- Spent pickle liquor from steel finishing operations in chlorine production.

K069 -- Emission control dust/sludge from secondary lead smelting.

K071 -- Brine purification muds from the mercury cells process in chlorine production, where separately prepurified brine is not used.

K073 -- Chlorinated hydrocarbon waste from the purification step of the diaphragm cell process using graphite anodes

K083 -- Distillation bottoms from aniline production.

K084 -- Wastewater treatment sludges generated during the production of veterinary pharmaceuticals from arsenic or organo-arsenic compounds.

K085 -- Distillation of fractionation column bottoms from the production of chlorobenzenes.

K086 -- Solvent washes and sludges; caustic washes and sludges, or water washes and sludges from cleaning tubs and equipment used in the formulation of ink from pigments, driers, soaps, and stabilizers containing chromium and lead.

K087 -- Decanter tank tar sludge from coking operations.

K099 -- Untreated wastewater from the production of 2,4-D.

K101 -- Distillation tar residues from the distillation of aniline-based compounds in the production of veterinary pharmaceuticals from arsenic or organo-arsenic compounds.

K102 -- Residue from the use of activated carbon for decolorization in the production of veterinary pharmaceuticals from arsenic or organo-arsenic compounds.

K103 -- Process residues from aniline extraction from the production of aniline.

K104 -- Combined wastewater streams generated from nitrobenzene/aniline production.

K106 -- Waste water treatment sludge from the mercury cell process in chlorine production.

§261.33(e) Wastes

P001 -- Warfarin, when present at concentration greater than 0.3%

P004 -- Aldrin

P005 -- Allyl alcohol

P010 -- Arsenic acid

P011 -- Arsenic (V) oxide

P012 -- Arsenic (III) oxide

P015 -- Beryllium dust

P016 -- Bis-(chloromethyl) ether

P018 -- Brucine

P020 -- Dinoseb

P030 --Soluble cyanide salts not elsewhere specified

P036 -- Dichlorophenylarsine

P037 -- Dieldrin

P039 -- Disulfoton

P041 -- Diethyl-p-nitrophenyl phosphate

P048 -- 2,4-Dinitrophenol

P050 -- Endosulfan

P058 -- Fluoracetic acid, sodium salt

P059 -- Heptachlor

P063 -- Hydrogen cyanide

P068 -- Methyl Hydrazine

P069 -- Methyllactonitrile

P070 -- Aldicarb

P071 -- Methyl parathion

P081 -- Nitroglycerine

P082 -- N-Nitrosodimethylamine

P084 -- N-Nitrosomethylvinylamine

P087 -- Osmium tetraoxide

P089 -- Parathion

P092 -- Phenylmercuric acetate

P094 -- Phorate

P097 -- Famphur

P102 -- Propargyl alcohol

P105 -- Sodium azide

P108 -- Strychnine and salts

P110 -- Tetraethyl lead

P115 -- Thallium (I) sulfate

P120 -- Vanadium pentoxide

P122 -- Zinc phosphide, when present at concentrations greater than 10%

P123 -- Toxaphene

§261.33(f) Wastes

U007 -- Acrylamide

U009 -- Acrylonitrile

U010 -- Mitomycin C

U012 -- Aniline

U016 -- Benz(c)acridine

U018 -- Benz(a)anthracene

U019 -- Benzene

U022 -- Benzo(a)pyrene

U029 -- Methyl bromide

U031 -- n-Butanol

U036 -- Chlordane, technical

U037 -- Chlorobenzene

U041 -- n-Chloro-2,3-epoxypropane

U043 -- Vinyl chloride

U044 -- Chloroform

U046 -- Chloromethyl methyl ether

U050 -- Chrysene

U051 -- Creosote

U053 -- Crotonaldehyde

U061 -- DDT

U063 -- Dibenzo (a, h) anthracene

U064 -- 1,2:7,8 Dibenzopyrene

U066 - -Dibromo-3-chloropropane 1,2-

U067 -- Ethylene dibromide

U074 -- 1,4-Dichloro-2-butene

U077 -- Ethane, 1,2-dichloro-

U078 -- Dichloroethylene,1,1-

U086 -- N,N Diethylhydrazine

U089 -- Diethylstilbestrol

U103 -- Dimethyl sulfate

U105 -- 2,4-Dinitrotoluene

U108 -- Dioxane,1,4-

U115 -- Ethylene oxide

U122 -- Formaldehyde

U124 -- Furan

U129 -- Lindane

U130 -- Hexachlorocyclopentadiene

U133 -- Hydrazine

U134 -- Hydrofluoric acid

U137 -- Indeno(1,2,3-cd)pyrene

U151 -- Mecury

U154 -- Methanol

U155 -- Methapyrilene

U157 -- 3-Methylcholanthrene

U158 -- 4,4-Methylene-bis-(2-chloroaniline)

U159 -- Methyl ethyl ketone

U171 -- Nitropropane, 2-

U177 -- N-Nitroso-N-methylurea

U180 -- N-Nitrosopyrrolidine

U185 -- Pentachloronitrobenzene

U188 -- Phenol

U192 -- Pronamide

U200 -- Reserpine

U209 -- Tetrachloroethane,1,1,2,2-

U210 -- Tetrachloroethylene

U211 -- Carbon tetrachloride

U219 -- Thiourea

U220 -- Toluene

U221 -- Toluenediamine

U223 -- Toluene diisocyanate

U226 -- Methylchloroform

U227 -- Trichloroethane,1,1,2-

U228 -- Trichloroethylene

U237 -- Uracil mustard

U238 -- Ethyl carbamate

U248 -- Warfarin, when present at concentrations of 0.3% or less

U249 -- Zinc phosphide, when present at concentrations of 10% or less

§268.11 Identification of wastes to be evaluated by June 8, 1989.

EPA will take action under sections 3004(g)(5) and 3004(m) of the Resource Conservation and Recovery Act, by June 8, 1989, for the following wastes (for ease of understanding the wastes have been listed by the section of 40 CFR Part 261 under which they were listed):

§261.31 Wastes

F010 -- Quenching bath sludge from oil baths from metal heat treating operations where cyanides are used in the process.

F011 -- Spent cyanide solutions from salt bath pot cleaning from metal heat treating operations.

F012 -- Quenching wastewater treatment sludges from metal heat operations where cyanides are used in the process.

F024 -- Wastes including but not limited to, distillation residues, heavy ends, tars and reactor clean-out wastes from the production of chlorinated aliphatic hydrocarbons, having carbon content from one to five, utilizing free radical catalyzed processes.

§261.32 Wastes

K009 -- Distillation bottoms from the production of acetaldehyde from ethylene.

K010 -- Distillation side cuts from the productions of acetaldehyde from ethylene.

K019 -- Heavy ends from the distillation of ethylene dichloride in ethylene dichloride production.

K025 -- Distillation bottoms from the production of nitrobenzene by the nitration of benzene.

K027 -- Centrifuge and distillation residues from toluene diisocyanate production.

K028 -- Spent catalyst from the hydrochlorinator reactor in the production of 1,1,1-trichloroethane.

K029 -- Waste from the product steam stripper in the production of 1,1,1-trichloroethane.

K038 -- Wastewater from the washing and stripping of phorate production.

K039 -- Filter cake from the filtration of diethylphosphoro-dithioic acid in the production of phorate.

K040 -- Wastewater treatment sludge from the production of phorate.

K041 -- Wastewater treatment sludge from the production of toxaphene.

K042 -- Heavy ends or distillation residues from the distillation of tetrachlorobenzene in the production of 2,4,5-T.

K043 -- 2,6-Dichlorophenol waste from the production of 2,4-D.

K095 -- Distillation bottoms from the production of 1,1,1-trichloroethane.

K096 -- Heavy ends from the heavy ends column from the production of 1,1,1-trichloroethane.

K097 -- Vacuum stripper discharge from the chlordane chlorinator in the production of chlordane.

K098 -- Untreated process wastewater from the production of toxaphene.

K105 -- Separated aqueous stream from the reactor product washing step in the production of chlorobenzenes.

§261.33(e) Wastes

P002 -- 1-Acetyl-2-thiourea
P003 -- Acrolein
P007 -- 5-(Aminoethyl)-3-isoxazolol
P008 -- 4-Aminopyridine
P014 -- -Thiophenol
P026 -- 1-(o-Chlorophenyl)thiourea
P027 -- Propanenitrile, 3-chloro
P029 -- Copper cyanides
P040 -- O,O-Diethyl o-pyrazinyl phosphorothioate
P043 -- Diisopropyl fluorophosphate
P044 -- Dimethoate
P049 -- 2,4-Dithiobiuret
P054 -- Aziridine
P057 -- Fluoracetamide
P060 -- Isodrin
P062 -- Hexaethyltetraphosphate
P066 -- Methomyl
P067 -- 2-Methylaziridine
P072 -- Alpha-naphthylthiourea (ANTU)
P074 -- Nickel cyanide
P085 -- Octamethylpyrophosphoramide
P098 -- Potassium cyanide
P104 -- Silver cyanide
P106 -- Sodium cyanide
P107 -- Strontium sulfide
P111 -- Tetraethylpyrophosphate
P112 -- Tetranitromethane
P113 -- Thallic oxide
P114 -- Thallium (I) selenite

§261.33(f) Wastes

U002 -- Acetone
U003 -- Acetonitrile
U005 -- o-Acetylaminofluorene
U008 -- Acrylic acid
U011 -- Amitrole
U014 -- Auramine
U015 -- Azaserine
U020 -- Benzenesulfonyl chloride
U021 -- Benzidine
U023 -- Benzotrichloride
U025 -- Dichloroethyl ether
U026 -- Chlornaphazine
U028 -- Bis-(2-ethylhexyl)phthalate
U032 -- Calcium chromate
U035 -- Chlorambucil
U047 -- Beta-chloronaphthalene
U049 -- 4-Chloro-o-toluidine, hydrochloride
U057 -- Cyclohexanone
U058 -- Cyclophosphamide
U059 -- Daunomycin
U060 -- DDD
U062 -- Diallate
U070 -- o-Dichlorobenzene
U073 -- Dichlorobenzidene,3,3-
U080 -- Methylene chloride

U083 -- Dichloropropane,1,2-
U092 -- Dimethylamine
U093 -- Dimethylaminoazobenzene
U094 -- Dimethylbenz(a)anthracene,7,12-
U095 -- Dimethylbenzidine,3,3'-
U097 -- Dimethylcarbamoyl chloride
U098 -- Dimethylhydrazine,1,1-
U099 -- Dimethylhydrazine,1,2-
U101 -- Dimethylphenol,2,4-
U106 -- Dinitrotoluene,2,6-
U107 -- Di-n-octyl phthalate
U109 -- 1,2,-Diphenylhydrazine
U110 -- Dipropylamine
U111 -- Di-N-Propylnitrosamine
U114 -- Ethylenebis-(dithiocarbamic acid)
U116 -- Ethylene thiourea
U119 -- Ethyl methanesulfonate
U127 -- Hexachlorobenzene
U128 -- Hexachlorobutadiene
U131 -- Hexachloroethane
U135 -- Hydrogen sulfide
U138 -- Methyl iodide
U140 -- Isobutyl alcohol
U142 -- Kepone
U143 -- Lasiocarpine
U144 -- Lead acetate
U146 -- Lead subacetate
U147 -- Maleic anhydride
U149 -- Malononitrile
U150 -- Melphalan
U161 -- Methyl isobutyl ketone
U162 -- Methyl methacrylate
U163 -- N-Methyl-N-nitro-N-nitrosoguanidine
U164 -- Methylthiouracil
U165 -- Naphthalene
U168 -- Napthylamine,2-
U169 -- Nitrobenzene
U170 -- p-Nitrophenol
U172 -- N-Nitroso-di-n-butylamine
U173 -- N-Nitroso-diethanolamine
U174 -- N-Nitroso-diethylamine
U176 -- N-Nitroso-N-ethylurea
U178 -- N-Nitroso-N-methylurethane
U179 -- N-Nitrosopiperidine
U189 -- Phosphorus sulfide
U193 -- 1,3-Propane sultone
U196 -- Pyridine
U203 -- Safrole
U205 -- Selenium disulfide
U206 -- Streptozotocin
U208 -- Terachloroethane,1,1,1,2-
U213 -- Tetrahydrofuran
U214 -- Thallium (I) acetate
U215 -- Thallium (I) carbonate
U216 -- Thallium (I) chloride
U217 -- Thallium (I) nitrate
U218 -- Thioacetamide
U235 -- Tris (2,3-Dibromopropyl) phosphate
U239 -- Xylene
U244 -- Thiram

§ 268.12 Identification of wastes to be evaluated by May 8, 1990.

(a) EPA will take action under sections 3004(g)(5) and 3004(m) of the Resource Conservation and Recovery Act, by May 8, 1990, for the following wastes (for ease of understanding, the wastes have been listed by the section of 40 CFR Part 261 under which they were listed):

§261.32 Wastes

K002 -- Wastewater treatment sludge from the production of chrome yellow and orange pigments.

K003 -- Wastewater treatment sludge from the production of molybdate orange pigments.

K005 -- Wastewater treatment sludge from the production of chrome green pigments.

K006 -- Wastewater treatment sludge from the production of chrome oxide green pigments (anhydrous and hydrated).

K007 -- Wastewater treatment sludge from the production of iron blue pigments.

K023 -- Distillation light ends from the production of phthalic anhydride from naphthalene.

K026 -- Stripping still tails from the production of methyl ethyl pyridines.

K032 -- Wastewater treatment sludge from the production of chlordane.

K033 -- Wastewater and scrub water from the chlorination of cyclopentadiene in the production of chlordane.

K034 -- Filter solids from the hexachlorocyclopentadiene in the production of chlordane.

K048 -- Dissolved air flotation (DAF) float from the petroleum refining industry.

K049 -- Slop oil emulsion solids from the petroleum refining industry. K050 -- Heat exchanger bundle cleaning sludge from the petroleum refining industry.

K051 -- API separator sludge from the petroleum refining industry.

K052 -- Tank bottoms (leaded) from the petroleum refining industry.

K093 -- Distillation light ends from the production of phthalic anhydride from orthoxylene.

K094 -- Distillation bottoms from the production of phthalic anhydride from orthoxylene.

K100 -- Waste leaching solution from acid leaching of emission control dust/sludge from secondary lead smelting.

§261.33(e) Wastes

P006 -- Aluminum phosphide
P009 -- Ammonium picrate
P013 -- Barium cyanide
P017 -- Bromoacetone
P021--Calcium cyanide

P022--Carbon disulfide
P023 -- Chloroacetaldehyde
P024--p-Chloroaniline
P028--Benzyl chloride
P031 -- Cyanogen
P033 -- Cyanogen chloride
P034 -- 4,6-Dinitro-o-cyclohexylphenol
P038 -- Diethylarsine
P042 -- Epinephrine
P045 -- Thiofanox
P046 -- Alpha, alpha-Dimethylphenethylamine
P047 -- 4,6-Dinitro-o-cresol and salts
P051 -- Endrin
P056 -- Fluorine
P064 -- Methyl isocyanate
P065 -- Mercury fulminate
P073 -- Nickel carbonyl
P075 -- Nicotine and salts
P076 -- Nitric oxide
P077 -- p-Nitroaniline
P078 -- Nitrogen dioxide
P088 -- Endothall
P093 -- N-Phenylthiourea
P095 -- Phosgene
P096 -- Phosphine
P099 -- Potassium silver cyanide
P101 -- Propanenitrile
P103 -- Selenourea
P109 -- Tetraethyldithiopyrophosphate
P116 -- Thiosemicarbazide
P118 -- Trichloromethanethiol
P119 -- Ammonium vanadate
P121 -- Zinc cyanide

§261.33(f) Wastes

U001 -- Acetaldehyde
U004 -- Acetophenone
U006 -- Acetyl chloride
U017 -- Benzal chloride
U024 -- Bis(2-chloroethoxy)methane
U027 -- Bis(2-chloroisopropyl)ether
U030 -- Benzene, 1-bromo-4-phenoxy
U033 -- Carbonyl fluoride
U034 -- Chloral
U038 -- Ethyl-4-4'-dichlorobenzilate
U039 -- 4-Chloro-m-cresol
U042 -- Vinyl ether, 2-chloroethyl
U045 -- Methyl chloride
U048 -- o-Chlorophenol
U052 -- Cresols
U055 -- Cumene
U056 -- Cyclohexane
U068 -- Methane, dibromo
U069 -- Dibutyl phthalate
U071 -- m-Dichlorobenzene
U072 -- p-Dichlorobenzene
U075 -- Dichlorodifluoromethane
U076 -- Ethane, 1,1-dichloro-
U079 -- 1,2-Dichlorethylene
U081 -- 2,4-Dichlorophenol
U082 -- 2,6-Dichlorophenol
U084 -- 1,3-Dichloropropene

U085 -- 2,2'-Bioxirane
U087 -- 0,0,-Diethyl-S-methyl-dithiophosphate
U088 -- Diethyl phthalate
U090 -- Dihydrosafrole
U091 -- 3,3'-Dimethoxybenzidine
U096 -- alpha,alpha-Dimethylbenzyl-hydroxyperoxide
U102 -- Dimethyl phthalate
U112 -- Ethyl acetate
U113 -- Ethyl acrylate
U117 -- Ethyl ether
U118 -- Ethylmethacrylate
U120 -- Fluoranthene
U121 -- Trichloromonofluoromethane
U123 -- Formic acid
U125 -- Furfural
U126 -- Glycidylaldehyde
U132 -- Hexachlorophene
U136 -- Cacodylic acid
U139 -- Iron dextran
U141 -- Isosafrole
U145 -- Lead phosphate
U148 -- Maleic hydrazide
U152 -- Methacrylonitrile
U153 -- Methanethiol
U156 -- Methyl chlorocarbonate
U160 -- Methyl ethyl ketone peroxide
U166 -- 1,4-Naphthaquinone
U167 -- 1-Naphthylamine
U181 -- 5-Nitro-o-toluidine
U182 -- Paraldehyde
U183 -- Pentachlorobenzene
U184 -- Pentachloroethane
U186 -- 1,3-Pentadiene
U187 -- Phenacetin
U190 -- Phthalic anhydride
U191 -- 2-Picoline
U194 -- 1-Propanamine
U197 -- p-Benzoquinone
U201 -- Resorcinol
U202 -- Saccharin and salts
U204 -- Selenious acid
U207 -- 1,2,4,5-tetrachlorobenzene
U222 -- o-Toluidine hydrochloride
U225 -- Bromoform
U234 -- Sym-Trinitrobenzene
U236 -- Trypan blue
U240 -- 2,4-D, salts and esters
U243 -- Hexachloropropene
U246 -- Cyanogen bromide
U247 -- Methoxychlor

Wastes identified as hazardous based on a characteristic alone] (i.e.,corrosivity, reactivity, ignitability and EP toxicity).

(b) Wastewater residues (less than 1% total organic carbon and less than 1% total suspended solids) resulting from the following well-designed and well-operated treatment methods for wastes listed in §§268.10 and 268.11 for which EPA has not promulgated wastewater treatment standards: metals recovery, metals precipitation, cyanide destruction, carbon adsorption, chemical oxidation, steam stripping, biodegradation, and incineration or other direct thermal destruction.

(c) Hazardous wastes listed in §§268.10 and 268.11 that are mixed hazardous/radioactive wastes.

(d) Multi-source leachate that is derived from disposal of any listed waste, except from Hazardous Wastes F020, F021, F022, F023, F026, F027, or F028.

(e) Nonwastewater forms of wastes listed in §268.10 that were originally disposed before August 17,1988 and for which EPA has promulgated "no land disposal" as the treatment standard (§268.43, Table CCW, No Land Disposal Subtable). This provision does not apply to waste codes K044, K045, K047, and K061 (high zinc subcategory).

(f) Nonwastewater forms of wastes listed in §268.10 for which EPA has promulgated "no land disposal" as the treatment standard (§268.43, Table CCW, No Land Disposal Subtable) that are generated in the course of treating wastewater forms of the wastes. This provision does not apply to waste codes K044, K045, K047, and K061 (high zinc subcategory).

(g) Nonwastewater forms of waste codes K015 and K083.

§ 268.13 Schedule for wastes identified or listed after November 8, 1984.

In the case of any hazardous waste iden-tified or listed under section 3001 after Nov-ember 8, 1984, the Administrator shall make a land disposal prohibition determina-tion within 6 months after the date of identi-fication or listing.

Subpart C -- Prohibitions on Land Disposal

§ 268.30 Waste specific prohibitions -- Solvent wastes.

(a) Effective November 8, 1986, the spent solvent wastes specified in 40 CFR 261.31 as EPA Hazardous Waste Nos. F001, F002, F003, F004, and F005, are prohibited under this part from land disposal (except in an injection well) unless one or more of the following conditions apply:

(1) The generator of the solvent waste is a small quantity generator of 100-1000 kilograms of hazardous waste per month; or

(2) The solvent waste is generated from any response action taken under the Comprehensive Environmental Response, Compensation and Liability Act of 1980 (CERCLA) or any corrective action taken under the Resource Conservation and Recovery Act (RCRA), except where the waste is contaminated soil or debris not subject to the provisions of this chapter until November 8, 1988; or

(3) The initial generator's solvent waste is a solvent-water mixture, solvent-containing sludge or solid, or solvent-contaminated soil (non-CERCLA or RCRA corrective action) containing less than 1 percent total F001-F005 solvent constituents listed in Table CCWE of §268.41 of this part; or

(4) The solvent waste is a residue from treating a waste described in paragraph (a)(1), (a)(2), or (a)(3) of this section; or the solvent waste is a residue from treating a waste not described in paragraph (a)(1), (a)(2), or (a)(3) of this section provided such residue belongs to a different treatability group than the waste as initially generated and wastes belonging to such a treatability group are described in paragraph (a)(3) of this section.

(b) Effective November 8, 1988, the F001-F005 solvent wastes listed in paragraphs (a) (1), (2), (3),and (4) of this section are prohibited from land disposal.

(c) Effective November 8, 1990, the F001-F005 solvent wastes which are contaminated soil and debris resulting from a response action taken under section 104 or 106 of the Comprehensive Environmental Response, Compensation, and Liability Act of 1980 (CERCLA) or a corrective action required under subtitle C of the Resource Conservation and Recovery Act (RCRA) and the residues from treating these wastes are prohibited from land disposal. Between November 8, 1988, and November 8, 1990, these wastes may be disposed in a landfill or surface impoundment only if such unit is in compliance with the requirements specified in §268.5(h)(2).

(d) The requirements of paragraphs (a), (b), and (c) of this section do not apply if:

(1) The wastes meet the standards of Subpart D of this part; or

(2) Persons have been granted an exemption from a prohibition pursuant to a petition under §268.6, with respect to those wastes and units covered by the petition; or

(3) Persons who have been granted an extension to the effective date of a prohibition pursuant to §268.5, with respect to those wastes and units covered by the extension.

§ 268.31 Waste specific prohibitions -- Dioxin-containing wastes.

(a) Effective November 8, 1988, the dioxin-containing wastes specified in 40 CFR 261.31 as EPA Hazardous Waste Nos. F020, F021, F022, F023, F026, F027, and F028, are prohibited from land disposal unless the following condition applies:

(1) The F020-F023 and F026-F028 dioxin-containing waste is contaminated soil and debris resulting from a response action taken under section 104 or 106 of the Comprehensive Environmental Response, Compensation, and Liability Act of 1980 (CERCLA) or a corrective action taken under subtitle C of the Resource Conservation and Recovery Act (RCRA).

(b) Effective November 8, 1990, the F020-F023 and F026-F028 dioxin-containing wastes listed in paragraph (a)(1) of this section are prohibited from land disposal.

(c) Between November 8, 1988, and November 8, 1990, wastes included in paragraph (a)(1) of this section may be disposed in a landfill or surface impoundment only if such unit is in compliance with the requirements specified in §268.5(h)(2) and all other applicable requirements of Parts 264 and 265 of this chapter.

(d) The requirements of paragraphs (a) and (b) of this section do not apply if:

(1) The wastes meet the standards of Subpart D of this part; or

(2) Persons have been granted an exemption from a prohibition pursuant to a petition under §268.6, with respect to those wastes and units covered by the petition; or

(3) Persons have been granted an extension to the effective date of a prohibition pursuant to §268.5, with respect to those wastes covered by the extension.

§ 268.32 Waste specific prohibitions -- California list wastes.

(a) Effective July 8, 1987, the following hazardous wastes are prohibited from land disposal (except in injection wells):

(1) Liquid hazardous wastes having a pH less than or equal to two (2.0);

(2) Liquid hazardous wastes containing polychlorinated biphenyls (PCBs) at concentrations greater than or equal to 50 ppm;

(3) Liquid hazardous wastes that are primarily water and contain halogenated organic compounds (HOCs) in total concentration greater than or equal to 1,000 mg/l and less than 10,000 mg/l HOCs.

(b)--(c) [Reserved]

(d) The requirements of paragraphs (a) and (e) of this section do not apply until:

(1) July 8, 1989 where the wastes are contaminated soil or debris not resulting from a response action taken under section 104 or 106 of the Comprehensive Environmental Response, Compensation, and Liability Act (CERCLA) or a corrective action taken under Subtitle C of the Resource Conservation and Recovery Act (RCRA). Between July 8,1987 and July 8, 1989, the wastes may be disposed in a landfill or surface impoundment only if such disposal is incompliance with the requirements specified in §268.5(h)(2).

(2) November 8, 1990 where the wastes are contaminated soil or debris resulting from a response action taken under section 104 or 106 of CERCLA or a corrective action required under Subtitle C of RCRA. Between November 8,1988 and November 8,1990, the wastes may be disposed in a landfill or surface impoundment only if such unit is in compliance with the requirements specified in §268.5(h)(2).

(e) Effective November 8, 1988, the following hazardous wastes are prohibited from land disposal (subject to any regulations that may be promulgated with respect to disposal in injection wells):

(1) Liquid hazardous wastes that contain HOCs in total concentration greater than or equal to 1,000 mg/l and are not prohibited under paragraph (a)(3) of this section; and

(2) Nonliquid hazardous wastes containing HOCs in total concentration greater than or equal to 1,000 mg/kg and are not wastes described in paragraph(d) of this section.

(f) Between July 8, 1987 and November 8, 1988, the wastes included in paragraphs (e)(1)

and (e)(2) of this section may be disposed in a landfill or surface impoundment only if such unit is in compliance with the requirements specified in §268.5(h)(2).

(g) The requirements of paragraphs (a),(d) and (e) of this section do not apply if:

(1) Persons have been granted an exemption from a prohibition pursuant to a petition under §268.6, with respect to those wastes and units covered by the petition (except for liquid hazardous wastes containing polychlorinated biphenyls at concentrations greater than or equal to 500 ppm which are not eligible for such exemptions); or

(2) Persons have been granted an extension to the effective date of a prohibition pursuant to §268.5, with respect to those wastes covered by the extension; or

(3) The wastes meet the applicable standards specified in Subpart D of this part or, where treatment standards are not specified, the wastes are in compliance with the applicable prohibitions set forth in this section or RCRA section 3004(d).

(h) The prohibitions and effective dates specified in paragraphs (a)(3),(d),and (e) of this section do not apply where the waste is subject to a Part 268 Subpart C prohibition and effective date for a specified HOC (such as a hazardous waste chlorinated solvent, see e.g., §268.30(a)).

(i) To determine whether or not a waste is a liquid under paragraphs (a) and (e) of this section and under RCRA section 3004(d), the following test must be used: Method 9095 (Paint Filter Liquids Test) as described in "Test Methods for Evaluating Solid Wastes, Physical/Chemical Methods," EPA Publication No. SW-846. (Incorporated by reference, see §260.11(a) of this chapter.)

(j) Except as otherwise provided in this paragraph, the waste analysis and recordkeeping requirements of §268.7 are applicable to wastes prohibited under this part or RCRA section 3004(d):

(1) The initial generator of a liquid hazardous waste must test his waste (not an extract or filtrate) in accordance with the procedures specified in §261.22(a)(1), or use knowledge of the waste, to determine if the waste has a pH less than or equal to two (2.0). If the liquid waste has a pH less than or equal to two (2.0), it is restricted from land disposal and all requirements of Part 268 are applicable, except as otherwise specified in this section.

(2) The initial generator of either a liquid hazardous waste containing polychlorinated biphenyls (PCBs) or a liquid or nonliquid hazardous waste containing halogenated organic compounds (HOCs) must test his waste (not an extract or filtrate), or use knowledge of the waste, to determine whether the concentration levels in the waste equal or exceed the prohibition levels specified in this section. If the concentration of PCBs or HOCs in the waste is greater than or equal to the prohibition levels specified in this section, the waste is restricted from land disposal and all requirements of Part 268 are applicable, except as otherwise specified in this section.

§ 268.33 Waste specific prohibitions -- First Third wastes

(a) Effective August 8, 1988, the wastes specified in 40 CFR 261.32 as EPA Hazardous Waste Nos. F006 (nonwastewater), K001, K004 wastes specified in §268.43(a), K008 wastes specified in §268.43(a), K016, K018, K019, K020, K021 wastes specified in §268.43(a), K022, (nonwastewater), K024, K025 nonwastewaters specified in §268.43(a), K030, K036 (nonwastewater), K037, K044, K045, nonexplosive K046 (nonwastewater), K047, K060 (nonwastewater), K061 (nonwastewaters containing less than 15% zinc), K062, non CaSO4 K069 (nonwastewater), K086 (solvent washes), K087, K099, K100 nonwastewaters specified in §268.43(a), K101 (wastewater), K101 (nonwastewater, low arsenic subcategory--less than 1% total arsenic), K102 (wastewater), K102 (nonwastewater, low arsenic subcategory--less than 1% total arsenic), K103, and K104 are prohibited from land disposal (except in an injection well).

(1) Effective August 8, 1988 and continuing until August 7, 1990, K061 wastes containing 15% zinc or greater are prohibited from land disposal pursuant to the treatment standards specified in §268.41 applicable to K061 wastes that contain less than 15% zinc.

(b) Effective August 8, 1990, the waste specified in 40 CFR 261.32 as EPA Hazardous Waste Nos. K071 is prohibited from land disposal.

(c) Effective August 8, 1990, the wastes specified in 40 CFR 268.10

having a treatment standard in Subpart D of this part based on incineration and which are contaminated soil and debris are prohibited from land disposal.

(d) Between November 8, 1988 and August 8, 1990, wastes included in paragraphs (b) and (c) of this section may be disposed of in a landfill or surface impoundment only if such unit is in compliance with the requirements specified in §268.5(h)(2).

(e) The requirements of paragraphs (a), (b), (c), and (d) of this section do not apply if:

(1) The wastes meet the applicable standards specified in Subpart D of this Part; or

(2) Persons have been granted an exemption from a prohibition pursuant to a petition under §268.6, with respect to those wastes and units covered by the petition; or

(3) Persons have been granted an extension to the effective date of a prohibition pursuant to §268.5, with respect to those wastes covered by the extension.

(f) Between August 8, 1988, and May 8, 1990, the wastes specified in §268.10 for which treatment standards under Subpart D of this Part have not been promulgated including those wastes which are subject to the statutory prohibitions of RCRA section 3004(d) or codified prohibitions under §268.32 of this Part, but not including wastes subject to a treatment standard under §268.42 of this Part, are prohibited from disposal in a landfill or surface impoundment unless a demonstration and certification have been submitted to §268.8.

(g) To determine whether a hazardous waste listed in §268.10 exceeds the applicable treatment standards specified in §268.41 and §268.43 , the initial generator must test a representative sample of the waste extract or the entire waste depending on whether the treatment standards are expressed as concentrations in the waste extract or the waste, or the generator may use knowledge of the waste. If the waste contains constituents in excess of the applicable Subpart D levels, the waste is prohibited from land disposal and all requirements of Part 268 are applicable, except as otherwise specified.

§ 268.34 Waste specific prohibitions -- second third wastes.

(a) Effective June 8, 1989, the following wastes specified in 40 CFR 261.31 as EPA Hazardous Waste Nos. F010; F024; the wastes specified in 40 CFR 261.32 as EPA Hazardous Waste Nos. K005, K007; K009 (nonwastewaters), K010, K023; K027; K028; K029 (nonwastewaters); K036; (wastewaters); K038; K039; K040; K043; K093; K094; K095 (nonwastewaters); K096 (nonwastewaters); K113; K114; K115; K116; and the wastes specified in 40 CFR 261.33 as EPA Hazardous Waste Nos. P013; P021; P029; P030; P039; P040; P041; P043; P044; P062; P063; P071; P074; P085; P089; P094; P097; P098; P099; P104; P106; P109; P111; P121; U028; U058; U069; U087; U088; U102; U107; U221; U223; and U235 are prohibited from land disposal.

(b) Effective June 8, 1989, the following wastes specified in 40 CFR 261.32 as EPA Hazardous Waste Nos. K009 (wastewaters), K011 (non wastewaters), K013 (nonwastewaters), and K014 (nonwastewaters) are prohibited from land disposal except when they are underground injected pursuant to 40 CFR 148.14(f) and 148.15(d).

(c) Effective July 8, 1989, the wastes specified in 40 CFR 261.31 as EPA Hazardous Waste Nos. F006 - cyanide (nonwastewater); F008; F009; F011 (wastewaters) and F012 (wastewaters) are prohibited from land disposal.

(1) Effective July 8, 1989, the following waste specified in 40 CFR 261.31 as EPA Hazardous Waste No. F007 is prohibited from land disposal except when it is underground injected pursuant to 40 CFR 148.14(f).

(2) Effective July 8, 1989 and continuing until December 8, 1989, F011 (nonwastewaters) and F012 (nonwastewaters) are prohibited from land disposal pursuant to the treatment standards specified in §§268.41 and 268.43 applicable to F007, F008, and F009 nonwastewaters. Effective December 8, 1989 F011 (nowastewaters) and F012 (nonwastewaters) are prohibited from land disposal pursuant to the treatment standards specified in §§268.41 and 268.43 applicable to

F011 (nonwastewaters) and F012 (nonwastewaters).

(d) Effective June 8, 1991, the wastes specified in this section having a treatment standard in Subpart D of this part based on incineration, and which are contaminated soil and debris are prohibited from land disposal.

(e) Between June 8, 1989 and June 8, 1991, (for wastes F007, F008, F009, F011, and F012 between June 8, 1989 and July 8, 1989) wastes included in paragraphs (c) and (d) of this section may be disposed in a landfill or surface impoundment, regardless whether such unit is a new, replacement, or lateral expansion unit, only if such unit is in compliance with the technical requirements specified in §268.5(h)(2).

(f) The requirements of paragraphs (a), (b), (c), and (d) of this section do not apply if:

(1) The wastes meet the applicable standards specified in Subpart D of this Part; or

(2) Persons have been granted an exemption from a prohibition pursuant to a petition under §268.6, with respect those wastes and units covered by the petition.

(g) The requirements of paragraphs (a), (b), and (c) of this section do not apply if persons have been granted an extension to the effective date of a prohibition pursuant to §268.5, with respect to those wastes covered by the extension.

(h) Between June 8, 1989 and May 8, 1990, the wastes specified in §268.11 for which treatment standards under Subpart D of this Part are not applicable, including California list wastes subject to the statutory prohibitions of RCRA section 3004(d) or codified prohibitions under §268.32, are prohibited from disposal in a landfill or surface impoundment unless the wastes are the subject of a valid demonstration and certification pursuant to §268.8.

(i) To determine whether a hazardous waste listed in §§268.10, 268.11, and 268.12 exceeds the applicable treatment standards specified in §§ 268.41 and 268.43, the initial generator must test a representative sample of the waste extract or the entire waste, depending on whether the treatment standards are expressed as concentrations in the waste extract or the waste, or the generator may use knowledge of the waste. If the waste contains constituents in excess of the applicable Subpart D levels, the waste is prohibited from land disposal and all requirements of Part 268 are applicable, except as otherwise specified.

§ 268.35 Waste specific prohibitions-- Third Third wastes.

(a) Effective August 8, 1990, the following wastes specified in 40 CFR 261.31 as EPA Hazardous Waste Numbers F002 (1,1,2-trichloroethane), F005 (benzene), F005 (2-ethoxy ethanol) F005 (2-nitropropane), F006 (wastewaters), F019, F025, and F039 (wastewaters); the wastes specified in 40 CFR 261.32 as EPA Hazardous Waste Numbers K002; K003; K004 (wastewaters); K005 (wastewaters); K006; K008 (wastewaters); K011 (wastewaters); K013 (wastewaters); K014 (wastewaters); K015 (wastewaters); K017; K021 (wastewaters); K022 (wastewaters); K025 (wastewaters); K026; K029 (wastewaters); K031 (wastewaters); K032; K033; K034; K035; K041; K042; K046 (wastewaters, reactive nonwastewaters); K048 (wastewaters); K049 (wastewaters); K050 (wastewaters); K051 (wastewaters); K052 (wastewaters); K060 (wastewaters); K061 (wastewaters) and (high zinc subcategory >15% zinc); K069 (wastewaters, calcium sulfate nonwastewaters); K073, K083; K084 (wastewaters); K085; K095 (wastewaters); K096 (wastewaters); K097; K098; K100 (wastewaters); K101 (wastewaters); K102 (wastewaters); K105; and K106 (wastewaters); the wastes specified in 40 CFR 261.33(e) as EPA Hazardous Waste Numbers P001; P002; P003; P004; P005; P006; P007; P008; P009; P010 (wastewaters); P011 (wastewaters); P012 (wastewaters); P014; P015; P016; P017; P018; P020; P022; P023; P024; P026; P027; P028; P031; P033; P034; P036 (wastewaters); P037; P038 (wastewaters); P042; P045; P046; P047; P048; P049; P050; P051; P054; P056; P057; P058; P059; P060; P064; P065 (wastewaters); P066; P067; P068; P069; P070; P072; P073; P075; P076; P077; P078; P081; P082; P084; P088; P092 (wastewaters); P093; P095; P096; P101; P102; P103; P105; P108; P110; P112; P113; P114; P115; P116; P118; P119; P120; P122; and P123; and the wastes specified in 40 CFR 261.33(f) as EPA Hazardous Waste Numbers U001; U002; U003; U004; U005; U006; U007; U008 ; U009; U010; U011; U012; U014; U015; U016; U017; U018; U019; U020; U021; U022; U023; U024; U025; U026; U027; U029; U030; U031; U032; U033; U034; U035; U036; U037; U038; U039; U041; U042; U043; U044; U045; U046; U047; U048; U049; U050; U051; U052; U053; U055; U056; U057; U059; U060; U061; U062; U063; U064; U066; U067; U068; U070; U071; U072; U073; U074; U075; U076; U077; U078; U079; U080; U081; U082; U083; U084; U085;U086; U089; U090; U091; U092; U093; U094; U095; U096; U097; U098; U099; U101; U103; U105; U106; U108; U109; U110; U111; U112; U113; U114; U115; U116; U117; U118; U119; U120; U121; U122; U123; U124; U125; U126; U127; U128; U129; U130; U131; U132; U133; U134; U135; U136 (wastewaters); U137; U138; U140; U141; U142; U143; U144; U145; U146; U147; U148; U149; U150; U151 (wastewaters); U152; U153; U154; U155; U156; U157; U158; U159; U160; U161; U162; U163; U164; U165; U166; U167; U168; U169; U170; U171; U172; U173; U174; U176; U177; U178; U179; U180; U181; U182; U183; U184; U185; U186; U187; U188; U189; U191; U192; U193; U194; U196; U197; U200; U201; U202; U203; U204; U205; U206; U207; U208; U209; U210; U211; U213; U214; U215; U216; U217; U218; U219; U220; U222; U225; U226; U227; U228; U234; U236; U237; U238; U239; U240; U243; U244; U246; U247; U248; U249; and the following wastes identified as hazardous based on a characteristic alone: D001; D002; D003; D004 (wastewaters), D005; D006; D007; D008 (except for lead materials stored before secondary smelting), D009 (wastewaters), D010, D011, D012, D013, D014, D015, D016, and D017 are prohibited from land disposal.

(b) Effective November 8, 1990, the following wastes specified in 40 CFR 261.32 as EPA Haz-ardous Waste Numbers K048 (nonwastewaters), K049 (nonwastewaters), K050 (nonwastewaters), and K052 (nonwastewaters) are prohibited from land disposal.

(c) Effective May 8, 1992, the following waste specified in 40 CFR 261.31 as EPA Hazardous Waste Numbers F039 (nonwastewaters); the wastes specified in 40 CFR 261.32 as EPA Hazardous Waste Numbers K031 (nonwastewaters); K084 (nonwastewaters); K101 (nonwastewaters); K102 (nonwastewaters); K106 (nonwastewaters); the wastes specified in 40 CFR 261.33(e) as EPA Hazardous Waste Numbers P010 (nonwastewaters); P011 (nonwastewaters); P012 (nonwastewaters); P036 (non-wastewaters); P038 (nonwastewaters); P065 (nonwastewaters); P087; and P092 (non-wastewaters); the wastes specified in 40 CFR 261.33(f) as EPA Hazardous Waste Numbers U136 (nonwastewaters); and U151 (nonwaste waters); the following wastes identified as hazardous based on a characteristic alone: D004 (nonwastewaters); D008 (lead materials stored before secondary smelting); and D009 (nonwastewaters); inorganic solid debris as defined in 40 CFR 268.2(g) (which also applies to chromium refractory bricks carrying the EPA Hazardous Waste Numbers K048-K052); and RCRA hazardous wastes that contain naturally occurring radioactive materials are prohibited from land disposal.

(d) Effective May 8, 1992, hazardous wastes listed in 40 CFR 268.10, 268.11, and 268.12 that are mixed radioactive/hazardous wastes, and soil or debris contaminated with hazardous wastes listed in 40 CFR 268.10, 268.11, and 268.12 that are mixed radioactive/hazardous wastes, are prohibited from land disposal.

(e) Effective May 8, 1992, the wastes specified in this section having a treatment standard in Subpart D of this Part based on incineration, mercury retorting, vitrification, acid leaching followed by chemical precipitation, or thermal recovery of metals, and which are contaminated soil or debris, are prohibited from land disposal.

(f) Between May 8, 1990 and August 8, 1990, the wastes included in paragraph (a) may be disposed of in a landfill or surface impoundment only if such unit is in compliance with the requirements specified in §268.5(h)(2).

(g) Between May 8, 1990 and November 8, 1990, wastes included in paragraph (b) of this section may be disposed of in a landfill or surface impoundment only if such unit is in compliance with the requirements specified in §268.5(h)(2).

(h) Between May 8, 1990, and May 8, 1992, wastes included in paragraphs (c), (d), and (e) of this section may be disposed of in a landfill or surface impoundment only if such unit is in compliance with the requirements specified in §268.5(h)(2).

(i) The requirements of paragraphs (a), (b), (c), (d), and (e) of this section do not apply if:

(1) The wastes meet the applicable standards specified in subpart D of this part;

(2) Persons have been granted an exemption from a prohibition pursuant to a petition under §268.6, with respect to those wastes and units covered by the petition;

(3) The wastes meet the applicable alternate standards established pursuant to a petition granted under §268.44;

(4) Persons have been granted an extension to the effective date of a prohibition pursuant to §268.5, with respect to these wastes covered by the extension.

(j) To determine whether a hazardous waste listed in §§268.10, 268.11, and 268.12 exceeds the applicable treatment standards specified in §§268.41 and 268.43, the initial generator must test a representative sample of the waste extract or the entire waste, depending on whether the treatment standards are expressed as concentrations in the waste extract or the waste, or the generator may use knowledge of the waste. If the waste contains constituents in excess of the applicable subpart D levels, the waste is prohibited from land disposal, and all requirements of part 268 are applicable, except as otherwise specified.

Subpart D -- Treatment Standards

§ 268.40 Applicability of treatment standards.

(a) A restricted waste identified in §268.41 may be land disposed only if an extract of the waste or of the treatment residue of the waste developed using the test method in Appendix II of Part 261 does not exceed the value shown in Table CCWE of §268.41 for any hazardous constituent listed in Table CCWE for that waste, with the following exceptions: D004, D008, K031, K084, K101, K102, P010, P011, P012, P036, P038, and U136. These wastes may be land disposed only if an extract of the waste or of the treatment residue of the waste developed using either the test method in 40 CFR part 261, appendix II, or the test method in appendix IX of this part, does not exceed the concentrations shown in Table CCWE of §268.41 for any hazardous constituent listed in Table CCWE for that waste.

(b) A restricted waste for which a treatment technology is specified under §268.42(a) may be land disposed after it is treated using that specified technology or an equivalent treatment method approved by the Administrator under the procedures set forth in §268.42(b).

(c) Except as otherwise specified in §268.43(c), a restricted waste identified in §268.43 may be land disposed only if the constituent concentrations in the waste or treatment residue of the waste do not exceed the value shown in Table CCW of §268.43 for any hazardous constituents listed in Table CCW for that waste.

§ 268.41 Treatment standards expressed as concentrations in waste extract.

(a) Table CCWE identifies the restricted wastes and concentrations of their associated constituents which may not be exceeded by the extract of a waste or waste treatment residual developed using the test method in Appendix 1 of this part for the allowable land disposal of such wastes, with the exception of wastes D004, D008, K031, K084, K101, K102, P010, P011, P012, P036, P038, and U136. Table CCWE iden-

tifies the restricted wastes D004, D008, K031, K084, K101, K102, P010, P011, P012, P036, P038, and U136 and the concentrations of their associated constituents which may not be exceeded by the extract of a waste or waste treatment residual developed using the test method in Appendix I of this part or appendix II of 40 CFR part 261 for the allowable land disposal of such wastes. (Appendix II of this part provides Agency guidance on treatment methods that have been shown to achieve the Table CCWE levels for the respective wastes. Appendix II of this part is not a regulatory requirement but is provided to assist generators and owners/operators in their selection of appropriate treatment methods.) Compliance with these concentrations is required based upon grab samples.

§ 268.41 Treatment standards expressed as concentrations in waste extract.

(a) Table CCWE identifies the restricted wastes and concentrations of their associated constituents which may not be exceeded by the extract of a waste or waste treatment residual developed using the test method in Appendix I of this part or appendix II of 40 CFR part 261 for the allowable land disposal of such wastes, with the exception of wastes D004, D008, K031, K084, K101, K102, P010, P011, P012, P036, P038, and U136. Table CCWE identifies the restricted wastes D004, D008, K031, K084, K101, K102, P010, P011, P012, P036, P038, and U136 and the concentrations of their associated constituents which may not be exceeded by the extract of a waste or waste treatment residual developed using the test method in Appendix I of this part or appendix II of 40 CFR part 261 for the allowable land disposal of such wastes. (Appendix II of this part provides Agency guidance on treatment methods that have been shown to achieve the Table CCWE levels for the respective wastes. Appendix II of this part is not a regulatory requirement but is provided to assist generators and owners/operators in their selection of appropriate treatment methods.) Compliance with these concentrations is required based upon grab samples.

Waste code	Commercial chemical name	See also	Regulated Hazardous Constituent	CAS No. for regulated hazardous constituent	Wastewaters Concentration (mg/l)	Notes	Nonwastewaters Concentration (mg/l)	Notes
D004..............	NA......................	Table CCW in 268.43	Arsenic..................................	7440-38-2	NA		5.0	[1]
D005..............	NA......................	Table CCW in 268.43	Barium	7440-39-3	NA		100	
D006..............	NA......................	Table CCW in 268.43	Cadmium...................................	7440-43-9	NA		1.0	
D007..............	NA......................	Table CCW in 268.43	Chromium (Total)..............	7440-47-32	NA		5.0	
D008..............	NA......................	Table CCW in 268.43	Lead	7439-92-1	NA		5.0	[1]
D009 (Low Mercury Subcategory-- less than 260 mg/kg Mercury).	NA......................	Table 2 in 268.42 and Table CCW in 268.43	Mercury	7439-97-6	NA		0.20	
D010..............	NA......................	Table CCW in 268.43	Selenium..................................	7782-49-2	NA		5.7	
D011..............	NA......................	Table CCW in 268.43	Silver	7440-22-4	NA		5.0	
F001-F005.......... spent solvents	NA......................	Table 2 in 268.42 and Table CCW in 268.43	Acetone	67-64-1	0.05		0.59	
			n-Butyl alcohol...................	71-36-3	5.0		5.0	
			Carbon disulfide...................	75-15-0	1.05		4.81	
			Carbon tetrachloride...........	56-23-5	0.05		0.96	
			Chlorobenzene.......................	108-90-7	0.15		0.05	
			Cresols (and cresylic acid)......................		2.82		0.75	
			Cyclohexanone......................	108-94-1	0.125		0.75	
			1,2-Dichlorobenzene	95-50-1	0.65		0.125	
			Ethyl acetate..........................	141-78-6	0.05		0.75	
			Ethylbenzene.........................	100-41-4	0.05		0.053	
			Ethyl ether............................	60-29-7	0.05		0.75	
			Isobutanol..............................	78-83-1	5.0		5.0	
			Methanol.................................	67-56-1	0.25		0.75	
			Methylene chloride................	75-9-2	0.20		0.96	
			Methyl ethyl ketone..............	78-93-3	0.05		0.75	
			Methyl isobutyl ketone..........	108-10-1	0.05		0.33	
			Nitrobenzene	98-95-3	0.66		0.125	
			Pyridine	110-86-1	1.12		0.33	
			Tetrachloroethylene...............	127-18-4	0.079		0.05	
			Toluene...................................	108-88-3	1.12		0.33	
			1,1,1-Trichloroethane.............	71-55-6	1.05		0.41	
			1,1,2-Trichloro- 1,1,2- Trifluorethane........................	76-13-1	1.05		0.96	
			Trichloroethylene..................	79-01-6	0.062		0.091	
			Trichlorofluoromethane........	75-69-4	0.05		0.96	
			Xylene.....................................		0.05		0.15	
F006.....................	NA......................	Table CCW in 268.43	Cadmium.................................	7440-43-9	NA		0.066	
			Chromium (Total)...................	7440-47-32	NA		5.2	
			Lead..	7439-92-1	NA		0.51	
			Nickel.....................................	7440-02-0	NA		0.32	
			Silver......................................	7440-22-4	NA		0.072	
F007.....................	NA......................	Table CCW in 268.43	Cadmium.................................	7440-43-9	NA		0.066	
			Chromium (Total)...................	7440-47-32	NA		5.2	
			Lead..	7439-92-1	NA		0.51	
			Nickel.....................................	7440-02-0	NA		0.32	
			Silver......................................	7440-22-4	NA		0.072	
F008.....................	NA......................	Table CCW in 268.43	Cadmium.................................	7440-43-9	NA		0.066	
			Chromium (Total)...................	7440-47-32	NA		5.2	
			Lead..	7439-92-1	NA		0.51	
			Nickel.....................................	7440-02-0	NA		0.32	
			Silver......................................	7440-22-4	NA		0.072	
F009.....................	NA......................	Table CCW in 268.43	Cadmium.................................	7440-43-9	NA		0.066	
			Chromium (Total)...................	7440-47-32	NA		5.2	
			Lead..	7439-92-1	NA		0.51	
			Nickel.....................................	7440-02-0	NA		0.32	
			Silver......................................	7440-22-4	NA		0.072	
F011.....................	NA......................	Table CCW in 268.43	Cadmium.................................	7440-43-9	NA		0.066	
			Chromium (Total)...............	7440-47-32	NA		5.2	
			Lead..	7439-92-1	NA		0.51	
			Nickel.....................................	7440-02-0	NA		0.32	
			Silver......................................	7440-22-4	NA		0.072	
F012.....................	NA......................	Table CCW in 268.43	Cadmium.................................	7440-43-9	NA		0.066	
			Chromium (Total)...................	7440-47-32	NA		5.2	
			Lead..	7439-92-1	NA		0.51	
			Nickel.....................................	7440-02-0	NA		0.32	
			Silver......................................	7440-22-4	NA		0.072	
F019.....................	NA......................	Table CCW in 268.43	Chromium (Total)	7440-47-32	NA		5.2	

Waste code	Commercial chemical name	See also	Regulated Hazardous Constituent	CAS No. for regulated hazardous constituent	Wastewaters Concentration (mg/l)	Notes	Nonwastewaters Concentration (mg/l)	Notes
F020-F023 and F026-F028 dioxin containing wastes[2]	NA	NA	HxCDD-All Hexachloro-dibenzo-p-dioxins		<1 ppb		<1 ppb	
			HxCDF-All hexachloro-dibenzofurans		<1 ppb		<1 ppb	
			PeCDD-All Pentachloro-dibenzo-p-dioxins		<1 ppb		<1 ppb	
			PeCDF-All Pentachloro-dibenzofurans		<1 ppb		<1 ppb	
			TCDD-All Tetrachloro-dibenzo-p-dioxins		<1 ppb		<1 ppb	
			TCDF-All Tetrachloro-dibenzofurans					
			2,4,5-Trichlorophenol	95-95-4	<1 ppb		<1 ppb	
			2,4,6-Trihlorophenol	88-06-2	< 0.05 ppm		< 0.05 ppm	
			2,3,4,6-Tetrachloro-phenol	58-90-2	< 0.05 ppm		< 0.05 ppm	
			Pentachlorophenol	87-86-5	< 0.01 ppm		< 0.01 ppm	
F024	NA	Table CCW in 268.43	Chromium (Total)	7440-47-32	NA		0.073	
			Lead	7439-92-1	NA		[Reserved]	
			Nickel	7440-02-0	NA		0.088	
F039	NA	Table CCW in 268.43	Antimony	7440-36-0	NA		0.23	
			Arsenic	7440-38-2	NA		5.0	
			Barium	7440-39-3	NA		52	
			Cadmium	7440-43-9	NA		0.066	
			Chromium. (Total)	7440-47-32	NA		5.2	
			Lead	7439-92-1	NA		0.51	
			Mercury	7439-97-6	NA		0.025	
			Nickel	7440-02-0	NA		0.32	
			Selenium	7782-49-2	NA		5.7	
			Silver	7440-22-4	NA		0.072	
K001	NA	Table CCW in 268.43	Lead	7439-92-1	NA		0.51	
K002	NA	Table CCW in 268.43	Chromium (Total)	440-47-32	NA		0.094	
			Lead	7439-92-1	NA		0.37	
K003	NA	Table CCW in 268.43	Chromium (Total)	7440-47-32	NA		0.094	
			Lead	7439-92-1	NA		0.37	
K004	NA	Table CCW	Chromium (Total)	7440-47-32	NA		0.094	
			Lead	7439-92-1	NA		0.37	
K005	NA	Table CCW in 268.43	Chromium (Total)	7440-47-32	NA		0.094	
			Lead	7439-92-1	NA		0.37	
K006 (anhydrous)	NA	Table CCW in 268.43	Chromium (Total)	7440-47-32	NA		0.094	
			Lead	7439-92-1	NA		0.37	
K006 (hydrated)	NA	Table CCW in 268.43	Chromium (Total)	7440-47-32	NA		5.2	
K007	NA	Table CCW in 268.43	Chromium (Total)	7440-47-32	NA		0.094	
			Lead	7439-92-1	NA		0.37	
K008	NA	Table CCW in 268.43	Chromium (Total)	7440-47-32	NA		0.094	
			Lead	7439-92-1	NA		0.37	
K015	NA	Table CCW in 268.43	Chromium (Total)	7440-47-32	NA		1.7	
			Nickel	7440-02-0	NA		0.2	
K021	NA	Table CCW in 268.43	Antimony	7440-36-0	NA		0.23	
K022	NA	Table CCW in 268.43	Chromium (Total)	7440-47-32	NA		5.2	
			Nickel	7440-02-0	NA		0.32	
K028	NA	Table CCW in 268.43	Chromium (Total)	7440-47-32	NA		0.073	
			Lead	7439-92-1	NA		0.021	
			Nickel	7440-02-0	NA		0.088	
K031	NA	Table CCW in 268.43	Arsenic	7440-38-2	NA		5.6	(1)
K046	NA	Table CCW in 268.43	Lead	7439-92-1	NA		0.18	
K048	NA	Table CCW in 268.43	Chromium (Total)	7440-47-32	NA		1.7	
			Nickel	7440-02-0	NA		0.20	
K049	NA	Table CCW in 268.43	Chromium (Total)	7440-47-32	NA		1.7	
			Nickel	7440-02-0	NA		0.20	
K050	NA	Table CCW in 268.43	Chromium (Total)	7440-47-32	NA		1.7	
			Nickel	7440-02-0	NA		0.20	
K051	NA	Table CCW in 268.43	Chromium . (Total)	7440-47-32	NA		1.7	
			Nickel	7440-02-0	NA		0.20	
K052	NA	Table CCW in 268.43	Chromium (Total)	7440-47-32	NA		1.7	
			Nickel	7440-02-0	NA		0.20	

Waste code	Commercial chemical name	See also	Regulated Hazardous Constituent	CAS No. for regulated hazardous constituent	Wastewaters Concentration (mg/l)	Notes	Nonwastewaters Concentration (mg/l)	Notes
K061 (Low Zinc Sub-category less than 15 % Total Zinc)......	N A	Table CCW in 268.43	Cadmium................................ Chromium (Total)................. Lead..................................... Nickel..................................	7440-43-9 7440-47-32 7439-92-1 7440-02-0	NA NA NA NA		0.14 5.2 0.24 0.32	
K061, High Zinc Subcategory	Electric Arc Furnace Dust..................	Table CCW in 268.43	Antimony............................... Arsenic................................. Barium.................................. Beryllium.............................. Cadmium............................... Chromium (Total)................. Lead..................................... Mercury................................ Nickel.................................. Selenium............................... Silver................................... Thallium............................... Vanadium.............................. Zinc......................................		NA NA NA NA NA NA NA NA NA NA NA NA NA NA		2.1 0.055 7.6 0.014 0.19 0.33 0.37 0.009 5 0.16 0.3 0.078 Reserved 5.3	
K062..............	NA......................	Table CCW in 268.43	Chromium (Total)................. Lead.....................................	7440-47-32 7439-92-1	NA NA		0.094 0.37	
K069.............. (Calcium Sulfate Subcategory)	NA......................	Table 2 in 268.42 and Table CCW in 268.43	Cadmium............................... Lead.....................................	7440-43-9 7439-92-1	NA NA		0.14 0.24	
K071..............	NA......................	Table CCW in 268.43	Mercury................................	7439-97-6	NA		0.025	
K083..............	NA......................	Table CCW in 268.43	Nickel..................................	7440-02-2	NA		0.088	
K084..............	NA......................	Table CCW in 268.43	Arsenic.................................	7440-38-2	NA		5.6	@
K086..............	NA......................	Table CCW in 268.43	Chromium (Total)................. Lead.....................................	7440-47-32 7439-92-1	NA NA		0.094 0.37	
K087..............	NA......................	Table CCW in 268.43	Lead.....................................	7439-92-1	NA		0.51	
K100..............	NA......................	Table CCW in 268.43	Cadmium............................... Chromium (Total)................. Lead.....................................	7440-43-9 7440-47-32 7439-92-1	NA NA NA		0.066 5.2 0.51	
K101..............	NA......................	Table CCW in 268.43	Arsenic.................................	7440-38-2	NA		5.6	@
K102..............	NA......................	Table CCW in 268.43	Arsenic.................................	7440-38-2	NA		5.6	@
K106.............. (Low Mercury Subcategory less than 260 mg/kg Mercury-residues from RMERC).	NA......................	Table 2 in 268.42 and Table CCW in 268.43	Mercury................................	7439-97-6	NA		0.020	
K106.............. (Low Mercury Subcategory-- less than 260 mg/kg Mercury-- that are not residues from RMERC).	NA......................	Table 2 in 268.42 and Table CCW in 268.43	Mercury................................ ..	7439-97-6	NA		0.025	
K115..............	NA......................	Table CCW in 268.43	Nickel	7440-02-0	NA		0.32	
P010..............	Arsenic acid......	Table CCW in 268.43	Arsenic.................................	7440-38-2	NA		5.6	[1]
P011..............	Arsenic pentoxide..........	Table CCW in 268.43	Arsenic.................................	7440-38-2	NA		5.6	[1]
P012..............	Arsenic trioxide..............	Table CCW in 268.43	Arsenic.................................	7440-38-2	NA		5.6	[1]
P013..............	Barium cyanide..............	Table CCW in 268.43	Barium..................................	7440-39-3	NA		52	
P036..............	Dichloro-phenylarsine	Table CCW in 268.43	Arsenic.................................	7440-38-2	NA		5.6	[1]
P038..............	Diethylarsine.	Table CCW in 268.43	Arsenic.................................	7440-38-2	NA		5.6	[1]
P065.............. (Low Mercury Subcategory - Less than 260 mg/kg Mercury- residues from RMERC)	Mercury.............. fulminate	Table 2 in 268.42 and Table CCW in 268.43	Mercury................................	7439-97-6	NA		0.20	

Waste code	Commercial chemical name	See also	Regulated Hazardous Constituent	CAS No. for regulated hazardous constituent	Wastewaters		Nonwastewaters	
					Concentration (mg/l)	Notes	Concentration (mg/l)	Notes
P065 (Low-Mercury Subcategory-Less than 260 kg/mg Mercury-incinerator residues (and are not residues from RMERC)	Mercury fulminate............	Table 2 in 268.42 and Table CCW in 268.43	Mercury.................................	7439-97-6	NA		0.025	
P073.................	Nickel carbonyl..............	Table1 CCW in 268.43	Nickel....................................	7440-02-0	NA		0.32	
P074.................	Nickel cyanide...............	Table CCW in 268.43	Nickel....................................	7440-02-0	NA		0.32	
P092 (Low Mercury Subcategory-Less than 260 mg/kg Mercury-residues from RMERC)	Phenyl mercury acetate...............	Table 2 in 268.42 and Table CCW in 268.43	Mercury.................................	7439-97-6	NA		0.20	
P092 (Low Mercury Subcategory-Less than 260 mg/kg Mercury residues (and are not residues from RMERC)	Phenyl mercury acetate...............	Table 2 in 268.42 and Table CCW in 268.43	Mercury.................................	7439-97-6	NA		0.025	
P099.................	Potassium silver cyanide...	Table CCW in 268.43	Silver....................................	7440-22-4	NA		0.072	
P103.................	Selenourea........	Table CCW in 268.43	Selenium................................	7782-49-2	NA		5.7	
P104.................	Silver cyanide.....	Table CCW in 268.43	Silver....................................	7440-22-4	NA		0.072	
P110.................	Tetraethyl lead.....................	Table CCW in 268.43	Lead......................................	7439-92-1	NA		0.51	
P114.................	Thallium selenite..............	Table CCW in 268.43	Selenium................................	7782-49-2	NA		5.7	
U032.................	Calcium chromate..........	Table CCW in 268.43	Chromium (Total)..................	7440-47-32	NA		0.094	
U051.................	Creosote............	Table CCW in 268.43	Lead......................................	7439-92-1	NA		0.51	
U136.................	Cacodylic acid	Table CCW in 268.43	Arsenic..................................	7440-38-2	NA		5.6	(1)
U144.................	Lead acetate.......	Table CCW in 268.43	Lead......................................	7439-92-1	NA		0.51	
U145.................	Lead phosphate.........	Table CCW in 268.43	Lead......................................	7439-92-1	NA		0.51	
U146.................	Lead subacetate........	Table CCW in 268.43	Lead......................................	7439-92-1	NA		0.51	
U151 (Low Mercury Subcategory-Less than 260 mg/kg Mercury-residues from RMERC)	Mercury............	Table CCW in 268.43 and Table 2 in 268.42	Mercury.................................	7439-97-6	NA		0.20	
U151 (Low Mercury Subcategory--Less than 260 mg/kg Mercury--that are not resdues from RMERC.)	Mercury............	Table CCW in 268.43 and Table 2 in 268.42	Mercury.................................	7439-97-6	NA		0.025	
U204.................	Selenium dioxide.............	Table CCW in 268.43	Selenium................................	7782-49-2	NA		5.7	
U205.................	Selenium sulfide...............	Table CCW in 268.43	Selenium................................	7782-49-2	NA		5.7	

[1] These treatment standards have been based on EP Leachate analysis but this does not preclude the use of TCLP analysis.

[2] These waste codes are not subcategorized into wastewaters and nonwastewaters.

NOTE: NA means Not Applicable.

@ means original text was not readable.

(b) When wastes with differing treatment standards for a constituent of concern are combined for purposes of treatment, the treatment residue must meet the lowest treatment standard for the constituent of concern, except that mixtures of high and low zinc nonwaste water K061 are subject to the treatment standard for high zinc K061.

§ 268.42 Treatment standards expressed as specified technologies.

(a) The following wastes in paragraphs (a)(1) and (a)(2) of this section and in Table 2 and Table 3 of this section must be treated using the technology or technologies specified in paragraphs (a)(1) and (a)(2) and Table 1 of this section.

(1) Liquid hazardous wastes containing polychlorinated biphenyls (PCBs) at concentrations greater than or equal to 50 ppm but less than 500 ppm must be incinerated in accordance with the technical requirements of 40 CFR 761.70 or burned in high efficiency boil-ers in accordance with the technical requirements of 40 CFR 761.60. Liquid hazardous wastes containing polychlorinated biphenyls (PCBs) at concentrations greater than or equal to 500 ppm must be incinerated in accordance with the technical requirements of 40 CFR 761.70. Thermal treatment under this section must also be in compliance with applicable regulations in Parts 264, 265, and 266.

(2) Nonliquid hazardous wastes containing halogenated organic compounds (HOCs) in total concentration greater than or equal to 1,000 mg/kg and liquid HOC-containing wastes that are prohibited under §268.32(e)(1) of this part must be incinerated in accordance with the requirements of 40 CFR part 264, subpart O, or 40 CFR part 265, subpart O. These treatment standards do not apply where the waste is subject to a part 268, subpart D, treatment standard for specific HOC (such as a hazardous waste chlorinated solvent for which a treatment standard is established under §268.41(a)).

(3) A mixture consisting of wastewater, the discharge of which is subject to regulation under either section 402 or section 307(b) of the Clean Water Act, and *de minimis* losses of materials from manufacturing operations in which these materials are used as raw materials or are produced as products in the manufacturing process, and that meet the criteria of the D001 ignitable liquids containing greater than 10 % total organic constituents (TOC) subcategory, is subject to the DEACT treatment standard described in Table 1 of this section. For purposes of this paragraph, *de minimis* losses include those from normal material handling operations (e.g., spills from the unloading or transfer of materials from bins or other containers, leaks from pipes, valves or other devices used to transfer materials); minor leaks from process equipment storage tanks, or containers; leaks from well-maintained pump packings and seals; sample purgings; and relief device discharges.

TABLE 1.--TECHNOLOGY CODES AND DESCRIPTION OF TECHNOLOGY-BASED STANDARDS

Technology Code	Description of technology-based standard
ADGAS:	Venting of compressed gases into an absorbing or reacting media (i.e., solid or liquid)--venting can be accomplished through physical release utilizing values/piping; physical penetration of the container; and/or penetration through detonation.
AMLGM:	Amalgamation of liquid, elemental mercury contaminated with radioactive materials utilizing inorganic reagents such as copper, zinc, nickel, gold, and sulfur that result in a nonliquid, semi-solid amalgam and thereby reducing potential emissions of elemental mercury vapors to the air.
BIODG:	Biodegradation of organics or non-metallic inorganics (i.e., degradable inorganics that contain the elements of phosphorus, nitrogen, and sulfur) in units operated under either aerobic or anaerobic conditions such that a surrogate compound or indicator parameter has been substantially reduced in concentration in the residuals (e.g., Total Organic Carbon can often be used as an indicator parameter for the biodegradation of many organic constituents that cannot be directly analyzed in wastewater residues).
CARBN:	Carbon adsorption (granulated or powdered) of non-metallic inorganics, organo-metallics, and/or organic constituents, operated such that a surrogate compound or indicator parameter has not undergone breakthrough (e.g., Total Organic Carbon can often be used as an indicator parameter for the adsorption of many organic constituents that cannot be directly analyzed in wastewater residues). Breakthrough occurs when the carbon has become saturated with the constituent (or indicator parameter) and substantial change in adsorption rate associated with that constituent occurs.
CHOXD:	Chemical or electrolytic oxidation utilizing the following oxidation reagents (or waste reagents) or combinations of reagents: (1) Hypochlorite (e.g. bleach); (2) chlorine; (3) chlorine dioxide; (4) ozone or UV (ultra- violet light) assisted ozone; (5) peroxides; (6) persulfates; (7) perchlorates; (8) permangantes; and/or (9) other oxidizing reagents of equivalent efficiency, performed in units operated such that a surrogate compound or indicator parameter has been substantially reduced in concentration in the residuals (e.g., Total Organic Carbon can often be used as an indicator parameter for the oxidation of many organic constituents that cannot be directly analyzed in wastewater residues). Chemical oxidation specifically includes what is commonly referred to as alkaline chlorination.
CHRED:	Chemical reduction utilizing the following reducing reagents (or waste reagents) or combinations of reagents: (1) Sulfur dioxide; (2) sodium, potassium, or alkali salts or sulfites, bisulfites, metabisulfites, and polyethylene glycols (e.g., NaPEG and KPEG); (3) sodium hydrosulfide; (4) ferrous salts; and/or (5) other reducing reagents of equivalent efficiency, performed in units operated such that a surrogate compound or indicator parameter has been substantially reduced in concentration in the residuals (e.g., Total Organic Halogens can often be used as an indicator parameter for the reduction of many halogenated organic constituents that cannot be directly analyzed in wastewater residues). Chemical reduction is commonly used for the reduction of hexavalent chromium to the trivalent state.
DEACT:	Deactivation to remove the hazardous characteristics of a waste due to its ignitability, corrosivity, and/or reactivity.
FSUBS:	Fuel substitution in units operated in accordance with applicable technical operating requirements.
HLVIT:	Vitrification of high level mixed radioactive wastes in units in compliance with all applicable radioactive protection requirements under control of the Nuclear Regulatory Commission.
IMERC:	Incineration of wastes containing organics and mercury in units operated in accordance with the technical operating requirements of 40 CFR part 264 subpart O and 40 CFR part 265 subpart O. All wastewater and nonwastewater residues derived from this process must then comply with the corresponding treatment standards per waste code with consideration of any applicable subcategories (e.g., High or Low Mercury Subcategories).
INCIN:	Incineration in units operated in accordance with the technical operating requirements of 40 CFR part 264 subpart O and 40 CFR part 265 subpart O.
LLEXT:	Liquid-liquid extraction (often referred to as solvent extraction) of organics from liquid wastes into an immiscible solvent for which the hazardous constituents have a greater solvent affinity, resulting in an extract high in organics that must undergo either incineration, reuse as a fuel, or other recovery/reuse and a raffinate (extracted liquid waste) proportionately low in organics that must undergo further treatment as specified in the standard.
MACRO:	Macroencapsulation with surface coating materials such as polymeric organics (e.g. resins and plastics) or with a jacket of inert inorganic materials to substantially reduce surface exposure to potential leaching media. Macroencapsulation specifically does not include any material that would be classified as a tank or container according to 40 CFR 260.10.

Technology Code	Description of technology-based standard
NEUTR:	Neutralization with the following reagents (or waste reagents) or combinations of reagents: (1) Acids; (2) bases; or (3) water (including wastewaters) resulting in a pH greater than 2 but less than 12.5 as measured in the aqueous residuals.
NLDBR:	No land disposal based on recycling.
PRECP:	Chemical precipitation of metals and other inorganics as insoluble precipitates of oxides, hydroxides, carbonates, sulfides, sulfates, chlorides, flourides, or phosphates. The following reagents (or waste reagents) are typically used alone or in combination: (1) Lime (i.e., containing oxides and/or hydroxides of calcium and/or magnesium); (2) caustic (i.e., sodium and/or potassium hydroxides); (3) soda ash (i.e., sodium carbonate); (4) sodium sulfide; (5) ferric sulfate or ferric chloride; (6) alum; or (7) sodium sulfate. Additional floculating, coagulation or similar reagents/processes that enhance sludge dewatering characteristics are not precluded from use.
RBERY:	Thermal recovery of Beryllium.
RCGAS:	Recovery/reuse of compressed gases including techniques such as reprocessing of the gases for reuse/resale; filtering/adsorption of impurities; remixing for direct reuse or resale; and use of the gas as a fuel source.
RCORR:	Recovery of acids or bases utilizing one or more of the following recovery technologies: (1) Distillation (i.e., thermal concentration); (2) ion exchange; (3) resin or solid adsorption; (4) reverse osmosis; and/or (5) incineration for the recovery of acid--Note: this does not preclude the use of other physical phase separation or concentration techniques such as decantation, filtration (including ultrafiltration), and centrifugation, when used in conjunction with the above listed recovery technologies.
RLEAD:	Thermal recovery of lead in secondary lead smelters.
RMERC:	Retorting or roasting in a thermal processing unit capable of volatilizing mercury and subsequently condensing the volatilized mercury for recovery. The retorting or roasting unit (or facility) must be subject to one or more of the following: (a) a National Emissions Standard for Hazardous Air Pollutants (NESHAP) for mercury; (b) a Best Available Control Technology (BACT) or a Lowest Achievable Emission Rate (LAER) standard for mercury imposed pursuant to a Prevention of Significant Deterioration (PSD) permit; or (c) a state permit that establishes emission limitations (within meaning of section 302 of the Clean Air Act) for mercury. All wastewater and nonwastewater residues derived from this process must then comply with the corresponding treatment standards per waste code with consideration of any applicable subcategories (e.g., High or Low Mercury Subcategories).
RMETL:	Recovery of metals or inorganics utilizing one or more of the following direct physical/removal technologies: (1) Ion exchange; (2) resin or solid (i.e., zeolites) adsorption; (3) reverse osmosis; (4) chelation/solvent extraction; (5) freeze crystalization; (6) ultrafiltration and/or (7) simple precipitation (i.e., crystalization)--Note: This does not preclude the use of other physical phase separation or concentration techniques such as decantation, filtration (including ultrafiltration), and centrifugation, when used in conjunction with the above listed recovery technologies.
RORGS:	Recovery of organics utilizing one or more of the following technologies: (1) Distillation; (2) thin film evaporation; (3) steam stripping; (4) carbon adsorption; (5) critical fluid extraction; (6) liquid-liquid extraction; (7) precipitation/crystallization (including freeze crystallization); or (8) chemical phase separation techniques (i.e., addition of acids, bases, demulsifiers, or similar chemicals);--Note: This does not preclude the use of other physical phase separation techniques such as decantation, filtration (including ultrafiltration), and centrifugation, when used in conjunction with the above listed recovery technologies.
RTHRM:	Thermal recovery of metals or inorganics from nonwastewaters in units identified as industrial furnaces according to 40 CFR 260.10, (1), (6), (7), (11), and (12) under the definition of "industrial furnaces".
RZINC:	Resmelting in high temperature metal recovery units for the purpose of recovery of zinc.
STABL:	Stabilization with the following reagents (or waste reagents) or combinations of reagents: (1) Portland cement; or (2) lime/pozzolans (e.g., fly ash and cement kiln dust)--this does not preclude the addition of reagents (e.g., iron salts, silicates, and clays) designed to enhance the set/cure time and/or compressive strength, or to overall reduce the leachability of the metal or inorganic.
SSTRP:	Steam stripping of organics from liquid wastes utilizing direct application of steam to the wastes operated such that liquid and vapor flow rates, as well as, temperature and pressure ranges have been optimized, monitored, and maintained. These operating parameters are dependent upon the design parameters of the unit such as, the number of separation stages and the internal column design. Thus, resulting in a condensed extract high in organics that must undergo either incineration, reuse as a fuel, or other recovery/reuse and an extracted wastewater that must undergo further treatment as specified in the standard.
WETOX:	Wet air oxidation performed in units operated such that a surrogate compound or indicator parameter has been substantially reduced in concentration in the residuals (e.g., Total Organic Carbon can often be used as an indicator parameter for the oxidation of many organic constituents that cannot be directly analyzed in wastewater residuals).
WTRRX:	Controlled reaction with water for highly reactive inorganic or organic chemicals with precautionary controls for protection of workers from potential violent reactions as well as precautionary controls for potential emissions of toxic/ignitable levels of gases released during the reaction.

Note 1: When a combination of these technologies (i.e., a treatment train) is specified as a single treatment standard, the order of application is specified in 268.42, Table 2 by indicating the five letter technology code that must be applied first, then the designation "fb." (an abbreviation for "followed by"), then the five letter technology code for the technology that must be applied next, and so on.

Note 2: When more than one technology (or treatment train) are specified as *alternative* treatment standards, the five letter technology codes (or the treatment trains) are separated by a semicolon (;) with the last technology preceded by the word "OR". This indicates that any one of these BDAT technologies or treatment trains can be used for compliance with the standard.

Waste Code	See Also	Waste descriptions and/or treatment subcategory	CAS No. for regulated hazardous constituents	Technology Code	
				Wastewaters	Nonwastewaters
D001	NA..........................	Ignitable Liquids based on 261.21(a)(1)--Wastewaters...............	NA	DEACT..........................	NA.
D001	NA..........................	Ignitable Liquids based on 261.21(a)(1) -- Low TOC Ignitable Liquids Sub-category--Less than 10 % total organic carbon...........................	NA	NA......................................	DEACT.
D001	NA..........................	Ignitable Liquids based on 261.21(a)(1) -- High TOC Ignitable Liquids Sub-category--Greater than or equal to 10 % total organic carbon...........................	NA	NA......................................	FSUBS; RORGS; or INCIN.
D001	NA..........................	Ignitable compressed gases based on 261.21(a)(3)......................	NA	NA......................................	DEACT.[2]
D001	NA..........................	Ignitable reactives based on 261.21(a)(2)...........................	NA	NA......................................	DEACT.
D001	NA..........................	Oxidizers based on 261.21(a)(4)...........................	NA	DEACT..........................	DEACT.
D002	NA..........................	Acid subcategory based on 261.22(a)(1)...........................	NA	DEACT..........................	DEACT.
D002	NA..........................	Alkaline subcategory based on 261.22(a)(1)........................	NA	DEACT..........................	DEACT.
D002	NA..........................	Other corrosives based on 261.22(a)(2)...........................	NA	DEACT..........................	DEACT.
D003	NA..........................	Reactive sulfides based on 261.23(a)(5)...........................	NA	DEACT (may not be diluted)...........	DEACT (may not be diluted).
D003	NA..........................	Explosives based on 261.23(a)(6), (7), and (8)............	NA	DEACT..........................	DEACT.
D003	NA..........................	Water reactives based on 261.23(a)(2), (3), and (4).....................	NA	NA......................................	DEACT.
D003	NA..........................	Other reactives based on 261.23(a)(1)...........................	NA	DEACT..........................	DEACT.
D006	NA..........................	Cadmium containing batteries....................	7440-43-9	NA......................................	RTHRM.
D008	NA..........................	Lead acid batteries (Note: This standard only applies to lead acid batteries that are identified as RCRA hazardous wastes and that are not excluded elsewhere from regulation under the land disposal restrictions of 40 CFR 268 or exempted under other EPA regula-tions (see 40 CFR 266.80.)................	7439-92-1	NA......................................	RLEAD.
D009	Table CCWE in 268.41 and Table CCW in 268.43....................	Mercury: (High Mercury Subcategory--greater than or equal to 260 mg/kg total Mercury--contains mercury and organics (and are not incinerator residues))....................	7439-97-6	NA......................................	IMERC; or RMERC.
D009	Table CCWE in 268.41 and Table CCW in 268.43....................	Mercury: (High Mercury Subcategory--greater than or equal to 260 mg/kg total Mercury--inorganics (including incinerator residues and residues from RMERC).........	7439-97-6	NA......................................	RMERC.
D012	Table CCW in 268.43...........	Endrin....................................	72-20-8	BIODG; or INCIN............	NA.
D013	Table CCW in 268.43...........	Lindane................................	58-89-9	CARBN; or INCIN...........	NA.
D014	Table CCW in 268.43...........	Methoxychlor....................................	72-43-5	WETOX; or INCIN...........	NA.
D015	Table CCW in 268.43...........	Toxaphene................................	8001-35-1	BIODG; or INCIN............	NA.
D016	Table CCW in 268.43...........	2,4-D....................................	94-75-7	CHOXD; BIODG; or INCIN............	NA.
D017	Table CCW in 268.43...........	2,4,5-TP....................................	93-72-1	CHOXD; or INCIN............	NA.
F005	Table CCWE in 268.41 and Table CCW in 268.43....................	2-Nitropropane...........................	79-46-9	(WETOX or CHOXD) fb CARBN; or INCIN.	INCIN.
F005	Table CCWE in 268.41 and Table CCW in 268.43....................	2-Ethoxyethanol.................	110-80-5	BIODG; or INCIN............	INCIN.
F024	Table CCWE in 268.41 and Table CCW in 268.43....................	....	NA	INCIN............................	INCIN.
K025	NA..........................	Distillation bottoms from the production of nitrobenzene by the nitration of benzene............	NA	LLEXT fb SSTRP fb CARBN; or INCIN.	INCIN.

164

Waste Code	See Also	Waste descriptions and/or treatment subcategory	CAS No. for regulated hazardous constituents	Technology Code	
				Wastewaters	Nonwastewaters
K026	NA....................................	Stripping still tails from the productioin of methyl ethyl pyridines.	NA	INCIN................................	INCIN.
K027	NA....................................	Centrifuge and distillation residues from toluene diisocyanate production..................	NA	CARBN; or INCIN..........	FSUBS; or INCIN
K039	NA....................................	Filter cake from the filtration of diethylphosphorodithioc acid in the production of phorate.	NA	CARBN; or INCIN..........	FSUBS; or INCIN.
K044	NA....................................	Wastewater treatment sludges from the manufac- turing and processing of explosives.	NA	DEACT................................	DEACT.
K045	NA....................................	Spent carbon from the treatment of wastewater containing explosives........................	NA	DEACT................................	DEACT.
K047	NA....................................	Pink/red water from TNT operations.	NA	DEACT................................	DEACT.
K069	Table CCWE in 268.41 and Table CCW in 268.43...................	Emission control dust/sludge from secondary lead smelting; Non-Calcium Sulfate Subcategory......................	NA	NA....................................	RLEAD.
K106	Table CCWE in 268.41 and Table CCW in 268.43...................	Wastewater treatment sludge from the mercury cell process in chlorine production: (High Mercury subcategory--greater than or equal to 260 mg/kg total mercury)...................	NA	NA....................................	RMERC.
K113	NA....................................	Condensed liquid light ends from the purification of toluenediamine in the production of toluenediamine via hydro- genation of dinitrotoluene..............	NA	CARBN; or INCIN..........	FSUBS; or INCIN.
K114	NA....................................	Vicinals from the purifica- tion of toluenediamine in the production of toluenedia- mine via hydrogenation of dinitrotoluene.	NA	CARBN; or INCIN..........	FSUBS; or INCIN.
K115	NA....................................	Heavy ends from the purifi- cation of toluenediamine in the production of toluenedia- mine via hydrogenation of dinitrotoluene......................	NA	CARBN; or INCIN..........	FSUBS; or INCIN.
K116	NA....................................	Organic condensate from the solvent recovery colunm in the production of toluene diisocyanate via phosgenation of toluenediamine.	NA	CARBN; or INCIN..........	FSUBS; or INCIN.
P001	NA....................................	Warfarin (>0.3%)...................	81-81-2	(WETOX or CHOXD) fb CARBN; or INCIN	FSUBS; or INCIN.
P002	NA....................................	1-Acetyl-2-thiourea...............	591-08-2	(WETOX or CHOXD) fb CARBN; or INCIN.....	INCIN.
P003	NA....................................	Acrolein............................	107-02-8	NA....................................	FSUBS; or INCIN.
P005	NA....................................	Allyl alcohol......................	107-18-6	(WETOX or CHOXD) fb CARBN; or INCIN.....	FSUBS; or INCIN.
P006	NA....................................	Aluminum phosphide.....................	20859-73-8	CHOXD; CHRED; or INCIN.	CHOXD; CHRED, or INCIN.
P007	NA....................................	5-Aminoethyl 3-isoxazolol...............	2763-96-4	(WETOX or CHOXD) fb CARBN; or INCIN.....	INCIN.
P008	NA....................................	4-Aminopyridine.....................	504-24-5	(WETOX or CHOXD) fb CARBN; or INCIN.....	INCIN.
P009	NA....................................	Ammonium picrate........................	131-74-8	CHOXD; CHRED, CARBN; BIODG; or INCIN..........................	FSUBS; CHOXD; CHRED; or INCIN.
P014	NA....................................	Thiophenol (Benzene thiol).............	108-98-5	(WETOX or CHOXD) fb CARBN; or INCIN.....	INCIN.
P015	NA....................................	Beryllium dust....................	7440-41-7	RMETL; or RTHRM..........	RMETL; or RTHRM.
P016	NA....................................	Bis(chloromethyl)ether.....................	542-88-1	(WETOX or CHOXD) fb CARBN; or INCIN.....	INCIN.
P017	NA....................................	Bromoacetone......................	598-31-2	(WETOX or CHOXD) fb CARBN; or INCIN.....	INCIN.
P018	NA....................................	Brucine............................	357-57-3	(WETOX or CHOXD) fb CARBN; or INCIN.....	INCIN.
P022	Table CCW in 268.43............	Carbon disulfide...................	75-15-0	NA.................................... .	INCIN.
P023	NA....................................	Chloroacetaldehyde......................	107-20-0	(WETOX or CHOXD) fb CARBN; or INCIN.....	INCIN.

Waste Code	See Also	Waste descriptions and/or treatment subcategory	CAS No. for regulated hazardous constituents	Technology Code Wastewaters	Technology Code Nonwastewaters
P026	NA....................................	1-(o-Chlorophenyl) thiourea............	5344-82-1	(WETOX or CHOXD) fb CARBN; or INCIN.....	INCIN.
P027	NA....................................	3-Chloropropionitrile........................	542-76-7	(WETOX or CHOXD) fb CARBN; or INCIN....	INCIN.
P028	NA....................................	Benzyl chloride................................	100-44-7	(WETOX or CHOXD) fb CARBN; or INCIN....	INCIN.
P031	NA....................................	Cyanogen...	460-19-5	CHOXD; WETOX or INCIN.........................	CHOXD; WETOX or INCIN.
P033	NA....................................	Cyanogen chloride............................	506-77-4	CHOXD; WETOX or INCIN.........................	CHOXD; WETOX or INCIN.
P034	NA....................................	2-Cyclohexyl-4,6-dinitrophenol	131-89-5	(WETOX or CHOXD) fb CARBN; or INCIN.....	INCIN.
P040	NA....................................	O,O-Diethyl O-pyrazinyl phosphorothioate...........................	297-97-2	CARBN; or INCIN...........	FSUBS; or INCIN.
P041	NA....................................	Diethyl-p-nitrophenyl phosphate....	311-45-5	CARBN; or INCIN...........	FSUBS; or INCIN.
P042	NA....................................	Epinephrine......................................	51-43-4	(WETOX or CHOXD) fb CARBN; or INCIN.....	INCIN.
P043	NA....................................	Diisopropyl fluorophosphate (DFP)...	55-91-4	CARBN; or INCIN...........	FSUBS; or INCIN.
P044	NA....................................	Dimethoate......................................	60-51-5	CARBN; or INCIN...........	FSUBS; or INCIN.
P045	NA....................................	Thiofanox...	39196-18-4	(WETOX or CHOXD) fb CARBN; or INCIN....	INCIN.
P046	NA....................................	alpha, alpha-Dimethylphen-ethylamine....................................	122-09-8	(WETOX or CHOXD) fb CARBN; or INCIN...	INCIN.
P047	NA....................................	4,6-Dinitro-o-cresol salts.................	534-52-1	(WETOX or CHOXD) fb CARBN; or INCIN....	INCIN.
P049	NA....................................	2,4-Dithiobiuret................................	541-53-7	(WETOX or CHOXD) fb CARBN; or INCIN....	INCIN.
P054	NA....................................	Aziridine..	151-56-4	(WETOX or CHOXD) fb CARBN; or INCIN.....	INCIN.
P056	Table CCW in 268.43...........	Fluorine...	7782-41-4	NA....................................	ADGAS fb NEUTR.
P057	NA....................................	Fluoroacetamide..............................	640-19-7	(WETOX or CHOXD) fb CARBN; or INCIN....	INCIN.
P058	NA....................................	Fluoroacetic acid, sodium salt........	62-74-8	(WETOX or CHOXD) fb CARBN; or INCIN...	INCIN.
P062	NA....................................	Hexaethyltetraphosphate................	757-58-4	CARBN; or INCIN..........	FSUBS; or INCIN
P064	NA....................................	Isocyanic acid, ethyl ester..............	624-83-9	(WETOX or CHOXD) fb CARBN; or INCIN.....	INCIN.
P065	Table CCWE in 268.41 and Table CCW in 268.43....................	Mercury fulminate: (High Mercury Subcategory — greater than or equal to 260 mg/kg total Mercury—either incinerator residues or residues from RMERC)...............................	628-86-4	NA....................................	RMERC.
P065	Table CCWE in 268.41 and Table CCW in 268.43....................	Mercury fulminate: (All Nonwastewaters that are not incinerator residues or are not residues from RMERC; regardless of Mercury Content)...	628-86-4	NA....................................	IMERC.
P066	NA....................................	Methomyl...	16752-77-5	(WETOX or CHOXD) fb CARBN; or INCIN....	INCIN.
P067	NA....................................	2-Methylaziridine.............................	75-55-8	(WETOX or CHOXD) fb CARBN; or INCIN....	INCIN.
P068	NA....................................	Methyl hydrazine.............................	60-34-4	CHOXD; CHRED; CARBN; BIODG; or INCIN.........................	FSUBS; CHOXD; CHRED; or INCIN.
P069	NA....................................	Methyllactonitrile............................	75-86-5	(WETOX or CHOXD) fb CARBN; or INCIN.....	INCIN.
P070	NA....................................	Aldicarb...	116-06-3	(WETOX or CHOXD) fb CARBN; or INCIN....	INCIN.
P072	NA....................................	1-Naphthyl-2-thiourea......................	86-88-4	(WETOX or CHOXD) fb CARBN; or INCIN....	INCIN.
P075	NA....................................	Nicotine and salts............................	1 54-11-5	(WETOX or CHOXD) fb CARBN; or INCIN....	INCIN.
P076	NA....................................	Nitric oxide......................................	10102-43-9	ADGAS............................	ADGAS.
P078	NA....................................	Nitrogen dioxide..............................	10102-44-0	ADGAS............................	ADGAS.
P081	NA....................................	Nitroglycerin....................................	55-63-0	CHOXD; CHRED; CARBN; BIODG; or INCIN........................	FSUBS; CHOXD; CHRED; or INCIN.
P082	Table CCW in 268.43...........	N-Nitrosodimethylamine.................	62-75-9	NA....................................	INCIN.
P084	NA....................................	N-Nitrosomethylvinylamine...........	4549-40-0	(WETOX or CHOXD) fb CARBN; or INCIN.....	INCIN.
P085	NA....................................	Octamethylpyrophosphoramide.....	152-16-9	CARBN; or INCIN...........	FSUBS; or INCIN
P087	NA....................................	Osmium tetroxide...........................	20816-12-0	RMETL; or RTHRM.........	RMETL; or RTHRM
P088	NA....................................	Endothall..	145-73-3	(WETOX or CHOXD) fb CARBN; or INCIN.....	FSUBS; or INCIN.

Waste Code	See Also	Waste descriptions and/or treatment subcategory	CAS No. for regulated hazardous constituents	Technology Code	
				Wastewaters	Nonwastewaters
P092	Table CCWE in 268.41 and Table CCW in 268.43..............	Phenyl mercury acetate: (High Mercury Subcategory— greater than or equal to 260 mg/kg total Mercury— either incinerator residues or residues from RMERC)...................	62-38-4	NA..................................	RMERC.
P092	Table CCWE in 268.41 and Table CCW in 268.43..............	Phenyl mercury acetate: (All nonwastewaters that are not incinerator residues and are not residues from RMERC: regardless of Mercury Content).	62-38-4	NA..................................	IMERC; or RMERC.
P093	NA.......................................	N-Phenylthiourea.............................	103-85-5	(WETOX or CHOXD) fb CARBN; or INCIN.....	INCIN.
P095	NA.......................................	Phosgene........................	75-44-5	(WETOX or CHOXD) fb CARBN; or INCIN.....	INCIN.
P096	NA.......................................	Phosphine........................	7803-51-2	CHOXD; CHRED; or INCIN......................	CHOXD; CHRED; or INCIN.
P102	NA.......................................	Propargyl alcohol............................	107-19-7	(WETOX or CHOXD) fb CARBN; or INCIN.....	FSUBS; or INCIN.
P105	NA.......................................	Sodium azide...................	26628-22-8	CHOXD; CHRED; CARBN; BIODG; or INCIN.	FSUBS; CHOXD; CHRED; or INCIN.
P108	NA.......................................	Strychnine and salts......................	1 57-24-9	(WETOX or CHOXD) fb CARBN; or INCIN.....	INCIN.
P109	NA.......................................	Tetraethyldithiopyrophosphate	3689-24-5	CARBN; or INCIN...........	FSUBS; or INCIN.
P112	NA.......................................	Tetranitromethane.......................	509-14-8	CHOXD; CHRED; CARBN; BIODG; or INCIN........................	FSUBS; CHOXD; CHRED; or INCIN.
P113	Table CCW in 268.43........	Thallic oxide................	1314-32-5	NA..................................	RTHRM; or STABL.
P115	Table CCW in 268.43........	Thallium (1) sulfate............	7446-18-6	NA..................................	RTHRM; or STABL.
P116	NA.......................................	Thiosemicarbazide....................	79-19-6	(WETOX or CHOXD) fb CARBN; or INCIN.....	INCIN.
P118	NA.......................................	Trichloromethanethiol..................	75-70-7	(WETOX or CHOXD) fb CARBN; or INCIN.....	INCIN.
P119	Table CCW in 268.43..........	Ammonium vanadate....................	7803-55-6	NA..................................	STABL.
P120	Table CCW in 268.43..........	Vanadium pentoxide..................	1314-62-1	NA..................................	STABL.
P122	NA.......................................	Zinc Phosphide (>10%).............	1314-84-7	CHOXD; CHRED; or INCIN......................	CHOXD; CHRED ; or INCIN
U001	NA.......................................	Acetaldehyde................................	75-07-0	(WETOX or CHOXD) fb CARBN; or INCIN.....	INCIN.
U003	Table CCW in 268.43..........	Acetonitrile................	75-05-8	NA..................................	INCIN.
U006	NA.......................................	Acetyl Chloride................	75-36-5	(WETOX or CHOXD) fb CARBN; or INCIN.....	INCIN.
U007	NA.......................................	Acrylamide........................	79-06-1	(WETOX or CHOXD) fb CARBN; or INCIN.....	INCIN.
U008	NA.......................................	Acrylic acid......................	79-10-7	(WETOX or CHOXD) fb CARBN; or INCIN.....	FSUBS; or INCIN.
U010	NA.......................................	Mitomycin C...................	50-07-7	(WETOX or CHOXD) fb CARBN; or INCIN.....	INCIN.
U011	NA.......................................	Amitrole............	61-82-5	(WETOX or CHOXD) fb CARBN; or INCIN.....	INCIN.
U014	NA.......................................	Auramine........................	492-80-8	(WETOX or CHOXD) fb CARBN; or INCIN.....	INCIN.
U015	NA.......................................	Azaserine........................	115-02-6	(WETOX or CHOXD) fb CARBN; or INCIN.....	INCIN.
U016	NA.......................................	Benz(c)acridine....................	225-51-4	(WETOX or CHOXD) fb CARBN; or INCIN.....	FSUBS; or INCIN.
U017	NA.......................................	Benzal chloride................	98-87-3	(WETOX or CHOXD) fb CARBN; or INCIN.....	INCIN.
U020	NA.......................................	Benzenesulfonyl chloride................	98-09-0	(WETOX or CHOXD) fb CARBN; or INCIN.....	INCIN.
U021	NA.......................................	Benzidine........................	92-87-5	(WETOX or CHOXD) fb CARBN; or INCIN.....	INCIN.
U023	NA.......................................	Benzotrichloride........................	98-07-7	CHOXD; CHRED; CARBN; BIODG; or INCIN.	FSUBS; CHOXD; CHRED; or INCIN.
U026	NA.......................................	Chlornaphazin....................	494-03-1	(WETOX or CHOXD) fb CARBN; or INCIN.....	INCIN.
U033	NA.......................................	Carbonyl fluoride............................	353-50-4	(WETOX or CHOXD) fb CARBN; or INCIN.....	INCIN.
U034	NA.......................................	Trichloroacetaldehyde (Chloral).....	75-87-6	(WETOX or CHOXD) fb CARBN; or INCIN.....	INCIN.
U035	NA.......................................	Chlorambucil........................	305-03-3	(WETOX or CHOXD) fb CARBN; or INCIN.....	INCIN.
U038	Table CCW in 268.43..........	Chlorobenzilate........................	510-15-6	NA..................................	INCIN.
U041	NA.......................................	1-Chloro-2,3-epoxypropane (Epichlorohydrin).	106-89-8	(WETOX or CHOXD) fb CARBN; or INCIN....	INCIN.
U042	Table CCW in 268.43..........	2-Chloroethyl vinyl ether.................	110-75-8	NA..................................	INCIN.
U046	NA.......................................	Chloromethyl methyl ether.............	107-30-2	(WETOX or CHOXD) fb CARBN; or INCIN.....	INCIN.

167

Waste Code	See Also	Waste descriptions and/or treatment subcategory	CAS No. for regulated hazardous constituents	Technology Code	
				Wastewaters	Nonwastewaters
U049	NA..........................	4-Chloro-o-toluidine hydrochloride	3165-93-3	(WETOX or CHOXD) fb CARBN; or INCIN.....	INCIN.
U053	NA..........................	Crotonaldehyde...............................	4170-30-3	(WETOX or CHOXD) fb CARBN; or INCIN.....	FSUBS; or INCIN.
U055	NA..........................	Cumene..	98-82-8	(WETOX or CHOXD) fb CARBN; or INCIN.....	FSUBS; or INCIN.
U056	NA..........................	Cyclohexane....................................	110-82-7	(WETOX or CHOXD) fb CARBN; or INCIN.....	FSUBS; or INCIN.
U057	Table CCW in 268.43............	Cyclohexanone.................................	108-94-1	NA..........................	FSUBS; or INCIN
U058	NA..........................	Cyclophosphamide.............................	50-18-0	CARBN; or INCIN............	FUSBS; or INCIN
U059	NA..........................	Daunomycin....................................	20830-81-3	(WETOX or CHOXD) fb CARBN; or INCIN.....	INCIN.
U062	NA..........................	Diallate..	2303-16-4	(WETOX or CHOXD) fb CARBN; or INCIN.....	INCIN.
U064	NA..........................	1,2,7,8-Dibenzopyrene......................	189-55-9	(WETOX or CHOXD) fb CARBN; or INCIN.....	FSUBS; or INCIN.
U073	NA..........................	3,3'-Dichlorobenzidine.......................	91-94-1	(WETOX or CHOXD) fb CARBN; or INCIN.....	INCIN.
U074	NA..........................	cis-1,4-Dichloro-2-butylene...............	1476-11-5	(WETOX or CHOXD) fb CARBN; or INCIN.....	INCIN.
		trans-1,4-Dichloro-2-butylene..........		(WETOX or CHOXD) fb CARBN; or INCIN.....	INCIN.
U085	NA..........................	1,2:3,4-Diepoxybutane......................	1464-53-5	(WETOX or CHOXD) fb CARBN; or INCIN.....	FSUBS; or INCIN.
U086	NA..........................	N,N-Diethylhydrazine	1615-80-1	CHOXD; CHRED; CARBN; BIODG; or INCIN.	FSUBS; CHOXD; CHRED; or INCIN.
U087	NA..........................	O,O-Diethyl S-methyldithio-phosphate.	3288-58-2	CARBN; or INCIN............	FSUBS; or INCIN.
U089	NA..........................	Diethyl stilbestrol.............................	56-53-1	(WETOX or CHOXD) fb CARBN; or INCIN.....	FSUBS; or INCIN.
U090	NA..........................	Dihydrosafrole.................................	94-58-6	(WETOX or CHOXD) fb CARBN; or INCIN.....	FSUBS; or INCIN.
U091	NA..........................	3,3'-Dimethoxybenzidine..................	119-90-4	(WETOX or CHOXD) fb CARBN; or INCIN.....	INCIN.
U092	NA..........................	Dimethylamine.................................	124-40-3	(WETOX or CHOXD) fb CARBN; or INCIN.....	INCIN.
U093	Table CCW in 268.43	p-Dimethylaminoazobenzene........	621-90-9	NA..........................	INCIN.
U094	NA..........................	7,12-Dimethyl benz(a)anthracene...	57-97-6	(WETOX or CHOXD) fb CARBN; or INCIN.....	FSUBS; or INCIN.
U095	NA..........................	3,3'-Dimethylbenzidine....................	119-93-7	(WETOX or CHOXD) fb CARBN; or INCIN.....	INCIN.
U096	NA..........................	a,a-Dimethyl benzyl hydroperoxyide.	80-15-9	CHOXD; CHRED; CARBN; BIODG; or INCIN.	FSUBS; CHOXD; CHRED; or INCIN.
U097	NA..........................	Dimethylcarbomyl chloride.............	79-44-7	(WETOX or CHOXD) fb CARBN; or INCIN.....	INCIN.
U098	NA..........................	1,1-Dimethylhydrazine......................	57-14-7	CHOXD; CHRED; CARBN; BIODG; or INCIN.	FSUBS; CHOXD; CHRED; or INCIN.
U099	NA..........................	1,2-Dimethylhydrzaine......................	540-73-8	CHOXD; CHRED; CARBN; BIODG; or INCIN.	FSUBS; CHOXD; CHRED; or INCIN.
U103	NA..........................	Dimethyl sulfate.............................	77-78-1	CHOXD; CHRED; CARBN; BIODG; or INCIN.	FSUBS; CHOXD; CHRED; or INCIN.
U109	NA..........................	1,2-Diphenylhydrazine......................	122-66-7	CHOXD; CHRED; CARBN; BIODG; or INCIN.	FSUBS; CHOXD; CHRED; or INCIN.
U110	NA..........................	Dipropylamine.................................	142-84-7	(WETOX or CHOXD) fb CARBN; or INCIN.....	INCIN.
U113	NA..........................	Ethyl acrylate.................................	140-88-5	(WETOX or CHOXD) fb CARBN; or INCIN.....	FSUBS; or INCIN.
U114	NA..........................	Ethylene bis-dithiocarbamic acid...	111-54-6	(WETOX or CHOXD) fb CARBN; or INCIN.....	INCIN.
U115	NA..........................	Ethylene oxide................................	75-21-8	(WETOX or CHOXD) fb CARBN; or INCIN.....	CHOXD; or INCIN.
U116	NA..........................	Ethylene thiourea............................	96-45-7	(WETOX or CHOXD) fb CARBN; or INCIN.....	INCIN.
U119	NA..........................	Ethyl methane sulfonate..................	62-50-0	(WETOX or CHOXD) fb CARBN; or INCIN.....	INCIN.
U122	NA..........................	Formaldehyde..................................	50-00-0	(WETOX or CHOXD) fb CARBN; or INCIN.....	FSUBS; or INCIN.
U123	NA..........................	Formic acid.....................................	64-18-6	(WETOX or CHOXD) fb CARBN; or INCIN.....	FSUBS; or INCIN.
U124	NA..........................	Furan...	110-00-9	(WETOX or CHOXD) fb CARBN; or INCIN.....	FSUBS; or INCIN.
U125	NA..........................	Furfural..	98-01-1	(WETOX or CHOXD) fb CARBN; or INCIN.....	FSUBS; or INCIN.
U126	NA..........................	Glycidaldehyde................................	765-34-4	(WETOX or CHOXD) fb CARBN; or INCIN.....	FSUBS; or INCIN.

168

Waste Code	See Also	Waste descriptions and/or treatment subcategory	CAS No. for regulated hazardous constituents	Technology Code	
				Wastewaters	Nonwastewaters
U132	NA	Hexachlorophenene	70-30-4	(WETOX or CHOXD) fb CARBN; or INCIN	INCIN.
U133	NA	Hydrzaine	302-01-2	CHOXD; CHRED; CARBN; BIODG; or INCIN.	FSUBS; CHOXD; CHRED; or INCIN.
U134	Table CCW in 268.43	Hydrogen Fluoride	7664-39-3	NA	ADGAS fb NEUTR; or NEUTR.
U135	NA	Hydrogen Sulfide	7783-06-4	CHOXD; CHRED; or INCIN.	CHOXD; CHRED; or INCIN.
U143	NA	Lasiocarpine	303-34-4	(WETOX or CHOXD) fb CARBN; or INCIN	INCIN.
U147	NA	Maleic anhydride	108-31-6	(WETOX or CHOXD) fb CARBN; or INCIN	FSUBS; or INCIN.
U148	NA	Maleic hydrazide	123-33-1	(WETOX or CHOXD) fb CARBN; or INCIN	INCIN.
U149	NA	Malononitrile	109-77-3	(WETOX or CHOXD) fb CARBN; or INCIN	INCIN.
U150	NA	Melphalan	148-82-3	(WETOX or CHOXD) fb CARBN; or INCIN	INCIN.
U151	Table CCWE in 268.41 and Table CCW in 268.43	Mercury: (High Mercury Subcategory—greater than or equal to 260 mg/kg total Mercury).	7439-97-6	NA	RMERC.
U153	NA	Methane thiol	74-93-1	(WETOX or CHOXD) fb CARBN; or INCIN	INCIN.
U154	NA	Methanol	67-56-1	(WETOX or CHOXD) fb CARBN; or INCIN	FSUBS; or INCIN.
U156	NA	Methyl chlorocarbonate	79-22-1	(WETOX or CHOXD) fb CARBN; or INCIN	INCIN.
U160	NA	Methyl ethyl ketone peroxide	1338-23-4	CHOXD; CHRED; CARBN; BIODG; or INCIN.	FSUBS, CHOXD; CHRED; or INCIN.
U163	NA	N-Methyl N'-nitro N-Nitroso-guanidine	70-25-7	(WETOX or CHOXD) fb CARBN; or INCIN	INCIN.
U164	NA	Methylthiouracil	56-04-2	(WETOX or CHOXD) fb CARBN; or INCIN	INCIN.
U166	NA	1,4-Naphthoquinone	130-15-4	(WETOX or CHOXD) fb CARBN; or INCIN	FSUBS; or INCIN.
U167	NA	1-Naphthylamine	134-32-7	(WETOX or CHOXD) fb CARBN; or INCIN	INCIN.
U168	Table CCW in 268.43	2-Naphthlyamine	91-59-8	NA	INCIN.
U171	NA	2-Nitropropane	79-46-9	(WETOX or CHOXD) fb CARBN; or INCIN	INCIN.
U-173	NA	N-Nitroso-di-n-ethanolamine	1116-54-7	(WETOX or CHOXD) fb CARBN; or INCIN	INCIN.
U-176	NA	N-Nitroso-N-ethylurea	759-73-9	(WETOX or CHOXD) fb CARBN; or INCIN	INCIN.
U-177	NA	N-Nitroso-N-methylurea	684-93-5	(WETOX or CHOXD) fb CARBN; or INCIN	INCIN.
U178	NA	N-Nitroso-N-methylurethane	615-53-2	(WETOX or CHOXD) fb CARBN; or INCIN	INCIN.
U182	NA	Paraldehyde	123-63-7	(WETOX or CHOXD) fb CARBN; or INCIN	FSUBS; or INCIN.
U184	NA	Pentachloroethane	76-01-7	(WETOX or CHOXD) fb CARBN; or INCIN	INCIN.
U186	NA	1,3-Pentadiene	504-60-9	(WETOX or CHOXD) fb CARBN; or INCIN	FSUBS; or INCIN.
U189	NA	Phosphorus sulfide	1314-80-3	CHOXD; CHRED; or INCIN	CHOXD; CHRED; or INCIN
U191	NA	2-Picoline	109-06-8	(WETOX or CHOXD) fb CARBN; or INCIN	INCIN.
U193	NA	1,3-Propane sultone	1120-71-4	(WETOX or CHOXD) fb CARBN; or INCIN	INCIN.
U194	NA	n-Propylamine	107-10-8	(WETOX or CHOXD) fb CARBN; or INCIN	INCIN.
U197	NA	p-Benzoquinone	106-51-4	(WETOX or CHOXD) fb CARBN; or INCIN	FSUBS; or INCIN.
U200	NA	Reserpine	50-55-5	(WETOX or CHOXD) fb CARBN; or INCIN	INCIN.
U201	NA	Resorcinol	108-46-3	(WETOX or CHOXD) fb CARBN; or INCIN	FSUBS; or INCIN.
U202	NA	Saccharin and salts	181-07-2	(WETOX or CHOXD) fb CARBN; or INCIN	INCIN.
U206	NA	Streptozatocin	18883-66-4	(WETOX or CHOXD) fb CARBN; or INCIN	INCIN.
U213	NA	Tetrahydrofuran	109-99-9	(WETOX or CHOXD) fb CARBN; or INCIN	FSUBS; or INCIN.

Waste Code	See Also	Waste descriptions and/or treatment subcategory	CAS No. for regulated hazardous constituents	Technology Code	
				Wastewaters	Nonwastewaters
U214	Table CCW in 268.43..........	Thallium (I) acetate...........................	563-68-8	NA...........................	RTHRM; or STABL.
U215	Table CCW in 268.43..........	Thallium (I) carbonate....................	6533-73-9	NA...........................	RTHRM; or STABL.
U216	Table CCW in 268.43..........	Thallium (I) chloride........................	7791-12-0	NA...........................	RTHRM; or STABL.
U217	Table CCW in 268.43..........	Thallium (I) nitrate.........................	10102-45-1	NA...........................	RTHRM; or STABL.
U218	NA..........	Thioacetamide...................	62-55-5	(WETOX or CHOXD) fb CARBN; or INCIN.....	INCIN.
U219	NA..........	Thiourea...................	62-56-6	(WETOX or CHOXD) fb CARBN; or INCIN.....	INCIN.
U221	NA..........	Toluenediamine...................	25376-45-8	CARBN; or INCIN..........	FSUBS; or INCIN.
U222	NA..........	o-Toluidine hydrochloride................	636-21-5	(WETOX or CHOXD) fb CARBN; or INCIN.....	INCIN.
U223	NA..........	Toluene diisocyanate................	26471-62-5	CARBN; or INCIN..........	FSUBS; or INCIN.
U234	NA..........	sym-Trinitrobenzene................	99-35-4	(WETOX or CHOXD) fb CARBN; or INCIN.....	INCIN.
U236	NA..........	Trypan Blue...................	72-57-1	(WETOX or CHOXD) fb CARBN; or INCIN.....	INCIN.
U237	NA..........	Uracil mustard...................	66-75-1	(WETOX or CHOXD) fb CARBN; or INCIN.....	INCIN.
U238	NA..........	Ethyl carbamate...................	51-79-6	(WETOX or CHOXD) fb CARBN; or INCIN.....	INCIN.
U240	NA..........	2,4-Dichlorophenoxyacetic (salts and esters)...............	194-75-7	(WETOX or CHOXD) fb CARBN; or INCIN.....	INCIN.
U244	NA..........	Thiram...................	137-26-8	(WETOX or CHOXD) fb CARBN; or INCIN.....	INCIN.
U246	NA..........	Cyanogen bromide...................	506-68-3	CHOXD; WETOX; or INCIN................	CHOXD; WETOX; or INCIN.
U248	NA..........	Warfarin (.3% or less).................	81-81-2	(WETOX or CHOXD) fb CARBN; or INCIN.....	FSUBS; or INCIN.
U249	NA..........	Zinc Phosphide (<10%).................	1314-84-7	CHOXD; CHRED; or INCIN................	CHOXD; CHRED; or INCIN

1 CAS Number given for parent compound only.
2 This waste code exists in gaseous form and is not categorized as wastewater or nonwastewater forms.
NOTE: NA means Not Applicable.

268.42 TABLE 3.--TECHNOLOGY-BASED STANDARDS FOR SPECIFIC RADIOACTIVE HAZARDOUS MIXED WASTE

Waste Code	Waste descriptions and/or treatment category	CAS No.	Technology Code	
			Wastewaters	Nonwastewaters
D002	Radioactive high level wastes generated during the reprocessing of fuel rods subcategory...................	NA..................	NA...........................	HLVIT.
D004	Radioactive high level wastes generated during the reprocessing of fuel rods subcategory...................	NA..................	NA...........................	HLVIT.
D005	Radioactive high level wastes generated during the reprocessing of fuel rods subcategory...................	NA..................	NA...........................	HLVIT.
D006	Radioactive high level wastes generated during the reprocessing of fuel rods subcategory...................	NA..................	NA...........................	HLVIT.
D007	Radioactive high level wastes generated during the reprocessing of fuel rods subcategory...................	NA..................	NA...........................	HLVIT.
D008	Radioactive lead solids subcategory (Note: these lead solids include but are not limited to, all forms of lead shielding, and other elemental forms of lead. These lead solids do not include treatment residuals such as hydroxide sludges, other wastewater treatment residuals, or incinerator ashes that can undergo conventional pozzolanic stabilization, nor do they include organo-lead materials that can be incinerated and stabilized as ash........	7439-92-1........	NA...........................	MACRO.
D008	Radioactive high level wastes generated during the reprocessing of fuel rods subcategory...................	NA..................	NA...........................	HLVIT.
D009	Elemental mercury contaminated with radioactive materials......	7439-97-6........	NA...........................	AMLGM.
D009	Hydraulic oil contaminated with mercury; radioactive materials subcategory...................	7439-97-6........	NA...........................	IMERC.
D009	Radioactive high level wastes generated during the reprocessing of fuel rods subcategory...................	NA..................	NA...........................	HLVIT.
D010	Radioactive high level wastes generated during the reprocessing of fuel rods subcategory...................	NA..................	NA...........................	HLVIT.
D011	Radioactive high level wastes generated during the reprocessing of fuel rods subcategory...................	NA..................	NA...........................	HLVIT.
U151	Mercury: Elemental mercury contaminated with radioactive materials...................	7439-97-6........	NA...........................	AMLGM.

NOTE: NA means Not Applicable.

(b) Any person may submit an application to the Administrator demonstrating that an alternative treatment method can achieve a measure of performance equivalent to that achievable by methods specified in paragraphs (a), (c), and (d) of this section. The applicant must submit information demonstrating that his treatment method is in compliance with federal, state, and local requirements and is protective of human health and the environment. On the basis of such information and any other available information, the Administrator may approve the use of the alternative treatment method if he finds that the alternative treatment method provides a measure of performance equivalent to that achieved by methods specified in paragraphs (a), (c), and (d) of this section. Any approval must be stated in writing and may contain such provisions and conditions as the Administrator deems appropriate. The person

to whom such approval is issued must comply with all limitations contained in such a determination.

(c) As an alternative to the otherwise applicable subpart D treatment standards, lab packs are eligible for land disposal provided the following requirements are met:

(1) The lab packs comply with the applicable provisions of 40 CFR 264.316 and 40 CFR 265.316;

(2) All hazardous wastes contained in such lab packs are specified in appendix IV or appendix V to part 268;

(3) The lab packs are incinerated in accordance with the requirements of 40 CFR part 264, subpart O or 40 CFR part 265, subpart O; and

(4) Any incinerator residues from lab packs containing D004, D005, D006, D007, D008, D010, and D011 are treated in compliance with the applicable treatment standards specified for such wastes in subpart D of this part.

(d) Radioactive hazardous mixed wastes with treatment standards specified in Table 3 of this section are not subject to any treatment standards specified in §268.41, §268.43, or Table 2 of this section. Radioactive hazardous mixed wastes not subject to treatment standards in Table 3 of this section remain subject to all applicable treatment standards specified in §268.41, §268.43, and Table 2 of this section.

§ 268.43 Treatment standards expressed as waste concentrations.

(a) Table CCW identifies the restricted wastes and the concentrations of their associated hazardous constituents which may not be exceeded by the waste or treatment residual (not an extract of such waste or residual) for the allowable land disposal of such waste or residual. Compliance with these concentrations is required based upon grab samples, unless otherwise noted in the following Table CCW.

268.43 TABLE CCW.--CONSTITUENT CONCENTRATIONS IN WASTE

Waste code	Commercial chemical name	See also	Regulated Hazardous Constituent	CAS No. for regulated hazardous constituent	Wastewaters Concentration (mg/l)	Notes	Nonwastewaters Concentration (mg/l)	Notes
D003 (Reactive Cyanides Subcategory based on 261.23(a)(5)	NA	NA	Cyanides (Total)	57-12-5	(4)		590	(3)
			Cyanides (Amenable)	57-12-5	0.86		30	
D004	NA	Table CCWE in 268.41	Arsenic	7440-38-2	5.0		NA	
D005	NA	Table CCWE in 268.41	Barium	7440-39-3	100		NA	
D006	NA	Table CCWE in 268.41	Cadmium	7440-43-9	1.0		NA	
D007	NA	Table CCWE in 268.41	Chromium (Total)	7440-47-32	5.0		NA	
D008	NA	Table CCWE om 268.41	Lead	7439-92-1	5.0		NA	
D009	NA	Table CCWE in 268.41	Mercury	7439-97-6	0.20		NA	
D010	NA	Table CCWE in 268.41	Selenium	7782-49-2	1.0		NA	
D011	NA	Table CCWE in 268.41	Silver	7440-22-4	5.0		NA	
D012	NA	Table 2 in 268.42	Endrin	720-20-8	NA		0.13	(1)
D013	NA	Table 2 in 268.42	Lindane	58-89-9	NA		0.066	(1)
D014	NA	Table 2 in 268.42	Methoxychlor	72-43-5	NA		0.18	(1)
D015	NA	Table 2 in 268.42	Toxaphene	8001-35-1	NA		1.3	(1)
D016	NA	Table 2 in 268.42	2,4-D	94-75-7	NA		10.0	(1)
D017	NA	Table 2 in 268.42	2,4,5-TP (Silvex)	93-76-5	NA		7.9	(1)
F001-F005 spent solvents	NA	Table CCWE in 268.41 and Table 2 in 268.42	1,1,2-Trichloroethane	71-55-6	0.030		7.6	(1)
			Benzene	71-43-2	0.070		3.7	(1)
F001-F005 spent solvents (Pharmaceutical Industry-Wastewater Subcategory).	NA	NA	Methylene chloride	75-09-2	0.44		NA	
F006	NA	Table CCWE in 268.41	Cyanides (Total)	57-12-5	1.2		590	
			Cyanides (Amenable)	57-12-5	0.86		30	
			Cadmium	7440-43-9	1.6		NA	
			Chromium	7440-47-32	0.32		NA	
			Lead	7439-92-1	0.040		NA	
			Nickel	7440-02-0	0.44		NA	

Waste code	Commercial chemical name	See also	Regulated Hazardous Constituent	CAS No. for regulated hazardous constituent	Wastewaters		Nonwastewaters	
					Concentration (mg/l)	Notes	Concentration (mg/l)	Notes
F007	NA	Table CCWE in 268.41	Cyanides (Total)	57-12-5	1.9	....	590	....
			Cyanides (Amenable)	57-12-5	0.1	....	30	....
			Chromium (Total)	7440-47-32	0.32	....	NA	....
			Lead	7439-92-1	0.04	....	NA	....
			Nickel	7440-02-0	0.44	....	NA	....
F008	NA	Table CCWE in 268.41	Cyanides (Total)	57-12-5	1.9	....	590	....
			Cyanides (Amenable)	57-12-5	0.1	....	30	....
			Chromium	7440-47-32	0.32	....	NA	....
			Lead	7439-92-1	0.04	....	NA	....
			Nickel	7440-02-0	0.44	....	NA	....
F009	NA	Table CCWE in 268.41	Cyanides (Total)	57-12-5	1.9	....	590	....
			Cyanides (Amenable)	57-12-5	0.1	....	30	....
			Chromium	7440-47-32	0.32	....	NA	....
			Lead	7439-92-1	0.04	....	NA	....
			Nickel	7440-02-0	0.44	....	NA	....
F010	NA	NA	Cyanides (Total)	57-12-5	1.9		1.5	....
			Cyanides (Amenable)	57-12-5	0.1		NA	....
F011	NA	Table CCWE in 268.41	Cyanides (Total)	57-12-5	1.9		110	....
			Cyanides (Amenable)	57-12-5	0.1		9.1	....
			Chromium (Total)	7440-47-32	0.32		NA	....
			Lead	7439-92-1	0.04		NA	....
			Nickel	7440-02-0	0.44		NA	....
F012	NA	Table CCWE in 268.41	Cyanides (Total)	57-12-5	1.9	....	110	....
			Cyanides (Amenable)	57-12-5	0.1	....	9.1	....
			Chromium (Total)	7440-47-32	0.32	....	NA	....
			Lead	7439-92-1	0.04	....	NA	....
			Nickel	7440-02-0	0.44	....	NA	....
F019	NA	Table CCWE in 268.41	Cyanides (Total)	57-12-5	1.2	....	590	(3)
			Cyanides (Amenable)	57-12-5	0.86	....	30	(3)
			Chromium (Total)	7440-47-32	0.32	....	NA	....
F024	NA	Table CCWE in 268.41 and Table 2 in 268.42 (Note: F024 organic standards must be treated via incineration (INCIN))	2-Chloro-1,3-butadiene	126-99-8	0.28	(1)	0.28	(1)
			3-Chloropropene	107-05-	0.28	(1)	0.28	(1)
			1,1-Dichloroethane	75-34-3	0.014	(1)	0.014	(1)
			1,2-Dichloroethane	107-06-2	0.014	(1)	0.014	(1)
			1,2-Dichloropropane	78-87-5	0.014	(1)	0.014	(1)
			cis-1,3-Dichloropropene	10061-01-5	0.014	(1)	0.014	(1)
			trans-1,3-Dichloropropene	10061-02-6	0.014	(1)	0.014	(1)
			Bis(2-ethylhexyl)-phthalate	117-81-7	0.036	(1)	1.8	(1)
			Hexachloroethane	67-72-1	0.036	(1)	1.8	(1)
			Chromium (Total)	7440-47-32	0.35	....	NA	....
			Nickel	7440-02-0	0.47	....	NA	....
F025 (Light Ends Sub-category)	NA	NA	Chloroform	67-66-3	0.046	(2)	6.2	(1)
			1,2-Dichloroethane	107-06-2	0.21	(2)	6.2	(1)
			1,1-Dichloroethylene	75-35-4	0.025	(2)	6.2	(1)
			Methylene chloride	75-9-2	0.089	(2)	31	(1)
			Carbon tetrachloride	56-23-5	0.057	(2)	6.2	(1)
			1,1,2-Trichloethane	79-00-5	0.054	(2)	6.2	(1)
			Trichloroethylene	79-01-6	0.054	(2)	5.6	(1)
			Vinyl chloride	75-01-4	0.27	(2)	33	(1)

Waste code	Commercial chemical name	See also	Regulated Hazardous Constituent	CAS No. for regulated hazardous constituent	Wastewaters		Nonwastewaters	
					Concentration (mg/l)	Notes	Concentration (mg/l)	Notes
F025 (Spent Filters or Acids and Desicants Subcategory)..	NA.................	NA.................	Chloroform................................	67-66-5	0.046	(2)	6.2	(1)
			Methylene chloride.................	75-9-2	0.089	(2)	31	(1)
			Carbon tetrachloride.............	56-23-5	0.057	(2)	6.2	(1)
			1,1,2-Trichloethane.................	79-00-5	0.054	(2)	6.2	(1)
			Trichloroethylene...................	79-01-6	0.054	(2)	5.6	(1)
			Vinyl chloride..........................	75-01-4	0.27	(2)	33	(1)
			Hexachlorobenzene................	118-74-1	0.055	(2)	37	(1)
			Hexachlorobutadiene.............	87-68-3	0.055	(2)	28	(1)
			Hexachoroethane....................	67-72-1	0.055	(2)	30	(1)
F039..................	NA.................	Table CCWE in 268.41.................	Acetone....................................	67-64-1	0.28	(2)	160	(1)
			Acenaphthalene......................	208-96-8	0.059	(2)	3.4	(1)
			Acenaphthene..........................	83-32-9	0.059	(2)	4.0	(1)
			Acetonitrile..............................	75-05-8	0.17	(2)	NA	....
			Acetophenone..........................	96-86-2	0.010	(2)	9.7	(1)
			2-	53-96-3	0.059	(2)	140	(1)
			Acetylaminofluorene...........	107-02-8	0.29	(2)	NA	....
			Acrolein....................................	107-13-1	0.24	(2)	84	(1)
			Acrylonitrile............................	309-00-2	0.021	(2)	0.066	(1)
			Aldrin..					
			4-Aminobiphenyl....................	92-67-1	0.13	(2)	NA	....
			Aniline......................................	62-53-3	0.81	(2)	14	(1)
			Anthracene..............................	120-12-7	0.059	(2)	4.0	(1)
			Aramite.....................................	140-57-8	0.36	(2)	NA	....
			Aroclor 1016............................	12674-11-2	0.013	(2)	0.92	(1)
			Aroclor 1221............................	11104-28-2	0.014	(2)	0.92	(1)
			Aroclor 1232............................	11141-16-5	0.013	(2)	0.92	(1)
			Aroclor 1242............................	53469-21-9	0.017	(2)	0.92	(1)
			Aroclor 1248............................	12672-29-6	0.013	(2)	0.92	(1)
			Aroclor 1254............................	11097-69-1	0.014	(2)	1.8	(1)
			Aroclor 1260............................	11096-82-5	0.014	(2)	1.8	(1)
			alpha-BHC................................	319-84-6	0.00014	(2)	0.066	(1)
			beta-BHC..................................	319-85-7	0.00014	(2)	0.066	(1)
			delta-BHC.................................	319-86-8	0.023	(2)	0.066	(1)
			gamma-BHC.............................	58-89-9	0.0017	(2)	0.066	(1)
			Benzene....................................	71-43-2	0.14	(2)	36	(1)
			Benz(a)anthracene.................	56-55-3	0.059	(2)	8.2	(1)
			Benzo(b)fluoranthene............	205-99-2	0.055	(2)	3.4	(1)
			Benzo(k)fluoranthene	207-08-9	0.059	(2)	3.4	(1)
			Benzo(g,h,i)perylene..............	191-24-2	0.0055	(2)	1.5	(1)
			Benzo(a)pyrene.......................	50-32-8	0.061	(2)	8.2	(1)
			Bromodichloromethane........	75-27-4	0.35	(2)	15	(1)
			Bromoform (Tribromo- methane).................................	75-25-2	0.63	(2)	15	(1)
			Bromomethane (methyl bromide).................................	74-83-9	0.11	(2)	15	(1)
			4-Bromophenyl phenyl ether..	101-55-3	0.055	(2)	15	(1)
			n-Butyl alcohol........................	71-36-3	5.6	(2)	2.6	(1)
			Butyl benzyl phthalate............	85-68-7	0.017	(2)	7.9	(1)
			2-sec-Butyl-4,6- dinitrophenol........................	88-85-7	0.066	(2)	2.5	(1)
			Carbon tetrachloride.............	56-23-5	0.057	(2)	5.6	(1)
			Carbon disulfide.....................	75-15-0	0.014	(2)	NA	....
			Chlordane................................	57-74-9	0.0033	(2)	0.13	(1)
			p-Chloroaniline.......................	106-47-8	0.46	(2)	16	(1)
			Chlorobenzene........................	108-90-7	0.057	(2)	5.7	(1)
			Chlorobenzilate......................	510-15-6	0.10	(2)	NA	....
			2-Chloro-1,3-butadiene...........	126-99-8	0.057	(2)	NA	....
			Chlorodibromomethane........	124-48-1	0.057	(2)	15	(1)
			Chloroethane	75-00-3	0.27	(2)	6.0	(1)

173

Waste code	Commercial chemical name	See also	Regulated Hazardous Constituent	CAS No. for regulated hazardous constituent	Wastewaters		Nonwastewaters	
					Concentration (mg/l)	Notes	Concentration (mg/l)	Notes
			bis(2-Chloroethoxy) methane................................	111-91-1	0.036	(2)	7.2	(1)
			bis(2-Chloroethyl) ether..	111-44-4	0.033	(2)	7.2	(1)
			Chloroform.................................	67-66-3	0.046	(2)	5.6	(1)
			bis(2-Chloroisopropyl) ether..	39638-32-9	0.055	(2)	7.2	(1)
			p-Chloro-m-cresol....................	59-50-7	0.018	(2)	14	(1)
			Chloromethane (Methyl chloride)...................	74-87-3.	0.19	(2)	33	(1)
			2-Chloronaphthalene.............	91-8-7	0.055	(2)	5.6	(1)
			2-Chlorophenol........................	95-57-8.	0.044	(2)	5.7	(1)
			3-Chloropropylene....................	107-05-1	0.036	(2)	28	(1)
			Chrysene....................................	218-01-9	0.059	(2)	8.2	(1)
			o-Cresol....................................	95-48-7	0.11	(2)	5.6	(1)
			Cresol (m- and p-isomers).....	....	0.77	(2)	3.2	(1)
			Cyclohexanone........................	108-94-1	0.36	(2)	N A	....
			1,2-Dibromo-3-chloropropane	96-12-8	0.11	(2)	15	(1)
			1,2-Dibromoethane (Ethylene dibromide)...............	106-93-4	0.028	(2)	15	(1)
			Dibromomethane....................	74-95-3	0.11	(2)	15	(1)
			2,4-Dichlorophenoxy acetic acid (2, 4-D).................	94-75-7	0.72	(2)	10	(1)
			o,p'-DDD...................................	53-19-0	0.023	(2)	0.087	(1)
			p,p'-DDD...................................	72-54-8	0.023	(2)	0.087	(1)
			o,p'-DDE...................................	3424-82-6	0.031	(2)	0.087	(1)
			p,p'-DDE...................................	72-55-9	0.031	(2)	0.087	(1)
			o,p'-DDT...................................	789-02-6	0.0039	(2)	0.087	(1)
			p,p'-DDT...................................	50-29-3	0.0039	(2)	0.087	(1)
			Dibenz(a,h) anthracene..........	53-70-3	0.055	(2)	8.2	(1)
			Dibenzo(a,e) pyrene...............	192-65-4	0.061	(2)	N A	....
			m-Dichlorobenzene.................	541-73-1	0.036	(2)	6.2	(1)
			o-Dichlorobenzene..................	95-50-1	0.088	(2)	6.2	(1)
			p-Dichlorobenzene..................	106-46-7	0.090	(2)	6.2	(1)
			Dichlorodifluoromethane......	75-71-8	0.23	(2)	7.2	(1)
			1,1-Dichloroethane.................	75-34-3	0.059	(2)	7.2	(1)
			1,2-Dichloroethane.................	107-06-2	0.21	(2)	7.2	(1)
			1,1-Dichloroethylene..............	75-35-4	0.025	(2)	33	(1)
			trans-1,2-Dichloroethylene....	....	0.054	(2)	33	(1)
			2,4-Dichlorophenol.................	120-83-2	0.044	(2)	14	(1)
			2,6-Dichlorophenol.................	87-65-0	0.044	(2)	14	(1)
			1,2-Dichloropropane..............	78-87-5	0.85	(2)	18	(1)
			cis-1,3-Dichloropropene........	10061-01-5	0.036	(2)	18	(1)

Waste code	Commercial chemical name	See also	Regulated Hazardous Constituent	CAS No. for regulated hazardous constituent	Wastewaters		Nonwastewaters	
					Concentration (mg/l)	Notes	Concentration (mg/l)	Notes
			trans-1,3-Dichloropropene...	10061-02-6	0.036	(2)	18	(1)
			Dieldrin.................................	60-57-1	0.017	(2)	0.13	(1)
			Diethyl phthalate....................	84-66-2	0.20	(2)	28	(1)
			2,4-Dimethyl phenol...............	105-67-9	0.036	(2)	14	(1)
			Dimethyl phthalate................	131-11-3	0.047	(2)	28	(1)
			Di-n-butyl phthalate..............	84-74-2	0.057	(2)	28	(1)
			1,4-Dinitrobenzene.................	100-25-4	0.32	(2)	2.3	(1)
			4,6-Dinitro-o-cresol...............	534-52-1	0.28	(2)	160	(1)
			2,4-Dinitrophenol..................	51-28-5	0.12	(2)	160	(1)
			2,4-Dinitrotoluene.................	121-14-2	0.32	(2)	140	(1)
			2,6-Dinitrotoluene.................	606-20-2	0.55	(2)	28	(1)
			Di-n-octyl phthalate..............	117-84-0	0.017	(2)	28	(1)
			Di-n-propylnitrosoamine......	621-64-7	0.40	(2)	14	(1)
			Diphenylamine......................	122-39-4	0.52	(2)	NA	....
			1,2-Diphenyl hydrazine........	122-66-7	0.087	(2)	NA	....
			Diphenyl nitrosamine..........	621-64-7	0.40	(2)	NA	....
			1,4-Dioxane...........................	123-91-1	0.12	(2)	170	(1)
			Disulfoton.............................	298-04-4	0.017	(2)	6.2	(1)
			Endosulfan I.........................	939-98-8	0.023	(2)	0.066	(1)
			Endosulfan II........................	33213-6-5	0.029	(2)	0.13	(1)
			Endosulfan sulfate................	1031-07-8	0.029	(2)	0.13	(1)
			Endrin....................................	72-20-8	0.0028	(2)	0.13	(1)
			Endrin aldehyde....................	7421-93-4	0.025	(2)	0.13	(1)
			Ethyl acetate.........................	141-78-6	0.34	(2)	33	(1)
			Ethyl cyanide.........................	107-12-0	0.24	(2)	360	(1)
			Ethyl benzene........................	100-41-4	0.057	(2)	6.0	(1)
			Ethyl ether............................	60-29-7	0.12	(2)	160	(1)
			bis(2-Ethylhexyl) phthalate..	117-81-7	0.28	(2)	28	(1)
			Ethyl methacrylate................	97-63-2	0.14	(2)	160	(1)
			Ethylene oxide.......................	75-21-8	0.12	(2)	NA	....
			Famphur................................	52-85-7	0.017	(2)	15	(1)
			Fluoranthene.........................	206-44-0	0.068	(2)	8.2	(1)
			Fluorene.................................	86-73-7	0.059	(2)	4.0	(1)
			Fluorotrichloromethane.......	75-69-4	0.020	(2)	33	(1)
			Heptachlor.............................	76-44-8	0.0012	(2)	0.066	(1)
			Heptachlor epoxide................	1024-57-3	0.016	(2)	0.066	(1)
			Hexachlorobenzene................	118-74-1	0.055	(2)	37	(1)
			Hexachlorobutadiene.............	87-68-3	0.055	(2)	28	(1)
			Hexachlorocyclopentadiene.	77-47-4	0.057	(2)	3.6	(1)
			Hexachlorodibenzo-furans...		0.000063	(2)	0.001	(1)
			Hexachlorodibenzo-p-dioxins...............................		0.000063	(2)	0.001	(1)
			Hexachloroethane.................	67-72-1	0.055	(2)	28	(1)
			Hexachloropropene...............	1888-71-7	0.035	(2)	28	(1)
			Indeno(1,2,3-c,d)pyrene........	193-39-5	0.0055	(2)	8.2	(1)
			Iodomethane..........................	74-86-4	0.19	(2)	65	(1)
			Isobutanol.............................	78-83-1	5.6	(2)	170	(1)
			Isodrin...................................	465-73-6	0.021	(2)	0.066	(1)
			Isosafrole..............................	120-58-1	0.081	(2)	2.6	(1)
			Kepone...................................	143-50-8	0.0011	(2)	0.13	(1)
			Methacrylonitrile..................	126-98-7	0.24	(2)	84	(1)
			Methanol................................	67-56-1	5.6	(2)	NA	....
			Methapyrilene.......................	91-80-5	0.081	(2)	1.5	(1)
			Methoxychlor.........................	72-43-5	0.25	(2)	0.18	@

175

Waste code	Commercial chemical name	See also	Regulated Hazardous Constituent	CAS No. for regulated hazardous constituent	Wastewaters Concentration (mg/l)	Notes	Nonwastewaters Concentration (mg/l)	Notes
			3-Methylcholanthrene..........	56-49-5	0.0055	(2)	15	(1)
			4,4-Methylene-bis-(2-chloro-aniline)....................	101-14-4	0.50	(2)	35	(1)
			Methylene chloride................	75-09-2	0.089	(2)	33	(1)
			Methyl ethyl ketone...............	78-93-3	0.28	(2)	36	(1)
			Methyl isobutyl ketone...........	108-10-1	0.14	(2)	33	(1)
			Methyl methacrylate..............	80-62-6	0.14	(2)	160	(1)
			Methyl methansulfonate......	66-27-3	0.018	(2)	NA	....
			Methyl parathion...................	298-00-0	0.014	(2)	4.6	(1)
			Naphthalene........................	91-20-3	0.059	(2)	3.1	(1)
			2-Naphthylamine..................	91-59-8	0.52	(2)	NA	....
			p-Nitroaniline......................	100-01-6	0.028	(2)	28	(1)
			Nitrobenzene........................	98-95-3	0.068	(2)	14	(1)
			5-Nitro-o-toluidine................	99-55-8	0.32	(2)	28	(1)
			4-Nitrophenol......................	100-02-7	0.12	(2)	29	(1)
			N-Nitrosodiethylamine.........	55-18-5	0.40	(2)	28	(1)
			N-Nitrosodimethylamine.....	62-75-9	0.40	(2)	NA	....
			N-Nitroso-di-n-butylamine...	924-16-3	0.40	(2)	17	(1)
			N-Nitrosomethylethylamine	10595-95-6	0.40	(2)	2.3	(1)
			N-Nitrosomorpholine............	59-89-2	0.40	(2)	2.3	(1)
			N-Nitrosopiperidine..............	100-75-4	0.013	(2)	35	(1)
			N-Nitrosopyrrolidine.............	930-55-2	0.013	(2)	35	(1)
			Parathion.............................	56-38-2	0.014	(2)	4.6	(1)
			Pentachlorobenzene..............	608-93-5	0.055	(2)	37	(1)
			Pentachlorodibenzo-furans..	....	0.000063	(2)	0.001	(1)
			Pentachlorodibenzo-p-dioxins...................	....	0.000063	(2)	0.001	(1)
			Pentochloronitrobenzene......	82-68-8	0.055	(2)	4.8	(1)
			Pentachlorophenol................	87-86-5	0.089	(2)	7.4	(1)
			Phenacetin...........................	62-44-2	0.081	(2)	16	(1)
			Phenanthrene.......................	85-01-8	0.059	(2)	3.1	(1)
			Phenol.................................	108-95-2	0.039	(2)	6.2	(1)
			Phorate................................	298-02-2	0.021	(2)	4.6	(1)
			Phthalic anhydride...............	85-44-9	0.069	(2)	NA	....
			Pronamide...........................	23950-58-5	0.093	(2)	1.5	(1)
			Pyrene.................................	129-00-0	0.067	(2)	8.2	(1)
			Pyridine...............................	110-86-1	0.014	(2)	16	(1)
			Safrole.................................	94-59-7	0.081	(2)	22	(1)
			Silvex(2,4,5-TP).....................	93-72-1	0.72	(2)	7.9	(1)
			2,4,5-T.................................	93-76-5	0.72	(2)	7.9	(1)
			1,2,4,5-Tetrachlorobenzene...	95-94-3	0.055	(2)	19	(1)
			Tetrachlorodibenzo-furans..	....	0.000063	(2)	0.001	(1)
			Tetrachlorodibenzo-p-dioxins...................	....	0.000063	(2)	0.001	(1)
			1,1,1,2-Tetrachloroethane......	630-20-6	0.057	(2)	42	(1)

Waste code	Commercial chemical name	See also	Regulated Hazardous Constituent	CAS No. for regulated hazardous constituent	Wastewaters		Nonwastewaters	
					Concentration (mg/l)	Notes	Concentration (mg/l)	Notes
			1,1,2,2-Tetrachloroethane.....	79-34-6	0.057	(2)	42	(1)
			Tetrachloroethylene.............	127-18-4	0.056	(2)	5.6	(1)
			2,3,4,6-Tetrachlorophenol......	58-90-2	0.030	(2)	37	(1)
			Toluene....................................	108-88-3	0.080	(2)	28	(1)
			Toxaphene...............................	8001-35-1	0.0095	(2)	1.3	(1)
			1,2,4-Trichlorobenzene...........	120-82-1	0.055	(2)	19	(1)
			1,1,1-Trichloroethane.............	71-55-6	0.054	(2)	5.6	(1)
			1,1,2-Trichloroethane.............	79-00-5	0.054	(2)	5.6	(1)
			Trichloroethylene....................	79-01-6	0.054	(2)	5.6	(1)
			2,4,5-Trichlorophenol.............	95-95-4	0.18	(2)	37	(1)
			2,4,6-Trichlorophenol.............	88-06-2	0.035	(2)	37	(1)
			1,2,3-Trichloropropane..........	96-18-4	0.85	(2)	28	(1)
			1,1,2-Trichloro-1,2,2-trifluoroethane............	76-13-1	0.057	(2)	28	(1)
			Tris (2,3-dibromopropyl) phosphate............................	126-72-7	0.11	(2)	NA	....
			Vinyl chloride........................	75-01-4	0.27	(2)	33	(1)
			Xylene(s)..............................	....	0.32	(2)	28	(1)
			Cyanides (Total).....................	57-12-5	1.2	(2)	1.8	(1)
			Fluoride..................................	16964-48-8	35	(2)	NA	....
			Sulfide....................................	8496-25-8	14	(2)	NA	....
			Antimony................................	7440-36-0	1.9	(2)	NA	....
			Arsenic...................................	7440-38-2	1.4	(2)	NA	....
			Barium....................................	7440-39-3	1.2	(2)	NA	....
			Beryllium................................	7440-41-7	0.82	(2)	NA	....
			Cadmium................................	7440-43-9	0.20	(2)	NA	....
			Chromium (Total)..................	7440-47-32	0.37	(2)	NA	....
			Copper....................................	7440-50-8	1.3	(2)	NA	....
			Lead..	7439-92-1	0.28	(2)	NA	....
			Mercury...................................	7439-97-6	0.15	(2)	NA	....
			Nickel.....................................	7440-02-0	0.55	(2)	NA	....
			Selenium.................................	7782-49-2	0.82	(2)	NA	....
			Silver......................................	7440-22-4	0.29	(2)	NA	....
			Thallium.................................	7440-28-0	1.4	(2)	NA	....
			Vanadium...............................	7440-62-2	0.042	(2)	NA	....
			Zinc..	7440-66-6	1.0	(2)	NA	....
K001..................	NA.....................	Table CCWE in 268.41.................	Naphthalene...........................	91-20-3	0.031	(1)	1.5	(1)
			Pentachlorophenol..................	87-86-5	0.18	(1)	7.4	(1)
			Phenanthrene..........................	85-01-8	0.031	(1)	1.5	(1)
			Pyrene....................................	129-00-0	0.028	(1)	1.5	(1)
			Toluene....................................	108-88-3	0.028	(1)	28	(1)
			Xylenes (Total).......................	....	0.032	(1)	33	(1)
			Lead..	7439-92-1	0.037	....	NA	....
K002..................	NA.....................	Table CCWE in 268.41.................	Chromium (Total)..................	7440-47-32	0.9	(2)	NA	....
			Lead..	7439-92-1	3.4	(2)	NA	....
K003..................	NA.....................	Table CCWE in 268.41.................	Chromium (Total)..................	7440-47-32	0.9	(2)	NA	....
			Lead..	7439-92-1	3.4	(2)	NA	....
K004..................	NA.....................	Table CCWE in	Chromium (Total)..................	7440-47-32	0.9	(2)	NA	....
		268.41.................	Lead..	7439-92-1	3.4	(2)	NA	@
K005..................	NA.....................	Table CCWE in 268.41.................	Chromium (Total)..................	7440-47-32	0.9	(2)	NA	....
			Lead..	7439-92-1	3.4	(2)	NA	....
			Cyanides (Total).....................	57-12-5	0.74	(2)	(4)	....
K006..................	NA.....................	Table CCWE in 268.41.................	Chromium (Total)..................	7440-47-32	0.9	3.4	(2)	NA
			Lead..	7439-92-1			(2)	NA
K007..................	NA.....................	Table CCWE in 268.41.................	Chromium (Total)..................	7440-47-32	0.9	(2)	NA	....
			Lead..	7439-92-1	3.4	(2)	NA	....
			Cyanides (Total).....................	57-12-5	0.74	(2)	(4)	....
K008..................	NA.....................	Table CCWE in 268.41.................	Chromium (Total)..................	7440-47-32	0.9	(2)	NA	....
			Lead..	7439-92-1	3.4	(2)	NA	....
K009..................	NA.....................	NA.....................	Chloroform............................	67-66-3	0.1	....	6.0	(1)
K010..................	NA.....................	NA.....................	Chloroform............................	67-66-3	0.1	....	6.0	(1)

177

Waste code	Commercial chemical name	See also	Regulated Hazardous Constituent	CAS No. for regulated hazardous constituent	Wastewaters		Nonwastewaters	
					Concentration (mg/l)	Notes	Concentration (mg/l)	Notes
K011	NA	NA	Acetonitrile	75-05-8	38	....	1.8	(1)
			Acrylonitrile	107-13-1	0.06	....	1.4	(1)
			Acrylamide	79-06-1	19	....	23	(1)
			Benzene	71-43-2	0.02	....	0.03	(1)
			Cyanide (Total)	57-12-5	21	....	57	....
K013	NA	NA	Acetonitrile	75-05-8	38	....	1.8	(1)
			Acrylonitrile	107-13-1	0.06	....	1.4	(1)
			Acrylamide	79-06-1	19	....	23	(1)
			Benzene	71-43-2	0.02	....	0.03	(1)
			Cyanide (Total)	57-12-5	21	....	57	....
K014	NA	NA	Acetonitrile	75-05-8	38	....	1.8	(1)
			Acrylonitrile	107-13-1	0.06	....	1.4	(1)
			Acrylamide	79-06-1	19	....	23	(1)
			Benzene	71-43-2	0.02	....	0.03	(1)
			Cyanide (Total)	57-12-5	21	....	57	....
K015	NA	Table CCWE in 268.41	Anthracene	120-12-7	1.0	....	3.4	(1)
			Benzal Chloride	98-87-3	0.28	....	6.2	(1)
			Sum of Benzo(b) fluoranthene and Benzo(k) fluoranthene	205-99-2 207-08-9	0.29	....	3.4	(1)
			Phenanthrene	85-01-8	0.27		3.4	(1)
			Toluene	108-88-3	0.15		6.0	(1)
			Chromium (Total)	7440-47-32	0.32	....	NA	....
			Nickel	7440-02-0	0.44	....	NA	....
K016	NA	NA	Hexachlorobenzene	118-74-1	0.033	(1)	28	(1)
			Hexachlorobutadiene	87-68-3	0.007	(1)	5.6	(1)
			Hexachlorocyclopentadiene	77-47-4	0.007	(1)	5.6	(1)
			Hexachloroethane	67-72-1	0.033	(1)	28	(1)
			Tetrachloroethene	127-18-4	0.007	(1)	6.0	(1)
K017	NA	NA	1,2-Dichloropropane	78-87-5	0.85	(1,2)	18	(1)
			1,2,3-Trichloropropane	96-18-4	0.85	(1,2)	28	(1)
			Bis(2-chloroethyl)ether	111-44-4	0.033	(1,2)	7.2	(1)
K018	NA	NA	Chloroethane	75-00-3	0.007	(1)	6.0	(1)
			Chloromethane	74-87-3	0.007	(1)	NA	....
			1,1-Dichloroethane	75-34-3	0.007	(1)	6.0	(1)
			1,2-Dichloroethane	107-06-2	0.007	(1)	6.0	(1)
			Hexachlorobenzene	118-74-1	0.033	(1)	28	(1)
			Hexachlorobutadiene	87-68-3	0.007	(1)	5.6	(1)
			Hexachloroethane	67-72-1	NA	....	28	(1)
			Pentachloroethane	76-01-7	0.007	(1)	5.6	(1)
			1,1,1-Trichloroethane	71-55-6	0.007	(1)	6.0	(1)
K019	NA	NA	Bis(2-chloroethyl)ether	111-44-4	0.007	(1)	5.6	(1)
			Chlorobenzene	108-90-7	0.006	(1)	6.0	(1)
			Chloroform	67-66-3	0.007	(1)	6.0	(1)
			p-Dichlorobenzene	106-46-7	0.008	(1)	NA	....
			1,2-Dichloroethane	107-06-2	0.007	(1)	6.0	(1)
			Fluorene	86-73-7	0.007	(1)	NA	....
			Hexachloroethane	67-72-1	0.033	(1)	28	(1)
			Naphthalene	91-20-3	0.007	(1)	5.6	(1)
			Phenanthrene	85-01-8	0.007	(1)	5.6	(1)
			1,2,4,5-Tetrachlorobenzene	95-94-3	0.017	(1)	NA	....
			Tetrachloroethene	127-18-4	0.007	(1)	6.0	(1)

178

Waste code	Commercial chemical name	See also	Regulated Hazardous Constituent	CAS No. for regulated hazardous constituent	Wastewaters Concentration (mg/l)	Notes	Nonwastewaters Concentration (mg/l)	Notes
			1,2,4-Trichlorobenzene..........	120-82-1	0.023	(1)	19	(1)
			1,1,1-Trichloroethane............	71-55-6	0.007	(1)	6.0	(1)
K020..................	NA..................	NA......................	1,2-Dichloroethane...............	107-06-2	0.007	(1)	6.0	(1)
			1,1,2,2-Tetrachloroethane......	79-34-6	0.007	(1)	5.6	(1)
			Tetrachloroethene................	127-18-4	0.007	(1)	6.0	(1)
K021......................	NA..................	Table CCWE in	Chloroform.........................	67-66-3	0.046	(2)	6.2	(1)
		268.41................	Carbon tetrachloride............	56-23-5	0.057	(2)	6.2	(1)
			Antimony................................	7440-36-0	0.60	(2)	NA	(1)
K022..................	NA..................	Table CCWE in	Toluene...............................	108-88-3	0.080	(2)	0.034	(1)
		268.41................	Acetophenone...................	96-86-2	0.010		19	(1)
			Diphenylamine......................	22-39-4	0.52	(2)	NA	
			Diphenylnitrosamine............	86-30-6	0.40	(2)	NA	
			Sum of Diphenylamine and Diphenylnitrosamine..........	....	NA		13	(1)
			Phenol...............................	108-95-2	0.039		12	(1)
			Chromium (Total)..................	7440-47-32	0.35		NA	
			Nickel...............................	7440-02-0	0.47		NA	
K023..................	NA..................	NA......................	Phthalic anhydride (measured as Phthalic acid)........	85-44-9	0.54	(1)	28	(1)
K024..................	NA..................	NA......................	Phthalic anhydride (measured as Phthalic acid)........	85-44-9	0.54	(1)	28	(1)
K028..................	NA..................	Table CCWE in	1,1-Dichloroethane................	75-34-3	0.007	(1)	6.0	(1)
		268.41................	trans-1,2-Dichloroethane.....	....	0.033	(1)	6.0	(1)
			Hexachlorobutadiene............	87-68-3	0.007	(1)	5.6	(1)
			Hexachloroethane................	67-72-1	0.033	(1)	28	(1)
			Pentachloroethane................	76-01-7	0.033	(1)	5.6	(1)
			1,1,1,2-Tetrachloroethane.....	630-20-6	0.007	(1)	5.6	(1)
			1,1,2,2-Tetrachloroethane......	79-34-6	0.007	(1)	5.6	(1)
			1,1,1-Trichloroethane............	71-55-6	0.007	(1)	6.0	(1)
			1,1,2-Trichloroethane............	79-00-5	0.007	(1)	6.0	(1)
			Tetrachloroethylene..............	127-18-4	0.007	(1)	6.0	(1)
			Cadmium................................	7440-43-9	6.4		NA	
			Chromium (Total)..................	7440-47-32	0.35		NA	
			Lead..................................	7439-92-1	0.037		NA	
			Nickel...............................	7440-02-0	0.47		NA	
K029..................	NA..................	NA......................	Chloroform.........................	67-66-3	0.046		6.0	(1)
			1,2-Dichloroethane...............	107-06-2	0.21		6.0	(1)
			1,1-Dichloroethylene..............	75-35-4	0.025		6.0	(1)
			1,1,1-Trichloroethane............	71-55-6	0.054		6.0	(1)
			Vinyl chloride.........................	75-01-4	0.27		6.0	(1)
K030..................	NA..................	NA......................	o-Dichlorobenzene..............	95-50-1	0.008	(1)	NA	
			p-Dichlorobenzene.................	106-46-7	0.008	(1)	NA	

Waste code	Commercial chemical name	See also	Regulated Hazardous Constituent	CAS No. for regulated hazardous constituent	Wastewaters Concentration (mg/l)	Notes	Nonwastewaters Concentration (mg/l)	Notes
			Hexachlorobutadiene	87 68 3	0.007	(1)	5.6	(1)
			Hexachloroethane	67-72-1	0.033	(1)	28	(1)
			Hexachloropropene	1888-71-7	NA	....	19	(1)
			Pentachlorobenzene	608-93-5	NA	....	28	(1)
			Pentachloroethane	76-01-7	0.007	(1)	5.6	(1)
			1,2,4,5-Tetrachlorobenzene	95-94-3	0.017	(1)	14	(1)
			Tetrachloroethene	127-18-4	0.007	(1)	6.0	(1)
			1,2,4-Trichlorobenzene	120-82-1	0.023	(1)	19	(1)
K031	NA	Table CCWE in	Arsenic	7440-38-2	0.79	....	NA	(1)
K032	NA	NA	Hexachloropentadiene	77-47-4	0.057	(2)	2.4	(1)
			Chlordane	57-74-9	0.0033	(2)	0.26	(1)
			Heptachlor	76-44-8	0.0012	(2)	0.066	(1)
			Heptachlor epoxide	1024-57-3	0.016	(2)	0.066	(1)
K033	NA	NA	Hexachlorocyclopenta-diene	77-47-4	0.057	(2)	2.4	(1)
K034	NA	NA	Hexachlorocyclopenta-diene	77-47-4	0.057	(2)	2.4	(1)
K035	NA	NA	Acenaphthene	83-32-9	NA	....	3.4	(1)
			Anthracene	120-12-7	NA	....	3.4	(1)
			Benz(a)anthracene	56-55-3	0.059	(2)	3.4	(1)
			Benzo(a)pyrene	50-32-8	NA	....	3.4	(1)
			Chrysene	218-01-9	0.059	(2)	3.4	(1)
			Dibenz(a,h)anthracene	53-70-3	NA	....	3.4	(1)
			Fluoranthene	206-44-0	0.068	(2)	3.4	(1)
			Fluorene	86-73-7	NA	....	3.4	(1)
			Indeno(1,2,3-cd)pyrene	193-39-5	NA	....	3.4	(1)
			Cresols (m- and p-isomers)	....	0.77	(2)	NA	....
			Naphthalene	91-20-3	0.059	(2)	3.4	(1)
			o-cresol	95-48-7	0.11	(2)	NA	....
			Phenanthrene	85-01-8	0.059	(2)	3.4	(1)
			Phenol	108-95-2	0.039	....	NA	....
			Pyrene	129-00-0	0.067	(2)	8-2	(1)
K036	NA	NA	Disulfoton	298-04-4	0.025	(2)	0.1	(1)
K037	NA	NA	Disulfoton	298-04-4	0.025	(2)	0.1	(1)
			Toluene	108-88-3	0.080	(2)	28	(1)
K038	NA	NA	Phorate	298-02-2	0.025	(2)	0.1	(1)
K040	NA	NA	Phorate	298-02-2	0.025	(2)	0.1	(1)
K041	NA	NA	Toxaphene	8001-35-1	0.0095	(2)	2.6	(1)
K042	NA	NA	1,2,4,5-Tetrachlorobenzene	95-94-3	0.055	(2)	4.4	(1)
			o-Dichlorobenzene	95-50-1	0.088	(2)	4.4	(1)
			p-Dichlorobenzene	106-46-7	0.090	(2)	4.4	(1)
			Pentachlorobenzene	608-93-5	0.055	(2)	4.4	(1)
			1,2,4-Trichlorobenzene	120-82-1	0.055	(2)	4.4	(1)
K043	NA	NA	2,4-Dichlorophenol	120-83-2	0.049	(1)	0.38	(1)
			2,6-Dichlorophenol	87-65-0	0.013	(1)	0.34	(1)
			2,4,5-Trichlorophenol	95-95-4	0.016	(1)	8.2	(1)
			2,4,6-Trichlorophenol	86-06-2	0.039	(1)	7.6	(1)
			Tetrachlorophenols (Total)	....	0.018	(1)	0.68	(1)

Waste code	Commercial chemical name	See also	Regulated Hazardous Constituent	CAS No. for regulated hazardous constituent	Wastewaters		Nonwastewaters	
					Concentration (mg/l)	Notes	Concentration (mg/l)	Notes
			Pentachlorophenol...............	87-86-5	0.022	(1)	1.9	(1)
			Tetrachloroethene.................	79-01-6	0.006	(1)	1.7	(1)
			Hexachlorodibenzo-p-dioxins...............	....	0.001	(1)	0.001	(1)
			Hexachlorodibenzo-furans...	....	0.001	(1)	0.001	(1)
			Pentachlorodibenzo-p-dioxins...............	....	0.001	(1)	0.001	(1)
			Pentachlorodibenzo-furans..	....	0.001	(1)	0.001	(1)
			Tetrachlorodibenzo-p-dioxins...............	....	0.001	(1)	0.001	(1)
			Tetrachlorodibenzo-furans..	....	0.001	(1)	0.001	(1)
K046.................	NA.....................	Table CCWE in 268.41.................	Lead...............................	7439-92-1	0.037	....	NA	....
K048.................	NA.....................	Table CCWE in 268.41.................	Benzene..............................	71-43-2	0.011	(1)	14	(1)
			Benzo(a)pyrene..................	50-32-8	0.047	(1)	12	(1)
			Bis(2-ethylhexyl) phthalate..	117-81-7	0.043	(1)	7.3	(1)
			Chrysene..........................	218-01-9	0.043	(1)	15	(1)
			Di-n-butyl phthalate...............	84-74-2	0.06	(1)	3.6	(1)
			Ethylbenzene.....................	100-41-4	0.011	(1)	14	(1)
			Fluorene..........................	86-73-7	0.005	(1)	NA	....
			Naphthalene.....................	91-20-3	0.033	(1)	42	(1)
			Phenanthrene....................	85-01-8	0.039	(1)	34	(1)
			Phenol............................	108-95-2	0.047	(1)	3.6	(1)
			Pyrene............................	129-00-0	0.045	(1)	36	(1)
			Toluene...........................	108-88-3	0.011	(1)	14	(1)
			Xylene(s)..........................		0.011	(1)	22	(1)
			Cyanides (Total).....................	57-12-5	0.028	(1)	1.8	(1)
			Chromium (Total).................	7440-47-32	0.2	....	NA	....
			Lead...............................	7439-92-1	0.037	....	NA	....
K049.................	NA.....................	Table CCWE in 268.41.................	Anthracene........................	120-12-7	0.039	(1)	28	(1)
			Benzene..............................	71-43-2	0.011	(1)	14	(1)
			Benzo(a)pyrene..................	50-32-8	0.047	(1)	12	(1)
			Bis(2-ethylhexyl) phthalate..	117-81-7	0.043	(1)	7.3	(1)
			Carbon disulfide..................	75-15-0	0.011	(1)	NA	....
			Chrysene..........................	2218-01-9	0.043	(1)	15	(1)
			2,4-Dimethylphenol...............	105-67-9	0.033	(1)	NA	....
			Ethylbenzene.....................	100-41-4	0.011	(1)	14	(1)
			Naphthalene.....................	91-20-3	0.033	(1)	42	(1)
			Phenanthrene....................	85-01-8	0.039	(1)	34	(1)
			Phenol............................	108-95-2	0.047	(1)	3.6	(1)
			Pyrene............................	129-00-0	0.045	(1)	36	(1)
			Toluene...........................	108-88-3	0.011	(1)	14	(1)
			Xylene(s)..........................		0.011	(1)	22	(1)
			Cyanides (Total).....................	57-12-5	0.028	(1)	1.8	(1)
			Chromium (Total).................	7440-47-32	0.2	....	NA	....
			Lead...............................	7439-92-1	0.037	(1)	NA	....
K050.................	NA.....................	Table CCWE in 268.41.................	Benzo(a)pyrene..................	50-32-8	0.047	(1)	12	(1)
			Phenol............................	108-95-2	0.047	(1)	3.6	(1)
			Cyanides (Total).....................	57-12-5	0.028	(1)	1.8	(1)
			Chromium (Total).................	7440-47-32	0.2	....	NA	....
			Lead...............................	7439-92-1	0.037	....	NA	....

181

Waste code	Commercial chemical name	See also	Regulated Hazardous Constituent	CAS No. for regulated hazardous constituent	Wastewaters Concentration (mg/l)	Notes	Nonwastewaters Concentration (mg/l)	Notes
K051	NA	Table CCWE in 268.41	Acenaphtene	208-96-8	0.05	(1)	NA	....
			Anthracene	120-12-7	0.039	(1)	28	(1)
			Benzene	71-43-2	0.011	(1)	14	(1)
			Benzo(a)anthracene	50-32-8	0.043	(1)	20	(1)
			Benzo(a)pyrene	117-81-7	0.047	(1)	12	(1)
			Bis(2-ethylhexyl) phthalate..	75-15-0	0.043	(1)	7.3	(1)
			Chrysene	2218-01-09				
			Di-n-butyl	105-67-9	0.043	(1)	15	(1)
			phthalate		0.06	(1)	3.6	(1)
			Ethylbenzene	100-41-4				
			Fluorence	86-73-7	0.011	(1)	14	(1)
			Naphthalene	91-20-3	0.05	(1)	NA	....
			Phenanthrene	85-01-8	0.033	(1)	42	(1)
			Phenol	108-95-2	0.039	(1)	34	(1)
			Pyrene	129-00-0	0.047	(1)	3.6	(1)
			Toluene	108-88-3	0.045	(1)	36	(1)
			Xylene(s)	....	0.011	(1)	14	(1)
			Cyanides (Total)	57-12-5	0.011	(1)	22	(1)
			Chromium (Total)	7440-47-32	0.028	(1)	1.8	(1)
			Lead	7439-92-1	0.2	....	NA	....
					0.037	....	NA	....
K052	NA	Table CCWE in 268.41	Benzene	71-43-2	0.011	(1)	14	(1)
			Benzo(a)pyrene	50-32-8	0.047	(1)	12	(1)
			o-Cresol	95-48-7	0.011	(1)	6.2	(1)
			p-cresol	106-44-5	0.011	(1)	6.2	(1)
			2,4-Dimethylphenol	105-67-9	0.033	(1)	NA	....
			Ethylbenzene	100-41-4	0.011	(1)	14	(1)
			Naphthalene	91-20-3	0.033	(1)	42	(1)
			Phenanthrene	85-01-8	0.039	(1)	34	(1)
			Phenol	108-95-2	0.047	(1)	3.6	(1)
			Toluene	108-88-3	0.011	(1)	14	(1)
			Xylenes	....	0.011	(1)	22	(1)
			Cyanides (Total)	57-12-5	0.028	(1)	1.8	(1)
			Chromium (Total)	7440-47-32	0.2	....	NA	....
			Lead	7439-92-1	0.037	....	NA	....
K060	NA	NA	Benzene	71-43-2	0.17	(1,2)	0.071	(1)
			Benzo(a)pyrene	50-32-8	0.035	(1,2)	3.6	(1)
			Naphthalene	91-20-3	0.028	(1,2)	3.4	(1)
			Phenol	108-95-2	0.042	(1,2)	3.4	(1)
			Cyanides (Total)	57-12-5	1.9		1.2	....
K061	NA	Table CCWE in 268.41	Cadmium	7440-43-9	1.61	....	NA	....
			Chromium (Total)	7440-47-32	0.32	....	NA	....
			Lead	7439-92-1	0.51	....	NA	....
			Nickel	7440-02-0	0.44	....	NA	....
K062	NA	Table CCWE in 268.41	Chromium (Total)	7440-47-32	0.32	....	NA	....
			Lead	7439-92-1	0.04	....	NA	....
			Nickel	7440-02-0	0.44	....	NA	....
K069	NA	Table CCWE in 268.41 and Table 2 in 268.42	Cadmium	7440-43-9	1.6	....	NA	....
			Lead	7439-92-1	0.51	....	NA	....
K071	NA	Table CCWE in 268.41	Mercury	7439-97-6	0.030	....	NA	....
K073	NA	NA	Carbon tetrachloride	56-23-5	0.057	(2)	6.2	(1)
			Chloroform	67-66-3	0.046	(2)	6.2	(1)
			Hexachloroethane	67-72-1	0.055	(2)	30	(1)
			Tetrachloroethane	127-18-4	0.056	(2)	6.2	(1)
			1,1,1-Trichloroethane	71-55-6	0.054	(2)	6.2	(1)

182

Waste code	Commercial chemical name	See also	Regulated Hazardous Constituent	CAS No. for regulated hazardous constituent	Wastewaters		Nonwastewaters	
					Concentration (mg/l)	Notes	Concentration (mg/l)	Notes
K083...............	NA.....................	Table CCWE in	Benzene....................	71-43-2	0.14	(2)	6.6	(1)
		268.41................	Aniline....................	62-53-3	0.81	....	14	(1)
			Diphenylamine........................	22-39-4	0.52	(2)	N A	....
			Diphenylnitrosamine............	86-30-6	0.40	(2)	N A	....
			Sum of Diphenylamine and Diphenylnitrosamine...	....	N A	....	14	(1)
			Nitrobenzene............................	98-95-3	0.068	(2)	14	(1)
			Phenol..	108-95-2	0.039	....	5.6	(1)
			Cyclohexanone........................	108-94-1	0.36	....	N A	....
			Nickel..	7440-02-0	0.47	....	N A	....
K084...............	NA.....................	NA.....................	Arsenic........................	7440-38-2	0.79	....	N A	....
K085...............	NA.....................	NA.....................	Benzene....................	71-43-2	0.14	(2)	4.4	(1)
			Chlorobenzene........................	108-90-7	0.057	(2)	4.4	(1)
			o-Dichlorobenzene.................	95-50-1	0.088	(2)	4.4	(1)
			m-Dichlorobenzene.................	541-73-1	0.036	(2)	4.4	@
			p-Dichlorobenzene.................	106-46-7	0.090	(2)	4.4	@
			1,2,4-Trichlorobenzene..........	120-82-1	0.055	(2)	4.4	@
			1,2,4,5-Tetrachlorobenzene...	95-94-3	0.055	(2)	4.4	@
			Pentachlorobenzene...............	608-93-5	0.055	(2)	4.4	@
			Hexachlorobenzene	118-74-1	0.055	(2)	4.4	(1)
			Aroclor 1016................	12674-11-2	0.013	(2)	0.92	(1)
			Aroclor 1221	11104-28-2	0.014	(2)	0.92	(1)
			Aroclor 1232...........................	11141-16-5	0.013	(2)	0.92	(1)
			Aroclor 1242............................	53469-21-9	0.017	(2)	0.92	(1)
			Aroclor 1248............................	12672-29-6	0.013	(2)	0.92	(1)
			Aroclor 1254...........................	11097-69-1	0.014	(2)	1.8	(1)
			Aroclor 1260...........................	11096-82-5	0.014	(2)	1.8	(1)

Waste code	Commercial chemical name	See also	Regulated Hazardous Constituent	CAS No. for regulated hazardous constituent	Wastewaters		Nonwastewaters	
					Concentration (mg/l)	Notes	Concentration (mg/l)	Notes
K086	NA	Table CCWE in	Acetone	67-64-1	0.28	....	160	(1)
		268.41	Acetophenone	96-86-2	0.010	....	9.7	(1)
			Bis(2-ethylhexyl)	117-81-7	0.28	(2)	28	(1)
			phthalate					(1)
			n-Butyl alcohol	71-36-3	5.6	....	2.6	(1)
			Butylbenzylphthalate	85-68-7	0.017	(2)	7.9	....
			Cycloghexanone	108-94-1	0.36	....	NA	(1)
			1,2-Dichlorobenzene	95-50-1	0.088	....	6.2	(1)
			Diethyl phthalate	84-66-2	0.20	(2)	28	(1)
			Dimethyl phthalate	131-11-3	0.047	(2)	28	(1)
			Di-n-butyl phthalate	84-74-2	0.057	(2)	28	(1)
			Di-n-octyl phthalate	117-84-0	0.017	(2)	28	(1)
			Ethyl acetate	141-78-6	0.34	(2)	33	(1)
			Ethylbenzene	100-41-4	0.057	(2)	6.0	....
			Methanol	67-56-1	5.6	(2)	NA	(1)
			Methyl isobutyl ketone	108-10-1	0.14	....	33	(1)
			Methyl ethyl ketone	78-93-3	0.28	....	36	(1)
			Methylene chloride	75-09-2	0.089	(2)	33	(1)
			Naphthalene	91-20-3	0.059	(2)	3.1	(1)
			Nitrobenzene	98-95-3	0.068	(2)	14	(1)
			Toluene	108-88-3	0.080	(2)	28	(1)
			1,1,1-Trichloroethane	71-55-6	0.054	(2)	5.6	(1)
			Trichloroethylene	79-01-6	0.054	(2)	5.6	(1)
			Xylenes (Total)		0.32	(2)	28	(1)
			Cyanides (Total)	57-12-5	1.9	....	1.5	....
			Chromium (Total)	7440-47-32	0.32	....	NA	....
			Lead	7439-92-1	0.037	....	NA	
K087	NA	Table CCWE in	Acenaphthalene	208-96-8	0.028	(1)	3.4	(1)
		268.41	Benzene	71-43-2	0.014	(1)	0.071	(1)
			Chrysene	218-01-9	0.028	(1)	3.4	(1)
			Fluoranthene	206-44-0	0.028	(1)	3.4	(1)
			Indeno(1,2,3-cd)pyrene	193-39-5	0.028	(1)	3.4	(1)
			Naphthalene	91-20-3	0.028	(1)	3.4	(1)
			Phenanthrene	85-01-8	0.028	(1)	3.4	(1)
			Toluene	108-88-3	0.008	(1)	0.65	(1)
			Xylenes		0.014	(1)	0.07	(1)
			Lead	7439-92-1	0.037	....	NA	....
K093	NA	NA	Phthalic anhydride (measured as Phthalic acid)	85-44-9	0.54	(1)	28	(1)
K094	NA	NA	Phthalic anhydride (measured as Phthalic acid)	85-44-9	0.54	(1)	28	(1)
K095	NA	NA	1,1,1,2-Tetrachloroethane	630-20-6	0.057	....	5.6	(1)
			1,1,2,2-Tetrachloroethane	79-34-6	0.057	....	5.6	(1)
			Tetrachloroethene	127-18-4	0.056	....	6.0	(1)
			1,1,2-Trichloroethane	79-00-5	0.054	....	6.0	(1)
			Trichloroethylene	79-01-6	0.054	....	5.6	(1)
			Hexachloroethane	67-72-1	0.055	....	28	(1)
			Pentachloroethane	76-01-7	0.055	....	5.6	(1)
K096	NA	NA	1,1,1,2-Tetrachloroethane	630-20-6	0.057	....	5.6	(1)
			1,1,2,2-Tetrachloroethane	79-34-6	0.057	....	5.6	(1)

Waste code	Commercial chemical name	See also	Regulated Hazardous Constituent	CAS No. for regulated hazardous constituent	Wastewaters		Nonwastewaters	
					Concentration (mg/l)	Notes	Concentration (mg/l)	Notes
			Tetrachloroethene...............	127-18-4	0.056	....	6.0	(1)
			1,1,2-Trichloroethane............	79-00-5	0.054	....	6.0	(1)
			Trichloroethene......................	79-01-6	0.054	....	6.6	(1)
			Trichloroethylene..................	79-01-6	0.054	....	5.6	(1)
			1,3-Dichlorobenzene..............	541-73-1	0.036	....	5.6	(1)
			Pentachloroethane.................	76-01-7	0.055	....	5.6	(1)
			1,2,4-Trichlorobenzene.........	120-82-1	0.055	....	19	(1)
K097................	NA................	NA................	Hexachlorocyclopentadiene.	77-47-4	0.057	(2)	24	(1)
			Chlordane............................	57-74-9	0.0033	(2)	0.26	(1)
			Heptachlor..........................	76-44-8	0.0012	(2)	0.066	(1)
			Heptachlor epoxide...............	1024-57-3	0.016	(2)	0.066	(1)
K098................	NA................	NA................	Toxaphene..........................	8001-35-1	0.0095	(2)	2.6	(1)
K099................	NA................	NA................	2,4-Dichlorophenoxyacetic acid................	94-75-7	1.0	(1)	1.0	(1)
			Hexachlorodibenzo-p dioxins................	....	0.001	(1)	0.001	(1)
			Hexachlorodibenzofurans..	....	0.001	(1)	0.001	(1)
			Pentachlorodibenzo-p-dioxins................	....	0.001	(1)	0.001	(1)
			Pentachlorodibenzofurans...	....	0.001	(1)	0.001	(1)
			Tetrachlorodibenzo-p-dioxins	....	0.001	(1)	0.001	(1)
			Tetrachlorodibenzofurans...	....	0.001	(1)	0.001	(1)
K100................	NA................	Table CCWE in 268.41................	Cadmium............................	7440-43-9	1.6	....	NA	....
			Chromium (Total)..................	7440-47-32	0.32	....	NA	....
			Lead...................................	7439-92-1	0.51	....	NA	....
K101................	NA................	NA................	o-Nitroaniline......................		0.27	(1)	14	(1)
			Arsenic...............................	7440-38-2	0.79	....	NA	....
			Cadmium............................	7440-43-9	0.24	....	NA	....
			Lead...................................	7439-92-1	0.17	....	NA	....
			Mercury..............................	7439-97-6	0.082	....	NA	....
K102................	NA................	Table CCWE in 268.41................	o-Nitrophenol......................		0.028	(1)	13	(1)
			Arsenic...............................	7440-38-2	0.79	....	NA	....
			Cadmium............................	7440-43-9	0.24	....	NA	....
			Lead...................................	7439-92-1	0.17	....	NA	....
			Mercury..............................	7439-97-6	0.082	....	NA	....
K103................	NA................	NA................	Aniline................................	62-53-3	4.5	....	5.6	(1)
			Benzene..............................	71-43-2	0.15	....	6.0	(1)
			2,4-Dinitrophenol..................	51-28-5	0.61	....	5.6	(1)
			Nitrobenzene.......................	98-95-3	0.073	....	5.6	(1)
			Phenol................................	108-95-2	1.4	....	5.6	(1)
K104................	NA................	NA................	Aniline................................	62-53-3	4.5	....	5.6	(1)
			Benzene..............................	71-43-2	0.15	....	6.0	(1)
			2,4-Dinitrophenol..................	51-28-5	0.61	....	5.6	(1)
			Nitrobenzene.......................	98-95-3	0.073	....	5.6	(1)
			Phenol................................	108-95-2	1.4	....	5.6	(1)
			Cyanides (Total)....................	57-12-5	2.7	....	1.8	(1)
K105................	NA................	NA................	Benzene..............................	71-43-2	0.14	....	4.4	(1)
			Chlorobenzene.....................	108-90-7	0.057	....	4.4	(1)
			o-Dichlorobenzene................	95-50-1	0.088	....	4.4	(1)
			p-Dichlorobenzene................	106-46-7	0.090	....	4.4	(1)
			2,4,5-Trichlorophenol............	95-95-4	0.18	....	4.4	(1)
			2,4,6-Trichlorophenol............	88-06-2	0.035	....	4.4	(1)
			2-Chlorophenol.....................	95-57-8	0.044	....	4.4	(1)
			Phenol................................	08-95-2	0.039	....	4.4	(1)

Waste code	Commercial chemical name	See also	Regulated Hazardous Constituent	CAS No. for regulated hazardous constituent	Wastewaters Concentration (mg/l)	Notes	Nonwastewaters Concentration (mg/l)	Notes
K106	NA	Table CCWE in 268.41 and Table 2 in 268.42	Mercury	7439-97-6	0.030	....	NA	....
K115	NA	Table CCWE in 268.41	Nickel	7440-02-0	0.47	....	NA	....
P004	Aldrin	NA	Aldrin	309-00-2	0.021	(2)	0.066	(1)
P010	Arsenic acid	Table CCWE in 268.41	Arsenic	7440-38-2	0.79	....	NA	....
P011	Arsenic pentoxide	Table CCWE in 268.41	Arsenic	7440-38-2	0.79	....	NA	....
P012	Arsenic trioxide	Table CCWE in 268.41	Arsenic	7440-38-2	0.79	....	NA	....
P013	Barium cyanide	Table CCWE in 268.41	Cyanides (Total)	57-12-5	1.9	....	110	....
			Cyanides (Amenable)	57-12-5	0.1	....	9.1	....
P020	2-sec-Butyl-4,6-dinitrophenol (Dinoseb)	NA	2-sec-Butyl-4,6-dinitrophenol (Dinoseb)	88-85-7	0.066	....	2.5	(1)
P021	Calcium cyanide	NA	Cyanides (Total)	57-12-5	1.9	....	110	....
			Cyanides (Amenable)	57-12-5	0.1	....	9.1	....
P022	Carbon disulfide	Table 2 in 268.42	Carbon disulfide	75-15-0	0.014	....	NA	....
P024	p-Chloroaniline	NA	p-Chloroaniline	106-47-8	0.46	....	16	(1)
P029	Copper cyanide	NA	Cyanides (Total)	57-12-5	1.9	....	110	....
			Cyanides (Amenable)	57-12-5	0.1	....	9.1	....
P030	Cyanides (soluble salts & complexes)	NA	Cyanides (Total)	57-12-5	1.9	....	110	....
			Cyanides (Amenable)	57-12-5	0.1	....	9.1	....
P036	Dichloro-phenylarsine	Table CCWE in 268.41	Arsenic	7440-38-2	0.79	....	NA	....
P037	Dieldrin	NA	Dieldrin	60-57-1	0.017	(2)	0.13	(1)
P038	Diethylarsine	Table CCWE in 268.41	Arsenic	7440-38-2	0.79	....	NA	....
P039	Disulfoton	NA	Disulfoton	298-04-4	0.017	....	0.1	(1)
P047	4,6-Dinitro-o-cresol	NA	4,6-Dinitro-o-cresol	534-52-1	0.28	(2)	160	(1)
P048	2,4-Dinitrophenol	NA	2,4-Dinitrophenol	51-28-5	0.12	(2)	160	(1)
P050	Endosulfan	NA	Endosulfan I	939-98-8	0.023	(2)	0.066	(1)
			Endosulfan II	33213-6-5	0.029	(2)	0.13	(1)
			Endosulfan sulfate	1031-07-8	0.029	(2)	0.13	(1)
P051	Endrin	NA	Endrin	72-20-8	0.0028	(2)	0.13	(1)
			Endrin aldehyde	7421-93-4	0.025	(2)	0.13	(1)
P056	Fluoride	Table 2 in 268.42	Fluoride	16964-48-8	35	....	NA	....
P059	Heptachlor	NA	Heptachlor	76-44-8	0.0012	(2)	0.066	(1)
			Heptachlor epoxide	1024-57-3	0.016	(2)	0.066	(1)
P060	Isodrin	NA	Isodrin	465-73-6	0.021	(2)	0.066	(1)
P063	Hydrogen cyanide	NA	Cyanides (Total)	57-12-5	1.9	....	110	....
			Cyanides (Amenable)	57-12-5	0.1	....	9.1	....
P065	Mercury fulminate	Table CCWE in 268.41 and Table 2 in 268.42	Mercury	7439-97-6	0.030	....	NA	....
P071	Methyl parathion	NA	Methyl parathion	298-00-0	0.025	....	0.1	(1)
P073	Nickel carbonyl	Table CCWE in 268.41	Nickel	7440-02-0	0.32	....	NA	....
P074	Nickel cyanide	Table CCWE in 268.41	Cyanides (Total)	57-12-5	1.9	....	110	....
			Cyanides (Amenable)	57-12-5	0.1	....	9.1	....
			Nickel	7440-02-0	0.44	....	NA	....
P077	p-Nitroaniline	NA	p-Nitroaniline	100-01-6	0.028	(2)	28	(1)
P082	N-Nitrosodimethylamine	Table 2 in 268.42	N-Nitrosodimethylamine	62-75-9	0.40	(2)	NA	....
P089	Parathion	NA	Parathion	56-38-2	0.025	....	0.1	(1)
P092	Phenylmercury acetate	Table CCWE in 268.41 and Table 2 in 268.42	Mercury	7439-97-6	0.030	....	NA	....
P094	Phorate	NA	Phorate	298-02-2	0.025	....	0.1	(1)
P097	Famphur	NA	Famphur	52-85-7	0.025	....	0.1	(1)
P098	Potassium cyanide	NA	Cyanides (Total)	57-12-5	1.9	....	110	....
			Cyanides (Amenable)	57-12-5	0.10	....	9.1	....

Waste code	Commercial chemical name	See also	Regulated Hazardous Constituent	CAS No. for regulated hazardous constituent	Wastewaters Concentration (mg/l)	Notes	Nonwastewaters Concentration (mg/l)	Notes
P099	Potassium silver cyanide	Table CCWE in 268.41	Cyanides (Total)	57-12-5	1.9	....	110	....
			Cyanides (Amenable)	57-12-5	0.1	....	9.1	....
			Silver	7440-22-4	0.29	....	NA	....
P101	Ethyl cyanide	NA	Ethyl Cyanide (Propane-nitrile)	107-12-0	0.24	(2)	360	(1)
P103	Selenourea	Table CCWE in 268.41	Selenium	7782-49-2	1.0	(2)	NA	....
P104	Silver cyanide	Table CCWE in 268.41	Cyanides (Total)	57-12-5	1.9	....	110	....
			Cyanides (Amenable)	57-12-5	0.10	....	9.1	....
			Silver	7440-22-4	0.29	....	NA	....
P106	Sodium cyanide	NA	Cyanides (Total)	57-12-5	1.9	....	110	....
			Cyanides (Amenable)	57-12-5	0.10	....	9.1	....
P110	Tetraethyl lead	Table CCWE in 268.41 and Table 2 in 268.42	Lead	7439-92-1	0.040	....	NA	....
P113	Thallic oxide	Table 2 in 268.42	Thallium	7440-28-0	0.14	(2)	NA	....
P114	Thallium selenite	Table CCWE in 268.41	Selenium	7782-49-2	1.0	....	NA	....
P115	Thallium(I)-sulfate	Table 2 in 268.42	Thallium	7440-28-0	0.14	(2)	NA	....
P119	Ammonia vandate	Table 2 in 268.42	Vanadium	7440-62-2	28	(2)	NA	....
P120	Vanadium pentoxide	Table 2 in 268.42	Vanadium	7440-62-2	28	(2)	NA	....
P121	Zinc cyanide	NA	Cyanides (Total)	57-12-5	1.9	....	110	....
			Cyanides (Amenable)	57-12-5	0.10	....	9.1	....
P123	Toxaphene	NA	Toxaphene	8001-35-1	0.0095	(2)	1.3	(1)
U002	Acetone	NA	Acetone	67-64-1	0.28	....	160	(1)
U003	Acetonitrile	Table 2 in 268.42	Acetonitrile	75-05-8	0.17	....	0.17	....
U004	Acetophenone	NA	Acetophenone	98-86-2	0.010	(1)	9.7	(1)
U005	2-Acetylamino-fluorene	NA	2-Acetylaminofluorene	53-96-3	0.059	(2)	140	(1)
U009	Acrylonitrile	NA	Acrylonitrile	107-13-1	0.24	(2)	84	(1)
U012	Aniline	NA	Aniline	62-53-3	0.81	....	14	(1)
U018	Benz(a)-anthracene	NA	Benz(a)anthracene	56-55-3	0.059	(2)	8.2	(1)
U019	Benzene	NA	Benzene	71-43-2	0.14	(2)	36	(1)
U022	Benzo(a)pyrene	NA	Benzo(a)pyrene	50-32-8	0.061	(2)	8.2	(1)
U024	Bis(2-chloroethoxy) methane	NA	Bis(2-chloroethoxy) methane	111-91-1	0.036	....	7.2	(1)
U025	Bis(2-chloroethyl) ether	NA	Bis(2-chloroethyl) ether	111-44-4	0.033	....	7.2	(1)
U027	Bis(2-chloroisopropyl)	NA	Bis(2-chloroisopropyl) ether	39638-32-9	0.055	(2)	7.2	(1)
U028	Bis(2-ethylhexyl) phthalate	NA	Bis(2-ethylhexyl) phthalate	117-81-7	0.54	(1)	28	(1)
U029	Bromomethane (Methyl bromide)	NA	Bromomethane (Methyl Bromice)	74-83-9	0.11	(1)	15	(1)
U030	4-Bromophenyl phenyl ether	NA	4-Bromophenyl phenyl ether	101-55-3	0.055	(1)	15	(1)
U031	n-Butyl alcohol	NA	n-Butyl alcohol	71-36-3	5.6	....	2.6	(1)
U032	Calcium chromate	Table CCWE in 268.41	Chromium (Total)	7440-47-32	0.32	....	NA	....
U036	Chlordane (alpha and gamma)	NA	Chlordane (alpha and gamma)	57-74-9	0.0033	(2)	0.13	(1)
U037	Chlorobenzene	NA	Chlorobenzene	108-90-7	0.057	(2)	5.7	(1)
U038	Chlorobenzilate	Table 2 in 268.42	Chlorobenzilate	510-15-6	0.10	(2)	NA	....
U039	p-Chloro-m-cresol	NA	p-Chloro-m-cresol	59-50-7	0.018	(2)	14	(1)
U042	2-Chloroethyl vinyl	Table 2 in 268.42	2-Chloroethyl vinyl	110-75-8	0.057	....	NA	....
U043	Vinyl chloride	NA	Vinyl chloride	75-01-4	0.27	(2)	33	(1)
U044	Chloroform	NA	Chloroform	67-66-3	0.046	(2)	5.6	(1)
U045	Chloromethane (Methyl chloride)	NA	Chloromethane (Methyl chloride)	74-87-3	0.19	(2)	33	(1)
U047	2-Chloro-naphthalene	NA	2-Chloro-naphthalene	91-58-7	0.055	(2)	5.6	@
U048	2-Chlorophenol	NA	2-Chlorophenol	95-57-8	0.044	(2)	5.7	@
U050	Chrysene	NA	Chrysene	218-01-9	0.059	(2)	8.2	(1)

187

Waste code	Commercial chemical name	See also	Regulated Hazardous Constituent	CAS No. for regulated hazardous constituent	Wastewaters		Nonwastewaters	
					Concentration (mg/l)	Notes	Concentration (mg/l)	Notes
U051	Creosote	Table CCWE in 268.41	Naphthalene	91-20-3	0.031		1.5	(1)
			Pentachlorophenol	87-86-5	0.18		7.4	(1)
			Phenanthrene	85-01-8	0.031		1.5	(1)
			Pyrene	129-00-0	0.028		1.5	(1)
			Toluene	108-88-3	0.028		28	(1)
			Xylenes (Total)		0.032		33	(1)
			Lead	7439-92-1	0.037		NA	
U052	Cresols (Cresylic acid)	NA	o-Cresol	95-48-7	0.11	(2)	5.6	(1)
			Cresols (m- and p- isomers)		0.77	(2)	3.2	(1)
U057	Cyclohexanone	Table 2 in 268.42	Cyclohexanone	108-94-1	0.36		NA	
U060	DDD	NA	o,p'-DDD	53-19-0	0.023		0.087	(1)
			p,p'-DDD	72-54-8	0.023		0.087	(1)
U061	DDT	NA	o,p'-DDT	789-02-6	0.0039	(2)	0.087	(1)
			p,p'-DDT	50-29-3	0.0039	(2)	0.087	(1)
			o,p'-DDD	53-19-0	0.023	(2)	0.087	(1)
			p,p'-DDD	72-54-8	0.023	(2)	0.087	(1)
			o,p'-DDE	3424-82-6	0.031	(2)	0.087	(1)
			p,p'-DDE	72-55-9	0.031	(2)	0.087	(1)
U063	Dibenzo(a,h) anthracene	NA	Dibenzo(a,h)anthracene	53-70-3	0.055	(2)	8.2	(1)
U066	1,2-Dibromo-3-chloropropane	NA	1,2-Dibromo-3-chloropropane	96-12-8	0.11	(2)	15	(1)
U067	1,2-Dibromo ethane (Ethylene dibromide)	NA	1,2-Dibromoethane (Ethylene dibromide)	106-93-4	0.028	(2)	15	(1)
U068	Dibromomethane	NA	Dibromomethane	74-95-3	0.11	(2)	15	(1)
U069	Di-n-butyl phthalate	NA	Di-n-butyl phthalate	84-74-2	0.54	(1)	28	(1)
U070	o-Dichlorobenzene	NA	o-Dichlorobenzene	95-50-1	0.088	(2)	6.2	(1)
U071	m-Dichlorobenzene	.NA	m-Dichlorobenzene	541-73-1	0.036		6.2	(1)
U072	p-Dichloro benzene	NA	p-Dichlorobenzene	104-46-7	0.090	(2)	6.2	(1)
U075	Dichlorodifluoromethane	NA	Dichlorodifluoromethane	75-71-8	0.23	(2)	7.2	(1)
U076	1,1-Dichloroethane	NA	1,1-Dichloroethane	75-34-3	0.059	(2)	7.2	(1)
U077	1,2-Dichloroethane	NA	1,2-Dichloroethane	107-06-2	0.21	(2)	7.2	(1)
U078	1,1-Dichloroethylene	NA	1,1-Dichloroethylene	75-34-4	0.025	(2)	33	(1)
U079	1,2-Dichloroethylene	NA	trans-1,2-Dichloroethylene	156-60-5	0.054	(2)	33	(1)
U080	Methylene chloride	NA	Methylene chloride	@	0.089	(2)	33	(1)
U081	2,4-Dichlorophenol	NA	2,4-Dichlorophenol	120-83-2	0.044	(2)	14	(1)
U082	2,6-Dichlorophenol	NA	2,6-Dichlorophenol	87-65-0	0.044	(2)	14	(1)
U083	1,2-Dichloropropane	NA	1,2-Dichloropropane	78-87-5	0.85	(2)	18	(1)
U084	1,3-Dichloropropene	NA	cis-1,3-Dichloropropylene	@	0.036	(2)	18	(1)
			trans-1,3 Dichloropropylene	10061-02-6	0.036	(2)	18	(1)
U088	Diethyl phthalate	NA	Diethyl phthalate	84-66-2	0.54	(2)	28	(1)
U093	p-Dimethylaminoazobenzene	Table 2 in 268.42	p-Dimethylaminoazobenzene	60-11-7	0.13	(2)	NA	
U101	2,4-Dimethylphenol	NA	2,4-Dimethylphenol	105-67-9	0.036	(2)	14	(1)
U102	Dimethyl phthalate	NA	Dimethyl phthalate	131-11-3	0.54	(1)	28	(1)
U105	2,4-Dinitrotoluene	NA	2,4-Dinitrotoluene	121-14-2	0.32	(2)	140	(1)
U106	2,6-Dinitrotoluene	NA	2,6-Dinitrotoluene	606-20-2	0.55	(2)	28	(1)

Waste code	Commercial chemical name	See also	Regulated Hazardous Constituent	CAS No. for regulated hazardous constituent	Wastewaters Concentration (mg/l)	Notes	Nonwastewaters Concentration (mg/l)	Notes
U107	Di-n-octyl phthalate	NA	Di-n-octyl phthalate	117-84-0	0.54	(1)	228	(1)
U108	1,4-Dioxane	NA	1,4-Dioxane	123-91-1	0.12	(2)	170	(1)
U111	Di-n-propyl-nitrosoamine	NA	Di-n-propylnitrosoamine	621-64-7	0.40	(2)	14	(1)
U112	Ethyl acetate	NA	Ethyl acetate	141-78-6	0.34	(2)	33	(1)
U117	Ethyl ether	NA	Ethyl ether	60-29-7	0.12	(2)	160	(1)
U118	Ethyl methacrylate	NA	Ethyl methacrylate	97-63-2	0.14	(2)	160	(1)
U120	Fluoranthene	NA	Fluoranthene	206-44-0	0.068	(2)	8.2	(1)
U121	Trichloromono-flouromethane	NA	Trichloromonofluoro-methane	75-69-4	0.020	(2)	33	(1)
U127	Hexachloro-benzene	NA	Hexachlorobenzene	118-74-1	0.055	(2)	37	(1)
U128	Hexachloro-butadiene	NA	Hexachlorobutadiene	87-68-3	0.055	(2)	28	(1)
U129	Lindane	NA	alpha-BHC	319-84-6	0.00014	(2)	0.66	(1)
			beta-BHC	319-85-7	0.00014	(2)	0.66	(1)
			Delta-BHC	319-86-8	0.023	(2)	0.66	(1)
			gamma-BHC (Lindane)	58-89-9	0.0017	(2)	0.66	(1)
U130	Hexachlorocy-clopentadiene	NA	Hexachlorocyclopentadiene	77-47-7	0.057	(2)	3.6	(1)
U131	Hexachloro-ethane	NA	Hexachloroethane	67-72-1	0.055	(2)	28	(1)
U134	Hydrogen fluoride	Table 2 in 268.42	Fluoride	16964-48-8	35	....	NA	....
U136	Cacodylic acid	Table CCWE in 268.41	Arsenic	7440-38-2	0.79	....	NA	....
U137	Indeno(1,2,3-c,d)pyrene	NA	Indeno(1,2,3-c,d)pyrene	193-39-5	0.0055	(2)	8.2	(1)
U138	Iodomethane	NA	Iodomethane	74-88-4	0.19	(2)	65	(1)
U140	Isobutyl alcohol	NA	Isobutyl alcohol	78-83-1	5.6	....	170	(1)
U141	Isosafrole	NA	Isosafrole	120-58-1	0.081	....	2.6	(1)
U142	Kepone	NA	Kepone	143-50-8	0.0011	....	0.13	(1)
U144	Lead acetate	Table CCWE in 268.41	Lead	7439-92-1	0.040	....	NA	....
U145	Lead phosphate	Table CCWE in 268.41	Lead	7439-92-1	0.040	....	NA	....
U146	Lead subacetate	Table CCWE in 268.41	Lead	7439-92-1	0.040	....	NA	....
U151	Mercury	Table CCWE in 268.41 and Table 2 in 268.42	Mercury	7439-97-6	0.030	....	NA	....
U152	Methacrylo-nitrile	NA	Methacrylonitrile	126-98-7	0.24	(2)	84	(1)
U154	Methanol	NA	Methanol	67-56-1	5.6	....	NA	....
U155	Methapyrilene	NA	Methapyrilene	91-80-5	0.081	....	1.5	(1)
U157	3-Methylchol-anthrene	NA	3-Methylcholanthrene	56-49-5	0.0055	(2)	15	(1)
U158	4,4'-Methylene-bis(2-chloro-aniline)	NA	4,4'-Methylene-bis(2-chloroaniline)	@	0.50	(2)	35	@
U159	Methyl ethyl ketone	NA	Methyl ethyl ketone	@	0.28	....	36	@
U161	Methyl isobutyl ketone	NA	Methyl isobutyl ketone	@	0.14	....	@	@
U162	Methyl metha-crylate	NA	Methyl methacrylate	@	0.14	....	@	@
U165	Naphthalene	NA	Naphthalene	91-20-3	0.059	(2)	@	@
U168	2-Naphthyla-mine	Table 2 in 268.42	2-Naphthylamine	91-59-8	0.52	(2)	NA	....
U169	Nitrobenzene	NA	Nitrobenzene	98-95-3	0.068	(2)	@	@
U170	4-Nitrophenol	NA	4-Nitrophenol	@	0.12	(2)	@	@
U172	n-Nitrosodi-n-butylamine	NA	n-Nitrosodi-n-butylamine	@	0.40	(2)	@	@
U174	N-Nitrosodie-thylamine	NA	N-Nitrosodiethylamine	@	0.40	(2)	@	@
U179	N-Nitrosopi-pendine	NA	n-Nitrosopipendine	@	0.013	(2)	@	@
U180	N-Nitroso-pyrrolidine	NA	n-Nitrosopyrrolidine	930-55-2	0.013	(2)	35	(1)
U181	5-Nitro-o-toluidine	NA	5-Nitro-o-toluidine	99-55-8	0.32	(2)	28	(1)
U183	Pentachloro-benzene	NA	Pentachlorobenzene	608-93-5	0.055	(2)	37	(1)

Waste code	Commercial chemical name	See also	Regulated Hazardous Constituent	CAS No. for regulated hazardous constituent	Wastewaters		Nonwastewaters	
					Concentration (mg/l)	Notes	Concentration (mg/l)	Notes
U185	Pentachloro-nitrobenzene	NA	Pentachloronitrobenzene	82-68-8	0.055	(2)	4.8	(1)
U187	Phenacetin	NA	Phenacetin	62-44-2	0.081		16	(1)
U188	Phenol	NA	Phenol	108-95-2	0.039		6.2	(1)
U190	Phthalic anhy-dride (meas-ured as Phth-alic acid)	NA	Phthalic anhydride (measured as Phthalic acid)	85-44-9	0.54	(1)	28	(1)
U192	Pronamide	NA	Pronamide	23950-58-5	0.093		1.5	(1)
U196	Pyridine	NA	Pyridine	110-86-1	0.014	(2)	16	(1)
U203	Safrole	NA	Safrole	94-59-7	0.081		22	(1)
U204	Selenium dioxide	Table CCWE in 268.41	Selenium	7782-49-2	1.0		NA	
U205	Selenium sulfide	Table CCWE in 268.41	Selenium	7782-49-2	1.0		NA	
U207	1,2,4,5-Tetra-chlorobenzene	NA	1,2,4,5-Tetrachlorobenzene	95-94-3	0.055	(2)	19	(1)
U208	1,1,1,2-Tetra-chloroethane	NA	1,1,1,2-Tetrachloroethane	630-20-6	0.057		42	(1)
U209	1,1,2,2-Tetra-chloroethane	NA	1,1,2,2-Tetrachloroethane	79-34-5	0.057	(2)	42	(1)
U210	Tetrachloro-ethylene	NA	Tetrachloroethylene	127-18-4	0.056	(2)	5.6	(1)
U211	Carbon tetrachloride	NA	Carbon tetrachloride	56-23-5	0.057	(2)	5.6	(1)
U214	Thallium(I)-acetate	Table 2 in 268.42	Thallium	7440-28-0	0.14	(2)	NA	
U215	Thallium(I)-carbonate	Table 2 in 268.42	Thallium	7440-28-0	0.14	(2)	NA	
U216	Thallium(I)-chloride	Table 2 in 268.42	Thallium	7440-28-0	0.14	(2)	NA	
U217	Thallium(I)-nitrate	Table 2 in 268.42	Thallium	7440-28-0	0.14	(2)	NA	
U220	Toluene	NA	Toluene	108-88-3	0.080	(2)	28	(1)
U225	Tribromo-methane (Bromoform)	NA	Tribromomethane (Bromoform)	75-25-2	0.63	(2)	15	(1)
U226	1,1,1-Trichloro-ethane	NA	1,1,1-Trichloroethane	71-55-6	0.054	(2)	5.6	(1)
U227	1,1,2-Trichloro-ethane	NA	1,1,2-Trichloroethane	79-00-5	0.054	(2)	5.6	(1)
U228	Trichloro-ethylene	NA	Trichloroethylene	79-01-6	0.054	(2)	5.6	(1)
U235	tris-(2,3-Dibro-mopropyl)-phosphate	NA	tris-(2,3-Dibromopropyl)-phosphate	126-72-7	0.025		0.10	(1)
U239	Xylenes	NA	Xylenes		0.32	(2)	28	(1)
U240	2,4-Dichloro-phenoxyacetic acid	NA	2,4-Dichlorophenoxyacetic acid	94-75-7	0.72		10	(1)
U243	Hexachloro-propene	NA	Hexachloropropene	1888-71-7	0.035	(2)	28	
U247	Methoxychlor	NA	Methoxychlor	72-43-5	0.25	(2)	0.18	(1)

1 Treatment standards for this organic constituent were established based upon incineration in units operated in accordance with the technical requirements of 40 CFR Part 264 Subpart O or Part 265 Subpart O, or based upon combustion in fuel substitution units operating in accordance with applicable technical requirements. A facility may certify compliance with these treatment standards according to provisions in 40 CFR Section 268.7.

2 Based on analysis of composite samples.

3 As analyzed using SW-846 Method 9010 or 9012; sample size 10 gram; distillation time: one hour and fifteen minutes.

4 Reserved.

Note: NA means Not Applicaable.

@ means original copy was not readable.

NO LAND DISPOSAL for:

K005 Nonwastewaters generated by the process described in the waste listing description, and disposed after June 8, 1989, and not generated in the course of treating wastewater forms of these wastes. (Based on No Generation)

K007 Nonwastewaters generated by the process described in the waste listing description, and disposed after June 8, 1989, and not generated in the course of treating wastewater forms of these wastes. (Based on No Generation)

K021 Nonwastewater forms of these wastes generated by the process described in the waste listing description and disposed after August 17, 1988, and not generated in the course of treating wastewater forms of these wastes (Based on No Generation)

K025 Nonwastewater forms of these wastes generated by the process described in the waste listing description and disposed after August 17, 1988, and not generated in the course of treating wastewater forms of these wastes (Based on No Generation)

K036 Nonwastewater forms of these wastes generated by the process described in the waste listind description and disposed after August 17, 1988, and not generated in the course of treating wastewater forms of these wastes (Based on No Generation)

K044 (Based on Reactivity)

K045 (Based on Reactivity)

K047 (Based on Reactivity)

K060 Nonwastewater forms of these wastes generated by the process described in the waste listing description and disposed after August 17, 1988, and not generated in the course of treating wastewater forms of these wastes (Based on No Generation)

K061 Nonwastewaters -- High Zinc Subcategory (greater than or equal to 15% total zinc) (Based on No Generation)

K069 Non-Calcium Sulfate Subcategory Nonwastewater forms of those wastes generated by the process described in the waste listing description and disposed after August 17, 1988, and not generated in the course of treating wastewater forms of these wastes (Based on Recycling)

K100 Nonwastewater forms of those wastes generated by the process described in the waste listing description and disposed after August 17, 1988, and not generated in the course of treating wastewater forms of these wastes (Based on No Generation)

(b) When wastes with differing treatment standards for a constituent of concern are combined for purposes of treatment, the treatment residue must meet the lowest treatment standard for the constituent of concern.

(c) Nonwithstanding the prohibi-tions specified in paragraph (a) of this section, treatment and disposal facilities may demonstrate (and certify pursuant to §268.7(b)(5)) compliance with the treatment standards for organic constituents specified by a footnote in Table CCW in this section, provided the following conditions are satisfied:

(1) The treatment standards for the organic constituents were established based on incineration in units operated in accordance with the technical requirements of 40 CFR subpart 264, subpart O, or part 265, subpart O, or based on combustion in fuel substitution units operating in accordance with applicable technical requirements;

(2) The treatment or disposal facility has used the methods referenced in paragraph (c)(1) of this section to treat the organic constituents; and

(3) The treatment or disposal facility has been unable to detect the organic constituents despite using its best goodfaith efforts as defined by applicable Agency guidance standards. Until such guidance or standards are developed, the treatment or disposal facility may demonstrate such good-faith efforts by achieving detection limits for the regulated organic constituents that do not exceed an order of magnitude of the treatment standards specified in this section.

§ 268.44 Variance from a treatment standard.

(a) Where the treatment standard is expressed as a concentration in a waste or waste extract and a waste cannot be treated to the specified level, or where the treatment technology is not appropriate to the waste, the generator or treatment facility may petition the Administrator for a variance from the treatment standard. The petitioner must demonstrate that because the physical or chemical properties of the waste differs significantly from wastes analyzed in developing the treatment standard, the waste cannot be treated to specified levels or by the specified methods.

(b) Each petition must be submitted in accordance with the procedures in §260.20.

(c) Each petition must include the following statement signed by the petitioner or an authorized representative:

I certify under penalty of law that I have personally examined and am familiar with the information submitted in this petition and all attached documents, and that, based on my inquiry of those individuals immediately responsible for obtaining the information, I believe that the submitted information is true, accurate, and complete. I am aware that these are significant penalties for submitting false information, including the possibility of fine and imprisonment.

(d) After receiving a petition for variance from a treatment standard, the Administrator may request any additional information or samples which he may require to evaluate the petition. Additional copies of the complete petition may be requested as needed to send to affected states and Regional Offices.

(e) The Administrator will give public notice in the FEDERAL REGISTER of the intent to approve or deny a petition and provide an opportunity for public comment. The final decision on a variance from a treatment standard will be published in the FEDERAL REGISTER.

(f) A generator, treatment facility, or disposal facility that is managing a waste covered by a variance from the treatment standards must comply with the waste analysis requirements for restricted wastes found under §268.7.

(g) During the petition review process, the applicant is required to comply with all restrictions on land disposal under this part once the effective date for the waste has been reached.

(h) Where the treatment standard is expressed as a concentration in a waste or waste extract and a waste generated under conditions specific to only one site cannot be treated to the specified level, or where the treatment technology is not appropriate to the waste, the generator or treatment facility may apply to the Administrator, or his delegated representative, for a site-specific variance from a treatment standard. The applicant for a site-specific variance must demonstrate that because the physical or chemical properties of the waste differs significantly from the waste analyzed in developing the treatment standard, the waste cannot be treated to specified levels or by the specified methods.

(i) Each application for a site-specific variance from a treatment standard must include the information in §260.20(b)(1)-(4);

(j) After receiving an application for a site-specific variance from a treatment standard, the Assistant Administrator, or his delegated representative, may request any additional information or samples which may be required to evaluate the application.

(k) A generator, treatment facility, or disposal facility that is managing a waste covered by a site-specific variance from a treatment standard must comply with the waste analysis requirements for restricted wastes found under §268.7.

(l) During the application review process, the applicant for a site-specific variance must comply with all restrictions on land disposal under this part once the effective date for the waste has been reached.

(m) [Reserved]

(n) [Reserved]

(o) The following facilities are excluded from the treatment standard under §268.43(a), Table CCW, and are subject to the following constituent concentrations:

Facility name[1] and address	Waste[1] code	See also	Regulated hazardous constituent	Wastewaters Concentration (mg/l)	Notes	Nonwastewaters Concentration (mg/l)	Notes
Craftsman Plating and Tinning, Corp., Chicago, IL	F006	Table CCWE in 268.41.............	Cyanides (Total)...	1.2	(2)	1800	(4)
			Cyanides (Amenable)	.86	(2 and 3)	30	(4)
			Cadmium.................	1.6	....	NA	....
			Chromium...............	.32	....	NA	....
			Lead..........................	.040	....	NA	....
			Nickel.....................	.44	....	NA	....
Northwestern Plating Works	F006	Table CCWE in 268.41.............	Cyanides (Total)......	1.2	(2 and 3)	970	(4)
			Cyanides (Amenable)	.86	(2)	30	(4)
			Cadmium.................	1.6	....	NA	....
			Chromium...............	.32	....	NA	....
			Lead..........................	.040	....	NA	

(1) -- A facility may certify compliance with these treatment standards according to provisions in 40 CFR 268.7.

(2) -- Cyanide Wastewater Standards for F006 are based on analysis of composite samples.

(3) -- These facilities must comply with 0.86 mg/l for amenable cyanides in the wastewater exiting the alkaline chlorination system.
  These facilities must also comply with 40 CFR 268.7(a)(4) for appropriate monitoring frequency consistent with the facilities' waste analysis plan.

(4) -- Cyanide nonwastewaters are analyzed using SW-846 Method 9010 or 9012, sample size 10 grams, distillation time, 1 hour and 15 minutes.

Subpart E--Prohibitions on Storage

§ 268.50 Prohibitions on storage of restricted wastes.

(a) Except as provided in this section, the storage of hazardous wastes restricted from land disposal under Subpart C of this part of RCRA section 3004 is prohibited, unless the following conditions are met:

(1) A generator stores such wastes in tanks or containers on-site solely for the purpose of the accumulation of such quantities of hazardous waste as necessary to facilitate proper recovery, treatment, or disposal and the generator complies with the requirements in §262.34 of this chapter. (A generator who is in existence on the effective date of a regulation under this part and who must store hazardous wastes for longer than 90 days due to the regulations under this Part becomes an owner/operator of a storage facility and must obtain a RCRA permit. Such a facility may qualify for interim status upon compliance with the regulations governing interim status under 40 CFR 270.70).

(2) An owner/operator of a hazardous waste treatment, storage, or disposal facility stores such wastes in tanks or containers solely for the purpose of the accumulation of such quantities of hazardous waste as necessary to facilitate proper recovery, treatment, or disposal and:

(i) Each container is clearly marked to identify its contents and the date each period of accumulation begins;

(ii) Each tank is clearly marked with a description of its contents, the quantity of each hazardous waste received, and the date each period of accumulation begins, or such information for each tank is recorded and maintained in the operating record at that facility. Regardless of whether the tank itself is marked, an owner/operator must comply with the operating record requirements specified in §§264.73 or 265.73.

(3) A transporter stores manifested shipments of such wastes at a transfer facility for 10 days or less.

(b) An owner/operator of a treatment, storage or disposal facility may store such wastes for up to one year unless the Agency can demonstrate that such storage was not solely for the purpose of accumulation of such quantities of hazardous waste as are necessary to facilitate proper recovery, treatment, or disposal.

(c) An owner/operator of a treatment, storage or disposal facility may store such wastes beyond one year; however, the owner/operator bears the burden of proving that such storage was solely for the purpose of accumulation of such quantities of hazardous waste as are necessary to facilitate proper recovery, treatment, or disposal.

(d) If a generator's waste is exempt from a prohibition on the type of land disposal utilized for the waste (for example, because of an approved case-by-case extension under §268.5, an approved §268.6 petition, or a national capacity variance under subpart C), the prohibition in paragraph (a) of this section does not apply during the period of such exemption.

(e) The prohibition in paragraph (a) of this section does not apply to hazardous wastes that meet the treatment standards specified under §§268.41, 268.42, and 268.43 or the treatment standards specified under the variance in §268.44, or, where treatment standards have not been specified, is in compliance with the applicable prohibitions specified in §268.32 or RCRA section 3004.

(f) Liquid hazardous wastes containing polychlorinated biphenyls (PCBs) at concentrations greater than or equal to 50 ppm must be stored at a facility that meets the requirements of 40 CFR 761.65(b) and must be removed from storage and treated or disposed as required by this part within one year of the date when such wastes are first placed into storage. The provisions of paragraph (c) of this section do not apply to such PCB wastes prohibited under §268.32 of this part.

192

KEY TO LAND DISPOSAL RESTRICTION CERTIFICATIONS FOR GENERATORS OF RESTRICTED WASTES

Note: Using knowledge or appropriate test methods, a generator must determine if he or she is producing a restricted hazardous waste *at the point of generation.* Test results or other basis for determination must be documented and kept on file for five years. All hazardous wastes are restricted with the exception of the following:

- Wastes generated by conditionally exempt small quantity generators,
- waste pesticides that a farmer disposes of pursuant to § 262.70, and
- wastes identified or listed as hazardous after November 8, 1984 for which EPA has not promulgated land disposal prohibitions or treatment standards.

1. Are you managing a restricted waste at the point of generation (See Table 1) that is excluded from the definition of hazardous or solid waste or exempt from Subtitle C regulation under 40 CFR 261.2-261.6 subsequent to the point of generation?

    Notes: (1) Exempt wastes include those which are discharged to POTWs under a domestic sewage exemp-tion. See Chapter II for solid and hazardous waste ex-emptions. (2) Dilution is prohibited as a substitute for treatment to achieve a treatment standard or avoid a land disposal prohibition unless dilution occurs as part of treatment of a characteristic waste in a treatment sys-tem which subsequently discharges the waste pursuant to a permit issued under section 402 of the Clean Water Act or pretreatment requirements under section 307 of the Clean Water Act unless a method has been specified as the treatment standard in 268.42. Figure 1 on page E-61 identifies situations when dilution is prohibited. (3) Newly identified Toxicity Characteristic hazardous wastes are not currently restricted and subject to land disposal prohibitions and notifications.

    YES: Place a one-time notice in your facility's waste management file identifying the waste genera-tion, the subsequent exclusion from the defini-tion of solid or hazardous waste or exemption from Subtitle C regulation, and the disposition of the waste. Maintain this record for at least five years from the date the waste was last treated, stored, or disposed of. Go to 2.

    NO: Go to 2

2. Have you generated a restricted hazardous waste?

    YES: Go to 3
    NO: Waste is not subject to land disposal restrictions.

3. Does the restricted hazardous waste, as generated, meet the treatment standards published in 40 CFR 268 Subpart D?

    YES: Go to 4.
    NO: Go to 5.

4. Is the untreated waste, which does meet the treatment standard, shipped off-site to a treatment, storage, or disposal facility?

    YES: Complete notification form section 2, sign the certification statement, and submit the form to the off-site treatment, storage or disposal facility. Maintain a copy of the form for at least five years from the date the waste was last sent off-site.

    NO: You must retain on-site a copy of all demonstrations, waste analysis data and other documentation pursuant to your determination that the waste meets the treatment standard for at least five years from the date that the waste was sent to on-site treatment, storage, or disposal.

5. Is the hazardous waste subject to a national capacity variance (see Table 2), a case-by-case extension under 40 CFR 268.5, or a no-migration petition under 40 CFR 268.6?

    YES: Hazardous waste may be land disposed. Complete notification form section 3, check applicable extension, variance or petition box, and submit the form to the off-site treatment, storage or disposal facility. Maintain a copy of the form for at least five years from the date the waste was last sent off-site.
    NO: Go to 6.

6. Have you treated the hazardous waste on-site in tanks or containers to meet a treatment standard and/or eliminate a waste characteristic?

YES: Generators, including small quantity generators, who treat hazardous waste on-site in tanks or containers to meet a treatment standard must develop and follow a written waste analysis plan based on a detailed analysis of the prohibited waste being treated. This plan must be sent to the EPA Regional Administrator 30 days prior to treatment with delivery verified. Go to 7.
Note: Operators of wastewater treatment units subject to regulation under sections 403 or 307(b) of the Clean Water Act are not required to submit waste analysis plans.

NO : Go to 8.

7. Is the waste no longer hazardous due to the elimination of a hazardous waste characteristic?

YES: Waste may be shipped to a RCRA Subtitle D facility. Complete the notification form section 4, sign the certification statement, and submit form to the appropriate EPA Regional Administrator or to your authorized state. Maintain a copy of the form for at least five years from the date the waste was last sent off-site.

Note: Do not complete form if waste is discharged to a POTW or under a NPDES permit.

NO: Complete the notification form section 2, sign certification statement, and submit form to the off-site treatment, storage or disposal facility. Maintain a copy of the form for at least 5 years from the date the waste was last sent off-site.

8. Is the waste generated by a small quantity generator and subject to a tolling agreement pursuant to 40 CFR 262.20?

YES: Complete notification form section 1 and submit the form to the recycling facility with the initial shipment. Maintain a copy of the form, as well as the tolling agreement, for at least three years after termination of the agreement.

NO: Go to 9.

9. Is the waste a lab pack that you wish to have treated off-site using the alternate treatment standard under 268.42?

YES: If the lab pack contains only nonhazardous wastes and/or organometallic wastes listed in 40 CFR 268 Appendix IV, complete notification form section 5 and sign the certification. If the lab pack contains only nonhazardous wastes and/or organic wastes listed in 40 CFR 268 Appendix V, complete notification form section 6 and sign the certification. Maintain a copy of the form for at least five years from the date the waste was last sent off-site.

NO: Complete notification form section 1 and submit the form to treatment, storage or disposal facility with each shipment. Maintain a copy of the form for at least five years from the date the waste was last sent off-site.

TABLE 1
All Restricted Wastes

D001-D017

F001 - F012, F019 - F028, F039

K001 - K011, K013 - K052, K060 - K062, K069 , K071, K073, K083 - K087, K093 - K106, K113 - K116

P001 - P018, P020 - P024, P026 - P031, P033, P034, P036 - P051, P054, P056 - P060, P062-P078, P081, P082, P084 - P089, P092 - P099, P101 - P106, P108 -P116, P118 -P123

U001- U012, U014 - U037 - U039, U041 - U053, U055 - U064, U066 -U099, U101 - U103, U105 -U138, U140 - U174, U176 - U194, U196 - U197, U200 -U211, U213 - U223, U225 - U228, U234 - U240, U243 - U244, U246 - U249.

California List (all applicable RCRA codes)

1. Liquid hazardous waste having a pH less than or equal to 2.

2. Liquid hazardous waste containing PCBs at a concentration greater or equal to 50 ppm.

3. Liquid hazardous waste that is primarily water and contains halogenated organic compounds (HOCs) in total concentration greater than or equal to 1,000 mg/l and less than 10,000 mg/l.

4. Liquid hazardous waste containing HOCs in total concentration greater than or equal to 1,000 mg/l.

5. Non-liquid hazardous waste containing HOCs in total concentration greater than or equal to 1,000 mg/kg.

6. Liquid hazardous waste including free liquids associated with any solid or sludge, containing the following metals or compounds of these metals at concentrations greater than or equal to those specified below:

Arsenic (As)	500 ppm
Cadmium (Cd)	100
Chromium (Cr^{+6})	500
Lead (Pb)	500
Mercury (Hg)	200
Nickel (Ni)	134
Selenium (Se)	100
Thallium (Tl)	130

7. Liquid hazardous waste, including free liquids associated with any solid or sludge containing free cyanide at concentrations greater than or equal to 1,000 mg/l.

TABLE 2
Waste Subject to National Capacity Variances

National Capacity variance expires May 8, 1992 for:

- Listed hazardous wastes with the following waste codes: F039*, K031*, K084*, K101*, K102*, K106*, P010*, P036*, P038*, P065*, P087*, P092*, U136*, U151*,

- Characteristically hazardous wastes with the following waste codes: D004*, D008 (lead materials which are stored be-fore secondary smelting), D009*, inorganic solid debris, and RCRA hazardous wastes that contain naturally occurring radioactive materials.

- Hazardous wastes that are listed in 40 CFR 268.10, 268.11, and 268.12 that are mixed radioactive/hazardous wastes and mixed soil or debris/radioactive/hazardous wastes.

- Third third wastes identified in 268.35 having a treatment standard based on incineration, mercury retorting, vitrification, acid leaching followed by chemical precipitation, or thermal recovery of metals, and which are contaminated soil or debris.

Definitions:

Nonwastewaters:	all materials which are not wastewaters.
Wastewaters:	materials containing less than 1% total organic carbon and less than 1% filterable solids (except F001 - F005, K011, K013, K014, K103, K104).
Inorganic Solid Debris:	nonfriable inorganic solids contaminated by D004-D011 hazardous wastes that are incapable of passing through a 9.5 mm standard sieve; and that require cutting, or crushing and grinding in mechanical sizing equipment prior to stabilization; and, are limited to the following inorganic or metal materials: metal slag, glassified slag, glass, concrete (excluding cementitious or pozzolanic stabilized hazardous wastes), masonry and refractory brick, metal cans, containers, drums, or tanks, metal nuts, bolts, pipes, pumps, valves, appliances or industrial equipment, and scrap metal as defined in 40 CFR 268.1(c)(6).

Note: This table does not identify the national capacity variances expiring on or before June 8, 1991.

*nonwastewaters

FIGURE I
EPA's Logic Diagram for Dilution Under the Land Disposal Regulations

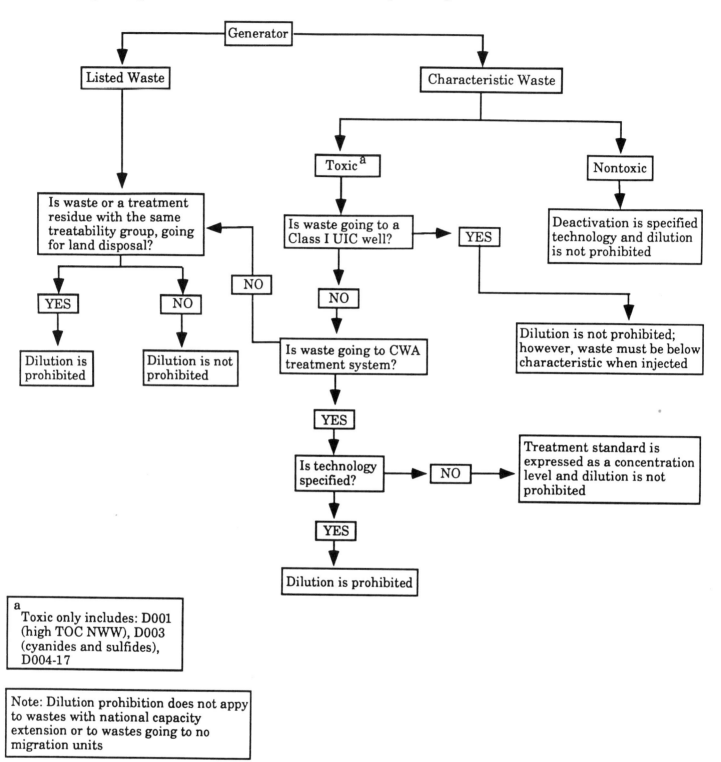

Source: Office of the Federal Register, *Federal Register — Rules and Regulations*, Vol. 56, No. 21, page 3875, Washington, D.C., January 31, 1991

NOTIFICATIONS AND CERTIFICATIONS FOR WASTES RESTRICTED FROM LAND DISPOSAL

GENERATOR'S NAME: _____ MANIFEST NUMBER: _____

GENERATOR EPA ID #: _____ TSD/STATE STREAM # (if required): _____

Section 1: RESTRICTED WASTE REQUIRING TREATMENT

❑   I am the initial generator of an untreated waste restricted from land disposal under 40 CFR 268. This waste, identified below, may not be land disposed unless it is first treated to the appropriate treatment standard(s), and prohibition level(s) identified below.

Treatability Group (Check one)   ❑ Wastewater   ❑ Nonwastewater

EPA Waste Code	Waste Subcategory (if any)	Treatment Technology Code (Table 1 of 268.42)	40 CFR 268 Reference
_____	_____	_____	_____
_____	_____	_____	_____
_____	_____	_____	_____
_____	_____	_____	_____

Note: Corresponding treatment standards must be attached for F001-F005, F039 and California list wastes.
❑ I have attached waste analysis data.   ❑ Waste analysis data is not available.

Section 2: RESTRICTED WASTE NOT REQUIRING TREATMENT

❑   The following waste, as generated, meets the applicable treatment standards under 40 CFR 268 Subpart D.
Treatability Group (Check one)   ❑ Wastewater   ❑ Nonwastewater

EPA Waste Code	Waste Subcategory (if any)	Treatment Technology Code (Table 1 of 268.42)	40 CFR 268 Reference
_____	_____	_____	_____
_____	_____	_____	_____
_____	_____	_____	_____
_____	_____	_____	_____

Note: Corresponding treatment standards must be attached for F001-F005, F039 and California list wastes.
❑ I have attached waste analysis data.   ❑ Waste analysis data is not available.

I certify under penalty of law that I personally have examined and am familiar with the waste through analysis and testing or through knowledge of the waste to support this certification that the waste complies with the treatment standards specified in 40 CFR Part 268, Subpart D and all applicable prohibitions set forth in 40 CFR 268.32 or RCRA section 3004(d). I believe that the information I submitted is true, accurate and complete. I am aware that there are significant penalties for submitting a false certification, including the possibility of a fine and imprisonment.

Signature _____ Name (Print) _____ Date _____

197

Section 3: RESTRICTED WASTE SUBJECT TO EXTENSION, PETITION, OR VARIANCE

❏   The following waste, as generated, is subject to: ❏ (a) A nationwide capacity variance under 40 CFR 268, Subpart C, ❏ (b) A case-by-case extension under 40 CFR 268.5, ❏ (c) A no migration petition under 40 CFR 268.6.

Treatability Group (Check one)   ❏ Wastewater   ❏ Nonwastewater

EPA Waste Code	Waste Subcategory (if any)	Treatment Technology Code (Table 1 of 268.42)	40 CFR 268 Reference
___	_____	_____	_____
___	_____	_____	_____
___	_____	_____	_____
___	_____	_____	_____

Note: Corresponding treatment standards must be attached for F001-F005, F039 and California list wastes.
    ❏ I have attached waste analysis data.   ❏ Waste analysis data is not available.

The variance, extension, or petition applicable to the described waste expires on the following date _____.

Section 4: TREATED WASTE SHIPPED TO A SUBTITLE D FACILITY

❏   The following waste, no longer exhibits a hazardous waste characteristic and is not hazardous per 40 CFR Part 261.

Name and address of Subtitle D Facility Receiving the Waste: _____

_____

Treatability Group (Check one)   ❏   Wastewater   ❏ Nonwastewater

Initial EPA Waste Code	Waste Subcategory and Treatability Group	Treatment Standards at Initial Point of Generation
___	_____	_____
___	_____	_____

I certify under penalty of law that I personally have examined and am familiar with the the treatment technology and operation of the treatment process used to support this certification and that, based on my inquiry of those individuals immediately responsible for obtaining this information, I believe that the treatment process has been operated and maintained properly so as to comply with the performance levels specified in 40 CFR Part 268, Subpart D, and all applicable prohibitions set forth in 40 CFR 268.32 or RCRA section 3004(d) without impermissible dilution of the prohibited waste. I am aware that there are significant penalties for submitting a false certification, including the possibility of a fine and imprisonment.

Signature _____ Name (Print) _____ Date _____

198

Section 5: ORGANOMETALLIC LAB PACK WASTE REQUIRING TREATMENT

☐   I am the initial generator of an untreated waste restricted from land disposal under 40 CFR 268. This waste, identified below, may not be land disposed unless it is first treated to the appropriate treatment standard(s), and prohibition level(s) identified below.

Treatability Group (Check one)   ☐   Wastewater   ☐   Nonwastewater

EPA Waste Code	Waste Subcategory (if any)	Treatment Technology Code (Table 1 of 268.42)	40 CFR 268 Reference
_____	_____	_____	_____
_____	_____	_____	_____
_____	_____	_____	_____

Note: Corresponding treatment standards must be attached for F001-F005, F039 and California list wastes.
   ☐ I have attached waste analysis data.   ☐ Waste analysis data is not available.

I certify under penalty of law that I have personally examined and am familiar with the waste and that the lab pack contains only the wastes specified in appendix IV to part 268 or solid wastes not subject to regulation under 40 CFR part 261. I am aware that there are significant penalties for submitting a false certification, including the possibility of a fine and imprisonment.

Signature _____ Name (Print) _____ Date _____

Section 6: ORGANIC LAB PACK WASTE REQUIRING TREATMENT

☐   I am the initial generator of an untreated waste restricted from land disposal under 40 CFR 268. This waste, identified below, may not be land disposed unless it is first treated to the appropriate treatment standard(s), and prohibition level(s) identified below.

Treatability Group (Check one)   ☐   Wastewater   ☐   Nonwastewater

EPA Waste Code	Waste Subcategory (if any)	Treatment Technology Code (Table 1 of 268.42)	40 CFR 268 Reference
_____	_____	_____	_____
_____	_____	_____	_____
_____	_____	_____	_____

Note: Corresponding treatment standards must be attached for F001-F005, F039 and California list wastes.
   ☐ I have attached waste analysis data.   ☐ Waste analysis data is not available.

I certify under penalty of law that I have personally examined and am familiar with the waste through analysis and testing or through knowledge of the waste and that the lab pack contains only organic wastes specified in appendix V to part 268 or solid wastes not subject to regulation under 40 CFR part 261. I am aware that there are significant penalties for submitting a false certification, including the possibility of a fine and imprisonment.

Signature _____ Name (Print) _____ Date _____

Appendix D

DOT Hazardous Materials Tables and List of Hazardous Substances

Note: There are two DOT Hazardous Materials Tables reproduced in Appendix D. The first table may be used to determine proper shipping descriptions for domestic shipments of hazardous waste and hazardous materials until October 1, 1993, and to identify packaging requirements until October 1, 1996, unless the waste or material is considered to be poisonous by inhalation, a new explosive, or an infectious substance (see Table 4.6 of this manual). The second DOT Hazardous Materials Table was printed in the rule entitled HM-181 (published in the Federal Register on December 21, 1990). This table must be used to determine the proper shipping descriptions and marking and labeling requirements for new explosives and infectious substances as of October 1, 1991. The new table must also be used by October 1, 1992 for materials which are poisonous by inhalation.

1990 DOT Hazardous Materials Table

(1) +/A/W	(2) Hazardous materials descriptions and proper shipping names	(3) Hazard class	(3A) Identification number	(4) Label(s) required (if not excepted)	(5) Packaging (a) Exceptions	(5) Packaging (b) Specific requirements	(6) Maximum net quantity in one package (a) Passenger carrying aircraft or railcar	(6) (b) Cargo only aircraft	(7) Water shipments (a) Cargo vessel	(7) (b) Passenger vessel	(7) (c) Other requirements
	Accumulator, pressurized (pneumatic or hydraulic), containing nonflammable gas	Nonflammable gas	NA1956	Nonflammable gas	173.306		No limit	No limit	1,2	1,2	
	Acetal	Flammable liquid	UN1088	Flammable liquid	173.118	173.119	1 quart	10 gallons	1,3	4	
	Acetaldehyde (ethyl aldehyde)	Flammable liquid	UN1089	Flammable liquid	None	173.119	Forbidden	10 gallons	1,3	5	
A	Acetaldehyde ammonia	ORM-A	UN1841	None	173.505	173.510	No limit	No limit	1,2	1,2	
	Acetic acid (aqueous solution)	Corrosive material	UN2790	Corrosive	173.244	173.245	1 quart	10 gallons	1,2	1,2	Stow separate from nitric acid or oxidizing materials
	Acetic acid, glacial	Corrosive material	UN2789	Corrosive	173.244	173.245	1 quart	10 gallons	1,2	1,2	Stow separate from nitric acid or oxidizing materials.
	Acetic anhydride	Corrosive material	UN1715	Corrosive	173.244	173.245	1 quart	1 gallon	1,2	1,2	
	Acetone	Flammable liquid	UN1090	Flammable liquid	173.118	173.119	1 quart	10 gallons	1,3	4	
	Acetone cyanohydrin	Poison B	UN1541	Poison	None	173.346 173.3a	Forbidden	55 gallons	1	5	Shade from radiant heat. Stow away from corrosive materials
	Acetone oil	Flammable liquid	UN1091	Flammable liquid	173.118	173.119	1 quart	10 gallons	1,2	1	
	Acetonitrile	Flammable liquid	NA1648	Flammable liquid	173.118	173.119	1 quart	10 gallons	1	4	Shade from radiant heat
	Acetyl acetone peroxide, in solution with not more than 9% by weight active oxygen. See **Organic peroxide, liquid or solution, n.o.s.**		UN2080								
	Acetyl acetone peroxide with more than 9% by weight active oxygen	Forbidden									
	Acetyl benzoyl peroxide, not more than 40% in solution. See **Acetyl benzoyl peroxide solution, not over 40% peroxide**		UN2081								
	Acetyl benzoyl peroxide, solid, or more than 40% in solution	Forbidden									
	Acetyl benzoyl peroxide solution, not over 40% peroxide	Organic peroxide	UN2081	Organic peroxide	None	173.222	Forbidden	1 quart	1,2	1	
	Acetyl bromide	Corrosive Material	UN1716	Corrosive	173.244	173.247	1 quart	1 gallon	1	1	Keep dry. Glass carboys not permitted on passenger vessels
	Acetyl chloride	Flammable liquid	UN1717	Flammable liquid	173.244	173.247	1 quart	1 gallon	1	1	Stow away from alcohols. Keep cool and dry. Separate longitudinally by an intervening complete compartment or hold from explosives
	Acetyl cyclohexanesulfonyl peroxide, more than 82%, wetted with less than 12% water	Forbidden									
	Acetyl cyclohexanesulphonyl peroxide, not more than 82%, wetted with not less than 12% water. See **Organic peroxide, solid, n.o.s.**		UN2082								
	Acetyl cyclohexanesulphonyl peroxide, not more than 32% in solution. See **Organic peroxide, liquid or solution, n.o.s.**		UN2083								
	Acetylene	Flammable gas	UN1001	Flammable gas	None	173.303	Forbidden	300 pounds	1	1	Shade from radiant heat
	Acetylene (liquid)	Forbidden									
	Acetylene silver nitrate	Forbidden									
A	Acetylene tetrabromide	ORM-A	UN2504	None	173.505	173.510	10 gallons	55 gallons			
	Acetyl iodide	Corrosive material	UN1898	Corrosive	173.244	173.247	1 quart	1 gallon	1	1	Keep dry. Glass carboys not permitted on passenger vessels
	Acetyl peroxide, not more than 25% in solution. See **Acetyl peroxide solution, not over 25% peroxide**		UN2084								
	Acetyl peroxide, solid, or more than 25% in solution	Forbidden									
	Acetyl peroxide solution, not over 25% peroxide	Organic peroxide	UN2084	Organic peroxide	173.153	173.222	Forbidden	1 quart	1,2	1	
	Acid butyl phosphate	Corrosive material	UN1718	Corrosive	173.244	173.245	1 quart	5 gallons	1,2	1,2	Glass carboys in hampers not permitted under deck
	Acid carboy, empty. See **Carboy, empty.**										
	Acid, liquid, n.o.s.	Corrosive material	NA1760	Corrosive	173.244	173.245	1 quart	5 pints	1	4	Keep cool
+	Acrolein, inhibited	Flammable liquid	UN1092	Flammable liquid and Poison	None	173.122	Forbidden	1 quart	1,2	5	Keep cool. Stow away from living quarters
	Acrylic acid	Corrosive material	UN2218	Corrosive	173.244	173.245	1 quart	5 pints	1	1	
	Acrylonitrile	Flammable liquid	UN1093	Flammable liquid and Poison	None	173.119	Forbidden	1 quart	1,2	5	Keep cool
	Actuating cartridge, explosive (fire extinguisher, or valve)	Class C explosive		Explosive C	173.114		50 pounds	150 pounds	1,2	1,2	Keep cool and dry

(1) A/W	(2) Hazardous materials descriptions and proper shipping names	(3) Hazard class	(3A) Identification number	(4) Label(s) required (if not excepted)	(5) Packaging (a) Exceptions	(5) Packaging (b) Specific requirements	(6) Maximum net quantity in one package (a) Passenger carrying aircraft or railcar	(6) (b) Cargo only aircraft	(7) Water shipments (a) Cargo vessel	(7) (b) Passenger vessel	(7) (c) Other requirements
	Adhesive	Combustible liquid	UN1133	None	173.118a	None	No limit	No limit	1,2	1,2	
	Adhesive	Flammable liquid	UN1133	Flammable liquid	173.118	173.132	1 quart	10 gallons	1,2	1	
	Aerosol product. See Compressed gas, n.o.s.										
	Air, compressed	Nonflammable gas	UN1002	Nonflammable gas	173.306	173.302	150 pounds	300 pounds	1,2	1,2	
	Air, refrigerated liquid (cryogenic liquid).	Nonflammable Gas	UN1003	Nonflammable Gas	173.320	173.316 173.318	Forbidden	300 pounds	1,2	1,2	Stow separate from flammables. Do not overstow with other cargo.
	Air conditioning machine. See Refrigerating machine										
	Airplane flare. See Fireworks, special										
	Alcoholic beverage	Flammable liquid	UN1170	Flammable liquid	173.118	173.125	See 173.118(c)	10 gallons	1,2	1	
	Alcoholic beverage	Combustible liquid	UN1170	None	173.118a	None	No limit	No limit	1,2	1,2	
	Alcohol, n.o.s.	Flammable liquid	UN1987	Flammable liquid	173.118	173.125	1 quart	10 gallons	1,2	1	
	Alcohol, n.o.s.	Combustible liquid	UN1987	None	173.118a	None	No limit	1,2	1,2		
	Aldrin	Poison B	NA2761	Poison	173.364	173.376	50 pounds	200 pounds	1,2	1,2	
A	Aldrin, cast solid	ORM-A	NA2761	None	173.505	173.510	No limit	No limit	1,2	1,2	
	Aldrin mixture, dry (with more than 65% aldrin)	Poison B	NA2761	Poison	173.364	173.376	50 pounds	200 pounds	1,2	1,2	
A	Aldrin mixture, dry, with 65% or less aldrin	ORM-A	NA2761	None	173.505	173.510	No limit	No limit	1,2	1,2	
	Aldrin mixture, liquid (with more than 60% aldrin)	Poison B	NA2762	Poison	173.345	173.361	1 quart	55 gallons	1,2	1,2	If flash point less than 141 deg. F, segregation same as for flammable liquids
A	Aldrin mixture, liquid, with 60% or less aldrin	ORM-A	NA2762	None	173.505	173.510	No limit	No limit	1,2	1,2	
	Alkaline (corrosive) liquid, n.o.s.	Corrosive material	NA1719	Corrosive	173.244	173.249	1 quart	5 gallons	1,2	1,2	
	Alkanesulfonic acid	Corrosive material	UN2584	Corrosive	173.244	173.245	5 pints	1 gallon	1,2	1	
	Alkyl aluminum halides. See Pyrophoric liquid, n.o.s.										
A	Allethrin	ORM-A	NA2902	None	173.505	173.510	No limit	No limit			
	Allyl alcohol	Flammable liquid	UN1098	Flammable liquid and Poison	None	173.119 173.3a	1 quart	10 gallons	1,2	1	
	Allyl bromide	Flammable liquid	UN1099	Flammable liquid	173.118	173.119	Forbidden	10 gallons	1,2	1	
	Allyl chloride	Flammable liquid	UN1100	Flammable liquid	None	173.119	Forbidden	10 gallons	1,3	5	
	Allyl chlorocarbonate	Flammable liquid	UN1722	Flammable liquid	None	173.288	Forbidden	5 pints	1	5	Keey dry. Separate longitudinally by an intervening complete hold or compartment from explosives. Segregation same as for corrosive materials
	Allyl chloroformate, See Allyl chlorocarbonate										
	Allyl trichlorosilane	Corrosive material	UN1724	Corrosive	None	173.280	Forbidden	10 gallons	1	1	Keep dry
	Aluminum alkyl. See Pyrophoric liquid. n.o.s.										
	Aluminum bromide, anhydrous	Corrosive material	UN1725	Corrosive	173.244	173.245b	25 pounds	100 pounds	1,2	1,2	Keep dry
	Aluminum chloride, anhydrous	Corrosive material	UN1726	Corrosive	173.244	173.245b	25 pounds	100 pounds	1,2	1,2	Keep dry
	Aluminum dross, wet or hot. See 173.173	Forbidden									
	Aluminum hydride	Flammable solid	UN2463	Flammable solid and Dangerous when wet	None	173.206	Forbidden	25 pounds	1,2	5	Segregation same as for flammable solid labeled Dangerous When Wet
	Aluminum. metallic, powder	Flammable solid	UN1396	Flammable solid	173.232	173.232	25 pounds	100 pounds	1,2	1,2	Keep dry. Segregation same as for flammable solids labeled dangerous when wet
	Aluminum nitrate	Oxidizer	UN1438	Oxidizer	173.153	173.182	25 pounds	100 pounds	1,2	1,2	
	Aluminum phosphate solution	Corrosive material	NA1760	Corrosive	173.244	173.245	1 quart	10 gallons	1,2	1,2	
	Aluminum phosphide	Flammable solid	UN1397	Flammable solid and Dangerous when wet	None	173.154	Forbidden	25 pounds	1,2	1,2	Stow away from acids and oxidizing materials

202

(1) +/ A/ W	(2) Hazardous materials descriptions and proper shipping names	(3) Hazard class	(3A) Identi- fication number	(4) Label(s) required (if not excepted)	(5) Packaging		(6) Maximum net quan- tity in one package		(7) Water shipments		
					(a) Exceptions	(b) Specific require- ments	(a) Passenger carrying aircraft or railcar	(b) Cargo only aircraft	(a) Cargo vessel	(b) Pas- senger vessel	(c) Other requirements
A	Aluminum sulfate solution	ORM-B	NA1760	None	173.505	173.510	25 pounds	100 pounds	1,2	1,2	
	Amatol. See High explosive										
	2-(2-Aminoethoxy) ethanol	Corrosive material	NA1760	Corrosive	173.244	173.245	1 quart	10 gallons	1,2	1,2	
	N-Aminoethylpiperazine	Corrosive material	UN2815	Corrosive	173.244	173.245	1 quart	10 gallons	1,2	1,2	
	Aminopropyldiethanolamine	Corrosive material	NA1760	Corrosive	173.244	173.245	1 quart	10 gallons	1,2	1,2	
	N-Aminopropylmorpholine	Corrosive material	NA1760	Corrosive	173.244	173.245	1 quart	10 gallons	1,2	1,2	
	bis (Aminopropyl) piperazine	Corrosive material	NA1760	Corrosive	173.244	173.245	1 quart	10 gallons	1,2	1,2	
	Ammonia, anhydrous	Nonflammable gas	UN1005	Nonflammable gas	173.306	173.304 173.314 173.315	Forbidden	300 pounds	1,2	4	Stow in well ventilated space.
	Ammonia solution (containing more than 44% ammonia)	Nonflammable gas	UN2073	Nonflammable gas	173.306	173.304 173.314 173.315ᵃ	Forbidden	300 pounds	1,2	4	Stow in well ventilated space.
	Ammonia solution (containing 44% or less ammonia in water). See Ammonium hydroxide										
	Ammonium arsenate, solid	Poison B	UN1546	Poison	173.364	173.365	50 pounds	200 pounds	1,2	1,2	Stow away from alkaline corrosives.
	Ammonium azide	Forbidden									
	Ammonium bifluoride, solid or solution. See Ammonium hydrogen fluoride, solid or solution										
A	Ammonium bisulfite, solid	ORM-B	NA2693	None	173.505	173.510	25 pounds	100 pounds	1,2	1,2	
	Ammonium bisulfite solution	Corrosive material	NA2693	Corrosive	173.244	173.245	1 quart	5 gallons	1,2	1,2	
	Ammonium bromate	Forbidden									
A	Ammonium carbamate	ORM-A	NA9083	None	173.505	173.510	50 pounds	No limit	1,2	1,2	Keep away from heat.
A	Ammonium carbonate	ORM-A	NA9084	None	173.505	173.510	50 pounds	No limit	1,2	1,2	Keep away from heat, acids, alum and salts of iron or zinc.
	Ammonium chlorate	Forbidden									
	Ammonium dichromate (ammonium bichromate)	Oxidizer	UN1439	Oxidizer	173.153	173.154 173.235	25 pounds	100 pounds	1,2	1,2	
A	Ammonium fluoborate	ORM-B	NA9088	None	None	173.510	25 pounds	100 pounds	1,2	1,2	
A	Ammonium fluoride	ORM-B	UN2505	None	173.505	173.800	25 pounds	100 pounds	1,2	1,2	
	Ammonium fulminate	Forbidden									
	Ammonium hydrogen fluoride, solid	Corrosive material	UN1727	Corrosive	173.244	173.245b	25 pounds	100 pounds	1,2	1,2	Keep dry
	Ammonium hydrogen fluoride solution	Corrosive material	UN2817	Corrosive	173.244	173.245	1 quart	5 gallons	1,2	1,2	Keep dry
A	Ammonium hydrogen sulfate	ORM-B	UN2506	None	173.505	173.800	25 pounds	100 pounds			
A	Ammonium hydrosulfide solution	ORM-A	NA2683	None	173.505	173.605	10 gallons	55 gallons			
	Ammonium hydroxide (containing not less than 12% but not more than 44% ammonia)	Corrosive material	NA2672	Corrosive	173.244	173.245	2 gallons	2 gallons	1	4	
AW	Ammonium hydroxide (containing less than 12% ammonia)	ORM-A	NA2672	None	173.505	173.510	10 gallons	55 gallons	1	1	
	Ammonium nitrate-carbonate mixture	Oxidizer	UN2068	Oxidizer	173.153	173.182	25 pounds	100 pounds	1,2	1,2	
	Ammonium nitrate fertilizer, containing no more than 0.2% carbon	Oxidizer	UN2067	Oxidizer	173.153	173.182	25 pounds	100 pounds	1,2	1,2	
	Ammonium nitrate - fuel oil mixture. See High explosive										
	Ammonium nitrate - fuel oil mixture (con- taining only prilled ammonium nitrate and fuel oil)	Blasting agent		Blasting agent	None	173.114a	Forbidden	100 pounds	1,2	1,2	
	Ammonium nitrate mixed fertilizer	Oxidizer	UN2069	Oxidizer	173.153	173.182	25 pounds	100 pounds	1,2	1,2	
	Ammonium nitrate (no organic coating)	Oxidizer	UN1942	Oxidizer	173.153	173.182	25 pounds	100 pounds	1,2	1,2	
	Ammonium nitrate (organic coating)	Oxidizer	NA1942	Oxidizer	173.153	173.182	25 pounds	100 pounds	1,2	1,2	
	Ammonium nitrate-phosphate	Oxidizer	UN2070	Oxidizer	173.153	173.182	25 pounds	100 pounds	1,2	1,2	
	Ammonium nitrate, solution (containing 35% or less water). See 173.154(a)(4) and 173.154(a)(17)	Oxidizer	UN2426	Oxidizer							
	Ammonium nitrite	Forbidden									

(1) +/A/W	(2) Hazardous materials descriptions and proper shipping names	(3) Hazard class	(3A) Identi-fication number	(4) Label(s) required (if not excepted)	(5) Packaging (a) Exceptions	(b) Specific require-ments	(6) Maximum net quantity in one package (a) Passenger carrying aircraft or railcar	(b) Cargo only aircraft	(7) Water shipments (a) Cargo vessel	(b) Pas-senger vessel	(c) Other requirements
	Ammonium oxalate	ORM-A	NA2449	None	173.505	173.510	50 pounds	200 pounds	1,2	1,2	
	Ammonium perchlorate	Oxidizer	UN1442	Oxidizer	173.153	173.239a	25 pounds	100 pounds	1,2	4	Stow away from powdered metals
	Ammonium perchlorate. See High explosive										
	Ammonium permanganate	Oxidizer	NA9190	Oxidizer	None	173.154	Forbidden	Forbidden	1,2	1,2	Separate from ammonium com-pounds and hydrogen peroxide. This material may be forbidden in water transpor-tation by certain countries
	Ammonium persulfate	Oxidizer	UN1444	Oxidizer	173.153	178.154	50 pounds	200 pounds	1,2	1,2	
	Ammonium picrate, dry. See High explosive										
	Ammonium picrate, wet (with 10% or more water)	Flammable solid	UN1310	Flammable solid	173.192		1 pound	1 pound	1	4	Stow away from heavy metals and their compounds
	Ammonium picrate, wet, with 10% or more water, over 16 ounces in one outside packaging. See High explosive										
A	Ammonium polysulfide solution	ORM-A	UN2818	None	173.505	173.605	10 gallons	55 gallons	1,2	1,2	
A	Ammonium silicofluoride	ORM-B	UN2854	None	173.505	173.510	25 pounds	100 pounds	1,2	1,2	
W	Ammonium sulfate nitrate	ORM-C	NA1477	None	173.505	173.910			1,2	1,2	Must not be accepted for transportation while hot. Separate by an intervening hold or com-partment from Class A explosives. Separate from other explosives, corrosive materials, flammable solids, liquids, or gases, oxidizing materials, organic peroxides, or organic materials
	Ammonium sulfide solution	Flammable liquid	UN2683	Flammable liquid	173.118	173.119	1 quart	10 gallons	1,2	1,2	
	Ammunition, chemical (containing a Poison A liquid or gas). See Chemical ammuni-tion, nonexplosive (containing a Poison A material)										
	Ammunition, chemical (containing a Poison B material). See Chemical ammunition, nonexplosive (containing a Poison B material)										
	Ammunition, chemical (containing an irritat-ing liquid or solid). See Chemical ammu-nition, nonexplosive (containing an irri-tating material)										
	Ammunition, chemical, explosive, with Poi-son A material	Class A explosive		Explosive A and Poison gas	None	173.59	Forbidden	Forbidden	6	5	No other cargo may be stowed in the same hold with these items
	Ammunition, chemical, explosive, with Poi-son B material	Class A explosive		Explosive A and Poison	None	173.59	Forbidden	Forbidden	6	5	No other cargo may be stowed in the same hold with these items
	Ammunition, chemical, explosive, with irritant	Class A explosive		Explosive A and Irritant	None	173.59	Forbidden	Forbidden	6	5	No other cargo may be stowed in the same hold with these items
	Ammunition for cannon with empty projectile	Class B explosive		Explosive B	None	173.89	Forbidden	Forbidden	1,2	5	
	Ammunition for cannon with explosive projectile	Class A explosive		Explosive A	None	173.54	Forbidden	Forbidden	6	5	
	Ammunition for cannon with gas projectile	Class A explosive		Explosive A	None	173.54	Forbidden	Forbidden	6	5	
	Ammunition for cannon with illuminating projectile	Class A explosive		Explosive A	None	173.54	Forbidden	Forbidden	6	5	
	Ammunition for cannon with incendiary projectile	Class A explosive		Explosive A	None	173.54	Forbidden	Forbidden	6	5	
	Ammunition for cannon with inert loaded projectile	Class B explosive		Explosive B	None	173.89	Forbidden	Forbidden	1,2	5	
	Ammunition for cannon without projectile	Class B Explosive		Explosive B	None	173.89	Forbidden	Forbidden	1,2	5	
	Ammunition for cannon with smoke projectile	Class A explosive		Explosive A	None	173.54	Forbidden	Forbidden	6	5	
	Ammunition for cannon with solid projectile	Class B explosive		Explosive B	None	173.89	Forbidden	Forbidden	1,2	5	
	Ammunition for cannon with tear gas projectile	Class A explosive		Explosive A	None	173.54	Forbidden	Forbidden	6	5	
	Ammunition for cannon with tear gas projectile	Class B explosive		Explosive B	None	173.89	Forbidden	Forbidden	1,2	5	
	Ammunition for small-arms with explosive projectile	Class A explosive		Explosive A	None	173.58	Forbidden	Forbidden	6	5	
	Ammunition for small-arms with incendiary projectile	Class A explosive		Explosive A	None	173.58	Forbidden	Forbidden	6	5	
	Ammunition, non-explosive. See 173.55										
	Ammunition, rocket. See Rocket ammunition with...										

(1)	(2)	(3)	(3A)	(4)	(5) Packaging		(6) Maximum net quantity in one package		(7) Water shipments		
+/ A/ W	Hazardous materials descriptions and proper shipping names	Hazard class	Identification number	Label(s) required (if not excepted)	(a) Exceptions	(b) Specific requirements	(a) Passenger carrying aircraft or railcar	(b) Cargo only aircraft	(a) Cargo vessel	(b) Passenger vessel	(c) Other requirements
	Ammunition, small-arms. See Small-arms ammunition										
	Amyl acetate	Flammable liquid	UN1104	Flammable liquid	173.118	173.119	1 quart	10 gallons	1,2	1,2	
	Amyl acid phosphate	Corrosive material	UN2819	Corrosive	173.244	173.245	1 quart	10 gallons	1,2	1,2	
	Amylamine	Flammable liquid	UN1106	Flammable liquid	173.118	173.119	1 quart	10 gallons	1,2	1	
	Amyl chloride	Flammable liquid	UN1107	Flammable liquid	173.118	173.119	1 quart	10 gallons	1,2	1	
	Amylene, normal	Flammable liquid	UN1108	Flammable liquid	173.118	173.119	1 quart	10 gallons	1,3	1,3	
	Amyl formate	Flammable liquid	UN1109	Flammable liquid	173.118	173.119	1 quart	10 gallons	1,2	1	
	Amyl mercaptan	Flammable liquid	UN1111	Flammable liquid	None	173.141	Forbidden	10 gallons	1,2	1	
	Amyl nitrite	Flammable liquid	UN1113	Flammable liquid	173.118	173.119	1 quart	10 gallons	1,3	4	
	tert-Amyl peroxy-2-ethylhexanoate, technically pure. See Organic peroxide, liquid or solution, n.o.s.		UN2898								
	tert-Amyl peroxyneodecanoate, not more than 75% with phlegmatizer. See Organic peroxide, liquid or solution, n.o.s.		UN2891								
	Amyl trichorosilane	Corrosive material	UN1728	Corrosive	None	173.280	Forbidden	10 gallons	1	5	Keep dry.
	Anhydrous ammonia. See Ammonia, anhydrous										
	Anhydrous hydrazine. See Hydrazine, anhydrous										
	Anhydrous hydrofluoric acid. See Hydrogen fluoride										
	Aniline oil drum, empty. See 173.347(d)	Poison B							1,2	1	Do not accept unless returnable package notice is on drum and the instructions thereon have been carried out.
+	Aniline oil, liquid	Poison B	UN1547	Poison	None	173.347	Forbidden	55 gallons	1,2	1,2	Stow away from oxidizing materials and acids.
	Anisoyl chloride	Corrosive material	UN1729	Corrosive	173.244	173.279	1 quart	1 quart	1	1	Keep dry.
	Antimonous chloride. See Antimony trichloride										
A	Antimony lactate, solid	ORM-A	UN1550	None	173.505	173.510	No limit	No limit			
	Antimony pentachloride	Corrosive material	UN1730	Corrosive	None	173.247	1 quart	1 quart	1	1	Keep dry. Glass carboys not permitted on passenger vessels.
	Antimony pentachloride solution	Corrosive material	UN1731	Corrosive	173.244	173.245	1 quart	5 pints	1	1	Keep dry. Glass carboys not permitted on passenger vessels.
	Antimony pentafluoride	Corrosive material	UN1732	Corrosive	None	173.246	Forbidden	25 pounds	1	5	Keep dry.
A	Antimony potassium tartrate, solid	ORM-A	UN1551	None	173.505	173.510	No limit	No limit	1,2	1,2	
	Antimony sulfide and a chlorate, mixtures of	Forbidden									
A	Antimony sulfide, solid	ORM-A	NA1325	None	173.505	173.510	No limit	No limit			
	Antimony tribromide, solid	Corrosive material	NA1549	Corrosive	173.244	173.245b	25 pounds	100 pounds	1,2	1,2	Keep dry
	Antimony tribromide solution	Corrosive material	NA1549	Corrosive	173.244	173.245	1 quart	5 pints	1	1	Keep dry
	Antimony trichloride, solid	Corrosive material	UN1733	Corrosive	173.244	173.245b	25 pounds	100 pounds	1,2	1,2	Keep dry
	Antimony trichloride solution	Corrosive material	UN1733	Corrosive	173.244	173.245	1 quart	5 pints	1	1	Keep dry
	Antimony trifluoride, solid	Corrosive material	NA1549	Corrosive	173.244	173.245b	25 pounds	100 pounds	1,2	1,2	Keep dry
	Antimony trifluoride solution	Corrosive material	NA1549	Corrosive	173.244	173.245	1 quart	5 pints	1	1	Keep dry
	Aqua ammonia solution (containing 44% or less ammonia). See Ammonium hydroxide										
	Argon or Argon compressed	Nonflammable gas	UN1006	Nonflammable gas	173.306	173.302 173.314	150 pounds	300 pounds	1,2	1,3	
	Argon, refrigerated liquid, (cryogenic liquid)	Nonflammable gas	UN1951	Nonflammable gas	173.320	173.316 173.318	100 pounds	1,100 pounds	1,3	1,3	
	Arsenic acid, solid	Poison B	UN1554	Poison	173.364	173.366	50 pounds	200 pounds	1,2	1,2	
	Arsenic acid solution	Poison B	UN1553	Poison	173.345	173.348	1 quart	55 gallons	1,2	1,2	
	Arsenical compound, liquid, n.o.s., or Arsenical mixture, liquid, n.o.s.	Poison B	UN1556	Poison	173.345	173.346	1 quart	55 gallons	1,2	1,2	

(1) A. W	(2) Hazardous materials descriptions and proper shipping names	(3) Hazard class	(3A) Identification number	(4) Label(s) required (if not excepted)	(5) Packaging (a) Exceptions	(b) Specific requirements	(6) Maximum net quantity in one package (a) Passenger carrying aircraft or railcar	(b) Cargo only aircraft	(7) Water shipments (a) Cargo vessel	(b) Passenger vessel	(c) Other requirements
	Arsenical compound, solid, n.o.s., or Arsenical mixture, solid, n.o.s.	Poison B	UN1557	Poison	173.364	173.367	50 pounds	200 pounds	1,2	1,2	Keep dry
	Arsenical dip, liquid (sheep dip)	Poison B	NA1557	Poison	173.345	173.346	1 quart	55 gallons	1,2	1,2	
	Arsenical dust	Poison B	UN1562	Poison	173.364	173.368	50 pounds	200 pounds	1,2	1,2	
	Arsenical pesticide, liquid, n.o.s., (compounds and preparations)	Flammable liquid	UN2760	Flammable liquid	173.118	173.119	1 quart	10 gallons	1,2	1	
	Arsenical pesticide, liquid, n.o.s., (compounds and preparations)	Poison B	UN2759	Poison	173.345	173.346	1 quart	55 gallons	1,2	1,2	
	Arsenical pesticide, solid, n.o.s., (compounds and preparations)	Poison B	UN2759	Poison	173.364	173.367	50 pounds	200 pounds	1,2	1,2	
	Arsenic bromide, solid	Poison B	UN1555	Poison	173.364	173.365	50 pounds	200 pounds	1,2	1,2	
	Arsenic chloride, liquid. See Arsenic trichloride										
	Arsenic disulfide. See Arsenic sulfide, solid										
	Arsenic iodide, solid	Poison B	NA1557	Poison	173.364	173.365	50 pounds	200 pounds	1,2	1,2	
	Arsenic pentoxide, solid	Poison B	UN1559	Poison	173.364	173.365	50 pounds	200 pounds	1,2	1,2	
	Arsenic, solid	Poison B	UN1558	Poison	173.364	173.366	50 pounds	200 pounds	1,2	1,2	
	Arsenic sulfide and a chlorate, mixtures of	Forbidden									
	Arsenic sulfide, solid	Poison B	NA1557	Poison	173.364	173.365	50 pounds	200 pounds	1,2	1,2	Keep dry
	Arsenic trichloride, liquid	Poison B	UN1560	Poison	173.345	173.346	1 quart	55 gallons	1,2	1,2	
	Arsenic trioxide, solid	Poison B	UN1561	Poison	173.364	173.366 173.368	50 pounds	200 pounds	1,2	1,2	
	Arsenic trisulfide	Poison B	NA1557	Poison	173.364	173.365	50 pounds	200 pounds	1,2	1,2	
	Arsenic, white, solid. See Arsenic trioxide, solid										
	Arsenious acid, solid. See Arsenic trioxide, solid										
	Arsenious and mercuric iodide solution	Poison B	NA2810	Poison	173.345	173.346	1 quart	55 gallons	1,2	1,2	
	Arsine	Poison A	UN2188	Poison gas and Flammable gas	None	173.328	Forbidden	Forbidden	1	5	Segregation same as for flammable gases
	Asbestos	ORM-C		None	173.1090	173.1090	No limit	No limit	1,2	1,2	Stow and handle to avoid airborne particles
	Ascaridole (organic peroxide)	Forbidden									
W	Asphalt, at or above its flashpoint	ORM-C	NA1999	None	None	None	Forbidden	Forbidden	1	5	When applicable, no fire or residue thereof may be present in the furnace heating the substance while the vehicle is on board a cargo vehicle
	Asphalt, cut back	Flammable liquid	NA1999	Flammable liquid	173.118	173.131	1 quart	10 gallons	1,2	1	
	Asphalt, cut back	Combustible liquid	NA1999	None	173.118a	None	No limit	No limit	1,2	1,2	
	Automobile, motorcycle, tractor, or other self-propelled vehicle. See Motor vehicle										
	Automobile, motorcycle, tractor, or other self-propelled vehicle, engine, or other mechanical apparatus, with charged electric storage battery, wet. See Motor vehicle										
	Azaurolic acid (salt of), (dry)	Forbidden									
	3-Azido-1,2-Propylene glycol dinitrate	Forbidden									
	5-Azido-1-hydroxy tetrazole	Forbidden									
	Azidodithiocarbonic acid	Forbidden									
	Azidoethyl nitrate	Forbidden									
	Azido guanidine picrate (dry)	Forbidden									
	Azido hydroxy tetrazole (mercury and silver salts)	Forbidden									
	Azinphos methyl	Poison B	NA2783	Poison	173.364	173.365	50 pounds	200 pounds	1,2	4	
	Azinphos methyl mixture, liquid	Poison B	NA2783	Poison	173.345	173.346	1/2 pint	1 quart	1,2	5	
	1-Aziridinyl phosphine oxide (tris). See Tris-(1-aziridinyl) phosphine oxide										
	Azotetrasole (dry)	Forbidden									
	Bags, burlap, used, must be classed for the hazardous material previously contained in bag. See 173.28, 173.29										
	Barium azide, wet, 50% or more water	Flammable solid	UN1571	Flammable solid	None	173.239	Forbidden	1 pound	1,2	1,2	Stow away from heavy metals
	Barium chlorate	Oxidizer	UN1445	Oxidizer	173.153	173.163	25 pounds	100 pounds	1,2	1,2	Separate from ammonium compounds. Stow away from powdered metals.
	Barium chlorate, wet	Oxidizer	NA1445	Oxidizer	173.153	173.163	25 pounds	200 pounds	1,2	1,2	Separate from ammonium compounds. Stow away from powdered metals.
	Barium cyanide, solid	Poison B	UN1565	Poison	173.370	173.370	25 pounds	200 pounds	1,2	1,2	Stow away from acids
	Barium nitrate	Oxidizer	UN1446	Oxidizer	173.153	173.182	25 pounds	100 pounds	1,2	1,2	
A	Barium oxide	ORM-B	UN1884	None	173.505	173.800	25 pounds	100 pounds			
	Barium perchlorate	Oxidizer	UN1447	Oxidizer	173.153	173.154	25 pounds	100 pounds	1,2	1,2	Stow away from powdered metals

(1)	(2)	(3)	(3A)	(4)	(5) Packaging		(6) Maximum net quantity in one package		(7) Water shipments		
+/ A/ W	Hazardous materials descriptions and proper shipping names	Hazard class	Identi- fication number	Label(s) required (if not excepted)	(a) Exceptions	(b) Specific require- ments	(a) Passenger carrying aircraft or railcar	(b) Cargo only aircraft	(a) Cargo vessel	(b) Pas- senger vessel	(c) Other requirements
	Barium permanganate	Oxidizer	UN1448	Oxidizer	173.153	173.154	25 pounds	100 pounds	1,2	1,2	Separate from ammonium compounds and hydrogen peroxide
	Barium peroxide	Oxidizer	UN1449	Oxidizer	173.153	173.156	25 pounds	100 pounds	1,2	1,2	Keep dry
	Barium styphnate, monohydrate. See Initiating explosive.										
	Barrel, empty. See Drum, empty										
	Battery, dry. Not subject to Parts 170-189 of this subchapter										
	Battery, electric storage, dry (containing potassium hydroxide, dry solid, flake bead, or granular)	Corrosive material	NA1813	Corrosive	173.244	173.245b	25 pounds	100 pounds	1,2	1,2	Keep dry
	Battery, electric storage, wet, filled with acid	Corrosive material	UN2794	Corrosive	173.260	173.260	Forbidden	No limit	1,2	1,2	
	Battery, electric storage, wet, filled with acid, with automobile (or specifically named self-propelled vehicle or mechanical apparatus)	Corrosive material	NA2794	Corrosive	173.250	173.260	No limit	No limit	1,2	1,2	Keep dry
	Battery, electric storage, wet, filled with alkali, with automobile (or specifically named self-propelled vehicle or mechanical apparatus)	Corrosive material	NA2797	Corrosive	173.250	173.260	No limit	No limit	1,2	1,2	Keep dry
	Battery, electric storage, wet, with wheelchair	Corrosive material		Corrosive	173.250	173.250 175.10	No limit	No limit	1,2	1,2	Keep dry
	Battery, electric storage, wet, nonspillable. See 173.260(d).										
	Battery, electric storage, wet, filled with alkali	Corrosive material	UN2795	Corrosive	173.260	173.260	Forbidden	No limit	1,2	1,2	
	Battery fluid, acid	Corrosive material	UN2796	Corrosive	173.244	173.257	1 quart	5 gallons	1,2	1,2	
	Battery fluid, acid, with electronic equipment or actuating device	Corrosive material	NA2796	Corrosive	None	173.259	Forbidden	5 pints	1,2	1,2	
	Battery fluid, acid, with battery, electric storage, wet, empty, or dry	Corrosive material	NA2796	Corrosive	None	173.258	Forbidden	5 pints	1,2	1,2	
	Battery fluid, alkali	Corrosive material	UN2797	Corrosive	173.244	173.257	1 quart	5 gallons	1,2	1,2	
	Battery fluid, alkali, with electronic equipment or actuating device	Corrosive material	NA2797	Corrosive	None	173.259	Forbidden	5 pints	1,2	1,2	
	Battery fluid, alkali, with battery, electric storage wet, empty or dry	Corrosive material	UN2797	Corrosive	None	173.258	Forbidden	5 pints	1,2	1,2	
	Battery, lithium. See 173.206(f)										
W	Battery parts (plates, grids, etc. unwashed, exhausted)	ORM-C		None	173.505	173.915			1,2	4	

Reserved

(1) +/ A/ W	(2) Hazardous materials descriptions and proper shipping names	(3) Hazard class	(3A) Identification number	(4) Label(s) required (if not excepted)	(5) Packaging (a) Exceptions	(5) (b) Specific requirements	(6) Maximum net quantity in one package (a) Passenger carrying aircraft or railcar	(6) (b) Cargo only aircraft	(7) Water shipments (a) Cargo vessel	(7) (b) Passenger vessel	(7) (c) Other requirements
	Benzaldehyde	Combustible liquid	NA1989	None	173.118a	None	No limit	No limit	1,2	1,2	
	Benzene (benzol)	Flammable liquid	UN1114	Flammable liquid	173.118	173.119	1 quart	10 gallons	1,2	1	
	Benzene diazonium chloride (dry)	Forbidden									
	Benzene diazonium nitrate (dry)	Forbidden									
	Benzene phosphorus dichloride	Corrosive material	UN2798	Corrosive	None	173.250a	Forbidden	5 pints	1	5	
	Benzene phosphorus thiodichloride	Corrosive material	UN2799	Corrosive	None	173.250a	Forbidden	5 pints	1	5	
	Benzenethiol. See Phenyl mercaptan	Forbidden									
	Benzene triozonide	Forbidden									
	Benzidine	Poison B	UN1885	Poison	173.364	173.365	50 pounds	200 pounds	1,2	1	
	Benzine	Flammable liquid	UN1115	Flammable liquid	173.118	173.119	1 quart	10 gallons	1,2	1	
	Benzoic derivative pesticide, liquid, n.o.s., (compounds and preparations)	Flammable liquid	UN2770	Flammable liquid	173.118	173.119	1 quart	10 gallons	1,2	1	
	Benzoic derivative pesticide, liquid, n.o.s., (compounds and preparations)	Poison B	UN2769	Poison	173.345	173.346	1 quart	55 gallons	1,2	1,2	
	Benzoic derivative pesticide, solid, n.o.s., (compounds and preparations)	Poison B	UN2769	Poison	173.364	173.365	50 pounds	200 pounds	1,2	1,2	
	Benzonitrile	Combustible liquid	UN2224	None	173.118a	None	No limit	No limit	1,2	1,2	
	Benzoxidiazoles (dry)	Forbidden									
	Benzoyl azide	Forbidden									
	Benzoyl chloride	Corrosive material	UN1736	Corrosive	173.244	173.247	1 quart	1 quart	1	1	Keep dry. Glass carboys not permitted on passenger vessels
	Benzoyl peroxide	Organic peroxide	NA2085	Organic peroxide	None	173.157 173.158	Forbidden	25 pounds	1,2	1	
	Benzoyl peroxide, more than 77% but less than 95% with water. See Benzoyl peroxide.		UN2088								
	Benzoyl peroxide, not less than 30% but not more than 52% with inert solid. See Organic peroxide, solid, n.o.s.		UN2089								
	Benzoyl peroxide, not more than 72% as a paste. See Organic peroxide, solid, n.o.s.		UN2087								
	Benzoyl peroxide, not more than 77% with water. See Benzoyl peroxide.		UN2090								
	Benzoyl peroxide, technically pure or Benzoyl peroxide, more than 52% with inert solid. See Benzoyl peroxide.		UN2085								
	Benzyl bromide (bromotoluene, alpha)	Corrosive material	UN1737	Corrosive	None	173.281	Forbidden	5 pints	1	5	Keep dry
	Benzyl chloride	Corrosive material	UN1738	Corrosive	173.244	173.295	Forbidden	1 quart	1	4	Keep dry
	Benzyl chloroformate (benzyl chlorocarbonate)	Corrosive material	UN1739	Corrosive	None	173.288	Forbidden	5 pints	1	5	Keep dry
	Beryllium chloride	Poison B	NA1566	Poison	173.364	173.365	50 pounds	200 pounds	1,2	1,2	
	Beryllium compound, n.o.s.	Poison B	UN1566	Poison	173.364	173.365	50 pounds	200 pounds	1,2	1,2	
	Beryllium fluoride	Poison B	NA1566	Poison	173.364	173.365	50 pounds	200 pounds	1,2	1,2	
	Beryllium nitrate	Oxidizer	UN2464	Oxidizer	173.153	173.182	25 pounds	100 pounds	1,2	1,2	
	Biphenyl triozonide	Forbidden									
	Bipyridilium pesticide, liquid, n.o.s. (compounds and preparations)	Flammable liquid	UN2782	Flammable liquid	173.118	173.119	1 quart	10 gallons	1,2	1	
	Bipyridilium pesticide, liquid, n.o.s. (compounds and preparations)	Poison B	UN2781	Poison	173.345	173.346	1 quart	55 gallons	1,2	1,2	
	Bipyridilium pesticide, solid, n.o.s. (compounds and preparations)	Poison B	UN2781	Poison	173.364	173.365	50 pounds	200 pounds	1,2	1,2	
	Black powder	Class A explosive		Explosive A	None	173.60	Forbidden	Forbidden	6	5	
	Black powder igniter with empty cartridge bag	Class C explosive		Explosive C	None	173.106	50 pounds	150 pounds	1,3	1,3	
	Blasting agent, n.o.s.	Blasting agent		Blasting agent	None	173.114a	Forbidden	100 pounds	1,2	1,2	
	Blasting caps. See Detonators, Class A or Class C explosives										
	Blasting caps, electric. See Detonators, Class A or Class C explosives										
	Blasting caps, percussion activated. See Detonators, Class A or Class C explosives										
	Blasting caps with detonating cord. See Detonators, Class A or Class C explosives and Detonating primers, Class A or Class C Explosives										

209

A/W	(2) Hazardous materials descriptions and proper shipping names	(3) Hazard class	(3A) Identification number	(4) Label(s) required (if not excepted)	(5) Packaging (a) Exceptions	(5) (b) Specific requirements	(6) Maximum net quantity in one package (a) Passenger carrying aircraft or railcar	(6) (b) Cargo only aircraft	(7) Water shipments (a) Cargo vessel	(7) (b) Passenger vessel	(7) (c) Other requirements
	Blasting caps with metal clad mild detonating fuze. See **Detonators, Class A** or **Class C explosives**										
	Blasting caps with safety fuse. See **Detonators, Class A** or **Class C explosives**										
	Blasting caps with shock tubes. See **Detonators, Class A** or **Class C explosives**										
	Blasting gelatin. See **High explosive**										
	Blasting powder. See **Black powder**										
W	Bleaching powder, containing 39% or less available chlorine	ORM-C	UN2208	None	173.505	173.920			1,2	1,2	Keep dry. Stow separate from flammable liquids and acids. (Stow away from oils, grease, and similar organic materials.
	Bomb, explosive. See **Explosive bomb**										
	Bomb, explosive with gas, smoke, or incendiary material. See **Explosive bomb**										
	Bomb, fireworks. See **Fireworks, special**										
	Bomb, gas, smoke, or incendiary, nonexplosive. See **Chemical ammunition, nonexplosive**										
	Bomb, incendiary, or smoke without bursting charge. See **Fireworks, special**										
	Bomb, practice, with electric primer or electric squib (non-explosive). See 173.55										
	Bomb, sand-loaded or empty (non-explosive). See 173.55										
	Booster, explosive	Class A explosive		Explosive A	None	173.69	Forbidden	Forbidden	6	5	
	Bordeaux arsenite, liquid	Poison B	NA2759	Poison	173.345	173.346	1 quart	55 gallons	1,2	1,2	
	Bordeaux arsenite, solid	Poison B	NA2759	Poison	173.364	173.365	50 pounds	200 pounds	1,2	1,2	
	Boron tribromide	Corrosive material	UN2692	Corrosive	None	173.251	Forbidden	1 quart	1	5	
	Boron trichloride	Corrosive material	UN1741	Corrosive	None	173.251	Forbidden	1 quart	1,2	5	Stow in well ventilated space. Shade from radiant heat. Segregation same as for non-flammable gases.
	Boron trifluoride	Nonflammable gas	UN1008	Nonflammable gas and Poison	None	173.302	Forbidden	Forbidden	1	5	Stow away from living quarters and foodstuffs
	Boron trifluoride-acetic acid complex	Corrosive material	UN1742	Corrosive	173.244	173.247	1 quart	1 gallon	1,2	1,2	
	Bromine	Corrosive material	UN1744	Corrosive	None	173.252	Forbidden	1 quart	1	5	Keep cool
	Bromine azide	Forbidden									
	Bromine pentafluoride	Oxidizer	UN1745	Oxidizer	None	173.246	Forbidden	100 pounds	1	5	Shade from radiant heat. Segregation same as for corrosives
	Bromine trifluoride	Oxidizer	UN1746	Oxidizer and Poison	None	173.246	Forbidden	100 pounds	1	5	Shade from dadiant heat. Segregation same as for corrosives
	4-Bromo-1,2-dinitrobenzene (unstable at 59 deg C.)	Forbidden									
	Bromoacetic acid, solid	Corrosive material	UN1938	Corrosive	173.244	173.245b	25 pounds	100 pounds	1,2	1,2	Keep dry
	Bromoacetic acid solution	Corrosive material	UN1938	Corrosive	173.244	173.245	1 quart	1 quart	1,2	1,2	Glass carboys in hampers not permitted under deck
	Bromoacetone, liquid	Poison A	UN1569	Poison gas	None	173.329	Forbidden	Forbidden	1	5	Segregation same as for flammable liquids
	Bromobenzene	Combustible liquid	UN2514	None	173.118a	None	No limit	No limit	1,2	1,2	
A	Bromochloromethane	ORM-A	UN1887	None	173.505	173.605	10 gallons	55 gallons			
	Bromosilane	Forbidden									
	Bromotoluene, alpha. See **Benzyl bromide**										
	Bromotrifluoromethane (R-13B1 or H-13O1)	Nonflammable gas	UN1009	Nonflammable gas	173.306	173.304 173.314 173.315	150 pounds	300 pounds	1,2	1,2	
	Brucine, solid (dimethoxy strychnine)	Poison B	UN1570	Poison	173.364	173.365	50 pounds	200 pounds	1,2	1,2	
	Burnt cotton, not repicked	Flammable solid	NA1325	Flammable solid	None	173.159	Forbidden	Forbidden	1	5	Separate from flammable gases or liquids, oxidizing materials, or organic peroxides
	Burster, explosive	Class A explosive		Explosive A	None	173.69	Forbidden	Forbidden	6	5	
+	Butadiene, inhibited	Flammable gas	UN1010	Flammable gas	173.306	173.304 173.314 173.315	Forbidden	300 pounds	1,2	1	Stow away from living quarters
	Butane or Liquefied petroleum gas. See **Liquefied petroleum gas**										
	1,2,4-Butanetriol trinitrate	Forbidden									
	tert-Butoxycarbonyl azide	Forbidden									

210

(1) +/A/W	(2) Hazardous materials descriptions and proper shipping names	(3) Hazard class	(3A) Identification number	(4) Label(s) required (if not excepted)	(5) Packaging		(6) Maximum net quantity in one package		(7) Water shipments		
					(a) Exceptions	(b) Specific requirements	(a) Passenger carrying aircraft or railcar	(b) Cargo only aircraft	(a) Cargo vessel	(b) Passenger vessel	(c) Other requirements
	n-Butyl-4, 4-di-(tert-butylperoxy) valerate, *technically pure.* See Organic peroxide, liquid or solution, n.o.s.		UN2140								
	n-Butyl-4, 4-di-(tert-butylperoxy)valerate, *not more than 52% with inert solid.* See Organic peroxide, solution, n.o.s.		UN2141								
	Butyl acetate	Flammable liquid	UN1123	Flammable liquid	173.118	173.119	1 quart	10 gallons	1,2	1	
	n-Butyl acid phosphate. *See* Acid butyl phosphate										
	Butyl alcohol	Flammable liquid	NA1120	Flammable liquid	173.118	173.125	1 quart	10 gallons	1,2	1	
	Butylamine	Flammable liquid	UN1125	Flammable liquid	173.118	173.119	1 quart	10 gallons	1,2	1	
	Butyl bromide, *normal*	Flammable liquid	UN1126	Flammable liquid	173.118	173.119	1 quart	10 gallons	1,2	1	
	Butyl chloride	Flammable liquid	UN1127	Flammable liquid	173.118	173.119	1 quart	10 gallons	1,2	1	
	tert-Butyl cumyl peroxide, *technically pure* or tert-Butyl cumene peroxide, *technically pure.* See Organic peroxide, liquid or solution, n.o.s.										
	Butyl ether	Flammable liquid	UN1149	Flammable liquid	173.118	173.119	1 quart	10 gallons	1,2	1,2	
	Butyl formate	Flammable liquid	UN1128	Flammable liquid	173.118	173.119	1 quart	10 gallons	1,2	1	
	tert-Butyl hydroperoxide, *more than 72% but not more than 90% with water.* See Organic peroxide, liquid or solution, n.o.s.		UN2094								
	tert-Butyl hydroperoxide, *not more than 72% with water.* See Organic peroxide, liquid or solution, n.o.s.		UN2093								
	tert-Butyl hydroperoxide, *not more than 80% in di-tert-butyl peroxide and solvent.* See Organic peroxide, liquid or solution, n.o.s.		UN2092								
	tert-Butyl hydroperoxide, *not more than 80% in di-tert-butyl peroxide or solvent.* See Organic peroxide, liquid or solution, n.o.s.		UN2092								
	tert-Butyl hydroperoxide, *more than 90% with water*	Forbidden									
	n-Butyl isocyanate	Flammable liquid	UN2485	Flammable liquid and Poison	None	173.119 173.3a	1 quart	10 gallons	1,2	1	
	tert-Butyl isopropyl benzene hydroperoxide	Organic peroxide	NA2091	Organic peroxide	173.153	173.224	1 quart	1 quart	1,2	4	
	Butyl mercaptan	Flammable liquid	UN2347	Flammable liquid	None	173.141	Forbidden	10 gallons	1,3	5	
	tert-Butyl peroxy-2-ethylhexanoate, *technically pure.* See Organic peroxide, liquid or solution, n.o.s.		UN2143								
	tert-Butyl peroxy-2-ethylhexanoate, *not more than 30% with 2,2-Di-(tert-butylperoxy) butane, not more than 35%, with not less than 35% phlegmatizer.* See Organic peroxide, liquid or solution, n.o.s.		UN2886								
	tert-Butyl peroxy-2-ethylhexanoate, *not more than 12% with 2,2-Di-(tert-butylperoxy) butane, not more than 14% with not less than 14% phlegmatizer and 60% inert inorganic solid.* See Organic peroxide, solid, n.o.s.		UN2887								
	tert-Butyl peroxy-2-ethylhexanoate, *not more than 50% with phlegmatizer.* See Organic peroxide, liquid or solution, n.o.s.		UN2888								
	tert-Butyl peroxy-3,5,5-trimethylhexanoate or tert-Butyl peroxyisononanoate, *technically pure.* See Organic peroxide, liquid or solution, n.o.s.		UN2104								
	3-tert-Butyl peroxy-3-phenylphthalide, *technically pure.* See Organic peroxide, solid, n.o.s.		UN2596								
	tert-Butyl peroxyacetate, *not more than 76% in solution.* See Organic peroxide, liquid or solution, n.o.s.		UN2095								
	tert-Butyl peroxyacetate, *not more than 52% in solution.* See Organic peroxide, liquid or solution, n.o.s.		UN2096								
	tert-Butyl peroxyacetate, *more than 76% in solution*	Forbidden									

(1)	(2)	(3)	(3A)	(4)	(5) Packaging		(6) Maximum net quantity in one package		(7) Water shipments		
+/ A/ W	Hazardous materials descriptions and proper shipping names	Hazard class	Identi-fication number	Label(s) required (if not excepted)	(a) Exceptions	(b) Specific require-ments	(a) Passenger carrying aircraft or railcar	(b) Cargo only aircraft	(a) Cargo vessel	(b) Pas-senger vessel	(c) Other requirements
	tert-Butyl peroxybenzoate, not more than 75% in solution. See **Organic peroxide, liquid or solution, n.o.s.**		UN2098								
	tert-Butyl peroxybenzoate, not more than 50% with inert inorganic solid. See **Organic perox-ide, solid, n.o.s.**		UN2890								
	tert-Butyl peroxybenzoate, technically pure or tert-Butyl peroxybenzoate, more than 75% in solu-tion. See **Organic peroxide, liquid or solution, n.o.s.**		UN2097								
	tert-Butyl peroxycrotonate, not more than 76% in solution. See **Organic peroxide, liquid or solu-tion, n.o.s.**		UN2183								
	n-Butyl peroxydicarbonate, not more than 52% in solution. See **Organic peroxide, liquid or solu-tion, n.o.s.**		UN2169								
	n-Butyl peroxydicarbonate, not more than 27% in solution. See **Organic peroxide,, liquid or solu-tion, n.o.s.**		UN2170								
	n-Butyl peroxydicarbonate, more than 52% in solutions	Forbidden									
	tert-Butyl peroxydiethylacetate, 33% with tert-Butyl peroxybenzoate, 33%, and solvent. See **Organic peroxide, liquid or solution, n.o.s.**		UN2551								
	tert-Butyl peroxydiethylacetate, technically pure. See **Organic peroxide, liquid or solution, n.o.s.**		UN2144								
	tert-Butyl peroxyisobutyrate, more than 52% but not more than 77% in solution. See **Organic peroxide, liquid or solution, n.o.s.**		UN2142								
	tert-Butyl peroxyisobutyrate, not more than 52% in solution. See **Organic peroxide, liquid or solu-tion, n.o.s.**		UN2562								
	tert-Butyl peroxyisobutyrate, more than 77% in solution	Forbidden									
	tert-Butyl peroxyisopropyl carbonate, technically pure. See **Organic peroxide, liquid or solu-tion, n.o.s.**		UN2103								
	tert-Butyl peroxymaleate, not more than 55% in solution. See **Organic peroxide, liquid or solu-tion, n.o.s.**		UN2100								
	tert-Butyl peroxymaleate, not more than 55% as a paste. See **Organic peroxide, solid, n.o.s.**		UN2101								
	tert-Butyl peroxymaleate, technically pure. See **Organic peroxide, solid, n.o.s.**		UN2099								
	tert-Butyl peroxyneodecanoate, not more than 77% in solution. See **Organic peroxide, liquid or solution, n.o.s.**		UN2177								
	tert-Butyl peroxyneodecanoate, technically pure. See **Organic peroxide, liquid or solution, n.o.s.**		UN2594								
	tert-Butyl peroxyphthalate, technically pure. See **Organic peroxide, solid, n.o.s.**		UN2105								
	tert-Butyl peroxypivalate, not more than 77% in solution. See **Organic peroxide, liquid or solu-tion, n.o.s.**		UN2110								
	Butyl phosphoric acid. See **Acid butyl phosphate**										
	Butyl trichlorosilane	Corrosive material	UN1747	Corrosive	None	173.280	Forbidden	10 gallons	1	1	Keep dry
	Butyraldehyde	Flammable liquid	UN1129	Flammable liquid	173.118	173.119	1 quart	10 gallons	1,2	1	
	Butyric acid	Corrosive material	UN2820	Corrosive	173.244	173.245	1 quart	10 gallons	1,2	1,2	
	Carbazide	Forbidden									
	Calcium arsenate, solid	Poison B	UN1573	Poison	173.364	173.367 173.368	50 pounds	200 pounds	1,2	1,2	
	Calcium arsenite, solid	Poison B	NA1574	Poison	173.364	173.365	50 pounds	200 pounds	1,2	1,2	
	Calcium bisulfite solution. See **Calcium hydrogen sulfite solution**										
	Calcium carbide	Flammable solid	UN1402	Flammable solid and Dangerous when wet	None	173.178	Forbidden	25 pounds	1,2	1,2	Keep dry. stow away from copper, its alloys, and salts.
	Calcium chlorate	Oxidizer	UN1452	Oxidizer	173.153	173.163	25 pounds	100 pounds	1,2	1,2	Separate from ammonium com-pounds. Stow away from powdered metals and cyanide

(1) +/A/W	(2) Hazardous materials descriptions and proper shipping names	(3) Hazard class	(3A) Identification number	(4) Label(s) required (if not excepted)	(5) Packaging (a) Exceptions	(5) Packaging (b) Specific requirements	(6) Maximum net quantity in one package (a) Passenger carrying aircraft or railcar	(6) (b) Cargo only aircraft	(7) Water shipments (a) Cargo vessel	(7) (b) Passenger vessel	(7) (c) Other requirements
	Calcium chlorite	Oxidizer	UN1453	Oxidizer	None	173.160	Forbidden	100 pounds	1,2	1,2	Separate from ammonium compounds, powdered materials, and cyanides
AW	Calcium cyanamide, not hydrated (containing more than 0.1% calcium carbide)	ORM-C	UN1403	None	None	173.945	25 pounds	200 pounds	1,2	1,2	Segregation same as for flammable solids labeled Dangerous When Wet
	Calcium cyanide, solid or Calcium cyanide mixture, solid	Poison B	UN1575	Poison	173.370	173.370	25 pounds	200 pounds	1,2	1,2	Stow away from corrosive liquids. Keep dry
	Calcium hydrogen sulfite solution	Corrosive material	NA2693	Corrosive	173.244	173.245	1 quart	5 gallons	1,2	1,2	
	Calcium hypochlorite, hydrated (minimum 5.5% but not more than 10% water, and containing more than 39% available chlorine)	Oxidizer	UN2880	Oxidizer	173.153	173.217	50 pounds	100 pounds	1,2	1,2	
	Calcium hypochlorite mixture, dry, (Containing more than 39% available chlorine)	Oxidizer	UN1748	Oxidizer	173.153	173.217	50 pounds	100 pounds	1,2	1,2	Keep cool and dry
	Calcium, metal	Flammable solid	UN1401	Flammable solid and Dangerous when wet	173.153	173.154	25 pounds	100 pounds	1,2	4	Keep cool and dry. Segregation same as for flammable solids labeled Dangerous When Wet
	Calcium, metal, crystalline	Flammable solid	NA1401	Flammable solid and Dangerous When Wet	None	173.231	Forbidden	25 pounds	1,2	5	Keep cool and dry. Segregation same as for flammable solids labeled Dangerous When Wet
	Calcium nitrate (See 173.182(a) Note)	Oxidizer	UN1454	Oxidizer	173.153	173.182	25 pounds	100 pounds	1,2	1,2	
AW	Calcium oxide	ORM-B	UN1910	None	173.505	173.850	25 pounds	100 pounds	1,2	1,2	Keep dry. Stow away from explosives, acids, combustible materials, and ammonium salts
	Calcium permanganate	Oxidizer	UN1456	Oxidizer	173.153	173.154	25 pounds	100 pounds	1,2	1,2	Separate from ammonium compounds and hydrogen peroxide
	Calcium peroxide	Oxidizer	UN1457	Oxidizer	173.153	173.156	25 pounds	100 pounds	1,2	1,2	Keep dry
	Calcium phosphide	Flammable solid	UN1360	Flammable solid and Dangerous When Wet	None	173.161	Forbidden	25 pounds	1	5	Keep cool and dry. Segregation same as for flammable solids labeled Dangerous When Wet
	Calcium resinate	Flammable solid	UN1313	Flammable solid	None	173.166	Forbidden	125 pounds	1	5	
	Calcium resinate, fused	Flammable solid	UN1314	Flammable solid	None	173.166	Forbidden	125 pounds	1	5	
	Calcium silicon (powder)	Flammable solid	UN1406	Flammable solid and Dangerous when wet	173.153	173.178	Forbidden	25 pounds	1,2	4	Segregation same as for flammable solids labeled Dangerous When Wet
AW	Camphene	ORM-A	NA9011	None	173.505	173.610	No limit	No limit	1,3	1,3	Stow away from foodstuffs and living quarters
	Camphor oil	Combustible liquid	UN1130	None	173.118a	None	No limit	No limit	1,2	1,2	
	Cannon primer	Class C explosive		None	None	173.107	50 pounds	150 pounds	1,3	5	
	Caprylyl peroxide solution	Organic peroxide	NA2129	Organic peroxide	173.153	173.221	1 quart	1 quart	1,2	4	Keep cool. Stow separate from combustible materials, explosives, or acids
	Caps, blasting. See Detonators, Class A or Class C explosives										
	Caps, toy. See Toy caps										
	Carbamate pesticide, liquid, n.o.s., (compounds and preparations)	Flammable liquid	UN2758	Flammable liquid	173.118	173.119	1 quart	10 gallons	1,2	1	
	Carbamate pesticide, liquid, n.o.s., (compounds and preparations)	Poison B	UN2757	Poison	173.345	173.346	1 quart	55 gallons	1,2	1,2	
	Carbamate pesticide, solid, n.o.s., (compounds and preparations)	Poison B	UN2757	Poison	173.364	173.365	50 pounds	200 pounds	1,2	1,2	
A	Carbaryl	ORM-A	NA2757	None	173.505	173.510	No limit	No limit	1,2	1,2	
	Carbofuran	Poison B	NA2757	Poison	173.364	173.365	50 pounds	200 pounds	1,2	1,2	
	Carbofuran mixture, liquid	Poison B	NA2757	Poison	173.345	173.346	1 quart	55 gallons	1,2	1,2	
+	Carbolic acid. See Phenol										
	Carbolic acid, liquid (liquid tar acid containing over 50% phenol). See Phenol, liquid										
	Carbon bisulfide, or Carbon disulfide	Flammable liquid	UN1131	Flammable liquid	None	173.121	Forbidden	Forbidden	1	5	Keep cool. Not permitted on any vessel transporting explosives, except that quantities not exceeding 200 pounds may be transported on such vessels under conditions approved by the Captain of the Port.
	Carbon dioxide	Nonflammable gas	UN1013	Nonflammable gas	173.306	173.302 173.304	150 pounds	300 pounds	1,2	1,2	
	Carbon dioxide, refrigerated liquid	Nonflammable gas	UN2187	Nonflammable gas	173.306	173.314 173.315	150 pounds	300 pounds	1,2	1,2	
	Carbon dioxide-nitrous oxide mixture	Nonflammable gas	UN1015	Nonflammable gas	173.306	173.304	150 pounds	300 pounds	1,2	1,2	

(1)	(2)	(3)	(3A)	(4)	(5) Packaging		(6) Maximum net quantity in one package		(7) Water shipments		
+/ A/ W	Hazardous materials descriptions and proper shipping names	Hazard class	Identi- fication number	Label(s) required (if not excepted)	(a) Exceptions	(b) Specific require- ments	(a) Passenger carrying aircraft or railcar	(b) Cargo only aircraft	(a) Cargo vessel	(b) Pas- senger vessel	(c) Other requirements
	Carbon dioxide-oxygen mixture	Nonflammable gas	UN1014	Nonflammable gas	173.306	173.304	150 pounds	300 pounds	1,2	1,2	
AW	Carbon dioxide, solid, or Dry ice, or Carbonice	ORM-A	UN1845	None	None	173.615	440 pounds	440 pounds	1	1	Stow away from open ventilators. Stow away from cyanides or cyanide mixtures, liquid or dry
+	Carbon monoxide	Flammable gas	UN1016	Flammable gas	173.306	173.302	Forbidden	150 pounds	1	4	
	Carbon monoxide, cryogenic liquid	Flammable gas	NA9202	Flammable gas	None	173.318	Forbidden	Forbidden	1	5	Stow away from living quarters.
AW	Carbon tetrachloride	ORM-A	UN1846	None	173.505	173.620	1 quart	55 gallons	1,2	1,2	Stow away from living quarters
	Carbonyl chloride. See Phosgene										
	Carboys, empty, must be classed for the hazardous material previously contained in carboy. See 173.29										
	Cartridge bags, empty, with black powder igniter	Class C explosive		Explosive C	None	173.106	50 pounds	150 pounds	1,3	1,3	
	Cartridge, practice ammunition	Class C explosive		Explosive C	None	171.101a	50 pounds	150 pounds	1,2	1,2	
	Case oil. See Gasoline or Naptha										
	Casinghead gasoline. See Gasoline										
W	Castor Beans	ORM-C		None	173.505	173.952			1,2	1,2	Stow away from living quarters and foodstuffs. Bulk shipments permitted in tight vans or containers only on cargo vessels (Castor beans only)
W	Castor pomace. See Castor beans										
	Caustic, potash, dry, solid, flake, bead, or granular. See Potassium hydroxide, dry, etc.										
	Caustic potash, liquid or solution. See Potassium hydroxide solution.										
	Caustic soda, dry, solid, flake, bead, or granular. See Sodium hydroxide, dry, etc.										
	Caustic soda, liquid or solution. See Sodium hydroxide solution.										
W	Cellosolve. See Ethylene glycol monoethyl ether										
W	Cellosolve acetate. See Ethylene glycol monoethyl ether acetate.										
	Cement	Combustible liquid	NA1133	None	173.118a	None	No limit	No limit	1,2	1,2	
	Cement	Flammable liquid	NA1133	Flammable liquid	173.118	173.132	1 quart	10 gallons	1,2	1	
	Cement, adhesive, n.o.s. See Cement.										
	Cement, container, linoleum, tile, or wallboard, liquid	Flammable liquid	NA1133	Flammable liquid	173.118	173.132	1 quart	15 gallons	1,2	1	
	Cement, leather	Flammable liquid	NA1133	Flammable liquid	173.118	173.119	1 quart	10 gallons	1,2	1	
	Cement, pyroxylin	Flammable liquid	NA1133	Flammable liquid	173.118	173.132	1 quart	15 gallons	1,2	1	
	Cement, roofing, liquid	Flammable liquid	NA1133	Flammable liquid	173.118	173.119	1 quart	10 gallons	1,2	1	
	Cement, rubber	Flammable liquid	NA1133	Flammable liquid	173.118	173.132	1 quart	15 gallons	1,2	1	
	Cesium metal	Flammable solid	UN1407	Flammable solid and Dangerous when wet	None	173.206	Forbidden	25 pounds	1,2	5	Segregation same as for flammable solids labeled Dangerous When Wet
	Charcoal briquettes or briquets	Flammable solid	NA1361	Flammable solid	173.162	173.162	50 pounds	50 pounds	1,2	1,2	
	Charcoal screenings, made from 'pinon' wood	Flammable solid	NA1361	Flammable solid	173.162	173.162	25 pounds	200 pounds	1,2	1	
	Charcoal, shell	Flammable solid	NA1361	Flammable solid	173.162	173.162	25 pounds	200 pounds	1,2	1,2	
	Charcoal, wood, ground, crushed, granulated, or pulverized	Flammable solid	NA1361	Flammable solid	173.162	173.162	25 pounds	200 pounds	1,2	1,2	
	Charcoal, wood, lump	Flammable solid	NA1361	Flammable solid	173.162	173.162	50 pounds	50 pounds	1,2	1,2	
	Charcoal wood screenings, other than 'pinon' wood screenings	Flammable solid	NA1361	Flammable solid	None	173.162	Forbidden	Forbidden	1	1	
	Charged well casing jet perforating gun (total explosive contents in guns 20 pounds or more per motor vehicle)	Class A explosive		Explosive A	None	173.53 173.80	Forbidden	Forbidden			Forbidden
	Charged well casing jet perforating gun (total explosive contents in guns not ex- ceeding 20 pounds per motor vehicle or special offshore down hole tool pallet)	Class C explosive		Explosive C	None	173.53 173.110	Forbidden	Forbidden	1,2	5	
	Chemical ammunition, explosive. See Ammunition, chemical, explosive, with...										

214

(1) +/A/W	(2) Hazardous materials descriptions and proper shipping names	(3) Hazard class	(3A) Identification number	(4) Label(s) required (if not excepted)	(5) Packaging (a) Exceptions	(5) (b) Specific requirements	(6) Maximum net quantity in one package (a) Passenger carrying aircraft or railcar	(6) (b) Cargo only aircraft	(7) Water shipments (a) Cargo vessel	(7) (b) Passenger vessel	(7) (c) Other requirements
	Chemical ammunition, nonexplosive (containing a Poison B material)	Poison B	UN2016	Poison	173.345	173.350	Forbidden	55 gallons			See correct shipping name of applicable Poison B material for stowage, special segregation requirements
	Chemical ammunition, nonexplosive (containing a Poison B material)	Poison B	UN2016	Poison	173.345	173.350	Forbidden	55 gallons			See correct shipping name of applicable Poison B material for stowage, special segregation requirements
	Chemical ammunition, nonexplosive (containing a Poison A material)	Poison A	UN2016	Poison gas	None	173.330	Forbidden	Forbidden			See correct shipping name of applicable Poison A material for stowage, special handling, and special segregation requirements
	Chemical kit	Corrosive material	NA1760	Corrosive	173.286		1 quart	1 quart	1,3	1,3	
	Chlorate and borate mixture (containing more than 28% chlorate)	Oxidizer	UN1458	Oxidizer	173.153	173.229	25 pounds	100 pounds	1,2	4	Stow away from ammonium compounds and away from powdered metals
	Chlorate and magnesium chloride mixture (containing more than 28% chlorate)	Oxidizer	UN1459	Oxidizer	173.153	173.229	25 pounds	100 pounds	1,2	4	Stow away from ammonium compounds and away from powdered metals
	Chlorate explosive, dry. See High explosive										
	Chlorate, n.o.s.	Oxidizer	UN1461	Oxidizer	173.153	173.163	25 pounds	100 pounds	1,2	4	Stow away from ammonium compounds and away from powdered metals
	Chlorate, n.o.s., wet	Oxidizer	NA1461	Oxidizer	173.153	173.163	25 pounds	200 pounds	1,2	4	Stow away from ammonium compounds and away from powdered metals
	Chlorate of potash. See Potassium chlorate										
	Chlorate of soda. See Sodium chlorate										
	Chlorate powder. See High explosive										
	Chlordane, liquid	Flammable liquid	NA2762	Flammable liquid	173.118	173.119	1 quart	10 gallons	1,2	1	
	Chlordane, liquid	Combustible liquid	NA2762	None	173.118a	None	No limit	No limit	1,2	1,2	
	Chloric acid	Oxidizer	NA2626	Oxidizer and Poison	None	173.237	Forbidden	Forbidden			Forbidden
	Chloride of phosphorus. See Phosphorus trichloride										
	Chloride of sulfur. See Sulfur chloride										
W	Chlorinated lime (chloride of lime.) See Bleaching powder										
+	Chlorine	Nonflammable gas	UN1017	Nonflammable gas and Poison	None	173.304 173.314 173.315	Forbidden	Forbidden	1,2	5	Stow in a well-ventilated space. Stow away from organic materials
	Chlorine azide	Forbidden									
	Chlorine dioxide hydrate, frozen	Oxidizer	NA9191	Oxidizer and Poison	None	173.237	Forbidden	Forbidden			Forbidden
	Chlorine dioxide (not hydrate)	Forbidden									
	Chlorine trifluoride	Oxidizer	UN1749	Oxidizer and Poison	None	173.246	Forbidden	100 pounds	1,3	5	Stow in well ventilated area away from organic material
	Chloroacetic acid, liquid or solution	Corrosive material	UN1750	Corrosive	173.244	173.294	1 quart	1 quart	1,2	1,2	Glass carboys in hampers not permitted under deck
	Chloroacetic acid, solid	Corrosive material	UN1751	Corrosive	173.244	173.245b	25 pounds	100 pounds	1,2	1,2	Keep dry
	Chloroacetophenone, gas, liquid, or solid (CN)	Irritating material	UN1697	Irritant	None	173.382	Forbidden	75 pounds	1	5	
	Chloroacetyl chloride	Corrosive material	UN1752	Corrosive	None	173.253	Forbidden	1 quart	1	5	Keep dry
	Chlorobenzene	Flammable liquid	UN1134	Flammable liquid	173.118	173.119	1 quart	10 gallons	1,2	1,2	
	Chlorobenzol. See Chlorobenzene										
	p-Chlorobenzoyl peroxide	Organic peroxide	UN2113	Organic peroxide	None	173.157 173.158	Forbidden	25 pounds	1	1	
	p-Chlorobenzoyl peroxide, not more than 75% with water. See p-Chlorobenzoyl peroxide.		UN2113								
	p-Chlorobenzoyl peroxide, not more than 52% as a paste. See Organic peroxide, solid, n.o.s.		UN2114								
	p-Chlorobenzoyl peroxide, not more than 52% in solution. See Organic peroxide, liquid or solution, n.o.s.		UN2115								
	1-Chloro-1,1-difluoroethane. See Chlorodifluoroethane (R-142b)										
+	Chlorodifluoroethane (R-142b) or (1-Chloro-1,1-difluoroethane).	Flammable gas	UN2517	Flammable gas	173.306	173.304 173.314 173.315	Forbidden	300 pounds	1,2	1	
	Chlorodifluoromethane (R-22)	Nonflammable gas	UN1018	Nonflammable gas	173.306	173.304 173.314 173.315	150 pounds	300 pounds	1,2	1	

(1)	(2)	(3)	(3A)	(4)	(5) Packaging		(6) Maximum net quantity in one package		(7) Water shipments		
+/ A/ W	Hazardous materials descriptions and proper shipping names	Hazard class	Identi-fication number	Label(s) required (if not excepted)	(a) Exceptions	(b) Specific require-ments	(a) Passenger carrying aircraft or railcar	(b) Cargo only aircraft	(a) Cargo vessel	(b) Pas-senger vessel	(c) Other requirements
	Chlorodifluoromethane and chloropentafluoroe-thane mixture (constant boiling mixture) (R-502). See Refrigerant gas, n.o.s.										
	Chlorodinitrobenzene. See Dinitrochlorobenzene										
AW	Chloroform	ORM-A	UN1888	None	173.505	173.630	10 gallons	55 gallons	1,2	1,2	Stow away from living quarters and foodstuffs
+	4-Chloro-o-toluidine hydrochloride	Poison B	UN1579	Poison	None	173.362	Forbidden	1 quart	1,2	1,2	
+	Chloropentafluoroethane (R-115)	Nonflammable gas	UN1020	Nonflammable gas	173.306	173.304 173.314 173.315	150 pounds	300 pounds	1,2	1,2	
	3-Chloroperoxybenzoic acid, not more than 86% with 3-chlorobenzoic acid. See Organic perox-ide, solid, n.o.s.		UN2755								
	Chlorophenyltrichlorosilane	Corrosive material	UN1753	Corrosive	None	173.280	Forbidden	10 gallons	1	1	Keep dry
+	Chloropicrin, absorbed	Poison B	NA1583	Poison	None	173.357	Forbidden	Forbidden	1	5	Keep cool
+	Chloropicrin and methyl chloride mixture	Poison A	UN1582	Flammable gas and Poison gas	None	173.329	Forbidden	Forbidden	1	5	Keep cool. Segregation same as for flammable gases.
+	Chloropicrin and nonflammable, nonliquefied compressed gas mixture	Poison A	NA1955	Poison gas and Nonflammable gas	None	173.329	Forbidden	Forbidden	1	5	Keep cool
	Chloropicrin in mixture, flammable (pressure not exceeding 14.7 psia; flash point below 100 deg. F.)	Poison B	NA2929	Poison and Flammable liquid	None	173.357	Forbidden	Forbidden	1	5	Keep cool.
+	Chloropicrin, liquid	Poison B	UN1580	Poison	None	173.357	Forbidden	Forbidden	1	5	Keep cool
+	Chloropicrin mixture (containing no compressed gas or Poison A liquid)	Poison B	UN1583	Poison	None	173.357	Forbidden	Forbidden	1	5	Keep cool
A	Chloroplatinic acid, solid	ORM-B	UN2507	None	173.505	173.800	25 pounds	100 pounds			
	Chloroprene, inhibited	Flammable liquid	UN1991	Flammable liquid	173.118	173.119	1 quart	10 gallons	1,2	1	
	Chloroprene, uninhibited	Forbidden									
	2-Chloropropene	Flammable liquid	UN2456	Flammable liquid	None	173.119	Forbidden	10 gallons	1,2	5	
	Chlorosulfonic acid	Corrosive material	UN1754	Corrosive	173.244	173.254	1 quart	1 quart	1	1	Keep dry. Glass carboys not permit-ted on passenger vessels
	Chlorosulfonic acid-sulfur trioxide mixture	Corrosive material	UN1754	Corrosive	173.144	173.254	1 quart	1 quart	1	1	Keep dry. Glass carboys not permit-ted on passenger vessels
	Chlorotetrafluoroethane (R-124)	Nonflammable gas	UN1021	Nonflammable gas	173.306	173.304 173.314	150 pounds	300 pounds	1,2	1,2	
	Chlorotrifluoromethane (R-13)	Nonflammable gas	UN1022	Nonflammable gas	173.306	173.304 173.314 173.315	150 pounds	300 pounds	1,2	1,2	
A	Chlorpyrifos	ORM-A	NA2783	None	173.505	173.510	100 pounds	No limit	1,2	1,2	
	Chromic acid mixture, dry	Oxidizer	NA1463	Oxidizer	173.153	173.164	25 pounds	100 pounds	1,2	1,2	Stow away from foodstuffs
	Chromic acid, solid	Oxidizer	NA1463	Oxidizer	173.153	173.164	25 pounds	100 pounds	1,2	1,2	Stow away from foodstuffs. Stow separate from flammable liquids and solids
	Chromic acid solution	Corrosive material	UN1755	Corrosive	173.244	173.287	1 quart	1 gallon	1	1	
	Chromic anhydride. See Chromic acid, solid										
	Chromic fluoride, solid	Corrosive material	UN1756	Corrosive	173.244	173.245b	25 pounds	100 pounds	1,2	1,2	
	Chromic fluoride solution	Corrosive material	UN1757	Corrosive	173.244	173.245	1 quart	1 gallon	1,2	1,2	
	Chromic trioxide. See Chromic acid, solid										
	Chromium oxychloride or Chromyl chloride	Corrosive material	UN1758	Corrosive	None	173.247	Forbidden	1 gallon	1	1	Keep dry. Glass carboys not permit-ted on passenger vesssels
	Cigarette lighter (or other similar ignition device)	Flammable gas	UN1057	Flammable gas	173.21 175.10	173.308	21 ounces	25 pounds	1	1	
	Cigarette lighter (or other similar ignition device)	Flammable liquid	UN1226	Flammable liquid	173.21 175.10	173.118	Forbidden	Forbidden	1	1	
	Cigarette load	Class C explosive		Explosive C	None	173.111	50 pounds	150 pounds	1,2	1,2	
	Cloud gas cylinder. See Chemical ammunition, nonexplosive										
	Coal briquettesa, hot	Forbidden									
	Coal facings, See Coal ground bituminous, etc.										
	Coal gas. See Hydrocarbon gas, nonliquefied										
	Coal, ground bituminous, sea coal, or coal facings	Flammable solid	NA1361	Flammable solid	173.165	173.165	Forbidden	Forbidden	1	1	Separate from flammable gases or liquids, oxidizing materials, or organic peroxides
	Coal oil (export shipment only). See Kerosene										
	Coal tar distillate	Combustible liquid	UN1137	None	173.118a	None	No limit	No limit	1,2	1,2	

216

(1) +/A/W	(2) Hazardous materials descriptions and proper shipping names	(3) Hazard class	(3A) Identification number	(4) Label(s) required (if not excepted)	(5) Packaging (a) Exceptions	(5) Packaging (b) Specific requirements	(6) Maximum net quantity in one package (a) Passenger carrying aircraft or railcar	(6) (b) Cargo only aircraft	(7) Water shipments (a) Cargo vessel	(7) (b) Passenger vessel	(7) (c) Other requirements
	Coal tar distillate	Flammable liquid	UN1136	Flammable liquid	173.118	173.119	1 quart	10 gallons	1,2	1	
	Coal tar dye, liquid *(not otherwise specifically named in 172.101)*	Corrosive material	NA2801	Corrosive	173.244	173.249a	1 quart	10 gallons	1,2	1,2	
	Coating solution	Flammable liquid	UN1139	Flammable liquid	173.118	173.132	1 quart	15 gallons	1,2	1	
	Cobalt resinate, precipitated	Flammable solid	UN1318	Flammable solid	None	173.166	Forbidden	125 pounds	1,2	1,2	
	Cocculus, solid *(fishberry)*	Poison B	UN1584	Poison	173.364	173.365	50 pounds	200 pounds	1,2	1,2	
W	Coconut meal pellets *containing at least 6% and not more than 13% moisture and not more than 10% residual fat content*	ORM-C		None	173.505	173.955			1,2	4	Keep dry
	Coke, hot	Forbidden									
	Collodion	Flammable liquid	NA2059	Flammable liquid	173.118	173.119	1 quart	10 gallons	1,2	1	
	Combination fuze	Class C explosive		Explosive C	None	173.105	50 pounds	150 pounds	1,3	1,3	
	Combination primer	Class C explosive		None	None	173.107	50 pounds	150 pounds	1,3	5	
	Combustible liquid, n.o.s.	Combustible liquid	NA1993	None	173.118a	None	No limit	No limit	1,2	1,2	
	Commercial shaped charge. See **High explosive**										
	Common fireworks. See **Fireworks, common**										
	Compound, cleaning, liquid	Flammable liquid	NA1993	Flammable liquid	173.118	173.119	1 quart	10 gallons	1,2	1	
	Compound, cleaning, liquid	Corrosive material	NA1760	Corrosive	173.244	173.245	1 quart	1 quart	1,2	1,2	
	Compound, cleaning, liquid	Combustible liquid	NA1993	None	173.118a	None	No limit	No limit	1,2	1,2	
	Compound, cleaning, liquid *(containing phosphoric acid, acetic acid, sodium hydroxide or potassium hydroxide)*	Corrosive material	NA1760	Corrosive	173.244	173.249a	1 quart	1 quart	1,2	1,2	
	Compound, cleaning, liquid *(containing hydrochloric (muriatic) acid)*	Corrosive material	NA1789	Corrosive	173.244	173.263	1 quart	1 gallon	1	1	
	Compound, cleaning, liquid *(containing hydrofluoric acid)*	Corrosive material	NA1790	Corrosive	172.244	173.256	1 quart	1 gallon	1	4	
	Compound, polishing, liquid	Flammable liquid	NA1142	Flammable liquid	173.118	173.119	1 quart	55 gallons	1,2	1	
	Compound, rust preventing *or* Compound, rust removing	Corrosive material	NA1760	Corrosive	173.144	173.245	1 quart	1 gallon	1,2	1,2	
	Compound, tree *or* weed killing, liquid	Combustible liquid	NA1993	None	173.118a	None	No limit	No limit	1,2	1,2	
	Compound, tree *or* weed killing, liquid	Corrosive material	NA1760	Corrosive	173.244	173.245	1 quart	1 quart	1,2	1,2	
	Compound, tree *or* weed killing, liquid	Flammable liquid	NA1993	Flammable liquid	173.118	173.119	1 quart	10 gallons	1,2	1	
	Compound, tree *or* weed killing, liquid	Poison B	NA2810	Poison	173.345	173.346	1 quart	55 gallons	1,2	1,2	
	Compound, tree *or* weed killing, solid	Oxidizer	NA1479	Oxidizer	173.153	173.154 173.229	25 pounds	100 pounds			
	Compound, vulcanizing, liquid	Corrosive material	NA1760	Corrosive	173.244	173.245	1 quart	1 quart	1,2	1,2	
	Compound, vulcanizing, liquid	Flammable liquid	NA1142	Flammable liquid	173.118	173.119	1 quart	10 gallons	1,2	1	
	Compressed gas, n.o.s.	Flammable gas	UN1954	Flammable gas	173.306	173.302 173.304 173.305	Forbidden	300 pounds	1	4	
	Compressed gas, n.o.s.	Nonflammable gas	UN1956	Nonflammable gas	173.306 173.307	173.302 173.304 173.305	150 pounds	300 pounds	1,2	1,2	
	Consumer commodity	ORM-D		None	173.505(b)	173.510 173.1200	65 pounds gross	65 pounds gross			Not subject to requirements of Part 176
	Container, reused or empty, must be classed for the hazardous material previously contained. See 173.28, 173.29										
	Copper acetoarsenite, solid	Poison B	UN1585	Poison	173.364	173.367	50 pounds	200 pounds	1,2	1,2	
	Copper acetylide	Forbidden									
	Copper amine azide	Forbidden									
	Copper arsenite, solid	Poison B	UN1586	Poison	173.364	173.365	50 pounds	200 pounds	1,2	1	
	Copper based pesticide, liquid, n.o.s. *(compounds and preparations)*	Flammable liquid	UN2776	Flammable liquid	173.118	173.119	1 quart	10 gallons	1,2	1	

(1)	(2)	(3)	(3A)	(4)	(5) Packaging		(6) Maximum net quantity in one package		(7) Water shipments		
+/ A/ W	Hazardous materials descriptions and proper shipping names	Hazard class	Identification number	Label(s) required (if not excepted)	(a) Exceptions	(b) Specific requirements	(a) Passenger carrying aircraft or railcar	(b) Cargo only aircraft	(a) Cargo vessel	(b) Passenger vessel	(c) Other requirements
	Copper based pesticide, liquid, n.o.s. (compounds and preparations)	Poison B	UN2775	Poison	173.345	173.346	1 quart	55 gallons	1,2	1,2	
	Copper based pesticide, solid, n.o.s. (compounds and preparations)	Poison B	UN2775	Poison	173.364	173.365	50 pounds	200 pounds	1,2	1,2	
A	Copper chloride	ORM-B	UN2802	None	173.505	173.800	25 pounds	100 pounds	1,2	1,2	
	Copper cyanide	Poison B	UN1587	Poison	173.370	173.370	25 pounds	200 pounds	1,2	1,2	Stow away from acids
	Copper tetramine nitrate	Forbidden									
W	Copra	ORM-C	UN1363	None	173.505	173.960			1,2	1,2	Segregation same as for flammable solids. Separate from flammable gases or liquids, oxidizing materials, or organic peroxides
	Copra pellets. See Coconut meal pellets										
	Cord, detonating flexible	Class A explosive		Explosive A	173.81	173.81	Forbidden	Forbidden	6	5	
	Cord, detonating flexible	Class C explosive		Explosive C	None	173.104	Forbidden	150 pounds	1,3	1,3	
	Corrosive liquid, n.o.s.	Corrosive material	UN1760	Corrosive	173.244	173.245 173.245a	1 quart	1 quart	1	4	For material that meets only the corrosion to skin criteria of 49 CFR 173.240(a)(1), 'under deck' stowage is also authorized if the description includes the additional entry specified by 172.203(i)(2).
	Corrosive liquid, poisonous, n.o.s.	Corrosive material	UN2922	Corrosive and Poison	173.244	173.245	1 quart	1 quart	1	4	
	Corrosive solid, n.o.s.	Corrosive material	UN1759	Corrosive	173.244	173.245b	25 pounds	100 pounds	1	4	For material that meets only the corrosion to skin criteria of 49 CFR 173.240(a)(1), 'under deck' stowage is also authorized if the description includes the additional entry specified by 172.203(i)(2).
	Cosmetics, liquid, n.o.s.	Corrosive material	NA1760	Corrosive	173.244	173.245	1 quart	1 quart	1,2	1,2	
	Cosmetics, n.o.s.	Combustible liquid	NA1993	None	173.118a	None	No limit	No limit	1,2	1,2	
	Cosmetics, n.o.s.	Flammable liquid	NA1993	Flammable liquid	173.118	173.119	1 quart	10 gallons	1,2	1	
	Cosmetics, n.o.s.	Flammable solid	NA1325	Flammable solid	173.153	173.154	25 pounds	100 pounds	1,2	1,2	
	Cosmetics, n.o.s.	Oxidizer	NA1479	Oxidizer	173.153	173.154	25 pounds	100 pounds	1,2	1,2	
	Cosmetics, solid, n.o.s.	Corrosive material	NA1759	Corrosive	173.244	173.245b	25 pounds	100 pounds	1,2	1,2	Keep dry
W	Cotton	ORM-C		None	173.505	173.965			1,2	1,2	Segregation same as for flammable solids. See 176.900 to 176.904
	Coumaphos	Poison B	NA2783	Poison	173.364	173.365	50 pounds	200 pounds	1,2	1,2	
	Coumaphos mixture, liquid	Poison B	NA2783	Poison	173.345	173.346	1/2 pint	1 quart	1,2	5	
	Cresol	Corrosive material	UN2076	Corrosive	173.244	173.245	1 quart	10 gallons	1,2	1,2	
	Crotonaldehyde	Flammable liquid	UN1143	Flammable liquid and Poison	None	173.119 173.3a	1 quart	1 gallon	1,2	1	
	Crotonic acid	Corrosive material	UN2823	Corrosive	173.244	173.245	1 quart	10 gallons	1,2	1,2	
	Crotonylene	Flammable liquid	UN1144	Flammable liquid	173.118	173.119	1 quart	10 gallons	1,3	4	
	Crude oil, petroleum	Combustible liquid	UN1267	None	173.118a	None	No limit	No limit	1,2	1,2	
	Crude oil, petroleum	Flammable liquid	UN1267	Flammable liquid	173.118	173.119	1 quart	10 gallons	1,2	1	
	Cumene hydroperoxide	Organic peroxide	UN2116	Organic peroxide	173.153	173.224	1 quart	1 quart	1,2	4	
	Cumene hydroperoxide, technically pure. See Cumene hydroperoxide		UN2116								
	Cupric cyanide. See Copper cyanidone										
	Cupric nitrate	Oxidizer	NA1479	Oxidizer	173.153	173.182	25 pounds	100 pounds	1,2	1,2	
	Cupriethylene-diamine solution	Corrosive material	UN1761	Corrosive	173.244	173.249	1 quart	1 gallon	1,2	1,2	
	Cyanide or cyanide mixture, dry	Poison B	UN1588	Poison	173.364	173.370	25 pounds	200 pounds	1,2	1,2	Keep dry. Stow away from acids
	Cyanide solutions, n.o.s.	Poison B	UN1935	Poison	173.345	173.352	1 quart	55 gallons	1,2	1,2	Stow away from acids
	Cyanogen bromide	Poison B	UN1889	Poison	None	173.379	Forbidden	25 pounds	1	5	Shade from radiant heat. Segregation same as for corrosive materials.
	Cyanogen chloride containing less than 0.9% water	Poison A	UN1589	Poison gas and Nonflammable gas	None	173.328	Forbidden	Forbidden	1	5	Shade from radiant heat
	Cyanogen gas	Poison A	UN1026	Flammable gas and Poison gas	None	173.328	Forbidden	Forbidden	1	5	Segregation same as for flammable gases.

218

(1) +/A/W	(2) Hazardous materials descriptions and proper shipping names	(3) Hazard class	(3A) Identification number	(4) Label(s) required (if not excepted)	(5) Packaging		(6) Maximum net quantity in one package		(7) Water shipments		
					(a) Exceptions	(b) Specific requirements	(a) Passenger carrying aircraft or railcar	(b) Cargo only aircraft	(a) Cargo vessel	(b) Passenger vessel	(c) Other requirements
	Cyanuric triazide	Forbidden									
	Cyclohexane	Flammable liquid	UN1145	Flammable liquid	173.118	173.119	1 quart	10 gallons	1,3	4	
	Cyclohexanone peroxide, 50 to 85% peroxide	Organic peroxide	UN2119	Organic peroxide	173.157	173.158	Forbidden	25 pounds	1	1	
	Cyclohexanone peroxide, as a paste with not more than 9% by weight active oxygen. See Cyclohexanone peroxide, 50 to 85% peroxide.		UN2896								
	Cyclohexanone peroxide, in solution with not more than 9% by weight active oxygen. See Cyclohexanone peroxide, 50 to 85% peroxide.		UN2118								
	Cyclohexanone peroxide, not over 50% peroxide	Organic peroxide	UN2896	Organic peroxide	173.153	173.154	2 pounds	25 pounds	1,2	1,2	
	Cyclohexanone peroxide and di-(1-hydroxy cyclohexyl) peroxide mixture. See appropriate cyclohexanone peroxide entry.										
	Cyclohexenyl trichlorosilane	Corrosive material	UN1762	Corrosive	None	173.280	Forbidden	10 gallons	1	1	Keep dry
	Cyclohexylamine	Flammable liquid	UN2357	Flammable liquid	173.118	173.119	1 quart	10 gallons	1,2	1	
	Cyclohexyl trichlorosilane	Corrosive material	UN1763	Corrosive	None	173.280	Forbidden	10 gallons	1	1	Keep dry
	Cyclopentane	Flammable liquid	UN1146	Flammable liquid	173.118	173.119	1 quart	10 gallons	1,3	4	
	Cyclopentane, methyl	Flammable liquid	UN2298	Flammable liquid	173.118	173.119	1 quart	10 gallons	1,3	4	
+	Cyclopropane	Flammable gas	UN1027	Flammable gas	173.306	173.304	Forbidden	300 pounds	1,2	1	
	Cyclotetramethylene tetranitramine (dry)(HMX)	Forbidden									
	Cyclotetramethylene tetranitramine, wet with not less than 10% water. See High explosive.										
	Cyclotrimethylene trinitramine, desensitized. See High explosive.										
	Cyclotrimethylene trinitramine, wet with not less than 10% water. See High explosive.										
	Cylinder, empty, including ton tanks, must be classed for the hazardous material previously contained in cylinder. See 173.29										
A	2,4-D. See 2,4-Dichlorophenoxyacetic acid										
A	DDT or Dichlorodiphenyltrichloroethane	ORM-A	NA2761	None	173.505	173.510	No limit	No limit	1,2	1,2	
	Decarborane	Flammable solid	UN1868	Flammable solid and Poison	None	173.236	Forbidden	25 pounds	1,2	1,2	
	Decahydronaphthalene	Combustible liquid	UN1147	None	173.118a	None	No limit	No limit	1,2	1,2	
	Decalin. See Decahydronaphthalene										
	Decanol peroxide, technically pure. See Organic peroxide, solid, n.o.s.		UN2120								
	Delay connectors. See Detonators, Class A or Class C explosives and Detonating primers, Class A or Class C explosives.										
	Delay electric igniter	Class C explosive		Explosive C	None	173.106	50 pounds	150 pounds	1,3	1,3	
	Denatured alcohol	Flammable liquid	NA1986	Flammable liquid	173.118	173.125	1 quart	10 gallons	1,2	1	
	Depth bomb. See Explosive bomb.										
	Detonating fuze, Class A, with or without radio-active components.	Class A explosive		Explosive A	None	173.69	Forbidden	Forbidden	6	5	
	Detonating fuze, Class C explosive	Class C explosive		Explosive C	None	173.113	50 pounds	150 pounds	1,3	1,3	
	Detonating primers, Class A explosives. See 173.53	Class A explosive		Explosive A	None	173.68	Forbidden	Forbidden	6	5	Do not stow detonating primers, Class A explosives with any high explosives. Do not handle at the same time high explosives are being loaded.
	Detonating primers, Class C explosives. See 173.100	Class C explosive		Explosive C	None	173.68	173.103(d)	150 pounds	1,2	1,2	The maximum net quantity in one package for this material shipped aboard passenger vessel is limited to 50 pounds. Must not be stowed in portable magazine or metal locker. Do not stow detonating primers, Class C explosives with high explosives. Do not handle at the same time high explosives are being loaded.

219

(1) +/A/W	(2) Hazardous materials descriptions and proper shipping names	(3) Hazard class	(3A) Identification number	(4) Label(s) required (if not excepted)	(5) Packaging		(6) Maximum net quantity in one package		(7) Water shipments		
					(a) Exceptions	(b) Specific requirements	(a) Passenger carrying aircraft or railcar	(b) Cargo only aircraft	(a) Cargo vessel	(b) Passenger vessel	(c) Other requirements
	Detonators, Class A explosives. See 173.53.	Class A explosive		Explosive A	None	173.66	Forbidden	Forbidden	6	—	Do not stow detonators, Class A with any high explosives. Do not handle at the same time high explosives are being loaded.
	Detonators, Class C explosives. See 173.100	Class C explosive		Explosive C	None	173.66	173.103(d)	150 pounds	1,2	1,2	The maximum net quantity in one package for this material shipped aboard passenger vessel is limited to 50 pounds. Must be stowed in portable magazine or metal locker. Do not stow detonators, Class C explosives with high explosives. Do not handle at the same time high explosives are being loaded.
	Detonators, commercial. See Detonators, Class A or Class C explosives										
	Di-(1-hydroxycyclohexyl) peroxide, technically pure. See Organic peroxide, solid, n.o.s.		UN2148								
	Di-(1-hydroxytetrazole) (dry)	Forbidden									
	Di-(1-naphthoyl) peroxide	Forbidden									
	Di-(2-ethylhexyl) peroxydicarbonate, technically pure. See Organic peroxide, liquid or solution, n.o.s.		UN2122								
	Di-(2-ethylhexyl) peroxydicarbonate, not more than 77% in solution. See Organic peroxide, liquid or solution, n.o.s.		UN2123								
	Di-(2-ethylhexyl) phosphoric acid	Corrosive material	NA1902	Corrosive	173.244	173.245	1 quart	10 gallons	1,2	1,2	
	Di-(2-methylbenzoyl) peroxide, not more than 85% with water. See Organic peroxide, solid, n.o.s.		UN2593								
	1,3-Di-(2-tert-butylperoxyisopropyl) benzene, technically pure or more than 40% with inert solid. See Organic peroxide, solid, n.o.s.		UN2112								
	1,3-Di-(2-tert-butylperoxyisopropyl) benzene and 1,4-Di-(2-tert-butylperoxyisopropyl) benzene mixture, technically pure or more than 40% with inert solid. See Organic peroxide, solid, n.o.s.		UN2112								
	1,4-Di-(2-tert-butylperoxyisopropyl) benzene, technically pure or more than 40% with inert solid. See Organic peroxide, solid, n.o.s.		UN2112								
	Di-(3,5,5-trimethyl-1,2-dioxolanyl-3) peroxide, not more than 50% as a paste, with phlegmatizer. See Organic peroxide, solid, n.o.s.		UN2597								
	2,2-Di-(4,4-di-tert-butylperoxycyclohexyl) propane, not more than 42% with inert solid. See Organic peroxide, solid, n.o.s.		UN2168								
	2,2-Di-(4,4-di-tert-butylperoxycyclohexyl) propane, more than 42% with inert solid	Forbidden									
	Di-(4-tert-butylcyclohexyl) peroxydicarbonate, technically pure. See Organic peroxide, solid, n.o.s.		UN2154								
	Di-(4-tert-butylcyclohexyl) peroxydicarbonate, not more than 42% stable dispersion, in water. See Organic peroxide, liquid or solution, n.o.s.		UN2894								
	Diacetone alcohol	Combustible liquid	UN1148	None	173.118a	None	No limit	No limit	1,2	1,2	
	Diacetone alcohol	Flammable liquid	UN1148	Flammable liquid	173.118	173.119	1 quart	10 gallons	1,2	1	
	Diacetone alcohol peroxide, not more than 57% in solution with not more than 9% hydrogen peroxide, not less than 26% diacetone alcohol and not less than 9% water, total active oxygen content not more than 9%. See Organic peroxide, liquid or solution, n.o.s.		UN2163								
	Diacetone alcohol peroxide, more than 57% in solution with more than 9% hydrogen peroxide, less than 26% diacetone alcohol and less than 9% water, total active oxygen content more than 9% by weight.	Forbidden									
	Diacetyl	Flammable liquid	UN2346	Flammable liquid	173.118	173.119	1 quart	10 gallons	1,2	1	
	p-Diazidobenzene	Forbidden									
	1,2-Diazidoethane	Forbidden									
A	Diazinon	ORM-A	NA2783	None	173.505	173.510	No limit	No limit	1,2	1,2	
	1,1'-Diazoaminonaphthalene	Forbidden									
	Diazoaminotetrazole (dry)	Forbidden									
	Diazodinitrophenol. See Initiating explosive										
	Diazodinitrophenol (dry)	Forbidden									
	Diazodiphenylmethane	Forbidden									
	Diazonium nitrates (dry)	Forbidden									

(1) +/A/W	(2) Hazardous materials descriptions and proper shipping names	(3) Hazard class	(3A) Identi-fication number	(4) Label(s) required (if not excepted)	(5) Packaging		(6) Maximum net quan-tity in one package		(7) Water shipments		
					(a) Except-ions	(b) Specific require-ments	(a) Passenger carrying aircraft or railcar	(b) Cargo only aircraft	(a) Cargo vessel	(b) Pas-senger vessel	(c) Other requirements
	Diazonium perchlorates (dry)	Forbidden									
	1,3-Diazopropane	Forbidden									
	Dibenzyl peroxydicarbonate, *not more than 87% with water. See* **Organic peroxide, solid, n.o.s.**		UN2149								
	Dibenzyl peroxydicarbonate, more than 87% with water	Forbidden									
	Di-(beta-nitroxyethyl) ammonium nitrate	Forbidden									
+	**Diborane** or **diborane mixtures**	Flammable gas	UN1911	Flammable gas and Poison	None	173.302	Forbidden	Forbidden	1	5	Separate from Chlorine and materials bearing the oxidizer label
	Dibromoacetylene	Forbidden									
A	**Dibromodifluoromethane**	ORM-A	UN1941	None	173.505	173.605	10 gallons	55 gallons			
W	**1,2-Dibromoethane.** *See* **Ethylene dibromide**										
	Dicetyl peroxydicarbonate, *not more than 42%, stable dispersion, in water. See* **Organic peroxide, liquid or solution, n.o.s.**		UN2895								
	Dicetyl peroxydicarbonate, *technically pure. See* **Organic peroxide, solid, n.o.s.**		UN2164								
	N,N'-Dichlorazodicarbonamidine (salts of), (dry)	Forbidden									
	1,1-Dichloro-2,2-bis(parachlorophenyl) ethane. See TDE										
	Dichloroacetic acid	Corrosive material	UN1764	Corrosive	173.244	173.245	1 quart	1 quart	1,2	1,2	Glass carboys in hampers not permitted under deck
	Dichloroacetyl chloride	Corrosive material	UN1765	Corrosive	173.244	173.247	1 quart	1 gallon	1	4	Keep dry
	Dichloroacetylene	Forbidden									
A	**Dichlorobenzene, ortho, liquid**	ORM-A	UN1591	None	173.505	173.510	No limit	No limit	1,2	1,2	
A	**Dichlorobenzene, para, solid**	ORM-A	UN1592	None	173.505	173.510	No limit	No limit	1,2	1,2	
	2,4-Dichlorobenzoyl peroxide, *not more than 75% with water. See* **Organic per-oxide, solid, n.o.s.**		UN2137								
	2,4-Dichlorobenzoyl peroxide, *not more than 52% as a paste. See* **Organic per-oxide, solid, n.o.s.**		UN2138								
	2,4-Dichlorobenzoyl peroxide, *not more than 52% in solution. See* **Organic perox-ide, liquid or solution, n.o.s.**		UN2139								
	2,4-Dichlorobenzoyl peroxide, more than 75% with water	Forbidden									
	Dichlorobutene	Flammable liquid	NA2924	Flammable liquid	173.118	173.119	1 quart	10 gallons	1,2	1	
	Dichlorobutene	Corrosive material	NA2924	Corrosive	173.244	173.245 173.245a	1 quart	10 gallons	1	4	
A	**Dichlorodifluoroethylene**	ORM-A	NA9018	None	173.505	173.605	10 gallons	55 gallons			
	Dichlorodifluoromethane *(R-12)*	Nonflammable gas	UN1028	Nonflammable gas	173.306	173.304 173.314 173.315	150 pounds	300 pounds	1,2	1,2	
	Dichlorodifluoromethane and difluoroethane mixture *(constant boiling mixture)(R-500). See* **Refrigerant gas, n.o.s.** *or* **Dis-persant gas, n.o.s.**										
	Dichlorodifluoromethane *(R-12)* **and dichlo-rotetrafluoroethane** *(R-114)* **mixture.** *See* **Refrigerant gas, n.o.s.** *or* **Dispersant gas, n.o.s.**										
	Dichlorodifluoromethane *(R-12)* **and chloro-difluoromethane** *(R-22)* **mixture.** *See* **Refrigerant gas, n.o.s.** *or* **Dispersant gas, n.o.s.**										
	Dichlorodifluoromethane *(R-12)* **and trichlo-rofluoromethane** *(R-11)* **mixture.** *See* **Refrigerant gas, n.o.s.** *or* **Dispersant gas, n.o.s.**										
	Dichlorodifluoromethane *(R-12),* **trichloro-fluoromethane** *(R-11)* **and chlorodifluoromethane**(R-22) **mixture.** *See* **Refrigerant gas, n.o.s.** *or* **Dispersant gas, n.o.s.**										
	Dichlorodifluoromethane *(R-12)* **and trichlo-rotrifluoroethane** *(R-113)* **mixture.** *See* **Refrigerant gas, n.o.s.** *or* **Dispersant gas, n.o.s.**										
A	**Dichlorodiphenyltrichloroethane.** *See* DDT										
	Dichloroethylene	Flammable liquid	UN1150	Flammable liquid	173.118	173.119	1 quart	10 gallons	1,2	1	
	Dichloroisopropyl ether	Corrosive material	UN2490	Corrosive	173.244	173.254	1 quart	10 gallons	1,2	1,2	

221

(1) +/A/W	(2) Hazardous materials descriptions and proper shipping names	(3) Hazard class	(3A) Identification number	(4) Label(s) required (if not excepted)	(5) Packaging (a) Exceptions	(5) Packaging (b) Specific requirements	(6) Maximum net quantity in one package (a) Passenger carrying aircraft or railcar	(6) (b) Cargo only aircraft	(7) Water shipments (a) Cargo vessel	(7) (b) Passenger vessel	(7) (c) Other requirements
A	Dichloromethane or Methylene chloride	ORM-A	UN1593	None	173.505	173.605	10 gallons	55 gallons			
	Dichloropentane	Flammable liquid	UN1152	Flammable liquid	173.118	173.119	1 quart	10 gallons	1,2	1,2	
A	2,4-Dichlorophenoxyacetic acid	ORM-A	NA2765	None	173.505	173.510	50 pounds	No limit	1,2	1,2	
	Dichlorophenyltrichlorosilane	Corrosive material	UN1766	Corrosive	None	173.280	Forbidden	10 gallons	1	1	Keep dry
	Dichloropropane. See Propylene dichloride										
	Dichloropropene	Flammable liquid	UN2047	Flammable liquid	173.118	173.119	1 quart	10 gallons	1,2	1	
	Dichloropropene and propylene dichloride mixture	Flammable liquid	NA2047	Flammable liquid	173.118	173.119	1 quart	10 gallons	1,2	1	
	2,2-Dichloropropionic acid	Corrosive material	NA1760	Corrosive	173.244	173.245	1 quart	10 gallons	1,2	1,2	
	Dichlorvos	Poison B	NA2783	Poison	173.345	173.346	Forbidden	1 quart	1,2	1,2	
	Dichlorvos mixture, dry	Poison B	NA2783	Poison	173.364	173.365	50 pounds	200 pounds	1,2	1,2	
	Dicumyl peroxide 50% solution	Organic peroxide	NA2121	Organic peroxide	173.153	173.224	1 quart	1 quart	1,2	4	
	Dicumyl peroxide, technically pure or Dicumyl peroxide, with inert solid. See Dicumyl peroxide, dry		UN2121								
	Dicumyl peroxide, dry	Organic peroxide	UN2121	Organic peroxide	173.153	173.154	2 pounds	25 pounds	1,2	1,2	
	Dicyclohexyl peroxydicarbonate, technically pure. See Organic peroxide, solid, n.o.s.		UN2152								
	Dicycohexyl peroxydicarbonate, not more than 91% with water. See Organic peroxide, solid, n.o.s.		UN2153								
A	Dieldrin	ORM-A	NA2761	None	173.505	173.510	No limit	No limit	1,2	1,2	
	Diesel Fuel. See Fuel oil										
	Diethanol nitrosamine dinitrate (dry)	Forbidden									
	Diethylamine	Flammable liquid	UN1154	Flammable liquid	173.118	173.119	Forbidden	5 pints	1,3	4	
	Diethyl cellosolve. See Ethylene glycol diethyl ether										
	Diethyl dichlorosilane	Flammable liquid	UN1767	Flammable liquid	None	173.135	Forbidden	10 gallons	1	1	Keep dry. Segregation same as for corrosives
	Diethylene glycol dinitrate. See 173.51	Forbidden									
	Diethylgold bromide	Forbidden									
	Diethyl ketone	Flammable liquid	UN1156	Flammable liquid	173.118	173.119	1 quart	10 gallons	1,2	1	
	Diethyl peroxydicarbonate, not more than 27% in solution. See Organic peroxide, liquid or solution, n.o.s.		UN2175								
	Diethyl peroxydicarbonate, more than 27% in solution	Forbidden									
	Diethylzinc. See Pyrophoric liquid, n.o.s.										
	Diflurorethane (R-152a)	Flammable gas	UN1030	Flammable gas	173.306	173.304 173.314 173.315	Forbidden	300 pounds	1,2	1,2	
	1,1-Difluoroethylene	Flammable gas	UN1959	Flammable gas	173.306	173.304	Forbidden	300 pounds	1,2	5	Stow away from living quarters.
	Difluorophosphoric acid, anhydrous	Corrosive material	UN1768	Corrosive	None	173.275	Forbidden	1 gallon	1,2	1,2	
	2,2-Dihydroperoxy propane, not more than 25% with inert organic solid. See Organic peroxide, solid, n.o.s.		UN2178								
	Dihydropyran	Flammable liquid	UN2376	Flammable liquid	173.118	173.119	1 quart	10 gallons	1,2	4	
	1,8-Dihydroxy-2,4,5,7-tetranitroanthraquinone (chrysamminic acid)	Forbidden									
	Diiodoacetylene	Forbidden									
	Diisobutyl ketone	Combustible liquid	UN1157	None	173.118a	None	No limit	No limit	1,2	1,2	
	Diisobutyl peroxide, not more than 52% in solution. See Organic peroxide, liquid or solution, n.o.s.		UN2182								
	Diisooctyl acid phosphate	Corrosive material	UN1902	Corrosive	173.244	173.296	1 quart	1 quart	1,2	1,2	Glass carboys in hampers not permitted under deck
	Diisopropylamine	Flammable liquid	UN1158	Flammable liquid	173.118	173.119	1 quart	10 gallons	1,2	1	
	Diisopropylbenzene hydroperoxide solution, not over 72% peroxide	Organic peroxide	UN2171	Organic peroxide	173.153	173.224	1 quart	1 quart	1,2	4	
	Diisopropylbenzene hydroperoxide, not more than 72% in solution. See Diisopropylbenzene hydroperoxide solution, not more than 72% peroxide		UN2171								

222

(1) +/A/W	(2) Hazardous materials descriptions and proper shipping names	(3) Hazard class	(3A) Identification number	(4) Label(s) required (if not excepted)	(5) Packaging (a) Exceptions	(5) (b) Specific requirements	(6) Maximum net quantity in one package (a) Passenger carrying aircraft or railcar	(6) (b) Cargo only aircraft	(7) Water shipments (a) Cargo vessel	(7) (b) Passenger vessel	(7) (c) Other requirements
	Diisopropylbenzene hydroperoxide, more than 72% in solution	Forbidden									
	Diisopropyl ether	Flammable liquid	UN1159	Flammable liquid	173.118	173.119	1 quart	10 gallons	1,3	4	
	Diisotridecyl peroxydicarbonate, *technically pure. See* **Organic peroxide, liquid or solution, n.o.s.**		UN2889								
	2,5-Dimethyl-2,5-di-(2-ethylhexanoylperoxy) hexane, *technically pure. See* **Organic peroxide, liquid or solution, n.o.s.**		UN2157								
	2,5-Dimethyl-2,5-di-(benzoylperoxy) hexane, *technically pure. See* **Organic peroxide, solid, n.o.s.**		UN2172								
	2,5-Dimethyl-2,5-di-(benzoylperoxy) hexane, *not more than 82% with inert solid. See* **Organic peroxide, solid, n.o.s.**		UN2173								
	2,5-Dimethyl-2,5-dihydroperoxy hexane, *not more than 82% with water. See* **Dimethylhexane dihydroperoxide, with 18% or more water.**		UN2174								
	2,5-Dimethyl-2,5-dihydroperoxy hexane, more than 82% with water	Forbidden									
	2,5-Dimethyl-2,5-di-(tert-butylperoxy) hexane, *technically pure. See* **Organic peroxide, liquid or solution, n.o.s.**		UN2155								
	2,5-Dimethyl-2,5-di-(tert-butylperoxy) hexane, *not more than 52% with inert solid. See* **Organic peroxide, solid, n.o.s.**		UN2156								
	2,5-Dimethyl-2,5-di-(tert-butylperoxy) hexyne-3, *technically pure. See* **Organic peroxide, liquid or solution, n.o.s.**		UN2158								
	2,5-Dimethyl-2,5-di-(tert-butylperoxy) hexyne-3, *not more than 52% with inert solid. See* **Organic peroxide, solid, n.o.s.**		UN2159								
+	Dimethylamine, anhydrous	Flammable gas	UN1032	Flammable gas	173.306	173.304 173.314 173.315	Forbidden	300 pounds	1,2	4	
	Dimethylamine, aqueous solution	Flammable liquid	UN1160	Flammable liquid	173.118	173.119	1 quart	10 gallons	1,2	1	
	2,3-Dimethylbutane	Flammable liquid	UN2457	Flammable liquid	173.118	173.119	1 quart	10 gallons	1,3	4	
	Dimethyl carbonate	Flammable liquid	UN1161	Flammable liquid	173.118	173.119	1 quart	10 gallons	1,2	1	
	Dimethyl chlorothiophosphate. See **Dimethyl phosphorochloridothioate.**										
	1,4-Dimethylcyclohexane	Flammable liquid	UN2263	Flammable liquid	173.118	173.119	1 quart	10 gallons	1,2	1	
	Dimethyldichlorosilane	Flammable liquid	UN1162	Flammable liquid	None	173.135	Forbidden	5 pints	1,2	1	
+	Dimethyl ether	Flammable gas	UN1033	Flammable gas	173.306	173.304 173.314 173.315	Forbidden	300 pounds	1,2	1	
	Dimethylhexane dihydroperoxide (dry)	Forbidden									
	Dimethylhexane dihydroperoxide, (with 18% or more water)	Organic peroxide	UN2174	Organic peroxide	None	173.157	Forbidden	25 pounds	1	1	
	Dimethylhydrazine, unsymmetrical (UDMH)	Flammable liquid	UN1163	Flammable liquid and Poison	None	173.145	Forbidden	5 pints	1,2	1	Keep dry. Separate from corrosive and oxidizing materials, and organic peroxides.
	Dimethyl phosphorochloridothioate.	Corrosive material	NA2267	Corrosive and poison	173.244	173.245	1 quart	1 quart	1,2	4	
	Dimethyl sulfate	Corrosive material	UN1595	Corrosive	None	173.255	Forbidden	1 quart	1	5	Keep cool
	Dimethyl sulfide	Flammable liquid	UN1164	Flammable liquid	None	173.119	Forbidden	10 gallons	1,2	5	
	Dimyristyl peroxydicarbonate, *technically pure. See* **Organic peroxide, solid, n.o.s.**		UN2595								
	Dimyristyl peroxydicarbonate, *not more than 22%, stable dispersion, in water. See* **Organic peroxide, liquid or solution, n.o.s.**		UN2892								
	1,4-Dinitro-1,1,4,4-tetramethylolbutanetetranitrate (dry)	Forbidden									
	2,4-Dinitro-1,3,5-trimethylbenzene	Forbidden									
	1,3-Dinitro-4,5-dinitrosobenzene	Forbidden									
	1,3-Dinitro-5,5-Dimethyl hydantoin	Forbidden									
	Dinitro-7,8-dimethylglycoluril (dry)	Forbidden									
	Dinitrobenzene, solid, or Dinitrobenzol, solid (RQ-1000/454)	Poison B	UN1597	Poison	173.364	174.371	50 pounds	200 pounds	1,2	1,2	
	Dinitrobenzene solution	Poison B	UN1597	Poison	173.345	173.346	1 quart	55 gallons	1,2	1,2	
	Dinitrochlorobenzene	Poison B	UN1577	Poison	173.364	173.365	50 pounds	200 pounds	1,2	1,2	
A	Dinitrocyclohexylphenol	ORM-A	NA9026	None	173.505	173.510	No limit	No limit	1,2	1,2	

(1) +/A/W	(2) Hazardous materials descriptions and proper shipping names	(3) Hazard class	(3A) Identification number	(4) Label(s) required (if not excepted)	(5) Packaging		(6) Maximum net quantity in one package		(7) Water shipments		
					(a) Exceptions	(b) Specific requirements	(a) Passenger carrying aircraft or railcar	(b) Cargo only aircraft	(a) Cargo vessel	(b) Passenger vessel	(c) Other requirements
	1,2-Dinitroethane	Forbidden									
	1,1-Dinitroethane (dry)	Forbidden									
	Dinitroglycoluril	Forbidden									
	Dinitromethane	Forbidden									
	Dinitrophenol solution	Poison B	UN1599	Poison	173.345	173.362a	1 quart	65 pounds	1,2	1,2	Stow away from heavy metals and their compounds. If flash point is 141 deg F or less segregation same as for flammable liquids
	Dinitropropylene glycol	Forbidden									
	2,4-Dinitroresorcinol (heavy metal salts of), (dry)	Forbidden									
	4,6-Dinitroresorcinol (heavy metal salts of), (dry)	Forbidden									
	3,5-Dinitrosalicylic acid (lead salt), (dry)	Forbidden									
	Dinitrosobenzylamidine and salts of (dry)	Forbidden									
	2,2-dinitrostilbene	Forbidden									
	a,a'-Di-(nitroxy)methylether	Forbidden									
	1,9-Dinitroxy pentamethylene-2,4,6,8-tetramine (dry)	Forbidden									
	Di-n-propyl peroxydicarbonate, technically pure. See Organic peroxide, liquid, n.o.s.		UN2176								
	Dioxane	Flammable liquid	UN1165	Flammable liquid	173.118	173.119	1 quart	10 gallons	1,2	1	
	Dioxolane	Flammable liquid	UN1166	Flammable liquid	173.118	173.119	1 quart	10 gallons	1,2	1	
	Diphenylaminechloroarsine (DM)	Irritating material	UN1698	Irritant	None	173.382	Forbidden	75 pounds	1	5	
	Diphenyl dichlorosilane	Corrosive material	UN1769	Corrosive	None	173.280	Forbidden	10 gallons	1	1	
	Diphenyl methyl bromide, solid	Corrosive material	UN1770	Corrosive	173.244	173.245b	25 pounds	100 pounds	1	4	
	Diphenyl methyl bromide solution	Corrosive material	UN1770	Corrosive	173.244	173.247	1 quart	1 gallon	1,2	1,2	
	Diphosgene. See Phosgene										
	Di-sec-butyl peroxydicarbonate, technically pure. See Organic peroxide, liquid or solution, n.o.s.		UN2150								
	Di-sec-butyl peroxydicarbonate, not more than 52% in solution. See Organic peroxide, liquid or solution, n.o.s.		UN2151								
	Disinfectant, liquid	Corrosive material	UN1903	Corrosive	173.244	173.245	1 quart	10 gallons	1	4	
	Disinfectant, liquid	Poison B	UN1601	Poison	173.345	173.346	1 quart	55 gallons	1,2	1	
	Disinfectant, liquid, n.o.s.	Combustible liquid	NA1993	None	173.118a	None	No limit	No limit	1,2	1,2	
	Disinfectant, solid	Poison B	UN1601	Poison	173.364	173.365	50 pounds	200 pounds	1,2	1	
	Dispersant gas, n.o.s. See Refrigerant gas, n.o.s.										
	Distearyl peroxydicarbonate, not more than 85% with stearyl alcohol. See Organic peroxide, solid, n.o.s.		UN2592								
	Disulfoton	Poison B	NA2783	Poison	None	173.358	Forbidden	1 quart	1,2	5	
	Disulfoton mixture, dry	Poison B	NA2783	Poison	173.377	173.377	Forbidden	200 pounds	1,2	4	
	Disulfoton mixture, liquid	Poison B	NA2783	Poison	173.359	173.359	½ pint	1 quart	1,2	5	
	Di-tert-butyl peroxide, technically pure. See Organic peroxide, liquid or solution, n.o.s.		UN2102								
	1,1-Di-(tert-butylperoxy)-3,3,5-trimethyl cyclohexane, technically pure. See Organic peroxide, liquid or solution n.o.s.		UN2145								
	1,1-Di-(tert-butylperoxy)-3,3,5-trimethyl cyclohexane, not more than 57% in solution. See Organic peroxide, liquid or solution, n.o.s.		UN2146								
	1,1-Di-(tert-butylperoxy)-3,3,5-trimethyl cyclohexane, not more than 58% with inert solid. See Organic peroxide, solid, n.o.s.		UN2147								
	2,2-Di-(tert-butylperoxy) butane, not more than 55% in solution. See Organic peroxide, liquid or solution, n.o.s.		UN2111								
	2,2-Di-(tert-butylperoxy) butane, more than 55% in solution	Forbidden									
	1,1-Di-(tert-butylperoxy) cyclohexane, technically pure. See Organic peroxide, liquid or solution, n.o.s.		UN2179								
	1,1-Di-(tert-butylperoxy) cyclohexane, not more than 77% in solution. See Organic peroxide, liquid or solution, n.o.s.		UN2180								

224

(1)	(2)	(3)	(3A)	(4)	(5) Packaging		(6) Maximum net quantity in one package		(7) Water shipments		
+/ A/ W	Hazardous materials descriptions and proper shipping names	Hazard class	Identification number	Label(s) required (if not excepted)	(a) Exceptions	(b) Specific requirements	(a) Passenger carrying aircraft or railcar	(b) Cargo only aircraft	(a) Cargo vessel	(b) Passenger vessel	(c) Other requirements
	1,2-Di-(tert-butylperoxy) cyclohexane, not more than 77% in solution. See **Organic peroxide, liquid or solution, n.o.s.**		UN2181								
	1,1-Di-(tert-butylperoxy) cyclohexane, not more than 40% with inert inorganic solid, with not less than 13% phlegmatizer. See **Organic peroxide, solid, n.o.s.**		UN2885								
	1,1-Di-(tert-butylperoxy) cyclohexane, not more than 50% with phlegmatizer. See **Organic peroxide, liquid or solution, n.o.s.**		UN2897								
	Di-(tert-butylperoxy) phthalate, more than 55% in solution	Forbidden									
	Di-(tert-butylperoxy) phthalate, technically pure. See **Organic peroxide, solid, n.o.s.**		UN2106								
	Di-(tert-butylperoxy) phthalate, not more than 55% in solution. See **Organic peroxide, liquid or solution, n.o.s.**		UN2107								
	Di-(tert-butylperoxy) phthalate, not more than 55% as a paste. See **Organic peroxide, solid, n.o.s.**		UN2108								
	2,2-Di-(tert-butylperoxy) propane, not more than 50% with phlegmatizer. See **Organic peroxide, liquid or solution, n.o.s.**		UN2883								
	2,2-Di-(tert-butylperoxy) propane, not more than 40% with inert inorganic solid with not less than 13% phlegmatizer. See **Organic peroxide, solid, n.o.s.**		UN2884								
	Dithiocarbamate pesticide liquid, n.o.s. (compounds and preparations)	Flammable liquid	UN2772	Flammable liquid	173.118	173.119	1 quart	10 gallons	1,2	1	
	Dithiocarbamate pesticide liquid, n.o.s. (compounds and preparations)	Poison B	UN2771	Poison	173.345	173.346	1 quart	55 gallons	1,2	1,2	
	Dithiocarbamate pesticide solid, n.o.s. (compounds and preparations)	Poison B	UN2771	Poison	173.364	173.365	50 pounds	200 pounds	1,2	1,2	
	Divinyl ether	Flammable liquid	UN1167	Flammable liquid	None	173.119	Forbidden	10 gallons	1,3	5	
	Dodecylbenzenesulfonic acid	Corrosive material	NA2584	Corrosive	173.244	173.245	1 quart	10 gallons	1,2	1,2	
	Dodecyl trichlorosilane	Corrosive material	UN1771	Corrosive	None	173.280	Forbidden	10 gallons	1	1	Keep dry
	Driers, paint or varnish, liquid, n.o.s.	Combustible liquid	UN1168	None	173.118a	None	No limit	No limit	1,2	1,2	
	Driers, paint or varnish, liquid, n.o.s.	Flammable liquid	UN1168	Flammable liquid	173.118 173.128	173.128	1 quart	55 gallons	1,2	1	
	Drill cartridge. See 173.55										
	Drugs, n.o.s.	Combustible liquid	NA1993	None	173.118a	None	No limit	No limit	1,2	1,2	
	Drugs, n.o.s.	Flammable solid	NA1325	Flammable solid	173.153	173.154	25 pounds	100 pounds	1,2	1,2	
	Drugs, n.o.s.	Oxidizer	NA1479	Oxidizer	173.153	173.154	25 pounds	100 pounds	1,2	1,2	
	Drugs, n.o.s.	Flammable liquid	NA1993	Flammable liquid	173.118	173.119	1 quart	10 gallons	1,2	1	
	Drugs, n.o.s. liquid	Corrosive material	NA1760	Corrosive	173.244	173.245	1 quart	1 quart	1,2	1,2	
	Drugs, n.o.s. liquid	Poison B	NA2810	Poison	173.345	173.346	1 quart	55 gallons	1,3	1	
	Drugs, n.o.s. solid	Corrosive material	NA1759	Corrosive	173.244	173.245b	25 pounds	100 pounds	1,2	1,2	Keep dry
	Drugs, n.o.s. solid	Poison B	NA2811	Poison	173.364	173.365	50 pounds	200 pounds	1,3	1,3	
	Drums, empty, must be classed for the hazardous material previously contained in drum. See 173.29.										
	Dry ice. See **Carbon dioxide, solid**										
	Dye intermediate, liquid	Corrosive material	UN2801	Corrosive	173.244	173.249a	1 quart	10 gallons	1,2	1,2	Stow away from foodstuffs and living quarters
	Dynamite. See **High explosive**										
	Electric blasting caps. See **Detonators, Class A** or **Class C explosives**										
	Electric squib	Class C explosive			Explosive C	None	173.106	50 pounds	150 pounds	1,3	1,3	
	Electrolyte (acid) battery fluid (not over 47% acid) (RQ-1000/454). See **Battery fluid, acid.**										
	Empty cartridge bag with black powder igniter	Class C explosive			Explosive C	None	173.106	50 pounds	150 pounds	1,3	1,3	
	Endosulfan	Poison B	NA2761	Poison	173.364	173.365	1 pound	10 pounds	1,2	1,2	If stowed under deck, must be stowed in a recoverable location.
	Endosulfan mixture, liquid	Poison B	NA2761	Poison	173.345	173.346	1 quart	55 gallons	1,2	1,2	

225

(1)	(2)	(3)	(3A)	(4)	(5) Packaging		(6) Maximum net quantity in one package		(7) Water shipments		
+/ A/ W	Hazardous materials descriptions and proper shipping names	Hazard class	Identi- fication number	Label(s) required (if not excepted)	(a) Exceptions	(b) Specific require- ments	(a) Passenger carrying aircraft or railcar	(b) Cargo only aircraft	(a) Cargo vessel	(b) Pas- senger vessel	(c) Other requirements
	Endrin	Poison B	NA2761	Poison	173.364	173.365	1 pound	10 pounds	1,2	1,2	If stored under deck, must be stowed in a recoverable location.
	Endrin mixture, liquid	Poison B	NA2761	Poison	173.345	173.346	1 quart	55 gallons	1,2	1,2	
	Engine, internal combustion				173.120						
	Engine starting fluid	Flammable gas	UN1960	Flammable gas	None	173.304	Forbidden	60 pounds	1,2	5	
	Epichlorohydrin	Flammable liquid	UN2023	Flammable liquid	173.118	173.119	1 quart	10 gallons	1,2	1,2	
	Escape or Evacuation slide, inflatable. See Life rafts, inflatable										
	Etching acid, liquid, n.o.s.	Corrosive material	NA1790	Corrosive	None	173.299	Forbidden	10 pounds	1	5	
+	Ethane or Ethane, compressed	Flammable gas	UN1035	Flammable gas	173.306	173.304	Forbidden	300 pounds	1,2	4	Stow away from living quarters.
	Ethane, refrigerated liquid	Flammable gas	UN1961	Flammable gas	None	173.315	Forbidden	Forbidden	1	5	Stow away from living quarters.
	Ethane-Propane mixture, refrigerated liquid	Flammable gas	UN1961	Flammable gas	None	173.315	Forbidden	Forbidden	1	5	Stow away from living quarters.
	Ethanol. See Ethyl alcohol										
	Ethanol amine dinitrate	Forbidden									
	Ethion	Poison B	NA2783	Poison	173.345	173.346	Forbidden	1 quart	1,2	1,2	
	Ethion mixture, dry	Poison B	NA2783	Poison	173.364	173.365	50 pounds	200 pounds	1,2	1,2	
	Ethyl-3,3-di-(tert-butylperoxy) butyrate, techni- cally pure. See Organic peroxide, liquid or solution, n.o.s.		UN2184								
	Ethyl-3,3-di-(tert-butylperoxy) butyrate, not more than 77% in solution. See Organic peroxide, liquid or solution, n.o.s.		UN2185								
	Ethyl-3,3-di-(tert-butylperoxy) butyrate, not more than 50% with inert inorganic solid. See Organic peroxide, solid, n.o.s.		UN2598								
	Ethyl acetate	Flammable liquid	UN1173	Flammable liquid	173.118	173.119	1 quart	10 gallons	1,2	1	
	Ethyl acrylate, inhibited	Flammable liquid	UN1917	Flammable liquid	173.118	173.119	1 quart	10 gallons	1,2	1	
	Ethyl alcohol	Flammable liquid	UN1170	Flammable liquid	173.118	173.125	1 quart	10 gallons	1,2	1	
	Ethyl aldehyde. See Acetaldehyde										
	Ethyl benzene	Flammable liquid	UN1175	Flammable liquid	173.118	173.119	1 quart	10 gallons	1,2	1	
	Ethyl borate	Flammable liquid	UN1176	Flammable liquid	173.118	173.119	1 quart	10 gallons	1,2	1	Keep dry
	Ethyl butyl acetate	Combustible liquid	UN1177	None	173.118a	None	No limit	No limit	1,2	1,2	
	Ethyl butyl ether	Flammable liquid	UN1179	Flammable liquid	173.118	173.119	1 quart	10 gallons	1,2	1	
	Ethyl butyraldehyde	Flammable liquid	UN1178	Flammable liquid	173.118	173.119	1 quart	10 gallons	1,2	1	
	Ethyl butyrate	Flammable liquid	UN1180	Flammable liquid	173.118	173.119	1 quart	10 gallons	1,2	1,2	
	Ethyl chloride	Flammable liquid	UN1037	Flammable liquid	None	173.123	Forbidden	See 173.123	1,2	1	Segregation same as for flammable gases
	Ethyl chloroacetate	Combustible liquid	UN1181	None	173.118a	None	No limit	No limit	1,2	1,2	
	Ethyl chloroformate (chlorocarbonate)	Flammable liquid	UN1182	Flammable liquid and Poison	None	173.288	Forbidden	5 pints	1,2	1	
	Ethyl chlorothioformate	Corrosive material	UN2826	Corrosive	173.244	173.245 173.245a	1 quart	1 quart	1,2	1	
	Ethyl crotonate	Flammable liquid	UN1862	Flammable liquid	173.118	173.119	1 quart	10 gallons	1,2	1	
	Ethyl dichlorosilane	Flammable liquid	UN1183	Flammable liquid	None	173.135	Forbidden	5 pints	1,2	1	
+	Ethylene or Ethylene, compressed	Flammable gas	UN1962	Flammable gas	173.306	173.304	Forbidden	300 pounds	1,2	4	Stow away from living quarters.
	Ethylene chlorohydrin	Poison B	UN1135	Poison	173.345	173.346 173.3a	1 quart	55 gallons	1,2	1	Segregation same as for flammable liquids
	Ethylene, refrigerated liquid (cryogenic liquid)	Flammable gas	UN1038	Flammable gas	None	173.318 173.319	Forbidden	Forbidden	1	5	Stow away from living quarters.
	Ethylenediamine	Corrosive material	UN1604	Corrosive	173.244	173.245	1 quart	1 quart	1,2	1,2	
	Ethylene diamine diperchlorate	Forbidden									
AW	Ethylene dibromide	Poison B	UN1605	Poison	173.345	173.346	1 quart	55 gallons	1,2	1,2	Stow away from living quarters
	Ethylene dichloride	Flammable liquid	UN1184	Flammable liquid	173.118	173.119	1 quart	10 gallons	1,2	1	
	Ethylene glycol diethyl ether (diethyl Cellosolve)	Flammable liquid	UN1153	Flammable liquid	173.118	173.119	1 quart	10 gallons	1,2	1,2	
	Ethylene glycol dinitrate	Forbidden									

(1)	(2)	(3)	(3A)	(4)	(5) Packaging		(6) Maximum net quantity in one package		(7) Water shipments		
+/ A/ W	Hazardous materials descriptions and proper shipping names	Hazard class	Identification number	Label(s) required (if not excepted)	(a) Exceptions	(b) Specific requirements	(a) Passenger carrying aircraft or railcar	(b) Cargo only aircraft	(a) Cargo vessel	(b) Passenger vessel	(c) Other requirements
	Ethylene glycol monoethyl ether ('Cellosolve')	Combustible liquid	UN1171	None	173.118a	None	No limit	No limit	1,2	1,2	
	Ethylene glycol monoethyl ether acetate ('Cellosolve acetate')	Combustible liquid	UN1172	None	173.118a	None	No limit	No limit	1,2	1,2	
	Ethylene glycol monomethyl ether (methyl 'Cellosolve')	Combustible liquid	UN1188	None	173.118a	None	No limit	No limit	1,2	1,2	
	Ethylene glycol monomethyl ether acetate (methyl 'Cellosolve acetate')	Combustible liquid	UN1189	None	173.118a	None	No limit	No limit	1,2	1,2	
	Ethylene imine, inhibited	Flammable liquid	UN1185	Flammable liquid and Poison	None	173.139	Forbidden	5 pints	1,2	1	
	Ethylene oxide	Flammable liquid	UN1040	Flammable liquid	None	173.124	Forbidden	See 173.124	1,2	1	Segregation same as for flammable gases.
	Ethyl ether	Flammable liquid	UN1155	Flammable liquid	None	173.119	Forbidden	10 gallons	1,3	5	
	Ethyl formate	Flammable liquid	UN1190	Flammable liquid	173.118	173.119	1 quart	10 gallons	1,3	4	
	Ethylhexaldehyde	Combustible liquid	UN1191	None	173.118a	None	No limit	No limit	1,2	1,2	
	Ethyl hydroperoxide (explodes above 100 deg. C)	Forbidden									
	Ethyl lactate	Combustible liquid	UN1192	None	173.118a	None	No limit	No limit	1,2	1,2	
	Ethyl mercaptan	Flammable liquid	UN2363	Flammable liquid	None	173.141	Forbidden	10 gallons	1,2	1	
	Ethyl methyl ether	Flammable liquid	UN1039	Flammable liquid	None	173.119	Forbidden	10 gallons	1,3	1	Segregation same as for flammable gases.
	Ethyl methyl ketone	Flammable liquid	UN1193	Flammable liquid	173.118	173.119	1 quart	10 gallons	1,2	1	
	Ethyl nitrate (nitric ether)	Flammable liquid	NA1993	Flammable liquid	173.118	173.119	Forbidden	Forbidden	1,2	1	
	Ethyl nitrite (nitrous ether)	Flammable liquid	UN1194	Flammable liquid	None	173.119	Forbidden	Forbidden	1,3	5	
	Ethyl perchlorate	Forbidden									
	Ethyl phenyl dichlorosilane	Corrosive material	UN2435	Corrosive	None	173.280	Forbidden	10 gallons	1	5	
	Ethyl phosphonothioic dichloride, anhydrous	Corrosive material	NA1760	Corrosive	173.244	173.245 173.245a	1 quart	1 quart	1	4	
	Ethyl phosphonous dichloride. See Pyroforic liquid, n.o.s.										
	Ethyl phosphorodichloridate	Corrosive material	NA1760	Corrosive	173.244	173.245 173.245a	1 quart	1 quart	1	4	
	Ethyl propionate	Flammable liquid	UN1195	Flammable liquid	173.118	173.119	1 quart	10 gallons	1,2	1	
	Ethyl silicate (tetraethyl orthosilicate)	Combustible liquid	UN1292	None	173.118a	None	No limit	No limit	1,2	1,2	
	Ethyl trichlorosilane	Flammable liquid	UN1196	Flammable liquid	None	173.135	Forbidden	5 pints	1,2	1	
	Etiologic agent, n.o.s.	Etiologic agent	NA2814	Etiologic agent	173.386	173.387	50ml or 50g	4L or 4Kg.			Not permitted except under specific conditions approved by the Department.
	Explosive auto alarm	Class C explosive		Explosive C	None	173.111	50 pounds	150 pounds	1,2	1,2	
	Explosive bomb	Class A explosive		Explosive A	None	173.56	Forbidden	Forbidden	1,2	5	Magazine stowage authorized. No other cargo may be stowed in the same hold with these items.
	Explosive cable cutter	Class C explosive		Explosive C	None	173.102	50 pounds	150 pounds	1,3	1,3	
	Explosive, forbidden. See Sec. 173.51	Forbidden									
	Explosive mine	Class A explosive		Explosive A	None	173.56	Forbidden	Forbidden	1,2	5	Magazine stowage authorized. No other cargo may be stowed in the same hold with these items.
	Explosive, new approval and evaluation. See 173.86										
	Explosive pest control devices	Class C explosive		Explosive C	None	173.100	50 pounds	150 pounds	1,3	1,3	
	Explosive power device, Class B	Class B explosive		Explosive B	None	173.94	Forbidden	150 pounds	1,2	5	
	Explosive power device, Class C	Class C explosive		Explosive C	None	173.102	50 pounds	150 pounds	1,3	1,3	
	Explosive projectile	Class A explosive		Explosive A	None	173.56	Forbidden	Forbidden	1,2	5	Magazine stowage authorized. No other cargo may be stowed in the same hold with this material.
	Explosive release device	Class C explosive		Explosive C	None	173.102	50 pounds	150 pounds	1,3	1,3	
	Explosive rivet	Class C explosive		Explosive C	None	173.100	50 pounds	150 pounds	1,2	1,2	
	Explosive, sample for laboratory examination				173.86		Forbidden	See 173.86			

227

(1) +/A/W	(2) Hazardous materials descriptions and proper shipping names	(3) Hazard class	(3A) Identification number	(4) Label(s) required (if not excepted)	(5) Packaging		(6) Maximum net quantity in one package		(7) Water shipments		
					(a) Exceptions	(b) Specific requirements	(a) Passenger carrying aircraft or railcar	(b) Cargo only aircraft	(a) Cargo vessel	(b) Passenger vessel	(c) Other requirements
	Explosive torpedo	Class A explosive		Explosive A	None	173.56	Forbidden	Forbidden	1,2	5	Magazine stowage authorized. No other cargo may be stowed in the same hold with this material.
	Extract, liquid, flavoring	Flammable liquid	UN1197	Flammable liquid	173.118	173.119	1 quart	10 gallons	1,2	1	
	Ferric arsenate, solid	Poison B	UN1606	Poison	173.364	173.365	50 pounds	200 pounds	1,2	1,2	
	Ferric arsenite, solid	Poison B	UN1607	Poison	173.364	173.365	50 pounds	200 pounds	1,2	1,2	
A	Ferric chloride, solid, *anhydrous*	ORM-B	UN1773	None	173.505	173.510	25 pounds	100 pounds	1,2	1,2	
	Ferric chloride solution	Corrosive material	UN2582	Corrosive	173.244	173.245	1 quart	10 quarts	1,2	1,2	
	Ferric nitrate	Oxidizer	UN1466	Oxidizer	173.153	173.182	25 pounds	100 pounds	1,2	1,2	
W	Ferrochrome, exothermic	ORM-C		None	173.505	173.985			1	1	
W	Ferromanganese, exothermic. *See* Ferrochrome, exothermic										
W	Ferrophosphorus	ORM-A		None	173.505	173.635			1,2	1,2	Keep dry. Stow away from living quarters
AW	Ferrosilicon, *containing 30% or more but not more than 70% silicon*	ORM-A	UN1408	None	173.505	173.645	Forbidden	25 pounds	1,2	1,2	Keep dry stow away from living quarters. Segregation same as for flammable solids labeled Dangerous When Wet.
	Ferrous arsenate, solid	Poison B	UN1608	Poison	173.364	173.365	50 pounds	200 pounds	1,2	1,2	
A	Ferrous chloride, solid	ORM-B	NA1759	None	173.505	173.510	No limit	No limit	1,2	1,2	
	Ferrous chloride, solution	Corrosive material	NA1760	Corrosive	173.244	173.245	1 quart	5 gallons	1,2	1,2	
	Fertilizer ammoniating solution *containing free ammonia (more than 25.3 p.s.i.g.)*	Nonflammable gas	UN1043	Nonflammable gas	173.306	173.304 173.314	Forbidden	300 pounds	1,2	4	
W	Fibers *(jute, hemp, flax, sisal, coir, kapok, and similar vegetable fibers)*	ORM-C	NA1372	None	173.505	173.965			1,2	1,2	Stow away from animal or vegetable oils. Segregation same as for flammable solids.
	Film *(nitrocellulose)*	Flammable solid	NA1324	Flammable solid	None	173.177	50 pounds	200 pounds	1,3	1,3	Stow away from other flammable cargo or substances.
	Firecracker. *See* Fireworks, common *or* special										
	Firecracker salute. *See* Fireworks, common *or* special										
	Fire extinguisher	Nonflammable gas	UN1044	Nonflammable gas	173.306		150 pounds	300 pounds	1,2	1,2	
	Fire extinguisher charge *containing not more than 50 grains of propellant explosive per unit. Not subject to requirements of this subchapter.*										
	Fire extinguisher charge containing sulfuric acid	Corrosive material	UN1774	Corrosive	173.261		1 quart	1 gallon	1,2	1,2	
	Fireworks, common	Class C explosive		Explosive C	None	173.100 173.108	50 pounds	200 pounds	1,3	1,3	Passenger vessels in metal lockers only
	Fireworks, exhibition display piece. *See* Fireworks, special										
	Fireworks, special	Class B explosive		Explosive B	None	173.88 173.91	Forbidden	200 pounds	3	3	Passenger vessels in metal lockers only. Toy torpedoes must not be packed with other special fireworks.
W	Fish meal *or* fish scrap containing 6% to 12% water	ORM-C	NA2216	None	173.505	173.995			1,2	1,2	Segregation same as for flammable solids. Separate from flammable gases or liquids, oxidizing materials, or organic peroxides. *Use double strip stowage for cargo 6-12 percent moisture containing not more than 12 percent fat. Use single strip stowage for cargo 6-12 percent moisture containing 12-15 percent fat.*
	Fish meal *or* fish scrap containing less than 6% or more than 12% water	Flammable solid	NA1374	Flammable solid	None	173.171	Forbidden	Forbidden	1,2	1,2	Separate from flammable gases or liquids, oxidizing materials, or organic peroxides.
	Fissile radioactive material. *See* Radioactive material, fissile										
	Flame retardant compound liquid	Corrosive material	NA1760	Corrosive	173.244	173.291	1 quart	10 gallons	1,2	1,2	
	Flammable gas n.o.s. *See* Compressed gas, n.o.s.										
	Flammable liquid, corrosive, n.o.s.	Flammable liquid	UN2924	Flammable liquid and Corrosive	None	173.119	1 quart	1 quart	1,2	1	
	Flammable liquid, n.o.s.	Flammable liquid	UN1993	Flammable liquid	173.118	173.119	1 quart	10 gallons	1,2	1	

(1) +/A/W	(2) Hazardous materials descriptions and proper shipping names	(3) Hazard class	(3A) Identification number	(4) Label(s) required (if not excepted)	(5) Packaging (a) Exceptions	(5) (b) Specific requirements	(6) Maximum net quantity in one package (a) Passenger carrying aircraft or railcar	(6) (b) Cargo only aircraft	(7) Water shipments (a) Cargo vessel	(7) (b) Passenger vessel	(7) (c) Other requirements
	Flammable liquid, poisonous, n.o.s.	Flammable liquid	UN1992	Flammable liquid and Poison	None	173.119	1 quart	10 gallons	1,2	1	
	Flammable solid, corrosive, n.o.s.	Flammable solid	UN2925	Flammable solid and Corrosive	173.153	173.154	25 pounds	25 pounds	1	4	
	Flammable solid, n.o.s.	Flammable solid	UN1325	Flammable solid	173.153	173.154	25 pounds	25 pounds	1,2	1,2	
	Flammable solid, poisonous, n.o.s.	Flammable solid	UN2926	Flammable solid and Poison	173.153	173.154	25 pounds	25 pounds	1,2	1	
	Flare. See Fireworks, common										
	Flare, airplane. See Fireworks, special										
	Flash cartridge. See Fireworks, special or Low explosives										
	Flash cracker. See Fireworks, common or special										
	Flash powder. See Fireworks, special or Low explosives										
	Flexible linear shaped charge, metal clad	Class C explosive		Explosive C	None	173.104	50 pounds	300 pounds	1,3	1,3	
	Flowers of sulfur. See Sulfur										
	Flue dust, poisonous	Poison B	NA2811	Poison	173.364	173.368	50 pounds	200 pounds	1,2	1,2	
	Fluoboric acid	Corrosive material	UN1775	Corrosive	173.244	173.283	1 quart	1 gallon	1,2	1,2	
	Fluoric acid. See Hydrofluoric acid										
	Fluorine	Nonflammable gas	UN1045	Poison and Oxidizer	None	173.302	Forbidden	Forbidden	1	5	Stow in well ventilated space away from organic materials
	Fluorophosphoric acid, anhydrous. See Monofluorophosphoric acid, anhydrous										
	Fluosilicic acid	Corrosive material	UN1778	Corrosive	None	173.265	1 quart	1 gallon	1,2	1,2	
	Fluorosilicic acid. See Hydrofluorosilicic acid										
	Fluorosulfonic acid or Fluosulfonic acid	Corrosive material	UN1777	Corrosive	None	173.274	Forbidden	1 gallon	1	5	Keep dry
	Forbidden explosives. See 173.51	Forbidden									
	Forbidden materials. See 173.21	Forbidden									
AW	**Formaldehyde solution** *(flash point more than 141 deg F.; in containers of 110 gallons or less)*	ORM-A	UN2209	None	173.505	173.510	10 gallons	55 gallons	1,2	4	
	Formaldehyde solution *(flash point not more than 141 deg F.; in containers over 110 gallons)*	Combustible liquid	UN1198	None	173.118a	None	10 gallons	55 gallons	1,2	1,2	
AW	**Formaldehyde solution** *(flash point more than 141 deg F.; in containers of 110 gallons or less)*	ORM-A	UN1198	None	173.505	173.510	10 gallons	55 gallons	1,2	4	
	Formaldehyde solution *(flash point more than 141 deg F.; in containers over 110 gallons)*	Combustible liquid	UN2209	None	173.118a	None	10 gallons	55 gallons	1,2	1,2	
	Formalin. See Formaldehyde solution										
	Formic acid	Corrosive material	UN1779	Corrosive	173.244	173.245 173.289	1 quart	5 gallons	1,2	1,2	Glass carboys in hampers not permitted under deck
	Formic acid solution	Corrosive material	UN1779	Corrosive	173.244	173.245 173.289	1 quart	5 gallons	1,2	1,2	
	Fuel, aviation, turbine engine	Flammable liquid	UN1863	Flammable liquid	173.118	173.119	1 quart	10 gallons	1,2	1	
	Fuel, aviation, turbine engine	Combustible liquid	UN1863	None	173.118a	None	No limit	No limit	1,2	1,2	
	Fuel oil	Combustible liquid	NA1993	None	173.118a	None	No limit	No limit	1,2	1,2	
	Fuel oil, Diesel. See Fuel oil										
	Fuel oil, No. 1, 2, 4, 5 or 6	Combustible liquid	NA1993	None	173.118a	None	No limit	No limit	1,2	1,2	
	Fulminate of mercury (dry)	Forbidden									
	Fulminate of mercury, wet. See Initiating explosive										
	Fulminating gold	Forbidden									
	Fulminating mercury	Forbidden									
	Fulminating platinum	Forbidden									
	Fulminating silver	Forbidden									
	Fulminic acid	Forbidden									
	Fumaryl chloride	Corrosive material	UN1780	Corrosive	173.244	173.245	1 quart	1 quart	1	1	Glass carboys not permitted
	Fumigant. See 173.152(a) Note 1										
	Furan	Flammable liquid	UN2389	Flammable liquid	173.118	173.119	1 quart	10 gallons	1,2	1	
	Furfural	Combustible liquid	UN1199	None	173.118a	None	No limit	No limit	1,2	1	

229

(1) +/A/W	(2) Hazardous materials descriptions and proper shipping names	(3) Hazard class	(3A) Identification number	(4) Label(s) required (if not excepted)	(5) Packaging		(6) Maximum net quantity in one package		(7) Water shipments		
					(a) Exceptions	(b) Specific requirements	(a) Passenger carrying aircraft or railcar	(b) Cargo only aircraft	(a) Cargo vessel	(b) Passenger vessel	(c) Other requirements
	Fusee (railway or highway)	Flammable solid	NA1325	Flammable solid	None	173.154a	50 pounds	200 pounds	1,3	1,3	
	Fuse igniter	Class C explosive		Explosive C	None	173.106	50 pounds	150 pounds	1,3	1,3	
	Fuse, instantaneous	Class C explosive		Explosive C	173.100		50 pounds	150 pounds	1,2	1,2	
	Fuse lighter	Class C explosive		Explosive C	None	173.106	50 pounds	150 pounds	1,3	1,3	
	Fusel oil	Combustible liquid	UN1201	None	173.118a	None	No limit	No limit	1,2	1,2	
	Fuse, mild detonating, metal clad	Class C explosive		Explosive C	None	173.104	50 pounds	300 pounds	1,2	1,2	
	Fuse, safety	Class C explosive		Explosive C	173.100	173.100	50 pounds	300 pounds	1,2	1,2	
	Fuze, combination	Class C explosive		Explosive C	None	173.105	50 pounds	150 pounds	1,3	1,3	
	Fuze, detonating	Class A explosive		Explosive A	None	173.69	Forbidden	Forbidden	6	5	
	Fuze, detonating, Class C explosive	Class C explosive		Explosive C	None	173.113	50 pounds	150 pounds	1,3	1,3	
	Fuze, detonating, radioactive	Class A explosive		Explosive A	None	173.69	Forbidden	Forbidden	6	5	
	Fuze, percussion	Class C explosive		Explosive C	None	173.105	50 pounds	150 pounds	1,3	1,3	
	Fuze, time	Class C explosive		Explosive C	None	173.105	50 pounds	150 pounds	1,3	1,3	
	Fuze, tracer	Class C explosive		Explosive C	None	173.105	50 pounds	150 pounds	1,3	1,3	
	Galactsan trinitrate	Forbidden									
	Gallium metal, liquid	ORM-B	UN2803	None	None	173.861	Forbidden	Forbidden	1	5	None
	Gallium metal, solid	ORM-B	UN2803	None	None	173.862	40 pounds	40 pounds	1,3	1	Shade from radiant heat
	Gas cylinder, empty. See Cylinder, empty.										
	Gas drips, hydrocarbon	Combustible liquid	UN1864	None	173.118a	None	No limit	No limit	1,2	1,2	
	Gas drips, hydrocarbon	Flammable liquid	UN1864	Flammable liquid	173.118	173.119	1 quart	10 gallons	1,2	1	
	Gas identification set	Poison A	NA9035	Poison gas	None	173.331	Forbidden	Forbidden	1	5	
	Gas identification set	Irritating material	NA9035	Irritant	None	173.331	Forbidden	Forbidden	1	5	
	Gas Mine. See Explosive mine										
	Gasohol (gasoline mixed with ethyl alcohol containing 20% maximum alcohol). See Gasoline										
	Gasoline (including casing-head and natural)	Flammable liquid	UN1203	Flammable liquid	173.118	173.119	1 quart	10 gallons	1,2	4	
	Gelatine Dynamite. See High explosive										
	Germane	Poison A	UN2192	Poison gas and Flammable gas	None	173.328	Forbidden	Forbidden	1	5	Segregation same as for flammable gases
	Glycerol-1,3-dinitrate	Forbidden									
	Glycerol monogluconate trinitrate	Forbidden									
	Glycerol monolactate trinitrate	Forbidden									
	Grenade without bursting charge. (With incendiary material)	Class B explosive		Explosive B	None	173.91	Forbidden	Forbidden	3	3	Passenger vessels in metal lockers only
	Grenade without bursting charge. (With smoke charge) (Smoke grenade)	Class C explosive		Explosive C	None	173.108	50 pounds	150 pounds	1,3	1,3	
	Grenade without bursting charge. (With Poison A gas charge)	Poison A	NA2016	Poison gas	None	173.330	Forbidden	Forbidden			See correct shipping name of applicable Poison A material for stowage, special handling, and special segregation requirements
	Grenade without bursting charge. (With Poison B charge)	Poison B	NA2016	Poison	None	173.350	Forbidden	Forbidden			See correct shipping name of applicable Poison B material for stowage, special handling, and special segregation requirements
	Grenade, empty, primed	Class C explosive		None	None	173.107	50 pounds	150 pounds	1,3	1,3	
	Grenade, hand or rifle, explosive (with or without gas, smoke, or incendiary material)	Class A explosive		Explosive A	None	173.56	Forbidden	Forbidden	1,2	5	No other cargo may be stowed in the same hold with these items
	Grenade, tear gas	Irritating material	NA2017	Irritant	None	173.385	Forbidden	75 pounds	1,2	1	
	Guanidine nitrate	Oxidizer	UN1467	Oxidizer	173.153	173.182	25 pounds	100 pounds	1,2	1,2	Separate from nitro-compounds, chlorates, and acids
	Guanyl nitrosamino guanylidene hydrazine. See Initiating explosive										
	Guanyl nitrosamino guanylidene hydrazine (dry)	Forbidden									
	Guanyl nitrosamino guanyl tetrazene. See Initiating explosive										

230

(1)	(2)	(3)	(3A)	(4)	(5) Packaging		(6) Maximum net quantity in one package		(7) Water shipments		
+/ A W	Hazardous materials descriptions and proper shipping names	Hazard class	Identi-fication number	Label(s) required (if not excepted)	(a) Exceptions	(b) Specific require-ments	(a) Passenger carrying aircraft or railcar	(b) Cargo only aircraft	(a) Cargo vessel	(b) Pas-senger vessel	(c) Other requirements
	Guided missile, without warhead. See **Rocket motor, Class A explosive** *or* **Rocket motor, Class B explosive**										
	Guided missile with warhead. See **Rocket ammunition with explosive, illuminating, gas, incendiary, or smoke projectile**										
	Guncotton. See **High explosive**										
	Guthion. See **Azinphos methyl**										
	Guthion mixture, liquid. See **Azinphos methyl mixture, liquid**										
	Hafnium metal, dry. *(See 173.214 Note 3)*	Flammable solid	UN2545	Flammable solid	None	173.214	Forbidden	75 pounds	1	5	
	Hafnium metal, wet	Flammable solid	UN1326	Flammable solid	None	173.214	Forbidden	150 pounds	1,2	5	
	Hand signal device	Class C explosive		Explosive C	None	173.108	50 pounds	200 pounds	1,2	1,2	
	Hazardous substance, liquid or solid, n.o.s. or ORM-E, liquid or solid, n.o.s.	ORM-E	NA9188	None	None	173.1300	No limit	No limit	1,2	1,2	
	Hazardous waste, liquid or solid, n.o.s.	ORM-E	NA9189	None	None	173.1300	Forbidden	550 pounds	1,2	1,2	
	Hazardous waste, meeting the definition of a hazard class other than ORM-E. See 172.101(c)(10)										
	Heater for refrigerator car, liquid fuel type *(containing fuel)*	Flammable liquid	NA1993	Flammable liquid	173.146		Forbidden	Forbidden	1,2	1	
	Helium *or* Helium, compressed	Nonflammable gas	UN1046	Nonflammable gas	173.306	173.302 173.314	150 pounds	300 pounds	1,2	1,2	
	Helium, refrigerated liquid *(cryogenic liquid)*	Nonflammable gas	UN1963	Nonflammable gas	173.320	173.316 173.318	100 pounds	1,100 pounds	1,3	1,3	
	Helium-oxygen mixture	Nonflammable gas	NA1980	Nonflammable gas	173.306	173.302	150 pounds	300 pounds	1,2	1,2	
	Heptane	Flammable liquid	UN1206	Flammable liquid	173.118	173.119	1 quart	10 gallons	1,2	1	
	Hexachlorocyclopentadiene	Corrosive material	UN2646	Corrosive	173.244	173.245	1 quart	10 gallons	1,2	1,2	
W	Hexachloroethane	ORM-A	NA9037	None	173.505	173.650			1,2	1,2	
	Hexadecyltrichlorosilane	Corrosive material	UN1781	Corrosive	None	173.280	Forbidden	10 gallons	1	1	Keep dry
	Hexadiene	Flammable liquid	UN2458	Flammable liquid	None	173.119	Forbidden	10 gallons	1,2	5	
	Hexaethyl tetraphosphate and compressed gas mixture	Poison A	UN1612	Poison gas	None	173.334	Forbidden	Forbidden	1	5	Shade from radiant heat
	Hexaethyl tetraphosphate, liquid	Poison B	UN1611	Poison	None	173.358	Forbidden	1 quart	1	4	
	Hexaethyl tetraphosphate mixture, dry *(containing more than 2% hexaethyl tetraphosphate)*	Poison B	NA2783	Poison	None	173.377	Forbidden	200 pounds	1,2	5	
	Hexaethyl tetraphosphate mixture, dry *(containing not more than 2% hexaethyl tetraphosphate)*	Poison B	NA2783	Poison	173.377	173.377	50 pounds	200 pounds	1,2	4	
	Hexaethyl tetraphosphate mixture, liquid *(containing more than 25% hexaethyl tetraphosphate)*	Poison B	NA2783	Poison	None	173.359	Forbidden	1 quart	1,2	5	
	Hexaethyl tetraphosphate mixture, liquid *(containing not more than 25% hexaethyl tetraphosphate)*	Poison B	UN2783	Poison	173.359	173.359	1 quart	1 quart	1,2	4	
	Hexafluorophosphoric acid	Corrosive material	UN1782	Corrosive	None	173.275	Forbidden	1 gallon	1,2	1,2	
	Hexafluoropropylene	Nonflammable gas	UN1858	Nonflammable gas	173.306	173.304 173.314 173.315	150 pounds	300 pounds	1	4	
	Hexafluoropropylene oxide	Nonflammable gas	NA1956	Nonflammable gas	173.306	173.304 173.314	150 pounds	300 pounds	1,2	1,2	
	Hexaldehyde	Flammable liquid	UN1207	Flammable liquid	173.118	173.119	1 quart	10 gallons	1,2	1,2	
	3,3,6,6,9,9-Hexamethyl-1,2,4,5-tetraoxo-cyclononane, *technically pure. See* **Organic peroxide, solid, n.o.s.**		UN2165								
	3,3,6,6,9,9-Hexamethyl-1,2,4,5-tetraoxocyclononane, *not more than 52% with inert solid. See* **Organic peroxide, solid, n.o.s.**		UN2166								
	3,3,6,6,9,9-Hexamethyl-1,2,4,5-tetraoxocyclononane, *not more than 52% in solution. See* **Organic peroxide, liquid or solution, n.o.s.**		UN2167								
	Hexamethylenediamine, solid	Corrosive material	UN2280	Corrosive	173.244	173.245b	25 pounds	100 pounds	1,2	1,2	
	Hexamethylenediamine, solution	Corrosive material	UN1783	Corrosive	173.244	173.292	1 quart	10 gallons	1,2	1,2	

231

(1) +/A/W	(2) Hazardous materials descriptions and proper shipping names	(3) Hazard class	(3A) Identi-fication number	(4) Label(s) required (if not excepted)	(5) Packaging (a) Exceptions	(b) Specific require-ments	(6) Maximum net quantity in one package (a) Passenger carrying aircraft or railcar	(b) Cargo only aircraft	(7) Water shipments (a) Cargo vessel	(b) Pas-senger vessel	(c) Other requirements
	Hexamethyleneimine	Flammable liquid	UN2493	Flammable liquid and Corrosive	None	173.119	1 quart	1 gallons	1,2	1	
	Hexamethylene triperoxide diamine (dry)	Forbidden									
	Hexamethylol benzene hexanitrate	Forbidden									
	Hexane	Flammable liquid	UN1208	Flammable liquid	173.118	173.119	1 quart	10 gallons	1,3	4	
	2,2',4,4',6,6'-Hexanitro-3,3'-dihydroxyazobenzene (dry)	Forbidden									
	Hexanitroazoxy benzene	Forbidden									
	2,2',3',4,4',6-Hexanitrodiphenylamine	Forbidden									
	2,3',4,4',5,6'-Hexanitrodiphenylether	Forbidden									
	N,N'-(hexanitrodiphenyl)ethylene dinitramine (dry)	Forbidden									
	Hexanitrodiphenyl urea	Forbidden									
	Hexanitroethane	Forbidden									
	Hexanitrooxanilide	Forbidden									
	Hexanoic acid	Corrosive material	NA1760	Corrosive	173.244	173.245	1 quart	10 gallons	1,2	1,2	
	Hexyltrichlorosilane	Corrosive material	UN1784	Corrosive	None	173.280	Forbidden	10 gallons	1	1	Keep dry
	High explosive	Class A explosive		Explosive A	173.65	173.61 173.87	Forbidden	Forbidden	6	5	
	High explosive, liquid	Class A explosive		Explosive A	None	173.62	Forbidden	Forbidden	6	5	
	Hydraulic accumulator. See Accumulator, pressurized										
	Hydrazine, anhydrous	Flammable liquid	UN2029	Flammable liquid and Poison	None	173.276	Forbidden	5 pints	1	5	Segregation same as for corrosives
	Hydrazine, aqueous solution	Corrosive material	UN2030	Corrosive	None	173.276	Forbidden	5 pints	1	5	
	Hydrazine azide	Forbidden									
	Hydrazine chlorate	Forbidden									
	Hydrazine dicarbonic acid diazide	Forbidden									
	Hydrazine perchlorate	Forbidden									
	Hydrazine selenate	Forbidden									
	Hydriodic acid	Corrosive material	UN1787	Corrosive	173.244	173.245	1 quart	1 gallon	1	1	Glass carboys not permitted on passenger vessel
	Hydrobromic acid, more than 49% strength	Corrosive material	UN1788	Corrosive	None	173.262	Forbidden	Forbidden	1	1	Glass carboys not permitted on passenger vessel
	Hydrobromic acid, anhydrous. See Hydrogen bromide										
	Hydrobromic acid not more than 49% strength	Corrosive material	UN1788	Corrosive	173.244	173.262	1 quart	1 gallon	1	1	Glass carboys not permitted on passenger vessel
+	Hydrocarbon gas, liquefied	Flammable gas	UN1965	Flammable gas	173.306	173.304 173.314	Forbidden	300 pounds	1,2	1	
+	Hydrocarbon gas, nonliquefied	Flammable gas	UN1964	Flammable gas	173.306	173.302	Forbidden	300 pounds	1,2	1	
	Hydrochloric acid	Corrosive material	UN1789	Corrosive	173.244	173.263	1 quart	1 gallon	1	1	Glass carboys not permitted on passenger vessel
	Hydrochloric acid, anhydrous. See Hydrogen chloride										
	Hydrochloric acid mixture	Corrosive material	NA1789	Corrosive	173.244	173.263	1 quart	1 gallon	1	1	Glass carboys not permitted on passenger vessel
	Hydrochloric acid solution, inhibited	Corrosive material	UN1789	Corrosive	173.244	173.263	1 quart	1 gallon	1	1	Glass carboys not permitted on passenger vessel
	Hydrocyanic acid (prussic) solution (5% or more hydrocyanic acid)	Poison A	UN1613	Flammable gas and Poison gas	None	173.332	Forbidden	Forbidden	1	5	Shade from radiant heat. Aqueous solutions containing more than 20% hydrogen cyanide are not permitted in transportation by water. Segregation same as for flammable gases.
	Hydrocyanic acid, liquefied	Poison A	NA1051	Flammable gas and Poison gas	None	173.332	Forbidden	Forbidden	1	5	Segregation same as for flammable gases
	Hydrocyanic acid (prussic), unstabilized	Forbidden									
+	Hydrocyanic acid solution, less than 5% hydrocyanic acid	Poison B	UN1613	Poison	None	173.351	Forbidden	25 pounds	1	5	Shade from radiant heat
	Hydrofluoric acid, anhydrous. See Hydrogen fluoride										
	Hydrofluoric acid solution	Corrosive material	UN1790	Corrosive	173.244	173.264	1 quart	1 gallon	1	4	
	Hydrofluoric and sulfuric acid mixture	Corrosive material	UN1786	Corrosive	None	173.290	Forbidden	1 gallon	1	5	
	Hydrofluoroboric acid. See Fluoboric acid										
	Hydrofluorosilicic acid or Hydrofluosilicic acid	Corrosive material	NA1778	Corrosive	None	173.265	1 quart	1 gallon	1,2	1,2	

(1)	(2)	(3)	(3A)	(4)	(5) Packaging		(6) Maximum net quantity in one package		(7) Water shipments		
+/A/W	Hazardous materials descriptions and proper shipping names	Hazard class	Identification number	Label(s) required (if not excepted)	(a) Exceptions	(b) Specific requirements	(a) Passenger carrying aircraft or railcar	(b) Cargo only aircraft	(a) Cargo vessel	(b) Passenger vessel	(c) Other requirements
+	Hydrogen or Hydrogen, compressed	Flammable gas	UN1049	Flammable gas	173.306	173.302 173.314	Forbidden	300 pounds	1,2	4	Stow away from living quarters.
	Hydrogen bromide	Nonflammable gas	UN1048	Nonflammable gas	173.306	173.304	Forbidden	300 pounds	1	4	
	Hydrogen chloride or Hydrogen chloride, anhydrous	Nonflammable gas	UN1050	Nonflammable gas	173.306	173.304	Forbidden	300 pounds	1	4	Stow away from foodstuff and living quarters.
	Hydrogen chloride refrigerated liquid	Nonflammable gas	UN2186	Nonflammable gas	None	173.314 173.315	Forbidden	300 pounds	1,2	4	Stow in well ventilated space.
	Hydrogen, refrigerated liquid (cryogenic liquid)	Flammable gas	UN1966	Flammable gas	None	173.316 173.318 173.319	Forbidden	Forbidden	5	5	
	Hydrogen fluoride	Corrosive material	UN1052	Corrosive	None	173.264	Forbidden	110 pounds	1	5	Segregation same as for nonflammable gases
	Hydrogen iodide solution See Hydriodic acid										
	Hydrogen peroxide solution (40% to 52% peroxide)	Oxidizer	UN2014	Oxidizer	173.244	173.266	Forbidden	Forbidden	1	4	Shade from radiant heat. Separate from permanganates. Keep away from powdered metals.
	Hydrogen peroxide solution (8% to 40% peroxide)	Oxidizer	UN2014	Oxidizer	173.244	173.266	1 quart	1 gallon	1,2	1	Shade from radiant heat. Separate from permanganates. Keep away from powdered metals.
	Hydrogen peroxide solution (over 52% peroxide)	Oxidizer	UN2015	Oxidizer and Corrosive	None	173.266	Forbidden	Forbidden	1	5	Shade from radiant heat. Separate from permanganates. Keep away from powdered metals. Concentrations greater than 60% hydrogen peroxide not permitted on any vessel except under conditions approved by the Department.
+	Hydrogen selenide	Poison A	UN2202	Poison gas & Flammable gas	None	173.328	Forbidden	Forbidden	1	5	Stow away from living quarters.
	Hydrogen sulfate. See Sulfuric acid										
+	Hydrogen sulfide	Flammable gas	UN1053	Flammable gas and Poison	None	173.304 173.314	Forbidden	300 pounds	1	5	
	Hydrosilicofluoric acid. See Hydrofluorosilicic acid										
	Hydroxyl amine iodide	Forbidden									
	Hypochlorite solution containing more than 7% available chlorine by weight	Corrosive material	UN1791	Corrosive	173.244	173.277	1 quart	4 gallons	1,2	1	Glass carboys in hampers not permitted under deck
A	Hypochlorite solution containing not more than 7% available chlorine by weight	ORM-B	NA1791	None	173.505	173.510	No limit	No limit			
	Hyponitrous acid	Forbidden									
	Igniter	Class C explosive		Explosive C	None	173.106	50 pounds	150 pounds	1,3	1,3	
	Igniter cord	Class C explosive		Explosive C	None	173.100	50 pounds	150 pounds	1,3	1,3	
	Igniter fuse, metal clad	Class C explosive		Explosive C	None	173.106	50 pounds	150 pounds	1,3	1,3	
	Igniter, jet thrust (jato)	Class A explosive		Explosive A	None	173.79	Forbidden	Forbidden	6	5	
	Igniter, jet thrust (jato)	Class B explosive		Explosive B	None	173.92	Forbidden	550 pounds	1,3	5	
	Igniter, rocket motor	Class A explosive		Explosive A	None	173.79	Forbidden	Forbidden	6	5	
	Igniter, rocket motor	Class B explosive		Explosive B	None	173.92	Forbidden	550 pounds	1,3	5	
	Illuminating projectile. See Fireworks, special										
	Iminobispropylamine	Corrosive material	UN2269	Corrosive	173.244	173.245	1 quart	10 gallons	1,2	1,2	
	Infectious substances, affecting humans, See Etiologic agent, n.o.s.		UN2814								
	Initiating explosive barium styphnate, monohydrate, lead styphnate (lead trinitroresorcinate)	Class A explosive		Explosive A	None	173.74	Forbidden	Forbidden	6	5	
	Initiating explosive (diazodinitrophenol)	Class A explosive		Explosive A	None	173.70	Forbidden	Forbidden	6	5	
	Initiating explosive (fulminate of mercury)	Class A explosive		Explosive A	None	173.71	Forbidden	Forbidden	6	5	
	Initiating explosive (guanyl nitrosamino guanylidene hydrazine)	Class A explosive		Explosive A	None	173.72	Forbidden	Forbidden	6	5	
	Initiating explosive (lead azide, dextrinated type only)	Class A explosive		Explosive A	None	173.73	Forbidden	Forbidden	6	5	
	Initiating explosive (lead mononitroresorcinate)	Class A explosive		Explosive A	None	173.70	Forbidden	Forbidden	6	5	
	Initiating explosive (nitro mannite)	Class A explosive		Explosive A	None	173.75	Forbidden	Forbidden	6	5	
	Initiating explosive (nitrosoguanidine)	Class A explosive		Explosive A	None	173.76	Forbidden	Forbidden	6	5	
	Initiating explosive (pentaerythrite tetranitrate)	Class A explosive		Explosive A	None	173.77	Forbidden	Forbidden	6	5	

233

(1) +/A/W	(2) Hazardous materials descriptions and proper shipping names	(3) Hazard class	(3A) Identification number	(4) Label(s) required (if not excepted)	(5) Packaging		(6) Maximum net quantity in one package		(7) Water shipments		
					(a) Exceptions	(b) Specific requirements	(a) Passenger carrying aircraft or railcar	(b) Cargo only aircraft	(a) Cargo vessel	(b) Passenger vessel	(c) Other requirements
	Initiating explosive (tetrazene (guanyl nitrosamine guanyl tetrazene))	Class A explosive		Explosive A	None	173.78	Forbidden	Forbidden	6	5	
	Initiating explosives (dry)	Forbidden									
	Ink	Combustible liquid	UN1210	None	173.118a	None	No limit	No limit	1,2	1,2	
	Ink	Flammable liquid	UN1210	Flammable liquid	173.118	173.144	1 quart	10 gallons	1,2	1	
	Inositol hexanitrate (dry)	Forbidden									
	Insecticide, dry, n.o.s.	Poison B	NA2588	Poison	173.364	173.365	50 pounds	200 pounds	1,2	1,2	
	Insecticide, liquefied gas (containing no Poison A or B material)	Nonflammable gas	NA1968	Nonflammable gas	173.306	173.304	150 pounds	300 pounds	1,3	1,3	
	Insecticide, liquefied gas, containing Poison A material or Poison B material	Poison A	NA1967	Poison gas	None	173.329 173.334	Forbidden	Forbidden	1	5	Shade from radiant heat
	Insecticide, liquid, n.o.s.	Combustible liquid	NA1993	None	173.118a	None	No limit	No limit	1,2	1,2	
	Insecticide, liquid, n.o.s.	Flammable liquid	NA1993	Flammable liquid	173.118	173.119	1 quart	10 gallons	1,2	1	
	Insecticide, liquid, n.o.s.	Poison B	NA2902	Poison	173.345	173.346	1 quart	55 gallons	1,2	1,2	
	Inulin trinitrate (dry)	Forbidden									
	Iodine azide (dry)	Forbidden									
	Iodine monochloride	Corrosive material	UN1792	Corrosive	None	173.293	Forbidden	1 quart	1	5	Keep dry
	Iodine pentafluoride	Oxidizer	UN2495	Oxidizer and Poison	None	173.246	Forbidden	100 pounds	1	1	Keep dry
	Iodoxy compounds (dry)	Forbidden									
	Iridium nitratopentamine iridium nitrate	Forbidden									
	Iron chloride, solid. See Ferric chloride, solid										
	Iron mass or sponge, not properly oxidized	Flammable solid	NA1383	Flammable solid	None	173.174	Forbidden	Forbidden	1,2	5	Separate from flammable gases or liquids, oxidizing materials, or organic peroxides
	Iron mass or sponge, spent	Flammable solid	UN1376	Flammable solid	None	173.174	Forbidden	Forbidden	1,2	5	Separate from flammable gases or liquids, oxidizing materials, or organic peroxides
	Iron oxide, spent. See Iron mass or sponge, spent										
	Iron sesquichloride, solid. See Ferric chloride										
	Irritating agent, n.o.s.	Irritating material	NA1693	Irritant	None	173.382	Forbidden	75 pounds	1	1	Stow away from living quarters
	Isobutane or Liquefied petroleum gas. See Liquefied petroleum gas										
	Isobutyl acetate	Flammable liquid	UN1213	Flammable liquid	173.118	173.119	1 quart	10 gallons	1,2	1	
	Isobutylamine	Flammable liquid	UN1214	Flammable liquid	173.118	173.119	1 quart	10 gallons	1,2	1	
	Isobutylene or Liquefied petroleum gas. See Liquefied petroleum gas										
	Isobutyric acid	Corrosive material	UN2529	Corrosive	173.244	173.245	1 quart	10 gallons	1,2	1,2	
	Isobutyric anhydride	Corrosive material	UN2530	Corrosive	173.244	173.245	1 quart	10 gallons	1,2	1,2	
	Isononanyl peroxide, technically pure or Isononanyl peroxide, in solution. See Organic peroxide, liquid or solution, n.o.s.		UN2128								
	Isooctane	Flammable liquid	UN1262	Flammable liquid	173.118	173.119	1 quart	10 gallons	1,2	1	
	Isooctene	Flammable liquid	UN1216	Flammable liquid	173.118	173.119	1 quart	10 gallons	1,3	4	
	Isopentane	Flammable liquid	UN1265	Flammable liquid	173.118	173.119	Forbidden	10 gallons	1,3	4	
	Isopentanoic acid	Corrosive material	NA1760	Corrosive	173.244	173.245	1 quart	10 gallons	1,2	1,2	
	Isoprene	Flammable liquid	UN1218	Flammable liquid	173.118	173.119	Forbidden	10 gallons	1,3	4	
	Isopropanol	Flammable liquid	UN1219	Flammable liquid	173.118	173.125	1 quart	10 gallons	1,2	1	
	Isopropyl acetate	Flammable liquid	UN1220	Flammable liquid	173.118	173.119	1 quart	10 gallons	1,2	1	
	Isopropyl acid phosphate, solid	Corrosive material	UN1793	Corrosive	173.244	173.245b	25 pounds	100 pounds	1,2	1,2	
	Isopropyl alcohol. See Isopropanol										
	Isopropylamine	Flammable liquid	UN1221	Flammable liquid	None	173.119	Forbidden	10 gallons	1,3	5	
	Isopropyl mercaptan	Flammable liquid	NA2402	Flammable liquid	None	173.141	Forbidden	10 gallons	1,3	5	

(1) +/A/W	(2) Hazardous materials descriptions and proper shipping names	(3) Hazard class	(3A) Identification number	(4) Label(s) required (if not excepted)	(5) Packaging (a) Exceptions	(5) Packaging (b) Specific requirements	(6) Maximum net quantity in one package (a) Passenger carrying aircraft or railcar	(6) (b) Cargo only aircraft	(7) Water shipments (a) Cargo vessel	(7) (b) Passenger vessel	(7) (c) Other requirements
	Isopropyl nitrate	Flammable liquid	UN1222	Flammable liquid	173.118	173.119	1 quart	10 gallons	1,2	1	
	Isopropyl percarbonate, stabilized	Organic peroxide	NA2134	Organic peroxide	None	173.282	Forbidden	Forbidden	5	5	
	Isopropyl percarbonate, unstabilized	Organic peroxide	NA2133	Organic peroxide	None	173.218	Forbidden	Forbidden	5	5	
	Isopropyl peroxydicarbonate, *technically pure.* See Isopropyl percarbonate, unstabilized		UN2133								
	Isopropyl peroxydicarbonate, *not more than 52% in solution.* See Organic peroxide, liquid or solution, n.o.s.		UN2134								
	Isopropyl phosphoric acid, solid. See Isopropyl acid phosphate, solid										
	Isothiocyanic acid (polymerization hazard)	Forbidden									
	Jet thrust igniter. See Igniter, jet thrust										
	Jet thrust unit (jato)	Class A explosive		Explosive A	None	173.79	Forbidden	Forbidden	6	5	
	Jet thrust unit (jato)	Class B explosive		Explosive B	None	173.92	Forbidden	550 pounds	1,3	5	
	Kerosene	Combustible liquid	UN1223	None	173.118a	None	No limit	No limit	1,2	1,2	
	Lacquer base or Lacquer chips, plastic (Wet with alcohol or solvent)	Flammable liquid	UN1263	Flammable liquid	173.118	173.127	1 quart	25 pounds	1,2	1	
	Lacquer base or Lacquer chips, dry	Flammable solid	NA2557	Flammable solid	173.175	173.175	25 pounds	100 pounds	1	1	
	Lauroyl peroxide	Organic peroxide	UN2124	Organic peroxide	173.153	173.157 173.158	2 pounds	25 pounds	1,2	1	
	Lauroyl peroxide, *not more than 42%, stable dispersion, in water.* See Organic peroxide, liquid or solution, n.o.s.		UN2893								
	Lauroyl peroxide, *technically pure.* See Lauroyl peroxide		UN2124								
	Lead arsenate, solid	Poison B	UN1617	Poison	173.364	173.367	50 pounds	200 pounds	1,2	1,2	
	Lead arsenite, solid	Poison B	UN1618	Poison	173.364	173.365	50 pounds	200 pounds	1,2	1,2	
	Lead azide. See Initiating explosive										
	Lead azide (dry)	Forbidden									
A	Lead chloride	ORM-B	NA2291	None	173.505	173.800	25 pounds	100 pounds	1,2	1,2	
	Lead cyanide	Poison B	UN1620	Poison	173.370		25 pounds	No limit	1,2	1,2	Stow away from acids
W	Lead dross (containing 3% or more free acid)	ORM-C	NA1794	None	173.505	173.1010			1,2	1,2	Segregation same as for corrosive materials
A	Lead fluoborate	ORM-B	NA2291	None	173.505	173.510	25 pounds	100 pounds	1,2	1,2	
A	Lead fluoride	ORM-B	NA2811	None	173.505	173.510	25 pounds	100 pounds	1,2	1,2	
	Lead mononitroresorcinate. See Initiating explosive										
	Lead mononitroresorcinate (dry)	Forbidden									
	Lead nitrate	Oxidizer	UN1469	Oxidizer	173.153	173.182	25 pounds	100 pounds	1,2	1,2	Stow away from foodstuffs
	Lead peroxide	Oxidizer	UN1872	Oxidizer	173.153	173.154	25 pounds	100 pounds	1,2	1,2	Stow away from foodstuffs
	Lead picrate (dry)	Forbidden									
W	Lead scrap. See Lead dross										
	Lead styphnate (dry)	Forbidden									
	Lead styphnate (lead trinitroresorcinate). See Initiating explosive										
	Lead sulfate, solid (containing more than 3% free acid)	Corrosive material	UN1794	Corrosive	173.244	173.245b	25 pounds	100 pounds	1,2	1,2	
	Life-saving appliances, self-inflating	ORM-C	UN2990	None	None	173.906	1 per inaccessible cargo compartment	No limit	1,2	1,2	
	Lime-nitrogen. See Calcium cyanamide, not hydrated										
	Lime, unslaked. See Calcium oxide										
A	Lindane	ORM-A	NA2761	None	173.505	173.510	No limit	No limit	1,2	1,2	
-	Liquefied hydrocarbon gas. See Hydrocarbon gas, liquefied										

(1) +/A/W	(2) Hazardous materials descriptions and proper shipping names	(3) Hazard class	(3A) Identification number	(4) Label(s) required (if not excepted)	(5) Packaging (a) Exceptions	(b) Specific requirements	(6) Maximum net quantity in one package (a) Passenger carrying aircraft or railcar	(b) Cargo only aircraft	(7) Water shipments (a) Cargo vessel	(b) Passenger vessel	(c) Other requirements
	Liquefied nonflammable gas (charged with nitrogen, carbon dioxide, or air)	Nonflammable gas	NA1058	Nonflammable gas	173.306	173.304	300 pounds	300 pounds	1,2	1,2	
+	Liquefied petroleum gas	Flammable gas	UN1075	Flammable gas	173.306	173.304 173.314 173.315	Forbidden	300 pounds	1,2	1	
	Liquid other than one classed as flammable, corrosive, poison or irritant, charged with nitrogen, carbon dioxide, or air. See Compressed gas n.o.s.										
	Lithium acetylide-ethylene diamine complex	Flammable solid	NA2813	Flammable solid and Dangerous when wet	None	173.206	Forbidden	25 pounds	1,2	5	Segregation same as for flammable solid labeled Dangerous When Wet
	Lithium aluminum hydride	Flammable solid	UN1410	Flammable solid and Dangerous when wet	None	173.206	Forbidden	25 pounds	1,2	5	Segregation same as for flammable solid labeled Dangerous When Wet
	Lithium aluminum hydride, ethereal	Flammable liquid	UN1411	Flammable liquid	None	173.137	Forbidden	1 quart	1	5	Segregation same as for flammable solids labeled Dangerous When Wet
	Lithium amide, powdered	Flammable solid	UN1412	Flammable solid	173.153	173.168	25 pounds	100 pounds	1,2	4	Segregation same as for flammable solids labeled Dangerous When Wet
	Lithium battery. See 173.206(f).										
	Lithium batteries, for disposal	ORM-C		None	None	173.1015	Forbidden	Forbidden			
	Lithium borohydride	Flammable solid	UN1413	Flammable solid and Dangerous when wet	None	173.206	Forbidden	25 pounds	1,2	5	Segregation same as for flammable solids labeled Dangerous When Wet
	Lithium ferrosilicon	Flammable solid	UN2830	Flammable solid and Dangerous when wet	None	173.206	Forbidden	25 pounds	1,2	5	Segregation same as for flammable solids labeled Dangerous When Wet
	Lithium hydride	Flammable solid	UN1414	Flammable solid and Dangerous when wet	None	173.206	Forbidden	25 pounds	1,2	5	Segregation same as for flammable solids labeled Dangerous When Wet
	Lithium hydride in fused solid form	Flammable solid	UN2805	Flammable solid and Dangerous when wet	None	173.206	Forbidden	100 pounds	1,2	5	Segregation same as for flammable solids labeled Dangerous When Wet
	Lithium hypochlorite compound, dry (containing more than 39% available chlorine)	Oxidizer	UN1471	Oxidizer	173.153	173.217	50 pounds	100 pounds	1,2	1,2	
	Lithium metal	Flammable solid	UN1415	Flammable solid and Dangerous when wet	None	173.206	Forbidden	25 pounds	1,2	5	Segregation same as for flammable solids labeled Dangerous When Wet
	Lithium metal, in cartridges	Flammable solid	UN1415	Flammable solid and Dangerous when wet	173.206	173.206	1 pound	25 pounds	1,2	4	Segregation same as for flammable solids labeled Dangerous When Wet
	Lithium nitride	Flammable solid	UN2806	Flammable solid and Dangerous when wet	None	173.206	Forbidden	25 pounds	1,2	5	Segregation same as for flammable solids labeled Dangerous When Wet
	Lithium peroxide	Oxidizer	UN1472	Oxidizer	173.153	173.154	25 pounds	100 pounds	1,2	1,2	Keep dry
	Lithium silicon	Flammable solid	UN1417	Flammable solid and Dangerous when wet	None	173.206	Forbidden	25 pounds	1,2	1,2	Segregation same as for flammable solids labeled Dangerous When Wet
	London purple, solid	Poison B	UN1621	Poison	173.364	173.365	50 pounds	200 pounds	1,2	1,2	
	Low blasting explosive. See Low explosive										
	Low explosive	Class A explosive		Explosive A	None	173.60	Forbidden	Forbidden	6	5	
	Lye. See Sodium hydroxide, solid										
	Magnesium aluminum phosphide	Flammable solid	UN1419	Flammable solid and Dangerous when wet	None	173.206	Forbidden	25 pounds	1,2	1,2	Segregation same as for flammable solids labeled Dangerous When Wet
+	Magnesium arsenate, solid	Poison B	UN1622	Poison	173.364	173.367	50 pounds	200 pounds	1,2	1,2	
	Magnesium dross, wet or hot. See 173.173	Forbidden									
	Magnesium granules coated, particle size not less than 149 microns	Flammable solid	UN2950	Flammable solid and Dangerous when wet	173.153	173.178	25 pounds	100 pounds	1,2	1,2	Segregation same as for flammable solids labeled Dangerous when wet.
	Magnesium metal (powder, pellets, turnings, or ribbon) or Magnesium aluminum powder	Flammable solid	UN1869	Flammable solid and Dangerous when wet	173.153	173.220	25 pounds	100 pounds	1,2	1,2	Segregation same as for flammable solids labeled Dangerous when wet.
	Magnesium nitrate	Oxidizer	UN1474	Oxidizer	173.153	173.182	25 pounds	100 pounds	1,2	1,2	
	Magnesium perchlorate	Oxidizer	UN1475	Oxidizer	173.153	173.154	25 pounds	100 pounds	1,3	1,3	Stow away from powdered metals
	Magnesium peroxide, solid	Oxidizer	UN1476	Oxidizer	173.153	173.154	25 pounds	100 pounds	1,2	1,2	Keep dry

(1) +/A/W	(2) Hazardous materials descriptions and proper shipping names	(3) Hazard class	(3A) Identification number	(4) Label(s) required (if not excepted)	(5) Packaging (a) Exceptions	(5) (b) Specific requirements	(6) Maximum net quantity in one package (a) Passenger carrying aircraft or railcar	(6) (b) Cargo only aircraft	(7) Water shipments (a) Cargo vessel	(7) (b) Passenger vessel	(7) (c) Other requirements
	Magnesium scrap (borings, clippings, shavings, sheet, turnings or scalpings)	Flammable solid	NA1869	Flammable solid and Dangerous when wet	173.153	173.220	Forbidden	Forbidden	1,2	1,2	Segregation same as for flammable solids labeled Dangerous When Wet
A	Magnetized material. See 173.21(f)										
A	Malathion	ORM-A	NA2783	None	173.505	173.510	No limit	No limit	1,2	1,2	
A	Maleic acid	ORM-A	NA2215	None	173.505	173.510	50 pounds	200 pounds	1,2	1,2	Keep tightly closed.
AW	Maleic anhydride	ORM-A	UN2215	None	173.505	173.510	50 pounds	200 pounds	1,2	1,2	Stow away from foodstuffs
	Mannitan tetranitrate	Forbidden									
	Matches, block. See Matches, strike anywhere										
	Matches, safety, book, card, or strike-on box.	Flammable solid	UN1944	None	173.176	None	50 pounds	50 pounds	1,2	1,2	
	Matches, strike anywhere	Flammable solid	UN1331	Flammable solid	None	173.176a	Forbidden	Forbidden	1,2	1	
	Matting acid. See Sulfuric acid										
	Medicines, n.o.s.	Combustible liquid	UN1851	None	173.118a	None	No limit	No limit	1,2	1,2	
	Medicines, n.o.s.	Flammable liquid	UN1851	Flammable liquid	173.118	173.119	1 quart	10 gallons	1,2	1	
	Medicines, n.o.s.	Flammable solid	UN1851	Flammable solid	173.153	173.154	25 pounds	100 pounds	1,2	1,2	
	Medicines, n.o.s.	Oxidizer	UN1851	Oxidizer	173.153	173.154	25 pounds	100 pounds	1,2	1,2	
	Medicines, n.o.s., liquid	Corrosive material	UN1851	Corrosive	173.244	173.245	1 quart	1 quart	1,2	1,2	
	Medicines, n.o.s., liquid	Poison B	UN1851	Poison	173.345	173.346	1 quart	55 gallons	1,3	1	
	Medicines, n.o.s., solid	Corrosive material	UN1851	Corrosive	173.244	173.245b	25 pounds	100 pounds	1,2	1,2	Keep dry
	Medicines, n.o.s., solid	Poison B	UN1851	Poison	173.364	173.365	50 pounds	200 pounds	1,3	1,3	
	p-Menthane hydroperoxide, technically pure. See Paramethane hydroperoxide		UN2125								
	Mercaptan mixture, aliphatic	Flammable liquid	NA1228	Flammable liquid	None	173.141	Forbidden	10 gallonss	1,3	5	
	Mercaptan mixture, aliphatic (in containers over 110 gallons)	Combustible liquid	NA1228	None	173.118a	None	Forbidden	10 gallons	1,2	1,2	
AW	Mercaptan mixture, aliphatic (in containers of 110 gallons or less). See 173.141(b)	ORM-A	NA1228	None	173.505	173.510	Forbidden	10 gallons	1,3	5	Stow in well ventilated space away from living quarters
+	Mercuric acetate	Poison B	UN1629	Poison	173.364	173.365	50 pounds	200 pounds	1,2	1,2	
+	Mercuric ammonium chloride, solid	Poison B	UN1630	Poison	173.364	173.365	50 pounds	200 pounds	1,2	1,2	
+	Mercuric benzoate, solid	Poison B	UN1631	Poison	173.364	173.365	50 pounds	200 pounds	1,2	1,2	
+	Mercuric bromide, solid	Poison B	UN1634	Poison	173.364	173.365	Forbidden	25 pounds	1,2	1,2	
+	Mercuric chloride, solid	Poison B	UN1624	Poison	173.364	173.372	Forbidden	25 pounds	1,2	1,2	
+	Mercuric cyanide, solid	Poison B	UN1636	Poison	173.370	173.370	25 pounds	200 pounds	1,2	1,2	Stow away from acids
+	Mercuric iodide, solid	Poison B	UN1638	Poison	173.364	173.365	50 pounds	200 pounds	1,2	1,2	
	Mercuric iodide solution	Poison B	UN1638	Poison	173.345	173.346	1 quart	55 gallons	1,2	1,2	
	Mercuric nitrate	Oxidizer	UN1625	Oxidizer	173.153	173.182	25 pounds	100 pounds	1,2	1,2	If stowed under deck, must be stowed in a recoverable location.
+	Mercuric oleate, solid	Poison B	UN1640	Poison	173.364	173.365	50 pounds	200 pounds	1,2	1,2	
	Mercuric oxide, solid	Poison B	UN1641	Poison	173.364	173.365	50 pounds	200 pounds	1,2	1,2	
+	Mercuric oxycyanide, solid (desensitized)	Poison B	UN1642	Poison	173.364	173.365	25 pounds	200 pounds	1,2	1,2	Stow away from acids
+	Mercuric potassium cyanide, solid	Poison B	UN1626	Poison	173.364	173.365 173.370	25 pounds	200 pounds	1,2	1,2	Stow away from acids
+	Mercuric potassium iodide, solid	Poison B	UN1643	Poison	173.364	173.365	50 pounds	200 pounds	1,2	1,2	
+	Mercuric salicylate solid	Poison B	UN1644	Poison	173.364	173.365	50 pounds	200 pounds	1,2	1,2	
+	Mercuric subsulfate, solid	Poison B	NA2025	Poison	173.364	173.365	50 pounds	200 pounds	1,2	1,2	
+	Mercuric sulfate, solid	Poison B	UN1645	Poison	173.364	173.365	50 pounds	200 pounds	1,2	1,2	
+	Mercuric sulfocyanate, solid or Mercuric thiocyanate, solid	Poison B	UN1646	Poison	173.364	173.365	50 pounds	200 pounds	1,2	1,2	
+	Mercurol or Mercury nucleate, solid	Poison B	UN1639	Poison	173.364	173.365	50 pounds	200 pounds	1,2	1,2	
+	Mercurous acetate, solid	Poison B	UN1629	Poison	173.364	173.365	50 pounds	200 pounds	1,2	1,2	
	Mercurous azide	Forbidden									
+	Mercurous bromide, solid	Poison B	UN1634	Poison	173.364	173.365	50 pounds	200 pounds	1,2	1,2	
-	Mercurous gluconate, solid	Poison B	UN1637	Poison	173.364	173.365	50 pounds	200 pounds	1,2	1,2	
+	Mercurous iodide, solid	Poison B	UN1638	Poison	173.364	173.365	50 pounds	200 pounds	1,2	1,2	
	Mercurous nitrate, solid	Oxidizer	UN1627	Oxidizer	173.153	173.154	50 pounds	100 pounds	1,2	1,2	
+	Mercurous oxide, black, solid	Poison B	UN1641	Poison	173.364	173.365	50 pounds	200 pounds	1,2	1,2	
+	Mercurous sulfate, solid	Poison B	UN1628	Poison	173.364	173.365	50 pounds	200 pounds	1,2	1,2	
	Mercury acetylide	Forbidden									
	Mercury based pesticide, liquid, n.o.s. (compounds and preparations)	Flammable liquid	UN2778	Flammable liquid	173.118	173.119	1 quart	10 gallons	1,2	1	
	Mercury based pesticide, liquid, n.o.s. (compounds and preparations)	Poison B	UN2777	Poison	173.345	173.346	1 quart	55 gallons	1,2	1,2	

237

(1) +/A/W	(2) Hazardous materials descriptions and proper shipping names	(3) Hazard class	(3A) Identification number	(4) Label(s) required (if not excepted)	(5) Packaging		(6) Maximum net quantity in one package		(7) Water shipments		
					(a) Exceptions	(b) Specific requirements	(a) Passenger carrying aircraft or railcar	(b) Cargo only aircraft	(a) Cargo vessel	(b) Passenger vessel	(c) Other requirements
	Mercury based pesticide, solid, n.o.s. (compounds and preparations)	Poison B	UN2777	Poison	173.364	173.365	50 pounds	200 pounds	1,2	1,2	
	Mercury compound, solid, n.o.s.	Poison B	UN2025	Poison	173.364	173.365	50 pounds	200 pounds	1,2	1,2	
	Mercury fulminate. See Initiating explosive										
	Mercury iodide aquabasic ammonobasic (iodide of Million's base)	Forbidden									
A	Mercury, metallic	ORM-B	NA2809	None	None	173.860	173.860	See 173.860	1,2	1,2	
	Mercury nitride	Forbidden									
	Mercury oxycyanide	Forbidden									
	Mesityl oxide	Flammable liquid	UN1229	Flammable liquid	None	173.119	1 quart	10 gallons	1,2	1,2	
	Metal alkyl, solution, n.o.s.	Flammable liquid	NA9195	Flammable liquid	173.118	173.119	1 quart	1 gallon	1,2	1	
W	Metal borings, shavings, turnings, or cuttings (ferrous metals only, except stainless steel)	ORM-C	UN2793	None	173.505	173.1025			1,2	1,2	Keep dry, not permitted if temperature of material is at or above 130 deg. F.
	Metal salts of methyl nitramine (dry)	Forbidden									
+	Methane, compressed	Flammable gas	UN1971	Flammable gas	173.306	173.302	Forbidden	300 pounds	1,2	4	Stow away from living quarters.
+	Methane, refrigerated liquid (cryogenic liquid)	Flammable gas	UN1972	Flammable gas	None	173.318	Forbidden	Forbidden	1	5	Stow way from living quarters.
	Methanol. See Methyl alcohol										
	Methazoic acid	Forbidden									
	Methyl acetate	Flammable liquid	UN1231	Flammable liquid	173.118	173.119	1 quart	10 gallons	1,2	1	
	Methyl acetone	Flammable liquid	UN1232	Flammable liquid	173.118	173.119	1 quart	10 gallons	1,2	1	
+	Methylacetylene-propadiene, stabilized	Flammable gas	UN1060	Flammable gas	173.306	173.304 173.314 173.315	Forbidden	300 pounds	1,2	1	
	Methyl acrylate, inhibited	Flammable liquid	UN1919	Flammable liquid	173.118	173.119	1 quart	10 gallons	1,2	1	
	Methylal	Flammable liquid	UN1234	Flammable liquid	None	173.119	Forbidden	10 gallons	1,3	5	
	Methyl alcohol	Flammable liquid	UN1230	Flammable liquid	173.118	173.119	1 quart	10 gallons	1,2	1	
+	Methylamine, anhydrous	Flammable gas	UN1061	Flammable gas	173.306	173.304 173.314 173.315	Forbidden	300 pounds	1	4	
	Methylamine, aqueous solution	Flammable liquid	UN1235	Flammable liquid	173.118	173.119	1 quart	10 gallons	1,3	4	Stow away from mercury and its compounds
	Methylamine dinitramine and dry salts thereof	Forbidden									
	Methylamine nitroform	Forbidden									
	Methylamine perchlorate (dry)	Forbidden									
	Methylamyl acetate	Flammable liquid	UN1233	Flammable liquid	173.118	173.119	1 quart	10 gallons	1,2	1,2	
	Methyl amyl ketone	Combustible liquid	UN1110	None	173.118a	None	No limit	No limit	1,2	1,2	
+	Methyl bromide and more than 2% chloropicrin mixture, liquid	Poison B	NA1581	Poison	None	173.353	Forbidden	Forbidden	1	5	Shade from radiant heat
+	Methyl bromide and nonflammable, nonliquefied compressed gas mixture, liquid (including up to 2% chloropicrin)	Poison B	NA1955	Poison	None	173.353a	Forbidden	300 pounds	1	5	Stow away from living quarters
+	Methyl bromide - ethylene dibromide mixture, liquid	Poison B	UN1647	Poison	None	173.353	Forbidden	55 gallons	1	1	
+	Methyl bromide, liquid (including up to 2% chloropicrin)	Poison B	UN1062	Poison	None	173.353	Forbidden	55 gallons	1	5	Stow away from living quarters. Segregation same as for nonflammable gas.
	Methyl butene	Flammable liquid	UN2460	Flammable liquid	None	173.119	Forbidden	10 gallons	1,2	5	
	Methyl butyrate	Flammable liquid	UN1237	Flammable liquid	173.118	173.119	1 quart	10 gallons	1,2	1	
	Methyl cellosolve. See Ethylene glycol monomethyl ether										
	Methyl cellosolve acetate. See Ethylene glycol monomethyl ether acetate										
+	Methyl chloride	Flammable gas	UN1063	Flammable gas	173.306	173.304 173.314 173.315	Forbidden	300 pounds	1,2	4	
+	Methyl chloride-methylene chloride mixture	Flammable gas	UN1912	Flammable gas	173.306	173.304 173.314	Forbidden	300 pounds	1,2	4	
	Methyl chlorocarbonate. See Methyl chloroformate										
A	Methyl chloroform. See 1,1,1-Trichloroethane										
	Methyl chloroformate	Flammable liquid	UN1238	Flammable liquid and Poison	None	173.288	Forbidden	5 pints	1,2	1	

(1) +/A/W	(2) Hazardous materials descriptions and proper shipping names	(3) Hazard class	(3A) Identification number	(4) Label(s) required (if not excepted)	(5) Packaging (a) Exceptions	(5) Packaging (b) Specific requirements	(6) Maximum net quantity in one package (a) Passenger carrying aircraft or railcar	(6) (b) Cargo only aircraft	(7) Water shipments (a) Cargo vessel	(7) (b) Passenger vessel	(7) (c) Other requirements
	Methylchloromethyl ether, anhydrous	Flammable liquid	UN1239	Flammable liquid and Poison	None	173.143	Forbidden	Forbidden	1	5	Shade from radiant heat
	Methyl cyanide	Flammable liquid	UN1648	Flammable liquid	173.118	173.119	1 quart	10 gallons	1	4	Shade from radiant heat.
	Methylcyclohexane	Flammable liquid	UN2296	Flammable liquid	173.118	173.119	1 quart	10 gallons	1,2	1	
	Methylcyclopentane	Flammable liquid	UN2298	Flammable liquid	173.118	173.119	1 quart	10 gallons	1,3	4	
	Methyl dichloroacetate	Corrosive material	UN2299	Corrosive	173.244	173.245	1 quart	1 quart	1,2	1,2	
	Methyldichloroarsine	Poison A	NA1556	Poison gas	None	173.328	Forbidden	Forbidden	1	5	Shade from radiant heat
	Methyl dichlorosilane	Flammable liquid	UN1242	Flammable liquid	None	173.136	Forbidden	5 pints	1,2	1	
	Methylene chloride. See Dichloromethane										
	Methylene glycol dinitrate	Forbidden									
	Methyl ethyl ether. See Ethyl methyl ether										
	Methyl ethyl ketone	Flammable liquid	UN1193	Flammable liquid	173.118	173.119	1 quart	10 gallons	1,2	1	
	Methyl ethyl ketone peroxide, in solution with not more than 9% by weight active oxygen. See Organic peroxide, liquid, or solution, n.o.s.		UN2550								
	Methyl ethyl ketone peroxide, in solution with more than 9% by weight active oxygen	Forbidden									
	Methyl ethyl pyridine	Corrosive material	UN2300	Corrosive	173.244	173.245	1 quart	10 gallons	1,2	1,2	
	Methyl formate	Flammable liquid	UN1243	Flammable liquid	173.118	173.119	1 quart	10 gallons	1,3	4	
	Methylfuran	Flammable liquid	UN2301	Flammable liquid	173.118	173.119	1 quart	10 gallons	1,3	4	
	a-Methylglucoside tetranitrate	Forbidden									
	a-Methylglycerol trinitrate	Forbidden									
	Methylhydrazine	Flammable liquid	UN1244	Flammable liquid and Poison	None	173.145	Forbidden	5 pints	1,2	1	Stow separate from oxidizing materials and corrosives
	Methyl isobutyl ketone peroxide, in solution with not more than 9% by weight active oxygen. See Organic peroxide, liquid or solution, n.o.s.		UN2126								
	Methyl isobutyl ketone peroxide, in solution with more than 9% by weight active oxygen	Forbidden									
	Methyl isocyanate	Flammable liquid	UN2480	Flammable liquid and Poison	None	173.119 173.3a	Forbidden	10 gallons	1	5	Keep cool. Stow away from living quarters and sources of heat
	Methyl isopropenyl ketone, inhibited	Flammable liquid	UN1246	Flammable liquid	173.118	173.119	1 quart	10 gallons	1,2	1	
	Methyl magnesium bromide in ethyl ether not over 40% concentration	Flammable liquid	UN1928	Flammable liquid	None	173.149	Forbidden	Forbidden	1	1	Segregation same as for flammable solids. Separate from flammable gases or liquids, oxidizing materials or organic peroxides.
+	Methyl mercaptan	Flammable gas	UN1064	Flammable gas	173.306	173.304 173.314 173.315	Forbidden	300 pounds	1,2	1	
	Methyl methacrylate monomer, inhibited	Flammable liquid	UN1247	Flammable liquid	173.118	173.119	1 quart	10 gallons	1,2	1	
	Methyl methacrylate monomer, uninhibited (high-purity, if acceptable under 173.21 of this subchapter)	Flammable liquid	NA1247	Flammable liquid	173.118	173.119	Forbidden	Forbidden	1,2	1	
	Methyl nitrate	Forbidden									
	N-Methyl-N'-nitro-N-nitrosoguanidine (not exceeding 25 grams in one outside packaging)	Flammable solid	NA1325	Flammable solid	None	173.179	Forbidden	Forbidden	4	5	
	Methyl parathion, liquid	Poison B	NA2783	Poison	None	173.358	Forbidden	1 quart	1,3	1,3	
	Methyl parathion mixture, dry	Poison B	NA2783	Poison	173.377	173.377	50 pounds	200 pounds	1,2	1,2	
	Methyl parathion mixture, liquid, (containing 25% or less methyl parathion)	Poison B	NA2783	Poison	None	173.359	1/2 pint	1 quart	1,2	1,2	
	Methyl parathion mixture, liquid, (containing over 25% methyl parathion)	Poison B	NA2783	Poison	None	173.359	Forbidden	1 quart	1,2	1,2	
	Methylpentadiene	Flammable liquid	UN2461	Flammable liquid	173.118	173.119	1 quart	10 gallons	1,2	1	
	Methyl pentane	Flammable liquid	UN2462	Flammable liquid	173.118	173.119	1 quart	10 gallons	1,2	1	
	Methyl phosphonic dichloride	Corrosive	NA9206	Corrosive and Poison	None	173.271	Forbidden	1 quart	1	1	Keep dry. Glass carboys not permitted on passenger vessels.

239

(1) +/A/W	(2) Hazardous materials descriptions and proper shipping names	(3) Hazard class	(3A) Identification number	(4) Label(s) required (if not excepted)	(5) Packaging (a) Exceptions	(b) Specific requirements	(6) Maximum net quantity in one package (a) Passenger carrying aircraft or railcar	(b) Cargo only aircraft	(7) Water shipments (a) Cargo vessel	(b) Passenger vessel	(c) Other requirements
	Methyl phosphonothioic dichloride, anhydrous	Corrosive material	NA1760	Corrosive	173.244	173.245 173.245a	1 quart	1 quart	1	4	
	Methyl phosphonous dichloride. See Pyroforic liquid, n.o.s.										
	Methyl pictric acid (heavy metal salts of)	Forbidden									
	Methyl propionate	Flammable liquid	UN1248	Flammable liquid	173.118	173.119	1 quart	10 gallons	1,2	1	
	Methyl propyl ketone	Flammable liquid	UN1249	Flammable liquid	173.118	173.119	1 quart	10 gallons	1,2	1	
	Methyl sulfate. See Dimethyl sulfate										
	Methyl sulfide. See Dimethyl sulfide										
	Methyltrichlorosilane	Flammable liquid	UN1250	Flammable liquid	None	173.135	Forbidden	10 gallons	1,2	1	
	Methyl trimethylol methane trinitrate	Forbidden									
	Methyl vinyl ketone, inhibited	Flammable liquid	UN1251	Flammable liquid	173.147	173.147	4 ounces	10 gallons	1,2	1	
	Mevinphos	Poison B	NA2783	Poison	None	173.358	Forbidden	1 quart	1,2	5	
	Mevinphos mixture, dry	Poison B	NA2783	Poison	173.377	173.377	Forbidden	200 pounds	1,2	4	
	Mevinphos mixture, liquid	Poison B	NA2783	Poison	173.359	173.359	½ pint	1 quart	1,2	5	
	Mexacarbate	Poison B	NA2757	Poison	173.364	173.365	50 pounds	200 pounds	2	2	
	Mild detonating fuse, metal clad. See Fuse, mild detonating, metal clad										
	Mine, empty. See 173.55										
	Mine, explosive, with gaseous material. See Explosive mine										
	Mine rescue equipment containing carbon dioxide	Nonflammable gas	NA1956	Nonflammable gas	173.306		150 pounds	300 pounds	1,2	1,2	
	Mining reagent, liquid (containing 20% or more cresylic acid)	Corrosive material	NA2022	Corrosive	173.244	173.249a	1 quart	10 gallons	1,2	1,2	
A	Mipafox	ORM-A	UN2783	None	173.505	173.510	No limit	No limit			
	Mixed acid. See Nitrating acid										
A	Molybdenum pentachloride	ORM-B	UN2508	None	173.505	173.800	25 pounds	100 pounds			
	Monochloroacetone, stabilized or inhibited	Irritating material	UN1695	Irritant	None	173.384	Forbidden	5 gallons	1	1	Stay away from living quarters
	Monochloroacetone (unstabilized)	Forbidden									
	Monochloroethylene. See Vinyl chloride										
	Monoethanolamine	Corrosive material	UN2491	Corrosive	173.244	173.245	1 quart	10 gallons	1,2	1,2	
	Monoethylamine	Flammable liquid	UN1036	Flammable liquid	None	173.148	Forbidden	5 pints	1,2	5	Segregation same as for flammable gas
	Monofluorophosphoric acid, anhydrous	Corrosive material	UN1776	Corrosive	None	173.275	Forbidden	1 gallon	1,2	1,2	Keep dry
	Morpholine	Flammable liquid	UN2054	Flammable liquid	173.118	173.119	1 quart	10 gallons	1,2	1	
	Morpholine, aqueous, mixture	Flammable liquid	NA2054	Flammable liquid	173.118	173.119	1 quart	10 gallons	1,2	1	
	Morpholine, aqueous, mixture	Corrosive material	NA1760	Corrosive	173.244	173.245	1 quart	10 gallons	1	4	
	Moth balls. See Naphthalene										
	Motion picture film. See Film										
+	Motor fuel antiknock compound	Poison B	UN1649	Poison	None	173.354	Forbidden	55 gallons	1	5	If flashpoint less than 141 degrees F, Segregation same as for flammable liquids
	Motor, internal combustion				173.120						
	Motor vehicle, etc. including automobile, motorcycle, truck, tractor, and other self-propelled vehicle or equipment powered by internal combustion engine, when offered new or used for transportation and which contain fuel in the engine or fuel tank or the electric storage battery is connected to either terminal of the electrical system	ORM-C		None	173.120 173.250 173.257 173.306 175.305 176.905				1,2	1,2	
	Muriatic acid. See Hydrochloric acid										
	Naphtha	Combustible liquid	UN2553	None	173.118a	None	No limit	No limit	1,2	1,2	
	Naphtha	Flammable liquid	UN2553	Flammable liquid	173.118	173.119	1 quart	10 gallons	1,2	1	
AW	Naphthalene or Naphthalin	ORM-A	UN1334	None	173.505	173.655	25 pounds	300 pounds	1,2	1,2	Segregation same as for flammable solids
	Naphthalene diozonide	Forbidden									
	Naphtha petroleum. See Petroleum naphtha										
	Naphthyl amineperchlorate	Forbidden									

240

(1) +/A/W	(2) Hazardous materials descriptions and proper shipping names	(3) Hazard class	(3A) Identification number	(4) Label(s) required (if not excepted)	(5) Packaging (a) Exceptions	(5) Packaging (b) Specific requirements	(6) Maximum net quantity in one package (a) Passenger carrying aircraft or railcar	(6) (b) Cargo only aircraft	(7) Water shipments (a) Cargo vessel	(7) (b) Passenger vessel	(7) (c) Other requirements
	Natural gas, refrigerated liquid (with high methane content) (cryogenic liquid)	Flammable gas	UN1972	Flammable gas	None	173.318	Forbidden	Forbidden	1	5	Stow away from living quarters.
	Natural gasoline. See Gasoline										
	Neohexane	Flammable liquid	UN1208	Flammable liquid	173.118	173.119	1 quart	10 gallons	1,3	4	
	Neon or Neon, compressed	Nonflammable gas	UN1065	Nonflammable gas	173.306	173.302	150 pounds	300 pounds	1,2	1,2	
	Neon, refrigerated liquid (cryogenic liquid)	Nonflammable gas	UN1913	Nonflammable gas	173.320	173.316	100 pounds	1,100 pounds	1,3	1,3	
	New explosive or explosive device. See 173.51 and 173.86										
	Nickel carbonyl	Flammable liquid	UN1259	Flammable liquid and Poison	None	173.126	Forbidden	Forbidden	1	5	Shade from radiant heat. Segregation same as for flammable liquids. Not permitted on a vessel transporting explosives, except that quantities not exceeding 200 pounds may be transported on such vessels under conditions approved by the Captain of the Port.
+	Nickel cyanide, solid	Poison B	UN1653	Poison	173.370		25 pounds	200 pounds	1,2	1,2	Stow away from acids
	Nickel nitrate	Oxidizer	UN2725	Oxidizer	173.153	173.182	25 pounds	100 pounds	1,2	1,2	
	Nickel picrate	Forbidden									
	Nicotine hydrochloride	Poison B	UN1656	Poison	173.345	173.346	1 quart	55 gallons	1,2	1,2	
	Nicotine, liquid	Poison B	UN1654	Poison	None	173.346	Forbidden	55 gallons	1,2	1,2	
	Nicotine salicylate	Poison B	UN1657	Poison	173.364	173.365	50 pounds	200 pounds	1,2	1,2	
+	Nicotine sulfate, liquid	Poison B	UN1658	Poison	173.345	173.346	1 quart	55 gallons	1,2	1,2	
+	Nicotine sulfate, solid	Poison B	UN1658	Poison	173.364	173.365	50 pounds	200 pounds	1,2	1,2	
	Nicotine tartrate	Poison B	UN1659	Poison	173.364	173.365	50 pounds	200 pounds	1,2	1,2	
	Nitrated paper (unstable)	Forbidden									
	Nitrate, n.o.s.	Oxidizer	NA1477	Oxidizer	173.153	173.182	25 pounds	100 pounds	1,2	1,2	
	Nitrate of ammonia explosives. See High explosive										
	Nitrates of diazonium compounds	Forbidden									
	Nitrating acid, mixture with not more than 50% nitric acid.	Corrosive	UN1796	Corrosive	None	173.267	Forbidden	1 quart	1	5	Stow away from fluorides.
	Nitrating acid, mixture with more than 50% nitric acid.	Oxidizer	UN1796	Oxidizer and Corrosive	None	173.267	Forbidden	1 quart	1	5	Segregation same as for corrosive material. Stow away from fluorides.
	Nitrating acid, spent	Corrosive material	NA1826	Corrosive	None	173.248	Forbidden	1 quart	1	5	
	Nitric acid (over 40%)	Oxidizer	UN2031	Oxidizer and Corrosive	None	173.268	Forbidden	5 pints	1	5	Segregation same as for corrosive materials. Stow away from hydrazine, separate from diethylenetriamine
	Nitric acid, 40% or less	Corrosive material	NA1760	Corrosive	None	173.268	Forbidden	5 pints	1	5	Stow away from hydrazine, separate from diethylenetriamine
	Nitric acid, fuming	Oxidizer	UN2032	Oxidizer and Poison	None	173.268	Forbidden	Forbidden	1	5	Segregation same as for corrosive materials. Stow away from hydrazine, separate from diethylenetriamine
	Nitric ether. See Ethyl nitrate										
	Nitric oxide	Poison A	UN1660	Poison gas	None	173.337	Forbidden	Forbidden	1	5	
	2-Nitro-2-methylpropanol nitrate	Forbidden									
	6-Nitro-4-diazotoluene-3-sulfonic acid (dry)	Forbidden									
	p-Nitroaniline. See Nitroaniline										
	N-Nitroaniline	Forbidden									
+	Nitroaniline	Poison B	UN1661	Poison	173.364	173.373	50 pounds	200 pounds	1,2	1,2	
	m-Nitrobenzene diazonium perchlorate	Forbidden									
	Nitrobenzene, liquid or Nitrobenzol, liquid (oil of mirbane)	Poison B	UN1662	Poison	173.345	173.346	1 quart	55 gallons	1,2	1,2	
	Nitro carbonitrate. See Blasting agent, n.o.s.										
	Nitrocellulose, colloided, granular or flake, wet with not less than 20% alcohol or solvent, or block, wet with not less than 25% alcohol	Flammable liquid	NA2059	Flammable liquid	173.118	173.127	1 quart	25 pounds	1,3	1	
	Nitrocellulose, colloided, granular or flake, wet with not less than 20% water	Flammable solid	NA2555	Flammable solid	173.153	173.184	25 pounds	100 pounds	1,3	1	
	Nitrocellulose, dry. See High explosive										
	Nitrocellulose, wet with not less than 30% alcohol or solvent	Flammable liquid	NA2556	Flammable liquid	173.118	173.127	1 quart	25 pounds	1,3	1	
	Nitrocellulose, wet with not less than 20% water	Flammable solid	NA2555	Flammable solid	173.153	173.184	25 pounds	100 pounds	1,3	1	
+	Nitrochlorobenzene, meta or para, solid	Poison B	UN1578	Poison	173.364	173.374	50 pounds	200 pounds	1,2	1,2	
+	Nitrochlorobenzene, ortho, liquid	Poison B	UN1578	Poison	173.345	173.346	1 quart	55 gallons	1,2	1,2	
	Nitroethane	Flammable liquid	UN2842	Flammable liquid	173.118	173.119	15 gallon	55 gallons	1,2	1	
	Nitroethylene polymer	Forbidden									
	Nitroethyl nitrate	Forbidden									

241

+/ A/ W	Hazardous materials descriptions and proper shipping names	Hazard class	Identi-fication number	Label(s) required (if not excepted)	(a) Exceptions	(b) Specific require-ments	(a) Passenger carrying aircraft or railcar	(b) Cargo only aircraft	(a) Cargo vessel	(b) Pas-senger vessel	(c) Other requirements
	Nitrogen or Nitrogen, compressed	Nonflammable gas	UN1066	Nonflammable gas	173.306	173.302 173.314	150 pounds	300 pounds	1,2	1,2	
	Nitrogen, refrigerated liquid (cryogenic liquid)	Nonflammable gas	UN1977	Nonflammable gas	173.320	173.316 173.318	100 pounds	1,100 pounds	1,3	1,3	
	Nitrogen dioxide, liquid	Poison A	UN1067	Poison gas and Oxidizer	None	173.336	Forbidden	Forbidden	1	5	Segregation same as for nonflammable gases. Stow away from organic materials.
	Nitrogen peroxide, liquid	‑on A	NA1067	Poison gas and Oxidizer	None	173.336	Forbidden	Forbidden	1	5	Segregation same as for nonflammable gases. Stow away from organic materials.
	Nitrogen tetroxide, liquid	Poison A	NA1067	Poison gas and Oxidizer	None	173.336	Forbidden	Forbidden	1	5	Segregation same as for nonflammable gases. Stow away from organic materials.
	Nitrogen trichloride	Forbidden									
	Nitrogen trifluoride	Nonflammable gas	UN2451	Nonflammable gas	None	173.302	Forbidden	300 pounds	1	5	Stow away from living quarters and organic materials
	Nitrogen triiodide	Forbidden									
	Nitrogen triiodide monoamine	Forbidden									
	Nitroglycerin, liquid, desensitized. See High explosive, liquid										
	Nitroglycerin, liquid, not desensitized. See 173.51	Forbidden									
	Nitroglycerin, spirits of. See Spirits of nitroglycerin										
	Nitroguanidine, dry. See High explosive										
	Nitroguanidine nitrate	Forbidden									
	Nitroguanidine, wet with not less than 20% water	Flammable solid	UN1336	Flammable solid	173.153	173.184	25 pounds	100 pounds	1,2	4	
	1-Nitro hydantoin	Forbidden									
	Nitrohydrochloric acid	Corrosive material	UN1798	Corrosive	None	173.278	Forbidden	5 pints	1	5	
	Nitrohydrochloric acid, diluted	Corrosive material	UN1798	Corrosive	None	173.278	Forbidden	5 pints	1	5	
	Nitro isobutane triol trinitrate	Forbidden									
	Nitromannite. See High explosive										
	Nitromannite (dry)	Forbidden									
	Nitromethane	Flammable liquid	UN1261	Flammable liquid	173.118	173.149a	1 quart	10 gallons	1,2	1,2	
	Nitromuriatic acid. See Nitrohydrochloric acid										
	N-Nitro-N-methylglycolamide nitrate	Forbidden									
	Nitrophenol pesticide, substituted, liquid or solid, n.o.s. (compounds and preparations) See Substituted nitrophenol pesticide, liquid or solid, n.o.s. (compounds and preparations)										
	m-Nitrophenyldinitro methane	Forbidden									
	Nitropropane	Flammable liquid	UN2608	Flammable liquid	173.118	173.119	15 gallon	55 gallons	1,2	1	
	Nitrosoguanidine. See Initiating explosive										
	Nitrostarch, dry. See High explosive										
	Nitrostarch, wet with not less than 30% alcohol or solvent	Flammable liquid	UN1337	Flammable liquid	173.118	173.127	1 quart	25 pounds	1,2	1	
	Nitrostarch, wet with not less than 20% water	Flammable solid	UN1337	Flammable solid	173.153	173.184	25 pounds	100 pounds	1	4	
	Nitrosugars (dry)	Forbidden									
	Nitrosyl chloride	Nonflammable gas	UN1069	Nonflammable gas	173.306	173.304 173.314	Forbidden	300 pounds	1	4	
	Nitrourea. See High explosive										
	Nitrous oxide or Nitrous oxide, compressed	Nonflammable gas	UN1070	Nonflammable gas	173.306	173.304	150 pounds	300 pounds	1,2	1,2	Under deck stowage must be in well-ventilated space
	Nitrous oxide, refrigerated liquid	Nonflammable gas	UN2201	Nonflammable gas	173.306	173.315	Forbidden	Forbidden	1	1	Stow away from flammables. Do not overstow with other cargo.
+	Nitroxylol	Poison B	NA1665	Poison	173.345	173.346	1 quart	55 gallons	1,2	1	
	Nonflammable gas, n.o.s. See Compressed gas, n.o.s.										
+	Nonliquefied hydrocarbon gas. See Hydrocarbon gas, nonliquefied										
	Nonyltrichlorosilane	Corrosive material	UN1799	Corrosive	None	173.280	Forbidden	10 gallons	1	1	Keep dry
	Nordhausen acid. See Sulfuric acid										
	Octadecyltrichlorosilane	Corrosive material	UN1800	Corrosive	None	173.280	Forbidden	10 gallons	1	1	Keep dry
	1,7-Octadiene-3,5-diyne-1,8-dimethoxy-9-octadecynoic acid	Forbidden									
	Octane	Flammable liquid	UN1262	Flammable liquid	173.118	173.119	1 quart	10 gallons	1,2	1	

242

(1) +/A/W	(2) Hazardous materials descriptions and proper shipping names	(3) Hazard class	(3A) Identification number	(4) Label(s) required (if not excepted)	(5) Packaging (a) Exceptions	(b) Specific requirements	(6) Maximum net quantity in one package (a) Passenger carrying aircraft or railcar	(b) Cargo only aircraft	(7) Water shipments (a) Cargo vessel	(b) Passenger vessel	(c) Other requirements
	n-Octanoyl peroxide, *technically pure. See Organic peroxide, liquid or solution, n.o.s.*		UN2129								
	Octyltrichlorosilane	Corrosive material	UN1801	Corrosive	None	173.280	Forbidden	10 gallons	1	1	Keep dry
	Oil, *described as oil,* Oil, n.o.s., *Petroleum oil, or Petroleum oil, n.o.s.*	Combustible liquid	NA1270	None	173.118a	None	No limit	No limit	1,2	1,2	
	Oil, *described as oil,* Oil, n.o.s., *Petroleum oil, or Petroleum oil, n.o.s.*	Flammable liquid	NA1270	Flammable liquid	173.118	173.119	1 quart	10 gallons	1,2	1	
	Oil of mirbane *See Nitrobenzene, liquid*										
	Oil of vitriol. *See Sulfuric acid*										
	Oil well cartridge	Class C explosive		Class C explosive	None	173.112	50 pounds	150 pounds	1,3	1,3	
	Oleum *(fuming sulfuric acid)*	Corrosive material	NA1831	Corrosive	None	173.272	Forbidden	5 pints	1,2	1	Under deck stowage must be in metal drums only. Keep dry.
	Organic peroxide, liquid or solution, n.o.s.	Flammable liquid	NA1993	Flammable liquid and Organic peroxide	None	173.119	Forbidden	1 quart	1,2	5	Stow separate from combustible materials, explosives, or acids
	Organic peroxide, liquid or solution, n.o.s.	Organic peroxide	NA9183	Organic peroxide	173.153	173.221	Forbidden	1 quart	1,2	1,2	Stow separate from combustible materials, explosives, or acids.
	Organic peroxide, mixture. *See Organic peroxide, solid, n.o.s. or Organic peroxide, liquid or solution, n.o.s., as appropriate*		UN2756								
	Organic peroxide, sample, n.o.s. *See Organic peroxide, solid, n.o.s. or Organic peroxide, liquid or solution, n.o.s., as appropriate.*		UN2255								
	Organic peroxide, solid, n.o.s.	Organic peroxide	NA9187	Organic peroxide	173.153	173.154	Forbidden	25 pounds	1,2	1,2	Stow separate from combustible materials, explosives, or acids.
	Organic peroxide, trial quantity, n.o.s. *See Organic peroxide, solid, n.o.s. or Organic peroxide, liquid or solution, n.o.s., as appropriate*		UN2899								
	Organic phosphate mixture, Organic phosphate compound mixture, or Organic phosphorus compound mixture; liquid	Poison B	NA2783	Poison	173.359	173.359	1/2 pint	1 quart	1,2	5	
	Organic phosphate mixture, Organic phosphate compound mixture, or Organic phosphorus compound mixture; solid or dry	Poison B	NA2783	Poison	173.377	173.377	50 pounds	200 pounds	1,2	4	
	Organic phosphate, Organic phosphate compound, or Organic phosphorus compound; mixed with compressed gas	Poison A	NA1955	Poison gas	None	173.334	Forbidden	Forbidden	1	5	Shade from radiant heat
	Organic phosphate, Organic phosphate compound, or Organic phosphorus compound; liquid	Poison B	NA2783	Poison	None	173.358	Forbidden	1 quart	1,2	5	
	Organic phosphate, Organic phosphate compound, or Organic phosphorus compound; solid or dry	Poison B	NA2783	Poison	None	173.377	Forbidden	200 pounds	1,2	4	
	Organochlorine pesticide, liquid, n.o.s. (compounds and preparations)	Flammable liquid	UN2762	Flammable liquid	173.118	173.119	1 quart	10 gallons	1,2	1	
	Organochlorine pesticide, liquid, n.o.s. (compounds and preparations)	Poison B	UN2761	Poison	173.345	173.346	1 quart	55 gallons	1,2	1,2	
	Organochlorine pesticide, solid, n.o.s. (compounds and preparations)	Poison B	UN2761	Poison	173.364	173.365	50 pounds	200 pounds	1,2	1,2	
	Organophosphorus pesticide, liquid, n.o.s. (compounds and preparations)	Flammable liquid	UN2784	Flammable liquid	None	173.119	Forbidden	1 quart	1,2	5	
	Organophosphorus pesticide, liquid, n.o.s. (compounds and preparations)	Poison B	UN2783	Poison	173.359	173.359	Forbidden	1 quart	1,2	5	
	Organophosphorus pesticide, solid, n.o.s. (compounds and preparations)	Poison B	UN2783	Poison	173.377	173.377	Forbidden	200 pounds	1,2	4	
	Organotin pesticide, liquid, n.o.s. (compounds and preparations)	Flammable liquid	UN2787	Flammable liquid	173.118	173.119	1 quart	10 gallons	1,2	1	
	Organotin pesticide, liquid, n.o.s. (compounds and preparations)	Poison B	UN2786	Poison	173.345	173.346	1 quart	55 gallons	1,2	1,2	
	Organotin pesticide, solid, n.o.s. (compounds and preparations)	Poison	UN2786	Poison	173.364	173.365	50 pounds	200 pounds	1,2	1,2	
A	ORM-A, n.o.s.	ORM-A	NA1693	None	173.505	173.510	No limit	No limit			
A	ORM-B, n.o.s.	ORM-B	NA1760	None	173.505	173.510	No limit	No limit			
	ORM-C. *See 173.500 and 176.900*										
	ORM-E, liquid or solid, n.o.s. *See Hazardous substance, liquid or solid, n.o.s.*										
	Orthonitroaniline. *See Nitroaniline*										
	Oxidizer, corrosive, liquid, n.o.s.	Oxidizer	NA9193	Oxidizer and Corrosive	None	173.245	Forbidden	1 quart	1	5	
	Oxidizer, corrosive, solid, n.o.s.	Oxidizer	NA9194	Oxidizer and Corrosive	173.153	173.154	25 pounds	25 pounds	1	4	
	Oxidizer material packed with other articles. *See 173.152*										
	Oxidizer, n.o.s. or Oxidizing material, n.o.s.	Oxidizer	UN1479	Oxidizer	173.153	173.154	25 pounds	25 pounds	1,2	1,2	

243

(1) +/A/W	(2) Hazardous materials descriptions and proper shipping names	(3) Hazard class	(3A) Identification number	(4) Label(s) required (if not excepted)	(5) Packaging (a) Exceptions	(5) (b) Specific requirements	(6) Maximum net quantity in one package (a) Passenger carrying aircraft or railcar	(6) (b) Cargo only aircraft	(7) Water shipments (a) Cargo vessel	(7) (b) Passenger vessel	(7) (c) Other requirements
	Oxidizer, poisonous, solid, n.o.s.	Oxidizer	NA9200	Oxidizer and Poison	173.153	173.154	25 pounds	25 pounds	1,2	4	
	Oxygen or Oxygen, compressed	Nonflammable gas	UN1072	Oxidizer	173.306	173.302 173.314	150 pounds	300 pounds	1,2	1,2	Under deck stowage must be in well ventilated space.
	Oxygen, refrigerated liquid (cryogenic liquid)	Nonflammable gas	UN1073	Oxidizer	173.320	173.316 173.318	Forbidden	Forbidden	1	1	Stow separate from flammables. Do not overstow with other cargo.
	Paint	Combustible liquid	UN1263	None	173.118a	None	No limit	No limit	1,2	1,2	
	Paint	Flammable liquid	UN1263	Flammable liquid	173.118	173.128	1 quart	55 gallons	1,2	1	
	Paint or paint related material	Corrosive material	NA1760	Corrosive	173.244	173.245	1 quart	1 gallon	1,2	1,2	
	Paint related material	Combustible liquid	NA1263	None	173.118a	None	No limit	No limit	1,2	1,2	
	Paint related material	Flammable liquid	UN1263	Flammable liquid	173.118	173.128	1 quart	55 gallons			
	Paper caps. See Toy caps										
AW	Paraformaldehyde	ORM-A	UN2213	None	173.505	173.510	50 pounds	200 pounds	1,2	1,2	
	Paraldehyde	Flammable liquid	UN1264	Flammable liquid	173.118	173.119	1 quart	10 gallons	1,2	1	
	Paramenthane hydroperoxide	Organic peroxide	UN2125	Organic peroxide	173.153	173.224	1 quart	1 quart	1,2	4	
	Paranitroaniline, solid. See Nitroaniline										
	Parathion and compressed gas mixture	Poison A	NA1967	Poison gas	None	173.334	Forbidden	Forbidden	1,3	5	
	Parathion, liquid	Poison B	NA2783	Poison	None	173.358	Forbidden	1 quart	1,3	1,3	
	Parathion mixture, dry	Poison B	NA2783	Poison	173.377	173.377	50 pounds	200 pounds	1,3	1,3	
	Parathion mixture, liquid	Poison B	NA2783	Poison	None	173.359	Forbidden	1 quart	1,3	1,3	
	Paris green, solid. See Copper acetoarsenite, solid										
	Pelargonyl peroxide, technically pure. See Organic peroxide, solid, n.o.s.		UN2130								
	Pentaborane	Flammable liquid	UN1380	Flammable liquid and Poison	None	173.138	Forbidden	Forbidden	1	5	Segregation same as for flammable solids. Separate from flammable gases or liquids, oxidizing materials, or organic peroxides.
	Pentaerythrite tetranitrate. See Initiating explosive										
	Pentaerythrite tetranitrate, desensitized, wet. See High explosive										
	Pentaerythrite tetranitrate (dry)	Forbidden									
	Pentane	Flammable liquid	UN1265	Flammable liquid	173.118	173.119	Forbidden	10 gallons	1,3	4	
	Pentanitroaniline (dry)	Forbidden									
	Pentolite, dry. See High explosive										
	Peracetic acid solution not over 43% peracetic acid and not over 6% hydrogen peroxide	Organic peroxide	NA2131	Organic peroxide	173.223	173.223	1 pint	5 pints	1	4	Shade from radiant heat
	Perchlorate, n.o.s.	Oxidizer	NA1481	Oxidizer	173.153	173.154	25 pounds	100 pounds	1,3	1,3	Stow away from powdered metals
	Perchloric acid, exceeding 50% but not exceeding 72% strength	Oxidizer	UN1873	Oxidizer	None	173.269	Forbidden	5 pints	1	5	Segregation same as for corrosive materials. Stow away from hydrazine.
	Perchloric acid exceeding 72% strength	Forbidden									
	Perchloric acid, not over 50% acid	Oxidizer	UN1802	Oxidizer	173.244	173.269	Forbidden	5 pints	1	1	Segregation same as for corrosive materials. Stow away from hydrazine.
	Perchloroethylene See Tetrachloroethylene		NA1897								
+	Perchloromethyl mercaptan	Poison B	UN1670	Poison	173.345	173.360	Forbidden	10 pounds	1	4	
	Percussion cap	Class C explosive		None	None	173.107	50 pounds	150 pounds	1,3	1,3	
	Percussion fuze	Class C explosive		Explosive C	None	173.105	50 pounds	150 pounds	1,3	1,3	
A	Perfluoro-2-butene	ORM-A	NA2422	None	173.505	173.605	10 gallons	55 gallons			
	Permanganate, n.o.s.	Oxidizer	NA1482	Oxidizer	173.153	173.154	25 pounds	100 pounds	1,2	1,2	Segregate from ammonium compounds, hydrogen peroxide, and acids
	Permanganate of potash. See Potassium permanganate										
	Peroxide, organic. See Organic Peroxide										
	Peroxyacetic acid, not more than 43% and with not more than 6% hydrogen peroxide. See Peracetic acid solution, not over 43% peracetic acid and not over 6% hydrogen peroxide		UN2131								
	Peroxyacetic acid, more than 43% and with more than 6% hydrogen peroxide	Forbidden									

(1) +/A/W	(2) Hazardous materials descriptions and proper shipping names	(3) Hazard class	(3A) Identification number	(4) Label(s) required (if not excepted)	(5) Packaging (a) Exceptions	(5) (b) Specific requirements	(6) Maximum net quantity in one package (a) Passenger carrying aircraft or railcar	(6) (b) Cargo only aircraft	(7) Water shipments (a) Cargo vessel	(7) (b) Passenger vessel	(7) (c) Other requirements
W	Pesticide, water reactive, including but not limited to fungicides, and herbicides, etc., which contain manganese ethylenebisdithiocarbamate	ORM-C	NA2210	None	173.505	173.1040			2	2	Keep dry
W	Petroleum coke (uncalcined)	ORM-C		None	173.505	173.1045			1,2	1,2	Not permitted if temperature of material is at or above 130 deg F
	Petroleum distillate	Combustible liquid	UN1268	None	173.118a	None	No limit	No limit	1,2	1,2	
	Petroleum distillate	Flammable liquid	UN1268	Flammable liquid	173.118	173.119	1 quart	10 gallons	1,3	4	
	Petroleum ether	Flammable liquid	UN1271	Flammable liquid	173.118	173.119	1 quart	10 gallons	1,3	4	
	Petroleum gas, liquefied. See Liquefied petroleum gas										
	Petroleum naphtha	Combustible liquid	UN1255	None	173.118a	None	No limit	No limit	1,2	1,2	
	Petroleum naphtha	Flammable liquid	UN1255	Flammable liquid	173.118	173.119	1 quart	10 gallons	1,2	1	
	Petroleum oil, n.o.s. See Oil										
A	Phencapton	ORM-A	NA2783	None	173.505	173.510	No limit	No limit			
+	Phenol	Poison B	UN1671	Poison	173.364	173.369	50 pounds	250 pounds	1,2	1,2	
	Phenol, liquid or solution (liquid tar acid containing over 50% phenol)	Poison B	NA2821	Poison	173.345	173.349	1 quart	55 gallons	1,2	1,2	
	Phenoxy pesticide, liquid, n.o.s. (compounds and preparations)	Flammable liquid	UN2766	Flammable liquid	173.118	173.119	1 quart	10 gallons	1,2	1	
	Phenoxy pesticide, liquid, n.o.s. (compounds and preparations)	Poison B	UN2765	Poison	173.345	173.346	1 quart	55 gallons	1,2	1,2	
	Phenoxy pesticide, solid, n.o.s. (compounds and preparations)	Poison B	UN2765	Poison	173.364	173.365	50 pounds	200 pounds	1,2	1,2	
A	Phenyldiamine, meta or para, solid	ORM-A	UN1673	None	173.505	173.510	No limit	No limit			
	Phenyldichloroarsine	Poison B	NA1556	Poison	None	173.355	Forbidden	30 gallons	1	5	
	m-Phenylene diaminediperchlorate (dry)	Forbidden									
	Phenyl mercaptan	Poison B	UN2337	Poison	173.345	173.346	Forbidden	10 gallons	1,2	1	
	Phenyltrichlorosilane	Corrosive material	UN1804	Corrosive	None	173.280	Forbidden	10 gallons	1	1	Keep dry
	Phenylurea pesticide, liquid, n.o.s. (compounds and preparations)	Flammable liquid	UN2768	Flammable liquid	173.118	173.119	1 quart	10 gallons	1,2	1	
	Phenylurea pesticide, liquid, n.o.s. (compounds and preparations)	Poison B	UN2767	Poison	173.345	173.346	1 quart	55 gallons	1,2	1,2	
	Phenylurea pesticide, solid, n.o.s. (compounds and preparations)	Poison B	UN2767	Poison	173.364	173.365	50 pounds	200 pounds	1,2	1,2	
	Phosgene (diphosgene)	Poison A	UN1076	Poison gas	None	173.333	Forbidden	Forbidden	1	5	
	Phosphine	Poison A	UN2199	Poison gas and Flammable gas	None	173.328	Forbidden	Forbidden	1	5	Segregation same as for flammable gases
	Phosphoric acid	Corrosive material	UN1805	Corrosive	173.244	173.245	1 quart	10 gallons	1,2	1,2	Glass carboys in hampers not permitted under deck
	Phosphoric acid triethyleneimine. See Tris(I-aziridiyl) phosphine oxide										
	Phosphoric anhydride (phosphorus pentoxide)	Corrosive material	NA1807	Corrosive	None	173.188	Forbidden	100 pounds	1,2	1,2	Keep dry. Glass bottles not permitted under deck
	Phosphorus, amorphous, red	Flammable solid	UN1338	Flammable solid	None	173.189	Forbidden	11 pounds	1,2	1,2	
	Phosphorus bromide. See Phosphorus tribromide										
	Phosphorus chloride. See Phosphorus trichloride										
	Phosphorus heptasulfide	Flammable solid	UN1339	Flammable solid	None	173.225	Forbidden	10 pounds	1,2	1	Separate from oxidizing materials
	Phosphorus oxybromide	Corrosive material	UN1939	Corrosive	None	173.271	Forbidden	1 quart	1	1	Keep dry. Glass carboys not permitted on passenger vessels.
	Phosphorus oxychloride	Corrosive material	UN1810	Corrosive	None	173.271	Forbidden	1 quart	1	1	Keep dry. Glass carboys not permitted on passenger vessels.
	Phosphorus pentachloride, solid	Corrosive material	UN1806	Corrosive	None	173.191	Forbidden	5 pounds	1	1	Keep dry
	Phosphorus pentasulfide	Flammable solid	UN1340	Flammable solid and Dangerous when wet	None	173.225	Forbidden	11 pounds	1,2	1,2	Separate from oxidizing material
	Phosphorus sesquisulfide	Flammable solid	UN1341	Flammable solid and Dangerous when wet	None	173.225	Forbidden	11 pounds	1,2	1	Separate from oxidizing materials
	Phosphorus tribromide	Corrosive material	UN1808	Corrosive	None	173.270	Forbidden	1 quart	1	1	Keep dry. Glass carboys not permitted on passenger vessels.
	Phosphorus trichloride	Corrosive material	UN1809	Corrosive	None	173.271	Forbidden	1 quart	1	1	Keep dry. Glass carboys not permitted on passenger vessels.
	Phosphorus trisulfide	Flammable solid	UN1343	Flammable solid	None	173.225	Forbidden	10 pounds	1,2	1	Separate from oxidizing materials

(1)	(2)	(3)	(3A)	(4)	(5) Packaging		(6) Maximum net quantity in one package		(7) Water shipments		
+/A/W	Hazardous materials descriptions and proper shipping names	Hazard class	Identi-fication number	Label(s) required (if not excepted)	(a) Exceptions	(b) Specific require-ments	(a) Passenger carrying aircraft or railcar	(b) Cargo only aircraft	(a) Cargo vessel	(b) Pas-senger vessel	(c) Other requirements
	Phosphorus, white or yellow, dry	Flammable solid	UN1381	Flammable solid and Poison	None	173.190	Forbidden	Forbidden	1,2	5	Separate from flammable gases or liquids, oxidizing materials, or organic peroxides.
	Phosphorus, white or yellow, in water	Flammable solid	UN1381	Flammable solid and Poison	None	173.190	Forbidden	25 pounds	1,2	5	Separate from flammable gases or liquids, oxidizing materials, or organic peroxides.
	Phosphorus (white or red) and a chlorate, mixtures of	Forbidden									
	Phosphoryl chloride. See Phosphorus oxychloride										
	Photographic film. See Film										
	Photographic flash powder. See Fireworks, special or Low explosive										
	Phthalimide derivative pesticide, liquid, n.o.s. (compounds and preparations)	Flammable liquid	UN2774	Flammable liquid	173.118	173.119	1 quart	10 gallons	1,2	1	
	Phthalimide derivative pesticide, liquid, n.o.s. (compounds and preparations)	Poison B	UN2773	Poison	173.345	173.346	1 quart	55 gallons	1,2	1,2	
	Phthalimide derivative pesticide, solid, n.o.s. (compounds and preparations)	Poison B	UN2773	Poison	173.364	173.365	50 pounds	200 pounds	1,2	1,2	
	Picrate, dry. See High explosive										
	Picrate of ammonia. See High explosive										
	Picric acid, dry. See High explosive										
	Picric acid, wet, with not less than 10% water	Flammable solid	NA1344	Flammable solid	173.192	173.193	1 pound	25 pounds	1	5	Under deck stowage permitted on cargo vessels if wet with more than 30% water. Stow away from heavy metals and their compounds.
	Picric acid, wet with not less than 10% water, over 25 pounds. See High explosive										
	Pinane hydroperoxide, technically pure. See Organic peroxide, liquid or solution, n.o.s.		UN2162								
	Pinane hydroperoxide solution not over 45% peroxide	Organic peroxide	UN2162	Organic peroxide	173.153	173.224	1 quart	1 quart	1,2	4	
	Pinene	Flammable liquid	UN2368	Flammable liquid	173.118	173.119	1 quart	10 gallons	1,2	1	
	Pine oil	Combustible liquid	UN1272	None	173.118a	None	No limit	No limit	1,2	1,2	
	Pinwheels. See Fireworks, common										
	Pivaloyl chloride. See Trimethylacetyl chloride										
	Poisonous liquid or gas, n.o.s.	Poison A	NA1955	Poison gas	None	173.328	Forbidden	Forbidden	1	5	
	Poisonous liquid or gas, Flammable, n.o.s.	Poison A	NA1953	Poison gas and Flammable gas	None	173.328	Forbidden	Forbidden	1	5	Segregation same as for flammable gases
	Poisonous liquid, n.o.s. or Poison B, liquid, n.o.s.	Poison B	UN2810	Poison	173.345	173.346	1 quart	55 gallons	1,2	1	
	Poisonous solid, corrosive, n.o.s.	Poison B	UN2928	Poison and Corrosive	173.364	173.365	25 pounds	100 pounds	1	4	
	Poisonous solid, n.o.s. or Poison B, solid, n.o.s.	Poison B	UN2811	Poison	173.364	173.365	50 pounds	200 pounds	1,2	1	
	Polymerizable material. See 173.21										
	Potassium arsenate, solid	Poison B	UN1677	Poison	173.364	173.365	50 pounds	200 pounds	1,2	1,2	
	Potassium arsenite, solid	Poison B	UN1678	Poison	173.364	173.365	50 pounds	200 pounds	1,2	1,2	
	Potassium bifluoride solution. See Potassium hydrogen fluoride solution										
	Potassium bromate	Oxidizer	UN1484	Oxidizer	173.153	173.154	25 pounds	100 pounds	1,2	1,2	Separate from ammonium compounds. Stow away from powdered metals.
	Potassium carbonyl	Forbidden									
	Potassium chlorate (potash chlorate)	Oxidizer	UN1485	Oxidizer	173.153	173.163	25 pounds	100 pounds	1,2	1,2	Separate from ammonium compounds. Stow away from powdered metals.
	Potassium cyanide, solid	Poison B	UN1680	Poison	173.370	173.370	25 pounds	200 pounds	1,2	1,2	Stow away from acids
	Potassium cyanide solution	Poison B	UN1680	Poison	173.345	173.352	1 quart	55 gallons	1,2	1,2	Stow away from acids
	Potassium dichloro isocyanurate. See Potassium dichloro-s-triazinetrione										
	Potassium dichloro-s-triazinetrione, dry (containing more than 39% available chlorine)	Oxidizer	NA2465	Oxidizer	173.153	173.217	50 pounds	100 pounds	1,2	1,2	
A	Potassium dichromate	ORM-A	NA1479	None	173.505	173.510	No limit	No limit	1,2	1,2	
A	Potassium fluoride	ORM-B	UN1812	None	173.505	173.510	No limit	No limit			
	Potassium fluoride solution	Corrosive material	UN1812	Corrosive	173.244	173.249	1 quart	5 gallons	1,2	1,2	
	Potassium hydrate. See Potassium hydroxide										
	Potassium hydrogen fluoride solution	Corrosive material	NA1811	Corrosive	173.244	173.249	1 quart	5 gallons	1,2	1,2	
A	Potassium hydrogen sulfate, solid	ORM-B	UN2509	None	173.505	173.800	25 pounds	100 pounds			

(1)	(2)	(3)	(3A)	(4)	(5) Packaging		(6) Maximum net quantity in one package		(7) Water shipments		
+A W	Hazardous materials descriptions and proper shipping names	Hazard class	Identification number	Label(s) required (if not excepted)	(a) Exceptions	(b) Specific requirements	(a) Passenger carrying aircraft or railcar	(b) Cargo only aircraft	(a) Cargo vessel	(b) Passenger vessel	(c) Other requirements
	Potassium hydroxide, dry, solid, flake, bead, or granular	Corrosive material	UN1813	Corrosive	173.244	173.245b	25 pounds	100 pounds	1,2	1,2	Keep dry. Do not stow with metals or alloys such as brass, copper, tin, zinc, aluminum, solder, or lead
	Potassium hydroxide, liquid or solution	Corrosive material	UN1814	Corrosive	173.244	173.249	1 quart	10 gallons	1,2	1,2	
	Potassium hypochlorite solution. See Hypochlorite solutions containing more than 7% available chlorine by weight										
A	Potassium metabisulfite	ORM-B	NA2693	None	173.505	173.510	No limit	No limit			
	Potassium, metal or metallic	Flammable solid	UN2257	Flammable solid and Dangerous when wet	None	173.206	Forbidden	25 pounds	1,2	5	Segregation same as for flammable solids labeled Dangerous when wet
	Potassium, metal liquid alloy	Flammable solid	UN1420	Flammable solid and Dangerous when wet	None	173.202	Forbidden	1 pound	1,2	5	Segregation same as for flammable solids labeled Dangerous when wet
	Potassium nitrate	Oxidizer	UN1486	Oxidizer	173.153	173.182	25 pounds	100 pounds	1,2	1,2	
	Potassium nitrate mixed (fused) with sodium nitrite. See Sodium nitrite mixed (fused) with potassium nitrate										
	Potassium nitrite	Oxidizer	UN1488	Oxidizer	173.153	173.154	25 pounds	100 pounds	1,2	1,2	Separate from ammonium compounds and cyanides. Stow away from foodstuffs.
	Potassium perchlorate	Oxidizer	UN1489	Oxidizer	173.153	173.219	25 pounds	100 pounds	1,3	1,3	Stow away from powdered metals
	Potassium permanganate	Oxidizer	UN1490	Oxidizer	173.153	173.154 173.194	25 pounds	100 pounds	1,2	1,2	Separate from ammonium compounds and hydrogen peroxide
	Potassium peroxide	Oxidizer	UN1491	Oxidizer	None	173.187	Forbidden	100 pounds	1,2	1,2	Keep dry
	Potassium persulfate	Oxidizer	UN1492	Oxidizer	173.153	173.154	50 pounds	200 pounds	1,2	1,2	
	Potassium sulfide	Flammable solid	UN1382	Flammable solid	173.153	173.207	25 pounds	300 pounds	1,2	1,2	Separate from liquid acids, flammable gases or liquids, oxidizing materials or organic peroxides
	Potassium superoxide	Oxidizer	UN2466	Oxidizer	None	173.187	Forbidden	100 pounds	1,2	1	Keep dry. Stow away from powdered metals, permanganates and combustible packagings and cargo
	Pressurized product. See Compressed gas, n.o.s.										
	Primer. See Cannon primer, Combination primer, or Small-arms primer										
	Primer, detonating. See Detonating primers Class A or Class C explosives										
	Projectile, explosive. See Explosive projectile										
	Projectile, gas, nonexplosive. See Chemical ammunition, nonexplosive (containing a Poison A, Poison B or irritating material, as appropriate)										
	Projectile, gas, smoke, or incendiary, with burster or booster with or without detonating fuze. See Explosive projectile										
	Projectile, illuminating, incendiary or smoke, with expelling charge but without bursting charge. See Fireworks, special										
	Projectile, sand-loaded, empty or solid. See 173.55										
	Propane or Liquefied petroleum gas. See Liquefied petroleum gas										
	Propargyl alcohol	Flammable liquid	NA1986	Flammable liquid and Poison	None	173.119	Forbidden	1 quart	1,2	5	
	Propellant explosive	Class A explosive		Explosive A	None	173.64	Forbidden	Forbidden	6	5	
	Propellant explosive in water (smokeless powder)	Class B explosive		Explosive B	None	173.93	Forbidden	Forbidden	1,3	5	Magazine stowage authorized
	Propellant explosive in water, unstable, condemned or deteriorated (smokeless powder)	Class B explosive		Explosive B	None	173.93	Forbidden	Forbidden	1,3	5	Magazine stowage authorized
	Propellant explosive, liquid	Class B explosive		Explosive B	None	173.93	Forbidden	10 pounds	1,2	5	Magazine stowage authorized
	Propellant explosive, solid	Class B explosive		Explosive B	None	173.93	Forbidden	10 pounds	1,3	5	Magazine stowage authorized
	Propionaldehyde	Flammable liquid	UN1275	Flammable liquid	173.118	173.119	1 quart	10 gallons	1,2	1	
	Propionic acid	Corrosive material	UN1848	Corrosive	173.244	173.245	1 quart	5 gallons	1,2	1,2	Separated by a complete compartment or hold from organic peroxides
	Propionic acid solution	Corrosive material	UN1848	Corrosive	173.244	173.245	1 quart	10 gallons	1,2	1,2	Separated by a complete compartment or hold from organic peroxides
	Propionic anhydride	Corrosive material	UN2496	Corrosive	173.244	173.245	1 quart	1 quart	1,2	1	Keep dry
	Propionyl peroxide, not more than 28% in solution. See Organic peroxide, liquid or solution, n.o.s.		UN2132								

(1)	(2)	(3)	(3A)	(4)	(5) Packaging		(6) Maximum net quantity in one package		(7) Water shipments		
+/ A/ W	Hazardous materials descriptions and proper shipping names	Hazard class	Identi- fication number	Label(s) required (if not excepted)	(a) Exceptions	(b) Specific require- ments	(a) Passenger carrying aircraft or railcar	(b) Cargo only aircraft	(a) Cargo vessel	(b) Pas- senger vessel	(c) Other requirements
	Propionyl peroxide, more than 28% in solution	Forbidden									
	Propyl acetate	Flammable liquid	UN1276	Flammable liquid	173.118	173.119	1 quart	10 gallons	1,2	1	
	Propyl alcohol	Flammable liquid	UN1274	Flammable liquid	173.118	173.125	1 quart	10 gallons	1,2	1,2	
	Propylamine	Flammable liquid	UN1277	Flammable liquid	None	173.119	Forbidden	10 gallons	1,3	5	
	Propyl chloride	Flammable liquid	UN1278	Flammable liquid	None	173.119	Forbidden	10 gallons	1,3	5	
	Propylene *or* Liquefied petroleum gas. *See* Lique- fied petroleum gas										
	Propylenediamine	Flammable liquid	UN2258	Flammable liquid	173.118	173.119	1 quart	10 gallons	1,2	1	
	Propylene dichloride	Flammable liquid	UN1279	Flammable liquid	173.118	173.119	1 quart	10 gallons	1,2	1	
	Propyleneimine, inhibited	Flammable liquid	UN1921	Flammable liquid	None	173.139	Forbidden	5 pints	1,2	1	
	Propylene oxide	Flammable liquid	UN1280	Flammable liquid	173.118	173.119	Forbidden	1 gallon	1,3	4	
	Propyl formate	Flammable liquid	UN1281	Flammable liquid	173.118	173.119	1 quart	10 gallons	1,2	1	
	Propyl mercaptan	Flammable liquid	NA2402	Flammable liquid	None	173.141	Forbidden	10 gallons	1,2	5	
	Propyl trichlorosilane	Corrosive material	UN1816	Corrosive	None	173.280	Forbidden	10 gallons	1	1	Keep dry
	Prussic acid. See Hydrocyanic acid, *as appropriate*										
	Pyridine	Flammable liquid	UN1282	Flammable liquid	173.118	173.119	1 quart	10 gallons	1,2	1	
	Pyridine perchlorate	Forbidden									
	Pyrophoric liquid, n.o.s. *or* Pyroforic liquid, n.o.s.	Flammable liquid	UN2845	Flammable liquid	None	173.134	Forbidden	Forbidden	1	5	Shade from radiant heat. Separate from flammable gases or liquids, oxidizing materials, or organix peroxides.
	Pyrosulfuryl chloride	Corrosive material	UN1817	Corrosive	173.244	173.247	1 quart	1 quart	1	4	Keep dry. Glass carboys not permit- ted on passenger vessels.
	Pyroxylin plastic scrap	Flammable solid	NA1325	Flammable solid	None	173.195	Forbidden	Forbidden	1	5	Shade from radiant heat
	Pyroxylin plastics, rods, sheets, rolls, *or* tubes	Flammable solid	NA1325	Flammable solid	173.197	173.197	50 pounds	350 pounds	1,3	1	
	Pyrolidine	Flammable liquid	UN1922	Flammable liquid	173.118	173.119	Forbidden	10 gallons	1,2	1	
	Quebrachitol pentanitrate	Forbidden									
	Quicklime. *See* Calcium oxide										
	Radioactive material, empty packages	Radioactive material	UN2908	Empty	173.421-1 173.427	173.421-1 173.427			1,2	1,2	
	Radioactive material, fissile, n.o.s.	Radioactive material	UN2918	Radioactive	173.453	173.417			1,2	1,2	
	Radioactive material, articles, manufactured from natural *or* depleted uranium *or* natural tho- rium	Radioactive material	UN2909	None	173.421-1 173.424	173.421-1 173.424			1,2	1,2	
	Radioactive material, instruments *and* articles	Radioactive material	UN2911	None	173.421-1 173.424	173.421-1 173.422			1,2	1,2	
	Radioactive material, limited quantity, n.o.s.	Radioactive material	UN2910	None	173.421 173.421-1	173.421 173.421-1			1,2	1,2	
	Radioactive material, low specific activity *or* LSA, n.o.s.	Radioactive material	UN2912	Radioactive	173.421 173.422 173.424	173.425			1,2	1,2	
	Radioactive material, n.o.s.	Radioactive material	UN2982	Radioactive	173.421 173.422 173.424	173.415 173.416			1,2	1,2	
	Radioactive material, special form, n.o.s.	Radioactive material	UN2974	Radioactive	173.421 173.422	173.415 173.416			1,2	1,2	
	Railway Fusee. See Fusee										
	Railway torpedo. *See* Torpedo, railway										
	Refrigerant gas, n.o.s. *or* Dispersant gas, n.o.s.	Nonflammable gas	UN1078	Nonflammable gas	173.306	173.304 173.314 173.315	150 pounds	300 pounds	1,2	1,2	
	Refrigerant gas, n.o.s. *or* Dispersant gas, n.o.s.	Flammable gas	NA1954	Flammable gas	173.306	173.304 173.314 173.315	Forbidden	300 pounds	1,2	1,2	
	Refrigerating machine	Nonflammable gas	UN2857	Nonflammable gas	173.306 173.307		No limit	No limit	1,3	1,3	
	Refrigerating machine	Flammable gas	NA1954	Flammable gas	173.306		No limit	No limit	1,3	1,3	
	Refrigerating machine	Flammable liquid	NA1993	Flammable liquid	173.130 173.306		No limit	No limit	1,2	1	
	Resin solution *(resin compound, liquid)*	Flammable liquid	UN1866	Flammable liquid	173.118	173.119	1 quart	55 gallons	1,2	1	

248

(1) +/A/W	(2) Hazardous materials descriptions and proper shipping names	(3) Hazard class	(3A) Identification number	(4) Label(s) required (if not excepted)	(5) Packaging (a) Exceptions	(5) (b) Specific requirements	(6) Maximum net quantity in one package (a) Passenger carrying aircraft or railcar	(6) (b) Cargo only aircraft	(7) Water shipments (a) Cargo vessel	(7) (b) Passenger vessel	(7) (c) Other requirements
	Rifle grenade. See Grenade, hand *or* rifle, explosive										
	Rifle powder. See Propellant explosive *or* Black powder										
	Road asphalt or tar, liquid. See Asphalt, cut back										
	Road asphalt or tar (when heated to or above its flash point). See Asphalt										
	Rocket ammunition with empty projectile	Class B explosive		Explosive B	None	173.90	Forbidden	Forbidden	1,3	5	
	Rocket ammunition with empty, inert, or solid loaded projectile	Class A explosive		Explosive A	None	173.57	Forbidden	Forbidden	6	5	
	Rocket ammunition with explosive projectile	Class A explosive		Explosive A	None	173.57	Forbidden	Forbidden	6	5	
	Rocket ammunition with gas projectile	Class A explosive		Explosive A	None	173.57	Forbidden	Forbidden	6	5	
	Rocket ammunition with illuminating projectile	Class A explosive		Explosive A	None	173.57	Forbidden	Forbidden	6	5	
	Rocket ammunition with incendiary projectile	Class A explosive		Explosive A	None	173.57	Forbidden	Forbidden	6	5	
	Rocket ammunition with inert loaded projectile	Class B explosive		Explosive B	None	173.90	Forbidden	Forbidden	1,3	5	
	Rocket ammunition with smoke projectile	Class A explosive		Explosive A	None	173.57	Forbidden	Forbidden	6	5	
	Rocket ammunition with solid projectile	Class B explosive		Explosive B	None	173.90	Forbidden	Forbidden	1,3	5	
	Rocket body, with electric primer or electric squib. See 173.55										
	Rocket engine, liquid	Class B explosive		Explosive B	None	173.95	Forbidden	Forbidden	1,2	5	Magazine stowage authorized
	Rocket fireworks. See Fireworks, common										
	Rocket head. See Explosive projectile										
	Rocket motor	Class A explosive		Explosive A	None	173.79	Forbidden	Forbidden	6	5	
	Rocket motor	Class B explosive		Explosive B	None	173.92	Forbidden	550 pounds	1,3	5	
	Roman candle. See Fireworks, common										
	Rubidium metal	Flammable solid	UN1423	Flammable solid and Dangerous when wet	None	173.206	Forbidden	225 pounds	1,2	5	Segregation same as for flammable solid labeled Dangerous When Wet
	Rubidium metal, in cartridges	Flammable solid	UN1423	Flammable solid and Dangerous when wet	173.206		1 pound	25 pounds	1,2	4	Segregation same as for flammable solid labeled Dangerous When Wet
	Safety fuse. See Fuse, safety										
	Safety squib	Class C explosive		Explosive C	None	173.106	50 pounds	150 pounds	1,3	1,3	
	Salute. See Fireworks common *or* special										
	Samples. See 172.101(c)(12)										
	Sand acid. See Hydrofluorosilicic acid										
	Selenic acid, liquid	Corrosive material	UN1905	Corrosive	None	173.245	Forbidden	5 pints	1,2	1,2	
	Selenium nitride	Forbidden									
	Selenium oxide	Poison B	NA2811	Poison	173.364	173.365	50 pounds	200 pounds	1,2	1,2	
	Self-lighting cigarette	Flammable solid	UN1867	Flammable solid	173.21		Forbidden	Forbidden	1,2	1,2	Keep dry
	Self propelled vehicle. See Motor vehicle										
	Shaped charge, commercial. See High explosive : 173.65(h)										
	Shaped charges (commercial) containing more than 8 ounces of explosives	Forbidden									
	Shell, fireworks. See Fireworks, common *or* special										
	Ship, distress signal. See Fireworks, special										
	Signal flare	Class C explosive		Explosive C	None	173.108	50 pounds	200 pounds	1,2	1,2	
	Silicofluoric acid. See Hydrofluorosilicic acid										
	Silicon chloride *or* Silicon tetrachloride	Corrosive material	UN1818	Corrosive	173.244	173.247	1 quart	1 gallon	1	1	Keep dry. Glass carboys not permitted on passenger vessels.
	Silicon chrome, exothermic. See Ferrochrome, exothermic										
+	Silicon tetrafluoride	Nonflammable gas	UN1859	Nonflammable gas	173.306	173.302	Forbidden	300 pounds	1	4	Stow away from foodstuffs

(1)	(2)	(3)	(3A)	(4)	(5) Packaging		(6) Maximum net quantity in one package		(7) Water shipments		
+/ A/ W	Hazardous materials descriptions and proper shipping names	Hazard class	Identi- fication number	Label(s) required (if not excepted)	(a) Exceptions	(b) Specific require- ments	(a) Passenger carrying aircraft or railcar	(b) Cargo only aircraft	(a) Cargo vessel	(b) Pas- senger vessel	(c) Other requirements
	Silver acetylide (dry)	Forbidden									
	Silver azide (dry)	Forbidden									
	Silver chlorite (dry)	Forbidden									
+	Silver cyanide	Poison B	UN1684	Poison	173.370	173.370	25 pounds	200 pounds	1,2	1,2	Stow away from acids
	Silver fulminate (dry)	Forbidden									
	Silver nitrate	Oxidizer	UN1493	Oxidizer	173.153	173.182	25 pounds	100 pounds	1,2	1,2	Stow away from foodstuffs
	Silver oxalate (dry)	Forbidden									
	Silver picrate (dry)	Forbidden									
	Small arms ammunition	Class C explosive		None	173.101		50 pounds	150 pounds	1,3	1,3	
	Small arms ammunition	ORM-D		None	173.101	173.1201	65 pounds gross	65 pounds gross	—	—	
	Small arms ammunition, irritating (tear gas) cartridge	Class C explosive		Irritant	None	173.101	Forbidden	150 pounds	1,3	1,3	
	Small arms primer	Class C explosive		None	None	173.107	50 pounds	150 pounds	1,3	1,3	
	Smoke candle	Class C explosive		Explosive C	None	173.108	50 pounds	200 pounds	1,3	1,3	
	Smoke generator. See Chemical ammunition, nonexplosive (containing a Poison A, Poison B, or irritating material, as appropriate)										
	Smoke grenade	Class C explosive		Explosive C	None	173.108	50 pounds	150 pounds	1,3	1,3	
	Smokeless powder for cannon or small arms. See Propellant explosive, Class A or B, as appropriate										
	Smokeless powder for small arms (100 pounds or less)	Flammable solid	NA1325	Flammable solid	173.88	173.197a	Forbidden	Forbidden	1,3	1,3	Segregation same as for explosives
	Smoke pot	Class C explosive		Explosive C	None	173.108	50 pounds	200 pounds	1,3	1,3	
	Smoke projectile with bursting charge. See Explosive projectile										
	Smoke projectile with expelling charge but without bursting charge. See Fireworks, special										
	Smoke signal	Class C explosive		Explosive C	None	173.108	50 pounds	200 pounds	1,3	1,3	
	Soda amatol. See High explosive										
	Soda lime, solid	Corrosive material	UN1907	Corrosive	173.244	173.245b	25 pounds	100 pounds	1,2	1,2	Keep dry
	Sodium acid sulfate, solid or solution. See appropriate Sodium hydrogen sulfate entry										
A	Sodium aluminate, solid	ORM-B	UN2812	None	173.505	173.800	25 pounds	100 pounds			
	Sodium aluminate solution	Corrosive material	UN1819	Corrosive	173.244	173.249	1 quart	5 gallons	1,2	1,2	
	Sodium aluminum hydride	Flammable solid	UN2835	Flammable solid and Dangerous when wet	None	173.206	Forbidden	25 pounds	1,2	5	Segregation same as for flammable solids labeled Dangerous When Wet
	Sodium amide	Flammable solid	UN1425	Flammable solid and Dangerous when wet	None	173.206	Forbidden	25 pounds	1,2	5	Segregation same as for flammable solids labeled Dangerous When Wet
	Sodium arsenate	Poison B	UN1685	Poison	173.364	173.365 173.368	50 pounds	200 pounds	1,2	1,2	
	Sodium arsenite, liquid (solution)	Poison B	UN1686	Poison	173.345	173.346	1 quart	55 gallons	1,2	1,2	
+	Sodium azide	Poison B	UN1687	Poison	173.364	173.375	50 pounds	100 pounds	1,2	1,2	Stow away from heavy metals, especially lead and its compounds. Stow separate from acids.
	Sodium bifluoride, solid	Corrosive material	UN2439	Corrosive	173.244	173.245b	25 pounds	100 pounds	1,2	1,2	
	Sodium bifluoride, solution	Corrosive material	UN2439	Corrosive	173.244	173.245	1 quart	5 gallons	1,2	1,2	
	Sodium bisulfate, solid or solution. See Sodium hydrogen sulfate, solid or solution										
	Sodium bisulfite, solid or solution. See Sodium hydrogen sulfite, solid or solution.										
	Sodium bromate	Oxidizer	UN1494	Oxidizer	173.153	173.154	25 pounds	100 pounds	1,2	1,2	Stow separate from ammonium compounds. Stow away from powdered metals.
	Sodium chlorate (soda chlorate)	Oxidizer	UN1495	Oxidizer	173.153	173.163	25 pounds	100 pounds	1,2	1,2	Stow separate from ammonium compounds. Stow away from powdered metals.
	Sodium chlorite	Oxidizer	UN1496	Oxidizer	None	173.160	Forbidden	100 pounds	1,2	1,2	Stow separate from ammonium compounds. Stow away from powdered metals.
	Sodium chlorite solution (not exceeding 42% sodium chlorite)	Corrosive material	UN1908	Corrosive	173.244	173.263	1 quart	4 gallons	1,2	1	Glass carboys in hampers not permitted under deck
	Sodium cyanide, solid	Poison B	UN1689	Poison	173.370	173.370	25 pounds	200 pounds	1,2	1,2	Stow away from acids

250

(1) +/A/W	(2) Hazardous materials descriptions and proper shipping names	(3) Hazard class	(3A) Identification number	(4) Label(s) required (if not excepted)	(5) Packaging (a) Exceptions	(5) (b) Specific requirements	(6) Maximum net quantity in one package (a) Passenger carrying aircraft or railcar	(6) (b) Cargo only aircraft	(7) Water shipments (a) Cargo vessel	(7) (b) Passenger vessel	(7) (c) Other requirements
	Sodium cyanide solution	Poison B	UN1689	Poison	173.345	173.352	1 quart	55 gallons	1,2	1,2	Stow away from acids
	Sodium dichloroisocyanurate. See Sodium dichloro-s-triazinetrione										
	Sodium dichloro-s-triazinetrione (dry, containing more than 39% available chlorine)	Oxidizer	UN2465	Oxidizer	173.153	173.217	50 pounds	100 pounds	1,2	1,2	
A	Sodium dichromate	ORM-A	NA1479	None	173.505	173.510	No limit	No limit	1,2	1,2	
A	Sodium fluoride, solid	ORM-B	UN1690	None	173.505	173.510	No limit	No limit	1,2	1,2	
	Sodium fluoride solution	Corrosive material	UN1690	Corrosive	173.244	173.245	1 quart	5 gallons	1,2	1,2	Stow away from acids
	Sodium hydrate. See Sodium hydroxide.										
	Sodium hydride	Flammable solid	UN1427	Flammable solid and Dangerous when wet	None	173.198	Forbidden	25 pounds	1,2	5	Segregation same as for flammable solids labeled Dangerous When Wet
A	Sodium hydrogen sulfate, solid	ORM-B	UN1821	None	173.505	173.800	25 pounds	100 pounds			
	Sodium hydrogen sulfate solution	Corrosive material	UN2837	Corrosive	173.244	173.245	1 quart	1 gallon	1,2	1,2	
A	Sodium hydrogen sulfite, solid	ORM-B	NA2693	None	173.505	173.800	25 pounds	100 pounds	1,2	1,2	
	Sodium hydrogen sulfite, solution	Corrosive material	NA2693	Corrosive	173.244	173.245	1 quart	5 gallons	1,2	1,2	
	Sodium hydrosulfide, solid (with less than 25% water of crystalization)	Flammable solid	UN2318	Flammable solid	173.153	173.154	25 pounds	100 pounds	1,2	1,2	
	Sodium hydrosulfide, solid (with not less than 25% water of crystallization)	Corrosive material	NA2923	Corrosive	173.244	173.245b	25 pounds	100 pounds	1,2	1,2	
	Sodium hydrosulfide, solution	Corrosive material	NA2922	Corrosive	173.244	173.245	1 quart	5 gallons	1,2	1,2	
	Sodium hydrosulfite (sodium dithionite)	Flammable solid	UN1384	Flammable solid	173.153	173.204	25 pounds	100 pounds	1,2	1,2	Keep dry. Below deck storage in metal drums only. Separate from flammable gases, liquids, oxidizing materials, or organic peroxides.
	Sodium hydroxide, dry, solid, flake, bead, or granular	Corrosive material	UN1823	Corrosive	173.244	173.245b	25 pounds	200 pounds	1,2	1,2	Keep dry
	Sodium hydroxide, liquid or solution	Corrosive material	UN1824	Corrosive	173.244	173.249	1 quart	5 gallons	1,2	1,2	
	Sodium hypochlorite. See Hypochlorite solution or Hypochlorite solution containing not more than 7% available chlorine										
A	Sodium metabisulfite	ORM-B	NA2693	None	173.505	173.510	No limit	No limit			
	Sodium, metal or metallic	Flammable solid	UN1428	Flammable solid and Dangerous when wet	None	173.206	Forbidden	25 pounds	1,2	5	Segregation same as for flammable solids labeled Dangerous When Wet
	Sodium, metal dispersion in organic solvent	Flammable solid	UN1429	Flammable solid and Dangerous when wet	None	173.230	Forbidden	10 pounds	1,2	5	Segregation same as for flammable solids labeled Dangerous When Wet
	Sodium, metal liquid alloy	Flammable solid	NA1421	Flammable solid and Dangerous when wet	None	173.202	Forbidden	1 pound	1,2	5	Segregation same as for flammable solids labeled Dangerous When Wet
	Sodium methylate, alcohol mixture	Combustible liquid	NA1289	None	173.118a	None	No limit	No limit	1,2	1,2	
	Sodium methylate, alcohol mixture	Flammable liquid	NA1289	Flammable liquid	173.118	173.119	1 quart	10 gallons	1,2	1	
	Sodium methylate, alcohol mixture	Corrosive material	NA1289	Corrosive	173.244	173.245	1 quart	1 quart	1,2	1,2	
	Sodium methylate, dry	Flammable solid	UN1431	Flammable solid and Dangerous When Wet	173.153	173.154	25 pounds	100 pounds	1,2	1	
	Sodium monoxide, solid	Corrosive material	UN1825	Corrosive	173.244	173.245b	25 pounds	100 pounds	1,2	1,2	Keep dry
	Sodium nitrate	Oxidizer	UN1498	Oxidizer	173.153	173.182	25 pounds	100 pounds	1,2	1,2	
	Sodium nitrate bags. See Bags, sodium nitrate, empty and unwashed										
	Sodium nitrite	Oxidizer	UN1500	Oxidizer	173.153	173.234	25 pounds	100 pounds	1,2	1,2	Stow separate from ammonium compounds and cyanides. Bagged material not permitted on passenger vessels
	Sodium nitrite mixed (fused) with potassium nitrate	Oxidizer	UN1487	Oxidizer	173.153	173.183	25 pounds	100 pounds	1,2	1,2	Stow separate from ammonium compounds and cyanides
	Sodium nitrite mixture (sodium nitrate, sodium nitrite, and potassium nitrate)	Oxidizer	NA1487	Oxidizer	173.153	173.234	25 pounds	100 pounds	1,2	1,2	Stow separate from ammonium compounds and cyanides
A	Sodium pentachlorophenate	ORM-A	UN2567	None	173.505	173.510	No limit	No limit			
	Sodium perchlorate	Oxidizer	UN1502	Oxidizer	173.153	173.154	25 pounds	100 pounds	1,3	1,3	Stow away from powdered metals

251

(1) +/A/W	(2) Hazardous materials descriptions and proper shipping names	(3) Hazard class	(3A) Identification number	(4) Label(s) required (if not excepted)	(5) Packaging (a) Exceptions	(5) (b) Specific requirements	(6) Maximum net quantity in one package (a) Passenger carrying aircraft or railcar	(6) (b) Cargo only aircraft	(7) Water shipments (a) Cargo vessel	(7) (b) Passenger vessel	(7) (c) Other requirements
	Sodium permanganate	Oxidizer	UN1503	Oxidizer	173.153	173.154	25 pounds	100 pounds	1,2	1,2	Separate from ammonium compounds and hydrogen peroxide
	Sodium peroxide	Oxidizer	UN1504	Oxidizer	None	173.187	Forbidden	100 pounds	1,2	1	Keep dry Stow away from powdered metals, permanganates, combustible packing of other cargo, and combustible foodstuffs
	Sodium persulfate	Oxidizer	UN1505	Oxidizer	173.153	173.154	50 pounds	200 pounds	1,2	1,2	
	Sodium phenolate, solid	Corrosive material	UN2497	Corrosive	173.244	173.245b	25 pounds	100 pounds	1,2	1,2	
	Sodium phosphide	Flammable solid	UN1432	Flammable solid and Dangerous when wet	None	173.154	Forbidden	25 pounds	1	5	
	Sodium picramate, wet (with at least 20% water)	Flammable solid	UN1349	Flammable solid	None	173.205	Forbidden	25 pounds	1,2	5	Stow away from heavy metals, especially lead, and its compounds
	Sodium picryl peroxide	Forbidden									
	Sodium potassium alloy (liquid)	Flammable solid	UN1422	Flammable solid and Dangerous when wet	None	173.206	Forbidden	1 pound	1,2	5	Under deck stowage must be readily accessible. Segregation same as for flammable solids labeled Dangerous When Wet
	Sodium potassium alloy (solid)	Flammable solid	UN1422	Flammable solid and Dangerous when wet	None	173.206	Forbidden	25 pounds	1,2	5	Under deck stowage must be readily accessible. Segregation same as for flammable solids labeled Dangerous When Wet
	Sodium selenite	Poison B	UN2630	Poison	173.364	173.365	50 pounds	200 pounds	1,2	1,2	
	Sodium sulfide, anhydrous or Sodium sulfide with less than 30% water of crystalization	Flammable solid	UN1385	Flammable solid	173.153	173.207	25 pounds	100 pounds	1,2	1,2	Stow separated from liquid acids.
	Sodium sulfide, hydrated with not less than 30% water	Corrosive material	UN1849	Corrosive	173.244	173.245b	25 pounds	100 pounds	1,2	1,2	Stow away from acids.
	Sodium superoxide	Oxidizer	UN2547	Oxidizer	None	173.187	Forbidden	100 pounds	1,2	5	Keep dry. Stow away from powdered metals, permanganates and combustible packagings and cargo
	Sodium tetranitride	Forbidden									
	Sparklers. See Fireworks, common										
	Spent iron mass. See Iron mass, spent										
	Spent iron sponge. See Iron sponge, spent										
	Spent mixed acid. See Nitrating acid, spent										
	Spent sulfuric acid. See Sulfuric acid, spent										
	Spirits of nitroglycerin, (1 to 10%)	Flammable liquid	NA1204	Flammable liquid	None	173.133	Forbidden	6 quarts	1,2	5	Segregation same as for explosives
	Spirits of nitroglycerin, not exceeding 1% nitroglycerin by weight	Flammable liquid	NA1204	Flammable liquid	173.118	173.133	1 quart	6 quarts	1,2	1	
	Sporting powder. See Black powder or Propellant explosive, solid										
	Spray starting fluid. See Engine starting fluid										
	Spreader cartridge. See Fireworks, special										
	Squib, electric or safety. See Electric squib or Safety squib										
	Stannic phosphide	Flammable solid	UN1433	Flammable solid and Dangerous when wet	None	173.154	Forbidden	25 pounds	1	5	Segregation same as for flammable solid labeled Dangerous When Wet
A	Stannous chloride, solid	ORM-B	NA1759	None	173.505	173.510	No limit	No limit			
	Starter cartridge	Class B explosive		Explosive B	None	173.92	Forbidden	200 pounds	1,3	5	
	Starter cartridge	Class C explosive		Explosive C	None	173.102	50 pounds	150 pounds	1,3	1,3	
	Storage battery, wet. See Battery, electric storage, wet										
	Strontium arsenite, solid	Poison B	UN1691	Poison	173.364	173.365	50 pounds	200 pounds	1,2	1,2	
	Strontium chlorate	Oxidizer	UN1506	Oxidizer	173.153	173.163	25 pounds	100 pounds	1,2	1,2	Stow separate from ammonium compounds. Stow away from powdered metals
	Strontium chlorate, wet	Oxidizer	UN1506	Oxidizer	173.153	173.163	25 pounds	200 pounds	1,2	1,2	Stow separate from ammonium compounds. Stow away from powdered metals
	Strontium nitrate	Oxidizer	UN1507	Oxidizer	173.153	173.182	25 pounds	100 pounds	1,2	1,2	
	Strontium peroxide	Oxidizer	UN1509	Oxidizer	173.153	173.154	25 pounds	100 pounds	1,2	1,2	Keep dry
	Strychnine salt, solid	Poison B	UN1692	Poison	173.364	173.365	50 pounds	200 pounds	1,2	1,2	
	Strychnine, solid	Poison B	UN1692	Poison	173.364	173.365	Forbidden	200 pounds	1,2	1,2	
	Styphnate of lead. See Initiating explosive										
	Styrene monomer, inhibited	Flammable liquid	UN2055	Flammable liquid	173.118	173.119	1 quart	10 gallons	1,2	1,2	

(1) +/A/W	(2) Hazardous materials descriptions and proper shipping names	(3) Hazard class	(3A) Identification number	(4) Label(s) required (if not excepted)	(5)(a) Exceptions	(5)(b) Specific requirements	(6)(a) Passenger carrying aircraft or railcar	(6)(b) Cargo only aircraft	(7)(a) Cargo vessel	(7)(b) Passenger vessel	(7)(c) Other requirements
	Substituted nitrophenol pesticide, liquid, n.o.s., (compounds and preparations)	Flammable liquid	UN2780	Flammable liquid	173.118	173.119	1 quart	10 gallons	1,2	1	
	Substituted nitrophenol pesticide, liquid, n.o.s., (compounds and preparations)	Poison B	UN2779	Poison	173.345	173.346	1 quart	55 gallons	1,2	1,2	
	Substituted nitrophenol pesticide, solid, n.o.s., (compounds and preparations)	Poison B	UN2779	Poison	173.364	173.365	50 pounds	200 pounds	1,2	1,2	
	Succinic acid peroxide	Organic peroxide	UN2135	Organic peroxide	173.153	173.157 173.158	Forbidden	25 pounds	1	1	
	Succinic acid peroxide, technically pure. See Succinic acid peroxide		UN2135								
	Sucrose octanitrate (dry)	Forbidden									
	Sulfur and chlorate, loose mixtures of	Forbidden									
	Sulfur chloride (mono)	Corrosive material	UN1828	Corrosive	None	173.247	Forbidden	1 gallon	1	1	Keep dry. Glass carboys not permitted on passenger vessels.
	Sulfur chloride (di)	Corrosive material	UN1828	Corrosive	None	173.247	Forbidden	1 gallon	1	1	Keep dry. Glass carboys not permitted on passenger vessels.
	Sulfur dioxide	Nonflammable gas	UN1079	Nonflammable gas	173.306	173.304 173.314 173.315	Forbidden	300 pounds	1,2	4	Stow away from living quarters
	Sulfur flower. See Sulfur, solid										
	Sulfur hexafluoride	Nonflammable gas	UN1080	Nonflammable gas	173.306	173.304	150 pounds	300 pounds	1,2	1,2	
	Sulfuric acid (For fuming sulfuric acid, see Oleum)	Corrosive material	UN1830	Corrosive	173.244	173.272	1 quart	1 gallon	1	1	Keep dry. Under deck stowage is permitted on cargo vessels only in metal drums.
	Sulfuric acid, spent	Corrosive material	UN1832	Corrosive	None	173.248	Forbidden	1 quart	1	1	Under deck stowage is permitted on cargo vessels only in metal drums
	Sulfuric anhydride. See Sulfur trioxide										
	Sulfurous acid	Corrosive material	UN1833	Corrosive	173.244	173.245	2 gallons	2 gallons	1,2	1	Glass carboys in hampers not permitted under deck
	Sulfur, molten or Sulphur, molten	ORM-C	UN2448	None	173.505	173.1080	Forbidden	Forbidden	1	1	Stow away from oxidizers and living quarters.
W	Sulfur, solid	ORM-C	UN1350	None	173.505	173.1080			1,2	1,2	Protect from sparks and open flame. Stow separate from oxidizing materials. Segregation same as for flammable solids.
	Sulfur trioxide	Corrosive material	UN1829	Corrosive	173.244	173.273	Forbidden	1 gallon	1,2	1,2	Keep dry. Glass bottles not permitted under deck.
	Sulfuryl chloride	Corrosive material	UN1834	Corrosive	173.244	173.247	1 quart	1 quart	1	1	Keep dry. Glass carboys not permitted on passenger vessels.
	Sulfuryl fluoride	Nonflammable gas	UN2191	Nonflammable gas	173.306	173.304 173.314	150 pounds	300 pounds	1,3	1	
	Sulphur. See Sulfur, solid										
	Supplementary charge (explosive)	Class A explosive		Explosive A	None	173.69	Forbidden	Forbidden	6	5	
A	2,4,5-T. See 2,4,5-Trichlorophenoxyacetic acid										
	Tank car, containing residual phosphorus and filled with water or inert gas. See 173.190										
	Tank car, empty (previously used for a hazardous materials). See 173.29										
	Tank car, empty (previously used for a Poison A material). See 172.510 and 173.29.										
	Tank, portable, empty (previously used for a hazardous material). See 172.510, 172.514 & 173.29)										
	Tank truck, empty. See 172.510, 172.514 and 173.29.										
A	TDE (1,1-Dichloro-2,2-bis(p-chlorophenyl)ethane)	ORM-A	NA2761	None	173.505	173.510	50 pounds	No limit	1,2	1,2	
	Tear gas ammunition. See Chemical ammunition, nonexplosive (containing an irritant material)										
	Tear gas candle	Irritating material	UN1700	Irritant	None	173.385	Forbidden	75 pounds	1	5	Stow away from living quarters
	Tear gas cartridge. See Small arms ammunition, irritating (tear gas) cartridge										
	Tear gas device	Irritating material	NA1693	Irritant	None	173.385	Forbidden	75 pounds	1	5	Stow away from living quarters
	Tear gas grenade. See Grenade, tear gas.										
	Tertiary alcohol, n.o.s. See Alcohol, n.o.s.										
	Tetraazido benzene quinone	Forbidden									
AW	Tetrachloroethane	ORM-A	UN1702	None	173.505	173.620	1 quart	10 gallons	1,2	1,2	
A	Tetrachloroethylene	ORM-A	UN1897	None	173.505	173.605	10 gallons	55 gallons			
	Tetraethylammonium perchlorate (dry)	Flammable solid	NA1325	Flammable solid	173.153	173.154	25 pounds	25 pounds	1,2	1,2	
	Tetraethyl dithiopyrophosphate and compressed gas mixture	Poison A	UN1703	Poison gas	None	173.334	Forbidden	Forbidden	1	5	Shade from radiant heat. Stow away from living quarters. Segregation same as for nonflammable gases.

253

(1) +/ A/ W	(2) Hazardous materials descriptions and proper shipping names	(3) Hazard class	(3A) Identi- fication number	(4) Label(s) required (if not excepted)	(5) Packaging (a) Exceptions	(5) Packaging (b) Specific require- ments	(6) Maximum net quan- tity in one package (a) Passenger carrying aircraft or railcar	(6) (b) Cargo only aircraft	(7) Water shipments (a) Cargo vessel	(7) (b) Pas- senger vessel	(7) (c) Other requirements
	Tetraethyl dithiopyrophosphate, liquid	Poison B	UN1704	Poison	None	173.358	Forbidden	1 quart	1	5	
	Tetraethyl dithiophyrophosphate mixture, dry	Poison B	UN1704	Poison	None	173.377	Forbidden	200 pounds	1	5	
	Tetraethyl dithiopyrophosphate mixture, liquid	Poison B	UN1704	Poison	None	173.359	Forbidden	1 quart	1	5	
	Tetraethyl lead, liquid (including flash point for export shipment by water)	Poison B	NA1649	Poison	None	173.354	Forbidden	55 gallons	1	5	If flash point is 141 deg F. or less, segregation must be the same as for flammable liquids.
	Tetraethyl pyrophosphate and compressed gas mixture	Poison A	UN1705	Poison gas	None	173.334	Forbidden	Forbidden	1	5	Shade from radiant heat. Stow away from living quarters. Segre- gation same as for nonflammable gases.
	Tetraethyl pyrophosphate, liquid	Poison B	NA2783	Poison	None	173.358	Forbidden	1 quart	1,2	5	
	Tetraethyl pyrophosphate mixture, dry	Poison B	NA2783	Poison	None	173.377	Forbidden	200 pounds	1,2	5	
	Tetraethyl pyrophosphate mixture, liquid	Poison B	NA2783	Poison	None	173.359	Forbidden	1 quart	1,2	5	
+	Tetrafluoroethylene, inhibited	Flammable gas	UN1081	Flammable gas	173.306	173.304	Forbidden	300 pounds	1,2	1,2	Stow away from living quarters
	1,2,3,6-Tetrahydrobenzaldehyde	Corrosive material	UN2498	Corrosive	173.244	173.245	1 quart	10 gallons	1,2	1,2	
	Tetrahydrofuran	Flammable liquid	UN2056	Flammable liquid	None	173.119	Forbidden	10 gallons	1,3	5	
	Tetralin hydroperoxide, technically pure. See Organic peroxide, solid, n.o.s.		UN2136								
	Tetramethylammonium hydroxide, liquid	Corrosive material	UN1835	Corrosive	173.244	173.245	1 quart	10 gallons	1,2	1,2	
	1,1,3,3-Tetramethylbutyl hydroperoxide, technically pure. See Organic peroxide, liquid or solution, n.o.s.		UN2160								
	1,1,3,3-Tetramethylbutyl peroxy-2- ethylhexanoate, technically pure. See Organic peroxide, liquid or solution, n.o.s.		UN2161								
	Tetramethylene diperoxide dicarbamide	Forbidden									
A	Tetramethylmethylenediamine	ORM-A	NA9069	None	173.505	173.510	No limit	No limit			
	Tetranitro diglycerin	Forbidden									
	Tetranitromethane	Oxidizer	UN1510	Oxidizer	None	173.203	Forbidden	Forbidden	1	5	Shade from radiant heat. Stow away from foodstuffs.
	2,3,4,6-Tetranitrophenol	Forbidden									
	2,3,4,6-Tetranitrophenyl methyl nitramine	Forbidden									
	2,3,4,6-Tetranitrophenylnitramine	Forbidden									
	Tetranitroresorcinol (dry)	Forbidden									
	2,3,5,6-Tetranitroso-1,4-dinitrobenzene	Forbidden									
	2,3,5,6-Tetranitrosd nitrobenzene (dry)	Forbidden									
	Tetrazene (guanyl nitrosamino guanyltetra- zene). See Initiating explosive.										
	Tetrazine (dry)	Forbidden									
	Tetrazolyl azide (dry)	Forbidden									
	Tetryl. See High explosive										
	Textile treating compound or mixture, liquid	Corrosive material	NA1760	Corrosive	173.244	173.249a	1 quart	10 gallons	1,2	1,2	
	Thallium salt, solid, n.o.s.	Poison B	NA1707	Poison	173.364	173.365	50 pounds	200 pounds	1,2	1,2	
	Thallium sulfate, solid	Poison B	NA1707	Poison	173.364	173.365	50 pounds	200 pounds	1,2	1,2	
	Thinner for rust prevention. See Paint related material										
	Thiocarbonylchloride. See Thiophosgene										
	Thioglycolic acid	Corrosive material	UN1940	Corrosive	173.244	173.245	1 quart	1 gallon	1,2	1,2	Glass carboys in hampers not permitted under deck
	Thionyl chloride	Corrosive material	UN1836	Corrosive	None	173.247	Forbidden	1 gallon	1	1	Keep dry. Glass carboys not per- mitted on passenger vessels.
	Thiophenol. See Phenyl mercaptan										
+	Thiophosgene	Poison B	UN2474	Poison	None	173.356	Forbidden	1 gallon	1	5	Shade from radiant heat
	Thiophosphoryl chloride	Corrosive material	UN1837	Corrosive	None	173.271	Forbidden	1 quart	1	1	Keep dry. Glass carboys not per- mitted on passenger vessels.
A	Thiram	ORM-A	NA2771	None	173.505	173.510	No limit	No limit	1,2	1,2	
	Thorium metal, pyrophoric	Radioactive material	UN2975	Radioactive and Flammable solid	None	173.418	Forbidden	Forbidden	1,2	1,2	
	Thorium nitrate	Radioactive material	UN2976	Radioactive and Oxidizer	None	173.419	Forbidden	25 pounds	1,2	1,2	Separate longitudinally by a complete hold or compartment from explosives
	Time fuze. See Fuze, time										
	Tin chloride, fuming. See Tin tetrachloride, anhydrous										
	Tin perchloride. See Tin tetrachloride, anhydrous										
	Tin tetrachloride, anhydrous	Corrosive material	UN1827	Corrosive	173.244	173.247	1 quart	1 quart	1	1	Keep dry. Glass carboys not per- mitted on passenger vessels.

254

(1)	(2)	(3)	(3A)	(4)	(5) Packaging		(6) Maximum net quantity in one package		(7) Water shipments		
+/ A/ W	Hazardous materials descriptions and proper shipping names	Hazard class	Identification number	Label(s) required (if not excepted)	(a) Exceptions	(b) Specific requirements	(a) Passenger carrying aircraft or railcar	(b) Cargo only aircraft	(a) Cargo vessel	(b) Passenger vessel	(c) Other requirements
	Titanium metal powder, *dry or wet with less than 20% water*	Flammable solid	UN2546	Flammable solid	None	173.208	Forbidden	75 pounds	1,2	5	
	Titanium metal powder, *wet with 20% or more water*	Flammable solid	UN1352	Flammable solid	None	173.208	Forbidden	150 pounds	1,2	5	
	Titanium sulfate solution *containing not more than 45% sulfuric acid*	Corrosive material	NA1760	Corrosive	173.244	173.297	1 quart	1 gallon	1	4	Shade from radiant heat. Keep dry.
	Titanium tetrachloride	Corrosive material	UN1838	Corrosive	173.244	173.247	1 quart	10 gallons	1	1	Keep dry. Glass carboys not permitted on passenger vessels.
	Toluene *(toluol)*	Flammable liquid	UN1294	Flammable liquid	173.118	173.119	1 quart	10 gallons	1,2	1	
A	Toluenediamine	ORM-A	NA1709	None	173.505	173.510	No limit	No limit	1,2	1,2	
+	Toluene diisocyanate	Poison B	UN2078	Poison	173.345	173.346	Forbidden	55 gallons	1,3	1,3	Shade from radiant heat
	Toluene sulfonic acid, liquid	Corrosive material	UN2584	Corrosive	173.244	173.245	1 quart	10 gallons	1,2	1,2	
	Torch. See Fireworks, common										
	Torpedo, railway	Class B explosive		Explosive B	None	173.91	Forbidden	200 pounds	1,2	1,2	Passenger vessels in metal lockers only
A	Toxaphene	ORM-A	NA2761	None	173.505	173.510	25 pounds	100 pounds	1,2	1,2	
	Toy caps	Class C explosive		Explosive C	None	173.100 173.109	50 pounds	150 pounds	1,3	1,3	
	Toy propellant device	Class C explosive		Explosive C	None	173.111	50 pounds	150 pounds	1,3	1,3	
	Toy smoke device	Class C explosive		Explosive C	None	173.111	50 pounds	150 pounds	1,3	1,3	
	Toy torpedo. See Fireworks, special										
	2,4,5-TP ester. *See* 2,4,5-Trichlorophenoxypropionic acid										
	Tracer	Class C explosive		Explosive C	None	173.105	50 pounds	150 pounds	1,3	1,3	
	Tracer fuze	Class C explosive		Explosive C	None	173.105	50 pounds	150 pounds	1,3	1,3	
	Tractor. See Motor vehicle										
	Trailer or truck body with refrigeration or heating equipment. See Motor vehicle										
	Triazine pesticide, liquid, n.o.s., *(compounds and preparations)*	Flammable liquid	UN2764	Flammable liquid	173.118	173.119	1 quart	10 gallons	1,2	1	
	Triazine pesticide, liquid, n.o.s., *(compounds and preparations)*	Poison B	UN2763	Poison	173.345	173.346	1 quart	55 gallons	1,2	1,2	
	Triazine pesticide, solid, n.o.s., *(compounds and preparations)*	Poison B	UN2763	Poison	173.364	173.365	50 pounds	200 pounds	1,2	1,2	
	Tri-(b-nitroxethyl) ammonium nitrate	Forbidden									
A	Trichlorfon	ORM-A	NA2783	None	173.505	173.510	50 pounds	200 pounds	1,2	1,2	
	Trichloroacetic acid, solid	Corrosive material	UN1839	Corrosive	173.244	173.245b	25 pounds	100 pounds	1,2	1	
	Trichloroacetic acid solution	Corrosive material	UN2564	Corrosive	173.244	173.245	1 quart	1 quart	1,2	1,2	Glass carboys in hampers not permitted under deck
A	1,1,1-Trichloroethane	ORM-A	UN2831	None	173.505	173.605	10 gallons	55 gallons	1,2	1,2	
A	Trichloroethylene	ORM-A	UN1710	None	173.505	173.605	10 gallons	55 gallons	1,2	1,2	
	Trichloroisocyanuric acid, dry	Oxidizer	UN2468	Oxidizer	173.153	173.217	10 pounds	50 pounds	1,2	1,2	Shade from radiant heat. Keep dry, stow separated from nitrogen compounds.
	Trichloromethyl perchlorate	Forbidden									
A	Trichlorophenol	ORM-A	NA2020	None	173.505	173.510	100 pounds	No limit	1,2	1,2	
A	2,4,5-Trichlorophenoxyacetic acid	ORM-A	NA2765	None	173.505	173.510	50 pounds	No limit	1,2	1,2	
A	2,4,5-Trichlorophenoxypropionic acid	ORM-A	NA2765	None	173.505	173.510	50 pounds	No limit	1,2	1,2	
	Trichlorosilane	Flammable liquid	UN1295	Flammable liquid	None	173.136	Forbidden	10 gallons	1	5	Segregation same as for flammable solids labeled Dangerous When Wet
	Trichloro-s-triazinetrione dry, *containing over 39% available chlorine*	Oxidizer	NA2468	Oxidizer	173.153	173.217	50 pounds	100 pounds	1,2	1,2	Shade from radiant heat. Keey dry. Stow separated from nitrogen compounds.
	mono-(Trichloro) tetra-(monopotassium dichloro)-penta-s-triazinetrione, dry *(containing over 39% available chlorine)*	Oxidizer	NA2468	Oxidizer	173.153	173.217	50 pounds	100 pounds	1,3	1,3	Keep dry
	Trick matches	Class C explosive		Explosive C	None	173.111	Forbidden	Forbidden	1,3	1,3	
	Trick noise maker, explosive	Class C explosive		Explosive C	None	173.111	50 pounds	150 pounds	1,3	1,3	

255

(1) +/A/W	(2) Hazardous materials descriptions and proper shipping names	(3) Hazard class	(3A) Identi-fication number	(4) Label(s) required (If not excepted)	(5) Packaging		(6) Maximum net quantity in one package		(7) Water shipments		
					(a) Exceptions	(b) Specific require-ments	(a) Passenger carrying aircraft or railcar	(b) Cargo only aircraft	(a) Cargo vessel	(b) Pas-senger vessel	(c) Other requirements
	Triethylamine	Flammable liquid	UN1296	Flammable liquid	173.118	173.119	1 quart	10 gallons	1,2	1	
+	Trifluorochlorethylene	Flammable gas	UN1082	Flammable gas	173.306	173.304 173.314	Forbidden	10 gallons	1,2	1	
	Trifluoromethane and chlorotrifluoromethane mixture (constant boiling mixture)(R-503). See Refrigerant gas, n.o.s.										
	Triformoxime trinitrate	Forbidden									
	1,3,5-Trimethyl-2,4,6-trinitrobenzene	Forbidden									
	Trimethylacetyl chloride	Corrosive material	UN2438	Corrosive	173.244	173.247	1 quart	1 quart	1,2	1,2	
	Trimethylamine, anhydrous	Flammable gas	UN1083	Flammable gas	173.306	173.304 173.314 173.315	Forbidden	300 pounds	1	4	
	Trimethylamine, aqueous solution	Flammable liquid	UN1297	Flammable liquid	173.118	173.119	1 quart	10 gallons	1,2	1	Stow away from mercury and mercury compounds
	Trimethylchlorosilane	Flammable liquid	UN1298	Flammable liquid	None	173.135	Forbidden	10 gallons	1,2	1	
	Trimethylene glycol diperchlorate	Forbidden									
	Trimethylol nitromethane trinitrate	Forbidden									
	2,4,6-Trinitro-1,3,5-triazido benzene (dry)	Forbidden									
	2,4,6-Trinitro-1,3-diazobenzene	Forbidden									
	Trinitroacetic acid	Forbidden									
	Trinitroacetonitrile	Forbidden									
	Trinitroamine cobalt	Forbidden									
	Trinitrobenzene, dry. See High explosive										
	Trinitrobenzene, wet containing at least 10% water	Flammable solid	UN1354	Flammable solid	173.212		1 pound	1 pound	1	4	Stow away from heavy metals and their compounds
	Trinitrobenzene, wet, containing at least 10% water, over 16 ounces in one outside packaging. See High explosive										
	Trinitrobenzoic acid, dry. See High explosive										
	Trinitrobenzoic acid, wet, containing at least 10% water	Flammable solid	UN1355	Flammable solid	173.192	173.193	1 pound	25 pounds	1	5	Stow away from heavy metals and their compounds
	Trinitrobenzoic acid, wet, containing at least 10% water, over 25 pounds in one out-side packaging. See High explosives										
	Trinitroethanol	Forbidden									
	Trinitroethylnitrate	Forbidden									
	Trinitromethane	Forbidden									
	1,3,5-Trinitronaphthalene	Forbidden									
	2,4,6-Trinitrophenyl guanidine (dry)	Forbidden									
	2,4,6-Trinitrophenyl nitramine	Forbidden									
	2,4,6-Trinitrophenyl trimethylol methyl nitram-ine trinitrate (dry)	Forbidden									
	Trinitroresorcinol. See High explosive										
	2,4,6-Trinitroso-3-methyl nitraminoanisole	Forbidden									
	Trinitrotetramine cobalt nitrate	Forbidden									
	Trinitrotoluene, dry. See High explosive										
	Trinitrotoluene, wet containing at least 10% water	Flammable solid	UN1356	Flammable solid	173.212		1 pound	1 pound	1	4	Stow away from heavy metals and their compounds
	Trinitrotoluene, wet, containing at least 10% water, over 16 ounces in one outside packaging. See High explosive										
	Tris-(1-aziridinyl) phosphine oxide	Corrosive material	UN2501	Corrosive	173.244	173.299a	1 quart	1 gallon	1	1	Keep dry. Glass carboys not per-mitted on passenger vessels.
	Tris, bis-bifluoroamino diethoxy propane (TVOPA)	Forbidden									
	Tungsten hexafluoride	Corrosive material	UN2196	Corrosive	None	173.284	Forbidden	110 pounds	1	5	Segregation same as for nonflam-mable gases
	Turpentine	Combustible liquid	UN1299	None	173.118a	None	No limit	No limit	1,2	1,2	
	Turpentine	Flammable liquid	UN1299	Flammable liquid	173.118	173.119	1 quart	10 gallons	1,2	1,2	
	Uranium hexafluoride, fissile (containing more than 1% U-235)	Radioactive material	UN2977	Radioactive and Corrosive	173.453	173.417 173.420			1,2	1,2	
	Uranium hexafluoride, low specific activity	Radioactive material	UN2978	Radioactive and Corrosive	173.421-2	173.420 173.425			1,2	1,2	
	Uranium metal pyrophoric	Radioactive material	UN2979	Radioactive and Flammable solid	None	173.418	Forbidden	Forbidden	1,2	1,2	
	Uranyl acetate	Radioactive material	NA9180	Radioactive	173.421 173.425	173.415 173.416			1,2	1,2	

256

(1) +/A/W	(2) Hazardous materials descriptions and proper shipping names	(3) Hazard class	(3A) Identification number	(4) Label(s) required (if not excepted)	(5) Packaging		(6) Maximum net quantity in one package		(7) Water shipments		
					(a) Exceptions	(b) Specific requirements	(a) Passenger carrying aircraft or railcar	(b) Cargo only aircraft	(a) Cargo vessel	(b) Passenger vessel	(c) Other requirements
	Uranyl nitrate hexahydrate solution	Radioactive Material	UN2980	Radioactive and Corrosive	173.421 173.425	173.415 173.416 173.417			1,2	1,2	
	Uranyl nitrate, solid	Radioactive material	UN2981	Radioactive and Oxidizer	None	173.419	Forbidden	25 pounds	1,2	1,2	Separate longitudinally by an intervening hold or compartment from explosives
	Urea nitrate, dry. See **High explosive**										
	Urea nitrate, wet with 10% or more water	Flammable solid	UN1357	Flammable solid	173.192	173.193	1 pound	25 pounds	1,2	1,2	
	Urea nitrate, wet with 10% or more water, over 25 pounds in one outside packaging. See **High explosive**										
	Urea peroxide	Organic peroxide	NA1511	Organic peroxide	173.153	173.227	2 pounds	25 pounds	1	4	Keep dry. Shade from radiant heat.
	Valeric acid	Corrosive material	NA1760	Corrosive	173.244	173.245	1 quart	10 gallons	1,2	1,2	
	Valeryl chloride	Corrosive material	UN2502	Corrosive	173.244	173.245	1 quart	1 gallon	1,2	1,2	
	Vanadium oxytrichloride	Corrosive material	UN2443	Corrosive	173.244	173.247a	Forbidden	1 quart	1	4	Shade from radiant heat
	Vanadium oxytrichloride and titanium tetrachloride mixture	Corrosive material	NA2443	Corrosive	None	173.245 173.245a	Forbidden	1 quart	1	4	Shade from radiant heat
	Vanadium tetrachloride	Corrosive material	UN2444	Corrosive	173.244	173.247a	Forbidden	1 quart	1	4	Shade from radiant heat
	Very signal cartridge	Class C explosive		Explosive C	None	173.108	50 pounds	200 pounds	1,3	1,3	
	Vinyl acetate	Flammable liquid	UN1301	Flammable liquid	173.118	173.119	1 quart	10 gallons	1,2	1	
+	Vinyl chloride	Flammable gas	UN1086	Flammable gas	173.306	173.304 173.314 173.315	Forbidden	300 pounds	1,2	4	Stow away from living quarters
	Vinyl ethyl ether, inhibited	Flammable liquid	UN1302	Flammable liquid	None	173.119	Forbidden	1 gallon	1,3	5	
	Vinyl fluoride, inhibited	Flammable gas	UN1860	Flammable gas	173.306	173.304 173.314 173.315	Forbidden	300 pounds	1	4	
	Vinylidene chloride, inhibited	Flammable liquid	UN1303	Flammable liquid	173.118	173.119	1 quart	10 gallons	1,3	4	
	Vinyl isobutyl ether	Flammable liquid	UN1304	Flammable liquid	173.118	173.119	1 quart	10 gallons	1,2	1	
+	Vinyl methyl ether	Flammable gas	UN1087	Flammable gas	173.306	173.304 173.314 173.315	Forbidden	20 pounds	1,2	1	Stow away from living quarters
	Vinyl nitrate polymer	Forbidden									
	Vinyl trichlorosilane	Flammable liquid	UN1305	Flammable liquid	None	173.135	Forbidden	10 gallons	1,2	1	
	Vitriol, oil of. See **Sulfuric acid**										
	War head. See **Explosive projectile**										
	Waste, hazardous. See **Hazardous waste, liquid or solid, n.o.s.**										
	Water pump system *tank charged with compressed air or nitrogen*	Nonflammable gas	NA1956	None	173.306		Forbidden	Forbidden	1,2	1,2	
	Water reactive solid, n.o.s.	Flammable solid	UN2813	Flammable solid and Dangerous when wet	173.153	173.154	Forbidden	25 pounds	1,2	4	Segregation same as for flammable solids labeled Dangerous When Wet
	Wheelchair, battery-equipped. See **Battery, electric storage, wet with wheelchair.**										
	Xenon	Nonflammable gas	UN2036	Nonflammable gas	173.306	173.302	150 pounds	300 pounds	1,2	1,2	
	X-ray film. See **Film**										
	Xylene *(xylol)*	Flammable liquid	UN1307	Flammable liquid	173.118	173.119	1 quart	10 gallons	1,2	1	
A	Xylenol	ORM-A	UN2261	None	173.505	173.510	100 pounds	No limit	1,2	1,2	
	Xylyl bromide	Irritating material	UN1701	Irritant	None	173.382	Forbidden	75 pounds	1	5	Stow away from living quarters
	p-Xylyl diazide	Forbidden									
	Zinc ammonium nitrite	Oxidizer	UN1512	Oxidizer	None	173.228	25 pounds	100 pounds	1,3	5	This material may be forbidden in water transportation by certain countries
	Zinc arsenate	Poison B	UN1712	Poison	173.364	173.365	50 pounds	200 pounds	1,2	1,2	
	Zinc arsenite, solid	Poison B	UN1712	Poison	173.364	173.365	50 pounds	200 pounds	1,2	1,2	

(1) +/A/W	(2) Hazardous materials descriptions and proper shipping names	(3) Hazard class	(3A) Identification number	(4) Label(s) required (if not excepted)	(5) Packaging		(6) Maximum net quantity in one package		(7) Water shipments		
					(a) Exceptions	(b) Specific requirements	(a) Passenger carrying aircraft or railcar	(b) Cargo only aircraft	(a) Cargo vessel	(b) Passenger vessel	(c) Other requirements
	Zinc chlorate	Oxidizer	UN1513	Oxidizer	173.153	173.163	25 pounds	100 pounds	1,2	1,2	Stow separate from ammonium compounds and away from powdered metals
	Zinc chloride solution	Corrosive material	UN1840	Corrosive	173.244	173.245	1 quart	1 quart	1,2	1,2	
	Zinc cyanide	Poison B	UN1713	Poison	173.370	173.370	25 pounds	200 pounds	1,2	1,2	Stow away from acids
	Zinc ethyl. See Pyrophoric liquid, n.o.s.										
A	Zinc hydrosulfite	ORM-A	UN1931	None	173.505	173.510	50 pounds	100 pounds	1,2	1,2	Keep dry. Stow away from acids and oxidizers
	Zinc muriate solution. See Zinc chloride solution										
	Zinc nitrate	Oxidizer	UN1514	Oxidizer	173.153	173.182	25 pounds	100 pounds	1,2	1,2	
	Zinc permanganate	Oxidizer	UN1515	Oxidizer	173.153	173.154	25 pounds	100 pounds	1,2	1,2	Separate from ammonium compounds and hydrogen peroxide
	Zinc peroxide	Oxidizer	UN1516	Oxidizer	173.153	173.154	25 pounds	100 pounds	1,2	1,2	Keep dry
	Zinc phosphide	Poison B	UN1714	Poison	173.364	173.365	25 pounds	100 pounds	1,2	1,2	Stow away from acids and oxidizers
	Zirconium hydride	Flammable solid	UN1437	Flammable solid and Dangerous when wet	None	173.206	Forbidden	150 pounds	1,2	5	Segregation same as for flammable solids labeled Dangerous When Wet
	Zirconium metal, dry, *chemically produced, finer than 20 mesh particle size*	Flammable solid	UN2008	Flammable solid	None	173.214	Forbidden	75 pounds	1	5	Separate from flammable gases or liquids, oxidizing materials or organic peroxides
	Zirconium metal, dry, *mechanically produced, finer than 270 mesh particle size*	Flammable solid	UN2008	Flammable solid	None	173.214	Forbidden	75 pounds	1	5	Separate from flammable gases or liquids, oxidizing materials or organic peroxides
	Zirconium, metal, liquid, suspensions	Flammable liquid	UN1308	Flammable liquid	None	173.140	Forbidden	5 gallons	1	5	
	Zirconium metal, wet, *chemically produced, finer than 20 mesh particle size*	Flammable solid	UN1358	Flammable solid	None	173.214	Forbidden	150 pounds	1,2	5	
	Zirconium metal, wet, *mechanically produced, finer than 270 mesh particle size*	Flammable solid	UN1358	Flammable solid	None	173.214	Forbidden	150 pounds	1,2	5	
	Zirconium nitrate	Oxidizer	UN2728	Oxidizer	173.153	173.182	25 pounds	100 pounds	1,2	1,2	
	Zirconium picramate, wet *with at least 20% of water*	Flammable solid	UN1517	Flammable solid	None	173.216	Forbidden	25 pounds	1	1	Stow away from heavy metals and their salts
	Zirconium scrap *(borings, clippings, shavings, sheets, or turnings)*	Flammable solid	UN1932	Flammable solid	173.153	173.220	Forbidden	Forbidden	1	4	Separate from flammable gases or liquids, oxidizing materials, or organic peroxides
A	Zirconium sulfate	ORM-B	NA9163	None	None	173.510	100 pounds	No limit	1,2	1,2	
	Zirconium tetrachloride, solid	Corrosive material	UN2503	Corrosive	173.244	173.245b	25 pounds	100 pounds	1,2	1,2	

258

Appendix to §172.101 -
List of Hazardous Substances
and Reportable Quantities

1. This appendix lists materials and their corresponding reportable quantities (RQs) which are listed or designated as "hazardous substances" under section 101(14) of the Comprehensive Environmental Response, Compensation, and Liability Act (CERCLA; Pub. L. 96-510). This appendix is divided into 2 tables which are entitled "Table 1—Hazardous Substances Other Than Radionuclides" and "Table 2—Radionuclides". A material in this appendix is regulated as a hazardous material and a hazardous substance under this subchapter if it meets the definition of a hazardous substance in §171.8 of this subchapter.

2. The procedure for selecting a proper shipping name for a hazardous substance is set forth in §172.101(c)(9).

3. Column 1 of Table 1, entitled "Hazardous substance", contains the names of those elements and compounds which are hazardous substances. Following the listing of elements and compounds is a listing of waste streams. These waste streams appear on the list in numerical sequence and are referenced by the appropriate "F" or "K" numbers. Column 2 of Table 1, entitled "Synonyms", contains the names of synonyms for certain elements and compounds listed in Column 1. No synonyms are listed for waste streams. Synonyms are useful in identifying hazardous substances and in identifying proper shipping names. Column 3 of Table 1, entitled "Reportable quantity (RQ)", contains the reportable quantity (RQ), in pounds and kilograms, for each hazardous substance listed in Column 1 of Table 1.

4. A series of notes are used throughout Table 1 and Table 2 to provide additional information concerning certain hazardous substances. These notes are explained at the end of each Table.

5. Table 2 lists radionuclides which are hazardous substances and their corresponding RQs. The RQs in Table 2 for radionuclides are expressed in units of curies and terabecquerels, whereas those in Table 1 are expressed in units of pounds. If a material is listed in both Table 1 and Table 2, the lowest RQ shall apply. Radionuclides are listed in alphabetical order. The RQs for radionuclides are given in the radiological unit of measure of curie, abbreviated "Ci", followed, in parentheses, by an equivalent unit measured in terabecquerels, abbreviated "TBq".

6. For mixtures of radionuclides, the following determinations shall be used in determining if a package contains an RQ of a hazardous substance: (i) If the identity and quantity (in curies or terabecquerels) of each radionuclide in a mixture or solution is known, the ratio between the quantity per package (in curies or terabecquerels) and the RQ for the radionuclide must be determined for each radionuclide. A package contains an RQ of a hazardous substance when the sum of the ratios for the radionuclides in the mixture or solution is equal to or greater than one; (ii) if the identity of each radionuclide in a mixture or solution is known but the quantity per package (in curies or terabecquerels) of one or more of the radionuclides is unknown, an RQ of a hazardous substance is present in a package when the total quantity (in curies or terabecquerels) of the mixture or solution is equal to or greater than the lowest RQ of any individual radionuclide in the mixture or solution; and (iii) if the identity of one or more radionuclides in a mixture or solution is unknown (or if the identity of a radionuclide by itself is unknown), an RQ of a hazardous substance is present when the total quantity (in curies or terabecquerels) in a package is equal to or greater than either one curie or the lowest RQ of any known individual radionuclide in the mixture or solution, whichever is lower.

Table 1—Hazardous Substances Other Than Radionuclides

Hazardous Substances	Synonyms	Reportable Quantity (RQ) Pounds (Kilograms)
Acenaphthene		100 (45.4)
Acenaphthylene		5000 (2270)
Acetaldehyde*	Ethanal	1000 (454)
Acetaldehyde, chloro-	Chloroacetaldehyde	1000 (454)
Acetaldehyde, trichloro-	Chloral	5000 (2270)
Acetamide, N-(aminothioxomethyl)-	1-Acetyl-2-thiourea	1000 (454)
Acetamide, N-(4-ethoxyphenyl)-	Phenacetin	100 (45.4)
Acetamide, N-fluoren-2-yl-	2-Acetylaminofluorene	1 (0.454)
Acetamide, 2-fluoro-	Fluoroacetamide	100 (45.4)
Acetic acid*		5000 (2270)
Acetic acid (2,4-dichlorophenoxy)-	2,4-D, salts and esters	100 (45.4)
	2,4-D acid	
Acetic acid, ethyl ester	Ethyl acetate*	5000 (2270)
Acetic acid, fluoro-, sodium salt	Fluoroacetic acid, sodium salt	10 (4.54)
Acetic acid, lead (2+)salt	Lead acetate	5000 (2270)
Acetic acid, thallium(I) salt	Thallium(I) acetate	100 (45.4)
Acetic acid, (2,4,5-trichlorophenoxy)	2,4,5-T*	1000 (454)
	2,4,5-T acid	
Acetic anhydride*		5000 (2270)
Acetone*	2-Propanone	5000 (2270)
Acetone cyanohydrin*	Propanenitrile, 2-hydroxy-2-methyl-	10 (4.54)
	2-Methyllactonitrile	
Acetonitrile*	Ethanenitrile	5000 (2270)
Acetophenone	Ethanone, 1-phenyl-	5000 (2270)
2-Acetylaminofluorene	Acetamide, N-fluoren-2-yl-	1 (0.454)
Acetyl bromide*		5000 (2270)
Acetyl chloride*	Ethanoyl chloride	5000 (2270)
1-Acetyl-2-thiourea	Acetamide, N-(aminothioxomethyl)-	1000 (454)
Acrolein*	2-Propenal	1 (0.454)
Acrylamide	2-Propenamide	5000 (2270)
Acrylic acid*	2-Propenoic acid	5000 (2270)
Acrylonitrile*	2-Propenenitrile	100 (45.4)
Adipic acid		5000 (2270)
Aldicarb	Propanal, 2-methyl-2-(methylthio)-	1 (0.454)
	O-[(methyl-amino) carbonyl]oxime	

259

Hazardous Substances	Synonyms	Reportable Quantity (RQ) Pounds (Kilograms)
Aldrin*	1,2,3,4,10-10-Hexachloro-1,4,4a,5,8,8a- hexahydro- 1,4,5,8-endo, exodimethanonaphthalene 1,4,5,8-Dimethanonaphthalene, 1,2,3,4,10,10-hexachloro- 1,4,4a,5,8,8a- hexahydro-,(1alpha,4alpha,4abeta,5alpha,8a	1 (0.454)
Allyl alcohol*	2-Propen-1-ol	100 (45.4)
Allyl chloride*		1000 (454)
Aluminum phosphide*		100 (45.4)
Aluminum sulfate*		5000 (2270)
5-(Aminomethyl)-3-isoxazolol	3(2H)-Isoxazolone, 5-(aminomethyl)- Muscimol	1000 (454)
4-Aminopyridine	4-Pyridinamine	1000 (454)
Amitrole	1H-1,2,4-Triazol-3-amine	10 (4.54)
Ammonia*		100 (45.4)
Ammonium acetate		5000 (2270)
Ammonium benzoate		5000 (2270)
Ammonium bicarbonate		5000 (2270)
Ammonium bichromate	Ammonium dichromate @	10 (4.54)
Ammonium bifluoride*		100 (45.4)
Ammonium bisulfite*		5000 (2270)
Ammonium carbamate*		5000 (2270)
Ammonium carbonate*		5000 (2270)
Ammonium chloride		5000 (2270)
Ammonium chromate		10 (4.54)
Ammonium citrate, dibasic		5000 (2270)
Ammonium dichromate @	Ammonium bichromate	10 (4.54)
Ammonium fluoborate*		5000 (2270)
Ammonium fluoride*		100 (45.4)
Ammonium hydroxide*		1000 (454)
Ammonium oxalate*		5000 (2270)
Ammonium picrate*	Phenol, 2,4,6-trinitro-, ammonium salt	10 (4.54)
Ammonium silicofluoride*		1000 (454)
Ammonium sulfamate		5000 (2270)
Ammoniumsulfide*		100 (45.4)
Ammonium sulfite		5000 (2270)
Ammonium tartrate		5000 (2270)
Ammonium thiocyanate		5000 (2270)
Ammonium vanadate	Vanadic acid, ammonium salt	1000 (454)
Amyl acetate* iso-Amyl acetate sec-Amyl acetate tert-Amyl acetate		5000 (2270)
Aniline*	Benzenamine	5000 (2270)
Anthracene		5000 (2270)
Antimony¢		5000 (2270)
Antimony pentachloride*		1000 (454)
Antimony potassium tartrate*		100 (45.4)
Antimony tribromide*		1000 (454)
Antimony trichloride*		1000 (454)
Antimony trifluoride*		1000 (454)
Antimony trioxide		1000 (454)
Argentate(1-), bis(cyano-C)-, potassium	Potassium silver cyanide	1 (0.454)
Aroclor 1016	POLYCHLORINATED BIPHENYLS (PCBs)	1 (0.454)
Aroclor 1221	POLYCHLORINATED BIPHENYLS (PCBs)	1 (0.454)
Aroclor 1232	POLYCHLORINATED BIPHENYLS (PCBs)	1 (0.454)
Aroclor 1242	POLYCHLORINATED BIPHENYLS (PCBs)	1 (0.454)
Aroclor 1248	POLYCHLORINATED BIPHENYLS (PCBs)	1 (0.454)
Aroclor 1254	POLYCHLORINATED BIPHENYLS (PCBs)	1 (0.454)
Aroclor 1260	POLYCHLORINATED BIPHENYLS (PCBs)	1 (0.454)
Arsenic*¢		1 (0.454)
Arsenic acid*	Arsenic acid H3AsO4	1 (0.454)
Arsenic acid H3AsO4	Arsenic acid*	1 (0.454)
Arsenic disulfide*		1 (0.454)
Arsenic oxide As203	Arsenic trioxide*	1 (0.454)
Arsenic oxide As205	Arsenic pentoxide*	1 (0.454)
Arsenic pentoxide*	Arsenic oxide As205	1 (0.454)
Arsenic trichloride*		1 (0.454)
Arsenic trioxide*	Arsenic oxide As203	1 (0.454)
Arsenic trisulfide*		1 (0.454)
Arsine, diethyl-	Diethylarsine	1 (0.454)
Arsinic acid, dimethyl-	Cacodylic acid	1 (0.454)
Arsonous dichloride, phenyl-	Dichlorophenylarsine Phenyl dichloroarsine @	1 (0.454)

Hazardous Substances	Synonyms	Reportable Quantity (RQ) Pounds (Kilograms)
Asbestos* ¢¢	Benzenamine, 4,4'-carbonimidoylbis(N,N- dimethyl-	1 (0.454)
Auramine	L-Serine, diazoacetate (ester)	100 (45.4)
Azaserine	Guthion*	1 (0.454)
Azinphos methyl @	Ethylenimine-	1 (0.454)
Aziridine	Ethylene imine@	1 (0.454)
Aziridine, 2-methyl-	1,2-Propylenimine	1 (0.454)
Azirino(2',3',3',4)pytrolo(1,2-a)indole-4,7-dione, 6-amino-8-[((aminocarbonyl)oxy)methyl]-1,1a,2,8,8a,8b-hexahydro-8a-methoxy-5-methyl-, [1aS-[aalpha,8beta,8aalpha,8balpha)]-.	Mitomycin C	10 (4.54)
Barium cyanide*		10 (4.54)
Benz[j]aceanthrylene, 1,2-dihydro-3-methyl-	3-Methylcholanthrene	10 (4.54)
Benz[c]acridine	3,4-Benzacridine	100 (45.4)
3,4-Benzacridine	Benz[c]acridine	100 (45.4)
Benzal chloride	Benzene, dichloromethyl-	5000 (2270)
Benzamide,3,5-dichloro-N-(1,1-dimethyl-2-propynyl)	Pronamide	5000 (2270)
Benz[a]anthracene	1,2-Benzanthracene	10 (4.54)
	Benzo[a]anthracene	
1,2-Benzanthracene	Benz[a]anthracene	10 (4.54)
	Benzo[a]anthracene	
Benz[a]anthracene, 7,12-dimethyl-	7,12-Dimethylbenz[a]anthracene	1 (0.454)
Benzenamine	Aniline*	5000 (2270)
Benzenamine, 4,4'-carbonimidoylbis(N,N-dimethyl-	Auramine	100 (45.4)
Benzenamine, 4-chloro-	p-Chloroaniline	1000 (454)
Benzenamine, 4-chloro-2-methyl-,hydrochloride	4-Chloro-o-toluidine, hydrochloride	100 (45.4)
Benzenamine, N,N-dimethyl-4-(phenylazo)-	p-Dimethylaminoazobenzene	10 (4.54)
Benzenamine, 2-methyl-	o-Toluidine	100 (45.4)
Benzenamine, 4-methyl-	p-Toluidine	100 (45.4)
Benzenamine, 4,4'-methylenebis(2-chloro-	4,4'-Methylenebis(2-chloroaniline)	10 (4.54)
Benzenamine,2-methyl-, hydrochloride	o-Toluidine hydrochloride	100 (45.4)
Benzenamine,2-methyl-5-nitro-	5-Nitro-o-toluidine	100 (45.4)
Benzenamine,4-nitro-	p-Nitroaniline	5000 (2270)
Benzene*		10 (4.54)
Benzene, 1-bromo-4-phenoxy-	4-Bromophenyl phenyl ether	100 (45.4)
Benzene, chloro-	Chlorobenzene*	100 (45.4)
Benzene, chloromethyl-	Benzyl chloride*	100 (45.4)
Benzene,1,2-dichloro-	o-Dichlorobenzene*	100 (45.4)
	1,2-Dichlorobenzene	
Benzene, 1,3-dichloro-	m-Dichlorobenzene	100 (45.4)
	1,3-Dichlorobenzene	
Benzene, 1,4-dichloro-	p-Dichlorobenzene*	100 (45.4)
	1,4-Dichlorobenzene	
Benzene, 1,1'-(2,2-dichloroethylidene)bis[4-chloro	DDD	1 (0.454)
	TDE*	
	4,4'-DDD	
Benzene, dichloromethyl-	Benzal chloride	5000 (2270)
Benzene, 1,3-diisocyanatomethyl	Toluene diisocyanate*	100 (45.4)
Benzene, dimethyl	Xylene* (mixed)	1000 (454)
m-Benzene,dimethyl	m-Xylene	
o-Benzene,dimethyl	o-Xylene	
p-Benzene,dimethyl	p-Xylene	
Benzene, hexachloro-	Hexachlorobenzene	10 (4.54)
Benzene, hexahydro-	Cyclohexane*	1000 (454)
Benzene, hydroxy-	Phenol*	1000 (454)
Benzene, methyl-	Toluene*	1000 (454)
Benzene, 1-methyl-2,4-dinitro-	2,4-Dinitrotoluene	10 (4.54)
Benzene, 2-methyl-1,3-dinitro-	2,6-Dinitrotoluene	100 (45.4)
Benzene, 1-methylethyl-	Cumene	5000 (2270)
Benzene, nitro-	Nitrobenzene*	1000 (454)
Benzene, pentachloro-	Pentachlorobenzene	10 (4.54)
Benzene, pentachloronitro-	Pentachloronitrobenzene (PCNB)	100 (45.4)
Benzene, 1,2,4,5-tetrachloro-	1,2,4,5-Tetrachlorobenzene	5000 (2270)
Benzene, 1,1'-(2,2,2-trichloroethylidene)bis [4-chloro-	DDT*	1 (0.454)
	4,4'-DDT	
Benzene, 1,1'-(2,2,2-trichloroethylidene)bis [4-methoxy)-	Methoxychlor	1 (0.454)
Benzene, (trichloromethyl)	Benzotrichloride	10 (4.54)
Benzene, 1,3,5-trinitro-	1,3,5-Trinitrobenzene	10 (4.54)
Benzeneacetic acid, 4-chloro-alpha-(4-chlorophenyl)-alpha-hydroxy-, ethyl ester	Chlorobenzilate	10 (4.54)
Benzenebutanoic acid, 4-[bis(2-chloroethyl)amino]-	Chlorambucil	10 (4.54)
Benzenediamine, ar-methyl-	Toluenediamine*	10 (4.54)

261

Hazardous Substances	Synonyms	Reportable Quantity (RQ) Pounds (Kilograms)
1,2-Benzenedicarboxylic acid,[bis(2-ethylhexyl)] ester	Bis(2-ethylhexyl)phthalate-	100 (45.4)
	Diethylhexyl phthalate	
1,2-Benzenedicarboxylic acid,dibutyl ester	n-Butyl phthalate	10 (4.54)
	Dibutyl phthalate	
	Di-n-butyl phthalate	
1,2-Benzenedicarboxylic acid, diethyl ester	Diethyl phthalate	1000 (454)
1,2-Benzenedicarboxylic acid, dimethyl ester	Dimethyl phthalate	5000 (2270)
1,2-Benzenedicarboxylic acid, dioctyl ester	Di-n-octyl phthalate	5000 (2270)
1,3-Benzenediol	Resorcinol	5000 (2270)
1,2-Benzenediol,4-[1- hydroxy-2-(methylamino) ethyl]-	Epinephrine	1000 (454)
Benzeneethanamine, alpha,alpha-dimethyl-	alpha,alpha-Dimethylphenethylamine	5000 (2270)
Benzeneethanamine, alpha,alpha-dimethyl-	alpha,alpha-Dimethylphenethylamine	5000 (2270)
Benzenesulfonic acid chloride	Benzenesulfonyl chloride	100 (45.4)
Benzenesulfonyl chloride	Benzenesulfonic acid chloride	100 (45.4)
Benzenethiol	Phenyl mercaptan @	100 (45.4)
	Thiophenol	
Benzidine*	(1,1'-Biphenyl)-4,4' diamine	1 (0.454)
1,2-Benzisothiazol-3(2H)-one,1,1-dioxide	Saccharin and salts	100 (45.4)
Benzo[a]anthracene	Benz[a]anthracene	10 (4.54)
	1,2-Benzanthracene	
1,3-Benzodioxole, 5-(2-propenyl)-	Safrole	100 (45.4)
1,3-Benzodioxole, 5-(1-propenyl)-	Isosafrole	100 (45.4)
1,3-Benzodioxole, 5-propyl-	Dihydrosafrole	10 (4.54)
Benzo[b]fluoranthene		1 (0.454)
Benzo[k]fluoranthene		5000 (2270)
Benzo[j,k]fluorene	Fluoranthene	100 (45.4)
Benzoic acid		5000 (2270)
Benzonitrile*		5000 (2270)
Benzo[g,h,i]perylene		5000 (2270)
2H-1-Benzopyran-2-one, 4-hydroxy-3-(3-oxo-1-phenyl-butyl) -, & salts, when present at concentrations greater than 0.3%	Warfarin, & salts, when present at concentrations greater than 0.3%	100 (45.4)
Benzo[a]pyrene	3,4-Benzopyrene	1 (0.454)
3,4-Benzopyrene	Benzo[a]pyrene	1 (0.454)
p-Benzoquinone	2,5-Cyclohexadiene-1,4-dione	10 (4.54)
Benzo[rst]pentaphene	Dibenz[a,i]pyrene	10 (4.54)
Benzotrichloride	Benzene, (trichloromethyl)	10 (4.54)
Benzoyl chloride*		1000 (454)
1,2-Benzphenanthrene	Chrysene	100 (45.4)
Benzyl chloride*	Benzene, chloromethyl-	100 (45.4)
Beryllium ¢	Beryllium dust ¢	10 (4.54)
Beryllium chloride*		1 (0.454)
Beryllium dust ¢	Beryllium ¢	10 (4.54)
Beryllium fluoride*		1 (0.454)
Beryllium nitrate*		1 (0.454)
alpha - BHC		10 (4.54)
beta - BHC		1 (0.454)
delta - BHC		1 (0.454)
gamma - BHC	Hexachlorocyclohexane (gamma isomer)	1 (0.454)
	Lindane*	
	Cyclohexane,1,2,3,4,5,6-hexachloro-, (1alpha,2alpha,3beta,4alpha,5alpha,6beta)-	
2,2'-Bioxirane	1,2:3,4-Diepoxybutane	10 (4.54)
(1,1'-Biphenyl)-4,4' diamine	Benzidine*	1 (0.454)
(1,1'-Biphenyl)-4,4' diamine 3,3'dichloro-	3,3'-Dichlorobenzidine	1 (0.454)
(1,1'-Biphenyl)-4,4' diamine 3,3'-dimethoxy-	3,3'-Dimethoxybenzidine	10 (4.54)
(1,1'-Biphenyl)-4,4' diamine 3,3'-dimethyl-	3,3'-Dimethylbenzidine	10 (4.54)
Bis(2-chloroethoxy) methane	Ethane, 1,1'-[methylenebis (oxy)]bis(2-chloro-	1000 (454)
	Dichloromethoxy ethane	
Bis(2-chloroethyl) ether	Dichloroethyl ether	10 (4.54)
	Ethane, 1,1'-oxybis[2-chloro-	
Bis(2-ethylhexyl)phthalate	1,2-Benzenedicarboxylic acid, [bis(2-ethylhexyl)] ester	100 (45.4)
	Diethylhexyl phthalate-	
Bromoacetone*	2-Propanone, 1-bromo-	1000 (454)
Bromoform	Methane, tribromo-	100 (45.4)
4-Bromophenyl phenyl ether	Benzene, 1-bromo-4- phenoxy-	100 (45.4)
Brucine	Strychnidin-10-one, 2,3-dimethoxy-	100 (45.4)
1,3-Butadiene, 1,1,2,3,4,4-hexachloro-	Hexachlorobutadiene*	1 (0.454)
1-Butanamine, N-butyl-N-nitroso-	N-Nitrosodi-n-butylamine	10 (4.54)
1-Butanol	n-Butyl alcohol*	5000 (2270)
2-Butanone	Ethyl methyl ketone @	5000 (2270)
	Methyl ethyl ketone(MEK)*	

262

Hazardous Substances	Synonyms	Reportable Quantity (RQ) Pounds (Kilograms)
2-Butanone, 3,3-dimethyl-1-(methylthio)-,O-[(methylamino) carbonyl]oxime	Thiofanox	100 (45.4)
2-Butanone peroxide	Methyl ethyl ketone peroxide*	10 (4.54)
2-Butenal	Crotonaldehyde*	100 (45.4)
2-Butane, 1,4-dichloro-	1,4-Dichloro-2-butene	1 (0.454)
2-Butenoic acid, 2-methyl-,7[[2,3-dihydroxy-2-(1-methoxyethyl)-3-methyl-1-oxobutoxy]methyl]-2,3,5,7a-tetrahydro-1H-pyrrolizin-1-yl ester,[1S-[1alpha (Z),7(2S*,3R*),7aalpha]]-.	Lasiocarpine	10 (4.54)
Butyl acetate*		5000 (2270)
iso- Butyl acetate		
sec- Butyl acetate		
tert- Butyl acetate		
n-Butyl alcohol*	1-Butanol	5000 (2270)
Butylamine*		1000 (454)
iso- Butylamine		
sec- Butylamine		
tert- Butylamine		
Butyl benzyl phthalate		100 (45.4)
n-Butyl phthalate	Dibutyl phthalate	10 (4.54)
	Di-n-butyl phthalate	
	1,2-Benzenedicarboxylic acid,dibutyl ether	
Butyric acid*		5000 (2270)
iso-Butyric acid		
Cacodylic acid	Arsenic acid, dimethyl-	1 (0.454)
Cadmium ¢		10 (4.54)
Cadmium acetate		10 (4.54)
Cadmium bromide		10 (4.54)
Cadmium chloride		10 (4.54)
Calcium arsenate*		1 (0.454)
Calcium arsenite*		1 (0.454)
Calcium carbide*		10 (4.54)
Calcium chromate*	Chromic acid H2CrO4, calcium salt	10 (4.54)
Calcium cyanide*	Calcium Cyanide Ca(CN)2	10 (4.54)
Calcium cyanide Ca(CN)2	Calcium cyanide	10 (4.54)
Calcium dodecylbenzene sulfonate		1000 (454)
Calcium hyprochlorite*		10 (4.54)
Camphene, octachloro-	Toxaphene*	1 (0.454)
Captan		10 (4.54)
Carbamic acid, ethyl ester	Ethyl carbamate (Urethan)	100 (45.4)
Carbamic acid, methylnitroso-, ethyl ester	N-Nitroso-N-methylurethane	1 (0.454)
Carbamic chloride, dimethyl-	Dimethylcarbamoyl chloride	1 (0.454)
Carbamide, thio-	Thiourea	10 (4.54)
Carbamimidoselenoic acid	Selenourea	1000 (454)
Carbamothioic acid, bis (1-methylethyl)-, S-(2,3-dichloro-2-propenyl) ester	Diallate	100 (45.4)
Carbaryl*		100 (45.4)
Carbofuran*		10 (4.54)
Carbon bisulfide*	Carbon disulfide*	100 (45.4)
Carbon disulfide*	Carbon bisulfide*	100 (45.4)
Carbonic acid, dithallium (1+)	Thallium(I) carbonate	100 (45.4)
Carbonic dichloride	Phosgene*	10 (4.54)
Carbonic difluoride	Carbon oxyfluoride	1000 (454)
Carbonochloridic acid, methyl ester	Methyl chlorocarbonate*	1000 (454)
	Methyl chloroformate *	
Carbon oxyfluoride	Carbonic difluoride	1000 (454)
Carbon tetrachloride*	Methane, tetrachloro-	10 (4.54)
Chloral	Acetaldehyde, trichloro-	5000 (2270)
Chlorambucil	Benzenebutanoic acid, 4-[bis(2-chloroethyl)amino]-	10 (4.54)
Chlordane*	Chlordane, technical*	1 (0.454)
	4,7-Methano-1H-indene, 1,2,4,5,6,7,8,8-octachloro-2,3,3a,4,7,7a-hexahydro-	
	Chlordane, alpha & gamma isomers	
Chlordane, alpha & gamma isomers	Chlordane, technical	1 (0.454)
	Chlordane*	
	4,7-Methano-1H-indene, 1,2,4,5,6,7,8,8-octachloro-2,3,3a,4,7,7a-hexahydro-	
Chlordane, technical*	Chlordane*	1 (0.454)
	4,7-Methano-1H-indene, 1,2,4,5,6,7,8,8-octachloro-2,3,3a,4,7,7a-hexahydro-	
	Chlordane, alpha & gamma isomers	
Chlorine*		10 (4.54)
Chlornaphazine	Naphthylamine, N,N'-bis (2-chloroethyl)-	100 (45.4)

Hazardous Substances	Synonyms	Reportable Quantity (RQ) Pounds (Kilograms)
Chloroacetaldehyde	Acetaldehyde, chloro-	1000 (454)
p-Chloroaniline	Benzenamine, 4-chloro-	1000 (454)
Chlorobenzene*	Benzene, chloro-	100 (45.4)
Chlorobenzilate	Benzeneacetic acid, 4-chloro-alpha-(4-chlorophenyl)-alpha-hydroxy-, ethyl ester	10 (4.54)
4-Chloro-m-cresol	p-Chloro-m-cresol	5000 (2270)
	Phenol, 4-chloro-3-methyl-	
p-Chloro-m-cresol	Phenol, 4-chloro-3-methyl-	5000 (2270)
	4-Chloro-m-cresol	
Chlorodibromomethane		100 (45.4)
Chloroethane	Ethyl chloride @	100 (45.4)
2-Chloroethyl vinyl ether	Ethene, 2-chloroethoxy-	1000 (454)
Chloroform*	Methane, trichloro-	10 (4.54)
Chloromethane	Methane, chloro	100 (45.4)
	Methyl chloride*	
Chloromethyl methyl ether	Methane, chloromethoxy-	1 (0.454)
	Methylchloromethyl ether @	
beta-Chloronaphthalene	Naphthalene, 2-chloro-	5000 (2270)
	2-Chloronaphthalene	
2-Chloronaphthalene	beta-Chloronaphthalene	5000 (2270)
	Naphthalene, 2-chloro-	
2-Chlorophenol	o-Chlorophenol	100 (45.4)
	Phenol, 2-chloro-	
o-Chlorophenol	Phenol, 2-chloro-	100 (45.4)
	2-Chlorophenol	
4-Chlorophenyl phenyl ether		5000 (2270)
1-(o-Chlorophenyl)thiourea	Thiourea, (2-chlorophenyl)-	100 (45.4)
3-Chloropropionitrile	Propanenitrile, 3-chloro-	1000 (454)
Chlorosulfonic acid*		1000 (454)
4-Chloro-o-toluidine, hydrochloride	Benzenamine, 4-chloro-2-methyl hydrochloride	100 (45.4)
Chlorpyrifos*		1 (0.454)
Chromic acetate		1000 (454)
Chromic acid*		10 (4.54)
Chromic acid H2CrO4, calcium salt	Calcium chromate	10 (4.54)
Chromic sulfate		1000 (454)
Chromium ¢		5000 (2270)
Chromous chloride		1000 (454)
Chrysene	1,2-Benzphenanthrene	100 (45.4)
Cobaltous bromide		1000 (454)
Cobaltous formate		1000 (454)
Cobaltous sulfamate		1000 (454)
Coke Oven Emissions		1 (0.454)
Copper ¢		5000 (2270)
Copper chloride @	Cupric chloride	10 (4.54)
Copper cyanide*	Copper cyanide CuCN	10 (4.54)
Copper cyanide CuCN	Copper cyanide*	10 (4.54)
Coumaphos*		10 (4.54)
Creosote		1 (0.454)
Cresol(s)*	Cresylic acid	1000 (454)
	Phenol, methyl-	
m-Cresol	m-Cresylic acid	
o-Cresol	o-Cresylic acid	
p-Cresol	p-Cresylic acid	
Cresylic acid	Cresols*	1000 (454)
	Phenol, methyl-	
m-Cresol	m-Cresylic acid	
o-Cresol	o-Cresylic acid	
p-Cresol	p-Cresylic acid	
Crotonaldehyde*	2-Butenal	100 (45.4)
Cumene	Benzene, 1-methylethyl-	5000 (2270)
Cumene hydroperoxide @	alpha,alpha-Dimethylbenzylhydroperoxide	10 (4.54)
	Hydroperoxide, 1-methyl-1-phenylethyl-	
Cupric acetate		100 (45.4)
Cupric acetoarsenite*		1 (0.454)
Cupric chloride	Copper chloride@	10 (4.54)
Cupric nitrate*		100 (45.4)
Cupric oxalate		100 (45.4)
Cupric sulfate		10 (4.54)
Cupric sulfate ammoniated		100 (45.4)
Cupric tartrate		100 (45.4)
Cyanides (soluble cyanide salts), not elsewhere specified*		10 (4.54)
Cyanogen*	Ethanedinitrile	100 (45.4)

264

Hazardous Substances	Synonyms	Reportable Quantity (RQ) Pounds (Kilograms)
Cyanogen bromide*	Cyanogen bromide (CN)Br	1000 (454)
Cyanogen bromide (CN)Br	Cyanogen bromide*	1000 (454)
Cyanogen chloride*	Cyanogen Chloride (CN)Cl	10 (4.54)
Cyanogen chloride (CN)Cl	Cyanogen chloride*	10 (4.54)
2,5-Cyclohexadiene-1,4-dione	p-Benzoquinone	10 (4.54)
Cyclohexane*	Benzene, hexahydro-	1000 (454)
Cyclohexane, 1,2,3,4,5,6-hexachloro-, (1alpha,2alpha,3beta,4alpha,5alpha,6beta)-	gamma-BHC Hexachlorocyclohexane(gamma isomer) Lindane*	1 (0.454)
Cyclohexanone		5000 (2270)
2-Cyclohexyl-4,6-dinitrophenol	Phenol,2-cyclohexyl-4,6-dinitro-	100 (45.4)
1,3-Cyclopentadiene, 1,2,3,4,5,5-hexachloro-	Hexachlorocyclopentadiene*	10 (4.54)
Cyclophosphamide	2H-1,3,2-Oxazaphosphorin, 2-amine,N,N-bis((2-chloroethyl) tetrahydro-)2-oxide	10 (4.54)
2,4-D Acid	2,4-D*, salts and esters Acetic acid (2,4-dichlorophenoxy)-	100 (45.4)
2,4-D Ester		100 (45.4)
2,4-D*, salts and esters	2,4-D Acid Acetic acid (2,4-dichloro-phenoxy)-	100 (45.4)
Daunomycin	5,12-Naphthacenedione, 8-acetyl-10-[3-amino,2,3,6-trideoxy-alpha-L-lyxo-hexopyranosyl(oxy)-7,8,9,10-tetrahydro-6,8,11-trihydroxy-1-methoxy-(8S-cis)-	10 (4.54)
DDD	Benzene,1,1'-(2,2-dichloroethylidene)bis[4-chloro TDE* 4,4'-DDD	1 (0.454)
4,4'-DDD	DDD Dichlorodiphenyl dichloroethane TDE*	1 (0.454)
DDE	4,4' DDE	1 (0.454)
4,4' DDE	DDE	1 (0.454)
DDT*	Benzene, 1,1'-(2,2,2-trichloroethylidene)bis[4-chloro- 4,4'-DDT	1 (0.454)
4,4' DDT	DDT* Benzene,1,1'-(2,2,2-trichloroethylidene)bis[4-chloro-	1 (0.454)
Diallate	Carbamothioic acid, bis (1-methylethyl)-, S-(2,3-dichloro-2-propenyl) ester	100 (45.4)
Diamine	Hydrazine*	1 (0.454)
Diazinon*		1 (0.454)
Dibenz[a,h]anthracene	Dibenzo[a,h]anthracene 1,2:5,6-Dibenzanthracene	1 (0.454)
1,2:5,6-Dibenzanthracene	Dibenz[a,h]anthracene Dibenzo[a,h]anthracene	1 (0.454)
Dibenzo[a,h]anthracene	Dibenz[a,h]anthracene 1,2:5,6-Dibenzanthracene	1 (0.454)
Dibenz[a,i]pyrene	Bezo [rst]pentaphene	10 (4.54)
1,2-Dibromo-3-chloropropane	Propane, 1,2-dibromo-3-chloro-	1 (0.454)
Dibutyl phthalate	Di-n-butyl phthalate n-Butyl phthalate* 1,2-Benzenedicarboxylic acid, dibutyl ester	10 (4.54)
Di-n-butylphthalate	Dibutyl phthalate n-butyl phthalate* 1,2-Benzenedicarboxylic acid, dibutyl ester	10 (4.54)
Dicamba		1000 (454)
Dichlobenil		100 (45.4)
Dichlone		1 (0.454)
Dichlorobenzene		100 (45.4)
1,2-Dichlorobenzene	Benzene, 1,2-dichloro- o-Dichlorobenzene*	100 (45.4)
1,3-Dichlorobenzene	Benzene, 1,3-dichloro- m-Dichlorobenzene	100 (45.4)
1,4-Dichlorobenzene	Benzene, 1,4-dichloro- p-Dichlorobenzene*	100 (45.4)
m-Dichlorobenzene	Benzene, 1,3-dichloro- 1,3-Dichlorobenzene	100 (45.4)
o-Dichlorobenzene*	Benzene, 1,2-dichloro- 1,2-Dichlorobenzene	100 (45.4)
p-Dichlorobenzene*	Benzene, 1,4-dichloro- 1,4-Dichlorobenzene	100 (45.4)
3,3'-Dichlorobenzidine	(1,1'-Biphenyl)-4,4'diamine,3,3' dichloro-	1 (0.454)
Dichlorobromomethane		5000 (2270)
1,4-Dichloro-2-butene	2-Butene, 1,4-dichloro-	1 (0.454)

Hazardous Substances	Synonyms	Reportable Quantity (RQ) Pounds (Kilograms)
Dichlorodifluoromethane*	Methane, dichlorodifluoro-	5000 (2270)
1,1-Dichloroethane	Ethane, 1,1-dichloro-	1000 (454)
	Ethylidene dichloride	
1,2-Dichloroethane	Ethane, 1,2-dichloro-	100 (45.4)
	Ethylene dichloride*	
1,1-Dichloroethylene	Ethene, 1,1-dichloro*	100 (45.4)
	Vinylidene chloride*	
1,2-Dichloroethylene	Ethene, 1,2-dichloro-(E)	1000 (454)
1,3-Dichloropropene	1-Propene, 1,3-dichloro-	100 (45.4)
Dichloroethyl ether	Bis (2-chloroethyl) ether	10 (4.54)
	Ethane, 1,1'-oxybis(2-chloro-	
Dichloroisopropyl-ether	Propane,2,2'-oxybis [2-chloro-	1000 (454)
Dichloromethane@	Methane, dichloro-	1000 (454)
	Methylene chloride*	
Dichloromethoxy ethane	Bis(2-chloroethoxy)methane	1000 (454)
	Ethane, 1,1'-[methylenebis(oxy)]bis(2-chloro-	
Dichloromethyl ether	Methane, oxybis(chloro-	1 (0.454)
2,4-Dichlorophenol	Phenol, 2,4-dichloro-	100 (45.4)
2,6-Dichlorophenol	Phenol, 2,6-dichloro-	100 (45.4)
Dichlorophenylarsine	Phenyl dichloroarsine@	1 (0.454)
	Arsonous dichloride, phenyl-	
Dichloropropane*		1000 (454)
1,1-Dichloropropane		
1,3-Dichloropropane		
1,2-Dichloropropane	Propylene dichloride*	1000 (454)
	Propane, 1,2-dichloro-	
Dichloropropane - Dichloropropene (mixture)		100 (45.4)
Dichloropropene*		100 (45.4)
2,3-Dichloropropene		
2,2-Dichloropropionic acid*		5000 (2270)
Dichlorvos*		10 (4.54)
Dicofol		10 (4.54)
Dieldrin*	2,7:3,6-Dimethanonaphth[2,3-b]oxirene,3,4,5,6,9,9-hexachloro-1a,2,2a,3,6,6a,7,7a-octahydro-, (1alpha,2beta,2aalpha,3beta,6beta,6aalpha,7beta,7aalpha)-	1 (0.454)
1,2:3,4-Diepoxybutane	2,2'-Bioxirane	10 (4.54)
Diethylamine*		1000 (454)
Diethylarsine	Arsine, diethyl-	1 (0.454)
1,4-Diethylenedioxide	1,4-Dioxane	100 (45.4)
Diethylhexyl phthalate	1,2-Benzenedicarbolic acid, [bis(2-ethylhexyl)] ester	100 (45.4)
	Bis(2-ethylhexyl)phthalate	
N,N'-Diethylhydrazine	Hydrazine, 1,2-diethyl-	10 (4.54)
O,O-Diethyl S-methyl dithiophosphate	Phosphorodithioic acid, O'O>-diethylS-methyl ester	5000 (2270)
Diethyl-p-nitrophenyl phosphate	Phosphoric acid, diethyl p-nitrophenyl ester	100 (45.4)
Diethyl phthalate	1,2-Benzenedicarboxylic acid, diethyl ester	1000 (454)
O,O-Diethyl O-pyrazinyl phosphorothioate	Phosphorothioic acid, O,O-diethyl O-pyrazinyl ester	100 (45.4)
Diethylstilbestrol	Phenol, 4,4'-(1,2-diethyl-1,2-ethenediyl)bis-,(E)	1 (0.454)
Dihydrosafrole	Benzene, 1,2- methylenedioxy-4-propyl-	10 (4.54)
Diisopropyl fluorophosphate	Phosphorofluoridic acid, bis(1-methylethyl) ester	100 (45.4)
1,4,5,8-Dimethanonaphthalene,1,2,3,4,10,10-hexachloro-1,4,4a,5,8,8a-hexahydro,(1alpha,4alpha,4abeta,5abeta, 8beta,8abeta)-	Isodrin	1 (0.454)
1,4,5,8-Dimethanonaphthalene,1,2,3,4,10,10-10-hexachloro-1,4,4a,5,8,8a-hexahydro-, (1alpha,4alpha,4abeta,5alpha, 8alpha,8abeta)-	Aldrin*	1 (0.454)
	1,2,3,4,10-10-Hexachloro-1,4,4a,5,8,8a-hexahydro-1,4:5,8-endo,exo-dimethanonapthalene	
2,7:3,6-Dimethanonaphth[2,3-b]oxirene,3,4,5,6,9,9-hexachloro-1a,2,2a,3,6,6a,7,7a-octahydro-, (1aalpha,2beta,2abeta,3alpha, 6alpha,6abeta,7beta,7aalpha)-	Endrin*	1 (0.454)
	Endrin, and metabolites	
2,7:3,6-Dimethanonaphth[2,3-b]oxirene, 3,4,5,6,9,9-hexachloro-1a,2,2a,3,6,6a,7,7a-octahydro-,(1aalpha,2beta,2aalpha,3beta, 6beta,6aalpha,7beta,7aalpha)-	Dieldrin*	1 (0.454)
Dimethoate	Phosphorodithioic acid, O,O- dimethyl S-[2(methyl amino)-2-oxoethyl]ester	10 (4.54)
3,3'-Dimethoxybenzidine	(1,1'-Biphenyl)-4,4' diamine,3,3' dimethoxy-	10 (4.54)
Dimethylamine*	Methanamine, N-methyl-	1000 (454)
p-Dimethylaminoazobenzene	Benzenamine, N,N-dimethyl-4-(phenylazo)-	10 (4.54)
7,12-Dimethylbenz[a] anthracene	Benz[a]anthracene,7,12-dimethyl-	1 (0.454)
3,3'-Dimethylbenzidine	(1,1' Biphenyl)-4,4'-diamine,3,3'-dimethyl-	10 (4.54)

Hazardous Substances	Synonyms	Reportable Quantity (RQ) Pounds (Kilograms)
alpha,alpha-Dimethylbenzyl-hydroperoxide	Hydroperoxide,1-methyl-1-phenylethyl- Cumene hydroperoxide@	10 (4.54)
Dimethylcarbamoyl chloride	Carbamic chloride, dimethyl-	1 (0.454)
1,1-Dimethylhydrazine	Dimethylhydrazine, unsymmetrical @ Hydrazine, 1,1-dimethyl-	10 (4.54)
1,2-Dimethylhydrazine	Hydrazine, 1,2-dimethyl-	1 (0.454)
Dimethylhydrazine,unsymmetrical@	1,1-Dimethylhydrazine Hydrazine,1,1-dimethyl-	10 (4.54)
alpha,alpha-Dimethylphenethylamine	Benezeneethanamine, alpha,alpha-dimethyl-	5000 (2270)
2,4-Dimethylphenol	Phenol, 2,4-dimethyl-	100 (45.4)
Dimethyl phthalate	1,2-Benzenedicarboxylic acid, dimethyl ester	5000 (2270)
Dimethyl sulfate*	Sulfuric acid, dimethyl ester	100 (45.4)
Dinitrobenzene* (mixed)		100 (45.4)
m- Dinitrobenzene		
o- Dinitrobenzene		
p- Dinitrobenzene		
4,6-Dinitro-o-cresol and salts	Phenol,2-methyl-4,6-dinitro-	10 (4.54)
Dinitrophenol		10 (4.54)
2,5- Dinitrophenol		
2,6- Dinitrophenol		
2,4-Dinitrophenol	Phenol, 2,4-dinitro-	10 (4.54)
Dinitrotoluene		10 (4.54)
3,4-Dinitrotoluene		
2,4-Dinitrotoluene	Benzene, 1-methyl-2,4-dinitro-	10 (4.54)
2,6-Dinitrotoluene	Benzene, 2-methyl-1,3-dinitro-	100 (45.4)
Dinoseb	Phenol,2-(1-methylpropyl)-4,6-dinitro	1000 (454)
Di-n-octyl phthalate	1,2-Benzenedicarboxylic acid, dioctyl ester	5000 (2270)
1,4-Dioxane	1,4-Diethylene dioxide	100 (45.4)t
1,2-Diphenylhydrazine	Hydrazine, 1,2-diphenyl-	10 (4.54)
Diphosphoramide, octamethyl-	Octamethylpyrophosphoramide	100 (45.4)
Diphosphoric acid,tetraethyl ester	Tetraethyl pyrophosphate*	10 (4.54)
Dipropylamine	1-Propanamine, N-propyl-	5000 (2270)
Di-n-propylnitrosamine	1-Propanamine, N-nitroso-N-propyl	10 (4.54)
Diquat		1000 (454)
Disulfoton*	Phosphorodithioic acid, O,O-diethyl S-[2-(ethylthio) ethyl]ester	1 (0.454)
Dithiobiuret	Thioimidodicarbonic diamide[(H2N)C(S)]2NH	100 (45.4)
Diuron		100 (45.4)
Dodecylbenzenesulfonic acid*		1000 (454)
Endosulfan*	6-9-Methano-2,4,3-benzodioxathiepin, 6,7,8,9,10,10-hexachloro-1,5,5a,6,9,9a-hexahydro-, 3-oxide.	1 (0.454)
alpha - Endosulfan		1 (0.454)
beta - Endosulfan		1 (0.454)
Endosulfan sulfate		1 (0.454)
Endothall	7-Oxabicyclo[2,2,1]heptane-2,3-dicarboxylic acid	1000 (454)
Endrin*	2,7:3,6-Dimethanonaphth[2,3-b]oxirene, 3,4,5,6,9,9-hexachloro-1a,2,2a,3,6,6a,7,7a-octa-hydro-,(1aalpha,2beta,2abeta, 3alpha,6alpha,6abeta,7beta,7aalpha)-	1 (0.454)
Endrin, & metabolites	Endrin, & metabolites Endrin 2,7:3,6-Dimethanonaphth[2,3-b]oxirene, 3,4,5,6,9,9-hexachloro-1a,2,2a,3,6,6a,7,7a oct-hydro-, (1aalpha,2beta,2abeta,3alpha,6alpha, 6abeta,7beta,7aalpha)-	1 (0.454)
Endrin aldehyde		1 (0.454)
Epichlorohydrin*	Oxirane, (chloromethyl)-	100 (45.4)
Epinephrine	1,2-Benzenediol, 4- [1-hydroxy-2-(methylamino)ethyl]-	1000 (454)
Ethanal	Acetaldehyde*	1000 (454)
Ethanamine, N-ethyl-N-nitroso-	N-Nitrosodiethylamine	1 (0.454)
Ethane, 1,2-dibromo-	Ethylene dibromide*	1 (0.454)
Ethane, 1,1-dichloro-	Ethylidene dichloride 1,1-Dichloroethane	1000 (454)
Ethane, 1,2-dichloro-	Ethylene dichloride* 1,2-Dichloroethane	100 (45.4)
Ethane, hexachloro-	Hexachloroethane*	100 (45.4)
Ethane, 1,1'-[methylenebis(oxy)]bis(2-chloro-	Bis(2-chloroethoxy)methane Dichloromethoxy ethane	1000 (454)
Ethane, 1,1'-oxybis-	Ethyl ether*	100 (45.4)
Ethane, 1,1'-oxybis(2-chloro-	Bis (2-chloroethyl) ether Dichloroethyl ether	10 (4.54)
Ethane, pentachloro-	Pentachloroethane	10 (4.54)
Ethane, 1,1,1,2-tetrachloro-	1,1,1,2-Tetrachloroethane- Tetrachloroethane@	100 (45.4)
Ethane, 1,1,2,2-tetrachloro-	1,1,2,2-Tetrachloroethane- Tetrachloroethane@	100 (45.4)
Ethane, 1,1,2-trichloro-	1,1,2-Trichloroethane	100 (45.4)
Ethane, 1,1,1-trichloro-	Methyl chloroform 1,1,1-Trichloroethane*	1000 (454)

Hazardous Substances	Synonyms	Reportable Quantity (RQ) Pounds (Kilograms)
1,2-Ethanediamine, N,N-dimethyl-N'-2-pyridinyl-N'-(2-thienyl-methyl)-	Methapyrilene	5000 (2270)
Ethanedinitrile	Cyanogen*	100 (45.4)
Ethanenitrile	Acetonitrile*	5000 (2270)
Ethanethiobamide	Thioacetamide	10 (4.54)
Ethanimidothioic acid, N-[[(methylamino)carbonyl] oxy]-, methyl ester	Methomyl	100 (45.4)
Ethanol, 2-ethoxy-	Ethylene glycol monoethyl ether*	1000 (454)
Ethanol, 2,2'-(nitrosoimino)bis-	N-Nitrosodiethanolamine	1 (0.454)
Ethanone, 1-phenyl-	Acetophenone	5000 (2270)
Ethanoyl chloride	Acetyl chloride*	5000 (2270)
Ethene, chloro-	Vinyl chloride*	1 (0.454)
Ethene,2-chloroethoxy-	2-Chloroethyl vinyl ether	1000 (454)
Ethene, 1,1-dichloro-	Vinylidene chloride*	100 (45.4)
	1,1-Dichloroethylene	
Ethene, 1,2-dichloro-(E)	1,2-Dichloroethylene	1000 (454)
Ethene, tetrachloro-	Perchloroethylene	100 (45.4)
	Tetrachloroethene	
	Tetrachloroethylene	
Ethene, trichloro-	Trichloroethene	100 (45.4)
	Trichloroethylene	
Ethion*		10 (4.54)
Ethyl acetate*	Acetic acid, ethyl ester	5000 (2270)
Ethyl acrylate*	2-Propenoicacid, ethyl ester	1000 (454)
Ethylbenzene*		1000 (454)
Ethyl carbamate (Urethan)	Carbamic acid, ethyl ester	100 (45.4)
Ethyl chloride @	Chloroethane	100 (45.4)
Ethyl cyanide	Propanenitrile	10 (4.54)
Ethylene dibromide*	Ethane, 1,2-dibromo-	1 (0.454)
Ethylene dichloride*	1,2-Dichloroethane	100 (45.4)
	Ethane, 1,2-dichloro-	
Ethylene glycol monoethyl ether*	Ethanol, 2-ethoxy	1000 (454)
Ethylene imine@	Aziridine	1 (0.454)
	Ethylenimine	
Ethylene oxide*	Oxirane	10 (4.54)
Ethylenebisdithiocarbamic acid	Ethylenebisdithiocarbamic acid, salts and esters	5000 (2270)
Ethylenebisdithiocarbamic acid, salts and esters	Ethylenebisdithiocarbamic acid	5000 (2270)
Ethylenediamine*		5000 (2270)
Ethylenediamine tetraacetic acid (EDTA)		5000 (2270)
Ethylenethiourea	2-Imidazolidinethione	10 (4.54)
Ethylenimine	Aziridine-	1 (0.454)
	Ethylene imine@	
Ethyl ether*	Ethane, 1,1'-oxybis-	100 (45.4)
Ethylidene dichloride	Ethane, 1,1-dichloro-	1000 (454)
	1,1-Dichloroethane	
Ethyl methacrylate	2-Propenoic acid, 2-methyl-, ethyl ester	1000 (454)
Ethyl methanesulfonate	Methanesulfonic acid, ethyl ester	1 (0.454)
Ethyl methyl ketone @	2-Butanone	5000 (2270)
	Methyl ethyl ketone(MEK)*	
Famphur	Phosphorothioic acid, O,[4-[(dimethylamino)-sulfonyl]phenyl] O,O-dimethylester	1000 (454)
Ferric ammonium citrate		1000 (454)
Ferric ammonium oxalate		1000 (454)
Ferric chloride		1000 (454)
Ferric fluoride		100 (45.4)
Ferric nitrate*		1000 (454)
Ferric sulfate		1000 (454)
Ferrous ammonium sulfate		1000 (454)
Ferrous chloride*		100 (45.4)
Ferrous sulfate		1000 (454)
Fluoranthene	Benzo[j,k]fluorene	100 (45.4)
Fluorene		5000 (2270)
Fluorine*		10 (4.54)
Fluoroacetamide	Acetamide, 2-fluoro-	100 (45.4)
Fluoroacetic acid, sodium salt	Acetic acid, fluoro-, sodium salt	10 (4.54)
Formaldehyde*	Methylene oxide	100 (45.4)
Formic acid*	Methanoic acid	5000 (2270)
Fulminic acid, mercury(2+)salt	Mercury fulminate	10 (4.54)
Fumaric acid		5000 (2270)
Furan*	Furfuran	100 (45.4)
Furan, tetrahydro-	Tetrahydrofuran*	1000 (454)
2-Furancarboxaldehyde	Furfural*	5000 (2270)

Hazardous Substances	Synonyms	Reportable Quantity (RQ) Pounds (Kilograms)
2,5-Furandione	Maleic anhydride*	5000 (2270)
Furfural*	2-Furancarboxaldehyde	5000 (2270)
Furfuran	Furan*	100 (45.4)
Glucopyranose, 2-deoxy-2-(3-methyl-3-nitrosoureido)-	Streptozotocin	1 (0.454)
D-Glucose, 2-deoxy-2-[[(methylnitrosoamino)-carbonyl]amino]-	D-Glucose, 2-deoxy-2[[(methylnitrosoamino)-carbonyl]amino]- Streptozotocin Glucopyranose, 2-deoxy-2-(3-methyl-3-nitrosoureido)-	1 (0.454)
Glycidylaldehyde	Oxiranecarboxaldehyde	10 (4.54)
Guanidine, N-methyl-N'-nitro-N-nitroso-	MNNG	10 (4.54)
Guthion*	Azinphos methyl @	1 (0.454)
Heptachlor	4,7-Methano-1H-indene,1,4,5,6,7,8,8-heptachloro-3a,4,7,7a-tetrahydro-	1 (0.454)
Heptachlor epoxide		1 (0.454)
Hexachlorobenzene	Benzene, hexachloro-	10 (4.54)
Hexachlorobutadiene	1,3-Butadiene, 1,1,2,3,4,4- hexachloro-	1 (0.454)
Hexachlorocyclohexane (gamma isomer)	gamma - BHC Lindane* Cyclohexane,1,2,3,4,5,6-hexachloro-, (1alpha,2alpha,3beta,4alpha,5alpha,6beta)-	1 (0.454)
Hexachlorocyclopentadiene*	1,3-Cyclopentadiene, 1,2,3,4,5,5-hexachloro-	10 (4.54)
Hexachloroethane*	Ethane, hexachloro-	100 (45.4)
1,2,3,4,10-10-Hexachloro-1,4,4a,5,8,8a-hexahydro-1,4:5,8-endo,exo-dimethanonaphthalene	Aldrin* 1,4,5,8-Dimethanonaphthalene,1,2,3,4,10,10-hexachloro-1,4,4a,5,8,8a-hexahydro-, (1alpha,4alpha,4abeta,5alpha,8alpha,8abeta)-	1 (0.454)
Hexachlorophene	Phenol,2,2'-methylenebis[3,4,6-trichloro	100 (45.4)
Hexachloropropene	1-Propene, 1,1,2,3,3,3-hexachloro-	1000 (454)
Hexaethyl tetraphosphate*	Tetraphosphoric acid, hexaethyl ester	100 (45.4)
2,4-(1H,3H)-Pyrimidinedione, 5-[bis(2-chloroethyl) amino]-	Uracil mustard	10 (4.54)
Hydrazine*	Diamine	1 (0.454)
Hydrazine, 1,2-diethyl-	N,N'-Diethylhydrazine	10 (4.54)
Hydrazine, 1,1-dimethyl-	1,1-Dimethylhydrazine Dimethylhydrazine, unsymmetrical @	10 (4.54)
Hydrazine, 1,2-dimethyl-	1,2-Dimethylhydrazine	1 (0.454)
Hydrazine, 1,2-diphenyl-	1,2-Diphenylhydrazine	10 (4.54)
Hydrazine, methyl-	Methyl hydrazine*	10 (4.54)
Hydrazinecarbothioamide	Thiosemicarbazide	100 (45.4)
Hydrochloric acid*	Hydrogen chloride*	5000 (2270)
Hydrocyanic acid*	Hydrogen cyanide	10 (4.54)
Hydrofluoric acid*	Hydrogen fluoride*	100 (45.4)
Hydrogen chloride*	Hydrochloric acid*	5000 (2270)
Hydrogen cyanide*	Hydrocyanic acid*	10 (4.54)
Hydrogen fluoride*	Hydrofluoric acid*	100 (45.4)
Hydrogen phosphide	Phosphine*	100 (45.4)
Hydrogen sulfide*	Hydrogen sulfide H2S	100 (45.4)
Hydrogen sulfide H2S	Hydrogen sulfide	100 (45.4)
Hydroperoxide, 1-methyl-1-phenylethyl-	alpha,alpha-Dimethylbenzylhydroperoxide Cumene hydroperoxide @	10 (4.54)
2-Imidazolidinethione	Ethylenethiourea	10 (4.54)
Indeno(1,2,3-cd)pyrene	1,10-(1,2-Phenylene)pyrene	100 (45.4)
1,3-Isobenzofurandione	Phthalic anhydride	5000 (2270)
Isobutyl alcohol	1-Propanol, 2-methyl-	5000 (2270)
Isodrin	1,4,5,8-Dimethanonaphthalene, 1,2,3,4,10,10-hexachloro-1,4,4a,5,8,8a-hexahydro-,(1alpha,4alpha,4abeta,5beta,8beta,8abeta)-	1 (0.454)
Isophorone		5000 (2270)
Isoprene*		100 (45.4)
Isopropanolamine dodecylbenzene sulfonate		1000 (454)
Isosafrole	1,3-Benzodioxole,5-(-1propenyl)-	100 (45.4)
3(2H)-Isoxazolone, 5-(aminomethyl)-	5-(Aminomethyl)-3-isoxazolol Muscimol	1000 (454)
Kepone	1,3,4-Metheno-2H-cyclobutal[cd]-pentalen-2-one,1,1a,3,3a,4,5,5,5a,5b, 6-decachloroc-tahydro-	1 (0.454)
Lasiocarpine	2-Butenoic acid, 2-methyl-,7[[2,3-dihydroxy-2-(1-methoxyethyl)-3-methyl-1-oxobutoxy]methyl]-2,3,5,7a-tetrahydro-1H-pyrrolizin-1-yl ester,[1S-[1alpha(Z),7(2S*,3R*),7aalpha]]-	10 (4.54)
Lead ¢		1 (0.454)
Lead acetate	Acetic acid, lead salt	5000 (2270)
Lead arsenate*		1 (0.454)
Lead,bis(acetato-O)tetrahydroxytri	Lead subacetate	100 (45.4)
Lead chloride*		100 (45.4)
Lead fluoborate*		100 (45.4)
Lead fluoride*		100 (45.4)

Hazardous Substances	Synonyms	Reportable Quantity (RQ) Pounds (Kilograms)
Lead Iodide		100 (45.4)
Lead nitrate*		100 (45.4)
Lead phosphate	Phosphoric acid, lead(2+)salt(2:3)	1 (0.454)
Lead stearate		5000 (2270)
Lead subacetate	Lead,bis(acetato-O)tetrahydroxytri	100 (45.4)
Lead sulfate*		100 (45.4)
Lead sulfide		5000 (2270)
Lead thiocyanate		100 (45.4)
Lindane*	gamma - BHC Hexachlorocyclohexane (gamma isomer) Cyclohexene, 1,2,3,4,5,6-hexachloro-, (1alpha,2alpha,3beta,4alpha,5alpha,6beta)-	1 (0.454)
Lithium chromate		10 (4.54)
Malathion*		100 (45.4)
Maleic acid*		5000 (2270)
Maleic anhydride*	2,5-Furandione	5000 (2270)
Maleic hydrazide	3,6-Pyridazinedione, 1,2-dihydro-	5000 (2270)
Malononitrile	Propanedinitrile	1000 (454)
Melphalan	L-Phenylalenine, 4-[bis(2-chloroethyl)amino]	1 (0.454)
Mercaptodimethur		10 (4.54)
Mercuric cyanide*		1 (0.454)
Mercuric nitrate*		10 (4.54)
Mercuric sulfate*		10 (4.54)
Mercuric thiocyanate		10 (4.54)
Mercurous nitrate*		10 (4.54)
Mercury*		1 (0.454)
Mercury, (acetato-O)phenyl-	Phenylmercuric acetate	100 (45.4)
Mercury fulminate	Fulminic acid, mercury(2+)salt	10 (4.54)
Methacrylonitrile	2-Propenenitrile, 2-methyl-	1000 (454)
Methanamine, N-methyl-	Dimethylamine*	1000 (454)
Methanamine, N-methyl-N-nitroso	N-Nitrosodimethylamine	10 (4.54)
Methane, bromo-	Methyl bromide*	1000 (454)
Methane, chloro-	Chloromethane Methyl chloride*	100 (45.4)
Methane, chloromethoxy-	Chloromethyl methyl ether Methylchloromethyl ether @	1 (0.454)
Methane, dibromo-	Methylene bromide	1000 (454)
Methane, dichloro-	Methylene chloride* Dichloromethane@	1000 (454)
Methane, dichlorodifluoro-	Dichlorodifluoromethane*	5000 (2270)
Methane, iodo-	Methyl iodide	100 (45.4)
Methane, isocyanato-	Methyl isocyanate*	1 (0.454)
Methane, oxybis(chloro-	Dichloromethyl ether	1 (0.454)
Methane, tetrachloro-	Carbon tetrachloride*	10 (4.54)
Methane, tetranitro-	Tetranitromethane*	10 (4.54)
Methane, tribromo-	Bromoform	100 (45.4)
Methane, trichloro-	Chloroform*	10 (4.54)
Methane, trichlorofluoro-	Trichloromonofluoromethane	5000 (2270)
Methenesulfenyl chloride, trichloro	Perchloromethyl mercaptan @ Trichloromethane sulfenyl chloride	100 (45.4)
Methanesulfonic acid, ethyl ester	Ethyl methanesulfonate	1 (0.454)
Methanethiol	Methyl mercaptan* Thiomethanol	100 (45.4)
6,9-Methano-2,4,3-benzodioxathiepin, 6,7,8,9,10,10-hexachloro-1,5,5a,6,9,9a-hexahydro-, 3-oxide	Endosulfan*	1 (0.454)
Methanoic acid	Formic acid*	5000 (2270)
4,7-Methano-1H-indene, 1,4,5,6,7,8,8-heptachloro-3a,4,7,7a-tetrahydro-	Heptachlor	1 (0.454)
4,7-Methano-1H-indene,1,4,5,6,7,8,8-octachloro-2,3,3a,4,7,7a-hexahydro-	Chlordane* Chlordane, technical* Chlordane,alpha & gamma isomers	1 (0.454)
Methanol*	Methyl alcohol*	5000 (2270)
Methapyrilene	1,2-Ethanediamine,N-N-dimethyl-N'-2-pyridinyl-N'-(2-thienylmethyl)-	5000 (2270)
1,3,4-Metheno-2H-cyclobutal[cd]-pentalen-2-one, 1,1a,3,3a,4,5,5,5a,5b,6-decachloroctahydro-	Kepone*	1 (0.454)
Methomyl	Ethanimidothioic acid,N-[[(methylamino)carbonyl]oxy]-, methyl ester	100 (45.4)
Methoxychlor	Benzene, 1,1'-(2,2,2-trichloroethylidene) bis[4-methoxy-	1 (0.454)
Methyl alcohol*	Methanol*	5000 (2270)
Methylamine @	Monomethylamine	100 (45.4)
Methyl bromide*	Methane, bromo-	1000 (454)
1-Methylbutadiene	1,3-Pentadiene	100 (45.4)

Hazardous Substances	Synonyms	Reportable Quantity (RQ) Pounds (Kilograms)
Methyl chloride*	Chloromethane	100 (45.4)
	Methane, chloro-	
Methyl chlorocarbonate*	Carbonochloridic acid, methyl ester	1000 (414)
	Methyl chloroformate *	
Methyl chloroform*	1,1,1-Trichloroethane*	1000 (454)
	Ethane, 1,1,1-trichloro-	
Methyl chloroformate *	Carbonochloridic acid, methyl ester	1000 (454)
	Methyl chlorocarbonate*	
Methylchloromethyl ether @	Chloromethyl methyl ether	1 (0.454)
	Methene, chloromethoxy-	
3-Methylcholanthrene	Benz[j]aceanthrylene, 1,2-dihydro-3-methyl-	10 (4.54)
4,4'-Methylenebis(2-chloroaniline)	Benzenamine, 4,4'-methylenebis(2-chloro-	10 (4.54)
Methylene bromide	Methane, dibromo-	1000 (454)
Methylene chloride*	Methane, dichloro-	1000 (454)
	Dichloromethane@	
Methylene oxide	Formaldehyde*	100 (45.4)
Methyl ethyl ketone(MEK)*	2-Butanone	5000 (2270)
	Ethyl methyl ketone @	
Methyl ethyl ketone peroxide*	2-Butanone peroxide	10 (4.54)
Methyl hydrazine*	Hydrazine, methyl-	10 (4.54)
Methyl iodide	Methane, iodo-	100 (45.4)
Methyl isobutyl ketone	4-Methyl-2-pentanone	5000 (2270)
Methyl isocyanate*	Methane, isocynato-	1 (0.454)
2-Methyllactonitrile	Acetone cyanohydrin*	10 (4.54)
	Propanenitrile, 2-hydroxy-2- methyl-	
Methyl mercaptan*	Methonethiol	100 (45.4)
	Thiomethanol	
Methyl methacrylate*	2-Propenoic acid, 2-methyl-, methylester	1000 (454)
Methyl parathion*	Phosphorothioic acid, O,O-dimethyl O-(4-nitrophenyl) ester	100 (45.4)
4-Methyl-2-pentanone	Methyl isobutyl ketone	5000 (2270)
Methylthiouracil	4(1H)-Pyrimidinone, 2,3-dihydro-6-methyl-2-thioxo-	10 (4.54)
Mevinphos*		10 (4.54)
Mexacarbate*		1000 (454)
Mitomycin C	Azirino[2',3':3,4]pyrrolo [1,2-a]indole-4,7-dione,6-amino-8-[[(amino-carbonyl)oxy]methyl]-1,1a,2,8,8a,8b-hexahydro-8a-methoxy-5-methyl-, [1aS-(1aalpha,8beta,8aalpha,8alpha]-	10 (4.54)
MNNG	Guanidine,N-methyl-N'-nitro-N-nitroso-	10 (4.54)
Monoethylamine*		100 (45.4)
Monomethylamine	Methylamine @	100 (45.4)
Muscimol	5-(Aminomethyl)-3-isoxazolol	1000 (454)
	3(2H)-isoxazolone, 5-(aminomethyl)-	
Naled		10 (4.54)
5,12-Naphthacenedione, 8-acetyl-10-[3-amino-2,3,6-trideoxy-alpha-L-lyxo-hexopyranosyl)oxy]-7,8,9,10-tetrahydro-6,8,11-trihydroxy-1- methoxy-,(8S-cis)-	Daunomycin	10 (4.54)
Naphthalenamine,N,N-bis(2-chloroethyl)-	Chlornaphazine	100 (45.4)
Naphthalene*		100 (45.4)
Naphthalene, 2-chloro-	beta-Chloronaphthalene	5000 (2270)
	2-Chloronaphthalene	
1,4-Naphthalenedione	1,4-Naphthoquinone	5000 (2270)
2,7-Naphthalenedisulfonic acid,3,3'-[(3,3'-dimethyl- (1,1'-biphenyl)- 4,4'-diyl)-bis(azo)]bis(5-amino-4-hydroxy)-tetrasodium salt.	Trypan blue	10 (4.54)
Naphthenic acid		100 (45.4)
1,4-Naphthoquinone	1,4-Naphthalenedione	5000 (2270)
alpha-Naphthylamine	1-Naphthylamine	100 (45.4)
beta-Naphthylamine	2-Naphthylamine	1 (0.454)
1-Naphthylamine	alpha-Naphthylamine	100 (45.4)
2-Naphthylamine	beta-Naphthylamine	1 (0.454)
alpha-Naphthylthiourea	Thiourea, 1-naphthalenyl-	100 (45.4)
Nickel ¢		100 (45.4)
Nickel ammonium sulfate		100 (45.4)
Nickel carbonyl*	Nickel carbonyl Ni(CO)4,(T-4)-	10 (4.54)
Nickel carbonyl Ni(CO)4,(T-4)-	Nickel carbonyl*	10 (4.54)
Nickel chloride		100 (45.4)
Nickel cyanide*	Nickel cyanide Ni(CN)2	10 (4.54)
Nickel cyanide Ni(CN)2	Nickel cyanide*	10 (4.54)
Nickel hydroxide		10 (4.54)
Nickel nitrate*		100 (45.4)
Nickel sulfate		100 (45.4)
Nicotine* and salts*	Pyridine, 3-(1-methyl-2-pyrrolidinyl)-,(S)-	100 (45.4)
Nitric acid*		1000 (454)
Nitric acid, thallium(1+)salt	Thallium(I) nitrate	100 (45.4)

Hazardous Substances	Synonyms	Reportable Quantity (RQ) Pounds (Kilograms)
Nitric oxide*	Nitrogen oxide NO	10 (4.54)
p-Nitroaniline*	Benzenamine, 4-nitro-	5000 (2270)
Nitrobenzene*	Benzene, nitro-	1000 (454)
Nitrogen dioxide*	Nitrogen oxide NO2	10 (4.54)
	Nitrogen peroxide @	
	Nitrogen tetroxide @	
Nitrogen oxide NO	Nitric oxide*	10 (4.54)
Nitrogen oxide NO2	Nitrogen dioxide*	10 (4.54)
	Nitrogen peroxide @	
	Nitrogen tetroxide @	
Nitrogen peroxide @	Nitrogen dioxide*	10 (4.54)
	Nitrogen oxide NO2	
	Nitrogen tetroxide @	
Nitrogen tetroxide @	Nitrogen dioxide*	10 (4.54)
	Nitrogen oxide NO2	
	Nitrogen peroxide @	
Nitroglycerine*	1,2,3-Propanetriol, trinitrate-	10 (4.54)
Nitrophenol (mixed)		100 (45.4)
m-		
o-	2-Nitrophenol	
p-	4-Nitrophenol	
	Phenol, 4-nitro-	
o-Nitrophenol	2-Nitrophenol	100 (45.4)
p-Nitrophenol	Phenol, 4-nitro-	100 (45.4)
	4-Nitrophenol	
2-Nitrophenol	o-Nitrophenol	100 (45.4)
4-Nitrophenol	p-Nitrophenol	100 (45.4)
	Phenol, 4-nitro-	
2-Nitropropane	Propane, 2-nitro-	10 (4.54)
N-Nitrosodi-n-butylamine	1-Butanamine, N-butyl-N-nitroso-	10 (4.54)
N-Nitrosodiethanolamine	Ethanol, 2,2'- (nitrosimino)bis-	1 (0.454)
N-Nitrosodiethylamine	Ethanamine, N-ethyl-N- nitroso-	1 (0.454)
N-Nitrosodimethylamine	Methanemine, N-methyl-N-nitroso-	10 (4.54)
N-Nitrosodiphenylamine		100 (45.4)
N-Nitroso-N-ethylurea	Urea, N-ethyl-N-nitroso-	1 (0.454)
N-Nitroso-N-methylurea	Urea, N-methyl-N-nitroso-	1 (0.454)
N-Nitroso-N-methylurethane	Carbamic acid, methylnitroso-,ethyl ester	1 (0.454)
N-Nitrosomethylvinylamine	Vinylamine, N-methyl-N- nitroso-	10 (4.54)
N-Nitrosopiperidine	Piperidine, 1-nitroso-	10 (4.54)
N-Nitrosopyrrolidine	Pyrrolidine, 1-nitroso-	1 (0.454)
Nitrotoluene		1000 (454)
m-Nitrotoluene		
o-Nitrotoluene		
p-Nitrotoluene		
5-Nitro-o-toluidine	Benzenamine, 2-methyl-5-nitro-	100 (45.4)
Octamethylpyrophosphoramide	Diphosphoramide, octamethyl-	100 (45.4)
Osmium oxide OsO4 (T-4)-	Osmium tetroxide	1000 (454)
Osmium tetroxide	Osmium oxide OsO4(T-4)-	1000 (454)
7-Oxabicyclo[2.2.1]heptane-2,3-dicarboxylic acid	Endothall	1000 (454)
1,2-Oxathiolane, 2,2-dioxide	1,3-Propane sultone	10 (4.54)
2H-1,3,2-Oxazaphosphorin-2-amine, N,N-bis(2-chloroethyl)tetra hydro-,2-oxide	Cyclophosphamide	10 (4.54)
Oxirane	Ethylene oxide*	10 (4.54)
Oxiranecarboxyaldehyde	Glycidylaldehyde	10 (4.54)
Oxirane, (chloromethyl)-	Epichlorohydrin*	100 (45.4)
Paraformaldehyde*		1000 (454)
Paraldehyde*	1,3,5-Trioxane, 2,4,6- trimethyl-	1000 (454)
Parathion*	Phosphorothioic acid, O,O-diethyl O-(4-nitrophenyl) ester	10 (4.54)
Pentachlorobenzene	Benzene, pentachloro-	10 (4.54)
Pentachloroethane	Ethane,pentachloro-	10 (4.54)
Pentachloronitrobenzene (PCNB)	Benzene, pentachloronitro-	100 (45.4)
Pentachlorophenol	Phenol, pentachloro-	10 (4.54)
1,3-Pentadiene	1-Methylbutadiene	100 (45.4)
Perchloroethylene*	Ethene, tetrachloro	100 (45.4)
	Tetrachloroethene	
	Tetrachloroethylene*	
Perchloromethyl mercaptan @	Methanesulferyl chloride, trichloro-	100 (45.4)
	Trichloromethanesulferyl chloride	
Phenacetin	Acetamide, N-(4-ethoxyphenyl)-	100 (45.4)
Phenanthrene		5000 (2270)
Phenol*	Benzene, hydroxy-	1000 (454)

272

Hazardous Substances	Synonyms	Reportable Quantity (RQ) Pounds (Kilograms)
Phenol, 2-chloro-	2-Chlorophenol	100 (45.4)
	o-Chlorophenol	
Phenol, 4-chloro-3-methyl-	4-Chloro-m-cresol	5000 (2270)
	p-Chloro-m-cresol	
Phenol, 2-cyclohexyl-4,6-dinitro-	2-Cyclohexyl-4,6-dinitrophenol	100 (45.4)
Phenol, 2,4-dichloro-	2,4-Dichlorophenol	100 (45.4)
Phenol, 2,6-dichloro-	2,6-Dichlorophenol	100 (45.4)
Phenol, 4,4'-(1,2-diethyl-1,2-ethenediyl)bis-, (E)	Diethylstilbestrol	1 (0.454)
Phenol, 2,4-dimethyl-	2,4-Dimethylphenol	100 (45.4)
Phenol, 2,4-dinitro-	2,4-Dinitrophenol	10 (4.54)
Phenol, methyl-	Cresol(s)*	1000 (454)
	Cresylic acid	
m-Cresol	m-Cresylic acid	
o-Cresol	o-Cresylic acid	
p-Cresol	p-Cresylic acid	
Phenol,2-methyl-4,6-dinitro-	4,6-Dinitro-o-cresol and salts	10 (4.54)
Phenol, 2,2'-methylenebis[3,4,6-trichloro-	Hexachlorophene	100 (45.4)
Phenol, 2-(1-methylpropyl)-4,6-dintro	Dinoseb	1000 (454)
Phenol, 4-nitro-	p-Nitrophenol	100 (45.4)
	4-Nitrophenol	
Phenol, pentachloro-	Pentachlorophenol	10 (4.54)
Phenol, 2,3,4,6-tetrachloro-	2,3,4,6-Tetrachlorophenol	10 (4.54)
Phenol, 2,4,5-trichloro-	2,4,5-Trichlorophenol	10 (4.54)
Phenol, 2,4,6-trichloro-	2,4,6-Trichlorophenol	10 (4.54)
Phenol, 2,4,6-trinitro-, ammonium salt	Ammonium picrate*	10 (4.54)
L-Phenylalanine, 4-[bis(2-chloroethyl)aminol]	Melphalan	1 (0.454)
Phenyl dichloroarsine@	Dichlorophenylarsine-	1 (0.454)
	Arsonous dichloride, phenyl-	
1,10-(1,2-Phenylene)pyrene	Indeno(1,2,3-cd)pyrene	100 (45.4)
Phenyl mercaptan @	Benzenethiol	100 (45.4)
	Thiophenol*	
Phenylmercuric acetate	Mercury, (acetato-O) phenyl-	100 (45.4)
Phenylthiourea	Thiourea, phenyl-	100 (45.4)
Phorate	Phosphorodithioic acid, O,O- diethyl S-(ethylthio), methylester	10 (4.54)
Phosgene*	Carbonic dichloride	10 (4.54)
Phosphine*	Hydrogen phosphide	100 (45.4)
Phosphoric acid*		5000 (2270)
Phosphoric acid, diethyl 4-nitrophenyl ester	Diethyl-p-nitrophenyl phosphate	100 (45.4)
Phosphoric acid, lead(2+) salt(2:3)	Lead phosphate	1 (0.454)
Phosphorodithioic acid, O,O-diethyl S-[2-(ethylthio) ethyl]ester	Disulfoton*	1 (0.454)
Phosphorodithioic acid, O,O-diethyl S-(ethylthio), methyl ester	Phorate	10 (4.54)
Phosphorodithioic acid, O,O-diethyl S-methyl ester	O,O-Diethyl S-methyl dithiophosphate	5000 (2270)
Phosphorodithioic acid, O,O-dimethyl S-[2(methyl amino)-2- oxoethyl]ester	Dimethoate	10 (4.54)
Phosphorofluoridic acid, bis(1-methylethyl) ester	Diisopropyl fluorophosphate	100 (45.4)
Phosphorothioic acid, O,O-diethyl O-(4-nitrophenyl) ester	Parathion*	10 (4.54)
Phosphorothioic acid, O,O-diethyl O-pyrazinyl ester	O,O-Diethyl O-pyrazinyl phosphorothioate	100 (45.4)
Phosphorothioic acid, O,O-dimethyl O-(4-nitrophenyl) ester	Methyl parathion*	100 (45.4)
Phosphorothioic acid, O,[4-[(dimethylamino)sulfonyl] phenyl] O,O- dimethyl ester.	Famphur	1000 (454)
Phosphorus*		1 (0.454)
Phosphorus oxychloride*		1000 (454)
Phosphorus pentasulfide*	Phosphorus sulfide	100 (45.4)
	Sulfur phosphide	
Phosphorus sulfide	Phosphorus pentasulfide*	100 (45.4)
	Sulfur phosphide	
Phosphorus trichloride*		1000 (454)
Phthalate anhydride	1,3-Isobenzofurandione	5000 (2270)
2-Picoline	Pyridine,2-methyl-	5000 (2270)
Piperidine, 1-nitroso-	N-Nitrosopiperidine	10 (4.54)
Plumbane, tetraethyl-	Tetraethyl lead*	10 (4.54)
POLYCHLORINATED BIPHENYLS (PCBs)		1 (0.454)
	Aroclor 1016	
	Aroclor 1221	
	Aroclor 1232	
	Aroclor 1242	
	Aroclor 1248	
	Aroclor 1254	
	Aroclor 1260	
Potassium arsenate*		1 (0.454)
Potassium arsenite*		1 (0.454)
Potassium bichromate	Potassium dichromate @	10 (4.54)
Potassium chromate		10 (4.54)

Hazardous Substances	Synonyms	Reportable Quantity (RQ) Pounds (Kilograms)
Postassium cyanide*	Potassium cyanide K(CN)	10 (4.54)
Potassium cyanide K(CN)	Potassium cyanide	10 (4.54)
Potassium dichromate @	Potassium bichromate	10 (4.54)
Potassium hydroxide *		1000 (454)
Potassium permanganate *		100 (45.4)
Potassium silver cyanide	Argentate(1-), bis(cyano-C)-, potassium	1 (0.454)
Pronamide	Benzamide, 3,5-dichloro-N-(1,1-dimethyl-2-propynyl)-	5000 (2270)
Propanal, 2-methyl-2-(methylthio)-,O-[(methylamino) carbonyl] oxime	Aldicarb	1 (0.454)
1-Propanamine	n-Propylamine*	5000 (2270)
1-Propanamine, N-nitroso-N-propyl-	Di-n-propylnitrosamine	10 (4.54)
1-Propanamine, N-propyl-	Dipropylamine	5000 (2270)
Propane, 1,2-dibromo-3-chloro-	1,2-Dibromo-3- chloropropane	1 (0.454)
Propane, 1,2-dichloro-	1,2-Dichloropropane	1000 (454)
	Propylene dichloride*	
Propane, 2-nitro-	2-Nitropropane	10 (4.54)
Propane, 2,2'-oxybis[2-chloro-	Dichloroisopropyl ether	1000 (454)
1,3-Propane sultone	1,2-Oxathiolane, 2,2-dioxide	10 (4.54)
Propanedinitrile	Malononitrile	1000 (454)
Propanenitrile	Ethyl cyanide	10 (4.54)
Propanenitrile, 3-chloro-	3-Chloropropionitrile	1000 (454)
Propanenitrile, 2-hydroxy-2-methyl-	Acetone cyanohydrin*	10 (4.54)
	2-Methyllactonitrile	
1,2,3-Propanetriol, trinitrate-	Nitroglycerine*	10 (4.54)
1-Propanol, 2,3-dibromo-, phosphate (3:1)	Tris(2,3-dibromopropyl) phosphate	10 (4.54)
1-Propanol, 2-methyl-	Isobutyl alcohol	5000 (2270)
2-Propanone	Acetone*	5000 (2270)
2-Propanone, 1-bromo-	Bromoacetone*	1000 (454)
Propargite		10 (4.54)
Propargyl alcohol*	2-Propyn-1-ol	1000 (454)
2-Propenal	Acrolein*	1 (0.454)
2-Propenamide	Acrylamide	5000 (2270)
1-Propene, 1,3-dichloro-	1,3-Dichloropropene	100 (45.4)
1-Propene, 1,1,2,3,3,3-hexachloro-	Hexachloropropene	1000 (454)
2-Propenenitrile	Acrylonitrile*	100 (45.4)
2-Propenenitrile, 2-methyl-	Methacrylonitrile	1000 (454)
2-Propenoic acid	Acrylic acid*	5000 (2270)
2-Propenoic acid, ethyl ester	Ethyl acrylate*	1000 (454)
2-Propenoic acid, 2-methyl-, ethyl ester	Ethyl methacrylate	1000 (454)
2-Propenoic acid, 2-methyl-, methyl ester	Methyl methacrylate*	1000 (454)
2-Propen-1-ol	Allyl alcohol*	100 (45.4)
Propionic acid*		5000 (2270)
Propionic acid, 2-(2,4,5-trichlorophenoxy)-	Silvex (2,4,5-TP)	100 (45.4)
	2,4,5-TP @	
	2,4,5-TP acid	
Propionic anhydride		5000 (2270)
n-Propylamine*	1-Propanamine	5000 (2270)
Propylene dichloride*	1,2-Dichloropropane	1000 (454)
	Propane, 1,2-dichloro-	
Propylene oxide*		100 (45.4)
1,2-Propylenimine*	Aziridine, 2-methyl-	1 (0.454)
2-Propyn-1-ol	Propargyl alcohol*	1000 (454)
Pyrene		5000 (2270)
Pyrethrins		1 (0.454)
3,6-Pyridazinedione, 1,2-dihydro-	Maleic hydrazide	5000 (2270)
4-Pyridinamine	4-Aminopyridine	1000 (454)
Pyridine*		1000 (454)
Pyridine, 2-methyl-	2-Picoline	5000 (2270)
Pyridine, 3-(1-methyl-2-pyrrolidinyl)-, (S)	Nicotine* and salts*	100 (45.4)
4(1H)-Pyrimidinone, 2,3-dihydro-6-methyl-2-thioxo-	Methylthiouracil	10 (4.54)
Pyrrolidine, 1-nitroso-	N-Nitrosopyrrolidine	1 (0.454)
Quinoline		5000 (2270)
RADIONUCLIDES		See Table 2
Reserpine	Yohimban-16-carboxylic acid,11,17-dimethoxy-18- [(3,4,5-trimethoxy-benzoyl)oxy-, methyl ester-, (3beta,16beta,17alpha,18beta,20alpha)-	5000 (2270)
Resorcinol	1,3-Benzenediol	5000 (2270)
Saccharin and salts	1,2-Benzisothiazol-3(2H)-one,1,1-dioxide	100 (45.4)
Safrole	1,3-Benzodioxole,5-(2-propenyl)-	100 (45.4)
Selenious acid		10 (4.54)
Selenious acid, dithallium(1+)salt	Thallium selenite	1000 (454)
Selenium ¢		100 (45.4)

274

Hazardous Substances	Synonyms	Reportable Quantity (RQ) Pounds (Kilograms)
Selenium dioxide	Selenium oxide*	10 (4.54)
Selenium oxide*	Selenium dioxide	10 (4.54)
Selenium sulfide	Selenium sulfide SeS2	10 (4.54)
Selenium sulfide SeS2	Selenium sulfide	10 (4.54)
Selenourea	Carbamimidoselenoic acid	1000 (454)
L-Serine, diazoacetate (ester)	Azaserine	1 (0.454)
Silver ¢		1000 (454)
Silver cyanide*	Silver cyanide Ag(CN)	1 (0.454)
Silver cyanide Ag(CN)	Silver cyanide	1 (0.454)
Silver nitrate*		1 (0.454)
Silvex(2,4,5-TP)	Propionic acid, 2-(2,4,5-trichlorophenoxy)- 2,4,5-TP @ 2,4,5-TP acid	100 (45.4)
Sodium*		10 (4.54)
Sodium arsenate*		1 (0.454)
Sodium arsenite*		1 (0.454)
Sodium azide*		1000 (454)
Sodium bichromate	Sodium dichromate @	10 (4.54)
Sodium bifluoride*		100 (45.4)
Sodium bisulfite*		5000 (2270)
Sodium chromate		10 (4.54)
Sodium cyanide*		10 (4.54)
Sodium cyanide Na(CN)	Sodium cyanide	10 (4.54)
Sodium dichromate @	Sodium bichromate	10 (4.54)
Sodium dodecylbenzene sulfonate		1000 (454)
Sodium fluoride*		1000 (454)
Sodium hydrosulfide*		5000 (2270)
Sodium hydroxide*		1000 (454)
Sodium hypochlorite*		100(45.4)
Sodium methylate*		1000 (454)
Sodium nitrite*		100 (45.4)
Sodium phosphate, dibasic		5000 (2270)
Sodium phosphate, tribasic		5000 (2270)
Sodium selenite*		100 (45.4)
Streptozotocin	Glucopyranose, 2-deoxy-2-(3-methyl-3-nitrosoureido)- D-Glucose, 2-deoxy-2-[[(methylnitrosoamino)-carbonyl]amino]-	1 (0.454)
Strontium chromate		10 (4.54)
Strychnidin-10-one	Strychnine* and salts*	10 (4.54)
Strychnidin-10-one, 2,3-dimethoxy-	Brucine	100 (45.4)
Strychnine* and salts*	Strychnidin-10-one	10 (4.54)
Styrene		1000 (454)
Sulfur chloride@	Sulfur monochloride	1000 (454)
Sulfur monochloride	Sulfur chloride@	1000 (454)
Sulfur phosphide	Phosphorus pentasulfide* Phosphorus sulfide	100 (45.4)
Sulfuric acid*		1000 (454)
Sulfuric acid, dimethyl ester	Dimethyl sulfate*	100 (45.4)
Sulfuric acid, dithallium(I+)salt	Thallium(I) sulfate*	100 (45.4)
2,4,5-T*	2,4,5-T acid Acetic acid,(2,4,5-trichlorophenoxy)	1000 (454)
2,4,5-T acid	2,4,5-T* Acetic acid, (2,4,5-trichlorophenoxy)	1000 (454)
2,4,5-T amines		5000 (2270)
2,4,5-T esters		1000 (454)
2,4,5-T salts		1000 (454)
TDE*	DDD Benzene, 1,1'-(2,2-dichloroethylidene)bis[4-chloro- 4,4'-DDD	1 (0.454)
1,2,4,5-Tetrachlorobenzene	Benzene, 1,2,4,5-tetrachloro-	5000 (2270)
2,3,7,8-Tetrachlorodibenzo-p-dioxin (TCDD)		1 (0.454)
1,1,1,2-Tetrachloroethane	Ethane,1,1,1,2-tetrachloro- Tetrachloroethane@	100 (45.4)
1,1,2,2-Tetrachloroethane	Ethane,1,1,2,2-tetrachloro- Tetrachloroethane@	100 (45.4
Tetrachloroethane@	Ethane, 1,1,1,2-tetrachloro- Ethane, 1,1,2,2-tetrachloro- 1,1,1,2-Tetrachloroethane 1,1,2,-Tetrachloroethane	100 (45.4)
Tetrachloroethene	Ethene, tetrachloro- Perchloroethylene* Tetrachloroethylene*	100 (45.4)

Hazardous Substances	Synonyms	Reportable Quantity (RQ) Pounds (Kilograms)
Tetrachloroethylene*	Ethene, tetrachloro-	100 (45.4)
	Perchloroethylene*	
	Tetrachloroethene	
2,3,4,6-Tetrachlorophenol	Phenol, 2,3,4,6-tetrachloro-	10 (4.54)
Tetraethyl lead*	Plumbane, tetraethyl-	10 (4.54)
Tetraethyl pyrophosphate*	Diphosphoric acid, tetraethyl ester	10 (4.54)
Tetraethyldithiopyrophosphate	Thiodiphosphoric acid, tetraethyl ester	100 (45.4)
Tetrahydrofuran*	Furan, tetrahydro-	1000 (454)
Tetranitromethane*	Methane, tetranitro-	10 (4.54)
Tetraphosphoric acid, hexaethyl ester	Hexaethyl tetraphosphate*	100 (45.4)
Thallic oxide	Thallium oxide T1203	100 (45.4)
Thallium ¢		1000 (454)
Thallium(I) acetate	Acetic acid, thallium(I+)salt	100 (45.4)
Thallium(I) carbonate	Carbonic acid, dithallium (I+)	100 (45.4)
Thallium(I) chloride	Thallium chloride T1Cl	100 (45.4)
Thallium chloride TlCl	Thallium(I) chloride	100 (45.4)
Thallium(I) nitrate	Nitric acid, thallium(1+) salt	100 (45.4)
Thallium oxide T1203	Thallic oxide	100 (45.4)
Thallium selenite	Selenious acid, dithallium(1+)salt	1000 (454)
Thallium(I) sulfate*	Sulfuric acid, dithallium(I+) salt	100 (45.4)
Thioacetamide	Ethanethioamide	10 (4.54)
Thiodiphosphoric acid, tetraethyl ester	Tetraethyldithiopyrophosphate	100 (45.4)
Thiofanox	2-butanone, 3,3-Dimethyl-1-(methylthio)-, O-[(methylamino)carbonyl] oxime	100 (45.4)
Thioimidodicarbonic diamide [(H2N)C(S)]2NH	Dithiobiuret	100 (45.4)
Thiomethanol	Methanethiol	100 (45.4)
	Methyl mercaptan*	
Thioperoxydicarbonic diamide [(H2N)C(S)]2S2, tetramethyl-	Thiram	10 (4.54)
Thiophenol*	Benzenethiol	100 (45.4)
	Phenyl mercaptan @	
Thiosemicarbazide	Hydrazinecarbothioamide	100 (45.4)
Thiourea	Carbamide, thio-	10 (4.54)
Thiourea, (2-chlorophenyl)-	1-(o-Chlorophenyl)thiourea	100 (45.4)
Thiourea, 1-naphthalenyl-	alpha-Naphthylthiourea	100 (45.4)
Thiourea, phenyl-	Phenylthiourea	100 (45.4)
Thiram	Thioperoxydicarbonic diamide [(H2N)C(S)2S2, tetramethyl-	10 (4.54)
Toluene*	Benzene, methyl-	1000 (454)
Toluenediamine*	Benzenediamine, ar-methyl-	10 (4.54)
Toluene diisocyanate*	Benzene, 1,3- diisocyanatomethyl	100 (45.4)
o-Toluidine	2-Amino-1-methyl benzene	100 (45.4)
p-Toluidine	Benzenaminew, 4-methyl-	100 (45.4)
o-Toluidine hydrochloride	Benzenamine, 2-methyl-, hydrochloride	100 (45.4)
Toxaphene*	Camphene, octachloro-	1 (0.454)
2,4,5-TP @	Propionic acid, 2-(2,4,5-trichlorophenoxy)-	100 (45.4)
	Silvex (2,4,5-TP)	
	2,4,5-TP acid	
2,4,5-TP acid	Propionic acid, 2-(2,4,5-trichlorophenoxy)-	100 (45.4)
	Silvex (2,4,5-TP)	
	2,4,5-TP @	
2,4,5-TP acid esters		100 (45.4)
1H-1,2,4-Triazol-3-amine	Amitrole	10 (4.54)
Trichlorfon		100 (45.4)
1,2,4-Trichlorobenzene		100 (45.4)
1,1,1-Trichloroethane*	Methyl chloroform*	1000 (454)
	Ethane, 1,1,1-trichloro-	
1,1,2-Trichloroethane	Ethane, 1,1,2-trichloro-	100 (45.4)
Trichloroethene	Trichloroethylene*	100 (45.4)
	Ethene, trichloro-	
Trichloroethylene*	Trichloroethene	100 (45.4)
	Ethene, trichloro-	
Trichloromethanesulfenyl chloride	Methanesulfenyl chloride, trichloro-	100 (45.4)
	Perchloromethyl mercaptan @	
Trichloromonofluoromethane	Methane, trichlorofluoro-	5000 (2270)
Trichlorophenol*		10 (4.54)
2,3,4-Trichlorophenol		
2,3,5-Trichlorophenol		
2,3,6-Trichlorophenol		
2,4,5-Trichlorophenol	Phenol, 2,4,5-trichloro-	
2,4,6-Trichlorophenol	Phenol, 2,4,6-trichloro-	
3,4,5-Trichlorophenol		
2,4,5-Trichlorophenol	Phenol, 2,4,5-trichloro-	10 (4.54)
2,4,6-Trichlorophenol	Phenol, 2,4,6-trichloro-	10 (4.54)

276

Hazardous Substances	Synonyms	Reportable Quantity (RQ) Pounds (Kilograms)
Triethanolamine dodecylbenzene sulfonate		1000 (454)
Triethylamine		5000 (2270)
Trimethylamine*		100 (45.4)
1,3,5-Trinitrobenzene	Benzene, 1,3,5-trinitro-	10 (4.54)
1,3,5-Trioxane, 2,4,6-trimethyl-	Paraldehyde*	1000 (454)
Tris(2,3-dibromopropyl) phosphate	1-Propanol, 2,3-dibromo-, phosphate(3:1)	10 (4.54)
Trypan blue	2,7-Naphthalenedisulfonic acid, 3,3'-[(3,3'-di-methyl-(1,1'-biphenyl)-4,4'-diyl)-bis(azo)]bis (5-amino-4-hydroxy)-tetrasodium salt	10 (4.54)
Uracil mustard	2,4-(1H,3H)-Pyrimidinedione, 5-[bis(2-chloroethyl) amino]-	10 (4.54)
Uranyl acetate*		100 (45.4)
Uranyl nitrate*		100 (45.4)
Urea, N-ethyl-N-nitroso-	N-Nitroso-N-ethylurea	1 (0.454)
Urea, N-methyl-N-nitroso-	N-Nitroso-N-methylurea	1 (0.454)
Vanadic acid, ammonium salt	Ammonium vanadate	1000 (454)
Vanadium oxide V205	Vanadium pentoxide	1000 (454)
Vanadium pentoxide	Vanadium oxide V205	1000 (454)
Vanadyl sulfate		1000 (454)
Vinyl acetate*	Vinyl acetate monomer	5000 (2270)
Vinyl acetate monomer	Vinyl acetate-*	5000 (2270)
Vinylamine, N-methyl-N-nitroso-	N-nitrosomethylvinylamine	10 (4.54)
Vinyl chloride*	Ethene, chloro-	1 (0.454)
Vinylidene chloride*	Ethene, 1,1-dichloro- 1,1-Dichloroethylene	100 (45.4)
Warfarin, & salts, when present at concentrations greater than 0.3%	2H-1-Benzopyran-2-one, 4-hydroxy-3-(3oxo-1-phenyl-butyl)-, & salts, when present at concentrations greater than 0.3%	100 (45.4)
Xylene* (mixed)	Benzene, dimethyl	1000 (454)
m-Bezene, dimethyl	m-Xylene	
o-Benzene, dimethyl	o-Xylene	
p-Benzene, dimethyl	p-Xylene	
Xylenol*		1000 (454)
Yohimban-16-carboxylic acid, 11,17-dimethoxy-18-[(3,4,5-trimethoxybenzoyl)oxy]-, methyl ester (3beta,16beta,17alpha,18beta,20alpha)-	Reserpine	5000 (2270)
Zinc ¢		1000 (454)
Zinc acetate		1000 (454)
Zinc ammonium chloride		1000 (454)
Zinc borate		1000 (454)
Zinc bromide		1000 (454)
Zinc carbonate		1000 (454)
Zinc chloride		1000 (454)
Zinc cyanide*	Zinc cyanide Zn(CN)2	10 (4.54)
Zinc cyanide Zn(CN)2	Zinc cyanide	10 (4.54)
Zinc fluoride		1000 (454)
Zinc formate		1000 (454)
Zinc hydrosulfite*		1000 (454)
Zinc nitrate*		1000 (454)
Zinc phenolsulfonate		5000 (2270)
Zinc phosphide*	Zinc phosphide Zn3P2, when present at concentrations greater than 10%	100 (45.4)
Zinc phosphide Zn3P2, when present at concentrations greater than 10%	Zinc phosphide-*	100 (45.4)
Zinc silicofluoride		5000 (2270)
Zinc sulfate		1000 (454)
Zirconium nitrate*		5000 (2270)
Zirconium potassium fluoride		1000 (454)
Zirconium sulfate*		5000 (2270)
Zirconium tetrachloride*		5000 (2270)
D001 Unlisted Hazardous Wastes Characteristic of Ignitability		100 (45.4)
D002 Unlisted Hazardous Wastes Characteristic of Corrosivity		100 (45.4)
D003 Unlisted Hazardous Wastes Characteristic of Reactivity		100 (45.4)
D004-D043 Unlisted Hazardous Wastes Characteristic of Toxicity		
D004 Arsenic		1 (0.454)
D005 Barium		1000 (454)
D006 Cadmium		10 (4.54)
D007 Chromium		10 (4.54)
D008 Lead		1 (0.454)
D009 Mercury		1 (0.454)
D010 Selenium		10 (4.54)
D011 Silver		1 (0.454)
D012 Endrin		1 (0.454)
D013 Lindane		1 (0.454)
D014 Methoxyclor		1 (0.454)
D015 Toxaphene		1 (0.454)

277

Hazardous Substances	Synonyms	Reportable Quantity (RQ) Pounds (Kilograms)
D016 2,4-D		100 (45.4)
D017 2,4,5-TP		100 (45.4)
D018 Benzene		10 (4.54)
D019 Carbon tetrachloride		10 (4.54)
D020 Chlordane		1 (0.454)
D021 Chlorobenzene		100 (45.4)
D022 Chloroform		10 (4.54)
D023 o-Cresol		1000 (454)
D024 m-Cresol		1000 (454)
D025 p-Cresol		1000 (454)
D026 Cresol		1000 (454)
D027 1,4-Dichlorobenzene		100 (45.4)
D028 1,2-Dichloroethane		100 (45.4)
D029 1,1-Dichloroethylene		100 (45.4)
D030 2,4-Dinitrotoluene		10 (4.54)
D031 Heptachlor(and hydroxide)		1 (0.454)
D032 Hexachlorobenzene		10 (4.54)
D033 Hexachlorobutadiene		1 (0.454)
D034 Hexachloroethane		100 (45.4)
D035 Methyl ethyl ketone		5000 (2270)
D036 Nitrobenzene		1000 (454)
D037 Pentachlorophenol		10 (4.54)
D038 Pyridine		1000 (454)
D039 Tetrachloroethylene		100 (45.4)
D040 Trichloroethylene		100 (45.4)
D041 2,4,5-Trichloroethylene		10 (4.54)
D042 2,4,6-Trichlorophenol		10 (4.54)
D043 Vinyl Chloride		1 (0.454)
F001		10 (4.54)
The following spent halogenated solvents used in degreasing; all spent, solvent mixtures/blends used in degreasing containing, before use, a total of ten percent or more (by volume) of one or more of the below listed halogenated solvents or those solvents listed in F002, F004, and F005; and still bottoms from the recovery of these spent solvents and spent solvent mixtures.		
(a) Tetrachloroethylene		100 (45.4)
(b) Trichloroethylene		100 (45.4)
(c) Methylene chloride		1000 (454)
(d) 1,1,1-Trichloroethane		1000 (454)
(e) Carbon tetrachloride		10 (4.54)
(f) Chlorinated fluorocarbons		5000 (2270)
F002		10 (4.54)
The following spent halogenated solvents; all spent solvent mixtures/ blends containing, before use, a total of ten percent or more (by volume) of one or more of the below listed halogenated solvents or those listed in F001, F004, F005; and still bottoms from the recovery of these spent solvents and spent solvent mixtures.		
(a) Tetrachloroethylene		100 (45.4)
(b) Methylene chloride		1000 (454)
(c) Trichloroethylene		100 (45.4)
(d) 1,1,1-Trichloroethane		1000 (454)
(e) Chlorobenzene		100 (45.4)
(f) 1,1,2-Trichloro-1,2,2- trifluoroethane		5000 (2270)
(g) o-Dichlorobenzene		100 (45.4)
(h) Trichlorofluoromethane		5000 (2270)
(i) 1,1,2 Trichloroethane		100 (45.4)
F003		100 (45.4)
The following spent non-halogenated solvents and solvents:		
(a) Xylene		1000 (454)
(b) Acetone		5000 (2270)
(c) Ethyl acetate		5000 (2270)
(d) Ethylbenzene		1000 (454)
(e) Ethyl ether		100 (45.4)
(f) Methyl isobutyl ketone		5000 (2270)
(g) n-Butyl alcohol		5000 (2270)
(h) Cyclohexanone		5000 (2270)
(i) Methanol		5000 (2270)
F004		1000 (454)
The following spent non-halogenated solvents and the still bottoms from the recovery of these solvents:		
(a) Cresols/Cresylic acid		1000 (454)
(b) Nitrobenzene		1000 (454)

278

Hazardous Substances	Synonyms	Reportable Quantity (RQ) Pounds (Kilograms)
F005	....	100 (45.4)
The following spent non-halogenated solvents and the still bottoms from the recovery of these solvents:		
(a) Toluene	....	1000 (454)
(b) Methyl ethyl ketone	....	5000 (2270)
(c) Carbon disulfide	....	100 (45.4)
(d) Isobutanol	....	5000 (2270)
(e) Pyridine	....	1000 (454)
F006	....	10 (4.54)
Wastewater treatment sludges from electroplating operations except from the following processes: (1) sulfuric acid anodizing of aluminum; (2) tin plating on carbon steel; (3) zinc plating (segregated basis) on carbon steel; (4) aluminum or zinc-aluminum plating on carbon steel; (5) cleaning/stripping associated with tin, zinc and aluminum plating on carbon steel; and (6) chemical etching and milling of aluminum.		
F007	....	10 (4.54)
Spent cyanide plating bath solutions from electroplating operations.		
F008	....	10 (4.54)
Plating bath residues from the bottom of plating baths from electroplating operations where cyanides are used in the process.		
F009	....	10 (4.54)
Spent stripping and cleaning bath solutions from electroplating operations where cyanides are used in the process.		
F010	....	10 (4.54)
Quenching bath residues from oil baths from metal heat treating operations where cyanides are used in the process.		
F011	....	10 (4.54)
Spent cyanide solutions from salt bath pot cleaning from metal heat treating operations (except for precious metals heat treating spent cyanide solutions from salt bath pot cleaning).		
F012	....	10 (4.54)
Quenching wastewater treatment sludges from metal heat treating operations where cyanides are used in the process.		
F019	....	10 (4.54)
Wastewater treatment sludges from the chemical conversion coating of aluminum-except from zirconium phosphating in aluminum can washing when such phosphating is an exclusive conversion coating process.		
F020	....	1 (0.454)
Wastes (except wastewater and spent carbon from hydrogen chloride purification from the production or manufacturing use (as a reactant, chemical intermediate, or component in a formulating process) of tri- or tetrachlorophenol, or of intermediates used to produce their pesticide derivatives. (This listing does not include wastes from the production of hexachlorophene from highly purified 2,4,5-trichlorophenol.)		
F021	....	1 (0.454)
Wastes (except wastewater and spent carbon from hydrogen chloride purification) from the production or manufacturing use (as a reactant, chemical intermediate, or component in a formulating process) of pentachlorophenol, or of intermediates used to produce its derivatives.		
F022	....	1 (0.454)
Wastes (except wastewater and spent carbon from hydrogen chloride purification) from the manufacturing use (as a reactant, chemical intermediate, or component in a formulating process) of tetra-, penta-, or hexachlorobenzenes under alkaline conditions.		
F023	....	1 (0.454)
Wastes (except wastewater and spent carbon from hydrogen chloride purification) from the production of materials on equipment previously used for the production or manufacturing use (as a reactant, chemical intermediate, or component in a formulating process) of tri- and tetrachlorophenols. (This listing does not include wastes from equipment used only for the production or use of hexachlorophene from highly purified 2,4, 5-trichlorophenol.)		

Hazardous Substances	Synonyms	Reportable Quantity (RQ) Pounds (Kilograms)
F024 .... Wastes, including but not limited to distillation residues, heavy ends, tars, and reactor cleanout wastes, from the production of chlorinated aliphatic hydrocarbons, having carbon content from one to five, utilizing free radical catalyzed processes. (This listing does not include light ends, spent filters and filter aids, spent dessicants(sic), wastewater, wastewater treatment sludges, spent catalysts, and wastes listed in Section 261.32.)		1 (0.454)
F025 .... Condensed light ends, spent filters and filter aids, and spent desiccant wastes from the production of certain chlorinated aliphatic hydrocarbons, by free radical catalyzed processes. These chlorinated aliphatic hydro-carbons are those having carbon chain lengths ranging from one to and including five, with varying amounts and positions of chlorine substitution.		1 (0.454)
F026 .... Wastes (except wastewater and spent carbon from hydrogen chloride purification) from the production of materials on equipment previously used for the manufacturing use (as a reactant, chemical intermediate, or component in a formulating process) of tetra-, penta-, or hexach-lorobenzene under alkaline conditions.		1 (0.454)
F027 .... Discarded unused formulations containing tri-, tetra-, or pentachlo-rophenol or discarded unused formulations containing compounds derived from these chlorophenols. (This listing does not include formulations containing hexachlorophene synthesized from prepurified 2,4,5-trichlorophenol as the sole component.)		1 (0.454)
F028 .... Residues resulting from the incineration or thermal treatment of soil contaminated with EPA Hazardous Waste Nos. F020, F021, F022, F023, F026, and F027.		1 (0.454)
F039 .... Multi source leachate.		1 (0.454)
K001 .... Bottom sediment sludge from the treatment of wastewaters from wood preserving processes that use creosote and/or pentachlorophenol.		1 (0.454)
K002 .... Wastewater treatment sludge from the production of chrome yellow and orange pigments.		1 (0.454)
K003 .... Wastewater treatment sludge from the production of molybdate orange pigments.		1 (0.454)
K004 .... Wastewater treatment sludge from the production of zinc yellow pigments.		10 (4.54)
K005 .... Wastewater treatment sludge from the production of chrome green pigments.		1 (0.454)
K006 .... Wastewater treatment sludge from the production of chrome oxide green pigments (anhydrous and hydrated).		10 (4.54)
K007 .... Wastewater treatment sludge from the production of iron blue pigments.		10 (4.54)
K008 .... Oven residue from the production of chrome oxide green pigments.		10 (4.54)
K009 .... Distillation bottoms from the production of acetaldehyde from ethylene.		10 (4.54)
K010 .... Distillation side cuts from the production of acetaldehyde from ethylene.		10 (4.54)
K011 .... Bottom stream from the wastewater stripper in the production of acrylonitrile.		10 (4.54)

Hazardous Substances	Synonyms	Reportable Quantity (RQ) Pounds (Kilograms)
K013 Bottom stream from the acetonitrile column in the production of acrylonitrile.		10 (4.54)
K014 Bottoms from the acetonitrile purification column in the production of acrylonitrile.		5000 (2270)
K015 Still bottoms from the distillation of benzyl chloride.		10 (4.54)
K016 Heavy ends or distillation residues from the production of carbon tetrachloride.		1 (0.454)
K017 Heavy ends (still bottoms) from the purification column in the production of epichlorohydrin.		10 (4.54)
K018 Heavy ends from the fractionation column in ethyl chloride production.		1 (0.454)
K019 Heavy ends from the distillation of ethylene dichloride in ethylene dichloride production.		1 (0.454)
K020 Heavy ends from the distillation of vinyl chloride in vinyl chloride monomer production.		1 (0.454)
K021 Aqueous spent antimony catalyst waste from fluoromethanes production.		10 (4.54)
K022 Distillation bottom tars from the production of phenol/acetone from cumene.		1 (0.454)
K023 Distillation light ends from the production of phthalic anhydride from naphthalene.		5000 (2270)
K024 Distillation bottoms from the production of phthalic anhydride from naphthalene.		5000 (2270)
K025 Distillation bottoms from the production of nitrobenzene by the nitration of benzene.		10 (4.54)
K026 Stripping still tails from the production of methyl ethyl pyridines.		1000 (454)
K027 Centrifuge and distillation residues from toluene diisocyanate production.		10 (4.54)
K028 Spent catalyst from the hydrochlorinator reactor in the production of 1,1,1-trichloroethane.		1 (0.454)
K029 Waste from the product steam stripper in the production of 1,1,1-trichloroethane.		1 (0.454)
K030 Column bottoms or heavy ends from the combined production of trichloroethylene and perchloroethylene.		1 (0.454)
K031 By-product salts generated in the production of MSMA and cacodylic acid.		1 (0.454)
K032 Wastewater treatment sludge from the production of chlordane.		10 (4.54)
K033 Wastewater and scrub water from the chlorination of cyclopentadiene in the production of chlordane.		10 (4.54)
K034 Filter solids from the filtration of hexachlorocyclopentadiene in the production of chlordane.		10 (4.54)

281

Hazardous Substances	Synonyms	Reportable Quantity (RQ) Pounds (Kilograms)
K035 .... Wastewater treatment sludges generated in the production of creosote.		1 (0.454)
K036 .... Still bottoms from toluene reclamation distillation in the production of disulfoton.		1 (0.454)
K037 .... Wastewater treatment sludges from the production of disulfoton.		1 (0.454)
K038 .... Wastewater from the washing and stripping of phorate production.		10 (4.54)
K039 .... Filter cake from the filtration of diethylphosphorodithioic acid in the production of phorate.		10 (4.54)
K040 .... Wastewater treatment sludge from the production of phorate.		10 (4.54)
K041 .... Wastewater treatment sludge from the production of toxaphene.		1 (0.454)
K042 .... Heavy ends or distillation residues from the distillation of tetrachlorobenzene in the production of 2,4,5-T.		10 (4.54)
K043 .... 2,6-Dichlorophenol waste from the production of 2,4-D.		10 (4.54)
K044 .... Wastewater treatment sludges from the manufacturing and processing of explosives.		10 (4.54)
K045 .... Spent carbon from the treatment of wastewater containing explosives.		10 (4.54)
K046 .... Wastewater treatment sludges from the manufacturing, formulation and loading of lead-based initiating compounds.		100 (45.4)
K047 .... Pink/red water from TNT operations.		10 (4.54)
K048 .... Dissolved air flotation (DAF) float from the petroleum refining industry.		1 (0.454)
K049 .... Slop oil emulsion solids from the petroleum refining industry.		1 (0.454)
K050 .... Heat exchanger bundle cleaning sludge from the petroleum refining industry.		10 (4.54)
K051 .... API separator sludge from the petroleum refining industry.		1 (0.454)
K052 .... Tank bottoms (leaded) from the petroleum refining industry.		10 (4.54)
K060 .... Ammonia still lime sludge from coking operations.		1 (0.454)
K061 .... Emission control dust/sludge from the primary production of steel in electric furnaces.		1 (0.454)
K062 .... Spent pickle liquor generated by steel finishing operations of facilities whithin the iron and steel industry.		1 (0.454)
K064 .... Acid plant blowdown slurry/sludge resulting from thickening of blowdown slurry from primary copper production.		1 (0.454)
K065 .... Surface impoundment solids contained in and dredged from surface impoundments at primary lead smelting facilities.		1 (0.454)
K066 .... Sludge from treatment of process wastewater and/or acid plant blowdown from primary zinc production.		1 (0.454)
K069 .... Emission control dust/sludge from secondary lead smelting.		1 (0.454)

282

Hazardous Substances	Synonyms	Reportable Quantity (RQ) Pounds (Kilograms)
K071 .... Brine purification muds from the mercury cell process in chlorine production, where separately prepurified brine is not used.	....	1 (0.454)
K073 .... Chlorinated hydrocarbon waste from the purification step of the diaphragm cell process using graphite anodes in chlorine production.	....	10 (4.54)
K083 .... Distillation bottoms from aniline extraction.	....	100 (45.4)
K084 .... Wastewater treatment sludges generated during the production of veterinary pharmaceuticals from arsenic or organo-arsenic compounds.	....	1 (0.454)
K085 .... Distillation or fractionation column bottoms from the production of chlorobenzenes.	....	10 (4.54)
K086 .... Solvent washes and sludges, caustic washes and sludges, or water washes and sludges from cleaning tubs and equipment used in the formulation of ink from pigments, driers, soaps, and stabilizers containing chromium and lead.	....	1 (0.454)
K087 .... Decanter tank tar sludge from coking operations.	....	100 (45.4)
K088 .... Spent potliners from primary aluminum reduction.	....	1 (0.454)
K090 .... Emission control dust or sludge from ferrochromiumsilicon production.	....	1 (0.454)
K091 .... Emission control dust or sludge from ferrochromium production.	....	1 (0.454)
K093 .... Distillation light ends from the production of phthalic anhydride from ortho-xylene.	....	5000 (2270)
K094 .... Distillation bottoms from the production of phthalic anhydride from ortho-xylene.	....	5000 (2270)
K095 .... Distillation bottoms from the production of 1,1,1-trichloroethane.	....	100 (45.4)
K096 .... Heavy ends from the heavy ends column from the production of 1,1,1-trichloroethane.	....	100 (45.4)
K097 .... Vacuum stripper discharge from the chlordane chlorinator in the production of chlordane.	....	1 (0.454)
K098 .... Untreated process wastewater from the production of toxaphene.	....	1 (0.454)
K099 .... Untreated wastewater from the production of 2,4-D.	....	10 (4.54)
K100 .... Waste leaching solution from acid leaching of emission control dust/sludge from secondary lead smelting.	....	1 (0.454)
K101 .... Distillation tar residues from the distillation of aniline-based compounds in the production of veterinary phamaceuticals from arsenic or organo-arsenic compounds.	....	1 (0.454)
K102 .... Residue from the use of activated carbon for decolorization in the production of veterinary pharmaceuticals from arsenic or organo-arsenic compounds.	....	1 (0.454)
K103 .... Process residues from aniline extraction from the production of aniline.	....	100 (45.4)
K104 .... Combined wastewater streams generated from nitrobenzene/aniline chlorobenzenes.	....	10 (4.54)

Hazardous Substances	Synonyms	Reportable Quantity (RQ) Pounds (Kilograms)
K105... Separated aqueous stream from the reactor product washing step in the production of chlorobenzenes.		10 (4.54)
K106... Wastewater treatment sludge from the mercury cell process in chlorine production.		1 (0.454)
K107... Column bottoms from product seperation from the production of 1,1-dimethylhydrazine (UDMH) from carboxylic acid hydrazines.		10 (4.54)
K108... Condensed column overheads from product seperation and condensed reactor vent gases from the production of 1,1-dimethylhydrazine (UDMH) from carboxylic acid hydrazides.		`10 (4.54)
K109... Spent filter cartridges from product purification from the production of 1,1-dimethylhydrazine (UDMH), from carboxylic acid hydrazides.		10 (4.54)
K110... Condensed column overheads from intermediate separation from the production of 1,1-dimethylhydrazines (UDMH) from carboxylic acid hydrazides.		10 (4.54)
K111... Product washwaters from the production of dinitrotoluene via nitration of toluene.		10 (4.54)
K112... Reaction by-product water from the drying column in the production of toluenediamine via hydrogenation of dinitrotoluene.		10 (4.54)
K113... Condensed liquid light ends from the purification of toluenediamine in the production of toluenediamine via hydrogenation of dinitrotoluene.		10 (4.54)
K114... Vicinals from the purification of toluenediamine in the production of toluenediamine via hydrogenation of dinitrotoluene.		10 (4.54)
K115... Heavy ends from the purification of toluenediamine in the production of toluenediamine via hydrogenation of dinitrotoluene.		10 (4.54)
K116... Organic condensate from the solvent recovery column in the production of toluene diisocyanate via phosgenation of toluenediamine.		10 (4.54)
K117... Wastewater from the reaction vent gas scrubber in the production of ethylene bromide via bromination of ethene.		1 (0.454)
K118... Spent absorbent solids from purification of ethylene dibromide in the production of ethylene dibromide.		1 (0.454)
K123... Process wastewater (including supernates, filtrates, and washwaters) from the production of ethylenebisdithiocarbamic acid and its salts.		10 (4.54)
K124... Reactor vent scrubber water from the production of ethylenebisdi-thiocarbamic acid and it salts.		10 (4.54)
K125... Filtration, evaporation, and centrifugation solids from the production of ethylenebisdithiocarbamic acid and its salts.		10 (4.54)
K126... Baghouse dust and floor sweepings in milling and packaging operations from the production or formulation of ethylenebisdithiocarbamic acid and its salts.		10 (4.54)
K131... Waste water from the reactor and spent sulfuric acid from the acid dryer in the production of methyl bromide.		100 (45.4)
K132... Spent absorbent and wastewater solids from the production of methyl bromide.		1000 (454)

284

Hazardous Substances	Synonyms	Reportable Quantity (RQ) Pounds (Kilograms)
K136... Still bottoms from the purification of ethylene dibromide in the pro- duction of ethylene dibromide via bromination of ethene.	....	1 (0.454)

Footnotes:

¢ the RQ for these hazardous substances is limited to those pieces of the metal having a diameter smaller than 100 micrometers (0.004 inches)

¢¢ the RQ for asbestos is limited to friable forms only

@ indicates that the name was added by RSPA because (1) the name is a synonym for a specific hazardous substance and (2) the name appears in the Hazardous Materials Table as a proper shipping name.

* indicates that this material appears by name in the Hazardous Materials Table

Sym-bols	Hazardous materials descriptions and proper shipping names	Hazard class or Division	Identifi-cation Numbers	Packing group	Label(s) required (if not excepted)	Special provisions	(8) Packaging authorizations (§173.***)			(9) Quantity limitations		(10) Vessel stowage requirements	
							Excep-tions	Non-bulk pack-aging	Bulk pack-aging	Passenger aircraft or railcar	Cargo aircraft only	Vessel stow-ages	Other stowage provisions
(1)	(2)	(3)	(4)	(5)	(6)	(7)	(8A)	(8B)	(8C)	(9A)	(9B)	(10A)	(10B)
	Accellerene, see p-Nitrosodimethylaniline												
	Accumulators, electric, see Batteries, wet *etc.*												
D	Accumulators, pressurized, pneumatic *or* hydraulic *(containing non-flammable gas)*	2.2	NA1956		NONFLAMMABLE GAS		306	306	None	No limit	No limit	A	
	Acetal	3	UN1088	II	FLAMMABLE LIQUID	T7	150	202	242	5 L	60 L	E	
	Acetaldehyde	3	UN1089	I	FLAMMABLE LIQUID	A3, B16, T20, T26, T29	None	201	243	Forbidden	30 L	E	
A	Acetaldehyde ammonia	9	UN1841	III	CLASS 9		155	204	241	200 kg	200 kg	A	34
	Acetaldehyde oxime	3	UN2332	II	FLAMMABLE LIQUID	T8	150	202	242	5 L	60 L	A	
	Acetic acid, glacial *or* Acetic acid solution, *more than 80 per cent acid, by mass*	8	UN2789	II	CORROSIVE	A3, A6, A7, A10 B2, T8	154	202	242	1 L	30 L	A	12, 21, 48
	Acetic acid solution, *more than 10 per cent but not more than 80 per cent acid, by mass*	8	UN2790	II	CORROSIVE	A3, A6, A7, A10 B2, T8	154	202	242	1 L	30 L	A	112
	Acetic anhydride	8	UN1715	II	CORROSIVE	A3, A6, A7, A10, B2, T8	154	202	242	1 L	30 L	A	40
	Acetone	3	UN1090	II	FLAMMABLE LIQUID	T8	150	202	242	5 L	60 L	B	
	Acetone cyanohydrin, stabilized	6.1	UN1541	I	POISON	2, A3, B9, B14, B32, B74, B76, B77, N34, T38, T43, T45	None	227	244	Forbidden	30 L	D	25, 40, 49
	Acetone oils	3	UN1091	II	FLAMMABLE LIQUID	T7, T30	150	202	242	5 L	60 L	B	
	Acetonitrile, see Methyl cyanide												
	Acetyl acetone peroxide with more than 9% by mass active oxygen	Forbid-den											
	Acetyl benzoyl peroxide, solid, or more than 40% in solution	Forbid-den											
	Acetyl bromide	8	UN1716	II	CORROSIVE	B2, T12, T26	154	202	242	1 L	30 L	C	8, 40
	Acetyl chloride	3	UN1717	II	FLAMMABLE LIQUID, CORROSIVE	A3, A6, A7, N34, T18, T26	None	202	243	1 L	5 L	B	40
	Acetyl cyclohexanesulfonyl peroxide, more than 82 per cent wetted with less than 12 per cent water	Forbid-den											
	Acetyl iodide	8	UN1898	II	CORROSIVE	B2, T9	154	202	242	1 L	30 L	C	8, 40
	Acetyl methyl carbinol	3	UN2621	III	FLAMMABLE LIQUID	B1, T1	150	203	242	60 L	220 L	A	
	Acetyl peroxide, solid, or more than 25 percent in solution	Forbid-den											
	Acetylene, dissolved	2.1	UN1001		FLAMMABLE GAS		None	303	None	Forbidden	15 kg	D	25, 40, 57
	Acetylene (liquefied)	Forbid-den											
	Acetylene silver nitrate	Forbid-den											
	Acetylene tetrabromide, see Tetrabromoethane												
	Acid butyl phosphate, see Butyl acid phosphate												
	Acid, sludge, see Sludge acid												
	Acridine	6.1	UN2713	III	KEEP AWAY FROM FOOD		153	213	240	100 kg	200 kg	A	
	Acrolein dimer, stabilized	3	UN2607	III	FLAMMABLE LIQUID	B1, T1	150	203	242	60 L	220 L	A	40
+	Acrolein, inhibited	6.1	UN1092	I	POISON, FLAMMABLE LIQUID	1, B9, B12, B14, B30, B42, B72, B77, T38, T43, T45	None	226	244	Forbidden	Forbidden	D	40
	Acrylamide	6.1	UN2074	III	KEEP AWAY FROM FOOD	T8	153	213	240	100 kg	200 kg	A	12
	Acrylic acid, inhibited	8	UN2218	II	CORROSIVE	B2, T8	154	202	242	1 L	30 L	C	8, 12, 21, 25, 40
	Acrylonitrile, inhibited	3	UN1093	I	FLAMMABLE LIQUID, POISON	B9, T18, T26	None	201	243	Forbidden	30 L	E	40
	Actuating cartridge, explosive, see Cartridges, power device												
	Adhesives, *containing a flammable liquid*	3	UN1133	II	FLAMMABLE LIQUID	B52, T7, T30	150	173	242	5 L	60 L	B	
				III	FLAMMABLE LIQUID	B1, B52, T7, T30	150	173	242	60 L	220 L	A	
	Adiponitrile	6.1	UN2205	III	KEEP AWAY FROM FOOD	T1	153	203	241	60 L	220 L	A	25
	Aerosols, *corrosive, Packing Group II or III, (each not exceeding 1 L capacity)*	2.2	UN1950		NONFLAMMABLE GAS, CORROSIVE	A34	306	None	None	75 kg	150 kg	A	40, 48, 85
	Aerosols, *flammable, (each not exceeding 1 L capacity)*	2.1	UN1950		FLAMMABLE GAS	N82	306	None	None	75 kg	150 kg	A	40, 48, 85

Symbols	Hazardous materials descriptions and proper shipping names	Hazard class or Division	Identification Numbers	Packing group	Label(s) required (if not excepted)	Special provisions	Packaging authorizations (§173.***)			Quantity limitations		Vessel stowage requirements	
							Exceptions	Non-bulk packaging	Bulk packaging	Passenger aircraft or railcar	Cargo aircraft only	Vessel stowages	Other stowage provisions
(1)	(2)	(3)	(4)	(5)	(6)	(7)	(8A)	(8B)	(8C)	(9A)	(9B)	(10A)	(10B)
	Aerosols, *non-flammable, (each not exceeding 1 L capacity)*	2.2	UN1950		NONFLAMMABLE GAS		306, 307	None	None	75 kg	150 kg	A	48, 85
	Aerosols, *poison, each not exceeding 1 L capacity*	2.2	UN1950		NONFLAMMABLE GAS	3	306	None	None	Forbidden	Forbidden	A	40, 48, 85
D	Air bag inflators *or* Air bag modules *for supplemental restraint systems. See also Articles, pyrotechnic for technical purposes (UN0430, UN0431, UN0432)*	4.1	NA1325	III	FLAMMABLE SOLID		166	166	166	25 kg	100 kg	A	
	Air, compressed	2.2	UN1002		NONFLAMMABLE GAS		306	302	302	75 kg	150 kg	A	
	Air, refrigerated liquid (cryogenic liquid)	2.2	UN1003		NONFLAMMABLE GAS, OXIDIZER		320	316	318, 319	Forbidden	150 kg	A	51
	Air, refrigerated liquid, *(cryogenic liquid)non-pressurized*	2.2	UN1003		NONFLAMMABLE GAS, OXIDIZER		320	316	318, 319	Forbidden	Forbidden	A	85
	Aircraft evacuation slides, *see* Life saving appliances *etc.*												
D	Aircraft hydraulic power unit fuel tank *(containing a mixture of anhydrous hydrazine and monomethyl hydrazine) (M86 fuel)*	3	NA9302	I	FLAMMABLE LIQUID, POISON, CORROSIVE		None	172	None	Forbidden	30 L	E	
	Aircraft survival kits, *see* Life saving appliances *etc.*												
	Alcoholic beverages	3	UN3065	III	FLAMMABLE LIQUID	B1, N11, T1	150	203	242	5 L	60 L	A	
	Alcohols, n.o.s	3	UN1987	I	FLAMMABLE LIQUID	T8, T31	None	201	243	1 L	30 L	E	
				II	FLAMMABLE LIQUID	T8, T31	150	202	242	5 L	60 L	B	
				III	FLAMMABLE LIQUID	B1, T7, T30	150	203	242	60 L	220 L	A	
	Alcohols, toxic, n.o.s.	3	UN1986	I	FLAMMABLE LIQUID, POISON	T8, T31	None	201	243	Forbidden	30 L	E	40
				II	FLAMMABLE LIQUID, POISON	T8, T31	None	202	243	1 L	60 L	B	40
	Aldehydes, n.o.s.	3	UN1989	I	FLAMMABLE LIQUID	T8, T31	None	201	243	1 L	30 L	E	
				II	FLAMMABLE LIQUID	T8, T31	150	202	242	5 L	60 L	B	
				III	FLAMMABLE LIQUID	B1, T7, T30	150	203	242	60 L	220 L	A	
	Aldehydes, toxic, n.o.s.	3	UN1988	I	FLAMMABLE LIQUID, POISON	T8, T31	None	201	243	Forbidden	30 L	E	40
				II	FLAMMABLE LIQUID, POISON	T8, T31	None	202	243	1 L	60 L	B	40
	Aldol	6.1	UN2839	II	POISON	T8	None	202	243	5 L	60 L	A	48
D	Aldrin, *liquid*	6.1	NA2762	II	POISON		None	202	243	5 L	60 L	B	
D	Aldrin, *solid*	6.1	NA2761	II	POISON		None	212	242	25 kg	100 kg	A	40
	Alkali metal alloys, liquid, n.o.s.	4.3	UN1421	I	DANGEROUS WHEN WET	A2, A3, N34	None	201	244	Forbidden	1 L	D	
	Alkali metal amalgams	4.3	UN1389	I	DANGEROUS WHEN WET	A2, A3, N34	None	201	244	Forbidden	1 L	D	
	Alkali metal amides	4.3	UN1390	II	DANGEROUS WHEN WET	A6, A7, A8, A19, A20	None	212	241	15 kg	50 kg	E	40
	Alkali metal dispersions, *or* Alkaline earth metal dispersions	4.3	UN1391	I	DANGEROUS WHEN WET	A2, A3	None	201	244	Forbidden	1 L	D	
	Alkaline corrosive liquids, n.o.s., see Caustic alkali liquids, n.o.s.												
	Alkaline earth metal alloys, n.o.s.	4.3	UN1393	II	DANGEROUS WHEN WET	A19	None	212	241	15 kg	50 kg	E	
	Alkaline earth metal amalgams	4.3	UN1392	I	DANGEROUS WHEN WET	A19, N34, N40	None	211	242	Forbidden	15 kg	D	
	Alkaloids, liquid, *poisonous*, n.o.s., *or* Alkaloid salts, liquid, *poisonous*, n.o.s.	6.1	UN3140	I	POISON	A4, T42	None	201	243	1 L	30 L	A	
				II	POISON	T14	None	202	243	5 L	60 L	A	
				III	KEEP AWAY FROM FOOD	T7	153	203	241	60 L	220 L	A	
	Alkaloids, solid, n.o.s. *or* alkaloid salts, solid, n.o.s. *poisonous*	6.1	UN1544	I	POISON		None	211	242	5 kg	50 kg	A	
				II	POISON		None	212	242	25 kg	100 kg	A	
				III	KEEP AWAY FROM FOOD		153	213	240	100 kg	200 kg	A	
	Alkyl, Aryl *or* Toluene sulfonic acid, liquid, *with more than 5 per cent free sulfuric acid*	8	UN2584	II	CORROSIVE	B2, T8, T27	154	202	242	1 L	30 L	B	9
	Alkyl, Aryl *or* Toluene sulfonic acid, liquid, *with not more than 5 per cent free sulfuric acid*	8	UN2586	III	CORROSIVE	T8	154	203	241	5 L	60 L	B	9
	Alkyl, Aryl *or* Toluene sulfonic acid, solid, *with more than 5 per cent free sulfuric acid*	8	UN2583	II	CORROSIVE		154	212	240	15 kg	50 kg	A	

287

Sym-bols	Hazardous materials descriptions and proper shipping names	Hazard class or Division	Identifi-cation Numbers	Packing group	Label(s) required (if not excepted)	Special provisions	(8) Packaging authorizations (§173.***)			(9) Quantity limitations		(10) Vessel stowage requirements	
							Excep-tions	Non-bulk pack-aging	Bulk pack-aging	Passenger aircraft or railcar	Cargo aircraft only	Vessel stow-ages	Other stowage provisions
(1)	(2)	(3)	(4)	(5)	(6)	(7)	(8A)	(8B)	(8C)	(9A)	(9B)	(10A)	(10B)
	Alkyl, Aryl *or* Toluene sulfonic acid, solid, *with not more than 5 per cent free sulfuric acid*	8	UN2585	III	CORROSIVE		154	213	240	25 kg	100 kg	A	
	Alkyl phenols, liquid, n.o.s. *(including C2-C8 homologues)*	6.1	UN3145	III	KEEP AWAY FROM FOOD	T7	153	203	241	60 L	220 L	A	
	Alkyl phenols, solid, n.o.s. *(including C2-C8 homologues)*	6.1	UN2430	III	KEEP AWAY FROM FOOD		153	213	240	100 kg	200 kg	A	
	Alkylamines, n.o.s. *or* Polyalkylamines, n.o.s., corrosive	8	UN2735	I	CORROSIVE	A3, A6, B10, N34, T42	None	201	242	0.5 L	2.5 L	A	
				II	CORROSIVE	B2, T8	154	202	242	1 L	30 L	A	
				III	CORROSIVE	T8	154	203	241	5 L	60 L	A	
	Alkylamines, n.o.s. *or* Polyalkylamines, n.o.s.*corrosive, flammable*	8	UN2734	I	CORROSIVE, FLAMMABLE LIQUID	A3, A6, N34, T8, T31	None	201	243	0.5 L	2.5 L	A	48
				II	CORROSIVE, FLAMMABLE LIQUID	T8, T31	None	202	243	1 L	30 L	A	48
	Alkylamines, n.o.s. *or* Polyalkylamines, n.o.s. *flammable, corrosive*	3	UN2733	I	FLAMMABLE LIQUID, CORROSIVE	T42	None	201	243	0.5 L	2.5 L	D	40
				II	FLAMMABLE LIQUID, CORROSIVE	T8, T31	None	202	243	1 L	5 L	B	40
				III	FLAMMABLE LIQUID, CORROSIVE	B1, T8, T31	None	203	242	5 L	60 L	A	40
	Allethrin, see Pesticides, liquid, toxic, n.o.s.												
	Allyl acetate	3	UN2333	II	FLAMMABLE LIQUID, POISON	T8	None	202	243	1 L	60 L	E	40
	Allyl alcohol	6.1	UN1098	I	POISON, FLAMMABLE LIQUID	2, B9, B14, B32, B74, B77, T38, T43, T45	None	227	244	Forbidden	Forbidden	E	40
	Allyl bromide	3	UN1099	I	FLAMMABLE LIQUID, POISON	T18	None	201	243	Forbidden	30 L	B	40
	Allyl chloride	3	UN1100	I	FLAMMABLE LIQUID, POISON	T18, T26	None	201	243	Forbidden	30 L	E	40
	Allyl chlorocarbonate, see Allyl chloroformate												
+	Allyl chloroformate	8	UN1722	I	CORROSIVE, POISON	1, A3, B9, B14, B30, B72, N41, T38, T43, T44	None	226	244	Forbidden	2.5 L	D	21, 40, 48, 95
	Allyl ethyl ether	3	UN2335	II	FLAMMABLE LIQUID, POISON	T8	None	202	243	1 L	60 L	E	40
	Allyl formate	3	UN2336	I	FLAMMABLE LIQUID, POISON	T18, T26	None	201	243	Forbidden	30 L	E	40
	Allyl glycidyl ether	3	UN2219	III	FLAMMABLE LIQUID, POISON	B1, T7	150	203	242	60 L	220 L	A	
	Allyl iodide	3	UN1723	II	FLAMMABLE LIQUID, CORROSIVE	A3, A6, N34, T18	None	201	243	0.5 L	2.5 L	B	40
+	Allyl isothiocyanate, stabilized	6.1	UN1545	II	POISON	2, A3, A7, B9, B14, B32, B74, T38, T43, T45	None	227	244	Forbidden	60 L	D	40
	Allylamine	6.1	UN2334	I	POISON, FLAMMABLE LIQUID	2, B9, B14, B32, B74, T38, T43, T45	None	227	244	Forbidden	Forbidden	E	40
	Allyltrichlorosilane, stabilized	8	UN1724	II	CORROSIVE, FLAMMABLE LIQUID	A7, B2, B6, N34, T8, T26	None	202	242	Forbidden	30 L	C	12, 21, 40, 48
	Aluminum alkyl halides	4.2	UN3052	I	SPONTANEOUSLY COMBUSTIBLE	B9, B11, T28, T29, T40	None	181	244	Forbidden	Forbidden	D	
	Aluminum alkyl hydrides	4.2	UN3076	I	SPONTANEOUSLY COMBUSTIBLE	B9, B11, T28, T29, T40	None	181	244	Forbidden	Forbidden	D	
	Aluminum alkyls	4.2	UN3051	I	SPONTANEOUSLY COMBUSTIBLE	B9, B11, T28, T29, T40	None	181	244	Forbidden	Forbidden	D	
	Aluminum borohydride *or* Aluminum borohydride in devices	4.2	UN2870	I	SPONTANEOUSLY COMBUSTIBLE, DANGEROUS WHEN WET	B11	None	181	244	Forbidden	Forbidden	D	
	Aluminum bromide, anhydrous	8	UN1725	II	CORROSIVE		154	212	240	15 kg	50 kg	A	40
	Aluminum bromide, solution	8	UN2580	III	CORROSIVE	T8	154	203	241	5 L	60 L	A	
	Aluminum carbide	4.3	UN1394	II	DANGEROUS WHEN WET	A20, N41	None	212	242	15 kg	50 kg	A	
	Aluminum chloride, anhydrous	8	UN1726	II	CORROSIVE		154	212	240	15 kg	50 kg	A	40
	Aluminum chloride, solution	8	UN2581	III	CORROSIVE	T8	154	203	241	5 L	60 L	A	
	Aluminum dross, wet or hot	Forbid-den											
	Aluminum ferrosilicon powder	4.3	UN1395	II	DANGEROUS WHEN WET, POISON	A19	None	212	242	15 kg	50 kg	A	40, 85, 103
	Aluminum hydride	4.3	UN2463	I	DANGEROUS WHEN WET	A19, N40	None	211	242	Forbidden	15 kg	E	

288

Sym-bols	Hazardous materials descriptions and proper shipping names	Hazard class or Division	Identi-fi-cation Numbers	Packing group	Label(s) required (if not excepted)	Special provisions	(8) Packaging authorizations (§173.***)			(9) Quantity limitations		(10) Vessel stowage requirements	
							Excep-tions	Non-bulk pack-aging	Bulk pack-aging	Passenger aircraft or railcar	Cargo aircraft only	Vessel stow-ages	Other stowage provisions
(1)	(2)	(3)	(4)	(5)	(6)	(7)	(8A)	(8B)	(8C)	(9A)	(9B)	(10A)	(10B)
D	Aluminum, molten	9	NA9260	III	CLASS 9		None	None	247	Forbidden	Forbidden	D	
	Aluminum nitrate	5.1	UN1438	III	OXIDIZER	A1, A29	152	213	240	25 kg	100 kg	A	
	Aluminum phosphate solution, see Corrosive liquids, n.o.s.												
	Aluminum phosphide	4.3	UN1397	I	DANGEROUS WHEN WET, POISON	A8, A19, N40	None	211	242	Forbidden	15 kg	E	40, 85
	Aluminum phosphide pesticides	6.1	UN3048	I	POISON	A8	None	211	242	Forbidden	15 kg	E	40, 85
	Aluminum powder, coated	4.1	UN1309	II	FLAMMABLE SOLID		151	212	240	15 kg	50 kg	A	13, 39, 101
				III	FLAMMABLE SOLID		151	213	240	25 kg	100 kg	A	13, 39, 101
	Aluminum powder, uncoated	4.3	UN1396	II	DANGEROUS WHEN WET	A19, A20	None	212	242	15 kg	50 kg	A	39
	Aluminum resinate	4.1	UN2715	III	FLAMMABLE SOLID		151	213	240	25 kg	100 kg	A	
	Aluminum silicon powder, uncoated	4.3	UN1398	III	DANGEROUS WHEN WET	A1, A19	None	213	241	25 kg	100 kg	A	40, 85, 103
	Amatols, see Explosives, blasting, type B												
	2-Amino-4-chlorophenol	6.1	UN2673	II	POISON		None	212	242	25 kg	100 kg	A	
	2-Amino-5-diethylaminopentane	6.1	UN2946	III	KEEP AWAY FROM FOOD	T1	153	203	240	60 L	220 L	A	
	2-(2-Aminoethoxy) ethanol	8	UN3055	III	CORROSIVE	T2	154	203	241	5 L	60 L	A	
	N-Aminoethylpiperazine	8	UN2815	III	CORROSIVE	T7	154	203	241	5 L	60 L	A	12, 48
	Aminophenols (o-; m-; p-)	6.1	UN2512	III	KEEP AWAY FROM FOOD	T1	153	213	240	100 kg	200 kg	A	
	Aminopropyldiethanolamine, see Alkylamines, n.o.s.												
	n-Aminopropylmorpholine, see Alkylamines, n.o.s.												
	Aminopyridines (o-; m-; p-)	6.1	UN2671	II	POISON	T7	None	212	242	25 kg	100 kg	B	12, 40, 48
I	Ammonia, anhydrous, liquefied *or* Ammonia solutions *relative density less than 0.880 at 15 degrees C in water, with more than 50 per cent ammonia*	2.3	UN1005		POISON GAS	4	None	304	314, 315	Forbidden	25 kg	D	40, 57
D	Ammonia, anhydrous, liquefied *or* Ammonia solutions, relative density less than 0.880 at 15 degrees C in water, with more than 50 percent ammonia	2.2	UN1005		NONFLAMMABLE GAS	13	None	304	314, 315	Forbidden	25 kg	D	40, 57
	Ammonia solutions, *relative density between 0.880 and 0.957 at 15 degrees C in water, with more than 10 per cent but not more than 35 percent ammonia*	8	UN2672	III	CORROSIVE	T14	154	203	241	5 L	60 L	A	40, 85
	Ammonia solutions, *relative density less than 0.880 at 15 degrees C in water, with more than 35 per cent but not more than 50 per cent ammonia*	2.2	UN2073		NONFLAMMABLE GAS		306	304	314, 315	Forbidden	150 kg	E	40, 57
	Ammonium arsenate	6.1	UN1546	II	POISON		None	212	242	25 kg	100 kg	A	
	Ammonium azide	Forbid-den											
	Ammonium bifluoride, solid, see Ammonium hydrogen fluoride, solid												
	Ammonium bifluoride solution, see Ammonium hydrogen fluoride, solution												
	Ammonium bromate	Forbid-den											
	Ammonium chlorate	Forbid-den											
	Ammonium dichromate	5.1	UN1439	II	OXIDIZER		152	212	242	5 kg	25 kg	A	
	Ammonium dinitro-o-cresolate	6.1	UN1843	II	POISON	T8	None	212	242	25 kg	100 kg	B	36, 65, 66, 77
	Ammonium fluoride	6.1	UN2505	III	KEEP AWAY FROM FOOD		153	213	240	100 kg	200 kg	A	26
	Ammonium fluorosilicate	6.1	UN2854	III	KEEP AWAY FROM FOOD		153	213	240	100 kg	200 kg	A	26
	Ammonium fulminate	Forbid-den											
	Ammonium hydrogen fluoride, solid	8	UN1727	II	CORROSIVE	N34	154	212	240	15 kg	50 kg	A	25, 26, 40
	Ammonium hydrogen fluoride, solution	8	UN2817	II	CORROSIVE, POISON	N34, T15	None	202	243	1 L	30 L	B	40, 95
	Ammonium hydrogen sulfate	8	UN2506	II	CORROSIVE		154	212	240	15 kg	50 kg	A	40
	Ammonium hydrosulfide, solution, see Ammonium sulfide solution												
D	*Ammonium hydroxide, see Ammonia solutions, etc.*												
	Ammonium metavanadate	6.1	UN2859	II	POISON		None	212	242	25 kg	100 kg	A	
D	Ammonium nitrate fertilizers	5.1	NA2072	III	OXIDIZER	7	152	213	240	25 kg	100 kg	B	48, 59, 60, 117

289

Sym-bols	Hazardous materials descriptions and proper shipping names	Hazard class or Division	Identifi-cation Numbers	Packing group	Label(s) required (if not excepted)	Special provisions	Packaging authorizations (§173.***)			Quantity limitations		Vessel stowage requirements	
							Excep-tions	Non-bulk pack-aging	Bulk pack-aging	Passenger aircraft or railcar	Cargo aircraft only	Vessel stow-ages	Other stowage provisions
(1)	(2)	(3)	(4)	(5)	(6)	(7)	(8A)	(8B)	(8C)	(9A)	(9B)	(10A)	(10B)
AW	Ammonium nitrate fertilizers: uniform non-segregating mixtures of nitrogen/phosphate or nitrogen/potash types or complete fertilizers of nitrogen/phosphate/potash type, with not more than 70 per cent ammonium nitrate and not more than 0.4 per cent total added combustible material or with not more than 45 per cent ammonium nitrate with unrestricted combustible material	9	UN2071	III	CLASS 9		155	213	240	200 kg	200 kg	A	
D	Ammonium nitrate-fuel oil mixture (containing only prilled ammonium nitrate and fuel oil)	1.5D	NA0331	II	EXPLOSIVE 1.5D		None	62	None	Forbidden	Forbidden	B	1E, 5E, 19E
	Ammonium nitrate, liquid (hot concentrated solution)	5.1	UN2426		OXIDIZER	B5, B17, T25	None	None	243	Forbidden	Forbidden	D	59, 60
D	Ammonium nitrate mixed fertilizers	5.1	NA2069	III	OXIDIZER	10	152	213	240	25 kg	100 kg	B	48, 59, 60, 117
	Ammonium nitrate, with more than 0.2 per cent combustible substances, including any organic substance calculated as carbon, to the exclusion of any other added substance	1.1D	UN0222	II	EXPLOSIVE 1.1D		None	62	None	Forbidden	Forbidden	B	1E, 5E, 19E
	Ammonium nitrate, with not more than 0.2 per cent of combustible substances, including any organic substance calculated as carbon, to the exclusion of any other added substance	5.1	UN1942	III	OXIDIZER	A1, A29	152	213	240	25 kg	100 kg	A	48, 59, 60, 116
	Ammonium nitrite	Forbid-den											
	Ammonium perchlorate	5.1	UN1442	II	OXIDIZER	A9	152	212	242	5 kg	25 kg	E	58, 69, 106
	Ammonium perchlorate	1.1D	UN0402	II	EXPLOSIVE 1.1D	107	None	62	None	Forbidden	Forbidden	B	1E, 5E, 19E
	Ammonium permanganate, see Permanganates, inorganic, n.o.s.												
	Ammonium persulfate	5.1	UN1444	III	OXIDIZER	A1, A29	152	213	240	25 kg	100 kg	A	
	Ammonium picrate, dry or wetted with less than 10 per cent water, by mass	1.1D	UN0004	II	EXPLOSIVE 1.1D		None	62	None	Forbidden	Forbidden	B	1E, 5E, 19E
	Ammonium picrate, wetted with not less than 10 per cent water, by mass	4.1	UN1310	I	FLAMMABLE SOLID	A2, N41	None	211	None	0.5 kg	0.5 kg	D	28, 36
	Ammonium polysulfide, solution	8	UN2818	II	CORROSIVE, POISON	T14	None	202	243	1 L	30 L	B	12, 26, 40, 48, 95
	Ammonium polyvanadate	6.1	UN2861	II	POISON		None	212	242	25 kg	100 kg	A	
	Ammonium silicofluoride, see Ammonium fluorosilicate												
	Ammonium sulfide solution	8	UN2683	II	CORROSIVE, POISON, FLAMMABLE LIQUID	T14	None	202	243	1 L	30 L	B	12, 22, 26, 48, 100
	Ammunition, blank, see Cartridges for weapons, blank												
	Ammunition, illuminating with or without burster, expelling charge or propelling charge	1.2G	UN0171	II	EXPLOSIVE 1.2G		63(b)	62	None	Forbidden	Forbidden	B	
	Ammunition, illuminating with or without burster, expelling charge or propelling charge	1.3G	UN0254	II	EXPLOSIVE 1.3G		63(b)	62	None	Forbidden	Forbidden	B	
	Ammunition, illuminating with or without burster, expelling charge or propelling charge	1.4G	UN0297	II	EXPLOSIVE 1.4G		63(b)	62	None	Forbidden	75 kg	A	24E
	Ammunition, incendiary liquid or gel, with burster, expelling charge or propelling charge	1.3J	UN0247	II	EXPLOSIVE 1.3J		63(b)	62	None	Forbidden	Forbidden	E	7E, 13E, 23E
	Ammunition, incendiary (water-activated contrivances) with burster, expelling charge or propelling charge, see Contrivances, water-activated, etc.												
	Ammunition, incendiary, white phosphorus, with burster, expelling charge or propelling charge	1.2H	UN0243	II	EXPLOSIVE 1.2H		63(b)	62	None	Forbidden	Forbidden	E	8E, 14E, 15E
	Ammunition, incendiary, white phosphorus, with burster, expelling charge or propelling charge	1.3H	UN0244	II	EXPLOSIVE 1.3H		63(b)	62	None	Forbidden	Forbidden	E	8E, 14E, 15E
	Ammunition, incendiary with or without burster,expelling charge, or propelling charge	1.2G	UN0009	II	EXPLOSIVE 1.2G		63(b)	62	None	Forbidden	Forbidden	B	
	Ammunition, incendiary with or without burster, expelling charge, or propelling charge	1.3G	UN0010	II	EXPLOSIVE 1.3G		63(b)	62	None	Forbidden	Forbidden	B	
	Ammunition, incendiary with or without burster, expelling charge or propelling charge	1.4G	UN0300	II	EXPLOSIVE 1.4G		63(b)	62	None	Forbidden	75 kg	A	24E
	Ammunition, practice	1.4G	UN0362	II	EXPLOSIVE 1.4G		63(b)	62	None	Forbidden	75 kg	A	24E
	Ammunition, practice	1.3G	UN0488	II	EXPLOSIVE 1.3G		63(b)	62	None	Forbidden	Forbidden	B	1E, 7E, 25E

290

Sym-bols	Hazardous materials descriptions and proper shipping names	Hazard class or Division	Identifi-cation Numbers	Packing group	Label(s) required (if not excepted)	Special provisions	(8) Packaging authorizations (§173.***)			(9) Quantity limitations		(10) Vessel stowage requirements	
							Excep-tions	Non-bulk pack-aging	Bulk pack-aging	Passenger aircraft or railcar	Cargo aircraft only	Vessel stow-ages	Other stowage provisions
(1)	(2)	(3)	(4)	(5)	(6)	(7)	(8A)	(8B)	(8C)	(9A)	(9B)	(10A)	(10B)
	Ammunition, proof	1.4G	UN0363	II	EXPLOSIVE 1.4G		63(b)	62	None	Forbidden	75 kg	A	24E
	Ammunition, rocket, see Warheads, rocket *etc.*												
	Ammunition, SA (small arms), see Cartridges for weapons, *etc.*												
	Ammunition, smoke (water-activated contrivances), white phosphorus, with burster, expelling charge or propelling charge, see Contrivances, water-activated, *etc. (UN 0248)*												
	Ammunition, smoke (water-activated contrivances), without white phosphorus or phosphides, with burster, expelling charge or propelling charge, see Contrivances, water-activated, *etc. (UN 0249)*												
	Ammunition, smoke, white phosphorus *with burster, expelling charge, or propelling charge*	1.3H	UN0246	II	EXPLOSIVE 1.3H		63(b)	62	None	Forbidden	Forbidden	E	8E, 14E, 15E, 17E
	Ammunition smoke, white phosphorus *with burster, expelling charge, or propelling charge*	1.2H	UN0245	II	EXPLOSIVE 1.2H		63(b)	62	None	Forbidden	Forbidden	E	8E, 14E, 15E, 17E
	Ammunition, smoke *with or without burster, expelling charge or propelling charge*	1.3G	UN0016	II	EXPLOSIVE 1.3G, CORROSIVE		63(b)	62	None	Forbidden	Forbidden	E	20E
	Ammunition, smoke *with or without burster, expelling charge or propelling charge*	1.4G	UN0303	II	EXPLOSIVE 1.4G, CORROSIVE		63(b)	62	None	Forbidden	75 kg	E	20E
	Ammunition, smoke *with or without burster, expelling charge or propelling charge*	1.2G	UN0015	II	EXPLOSIVE 1.2G, CORROSIVE		63(b)	62	None	Forbidden	Forbidden	E	20E
	Ammunition, sporting, see Cartridges for weapons, *etc. (UN 0012; UN 0328; UN 0339)*												
	Ammunition, tear-producing, non-explosive, without burster or expelling charge, non-fuzed	6.1	UN2017	II	POISON, CORROSIVE		None	212	None	Forbidden	50 kg	E	13, 40
	Ammunition, tear-producing *with burster, expelling charge or propelling charge*	1.2G	UN0018	II	EXPLOSIVE 1.2G, CORROSIVE, POISON		63(b)	62	None	Forbidden	Forbidden	E	20E
	Ammunition, tear-producing *with burster, expelling charge or propelling charge*	1.3G	UN0019	II	EXPLOSIVE 1.3G, CORROSIVE, POISON		63(b)	62	None	Forbidden	Forbidden	E	20E
	Ammunition, tear-producing *with burster, expelling charge or propelling charge*	1.4G	UN0301	II	EXPLOSIVE 1.4G, CORROSIVE, POISON		63(b)	62	None	Forbidden	75 kg	E	20E
	Ammunition, toxic, nonexplosive, without burster or expelling charge, non-fuzed	6.1	UN2016	II	POISON		None	212	None	Forbidden	100 kg	E	13, 40
	Ammunition, toxic (water-activated contrivances), with burster, expelling charge or propelling charge, see Contrivances, water-activated, *etc.*												
	Ammunition, toxic *with burster, expelling charge, or propelling charge*	1.2K	UN0020	II	EXPLOSIVE 1.2K, POISON		63(b)	62	None	Forbidden	Forbidden	E	2E, 8E, 11E, 17E
	Ammunition, toxic *with burster, expelling charge, or propelling charge*	1.3K	UN0021	II	EXPLOSIVE 1.3K, POISON		63(b)	62	None	Forbidden	Forbidden	E	2E, 8E, 11E, 17E
	Amyl acetates	3	UN1104	III	FLAMMABLE LIQUID	B1, T1	150	203	241	60 L	220 L	A	
	Amyl acid phosphate	8	UN2819	III	CORROSIVE	T7	154	203	241	5 L	60 L	A	
	Amyl alcohols	3	UN1105	II	FLAMMABLE LIQUID	T1	150	202	242	5 L	60 L	B	
				III	FLAMMABLE LIQUID	B1, B3, T1	150	203	242	60 L	220 L	A	
	Amyl butyrates	3	UN2620	III	FLAMMABLE LIQUID	B1, T1	150	203	242	60 L	220 L	A	
	Amyl chlorides	3	UN1107	II	FLAMMABLE LIQUID	T1	150	202	242	5 L	60 L	B	
	Amyl formates	3	UN1109	III	FLAMMABLE LIQUID	B1, T1	150	203	242	60 L	220 L	A	
	Amyl mercaptans	3	UN1111	II	FLAMMABLE LIQUID	A3, T8	None	202	242	5 L	60 L	B	95, 102
	Amyl methyl ketone	3	UN1110	III	FLAMMABLE LIQUID	B1, T1	150	203	242	60 L	220 L	A	
	Amyl nitrate	3	UN1112	III	FLAMMABLE LIQUID	B1, T1	150	202	242	5 L	60 L	A	40
	Amyl nitrites	3	UN1113	II	FLAMMABLE LIQUID	T8	150	202	242	5 L	60 L	E	40
	Amylamines	3	UN1106	II	FLAMMABLE LIQUID	T1	150	202	242	5 L	60 L	B	
	n-Amylene	3	UN1108	I	FLAMMABLE LIQUID	T14	150	201	243	1 L	30 L	E	
	Amyltrichlorosilane	8	UN1728	II	CORROSIVE	A7, B2, B6, N34, T8, T26	None	202	242	Forbidden	30 L	C	40
	Anhydrous, ammonia see Ammonia, anhydrous, liquefied												
	Anhydrous hydrofluoric acid, see Hydrogen fluoride, anhydrous												

Sym-bols (1)	Hazardous materials descriptions and proper shipping names (2)	Hazard class or Division (3)	Identifi-cation Numbers (4)	Packing group (5)	Label(s) required (if not excepted) (6)	Special provisions (7)	(8) Packaging authorizations (§173.***) Excep-tions (8A)	Non-bulk pack-aging (8B)	Bulk pack-aging (8C)	(9) Quantity limitations Passenger aircraft or railcar (9A)	Cargo aircraft only (9B)	(10) Vessel stowage requirements Vessel stow-ages (10A)	Other stowage provisions (10B)
+	Aniline	6.1	UN1547	II	POISON	T8	None	202	243	5 L	60 L	A	40
	Aniline hydrochloride	6.1	UN1548	III	KEEP AWAY FROM FOOD		153	213	240	100 kg	200 kg	A	
	Aniline oil, see Aniline												
	Anisidines	6.1	UN2431	III	KEEP AWAY FROM FOOD	T1	153	203	241	60 L	220 L	A	
	Anisole	3	UN2222	III	FLAMMABLE LIQUID	B1, T1	150	203	242	60 L	220 L	A	
	Anisoyl chloride	8	UN1729	II	CORROSIVE	B2, T8	154	202	242	1 L	30 L	C	8, 40
	Anti-freeze, liquid, see Flammable liquids, n.o.s.												
	Antimonous chloride, see Antimony trichloride												
	Antimony compounds, inorganic, liquid, n.o.s.	6.1	UN3141	I	POISON	A4, T42	None	201	243	1 L	30 L	A	
				II	POISON	T14	None	202	243	5 L	60 L	A	
				III	KEEP AWAY FROM FOOD	T7	153	203	241	60 L	220 L	A	
	Antimony compounds, inorganic, solid, n.o.s.	6.1	UN1549	I	POISON		None	211	242	5 kg	50 kg	A	
				II	POISON		None	212	242	25 kg	100 kg	A	
				III	KEEP AWAY FROM FOOD		153	213	240	100 kg	200 kg	A	
	Antimony lactate	6.1	UN1550	III	KEEP AWAY FROM FOOD		153	213	240	100 kg	200 kg	A	
	Antimony pentachloride, liquid	8	UN1730	II	CORROSIVE	B2, T8, T26	None	202	242	1 L	30 L	C	8, 40
	Antimony pentachloride, solutions	8	UN1731	II	CORROSIVE	B2, T8, T27	154	202	242	1 L	30 L	C	8, 40
	Antimony pentafluoride	8	UN1732	II	CORROSIVE, POISON	A3, A6, A7, A10, N3, T12, T26	None	202	243	Forbidden	30 L	D	40, 95
	Antimony potassium tartrate	6.1	UN1551	III	KEEP AWAY FROM FOOD		153	213	240	100 kg	200 kg	A	
	Antimony powder	6.1	UN2871	III	KEEP AWAY FROM FOOD		153	213	240	100 kg	200 kg	A	
	Antimony sulfide and a chlorate, mixtures of	Forbid-den											
	Antimony sulfide, solid, see Antimony compounds, inorganic, n.o.s.												
D	Antimony tribromide, solid	8	NA1549	II	CORROSIVE		154	212	240	25 kg	100 kg	A	13
D	Antimony tribromide, solution	8	NA1549	II	CORROSIVE	B2	154	202	242	1 L	30 L	C	13
	Antimony trichloride, liquid	8	UN1733	II	CORROSIVE	B2	154	202	242	1 L	30 L	C	40
	Antimony trichloride, solid	8	UN1733	II	CORROSIVE		154	212	240	15 kg	50 kg	A	40
D	Antimony trifluoride, solid	8	NA1549	II	CORROSIVE		154	212	240	25 kg	25 kg	A	13
D	Antimony trifluoride solution	8	NA1549	II	CORROSIVE	B2	154	202	242	1 L	30 L	C	13
	Aqua ammonia, see Ammonia solution, *etc.*												
	Argon, compressed	2.2	UN1006		NONFLAMMABLE GAS		306	302	314, 315	75 kg	150 kg	A	
	Argon, refrigerated liquid (cryogenic liquid)	2.2	UN1951		NONFLAMMABLE GAS		320	316	318	50 kg	500 kg	B	
	Arsenic	6.1	UN1558	II	POISON		None	212	242	25 kg	100 kg	A	
	Arsenic acid, liquid	6.1	UN1553	I	POISON	T18, T27	None	201	243	1 L	30 L	B	
	Arsenic acid, solid	6.1	UN1554	II	POISON		None	212	242	25 kg	100 kg	A	
	Arsenic bromide	6.1	UN1555	II	POISON		None	212	242	25 kg	100 kg	A	12, 40
	Arsenic chloride, see Arsenic trichloride												
	Arsenic compounds, liquid, n.o.s. *including arsenates n.o.s.; arsenites, n.o.s.; arsenic sulfides, n.o.s.; and organic compounds of arsenic, n.o.s.*	6.1	UN1556	I	POISON		None	201	243	1 L	30 L	B	40
				II	POISON		None	202	243	5 L	60 L	B	40
				III	KEEP AWAY FROM FOOD		153	203	241	60 L	220 L	B	40
	Arsenic compounds, solid, n.o.s. *including arsenates, n.o.s.; arsenites, n.o.s.; arsenic sulfides, n.o.s.; and organic compounds of arsenic, n.o.s.*	6.1	UN1557	I	POISON		None	211	242	5 kg	50 kg	A	
				II	POISON		None	212	242	25 kg	100 kg	A	
				III	KEEP AWAY FROM FOOD		153	213	240	100 kg	200 kg	A	
	Arsenic pentoxide	6.1	UN1559	II	POISON		None	212	242	25 kg	100 kg	A	
D	Arsenic sulfide	6.1	NA1557	II	POISON		None	212	242	25 kg	100 kg	A	
	Arsenic sulfide and a chlorate, mixtures of	Forbid-den											
	Arsenic trichloride	6.1	UN1560	I	POISON	2, B9, B14, B32, B74, T38, T43, T45	None	227	244	1L	30L	B	40
	Arsenic trioxide	6.1	UN1561	II	POISON		None	212	242	25 kg	100 kg	A	
D	Arsenic trisulfide	6.1	NA1557	II	POISON		None	212	242	25 kg	100 kg	A	
	Arsenic, white, solid, see Arsenic trioxide												
	Arsenical dust	6.1	UN1562	II	POISON		None	212	242	25 kg	100 kg	A	
	Arsenical pesticides, liquid, flammable, toxic, n.o.s., *flash point less than 23 degrees C.*	3	UN2760	I	FLAMMABLE LIQUID, POISON		None	201	243	Forbidden	30 L	B	40
				II	FLAMMABLE LIQUID, POISON		None	202	243	1 L	60 L	B	40

Sym-bols	Hazardous materials descriptions and proper shipping names	Hazard class or Division	Identifi-cation Numbers	Packing group	Label(s) required (if not excepted)	Special provisions	Packaging authorizations (§173.***)			Quantity limitations		Vessel stowage requirements	
							(8)			(9)		(10)	
							Excep-tions	Non-bulk pack-aging	Bulk pack-aging	Passenger aircraft or railcar	Cargo aircraft only	Vessel stow-ages	Other stowage provisions
(1)	(2)	(3)	(4)	(5)	(6)	(7)	(8A)	(8B)	(8C)	(9A)	(9B)	(10A)	(10B)
	Arsenical pesticides, liquid, toxic, flammable, n.o.s. *flashpoint not less than 23 degrees C.*	6.1	UN2993	I	POISON, FLAMMABLE LIQUID	T42	None	201	243	1 L	30 L	B	40
				II	POISON, FLAMMABLE LIQUID	T14	None	202	243	5 L	60 L	B	40
				III	KEEP AWAY FROM FOOD, FLAMMABLE LIQUID	B1, T14	153	203	241	60 L	220 L	A	40
	Arsenical pesticides, liquid, toxic, n.o.s.	6.1	UN2994	I	POISON	T42	None	201	243	1 L	30 L	B	40
				II	POISON	T14	None	202	243	5 L	60 L	B	40
				III	KEEP AWAY FROM FOOD	T14	153	203	241	60 L	220 L	A	40
	Arsenical pesticides, solid, toxic, n.o.s.	6.1	UN2759	I	POISON		None	211	242	5 kg	50 kg	A	40
				II	POISON		None	212	242	25 kg	100 kg	A	40
				III	KEEP AWAY FROM FOOD		153	213	240	100 kg	200 kg	A	40
	Arsenious acid, solid, see Arsenic trioxide												
	Arsenious and mercuric iodide solution, see Arsenic compounds, liquid, n.o.s.												
	Arsine	2.3	UN2188		POISON GAS, FLAMMABLE GAS	1	None	192	245	Forbidden	Forbidden	D	40
	Articles, explosive, extremely insensitive *or* Articles, EEI	1.6N	UN0486	II	EXPLOSIVE 1.6N	101	None	62	None	Forbidden	Forbidden	B	
	Articles, explosive, n.o.s.	1.4S	UN0349	II	EXPLOSIVE 1.4S	101	None	62	None	25 kg	100 kg	A	9E
	Articles, explosive, n.o.s.	1.4B	UN0350	II	EXPLOSIVE 1.4B	101	None	62	None	Forbidden	Forbidden	A	24E
	Articles, explosive, n.o.s.	1.4C	UN0351	II	EXPLOSIVE 1.4C	101	None	62	None	Forbidden	Forbidden	A	24E
	Articles, explosive, n.o.s.	1.4D	UN0352	II	EXPLOSIVE 1.4D	101	None	62	None	Forbidden	Forbidden	A	24E
	Articles, explosive, n.o.s.	1.4G	UN0353	II	EXPLOSIVE 1.4G	101	None	62	None	Forbidden	Forbidden	A	24E
	Articles, explosive, n.o.s.	1.1L	UN0354	II	EXPLOSIVE 1.1L	101	None	62	None	Forbidden	Forbidden	E	2E, 8E, 17E
	Articles, explosive, n.o.s.	1.2L	UN0355	II	EXPLOSIVE 1.2L	101	None	62	None	Forbidden	Forbidden	E	2E, 8E, 17E
	Articles, explosive, n.o.s.	1.3L	UN0356	II	EXPLOSIVE 1.3L	101	None	62	None	Forbidden	Forbidden	E	2E, 8E, 17E
	Articles, explosive, n.o.s.	1.1C	UN0462	II	EXPLOSIVE 1.1C	101	None	62	None	Forbidden	Forbidden	B	
	Articles, explosive, n.o.s.	1.1D	UN0463	II	EXPLOSIVE 1.1D	101	None	62	None	Forbidden	Forbidden	B	
	Articles, explosive, n.o.s.	1.1E	UN0464	II	EXPLOSIVE 1.1E	101	None	62	None	Forbidden	Forbidden	B	
	Articles, explosive, n.o.s.	1.1F	UN0465	II	EXPLOSIVE 1.1F	101	None	62	None	Forbidden	Forbidden	E	
	Articles, explosive, n.o.s.	1.2C	UN0466	II	EXPLOSIVE 1.2C	101	None	62	None	Forbidden	Forbidden	B	
	Articles, explosive, n.o.s.	1.2D	UN0467	II	EXPLOSIVE 1.2D	101	None	62	None	Forbidden	Forbidden	B	
	Articles, explosive, n.o.s.	1.2E	UN0468	II	EXPLOSIVE 1.2E	101	None	62	None	Forbidden	Forbidden	B	
	Articles, explosive, n.o.s.	1.2F	UN0469	II	EXPLOSIVE 1.2F	101	None	62	None	Forbidden	Forbidden	E	
	Articles, explosive, n.o.s.	1.3C	UN0470	II	EXPLOSIVE 1.3C	101	None	62	None	Forbidden	Forbidden	B	
	Articles, explosive, n.o.s.	1.4E	UN0471	II	EXPLOSIVE 1.4E	101	None	62	None	Forbidden	75kg	A	24E
	Articles, explosive, n.o.s.	1.4F	UN0472	II	EXPLOSIVE 1.4F	101	None	62	None	Forbidden	Forbidden	E	
	Articles, pyrophoric	1.2L	UN0380	II	EXPLOSIVE 1.2L		None	62	None	Forbidden	Forbidden	E	2E, 8E, 17E
	Articles, pyrotechnic *for technical purposes*	1.1G	UN0428	II	EXPLOSIVE 1.1G		None	62	None	Forbidden	Forbidden	B	
	Articles, pyrotechnic *for technical purposes*	1.2G	UN0429	II	EXPLOSIVE 1.2G		None	62	None	Forbidden	Forbidden	B	
	Articles, pyrotechnic *for technical purposes*	1.3G	UN0430	II	EXPLOSIVE 1.3G		None	62	None	Forbidden	Forbidden	B	
	Articles, pyrotechnic *for technical purposes*	1.4G	UN0431	II	EXPLOSIVE 1.4G		None	62	None	Forbidden	75 kg	A	24E
	Articles, pyrotechnic *for technical purposes*	1.4S	UN0432	II	EXPLOSIVE 1.4S		None	62	None	25 kg	100 kg	A	9E
	Asbestos, blue or brown, see Blue asbestos *etc.*												
	Asbestos, white, see White asbestos *etc.*												
	Ascaridole (organic peroxide)	Forbid-den											
D	Asphalt, *at or above its flashpoint*	3	NA1999	III	FLAMMABLE LIQUID	B1	150	203	247	Forbidden	Forbidden	D	
D	Asphalt, cut back, *see* Tars, liquid, *etc.*												
	Automobile, motorcycle, tractor, or other self-propelled vehicle, engine, or other mechanical apparatus. see Vehicles, self-propelled												
	Azaurolic acid (salt of) (dry)	Forbid-den											
	Azido guanidine picrate (dry)	Forbid-den											
	5-Azido-1-hydroxy tetrazole	Forbid-den											
	Azido hydroxy tetrazole (mercury and silver salts)	Forbid-den											
	Azido hydroxy tetrazole (mercury and silver salts)	Forbid-den											
	3-Azido-1,2-Propylene glycol dinitrate	Forbid-den											

293

(1) Symbols	(2) Hazardous materials descriptions and proper shipping names	(3) Hazard class or Division	(4) Identification Numbers	(5) Packing group	(6) Label(s) required (if not excepted)	(7) Special provisions	(8A) Exceptions	(8B) Non-bulk packaging	(8C) Bulk packaging	(9A) Passenger aircraft or railcar	(9B) Cargo aircraft only	(10A) Vessel stowages	(10B) Other stowage provisions
	Azidodithiocarbonic acid	Forbidden											
	Azidoethyl nitrate	Forbidden											
	1-Aziridinyl phosphine oxide-(tris), see Tris-(1-aziridinyl) phosphine oxide, solution												
	2,2'-Azodi-(2,4-dimethyl-4-methoxyvaleronitrile)	4.1	UN2955	II	FLAMMABLE SOLID		None	224	None	Forbidden	Forbidden	D	2
	2,2'-Azodi-(2,4 dimethylvaleronitrile)	4.1	UN2953	II	FLAMMABLE SOLID		None	224	None	Forbidden	Forbidden	D	2
	1,1'-Azodi-(hexahydrobenzonitrile)	4.1	UN2954	II	FLAMMABLE SOLID		None	224	None	15 kg	50 kg	B	12, 61, 85
	2,2'-Azodi (2-methyl-butyronitrile)	4.1	UN3030	II	FLAMMABLE SOLID		None	224	None	Forbidden	Forbidden	D	2, 61
	Azodiisobutyronitrile	4.1	UN2952	II	FLAMMABLE SOLID, EXPLOSIVES	41, 53	None	224	None	Forbidden	Forbidden	D	2
	Azotetrazole (dry)	Forbidden											
	Barium	4.3	UN1400	II	DANGEROUS WHEN WET	A19	None	212	241	15 kg	50 kg	E	
	Barium alloys, pyrophoric	4.2	UN1854	I	SPONTANEOUSLY COMBUSTIBLE		None	181	None	Forbidden	Forbidden	D	
	Barium azide, *dry or wetted with less than 50 per cent water, by mass*	1.1A	UN0224	II	EXPLOSIVE 1.1A, Poison	111, 117	None	62	None	Forbidden	Forbidden	E	2E, 6E
	Barium azide, *wetted with not less than 50 per cent water, by mass*	4.1	UN1571	I	FLAMMABLE SOLID, POISON	A2	None	182	None	Forbidden	0.5 kg	D	28, 36
	Barium bromate	5.1	UN2719	II	OXIDIZER, POISON		None	212	242	5 kg	25 kg	A	56, 58, 106
	Barium chlorate	5.1	UN1445	II	OXIDIZER, POISON	A9, N34, T8	None	212	242	5 kg	25 kg	A	56, 58, 106
	Barium compounds, n.o.s.	6.1	UN1564	I	POISON		None	211	242	5 kg	50 kg	A	
				II	POISON		None	212	242	25 kg	100 kg	A	
				III	KEEP AWAY FROM FOOD		153	213	240	100 kg	200 kg	A	
	Barium cyanide	6.1	UN1565	I	POISON	N74, N75	None	211	242	5 kg	50 kg	A	26, 40
	Barium hypochlorite *with more than 22 per cent available chlorine*	5.1	UN2741	II	OXIDIZER	A7, A9, N34	152	212	None	5 kg	25 kg	B	56, 58, 106
	Barium nitrate	5.1	UN1446	II	OXIDIZER, POISON		None	212	242	5 kg	25 kg	A	
	Barium oxide	6.1	UN1884	III	KEEP AWAY FROM FOOD		153	213	240	100 kg	200 kg	A	
	Barium perchlorate	5.1	UN1447	II	OXIDIZER, POISON	T8	None	212	242	5 kg	25 kg	A	56, 58, 106
	Barium permanganate	5.1	UN1448	II	OXIDIZER, POISON		None	212	242	5 kg	25 kg	D	56, 58, 69, 106, 107
	Barium peroxide	5.1	UN1449	II	OXIDIZER, POISON		None	212	2	5 kg	25 kg	A	13, 75, 106
	Barium selenate, see Selenates *or* Selenites												
	Barium selenite, see Selenates *or* Selenites												
D	Barium styphnate	1.1A	NA0473	II	EXPLOSIVE 1.1A	111, 117	None	62	None	Forbidden	Forbidden	E	2E, 6E
	Batteries, dry, containing potassium hydroxide solid, *electric, storage*	8	UN3028	III	CORROSIVE		None	213	None	25 kg gross	230 kg gross	A	
	Batteries, wet, filled with acid, *electric storage*	8	UN2794	III	CORROSIVE		159	159	None	25 kg gross	No limit	A	
	Batteries, wet, filled with alkali, *electric storage*	8	UN2795	III	CORROSIVE		159	159	None	25 kg gross	No limit	A	
AW	Batteries, wet, non-spillable, *electric storage*	8	UN2800	III	CORROSIVE		159	159	None	No Limit	No Limit	A	
	Battery fluid, acid	8	UN2796	II	CORROSIVE	A3, A7, B2, B15, N6, N34, T9, T27	154	202	242	1 L	30 L	B	
	Battery fluid, alkali	8	UN2797	II	CORROSIVE	B2, N6, T8	154	202	242	1 L	30 L	A	
	Battery lithium type, see Lithium batteries *etc.*												
	Battery, wet, filled with acid or alkali with automobile (or named self-propelled vehicle or mechanical equipment containing internal combustion engine) see Vehicles, self-propelled *etc.*												
	Battery, wet, with wheelchair, see Wheelchair, electric												
	Benzene	3	UN1114	II	FLAMMABLE LIQUID	T8	150	202	242	5 L	60 L	B	40
	Benzene diazonium chloride (dry)	Forbidden											
	Benzene diazonium nitrate (dry)	Forbidden											

Symbols	Hazardous materials descriptions and proper shipping names	Hazard class or Division	Identification Numbers	Packing group	Label(s) required (if not excepted)	Special provisions	Packaging authorizations (§173.***)			Quantity limitations		Vessel stowage requirements	
							Exceptions	Non-bulk packaging	Bulk packaging	Passenger aircraft or railcar	Cargo aircraft only	Vessel stowages	Other stowage provisions
(1)	(2)	(3)	(4)	(5)	(6)	(7)	(8A)	(8B)	(8C)	(9A)	(9B)	(10A)	(10B)
	Benzene-1,3-disulfohydrazide, *not more than 52 per cent as a paste*	4.1	UN2971	II	FLAMMABLE SOLID		None	224	None	15 kg	50 kg	B	12, 61, 85
	Benzene phosphorus dichloride, see Phenyl phosphorus dichloride												
	Benzene phosphorus thiodichloride, see Phenyl phosphorus thiodichloride												
	Benzene sulfohydrazide	4.1	UN2970	II	FLAMMABLE SOLID		None	224	None	15 kg	50 kg	B	12, 61, 85
	Benzene sulfonyl chloride	8	UN2225	III	CORROSIVE	T8	154	203	241	5 L	60 L	A	40
	Benzene triozonide	Forbidden											
	Benzenethiol, see Phenyl mercaptan												
	Benzidine	6.1	UN1885	II	POISON		None	212	242	25 kg	100 kg	A	
	Benzoic derivative pesticides, liquid, flammable, toxic, n.o.s., *flash point less than 23 degrees C.*	3	UN2770	I	FLAMMABLE LIQUID, POISON		None	201	243	Forbidden	30 L	E	
				II	FLAMMABLE LIQUID, POISON		None	202	243	1 L	60 L	B	
	Benzoic derivative pesticides, liquid, toxic, flammable, n.o.s. *flashpoint not less than 23 degrees C.*	6.1	UN3003	I	POISON, FLAMMABLE LIQUID	T42	None	201	243	1 L	30 L	B	40
				II	POISON, FLAMMABLE LIQUID	T14	None	202	243	5 L	60 L	B	40
				III	KEEP AWAY FROM FOOD, FLAMMABLE LIQUID	T14	153	203	241	60 L	220 L	A	40
	Benzoic derivative pesticides, liquid, toxic, n.o.s.	6.1	UN3004	I	POISON	T42	None	201	243	1 L	30 L	B	40
				II	POISON	T14	None	202	243	5 L	60 L	B	40
				III	KEEP AWAY FROM FOOD	T14	153	203	241	60 L	220 L	A	40
	Benzoic derivative pesticides, solid, toxic, n.o.s.	6.1	UN2769	I	POISON		None	211	242	5 kg	50 kg	A	40
				II	POISON		None	212	242	25 kg	100 kg	A	
				III	KEEP AWAY FROM FOOD		153	213	240	100 kg	200 kg	A	
	Benzol, see Benzene												
	Benzonitrile	6.1	UN2224	II	POISON	T14	None	202	243	5 L	60 L	A	26, 40
	Benzoquinone	6.1	UN2587	II	POISON		None	212	242	25 kg	100 kg	A	
	Benzotrichloride	8	UN2226	II	CORROSIVE	B2, T15	154	202	242	1 L	30 L	A	40
	Benzotrifluoride	3	UN2338	II	FLAMMABLE LIQUID	T2	150	202	242	5 L	60 L	B	40
	Benzoxidiazoles (dry)	Forbidden											
	Benzoyl azide	Forbidden											
	Benzoyl chloride	8	UN1736	II	CORROSIVE	B2, T9, T26	154	202	242	1 L	30 L	C	8, 40
	Benzyl bromide	6.1	UN1737	II	POISON, CORROSIVE	A3, A7, N33, N34, T12, T26	None	202	243	1 L	30 L	D	13, 40
	Benzyl chloride	6.1	UN1738	II	POISON, CORROSIVE	A3, A7, B41, B70, N33, N43, T12, T26	None	202	243	1 L	30 L	D	13, 40
	Benzyl chloride *unstabilized*	6.1	UN1738	II	POISON, CORROSIVE	A3, A7, B8, B11, N33, N34, N43, T12, T26	None	202	243	1 L	30 L	D	13, 20
	Benzyl chloroformate	8	UN1739	I	CORROSIVE	A3, A6, B4, N41, T18, T26	None	201	242	Forbidden	2.5 L	D	40
	4-(Benzyl(ethyl)amino)-3-ethoxybenzenediazonium zinc chloride	4.1	UN3037	II	FLAMMABLE SOLID		None	224	None	Forbidden	Forbidden	D	2
	Benzyl iodide	6.1	UN2653	II	POISON	T8	None	202	243	5 L	60 L	B	12, 40, 48
	4-(Benzyl(methyl)amino)3-ethoxybenzenediazonium zinc chloride	4.1	UN3038	II	FLAMMABLE SOLID		None	224	None	Forbidden	Forbidden	D	2
	Benzyldimethylamine	8	UN2619	II	CORROSIVE	B2, T1	154	202	242	1 L	30 L	A	12, 21, 40, 48
	Benzylidene chloride	6.1	UN1886	II	POISON	T8	None	202	243	5 L	60 L	D	40
	Beryllium compounds, n.o.s.	6.1	UN1566	II	POISON		None	212	242	25 kg	100 kg	A	
	Beryllium nitrate	5.1	UN2464	II	OXIDIZER, POISON		None	212	242	5 kg	25 kg	A	
	Beryllium, powder	6.1	UN1567	II	POISON, FLAMMABLE SOLID		None	212	242	15 kg	50 kg	A	
	Bifluorides, n.o.s. *solid*	8	UN1740	II	CORROSIVE	N3, N34	None	212	240	15 kg	50 kg	A	25, 26, 40
	Bifluorides, n.o.s. *solutions*	8	UN1740	II	CORROSIVE	N3, N34	None	202	243	1 L	30 L	A	25, 26, 40
	Biphenyl triozonide	Forbidden											
	Bipyridilium pesticides, liquid, flammable, toxic, n.o.s., *flash point less than 23 degrees C.*	3	UN2782	I	FLAMMABLE LIQUID, POISON		None	201	243	Forbidden	30 L	E	
				II	FLAMMABLE LIQUID, POISON		None	202	243	1 L	60 L	B	

295

Symbols	Hazardous materials descriptions and proper shipping names	Hazard class or Division	Identification Numbers	Packing group	Label(s) required (if not excepted)	Special provisions	Exceptions	Non-bulk packaging	Bulk packaging	Passenger aircraft or railcar	Cargo aircraft only	Vessel stowages	Other stowage provisions
(1)	(2)	(3)	(4)	(5)	(6)	(7)	(8A)	(8B)	(8C)	(9A)	(9B)	(10A)	(10B)
	Bipyridilium pesticides, liquid, toxic, flammable, n.o.s. *flashpoint not less than 23 degrees C.*	6.1	UN3015	I	POISON, FLAMMABLE LIQUID	T42	None	201	243	1 L	30 L	B	21, 40, 48
				II	POISON, FLAMMABLE LIQUID	T14	None	202	243	5 L	60 L	B	21, 40, 48
				III	KEEP AWAY FROM FOOD, FLAMMABLE LIQUID	B1, T14	153	203	242	60 L	220 L	A	21, 40, 48
	Bipyridilium pesticides, liquid, toxic, n.o.s.	6.1	UN3016	I	POISON	T42	None	201	243	1 L	30 L	B	40
				II	POISON	T14	None	202	243	5 L	60 L	B	40
				III	KEEP AWAY FROM FOOD	T14	153	203	241	60 L	220 L	A	40
	Bipyridilium pesticides, solid, toxic, n.o.s.	6.1	UN2781	I	POISON		None	211	242	5 kg	50 kg	A	40
				II	POISON		None	212	242	25 kg	100 kg	A	40
				III	KEEP AWAY FROM FOOD		153	213	240	100 kg	200 kg	A	40
	bis (Aminopropyl) piperazine, see Corrosive liquid, n.o.s.												
	Bisulfites, inorganic, aqueous solutions, n.o.s.	8	UN2693	III	CORROSIVE	T8	154	203	241	1 L	30 L	A	8, 26, 40
	Black powder, compressed *or* Gunpowder, compressed *or* Black powder, in pellets *or* Gunpowder, in pellets	1.1D	UN0028	II	EXPLOSIVE 1.1D		None	62	None	Forbidden	Forbidden	B	1E, 5E
	Black powder *or* Gunpowder, *granular or as a meal*	1.1D	UN0027	II	EXPLOSIVE 1.1D		None	62	None	Forbidden	Forbidden	B	10E, 26E
	Blasting agent, n.o.s., see Explosives, blasting *etc.*												
	Blasting cap assemblies, see Detonator assemblies, non-electric, *for blasting*												
	Blasting caps, electric, see Detonators, electric *for blasting*												
	Blasting caps, non-electric, see Detonators, non-electric, *for blasting*												
	Bleaching powder, see Calcium hypochlorite mixtures, *etc.*												
	Blue Asbestos (*Crocidolite*) *or* Brown asbestos (amosite, mysorite)	9	UN2212	II	CLASS 9		155	216	240	Forbidden	Forbidden	A	34, 40
	Bombs, photo-flash	1.1F	UN0037	II	EXPLOSIVE 1.1F		63(b)	62	None	Forbidden	Forbidden	E	
	Bombs, photo-flash	1.1D	UN0038	II	EXPLOSIVE 1.1D		63(b)	62	None	Forbidden	Forbidden	B	
	Bombs, photo-flash	1.2G	UN0039	II	EXPLOSIVE 1.2G		63(b)	62	None	Forbidden	Forbidden	B	
	Bombs, photo-flash	1.3G	UN0299	II	EXPLOSIVE 1.3G		63(b)	62	None	Forbidden	Forbidden	B	
	Bombs, smoke, non-explosive, *with corrosive liquid, without initiating device*	8	UN2028	II	CORROSIVE		None	160	None	Forbidden	50 kg	E	40
	Bombs, *with bursting charge*	1.1F	UN0033	II	EXPLOSIVE 1.1F		63(b)	62	None	Forbiden	Forbidden	E	
	Bombs, *with bursting charge*	1.1D	UN0034	II	EXPLOSIVE 1.1D		63(b)	62	None	Forbidden	Forbidden	B	3E, 7E
	Bombs, *with bursting charge*	1.2D	UN0035	II	EXPLOSIVE 1.2D		63(b)	62	None	Forbidden	Forbidden	B	3E, 7E
	Bombs, *with bursting charge*	1.2F	UN0291	II	EXPLOSIVE 1.2F		63(b)	62	None	Forbidden	Forbidden	E	
	Bombs with flammable liquid, *with bursting charge*	1.1J	UN0399	II	EXPLOSIVE 1.1J		63(b)	62	None	Forbidden	Forbidden	E	7E, 16E, 23E
	Bombs with flammable liquid, *with bursting charge*	1.2J	UN0400	II	EXPLOSIVE 1.2J		63(b)	62	None	Forbidden	Forbidden	E	7E, 16E, 23E
	Boosters with detonator	1.1B	UN0225	II	EXPLOSIVE 1.1B		None	62	None	Forbidden	Forbidden	B	2E, 6E
	Boosters with detonator	1.2B	UN0268	II	EXPLOSIVE 1.2B		None	62	None	Forbidden	Forbidden	E	1E, 7E
D	Boosters with detonator	1.4B	NA0350	II	EXPLOSIVE 1.4B	115	None	62	None	Forbidden	75 kg	A	24E
	Boosters, *without detonator*	1.1D	UN0042	II	EXPLOSIVE 1.1D		None	62	None	Forbidden	Forbidden	B	
	Boosters, *without detonator*	1.2D	UN0283	II	EXPLOSIVE 1.2D		None	62	None	Forbidden	Forbidden	B	
	Borate and chlorate mixtures, see Chlorate and borate mixtures												
	Borneol	4.1	UN1312	III	FLAMMABLE SOLID	A1	None	213	240	25 kg	100 kg	A	
+	Boron tribromide	8	UN2692	I	CORROSIVE, POISON	2, A3, A7, B9, B14, B32, B74, N34, T38, T43, T45	None	227	244	Forbidden	2.5 L	C	12
	Boron trichloride	2.3	UN1741		POISON GAS, CORROSIVE	1, B9, B14	None	304	314	Forbidden	Forbidden	E	25, 40
	Boron trifluoride	2.3	UN1008		POISON GAS	2, B9, B14	None	302	314, 315	Forbidden	Forbidden	D	40
	Boron trifluoride acetic acid complex	8	UN1742	II	CORROSIVE	B2, B6, T9, T27	154	202	242	1 L	30 L	A	
	Boron trifluoride diethyl etherate	8	UN2604	I	CORROSIVE, FLAMMABLE LIQUID	A19, T8, T26	None	202	243	0.5 L	2.5 L	D	12, 21, 40, 48
	Boron trifluoride dihydrate	8	UN2851	II	CORROSIVE	T9, T27	154	212	240	15 kg	50 kg	B	12, 40, 48
	Boron trifluoride dimethyl etherate	4.3	UN2965	II	DANGEROUS WHEN WET, CORROSIVE, FLAMMABLE LIQUID	A19, T8, T26	None	202	243	1 L	5 L	D	21, 28, 40, 49, 100
	Boron trifluoride propionic acid complex	8	UN1743	II	CORROSIVE	B2, T9, T27	154	202	242	1 L	30 L	A	
	Box toe gum, see Nitrocellulose *etc.*												

296

Sym-bols	Hazardous materials descriptions and proper shipping names	Hazard class or Division	Identifi-cation Numbers	Packing group	Label(s) required (If not excepted)	Special provisions	Packaging authorizations (§173.***)			Quantity limitations		Vessel stowage requirements	
							Excep-tions	Non-bulk pack-aging	Bulk pack-aging	Passenger aircraft or railcar	Cargo aircraft only	Vessel stow-ages	Other stowage provisions
(1)	(2)	(3)	(4)	(5)	(6)	(7)	(8A)	(8B)	(8C)	(9A)	(9B)	(10A)	(10B)
	Brake fluid, hydraulic	3	UN1118	II	FLAMMABLE LIQUID	T7, T30	150	202	242	5 L	60 L	B	
				III	FLAMMABLE LIQUID	B1, T7, T30	150	203	242	60 L	220 L	A	
	Bromates, inorganic, n.o.s.	5.1	UN1450	II	OXIDIZER		152	212	242	5 kg	25 kg	A	56, 58, 106
	Bromine azide	Forbid-den											
+	Bromine or Bromine solutions	8	UN1744	I	CORROSIVE, POISON	1, A3, A6, B9, B12, B31, B64, B73, B85, N34, N43, T18, T41	None	226	249	Forbidden	2.5 L	D	12, 40, 66, 74, 89, 90, 95
	Bromine chloride	2.3	UN2901		POISON GAS, CORROSIVE, OXIDIZER	2, B9, B12, B14	None	304	314, 315	Forbidden	Forbidden	D	40, 89, 90
+	Bromine pentafluoride	5.1	UN1745	I	OXIDIZER, POISON, CORROSIVE	1, B9, B14, B30, B72, T38, T43, T44	None	228	244	Forbidden	Forbidden	D	25, 40, 66, 90
+	Bromine trifluoride	5.1	UN1746	I	OXIDIZER, POISON, CORROSIVE	2, B9, B14, B32, B74, T38, T43, T45	None	228	244	Forbidden	Forbidden	D	25, 40, 66, 90
	4-Bromo-1,2-dinitrobenzene	Forbid-den											
	4-Bromo-1,2-dinitrobenzene (unstable at 59 deg C.)	Forbid-den											
	1-Bromo-3-methylbutane	3	UN2341	III	FLAMMABLE LIQUID	B1, T7, T30	150	203	242	60 L	220 L	A	
	1-Bromo-3-nitrobenzene (unstable at 56 deg C)	Forbid-den											
	Bromoacetic acid, solid	8	UN1938	II	CORROSIVE	A7, N34, T9	154	212	240	15 kg	50 kg	A	
	Bromoacetic acid, solution	8	UN1938	II	CORROSIVE	B2, T9	154	202	242	1 L	30 L	A	40
+	Bromoacetone	6.1	UN1569	II	POISON	2	None	193	245	Forbidden	Forbidden	D	40
	Bromoacetyl bromide	8	UN2513	II	CORROSIVE	B2, T9, T26	154	202	242	1 L	30 L	C	8
	Bromobenzene	3	UN2514	III	FLAMMABLE LIQUID	B1, T1	150	203	242	60 L	220 L	A	
	Bromobenzyl cyanides, liquid	6.1	UN1694	I	POISON	T18	None	201	243	Forbidden	30 L	D	12, 40
	Bromobenzyl cyanides, solid	6.1	UN1694	I	POISON	T18	None	211	241	Forbidden	50 kg	D	12, 40
	2-Bromobutane	3	UN2339	II	FLAMMABLE LIQUID	B1, T1	150	202	242	5 L	60 L	B	40
	Bromochloromethane	6.1	UN1887	III	KEEP AWAY FROM FOOD	T7	153	203	241	60 L	220 L	A	
	2-Bromoethyl ethyl ether	3	UN2340	II	FLAMMABLE LIQUID	T7	150	202	242	5 L	60 L	B	40
	Bromoform	6.1	UN2515	III	KEEP AWAY FROM FOOD	T7	153	203	241	60 L	220 L	A	12, 40, 48
	Bromomethylpropanes	3	UN2342	II	FLAMMABLE LIQUID	T7, T30	150	202	242	5 L	60 L	B	
	2-Bromopentane	3	UN2343	II	FLAMMABLE LIQUID	T1	150	202	242	5 L	60 L	B	
	2-Bromopropane	3	UN2344	II	FLAMMABLE LIQUID	T7	150	202	242	5 L	60 L	B	40
	3-Bromopropyne	3	UN2345	II	FLAMMABLE LIQUID	T8	150	202	242	5 L	60 L	D	40
	Bromosilane	Forbid-den											
	Bromotoluene-alpha, see Benzyl bromide												
	Bromotrifluoroethylene	2.1	UN2419		FLAMMABLE GAS		None	304	314, 315	Forbidden	150 kg	B	40
	Bromotrifluoromethane, R13B1	2.2	UN1009		NONFLAMMABLE GAS		306	304	314, 315	75 kg	150 kg	A	
	Brucine	6.1	UN1570	I	POISON		None	212	242	5 kg	50 kg	A	
	Bursters, explosive	1.1D	UN0043	II	EXPLOSIVE 1.1D		None	62	None	Forbidden	Forbidden	B	
	Butadienes, inhibited	2.1	UN1010		FLAMMABLE GAS		306	304	314, 315	Forbidden	150 kg	B	40
	Butane or Butane mixtures see also Petroleum gases, liquefied	2.1	UN1011		FLAMMABLE GAS		306	304	314, 315	Forbidden	150 kg	E	40
	Butane, butane mixtures and mixtures having similar properties in cartridges each not exceeding 500 grams, see Receptacles, etc.												
	Butanedione	3	UN2346	II	FLAMMABLE LIQUID	T1	150	202	242	5 L	60 L	B	
	1,2,4-Butanetriol trinitrate	Forbid-den											
	Butanols	3	UN1120	II	FLAMMABLE LIQUID	T1	150	202	242	5 L	60 L	B	
				III	FLAMMABLE LIQUID	B1, T1	150	203	242	60 L	220 L	A	
	tert-Butoxycarbonyl azide	Forbid-den											

297

(1) Symbols	(2) Hazardous materials descriptions and proper shipping names	(3) Hazard class or Division	(4) Identification Numbers	(5) Packing group	(6) Label(s) required (If not excepted)	(7) Special provisions	(8) Packaging authorizations (§173.***)			(9) Quantity limitations		(10) Vessel stowage requirements	
							(8A) Exceptions	(8B) Non-bulk packaging	(8C) Bulk packaging	(9A) Passenger aircraft or railcar	(9B) Cargo aircraft only	(10A) Vessel stowages	(10B) Other stowage provisions
	Butoxyl	3	UN2708	III	FLAMMABLE LIQUID	B1, T1	150	203	241	60 L	220 L	A	
	Butyl acetates	3	UN1123	II	FLAMMABLE LIQUID	T1	150	202	242	5 L	60 L	B	
				III	FLAMMABLE LIQUID	B1, T1	150	202	241	60 L	220 L	A	
	Butyl acid phosphate	8	UN1718	III	CORROSIVE	T7	154	203	241	5 L	60 L	A	
	Butyl alcohols, see Butanols												
	Butyl benzenes	3	UN2709	III	FLAMMABLE LIQUID	B1, T1	150	203	242	60 L	220 L	A	
	n-Butyl bromide	3	UN1126	II	FLAMMABLE LIQUID	T1	150	202	242	5 L	60 L	B	
	n-Butyl chloride, see Chlorobutanes												
	n-Butyl chloroformate	6.1	UN2743	I	POISON, CORROSIVE	2, B9, B14, B32, B74, T38, T43, T45	None	227	244	1 L	30 L	A	12, 13, 22, 25, 40, 48, 100
D	sec-Butyl chloroformate	6.1	NA2742	I	POISON, FLAMMABLE LIQUID, CORROSIVE	2, B9, B14, B32, B74, T38, T43, T45	None	227	244	1 L	30 L	A	12, 13, 22, 25, 40, 48, 100
	Butyl ethers, see Dibutyl ethers												
	Butyl ethyl ether, see Ethyl butyl ether												
	n-Butyl formate	3	UN1128	II	FLAMMABLE LIQUID	T1	150	202	242	5 L	60 L	B	
	tert-Butyl hydroperoxide, more than 90 per cent with water	Forbid-den											
	N-n-Butyl imidazole	6.1	UN2690	II	POISON	T8	None	202	243	5 L	60 L	A	40
+	Tert-Butyl isocyanate	3	UN2484	I	FLAMMABLE LIQUID, POISON	1, A7, B9, B14, B30, B72, T38, T43, T44	None	226	244	Forbidden	30 L	D	40
+	n-Butyl isocyanate	3	UN2485	II	FLAMMABLE LIQUID, POISON	1, A7, B9, B14, B30, B72, B77, T38, T43, T44	None	226	244	Forbidden	60 L	D	40
	Butyl mercaptans	3	UN2347	II	FLAMMABLE LIQUID	A3, T8	150	202	242	5 L	60 L	B	26, 95, 102
	n-Butyl methacrylate	3	UN2227	III	FLAMMABLE LIQUID	B1, T1	150	203	242	60 L	220 L	A	
	Butyl methyl ether	3	UN2350	II	FLAMMABLE LIQUID	T8	150	202	242	5 L	60 L	B	
	Butyl nitrites	3	UN2351	I	FLAMMABLE LIQUID	T8	150	202	242	1 L	30 L	E	40
				II	FLAMMABLE LIQUID	T8	150	202	242	5 L	60 L	B	40
				III	FLAMMABLE LIQUID	B1, T8	150	202	242	60 L	220 L	A	40
	tert-Butyl peroxyacetate, more than 76 per cent in solution	Forbid-den											
	n-Butyl peroxydicarbonate, more than 52 percent in solution	Forbid-den											
	tert-Butyl peroxyisobutyrate, more than 77 per cent in solution	Forbid-den											
	Butyl phosphoric acid, see Butyl acid phosphate												
	5-tert-Butyl-2,4,6-trinitro-m-xylene or Musk xylene	4.1	UN2956	III	FLAMMABLE SOLID,		None	214	None	Forbidden	Forbidden	D	12
	Butyl vinyl ether, inhibited	3	UN2352	II	FLAMMABLE LIQUID	T7	150	202	242	5 L	60 L	B	40
	Butylacrylate	3	UN2348	III	FLAMMABLE LIQUID	B1, T8, T31	150	202	241	60 L	220 L	A	
	n-Butylamine	3	UN1125	II	FLAMMABLE LIQUID	T8	150	202	242	5 L	60 L	B	40
	N-Butylaniline	6.1	UN2738	II	POISON	T8	None	202	243	5 L	60 L	A	40
	tert-Butylcyclohexylchloroformate	6.1	UN2747	III	KEEP AWAY FROM FOOD	T8	153	203	241	60 L	220 L	A	12, 13, 25, 48
	Butylene see also Petroleum gases, liquefied	2.1	UN1012		FLAMMABLE GAS		None	304	314, 315	Forbidden	150 kg	E	40
	1,2-Butylene oxide, stabilized	3	UN3022	II	FLAMMABLE LIQUID	T8	150	202	242	5 L	60 L	B	49
	Butylphenols, liquid	6.1	UN2228	III	KEEP AWAY FROM FOOD	T7	153	203	241	60 L	220 L	A	
	Butylphenols, solid	6.1	UN2229	III	KEEP AWAY FROM FOOD	T7	153	213	240	100 kg	200 kg	A	
	Butylpropionate	3	UN1914	III	FLAMMABLE LIQUID	B1, T1	150	203	242	60 L	220 L	A	
	Butyltoluenes	6.1	UN2667	III	KEEP AWAY FROM FOOD	T2	153	203	241	60 L	220 L	A	
	Butyltrichlorosilane	8	UN1747	II	CORROSIVE	A7, B2, B6, N34, T8, T26	None	202	242	Forbidden	30 L	C	12, 21, 40, 48
	1,4-Butynediol	6.1	UN2716	III	KEEP AWAY FROM FOOD	A1	None	213	240	100 kg	200 kg	A	61, 70

298

Sym-bols	Hazardous materials descriptions and proper shipping names	Hazard class or Division	Identifi-cation Numbers	Packing group	Label(s) required (if not excepted)	Special provisions	(8) Packaging authorizations (§173.***)			(9) Quantity limitations		(10) Vessel stowage requirements	
							Excep-tions	Non-bulk pack-aging	Bulk pack-aging	Passenger aircraft or railcar	Cargo aircraft only	Vessel stow-ages	Other stowage provisions
(1)	(2)	(3)	(4)	(5)	(6)	(7)	(8A)	(8B)	(8C)	(9A)	(9B)	(10A)	(10B)
	Butyraldehyde	3	UN1129	II	FLAMMABLE LIQUID	T8	150	202	242	5 L	60 L	B	
	Butyraldoxime	3	UN2840	III	FLAMMABLE LIQUID	B1, T1	150	203	242	60 L	220 L	A	
	Butyric acid	8	UN2820	III	CORROSIVE	T1	154	203	241	5 L	60 L	A	12, 48
	Butyric anhydride	8	UN2739	III	CORROSIVE	T2	154	203	241	5 L	60 L	A	
	Butyronitrile	3	UN2411	II	FLAMMABLE LIQUID, POISON	T14	None	202	243	1 L	60 L	E	40
	Butyryl chloride	3	UN2353	II	FLAMMABLE LIQUID, CORROSIVE	T9, T26	None	202	243	1 L	5 L	C	40
	Cabazide	Forbid-den											
	Cacodylic acid	6.1	UN1572	II	POISON		None	212	242	25 kg	100 kg	E	26
	Cadmium compounds	6.1	UN2570	I	POISON		None	211	242	5 kg	50 kg	A	
				II	POISON		None	212	242	25 kg	100 kg	A	
				III	KEEP AWAY FROM FOOD		153	213	240	100 kg	200 kg	A	
	Caesium hydroxide, solid	8	UN2682	II	CORROSIVE		154	212	240	15 kg	50 kg	A	
	Caesium hydroxide solution	8	UN2681	II	CORROSIVE	B2, T8	154	202	242	1 L	30 L	A	
	Calcium	4.3	UN1401	II	DANGEROUS WHEN WET		None	212	241	15 kg	50 kg	E	
	Calcium arsenate	6.1	UN1573	II	POISON		None	212	242	25 kg	100 kg	A	
	Calcium arsenate and calcium arsenite, mixtures, solid	6.1	UN1574	II	POISON		None	212	242	25 kg	100 kg	A	
D	Calcium arsenite, solid	6.1	NA1574	II	POISON		None	212	242	25 kg	100 kg	A	
	Calcium bisulfite solution, see Bisulfites, inorganic, aqueous solutions, n.o.s.												
	Calcium carbide	4.3	UN1402	II	DANGEROUS WHEN WET	A1, A8, B55, N34	None	212	241	15 kg	50 kg	B	
	Calcium chlorate	5.1	UN1452	II	OXIDIZER	N34	152	212	242	5 kg	25 kg	A	56, 58, 106
	Calcium chlorate solution	5.1	UN2429	II	OXIDIZER	A2, N41, T8	152	202	242	1 L	5 L	B	56, 58, 106
	Calcium chlorite	5.1	UN1453	II	OXIDIZER	A9, N34	152	212	242	5 kg	25 kg	A	56, 58, 106
	Calcium cyanamide *with more than 0.1 per cent of calcium carbide*	4.3	UN1403	III	DANGEROUS WHEN WET	A1, A19	None	213	241	25 kg	100 kg	A	
	Calcium cyanide	6.1	UN1575	I	POISON	N79, N80	None	211	242	5 kg	50 kg	A	26, 40
	Calcium dithionite *or* Calcium hydrosulfite	4.2	UN1923	II	SPONTANEOUSLY COMBUSTIBLE	A19, A20	None	212	241	15 kg	50 kg	E	13
	Calcium hydride	4.3	UN1404	I	DANGEROUS WHEN WET	A19, N40	None	211	242	Forbidden	15 kg	E	
	Calcium hydrosulfite, *see* Calcium dithionite												
	Calcium hypochlorite, dry *or* Calcium hypochlorite mixtures dry *with more than 39 per cent available chlorine (8.8 per cent available oxygen)*	5.1	UN1748	II	OXIDIZER	A7, A9, N34	152	212	None	5 kg	25 kg	D	48, 56, 58, 69, 106, 118
	Calcium hypochlorite, hydrated *or* Calcium hypochlorite, hydrated mixtures, with not less than 5.5 per cent but not more than 10 per cent water	5.1	UN2880	II	OXIDIZER		152	212	240	5 kg	25 kg	A	50, 56, 58, 69, 106
	Calcium hypochlorite mixtures, dry, *with more than 10 per cent but not more than 39 per cent available chlorine*	5.1	UN2208	III	OXIDIZER	A1, A29, N34	152	213	240	25 kg	100 kg	A	56, 58, 69, 106
	Calcium manganese silicon	4.3	UN2844	III	DANGEROUS WHEN WET	A1, A19	None	213	241	25 kg	100 kg	A	85, 103
	Calcium nitrate	5.1	UN1454	III	OXIDIZER	T2	152	213	240	25 kg	100 kg	A	
A	Calcium oxide	8	UN1910	III	CORROSIVE		154	213	240	25 kg	100 kg	A	
	Calcium perchlorate	5.1	UN1455	II	OXIDIZER	T8	152	212	242	5 kg	25 kg	A	56, 58, 106
	Calcium permanganate	5.1	UN1456	II	OXIDIZER		152	212	242	5 kg	25 kg	D	56, 58, 69, 106, 107
	Calcium peroxide	5.1	UN1457	II	OXIDIZER		152	212	242	5 kg	25 kg	A	13, 75, 106
	Calcium phosphide	4.3	UN1360	I	DANGEROUS WHEN WET, POISON	A8, A19, N40	None	211	242	Forbidden	15 kg	E	40, 85
	Calcium, pyrophoric *or* Calcium alloys, pyrophoric	4.2	UN1855	I	SPONTANEOUSLY COMBUSTIBLE		None	187	None	Forbidden	Forbidden	D	
	Calcium resinate	4.1	UN1313	III	FLAMMABLE SOLID	A1, A19	None	213	240	25 kg	100 kg	A	
	Calcium resinate, fused	4.1	UN1314	III	FLAMMABLE SOLID	A1, A19	None	213	240	25 kg	100 kg	A	
	Calcium selenate, *see* Selenates *or* Selenites												
	Calcium silicide	4.3	UN1405	II	DANGEROUS WHEN WET	A19	None	212	241	15 kg	50 kg	B	85, 103
				III	DANGEROUS WHEN WET	A1, A19	None	213	241	25 kg	100 kg	B	85, 103

299

Sym-bols	Hazardous materials descriptions and proper shipping names	Hazard class or Division	Identifi-cation Numbers	Packing group	Label(s) required (if not excepted)	Special provisions	(8) Packaging authorizations (§173.***)			(9) Quantity limitations		(10) Vessel stowage requirements	
							Excep-tions	Non-bulk pack-aging	Bulk pack-aging	Passenger aircraft or railcar	Cargo aircraft only	Vessel stow-ages	Other stowage provisions
(1)	(2)	(3)	(4)	(5)	(6)	(7)	(8A)	(8B)	(8C)	(9A)	(9B)	(10A)	(10B)
	Camphor oil	3	UN1130	III	FLAMMABLE LIQUID	B1, T1	150	203	242	60 L	220 L	A	
	Camphor, *synthetic*	4.1	UN2717	III	FLAMMABLE SOLID	A1	None	213	240	25 kg	100 kg	A	
	Cannon primers, see Primers, tubular												
	Caproic acid	8	UN2829	III	CORROSIVE	T1	154	203	241	5 L	60 L	A	
	Caps, blasting, see Detonators, *etc.*												
	Carbamate pesticides, liquid, flammable, toxic, n.o.s., *flash point less than 23 degrees C.*	3	UN2758	I	FLAMMABLE LIQUID, POISON		None	201	243	Forbidden	30 L	B	40
				II	FLAMMABLE LIQUID, POISON		None	202	243	1 L	60 L	B	40
	Carbamate pesticides, liquid, toxic, flammable, n.o.s. *flash point not less than 23 degrees C.*	6.1	UN2991	I	POISON, FLAMMABLE LIQUID	T42	None	201	243	1 L	30 L	B	40
				II	POISON, FLAMMABLE LIQUID	T14	None	202	243	5 L	60 L	B	40
				III	KEEP AWAY FROM FOOD, FLAMMABLE LIQUID	B1, T14	153	203	242	60 L	220 L	A	40
	Carbamate pesticides, liquid, toxic, n.o.s.	6.1	UN2992	I	POISON	T42	None	201	243	1 L	30 L	B	40
				II	POISON	T14	None	202	243	5 L	60 L	B	40
				III	KEEP AWAY FROM FOOD	T14	153	203	241	60 L	220 L	A	40
	Carbamate pesticides, solid, toxic, n.o.s.	6.1	UN2757	I	POISON		None	211	242	5 kg	50 kg	A	40
				II	POISON		None	212	242	25 kg	100 kg	A	40
				III	KEEP AWAY FROM FOOD		153	213	240	100 kg	200 kg	A	40
	Carbolic acid, see Phenol, solid *or* Phenol, molten												
	Carbolic acid solutions, see Phenol solutions												
I	Carbon, activated	4.2	UN1362	III	SPONTANEOUSLY COMBUSTIBLE		None	213	241	0.5 kg	0.5 kg	A	12
I	Carbon, *animal or vegetable origin*	4.2	UN1361	III	SPONTANEOUSLY COMBUSTIBLE		None	213	241	Forbidden	Forbidden	A	12
	Carbon bisulfide, see Carbon disulfide												
	Carbon dioxide	2.2	UN1013		NONFLAMMABLE GAS		306	302, 304	302, 314, 315	75 kg	150 kg	A	
	Carbon dioxide and ethylene oxide mixtures *with more than 6 per cent but not more than 25 percent ethylene oxide*	2.1	UN1041		FLAMMABLE GAS		None	304	314, 315	Forbidden	25 kg	D	40
	Carbon dioxide and ethylene oxide mixtures *with more than 25 percent ethylene oxide*	2.3	UN1041		POISON GAS, FLAMMABLE GAS	6, B9, B14	None	304	314, 315	Forbidden	25 kg	D	40
	Carbon dioxide and ethylene oxide mixtures *with not more than 6 per cent ethylene oxide*	2.2	UN1952		NONFLAMMABLE GAS		None	304	314, 315	75 kg	150 kg	B	
	Carbon dioxide and nitrous oxide mixtures	2.2	UN1015		NONFLAMMABLE GAS		306	None	244	75 kg	150 kg	A	
	Carbon dioxide and oxygen mixtures	2.2	UN1014		NONFLAMMABLE GAS		306	None	244	75 kg	150 kg	A	
	Carbon dioxide, refrigerated liquid	2.2	UN2187		NONFLAMMABLE GAS	B43	306	None	314, 315	50 kg	500 kg	B	
AW	Carbon dioxide, solid *or* Dry ice	9	UN1845	III	None	B12	217	217	240	200 kg	200 kg	C	40
	Carbon disulfide	3	UN1131	I	FLAMMABLE LIQUID, POISON	B16, T18, T26, T29	None	201	243	Forbidden	Forbidden	D	18, 40, 115
	Carbon monoxide	2.3	UN1016		POISON GAS, FLAMMABLE GAS	4	None	302	None	Forbidden	25 kg	D	40
	Carbon monoxide and hydrogen mixture	2.1	UN2600		FLAMMABLE GAS	5	None	302	302	Forbidden	Forbidden	D	40
D	Carbon monoxide, refrigerated liquid *(cryogenic liquid)*	2.3	NA9202		POISON GAS, FLAMMABLE GAS	4	None	316	318	Forbidden	Forbidden	D	
	Carbon tetrabromide	6.1	UN2516	III	KEEP AWAY FROM FOOD		153	213	240	100 kg	200 kg	A	25
	Carbon tetrachloride	6.1	UN1846	II	POISON	N36, T8	None	202	243	5 L	60 L	A	40
	Carbonyl chloride, see Phosgene												
	Carbonyl fluoride	2.3	UN2417		POISON GAS	2	None	302	None	Forbidden	Forbidden	D	40
	Carbonyl sulfide	2.3	UN2204		POISON GAS, FLAMMABLE GAS	2, B9, B14	None	304	314, 315	Forbidden	25 kg	D	40
	Cartridge cases, empty primed, see Cases, cartridge, empty, with primer												
	Cartridges, actuating, for aircraft ejector seat catapult, fire extinguisher, canopy removal or apparatus, see Cartridges, power device												
	Cartridges, explosive, see Charges, demolition												
	Cartridges, flash	1.1G	UN0049	II	EXPLOSIVE 1.1G		None	62	None	Forbidden	Forbidden	B	
	Cartridges, flash	1.3G	UN0050	II	EXPLOSIVE 1.3G		None	62	None	Forbidden	75 kg	B	
	Cartridges for weapons, blank	1.1C	UN0326	II	EXPLOSIVE 1.1C		None	62	None	Forbidden	Forbidden	B	

(1) Symbols	(2) Hazardous materials descriptions and proper shipping names	(3) Hazard class or Division	(4) Identification Numbers	(5) Packing group	(6) Label(s) required (if not excepted)	(7) Special provisions	(8) Packaging authorizations (§173.***)			(9) Quantity limitations		(10) Vessel stowage requirements	
							(8A) Exceptions	(8B) Non-bulk packaging	(8C) Bulk packaging	(9A) Passenger aircraft or railcar	(9B) Cargo aircraft only	(10A) Vessel stowages	(10B) Other stowage provisions
	Cartridges for weapons, blank	1.2C	UN0413	II	EXPLOSIVE 1.2C		None	62	None	Forbidden	Forbidden	B	
	Cartridges for weapons, blank or Cartridges, small arms, blank	1.3C	UN0327	II	EXPLOSIVE 1.3C		None	62	None	Forbidden	Forbidden	B	
	Cartridges for weapons, blank or Cartridges, small arms, blank	1.4C	UN0338	II	EXPLOSIVE 1.4C		None	62	None	Forbidden	75 kg	A	24E
	Cartridges for weapons, blank or Cartridges, small arms, blank	1.4S	UN0014	II	None	112	None	62	None	25 kg	100 kg	A	9E
	Cartridges for weapons, inert projectile or Cartridges, small arms	1.2C	UN0328	II	EXPLOSIVE 1.2C		None	62	None	Forbidden	Forbidden	B	
	Cartridges for weapons, inert projectile or Cartridges, small arms	1.4C	UN0339	II	EXPLOSIVE 1.4C		None	62	None	Forbidden	75 kg	B	
	Cartridges for weapons, inert projectile or Cartridges, small arms	1.3C	UN0417	II	EXPLOSIVE 1.3C		None	62	None	Forbidden	Forbidden	B	
	Cartridges for weapons, inert projectile or Cartridges, small arms, other than blank	1.4S	UN0012	II	None	112	None	62	None	25 kg	100 kg	A	9E
	Cartridges for weapons, with bursting charge	1.1F	UN0005	II	EXPLOSIVE 1.1F		None	62	None	Forbidden	Forbidden	E	
	Cartridges for weapons, with bursting charge	1.2F	UN0007	II	EXPLOSIVE 1.2F		None	62	None	Forbidden	Forbidden	E	
	Cartridges for weapons, with bursting charge	1.4F	UN0348	II	EXPLOSIVE 1.4F		None	62	None	Forbidden	Forbidden	E	
	Cartridges for weapons, with bursting charge	1.4E	UN0412	II	EXPLOSIVE 1.4E		None	62	None	Forbidden	75 kg	A	24E
	Cartridges for weapons, with bursting charge	1.1E	UN0006	II	EXPLOSIVE 1.1E		None	62	None	Forbidden	Forbidden	B	
	Cartridges for weapons, with bursting charge	1.2E	UN0321	II	EXPLOSIVE 1.2E		None	62	None	Forbidden	Forbidden	B	
	Cartridges, oil well	1.3C	UN0277	II	EXPLOSIVE 1.3C		None	62	None	Forbidden	Forbidden	B	
	Cartridges, oil well	1.4C	UN0278	II	EXPLOSIVE 1.4C		None	62	None	Forbidden	75 kg	A	24E
	Cartridges, power device	1.3C	UN0275	II	EXPLOSIVE 1.3C		None	62	None	Forbidden	75 kg	B	
	Cartridges, power device	1.4C	UN0276	II	EXPLOSIVE 1.4C	110	None	62	None	Forbidden	75 kg	A	24E
	Cartridges, power device	1.2C	UN0381	II	EXPLOSIVE 1.2C		None	62	None	Forbidden	Forbidden	B	
	Cartridges, power device	1.4S	UN0323	II	EXPLOSIVE 1.4S	110, 112	None	62	None	25 kg	100 kg	A	9E
	Cartridges, safety, blank, see Cartridges for weapons, blank (UN 0014)												
	Cartridges, safety, see Cartridges for weapons, other than blank or Cartridges, power device (UN 0323)												
	Cartridges, signal	1.3G	UN0054	II	EXPLOSIVE 1.3G		None	62	None	Forbidden	75 kg	B	
	Cartridges, signal	1.4G	UN0312	II	EXPLOSIVE 1.4G		None	62	None	Forbidden	75 kg	A	24E
	Cartridges, signal	1.4S	UN0405	II	EXPLOSIVE 1.4S		None	62	None	25 kg	100 kg	A	9E
D	Cartridges, small arms	ORM-D	None		None	112	230	None	None	30 kg gross	30 kg gross	A	
	Cartridges, sporting, see Cartridges for weapons, other than blank												
	Cartridges, starter, jet engine, see Cartridges, power device												
I	Cases, cartridge, empty with primer	1.4S	UN0055	II	EXPLOSIVE 1.4S		None	62	None	25 kg	100 kg	A	9E
	Cases, cartridges, empty with primer	1.4C	UN0379	II	EXPLOSIVE 1.4C		None	62	None	Forbidden	75 kg	A	24E
	Cases, combustible, empty, without primer	1.3C	UN0447	II	EXPLOSIVE 1.3C		None	62	None	Forbidden	Forbidden	B	
	Cases, combustible, empty, without primer	1.4C	UN0446	II	EXPLOSIVE 1.4C		None	62	None	Forbidden	75 kg	A	24E
	Casinghead gasoline see Natural gasoline												
AW	Castor beans or Castor meal or Castor pomace or Castor flake	9	UN2969	II	None		155	204	240	No limit	No limit	E	34, 40, 44, 120
	Caustic alkali liquids, n.o.s.	8	UN1719	I	CORROSIVE	A7, B10, T42	None	201	242	0.5 L	2.5 L	A	
				II	CORROSIVE	B2, T14	154	202	242	1 L	30 L	A	
				III	CORROSIVE	T7	154	203	241	5 L	60 L	A	
	Caustic potash, see Potassium hydroxide etc.												
	Caustic soda, (etc.) see Sodium hydroxide etc.												
	Celluloid, in block, rods, rolls, sheets, tubes, etc., except scrap	4.1	UN2000	III	FLAMMABLE SOLID		None	213	240	25 kg	100 kg	A	
	Celluloid, scrap	4.2	UN2002	III	SPONTANEOUSLY COMBUSTIBLE		None	213	241	Forbidden	Forbidden	D	
	Cement, see Adhesives containing flammable liquid												
	Cerium, slabs, ingots, or rods	4.1	UN1333	II	FLAMMABLE SOLID	N34	None	212	240	15 kg	50 kg	A	74, 91
	Cerium, turnings or gritty powder	4.3	UN3078	II	DANGEROUS WHEN WET	A1	None	213	242	15 kg	50 kg	E	
	Cesium or Caesium	4.3	UN1407	I	DANGEROUS WHEN WET	A19, N34, N40	None	211	242	Forbidden	15 kg	D	
	Cesium nitrate or Caesium nitrate	5.1	UN1451	III	OXIDIZER	A1, A29	152	213	240	25 kg	100 kg	A	
D	Charcoal briquettes, shell, screenings, wood, etc.	4.2	NA1361	III	SPONTANEOUSLY COMBUSTIBLE		151	213	240	25 kg	100 kg	A	12
	Charges, bursting, plastics bonded	1.1D	UN0457	II	EXPLOSIVE 1.1D		None	62	None	Forbidden	Forbidden	B	
	Charges, bursting, plastics bonded	1.2D	UN0458	II	EXPLOSIVE 1.2D		None	62	None	Forbidden	Forbidden	B	
	Charges, bursting, plastics bonded	1.4D	UN0459	II	EXPLOSIVE 1.4D		None	62	None	Forbidden	75kg	A	24E

Sym-bols	Hazardous materials descriptions and proper shipping names	Hazard class or Division	Identifi-cation Numbers	Packing group	Label(s) required (if not excepted)	Special provisions	(8) Packaging authorizations (§173.***)			(9) Quantity limitations		(10) Vessel stowage requirements	
							Excep-tions	Non-bulk pack-aging	Bulk pack-aging	Passenger aircraft or railcar	Cargo aircraft only	Vessel stow-ages	Other stowage provisions
(1)	(2)	(3)	(4)	(5)	(6)	(7)	(8A)	(8B)	(8C)	(9A)	(9B)	(10A)	(10B)
	Charges, bursting, plastics bonded	1.4S	UN0460	II	EXPLOSIVE 1.4S		None	62	None	25 kg	100 kg	A	9E
	Charges, demolition	1.1D	UN0048	II	EXPLOSIVE 1.1D		None	62	None	Forbidden	Forbidden	B	
	Charges, depth	1.1D	UN0056	II	EXPLOSIVE 1.1D		None	62	None	Forbidden	Forbidden	B	3E, 7E
	Charges, expelling, explosive, for fire extinguishers, see Cartridges, power device												
	Charges, explosive, commercial without detonator	1.1D	UN0442	II	EXPLOSIVE 1.1D		None	62	None	Forbidden	Forbidden	B	
	Charges, explosive, commercial without detonator	1.2D	UN0443	II	EXPLOSIVE 1.2D		None	62	None	Forbidden	Forbidden	B	
	Charges, explosive, commercial without detonator	1.4D	UN0444	II	EXPLOSIVE 1.4D		None	62	None	Forbidden	75 kg	A	24E
	Charges, explosive, commercial without detonator	1.4S	UN0445	II	EXPLOSIVE 1.4S		None	62	None	25 kg	100 kg	A	9E
	Charges, propelling, for cannon	1.2C	UN0414	II	EXPLOSIVE 1.2C		None	62	None	Forbidden	Forbidden	B	1E, 5E
	Charges, propelling, for cannon	1.3C	UN0242	II	EXPLOSIVE 1.3C		None	62	None	Forbidden	Forbidden	B	1E, 5E
	Charges, propelling, for cannon	1.1C	UN0279	II	EXPLOSIVE 1.1C		None	62	None	Forbidden	Forbidden	B	1E, 5E
	Charges, propelling, for rocket motors	1.1C	UN0271	II	EXPLOSIVE 1.1C		None	62	None	Forbidden	Forbidden	B	
	Charges, propelling, for rocket motors	1.3C	UN0272	II	EXPLOSIVE 1.3C		None	62	None	Forbidden	Forbidden	B	
	Charges, propelling, for rocket motors	1.2C	UN0415	II	EXPLOSIVE 1.2C		None	62	None	Forbidden	Forbidden	B	
	Charges, propelling, for rocket motors, composite mixture	1.1C	UN0273	II	EXPLOSIVE 1.1C		None	62	None	Forbidden	Forbidden	B	
	Charges, propelling, for rocket motors, composite mixture	1.3C	UN0274	II	EXPLOSIVE 1.3C		None	62	None	Forbidden	Forbidden	B	
	Charges, propelling, for rocket motors, composite mixture	1.2C	UN0416	II	EXPLOSIVE 1.2C		None	62	None	Forbidden	Forbidden	B	
	Charges, shaped, commercial without detonator	1.2D	UN0439	II	EXPLOSIVE 1.2D		None	62	None	Forbidden	Forbidden	B	
	Charges, shaped, commercial without detonator	1.4D	UN0440	II	EXPLOSIVE 1.4D		None	62	None	Forbidden	75 kg	A	24E
	Charges, shaped, commercial without detonator	1.4S	UN0441	II	EXPLOSIVE 1.4S		None	62	None	25 kg	100 kg	A	9E
	Charges, shaped, commercial, without detonator	1.1D	UN0059	II	EXPLOSIVE 1.1D		None	62	None	Forbidden	Forbidden	B	
	Charges, shaped, flexible, linear	1.4D	UN0237	II	EXPLOSIVE 1.4D		None	62	None	Forbidden	75 kg	A	24E
	Charges, shaped, flexible, linear	1.1D	UN0288	II	EXPLOSIVE 1.1D	101	None	62	None	Forbidden	Forbidden	B	
	Charges, supplementary explosive	1.1D	UN0060	II	EXPLOSIVE 1.1D		None	62	None	Forbidden	Forbidden	B	1E, 5E
D	Chemical kit	8	NA1760	II	CORROSIVE		154	161	None	1 L	30 L	B	40
	Chemical kits (must be classified and labelled according to the hazard class of the constituent(s) and must meet the requirements of special provision 15 in 172.102(c)(1))												
	Chloral, anhydrous, inhibited	6.1	UN2075	II	POISON	T14	None	212	243	25 kg	100 kg	D	40
	Chlorate and borate mixtures	5.1	UN1458	II	OXIDIZER	A9, N34	152	212	240	5 kg	25 kg	A	56, 58, 106
	Chlorate and magnesium chloride mixtures	5.1	UN1459	II	OXIDIZER	A9, N34, T8	152	212	240	5 kg	25 kg	A	56, 58, 106
	Chlorate of potash, see Potassium chlorate												
	Chlorate of soda, see Sodium chlorate												
	Chlorates, inorganic, n.o.s.	5.1	UN1461	II	OXIDIZER	A9, N34	152	212	242	5 kg	25 kg	A	56, 58, 106
	Chloric acid solution, with not more than 10 per cent chloric acid	5.1	UN2626	I	OXIDIZER	T25	None	229	243	Forbidden	Forbidden	D	56, 58, 106
	Chloride of phosphorus, see Phosphorus trichloride												
	Chloride of sulfur, see Sulfur chloride												
	Chlorinated lime, see Calcium hypochlorite mixtures, etc.												
	Chlorine	2.3	UN1017		POISON GAS	2, B9, B14	None	304	314, 315	Forbidden	Forbidden	D	40, 51, 55, 62, 68
	Chlorine azide	Forbid-den											
D	Chlorine dioxide, hydrate, frozen	5.1	NA9191	II	OXIDIZER, POISON		None	229	None	Forbidden	Forbidden	E	
	Chlorine dioxide (not hydrate)	Forbid-den											
	Chlorine pentafluoride	2.3	UN2548		POISON GAS, OXIDIZER, CORROSIVE	1, B7, B9, B14	None	304	314	Forbidden	Forbidden	D	40, 89, 90
	Chlorine trifluoride	2.3	UN1749		POISON GAS, OXIDIZER, CORROSIVE	1, B7, B9, B14	None	304	314	Forbidden	Forbidden	D	40, 89, 90
	Chlorites, inorganic, n.o.s.	5.1	UN1462	II	OXIDIZER	A7, N34, T8	152	212	242	5 kg	25 kg	A	56, 58, 106
	1-Chloro-3-bromopropane	6.1	UN2688	III	KEEP AWAY FROM FOOD	T2	153	203	241	60 L	220 L	A	
	3-Chloro-4-diethylaminobenzenediazonium zinc chloride	4.1	UN3033	II	FLAMMABLE SOLID		None	224	None	15 kg	50 kg	C	

302

Sym-bols	Hazardous materials descriptions and proper shipping names	Hazard class or Division	Identifi-cation Numbers	Packing group	Label(s) required (if not excepted)	Special provisions	(8) Packaging authorizations (§173.***)			(9) Quantity limitations		(10) Vessel stowage requirements	
							Excep-tions	Non-bulk pack-aging	Bulk pack-aging	Passenger aircraft or railcar	Cargo aircraft only	Vessel stow-ages	Other stowage provisions
(1)	(2)	(3)	(4)	(5)	(6)	(7)	(8A)	(8B)	(8C)	(9A)	(9B)	(10A)	(10B)
	1-Chloro-1,1-difluoroethane, see Chlorodifluoroethanes												
	3-Chloro-4-methylphenylisocyanate	6.1	UN2236	II	POISON		None	202	243	5 L	60 L	B	40
	4-Chloro-o-toluidine hydrochloride	6.1	UN1579	III	KEEP AWAY FROM FOOD		153	213	241	100 kg	200 kg	A	
+	Chloroacetaldehyde	6.1	UN2232	II	POISON	2, B9, B14, B32, B74, T38, T43, T45	None	227	244	5 L	60 L	D	40
	Chloroacetic acid, liquid	8	UN1750	II	CORROSIVE, POISON	A7, N34, T9, T27	None	202	243	1 L	30 L	A	40
	Chloroacetic acid, solid	8	UN1751	II	CORROSIVE	A3, A7, N34	None	212	242	15 kg	50 kg	A	40
+	Chloroacetone, stabilized	6.1	UN1695	II	POISON	2, B9, B14, B32, B74, N12, N32, N34, T38, T43, T45	None	227	244	Forbidden	Forbidden	D	40
	Chloroacetone *(unstabilized)*	Forbid-den											
+	Chloroacetonitrile	6.1	UN2668	II	POISON	2, B9, B14, B32, B74, T38, T43, T45	None	227	244	Forbidden	60 L	A	12, 26, 40, 48
	Chloroacetophenone *(CN), liquid*	6.1	UN1697	II	POISON	A3, N12, N32, N33	None	202	242	Forbidden	60 L	D	12, 40
	Chloroacetophenone *(CN), solid*	6.1	UN1697	II	POISON	A3, N12, N32, N33, N34	None	212	None	Forbidden	100 kg	D	12, 40
+	Chloroacetyl chloride	8	UN1752	II	CORROSIVE, POISON	2, A3, A6, A7, B3, B8, B9, B14, B32, B74, B77, N34, N43, T38, T43, T45	None	227	244	Forbidden	Forbidden	D	40
	Chloroanilines, liquid	6.1	UN2019	II	POISON	T14	None	202	243	5 L	60 L	A	
	Chloroanilines, solid	6.1	UN2018	II	POISON	T14, T38	None	212	242	25 kg	100 kg	A	
	Chloroanisidines	6.1	UN2233	III	KEEP AWAY FROM FOOD		153	213	240	100 kg	200 kg	A	
	Chlorobenzene	3	UN1134	III	FLAMMABLE LIQUID	B1, T1	150	203	241	60 L	220 L	A	
	Chlorobenzol, see Chlorobenzene												
	Chlorobenzotrifluorides	3	UN2234	III	FLAMMABLE LIQUID	B1, T1	150	203	242	60 L	220 L	A	40
	Chlorobenzylchlorides	6.1	UN2235	III	KEEP AWAY FROM FOOD	T8	153	203	241	60 L	220 L	A	
	Chlorobutanes	3	UN1127	II	FLAMMABLE LIQUID	T8	150	202	242	5 L	60 L	B	
	Chlorocresols, *liquid*	6.1	UN2669	II	POISON	T8	None	202	243	5 L	60 L	A	12
	Chlorocresols, *solid*	6.1	UN2669	II	POISON		None	212	242	25 kg	100 kg	A	12
	Chlorodifluorobromomethane, *R12B1*	2.2	UN1974		NONFLAMMABLE GAS		306	304	314, 315	75 kg	150 kg	A	
	Chlorodifluoroethanes, R142b or Difluorochloroethanes, *R142b*	2.1	UN2517		FLAMMABLE GAS		306	304	314, 315	Forbidden	150 kg	B	40
	Chlorodifluoromethane and chloropentafluoroethane mixture *with fixed boiling point, with approximately 49 per cent chlorodifluoromethane, R502*	2.2	UN1973		NONFLAMMABLE GAS		306	304	314, 315	75 kg	150 kg	A	
	Chlorodifluoromethane, *R22*	2.2	UN1018		NONFLAMMABLE GAS		306	304	314, 315	75 kg	150 kg	A	
	Chlorodinitrobenzenes	6.1	UN1577	II	POISON	T14	None	212	242	25 kg	100 kg	A	91
	Chloroform	6.1	UN1888	II	POISON	N36, T14	None	202	243	5 L	60 L	A	40
	Chloroformates, n.o.s., *flash point not less than 23 degrees C.*	6.1	UN2742	II	POISON, CORROSIVE	5	None	202	243	1 L	30 L	A	12, 13, 22, 25, 40, 48, 100
	Chloromethyl ethyl ether	3	UN2354	II	FLAMMABLE LIQUID, POISON	T8	None	202	243	1 L	60 L	E	40
	Chloromethylchloroformate	6.1	UN2745	II	POISON, CORROSIVE	T18	None	202	243	1 L	30 L	A	12, 13, 22, 25, 40, 48, 100
	Chloronitroanilines	6.1	UN2237	III	KEEP AWAY FROM FOOD		153	213	240	100 kg	200 kg	A	
+	Chloronitrobenzene, *ortho, liquid*	6.1	UN1578	II	POISON	T14	None	202	243	5 L	60 L	A	
+	Chloronitrobenzenes *meta or para, solid*	6.1	UN1578	II	POISON	T14	None	212	242	25 kg	100 kg	A	
	Chloronitrotoluenes *liquid*	6.1	UN2433	III	KEEP AWAY FROM FOOD		153	203	241	60 L	220 L	A	
	Chloronitrotoluenes, *solid*	6.1	UN2433	III	KEEP AWAY FROM FOOD		153	213	240	100 kg	200 kg	A	
	Chloropentafluoroethane, *R115*	2.2	UN1020		NONFLAMMABLE GAS		306	304	314, 315	75 kg	150 kg	A	
	Chlorophenates, liquid	8	UN2904	III	CORROSIVE		154	203	241	5 L	60 L	A	
	Chlorophenates, solid	8	UN2905	III	CORROSIVE		154	213	240	25 kg	100 kg	A	
	Chlorophenols, liquid	6.1	UN2021	III	KEEP AWAY FROM FOOD	T7	153	203	241	60 L	220 L	A	
	Chlorophenols, solid	6.1	UN2020	III	KEEP AWAY FROM FOOD	T7	153	213	240	100 kg	200 kg	A	
	Chlorophenyltrichlorosilane	8	UN1753	II	CORROSIVE	A7, B2, B6, N34, T8, T26	None	202	242	Forbidden	30 L	C	40

303

Symbols	Hazardous materials descriptions and proper shipping names	Hazard class or Division	Identification Numbers	Packing group	Label(s) required (If not excepted)	Special provisions	Packaging authorizations (§173.***)			Quantity limitations		Vessel stowage requirements	
							Exceptions	Non-bulk packaging	Bulk packaging	Passenger aircraft or railcar	Cargo aircraft only	Vessel stowages	Other stowage provisions
(1)	(2)	(3)	(4)	(5)	(6)	(7)	(8A)	(8B)	(8C)	(9A)	(9B)	(10A)	(10B)
+	Chloropicrin	6.1	UN1580	I	POISON	2, B7, B9, B14, B32, B46, B74, T38, T43, T45	None	227	244	Forbidden	Forbidden	D	40
	Chloropicrin and methyl bromide mixtures	2.3	UN1581		POISON GAS	2, B9, B14	None	193	314, 315	Forbidden	Forbidden	D	25, 40
	Chloropicrin and methyl chloride mixtures	2.3	UN1582		POISON GAS	2	None	193	245	Forbidden	Forbidden	D	25, 40
	Chloropicrin mixture, flammable (pressure not exceeding 14.7 psia at 115 degrees F flash point below 100 deg F) see Poisonous liquids, flammable, n.o.s.												
	Chloropicrin mixtures, n.o.s.	6.1	UN1583	I	POISON	5	None	201	243	Forbidden	Forbidden	C	40
				II	POISON		None	202	243	Forbidden	Forbidden	C	40
				III	KEEP AWAY FROM FOOD		153	203	241	Forbidden	Forbidden	C	40
D	Chloropivaloyl chloride	6.1	NA9263	I	POISON, CORROSIVE	2, B9, B14, B32, B74, T38, T43, T45	None	227	244	Forbidden	Forbidden	B	40
	Chloroplatinic acid, solid	8	UN2507	III	CORROSIVE		154	213	240	25 kg	100 kg	A	
	Chloroprene, inhibited	3	UN1991	I	FLAMMABLE LIQUID, POISON	B57, T15	None	201	243	Forbidden	30 L	D	40
	Chloroprene, uninhibited	Forbidden											
	2-Chloropropane	3	UN2356	I	FLAMMABLE LIQUID	N36, T14	150	201	243	1 L	30 L	E	
	3-Chloropropanol-1	6.1	UN2849	III	KEEP AWAY FROM FOOD	T8	153	203	241	60 L	220 L	A	
	2-Chloropropene	3	UN2456	I	FLAMMABLE LIQUID	A3, N36, T20	150	201	243	1 L	30 L	E	
	alpha-Chloropropionic acid	8	UN2511	III	CORROSIVE	T8	154	203	241	5 L	60 L	A	8
	2-Chloropyridine	6.1	UN2822	II	POISON	T14	None	202	243	5 L	60 L	A	40
	Chlorosilanes, n.o.s.	8	UN2987	II	CORROSIVE	B2	154	202	242	1 L	30 L	C	40
	Chlorosilanes, n.o.s., flash point not less than 23 degrees C.	8	UN2986	II	CORROSIVE, FLAMMABLE LIQUID		None	202	243	1 L	30 L	C	23, 40
	Chlorosilanes, n.o.s. flashpoint less than 23 degrees C.	3	UN2985	II	FLAMMABLE LIQUID, CORROSIVE	T18, T26	None	201	243	1 L	5 L	B	40
	Chlorosilanes, n.o.s., which in contact with water emit flammable gases	4.3	UN2988	I	DANGEROUS WHEN WET, FLAMMABLE LIQUID, CORROSIVE	A2	None	201	244	Forbidden	1 L	D	21, 28, 40, 49, 100
+	Chlorosulfonic acid (with or without sulfur trioxide)	8	UN1754	I	CORROSIVE, POISON	2, A3, A6, A10, B10, B9, B14, B32, B74, T38, T43, T45	None	227	244	0.5 L	2.5 L	C	8, 40
	Chlorotetrafluoroethane, R124	2.2	UN1021		NONFLAMMABLE GAS		306	304	314, 315	75 kg	150 kg	A	
	Chlorotoluenes	3	UN2238	III	FLAMMABLE LIQUID	B1, T1	150	203	242	60 L	220 L	A	
	Chlorotoluidines liquid	6.1	UN2239	III	KEEP AWAY FROM FOOD	T7	153	203	241	60 L	220 L	A	
	Chlorotoluidines solid	6.1	UN2239	III	KEEP AWAY FROM FOOD		153	213	240	100 kg	200 kg	A	
	Chlorotrifluoroethane, R133a	2.2	UN1983		NONFLAMMABLE GAS		306	304	314, 315	75 kg	150 kg	A	
	Chlorotrifluoromethane and trifluoromethane azeotropic mixture with approximately 60 per cent chlorotrifluoromethane, R503	2.2	UN2599		NONFLAMMABLE GAS		306	304	314, 315	75 kg	150 kg	A	
	Chlorotrifluoromethane, R13	2.2	UN1022		NONFLAMMABLE GAS		306	304	314, 315	75 kg	150 kg	A	
D	Chromic acid, solid	5.1	NA1463	II	OXIDIZER, CORROSIVE		None	212	242	5 kg	25 kg	A	
	Chromic acid solution	8	UN1755	II	CORROSIVE	B2, T9, T27	154	202	242	1 L	30 L	C	40
	Chromic anhydride, see Chromium trioxide, anhydrous												
	Chromic fluoride, solid	8	UN1756	II	CORROSIVE		154	212	240	15 kg	50 kg	A	26
	Chromic fluoride, solution	8	UN1757	II	CORROSIVE	B2, T8	154	202	242	1 L	30 L	A	
	Chromium nitrate	5.1	UN2720	III	OXIDIZER	A1, A29	152	213	240	25 kg	100 kg	A	
	Chromium oxychloride	8	UN1758	I	CORROSIVE	A3, A6, A7, B10, N34, T12, T26	None	201	242	0.5 L	2.5 L	C	8, 40, 66, 74, 89, 90
	Chromium trioxide, anhydrous	5.1	UN1463	II	OXIDIZER, CORROSIVE		None	212	242	5 kg	25 kg	A	
	Chromosulfuric acid	8	UN2240	I	CORROSIVE	A3, A6, A7, B4, B6, N34, T12, T27	None	201	242	0.5 L	2.5 L	B	8, 9, 40, 66, 74, 89, 90
	Chromyl chloride, see Chromium oxychloride												
	Cigar and cigarette lighters, charged with fuel, see Lighters for cigars, cigarettes, etc.												
	Coal briquettes, hot	Forbidden											
	Coal gas	2.3	UN1023		POISON GAS, FLAMMABLE GAS	3	None	302	314, 315	Forbidden	25 kg	D	40

(1) Symbols	(2) Hazardous materials descriptions and proper shipping names	(3) Hazard class or Division	(4) Identification Numbers	(5) Packing group	(6) Label(s) required (if not excepted)	(7) Special provisions	(8A) Exceptions	(8B) Non-bulk packaging	(8C) Bulk packaging	(9A) Passenger aircraft or railcar	(9B) Cargo aircraft only	(10A) Vessel stowages	(10B) Other stowage provisions
	Coal tar distillates, flammable	3	UN1136	II	FLAMMABLE LIQUID	T8, T31	150	202	242	5 L	60 L	B	
				III	FLAMMABLE LIQUID	B1, T7, T30	150	203	242	60 L	220 L	A	
	Coal tar dye, corrosive, liquid, n.o.s., see Dyes, liquid or solid, n.o.s. or Dye intermediates, liquid or solid, n.o.s., corrosive												
	Coating solution	3	UN1139	II	FLAMMABLE LIQUID	T7, T30	150	202	242	5 L	60 L	B	
				III	FLAMMABLE LIQUID	B1, T7, T30	150	203	242	60 L	220 L	A	
	Cobalt naphthenates, powder	4.1	UN2001	III	FLAMMABLE SOLID	A19	151	213	240	25 kg	100 kg	A	
	Cobalt resinate, precipitated	4.1	UN1318	III	FLAMMABLE SOLID	A1, A19	151	213	240	25 kg	100 kg	A	
	Cocculus	6.1	UN1584	II	POISON		None	212	242	25 kg	100 kg	A	
	Coke, hot	Forbidden											
	Collodion, see Nitrocellulose etc.												
D	Compounds, cleaning liquid	8	NA1760	I	CORROSIVE	A7, B10, T42	None	201	242	0.5 L	2.5 L	B	40
				II	CORROSIVE	B2, N37, T14	154	202	242	1 L	30 L	B	40
				III	CORROSIVE	N37, T7	154	203	241	5 L	60 L	A	40
D	Compounds, cleaning liquid	3	NA1993	I	FLAMMABLE LIQUID	T42	150	201	243	1 L	30 L	E	
				II	FLAMMABLE LIQUID	T8, T31	150	202	242	5 L	60 L	B	
				III	FLAMMABLE LIQUID	B1, B52, T7, T30	150	203	242	60 L	220 L	A	
D	Compounds, tree or weed killing, liquid	8	NA1760	I	CORROSIVE	A7, B10, T42	None	201	242	0.5 L	2.5 L	B	40
				II	CORROSIVE	B2, N37, T14	154	202	242	1 L	30 L	B	40
				III	CORROSIVE	N37, T7	154	203	241	5 L	60 L	A	40
D	Compounds, tree or weed killing, liquid	3	NA1993	I	FLAMMABLE LIQUID	T42	150	201	243	1 L	30 L	E	
				II	FLAMMABLE LIQUID	T8, T31	150	202	242	5 L	60 L	B	
				III	FLAMMABLE LIQUID	B1, B52, T7, T30	150	203	242	60 L	220 L	A	
D	Compounds, tree or weed killing, liquid	6.1	NA2810	I	POISON		153	201	243	1 L	30 L	B	40
				II	POISON		153	202	243	5 L	60 L	B	40
				III	KEEP AWAY FROM FOOD		153	203	241	60 L	220 L	A	40
D	Combustible liquid, n.o.s.	Combustible liquid	NA1993	III	None	T1	150	203	241	60 L	220 L	A	
	Components, explosive train, n.o.s.	1.2B	UN0382	II	EXPLOSIVE 1.2B	101	None	62	None	Forbidden	Forbidden	B	1E, 6E
	Components, explosive train, n.o.s.	1.4B	UN0383	II	EXPLOSIVE 1.4B	101	None	62	None	Forbidden	75 kg	A	24E
	Components, explosive train, n.o.s.	1.4S	UN0384	II	EXPLOSIVE 1.4S	101	None	62	None	25 kg	100 kg	A	9E
	Components, explosive train, n.o.s.	1.1B	UN0461	II	EXPLOSIVE 1.1B	101	None	62	None	Forbidden	Forbidden	B	1E, 6E
	Composition B, see Hexolite, etc.												
	Compressed or Liquefied gases, flammable, n.o.s.	2.1	UN1954		FLAMMABLE GAS		306	302, 304, 305	314, 315	Forbidden	150 kg		40, 105
	Compressed or Liquefied gases, flammable, toxic, n.o.s. Inhalation hazard Zone A	2.3	UN1953		POISON GAS, FLAMMABLE GAS	1	None	192	245	Forbidden	Forbidden	D	40, 95
	Compressed or Liquefied gases, flammable, toxic, n.o.s. Inhalation Hazard Zone B	2.3	UN1953		POISON GAS, FLAMMABLE GAS	2, B9, B14	None	302, 304, 305	314, 315	Forbidden	Forbidden	D	40
	Compressed or Liquefied gases, flammable, toxic, n.o.s. Inhalation Hazard Zone C	2.3	UN1953		POISON GAS, FLAMMABLE GAS	3, B14	None	302, 304, 305	314, 315	Forbidden	Forbidden	D	40
	Compressed or Liquefied gases, flammable, toxic, n.o.s. Inhalation Hazard Zone D	2.3	UN1953		POISON GAS, FLAMMABLE GAS	4	None	302, 304, 305	314, 315	Forbidden	Forbidden	D	40
	Compressed or Liquefied gases, n.o.s.	2.2	UN1956		NONFLAMMABLE GAS		306, 307	302, 304, 305	314, 315	75 kg	150 kg	A	
	Compressed or Liquefied gases, toxic, n.o.s. Inhalation Hazard Zone A	2.3	UN1955		POISON GAS	1	None	192	245	Forbidden	Forbidden	D	40
	Compressed or Liquefied gases, toxic, n.o.s. Inhalation Hazard Zone B	2.3	UN1955		POISON GAS	2, B9, B14	None	302, 304, 305	314, 315	Forbidden	Forbidden	D	40
	Compressed or Liquefied gases, toxic, n.o.s. Inhalation Hazard Zone C	2.3	UN1955		POISON GAS	3, B14	None	302, 304, 305	314, 315	Forbidden	Forbidden	D	40
	Compressed or Liquefied gases, toxic, n.o.s. Inhalation Hazard Zone D	2.3	UN1955		POISON GAS	4	None	302, 304, 305	314, 315	Forbidden	Forbidden	D	40
D	Consumer commodity	ORM-D	None		None		156, 306	156, 306	None	30 kg gross	30 kg gross	A	
	Contrivances, water-activated, with burster, expelling charge or propelling charge	1.2L	UN0248	II	EXPLOSIVE 1.2L	101	None	62	None	Forbidden	Forbidden	E	2E, 8E, 11E, 17E
	Contrivances, water-activated, with burster, expelling charge or propelling charge	1.3L	UN0249	II	EXPLOSIVE 1.3L	101	None	62	None	Forbidden	Forbidden	E	2E, 8E, 11E, 17E
	Copper acetoarsenite	6.1	UN1585	II	POISON		None	212	242	25 kg	100 kg	A	
	Copper acetylide	Forbidden											
	Copper amine azide	Forbidden											
	Copper arsenite	6.1	UN1586	II	POISON		None	212	242	25 kg	100 kg	A	

Symbols (1)	Hazardous materials descriptions and proper shipping names (2)	Hazard class or Division (3)	Identification Numbers (4)	Packing group (5)	Label(s) required (if not excepted) (6)	Special provisions (7)	Packaging authorizations (§173.***) (8)			Quantity limitations (9)		Vessel stowage requirements (10)	
							Exceptions (8A)	Non-bulk packaging (8B)	Bulk packaging (8C)	Passenger aircraft or railcar (9A)	Cargo aircraft only (9B)	Vessel stowages (10A)	Other stowage provisions (10B)
	Copper based pesticides, liquid, flammable, toxic n.o.s., *flash point less than 23 degrees C.*	3	UN2776	I	FLAMMABLE LIQUID, POISON		None	201	243	Forbidden	30 L	B	40
				II	FLAMMABLE LIQUID, POISON		None	202	243	1 L	60 L	B	40
	Copper based pesticides, liquid, toxic, flammable, n.o.s. *flashpoint not less than 23 degrees C.*	6.1	UN3009	I	POISON, FLAMMABLE LIQUID	T42	None	201	243	1 L	30 L	B	40
				II	POISON, FLAMMABLE LIQUID	T14	None	202	243	5 L	60 L	B	40
				III	KEEP AWAY FROM FOOD, FLAMMABLE LIQUID	B1, T14	153	203	241	60 L	220 L	A	40
	Copper based pesticides, liquid, toxic, n.o.s.	6.1	UN3010	I	POISON	T42	None	201	243	1 L	30 L	B	40
				II	POISON	T14	None	202	243	5 L	60 L	B	40
				III	KEEP AWAY FROM FOOD	T14	153	203	241	60 L	220 L	A	40
	Copper based pesticides, solid, toxic, n.o.s.	6.1	UN2775	I	POISON		None	211	242	5 kg	50 kg	A	40
				II	POISON		None	212	242	25 kg	100 kg	A	40
				III	KEEP AWAY FROM FOOD		153	213	240	100 kg	200 kg	A	40
	Copper chlorate	5.1	UN2721	II	OXIDIZER	A1	152	212	242	5 kg	25 kg	A	56, 58, 106
	Copper chloride	8	UN2802	III	CORROSIVE		154	213	240	25 kg	100 kg	A	
	Copper cyanide	6.1	UN1587	II	POISON		None	204	242	25 kg	100 kg	A	26
	Copper selenate, *see* Selenates *or* Selenites												
	Copper selenite, *see* Selenates *or* Selenites												
	Copper tetramine nitrate	Forbidden											
AW	Copra	4.2	UN1363	III	SPONTANEOUSLY COMBUSTIBLE		None	213	241	Forbidden	Forbidden	A	13, 19, 48, 119
	Cord, detonating, *flexible*	1.1D	UN0065	II	EXPLOSIVE 1.1D	102	63(a)	62	None	Forbidden	Forbidden	B	
	Cord, detonating, *flexible*	1.4D	UN0289	II	EXPLOSIVE 1.4D		None	62	None	Forbidden	75 kg	A	24E
	Cord detonating *or* Fuse detonating *metal clad*	1.2D	UN0102	II	EXPLOSIVE 1.2D		None	62	None	Forbidden	Forbidden	B	
	Cord, detonating *or* Fuse, detonating *metal clad*	1.1D	UN0290	II	EXPLOSIVE 1.1D		None	62	None	Forbidden	Forbidden	B	
	Cord, detonating, mild effect *or* Fuse, detonating, mild effect *metal clad*	1.4D	UN0104	II	EXPLOSIVE 1.4D		None	62	None	Forbidden	75 kg	A	24E
	Cord, igniter	1.4G	UN0066	II	EXPLOSIVE 1.4G		None	62	None	Forbidden	75 kg	A	24E
	Cordeau detonant fuse, see Cord, detonating, *etc.;* Cord, detonating, *flexible*												
	Cordite, see Powder, smokeless												
	Corrosive liquids, flammable, n.o.s.	8	UN2920	I	CORROSIVE, FLAMMABLE LIQUID	B10, T42	None	201	243	0.5 L	2.5 L	C	12, 21, 25, 40, 48
				II	CORROSIVE, FLAMMABLE LIQUID	B2, T15, T26	None	202	243	1 L	30 L	C	12, 21, 25, 40, 48
	Corrosive liquids, n.o.s.	8	UN1760	I	CORROSIVE	A7, B10, T42	None	201	243	0.5 L	2.5 L	B	40
				II	CORROSIVE	B2, T14	154	202	242	1 L	30 L	B	40
				III	CORROSIVE	T7	154	203	241	5 L	60 L	A	40
	Corrosive liquids, oxidizing, n.o.s.	8	UN3093	I	CORROSIVE, OXIDIZER		None	201	243	Forbidden	2.5 L	C	89
				II	CORROSIVE, OXIDIZER		None	202	243	1 L	30 L	C	89
	Corrosive liquids, poisonous, n.o.s.	8	UN2922	I	CORROSIVE, POISON	A7, B10	None	201	243	0.5 L	2.5 L	B	40, 95
				II	CORROSIVE, POISON	B3	None	202	243	1 L	30 L	B	40, 95
	Corrosive liquids, which in contact with water emit flammable gases, n.o.s.	8	UN3094	I	CORROSIVE, DANGEROUS WHEN WET		None	201	243	Forbidden	1 L	E	
				II	CORROSIVE, DANGEROUS WHEN WET		None	202	243	1 L	5 L	E	
	Corrosive solids, flammable, n.o.s.	8	UN2921	I	CORROSIVE, FLAMMABLE SOLID		None	211	242	1 kg	25 kg	B	12, 24, 25, 48
				II	CORROSIVE, FLAMMABLE SOLID		None	212	242	15 kg	50 kg	B	12, 24, 25, 48
	Corrosive solids, n.o.s.	8	UN1759	I	CORROSIVE		None	211	242	1 kg	25 kg	B	
				II	CORROSIVE		154	212	240	15 kg	50 kg	A	
				III	CORROSIVE		154	213	240	25 kg	100 kg	A	
	Corrosive solids, oxidizing, n.o.s.	8	UN3084	I	CORROSIVE, OXIDIZER		None	211	240	1 kg	25 kg	C	89
				II	CORROSIVE, OXIDIZER		None	212	240	15 kg	50 kg	C	89

Symbols (1)	Hazardous materials descriptions and proper shipping names (2)	Hazard class or Division (3)	Identification Numbers (4)	Packing group (5)	Label(s) required (if not excepted) (6)	Special provisions (7)	(8) Packaging authorizations (§173.***)			(9) Quantity limitations		(10) Vessel stowage requirements	
							Exceptions (8A)	Non-bulk packaging (8B)	Bulk packaging (8C)	Passenger aircraft or railcar (9A)	Cargo aircraft only (9B)	Vessel stowages (10A)	Other stowage provisions (10B)
	Corrosive solids, poisonous, n.o.s.	8	UN2923	I	CORROSIVE, POISON		None	211	242	1 kg	25 kg	B	40, 95
				II	CORROSIVE, POISON		None	212	240	15 kg	50 kg	B	40, 95
	Corrosive solids, self heating, n.o.s.	8	UN3095	I	CORROSIVE, SPONTANEOUSLY COMBUSTIBLE		None	211	241	1 kg	25 kg	C	
				II	CORROSIVE, SPONTANEOUSLY COMBUSTIBLE		None	212	242	15 kg	50 kg	C	
	Corrosive solids, which in contact with water emit flammable gases, n.o.s.	8	UN3096	I	CORROSIVE, DANGEROUS WHEN WET		None	211	241	1 kg	25 kg	E	
				II	CORROSIVE, DANGEROUS WHEN WET		None	212	242	15 kg	50 kg	E	
DW	Cotton	9	NA1365			W41	None	None	None	No limit	No limit	A	
I	Cotton waste, oily	4.2	UN1364	III	SPONTANEOUSLY COMBUSTIBLE	N9	None	213	None	Forbidden	Forbidden	A	54
AIW	Cotton, wet	4.2	UN1365				None	204	241	Forbidden	Forbidden	A	
	Coumarin derivative pesticides, liquid, flammable, toxic, n.o.s., *flashpoint less than 23 deg C.*	3	UN3024	I	FLAMMABLE LIQUID, POISON		None	201	243	Forbidden	30 L	B	40
				II	FLAMMABLE LIQUID, POISON		None	202	243	1 L	60 L	B	40
	Coumarin derivative pesticides, liquid, toxic, flammable, n.o.s. *flashpoint not less than 23 degrees C.*	6.1	UN3025	I	POISON, FLAMMABLE LIQUID		None	201	243	1 L	30 L	B	40
				II	POISON, FLAMMABLE LIQUID		None	202	243	5 L	60 L	B	40
				III	KEEP AWAY FROM FOOD, FLAMMABLE LIQUID	B1	153	203	241	60 L	220 L	A	40
	Coumarin derivative pesticides, liquid, toxic, n.o.s.	6.1	UN3026	I	POISON		None	201	243	1 L	30 L	B	40
				II	POISON		None	202	243	5 L	60 L	B	40
				III	KEEP AWAY FROM FOOD		153	203	241	60 L	220 L	A	40
	Coumarin derivative pesticides, solid, toxic, n.o.s.	6.1	UN3027	I	POISON		None	211	242	5 kg	50 kg	A	40
				II	POISON		None	212	242	25 kg	100 kg	A	40
				III	KEEP AWAY FROM FOOD		153	213	240	100 kg	200 kg	A	40
	Cresols *(o-; m-; p-)*	6.1	UN2076	II	POISON	T8	None	202	243	5 L	60 L	A	
	Cresylic acid	6.1	UN2022	II	POISON	T8	None	202	243	5 L	60 L	A	
+	Crotonaldehyde, stabilized	3	UN1143	II	FLAMMABLE LIQUID, POISON	2, B9, B14, B32, B74, B77, T38, T43, T45	None	227	244	Forbidden	60 L	B	40
	Crotonic acid *liquid*	8	UN2823	III	CORROSIVE		154	203	240	5 L	60 L	A	12, 48
	Crotonic acid, *solid*	8	UN2823	III	CORROSIVE		154	213	240	25 kg	100 kg	A	12, 48
	Crotonylene	3	UN1144	I	FLAMMABLE LIQUID	T20	150	201	243	1 L	30 L	E	
	Cupriethylenediamine solution	8	UN1761	II	CORROSIVE, POISON	T8, T26	154	202	243	1 L	30 L	A	95
	Cutters, cable, explosive	1.4S	UN0070	II	EXPLOSIVE 1.4S		None	62	None	25 kg	100 kg	A	9E
	Cyanide or cyanide mixtures, dry, see Cyanides, inorganic, n.o.s.												
	Cyanide solutions	6.1	UN1935	I	POISON	B37, T18, T26	None	201	243	1 L	30 L	B	40, 52
				II	POISON	T18, T26	None	202	243	5 L	60 L	A	40, 52
				III	KEEP AWAY FROM FOOD	T18, T26	153	203	241	60 L	220 L	A	40, 52
	Cyanides, inorganic, n.o.s.	6.1	UN1588	I	POISON	N74, N75	None	211	242	5 kg	50 kg	A	52
				II	POISON	N74, N75	None	212	242	25 kg	100 kg	A	52
				III	KEEP AWAY FROM FOOD	N74, N75	153	203	241	100 kg	200 kg	A	52
	Cyanogen bromide	6.1	UN1889	I	POISON, CORROSIVE	1, A6, A8, B9, B14, B30, B72, T38, T43, T44	None	226	244	Forbidden	25 kg	D	40
	Cyanogen chloride, inhibited	2.3	UN1589		POISON GAS, FLAMMABLE GAS	1	None	192	245	Forbidden	Forbidden	D	40
	Cyanogen, liquefied	2.3	UN1026		POISON GAS, FLAMMABLE GAS	2	None	192	245	Forbidden	Forbidden	D	40
	Cyanuric chloride	8	UN2670	III	CORROSIVE		None	213	240	25 kg	100 kg	A	12, 40, 48
	Cyanuric triazide	Forbidden											
	Cyclobutane	2.1	UN2601		FLAMMABLE GAS		306	304	314, 315	Forbidden	150 kg	B	40
	Cyclobutylchloroformate	6.1	UN2744	II	POISON, CORROSIVE	T18	None	202	243	1 L	30 L	A	12, 13, 22, 25, 40, 48, 100

307

(1) Symbols	(2) Hazardous materials descriptions and proper shipping names	(3) Hazard class or Division	(4) Identification Numbers	(5) Packing group	(6) Label(s) required (if not excepted)	(7) Special provisions	(8) Packaging authorizations (§173.***)			(9) Quantity limitations		(10) Vessel stowage requirements	
							(8A) Exceptions	(8B) Non-bulk packaging	(8C) Bulk packaging	(9A) Passenger aircraft or railcar	(9B) Cargo aircraft only	(10A) Vessel stowages	(10B) Other stowage provisions
	1,5,9-Cyclododecatriene	6.1	UN2518	III	KEEP AWAY FROM FOOD	T7	153	203	241	60 L	220 L	A	40
	Cycloheptane	3	UN2241	II	FLAMMABLE LIQUID	T1	150	202	242	5 L	60 L	B	40
	Cycloheptatriene	3	UN2603	II	FLAMMABLE LIQUID, POISON	T14	None	202	243	1 L	60 L	E	40
	Cycloheptene	3	UN2242	II	FLAMMABLE LIQUID	T7	150	202	241	5 L	60 L	B	
	Cyclohexane	3	UN1145	II	FLAMMABLE LIQUID	T8	150	202	242	5 L	60 L	E	
	Cyclohexanone	3	UN1915	III	FLAMMABLE LIQUID	B1, T1	150	203	242	60 L	220 L	A	
	Cyclohexene	3	UN2256	II	FLAMMABLE LIQUID	T7	150	202	242	5 L	60 L	E	
	Cyclohexenyltrichlorosilane	8	UN1762	II	CORROSIVE	A7, B2, N34, T8, T26	None	202	242	Forbidden	30 L	C	40
	Cyclohexyl acetate	3	UN2243	III	FLAMMABLE LIQUID	B1, T1	150	203	242	60 L	220 L	A	
+	Cyclohexyl isocyanate	6.1	UN2488	II	POISON	2, B9, B14, B32, B74, B77, T38, T43, T45	None	227	244	5 L	60 L	D	40
	Cyclohexyl mercaptan	3	UN3054	III	FLAMMABLE LIQUID	B1, T1	150	203	242	60 L	220 L	A	40, 95, 102
	Cyclohexylamine	8	UN2357	II	CORROSIVE, FLAMMABLE LIQUID	T8, T26	None	202	243	1 L	30 L	A	12, 21, 40, 48
	Cyclohexyltrichlorosilane	8	UN1763	II	CORROSIVE	A7, B2, N34, T8, T26	None	202	242	Forbidden	30 L	C	40
	Cyclonite and cyclotetramethylenetetranitramine mixtures, wetted *or* desensitized *see* RDX and HMX mixtures, wetted *or* desensitized *etc.* ed												
	Cyclonite and HMX mixtures, wetted *or* desensitized *see* RDX and HMX mixtures, wetted *or* desensitized *etc.*												
	Cyclonite and octogen mixtures, wetted *or* desensitized *see* RDX and HMX mixtures, wetted *or* desensitized *etc.*												
	Cyclonite, *see* Cyclotrimethylenetrinitramine, *etc.*												
	Cyclooctadiene phosphines, *see* 9-Phosphabicyclononanes												
	Cyclooctadienes	3	UN2520	III	FLAMMABLE LIQUID	B1, T1	150	203	242	60 L	220 L	A	
	Cyclooctatetraene	3	UN2358	II	FLAMMABLE LIQUID	T8	150	202	242	5 L	60 L	B	
	Cyclopentane	3	UN1146	II	FLAMMABLE LIQUID	T14	150	202	242	5 L	60 L	E	
	Cyclopentane, methyl, *see* Methyl cyclopentane												
	Cyclopentanol	3	UN2244	III	FLAMMABLE LIQUID	B1, T1	150	203	242	60 L	220 L	A	
	Cyclopentanone	3	UN2245	III	FLAMMABLE LIQUID	B1, T1	150	203	242	60 L	220 L	A	
	Cyclopentene	3	UN2246	II	FLAMMABLE LIQUID	T13	150	202	242	5 L	60 L	E	
	Cyclopropane, liquified	2.1	UN1027		FLAMMABLE GAS		306	304	314, 315	Forbidden	150 kg	E	40
	Cyclotetramethylene tetranitramine (dry or unphlegmatized) (HMX)	Forbidden											
	Cyclotetramethylenetetranitramine, desensitized *or* Octogen, desensitized *or* HMX, desensitized	1.1D	UN0484	II	EXPLOSIVE 1.1D		None	62	None	Forbidden	Forbidden	B	1E, 5E
	Cyclotetramethylenetetranitramine, wetted *or* HMX, wetted *or* Octogen, wetted *with not less than 15 per cent water, by mass*	1.1D	UN0226	II	EXPLOSIVE 1.1D		None	62	None	Forbidden	Forbidden	B	1E, 5E
	Cyclotrimethylenenitramine and octogen, mixtures, wetted *or* desensitized *see* RDX and HMX mixtures, wetted *or* desensitized *etc.*												
	Cyclotrimethylenetrinitramele and cyclotetramethylenetetranitramine mixtures, wetted *or* desensitized *see* RDX and HMX mixtures, wetted *or* desensitized *etc.*												
	Cyclotrimethylenetrinitramine and HMX mixtures, wetted *or* desensitized *see* RDX and HMX mixtures, wetted *or* desensitized *etc.*												

308

Sym-bols	Hazardous materials descriptions and proper shipping names	Hazard class or Division	Identifi-cation Numbers	Packing group	Label(s) required (if not excepted)	Special provisions	(8) Packaging authorizations (§173.***)			(9) Quantity limitations		(10) Vessel stowage requirements	
							Excep-tions	Non-bulk pack-aging	Bulk pack-aging	Passenger aircraft or railcar	Cargo aircraft only	Vessel stow-ages	Other stowage provisions
(1)	(2)	(3)	(4)	(5)	(6)	(7)	(8A)	(8B)	(8C)	(9A)	(9B)	(10A)	(10B)
	Cyclotrimethylenetrinitramine, desensitized or Cyclonite, desensitized or Hexogen, desensitized or RDX, desensitized; Hexogen; RDX), desensitized	1.1D	UN0483	II	EXPLOSIVE 1.1D		None	62	None	Forbidden	Forbidden	B	1E, 5E
	Cyclotrimethylenetrinitramine, wetted or Cyclonite, wetted or Hexogen, wetted or RDX, wetted with not less than 15 percent water by mass	1.1D	UN0072	II	EXPLOSIVE 1.1D		None	62	None	Forbidden	Forbidden	B	1E, 5E
	Cymenes	3	UN2046	III	FLAMMABLE LIQUID	B1, T1	150	203	242	60 L	220 L	A	
	Decaborane	4.1	UN1868	II	FLAMMABLE SOLID, POISON	A19, A20	None	212	None	Forbidden	50 kg	A	
	Decahydronaphthalene	3	UN1147	III	FLAMMABLE LIQUID	B1, T1	150	203	242	60 L	220 L	A	
	n-Decane	3	UN2247	III	FLAMMABLE LIQUID	B1, T1	150	203	242	60 L	220 L	A	
	Deflagrating metal salts of aromatic nitroderivatives, n.o.s	1.3C	UN0132	II	EXPLOSIVE 1.3C		None	62	None	Forbidden	Forbidden	B	1E, 5E
	Delay electric igniter, see Igniters												
D	Denatured alcohol	3	NA1987	II	FLAMMABLE LIQUID	T8, T31	150	202	242	5 L	60 L	B	
				III	FLAMMABLE LIQUID	B1, T7, T30	150	203	242	60 L	220 L	A	
D	Denatured alcohol	3	NA1986	I	FLAMMABLE LIQUID, POISON	T8, T31	None	201	243	Forbidden	30 L	E	40
				II	FLAMMABLE LIQUID, POISON	T8, T31	150	202	243	1 L	60 L	E	40
	Depth charges, see Charges, depth												
	Detonating relays, see Detonators, etc.												
	Detonator assemblies, non-electric for blasting	1.1B	UN0360	II	EXPLOSIVE 1.1B		None	62	None	Forbidden	Forbidden	B	1E, 2E, 6E
	Detonator assemblies, non-electric, for blasting	1.4B	UN0361	II	EXPLOSIVE 1.4B	103	63(f), 63(g)	62	None	Forbidden	75 kg	A	1E, 2E, 6E, 24E
	Detonators, electric, for blasting	1.1B	UN0030	II	EXPLOSIVE 1.1B		63(f), 63(g)	62	None	Forbidden	Forbidden	B	
	Detonators, electric, for blasting	1.4B	UN0255	II	EXPLOSIVE 1.4B	103	63(f), 63(g)	62	None	Forbidden	75 kg	A	24E
	Detonators, electric for blasting	1.4S	UN0456	II	EXPLOSIVE 1.4S	104	63(f), 63(g)	62	None	25 kg	100 kg	A	9E
	Detonators for ammunition	1.1B	UN0073	II	EXPLOSIVE 1.1B		None	62	None	Forbidden	Forbidden	B	2E, 6E, 25E
	Detonators for ammunition	1.2B	UN0364	II	EXPLOSIVE 1.2B		None	62	None	Forbidden	Forbidden	B	2E, 6E
	Detonators for ammunition	1.4B	UN0365	II	EXPLOSIVE 1.4B	103	None	62	None	Forbidden	75 kg	A	24E
	Detonators for ammunition	1.4S	UN0366	II	EXPLOSIVE 1.4S	104	None	62	None	25 kg	100 kg	A	9E
	Detonators, non-electric, for blasting	1.1B	UN0029	II	EXPLOSIVE 1.1B		None	62	None	Forbidden	Forbidden	B	1E, 2E, 6E
	Detonators, non-electric, for blasting	1.4B	UN0267	II	EXPLOSIVE 1.4B	103	63(f), 63(g)	62	None	Forbidden	75 kg	B	
	Detonators, non-electric for blasting	1.4S	UN0455	II	EXPLOSIVE 1.4S	104	None	62	None	25 kg	100 kg	A	9E
	Deuterium	2.1	UN1957		FLAMMABLE GAS		306	302	None	Forbidden	150 kg	E	40
	Devices, small, hydrocarbon gas powered or hydrocarbon gas refills for small devices with release device	2.1	UN3150		FLAMMABLE GAS		306	304		Forbidden	150 kg	B	40
	Di-n-amylamine	6.1	UN2841	III	KEEP AWAY FROM FOOD	T8	153	203	241	60 L	220 L	A	
	Di-n-butyl peroxydicarbonate, more than 52 per cent in solution	Forbid-den											
	Di-n-butylamine	8	UN2248	II	CORROSIVE, FLAMMABLE LIQUID	T8	None	202	243	1 L	30 L	A	12, 21, 48
	2,2-Di-(tert-butylperoxy) butane, more than 55 per cent in solution	Forbid-den											
	Di-(tert-butylperoxy) phthalate, more than 55 per cent in solution	Forbid-den											
	2,2-Di-(4,4-di-tert-butylperoxycyclohexyl) propane, more than 42 per cent with inert solid	Forbid-den											
	Di-2,4-dichlorobenzoyl peroxide, more than 75 per cent with water	Forbid-den											
	1,2-Di-(dimethylamino) ethane	3	UN2372	II	FLAMMABLE LIQUID	T8	150	202	242	5 L	60 L	B	
	Di-2-ethylhexyl phosphoric acid, see Diisooctyl acid phosphate												
	Di-(1-hydroxytetrazole) (dry)	Forbid-den											
	Di-(1-naphthoyl) peroxide	Forbid-den											
	a,a'-Di-(nitroxy) methylether	Forbid-den											
	Di-(beta-nitroxyethyl) ammonium nitrate	Forbid-den											

309

Sym-bols	Hazardous materials descriptions and proper shipping names	Hazard class or Division	Identifi-cation Numbers	Packing group	Label(s) required (if not excepted)	Special provisions	(8) Packaging authorizations (§173.***)			(9) Quantity limitations		(10) Vessel stowage requirements	
							Excep-tions	Non-bulk pack-aging	Bulk pack-aging	Passenger aircraft or railcar	Cargo aircraft only	Vessel stow-ages	Other stowage provisions
(1)	(2)	(3)	(4)	(5)	(6)	(7)	(8A)	(8B)	(8C)	(9A)	(9B)	(10A)	(10B)
	Diacetone alcohol	3	UN1148	III	FLAMMABLE LIQUID	B1, T1	150	203	242	60 L	220 L	A	
	Diacetone alcohol peroxides, more than 57% in solution with more than 9% hydrogen peroxide, less than 26% diacetone alcohol and less than 9% water; total active oxygen content more than 9% by mass	Forbid-den											
	Diacetyl, see Butanedione												
	Diacetyl peroxide, solid, or more than 25% in solution	Forbid-den											
	Diallylamine	3	UN2359	II	FLAMMABLE LIQUID	T8	150	202	242	5 L	60 L	B	40
	Diallylether	3	UN2360	II	FLAMMABLE LIQUID, POISON	N12, T8	None	202	243	1 L	60 L	E	40
	4,4'-Diaminodiphenyl methane	6.1	UN2651	III	KEEP AWAY FROM FOOD		153	213	240	100 kg	200 kg	A	
	p-Diazidobenzene	Forbid-den											
	1,2-Diazidoethane	Forbid-den											
	2-Diazo-1-naphthol-4-sulpho-chloride	4.1	UN3042	II	FLAMMABLE SOLID, EXPLOSIVE	53	None	224	None	Forbidden	Forbidden	D	
	2-Diazo-1-naphthol-5-sulpho-chloride	4.1	UN3043	II	FLAMMABLE SOLID, EXPLOSIVE	53	None	224	None	Forbidden	Forbidden	D	
	1,1'-Diazoaminonaphthalene	Forbid-den											
	Diazoaminotetrazole (dry)	Forbid-den											
	Diazodinitrophenol (dry)	Forbid-den											
	Diazodinitrophenol, wetted *with not less than 40 per cent water or mixture of alcohol and water, by mass*	1.1A	UN0074	II	EXPLOSIVE 1.1A	111, 117	None	62	None	Forbidden	Forbidden	E	2E, 6E
	Diazodiphenylmethane	Forbid-den											
	Diazonium nitrates (dry)	Forbid-den											
	Diazonium perchlorates (dry)	Forbid-den											
	1,3-Diazopropane	Forbid-den											
	Dibenzyl peroxydicarbonate, more than 87 per cent with water	Forbid-den											
	Dibenzyldichlorosilane	8	UN2434	II	CORROSIVE	B2, T8, T26	154	202	242	1 L	30 L	C	40
	Diborane	2.3	UN1911		POISON GAS, FLAMMABLE GAS	1	None	302	None	Forbidden	Forbidden	D	40, 57
	Diborane mixtures	2.1	NA1911		FLAMMABLE GAS	5	None	302	245	Forbidden	Forbidden	D	40, 57
	Dibromoacetylene	Forbid-den											
	Dibromobenzene	3	UN2711	III	FLAMMABLE LIQUID	B1, T1	150	203	242	60 L	220 L	A	
	1,2-Dibromobutan-3-one	6.1	UN2648	II	POISON		None	202	243	5 L	60 L	B	40
	Dibromochloropropane	6.1	UN2872	III	KEEP AWAY FROM FOOD	T7	153	203	241	60 L	220 L	A	
A	Dibromodifluoromethane, *R12B2*	9	UN1941	III	None	T22	155	203	241	100 L	220 L	A	25
	1,2-Dibromoethane, see Ethylene dibromide												
	Dibromomethane	6.1	UN2664	III	KEEP AWAY FROM FOOD	T7	153	203	241	60 L	220 L	A	
	Dibutyl ethers	3	UN1149	III	FLAMMABLE LIQUID	B1, T1	150	203	242	60 L	220 L	A	
	Dibutylaminoethanol	6.1	UN2873	III	KEEP AWAY FROM FOOD	T1	153	203	241	60 L	220 L	A	
	N,N'-Dichlorazodicarbonamidine (salts of) (dry)	Forbid-den											
	1,1-Dichloro-1-nitroethane	6.1	UN2650	II	POISON	T8	None	202	243	5 L	60 L	A	12, 40, 48
D	3,5-Dichloro-2,4,6-trifluoropyridine	6.1	NA9264	I	POISON	2, B9, B14, B32, B74, T38, T43, T45	None	227	244	Forbidden	Forbidden	A	40, 95
	Dichloroacetic acid	8	UN1764	II	CORROSIVE	A3, A6, A7, B2, N34, T9, T27	154	202	242	1 L	30 L	A	
	1,3-Dichloroacetone	6.1	UN2649	II	POISON		None	212	243	25 kg	100 kg	B	12, 40, 48
	Dichloroacetyl chloride	8	UN1765	II	CORROSIVE	A3, A6, A7, B2, B6, N34, T8, T26	154	202	242	1 L	30 L	D	40
	Dichloroacetylene	Forbid-den											
	Dichloroanilines, solid *or* liquid	6.1	UN1590	II	POISON	T14	None	202	242	5 L	60 L	A	40
	o-Dichlorobenzene	6.1	UN1591	III	KEEP AWAY FROM FOOD	T7	153	203	241	60 L	220 L	A	
	p-Dichlorobenzene	6.1	UN1592	III	KEEP AWAY FROM FOOD		153	213	240	100 kg	200 kg	A	

310

Sym-bols	Hazardous materials descriptions and proper shipping names	Hazard class or Division	Identifi-cation Numbers	Packing group	Label(s) required (If not excepted)	Special provisions	Packaging authorizations (§173.***) Exceptions	Non-bulk pack-aging	Bulk pack-aging	Quantity limitations Passenger aircraft or railcar	Cargo aircraft only	Vessel stow-ages	Other stowage provisions
(1)	(2)	(3)	(4)	(5)	(6)	(7)	(8A)	(8B)	(8C)	(9A)	(9B)	(10A)	(10B)
D	Dichlorobutene	8	NA2920	I	CORROSIVE, FLAMMABLE LIQUID		None	201	243	0.5 L	2.5 L	C	12, 21, 25, 40, 48
	2,2-Dichlorodiethyl ether	6.1	UN1916	II	POISON, FLAMMABLE LIQUID	N33, N34, T8	None	202	243	5 L	60 L	A	
	Dichlorodifluoromethane and difluoroethane azeotropic mixture *with approximately 74 per cent dichlorodifluoromethane, R500*	2.2	UN2602		NONFLAMMABLE GAS		306	304	314, 315	75 kg	150 kg	A	
	Dichlorodifluoromethane and ethylene oxide mixture, *with not more than 12% ethylene oxide*	2.2	UN3070		NONFLAMMABLE GAS		None	304	314, 315	Forbidden	25 kg	D	40
	Dichlorodifluoromethane, *R12*	2.2	UN1028		NONFLAMMABLE GAS		306	304	314, 315	75 kg	150 kg	A	
	Dichlorodimethyl ether, symmetrical	6.1	UN2249	I	POISON	T25	None	201	243	Forbidden	Forbidden	D	40, 105
	1,1-Dichloroethane	3	UN2362	II	FLAMMABLE LIQUID	T7	150	202	242	5 L	60 L	B	40
	1,2-Dichloroethane, see Ethylene dichloride												
	Dichloroethyl sulfide	Forbid-den											
	Dichloroethylene	3	UN1150	II	FLAMMABLE LIQUID	T14	150	202	242	5 L	60 L	B	
	Dichlorofluoromethane, *R21*	2.2	UN1029		NONFLAMMABLE GAS		306	304	314, 315	75 kg	150 kg	A	
	Dichloroisocyanuric acid, dry *or* Dichloroisocyanuric acid salts	5.1	UN2465	II	OXIDIZER	28	152	212	240	5 kg	25 kg	A	13
	Dichloroisopropyl ether	6.1	UN2490	II	POISON	T8	None	202	243	5 L	60 L	B	
	Dichloromethane	6.1	UN1593	III	KEEP AWAY FROM FOOD	N36, T13	153	203	241	60 L	220 L	A	
	Dichloropentanes	3	UN1152	III	FLAMMABLE LIQUID	B1, T1	150	202	241	60 L	220 L	A	
	Dichlorophenyl isocyanates	6.1	UN2250	II	POISON		None	212	242	25 kg	100 kg	A	25, 40, 48
	Dichlorophenyltrichlorosilane	8	UN1766	II	CORROSIVE	A7, B2, B6, N34, T8, T26	None	202	242	Forbidden	30 L	C	40
	Dichloropropane, see Propylene dichloride												
	1,3-Dichloropropanol-2	6.1	UN2750	II	POISON	T8	None	202	243	5 L	60 L	A	12, 40, 48
	Dichloropropene	3	UN2047	II	FLAMMABLE LIQUID	T8	150	202	242	5 L	60 L	A	
	Dichloropropene and propylene dichloride mixture, see Propylene dichloride												
	Dichlorosilane	2.3	UN2189		POISON GAS, FLAMMABLE GAS	2, B9, B14	None	304	314, 315	Forbidden	Forbidden	D	40
	Dichlorotetrafluoroethane, *R114*	2.2	UN1958		NONFLAMMABLE GAS		306	304	314, 315	75 kg	150 kg	A	
	Dichlorovinylchloroarsine	Forbid-den											
	Dicycloheptadiene, see Norbornadiene												
	Dicyclohexylamine	8	UN2565	III	CORROSIVE	T8	154	203	241	5 L	60 L	A	
	Dicyclohexylammonium nitrite	4.1	UN2687	III	FLAMMABLE SOLID		153	213	240	25 kg	100 kg	A	48
	Dicyclopentadiene	3	UN2048	III	FLAMMABLE LIQUID	B1, T1	150	203	242	60 L	220 L	A	
	Didymium nitrate	5.1	UN1465	III	OXIDIZER	A1	152	213	240	25 kg	100 kg	A	
D	Dieldrin	6.1	NA2761	II	POISON		None	212	242	0.5 kg	5 kg	A	40
D	Diesel fuel	3	NA1993	III	None	B1	150	203	241	60 L	220 L	A	
	Diethanol nitrosamine dinitrate (dry)	Forbid-den											
	2,5-Diethoxy-4-morpholinobenzenediazonium zinc chloride	4.1	UN3036	II	FLAMMABLE SOLID		None	224	None	15 kg	50 kg	C	2
	Diethoxymethane	3	UN2373	II	FLAMMABLE LIQUID	T8	150	202	242	5 L	60 L	B	
	3,3-Diethoxypropene	3	UN2374	II	FLAMMABLE LIQUID	T1	150	202	242	5 L	60 L	B	
	N,N-Diethyl aniline	6.1	UN2432	III	KEEP AWAY FROM FOOD	T2	153	203	241	60 L	220 L	A	
	Diethyl carbonate	3	UN2366	III	FLAMMABLE LIQUID	B1, T1	150	203	242	60 L	220 L	A	
	Diethyl cellosolve, see Ethylene glycol diethyl ether												
	Diethyl ether *or* Ethyl ether	3	UN1155	I	FLAMMABLE LIQUID	T21	150	201	243	1 L	30 L	E	40
	Diethyl ketone	3	UN1156	II	FLAMMABLE LIQUID	T1	150	202	242	5 L	60 L	B	
	Diethyl peroxydicarbonate, more than 27 per cent in solution	Forbid-den											
	Diethyl sulfate	6.1	UN1594	II	POISON	T14	None	202	243	5 L	60 L	C	
	Diethyl sulfide	3	UN2375	II	FLAMMABLE LIQUID	T14	None	202	243	1 L	60 L	E	

311

Symbols	Hazardous materials descriptions and proper shipping names	Hazard class or Division	Identification Numbers	Packing group	Label(s) required (if not excepted)	Special provisions	Packaging authorizations (§173.***)			Quantity limitations		Vessel stowage requirements	
							Exceptions	Non-bulk packaging	Bulk packaging	Passenger aircraft or railcar	Cargo aircraft only	Vessel stowages	Other stowage provisions
(1)	(2)	(3)	(4)	(5)	(6)	(7)	(8A)	(8B)	(8C)	(9A)	(9B)	(10A)	(10B)
	Diethylamine	3	UN1154	II	FLAMMABLE LIQUID	N34, T8	150	202	242	5 L	60 L	E	
	Diethylaminoethanol	3	UN2686	III	FLAMMABLE LIQUID	B1, T1	150	203	242	60 L	220 L	A	
AW	Diethylaminopropylamine	8	UN2684	III	CORROSIVE, FLAMMABLE LIQUID	B1, B2, T8	154	203	243	5 L	60 L	A	12, 21, 48
	Diethylbenzene	3	UN2049	III	FLAMMABLE LIQUID	B1, T1	150	203	242	60 L	220 L	A	
	Diethyldichlorosilane	8	UN1767	II	CORROSIVE, FLAMMABLE LIQUID	A7, B6, N34, T8, T26	None	202	243	Forbidden	30 L	C	21, 40
	Diethylene glycol dinitrate	Forbidden											
	Diethyleneglycol dinitrate, desensitized *with not less than 25 percent non-volatile water-insoluble phlegmatizer, by mass*	1.1D	UN0075	II	EXPLOSIVE 1.1D		None	62	None	Forbidden	Forbidden	B	1E, 4E, 21E
	Diethylenetriamine	8	UN2079	II	CORROSIVE	B2, T8	154	202	242	1 L	30 L	A	40
	N,N-Diethylethylenediamine	8	UN2685	II	CORROSIVE, FLAMMABLE LIQUID	T8	None	202	243	1 L	30 L	A	12, 21, 48
	Diethylgold bromide	Forbidden											
	Diethylthiophosphoryl chloride	8	UN2751	II	CORROSIVE	B2, T8	None	202	242	15 kg	50 kg	D	12, 40
	Diethylzinc	4.2	UN1366	I	SPONTANEOUSLY COMBUSTIBLE	B11, T28, T40	None	181	244	Forbidden	Forbidden	D	18
	Difluorochloroethanes, see Chlorodifluoroethanes												
	Difluoroethane, *R152a*	2.1	UN1030		FLAMMABLE GAS		306	304	314, 315	Forbidden	150 kg	B	40
	1,1-Difluoroethylene, *R1132a*	2.1	UN1959		FLAMMABLE GAS		306	304	None	Forbidden	150 kg	E	40
	Difluorophosphoric acid, anhydrous	8	UN1768	II	CORROSIVE	A6, A7, B2, N5, N34, T9, T27	None	202	242	1 L	30 L	A	40
	2,3-Dihydropyran	3	UN2376	II	FLAMMABLE LIQUID	T7	150	202	242	5 L	60 L	B	
	1,8-Dihydroxy-2,4,5,7-tetranitroanthraquinone (chrysamminic acid)	Forbidden											
	Diiodoacetylene	Forbidden											
	Diisobutyl ketone	3	UN1157	III	FLAMMABLE LIQUID	B1, T1	150	203	242	60 L	220 L	A	
	Diisobutylamine	3	UN2361	III	FLAMMABLE LIQUID	B1, T1	150	203	242	60 L	220 L	A	
	Diisobutylene, isomeric compounds	3	UN2050	II	FLAMMABLE LIQUID	T1	150	202	242	5 L	60 L	B	
	Diisooctyl acid phosphate	8	UN1902	III	CORROSIVE	T7	154	203	241	5 L	60 L	A	
	Diisopropyl ether	3	UN1159	II	FLAMMABLE LIQUID	T8	150	202	242	5 L	60 L	E	40
	Diisopropylamine	3	UN1158	II	FLAMMABLE LIQUID	T8	150	202	242	5 L	60 L	B	
	Diisopropylbenzene hydroperoxide, more than 72 percent in solution	Forbidden											
+	Diketene, inhibited	3	UN2521	III	FLAMMABLE LIQUID, POISON	2, B9, B14, B32, B74, T38, T43, T45	None	227	244	60 L	220 L	A	49
	1,1-Dimethoxyethane	3	UN2377	II	FLAMMABLE LIQUID	T13	150	202	242	5 L	60 L	B	
	1,2-Dimethoxyethane	3	UN2252	II	FLAMMABLE LIQUID	T1	150	202	242	5 L	60 L	B	
	Dimethyl carbonate	3	UN1161	II	FLAMMABLE LIQUID	T8	150	202	242	5 L	60 L	B	
	Dimethyl chlorothiophosphate, see Dimethyl thiophosphoryl chloride												
	2,5-Dimethyl-2,5-dihydroperoxy hexane, more than 82 per cent with water	Forbidden											
	Dimethyl disulfide	3	UN2381	II	FLAMMABLE LIQUID	T8	150	202	242	5 L	60 L	B	40
	Dimethyl ether	2.1	UN1033		FLAMMABLE GAS		306	304	314, 315	Forbidden	150 kg	B	40
	Dimethyl-N-propylamine	3	UN2266		FLAMMABLE LIQUID, CORROSIVE	T14, T26	None	202	243	1 L	5 L	B	40
	Dimethyl sulfate	6.1	UN1595	I	POISON, CORROSIVE	2, B9, B14, B32, B74, B77, T38, T43, T45	None	227	244	Forbidden	2.5 L	D	40
	Dimethyl sulfide	3	UN1164	II	FLAMMABLE LIQUID	T14	None	201	243	1 L	30 L	E	40
	Dimethyl thiophosphoryl chloride	8	UN2267	III	CORROSIVE	T7	None	203	241	5 L	60 L	B	8
	Dimethylamine, anhydrous	2.1	UN1032		FLAMMABLE GAS		None	304	314, 315	Forbidden	Forbidden	D	40
	Dimethylamine solution	3	UN1160	II	FLAMMABLE LIQUID	T8	150	202	242	5 L	60 L	B	

Sym-bols (1)	Hazardous materials descriptions and proper shipping names (2)	Hazard class or Division (3)	Identifi-cation Numbers (4)	Packing group (5)	Label(s) required (if not excepted) (6)	Special provisions (7)	(8) Packaging authorizations (§173.***)			(9) Quantity limitations		(10) Vessel stowage requirements	
							Excep-tions (8A)	Non-bulk pack-aging (8B)	Bulk pack-aging (8C)	Passenger aircraft or railcar (9A)	Cargo aircraft only (9B)	Vessel stow-ages (10A)	Other stowage provisions (10B)
	4-Dimethylamino-6-(2-dimethylaminoethoxy) toluene-2-diazonium zinc chloride	4.1	UN3039	II	FLAMMABLE SOLID		None	224	None	Forbidden	Forbidden	D	2
	2-Dimethylaminoacetonitrile	3	UN2378	II	FLAMMABLE LIQUID, POISON	T8	None	202	243	1 L	60 L	A	26, 40
	Dimethylaminoethyl methacrylate	6.1	UN2522	II	POISON	T8	None	202	243	5 L	60 L	B	40
	N,N-Dimethylaniline	6.1	UN2253	II	POISON	T8	None	202	243	5 L	60 L	A	
	2,3-Dimethylbutane	3	UN2457	II	FLAMMABLE LIQUID	T13	150	202	242	5 L	60 L	E	
	1,3-Dimethylbutylamine	3	UN2379	II	FLAMMABLE LIQUID	T8	150	202	242	5 L	60 L	B	
	Dimethylcarbamoyl chloride	8	UN2262	II	CORROSIVE	B2, T8	154	202	242	1 L	30 L	A	40
	Dimethylcyclohexanes	3	UN2263	II	FLAMMABLE LIQUID	T1	150	202	242	5 L	60 L	B	
	Dimethylcyclohexylamine	8	UN2264	II	CORROSIVE	B2, T8	154	202	242	1 L	30 L	A	12, 21, 40, 48
	Dimethyldichlorosilane	3	UN1162	I	FLAMMABLE LIQUID, CORROSIVE	B77, T15, T26	None	201	243	Forbidden	Forbidden	B	40
	Dimethyldiethoxysilane	3	UN2380	II	FLAMMABLE LIQUID	T8	150	202	242	5 L	60 L	B	
	Dimethyldioxanes	3	UN2707	II	FLAMMABLE LIQUID	T8, T31	150	202	242	5 L	60 L	B	
				III	FLAMMABLE LIQUID	B1, T7, T30	150	203	242	60 L	220 L	A	
	Dimethylethanolamine	3	UN2051	III	FLAMMABLE LIQUID	B1, T1	150	203	242	60 L	220 L	A	
	N,N-Dimethylformamide	3	UN2265	III	FLAMMABLE LIQUID	B1, T1	150	203	242	60 L	220 L	A	
	Dimethylhexane dihydroperoxide (dry)	Forbid-den											
+	Dimethylhydrazine, symmetrical	3	UN2382	I	FLAMMABLE LIQUID, POISON	2, A7, B9, B14, B32, B74, B77, T38, T43, T45	None	227	244	Forbidden	30 L	E	40
	Dimethylhydrazine, unsymmetrical	6.1	UN1163	I	POISON, FLAMMABLE LIQUID, CORROSIVE	2, A7, B9, B14, B32, B58, B79, T38, T43, T45	None	227	244	Forbidden	Forbidden	D	21, 40, 49, 61, 100
	2,2-Dimethylpropane *other than pentane and isopentane*	2.1	UN2044		FLAMMABLE GAS		306	304	314, 315	Forbidden	150 kg	E	40
	Dimethylzinc	4.2	UN1370	I	SPONTANEOUSLY COMBUSTIBLE	B11, B16, T28, T29, T40	None	181	244	Forbidden	Forbidden	D	18
	Dinitro-o-cresol, *solid*	6.1	UN1598	II	POISON	T14	None	212	242	25 kg	100 kg	A	
	Dinitro-o-cresol, *solution*	6.1	UN1598	II	POISON	T14	None	202	243	5 L	60 L	A	
	1,3-Dinitro-5,5-dimethyl hydantoin	Forbid-den											
	Dinitro-7,8-dimethylglycoluril (dry)	Forbid-den											
	1,3-Dinitro-4,5-dinitrosobenzene	Forbid-den											
	1,4-Dinitro-1,1,4,4-tetramethylolbutanetetranitrate (dry)	Forbid-den											
	2,4-Dinitro-1,3,5-trimethylbenzene	Forbid-den											
	Dinitroanilines	6.1	UN1596	II	POISON	T14	None	212	242	25 kg	100 kg	A	91
	Dinitrobenzenes, *liquid*	6.1	UN1597	II	POISON	11, T14	None	202	243	5 L	60 L	A	91
	Dinitrobenzenes, *solid*	6.1	UN1597	II	POISON	11	None	212	242	25 kg	100 kg	A	91
	Dinitrochlorobenzene, see Chlorodinitrobenzene												
	1,2-Dinitroethane	Forbid-den											
	1,1-Dinitroethane (dry)	Forbid-den											
	Dinitrogen tetroxide, liquefied	2.3	UN1067		POISON GAS, OXIDIZER	1, B7, B12, B14, B45, B46, B61, B66, B67, B77	None	336	314	Forbidden	Forbidden	D	40, 43
	Dinitroglycoluril	Forbid-den											
	Dinitroglycoluril or Dingu	1.1D	UN0489	II	EXPLOSIVE 1.1D		None	62	None	Forbidden	Forbidden	B	1E, 5E, 25E
	Dinitromethane	Forbid-den											
	Dinitrophenol, *dry or wetted with less than 15 per cent water, by mass*	1.1D	UN0076	II	EXPLOSIVE 1.1D, POISON		None	62	None	Forbidden	Forbidden	B	1E, 5E
	Dinitrophenol solutions	6.1	UN1599	II	POISON	T8	None	202	243	5 L	60 L	A	36
	Dinitrophenol, wetted *with not less than 15 per cent water, by mass*	4.1	UN1320	I	FLAMMABLE SOLID, POISON	A8, A19, A20, N41	None	211	None	1 kg	15 kg	E	28, 36
	Dinitrophenolates *alkali metals, dry or wetted with less than 15 per cent water, by mass*	1.3C	UN0077	II	EXPLOSIVE 1.3C, POISON		None	62	None	Forbidden	Forbidden	B	1E, 5E

313

Sym-bols (1)	Hazardous materials descriptions and proper shipping names (2)	Hazard class or Division (3)	Identifi-cation Numbers (4)	Packing group (5)	Label(s) required (if not excepted) (6)	Special provisions (7)	Packaging authorizations (§173.***)			Quantity limitations		Vessel stowage requirements	
							Excep-tions (8A)	Non-bulk pack-aging (8B)	Bulk pack-aging (8C)	Passenger aircraft or railcar (9A)	Cargo aircraft only (9B)	Vessel stow-ages (10A)	Other stowage provisions (10B)
	Dinitrophenolates, wetted *with not less than 15 per cent water, by mass*	4.1	UN1321	I	FLAMMABLE SOLID, POISON	A8, A19, A20, N41	None	211	None	1 kg	15 kg	E	28, 36
	Dinitropropylene glycol	Forbid-den											
	Dinitroresorcinol, *dry or wetted with less than 15 per cent water, by mass*	1.1D	UN0078	II	EXPLOSIVE 1.1D		None	62	None	Forbidden	Forbidden	B	1E, 5E
	4,6-Dinitroresorcinol (heavy metal salts of) (dry)	Forbid-den											
	2,4-Dinitroresorcinol (heavy metal salts of) (dry)	Forbid-den											
	Dinitroresorcinol, wetted *with not less than 15 per cent water, by mass*	4.1	UN1322	I	FLAMMABLE SOLID	A8, A19, A20, N41	None	211	None	1 kg	15 kg	E	28, 36
	3,5-Dinitrosalicylic acid (lead salt) (dry)	Forbid-den											
	N,N'-Dinitroso-N,N'-dimethyl terephthalamide *not more than 72% as a paste*	4.1	UN2973	II	FLAMMABLE SOLID, EXPLOSIVE	41, 53	None	224	None	Forbidden	Forbidden	D	12, 61
	Dinitrosobenzene	1.3C	UN0406	II	EXPLOSIVE 1.3C		None	62	None	Forbidden	Forbidden	B	1E, 5E
	Dinitrosobenzylamidine and salts of (dry)	Forbid-den											
	N,N'-Dinitrosopentamethylenetetramine *not more than 82% with phlegmatizer*	4.1	UN2972	II	FLAMMABLE SOLID, EXPLOSIVE	41, 53	None	224	None	Forbidden	Forbidden	D	12, 61
	2,2-Dinitrostilbene	Forbid-den											
	Dinitrotoluenes, *liquid*	6.1	UN2038	II	POISON	T8	None	202	243	5 L	60 L	A	
	Dinitrotoluenes, molten	6.1	UN1600	II	POISON	T14	None	202	243	Forbidden	Forbidden	C	
	Dinitrotoluenes, *solid*	6.1	UN2038	II	POISON	T8	None	212	242	25 kg	100 kg	A	
	1,9-Dinitroxy pentamethylene-2,4,6,8-tetramine (dry)	Forbid-den											
	Dioxane	3	UN1165	II	FLAMMABLE LIQUID	T8	150	202	242	5 L	60 L	B	
	Dioxolane	3	UN1166	II	FLAMMABLE LIQUID	T8	150	202	242	5 L	60 L	B	40
	Dipentene	3	UN2052	III	FLAMMABLE LIQUID	B1, T1	150	203	242	60 L	220 L	A	
	Diphenylamine chloroarsine	6.1	UN1698	I	POISON		None	201	None	Forbidden	Forbidden	D	40
	Diphenylchloroarsine, solid *or* liquid	6.1	UN1699	I	POISON	A8, B14, B32, N33, N34	None	211	244	Forbidden	15 kg	D	40
	Diphenyldichlorosilane	8	UN1769	II	CORROSIVE	A7, B2, N34, T8, T26	None	202	244	Forbidden	30 L	C	40
	Diphenylmethane-4,4'diisocyanate	6.1	UN2489	III	KEEP AWAY FROM FOOD	T8	153	203	241	60 L	220 L	A	48, 108
	Diphenylmethyl bromide	8	UN1770	II	CORROSIVE		154	212	240	15 kg	50 kg	D	40
	Diphenyloxide-4,4'disulfohydrazide	4.1	UN2951	II	FLAMMABLE SOLID		None	224	None	15 kg	50 kg	B	12, 61, 85
	Dipicryl sulfide, *dry or wetted with less than 10 per cent water, by mass*	1.1D	UN0401	II	EXPLOSIVE 1.1D		None	62	None	Forbidden	Forbidden	B	1E, 5E, 19E
	Dipicryl sulfide, wetted *with not less than 10 per cent water, by mass*	4.1	UN2852	I	FLAMMABLE SOLID	A2, N41	None	211	None	Forbidden	0.5 kg	D	28, 36
	Dipicrylamine, *see* Hexanitrodiphenylamine												
	Dipropionyl peroxide, more than 28 per cent in solution	Forbid-den											
	Dipropyl ether	3	UN2384	II	FLAMMABLE LIQUID	T1	150	202	242	5 L	60 L	B	
	Dipropylamine	3	UN2383	II	FLAMMABLE LIQUID	T8	150	202	242	5 L	60 L	B	
	4-Dipropylaminobenzenediazonium zinc chloride	4.1	UN3034	II	FLAMMABLE SOLID		None	224	None	15 kg	50 kg	C	
	Dipropylketone	3	UN2710	III	FLAMMABLE LIQUID	B1, T1	150	203	242	60 L	220 L	A	
	Disinfectants, corrosive liquid, n.o.s.	8	UN1903	II	CORROSIVE	B2	154	202	242	1 L	30 L	A	
				III	CORROSIVE		154	203	241	5 L	60 L	A	40
	Disinfectants, liquid, n.o.s *poisonous*	6.1	UN3142	I	POISON	A4, T42	None	201	243	1 L	30 L	A	40
				II	POISON	T14	None	202	243	5 L	60 L	A	40
				III	KEEP AWAY FROM FOOD	T7	153	203	241	60 L	220 L	A	40
	Disinfectants, solid, n.o.s. *poisonous*	6.1	UN1601	II	POISON		None	212	242	25 kg	100 kg	A	40
				III	KEEP AWAY FROM FOOD		153	213	240	100 kg	200 kg	A	40
	Dispersant gases, n.o.s. *see* Refrigerant gases, n.o.s.												
	Dithiocarbamate pesticides, liquid, flammable, toxic, n.o.s., *flash point less than 23 degrees C.*	3	UN2772	I	FLAMMABLE LIQUID, POISON		None	201	243	Forbidden	30 L	B	40
				II	FLAMMABLE LIQUID, POISON		None	202	243	1 L	60 L	B	40

314

Sym-bols	Hazardous materials descriptions and proper shipping names	Hazard class or Division	Identifi-cation Numbers	Packing group	Label(s) required (if not excepted)	Special provisions	(8) Packaging authorizations (§173.***)			(9) Quantity limitations		(10) Vessel stowage requirements	
							Excep-tions	Non-bulk pack-aging	Bulk pack-aging	Passenger aircraft or railcar	Cargo aircraft only	Vessel stow-ages	Other stowage provisions
(1)	(2)	(3)	(4)	(5)	(6)	(7)	(8A)	(8B)	(8C)	(9A)	(9B)	(10A)	(10B)
	Dithiocarbamate pesticides, liquid, toxic, flammable, n.o.s. *flashpoint not less than 23 degrees C.*	6.1	UN3005	I	POISON, FLAMMABLE LIQUID	T42	None	201	243	1 L	30 L	B	40
				II	POISON, FLAMMABLE LIQUID	T14	None	202	243	5 L	60 L	B	40
				III	KEEP AWAY FROM FOOD, FLAMMABLE LIQUID	T14	153	203	241	60 L	220 L	A	40
	Dithiocarbamate pesticides, liquid, toxic, n.o.s.	6.1	UN3006	I	POISON	T42	None	201	243	1 L	30 L	B	40
				II	POISON	T14	None	202	243	5 L	60 L	B	40
				III	KEEP AWAY FROM FOOD	T14	153	203	241	60 L	220 L	A	40
	Dithiocarbamate pesticides, solid, toxic, n.o.s.	6.1	UN2771	I	POISON		None	211	242	5 kg	50 kg	A	40
				II	POISON		None	212	242	25 kg	100 kg	A	40
				III	KEEP AWAY FROM FOOD		153	213	240	100 kg	200 kg	A	40
	Divinyl ether, inhibited	3	UN1167	I	FLAMMABLE LIQUID	T14	None	202	241	5 L	60 L	E	40
D	Dodecylbenzenesulfonic acid	8	NA2584	II	CORROSIVE	B2	154	202	242	1 L	30 L	B	9
	Dodecyltrichlorosilane	8	UN1771	II	CORROSIVE	A7, B2, B6, N34, T8, T26	None	202	242	Forbidden	30 L	C	40
	Dry ice, *see* Carbon dioxide, solid												
	Dyes, liquid, n.o.s. *or* dye intermediates, liquid, n.o.s. *corrosive*	8	UN2801	II	CORROSIVE	11, B2, T14	154	202	242	1 L	30 L	A	23
				III	CORROSIVE	11, T7	154	203	241	5 L	60 L	A	23
	Dyes, liquid, n.o.s *or* dye intermediates, liquid, n.o.s. *poisonous*	6.1	UN1602	II	POISON		None	202	243	5 L	60 L	A	
				III	KEEP AWAY FROM FOOD		153	203	241	60 L	220	A	
	Dyes, solid, n.o.s. *or* Dye intermediates, solid, n.o.s. *corrosive*	8	UN3147	II	CORROSIVE		154	212	240	15 kg	50 kg	A	
				III	CORROSIVE		154	213	240	25 kg	100 kg	A	
	Dyes, solid, n.o.s. *or* dye intermediates, solid, n.o.s. *poisonous*	6.1	UN3143	I	POISON	A5	None	211	242	5kg	50kg	A	
				II	POISON		None	212	242	25 kg	100 kg	A	
				III	KEEP AWAY FROM FOOD		153	213	240	100 kg	200 kg	A	
	Dynamite, *see* Explosive, blasting, type A												
	Electrolyte (acid or alkali) for batteries, *see* Battery fluid, acid *or* Battery fluid, alkali												
D	Elevated temperature material, liquid, n.o.s. *(at or above 100°C (212°F) and below its flash point)*	9	NA9259	III	Class 9		None	None	247	Forbidden	Forbidden	D	M4
D	*Elevated temperature material at or above its flash point, see* Flammable liquid, elevated temperature material, n.o.s. *(see §173.247(d)(2))*												
D	*Elevated temperature material, solid, n.o.s. (see §173.247(d)(2))*												
	Engine starting fluid, *with flammable gas*	2.1	UN1960		FLAMMABLE GAS		None	304	None	Forbidden	150 kg	D	40
	Engines, internal combustion, *see* Vehicle, self-propelled												
	Environmentally hazardous substances, liquid, n.o.s.	9	UN3082	III	CLASS 9	8, T1	155	203	241	None	None	A	
	Environmentally hazardous substances, solid, n.o.s.	9	UN3077	III	CLASS 9	8, B54	155	213	240	None	None	A	
	Epibromohydrin	6.1	UN2558	I	POISON	T18, T26	None	201	243	Forbidden	Forbidden	D	40
	Epichlorohydrin	6.1	UN2023	II	POISON	T14	None	202	243	5 L	60 L	A	40
	1,2-Epoxy-3-ethoxypropane	3	UN2752	III	FLAMMABLE LIQUID	B1, T1	150	203	242	60 L	220 L	A	
	Etching acid, liquid, n.o.s., see Hydrofluoric acid, solution *etc.*												
	Ethane, compressed	2.1	UN1035		FLAMMABLE GAS		306	304	302	Forbidden	150 kg	E	40
D	Ethane-Propane mixture, refrigerated liquid	2.1	NA1961		FLAMMABLE GAS		None	316	314, 315	Forbidden	Forbidden	D	40
	Ethane, refrigerated liquid	2.1	UN1961		FLAMMABLE GAS		None	None	315	Forbidden	Forbidden	D	40
	Ethanol amine dinitrate	Forbid-den											
	Ethanol *or* Ethyl alcohol *or* Ethanol solutions *or* Ethyl alcohol solutions	3	UN1170	II	FLAMMABLE LIQUID	T1	150	202	242	5 L	60 L	A	
				III	FLAMMABLE LIQUID	B1, T1	150	203	242	60 L	220 L	A	
	Ethanolamine *or* Ethanolamine solutions	8	UN2491	III	CORROSIVE	T7	154	203	241	5 L	60 L	A	
	Ether, see Diethyl ether												
	Ethyl acetate	3	UN1173	II	FLAMMABLE LIQUID	T2	150	202	242	5 L	60 L	B	

315

Symbols	Hazardous materials descriptions and proper shipping names	Hazard class or Division	Identification Numbers	Packing group	Label(s) required (if not excepted)	Special provisions	Exceptions	Non-bulk packaging	Bulk packaging	Passenger aircraft or railcar	Cargo aircraft only	Vessel stowages	Other stowage provisions
(1)	(2)	(3)	(4)	(5)	(6)	(7)	(8A)	(8B)	(8C)	(9A)	(9B)	(10A)	(10B)
	Ethyl acrylate, inhibited	3	UN1917	II	FLAMMABLE LIQUID	T8	150	202	242	5 L	60 L	B	40
	Ethyl alcohol, see Ethanol												
	Ethyl aldehyde, see Acetaldehyde												
	Ethyl amyl ketone	3	UN2271	III	FLAMMABLE LIQUID	B1, T1	150	203	242	60 L	220 L	A	
	N-Ethyl-N-benzylaniline	6.1	UN2274	III	KEEP AWAY FROM FOOD	T2	153	203	241	60 L	220 L	A	
	Ethyl borate	3	UN1176	II	FLAMMABLE LIQUID	T8	150	202	242	5 L	60 L	B	
	Ethyl bromide	6.1	UN1891	II	POISON	T17	None	202	243	5 L	60 L	B	40
	Ethyl bromoacetate	6.1	UN1603	II	POISON	T14	None	202	243	Forbidden	Forbidden	D	40
	Ethyl butyl ether	3	UN1179	II	FLAMMABLE LIQUID	B1, T1	150	202	242	5 L	60 L	B	
	Ethyl butyrate	3	UN1180	III	FLAMMABLE LIQUID	B1, T1	150	202	242	5 L	60 L	A	
	Ethyl chloride	2.1	UN1037		FLAMMABLE GAS	B63, B77	None	322	314, 315	Forbidden	150 kg	B	40
	Ethyl chloroacetate	6.1	UN1181	II	POISON	T14	None	202	243	5 L	60 L	A	
	Ethyl chloroformate	6.1	UN1182	I	POISON, FLAMMABLE LIQUID, CORROSIVE	2, A3, A6, A7, B9, B14, B32, B74, N34, T38, T43, T45	None	227	244	Forbidden	Forbidden	D	21, 40, 100
	Ethyl-2-chloropropionate	3	UN2935	III	FLAMMABLE LIQUID	B1, T1	150	203	242	60 L	220 L	A	
+	Ethyl chlorothioformate	8	UN2826	II	CORROSIVE, POISON	2, B9, B14, B32, B74, T38, T43, T45	None	227	244	1 L	30 L	A	12, 21, 40, 48
	Ethyl crotonate	3	UN1862	II	FLAMMABLE LIQUID	T1	150	202	242	5 L	60 L	B	
	Ethyl cyanoacetate	6.1	UN2666	III	KEEP AWAY FROM FOOD	T8	153	203	241	60 L	220 L	A	26
	Ethyl ether, see Diethyl ether												
	Ethyl fluoride	2.1	UN2453		FLAMMABLE GAS		306	304	314, 315	75 kg	150 kg	E	40
	Ethyl formate	3	UN1190	II	FLAMMABLE LIQUID	T8	150	202	242	5 L	60 L	E	
	Ethyl hydroperoxide	Forbidden											
	Ethyl isobutyrate	3	UN2385	II	FLAMMABLE LIQUID	T1	150	202	242	5 L	60 L	B	
+	Ethyl isocyanate	3	UN2481	I	FLAMMABLE LIQUID, POISON	1, A7, B9, B14, B30, B72, T38, T43, T44	None	226	244	Forbidden	30 L	D	40
	Ethyl lactate	3	UN1192	III	FLAMMABLE LIQUID	B1, T1	150	203	242	60 L	220 L	A	
	Ethyl mercaptan	3	UN2363	I	FLAMMABLE LIQUID	T21	None	201	243	Forbidden	30 L	E	95, 102
	Ethyl methacrylate	3	UN2277	II	FLAMMABLE LIQUID	T1	150	202	242	5 L	60 L	B	
	Ethyl methyl ether	2.1	UN1039		FLAMMABLE GAS	B63	None	324	314, 315	Forbidden	150 kg	B	40
	Ethyl methyl ketone or Methyl ethyl ketone	3	UN1193	II	FLAMMABLE LIQUID	T8	150	202	242	5 L	60 L	B	
	Ethyl nitrite solutions	3	UN1194	I	FLAMMABLE LIQUID, POISON		None	201	None	Forbidden	Forbidden	E	40, 105
	Ethyl orthoformate	3	UN2524	III	FLAMMABLE LIQUID	B1, T7	150	203	242	60 L	220 L	A	
	Ethyl oxalate	6.1	UN2525	III	KEEP AWAY FROM FOOD	T1	153	203	241	60 L	220 L	A	
	Ethyl perchlorate	Forbidden											
D	Ethyl phosphonothioic dichloride, anhydrous	6.1	NA2927	I	POISON, CORROSIVE	2, B9, B14, B32, B74, T38, T43, T45	None	227	244	Forbidden	Forbidden	D	20, 40, 95
D	Ethyl phosphonous dichloride, anhydrous pyrophoric liquid	6.1	NA2845	I	POISON, SPONTANEOUSLY COMBUSTIBLE	2, B9, B14, B32, B74, T38, T43, T45	None	227	244	Forbidden	Forbidden	D	18
D	Ethyl phosphorodichloridate	6.1	NA2927	I	POISON, CORROSIVE	2, B9, B14, B32, B74, T38, T43, T45	None	227	244	Forbidden	Forbidden	D	20, 40, 95
	Ethyl propionate	3	UN1195	II	FLAMMABLE LIQUID	T1	150	202	242	5 L	60 L	B	
	Ethyl propyl ether	3	UN2615	II	FLAMMABLE LIQUID	T8	150	202	242	5 L	60 L	E	
	Ethyl silicate, see Tetraethyl silicate												
	Ethylacetylene, inhibited	2.1	UN2452		FLAMMABLE GAS		None	304	314, 315	Forbidden	150 kg	B	40
	Ethylamine	2.1	UN1036		FLAMMABLE GAS	B77	None	321	314, 315	Forbidden	Forbidden	D	40
	Ethylamine, aqueous solution with not less than 50 per cent but not more than 70 per cent ethylamine	3	UN2270	II	FLAMMABLE LIQUID	T14	150	202	242	5 L	60 L	B	40
	N-Ethylaniline	6.1	UN2272	III	KEEP AWAY FROM FOOD	T2	153	203	241	60 L	220 L	A	

316

Symbols	Hazardous materials descriptions and proper shipping names	Hazard class or Division	Identification Numbers	Packing group	Label(s) required (if not excepted)	Special provisions	Packaging authorizations (§173.***)			Quantity limitations		Vessel stowage requirements	
							Exceptions	Non-bulk packaging	Bulk packaging	Passenger aircraft or railcar	Cargo aircraft only	Vessel stowages	Other stowage provisions
(1)	(2)	(3)	(4)	(5)	(6)	(7)	(8A)	(8B)	(8C)	(9A)	(9B)	(10A)	(10B)
	2-Ethylaniline	6.1	UN2273	III	KEEP AWAY FROM FOOD	T2	153	203	241	60 L	220 L	A	
	Ethylbenzene	3	UN1175	II	FLAMMABLE LIQUID	T1	150	202	242	5 L	60 L	B	
	N-Ethylbenzyltoluidines solid or liquid	6.1	UN2753	III	KEEP AWAY FROM FOOD	T14	153	203	241	60 L	220 L	A	
	2-Ethylbutanol	3	UN2275	III	FLAMMABLE LIQUID	B1, T1	150	203	242	60 L	220 L	A	
	2-Ethylbutyl acetate	3	UN1177	III	FLAMMABLE LIQUID	B1, T1	150	203	242	60 L	220 L	A	
	2-Ethylbutyraldehyde	3	UN1178	II	FLAMMABLE LIQUID	B1, T1	150	202	242	5 L	60 L	B	
	Ethyldichloroarsine	6.1	UN1892	I	POISON	2, B9, B14, B32, B74, T38, T43, T45	None	227	244	Forbidden	Forbidden	D	40
	Ethyldichlorosilane	4.3	UN1183	I	DANGEROUS WHEN WET, CORROSIVE, FLAMMABLE LIQUID	A2, A3, A7, N34, T18, T26	None	201	244	Forbidden	1 L	D	21, 28, 40, 49, 100
	Ethylene, acetylene and propylene in mixtures, refrigerated liquid containing at least 71.5 per cent ethylene with not more than 22.5 per cent acetylene and not more than 6 per cent propylene	2.1	UN3138		FLAMMABLE GAS		None	304	314, 315	Forbidden	Forbidden	D	40
+	Ethylene chlorohydrin	6.1	UN1135	II	POISON	2, B9, B14, B32, B74, T38, T43, T45	None	227	244	Forbidden	60 L	A	40
	Ethylene, compressed	2.1	UN1962		FLAMMABLE GAS		306	304	302	Forbidden	150 kg	E	40
	Ethylene diamine diperchlorate	Forbidden											
+	Ethylene dibromide	6.1	UN1605	II	POISON	2, B9, B14, B32, B74, B77, T38, T43, T45	None	227	244	5 L	60 L	A	40
	Ethylene dibromide and methyl bromide liquid mixtures, see Methyl bromide and ethylene dibromide, liquid mixtures												
	Ethylene dichloride	3	UN1184	II	FLAMMABLE LIQUID, POISON	T14	None	202	243	1 L	60 L	B	40
	Ethylene glycol diethyl ether	3	UN1153	III	FLAMMABLE LIQUID	B1, T1	150	203	242	60 L	220 L	A	
	Ethylene glycol dinitrate	Forbidden											
	Ethylene glycol monobutyl ether	6.1	UN2369	III	KEEP AWAY FROM FOOD	T1	153	203	241	60 L	220 L	A	
	Ethylene glycol monoethyl ether	3	UN1171	III	FLAMMABLE LIQUID	B1, T1	150	203	242	60 L	220 L	A	
	Ethylene glycol monoethyl ether acetate	3	UN1172	III	FLAMMABLE LIQUID	B1, T1	150	203	242	60 L	220 L	A	
	Ethylene glycol monomethyl ether	3	UN1188	III	FLAMMABLE LIQUID	B1, T1	150	203	242	60 L	220 L	A	
	Ethylene glycol monomethyl ether acetate	3	UN1189	III	FLAMMABLE LIQUID	B1, T1	150	203	242	60 L	220 L	A	
	Ethylene oxide and carbon dioxide mixtures, see Carbon dioxide and ethylene oxide mixtures, etc.												
	Ethylene oxide and propylene oxide mixtures, not more than 30 per cent ethylene oxide	3	UN2983	I	FLAMMABLE LIQUID, POISON	5, A11, N4, N34, T24, T29	None	201	243	Forbidden	30 L	E	40
	Ethylene oxide, pure or with nitrogen	2.3	UN1040		POISON GAS, FLAMMABLE GAS	3	None	323	323	Forbidden	25 kg	D	40
	Ethylene, refrigerated liquid (cryogenic liquid)	2.1	UN1038		FLAMMABLE GAS		None	316	318, 319	Forbidden	Forbidden	D	40
	Ethylenediamine	8	UN1604	II	CORROSIVE, FLAMMABLE LIQUID	T14	154	202	243	1 L	30 L	A	12, 21, 40, 48
	Ethyleneimine, inhibited	6.1	UN1185	I	POISON, FLAMMABLE LIQUID	1, B9, B14, B30, B72, B77, N25, N32, T38, T43, T44	None	226	244	Forbidden	Forbidden	D	40
	Ethylhexaldehyde, see Octyl aldehydes etc.												
	2-Ethylhexylamine	8	UN2276	III	CORROSIVE	T2	154	203	241	5 L	60 L	A	12, 21, 40, 48
	2-Ethylhexylchloroformate	6.1	UN2748	II	POISON, CORROSIVE	T42	None	202	243	1 L	30 L	A	12, 13, 25, 40, 48, 95
	Ethylphenyldichlorosilane	8	UN2435	II	CORROSIVE	A7, B2, N34, T8, T26	None	202	242	Forbidden	30 L	C	
	1-Ethylpiperidine	3	UN2386	II	FLAMMABLE LIQUID	T8	150	202	242	5 L	60 L	B	
	Ethylsulfuric acid	8	UN2571	II	CORROSIVE	B2, T9, T27	154	202	242	1 L	30 L	C	14
	N-Ethyltoluidines	6.1	UN2754	II	POISON	T14	None	202	243	5 L	60 L	A	48
	Ethyltrichlorosilane	3	UN1196	II	FLAMMABLE LIQUID, CORROSIVE	A7, N34, T15, T26	None	201	243	Forbidden	2.5 L	B	40

317

Symbols	Hazardous materials descriptions and proper shipping names	Hazard class or Division	Identification Numbers	Packing group	Label(s) required (if not excepted)	Special provisions	Packaging authorizations (§173.***)			Quantity limitations		Vessel stowage requirements	
							Exceptions	Non-bulk packaging	Bulk packaging	Passenger aircraft or railcar	Cargo aircraft only	Vessel stowages	Other stowage provisions
(1)	(2)	(3)	(4)	(5)	(6)	(7)	(8A)	(8B)	(8C)	(9A)	(9B)	(10A)	(10B)
	Etiologic agent, see Infectious substances, *etc.*												
	Explosive articles, see Articles, explosive, n.o.s. *etc.*												
	Explosive, blasting, type A	1.1D	UN0081	II	EXPLOSIVE 1.1D		None	62	None	Forbidden	Forbidden	B	1E, 5E, 19E, 21E
	Explosive, blasting, type B	1.1D	UN0082	II	EXPLOSIVE 1.1D		None	62	None	Forbidden	Forbidden	B	1E, 5E, 19E
	Explosive, blasting, type B *or Agent blasting,* Type B	1.5D	UN0331	II	EXPLOSIVE 1.5D	105, 106	None	62	None	Forbidden	Forbidden	B	1E, 5E, 19E
	Explosive, blasting, type C	1.1D	UN0083	II	EXPLOSIVE 1.1D		None	62	None	Forbidden	Forbidden	B	1E, 5E, 22E
	Explosive, blasting, type D	1.1D	UN0084	II	EXPLOSIVE 1.1D		None	62	None	Forbidden	Forbidden	B	1E, 5E
	Explosive, blasting, type E	1.1D	UN0241	II	EXPLOSIVE 1.1D		None	62	None	Forbidden	Forbidden	B	1E, 5E, 19E
	Explosive, blasting, type E *or Agent blasting,* Type E	1.5D	UN0332	II	EXPLOSIVE 1.5D	105, 106	None	62	None	Forbidden	Forbidden	B	1E, 5E
	Explosive, forbidden. See Sec. 173.51	Forbidden											
D	Explosive pest control devices	1.1E	NA0006	II	EXPLOSIVE 1.1E		None	62	None	Forbidden	Forbidden	E	
D	Explosive pest control devices	1.4E	NA0412	II	EXPLOSIVE 1.4E		None	62	None	Forbidden	75 kg	A	24E
	Explosive substances, see Substances, explosive, n.o.s. *etc.*												
	Explosives, slurry, see Explosive, blasting, type E												
	Explosives, water gels, see Explosive, blasting, type E												
	Extracts, aromatic, liquid	3	UN1169	II	FLAMMABLE LIQUID	T7, T30	150	202	242	5 L	60 L	B	
				III	FLAMMABLE LIQUID	B1, T7, T30	150	203	242	60 L	220 L	A	
	Extracts, flavoring, liquid	3	UN1197	II	FLAMMABLE LIQUID	T7, T30	150	202	242	5 L	60 L	B	
				III	FLAMMABLE LIQUID	B1, T7, T30	150	203	242	60 L	220 L	A	
	Fabric with animal or vegetable oil, see Fibers or fabrics, *etc.*												
	Ferric arsenate	6.1	UN1606	II	POISON		None	212	242	25 kg	100 kg	A	
	Ferric arsenite	6.1	UN1607	II	POISON		None	212	242	25 kg	100 kg	A	
	Ferric chloride	8	UN1773	III	CORROSIVE		154	213	240	25 kg	100 kg	A	
	Ferric chloride, solution	8	UN2582	III	CORROSIVE	B15, T8	154	203	241	5 L	60 L	A	
	Ferric nitrate	5.1	UN1466	III	OXIDIZER	A1, A29	152	213	240	25 kg	100 kg	A	
	Ferrocerium	4.1	UN1323	II	FLAMMABLE SOLID	A19	151	212	240	15 kg	50 kg	A	
	Ferrosilicon, *with 30 percent or more but less than 90 percent silicon*	4.3	UN1408	III	DANGEROUS WHEN WET	A1, A19	None	213	240	25 kg	100 kg	A	13, 40, 85, 103
	Ferrous arsenate	6.1	UN1608	II	POISON		None	212	242	25 kg	100 kg	A	
D	Ferrous chloride, solid	8	NA1759	II	CORROSIVE		154	212	240	15 kg	50 kg	A	
D	Ferrous chloride, solution	8	NA1760	II	CORROSIVE	B3	154	202	242	1 L	30 L	B	40
	Ferrous metal borings, shavings, turnings *or* cuttings *in a form liable to self-heating*	4.2	UN2793	III	SPONTANEOUSLY COMBUSTIBLE	A1, A19	None	213	241	25 kg	100 kg	A	
	Fertilizer ammoniating solution *with free ammonia*	2.2	UN1043		NONFLAMMABLE GAS		306	304	314, 315	Forbidden	150 kg	E	40
AIW	Fibers *or* Fabrics, animal *or* vegetable, n.o.s. *with animal or vegetable oil*	4.2	UN1373	III	SPONTANEOUSLY COMBUSTIBLE		None	213	241	Forbidden	Forbidden	A	
	Films, nitrocellulose base, from which gelatine has been removed; film scrap, see Celluloid scrap												
	Films, nitrocellulose base, *gelatine coated (except scrap)*	4.1	UN1324	III	FLAMMABLE SOLID		None	183	None	25 kg	100 kg	D	91
	Fire extinguisher charges, *corrosive liquid*	8	UN1774	II	CORROSIVE	N41	154	202	None	1 L	30 L	A	
	Fire extinguisher charges, expelling, explosive, see Cartridges, power device												
	Fire extinguishers *containing compressed or liquefied gas*	2.2	UN1044		NONFLAMMABLE GAS		306	306	None	75 kg	150 kg	A	
	Firelighters, solid *with flammable liquid*	4.1	UN2623	II	FLAMMABLE SOLID	A19	None	212	None	15 kg	50 kg	A	119
				III	FLAMMABLE SOLID	A1, A19	None	213	None	25 kg	100 kg	A	119
	Fireworks	1.1G	UN0333	II	EXPLOSIVE 1.1G	108	None	62	None	Forbidden	Forbidden	B	
	Fireworks	1.2G	UN0334	II	EXPLOSIVE 1.2G	108	None	62	None	Forbidden	Forbidden	B	
	Fireworks	1.3G	UN0335	II	EXPLOSIVE 1.3G	108	None	62	None	Forbidden	Forbidden	B	
	Fireworks	1.4G	UN0336	II	EXPLOSIVE 1.4G	108	None	62	None	Forbidden	75 kg	A	24E
	Fireworks	1.4S	UN0337	II	EXPLOSIVE 1.4S	108	None	62	None	25 kg	100 kg	A	9E
W	Fish meal *or* Fish scrap stabilized	9	UN2216	III	None	A1	155	218	218	No limit	No limit	A	88, 120
	Fish meal, unstabilized *or* Fish scrap, unstabilized	4.2	UN1374	II	SPONTANEOUSLY COMBUSTIBLE	A1, A19	None	212	241	15 kg	50 kg	A	119, 120

Symbols	Hazardous materials descriptions and proper shipping names	Hazard class or Division	Identification Numbers	Packing group	Label(s) required (if not excepted)	Special provisions	Packaging authorizations (§173.***)			Quantity limitations		Vessel stowage requirements	
							Exceptions	Non-bulk packaging	Bulk packaging	Passenger aircraft or railcar	Cargo aircraft only	Vessel stowages	Other stowage provisions
(1)	(2)	(3)	(4)	(5)	(6)	(7)	(8A)	(8B)	(8C)	(9A)	(9B)	(10A)	(10B)
	Fissile radioactive materials, see Radioactive material, fissile, n.o.s.												
	Flammable compressed gas, see Compressed or Liquefied gas, flammable, *etc.*												
	Flammable compressed gas (small receptacles not fitted with a dispersion device, not refillable), see Receptacles, *etc.*												
	Flammable gas in lighters, see Lighters for cigars or cigarettes, *with flammable gas*												
	Flammable liquid, elevated temperature material, n.o.s.	3	NA9275	III	FLAMMABLE LIQUID		None	None	247	Forbidden	Forbidden	D	M4
	Flammable liquids, corrosive, n.o.s.	3	UN2924	I	FLAMMABLE LIQUID, CORROSIVE	T42	None	201	243	0.5 L	2.5 L	E	40
				II	FLAMMABLE LIQUID, CORROSIVE	T15, T26	None	202	243	1 L	5 L	B	40
				III	FLAMMABLE LIQUID, CORROSIVE	B1, T15, T26	150	203	242	5 L	60 L	A	40
	Flammable liquids, n.o.s.	3	UN1993	I	FLAMMABLE LIQUID	T42	150	201	243	1 L	30 L	E	
				II	FLAMMABLE LIQUID	T8, T31	150	202	242	5 L	60 L	B	
				III	FLAMMABLE LIQUID	B1, B52, T7, T30	150	203	242	60 L	220 L	A	
	Flammable liquids, poisonous, n.o.s.	3	UN1992	I	FLAMMABLE LIQUID, POISON	T42	None	201	243	Forbidden	30 L	E	40
				II	FLAMMABLE LIQUID, POISON	T18	None	202	243	1 L	60 L	B	40
	Flammable solids, corrosive, n.o.s.	4.1	UN2925	II	FLAMMABLE SOLID, CORROSIVE		None	212	242	15 kg	50 kg	D	40
				III	FLAMMABLE SOLID, CORROSIVE	A1	151	213	242	25 kg	100 kg	D	40
	Flammable solids, n.o.s.	4.1	UN1325	II	FLAMMABLE SOLID		151	212	240	15 kg	50 kg	B	
				III	FLAMMABLE SOLID		151	213	240	25 kg	100 kg	B	
	Flammable solids, poisonous, n.o.s.	4.1	UN2926	II	FLAMMABLE SOLID, POISON		None	212	242	15 kg	50 kg	B	40
				III	FLAMMABLE SOLID, KEEP AWAY FROM FOOD	A1	151	213	242	25 kg	100 kg	B	40
	Flares, aerial	1.3G	UN0093	II	EXPLOSIVE 1.3G		None	62	None	Forbidden	75 kg	B	
	Flares, aerial	1.4G	UN0403	II	EXPLOSIVE 1.4G		None	62	None	Forbidden	75 kg	A	24E
	Flares, aerial	1.4S	UN0404	II	EXPLOSIVE 1.4S		None	62	None	25 kg	100 kg	A	9E
	Flares, aerial	1.1G	UN0420	II	EXPLOSIVE 1.1G		None	62	None	Forbidden	Forbidden	B	
	Flares, aerial	1.2G	UN0421	II	EXPLOSIVE 1.2G		None	62	None	Forbidden	Forbidden	B	
	Flares, airplane, see Flares, aerial												
	Flares, signal, see Cartridges, signal												
	Flares surface	1.1G	UN0418	II	EXPLOSIVE 1.1G		None	62	None	Forbidden	Forbidden	B	
	Flares, surface	1.2G	UN0419	II	EXPLOSIVE 1.2G		None	62	None	Forbidden	Forbidden	B	
	Flares, surface	1.3G	UN0092	II	EXPLOSIVE 1.3G		None	62	None	Forbidden	75 kg	B	
	Flares, water-activated, see Contrivances, water-activated, *etc.*												
	Flash powder	1.1G	UN0094	II	EXPLOSIVE 1.1G		None	62	None	Forbidden	Forbidden	B	1E, 5E
	Flash powder	1.3G	UN0305	II	EXPLOSIVE 1.3G		None	62	None	Forbidden	Forbidden	B	1E, 5E
	Flue dusts, poisonous, see Arsenical dust												
	Fluoboric acid	8	UN1775	II	CORROSIVE	A6, A7, B2, B15, N3, N34, T15, T27	154	202	242	1 L	30 L	A	
	Fluoric acid, see Hydrofluoric acid, solution, *etc.*												
	Fluorine, compressed	2.3	UN1045		POISON GAS, OXIDIZER	1	None	302	None	Forbidden	Forbidden	D	40
	Fluoroacetic acid	6.1	UN2642	I	POISON		None	211	242	1 kg	15 kg	E	
	Fluoroanilines	6.1	UN2941	III	KEEP AWAY FROM FOOD	T8	153	203	241	60 L	220 L	A	
	Fluorobenzene	3	UN2387	II	FLAMMABLE LIQUID	T8	150	202	242	5 L	60 L	B	
	Fluorophosphoric acid anhydrous	8	UN1776	II	CORROSIVE	A6, A7, B2, N3, N34, T9, T27	None	202	242	1 L	30 L	A	
	Fluorosilicates, n.o.s.	6.1	UN2856	III	KEEP AWAY FROM FOOD		153	213	240	100 kg	200 kg	A	26
	Fluorosilicic acid	8	UN1778	II	CORROSIVE	A6, A7, B2, B15, N3, N34, T12, T27	None	202	242	1 L	30 L	A	
	Fluorosulfonic acid	8	UN1777	I	CORROSIVE	A3, A6, A7, A10, B6, B10, B41, N3, T9, T27	None	201	242	0.5 L	2.5 L	D	40

319

(1) Symbols	(2) Hazardous materials descriptions and proper shipping names	(3) Hazard class or Division	(4) Identification Numbers	(5) Packing group	(6) Label(s) required (if not excepted)	(7) Special provisions	(8) Packaging authorizations (§173.***)			(9) Quantity limitations		(10) Vessel stowage requirements	
							(8A) Exceptions	(8B) Non-bulk packaging	(8C) Bulk packaging	(9A) Passenger aircraft or railcar	(9B) Cargo aircraft only	(10A) Vessel stowages	(10B) Other stowage provisions
	Fluorotoluenes	3	UN2388	II	FLAMMABLE LIQUID	T8	150	202	242	5 L	60 L	B	40
	Forbidden materials. See 173.21	Forbidden											
	Formaldehyde, solutions	9	UN2209	III	None	T1	155	204	240	100 L	220 L	A	
	Formaldehyde, solutions, flammable	3	UN1198	III	FLAMMABLE LIQUID	B1, T8	150	203	242	60 L	220 L	A	40
	Formalin, see Formaldehyde, solutions												
	Formic acid	8	UN1779	II	CORROSIVE	B2, B12, B28, T8	154	202	242	1 L	30 L	A	40
	Fracturing devices, explosive, without detonators for oil wells	1.1D	UN0099	II	EXPLOSIVE 1.1D		None	62	None	Forbidden	Forbidden	B	
D	Fusee (railway or highway)	4.1	NA1325	II	FLAMMABLE SOLID		None	184	None	15 kg	50 kg	B	
	Fuel, aviation, turbine engine	3	UN1863	I	FLAMMABLE LIQUID	T7	150	201	243	1 L	30 L	E	
				II	FLAMMABLE LIQUID	T1	150	202	242	5 L	60 L	B	
				III	FLAMMABLE LIQUID	B1, T1	150	203	242	60 L	220 L	A	
D	Fuel oil (No. 1, 2, 4, 5, or 6)	3	NA1993	III	FLAMMABLE LIQUID	B1	150	203	241	60 L	220 L	A	
	Fulminate of mercury (dry)	Forbidden											
	Fulminate of mercury, wet, see Mercury fulminate, etc.												
	Fulminating gold	Forbidden											
	Fulminating mercury	Forbidden											
	Fulminating platinum	Forbidden											
	Fulminating silver	Forbidden											
	Fulminic acid	Forbidden											
	Fumaryl chloride	8	UN1780	II	CORROSIVE	B2, T8, T26	154	202	242	1 L	30 L	C	8, 40
	Furan	3	UN2389	I	FLAMMABLE LIQUID	T18	None	201	242	1 L	30 L	E	40
	Furfural	3	UN1199	III	FLAMMABLE LIQUID	B1, T1	150	203	241	60 L	220 L	A	
	Furfuryl alcohol	6.1	UN2874	III	KEEP AWAY FROM FOOD	T2	153	203	240	60 L	220 L	A	26, 74
	Furfurylamine	3	UN2526	III	FLAMMABLE LIQUID	B1, T1	150	203	241	60 L	220 L	A	40
	Fuse, detonating, metal clad, see Cord, detonating, metal clad												
	Fuse, detonating, mild effect, metal clad, see Cord, detonating, mild effect, metal clad												
	Fuse, igniter tubular metal clad	1.4G	UN0103	II	EXPLOSIVE 1.4G		None	62	None	Forbidden	75 kg	A	24E
	Fuse, instantaneous, non-detonating or Quickmatch	1.3G	UN0101	II	EXPLOSIVE 1.3G		None	62	None	Forbidden	Forbidden	B	
	Fuse, safety	1.4S	UN0105	II	EXPLOSIVE 1.4S		None	62	None	25 kg	100 kg	A	9E
	Fusel oil	3	UN1201	II	FLAMMABLE LIQUID	T1	150	202	242	5 L	60 L	B	
				III	FLAMMABLE LIQUID	B1, T1	150	203	242	60 L	220 L	A	
	Fuses, tracer, see Tracers for ammunition												
	Fuzes, combination, percussion and time, see Fuzes, detonating (UN 0257, UN 0367); Fuzes, igniting (UN 0317, UN 0368)												
	Fuzes, detonating	1.1B	UN0106	II	EXPLOSIVE 1.1B		None	62	None	Forbidden	Forbidden	B	2E, 6E
	Fuzes, detonating	1.2B	UN0107	II	EXPLOSIVE 1.2B		None	62	None	Forbidden	Forbidden	B	2E, 6E
	Fuzes, detonating	1.4B	UN0257	II	EXPLOSIVE 1.4B	116	None	62	None	Forbidden	75 kg	A	24E
	Fuzes, detonating	1.4S	UN0367	II	EXPLOSIVE 1.4S	116	None	62	None	25 kg	100 kg	A	9E
	Fuzes, detonating, with protective features	1.1D	UN0408	II	EXPLOSIVE 1.1D		None	62	None	Forbidden	Forbidden	B	
	Fuzes, detonating, with protective features	1.2D	UN0409	II	EXPLOSIVE 1.2D		None	62	None	Forbidden	Forbidden	B	
	Fuzes, detonating, with protective features	1.4D	UN0410	II	EXPLOSIVE 1.4D	116	None	62	None	Forbidden	75 kg	A	24E
	Fuzes, igniting	1.3G	UN0316	II	EXPLOSIVE 1.3G		None	62	None	Forbidden	Forbidden	B	
	Fuzes, igniting	1.4G	UN0317	II	EXPLOSIVE 1.4G		None	62	None	Forbidden	75 kg	B	
	Fuzes, igniting	1.4S	UN0368	II	EXPLOSIVE 1.4S		None	62	None	25 kg	100 kg	A	9E
	Galactsan trinitrate	Forbidden											
	Gallium	8	UN2803	III	CORROSIVE		None	162	240	20 kg	20 kg	B	48
	Gas drips, hydrocarbon	3	UN1864	II	FLAMMABLE LIQUID	T7, T30	150	202	242	5 L	60 L	B	
	Gas generator assemblies (aircraft), containing a non-flammable non-toxic gas and a propellant cartridge	2.2			NONFLAMMABLE GAS		None	335	None	75 kg	150 kg	A	

320

Sym-bols	Hazardous materials descriptions and proper shipping names	Hazard class or Division	Identifi-cation Numbers	Packing group	Label(s) required (if not excepted)	Special provisions	(8) Packaging authorizations (§173.***) Excep-tions (8A)	Non-bulk pack-aging (8B)	Bulk pack-aging (8C)	(9) Quantity limitations Passenger aircraft or railcar (9A)	Cargo aircraft only (9B)	(10) Vessel stowage requirements Vessel stow-ages (10A)	Other stowage provisions (10B)
(1)	(2)	(3)	(4)	(5)	(6)	(7)	(8A)	(8B)	(8C)	(9A)	(9B)	(10A)	(10B)
D	Gas identification set	2.3	NA9035		POISON GAS	6	None	194	None	Forbidden	Forbidden	D	
	Gas oil	3	UN1202	III	FLAMMABLE LIQUID	B1, T7, T30	150	203	242	60 L	220 L	A	
D	Gasohol (gasoline mixed with ethyl alcohol, max. 20% alcohol)	3	NA1203	II	FLAMMABLE LIQUID		150	202	242	5 L	50 L	E	
	Gasoline	3	UN1203	II	FLAMMABLE LIQUID	B33, T8	150	202	242	5 L	60 L	E	
	Gasoline, casinghead, see Natural gasoline												
	Gelatine, blasting, see Explosive, blasting, type A												
	Gelatine dynamites, see Explosive, blasting, type A												
	Germane	2.3	UN2192		POISON GAS, FLAMMABLE GAS	1	None	192	245	Forbidden	Forbidden	D	40
	Glycerol-1,3-dinitrate	Forbid-den											
	Glycerol gluconate trinitrate	Forbid-den											
	Glycerol lactate trinitrate	Forbid-den											
	Glycerol alpha-monochlorohydrin	6.1	UN2689	III	KEEP AWAY FROM FOOD	T2	153	203	241	60 L	220 L	A	
	Glyceryl trinitrate, see Nitroglycerin, etc.												
	Glycidaldehyde	3	UN2622	II	FLAMMABLE LIQUID, POISON	T8	150	202	243	1 L	60 L	A	40
D	Grenades, empty primed	1.4S	NA0349	II	None	None	None	62	None	25 kg	100 kg	A	9E
	Grenades, hand or rifle, with bursting charge	1.1D	UN0284	II	EXPLOSIVE 1.1D		63(b)	62	None	Forbidden	Forbidden	B	
	Grenades, hand or rifle, with bursting charge	1.2D	UN0285	II	EXPLOSIVE 1.2D		63(b)	62	None	Forbidden	Forbidden	B	
	Grenades, hand or rifle, with bursting charge	1.1F	UN0292	II	EXPLOSIVE 1.1F		63(b)	62	None	Forbidden	Forbidden	E	
	Grenades, hand or rifle, with bursting charge	1.2F	UN0293	II	EXPLOSIVE 1.2F		63(b)	62	None	Forbidden	Forbidden	E	
	Grenades, illuminating, see Ammunition, illuminating, etc.												
	Grenades practice Hand or rifle	1.4G	UN0452	II	EXPLOSIVE 1.4G		63(b)	62	None	Forbidden	75 kg	B	
	Grenades, practice, hand or rifle	1.4S	UN0110	II	EXPLOSIVE 1.4S		63(b)	62	None	25 kg	100 kg	A	9E
	Grenades, practice, hand or rifle	1.3G	UN0318	II	EXPLOSIVE 1.3G		63(b)	62	None	Forbidden	Forbidden	B	
	Grenades, practice, hand or rifle	1.2G	UN0372	II	EXPLOSIVE 1.2G		63(b)	62	None	Forbidden	Forbidden	B	
	Grenades, smoke, see Ammunition, smoke, etc.												
	Guanidine nitrate	5.1	UN1467	III	OXIDIZER	A1	152	213	240	25 kg	100 kg	A	73
	Guanyl nitrosaminoguanylidene hydrazine (dry)	Forbid-den											
	Guanyl nitrosaminoguanylidene hydrazine, wetted with not less than 30 per cent water, by mass	1.1A	UN0113	II	EXPLOSIVE 1.1A	111, 117	None	62	None	Forbidden	Forbidden	E	2E, 6E
	Guanyl nitrosaminoguanyltetrazene (dry)	Forbid-den											
	Guanyl nitrosaminoguanyltetrazene, wetted or Tetrazene, wetted with not less than 30 per cent water or mixture of alcohol and water, by mass	1.1A	UN0114	II	EXPLOSIVE 1.1A	111, 117	None	62	None	Forbidden	Forbidden	E	2E, 6E
	Gunpowder, compressed or Gunpowder in pellets, see Black powder (UN 0028)												
	Gunpowder, granular or as a meal, see Black powder (UN 0027)												
	Hafnium powder, dry	4.2	UN2545	I	SPONTANEOUSLY COMBUSTIBLE		None	211	242	Forbidden	Forbidden	D	
				II	SPONTANEOUSLY COMBUSTIBLE	A19, A20, N34	None	212	241	15 kg	50 kg	D	
				III	SPONTANEOUSLY COMBUSTIBLE		None	213	241	25 kg	100 kg	D	
	Hafnium powder, wetted with not less than 25 per cent water (a visible excess of water must be present) (a) mechanically produced, particle size less than 53 microns; (b) chemically produced, particle size less than 840 microns	4.1	UN1326	II	FLAMMABLE SOLID	A6, A19, A20, N34	None	212	241	15 kg	50 kg	E	
	Halogenated irritating liquids, n.o.s.	6.1	UN1610	I	POISON	T42	None	201	243	Forbidden	Forbidden	D	40
				II	POISON	T14	None	202	243	5 L	60 L	D	40
				III	KEEP AWAY FROM FOOD	T14	153	202	241	60 L	220 L	D	40
	Hand signal device, see Signal devices, hand												
	Hazardous substances, liquid or solid, n.o.s., see Environmentally hazardous substances, etc.												
D	Hazardous waste, liquid, n.o.s.	9	NA3082	III	CLASS 9		155	203	241	No limit	No limit	A	
D	Hazardous waste, solid, n.o.s.	9	NA3077	III	CLASS 9	B54	155	213	240	No limit	No limit	A	
	Helium, compressed	2.2	UN1046		NONFLAMMABLE GAS		306	302	302, 314	75 kg	150 kg	A	85

Symbols (1)	Hazardous materials descriptions and proper shipping names (2)	Hazard class or Division (3)	Identification Numbers (4)	Packing group (5)	Label(s) required (if not excepted) (6)	Special provisions (7)	Packaging authorizations (§173.***) Exceptions (8A)	Non-bulk packaging (8B)	Bulk packaging (8C)	Quantity limitations Passenger aircraft or railcar (9A)	Cargo aircraft only (9B)	Vessel stowage requirements Vessel stowages (10A)	Other stowage provisions (10B)
	Helium-oxygen mixture, see Rare gases and oxygen mixtures												
	Helium, refrigerated liquid (cryogenic liquid)	2.2	UN1963		NONFLAMMABLE GAS		320	316	318	50 kg	500 kg	B	
	n-Heptaldehyde	3	UN3056	III	FLAMMABLE LIQUID	B1, T1	150	203	242	60 L	220 L	A	
	Heptanes	3	UN1206	II	FLAMMABLE LIQUID	T2	150	202	242	5 L	60 L	B	
	n-Heptene	3	UN2278	II	FLAMMABLE LIQUID	T8	150	202	242	5 L	60 L	B	
	Hexachloroacetone	6.1	UN2661	III	KEEP AWAY FROM FOOD	T8	153	203	241	60 L	220 L	B	12, 40
	Hexachlorobenzene	6.1	UN2729	III	KEEP AWAY FROM FOOD		153	203	241	60 L	220 L	A	
	Hexachlorobutadiene	6.1	UN2279	III	KEEP AWAY FROM FOOD	T7	153	203	241	60 L	220 L	A	
	Hexachlorocyclopentadiene	6.1	UN2646	I	POISON	2, B9, B14, B32, B74, B77, T38, T43, T44	None	227	244	Forbidden	Forbidden	D	40
	Hexachlorophene	6.1	UN2875	III	KEEP AWAY FROM FOOD		153	213	240	100 kg	200 kg	A	
	Hexadecyltrichlorosilane	8	UN1781	II	CORROSIVE	A7, B2, B6, N34, T8	None	202	242	Forbidden	30 L	C	40
	Hexadienes	3	UN2458	II	FLAMMABLE LIQUID	T7	None	202	242	5 L	60 L	B	
	Hexaethyl tetraphosphate and compressed gas mixtures	2.3	UN1612		POISON GAS	3	None	334	None	Forbidden	Forbidden	D	40
	Hexaethyl tetraphosphate liquid	6.1	UN1611	I	POISON	A4	None	201	243	1 L	30 L	E	40
				II	POISON	N76	None	202	243	5 L	60 L	E	40
				III	KEEP AWAY FROM FOOD	N77	None	203	241	60 L	220 L	E	40
	Hexaethyl tetraphosphate, solid	6.1	UN1611	I	POISON		None	211	242	Forbidden	15 kg	E	95
				II	POISON	N76	None	212	242	25 kg	100 kg	E	95
				III	KEEP AWAY FROM FOOD	N77	153	213	240	100 kg	200 kg	E	34
	Hexafluoroacetone	2.3	UN2420		POISON GAS	2, B9, B14	None	304	314, 315	Forbidden	25 kg	D	40
	Hexafluoroacetone hydrate	6.1	UN2552	II	POISON	T14	None	202	243	5 L	60 L	B	40
	Hexafluoroethane, R116	2.2	UN2193		NONFLAMMABLE GAS		306	304	314, 315	75 kg	150 kg	A	
	Hexafluorophosphoric acid	8	UN1782	II	CORROSIVE	A6, A7, B2, N3, N34, T9, T27	None	202	242	1 L	30 L	A	
D	Hexafluoropropylene oxide	2.2	NA1956		NONFLAMMABLE GAS		306	304	314, 315	75 kg	150 kg	A	
	Hexafluoropropylene, R1216	2.2	UN1858		NONFLAMMABLE GAS		306	304	314, 315	75 kg	150 kg	A	
	Hexaldehyde	3	UN1207	III	FLAMMABLE LIQUID	B1, T1	150	203	242	60 L	220 L	A	
	Hexamethylene diisocyanate	6.1	UN2281	II	POISON	T14	None	202	243	5 L	60 L	B	13, 40
	Hexamethylene triperoxide diamine (dry)	Forbidden											
	Hexamethylenediamine, solid	8	UN2280	III	CORROSIVE		154	213	240	25 kg	100 kg	A	12, 48
	Hexamethylenediamine solution	8	UN1783	II	CORROSIVE	T8	None	202	243	1 L	30 L	A	
	Hexamethyleneimine	3	UN2493	II	FLAMMABLE LIQUID, CORROSIVE	T8	None	202	243	1 L	5 L	B	40
	Hexamethylol benzene hexanitrate	Forbidden											
	Hexamine	4.1	UN1328	III	FLAMMABLE SOLID	A1	151	213	240	25 kg	100 kg	A	
	Hexanes	3	UN1208	II	FLAMMABLE LIQUID	T8	150	202	242	5 L	60 L	E	
	2,2',4,4',6,6'-Hexanitro-3,3'-dihydroxyazobenzene (dry)	Forbidden											
	Hexanitroazoxy benzene	Forbidden											
	N,N'-(hexanitrodiphenyl) ethylene dinitramine (dry)	Forbidden											
	Hexanitrodiphenyl urea	Forbidden											
	2,2',3,4,4',6-Hexanitrodiphenylamine	Forbidden											
	Hexanitrodiphenylamine (Dipicrylamine; Hexyl)	1.1D	UN0079	II	EXPLOSIVE 1.1D		None	62	None	Forbidden	Forbidden	B	1E, 5E
	2,3',4,4',6,6'-Hexanitrodiphenylether	Forbidden											
	Hexanitroethane	Forbidden											
	Hexanitrooxanilide	Forbidden											

322

(1) Symbols	(2) Hazardous materials descriptions and proper shipping names	(3) Hazard class or Division	(4) Identification Numbers	(5) Packing group	(6) Label(s) required (if not excepted)	(7) Special provisions	(8A) Exceptions	(8B) Non-bulk packaging	(8C) Bulk packaging	(9A) Passenger aircraft or railcar	(9B) Cargo aircraft only	(10A) Vessel stowage	(10B) Other stowage provisions
	Hexanitrostilbene	1.1D	UN0392	II	EXPLOSIVE 1.1D		None	62	None	Forbidden	Forbidden	B	1E, 5E
	Hexanoic acid, see Corrosive liquids, n.o.s.												
	Hexanols	3	UN2282	III	FLAMMABLE LIQUID	B1, T1	150	203	242	60 L	220 L	A	
	Hexatonal, cast	1.1D	UN0393	II	EXPLOSIVE 1.1D		None	62	None	Forbidden	Forbidden	B	1E, 5E
	1-Hexene	3	UN2370	II	FLAMMABLE LIQUID	T8	150	202	242	5 L	60 L	E	
	Hexogen and cyclotetramethylenetetranitramine mixtures, wetted or desensitized see RDX and HMX mixtures, wetted or desensitized etc.												
	Hexogen and HMX mixtures, wetted or desensitized see RDX and HMX mixtures, wetted or desensitized etc.												
	Hexogen and octogen mixtures, wetted or desensitized see RDX and HMX mixtures, wetted or desensitized etc.												
	Hexogen, see Cyclotrimethylenetrinitramine, etc.												
	Hexolite, dry or wetted with less than 15 per cent water, by mass	1.1D	UN0118	II	EXPLOSIVE 1.1D		None	62	None	Forbidden	Forbidden	B	1E, 5E
	Hexyl, see Hexanitrodiphenylamine												
	Hexyltrichlorosilane	8	UN1784	II	CORROSIVE	A7, B2, B6, N34, T8, T26	None	202	242	Forbidden	30 L	C	40
	High explosives, see individual explosives' entries												
	HMX, see Cyclotetramethylene-tetranitramine, etc.												
	Hydrazine, anhydrous or Hydrazine aqueous solutions with more than 64 per cent hydrazine, by mass	3	UN2029	I	FLAMMABLE LIQUID, POISON, CORROSIVE	A3, A6, A7, A10, B16, B53, T25	None	201	243	Forbidden	2.5 L	D	21, 40, 42, 100
	Hydrazine azide	Forbidden											
	Hydrazine chlorate	Forbidden											
	Hydrazine dicarbonic acid diazide	Forbidden											
	Hydrazine hydrate or Hydrazine aqueous solutions, with not more than 64 per cent hydrazine, by mass	8	UN2030	II	CORROSIVE, POISON	B16, B53, T15	None	202	243	Forbidden	30 L	D	40, 42, 82
	Hydrazine perchlorate	Forbidden											
	Hydrazine selenate	Forbidden											
	Hydrides, metal, n.o.s.	4.3	UN1409	I	DANGEROUS WHEN WET	A19, N34, N40	None	211	242	Forbidden	15 kg	D	
	Hydriodic acid, anhydrous, see Hydrogen iodide, anhydrous												
	Hydriodic acid, solution	8	UN1787	II	CORROSIVE	A3, A6, B2, N41, T9, T27	154	202	242	1 L	30 L	C	8
	Hydrobromic acid, anhydrous, see Hydrogen bromide, anhydrous												
	Hydrobromic acid solution more than 49% hydrobromic acid	8	UN1788	II	CORROSIVE	B2, B15, N41, T9, T27	154	202	242	Forbidden	Forbidden	C	8
	Hydrobromic acid solution, not more than 49% hydrobromic acid	8	UN1788	II	CORROSIVE	A3, A6, B2, B15, N41, T9, T27	154	202	242	1 L	30 L	C	8
	Hydrocarbon gases, compressed, n.o.s. or Hydrocarbon gases mixtures, compressed, n.o.s.	2.1	UN1964		FLAMMABLE GAS		306	302	314, 315	Forbidden	150 kg	E	40
	Hydrocarbon gases, liquefied, n.o.s. or Hydrocarbon gases mixtures, liquefied, n.o.s.	2.1	UN1965		FLAMMABLE GAS		306	304	314, 315	Forbidden	150 kg	E	40
	Hydrochloric acid, anhydrous, see Hydrogen chloride, anhydrous												
	Hydrochloric acid, solution	8	UN1789	II	CORROSIVE	A3, A6, B2, B15, N41, T9, T27	154	202	242	1 L	30 L	C	8
	Hydrocyanic acid, anhydrous, see Hydrogen cyanide etc.												
D	Hydrocyanic acid, aqueous solutions less than 5% HCN	6.1	NA1613	II	POISON	B12, T18, T26	None	195	243	Forbidden	5 L	D	40
	Hydrocyanic acid, aqueous solutions not more than 20% hydrocyanic acid	6.1	UN1613	I	POISON	2, B12, B61, B65, B77, B82	None	195	244	Forbidden	Forbidden	D	40
	Hydrocyanic acid, liquefied, see Hydrogen cyanide, etc.												
	Hydrocyanic acid (prussic), unstabilized	Forbidden											

323

(1) Symbols	(2) Hazardous materials descriptions and proper shipping names	(3) Hazard class or Division	(4) Identification Numbers	(5) Packing group	(6) Label(s) required (if not excepted)	(7) Special provisions	(8) Packaging authorizations (§173.***)			(9) Quantity limitations		(10) Vessel stowage requirements	
							(8A) Exceptions	(8B) Non-bulk packaging	(8C) Bulk packaging	(9A) Passenger aircraft or railcar	(9B) Cargo aircraft only	(10A) Vessel stowages	(10B) Other stowage provisions
	Hydrofluoric acid and Sulfuric acid mixtures	8	UN1786	I	CORROSIVE, POISON	A6, A7, B15, B23, N5, N34, T18, T27	None	201	243	Forbidden	2.5 L	D	40, 95
	Hydrofluoric acid, anhydrous, see Hydrogen fluoride, anhydrous												
	Hydrofluoric acid, solution, more than 60 per cent strength	8	UN1790	I	CORROSIVE, POISON	A6, A7, B4, B12, B15, B23, N5, N34, T18, T27	None	201	243	0.5 L	2.5 L	D	12, 40, 48, 95
	Hydrofluoric acid, solution, not more than 60 per cent strength	8	UN1790	II	CORROSIVE, POISON	A6, A7, B12, B15, N5, N34, T18, T27	None	202	243	1 L	30 L	D	12, 40, 48, 95
	Hydrofluoroboric acid, see Fluoboric acid												
	Hydrofluorosilicic acid, see Fluorosilicic acid												
	Hydrogen and Methane mixtures, compressed	2.1	UN2034		FLAMMABLE GAS		306	302	302, 314, 315	Forbidden	150 kg	E	40
	Hydrogen bromide, anhydrous	2.3	UN1048		POISON GAS, CORROSIVE	3, B14	None	304	314, 315	Forbidden	25 kg	D	40
	Hydrogen chloride, anhydrous	2.3	UN1050		POISON GAS, CORROSIVE	3	None	304	None	Forbidden	Forbidden	D	40
	Hydrogen chloride, refrigerated liquid	2.3	UN2186		POISON GAS, CORROSIVE	3, B6, B43	None	None	314, 315	Forbidden	Forbidden	B	40
	Hydrogen, compressed	2.1	UN1049		FLAMMABLE GAS		306	302	302, 314	Forbidden	150 kg	E	40, 57
	Hydrogen cyanide, anhydrous, stabilized	6.1	UN1051	I	POISON, FLAMMABLE LIQUID	1, B12, B61, B65, B77, B82	None	195	244	Forbidden	Forbidden	D	40
	Hydrogen cyanide, anhydrous, stabilized, absorbed in a porous inert material	6.1	UN1614	I	POISON	5	None	195	None	Forbidden	Forbidden	D	25, 40
	Hydrogen fluoride, anhydrous	8	UN1052	I	CORROSIVE, POISON	3, B7, B12, B46, B71, B77, T24, T27	None	163	243	Forbidden	Forbidden	D	40, 95
	Hydrogen iodide, anhydrous	2.2	UN2197		NONFLAMMABLE GAS, CORROSIVE		306	304	314, 315	Forbidden	Forbidden	D	40
	Hydrogen iodide solution, see Hydriodic acid, solution												
	Hydrogen peroxide and peroxyacetic acid mixtures, with acids, water and not more than 5 per cent peroxyacetic acid, stabilized	5.1	UN3149	II	OXIDIZER, CORROSIVE	A2, A3, A6, B12, B53, T14	None	202	243	1 L	5 L	D	25, 66, 75, 106
	Hydrogen peroxide, aqueous solutions with more than 40 per cent but not more than 60 per cent hydrogen peroxide (stabilized as necessary)	5.1	UN2014	II	OXIDIZER, CORROSIVE	12, A3, A6, B12, BB53, B80, B81, B85, T14, T37	None	202	243	Forbidden	Forbidden	D	25, 66, 75, 106
	Hydrogen peroxide, aqueous solutions with not less than 8 per cent but less than 20 per cent hydrogen peroxide (stabilized as necessary)	5.1	UN2984	III	OXIDIZER	17, A1, T8, T37	152	203	241	2.5 L	30 L	B	25, 75, 106
	Hydrogen peroxide, aqueous solutions with not less than 20 per cent but not more than 40 per cent hydrogen peroxide (stabilized as necessary)	5.1	UN2014	II	OXIDIZER, CORROSIVE	A2, A3, A6, B12, B53, T14, T37	None	202	243	1 L	5 L	D	25, 66, 75, 106
	Hydrogen peroxide, stabilized or Hydrogen peroxide aqueous solutions, stabilized with more than 60 per cent hydrogen peroxide	5.1	UN2015	I	OXIDIZER, CORROSIVE	12, A3, A6, B12, B53, B80, B81, B85, T15, T37	None	201	243	Forbidden	Forbidden	D	25, 66, 75, 106
	Hydrogen, refrigerated liquid (cryogenic liquid)	2.1	UN1966		FLAMMABLE GAS		None	316	318, 319	Forbidden	Forbidden	D	40
	Hydrogen selenide, anhydrous	2.3	UN2202		POISON GAS, FLAMMABLE GAS	1	None	192	245	Forbidden	Forbidden	D	40
	Hydrogen sulfate, see Sulfuric acid												
	Hydrogen sulfide, liquefied	2.3	UN1053		POISON GAS, FLAMMABLE GAS	2, B9, B14	None	304	314, 315	Forbidden	Forbidden	D	40
	Hydroquinone, liquid	6.1	UN2662	III	KEEP AWAY FROM FOOD	T8	153	213	240	100 kg	200 kg	A	
	Hydroquinone, solid	6.1	UN2662	III	KEEP AWAY FROM FOOD		153	213	240	100 kg	200 kg	AA	
	Hydrosilicofluoric acid, see Fluorosilicic acid												
	3-(2-Hydroxyethoxy)-4-pyrrolidin-1-ylbenzenediazonium zinc chloride	4.1	UN3035	II	FLAMMABLE SOLID		None	224	240	Forbidden	Forbidden	D	2
	Hydroxyl amine iodide	Forbidden	*										
AW	Hydroxylamine sulfate	8	UN2865	III	CORROSIVE		154	213	240	25 kg	100 kg	A	
	Hypochlorite solutions with more than 5 per cent but less than 16 per cent available chlorine	8	UN1791	III	CORROSIVE	N34, T7	154	203	241	5 L	60 L	B	26
	Hypochlorite solutions with 16 per cent or more available chlorine	8	UN1791	II	CORROSIVE	A7, B2, B15, N34, T7	154	202	242	1 L	30 L	B	26
	Hyponitrous acid	Forbidden											
	Igniter fuse, metal clad, see Fuse, igniter, tubular, metal clad												
	Igniters	1.1G	UN0121	II	EXPLOSIVE 1.1G		None	62	None	Forbidden	Forbidden	B	
	Igniters	1.2G	UN0314	II	EXPLOSIVE 1.2G		None	62	None	Forbidden	Forbidden	B	
	Igniters	1.3G	UN0315	II	EXPLOSIVE 1.3G		None	62	None	Forbidden	Forbidden	A	
	Igniters	1.4G	UN0325	II	EXPLOSIVE 1.4G		None	62	None	Forbidden	75 kg	A	24E

Symbols (1)	Hazardous materials descriptions and proper shipping names (2)	Hazard class or Division (3)	Identification Numbers (4)	Packing group (5)	Label(s) required (if not excepted) (6)	Special provisions (7)	Packaging authorizations (§173.***) (8)			Quantity limitations (9)		Vessel stowage requirements (10)	
							Exceptions (8A)	Non-bulk packaging (8B)	Bulk packaging (8C)	Passenger aircraft or railcar (9A)	Cargo aircraft only (9B)	Vessel stowages (10A)	Other stowage provisions (10B)
	Igniters	1.4S	UN0454	II	EXPLOSIVE 1.4S		None	62	None	25 kg	100 kg	A	9E
	3,3'-Iminodipropylamine	8	UN2269	III	CORROSIVE	T8	154	203	241	5 L	60 ℓ	A	
	Infectious substances, affecting animals only	6.2	UN2900		INFECTIOUS SUBSTANCE		196	196	None	50 mL or 50 g	4 L or 4 kg	B	
	Infectious substances, affecting humans	6.2	UN2814		INFECTIOUS SUBSTANCE		196	196	None	50 mL or 50 g	4 L or 4 kg	B	
	Inflammable, see Flammable												
	Initiating explosives (dry)	Forbidden											
	Ink, printer's, flammable	3	UN1210	II	FLAMMABLE LIQUID	T7, T30,	150	173	242	5 L	60 L	B	
				III	FLAMMABLE LIQUID	B1, T7, T30	150	173	242	60 L	220 L	A	
	Inositol hexanitrate (dry)	Forbidden											
	Insecticide gases flammable n.o.s.	2.1	UN1968		FLAMMABLE GAS		306	304	314, 315	75 kg	150 kg	D	40
	Insecticide gases, n.o.s.	2.2	UN1968		NONFLAMMABLE GAS		306	304	314, 315	75 kg	150 kg	A	105
	Insecticide gases, toxic, n.o.s.	2.3	UN1967		POISON GAS	3	None	193, 334	245	Forbidden	Forbidden	D	40
	Inulin trinitrate (dry)	Forbidden											
	Iodine azide (dry)	Forbidden											
	Iodine monochloride	8	UN1792	II	CORROSIVE	B6, N41, T8, T26	None	202	242	Forbidden	50 kg	D	40, 66, 74, 89, 90
	Iodine pentafluoride	5.1	UN2495	I	OXIDIZER, POISON		None	205	243	Forbidden	2.5 L	D	25, 40, 66, 90
	2-Iodobutane	3	UN2390	II	FLAMMABLE LIQUID	T8	150	202	242	5 L	60 L	B	
	Iodomethylpropanes	3	UN2391	II	FLAMMABLE LIQUID	T8	150	202	242	5 L	60 L	B	
	Iodopropanes	3	UN2392	III	FLAMMABLE LIQUID	B1, T8	150	203	241	60 L	220 L	A	
	Iodoxy compounds (dry)	Forbidden											
	Iridium nitratopentamine iridium nitrate	Forbidden											
	Iron chloride, see Ferric chloride												
	Iron oxide, spent, or iron sponge, spent obtained from coal gas purification	4.2	UN1376	III	SPONTANEOUSLY COMBUSTIBLE	B18	None	213	240	Forbidden	Forbidden	E	
	Iron pentacarbonyl	6.1	UN1994	I	POISON, FLAMMABLE LIQUID	1, B9, B14, B30, B72, B77, T38, T43, T44	None	192	244	Forbidden	Forbidden	D	40
	Iron sesquichloride, see Ferric chloride												
	Irritating material, see Tear gas substances, etc.												
	Isobutane or Isobutane mixtures	2.1	UN1969		FLAMMABLE GAS		306	304	314, 315	Forbidden	150 kg	E	40
	Isobutanol or Isobutyl alcohol	3	UN1212	III	FLAMMABLE LIQUID	B1, T1	150	203	241	60 L	220 L	A	
	Isobutyl acetate	3	UN1213	II	FLAMMABLE LIQUID	T1	150	202	242	5 L	60 L	B	
	Isobutyl acrylate	3	UN2527	III	FLAMMABLE LIQUID	B1, T1	150	203	242	60 L	220 L	A	
	Isobutyl alcohol, see Isobutanol												
	Isobutyl aldehyde, see Isobutyraldehyde												
D	Isobutyl chloroformate	6.1	NA2742	I	POISON, FLAMMABLE LIQUID, CORROSIVE	2, B9, B14, B32, B74, T38, T43, T45	None	227	244	1 L	30 L	A	12, 13, 22, 25, 40, 48, 100
	Isobutyl formate	3	UN2393	II	FLAMMABLE LIQUID	T1	150	202	242	5 L	60 L	B	
	Isobutyl isobutyrate	3	UN2528	III	FLAMMABLE LIQUID	B1, T1	150	203	242	60 L	220 L	A	
+	Isobutyl isocyanate	3	UN2486	II	FLAMMABLE LIQUID, POISON	1, B9, B14, B30, B72, T38, T43, T44	None	226	244	1 L	60 L	D	40
	Isobutyl methacrylate	3	UN2283	III	FLAMMABLE LIQUID	B1, T1	150	203	242	60 L	220 L	A	
	Isobutyl propionate	3	UN2394	III	FLAMMABLE LIQUID	T1	150	203	242	60 L	220 L	B	
	Isobutylamine	3	UN1214	II	FLAMMABLE LIQUID	T8	150	202	242	5 L	60 L	B	40
	Isobutylene see also Petroleum gases, liquefied	2.1	UN1055		FLAMMABLE GAS		306	304	314, 315	Forbidden	150 kg	E	40
	Isobutyraldehyde or isobutyl aldehyde	3	UN2045	II	FLAMMABLE LIQUID	T8	150	202	242	5 L	60 L	E	40
	Isobutyric acid	3	UN2529	III	FLAMMABLE LIQUID	B1, T1	150	203	242	60 L	220 L	A	
	Isobutyric anhydride	3	UN2530	III	FLAMMABLE LIQUID	B1, T1	150	203	242	60 L	220 L	A	

Symbols	Hazardous materials descriptions and proper shipping names	Hazard class or Division	Identification Numbers	Packing group	Label(s) required (if not excepted)	Special provisions	Packaging authorizations (§173.***)			Quantity limitations		Vessel stowage requirements	
							Exceptions	Non-bulk packaging	Bulk packaging	Passenger aircraft or railcar	Cargo aircraft only	Vessel stowages	Other stowage provisions
(1)	(2)	(3)	(4)	(5)	(6)	(7)	(8A)	(8B)	(8C)	(9A)	(9B)	(10A)	(10B)
	Isobutyronitrile	3	UN2284	II	FLAMMABLE LIQUID, POISON	T17	None	202	243	1 L	60 L	E	40
	Isobutyryl chloride	3	UN2395	II	FLAMMABLE LIQUID, CORROSIVE	T9, T26	None	202	243	1 L	5 L	C	40
	Isocyanates, liquid or solid, n.o.s. or Isocyanate solutions, n.o.s. boiling point not less than 300 degrees C	6.1	UN2207	III	KEEP AWAY FROM FOOD		153	203	241	60 L	220 L	A	48
	Isocyanates, n.o.s. or Isocyanate solutions, n.o.s., flash point more than 61 degrees C and boiling point less than 300 degrees C	6.1	UN2206	II	POISON	T15	None	202	243	5 L	60 L	D	25, 40, 48
	Isocyanates, n.o.s. or Isocyanate solutions, n.o.s., flash point not less than 23 degrees C but not more than 61 degrees C and boiling point less than 300 degrees C	6.1	UN3080	II	POISON, FLAMMABLE LIQUID	T15	None	202	243	5 L	60 L	D	25, 40, 48
	Isocyanates, n.o.s. or Isocyanate solutions, n.o.s. (flashpoint less than 23 degrees C)	3	UN2478	II	FLAMMABLE LIQUID, POISON	5, A3, A7	None	202	243	1 L	60 L	D	40
	Isocyanatobenzotrifluorides	6.1	UN2285	II	POISON	5, T14	None	202	243	5 L	60 L	B	25, 40, 48
	Isoheptenes	3	UN2287	II	FLAMMABLE LIQUID	T7	150	202	242	5 L	60 L	B	
	Isohexenes	3	UN2288	II	FLAMMABLE LIQUID	T7	150	202	242	5 L	60 L	E	
	Isooctane, see Octanes												
	Isooctenes	3	UN1216	II	FLAMMABLE LIQUID	T8	150	202	242	5 L	60 L	B	
	Isopentane, see n-Pentane												
	Isopentanoic acid, see Corrosive liquids, n.o.s.												
	Isopentenes	3	UN2371	I	FLAMMABLE LIQUID	T20	150	201	243	1 L	30 L	E	
	Isophorone diisocyanate	6.1	UN2290	III	KEEP AWAY FROM FOOD	T7	153	203	241	60 L	220 L	B	40
AW	Isophoronediamine	8	UN2289	III	CORROSIVE	T8	154	203	241	5 L	60 L	A	8
	Isoprene, inhibited	3	UN1218	I	FLAMMABLE LIQUID	T20	150	201	243	1 L	30 L	E	
	Isopropanol or Isopropyl alcohol	3	UN1219	II	FLAMMABLE LIQUID	T1	150	202	242	5 L	60 L	B	
	Isopropenyl acetate	3	UN2403	II	FLAMMABLE LIQUID	T1	150	202	242	5 L	60 L	B	
	Isopropenylbenzene	3	UN2303	III	FLAMMABLE LIQUID	B1, T1	150	203	242	60 L	220 L	A	
	Isopropyl acetate	3	UN1220	II	FLAMMABLE LIQUID	T1	150	202	242	5 L	60 L	B	
	Isopropyl acid phosphate	8	UN1793	III	CORROSIVE	T7	154	213	240	25 kg	100 kg	A	
	Isopropyl alcohol, see Isopropanol												
	Isopropyl butyrate	3	UN2405	III	FLAMMABLE LIQUID	B1, T1	150	203	242	60 L	220 L	A	
	Isopropyl chloroacetate	3	UN2947	III	FLAMMABLE LIQUID	B1, T1	150	203	242	60 L	220 L	A	
+	Isopropyl chloroformate	3	UN2407	I	FLAMMABLE LIQUID, CORROSIVE, POISON	2, B9, B14, B32, B74, B77, T38, T43, T45	None	227	244	Forbidden	Forbidden	B	40
	Isopropyl-2-chloropropionate	3	UN2934	III	FLAMMABLE LIQUID	B1, T1	150	203	242	60 L	220 L	A	
	Isopropyl isobutyrate	3	UN2406	II	FLAMMABLE LIQUID	T1	150	202	242	5 L	60 L	B	
+	Isopropyl isocyanate	3	UN2483	I	FLAMMABLE LIQUID, POISON	1, B9, B14, B30, B72, T38, T43, T44	None	226	244	Forbidden	30 L	D	40
	Isopropyl mercaptan, see Propanethiols												
	Isopropyl nitrate	3	UN1222	II	FLAMMABLE LIQUID	T25	150	202	None	5 L	60 L	D	
	Isopropyl phosphoric acid, see Isopropyl acid phosphate												
	Isopropyl propionate	3	UN2409	II	FLAMMABLE LIQUID	T1	150	202	242	5 L	60 L	B	
	Isopropylamine	3	UN1221	I	FLAMMABLE LIQUID	T20	None	201	243	1 L	30 L	E	
	Isopropylbenzene	3	UN1918	III	FLAMMABLE LIQUID	B1, T1	150	203	242	60 L	220 L	A	
	Isopropylcumyl hydroperoxide, more than 72 per cent in solution	Forbidden											
	Isosorbide dinitrate mixture with not less than 60 per cent lactose, mannose, starch or calcium hydrogen phosphate	4.1	UN2907	II	FLAMMABLE SOLID		None	212	None	15 kg	50 kg	E	
	Isothiocyanic acid	Forbidden											

326

Symbols	Hazardous materials descriptions and proper shipping names	Hazard class or Division	Identification Numbers	Packing group	Label(s) required (If not excepted)	Special provisions	Packaging authorizations (§173.***)			Quantity limitations		Vessel stowage requirements	
							Exceptions	Non-bulk packaging	Bulk packaging	Passenger aircraft or railcar	Cargo aircraft only	Vessel stowages	Other stowage provisions
(1)	(2)	(3)	(4)	(5)	(6)	(7)	(8A)	(8B)	(8C)	(9A)	(9B)	(10A)	(10B)
	Jet fuel, see Fuel aviation, turbine engine												
	Jet perforating guns, charged oil well, without detonator	1.1D	UN0124	II	EXPLOSIVE 1.1D		None	62	None	Forbidden	Forbidden	B	
D	Jet perforating guns, charged oil well, without detonator	1.4D	NA0124	II	EXPLOSIVE 1.4D	114	None	62	None	Forbidden	Forbidden	A	24E
	Jet perforators, see Charges, shaped, commercial etc.												
	Jet tappers, without detonator, see Charges, shaped commercial, etc.												
	Jet thrust igniters, for rocket motors or Jato, see Igniters												
	Jet thrust unit (Jato), see Rocket motors												
	Kerosene	3	UN1223	III	FLAMMABLE LIQUID	B1, T1	150	203	242	60 L	220 L	A	
	Ketones, liquid, n.o.s.	3	UN1224	I	FLAMMABLE LIQUID	T8, T31	None	201	243	1 L	30 L	E	
				II	FLAMMABLE LIQUID	T8, T31	150	202	242	5 L	60 L	B	
				III	FLAMMABLE LIQUID	B1, T7, T30	150	203	242	60 L	220 L	A	
	Krypton, compressed	2.2	UN1056		NONFLAMMABLE GAS		306	302	None	75 kg	150 kg	A	
	Krypton, refrigerated liquid (cryogenic liquid)	2.2	UN1970		NONFLAMMABLE GAS		320	None	None	50 kg	500 kg	B	
	Lacquer base or lacquer chips, nitrocellulose, dry, see Nitrocellulose, etc. (UN 2557)												
	Lacquer base or lacquer chips, plastic, wet with alcohol or solvent, see Nitrocellulose (UN 2059, UN 2060, UN 2555, UN2556) or Paint etc. (UN1263)												
	Lead acetate	6.1	UN1616	III	KEEP AWAY FROM FOOD		153	213	240	100 kg	200 kg	A	
	Lead arsenates	6.1	UN1617	II	POISON		None	212	242	25 kg	100 kg	A	
	Lead arsenites	6.1	UN1618	II	POISON		None	212	242	25 kg	100 kg	A	
	Lead azide (dry)	Forbidden											
	Lead azide, wetted with not less than 20 per cent water or mixture of alcohol and water, by mass	1.1A	UN0129	II	EXPLOSIVE 1.1A	111, 117	None	62	None	Forbidden	Forbidden	E	2E, 6E
	Lead compounds, soluble, n.o.s.	6.1	UN2291	II	POISON		153	213	240	100 kg	200 kg	A	
	Lead cyanide	6.1	UN1620	II	POISON		None	212	242	25 kg	100 kg	A	26
	Lead dioxide	5.1	UN1872	III	OXIDIZER	A1	152	213	240	25 kg	100 kg	A	34
	Lead dross, see Lead sulphate, with more than 3% free acid												
D	Lead mononitroresorcinate	1.1A	NA0473	II	EXPLOSIVE 1.1A	111, 117	None	62	None	Forbidden	Forbidden	E	2E, 6E
	Lead nitrate	5.1	UN1469	II	OXIDIZER, POISON		None	212	242	5 kg	25 kg	A	
	Lead nitroresorcinate (dry)	Forbidden											
	Lead perchlorate, solid or solution	5.1	UN1470	II	OXIDIZER, POISON	T8	None	212	242	5 kg	25 kg	A	56, 58, 106
	Lead peroxide, see Lead dioxide												
	Lead phosphite, dibasic	4.1	UN2989	II	FLAMMABLE SOLID		None	212	240	5 kg	25 kg	B	34
				III	FLAMMABLE SOLID		151	213	240	15 kg	50 kg	B	34
	Lead picrate (dry)	Forbidden											
	Lead styphnate (dry)	Forbidden											
	Lead styphnate, wetted or Lead trinitroresorcinate, wetted with not less than 20 per cent water or mixture of alcohol and water, by mass	1.1A	UN0130	II	EXPLOSIVE 1.1A	111, 117	None	62	None	Forbidden	Forbidden	E	2E, 6E
	Lead sulfate with more than 3 per cent free acid	8	UN1794	II	CORROSIVE		154	212	240	15 kg	50 kg	A	
	Lead trinitroresorcinate, see Lead styphnate, etc.												
	Life-saving appliances, not self inflating containing dangerous goods as equipment	9	UN3072		None		None	219	None	No limit	No limit	A	120
	Life-saving appliances, self inflating	9	UN2990		None		None	219	None	No limit	No limit	A	120
	Lighter replacement cartridges containing liquefied petroleum gases (and similar devices, each not exceeding 65 grams), see Lighters for cigars, cigarettes, etc. with flammable gas												
D	Lighters for cigars, cigarettes, etc., with lighter fluids	3	NA1226	II	FLAMMABLE LIQUID	N10	None	21	None	Forbidden	Forbidden	B	

Sym-bols	Hazardous materials descriptions and proper shipping names	Hazard class or Division	Identifi-cation Numbers	Packing group	Label(s) required (if not excepted)	Special provisions	(8) Packaging authorizations (§173.***)			(9) Quantity limitations		(10) Vessel stowage requirements	
							Excep-tions	Non-bulk pack-aging	Bulk pack-aging	Passenger aircraft or railcar	Cargo aircraft only	Vessel stow-ages	Other stowage provisions
(1)	(2)	(3)	(4)	(5)	(6)	(7)	(8A)	(8B)	(8C)	(9A)	(9B)	(10A)	(10B)
	Lighters, fuse	1.4S	UN0131	II	EXPLOSIVE 1.4S		None	62	None	25 kg	100 kg	A	9E
	Lighters or Lighter refills (cigarettes) containing flammable gas	2.1	UN1057		FLAMMABLE GAS	N10	None	21, 308	None	1 kg	15 kg	B	40
	Lime, unslaked, see Calcium oxide												
	Liquefied gases, non-flammable charged with nitrogen, carbon dioxide or air	2.2	UN1058		NONFLAMMABLE GAS		306	304	None	75 kg	150 kg	A	
	Liquefied hydrocarbon gas, see Hydrocarbon gases, liquefied, n.o.s., etc.												
	Liquefied natural gas, see Methane, etc. (UN 1972)												
	Liquefied petroleum gas see Petroleum gases, liquefied												
	Lithium	4.3	UN1415	II	DANGEROUS WHEN WET	A7, A19, N45	None	212	244	Forbidden	50 kg	E	
	Lithium acetylide ethylenediamine complex, see Substances which in contact with water emit flammable gases												
	Lithium alkyls	4.2	UN2445	I	SPONTANEOUSLY COMBUSTIBLE	B11, T28, T40	None	181	244	Forbidden	Forbidden	D	
	Lithium aluminum hydride	4.3	UN1410	I	DANGEROUS WHEN WET	A19, N40	None	211	242	Forbidden	15 kg	E	
	Lithium aluminum hydride, ethereal	4.3	UN1411	I	DANGEROUS WHEN WET, FLAMMABLE LIQUID	A2, A3, A11, N34	None	201	244	Forbidden	1 L	D	40
	Lithium batteries, contained in equipment	9	UN3091	II	CLASS 9	18, A12	None	185	None	See A12	See A12	A	
	Lithium battery, liquid cathode	9	UN3090	II	CLASS 9	A12	None	185	None	See A12	0.5 kg	A	
	Lithium battery, solid cathode	9	UN3090	II	CLASS 9	A12	None	185	None	See A12	0.5 kg	A	
	Lithium borohydride	4.3	UN1413	I	DANGEROUS WHEN WET	A19, N40	None	211	242	Forbidden	15 kg	E	
	Lithium ferrosilicon	4.3	UN2830	II	DANGEROUS WHEN WET	A19	None	212	241	15 kg	50 kg	E	40, 85, 103
	Lithium hydride	4.3	UN1414	I	DANGEROUS WHEN WET	A19, N40	None	211	242	Forbidden	15 kg	E	
	Lithium hydride, fused solid	4.3	UN2805	II	DANGEROUS WHEN WET	A8, A19, A20	None	212	241	15 kg	50 kg	E	
	Lithium hydroxide, monohydrate or Lithium hydroxide, solid	8	UN2680	II	CORROSIVE		154	212	240	15 kg	50 kg	A	
	Lithium hydroxide, solution	8	UN2679	II	CORROSIVE	B2, T8	154	202	242	1 L	30 L	A	96
	Lithium hypochlorite, dry or Lithium hypochlorite mixtures, dry	5.1	UN1471	II	OXIDIZER	A9, N34	152	212	240	5 kg	25 kg	A	13, 48, 56, 58, 69, 106, 116
	Lithium in cartridges, see Lithium												
	Lithium nitrate	5.1	UN2722	III	OXIDIZER	A1	152	213	240	25 kg	100 kg	A	
	Lithium nitride	4.3	UN2806	I	DANGEROUS WHEN WET	A19, N40	None	211	242	Forbidden	15 kg	E	
	Lithium peroxide	5.1	UN1472	II	OXIDIZER	A9, N34	152	212	None	5 kg	25 kg	A	13, 75, 106
	Lithium silicon	4.3	UN1417	II	DANGEROUS WHEN WET	A19, A20	None	212	241	15 kg	50 kg	A	85, 103
	LNG, see Methane etc. (UN 1972)												
	London Purple	6.1	UN1621	II	POISON		None	212	242	25 kg	100 kg	A	
	LPG, see Petroleum gases, liquefied												
	Lye, see Sodium hydroxide, solutions												
	Magnesium alkyls	4.2	UN3053	I	SPONTANEOUSLY COMBUSTIBLE	B11, T28, T29, T40	None	181	244	Forbidden	Forbidden	D	18
	Magnesium aluminum phosphide	4.3	UN1419	I	DANGEROUS WHEN WET, POISON	A19, N34, N40	None	211	242	Forbidden	15 kg	E	40, 85
+	Magnesium arsenate	6.1	UN1622	II	POISON		None	212	242	25 kg	100 kg	A	
	Magnesium bisulfite solution, see Bisulfites, inorganic aqueous solutions, n.o.s.												
	Magnesium bromate	5.1	UN1473	II	OXIDIZER	A1	152	212	242	5 kg	25 kg	A	56, 58, 106
	Magnesium chlorate	5.1	UN2723	II	OXIDIZER		152	212	242	5 kg	25 kg	A	56, 58, 106
	Magnesium diamide	4.2	UN2004	II	SPONTANEOUSLY COMBUSTIBLE	A8, A19, A20	None	212	241	15 kg	50 kg	C	
	Magnesium diphenyl	4.2	UN2005	I	SPONTANEOUSLY COMBUSTIBLE		None	187	244	Forbidden	Forbidden	C	
	Magnesium dross, wet or hot	Forbid-den											
	Magnesium fluorosilicate	6.1	UN2853	III	KEEP AWAY FROM FOOD		153	213	240	100 kg	200 kg	A	26
	Magnesium granules, coated particle size not less than 149 microns	4.3	UN2950	III	DANGEROUS WHEN WET	A1, A19	None	213	240	25 kg	100 kg	A	
	Magnesium hydride	4.3	UN2010	I	DANGEROUS WHEN WET	A19, N40	None	211	242	Forbidden	15 kg	E	

328

(1) Sym-bols	(2) Hazardous materials descriptions and proper shipping names	(3) Hazard class or Division	(4) Identifi-cation Numbers	(5) Packing group	(6) Label(s) required (if not excepted)	(7) Special provisions	(8) Packaging authorizations (§173.***)			(9) Quantity limitations		(10) Vessel stowage requirements	
							(8A) Excep-tions	(8B) Non-bulk pack-aging	(8C) Bulk pack-aging	(9A) Passenger aircraft or railcar	(9B) Cargo aircraft only	(10A) Vessel stow-ages	(10B) Other stowage provisions
	Magnesium or Magnesium alloys with more than 50 per cent magnesium in pellets, turnings or ribbons	4.1	UN1869	III	FLAMMABLE SOLID	A1	151	213	240	25 kg	100 kg	A	39
	Magnesium nitrate	5.1	UN1474	III	OXIDIZER	A1, T2	152	213	240	25 kg	100 kg	A	
	Magnesium perchlorate	5.1	UN1475	II	OXIDIZER	T8	152	212	242	5 kg	25 kg	A	56, 58, 106
	Magnesium peroxide	5.1	UN1476	II	OXIDIZER		152	212	242	5 kg	25 kg	A	13, 75, 106
	Magnesium phosphide	4.3	UN2011	I	DANGEROUS WHEN WET, POISON	A19, N40	None	211	None	Forbidden	15 kg	E	40, 85
	Magnesium, powder or Magnesium alloys, powder	4.3	UN1418	II	DANGEROUS WHEN WET, SPONTANEOUSLY COMBUSTIBLE	A19, B56	None	212	241	15 kg	50 kg	A	39
	Magnesium scrap, see Magnesium, etc. (UN 1869)												
	Magnesium silicide	4.3	UN2624	II	DANGEROUS WHEN WET	A19, A20	None	212	241	15 kg	50 kg	B	85, 103
	Magnetized material, see section 173.21												
D	Maleic acid	8	NA2215	III	CORROSIVE		154	213	240	25 kg	100 kg	A	
	Maleic anhydride	8	UN2215	III	CORROSIVE	T7	154	213	240	25 kg	100 kg	A	
	Malononitrile	6.1	UN2647	II	POISON		None	212	242	25 kg	100 kg	A	12
	Maneb or Maneb preparations with not less than 60 per cent maneb	4.2	UN2210	III	SPONTANEOUSLY COMBUSTIBLE, DANGEROUS WHEN WET	A1, A19	None	213	242	25 kg	100 kg	A	34
	Maneb stabilized or Maneb preparations, stabilized against self-heating	4.3	UN2968	III	DANGEROUS WHEN WET	A1, A19	None	213	242	25 kg	100 kg	B	34
	Manganese nitrate	5.1	UN2724	III	OXIDIZER	A1	152	213	240	25 kg	100 kg	A	
	Manganese resinate	4.1	UN1330	III	FLAMMABLE SOLID	A1	151	213	240	25 kg	100 kg	A	
	Mannitan tetranitrate	Forbid-den											
	Mannitol hexanitrate (dry)	Forbid-den											
D	Mannitol hexanitrate (Nitromannite), wetted with not less than 40 percent water, by mass or mixture of alcohol and water	1.1A	NA0133	II	EXPLOSIVE 1.1A	111	None	62	None	Forbidden	Forbidden	E	1E, 5E
	Matches, block, see Matches, 'strike anywhere'												
	Matches, fusee	4.1	UN2254	III	FLAMMABLE SOLID		186	186	None	Forbidden	Forbidden	A	
	Matches, safety (book, card or strike on box)	4.1	UN1944	III	FLAMMABLE SOLID		186	186	None	25 kg	100 kg	A	
	Matches, strike anywhere	4.1	UN1331	III	FLAMMABLE SOLID		186	186	None	Forbidden	Forbidden	B	
	Matches, wax, Vesta	4.1	UN1945	III	FLAMMABLE SOLID		186	186	None	25 kg	100 kg	B	
	Matting acid, see Sulfuric acid												
D	Medicines, corrosive, liquid, n.o.s.	8	NA1760	II	CORROSIVE	B3	154	202	242	1 L	30 L	B	40
				III	CORROSIVE		154	203	241	5 L	60 L	A	40
D	Medicines, corrosive, solid, n.o.s.	8	NA1759	II	CORROSIVE		154	212	240	15 kg	50 kg	A	
				III	CORROSIVE		154	213	240	25 kg	100 kg	A	
D	Medicines, flammable, liquid, n.o.s.	3	NA1993	I	FLAMMABLE LIQUID		150	201	243	1 L	30 L	E	
				II	FLAMMABLE LIQUID		150	202	242	5 L	60 L	B	
				III	FLAMMABLE LIQUID	B1	150	203	242	60 L	220 L	A	
D	Medicines, flammable, solid, n.o.s.	4.1	NA1325	II	FLAMMABLE SOLID		151	212	240	15 kg	50 kg	B	
D	Medicines, oxidizing substance, solid, n.o.s.	5.1	NA1479	II	OXIDIZER		152	212	242	5 kg	25 kg	B	56, 58, 69, 106
D	Medicines, poisonous, liquid, n.o.s.	6.1	NA2810	I	POISON		153	201	243	1 L	30 L	B	40
				II	POISON		153	202	243	5 L	60 L	B	40
				III	KEEP AWAY FROM FOOD		153	203	241	60 L	220 L	A	40
D	Medicines, poisonous, solid, n.o.s.	6.1	NA2811	I	POISON		153	211	242	5 kg	50 kg	B	
				II	POISON		153	212	242	25 kg	100 kg	B	
				III	KEEP AWAY FROM FOOD		153	213	240	100 kg	200 kg	A	
	Memtetrahydrophthalic anhydride, see Corrosive liquids, n.o.s.												
	Mercaptans, liquid, n.o.s. or Mercaptan mixtures, liquid, n.o.s.	3	UN1228	II	FLAMMABLE LIQUID, POISON	T14	None	202	243	Forbidden	60 L	B	40, 95, 102
	Mercaptans, liquid n.o.s. or Mercaptan mixtures, liquid, n.o.s., flash point not less than 23 degrees C	6.1	UN3071	II	POISON, FLAMMABLE LIQUID	T14	None	202	243	5 L	60 L	C	40, 121
	5-Mercaptotetrazol-1-acetic acidd	1.4C	UN0448	II	EXPLOSIVE 1.4C		None	62	None	Forbidden	75 kg	E	1E, 5E

329

(1) Sym-bols	(2) Hazardous materials descriptions and proper shipping names	(3) Hazard class or Division	(4) Identifi-cation Numbers	(5) Packing group	(6) Label(s) required (If not excepted)	(7) Special provisions	(8A) Excep-tions	(8B) Non-bulk pack-aging	(8C) Bulk pack-aging	(9A) Passenger aircraft or railcar	(9B) Cargo aircraft only	(10A) Vessel stow-ages	(10B) Other stowage provisions
	Mercuric arsenate	6.1	UN1623	II	POISON		None	212	242	25 kg	100 kg	A	
	Mercuric chloride	6.1	UN1624	II	POISON		None	212	242	25 kg	100 kg	A	
	Mercuric compounds, see Mercury compounds, etc.												
	Mercuric nitrate	6.1	UN1625	II	POISON	N73	None	212	242	25 kg	100 kg	A	
+	Mercuric potassium cyanide	6.1	UN1626	I	POISON	N74, N75	None	211	242	5 kg	50 kg	A	26
	Mercuric sulfocyanate, see Mercury thiocyanate												
	Mercurol, see Mercury nucleate												
	Mercurous azide	Forbid-den											
	Mercurous compounds, see Mercury compounds, etc.												
	Mercurous nitrate	6.1	UN1627	II	POISON		None	212	242	25 kg	100 kg	A	
A W	Mercury	8	UN2809	III	CORROSIVE		164	164	240	35 kg	35 kg	B	40, 97
	Mercury acetate	6.1	UN1629	II	POISON		None	212	242	25 kg	100 kg	A	
	Mercury acetylide	Forbid-den											
	Mercury ammonium chloride	6.1	UN1630	II	POISON		None	212	242	25 kg	100 kg	A	
	Mercury based pesticides, liquid, flammable, toxic, n.o.s. *flash point less than 23 deg C*	3	UN2778	I	FLAMMABLE LIQUID, POISON		None	201	243	Forbidden	30 L	B	40
				II	FLAMMABLE LIQUID, POISON		None	202	243	1 L	60 L	B	40
	Mercury based pesticides, liquid, toxic, flammable, n.o.s. *flashpoint not less than 23 degrees C*	6.1	UN3011	I	POISON, FLAMMABLE LIQUID	T42	None	201	243	1 L	30 L	B	40
				II	POISON, FLAMMABLE LIQUID	T14	None	202	243	5 L	60 L	B	40
				III	KEEP AWAY FROM FOOD, FLAMMABLE LIQUID	T14	153	202	241	60 L	220 L	A	40
	Mercury based pesticides, liquid, toxic, n.o.s.	6.1	UN3012	I	POISON	T42	None	201	243	1 L	30 L	B	40
				II	POISON	T14	None	202	243	5 L	60 L	B	40
				III	KEEP AWAY FROM FOOD	T14	153	203	241	60 L	220 L	A	40
	Mercury based pesticides, solid, toxic, n.o.s.	6.1	UN2777	I	POISON		None	211	242	5 kg	50 kg	A	40
				II	POSION		None	212	242	25 kg	100 kg	A	40
				III	KEEP AWAY FROM FOOD		153	213	240	100 kg	200 kg	A	40
	Mercury benzoate	6.1	UN1631	II	POISON		None	212	242	25 kg	100 kg	A	
	Mercury bromides	6.1	UN1634	II	POISON		None	212	242	25 kg	100 kg	A	
	Mercury compounds, liquid, n.o.s.	6.1	UN2024	I	POISON		None	201	243	1 L	30 L	B	40
				II	POISON		None	202	243	5 L	60 L	B	40
				III	KEEP AWAY FROM FOOD		153	203	241	60 L	220 L	B	40
	Mercury compounds, solid, n.o.s.	6.1	UN2025	I	POISON		None	211	242	5 kg	50 kg	A	
				II	POISON		None	212	242	25 kg	100 kg	A	
				III	KEEP AWAY FROM FOOD		153	213	240	100 kg	200 kg	A	
A	Mercury contained in manufactured articles	8	UN2809	I	CORROSIVE		None	164	None	No limit	No limit	B	40
	Mercury cyanide	6.1	UN1636	II	POISON	N74, N75	None	212	242	25 kg	100 kg	A	26
	Mercury fulminate, wetted *with not less than 20 per cent water, or mixture of alcohol and water, by mass*	1.1A	UN0135	II	EXPLOSIVE 1.1A	111, 117	None	62	None	Forbidden	Forbidden	E	2E, 6E
	Mercury gluconate	6.1	UN1637	II	POISON		None	212	242	25 kg	100 kg	A	
	Mercury iodide	6.1	UN1638	II	POISON		None	212	242	25 kg	100 kg	A	
	Mercury iodide aquabasic ammonobasic (iodide of Millon's base)	Forbid-den											
	Mercury iodide, solution	6.1	UN1638	II	POISON		None	202	243	5 L	60 L	A	
	Mercury nitride	Forbid-den											
	Mercury nucleate	6.1	UN1639	II	POISON		None	212	242	25 kg	100 kg	A	
	Mercury oleate	6.1	UN1640	II	POISON		None	212	242	25 kg	100 kg	A	
	Mercury oxide	6.1	UN1641	II	POISON		None	212	242	25 kg	100 kg	A	
	Mercury oxycyanide	Forbid-den											
	Mercury oxycyanide, desensitized	6.1	UN1642	II	POISON		None	212	242	25 kg	100 kg	A	26, 91
	Mercury potassium iodide	6.1	UN1643	II	POISON		None	212	242	25 kg	100 kg	A	
	Mercury salicylate	6.1	UN1644	II	POISON		None	212	242	25 kg	100 kg	A	
+	Mercury sulfates	6.1	UN1645	II	POISON		None	212	242	25 kg	100 kg	A	
	Mercury thiocyanate	6.1	UN1646	II	POISON		None	212	242	25 kg	100 kg	A	
	Mesityl oxide	3	UN1229	III	FLAMMABLE LIQUID	B1, T1	None	203	242	60 L	220 L	A	
	Metal alkyl halides, n.o.s.	4.2	UN3049	I	SPONTANEOUSLY COMBUSTIBLE	B9, B11, T28, T29, T40	None	181	244	Forbidden	Forbidden	D	

330

Sym-bols	Hazardous materials descriptions and proper shipping names	Hazard class or Division	Identi-fi-cation Numbers	Packing group	Label(s) required (if not excepted)	Special provisions	(8) Packaging authorizations (§173.***)			(9) Quantity limitations		(10) Vessel stowage requirements	
							Excep-tions	Non-bulk pack-aging	Bulk pack-aging	Passenger aircraft or railcar	Cargo aircraft only	Vessel stow-ages	Other stowage provisions
(1)	(2)	(3)	(4)	(5)	(6)	(7)	(8A)	(8B)	(8C)	(9A)	(9B)	(10A)	(10B)
	Metal alkyl hydrides, n.o.s.	4.2	UN3050	I	SPONTANEOUSLY COMBUSTIBLE	B9, B11, T28, T29, T40	None	181	244	Forbidden	Forbidden	D	
D	Metal alkyl, solution, n.o.s.	3	NA9195	II	FLAMMABLE LIQUID		150	202	242	1 L	4 L	B	
	Metal alkyls, n.o.s.	4.2	UN2003	I	SPONTANEOUSLY COMBUSTIBLE	B11, T42	None	181	244	Forbidden	Forbidden	D	
	Metal catalyst, dry	4.2	UN2881	I	SPONTANEOUSLY COMBUSTIBLE	N34	None	187	None	Forbidden	Forbidden	B	
	Metal catalyst, wetted with not less than 40 per cent water or other suitable liquid, by mass, finely divided, activated or spent	4.2	UN1378	II	SPONTANEOUSLY COMBUSTIBLE	A2, A8, N34	None	212	None	Forbidden	50 kg	C	
	Metal powders, flammable, n.o.s.	4.1	UN3089	II	FLAMMABLE SOLID		151	212	240	15 kg	50 kg	B	
				III	FLAMMABLE SOLID		151	212	140	25 kg	100 kg	B	
	Metal salts of methyl nitramine (dry)	Forbid-den											
	Metaldehyde	4.1	UN1332	III	FLAMMABLE SOLID	A1	151	213	240	25 kg	100 kg	A	
	Methacrylaldehyde	3	UN2396	II	FLAMMABLE LIQUID, POISON	T8	None	202	243	1 L	60 L	E	40
	Methacrylic acid, inhibited	8	UN2531	III	CORROSIVE	T8	154	203	241	5 L	60 L	A	8, 12, 48
	Methacrylonitrile, inhibited	3	UN3079	I	FLAMMABLE LIQUID, POISON		None	201	243	Forbidden	30 L	D	12, 40, 48
	Methallyl alcohol	3	UN2614	III	FLAMMABLE LIQUID	B1, T1	150	203	242	60 L	220 L	A	
	Methane and hydrogen, mixtures, see Hydrogen and methane, mixtures, etc.												
	Methane, compressed or Natural gas, compressed (with high methane content)	2.1	UN1971		FLAMMABLE GAS		306	302	302	Forbidden	150 kg	E	40
	Methane, refrigerated liquid (cryogenic liquid)or Natural gas, refrigerated liquid (cryogenic liquid)(with high methane content)	2.1	UN1972		FLAMMABLE GAS		None	None	318	Forbidden	Forbidden	D	40
	Methanol, or Methyl alcohol	3	UN1230	II	FLAMMABLE LIQUID, POISON	T8	None	202	243	1 L	60 L	B	40
	Methazoic acid	Forbid-den											
	4-Methoxy-4-methylpentan-2-one	3	UN2293	III	FLAMMABLE LIQUID	B1, T1	150	203	242	60 L	220 L	A	
	1-Methoxy-2-proponal	3	UN3092	III	FLAMMABLE LIQUID	B1, T1	150	203	242	60 L	220 L	A	44
+	Methoxymethyl isocyanate	3	UN2605	I	FLAMMABLE LIQUID, POISON	1, B9, B14, B30, B72, T38, T43, T44	None	226	244	Forbidden	30 L	D	40
	Methyl acetate	3	UN1231	II	FLAMMABLE LIQUID	T8	150	202	242	5 L	60 L	B	
	Methyl acrylate, inhibited	3	UN1919	II	FLAMMABLE LIQUID	T8	150	202	242	5 L	60 L	B	
	Methyl alcohol, see Methanol												
	Methyl allyl chloride	3	UN2554	II	FLAMMABLE LIQUID	T8	150	202	242	5 L	60 L	E	
	Methyl amyl ketone, see Amyl methyl ketone												
	Methyl benzoate	6.1	UN2938	III	KEEP AWAY FROM FOOD	T1	153	203	240	60 L	220 L	A	
	Methyl bromide	2.3	UN1062		POISON GAS	3, B14	None	193	314, 315	Forbidden	25 kg	D	40
	Methyl bromide and chloropicrin mixtures with more than 2 per cent chloropicrin, see Chloropicrin and methyl bromide mixtures												
	Methyl bromide and chloropicrin mixtures with not more than 2 per cent chloropicrin, see Methyl bromide												
	Methyl bromide and ethylene dibromide mixtures, liquid	6.1	UN1647	I	POISON	2, B9, B14, B32, B74, N65, T38, T43, T45	None	227	244	Forbidden	30 L	C	40
	Methyl bromoacetate	6.1	UN2643	II	POISON	T8	None	202	243	5 L	60 L	D	40
	3-Methyl-1-butene	3	UN2561	I	FLAMMABLE LIQUID	T20	None	201	243	1 L	30 L	E	
	2-Methyl-1-butene	3	UN2459	I	FLAMMABLE LIQUID	T14	None	201	243	1 L	30 L	E	
	2-Methyl-2-butene	3	UN2460	II	FLAMMABLE LIQUID	T14	None	202	242	5 L	60 L	E	
	Methyl tert butyl ether	3	UN2398	II	FLAMMABLE LIQUID	T14	150	202	242	5 L	60 L	E	
	Methyl butyrate	3	UN1237	II	FLAMMABLE LIQUID	T1	150	202	242	5 L	60 L	B	
	Methyl chloride	2.1	UN1063		FLAMMABLE GAS		306	304	314, 315	Forbidden	25 kg	D	40
	Methyl chloride and chloropicrin mixtures, see Chloropicrin and methyl chloride mixtures												

331

Sym-bols	Hazardous materials descriptions and proper shipping names	Hazard class or Division	Identifi-cation Numbers	Packing group	Label(s) required (if not excepted)	Special provisions	Packaging authorizations (§173.***)			Quantity limitations		Vessel stowage requirements	
							Excep-tions	Non-bulk pack-aging	Bulk pack-aging	Passenger aircraft or railcar	Cargo aircraft only	Vessel stow-ages	Other stowage provisions
(1)	(2)	(3)	(4)	(5)	(6)	(7)	(8A)	(8B)	(8C)	(9A)	(9B)	(10A)	(10B)
	Methyl chloride and methylene chloride mixtures	2.1	UN1912		FLAMMABLE GAS		306	304	314, 315	Forbidden	150 kg	D	40
	Methyl chloroacetate	6.1	UN2295	II	POISON	T11	None	202	243	5 L	60 L	C	
	Methyl chlorocarbonate, see Methyl chloroformate												
	Methyl chloroform, see 1,1,1-Trichloroethane												
	Methyl chloroformate	6.1	UN1238	I	POISON, FLAMMABLE LIQUID, CORROSIVE	1, A3, A6, A7, B9, B14, B30, B72, N34, T38, T43, T44	None	226	244	Forbidden	Forbidden	D	21, 40, 100
	Methyl-2-chloropropionate	3	UN2933	III	FLAMMABLE LIQUID	B1, T7	150	203	242	60 L	220 L	A	
	Methyl cyanide	3	UN1648	II	FLAMMABLE LIQUID, POISON	T14	None	202	243	1 L	60 L	B	40
	Methyl cyclohexane	3	UN2296	II	FLAMMABLE LIQUID	B1, T1	150	202	242	5 L	60 L	B	
	Methyl cyclohexanols, *flash point not more than 60.5 degrees C*	3	UN2617	III	FLAMMABLE LIQUID	B1, T2	150	203	242	60 L	220 L	A	
	Methyl cyclohexanone	3	UN2297	III	FLAMMABLE LIQUID	B1, T1	150	203	242	60 L	220 L	A	
	Methyl cyclopentane	3	UN2298	II	FLAMMABLE LIQUID	T8	150	202	242	5 L	60 L	B	
	Methyl dichloroacetate	6.1	UN2299	III	KEEP AWAY FROM FOOD	T1	153	203	241	60 L	220 L	A	
	Methyl ethyl ether, see Ethyl methyl ether												
	Methyl ethyl ketone, see Ethyl methyl ketone												
	Methyl ethyl ketone peroxide, in solution with more than 9 per cent by mass active oxygen	Forbid-den											
	2-Methyl-5-ethylpyridine	6.1	UN2300	III	KEEP AWAY FROM FOOD	T7	153	203	241	60 L	220 L	A	
	Methyl fluoride	2.1	UN2454		FLAMMABLE GAS		306	304	314, 315	Forbidden	150 kg	E	40
	Methyl formate	3	UN1243	I	FLAMMABLE LIQUID	T20	150	201	243	1 L	30 L	E	
+	Methyl iodide	6.1	UN2644	II	POISON	2, B9, B14, B32, B74, T38, T43, T45	None	227	244	5 L	60 L	A	12, 40, 48
	Methyl isobutyl carbinol	3	UN2053	III	FLAMMABLE LIQUID	B1, T1	150	203	242	60 L	220 L	A	
	Methyl isobutyl ketone	3	UN1245	II	FLAMMABLE LIQUID	T1	150	202	242	5 L	60 L	B	
	Methyl isobutyl ketone peroxide, in solution with more than 9 per cent by mass active oxygen	Forbid-den											
	Methyl isocyanate	6.1	UN2480	I	POISON, FLAMMABLE LIQUID	1, A7, B9, B14, B30, B72, T38, T43, T44	None	226	244	Forbidden	Forbidden	D	26, 40
	Methyl isopropenyl ketone, inhibited	3	UN1246	II	FLAMMABLE LIQUID	T7	150	202	242	5 L	60 L	B	
+	Methyl isothiocyanate	3	UN2477	II	FLAMMABLE LIQUID, POISON	1, B9, B14, B30, B72, T38, T43, T44	None	226	244	Forbidden	60 L	A	
	Methyl isovalerate	3	UN2400	II	FLAMMABLE LIQUID	T1	150	202	242	5 L	60 L	B	
	Methyl magnesium bromide, in ethyl ether	4.3	UN1928	I	DANGEROUS WHEN WET, FLAMMABLE LIQUID		None	201	243	Forbidden	1 L	D	
	Methyl mercaptan	2.3	UN1064		POISON GAS, FLAMMABLE GAS	2, B7, B9, B14	None	304	314, 315	Forbidden	25 kg	D	40
	Methyl mercaptopropionaldehyde, see Thia-4-pentanal												
	Methyl methacrylate monomer, inhibited	3	UN1247	II	FLAMMABLE LIQUID	T8	150	202	242	5 L	60 L	B	40
	Methyl nitramine (dry)	Forbid-den											
	Methyl nitrate	Forbid-den											
	Methyl nitrite	Forbid-den											
	Methyl norbornene dicarboxylic anhydride, see Corrosive liquids, n.o.s.												
+	Methyl orthosilicate	3	UN2606	I	FLAMMABLE LIQUID, POISON	2, B9, B14, B32, B74, T38, T43, T45	None	227	244	Forbidden	30L	E	40
D	Methyl parathion *liquid*	6.1	NA3018	II	POISON	N76, T14	None	202	243	Forbidden	1 L	A	40
D	Methyl parathion *solid*	6.1	NA2783	II	POISON	N77	None	212	242	25 kg	100 kg	A	40
D	Methyl phosphonic dichloride	6.1	NA9206	I	POISON, CORROSIVE	2, A3, B9, B14, B32, B74, N34, N43, T38, T43, T45	None	227	244	Forbidden	Forbidden	C	

332

Sym-bols	Hazardous materials descriptions and proper shipping names	Hazard class or Division	Identifi-cation Numbers	Packing group	Label(s) required (if not excepted)	Special provisions	(8) Packaging authorizations (§173.***)			(9) Quantity limitations		(10) Vessel stowage requirements	
							Excep-tions	Non-bulk pack-aging	Bulk pack-aging	Passenger aircraft or railcar	Cargo aircraft only	Vessel stow-ages	Other stowage provisions
(1)	(2)	(3)	(4)	(5)	(6)	(7)	(8A)	(8B)	(8C)	(9A)	(9B)	(10A)	(10B)
	Methyl phosphonothioic dichloride, anhydrous, see Corrosive liquid, n.o.s.												
D	Methyl phosphonous dichloride, pyrophoric liquid	6.1	NA2845	I	POISON, SPONTANEOUSLY COMBUSTIBLE	2, B9, B14, B16, B32, B74, T38, T43, T45	None	227	244	Forbidden	Forbidden	D	18
	Methyl picric acid (heavy metal salts of)	Forbid-den											
	Methyl propionate	3	UN1248	II	FLAMMABLE LIQUID	T2	150	202	242	5 L	60 L	B	
	Methyl propyl ether	3	UN2612	II	FLAMMABLE LIQUID	T14	150	202	242	5 L	60 L	E	40
	Methyl propyl ketone	3	UN1249	II	FLAMMABLE LIQUID	T1	150	202	242	5 L	60 L	B	
	Methyl sulfate, see Dimethyl sulfate												
	Methyl sulfide, see Dimethyl sulfide												
	Methyl trichloroacetate	6.1	UN2533	III	KEEP AWAY FROM FOOD	T1	153	203	241	60 L	220 L	A	
	Methyl trimethylol methane trinitrate	Forbid-den											
	Methyl vinyl ketone	3	UN1251	II	FLAMMABLE LIQUID	T8	150	202	242	5 L	60 L	B	
	Methylacetylene and propadiene mixtures, stabilized	2.1	UN1060		FLAMMABLE GAS		306	304	314, 315	Forbidden	150 kg	B	40
	Methylal	3	UN1234	II	FLAMMABLE LIQUID	T14	None	202	242	5L	60 L	E	
	Methylamine, anhydrous	2.3	UN1061		POISON GAS, FLAMMABLE GAS	3, B14	None	304	314, 315	Forbidden	150 kg	B	40
	Methylamine, aqueous solution	3	UN1235	II	FLAMMABLE LIQUID, CORROSIVE	B1, T8	150	202	242	5 L	60 L	E	41
	Methylamine dinitramine and dry salts thereof	Forbid-den											
	Methylamine nitroform	Forbid-den											
	Methylamine perchlorate (dry)	Forbid-den											
	Methylamyl acetate	3	UN1233	III	FLAMMABLE LIQUID	B1, T1	150	203	242	60 L	220 L	A	
	N-Methylaniline	6.1	UN2294	III	KEEP AWAY FROM FOOD	T7	153	203	241	60 L	220 L	A	
	alpha-Methylbenzyl alcohol	6.1	UN2937	III	KEEP AWAY FROM FOOD	T1	153	203	241	60 L	220 L	A	
	3-Methylbutan-2-one	3	UN2397	II	FLAMMABLE LIQUID	T1	150	202	242	5 L	60 L	B	
	N-Methylbutylamine	3	UN2945	II	FLAMMABLE LIQUID	T8	150	202	242	5 L	60 L	B	40
	Methylchloromethyl ether	6.1	UN1239	I	POISON, FLAMMABLE LIQUID	1, B9, B14, B30, B72, T38, T43, T44	None	226	244	Forbidden	Forbidden	D	40
	Methylchlorosilane	2.3	UN2534		POISON GAS, FLAMMABLE GAS	2, A2, A3, A7, B9, B14, N34	None	226	314, 315	Forbidden	25 kg	D	40
D	Methyldichloroarsine	6.1	NA1556	I	POISON	2	None	192	None	Forbidden	Forbidden	D	40, 95
	Methyldichlorosilane	4.3	UN1242	I	DANGEROUS WHEN WET, CORROSIVE, FLAMMABLE LIQUID	A2, A3, A7, B6, B77, N34, T16, T26	None	201	243	Forbidden	1 L	D	21, 28, 40, 49, 100
	Methylene chloride, see Dichloromethane												
	Methylene glycol dinitrate	Forbid-den											
	2-Methylfuran	3	UN2301	II	FLAMMABLE LIQUID	T7	150	202	242	5 L	60 L	E	
	a-Methylglucoside tetranitrate	Forbid-den											
	a-Methylglycerol trinitrate	Forbid-den											
	5-Methylhexan-2-one	3	UN2302	III	FLAMMABLE LIQUID	B1, T1	150	203	242	60 L	220 L	A	
	Methylhydrazine	6.1	UN1244	I	POISON, FLAMMABLE LIQUID, CORROSIVE	1, B9, B14, B30, B72, B77, N34, T38, T43, T44	None	227	244	Forbidden	Forbidden	D	21, 49, 100
	Methylmorpholine	3	UN2535	II	FLAMMABLE LIQUID, CORROSIVE	B6, T8	None	202	243	1 L	5 L	B	40
	Methylpentadienes	3	UN2461	II	FLAMMABLE LIQUID	T7	150	202	241	5 L	60 L	E	
	2-Methylpentan-2-ol	3	UN2560	III	FLAMMABLE LIQUID	B1, T1	150	203	242	60 L	220 L	A	

333

Sym-bols	Hazardous materials descriptions and proper shipping names	Hazard class or Division	Identifi-cation Numbers	Packing group	Label(s) required (If not excepted)	Special provisions	(8) Packaging authorizations (§173.***)			(9) Quantity limitations		(10) Vessel stowage requirements	
							Excep-tions	Non-bulk pack-aging	Bulk pack-aging	Passenger aircraft or railcar	Cargo aircraft only	Vessel stow-ages	Other stowage provisions
(1)	(2)	(3)	(4)	(5)	(6)	(7)	(8A)	(8B)	(8C)	(9A)	(9B)	(10A)	(10B)
	Methylpentanes, see Hexanes												
	Methylphenyldichlorosilane	8	UN2437	II	CORROSIVE	T8, T26	154	202	242	1 L	30 L	C	40
	1-Methylpiperidine	3	UN2399	II	FLAMMABLE LIQUID	T8	150	202	242	5 L	60 L	B	
	Methyltetrahydrofuran	3	UN2536	II	FLAMMABLE LIQUID	T7	150	202	242	5 L	60 L	B	
	Methyltrichlorosilane	3	UN1250	I	FLAMMABLE LIQUID, CORROSIVE	A7, B6, B77, N34, T14, T26	None	201	243	Forbidden	2.5 L	B	40
	alpha-Methylvaleraldehyde	3	UN2367	II	FLAMMABLE LIQUID	B1, T1	150	203	242	60 L	220 L	B	
	Mine rescue equipment containing carbon dioxide, see Carbon dioxide												
	Mines with bursting charge	1.1F	UN0136	II	EXPLOSIVE 1.1F		63(b)	62	None	Forbidden	Forbidden	E	
	Mines with bursting charge	1.1D	UN0137	II	EXPLOSIVE 1.1D		63(b)	62	None	Forbidden	Forbidden	B	3E, 7E
	Mines with bursting charge	1.2D	UN0138	II	EXPLOSIVE 1.2D		63(b)	62	None	Forbidden	Forbidden	B	3E, 7E
	Mines with bursting charge	1.2F	UN0294	II	EXPLOSIVE 1.2F		63(b)	62	None	Forbidden	Forbidden	E	
	Mixed acid, see Nitrating acid, mixtures etc.												
	Molybdenum pentachloride	8	UN2508	III	CORROSIVE	T8, T26	154	213	240	25 kg	100 kg	C	40
	Monochloroacetone (unstabilized)	Forbid-den											
	Monochloroethylene, see Vinyl chloride, inhibited												
	Monoethanolamine, see Ethanolamine, solutions												
	Monoethylamine, see Ethylamine												
	Morpholine	3	UN2054	III	FLAMMABLE LIQUID	B1, T1	150	203	242	60 L	220 L	A	
	Morpholine, aqueous, mixture, see Corrosive liquids, n.o.s.												
	Motor fuel anti-knock compounds see Motor fuel anti-knock mixtures												
+	Motor fuel anti-knock mixtures	6.1	UN1649	I	POISON, FLAMMABLE LIQUID	14, B9, B12, B90, T26, T39	None	201	244	Forbidden	30 L	E	40
	Motor spirit, see Gasoline												
	Motor vehicle, see Vehicles, self-propelled												
	Motorcycles, see Vehicles, self-propelled												
	Muriatic acid, see Hydrochloric acid solution												
	Musk xylene, see 5-tert-Butyl2,4,6-trinitro-m-xylene												
	Naphtha	3	UN2553	II	FLAMMABLE LIQUID	T8, T31	150	202	242	5 L	60 L	B	
				III	FLAMMABLE LIQUID	B1, T7, T30	150	203	242	60 L	220 L	A	
	Naphtha, petroleum	3	UN1255	I	FLAMMABLE LIQUID	T8	150	201	243	1 L	30 L	E	
				II	FLAMMABLE LIQUID	T8	150	202	242	5 L	60 L	B	
	Naphtha, solvent	3	UN1256	II	FLAMMABLE LIQUID	T8, T31	150	202	242	5 L	60 L	B	
				III	FLAMMABLE LIQUID	B1, T7, T30	150	203	242	60 L	220 L	A	
	Naphthalene, crude or refined	4.1	UN1334	III	FLAMMABLE SOLID	A1	151	213	240	25 kg	100 kg	A	
	Naphthalene diozonide	Forbid-den											
	Naphthalene, molten	4.1	UN2304	III	FLAMMABLE SOLID	A1, T8	151	213	241	25 kg	100 kg	C	
	Naphthyl amineperchlorate	Forbid-den											
	alpha-Naphthylamine	6.1	UN2077	III	KEEP AWAY FROM FOOD	T7	153	213	240	100 kg	200 kg	A	
	beta-Naphthylamine	6.1	UN1650	II	POISON	T12, T26	None	212	242	25 kg	100 kg	A	
	Naphthylthiourea	6.1	UN1651	II	POISON		None	212	242	25 kg	100 kg	A	
	Naphthylurea	6.1	UN1652	II	POISON		None	212	242	25 kg	100 kg	A	
	Natural gases (with high methane content), see Methane, etc. (UN 1971, UN 1972)												
	Natural gasoline	3	UN1257	I	FLAMMABLE LIQUID	T8	150	201	243	1 L	30 L	E	
				II	FLAMMABLE LIQUID	T8	150	202	242	5 L	60 L	E	
	Neohexane, see Hexanes												
	Neon, compressed	2.2	UN1065		NONFLAMMABLE GAS		306	302	302	75 kg	150 kg	A	
	Neon, refrigerated liquid (cryogenic liquid)	2.2	UN1913		NONFLAMMABLE GAS		320	316	None	50 kg	500 kg	B	

Sym-bols	Hazardous materials descriptions and proper shipping names	Hazard class or Division	Identifi-cation Numbers	Packing group	Label(s) required (If not excepted)	Special provisions	(8) Packaging authorizations (§173.***)			(9) Quantity limitations		(10) Vessel stowage requirements	
							Excep-tions	Non-bulk pack-aging	Bulk pack-aging	Passenger aircraft or railcar	Cargo aircraft only	Vessel stow-ages	Other stowage provisions
(1)	(2)	(3)	(4)	(5)	(6)	(7)	(8A)	(8B)	(8C)	(9A)	(9B)	(10A)	(10B)
	New explosive or explosive device, see sections 173.51 and 173.56												
	Nickel carbonyl	6.1	UN1259	I	POISON, FLAMMABLE LIQUID	1	None	198	None	Forbidden	Forbidden	D	18, 40
	Nickel cyanide	6.1	UN1653	II	POISON	N74, N75	None	212	242	25 kg	100 kg	A	26
	Nickel nitrate	5.1	UN2725	III	OXIDIZER	A1	152	213	240	25 kg	100 kg	A	
	Nickel nitrite	5.1	UN2726	III	OXIDIZER	A1	152	213	240	25 kg	100 kg	A	56, 58
	Nickel picrate	Forbid-den											
	Nicotine	6.1	UN1654	II	POISON		None	202	243	5 L	60 L	A	
	Nicotine compounds, liquid, n.o.s. or Nicotine preparations, liquid, n.o.s.	6.1	UN3144	I	POISON	A4, T42	None	201	243	1 L	30 L	B	40
				II	POISON	T14	None	202	243	5 L	60 L	B	40
				III	KEEP AWAY FROM FOOD	T7	153	203	241	60 L	220 L	B	40
	Nicotine compounds, solid, n.o.s. or Nicotine preparations, solid, n.o.s.	6.1	UN1655	I	POISON		None	211	242	5 kg	50 kg	B	
				II	POISON		None	212	242	25 kg	100 kg	A	
				III	KEEP AWAY FROM FOOD		153	213	240	100 kg	200 kg	A	
	Nicotine hydrochloride or Nicotine hydrochloride solution	6.1	UN1656	II	POISON		None	202	243	5 L	60 L	A	
	Nicotine salicylate	6.1	UN1657	II	POISON		None	212	242	25 kg	100 kg	A	
	Nicotine sulfate, *solid*	6.1	UN1658	II	POISON		None	212	242	25 kg	100 kg	A	
	Nicotine sulfate, *solution*	6.1	UN1658	II	POISON	T14	None	202	243	5 L	60 L	A	
	Nicotine tartrate	6.1	UN1659	II	POISON		None	212	242	25 kg	100 kg	A	
	Nitrated paper (unstable)	Forbid-den											
	Nitrates, inorganic, n.o.s.	5.1	UN1477	II	OXIDIZER		152	212	240	5 kg	25 kg	A	46
	Nitrates of diazonium compounds	Forbid-den											
	Nitrating acid mixtures spent *with not more than 50 per cent nitric acid*	8	UN1826	II	CORROSIVE	B2, T12, T27	None	158	242	Forbidden	30 L	D	40
	Nitrating acid mixtures, spent *with 50 per cent or more nitric acid*	8	UN1826	I	CORROSIVE, OXIDIZER	T12, T27	None	158	243	Forbidden	2.5 L	D	40, 66, 89
	Nitrating acid mixtures *with not more than 50 per cent nitric acid*	8	UN1796	II	CORROSIVE	B2, T12, T27	None	158	242	Forbidden	30 L	D	40
	Nitrating acid mixtures *with 50 per cent or more nitric acid*	8	UN1796	I	CORROSIVE, OXIDIZER	T12, T27	None	158	243	Forbidden	2.5 L	D	40, 66, 89
	Nitric acid *other than red fuming with more than 70 percent nitric acid*	8	UN2031	I	CORROSIVE	B12, B53, T9, T27	None	158	243	Forbidden	2.5 L	D	110, 111
	Nitric acid *other than red fuming, with not more than 70 percent nitric acid*	8	UN2031	II	CORROSIVE	B2, B12, B53, T9, T27	None	158	242	Forbidden	30 L	D	110, 111
+	Nitric acid, red fuming	8	UN2032	I	CORROSIVE, OXIDIZER, POISON	2, B9, B32, B74, T38, T43, T45	None	227	244	Forbidden	Forbidden	D	40, 66, 74, 89, 90, 95
	Nitric oxide	2.3	UN1660		POISON GAS	2, B12, B37, B46, B50, B60, B77	None	337	None	Forbidden	Forbidden	D	40
	Nitric oxide and dinitrogen tetroxide mixtures (Nitric oxide and nitrogen dioxide mixtures)	2.3	UN1975		POISON GAS, OXIDIZER	2, B7, B9, B12, B14, B45, B46, B61, B66, B67, B77	None	337	None	Forbidden	Forbidden	D	40
	Nitrites, inorganic, n.o.s.	5.1	UN2627	II	OXIDIZER	A33	152	212	None	5 kg	25 kg	A	46, 56, 58
	3-Nitro-4-chlorobenzotrifluoride	6.1	UN2307	II	POISON	T8	None	202	243	5 L	60 L	A	40
	6-Nitro-4-diazotoluene-3-sulfonic acid (dry)	Forbid-den											
	Nitro isobutane triol trinitrate	Forbid-den											
	N-Nitro-N-methylglycolamide nitrate	Forbid-den											
	2-Nitro-2-methylpropanol nitrate	Forbid-den											
	Nitro urea	1.1D	UN0147	II	EXPLOSIVE 1.1D		None	62	None	Forbidden	Forbidden	B	1E, 5E
	N-Nitroaniline	Forbid-den											
	Nitroanilines (o-; m-; p-;)	6.1	UN1661	II	POISON	T14	None	212	242	25 kg	100 kg	A	
	Nitroanisole	6.1	UN2730	III	KEEP AWAY FROM FOOD	T8	153	213	240	100 kg	200 kg	A	
	Nitrobenzene	6.1	UN1662	II	POISON	T14	None	202	243	5 L	60 L	A	40
	m-Nitrobenzene diazonium perchlorate	Forbid-den											
	Nitrobenzenesulfonic acid	8	UN2305	II	CORROSIVE		154	212	240	1 L	30 L	A	
	Nitrobenzol, see Nitrobenzene												
	5-Nitrobenzotriazol	1.1D	UN0385	II	EXPLOSIVE 1.1D		None	62	None	Forbidden	Forbidden	B	1E, 5E, 19E
	Nitrobenzotrifluorides	6.1	UN2306	II	POISON	T8	None	202	243	5 L	60 L	A	40
	Nitrobromobenzenes *liquid*	6.1	UN2732	III	KEEP AWAY FROM FOOD	T8, T38	153	203	241	60 L	220 L	A	48

Sym-bols	Hazardous materials descriptions and proper shipping names	Hazard class or Division	Identifi-cation Numbers	Packing group	Label(s) required (if not excepted)	Special provisions	(8) Packaging authorizations (§173.***)			(9) Quantity limitations		(10) Vessel stowage requirements	
							Excep-tions	Non-bulk pack-aging	Bulk pack-aging	Passenger aircraft or railcar	Cargo aircraft only	Vessel stow-ages	Other stowage provisions
(1)	(2)	(3)	(4)	(5)	(6)	(7)	(8A)	(8B)	(8C)	(9A)	(9B)	(10A)	(10B)
	Nitrobromobenzenes solid	6.1	UN2732	III	KEEP AWAY FROM FOOD		153	213	240	100 kg	200 kg	A	48
	Nitrocellulose, dry or wetted with less than 25 per cent water (or alcohol), by mass	1.1D	UN0340	II	EXPLOSIVE 1.1D		None	62	None	Forbidden	Forbidden	B	4E, 27E
	Nitrocellulose, plasticized with not less than 18 per cent plasticizing substance, by mass	1.3C	UN0343	II	EXPLOSIVE 1.3C		None	62	None	Forbidden	Forbidden	B	1E, 5E
	Nitrocellulose, solution, flammable with not more than 12.6 per cent nitrogen, by mass, and not more than 55 per cent nitrocellulose	3	UN2059	II	FLAMMABLE LIQUID	T8, T31	150	202	242	5 L	60 L	B	
				III	FLAMMABLE LIQUID	B1, T7, T30	150	203	242	60 L	220 L	A	
	Nitrocellulose, unmodified or plasticized with less than 18 per cent plasticizing substance, by mass	1.1D	UN0341	II	EXPLOSIVE 1.1D		None	62	None	Forbidden	Forbidden	B	4E, 27E
	Nitrocellulose, wetted with not less than 25 per cent alcohol, by mass	1.3C	UN0342	II	EXPLOSIVE 1.3C		None	62	None	Forbidden	Forbidden	B	1E, 5E
	Nitrocellulose with alcohol not less than 25 per cent alcohol by mass, and not more than 12.6 per cent nitrogen, by dry mass	4.1	UN2556	II	FLAMMABLE SOLID		151	212	None	1 kg	15 kg	D	28
	Nitrocellulose with plasticizing not less than 18 per cent, plasticizing substance, by mass, and not more than 12.6 per cent nitrogen, by dry mass	4.1	UN2557	II	FLAMMABLE SOLID		151	212	None	1 kg	15 kg	D	28
	Nitrocellulose with water not less than 25 per cent water, by mass	4.1	UN2555	II	FLAMMABLE SOLID		151	212	None	15 kg	50 kg	E	28
	Nitrochlorobenzene, see Chloronitrobenzenes etc.												
	Nitrocresols	6.1	UN2446	III	KEEP AWAY FROM FOODS		153	213	240	100 kg	200 kg	A	
	Nitroethane	3	UN2842	III	FLAMMABLE LIQUID	B1, T8	150	203	242	60 L	220 L	A	
	Nitroethyl nitrate	Forbid-den											
	Nitroethylene polymer	Forbid-den											
	Nitrogen, compressed	2.2	UN1066		NONFLAMMABLE GAS		306	302	314, 315	75 kg	150 kg	A	
	Nitrogen dioxide, liquefied see Dinitrogen tetroxide, liquefied												
	Nitrogen fertilizer solution, see Fertilizer ammoniating solution etc.												
	Nitrogen, mixtures with rare gases, see Rare gases and nitrogen mixtures												
	Nitrogen peroxide, see Dinitrogen tetroxide, liquefied												
	Nitrogen, refrigerated liquid (cryogenic liquid)	2.2	UN1977		NONFLAMMABLE GAS		320	316	318	50 kg	500 kg	A	
	Nitrogen tetroxide and nitric oxide mixtures, see Nitric oxide and nitrogen tetroxide mixtures												
	Nitrogen tetroxide, see Dinitrogen tetroxide, liquefied												
	Nitrogen trichloride	Forbid-den											
	Nitrogen trifluoride	2.2	UN2451		NONFLAMMABLE GAS, OXIDIZER		None	302	None	Forbidden	25 kg	D	40
	Nitrogen triiodide	Forbid-den											
	Nitrogen triiodide monoamine	Forbid-den											
	Nitrogen trioxide	2.3	UN2421		POISON GAS, OXIDIZER		None	336	245	Forbidden	Forbidden	D	40
	Nitroglycerin, desensitized with not less than 40 per cent non-volatile water insoluble phlegmatizer, by mass	1.1D	UN0143	II	EXPLOSIVE 1.1D, POISON		None	62	None	Forbidden	Forbidden	B	1E, 4E, 21E
	Nitroglycerin, liquid, not desensitized	Forbid-den											
	Nitroglycerin, solution in alcohol, with more than 1% but not more than 5% nitroglycerin	3	UN3064	II	FLAMMABLE LIQUID	N8	None	202	None	Forbidden	5 L	E	
	Nitroglycerin, solution in alcohol, with more than 1 percent but not more than 10 percent nitroglycerin	1.1D	UN0144	II	EXPLOSIVE 1.1D	20	None	62	None	Forbidden	Forbidden	B	1E, 4E, 21E
	Nitroglycerin solution in alcohol with not more than 1 per cent nitroglycerin	3	UN1204	II	FLAMMABLE LIQUID	N34, T25	None	202	None	5 L	60 L	B	
	Nitroguanidine nitrate	Forbid-den											

336

Sym-bols	Hazardous materials descriptions and proper shipping names	Hazard class or Division	Identifi-cation Numbers	Packing group	Label(s) required (if not excepted)	Special provisions	(8) Packaging authorizations (§173.***)			(9) Quantity limitations		(10) Vessel stowage requirements	
							Excep-tions	Non-bulk pack-aging	Bulk pack-aging	Passenger aircraft or railcar	Cargo aircraft only	Vessel stow-ages	Other stowage provisions
(1)	(2)	(3)	(4)	(5)	(6)	(7)	(8A)	(8B)	(8C)	(9A)	(9B)	(10A)	(10B)
	Nitroguanidine or Picrite, dry or wetted with less than 20 per cent water, by mass	1.1D	UN0282	II	EXPLOSIVE 1.1D		None	62	None	Forbidden	Forbidden	B	1E, 5E
	Nitroguanidine, wetted or Picrite, wetted with not less than 20 per cent water, by mass	4.1	UN1336	I	FLAMMABLE SOLID	A8, A19, A20, N41	None	211	None	1 kg	15 kg	E	28
	1-Nitrohydantoin	Forbid-den											
	Nitrohydrochloric acid	8	UN1798	I	CORROSIVE	A3, B10, N41, T18, T27	None	201	242	Forbidden	2.5 L	D	40, 66, 74, 89, 90
	Nitromannite (dry)	Forbid-den											
	Nitromannite, wetted, see Mannitol hexanitrate, etc.												
	Nitromethane	3	UN1261	II	FLAMMABLE LIQUID	T25	150	202	None	Forbidden	60 L	A	
	Nitromuriatic acid, see Nitrohydrochloric acid												
	Nitronaphthalene	4.1	UN2538	III	FLAMMABLE SOLID	A1	151	213	240	25 kg	100 kg	A	
	Nitrophenols (o-; m-; p-;)	6.1	UN1663	III	KEEP AWAY FROM FOOD	T8, T38	153	213	240	100 kg	200 kg	A	
	m-Nitrophenyldinitro methane	Forbid-den											
	Nitropropanes	3	UN2608	III	FLAMMABLE LIQUID	B1, T1	150	203	242	60 L	220 L	A	
	p-Nitrosodimethylaniline	4.2	UN1369	II	SPONTANEOUSLY COMBUSTIBLE	A19, A20, N34	None	212	241	15 kg	50 kg	D	34
D	Nitrosoguanidine	1.1A	NA0473	II	EXPLOSIVE 1.1A	111, 117	None	62	None	Forbidden	Forbidden	E	2E, 6E
	Nitrostarch, dry or wetted with less than 20 per cent water, by mass	1.1D	UN0146	II	EXPLOSIVE 1.1D		None	62	None	Forbidden	Forbidden	B	1E, 5E
	Nitrostarch, wetted with not less than 20 per cent water, by mass	4.1	UN1337	I	FLAMMABLE SOLID	A8, A19, A20, N41	None	211	None	1 kg	15 kg	D	28
	Nitrosugars (dry)	Forbid-den											
	Nitrosyl chloride	2.3	UN1069		POISON GAS, CORROSIVE	3, B14	None	304	314, 315	Forbidden	Forbidden	D	40
	Nitrosylsulfuric acid	8	UN2308	II	CORROSIVE	A3, A6, A7, B2, N34, T9, T27	154	202	242	1 L	30 L	D	40, 66, 74, 89, 90
	Nitrotoluenes, liquid o-; m-; p-;	6.1	UN1664	II	POISON	T14	None	202	243	5 L	60 L	A	
	Nitrotoluenes, solid m-, p-	6.1	UN1664	II	POISON	T14	None	212	242	25 kg	100 kg	A	
	Nitrotoluidines (mono)	6.1	UN2660	III	KEEP AWAY FROM FOOD		153	213	240	100 kg	200 kg	A	
	Nitrotriazolone or NTO	1.1D	UN0490	II	EXPLOSIVE 1.1D		None	62		Forbidden	Forbidden	B	1E, 5E, 25E
	Nitrous oxide and carbon dioxide mixtures, see Carbon dioxide and nitrous oxide mixtures												
	Nitrous oxide, compressed	2.2	UN1070		NONFLAMMABLE GAS		306	304	314, 315	75 kg	150 kg	A	40
	Nitrous oxide, refrigerated liquid	2.2	UN2201		NONFLAMMABLE GAS	B6	None	None	314, 315	75 kg	150 kg	B	40
	Nitroxylenes, (o-; m-; p-)	6.1	UN1665	II	POISON	T14	None	202	243	5 L	60 L	A	
	Nitroxylol, see Nitroxylenes												
	Nonanes	3	UN1920	III	FLAMMABLE LIQUID	B1, T1	150	203	242	60 L	220 L	A	
	Nonflammable gas, n.o.s., see Compressed or Liquefied gases, etc. (UN 1955, UN 1956)												
	Nonliquefied gases, see Compressed gases, etc.												
	Nonliquefied hydrocarbon gas, see Hydrocarbon gases, compressed, n.o.s.												
	Nonyltrichlorosilane	8	UN1799	II	CORROSIVE	A7, B2, B6, N34, T8, T26	None	202	242	Forbidden	30 L	C	40
	2,5 Norbornadiene (Dicycloheptadiene)	3	UN2251	II	FLAMMABLE LIQUID		150	202	241	5 L	60 L	D	
	Nordhausen acid, see Sulfuric acid, fuming etc.												
	Octadecyltrichlorosilane	8	UN1800	II	CORROSIVE	A7, B2, B6 N34, T8	None	202	242	Forbidden	30 L	C	40
	Octadiene	3	UN2309	II	FLAMMABLE LIQUID	B1, T1	150	202	242	5 L	60 L	B	
	1,7-Octadine-3,5-diyne-1,8-dimethoxy-9-octadecynoic acid	Forbid-den											
	Octafluorobut-2-ene	2.2	UN2422		NONFLAMMABLE GAS		None	304	314, 315	75 kg	150 kg	A	
	Octafluorocyclobutane, RC318	2.2	UN1976		NONFLAMMABLE GAS		None	304	314, 315	75 kg	150 kg	A	
	Octafluoropropane, R218	2.2	UN2424		NONFLAMMABLE GAS		None	304	314, 315	75 kg	150 kg	A	
	Octanes	3	UN1262	II	FLAMMABLE LIQUID	T1	150	202	242	5 L	60 L	B	

337

Symbols (1)	Hazardous materials descriptions and proper shipping names (2)	Hazard class or Division (3)	Identification Numbers (4)	Packing group (5)	Label(s) required (if not excepted) (6)	Special provisions (7)	Exceptions (8A)	Non-bulk packaging (8B)	Bulk packaging (8C)	Passenger aircraft or railcar (9A)	Cargo aircraft only (9B)	Vessel stowages (10A)	Other stowage provisions (10B)
	Octogen, see Cyclotetramethylene tetranitramine, etc.												
	Octolite or Octol, dry or wetted with less than 15 per cent water, by mass	1.1D	UN0266	II	EXPLOSIVE 1.1D		None	62		Forbidden	Forbidden	B	1E, 5E
	Octyl aldehydes, flammable	3	UN1191	III	FLAMMABLE LIQUID	B1, T1	150	203	242	60 L	220 L	A	
+	tert-Octylmercaptan	6.1	UN3023	II	POISON, FLAMMABLE LIQUID	2, B9, B14, B32, B74, T38, T43, T45	None	227	244	Forbidden	60 L	B	40
	Octyltrichlorosilane	8	UN1801	II	CORROSIVE	A7, B2, B6, N34, T8, T26	None	202	242	Forbidden	30 L	C	40
	Oil gas	2.1	UN1071		FLAMMABLE GAS		None	304	314, 315	Forbidden	150 kg	D	40
	Oleum, see Sulfuric acid, fuming												
	Organic peroxide type A, liquid or solid	Forbidden											
	Organic peroxide type B, liquid	5.2	UN3101	II	ORGANIC PEROXIDE EXPLOSIVE	53	None	225	None	Forbidden	Forbidden	D	12, 40
	Organic peroxide type B, liquid, temperature controlled	5.2	UN3111	II	ORGANIC PEROXIDE EXPLOSIVE	53	None	225	None	Forbidden	Forbidden	D	2, 40
	Organic peroxide type B, solid	5.2	UN3102	II	ORGANIC PEROXIDE EXPLOSIVE	53	None	225	None	Forbidden	Forbidden	D	12, 40
	Organic peroxide type B, solid, temperature controlled	5.2	UN3112	II	ORGANIC PEROXIDE EXPLOSIVE	53	None	225	None	Forbidden	Forbidden	D	2, 40
	Organic peroxide type C, liquid	5.2	UN3103	II	ORGANIC PEROXIDE		152	225	None	5 L	10 L	D	12, 40
	Organic peroxide type C, liquid, temperature controlled	5.2	UN3113	II	ORGANIC PEROXIDE		None	225	None	Forbidden	Forbidden	D	2, 40
	Organic peroxide type C, solid	5.2	UN3104	II	ORGANIC PEROXIDE		152	225	None	5 kg	10 kg	D	12, 40
	Organic peroxide type C, solid, temperature controlled	5.2	UN3114	II	ORGANIC PEROXIDE		None	225	None	Forbidden	Forbidden	D	2, 40
	Organic peroxide type D, liquid	5.2	UN3105	II	ORGANIC PEROXIDE		152	225	None	5 L	10 L	D	12, 40
	Organic peroxide type D, liquid, temperature controlled	5.2	UN3115	II	ORGANIC PEROXIDE		None	225	None	Forbidden	Forbidden	D	2, 40
	Organic peroxide type D, solid	5.2	UN3106	II	ORGANIC PEROXIDE		152	225	None	5 kg	10 kg	D	12, 40
	Organic peroxide type D, solid, temperature controlled	5.2	UN3116	II	ORGANIC PEROXIDE		None	225	None	Forbidden	Forbidden	D	2, 40
	Organic peroxide type E, liquid	5.2	UN3107	II	ORGANIC PEROXIDE		152	225	None	10 L	25 L	D	12, 40
	Organic peroxide type E, liquid, temperature controlled	5.2	UN3117	II	ORGANIC PEROXIDE		None	225	None	Forbidden	Forbidden	D	2, 40
	Organic peroxide type E, solid	5.2	UN3108	II	ORGANIC PEROXIDE		152	225	None	10 kg	25 kg	D	12, 40
	Organic peroxide type E, solid, temperature controlled	5.2	UN3118	II	ORGANIC PEROXIDE		None	225	None	Forbidden	Forbidden	D	2, 40
	Organic peroxide type F, liquid	5.2	UN3109	II	ORGANIC PEROXIDE		152	225	225	10 L	25 L	D	12, 40
	Organic peroxide type F, liquid, temperature controlled	5.2	UN3119	II	ORGANIC PEROXIDE		None	225	None	Forbidden	Forbidden	D	2, 40
	Organic peroxide type F, solid	5.2	UN3110	II	ORGANIC PEROXIDE	T42	152	225	None	10 kg	25 kg	D	12, 40
	Organic peroxide type F, solid, temperature controlled	5.2	UN3120	II	ORGANIC PEROXIDE		None	225	None	Forbidden	Forbidden	D	2, 40
D	Organic phosphate, Organic phosphate compound, or Organic phosphorus compound; mixed with compressed gas	2.3	NA1955		POISON GAS	3	None	334	None	Forbidden	Forbidden	D	40
	Organochlorine pesticides liquid, flammable, toxic, n.o.s. flash point less than 23 degrees C.	3	UN2762	I	FLAMMABLE LIQUID, POISON		None	201	243	Forbidden	30 L	B	
				II	FLAMMABLE LIQUID, POISON		None	202	243	1 L	60 L	B	
	Organochlorine pesticides, liquid, toxic, flammable, n.o.s. flashpoint not less than 23 degrees C.	6.1	UN2995	I	POISON, FLAMMABLE LIQUID	T42	None	201	243	1 L	30 L	B	40
				II	POISON, FLAMMABLE LIQUID	T14	None	202	243	5 L	60 L	B	40
				III	KEEP AWAY FROM FOOD, FLAMMABLE LIQUID	B1, T14	153	203	242	60 L	220 L	A	40
	Organochlorine pesticides, liquid, toxic, n.o.s.	6.1	UN2996	I	POISON	T42	None	201	243	1 L	30 L	B	40
				II	POISON	T14	None	202	242	5 L	60 L	B	40
				III	KEEP AWAY FROM FOOD	T14	153	203	241	60 L	220 L	A	40

Sym-bols	Hazardous materials descriptions and proper shipping names	Hazard class or Division	Identifi-cation Numbers	Packing group	Label(s) required (if not excepted)	Special provisions	Excep-tions	Non-bulk pack-aging	Bulk pack-aging	Passenger aircraft or railcar	Cargo aircraft only	Vessel stow-ages	Other stowage provisions
								(8) Packaging authorizations (§173.***)		(9) Quantity limitations		(10) Vessel stowage requirements	
(1)	(2)	(3)	(4)	(5)	(6)	(7)	(8A)	(8B)	(8C)	(9A)	(9B)	(10A)	(10B)
	Organochlorine pesticides, solid toxic n.o.s.	6.1	UN2761	I	POISON		None	211	242	5 kg	50 kg	A	40
				II	POISON		None	212	242	25 kg	100 kg	A	40
				III	KEEP AWAY FROM FOOD		153	213	240	100 kg	200 kg	A	40
	Organophosphorus pesticides, liquid, flammable, toxic, n.o.s., *flash point less than 23 degrees C.*	3	UN2784	I	FLAMMABLE LIQUID, POISON		None	201	243	Forbidden	30 L	B	
				II	FLAMMABLE LIQUID, POISON		None	202	243	1 L	60 L	B	
	Organophosphorus pesticides, liquid, toxic, flammable, n.o.s. *flashpoint not less than 23 degrees C.*	6.1	UN3017	I	POISON, FLAMMABLE LIQUID	N76, T42	None	201	243	1 L	30 L	B	40
				II	POISON, FLAMMABLE LIQUID	N76, T14	None	202	243	5 L	60 L	B	40
				III	KEEP AWAY FROM FOOD, FLAMMABLE LIQUID	B1, N76, T14	153	203	242	60 L	220 L	A	40
	Organophosphorus pesticides, liquid, toxic, n.o.s.	6.1	UN3018	I	POISON	N76, T42	None	201	243	1 L	30 L	B	40
				II	POISON	N76, T14	None	202	243	5 L	60 L	B	40
				III	KEEP AWAY FROM FOOD	N76, T14	153	203	241	60 L	220 L	A	40
	Organophosphorus pesticides, solid, toxic, n.o.s.	6.1	UN2783	I	POISON	N77	None	211	242	5 kg	50 kg	A	40
				II	POISON	N77	None	212	242	25 kg	100 kg	A	40
				III	KEEP AWAY FROM FOOD	N77	153	213	240	100 kg	200 kg	A	40
	Organotin compounds, liquid, n.o.s.	6.1	UN2788	I	POISON	A3, N33, N34, T42	None	201	243	1 L	30 L	B	40
				II	POISON	A3, N33, N34, T14	None	202	243	5 L	60 L	A	40
				III	KEEP AWAY FROM FOOD	T14	153	203	241	60 L	220 L	A	40
	Organotin compounds, solid, n.o.s.	6.1	UN3146	I	POISON	A5	None	211	242	5 kg	50 kg	B	40
				II	POISON		None	212	242	25 kg	100 kg	A	40
				III	KEEP AWAY FROM FOOD		153	213	240	100 kg	200 kg	A	40
	Organotin pesticides, liquid, flammable, toxic, n.o.s., *flash point less than 23deg C*	3	UN2787	I	FLAMMABLE LIQUID, POISON		None	201	243	Forbidden	30 L	B	
				II	FLAMMABLE LIQUID, POISON		None	202	243	1 L	60 L	B	
	Organotin pesticides, liquid, toxic, flammable, n.o.s. *flashpoint not less than 23 degrees C*	6.1	UN3019	I	POISON, FLAMMABLE LIQUID	T42	None	201	243	1 L	30 L	B	40
				II	POISON, FLAMMABLE LIQUID	T14	None	202	243	5 L	60 L	B	40
				III	KEEP AWAY FROM FOOD, FLAMMABLE LIQUID	B1, T14	153	203	242	60 L	220 L	A	40
	Organotin pesticides, liquid, toxic, n.o.s.	6.1	UN3020	I	POISON	T42	None	201	243	1 L	30 L	B	40
				II	POISON	T14	None	202	243	5 L	60 L	B	40
				III	KEEP AWAY FROM FOOD	T14	153	203	241	60 L	220 L	A	40
	Organotin pesticides, solid, toxic, n.o.s.	6.1	UN2786	I	POISON		None	211	242	5 kg	50 kg	A	40
				II	POISON		None	212	242	25 kg	100 kg	A	40
				III	KEEP AWAY FROM FOOD		153	213	240	100 kg	200 kg	A	40
	Orthonitroaniline, see Nitroanilines etc.												
	Osmium tetroxide	6.1	UN2471	I	POISON	A8, N33, N34	None	211	242	5 kg	50 kg	B	40
AD	Other regulated substances, liquid, n.o.s.	9	NA3082	III	CLASS 9		155	203	241	No limit	No limit	A	
AD	Other regulated substances, solid, n.o.s.	9	NA3077	III	CLASS 9		155	213	240	No limit	No limit	A	
	Oxalates, water soluble	6.1	UN2449	III	KEEP AWAY FROM FOOD		153	213	240	100 kg	200 kg	A	
	Oxidizing substances, liquid, corrosive, n.o.s.	5.1	UN3098	I	OXIDIZER, CORROSIVE		None	201	244	Forbidden	2.5 L	B	34, 56, 58, 69, 106
				II	OXIDIZER, CORROSIVE		None	202	243	1 L	5 L	D	34, 56, 58, 69, 106
				III	OXIDIZER, CORROSIVE		152	203	242	2.5 L	30 L	B	34, 56, 58, 69, 106
	Oxidizing substances, liquid, n.o.s.	5.1	UN3139	II	OXIDIZER	A2	152	202	242	1 L	5 L	B	56, 58, 69, 106
	Oxidizing substances, liquid, poisonous, n.o.s.	5.1	UN3099	I	OXIDIZER, POISON		None	201	244	Forbidden	2.5 L	D	56, 58, 95, 106
				II	OXIDIZER, POISON		None	202	243	1 L	5 L	B	56, 58, 95, 106
				III	OXIDIZER, KEEP AWAY FROM FOOD		152	203	242	2.5L	30L	B	56, 58, 95, 106

Symbols (1)	Hazardous materials descriptions and proper shipping names (2)	Hazard class or Division (3)	Identification Numbers (4)	Packing group (5)	Label(s) required (if not excepted) (6)	Special provisions (7)	(8) Packaging authorizations (§173.***) Exceptions (8A)	Non-bulk packaging (8B)	Bulk packaging (8C)	(9) Quantity limitations Passenger aircraft or railcar (9A)	Cargo aircraft only (9B)	(10) Vessel stowage requirements Vessel stowages (10A)	Other stowage provisions (10B)
	Oxidizing substances, solid, corrosive, n.o.s.	5.1	UN3085	I	OXIDIZER, CORROSIVE		None	211	242	1 kg	15 kg	D	13, 34, 56, 58, 69, 106
				II	OXIDIZER, CORROSIVE		None	212	242	5 kg	25 kg	B	13, 34, 56, 58, 69, 106
				III	OXIDIZER, CORROSIVE		152	213	240	25 kg	100 kg	B	13, 34, 56, 58, 69, 106
	Oxidizing substances, solid, flammable, n.o.s.	5.1	UN3137		OXIDIZER, FLAMMABLE SOLID		None	214	214	Forbidden	Forbidden		
	Oxidizing substances, solid, n.o.s.	5.1	UN1479	I	OXIDIZER		152	211	242	1 kg	15 kg	B	56, 58, 69, 106
				II	OXIDIZER		152	212	240	5 kg	25 kg	D	56, 58, 69, 106
				III	OXIDIZER		152	213	240	25 kg	100 kg	B	56, 58, 69, 106
	Oxidizing substances, solid, poisonous, n.o.s.	5.1	UN3087	I	OXIDIZER, POISON		None	211	242	1 kg	15 kg	D	56, 58, 69, 95, 106
				II	OXIDIZER, POISON		None	212	242	5 kg	25 kg	B	56, 58, 69, 95, 106
				III	OXIDIZER, KEEP AWAY FROM FOOD		152	213	240	25 kg	100 kg	B	56, 58, 69, 95, 106
	Oxidizing substances, solid, self heating, n.o.s.	5.1	UN3100		OXIDIZER, SPONTANEOUSLY COMBUSTIBLE		None	214	214	Forbidden	Forbidden		
	Oxidizing substances, solid, which in contact with water emit flammable gases, n.o.s.	5.1	UN3121		OXIDIZER, DANGEROUS WHEN WET		None	214	214	Forbidden	Forbidden		
	Oxygen and carbon dioxide mixtures, see Carbon dioxide and oxygen mixtures												
	Oxygen, compressed	2.2	UN1072		NONFLAMMABLE GAS, OXIDIZER		306	302	314, 315	75 kg	150 kg	A	
	Oxygen difluoride	2.3	UN2190		POISON GAS, OXIDIZER	1	None	304	None	Forbidden	Forbidden	D	13, 40
	Oxygen, mixtures with rare gases, see Rare gases and oxygen mixtures												
	Oxygen, refrigerated liquid (cryogenic liquid)	2.2	UN1073		NONFLAMMABLE GAS, OXIDIZER		320	316	318	Forbidden	Forbidden	D	
	Paint including paint, lacquer, enamel, stain, shellac solutions, varnish, polish, liquid filler, and liquid lacquer base	3	UN1263	II	FLAMMABLE LIQUID	B52, T7, T30	150	173	242	5 L	60 L	B	
				III	FLAMMABLE LIQUID	B1, B52, T7, T30	150	173	242	60 L	220 L	A	
	Paint or Paint related material	8	UN3066	II	CORROSIVE	B2, N71, T7	154	202	242	1 L	30 L	A	
				III	CORROSIVE	B52, N71, T7	154	203	241	5 L	60 L	A	
	Paint related material including paint thinning, drying, removing, or reducing compound	3	UN1263	II	FLAMMABLE LIQUID	B52, T7, T30	150	173	242	5 L	60 L	B	
				III	FLAMMABLE LIQUID	B1, B52, T7, T30	150	173	242	60 L	220 L	A	
	Paper, unsaturated oil treated incompletely dried (including carbon paper)	4.2	UN1379	III	SPONTANEOUSLY COMBUSTIBLE		None	213	241	Forbidden	Forbidden	A	
	Paraformaldehyde	4.1	UN2213	III	NONE	A1	151	213	240	25 kg	100 kg	A	
	Paraldehyde	3	UN1264	III	FLAMMABLE LIQUID	B1, T1	150	203	242	60 L	220 L	A	
	Paranitroaniline, solid, see Nitroanilines etc.												
D	Parathion	6.1	NA2783	I	POISON	T42	None	201	243	Forbidden	1 L	A	40
D				II	POISON	T14	None	202	243	Forbidden	5 L	A	40
D	Parathion and compressed gas mixture	2.3	NA1967		POISON GAS	3	None	334	245	Forbidden	Forbidden	E	40
	Paris green, solid, see Copper acetoarsenite												
D	PCB, see Polychlorinated biphenyls												
+	Pentaborane	4.2	UN1380	I	SPONTANEOUSLY COMBUSTIBLE, POISON	1	None	205	245	Forbidden	Forbidden	D	
	Pentachloroethane	6.1	UN1669	II	POISON	T14	None	202	243	5 L	60 L	A	40
	Pentaerythrite tetranitrate (dry)	Forbidden											
D	Pentaerythrite tetranitrate or Pentaerythritol tetranitrate or PETN, wetted with not less than 25 per cent water, by mass, or Pentaerythrite tetranitrate or Pentaerythritol tetranitrate or PETN, desensitized with not less than 15 per cent phlegmatizer by mass	1.1A	NA0150	II	EXPLOSIVE 1.1A	111, 117	None	62	None	Forbidden	Forbidden	B	1E, 5E
	Pentaerythrite tetranitrate or Pentaerythritol tetranitrate or PETN, with not less than 7 per cent wax by mass	1.1D	UN0411	II	EXPLOSIVE 1.1D		None	62	None	Forbidden	Forbidden	B	1E, 5E
	Pentaerythritol tetranitrate, see Pentaerythrite tetranitrate, etc.												
	Pentamethylheptane	3	UN2286	III	FLAMMABLE LIQUID	B1, T1	150	203	242	60 L	220 L	A	
	Pentan-2,4-Dione	3	UN2310	III	FLAMMABLE LIQUID	B1, T1	150	203	242	60 L	220 L	A	

340

Symbols (1)	Hazardous materials descriptions and proper shipping names (2)	Hazard class or Division (3)	Identification Numbers (4)	Packing group (5)	Label(s) required (If not excepted) (6)	Special provisions (7)	Exceptions (8A)	Non-bulk packaging (8B)	Bulk packaging (8C)	Passenger aircraft or railcar (9A)	Cargo aircraft only (9B)	Vessel stowages (10A)	Other stowage provisions (10B)
	n-Pentanes or isopentane	3	UN1265	I	FLAMMABLE LIQUID	T20	150	201	243	1 L	30 L	E	
	Pentanitroaniline (dry)	Forbidden											
	1-Pentol	8	UN2705	II	CORROSIVE	B2, T8	154	202	242	1 L	30 L	B	38
	Pentolite, *dry or wetted with less than 15 per cent water, by mass*	1.1D	UN0151	II	EXPLOSIVE 1.1D		None	62	None	Forbidden	Forbidden	B	1E, 5E
	Perchlorates, inorganic, n.o.s.	5.1	UN1481	II	OXIDIZER		152	212	242	5 kg	25 kg	A	46, 56
	Perchloric acid, more than 72 per cent acid by mass	Forbidden											
	Perchloric acid more than 50 per cent but not more than 72 per cent acid, by mass	5.1	UN1873	I	OXIDIZER, CORROSIVE	A2, A3, N41, T9, T27	None	201	243	Forbidden	2.5 L	D	66
	Perchloric acid not more than 50 per cent acid by mass	8	UN1802	II	CORROSIVE, OXIDIZER	N41, T9	None	202	243	Forbidden	30 L	C	66, 89
	Perchloroethylene, see Tetrachloroethylene												
	Perchloromethylmercaptan	6.1	UN1670	I	POISON	2, A3, A7, B9, B14, B32, B74, N34, T38, T43, T45	None	227	244	Forbidden	30 L	D	40
	Perchloryl fluoride	2.3	UN3083		POISON GAS, OXIDIZER	3, B12, B14	None	302	314, 315	Forbidden	Forbidden	D	40, 43, 95
	Percussion caps, see Primers, cap type												
	Perfluoro-2-butene, see Octafluorobut-2-ene												
	Perfluoroethylvinyl ether	2.1	UN3154		FLAMMABLE GAS		306	302, 304, 305	314, 315	Forbidden	150 kg	E	40
	Perfluoromethylvinyl ether	2.1	UN3153		FLAMMABLE GAS		306	302, 304, 305	314, 315	Forbidden	150 kg	E	40
	Perfumery products *with flammable solvents*	3	UN1266	II	FLAMMABLE LIQUID	T7, T30	150	202	242	15 L	60 L	B	
				III	FLAMMABLE LIQUID	B1, T7, T30	150	203	242	60 L	220 L	A	
	Permanganates, inorganic, n.o.s. (except ammonium permanganate, the transport of which is prohibited except when approved by the Associate Administrator for Hazardous Materials Safety.y the competent authorities)	5.1	UN1482	II	OXIDIZER	A30	152	212	242	5 kg	25 kg	D	56, 58, 69, 106, 107
	Peroxides, inorganic, n.o.s.	5.1	UN1483	II	OXIDIZER	A7, A20, N34	None	212	242	5 kg	25 kg	A	13, 75, 106
	Peroxyacetic acid, more than 43 per cent and with more than 6 per cent hydrogen peroxide	Forbidden											
	Pesticides, liquid, flammable, toxic, n.o.s. (flashpoint less than 23 degrees C.)	3	UN3021	I	FLAMMABLE LIQUID, POISON	B5	None	201	243	Forbidden	30 L	B	
				II	FLAMMABLE LIQUID, POISON		None	202	243	1 L	60 L	B	
	Pesticides, liquid, toxic, flammable, n.o.s. *flashpoint not less than 23 degrees C.*	6.1	UN2903	I	POISON, FLAMMABLE LIQUID	T42	None	201	243	1 L	30 L	B	40
				II	POISON, FLAMMABLE LIQUID	T14	None	202	243	5 L	60 L	B	40
				III	KEEP AWAY FROM FOOD, FLAMMABLE LIQUID	B1, T14	153	203	242	60 L	220 L	A	40
	Pesticides, liquid, toxic, n.o.s.	6.1	UN2902	I	POISON	T42	None	201	243	1 L	30 L	B	40
				II	POISON	T14	None	202	243	5 L	60 L	B	40
				III	KEEP AWAY FROM FOOD	T14	153	203	241	60 L	220 L	A	40
	Pesticides, solid, toxic, n.o.s.	6.1	UN2588	I	POISON		None	211	242	5 kg	50 kg	A	40
				II	POISON		None	212	242	25 kg	100 kg	A	40
				III	KEEP AWAY FROM FOOD		153	213	240	100 kg	200 kg	A	40
	PETN, see Pentaerythrite tetranitrate												
	PETN/TNT, see Pentolite, etc.												
	Petrol, see Gasoline												
	Petroleum crude oil	3	UN1267	I	FLAMMABLE LIQUID	T8, T31	None	201	243	1 L	30 L	E	
				II	FLAMMABLE LIQUID	T8, T31	150	202	242	5 L	60 L	B	
				III	FLAMMABLE LIQUID	B1, T7, T30	150	203	242	60 L	220 L	A	
	Petroleum distillates, n.o.s.	3	UN1268	I	FLAMMABLE LIQUID	T8, T31	150	201	243	1 L	30 L	E	
				II	FLAMMABLE LIQUID	T8, T31	150	202	242	5 L	60 L	B	
				III	FLAMMABLE LIQUID	B1, T7, T30	150	203	242	60 L	220 L	A	
	Petroleum ether, see Petroleum spirit												
	Petroleum gases, liquefied *or* Liquefied petroleum gas	2.1	UN1075		FLAMMABLE GAS		306	304	314, 315	Forbidden	150 kg	E	40

Sym-bols (1)	Hazardous materials descriptions and proper shipping names (2)	Hazard class or Division (3)	Identifi-cation Numbers (4)	Packing group (5)	Label(s) required (if not excepted) (6)	Special provisions (7)	Exceptions (8A)	Non-bulk pack-aging (8B)	Bulk pack-aging (8C)	Passenger aircraft or railcar (9A)	Cargo aircraft only (9B)	Vessel stow-ages (10A)	Other stowage provisions (10B)
	Petroleum naphtha, see Naphtha, petroleum												
	Petroleum oil	3	UN1270	I	FLAMMABLE LIQUID	T8, T31	None	201	243	1 L	30 L	E	
				II	FLAMMABLE LIQUID	T8, T31	150	202	242	5 L	60 L	B	
				III	FLAMMABLE LIQUID	B1, T7, T30	150	203	242	60 L	220 L	A	
	Petroleum spirit	3	UN1271	I	FLAMMABLE LIQUID	T8	150	201	243	1 L	30 L	E	
				II	FLAMMABLE LIQUID	B1, T8	150	202	242	5 L	60 L	B	
	Phenacyl bromide	6.1	UN2645	II	POISON		None	212	242	25 kg	100 kg	B	40, 48
	Phenetidines	6.1	UN2311	III	KEEP AWAY FROM FOOD	T7	153	203	241	60 L	220 L	A	
	Phenol, molten	6.1	UN2312	II	POISON	B14, T8	None	202	243	Forbidden	Forbidden	B	40
+	Phenol, solid	6.1	UN1671	II	POISON	N78, T14	None	212	240	25 kg	100 kg	A	
	Phenol solutions	6.1	UN2821	II	POISON	T14	None	202	243	5 L	60 L	A	
	Phenolsulfonic acid, liquid	8	UN1803	II	CORROSIVE	B2, N41, T8	154	202	242	1 L	30 L	C	14
	Phenoxy pesticides, liquid, flammable, toxic n.o.s., *flash point less than 23 degrees C.*	3	UN2766	I	FLAMMABLE LIQUID, POISON		None	201	243	Forbidden	30 L	B	
				II	FLAMMABLE LIQUID, POISON		None	202	243	1 L	60 L	B	
	Phenoxy pesticides, liquid, toxic, flammable, n.o.s. *flashpoint not less than 23 degrees C.*	6.1	UN2999	I	POISON, FLAMMABLE LIQUID	T42	None	201	243	1 L	30 L	B	40
				II	POISON, FLAMMABLE LIQUID	T14	None	202	243	5 L	60 L	B	40
				III	KEEP AWAY FROM FOOD, FLAMMABLE LIQUID	B1, T14	153	203	242	60 L	220 L	A	40
	Phenoxy pesticides, liquid, toxic, n.o.s.	6.1	UN3000	I	POISON	T42	None	201	243	1 L	30 L	B	40
				II	POISON	T14	None	202	243	5 L	60 L	B	40
				III	KEEP AWAY FROM FOOD	T14	153	203	241	60 L	220 L	A	40
	Phenoxy pesticides, solid, toxic, n.o.s.	6.1	UN2765	I	POISON		None	211	242	5 kg	50 kg	A	40
				II	POISON		None	212	242	25 kg	100 kg	A	40
				III	KEEP AWAY FROM FOOD		153	213	240	100 kg	200 kg	A	40
+	Phenyl isocyanate	6.1	UN2487	II	POISON	2, A3, B9, B14, B32, B74, B77, N33, N34, T38, T43, T45	None	227	244	5 L	60 L	D	40
+	Phenyl mercaptan	6.1	UN2337	II	POISON, FLAMMABLE LIQUID	2, B9, B14, B32, B74, B77, T38, T43, T45	None	227	244	5 L	60 L	B	26, 40
	Phenyl phosphorus dichloride	8	UN2798	II	CORROSIVE	B2, B15, T8, T26	154	202	242	Forbidden	30 L	B	40
	Phenyl phosphorus thiodichloride	8	UN2799	II	CORROSIVE	B2, B15, T8, T26	154	202	242	Forbidden	30 L	B	40
	Phenyl urea pesticides, liquid, flammable, toxic, n.o.s., *flash point less than 23 degrees C.*	3	UN2768	I	FLAMMABLE LIQUID, POISON		None	201	243	Forbidden	30 L	B	
				II	FLAMMABLE LIQUID, POISON		None	202	243	1 L	60 L	B	
	Phenyl urea pesticides, liquid, toxic, flammable, n.o.s., *flash point not less than 23 degrees C.*	6.1	UN3001	I	POISON, FLAMMABLE LIQUID	T42	None	201	243	1 L	30 L	B	40
				II	POISON, FLAMMABLE LIQUID	T14	None	202	243	5 L	60 L	B	40
				III	KEEP AWAY FROM FOOD, FLAMMABLE LIQUID	B1, T14	153	203	242	60 L	220 L	A	40
	Phenyl urea pesticides, liquid, toxic, n.o.s.	6.1	UN3002	I	POISON	T42	None	201	243	1 L	30 L	B	40
				II	POISON	T14	None	202	243	5 L	60 L	B	40
				III	KEEP AWAY FROM FOOD	T14	153	203	241	60 L	220 L	A	40
	Phenyl urea pesticides, solid, toxic, n.o.s.	6.1	UN2767	I	POISON		None	211	242	5 kg	50 kg	A	40
				II	POISON		None	212	242	25 kg	100 kg	A	40
				III	KEEP AWAY FROM FOOD		153	213	240	100 kg	200 kg	A	40
	Phenylacetonitrile, liquid	6.1	UN2470	III	KEEP AWAY FROM FOOD	T8	153	203	241	60 L	220 L	A	26
	Phenylacetyl chloride	8	UN2577	II	CORROSIVE	B2, T8, T26	154	202	242	1 L	30 L	C	40
	Phenylcarbylamine chloride	6.1	UN1672	I	POISON	2, B9, B14, B32, B74, T38, T43, T45	None	227	244	Forbidden	Forbidden	D	40
	Phenylchloroformate	6.1	UN2746	II	POISON, CORROSIVE	T12	None	202	243	1 L	30 L	A	12, 13, 25, 40, 48
	m-Phenylene diaminediperchlorate (dry)	Forbid-den											
	Phenylenediamines (*o-; m-; p-;*)	6.1	UN1673	III	KEEP AWAY FROM FOOD		153	213	240	100 kg	200 kg	A	108

Sym-bols (1)	Hazardous materials descriptions and proper shipping names (2)	Hazard class or Division (3)	Identifi-cation Numbers (4)	Packing group (5)	Label(s) required (if not excepted) (6)	Special provisions (7)	Packaging authorizations (§173.***)			Quantity limitations		Vessel stowage requirements	
							Excep-tions (8A)	Non-bulk pack-aging (8B)	Bulk pack-aging (8C)	Passenger aircraft or railcar (9A)	Cargo aircraft only (9B)	Vessel stow-ages (10A)	Other stowage provisions (10B)
	Phenylhydrazine	6.1	UN2572	II	POISON	T8	None	202	243	5 L	60 L	A	40
	Phenylmercuric acetate	6.1	UN1674	II	POISON		None	212	242	25 kg	100 kg	A	
	Phenylmercuric compounds, n.o.s.	6.1	UN2026	I	POISON		None	211	242	5 kg	50 kg	A	
				II	POISON		None	212	242	25 kg	100 kg	A	
				III	KEEP AWAY FROM FOOD		153	213	240	100 kg	200 kg	A	
	Phenylmercuric hydroxide	6.1	UN1894	II	POISON		None	212	242	25 kg	100 kg	A	
	Phenylmercuric nitrate	6.1	UN1895	II	POISON		None	212	242	25 kg	100 kg	A	
	Phenyltrichlorosilane	8	UN1804	II	CORROSIVE	A7, B6, N34, T8	None	202	242	Forbidden	30 L	C	40
	Phosgene	2.3	UN1076		POISON GAS, CORROSIVE	1, B7, B46	None	192	314	Forbidden	Forbidden	D	40
	9-Phosphabicyclononanes or Cyclooctadiene phosphines	4.2	UN2940	II	SPONTANEOUSLY COMBUSTIBLE	A19	None	212	241	15 kg	50 kg	A	
	Phosphine	2.3	UN2199		POISON GAS, FLAMMABLE GAS	1	None	192	245	Forbidden	Forbidden	D	40
	Phosphoric acid	8	UN1805	III	CORROSIVE	A7, N34, T7	154	203	241	5 L	60 L	A	
	Phosphoric acid triethyleneimine, see Tri-(1-aziridiyl) phosphine oxide, solution												
	Phosphoric anhydride, see Phosphorus pentoxide												
	Phosphorous acid, ortho	8	UN2834	III	CORROSIVE	T7	154	213	240	25 kg	100 kg	A	48
	Phosphorus, amorphous	4.1	UN1338	III	FLAMMABLE SOLID	A1, A19, B1, B9, B12, B26	None	213	243	25 kg	100 kg	A	74
	Phosphorus bromide, see Phosphorus tribromide												
	Phosphorus chloride, see Phosphorus trichloride												
	Phosphorus heptasulfide, *free from yellow or white phosphorus*	4.1	UN1339	II	FLAMMABLE SOLID	A20, N34	None	212	240	15 kg	50 kg	B	74
	Phosphorus oxybromide	8	UN1939	II	CORROSIVE	B8, N41, N43	None	212	240	Forbidden	50 kg	C	12, 40, 48
	Phosphorus oxybromide, molten	8	UN2576	II	CORROSIVE	B2, B8, N41, N43, T8, T27	None	202	242	Forbidden	Forbidden	C	40
+	Phosphorus oxychloride	8	UN1810	II	CORROSIVE, POISON	2, A7, B9, B14, B32, B74, B77, N34, T38, T43, T45	None	227	244	Forbidden	30 L	C	8, 40
	Phosphorus pentabromide	8	UN2691	II	CORROSIVE	A7, N34	154	202	240	Forbidden	50 kg	B	12, 40, 48
	Phosphorus pentachloride	8	UN1806	II	CORROSIVE	A7, N34	None	202	240	Forbidden	50 kg	C	40
	Phosphorus pentafluoride	2.3	UN2198		POISON GAS	1	None	302	None	Forbidden	Forbidden	D	40
	Phosphorus pentasulfide, *free from yellow or white phosphorus*	4.3	UN1340	II	DANGEROUS WHEN WET	A20, B59	None	212	243	15 kg	50 kg	B	74
	Phosphorus pentoxide	8	UN1807	II	CORROSIVE	A7, N34	154	212	240	15 kg	50 kg	A	10
	Phosphorus sesquisulfide, *free from yellow or white phosphorous*	4.1	UN1341	II	FLAMMABLE SOLID	A20, N34	None	212	240	15 kg	50 kg	B	74
	Phosphorus tribromide	8	UN1808	II	CORROSIVE	A3, A6, A7, B2, B25, N34, N43, T8	None	202	242	Forbidden	30 L	C	8, 40
+	Phosphorus trichloride	8	UN1809	II	CORROSIVE, POISON	2, A3, A7, B9, B14, B15, B32, B74, B77, N34, T38, T43, T45	None	227	244	Forbidden	30L	C	8, 40
	Phosphorus trioxide	8	UN2578	III	CORROSIVE		154	213	241	25 kg	100 kg	A	12, 48
	Phosphorus trisulfide, *free from yellow or white phosphorus*	4.1	UN1343	II	FLAMMABLE SOLID	A20, N34	None	212	240	15 kg	50 kg	B	74
	Phosphorus white, molten	4.2	UN2447	I	SPONTANEOUSLY COMBUSTIBLE, POISON	B9, B12, B26, N34, T15, T26, T29	None	188	243	Forbidden	Forbidden	D	
	Phosphorus (white or red) and a chlorate, mixtures of	Forbid-den											
	Phosphorus, white or yellow dry or under water or in solution	4.2	UN1381	I	SPONTANEOUSLY COMBUSTIBLE, POISON	B9, B12, B26, N34, T15, T26, T33	None	188	243	Forbidden	Forbidden	E	
	Phosphoryl chloride, see Phosphorus oxychloride												
	Phthalic anhydride with more than .05 per cent maleic anhydride	8	UN2214	III	CORROSIVE	T7	154	213	240	25 kg	100 kg	A	
	Phthalimide derivative pesticides, liquid, flammable, toxic, n.o.s., *flash point less than 23 degrees C.*	3	UN2774	I	FLAMMABLE LIQUID, POISON		None	201	243	Forbidden	30 L	B	
				II	FLAMMABLE LIQUID, POISON		None	202	243	1 L	60 L	B	
	Phthalimide derivative pesticides, liquid, toxic, flammable, n.o.s. *flashpoint not less than 23 degrees C.*	6.1	UN3007	I	POISON, FLAMMABLE LIQUID	T42	None	201	243	1 L	30 L	B	40
				II	POISON, FLAMMABLE LIQUID	T14	None	202	243	5 L	60 L	B	40
				III	KEEP AWAY FROM FOOD, FLAMMABLE LIQUID	T14	153	203	242	60 L	220 L	A	40

343

Sym-bols	Hazardous materials descriptions and proper shipping names	Hazard class or Division	Identifi-cation Numbers	Packing group	Label(s) required (if not excepted)	Special provisions	(8) Packaging authorizations (§173.***)			(9) Quantity limitations		(10) Vessel stowage requirements	
							Excep-tions	Non-bulk pack-aging	Bulk pack-aging	Passenger aircraft or railcar	Cargo aircraft only	Vessel stow-ages	Other stowage provisions
(1)	(2)	(3)	(4)	(5)	(6)	(7)	(8A)	(8B)	(8C)	(9A)	(9B)	(10A)	(10B)
	Phthalimide derivative pesticides, liquid, toxic, n.o.s.	6.1	UN3008	I	POISON	T42	None	201	243	1 L	30 L	B	40
				II	POISON	T14	None	202	243	5 L	60 L	B	40
				III	KEEP AWAY FROM FOOD	T14	153	203	241	60 L	220 L	A	40
	Phthalimide derivative pesticides, solid, toxic, n.o.s.	6.1	UN2773	I	POISON		None	211	242	5 kg	50 kg	A	40
				II	POISON		None	212	242	25 kg	100 kg	A	40
				III	KEEP AWAY FROM FOOD		153	213	240	100 kg	200 kg	A	40
	Picolines	3	UN2313	III	FLAMMABLE LIQUID	B1, T8	150	202	242	5 L	60 L	A	40
	Picric acid, see Trinitrophenol, etc.												
D	Picric acid, wet, with not less than 10% water	4.1	NA1344	I	FLAMMABLE SOLID	A19, A20, N41	None	211	None	Forbidden	Forbidden	D	
	Picrite, see Nitroguanidine, etc.												
	Picryl chloride, see Trinitrochlorobenzene												
	Pine oil	3	UN1272	III	FLAMMABLE LIQUID	B1, T1	150	203	242	60 L	220 L	A	
	alpha-Pinene	3	UN2368	III	FLAMMABLE LIQUID	B1, T1	150	203	242	60 L	220 L	A	
	Piperazine	8	UN2579	III	CORROSIVE	T7	154	213	240	25 kg	100 kg	A	12, 48
	Piperidine	3	UN2401	II	FLAMMABLE LIQUID	T2	150	202	242	5 L	60 L	B	
	Pivaloyl chloride, see Trimethyl acetyl chloride												
A	Plastic molding material in dough, sheet or extruded rope form	9		III	CLASS 9		155	213	None	100 kg	200 kg	A	
	Plastic solvent, n.o.s., see Flammable liquids, n.o.s.												
	Plastics, nitrocellulose based, spontaneously combustible, n.o.s.	4.2	UN2006	III	SPONTANEOUSLY COMBUSTIBLE		None	213	None	Forbidden	Forbidden	C	
	Poisonous gases, n.o.s., see Compressed or liquefied gases, flammable or toxic, n.o.s.												
	Poisonous liquids, corrosive, n.o.s.	6.1	UN2927	I	POISON, CORROSIVE	T42	None	201	243	0.5 L	2.5 L	B	40
				II	POISON, CORROSIVE		None	202	243	1 L	30 L	B	40
	Poisonous liquids, corrosive, n.o.s., inhalation hazard, Packing Group I, Zone A	6.1	UN2927	I	POISON, CORROSIVE	1, B9, B14, B30, B72, T38, T43, T44	None	226	244	Forbidden	Forbidden	D	20, 40, 95
	Poisonous liquids, corrosive, n.o.s., inhalation hazard, Packing Group I, Zone B	6.1	UN2927	I	POISON, CORROSIVE	2, B9, B14, B32, B74, T38, T43, T45	None	227	244	Forbidden	Forbidden	D	20, 40, 95
	Poisonous liquids, flammable, n.o.s.	6.1	UN2929	I	POISON, FLAMMABLE LIQUID	T42	None	201	243	1 L	30 L	B	40
				II	POISON, FLAMMABLE LIQUID	T15	None	202	243	5 L	60 L	B	40
	Poisonous liquids, flammable, n.o.s., inhalation hazard, Packing Group I, Zone A	6.1	UN2929	I	POISON, FLAMMABLE LIQUID	1, B9, B14, B30, B72, T38, T43, T44	None	226	244	Forbidden	Forbidden	D	20, 40, 95
	Poisonous liquids, flammable, n.o.s., inhalation hazard, Packing Group I, Zone B	6.1	UN2929	I	POISON, FLAMMABLE LIQUID	2, B9, B14, B32, B74, T38, T43, T45	None	227	244	Forbidden	Forbidden	D	20, 40, 95
	Poisonous liquids, n.o.s.	6.1	UN2810	I	POISON	T42	None	201	243	1 L	30 L	B	40
				II	POISON	T14	None	202	243	5 L	60 L	B	40
				III	KEEP AWAY FROM FOOD	T7	153	203	241	60 L	220 L	A	40
	Poisonous liquids, n.o.s. inhalation hazard, Packing Group I, Zone A	6.1	UN2810	I	POISON	1, B9, B14, B30, B72, T38, T43, T44	None	226	244	Forbidden	Forbidden	D	20, 40, 95
	Poisonous liquids, n.o.s. inhalation hazard, Packing Group I, Zone B	6.1	UN2810	I	POISON	2, B9, B14, B32, B74, T38, T43, T45	None	227	244	Forbidden	Forbidden	D	20, 40, 95
	Poisonous liquids, oxidizing, n.o.s.	6.1	UN3122	I	POISON, OXIDIZER	A4	None	201	243	Forbidden	2.5 L	C	89
				II	POISON, OXIDIZER		None	202	243	1 L	5 L	C	89
	Poisonous liquids, oxidizing, n.o.s. inhalation hazard, packing group I, Zone A	6.1	UN3122	I	POISON, OXIDIZER	1, B9, B14, B30, B72, T38, T43, T44	None	226	244	Forbidden	2.5 L	C	89
	Poisonous liquids, oxidizing, n.o.s. inhalation Hazard, Packing Group I, Zone B	6.1	UN3122	I	POISON, OXIDIZER	2, B9, B14, B32, T38, T43, T45	None	227	244	Forbidden	Forbidden	C	89
	Poisonous liquids which in contact with water emit flammable gases, n.o.s.	6.1	UN3123	I	POISON, DANGEROUS WHEN WET	A4	None	201	243	Forbidden	1 L	E	
				II	POISON, DANGEROUS WHEN WET		None	202	243	1 L	5 L	E	
	Poisonous solids, corrosive, n.o.s.	6.1	UN2928	I	POISON, CORROSIVE		None	211	242	1 kg	25 kg	B	40
				II	POISON, CORROSIVE		None	212	242	15 kg	50 kg	B	40

344

Sym-bols	Hazardous materials descriptions and proper shipping names	Hazard class or Division	Identifi-cation Numbers	Packing group	Label(s) required (If not excepted)	Special provisions	(8) Packaging authorizations (§173.***)			(9) Quantity limitations		(10) Vessel stowage requirements	
							Excep-tions	Non-bulk pack-aging	Bulk pack-aging	Passenger aircraft or railcar	Cargo aircraft only	Vessel stow-ages	Other stowage provisions
(1)	(2)	(3)	(4)	(5)	(6)	(7)	(8A)	(8B)	(8C)	(9A)	(9B)	(10A)	(10B)
	Poisonous solids, flammable, n.o.s.	6.1	UN2930	I	POISON, FLAMMABLE SOLID		None	211	242	1 kg	15 kg	B	
				II	POISON, FLAMMABLE SOLID		None	212	242	15 kg	50 kg	B	
	Poisonous solids, n.o.s.	6.1	UN2811	I	POISON		None	211	242	5 kg	50 kg	B	
				II	POISON		None	212	242	25 kg	100 kg	B	
				III	KEEP AWAY FROM FOOD		153	213	240	100 kg	200 kg	A	
	Poisonous solids, oxidizing, n.o.s.	6.1	UN3086	I	POISON, OXIDIZER		None	211	242	1 kg	15 kg	C	89
				II	POISON, OXIDIZER		None	212	242	15 kg	50 kg	C	89
	Poisonous, solids, self heating, n.o.s.	6.1	UN3124	I	POISON, SPONTANEOUSLY COMBUSTIBLE	A5	None	211	241	5 kg	15 kg	C	
				II	POISON, SPONTANEOUSLY COMBUSTIBLE		None	212	242	15 kg	50 kg	C	
	Poisonous, solids, which in contact with water emit flammable gases, n.o.s.	6.1	UN3125	I	POISON, DANGEROUS WHEN WET	A5	None	211	241	5 kg	15 kg	E	
				II	POISON, DANGEROUS WHEN WET		None	212	242	15 kg	50 kg	E	
	Polyalkylamines, n.o.s., see Alkylamines, etc.												
AW	Polychlorinated biphenyls	9	UN2315	II	CLASS 9	9, N81	155	202	241	100 L	220 L	A	34
D	Polyester resin kits	5.2	NA2255	II	ORGANIC PEROXIDE		None	225	246	5 kg	5 kg	D	
	Polyhalogenated biphenyls, liquid or Polyhalogenated terphenyls liquid	9	UN3151	II	CLASS 9		155	204	241	100 L	220 L	A	34
	Polyhalogenated biphenyls, solid or Polyhalogenated terphenyls, solid	9	UN3152	II	CLASS 9		155	204	241	100 kg	200 kg	A	34
	Polystyrene beads, expandable, evolving flammable vapor.	9	UN2211	III	None		221	221	240	100 kg	200 kg	A	85, 87
	Potassium	4.3	UN2257	II	DANGEROUS WHEN WET	A19, A20, B27, N6, N34, T15, T26	None	212	244	Forbidden	50 kg	D	
	Potassium arsenate	6.1	UN1677	II	POISON		None	212	242	25 kg	100 kg	A	
	Potassium arsenite	6.1	UN1678	II	POISON		None	212	242	25 kg	100 kg	A	
	Potassium bifluoride, solid	8	UN1811	II	CORROSIVE, POISON	N3, N34, T8	154	212	242	15 kg	50 kg	A	25, 26, 40, 95
	Potassium bifluoride, solution	8	UN1811	II	CORROSIVE, POISON	N3, N34, T8	154	202	242	1 L	30 L	A	26, 40, 95
	Potassium bisulfite solution, see Bisulfites, inorganic, aqueous solutions, n.o.s.												
	Potassium borohydride	4.3	UN1870	I	DANGEROUS WHEN WET	A19, N40	None	211	242	Forbidden	15 kg	E	
	Potassium bromate	5.1	UN1484	II	OXIDIZER		152	212	242	5 kg	25 kg	A	56, 58, 106
	Potassium carbonyl	Forbid-den											
	Potassium chlorate	5.1	UN1485	II	OXIDIZER	A9, N34	152	212	242	5 kg	25 kg	A	56, 58, 106
	Potassium chlorate mixed with mineral oil, see Explosive, blasting, type C												
	Potassium chlorate, solution	5.1	UN2427	II	OXIDIZER	A2, T8	152	202	241	1 L	5 L	B	56, 58, 106
	Potassium cuprocyanide	6.1	UN1679	II	POISON		None	212	242	25 kg	100 kg	A	26
	Potassium cyanide	6.1	UN1680	I	POISON	B69, B77, N74, N75, T18, T26	None	211	242	5 kg	50 kg	B	52
	Potassium dichloro isocyanurate or Potassium dichloro-s-triazinetrione, see Dichloroisocyanuric acid, dry or Dichloroisocyanuric acid salts etc.												
	Potassium dithionite or Potassium hydrosulfite	4.2	UN1929	II	SPONTANEOUSLY COMBUSTIBLE	A8, A19, A20	None	212	241	15 kg	50 kg	E	13
	Potassium fluoride	6.1	UN1812	III	KEEP AWAY FROM FOOD	T8	153	213	240	100 kg	200 kg	A	26
	Potassium fluoroacetate	6.1	UN2628	I	POISON		None	211	242	5 kg	50 kg	E	
	Potassium fluorosilicate	6.1	UN2655	III	KEEP AWAY FROM FOOD		153	213	240	100 kg	200 kg	A	26
	Potassium hydrate, see Potassium hydroxide, solid												
	Potassium hydrogen fluoride, see Potassium bifluoride												
	Potassium hydrogen fluoride solution, see Corrosive liquid, n.o.s.												

345

Symbols (1)	Hazardous materials descriptions and proper shipping names (2)	Hazard class or Division (3)	Identification Numbers (4)	Packing group (5)	Label(s) required (if not excepted) (6)	Special provisions (7)	(8) Packaging authorizations (§173.***)			(9) Quantity limitations		(10) Vessel stowage requirements	
							Exceptions (8A)	Non-bulk packaging (8B)	Bulk packaging (8C)	Passenger aircraft or railcar (9A)	Cargo aircraft only (9B)	Vessel stowages (10A)	Other stowage provisions (10B)
	Potassium hydrogen sulfate	8	UN2509	II	CORROSIVE	A7, N34	154	212	240	15 kg	50 kg	A	
	Potassium hydrosulfite, see Potassium dithionite												
	Potassium hydroxide, liquid, see Potassium hydroxide solution												
	Potassium hydroxide, solid	8	UN1813	II	CORROSIVE		154	212	240	15 kg	50 kg	A	
	Potassium hydroxide, solution	8	UN1814	II	CORROSIVE	B2, T8	154	202	242	1 L	30 L	A	
	Potassium hypochlorite, solution, see Hypochlorite solutions, etc.												
	Potassium, metal alloys	4.3	UN1420	I	DANGEROUS WHEN WET	A19, A20, B27	None	212	244	Forbidden	50 kg	D	
	Potassium metal, liquid alloy, see Alkali metal alloys, liquid												
	Potassium metavanadate	6.1	UN2864	II	POISON		None	212	242	25 kg	100 kg	A	
	Potassium monoxide	8	UN2033	II	CORROSIVE		154	212	240	15 kg	50 kg	A	
	Potassium nitrate	5.1	UN1486	III	OXIDIZER	A1, A29	152	212	240	25 kg	100 kg	A	
	Potassium nitrate and sodium nitrite mixtures	5.1	UN1487	II	OXIDIZER	B12, B78	152	212	240	5 kg	25 kg	A	56, 58
	Potassium nitrite	5.1	UN1488	II	OXIDIZER		152	212	242	5 kg	25 kg	A	56, 58
	Potassium perchlorate, solid or solution	5.1	UN1489	II	OXIDIZER	T8	152	212	242	5 kg	25 kg	A	56, 58, 106
	Potassium permanganate	5.1	UN1490	II	OXIDIZER	B12	152	212	242	5 kg	25 kg	D	56, 58, 69, 106, 107
	Potassium peroxide	5.1	UN1491	I	OXIDIZER	A20, N34	None	211	None	Forbidden	15 kg	B	13, 75, 106
	Potassium persulfate	5.1	UN1492	III	OXIDIZER	A1, A29	152	213	240	25 kg	100 kg	A	
	Potassium phosphide	4.3	UN2012	I	DANGEROUS WHEN WET, POISON	A19, N40	None	211	None	Forbidden	15 kg	E	40, 85
	Potassium salts of aromatic nitro-derivatives, explosive	1.3C	UN0158	II	EXPLOSIVE 1.3C		None	62	None	Forbidden	Forbidden	B	1E, 5E
	Potassium selenate, see Selenates or Selenites												
	Potassium selenite, see Selenates or Selenites												
	Potassium sodium alloys	4.3	UN1422	I	DANGEROUS WHEN WET	A19, B27, N34, N40, T15, T26	None	201	244	Forbidden	15 kg	D	
	Potassium sulfide, anhydrous or Potassium sulfide with less than 30 per cent water of crystallization	4.2	UN1382	II	SPONTANEOUSLY COMBUSTIBLE	A19, A20, B16, N34	None	212	241	15 kg	50 kg	A	
	Potassium sulfide, hydrated with not less than 30 per cent water of crystallization	8	UN1847	II	CORROSIVE		154	212	240	15 kg	50 kg	A	26
	Potassium superoxide	5.1	UN2466	I	OXIDIZER	A20	None	211	None	Forbidden	15 kg	B	13, 75, 106
	Powder cake, wetted or Powder paste, wetted with not less than 25 per cent water, by mass	1.3C	UN0159	II	EXPLOSIVE 1.3C		None	62	None	Forbidden	Forbidden	B	1E, 5E
	Powder cake, wetted or Powder paste, wetted with not less than 17 percent alcohol by mass	1.1C	UN0433	II	EXPLOSIVE 1.1C		None	62	None	Forbidden	Forbidden	B	1E, 5E
	Powder paste, see Powder cake, etc.												
	Powder, smokeless	1.1C	UN0160	II	EXPLOSIVE 1.1C		None	62	None	Forbidden	Forbidden	B	10E, 26E
	Powder, smokeless	1.3C	UN0161	II	EXPLOSIVE 1.3C		None	62	None	Forbidden	Forbidden	B	10E, 26E
	Power device, explosive, see Cartridges, power device												
	Primers, cap type	1.4S	UN0044	II	None		None	62	None	25 kg	100 kg	A	9E
	Primers, cap type	1.1B	UN0377	II	EXPLOSIVE 1.1B		None	62	None	Forbidden	Forbidden	B	2E, 6E
	Primers, cap type	1.4B	UN0378	II	EXPLOSIVE 1.4B		None	62	None	Forbidden	75 kg	B	
	Primers, small arms, see Primers, cap type												
	Primers, tubular	1.3G	UN0319	II	EXPLOSIVE 1.3G		None	62	None	Forbidden	Forbidden	B	
	Primers, tubular	1.4G	UN0320	II	EXPLOSIVE 1.4G		None	62	None	Forbidden	75 kg	A	24E
	Primers, tubular	1.4S	UN0376	II	None		None	62	None	25 kg	100 kg	A	9E
	Projectiles, illuminating, see Ammunition, illuminating, etc.												
	Projectiles, inert with tracer	1.4S	UN0345	II	EXPLOSIVE 1.4S		63(b)	62	None	25 kg	100 kg	A	3E, 7E, 9E
	Projectiles, inert, with tracer	1.3G	UN0424	II	EXPLOSIVE 1.3G		63(b)	62	None	Forbidden	Forbidden	B	3E, 7E
	Projectiles, inert, with tracer	1.4G	UN0425	II	EXPLOSIVE 1.4G		63(b)	62	None	Forbidden	75 kg	A	3E, 7E, 24E
	Projectiles, with burster or expelling charge	1.2D	UN0346	II	EXPLOSIVE 1.2D		63(b)	62	None	Forbidden	Forbidden	B	3E, 7E
	Projectiles, with burster or expelling charge	1.4D	UN0347	II	EXPLOSIVE 1.4D		63(b)	62	None	Forbidden	75 kg	A	3E, 7E, 24E
	Projectiles, with burster or expelling charge	1.2F	UN0426	II	EXPLOSIVE 1.2F		63(b)	62	None	Forbidden	Forbidden	E	
	Projectiles, with burster or expelling charge	1.4F	UN0427	II	EXPLOSIVE 1.4F		63(b)	62	None	Forbidden	Forbidden	E	
	Projectiles, with burster or expelling charge	1.2G	UN0434	II	EXPLOSIVE 1.2G		63(b)	62	None	Forbidden	Forbidden	B	3E, 7E
	Projectiles, with burster or expelling charge	1.4G	UN0435	II	EXPLOSIVE 1.4G		63(b)	62	None	Forbidden	75 kg	A	3E, 7E, 24E
	Projectiles, with bursting charge	1.1F	UN0167	II	EXPLOSIVE 1.1F		63(b)	62	None	Forbidden	Forbidden	E	
	Projectiles, with bursting charge	1.1D	UN0168	II	EXPLOSIVE 1.1D		63(b)	62	None	Forbidden	Forbidden	B	3E, 7E
	Projectiles, with bursting charge	1.2D	UN0169	II	EXPLOSIVE 1.2D		63(b)	62	None	Forbidden	Forbidden	B	3E, 7E

Symbols	Hazardous materials descriptions and proper shipping names	Hazard class or Division	Identification Numbers	Packing group	Label(s) required (if not excepted)	Special provisions	(8) Packaging authorizations (§173.***) Exceptions	Non-bulk packaging	Bulk packaging	(9) Quantity limitations Passenger aircraft or railcar	Cargo aircraft only	(10) Vessel stowage requirements Vessel stowages	Other stowage provisions
(1)	(2)	(3)	(4)	(5)	(6)	(7)	(8A)	(8B)	(8C)	(9A)	(9B)	(10A)	(10B)
	Projectiles, *with bursting charge*	1.2F	UN0324	II	EXPLOSIVE 1.2F		63(b)	62	None	Forbidden	Forbidden	E	
	Projectiles, *with bursting charge*	1.4D	UN0344	II	EXPLOSIVE 1.4D		63(b)	62	None	Forbidden	75 kg	A	3E, 7E, 24E
	Propadiene, inhibited.	2.1	UN2200		FLAMMABLE GAS		None	304	314, 315	Forbidden	150 kg	B	40
	Propadiene mixed with methyl acetylene, see Methyl acetylene and propadiene mixtures, stabilized												
	Propane see also Petroleum gases, liquefied	2.1	UN1978		FLAMMABLE GAS		306	304	314, 315	Forbidden	150 kg	E	40
	Propanethiols	3	UN2402	II	FLAMMABLE LIQUID	T8	150	202	242	5 L	60 L	E	95, 102
	n-Propanol or Propyl alcohol normal	3	UN1274	II	FLAMMABLE LIQUID	B1, T1	150	202	242	5 L	60 L	B	
D	Propargyl alcohol	3	NA1986	II	FLAMMABLE LIQUID, POISON		None	202	243	Forbidden	1 L	B	40
D	Propellant explosive, liquid	1.1C	NA0474	II	EXPLOSIVE 1.1C		None	62	None	Forbidden	Forbidden	B	1E, 5E
D	Propellant explosive, liquid	1.3C	NA0477	II	EXPLOSIVE 1.3C		None	62	None	Forbidden	Forbidden	B	1E, 5E
D	Propellant explosive, solid	1.1C	NA0273	II	EXPLOSIVE 1.1C		None	62	None	Forbidden	5 kg	B	
D	Propellant explosive, solid	1.3C	NA0274	II	EXPLOSIVE 1.3C		None	62	None	Forbidden	5 kg	B	
	Propionaldehyde	3	UN1275	II	FLAMMABLE LIQUID	T14	150	202	242	5 L	60 L	E	
	Propionic acid	8	UN1848	III	CORROSIVE	T7	154	203	241	5 L	60 L	A	22, 48
	Propionic anhydride	8	UN2496	III	CORROSIVE	T2	154	203	241	5 L	60 L	A	8
	Propionitrile	3	UN2404	II	FLAMMABLE LIQUID, POISON	T14	None	201	243	Forbidden	60 L	E	40
	Propionyl chloride	3	UN1815	II	FLAMMABLE LIQUID, CORROSIVE	T8, T26	None	202	243	1 L	5 L	B	40
	n-Propyl acetate	3	UN1276	II	FLAMMABLE LIQUID	T1	150	202	242	5 L	60 L	B	
	Propyl alcohol, see Propanol												
	n-Propyl benzene	3	UN2364	III	FLAMMABLE LIQUID	B1, T1	150	203	242	60 L	220 L	A	
	Propyl chloride	3	UN1278	II	FLAMMABLE LIQUID	N34, T14	None	202	242	Forbidden	60 L	E	
	n-Propyl chloroformate	6.1	UN2740	I	POISON, FLAMMABLE LIQUID, CORROSIVE	2, A3, A6, A7, B9, B14, B32, B74, B77, N34, T38, T43, T45	None	227	244	Forbidden	2.5 L	B	21, 40, 48, 100
	Propyl formates	3	UN1281	II	FLAMMABLE LIQUID	T8	150	202	242	5 L	60 L	B	
+	n-Propyl isocyanate	3	UN2482	I	FLAMMABLE LIQUID, POISON	1, A7, B9, B14, B30, B72, T38, T43, T44	None	226	244	Forbidden	30 L	D	40
	Propyl mercaptan, see Propanethiols												
	n-Propyl nitrate	3	UN1865	II	FLAMMABLE LIQUID	T25	150	202	None	5 L	60 L	D	
	Propylamine	3	UN1277	II	FLAMMABLE LIQUID, CORROSIVE	N34, T14	None	202	242	5.L	60 L	E	40
	Propylene see also Petroleum gases, liquefied	2.1	UN1077		FLAMMABLE GAS		306	304	314, 315	Forbidden	150 kg	E	40
	Propylene chlorohydrin	6.1	UN2611	II	POISON	T9	None	202	243	5 L	60 L	A	12, 40, 48
	Propylene dichloride	3	UN1279	II	FLAMMABLE LIQUID	N36, T1	150	202	242	5 L	60 L	B	
	Propylene oxide	3	UN1280	I	FLAMMABLE LIQUID	A3, N34, T20, T29	None	201	243	1 L	30 L	E	40
	Propylene tetramer	3	UN2850	III	FLAMMABLE LIQUID	B1, T1	150	203	242	60 L	220 L	A	
	1,2-Propylenediamine	8	UN2258	III	CORROSIVE	A3, A6, N34, T8	None	203	243	1 L	30 L	A	12, 20, 40, 48
	Propyleneimine, inhibited	3	UN1921	I	FLAMMABLE LIQUID	A3, N34, T25	None	201	243	1 L	30 L	B	40
	Propyltrichlorosilane	8	UN1816	II	CORROSIVE	A7, B2, B6, N34, T8, T26	None	202	242	Forbidden	30 L	C	12, 21, 40, 48
	Prussic acid, see Hydrogen cyanide												
	Pyridine	3	UN1282	II	FLAMMABLE LIQUID, POISON	T8	None	202	243	1 L	60 L	B	21, 100
	Pyridine perchlorate	Forbidden											
	Pyrophoric liquids, n.o.s.	4.2	UN2845	I	SPONTANEOUSLY COMBUSTIBLE	B11, T42	None	181	244	Forbidden	Forbidden	D	18
	Pyrophoric metals, n.o.s., or Pyrophoric alloys, n.o.s.	4.2	UN1383	I	SPONTANEOUSLY COMBUSTIBLE	B11	None	187	242	Forbidden	Forbidden	D	
	Pyrophoric solids, n.o.s.	4.2	UN2846	I	SPONTANEOUSLY COMBUSTIBLE		None	187	242	Forbidden	Forbidden	D	
	Pyrosulfuryl chloride	8	UN1817	II	CORROSIVE	B2, T9, T27	154	202	242	1 L	30 L	C	8, 40
	Pyroxylin solution or solvent, see Nitrocellulose												
	Pyrrolidine	3	UN1922	II	FLAMMABLE LIQUID	T1	150	202	242	5 L	60 L	B	40

347

Symbols (1)	Hazardous materials descriptions and proper shipping names (2)	Hazard class or Division (3)	Identification Numbers (4)	Packing group (5)	Label(s) required (if not excepted) (6)	Special provisions (7)	Packaging authorizations (§173.***)			Quantity limitations		Vessel stowage requirements	
							Exceptions (8A)	Non-bulk packaging (8B)	Bulk packaging (8C)	Passenger aircraft or railcar (9A)	Cargo aircraft only (9B)	Vessel stowages (10A)	Other stowage provisions (10B)
	Quebrachitol pentanitrate	Forbidden											
	Quicklime, see Calcium oxide												
	Quinoline	6.1	UN2656	III	KEEP AWAY FROM FOOD	T8	153	203	241	60 L	220 L	A	12, 48
	R 114, see Dichlorotetrafluoroethane												
	R 115, see Chloropentafluoroethane												
	R 116, see Hexafluoroethane												
	R 124, see Chlorotetrafluoroethane												
	R 133a, see Chlorotrifluoroethane												
	R 152a, see Difluoroethane												
	R 500, see Dichlorodifluoromethane and difluorethane, *etc.*												
	R 502, see Chlorodifluoromethane and chloropentafluoroethane mixture, *etc.*												
	R 503, see Chlorotrifluoromethane and trifluoromethane, *etc.*												
	R 12, see Dichlorodifluoromethane												
	R 12B1, see Chlorodifluorobromomethane												
	R 13, see Chlorotrifluoromethane												
	R 13B1, see Bromotrifluoromethane												
	R 14, see Tetrafluoromethane												
	R 21, see Dichlorofluoromethane												
	R 22, see Chlorodifluoromethane												
	Radioactive material, excepted package-articles manufactured from natural or depleted uranium or natural thorium	7	UN2910		None		421-1, 424	421-1, 424	421-1, 424			A	
	Radioactive material, excepted package-empty packaging	7	UN2910		EMPTY		427	427	427			A	
	Radioactive material, excepted package-instruments or articles	7	UN2910		None		421-1, 422	421-1, 422	421-1, 422			A	
	Radioactive material, excepted package-limited quantity of material	7	UN2910		None		421, 421-1	421, 421-1	421, 421-1			A	
	Radioactive material, fissile, n.o.s.	7	UN2918		RADIOACTIVE		453	417	417			A	40, 95
	Radioactive material, low specific activity *LSA*, n.o.s.	7	UN2912		RADIOACTIVE		421, 422, 424	425	425			A	
	Radioactive material, n.o.s.	7	UN2982		RADIOACTIVE		421, 422, 424	415, 416	415, 416			A	40, 95
	Radioactive material, special form, n.o.s.	7	UN2974		RADIOACTIVE		421, 422	415, 416	415, 416			A	
	Railway torpedo, see Signals, railway track, explosive												
	Rare gases and nitrogen mixtures	2.2	UN1981		NONFLAMMABLE GAS		306	302	None	75 kg	150 kg	A	
	Rare gases and oxygen mixtures	2.2	UN1980		NONFLAMMABLE GAS		306	302	None	75 kg	150 kg	A	
	Rare gases, mixtures	2.2	UN1979		NONFLAMMABLE GAS		306	302	None	75 kg	150 kg	A	
	RC 318, see Octafluorocyclobutane												
	RDX and cyclotetramethylenetetranitramine, wetted or desensitized *see* RDX and HMX mixtures, wetted or desensitized												
	RDX and HMX mixtures, wetted *with not less than 15 percent water by mass or* RDX and HMX mixtures, desensitized *with not less than 10 percent phlegmatizer by mass*	1.1D	UN0391	II	EXPLOSIVE 1.1D		None	62	None	Forbidden	Forbidden	B	1E, 5E
	RDX and Octogen mixtures, wetted or desensitized *see* RDX and HMX mixtures, wetted or desensitized *etc.*												
	RDX and Octogen mixtures, wetted or desensitized *see* RDX and HMX mixtures, wetted or desensitized *etc.*												
	RDX, see Cyclotrimethylene trinitramine, *etc.*												
	Receptacles, small, containing gas *flammable, without release device, not refillable and not exceeding 1 L capacity*	2.1	UN2037		FLAMMABLE GAS		306	304	None	1 kg	15 kg	B	40
	Receptacles, small, containing gas *nonflammable, without release device, not refillable and not exceeding 1 L capacity*	2.2	UN2037		NONFLAMMABLE GAS		306	304	None	1 kg	15 kg	B	40
	Red phosphorus, see Phosphorus, amorphous												
	Refrigerant gases, n.o.s.	2.2	UN1078		NONFLAMMABLE GAS		306	304	314, 315	75 kg	150 kg	A	
D	Refrigerant gases, n.o.s. *or* Dispersant gases, n.o.s.	2.1	NA1954		FLAMMABLE GAS		306	304	314, 315	Forbidden	150 kg	C	40
D	Refrigerating machine	3	NA1993	III	FLAMMABLE LIQUID		174	174	None	10 L	10 L	A	
D	Refrigerating machines, *containing flammable, non-poisonous, liquefied gas*	2.1	NA1954		FLAMMABLE GAS		306	306	306	Forbidden	25 kg	C	40
	Refrigerating machines, *containing non-flammable, non-poisonous, liquefied gas*	2.2	UN2857		NONFLAMMABLE GAS		306, 307	306	306, 307	Forbidden	450 kg	A	

348

Symbols (1)	Hazardous materials descriptions and proper shipping names (2)	Hazard class or Division (3)	Identification Numbers (4)	Packing group (5)	Label(s) required (if not excepted) (6)	Special provisions (7)	(8) Packaging authorizations (§173.***)			(9) Quantity limitations		(10) Vessel stowage requirements	
							Exceptions (8A)	Non-bulk packaging (8B)	Bulk packaging (8C)	Passenger aircraft or railcar (9A)	Cargo aircraft only (9B)	Vessel stowages (10A)	Other stowage provisions (10B)
D	Regulated medical waste	6.2	NA9275	II	INFECTIOUS SUBSTANCE		197	197	None	Forbidden	Forbidden	E	
	Release devices, explosive	1.4S	UN0173	II	EXPLOSIVE 1.4S		None	62	None	25 kg	100 kg	A	24E
	Resin solution, *flammable*	3	UN1866	II	FLAMMABLE LIQUID	B52, T7, T30	150	202	242	5 L	60 L	B	
				III	FLAMMABLE LIQUID	B1, B52, T7, T30	150	203	242	60 L	220 L	A	
	Resorcinol	6.1	UN2876	III	KEEP AWAY FROM FOOD		153	213	240	100 kg	200 kg	A	
	Rifle grenade, see Grenades, hand or rifle, etc.												
	Rifle powder, see Powder, smokeless (UN 0160)												
	Rivets, explosive	1.4S	UN0174	II	EXPLOSIVE 1.4S		None	62	None	25 kg	100 kg	A	9E
	Road asphalt or tar liquid, see Tars, liquid, etc.												
	Rocket motors	1.3C	UN0186	II	EXPLOSIVE 1.3C	109	None	62	None	Forbidden	220 kg	B	9E
	Rocket motors	1.1C	UN0280	II	EXPLOSIVE 1.1C	109	None	62	None	Forbidden	Forbidden	B	
	Rocket motors	1.2C	UN0281	II	EXPLOSIVE 1.2C	109	None	62	None	Forbidden	Forbidden	B	
	Rocket motors, liquid fueled	1.2J	UN0395	II	EXPLOSIVE 1.2J	109	None	62	None	Forbidden	Forbidden	E	7E, 16E, 23E
	Rocket motors, liquid fueled	1.3J	UN0396	II	EXPLOSIVE 1.3J	109	None	62	None	Forbidden	Forbidden	E	7E, 16E, 23E
	Rocket motors with hypergolic liquids *with or without an expelling charge*	1.3L	UN0250	II	EXPLOSIVE 1.3L	109	None	62	None	Forbidden	Forbidden	E	2E, 8E, 11E, 17E
	Rocket motors with hypergolic liquids *with or without an expelling charge*	1.2L	UN0322	II	EXPLOSIVE 1.2L	109	None	62	None	Forbidden	Forbidden	E	2E, 8E, 11E, 17E
	Rockets, line throwing	1.4G	UN0453	II	EXPLOSIVE 1.4G		None	62	None	Forbidden	75 kg	B	
	Rockets, line-throwing	1.2G	UN0238	II	EXPLOSIVE 1.2G		None	62	None	Forbidden	Forbidden	B	
	Rockets, line-throwing	1.3G	UN0240	II	EXPLOSIVE 1.3G		None	62	None	Forbidden	75 kg	B	
	Rockets, liquid fueled *with bursting charge*	1.2J	UN0398	II	EXPLOSIVE 1.2J		None	62	None	Forbidden	Forbidden	E	7E, 16E, 23E
	Rockets, liquid fueled *with bursting charge*	1.1J	UN0397	II	EXPLOSIVE 1.1J		None	62	None	Forbidden	Forbidden	E	7E, 16E, 23E
	Rockets, *with bursting charge*	1.1F	UN0180	II	EXPLOSIVE 1.1F		None	62	None	Forbidden	Forbidden	E	
	Rockets, *with bursting charge*	1.1E	UN0181	II	EXPLOSIVE 1.1E		None	62	None	Forbidden	Forbidden	B	
	Rockets, *with bursting charge*	1.2E	UN0182	II	EXPLOSIVE 1.2E		None	62	None	Forbidden	Forbidden	B	
	Rockets, *with bursting charge*	1.2F	UN0295	II	EXPLOSIVE 1.2F		None	62	None	Forbidden	Forbidden	E	
	Rockets, *with expelling charge*	1.2C	UN0436	II	EXPLOSIVE 1.2C		None	62	None	Forbidden	Forbidden	B	
	Rockets, *with expelling charge*	1.3C	UN0437	II	EXPLOSIVE 1.3C		None	62	None	Forbidden	Forbidden	B	
	Rockets, *with expelling charge*	1.4C	UN0438	II	EXPLOSIVE 1.4C		None	62	None	Forbidden	75 kg	A	24E
	Rockets, *with inert head*	1.3C	UN0183	II	EXPLOSIVE 1.3C		None	62	None	Forbidden	Forbidden	B	
	Rosin oil	3	UN1286	II	FLAMMABLE LIQUID	T7	150	202	242	5 L	60 L	B	
				III	FLAMMABLE LIQUID	B1, T1	150	203	242	60 L	220 L	A	
	Rubber solution	3	UN1287	II	FLAMMABLE LIQUID	T7, T30	150	202	242	5 L	60 L	B	
				III	FLAMMABLE LIQUID	B1, T7, T30	150	203	242	60 L	220 L	A	
	Rubidium	4.3	UN1423	I	DANGEROUS WHEN WET	22, A7, A19, N34, N40, N45	None	211	242	Forbidden	15 kg	D	
	Rubidium hydroxide	8	UN2678	II	CORROSIVE	T8	154	212	240	15 kg	50 kg	A	
	Rubidium hydroxide solution	8	UN2677	II	CORROSIVE	B2, T8	154	202	242	1 L	30 L	A	
	Safety fuse, see Fuse, safety												
	Samples, explosive, *other than initiating explosives*		UN0190			113		62	None	Forbidden	Forbidden	E	12E
	Sand acid, see Fluorosilicic acid												
	Seed cake, containing vegetable oil solvent extractions and expelled seeds, containing not more than 10% of oil and when the amount of moisture is higher than 11%, not more than 20% of oil and moisture combined.	4.2	UN1386	III	None	N7	None	213	241	Forbidden	Forbidden	A	13
I	Seed cake with more than 1.5 percent oil and not more than 11 percent moisture	4.2	UN1386	III	None	N7	None	213	241	Forbidden	Forbidden	E	13
I	Seed cake with not more than 1.5 percent oil and not more than 11 percent moisture	4.2	UN2217	III	None	N7	None	213	241	Forbidden	Forbidden	A	13
	Selenates or Selenites	6.1	UN2630	I	POISON		None	211	242	5 kg	50 kg	E	
	Selenic acid	8	UN1905	I	CORROSIVE	N34	None	211	242	Forbidden	25 kg	A	
	Selenites, see Selenates or Selenites												
	Selenium disulfide	6.1	UN2657	II	POISON		None	212	242	25 kg	100 kg	A	
	Selenium hexafluoride	2.3	UN2194		POISON GAS	1	None	302	None	Forbidden	Forbidden	D	40
	Selenium nitride	Forbidden											
D	Selenium oxide	6.1	NA2811	I	POISON		None	211	242	5 kg	50 kg	B	
	Selenium oxychloride	8	UN2879	I	CORROSIVE, POISON	A3, A6, A7, N34, T12, T27	None	201	243	0.5 L	2.5 L	E	40, 95

Sym-bols	Hazardous materials descriptions and proper shipping names	Hazard class or Division	Identifi-cation Numbers	Packing group	Label(s) required (if not excepted)	Special provisions	(8) Packaging authorizations (§173.***)			(9) Quantity limitations		(10) Vessel stowage requirements	
							Excep-tions	Non-bulk pack-aging	Bulk pack-aging	Passenger aircraft or railcar	Cargo aircraft only	Vessel stow-ages	Other stowage provisions
(1)	(2)	(3)	(4)	(5)	(6)	(7)	(8A)	(8B)	(8C)	(9A)	(9B)	(10A)	(10B)
	Selenium powder	6.1	UN2658	III	KEEP AWAY FROM FOOD		153	213	240	100 kg	200 kg	A	
	Self-heating substances, solid, corrosive, n.o.s.	4.2	UN3126	II	SPONTANEOUSLY COMBUSTIBLE, CORROSIVE		None	212	242	15 kg	50 kg	C	
				III	SPONTANEOUSLY COMBUSTIBLE, CORROSIVE		None	213	242	25 kg	100 kg	C	
	Self-heating substances, solid, n.o.s.	4.2	UN3088	II	SPONTANEOUSLY COMBUSTIBLE		None	212	241	15 kg	50 kg	C	
				III	SPONTANEOUSLY COMBUSTIBLE		None	213	241	25 kg	100 kg	C	
	Self-heating substances, solid, oxidizing, n.o.s.	4.2	UN3127		SPONTANEOUSLY COMBUSTIBLE, OXIDIZER		None	214	214	Forbidden	Forbidden		
	Self-heating substances, solid, poisonous, n.o.s.	4.2	UN3128	II	SPONTANEOUSLY COMBUSTIBLE, POISON		None	212	242	15 kg	50 kg	C	
				III	SPONTANEOUSLY COMBUSTIBLE, KEEP AWAY FROM FOOD		None	213	242	25 kg	100 kg	C	
	Self-propelled vehicle, see Vehicles, self-propelled												
	Self-reactive substances (aliphatic azocompounds, aromatic sulphohydrazides, N-nitroso compounds, diazonium salts) Sample, n.o.s.	4.1	UN3031	II	FLAMMABLE SOLID		None	214	None	Forbidden	Forbidden	D	
	Self-reactive substances (aliphatic azocompounds, aromatic sulphohydrazides, N-nitroso compounds, diazonium salts), Trial quantities, n.o.s.	4.1	UN3032	II	FLAMMABLE SOLID		None	214	None	Forbidden	Forbidden	D	
	Shale oil	3	UN1288	I	FLAMMABLE LIQUID	T7	None	201	243	1 L	30 L	B	
				II	FLAMMABLE LIQUID	T7, T30	150	202	242	5 L	60 L	B	
				III	FLAMMABLE LIQUID	B1, T7, T30	150	203	242	60 L	220 L	A	
	Shaped charges, commercial, see Charges, shaped, commercial etc.												
	Signal devices, hand	1.4G	UN0191	II	EXPLOSIVE 1.4G		None	62	None	Forbidden	75 kg	A	24E
	Signal devices, hand	1.4S	UN0373	II	EXPLOSIVE 1.4S		None	62	None	25 kg	100 kg	A	9E
	Signals, distress, ship	1.1G	UN0194	II	EXPLOSIVE 1.1G		None	62	None	Forbidden	Forbidden	B	
	Signals, distress, ship	1.3G	UN0195	II	EXPLOSIVE 1.3G		None	62	None	Forbidden	75 kg	B	
	Signals, highway, see Signal devices, hand; Fireworks, type D												
	Signals, railway track, explosive	1.1G	UN0192	II	EXPLOSIVE 1.1G		None	62	None	Forbidden	Forbidden	B	
	Signals, railway track, explosive	1.4S	UN0193	II	EXPLOSIVE 1.4S		None	62	None	25 kg	100 kg	A	9E
	Signals, ship distress, wateractivated, see Contrivances, water-activated, etc.												
	Signals, smoke	1.1G	UN0196	II	EXPLOSIVE 1.1G		None	62	None	Forbidden	Forbidden	B	
	Signals, smoke	1.2G	UN0313	II	EXPLOSIVE 1.2G		None	62	None	Forbidden	Forbidden	B	
	Signals, smoke	1.4G	UN0197	II	EXPLOSIVE 1.4G		None	62	None	Forbidden	75 kg	A	24E
	Signals, smoke	1.3G	UN0487	II	EXPLOSIVE 1.3G		None	62	None	Forbidden	Forbidden	B	1E, 7E, 25E
	Silane	2.1	UN2203		FLAMMABLE GAS		None	302	None	Forbidden	Forbidden	E	40, 57, 104
	Silicofluoric acid, see Fluorosilicic acid												
	Silicon chloride, see Silicon tetrachloride												
	Silicon powder, amorphous	4.1	UN1346	III	FLAMMABLE SOLID	A1	None	213	240	25 kg	100 kg	A	
	Silicon tetrachloride	8	UN1818	II	CORROSIVE	A3, A6, B2, B6, N41, T18, T26, T29	154	202	242	1 L	30 L	C	8, 40
	Silicon tetrafluoride	2.3	UN1859		POISON GAS, CORROSIVE	4	None	302	None	Forbidden	25 kg	D	40
	Silver acetylide (dry)	Forbid-den											
	Silver arsenite	6.1	UN1683	II	POISON		None	212	242	25 kg	100 kg	A	
	Silver azide (dry)	Forbid-den											
	Silver chlorite (dry)	Forbid-den											
	Silver cyanide	6.1	UN1684	II	POISON		None	212	242	25 kg	100 kg	A	26, 40
	Silver fulminate (dry)	Forbid-den											
	Silver nitrate	5.1	UN1493	II	OXIDIZER		152	212	242	5 kg	25 kg	A	
	Silver oxalate (dry)	Forbid-den											
	Silver picrate (dry)	Forbid-den											

350

Symbols (1)	Hazardous materials descriptions and proper shipping names (2)	Hazard class or Division (3)	Identification Numbers (4)	Packing group (5)	Label(s) required (if not excepted) (6)	Special provisions (7)	(8) Packaging authorizations (§173.***)			(9) Quantity limitations		(10) Vessel stowage requirements	
							Exceptions (8A)	Non-bulk packaging (8B)	Bulk packaging (8C)	Passenger aircraft or railcar (9A)	Cargo aircraft only (9B)	Vessel stowages (10A)	Other stowage provisions (10B)
	Silver picrate, wetted with not less than 30 per cent water, by mass	4.1	UN1347	I	FLAMMABLE SOLID		None	211	None	Forbidden	Forbidden	D	28, 36
	Sludge, acid	8	UN1906	II	CORROSIVE	A3, A7, B2, N34, T9, T27	None	202	242	Forbidden	30 L	C	14
D	Smokeless powder for small arms (100 pounds or less)	4.1	NA1325	I	FLAMMABLE SOLID	16	None	171	None	Forbidden	Forbidden	A	
	Soda lime with more than 4 per cent sodium hydroxide	8	UN1907	III	CORROSIVE		154	213	240	25 kg	100 kg	A	
	Sodium	4.3	UN1428	II	DANGEROUS WHEN WET	A7, A8, A19, A20, B9, B28, B68, N34, T15, T28, T29	None	212	244	Forbidden	50 kg	D	
	Sodium aluminate, solid	8	UN2812	III	CORROSIVE		154	213	240	25 kg	100 kg	A	
	Sodium aluminate, solution	8	UN1819	II	CORROSIVE	B2, T8	154	202	242	1 L	30 L	A	
	Sodium aluminum hydride	4.3	UN2835	II	DANGEROUS WHEN WET	A8, A19, A20	None	212	242	Forbidden	50 kg	E	
	Sodium ammonium vanadate	6.1	UN2863	II	POISON		None	212	242	25 kg	100 kg	A	
	Sodium arsanilate	6.1	UN2473	III	KEEP AWAY FROM FOOD		153	213	240	100 kg	200 kg	A	
	Sodium arsenate	6.1	UN1685	II	POISON		None	212	240	25 kg	100 kg	A	
	Sodium arsenite, aqueous solutions	6.1	UN1686	II	POISON	T15	None	202	243	5 L	60 L	A	
				III	KEEP AWAY FROM FOOD	T15	153	203	241	60 L	220 L	A	
	Sodium arsenite, solid	6.1	UN2027	II	POISON		None	212	242	25 kg	100 kg	A	
	Sodium azide	6.1	UN1687	II	POISON	B28	None	212	242	25 kg	100 kg	A	36, 52, 91
	Sodium bifluoride, see Sodium hydrogen fluoride												
	Sodium bisulfate, solid or solution, see Sodium hydrogen sulfate, solid or solution												
	Sodium bisulfite, solution, see Bisulfites, inorganic, aqueous solutions, n.o.s.												
	Sodium borohydride	4.3	UN1426	I	DANGEROUS WHEN WET	N40	None	211	242	Forbidden	15 kg	E	
	Sodium bromate	5.1	UN1494	II	OXIDIZER		152	212	242	5 kg	25 kg	A	56, 58, 106
	Sodium cacodylate	6.1	UN1688	II	POISON		None	212	242	25 kg	100 kg	A	26
	Sodium chlorate	5.1	UN1495	II	OXIDIZER	A9, N34, T8	152	212	240	5 kg	25 kg	A	56, 58, 106
	Sodium chlorate mixed with dinitrotoluene, see Explosive blasting, type C												
	Sodium chlorate, solution	5.1	UN2428	II	OXIDIZER	A2, B6, T8	152	202	241	1 L	5 L	B	56, 58, 106
	Sodium chlorite	5.1	UN1496	II	OXIDIZER	A9, N34, T8	None	212	242	5 kg	25 kg	A	56, 58, 106
	Sodium chlorite solution with more than 5 per cent available chlorine	8	UN1908	II	CORROSIVE	A3, A6, A7, B2, N34, T8	154	202	242	1 L	30 L	B	26
	Sodium chloroacetate	6.1	UN2659	III	KEEP AWAY FROM FOOD		153	213	240	100 kg	200 kg	A	
	Sodium cuprocyanide, solid	6.1	UN2316	I	POISON		None	211	242	5 kg	50 kg	A	26
	Sodium cuprocyanide, solution	6.1	UN2317	I	POISON	T8, T26	None	201	243	1 L	30 L	B	26, 40
	Sodium cyanide	6.1	UN1689	I	POISON	B69, B77, N74, N75, T42	None	211	242	5 kg	50 kg	B	52
	Sodium 2-diazo-1-naphthol-4-sulphonate	4.1	UN3040	II	FLAMMABLE SOLID		None	224	None	15 kg	50 kg	C	61
	Sodium 2-diazo-1-naphthol-5-sulphonate	4.1	UN3041	II	FLAMMABLE SOLID		None	224	None	15 kg	50 kg	C	61
	Sodium dichloroisocyanurate or Sodium dichloro-s-triazinetrione, see Dichloroisocyanuric acid etc.												
	Sodium dinitro-o-cresolate, dry or wetted with less than 15 per cent water, by mass	1.3C	UN0234	II	EXPLOSIVE 1.3C		None	62	None	Forbidden	Forbidden	B	1E, 5E
	Sodium dinitro-ortho-cresolate, wetted with not less than 15 per cent water, by mass	4.1	UN1348	I	FLAMMABLE SOLID, POISON	A8, A19, A20, N41	None	211	None	1 kg	15 kg	E	28, 36
	Sodium dithionite or Sodium hydrosulfite	4.2	UN1384	II	SPONTANEOUSLY COMBUSTIBLE	A19, A20	None	212	241	15 kg	50 kg	E	13
	Sodium fluoride	6.1	UN1690	III	KEEP AWAY FROM FOOD	T8	153	213	240	100 kg	200 kg	A	26
	Sodium fluoroacetate	6.1	UN2629	I	POISON		None	211	242	5 kg	50 kg	E	
	Sodium fluorosilicate	6.1	UN2674	III	KEEP AWAY FROM FOOD		153	213	240	100 kg	200 kg	A	26
	Sodium hydrate, see Sodium hydroxide, solid												
	Sodium hydride	4.3	UN1427	I	DANGEROUS WHEN WET	A19, N40	None	211	242	Forbidden	15 kg	E	
	Sodium hydrogen fluoride	8	UN2439	II	CORROSIVE	N3, N34	154	212	240	15 kg	50 kg	A	12, 25, 26, 40, 48
	Sodium hydrogen fluoride, solution	8	UN2439	II	CORROSIVE	N3, N34	154	202	242	1 L	30 L	A	12, 25, 26, 40
	Sodium hydrogen sulfate, solid	8	UN1821	III	CORROSIVE		154	213	240	25 kg	100 kg	A	
	Sodium hydrogen sulfate, solution	8	UN2837	II	CORROSIVE	A7, B2, N34, T8, T26	154	202	242	1 L	30 L	A	

351

Sym-bols	Hazardous materials descriptions and proper shipping names	Hazard class or Division	Identifi-cation Numbers	Packing group	Label(s) required (if not excepted)	Special provisions	Exceptions	Non-bulk packaging	Bulk packaging	Passenger aircraft or railcar	Cargo aircraft only	Vessel stowages	Other stowage provisions
(1)	(2)	(3)	(4)	(5)	(6)	(7)	(8A)	(8B)	(8C)	(9A)	(9B)	(10A)	(10B)
D	Sodium hydrosulfide, solution	8	NA2922	II	CORROSIVE, POISON	B2	154	202	242	1 L	30 L	B	40, 95
	Sodium hydrosulfide, with less than 25 per cent water of crystallization	4.2	UN2318	II	SPONTANEOUSLY COMBUSTIBLE	A7, A19, A20	None	212	241	15 kg	50 kg	A	
	Sodium hydrosulfide with not less than 25 per cent water of crystallization	8	UN2949	II	CORROSIVE	A7	154	212	240	15 kg	50 kg	A	26
	Sodium hydrosulfite, see Sodium dithionite												
	Sodium hydroxide, solid	8	UN1823	II	CORROSIVE		154	212	240	15 kg	50 kg	A	
	Sodium hydroxide solution	8	UN1824	II	CORROSIVE	B2, N34, T8	154	202	242	1 L	30 L	A	
	Sodium hypochlorite, solution, see Hypochlorite solutions etc.												
	Sodium metal, liquid alloy, see Alkali metal alloys, liquid, n.o.s.												
	Sodium methylate	4.2	UN1431	II	SPONTANEOUSLY COMBUSTIBLE, CORROSIVE	A19	None	211	242	15kg	50 kg	B	
	Sodium methylate solutions in alcohol	3	UN1289	II	FLAMMABLE LIQUID	T8, T31	150	202	242	5 L	60 L	B	
				III	FLAMMABLE LIQUID	B1, T7, T30	150	202	242	60 L	220 L	A	
	Sodium monoxide	8	UN1825	II	CORROSIVE		154	212	240	15 kg	50 kg	A	
	Sodium nitrate	5.1	UN1498	III	OXIDIZER	A1, A29	152	213	240	25 kg	100 kg	A	
	Sodium nitrate and potassium nitrate mixtures	5.1	UN1499	III	OXIDIZER	A1, A29	152	213	240	25 kg	100 kg	A	
	Sodium nitrite	5.1	UN1500	III	OXIDIZER	A1, A29	152	213	240	25 kg	100 kg	A	56, 58
	Sodium pentachlorophenate	6.1	UN2567	II	POISON		None	212	242	25 kg	100 kg	A	
	Sodium percarbonate	5.1	UN2467	III	OXIDIZER	27, A1, A29	152	213	240	25 kg	100 kg	A	13
	Sodium perchlorate	5.1	UN1502	II	OXIDIZER	T8	152	212	242	5 kg	25 kg	A	56, 58, 106
	Sodium permanganate	5.1	UN1503	II	OXIDIZER		152	212	242	5 kg	25 kg	D	56, 58, 69, 106, 107
	Sodium peroxide	5.1	UN1504	I	OXIDIZER	A20, N34	None	211	None	Forbidden	15 kg	B	13, 75, 106
	Sodium persulfate	5.1	UN1505	III	OXIDIZER	A1	152	213	240	25 kg	100 kg	A	
	Sodium phenolate, solid	8	UN2497	III	CORROSIVE		154	213	240	25 kg	100 kg	A	
	Sodium phosphide	4.3	UN1432	I	DANGEROUS WHEN WET, POISON	A19, N40	None	211	None	Forbidden	15 kg	E	40, 85
	Sodium picramate, dry or wetted with less than 20 per cent water, by mass	1.3C	UN0235	II	EXPLOSIVE 1.3C		None	62	None	Forbidden	Forbidden	B	1E, 5E
	Sodium picramate, wetted with not less than 20 per cent water, by mass	4.1	UN1349	I	FLAMMABLE SOLID	A8, A19, N41	None	211	None	Forbidden	15 kg	E	28, 36
	Sodium picryl peroxide	Forbid-den											
	Sodium potassium alloys, see Potassium sodium alloys												
	Sodium salts of aromatic nitro-derivatives, n.o.s.explosive	1.3C	UN0203	II	EXPLOSIVE 1.3C		None	62	None	Forbidden	Forbidden	B	1E, 5E
	Sodium selenate, see Selenates or Selenites												
D	Sodium selenite	6.1	NA2630	II	POISON		None	212	242	25 kg	100 kg	E	
	Sodium sulfide, anhydrous or Sodium sulfide with less than 30 per cent water of crystallization	4.2	UN1385	II	SPONTANEOUSLY COMBUSTIBLE	A19, A20, N34	None	212	241	15 kg	50 kg	A	
	Sodium sulfide, hydrated with at least 30 per cent water	8	UN1849	II	CORROSIVE	T8	154	212	240	15 kg	50 kg	A	26
	Sodium superoxide	5.1	UN2547	I	OXIDIZER	A20, N34	None	211	None	Forbidden	15 kg	E	13, 75, 106
	Sodium tetranitride	Forbid-den											
	Sounding devices, explosive	1.2F	UN0204	II	EXPLOSIVE 1.2F		None	62	None	Forbidden	Forbidden	E	
	Sounding devices, explosive	1.1F	UN0296	II	EXPLOSIVE 1.1F		None	62	None	Forbidden	Forbidden	E	
	Sounding devices, explosive	1.1D	UN0374	II	EXPLOSIVE 1.1D		None	62	None	Forbidden	Forbidden	B	
	Sounding devices, explosive	1.2D	UN0375	II	EXPLOSIVE 1.2D		None	62	None	Forbidden	Forbidden	B	
	Spirits of salt, see Hydrochloric acid												
	Squibs, see Igniters etc.												
	Stannic chloride, anhydrous	8	UN1827	II	CORROSIVE	B2, T8, T26	154	202	242	1 L	30 L	C	8
	Stannic chloride, pentahydrate	8	UN2440	III	CORROSIVE		154	213	240	25 kg	100 kg	A	
	Stannic phosphide	4.3	UN1433	I	DANGEROUS WHEN WET, POISON	A19, N40	None	211	242	Forbidden	15 kg	E	40, 85
	Steel swarf, see Ferrous metal borings, etc.												
	Stibine	2.3	UN2676		POISON GAS, FLAMMABLE GAS	1	None	304	None	Forbidden	Forbidden	D	40
	Storage batteries, wet, see Batteries, wet etc.												
	Strontium arsenite	6.1	UN1691	II	POISON		None	212	242	25 kg	100 kg	A	
	Strontium chlorate, solid or solution	5.1	UN1506	II	OXIDIZER	A1, A9, N34, T8	152	212	242	5 kg	25 kg	A	56, 58, 106

352

Symbols	Hazardous materials descriptions and proper shipping names	Hazard class or Division	Identification Numbers	Packing group	Label(s) required (if not excepted)	Special provisions	Exceptions	Non-bulk packaging	Bulk packaging	Passenger aircraft or railcar	Cargo aircraft only	Vessel stowages	Other stowage provisions
(1)	(2)	(3)	(4)	(5)	(6)	(7)	(8A)	(8B)	(8C)	(9A)	(9B)	(10A)	(10B)
	Strontium nitrate	5.1	UN1507	III	OXIDIZER	A1, A29	152	213	240	25 kg	100 kg	A	
	Strontium perchlorate	5.1	UN1508	II	OXIDIZER	T8	152	212	242	5 kg	25 kg	A	56, 58, 106
	Strontium peroxide	5.1	UN1509	II	OXIDIZER		152	212	242	5 kg	25 kg	A	13, 75, 106
	Strontium phosphide	4.3	UN2013	I	DANGEROUS WHEN WET, POISON	A19, N40	None	211	None	Forbidden	15 kg	E	40, 85
	Strychnine or Strychnine salts	6.1	UN1692	I	POISON		None	211	242	5 kg	50 kg	A	40
	Styphnic acid, see Trinitroresorcinol, etc.												
	Styrene monomer, inhibited	3	UN2055	III	FLAMMABLE LIQUID	B1, T1	150	203	242	60 L	220 L	A	
	Substances, explosive, n.o.s.	1.1L	UN0357	II	EXPLOSIVE 1.1L	101	None	62	None	Forbidden	Forbidden	E	2E, 8E, 11E, 17E
	Substances, explosive, n.o.s.	1.2L	UN0358	II	EXPLOSIVE 1.2L	101	None	62	None	Forbidden	Forbidden	E	2E, 8E, 11E, 17E
	Substances, explosive, n.o.s.	1.3L	UN0359	II	EXPLOSIVE 1.3L	101	None	62	None	Forbidden	Forbidden	E	2E, 8E, 11E, 17E
	Substances, explosive, n.o.s.	1.1A	UN0473	II	EXPLOSIVE 1.1A	101, 111	None	62	None	Forbidden	Forbidden	E	2E, 6E
	Substances, explosive, n.o.s.	1.1C	UN0474	II	EXPLOSIVE 1.1C	101	None	62	None	Forbidden	Forbidden	B	1E, 5E
	Substances, explosive, n.o.s.	1.1D	UN0475	II	EXPLOSIVE 1.1D	101	None	62	None	Forbidden	Forbidden	B	1E, 5E
	Substances, explosive, n.o.s.	1.1G	UN0476	II	EXPLOSIVE 1.1G	101	None	62	None	Forbidden	Forbidden	B	1E, 5E
	Substances, explosive, n.o.s.	1.3C	UN0477	II	EXPLOSIVE 1.3C	101	None	62	None	Forbidden	Forbidden	E	1E, 8E
	Substances, explosive, n.o.s.	1.3G	UN0478	II	EXPLOSIVE 1.3G	101	None	62	None	Forbidden	Forbidden	E	1E, 8E
	Substances, explosive, n.o.s..	1.4G	UN0485	II	EXPLOSIVE 1.4G	101	None	62	None	Forbidden	75 kg	E	1E, 5E
	Substances, explosive, n.o.s.	1.4S	UN0481	II	EXPLOSIVE 1.4S	101	None	62	None	25 kg	75 kg	A	1E, 5E
	Substances, explosive, very insensitive, n.o.s., or Substances, EVI, n.o.s.	1.5D	UN0482	II	EXPLOSIVE 1.5D	101	None	62	None	Forbidden	Forbidden	B	1E, 5E
	Substances, explosives, n.o.s.	1.4C	UN0479	II	EXPLOSIVE 1.4C	101	None	62	None	Forbidden	75 kg	A	1E, 5E
	Substances, explosives, n.o.s.	1.4D	UN0480	II	EXPLOSIVE 1.4D	101	None	62	None	Forbidden	75 kg	A	1E, 5E
	Substances which in contact with water emit flammable gases, liquid, corrosive, n.o.s.	4.3	UN3129	I	DANGEROUS WHEN WET, CORROSIVE		None	201	243	Forbidden	1 L	E	
				II	DANGEROUS WHEN WET, CORROSIVE		None	202	243	1 L	5 L	E	
				III	DANGEROUS WHEN WET, CORROSIVE		None	203	242	5 L	60 L	E	
	Substances which in contact with water emit flammable gases, liquid n.o.s.	4.3	UN3148	I	DANGEROUS WHEN WET		None	201	244	Forbidden	1 L	E	40
				II	DANGEROUS WHEN WET		None	202	243	1 L	5 L	E	40
				III	DANGEROUS WHEN WET		None	203	243	5 L	60 L	E	40
	Substances which in contact with water emit flammable gases, liquid, poisonous, n.o.s.	4.3	UN3130	I	DANGEROUS WHEN WET, POISON	A4	None	201	243	Forbidden	1 L	E	
				II	DANGEROUS WHEN WET, POISON		None	202	243	1 L	5 L	E	
				III	DANGEROUS WHEN WET, KEEP AWAY FROM FOOD		None	203	242	5 L	60 L	E	
	Substances which in contact with water emit flammable gases, solid, corrosive, n.o.s.	4.3	UN3131	I	DANGEROUS WHEN WET, CORROSIVE	N40	None	211	242	Forbidden	15 kg	E	
				II	DANGEROUS WHEN WET, CORROSIVE		None	212	242	15 kg	50 kg	E	
				III	DANGEROUS WHEN WET, CORROSIVE		None	213	241	25 kg	100 kg	E	
	Substances which in contact with water emit flammable gases, solid, flammable n.o.s.	4.3	UN3132	I	DANGEROUS WHEN WET, FLAMMABLE SOLID	N40	None	211	242	Forbidden	15 kg	E	
				II	DANGEROUS WHEN WET, FLAMMABLE SOLID		None	212	242	15 kg	50 kg	E	
				III	DANGEROUS WHEN WET, FLAMMABLE SOLID		None	213	241	25 kg	100 kg	E	
I	Substances which in contact with water emit flammable gases, solid n.o.s.	4.3	UN2813	I	DANGEROUS WHEN WET	N40	None	211	242	Forbidden	15kg	E	40
				II	DANGEROUS WHEN WET		None	212	242	15kg	50kg	E	40
				III	DANGEROUS WHEN WET		None	213	242	25kg	100kg	E	40

353

Sym-bols	Hazardous materials descriptions and proper shipping names	Hazard class or Division	Identification Numbers	Packing group	Label(s) required (if not excepted)	Special provisions	Exceptions (8A)	Non-bulk pack-aging (8B)	Bulk pack-aging (8C)	Passenger aircraft or railcar (9A)	Cargo aircraft only (9B)	Vessel stow-ages (10A)	Other stowage provisions (10B)
(1)	(2)	(3)	(4)	(5)	(6)	(7)	(8A)	(8B)	(8C)	(9A)	(9B)	(10A)	(10B)
	Substances which in contact with water emit flammable gases, solid, oxidizing, n.o.s.	4.3	UN3133		DANGEROUS WHEN WET, OXIDIZER		None	214	214	Forbidden	Forbidden		
	Substances which in contact with water, emit flammable gases, solid, poisonous, n.o.s.	4.3	UN3134	I	DANGEROUS WHEN WET, POISON	A5, N40	None	211	242	Forbidden	15kg	E	
				II	DANGEROUS WHEN WET, POISON		None	212	242	15kg	50kg	E	
				III	DANGEROUS WHEN WET, KEEP AWAY FROM FOOD		None	213	241	25kg	100kg	E	
	Substances which in contact with water emit flammable gases, solid, self-heating, n.o.s.	4.3	UN3135	I	DANGEROUS WHEN WET, SPONTANEOUSLY COMBUSTIBLE	N40	None	211	242	Forbidden	15 kg	E	
				II	DANGEROUS WHEN WET, SPONTANEOUSLY COMBUSTIBLE		None	212	242	15 kg	50 kg	E	
				III	DANGEROUS WHEN WET, SPONTANEOUSLY COMBUSTIBLE		None	213	241	25 kg	100 kg	E	
	Substituted nitrophenol pesticides, liquid, flammable, toxic, n.o.s., *flash point less than 23 degrees C.*	3	UN2780	I	FLAMMABLE LIQUID, POISON		None	201	243	Forbidden	30 L	B	
				II	FLAMMABLE LIQUID, POISON		None	202	243	1 L	60 L	B	
	Substituted nitrophenol pesticides, liquid, toxic, flammable, n.o.s., *flashpoint not less than 23 degrees C.*	6.1	UN3013	I	POISON, FLAMMABLE LIQUID	T42	None	201	243	1 L	30 L	B	40
				II	POISON, FLAMMABLE LIQUID	T14	None	202	243	5 L	60 L	B	40
				III	KEEP AWAY FROM FOOD, FLAMMABLE LIQUID	B1, T14	153	203	242	60 L	220 L	A	40
	Substituted nitrophenol pesticides, liquid, toxic, n.o.s.	6.1	UN3014	I	POISON	T42	None	201	243	1 L	30 L	B	40
				II	POISON	T14	None	202	243	5 L	60 L	B	40
				III	KEEP AWAY FROM FOOD	T14	153	203	241	60 L	220 L	A	40
	Substituted nitrophenol pesticides, solid, toxic, n.o.s.	6.1	UN2779	I	POISON		None	211	242	5 kg	50 kg	A	40
				II	POISON		None	212	242	25 kg	100 kg	A	40
				III	KEEP AWAY FROM FOOD		153	213	240	100 kg	200 kg	A	40
	Sucrose octanitrate (dry)	Forbid-den											
	Sulfamic acid	8	UN2967	III	CORROSIVE		154	213	240	25 kg	100 kg	A	
I	Sulfur	4.1	UN1350	III	FLAMMABLE SOLID	A1, N20	151	213	240	25 kg	100 kg	A	19, 74
D	Sulfur	9	NA1350	III	CLASS 9	A1, N20	151	213	240	25 kg	100 kg	A	19, 74
	Sulfur and chlorate, loose mixtures of	Forbid-den											
	Sulfur chlorides	8	UN1828	I	CORROSIVE	5, A3, B10, B77, N34	None	201	243	Forbidden	2.5 L	C	8, 40
	Sulfur dichloride, see Sulfur chlorides												
	Sulfur dioxide, liquefied	2.3	UN1079		POISON GAS	3, B14	None	304	314, 315	Forbidden	25 kg	D	40
	Sulfur dioxide solution, see Sulfurous acid												
	Sulfur hexafluoride	2.2	UN1080		NONFLAMMABLE GAS		306	304	314, 315	75 kg	150 kg	A	
I	Sulfur, molten	4.1	UN2448	III	FLAMMABLE SOLID	B12, B85, T9	None	213	241	Forbidden	Forbidden	C	61
D	Sulfur, molten	9	NA2448	III	CLASS 9	B12, B85, T9	None	213	241	Forbidden	Forbidden	C	61
	Sulfur tetrafluoride	2.3	UN2418		POISON GAS	1	None	302	245	Forbidden	25 kg	D	40
+	Sulfur trioxide, inhibited	8	UN1829	I	CORROSIVE, POISON	2, A7, B9, B12, B14, B32, B49, B74, B77, N34, T38, T43, T45	None	227	244	Forbidden	25 kg	A	10, 40
+,D	Sulfur trioxide, uninhibited	8	NA1829	I	CORROSIVE, POISON	2, A7, B9, B12, B14, B32, B49, B74, B77, N34, T38, T43, T45	None	227	244	Forbidden	25 kg	A	10, 40
	Sulfuretted hydrogen, see Hydrogen sulfide, liquefied												
	Sulfuric acid	8	UN1830	II	CORROSIVE	A3, A7, B2, B83, B84, N34, T9, T27	154	202	242	1 L	30 L	C	14

354

Sym-bols (1)	Hazardous materials descriptions and proper shipping names (2)	Hazard class or Division (3)	Identification Numbers (4)	Packing group (5)	Label(s) required (if not excepted) (6)	Special provisions (7)	(8) Packaging authorizations (§173.***) Exceptions (8A)	Non-bulk packaging (8B)	Bulk packaging (8C)	(9) Quantity limitations Passenger aircraft or railcar (9A)	Cargo aircraft only (9B)	(10) Vessel stowage requirements Vessel stowages (10A)	Other stowage provisions (10B)
+	Sulfuric acid, fuming greater than or equal to 30 percent free sulfur trioxide	8	UN1831	I	CORROSIVE, POISON	2, A3, A6, A7, B9, B14, B32, B74, B77, B84, N34, T38, T43, T45	None	227	244	Forbidden	2.5 L	C	14, 40
	Sulfuric acid, fuming less than 30 percent free sulfur trioxide	8	UN1831	I	CORROSIVE, POISON	A3, A7, B84, N34, T18, T27	None	201	243	Forbidden	2.5 L	C	14, 40
	Sulfuric acid, spent	8	UN1832	II	CORROSIVE	A3, A7, B2, B83, B84, N34, T9, T27	None	202	242	Forbidden	30 L	C	14
	Sulfuric and hydrofluoric acid mixtures, see Hydrofluoric and sulfuric acid mixtures												
	Sulfuric anhydride, see Sulfur trioxide, inhibited												
	Sulfurous acid	8	UN1833	II	CORROSIVE	B3, T8	154	202	242	1 L	30 L	B	40
+	Sulfuryl chloride	8	UN1834	I	CORROSIVE, POISON	1, A3, B6, B9, B10, B14, B32, B74, B77, N34, T38, T43, T44	None	226	244	0.5 L	2.5 L	C	8, 40
	Sulfuryl fluoride	2.3	UN2191		POISON GAS	4	None	304	314, 315	Forbidden	25 kg	D	40
	Tars, liquid including road asphalt and oils, bitumen and cut backs	3	UN1999	II	FLAMMABLE LIQUID	T7, T30	150	202	242	5 L	60 L	B	
				III	FLAMMABLE LIQUID	B1, T7, T30	150	203	242	60 L	220 L	A	
	Tear gas candles	6.1	UN1700	II	POISON, FLAMMABLE SOLID		None	340	None	Forbidden	50 kg	D	40
	Tear gas cartridges, see Ammunition, tear-producing, etc.												
D	Tear gas devices with more than 2 per cent tear gas substances, by mass	6.1	NA1693	I	POISON		None	340	None	Forbidden	Forbidden	D	40, 95
				II	POISON		None	340	None	Forbidden	Forbidden	D	40, 95
	Tear gas devices, with not more than 2 per cent tear gas substances, by mass, see Aerosols, etc.												
	Tear gas grenades, see Tear gas candles												
	Tear gas substances, n.o.s., liquid	6.1	UN1693	I	POISON		None	201	None	Forbidden	Forbidden	D	40
				II	POISON		None	202	None	Forbidden	5 L	D	40
	Tear gas substances, n.o.s., solid	6.1	UN1693	I	POISON		None	211	None	Forbidden	Forbidden	D	40
				II	POISON		None	212	None	Forbidden	25 kg	D	40
	Tellurium hexafluoride	2.3	UN2195		POISON GAS	1	None	302	None	Forbidden	Forbidden	D	40
	Terpene hydrocarbons, n.o.s.	3	UN2319	III	FLAMMABLE LIQUID	B1, T1	150	203	242	60 L	220 L	A	
	Terpinolene	3	UN2541	III	FLAMMABLE LIQUID	B1, T1	150	203	242	60 L	220 L	A	
	Tetraazido benzene quinone	Forbidden											
	Tetrabromoethane	6.1	UN2504	III	KEEP AWAY FROM FOOD	T7	153	203	241	60 L	220 L	A	
	Tetrachloroethane	6.1	UN1702	II	POISON	N36, T14	None	202	243	5 L	60 L	A	40
	Tetrachloroethylene	6.1	UN1897	III	KEEP AWAY FROM FOOD	N36, T1	153	203	241	60 L	220 L	A	40
	Tetraethyl dithiopyrophosphate	6.1	UN1704	II	POISON		None	212	242	25 kg	100 kg	D	40
	Tetraethyl dithiopyrophosphate and gases in solution or tetraethyl dithiopyrophosphate and gas mixtures LC50 over 200 but not greater than 5000 ppm	2.3	UN1703		POISON GAS	6	None	334	245	Forbidden	Forbidden	D	40
	Tetraethyl dithiopyrophosphate and gases in solution or Tetraethyl dithiopyrophosphate and gases mixtures LC50 less than or equal to 200 ppm	2.3	UN1703		POISON GAS	1	None	334	245	Forbidden	Forbidden	D	40, 85, 95
D	Tetraethyl lead, liquid	6.1	NA1649	I	POISON, FLAMMABLE LIQUID		None	201	None	Forbidden	Forbidden	E	40
	Tetraethyl pyrophosphate and compressed gas mixtures LC50 less than or equal to 200 ppm	2.3	UN1705		POISON GAS	1	None	334	245	Forbidden	Forbidden	D	40, 85, 95
	Tetraethyl pyrophosphate and compressed gas mixtures LC50 over 200 ppm but not greater than 5000 ppm	2.3	UN1705		POISON GAS	6, B9, B14	None	334	314, 315	Forbidden	Forbidden	D	40
D	Tetraethyl pyrophosphate, liquid	6.1	NA3018	I	POISON		None	201	243	Forbidden	1 L	A	40
D	Tetraethyl pyrophosphate solid	6.1	NA2783	I	POISON	N77	None	211	242	Forbidden	50 kg	A	40
	Tetraethyl silicate	3	UN1292	III	FLAMMABLE LIQUID	B1, T1	150	203	241	60 L	220 L	A	
	Tetraethylammonium perchlorate (dry)	Forbidden											
	Tetraethylenepentamine	8	UN2320	III	CORROSIVE	T2	154	203	241	5 L	60 L	A	8
	Tetrafluoroethylene, inhibited	2.1	UN1081		FLAMMABLE GAS		306	304	None	Forbidden	150 kg	E	40
	Tetrafluoromethane, R14	2.2	UN1982		NONFLAMMABLE GAS		None	302	None	75 kg	150 kg	A	
	1,2,3,6-Tetrahydrobenzaldehyde	3	UN2498	III	FLAMMABLE LIQUID	B1, T1	150	203	242	60 L	220 L	A	

355

Sym-bols (1)	Hazardous materials descriptions and proper shipping names (2)	Hazard class or Division (3)	Identification Numbers (4)	Packing group (5)	Label(s) required (if not excepted) (6)	Special provisions (7)	(8) Packaging authorizations (§173.***)			(9) Quantity limitations		(10) Vessel stowage requirements	
							Exceptions (8A)	Non-bulk packaging (8B)	Bulk packaging (8C)	Passenger aircraft or railcar (9A)	Cargo aircraft only (9B)	Vessel stowages (10A)	Other stowage provisions (10B)
	Tetrahydrofuran	3	UN2056	II	FLAMMABLE LIQUID	T8	None	202	242	5 L	60 L	B	
	Tetrahydrofurfurylamine	3	UN2943	III	FLAMMABLE LIQUID	B1, T1	150	203	242	60 L	220 L	A	
	Tetrahydrophthalic anhydrides with more than 0.05 percent of maleic anhydride	8	UN2698	III	CORROSIVE		154	213	240	25 kg	100 kg	A	
	1,2,3,6-Tetrahydropyridine	3	UN2410	II	FLAMMABLE LIQUID	T8	150	202	242	5 L	60 L	B	
	Tetrahydrothiophene	3	UN2412	II	FLAMMABLE LIQUID	T7	150	202	242	5 L	60 L	B	
	Tetramethylammonium hydroxide	8	UN1835	II	CORROSIVE	B2, T8	154	202	242	1 L	30 L	A	
	Tetramethylene diperoxide dicarbamide	Forbidden											
	Tetramethylsilane	3	UN2749	I	FLAMMABLE LIQUID	T21, T26	None	201	243	Forbidden	30 L	D	
	Tetranitro diglycerin	Forbidden											
	Tetranitroaniline	1.1D	UN0207	II	EXPLOSIVE 1.1D		None	62	None	Forbidden	Forbidden	B	1E, 5E, 19E
+	Tetranitromethane	5.1	UN1510	I	OXIDIZER, POISON	2, B9, B14, B32, B74, T38, T43, T45	None	227	None	Forbidden	Forbidden	D	40, 66, 106
	2,3,4,6-Tetranitrophenol	Forbidden											
	2,3,4,6-Tetranitrophenyl methyl nitramine	Forbidden											
	2,3,4,6-Tetranitrophenylnitramine	Forbidden											
	Tetranitroresorcinol (dry)	Forbidden											
	2,3,5,6-Tetranitroso-1,4-dinitrobenzene	Forbidden											
	2,3,5,6-Tetranitroso nitrobenzene (dry)	Forbidden											
	Tetrapropylorthotitanate	3	UN2413	III	FLAMMABLE LIQUID	B1, T8	150	202	242	5 L	60 L	A	
	Tetrazene, see Guanyl nitrosaminoguanyltetrazene												
	Tetrazine (dry)	Forbidden											
	Tetrazol-1-acetic acid	1.4C	UN0407	II	EXPLOSIVE 1.4C		None	62	None	Forbidden	75 kg	A	1E, 5E
	Tetrazolyl azide (dry)	Forbidden											
	Tetryl, see Trinitrophenylmethylnitramine												
	Thallium chlorate	5.1	UN2573	II	OXIDIZER, POISON		None	212	242	5 kg	25 kg	A	56, 58, 106
	Thallium compounds, n.o.s.	6.1	UN1707	II	POISON		None	212	242	25 kg	100 kg	A	
	Thallium nitrate	6.1	UN2727	II	POISON, OXIDIZER		None	212	242	5 kg	25 kg	A	89
D	Thallium sulfate, solid	6.1	NA1707	II	POISON		None	211	242	5 kg	50 kg	A	
	Thia-4-pentanal	6.1	UN2785	III	KEEP AWAY FROM FOOD	T8	153	203	241	60 L	220 L	D	25, 49
	Thioacetic acid	3	UN2436	II	FLAMMABLE LIQUID	T8	150	202	242	5 L	60 L	B	
	Thiocarbonylchloride, see Thiophosgene												
	Thioglycol	6.1	UN2966	II	POISON	T8	None	202	243	5 L	60 L	A	
	Thioglycolic acid	8	UN1940	II	CORROSIVE	A7, B2, N34, T8	154	202	242	1 L	30 L	A	
	Thiolactic acid	6.1	UN2936	II	POISON	T8	None	212	242	25 kg	100 kg	A	
+	Thionyl chloride	8	UN1836	I	CORROSIVE, POISON	2, A3, A10, B6, B9, B14, B32, B74, B77, N34, T38, T43, T45	None	227	244	Forbidden	2.5 L	C	8, 40
	Thiophene	3	UN2414	II	FLAMMABLE LIQUID	T2	150	202	242	5 L	60 L	B	40
+	Thiophosgene	6.1	UN2474	II	POISON	2, A7, B9, B14, B32, B74, N33, N34, T38, T43, T45	None	227	244	Forbidden	60 L	B	26, 40
	Thiophosphoryl chloride	8	UN1837	II	CORROSIVE	A3, A7, B2, B8, B25, N34, T12	None	202	242	Forbidden	30 L	C	8, 40
	Thorium metal, pyrophoric	7	UN2975		RADIOACTIVE, SPONTANEOUSLY COMBUSTIBLE		None	418	None	Forbidden	Forbidden	D	
	Thorium nitrate, solid	7	UN2976		RADIOACTIVE, OXIDIZER		None	419	None	Forbidden	15 kg	A	
	Tin chloride, fuming, see Stannic chloride, anhydrous												
	Tin perchloride or Tin tetrachloride, see Stannic chloride, anhydrous												

356

Sym-bols	Hazardous materials descriptions and proper shipping names	Hazard class or Division	Identifi-cation Numbers	Packing group	Label(s) required (if not excepted)	Special provisions	Excep-tions (8A)	Non-bulk pack-aging (8B)	Bulk pack-aging (8C)	Passenger aircraft or railcar (9A)	Cargo aircraft only (9B)	Vessel stow-ages (10A)	Other stowage provisions (10B)
(1)	(2)	(3)	(4)	(5)	(6)	(7)	(8A)	(8B)	(8C)	(9A)	(9B)	(10A)	(10B)
	Tinctures, medicinal	3	UN1293	II	FLAMMABLE LIQUID	T8, T31	150	202	242	5 L	60 L	B	
				III	FLAMMABLE LIQUID	B1, T7, T30	150	203	241	60 L	220 L	A	
	Tinning flux, see Zinc chloride												
	Titanium hydride	4.1	UN1871	II	FLAMMABLE SOLID	A19, A20, N34	None	212	241	15 kg	50 kg	E	
	Titanium powder, dry	4.2	UN2546	I	SPONTANEOUSLY COMBUSTIBLE		None	211	242	Forbidden	Forbidden	D	
				II	SPONTANEOUSLY COMBUSTIBLE	A19, A20, N5, N34	None	212	241	15 kg	50 kg	D	
				III	SPONTANEOUSLY COMBUSTIBLE		None	213	241	25 kg	100 kg	D	
	Titanium powder, wetted *with not less than 25 per cent water (a visible excess of water must be present) (a) mechanically produced, particle size less than 53 microns; (b) chemically produced, particle size less than 840 microns*	4.1	UN1352	II	FLAMMABLE SOLID	A19, A20, N34	None	212	240	15 kg	50 kg	E	
	Titanium sponge granules or Titanium sponge powders	4.1	UN2878	III	FLAMMABLE SOLID	A1	None	213	240	25 kg	100 kg	D	
D	Titanium sulfate solution	8	NA1760	II	CORROSIVE	B2, B15	None	213	242	1 L	30 L	B	40
+	Titanium tetrachloride	8	UN1838	II	CORROSIVE, POISON	2, A3, A6, B7, B9, B14, B32, B41, B74, N41, T38, T43, T45	None	227	244	Forbidden	30 L	C	8, 40
	Titanium trichloride mixtures	8	UN2869	II	CORROSIVE	A7, N34	154	212	240	15 kg	50 kg	A	40
	Titanium trichloride, pyrophoric or Titanium trichloride mixtures, pyrophoric	4.2	UN2441	I	SPONTANEOUSLY COMBUSTIBLE, CORROSIVE	A7, A8, A19, A20, N34	None	181	244	Forbidden	Forbidden	D	40
	TNT mixed with aluminum, see Tritonal												
	TNT, see Trinitrotoluene, etc.												
	Toe puffs, *nitrocellulose base*	4.1	UN1353	III	FLAMMABLE SOLID	A1	None	213	240	25 kg	100 kg	D	
	Toluene	3	UN1294	II	FLAMMABLE LIQUID	T1	150	202	242	5 L	60 L	B	
	Toluene diisocyanate	6.1	UN2078	II	POISON	T14	None	202	243	5 L	60 L	B	25, 40
	Toluene sulfonic acid, see Alkyl, Aryl or Toluene sulfonic acid etc.												
	Toluidines *liquid*	6.1	UN1708	II	POISON	T14	None	202	243	5 L	60 L	A	
	Toluidines *solid*	6.1	UN1708	II	POISON		None	212	241	25 kg	100 kg	A	
	2,4-Toluylenediamine or 2,4-Toluenediamine	6.1	UN1709	III	KEEP AWAY FROM FOOD	T7	153	213	240	100 kg	200 kg	A	
	Torpedoes, liquid fuelled, *with inert head*	1.3J	UN0450	II	EXPLOSIVE 1.3J		63(b)	62	None	Forbidden	Forbidden	E	7E, 16E, 23E
	Torpedoes, liquid fuelled, *with or without bursting charge*	1.1J	UN0449	II	EXPLOSIVE 1.1J		63(b)	62	None	Forbidden	Forbidden	E	7E, 16E, 23E
	Torpedoes *with bursting charge*	1.1E	UN0329	II	EXPLOSIVE 1.1E		63(b)	62	None	Forbidden	Forbidden	B	
	Torpedoes *with bursting charge*	1.1F	UN0330	II	EXPLOSIVE 1.1F		63(b)	62	None	Forbidden	Forbidden	B	
	Torpedoes *with bursting charge*	1.1D	UN0451	II	EXPLOSIVE 1.1D		63(b)	62	None	Forbidden	Forbidden	B	
	Tracers for ammunition	1.3G	UN0212	II	EXPLOSIVE 1.3G		None	62	None	Forbidden	Forbidden	B	
	Tracers for ammunition	1.4G	UN0306	II	EXPLOSIVE 1.4G		None	62	None	Forbidden	75 kg	A	24E
	Tractors, see Vehicles, self propelled												
	Tri-(b-nitroxyethyl) ammonium nitrate	Forbid-den											
	Triallyl borate	6.1	UN2609	III	KEEP AWAY FROM FOOD		153	203	241	60 L	220 L	A	13
	Triallylamine	3	UN2610	III	FLAMMABLE LIQUID	B1, T1	150	203	242	60 L	220 L	A	40
	Triazine pesticides, liquid, flammable, toxic, n.o.s., *flash point less than 23 deg C.*	3	UN2764	I	FLAMMABLE LIQUID, POISON		None	201	243	Forbidden	30 L	B	
				II	FLAMMABLE LIQUID, POISON		None	202	243	1 L	60 L	B	
	Triazine pesticides, liquid, toxic, flammable, n.o.s. *flashpoint not less than 23 degrees C.*	6.1	UN2997	I	POISON, FLAMMABLE LIQUID	T42	None	201	243	1 L	30 L	B	40
				II	POISON, FLAMMABLE LIQUID	T14	None	202	243	5 L	60 L	B	40
				III	KEEP AWAY FROM FOOD, FLAMMABLE LIQUID	T14	153	203	242	60 L	220 L	A	40
	Triazine pesticides, liquid, toxic, n.o.s.	6.1	UN2998	I	POISON	T42	None	201	243	1 L	30 L	B	40
				II	POISON	T14	None	202	243	5 L	60 L	B	40
				III	KEEP AWAY FROM FOOD	T14	153	203	241	60 L	220 L	A	40
	Triazine pesticides, solid, toxic, n.o.s.	6.1	UN2763	I	POISON		None	211	242	5 kg	50 kg	A	40
				II	POISON		None	212	242	25 kg	100 kg	A	40
				III	KEEP AWAY FROM FOOD		153	213	240	100 kg	200 kg	A	40

Sym-bols	Hazardous materials descriptions and proper shipping names	Hazard class or Division	Identifi-cation Numbers	Packing group	Label(s) required (If not excepted)	Special provisions	Exceptions	Non-bulk pack-aging	Bulk pack-aging	Passenger aircraft or railcar	Cargo aircraft only	Vessel stow-ages	Other stowage provisions
							(8A)	(8B)	(8C)	(9A)	(9B)	(10A)	(10B)
(1)	(2)	(3)	(4)	(5)	(6)	(7)							
	Tributylamine	8	UN2542	III	CORROSIVE	T2	None	203	241	5 L	60 L	A	
D	(mono-(Trichloro) tetra-(monopotassium dichloro)-penta-s-triazinetrione, dry (containing over 39% available chlorine)	5.1	NA2468	II	OXIDIZER		152	212	240	5 kg	25 kg	A	13
	Trichloro-s-triazinetrione dry, containing over 39% available chlorine, see Trichloroisocyanuric acid, dry												
	Trichloroacetic acid	8	UN1839	II	CORROSIVE	A7, N34	154	212	240	15 kg	50 kg	A	
	Trichloroacetic acid, solution	8	UN2564	II	CORROSIVE	A3, A6, A7, B2, N34, T8	154	202	242	1 L	30 L	B	8
+	Trichloroacetyl chloride	8	UN2442	II	CORROSIVE, POISON	1, A3, A7, B9, B14, B30, B72, N34, T38, T43, T44	None	226	244	Forbidden	Forbidden	D	40
	Trichlorobenzenes, liquid	6.1	UN2321	III	KEEP AWAY FROM FOOD	T7	153	203	241	60 L	220 L	A	
	Trichlorobutene	6.1	UN2322	II	POISON	T8	None	202	243	5 L	60 L	A	25, 40, 48
	1,1,1-Trichloroethane	6.1	UN2831	III	KEEP AWAY FROM FOOD	N36, T7	153	203	241	60 L	220 L	A	40
	Trichloroethylene	6.1	UN1710	III	KEEP AWAY FROM FOOD	N36, T1	153	203	241	60 L	220 L	A	40
	Trichloroisocyanuric acid, dry	5.1	UN2468	II	OXIDIZER		152	212	240	5 kg	25 kg	A	13
	Trichloromethyl perchlorate	Forbidden											
	Trichlorosilane	4.3	UN1295	I	DANGEROUS WHEN WET, FLAMMABLE LIQUID, CORROSIVE	A7, N34, T24, T26	None	201	244	Forbidden	Forbidden	D	21, 28, 40, 49, 100
	Tricresyl phosphate with more than 3 per cent ortho isomer	6.1	UN2574	II	POISON	A3, N33, N34, T8	None	202	243	5 L	60 L	A	
	Triethyl phosphite	3	UN2323	III	FLAMMABLE LIQUID	B1, T1	150	203	242	60 L	220 L	A	
	Triethylamine	3	UN1296	II	FLAMMABLE LIQUID	T8	150	202	242	5 L	60 L	B	40
	Triethylenetetramine	8	UN2259	II	CORROSIVE	B2, T8	154	202	242	1 L	30 L	B	40
	Trifluoroacetic acid	8	UN2699	I	CORROSIVE	A3, A6, A7, B4, N3, N34, T18, T27	None	201	242	0.5 L	2.5 L	B	12, 40, 48
	Trifluoroacetylchloride	2.2	UN3057		NONFLAMMABLE GAS, CORROSIVE	B44	None	304	314, 315	Forbidden	25kg	D	40
	Trifluorochloroethylene, inhibited, R1113	2.1	UN1082		FLAMMABLE GAS		306	304	314, 315	Forbidden	150 kg	B	40
	Trifluoroethane, compressed, R143	2.1	UN2035		FLAMMABLE GAS		306	304	314, 315	Forbidden	150 kg	B	40
	Trifluoromethane	2.2	UN1984		NONFLAMMABLE GAS		306	304	314, 315	75 kg	150 kg	A	
D	Trifluoromethane and chlorotrifluoromethane mixture (constant boiling mixture) (R-503). See Refrigerant gases, n.o.s.												
	Trifluoromethane, refrigerated, liquid	2.2	UN3136		NONFLAMMABLE GAS		306	None	314, 315	50 kg	500 kg	A	
	3-Trifluoromethylaniline	6.1	UN2948	II	POISON	T14	None	202	243	5 L	60 L	A	40
	2-Trifluoromethylaniline	6.1	UN2942	III	KEEP AWAY FROM FOOD		153	203	241	60 L	220 L	A	
	Triformoxime trinitrate	Forbidden											
	Triisobutylene	3	UN2324	III	FLAMMABLE LIQUID	B1, T7, T30	150	203	242	60 L	220 L	A	
	Triisocyanatoisocyanurate of Isophoronediisocyanate, solution, 70 per cent, by mass	3	UN2906	III	FLAMMABLE LIQUID	B1, T1	150	203	242	60 L	220 L	A	
	Triisopropyl borate	3	UN2616	III	FLAMMABLE LIQUID	B1, T8, T31	150	202	242	60 L	220 L	A	
D	Trimethoxysilane	6.1	NA9269	I	POISON, FLAMMABLE LIQUID	2, B9, B14, B32, B74, T38, T43, T45	None	227	244	Forbidden	Forbidden	E	40
	Trimethyl borate	3	UN2416	II	FLAMMABLE LIQUID	T14	150	202	242	5 L	60 L	B	
	Trimethyl phosphite	3	UN2329	III	FLAMMABLE LIQUID	T1	150	203	242	60 L	220 L	A	
	1,3,5-Trimethyl-2,4,6-trinitrobenzene	Forbidden											
+	Trimethylacetyl chloride	8	UN2438	II	CORROSIVE, FLAMMABLE LIQUID, POISON	2, A3, A6, A7, B3, B9, B14, B32, B74, N34, T38, T43, T45	None	227	244	1 L	30 L	D	12, 21, 25, 40, 48
	Trimethylamine, anhydrous	2.1	UN1083		FLAMMABLE GAS		306	304	314, 315	Forbidden	150 kg	B	40
	Trimethylamine, aqueous solutions not more than 50 per cent trimethylamine by mass	3	UN1297	I	FLAMMABLE LIQUID	T42	150	202	242	5 L	60 L	D	40, 41
				II	FLAMMABLE LIQUID	B1, T14	150	203	242	60 L	220 L	B	40, 41
	1,3,5-Trimethylbenzene	3	UN2325	III	FLAMMABLE LIQUID	B1, T1	None	203	242	60 L	220 L	A	

358

Sym-bols (1)	Hazardous materials descriptions and proper shipping names (2)	Hazard class or Division (3)	Identifi-cation Numbers (4)	Packing group (5)	Label(s) required (if not excepted) (6)	Special provisions (7)	Excep-tions (8A)	Non-bulk pack-aging (8B)	Bulk pack-aging (8C)	Passenger aircraft or railcar (9A)	Cargo aircraft only (9B)	Vessel stow-ages (10A)	Other stowage provisions (10B)
	Trimethylchlorosilane	3	UN1298	I	FLAMMABLE LIQUID, CORROSIVE	A3, A7, B77, N34, T14, T26	None	201	243	Forbidden	2.5 L	E	40
	Trimethylcyclohexylamine	8	UN2326	III	CORROSIVE	T2	154	203	241	5 L	60 L	A	8
	Trimethylene glycol diperchlorate	Forbid-den											
	Trimethylhexamethylene diisocyanate	6.1	UN2328	III	KEEP AWAY FROM FOOD	T8	153	203	241	60 L	220 L	B	
	Trimethylhexamethylenediamines	8	UN2327	III	CORROSIVE	T7	154	203	241	5 L	60 L	A	8
	Trimethylol nitromethane trinitrate	Forbid-den											
	Trinitro-meta-cresol	1.1D	UN0216	II	EXPLOSIVE 1.1D		None	62	None	Forbidden	Forbidden	B	1E, 5E
	2,4,6-Trinitro-1,3-diazobenzene	Forbid-den											
	2,4,6-Trinitro-1,3,5-triazido benzene (dry)	Forbid-den											
	Trinitroacetic acid	Forbid-den											
	Trinitroacetonitrile	Forbid-den											
	Trinitroamine cobalt	Forbid-den											
	Trinitroaniline or Picramide	1.1D	UN0153	II	EXPLOSIVE 1.1D		None	62	None	Forbidden	Forbidden	B	1E, 5E, 19E
	Trinitroanisole	1.1D	UN0213	II	EXPLOSIVE 1.1D		None	62	None	Forbidden	Forbidden	B	1E, 5E, 19E
	Trinitrobenzene, dry or wetted with less than 30 per cent water, by mass	1.1D	UN0214	II	EXPLOSIVE 1.1D		None	62	None	Forbidden	Forbidden	B	1E, 5E, 19E
	Trinitrobenzene, wetted with not less than 30 per cent water, by mass	4.1	UN1354	I	FLAMMABLE SOLID	A2, A8, A19, N41	None	211	None	0.5 kg	0.5 kg	E	28, 36
	Trinitrobenzenesulfonic acid	1.1D	UN0386	II	EXPLOSIVE 1.1D		None	62	None	Forbidden	Forbidden	E	1E, 5E, 19E
	Trinitrobenzoic acid, dry or wetted with less than 30 per cent water, by mass	1.1D	UN0215	II	EXPLOSIVE 1.1D		None	62	None	Forbidden	Forbidden	B	1E, 5E
	Trinitrobenzoic acid, wetted with not less than 30 per cent water, by mass	4.1	UN1355	I	FLAMMABLE SOLID	A2, A8, A19, N41	None	211	None	0.5 kg	0.5 kg	E	28, 36
	Trinitrochlorobenzene or Picryl chloride	1.1D	UN0155	II	EXPLOSIVE 1.1D		None	62	None	Forbidden	Forbidden	B	1E, 5E
	Trinitroethanol	Forbid-den											
	Trinitroethylnitrate	Forbid-den											
	Trinitrofluorenone	1.1D	UN0387	II	EXPLOSIVE 1.1D		None	62	None	Forbidden	Forbidden	B	1E, 5E, 19E
	Trinitromethane	Forbid-den											
	1,3,5-Trinitronaphthalene	Forbid-den											
	Trinitronaphthalene	1.1D	UN0217	II	EXPLOSIVE 1.1D		None	62	None	Forbidden	Forbidden	B	1E, 5E, 19E
	Trinitrophenetole	1.1D	UN0218	II	EXPLOSIVE 1.1D		None	62	None	Forbidden	Forbidden	B	1E, 5E, 19E
	Trinitrophenol or Picric acid, dry or wetted with less than 30 per cent water, by mass	1.1D	UN0154	II	EXPLOSIVE 1.1D		None	62	None	Forbidden	Forbidden	B	1E, 5E
	Trinitrophenol, wetted with not less than 30 per cent water, by mass	4.1	UN1344	I	FLAMMABLE SOLID	A8, A19, N41	None	211	None	1 kg	15 kg	E	28, 36, 48
	2,4,6-Trinitrophenyl guanidine (dry)	Forbid-den											
	2,4,6-Trinitrophenyl nitramine	Forbid-den											
	2,4,6-Trinitrophenyl trimethylol methyl nitramine trinitrate (dry)	Forbid-den											
	Trinitrophenylmethylnitramine or Tetryl	1.1D	UN0208	II	EXPLOSIVE 1.1D		None	62	None	Forbidden	Forbidden	B	1E, 5E
	Trinitroresorcinol or Styphnic acid, dry or wetted with less than 20 per cent water, or mixture of alcohol and water, by mass	1.1D	UN0219	II	EXPLOSIVE 1.1D		None	62	None	Forbidden	Forbidden	B	1E, 5E
	Trinitroresorcinol, wetted or Styphnic acid, wetted with not less than 20 per cent water, or mixture of alcohol and water by mass	1.1D	UN0394	II	EXPLOSIVE 1.1D		None	62	None	Forbidden	Forbidden	B	1E, 5E
	2,4,6-Trinitroso-3-methyl nitraminoanisole	Forbid-den											
	Trinitrotetramine cobalt nitrate	Forbid-den											
	Trinitrotoluene and Trinitrobenzene mixtures or Trinitrotoluene or TNT and trinitrobenzene mixtures or TNT and hexanitrostilbene mixturesand Hexanitrostilbene mixtures	1.1D	UN0388	II	EXPLOSIVE 1.1D		None	62	None	Forbidden	Forbidden	B	1E, 5E, 19E

Sym-bols	Hazardous materials descriptions and proper shipping names	Hazard class or Division	Identifi-cation Numbers	Packing group	Label(s) required (if not excepted)	Special provisions	(8) Packaging authorizations (§173.***)			(9) Quantity limitations		(10) Vessel stowage requirements	
							Excep-tions	Non-bulk pack-aging	Bulk pack-aging	Passenger aircraft or railcar	Cargo aircraft only	Vessel stow-ages	Other stowage provisions
(1)	(2)	(3)	(4)	(5)	(6)	(7)	(8A)	(8B)	(8C)	(9A)	(9B)	(10A)	(10B)
	Trinitrotoluene mixtures containing Trinitrobenzene and Hexanitrostilbene or TNT mixtures containing trinitrobenzene and hexanitrostilbene	1.1D	UN0389	II	EXPLOSIVE 1.1D		None	62	None	Forbidden	Forbidden	B	1E, 5E
	Trinitrotoluene or TNT, dry or wetted with less than 30 per cent water, by mass	1.1D	UN0209	II	EXPLOSIVE 1.1D		None	62	None	Forbidden	Forbidden	B	1E, 5E
	Trinitrotoluene, wetted with not less than 30 per cent water, by mass	4.1	UN1356	I	FLAMMABLE SOLID	A2, A8, A19, N41	None	211	None	0.5 kg	0.5 kg	E	28, 36
	Tripropylamine	3	UN2260	III	FLAMMABLE LIQUID, CORROSIVE	B1, T8	None	202	243	1 L	5 L	A	40
	Tripropylene	3	UN2057	II	FLAMMABLE LIQUID	T1	150	202	242	5 L	60 L	B	
				III	FLAMMABLE LIQUID	B1, T1	150	203	242	60 L	220 L	A	
	Tris-(1-aziridinyl)phosphine oxide, solution	6.1	UN2501	II	POISON	T8	None	202	243	5 L	60 L	A	
	Tris, bis-bifluoroamino diethoxy propane (TVOPA)	Forbid-den											
	Tritonal	1.1D	UN0390	II	EXPLOSIVE 1.1D		None	62	None	Forbidden	Forbidden	B	1E, 5E
	Tungsten hexafluoride	2.3	UN2196		POISON GAS	3	None	338	None	Forbidden	Forbidden	D	40
	Turpentine	3	UN1299	III	FLAMMABLE LIQUID	B1, T1	150	203	242	60 L	220 L	A	
I	Turpentine substitute	3	UN1300	I	FLAMMABLE LIQUID	T1	None	201	243	1 L	30 L	B	
				II	FLAMMABLE LIQUID	T1	150	202	242	5 L	60 L	B	
				III	FLAMMABLE LIQUID	B1, T1	150	203	242	60 L	220 L	A	
	Undecane	3	UN2330	III	FLAMMABLE LIQUID	B1, T1	150	203	242	60 L	220 L	A	
	Uranium hexafluoride, fissile (containing more than 1% U-235)	7	UN2977		RADIOACTIVE, CORROSIVE		453	417	417			A	
	Uranium hexafluoride, fissile excepted or non-fissile	7	UN2978		RADIOACTIVE, CORROSIVE		421	425	425				
	Uranium metal, pyrophoric	7	UN2979		RADIOACTIVE, SPONTANEOUSLY COMBUSTIBLE		None	418	None			D	
	Uranyl nitrate hexahydrate solution	7	UN2980		RADIOACTIVE, CORROSIVE		421, 425	415, 416, 417	415, 416, 417			D	
	Uranyl nitrate, solid	7	UN2981		RADIOACTIVE, OXIDIZER		None	419	None	Forbidden	15 kg	A	
	Urea hydrogen peroxide	5.1	UN1511	III	OXIDIZER	A1, A7, A29	152	213	240	25 kg	100 kg	A	13
	Urea nitrate, dry or wetted with less than 20 per cent water, by mass	1.1D	UN0220	II	EXPLOSIVE 1.1D		None	62	None	Forbidden	Forbidden	B	1E, 5E
	Urea nitrate, wetted with not less than 20 per cent water, by mass	4.1	UN1357	I	FLAMMABLE SOLID	A8, A19, N41	None	211	None	1 kg	15 kg	A	28
	Urea peroxide, see Urea hydrogen peroxide												
	Valeraldehyde	3	UN2058	II	FLAMMABLE LIQUID	T1	150	202	242	5 L	60 L	B	
	Valeric acid, see Corrosive liquids, n.o.s.												
	Valeryl chloride	8	UN2502	II	CORROSIVE	A3, A6, A7, B2, N34, T8	154	202	242	1 L	30 L	C	23, 40
	Vanadium oxytrichloride	8	UN2443	II	CORROSIVE	A3, A6, A7, B2, B16, N34, T8, T26	154	202	242	Forbidden	30 L	C	40
	Vanadium pentoxide, nonfused form	6.1	UN2862	II	POISON		None	212	242	25 kg	2.5 L	A	
	Vanadium tetrachloride	8	UN2444	I	CORROSIVE	A3, A6, A7, B4, N34, T8, T26	None	201	242	Forbidden	2.5 L	C	8, 40
AW	Vanadium trichloride	8	UN2475	III	CORROSIVE		154	213	240	25 kg	100 kg	A	40
	Vanadium trioxide, nonfused form	6.1	UN2860	II	POISON		None	212	242	25 kg	100 kg	A	
	Vanadyl sulfate	6.1	UN2931	II	POISON		None	212	242	25 kg	100 kg	A	
D	Vehicles, self-propelled including internal combustion engines or other apparatus containing an internal combustion engine or electric storage battery(see also Wheel chair, electric)	9	None	III	CLASS 9		220	220	None	No limit	No limit	A	
	Very signal cartridge, see Cartridges, signal												
	Vinyl acetate, inhibited	3	UN1301	II	FLAMMABLE LIQUID	T8	150	202	242	5 L	60 L	B	
	Vinyl bromide, inhibited	2.1	UN1085		FLAMMABLE GAS		306	304	None	Forbidden	150 kg	B	40
	Vinyl butyrate, inhibited	3	UN2838	II	FLAMMABLE LIQUID	T7	150	202	242	5 L	60 L	B	
	Vinyl chloride, inhibited	2.1	UN1086		FLAMMABLE GAS	B44	306	304	314, 315	Forbidden	150 kg	B	40
	Vinyl chloroacetate	6.1	UN2589	II	POISON, FLAMMABLE LIQUID	T14	None	202	243	5 L	60 L	A	
	Vinyl ethyl ether, inhibited	3	UN1302	II	FLAMMABLE LIQUID	A3, T14	None	201	243	1 L	30 L	E	

360

Sym-bols	Hazardous materials descriptions and proper shipping names	Hazard class or Division	Identifi-cation Numbers	Packing group	Label(s) required (if not excepted)	Special provisions	(8) Packaging authorizations (§173.***)			(9) Quantity limitations		(10) Vessel stowage requirements	
							Excep-tions	Non-bulk pack-aging	Bulk pack-aging	Passenger aircraft or railcar	Cargo aircraft only	Vessel stow-ages	Other stowage provisions
(1)	(2)	(3)	(4)	(5)	(6)	(7)	(8A)	(8B)	(8C)	(9A)	(9B)	(10A)	(10B)
	Vinyl fluoride, inhibited	2.1	UN1860		FLAMMABLE GAS	B43	306	304	314, 315	Forbidden	150 kg	E	40
	Vinyl isobutyl ether, inhibited	3	UN1304	II	FLAMMABLE LIQUID	T8	150	202	242	5 L	60 L	B	
	Vinyl methyl ether, inhibited	2.1	UN1087		FLAMMABLE GAS	B44	306	304	314, 315	Forbidden	150 kg	B	40
	Vinyl nitrate polymer	Forbid-den											
	Vinyl toluene, inhibited *mixed isomers*	3	UN2618	III	FLAMMABLE LIQUID	B1, T1	150	203	242	60 L	220 L	A	
	Vinylidene chloride, inhibited	3	UN1303	I	FLAMMABLE LIQUID	T23, T29	150	201	243	1 L	30 L	E	40
	Vinylpyridenes, inhibited	6.1	UN3073	II	POISON, FLAMMABLE LIQUID	T8	None	212	243	5 L	60 L	B	40
	Vinyltrichlorosilane	3	UN1305	I	FLAMMABLE LIQUID, CORROSIVE	A3, A7, B6, N34, T14, T26	None	201	243	Forbidden	2.5 L	B	40
	Warheads, rocket *with burster or expelling charge*	1.4D	UN0370	II	EXPLOSIVE 1.4D		None	62	None	Forbidden	75 kg	A	3E, 7E, 24E
	Warheads, rocket *with burster or expelling charge*	1.4F	UN0371	II	EXPLOSIVE 1.4F		None	62	None	Forbidden	Forbidden	E	
	Warheads, rocket *with bursting charge*	1.1D	UN0286	II	EXPLOSIVE 1.1D		None	62	None	Forbidden	Forbidden	B	3E, 7E
	Warheads, rocket *with bursting charge*	1.2D	UN0287	II	EXPLOSIVE 1.2D		None	62	None	Forbidden	Forbidden	B	3E, 7E
	Warheads, rocket *with bursting charge*	1.1F	UN0369	II	EXPLOSIVE 1.1F		None	62	None	Forbidden	Forbidden	E	
	Warheads, torpedo *with bursting charge*	1.1D	UN0221	II	EXPLOSIVE 1.1D		None	62	None	Forbidden	Forbidden	B	3E, 7E
	Water reactive substances, n.o.s., see Substances which in contact with water, etc.												
AD	Wheel chair, electric (*spillable or non-spillable type batteries*)	9	None	III	CLASS 9		222	222	None	No limit	No limit	A	
	White acid, see Hydrofluoric acid mixtures												
	White asbestos, (chrysotile, actinolite, anthophyllite, tremolite)	9	UN2590	III	CLASS 9		155	216	240	200 kg	200 kg	A	34, 40
	Wood preservatives, liquid	3	UN1306	II	FLAMMABLE LIQUID	T7, T30	150	202	242	5 L	60 L	B	40
				III	FLAMMABLE LIQUID	B1, T7, T30	150	203	242	60 L	220 L	A	40
	Xenon	2.2	UN2036		NONFLAMMABLE GAS		306	302	None	75 kg	150 kg	A	
	Xenon, refrigerated liquid (*cryogenic liquids*)	2.2	UN2591		NONFLAMMABLE GAS		320	None	None	50 kg	500 kg	B	
	Xylenes	3	UN1307	II	FLAMMABLE LIQUID	T1	150	202	242	5 L	60 L	B	
				III	FLAMMABLE LIQUID	B1, T1	150	203	242	60 L	220 L	A	
	Xylenols	6.1	UN2261	II	POISON	T8	None	212	243	25 kg	100 kg	A	
	Xylidines, solid *or solution*	6.1	UN1711	II	POISON	T14	None	202	243	5 L	60 L	A	
	Xylyl bromide	6.1	UN1701	II	POISON	A3, A6, A7, N33	None	340	None	Forbidden	60 L	D	40
	p-Xylyl diazide	Forbid-den											
	Zinc ammonium nitrite	5.1	UN1512	II	OXIDIZER		None	212	242	5 kg	25 kg	E	
	Zinc arsenate *or Zinc arsenite or Zinc arsenate and Zinc arsenite mixtures.*	6.1	UN1712	II	POISON		None	212	242	25 kg	100 kg	A	
	Zinc ashes	4.3	UN1435	III	DANGEROUS WHEN WET	A1, A19	None	213	241	25 kg	100 kg	A	
	Zinc bisulfite solution see Bisulfites, inorganic aqueous solutions, n.o.s.												
	Zinc bromate	5.1	UN2469	III	OXIDIZER	A1, A29	152	213	240	25 kg	100 kg	A	56, 58, 106
	Zinc chlorate	5.1	UN1513	II	OXIDIZER	A9, N34	152	212	242	5 kg	25 kg	A	56, 58, 106
	Zinc chloride, anhydrous	8	UN2331	III	CORROSIVE		None	213	240	25 kg	100 kg	A	
	Zinc chloride, solution	8	UN1840	III	CORROSIVE	T7	154	203	241	5 L	60 L	A	
	Zinc cyanide	6.1	UN1713	I	POISON		None	211	242	5 kg	50 kg	A	26
	Zinc dithionite *or Zinc hydrosulfite*	9	UN1931	III	None		155	204	240	100 kg	200 kg	A	13, 49, 102
	Zinc ethyl, see Diethylzinc												
	Zinc fluorosilicate	6.1	UN2855	III	KEEP AWAY FROM FOOD		153	213	240	100 kg	200 kg	A	26
	Zinc hydrosulfite, see Zinc dithionite												
	Zinc muriate solution, see Zinc chloride, solution												

Sym-bols	Hazardous materials descriptions and proper shipping names	Hazard class or Division	Identifi-cation Numbers	Packing group	Label(s) required (if not excepted)	Special provisions	Excep-tions	Non-bulk pack-aging	Bulk pack-aging	Passenger aircraft or railcar	Cargo aircraft only	Vessel stow-ages	Other stowage provisions
(1)	(2)	(3)	(4)	(5)	(6)	(7)	(8A)	(8B)	(8C)	(9A)	(9B)	(10A)	(10B)
	Zinc nitrate	5.1	UN1514	II	OXIDIZER		152	212	240	5 kg	25 kg	A	
	Zinc permanganate	5.1	UN1515	II	OXIDIZER		152	212	242	5 kg	25 kg	D	56, 58, 69, 106, 107
	Zinc peroxide	5.1	UN1516	II	OXIDIZER		152	212	242	5 kg	25 kg	A	13, 75, 106
	Zinc phosphide	4.3	UN1714	I	DANGEROUS WHEN WET, POISON	A19, N40	None	211	None	Forbidden	15 kg	E	40, 85
	Zinc powder or Zinc dust	4.3	UN1436	I	DANGEROUS WHEN WET, SPONTANEOUSLY COMBUSTIBLE	A19, N40	None	211	242	Forbidden	15kg	A	
				II	DANGEROUS WHEN WET, SPONTANEOUSLY COMBUSTIBLE	A19	None	212	242	15 kg	50 kg	A	
				III	DANGEROUS WHEN WET, SPONTANEOUSLY COMBUSTIBLE		None	213	242	25kg	100kg	A	
	Zinc resinate	4.1	UN2714	III	FLAMMABLE SOLID	A1	151	213	240	25 kg	100 kg	A	
	Zinc selenate, see Selenates or Selenites												
	Zinc selenite, see Selenates or Selenites												
	Zinc silicofluoride, see Zinc fluorosilicate												
	Zirconium, dry, coiled wire, finished metal sheets, strip (thinner than 254 microns but not thinner than 18 microns)	4.1	UN2858	III	FLAMMABLE SOLID	A1	151	213	240	25 kg	100 kg	A	
	Zirconium, dry, finished sheets, strip or coiled wire	4.2	UN2009	III	SPONTANEOUSLY COMBUSTIBLE	A1, A19	None	213	240	25 kg	100 kg	D	
	Zirconium hydride	4.1	UN1437	II	FLAMMABLE SOLID	A19, A20, N34	None	212	240	15 kg	50 kg	E	
	Zirconium nitrate	5.1	UN2728	III	OXIDIZER	A1, A29	152	213	240	25 kg	100 kg	A	
	Zirconium picramate, dry or wetted with less than 20 per cent water, by mass	1.3C	UN0236	II	EXPLOSIVE 1.3C		None	62	None	Forbidden	Forbidden	B	1E, 5E
	Zirconium picramate, wetted with not less than 20 per cent water, by mass	4.1	UN1517	I	FLAMMABLE SOLID	N41	None	211	None	1 kg	15 kg	D	28, 36
	Zirconium powder, dry	4.2	UN2008	I	SPONTANEOUSLY COMBUSTIBLE		None	211	242	Forbidden	Forbidden	D	
				II	SPONTANEOUSLY COMBUSTIBLE	A19, A20, N5, N34	None	212	241	15 kg	50 kg	D	
				III	SPONTANEOUSLY COMBUSTIBLE		None	213	241	25kg	100kg	D	
	Zirconium powder, wetted with not less than 25 per cent water (a visible excess of water must be present) (a) mechanically produced, particle size less than 53 microns; (b) chemically produced, particle size less than 840 microns	4.1	UN1358	II	FLAMMABLE SOLID	A19, A20, N34	None	212	241	15 kg	50 kg	E	
	Zirconium scrap	4.2	UN1932	III	SPONTANEOUSLY COMBUSTIBLE	N34	None	213	240	Forbidden	Forbidden	D	
D	Zirconium sulfate	8	NA9163	III	CORROSIVE	N34	None	213	240	50 kg	No limit	A	
	Zirconium suspended in a liquid	3	UN1308	II	FLAMMABLE LIQUID		None	202	242	Forbidden	60 L	B	
	Zirconium tetrachloride	8	UN2503	III	CORROSIVE		154	213	240	25 kg	100 kg	A	

Appendix E

Environmental Protection Agency Hazardous Waste Management Regulations

Including 40 CFR Parts:
261
262
263
265.16
265 Subpart C
265 Subpart D
265 Subpart I
265 Subpart J
266

ENVIRONMENTAL PROTECTION AGENCY REGULATIONS FOR IDENTIFYING HAZARDOUS WASTE

40 CFR 261

Subpart A -- General

§ 261.1 Purpose and scope.

(a) This part identifies those solid wastes which are subject to regulation as hazardous wastes under Parts 262 through 265, 268, and Parts 270, 271, and 124 of this chapter and which are subject to the notification requirements of section 3010 of RCRA. In this part:

(1) Subpart A defines the terms "solid waste" and "hazardous waste", identifies those wastes which are excluded from regulation under Parts 262 through 266, 268 and 270 and establishes special management requirements for hazardous waste produced by conditionally exempt small quantity generators and hazardous waste which is recycled.

(2) Subpart B sets forth the criteria used by EPA to identify characteristics of hazardous waste and to list particular hazardous wastes.

(3) Subpart C identifies characteristics of hazardous waste.

(4) Subpart D lists particular hazardous wastes.

(b)(1) The definition of solid waste contained in this part applies only to wastes that also are hazardous for purposes of the regulations implementing Subtitle C of RCRA. For example, it does not apply to materials (such as non-hazardous scrap, paper, textiles, or rubber) that are not otherwise hazardous wastes and that are recycled.

(2) This part identifies only some of the materials which are solid wastes and hazardous wastes under sections 3007, 3013, and 7003 of RCRA. A material which is not defined as a solid waste in this part, or is not a hazardous waste identified or listed in this part, is still a solid waste and a hazardous waste for purposes of these sections if:

(i) In the case of sections 3007 and 3013, EPA has reason to believe that the material may be a solid waste within the meaning of section 1004(27) of RCRA and a hazardous waste within the meaning of section 1004(5) of RCRA; or

(ii) In the case of section 7003, the statutory elements are established.

(c) For the purposes of §261.2 and §261.6:

(1) A "spent material" is any material that has been used and as a result of contamination can no longer serve the purpose for which it was produced without processing;

(2) "Sludge" has the same meaning used in §260.10 of this chapter;

(3) A "by-product" is a material that is not one of the primary products of a production process and is not solely or separately produced by the production process. Examples are process residues such as slags or distillation column bottoms. The term does not include a co-product that is produced for the general public's use and is ordinarily used in the form it is produced by the process.

(4) A material is "reclaimed" if it is processed to recover a usable product, or if it is regenerated. Examples are recovery of lead values from spent batteries and regeneration of spent solvents.

(5) A material is "used or reused" if it is either:

(i) Employed as an ingredient (including use as an intermediate) in an industrial process to make a product (for example, distillation bottoms from one process used as feedstock in another process). However, a material will not satisfy this condition if distinct components of the material are recovered as separate end products (as when metals are recovered from metal-containing secondary materials); or

(ii) Employed in a particular function or application as an effective substitute for a commercial product (for example, spent pickle liquor used as phosphorous precipitant and sludge conditioner in wastewater treatment).

(6) "Scrap metal" is bits and pieces of metal parts (e.g.,) bars, turnings, rods, sheets, wire) or metal pieces that may be combined together with bolts or soldering (e.g., radiators, scrap automobiles, railroad box cars), which when worn or superfluous can be recycled.

(7) A material is "recycled" if it is used, reused, or reclaimed.

(8) A material is "accumulated speculatively" if it is accumulated before being recycled. A material is not accumulated speculatively, however, if the person accumulating it can show that the material is potentially recyclable and has a feasible means of being recycled; and that--during the calendar year (commencing on January 1)--the amount of material that is recycled, or transferred to a different site for recycling, equals at least 75 percent by weight or volume of the amount of that material accumulated at the beginning of the period. In calculating the percentage of turnover, the 75 percent requirement is to be applied to each material of the same type (e.g., slags from a single smelting process) that is recycled in the same way (i.e., from which the same material is recovered or that is used in the same way). Materials accumulating in units that would be exempt from regulation under §261.4(c) are not be included in making the calculation. (Materials that are already defined as solid wastes also are not to be included in making the calculation.) Materials are no longer in this category once they are removed from accumulation for recycling, however.

§ 261.2 Definition of solid waste.

(a)(1) A *solid waste* is any discarded material that is not excluded by §261.4(a) or that is not excluded by variance granted under §260 .30 and §260.31.

(2) A *discarded material* is any material which is:

(i) *Abandoned,* as explained in paragraph (b) of this section; or

(ii) *Recycled,* as explained in paragraph (c) of this section; or

(iii) Considered *inherently waste-like,* as explained in paragraph (d) of this section.

(b) Materials are solid waste if they are *abandoned* by being:

(1) Disposed of; or

(2) Burned or incinerated; or

(3) Accumulated, stored, or treated (but not recycled) before or in lieu of being abandoned by being disposed of, burned, or incinerated.

(c) Materials are solid wastes if they are *recycled*--or accumulated, stored, or treated before recycling--as specified in paragraphs (c)(1) through (4) of this section.

(1) *Used in a manner constituting disposal.* (i) Materials noted with a "*" in Column 1 of Table I are solid wastes when they are:

(A) Applied to or placed on the land in a manner that constitutes disposal; or

(B) Used to produce products that are applied to or placed on the land or are other-wise contained in products that are applied to or placed on the land (in which cases the product itself remains a solid waste).

(ii) However, commercial chemical products listed in §261.33 are not solid wastes if they are applied to the land and that is their ordinary manner of use.

(2) *Burning for energy recovery.* (i) Materials noted with a "*" in column 2 of Table 1 are solid wastes when they are:

(A) Burned to recover energy;

(B) Used to produce a fuel or are otherwise contained in fuels (in which cases the fuel itself remains a solid waste).

(iii) However, commercial chemical products listed in §261.33 are not solid wastes if they are themselves fuels.

(3) *Reclaimed.* Materials noted with a "*" in column 3 of Table 1 are solid wastes when reclaimed.

(4) *Accumulated speculatively.* Materials noted with a "*" in column 4 of Table 1 are solid wastes when accumulated speculatively.

TABLE 1

	Use constituting disposal (261.2(c)(1)) (1)	Energy recovery/ fuel (261.2(c)(2)) (2)	Relcama-tion (261.2(c)(3)) (3)	Speculative accumula-tion (261.2(c)(4)) (4)
Spent Materials..	(*)	(*)	(*)	(*)
Sludges (listed in 40 CFR Part 261.31 or .32).........................	(*)	(*)	(*)	(*)
Sludges exhibiting a characteristic of hazardous waste............	(*)	(*)	....	(*)
By-products (listed in 40 CFR Part 261.31 or 261.32).............	(*)	(*)	(*)	(*)
By-products exhibiting a characteristic of hazardous waste....	(*)	(*)	....	(*)
Commercial chemical products listed in 40 CFR §261.33........	(*)	(*)	....	....
Scrap Metal...	(*)	(*)	(*)	(*)

Note--The terms "spent materials", "sludges", "by products", and "scrap metal" are defined in §261.1.

(d) *Inherently waste-like materials.* The following materials are solid wastes when they are recycled in any manner:

(1) Hazardous Waste Nos. F020, F021 (unless used as an ingredient to make a product at the site of generation), F022, F023, F026, and F028.

(2) Secondary materials fed to a halogen acid furnace that exhibit a characteristic of a hazardous waste or are listed as a hazardous waste as defined in subparts C or D of this part, except for brominated material that meets the following criteria:

(i) The material must contain a bromine concentration of at least 45%; and

(ii) The material must contain less than a total of 1 % of toxic organic compounds listed in appendix VIII; and

(iii) The material is processed continually on-site in the halogen acid furnace via direct conveyance (hard piping).

(3) The Administrator will use the following criteria to add wastes to that list:

(i)(A) The materials are ordinarily disposed of, burned, or incinerated; or

(B) The materials contain toxic constituents listed in Appendix VIII of Part 261 and these constituents are not ordinarily found in raw materials or products for which the materials sub-stitute (or are found in raw materials or products in smaller concentrations) and are not used or reused during the recycling process; and

(ii) The material may pose a substantial hazard to human health and the environment when recycled.

(e) *Materials that are not solid waste when recycled.* (1) Materials are not solid wastes when they can be shown to be recycled by being:

(i) Used or reused as ingredients in an industrial process to make a product, provided the materials are not being reclaimed; or

(ii) Used or reused as effective substitutes for commercial products; or

(iii) Returned to the original process from which they are generated, without first being reclaimed. The material must be returned as a substitute for raw material feedstock, and the process must use raw materials as principal feedstocks.

(2) The following materials are solid wastes, even if the recycling involves use, reuse, or return to the original process (described in paragraphs (i) through (iii) of this section):

(i) Materials used in a manner constituting disposal, or used to produce products that are applied to the land; or

(ii) Materials burned for energy recovery, used to produce a fuel, or contained in fuels; or

(iii) Materials accumulated speculatively; or

(iv) Materials listed in paragraph (d)(1) of this section.

(f) *Documentation of claims that materials are not solid wastes or are conditionally exempt from regulation.* Respondents in actions to enforce regulations implementing Subtitle C of RCRA who raise a claim that a certain material is not a solid waste, or is conditionally exempt from regulation, must demonstrate that there is a known market or disposition for the material, and that they meet the terms of the exclusion or exemption. In doing so, they must provide appropriate documentation (such as contracts showing that a second person uses the material as an ingredient in a production process) to demonstrate that the material is not a waste, or is exempt from regulation. In addition, owners or operators of facilities claiming that they actually are recycling materials must show that they have the necessary equipment to do so.

§ 261.3 Definition of hazardous waste.

(a) A solid waste, as defined in §261.2, is a hazardous waste if:

(1) It is not excluded from regulation as

a hazardous waste under §261.4(b); and

(2) It meets any of the following criteria:

(i) It exhibits any of the characteristics of hazardous waste identified in subpart C except that any mixture of a waste from the extraction, beneficiation, and processing of ores and minerals excluded under §261.4(b)(7) and any other solid waste exhibiting a characteristic of hazardous waste under subpart C of this part only if it exhibits a characteristic that would not have been exhibited by the excluded waste alone if such mixture had not occurred or if it continues to exhibit any of the characteristics exhibited by the non-excluded wastes prior to mixture. Further, for the purposes of applying the Extraction Procedure Toxicity characteristic to such mixtures, the mixture is also a hazardous waste if it exceeds the maximum concentration for any contaminant listed in table I to §261.24 that would not have been exceeded by the excluded waste alone if the mixture had not occurred or if it continues to exceed the maximum concentration for any contaminant exceeded by the nonexempt waste prior to mixture.

(ii) It is listed in Subpart D and has not been excluded from the lists in Subpart D under §§260.20 and 260.22 of this chapter.

(iii) It is a mixture of a solid waste and a hazardous waste that is listed in subpart D of this part solely because it exhibits one or more of the characteristics of hazardous waste identified in subpart C, unless the resultant mixture no longer exhibits any characteristic of hazardous waste identified in subpart C of this part or unless the solid waste is excluded from regulation under §261.4(b)(7) and the resultant mixture no longer exhibits any characteristic of hazardous waste identified in subpart C of this part for which the hazardous waste listed in subpart D of this part was listed.

(iv) It is a mixture of solid waste and one or more hazardous wastes listed in Subpart D and has not been excluded from this paragraph under §§260.20 and 260.22 of this chapter; however, the following mixtures of solid wastes and hazardous wastes listed in Subpart D are not hazardous wastes (except by application of paragraph (a)(2)(i) or (ii) of this section) if the generator can demonstrate that the mixture consists of wastewater the discharge of which is subject to regulation under either section 402 or section 307(b) of the Clean Water Act (including wastewater at facilities which have eliminated the discharge of wastewater) and:

(A) One or more of the following spent solvents listed in §261.31--carbon tetrachloride, tetrachloroethylene, trichloroethylene--provided that the maximum total weekly usage of these solvents (other than the amounts that can be demonstrated not to be discharged to wastewater) divided by the average weekly flow of wastewater into the head works of the facility's wastewater treatment or pretreatment system does not exceed 1 part per million; or

(B) One or more of the following spent solvents listed in §261.31--methylene chloride, 1,1,1-trichloroethane, chlorobenzene, o-dichlorobenzene, cresols, cresylic acid, nitrobenzene, toluene, methyl ethyl ketone, carbon disulfide, isobutanol, pyridine, spent chlorofluorocarbon solvents--provided that the maximum total weekly usage of these solvents (other than the amounts that can be demonstrated not to be discharged to wastewater) divided by the average weekly flow of wastewater into the headworks of the facility's wastewater treatment or pre-treatment system does not exceed 25 parts per million; or

(C) One of the following wastes listed in §261.32--heat exchanger bundle cleaning sludge from the petroleum refining industry (EPA Hazardous Waste No. K050); or

(D) A discarded commercial chemical product, or chemical intermediate listed in §261.33, arising from de minimis losses of these materials from manufacturing operations in which these materials are used as raw materials or are produced in the manufacturing process. For purposes of this subparagraph, "de minimis" losses include those from normal material handling operations (e.g. spills from the unloading or transfer of materials from bins or other containers, leaks from pipes, valves or other devices used to transfer materials); minor leaks of process equipment, storage tanks or containers; leaks from well-maintained pump packings and seals; sample purgings; relief device discharges; discharges from safety showers and rinsing and cleaning of personal safety equipment; and rinsate from empty containers or from containers that are rendered empty by that rinsing; or

(E) Wastewater resulting from laboratory operations containing toxic (T) wastes listed in Subpart D, provided that the annualized average flow of laboratory wastewater does not exceed one percent of total wastewater flow into the headworks of the facility's wastewater treatment or pre-treatment system, or provided the wastes, combined annualized average concentration does not exceed one part per million in the headworks of the facility's wastewater treatment or pre-treatment facility. Toxic (T) wastes used in laboratories that are demonstrated not to be discharged to wastewater are not to be included in this calculation.

(b) A solid waste which is not excluded from regulation under paragraph (a)(1) of this section becomes a hazardous waste when any of the following events occur:

(1) In the case of a waste listed in Subpart D, when the waste first meets the listing description set forth in Subpart D.

(2) In the case of a mixture of solid waste and one or more listed hazardous wastes, when a hazardous waste listed in Subpart D is first added to the solid waste.

(3) In the case of any other waste (including a waste mixture), when the waste exhibits any of the characteristics identified in Subpart C.

(c) Unless and until it meets the criteria of paragraph (d):

(1) A hazardous waste will remain a hazardous waste.

(i) Except as otherwise provided in paragraph (c)(2)(ii) of this section, any solid waste generated from the treatment, storage, or disposal of a hazardous waste, including any sludge, spill residue, ash, emission control dust, or leachate (but not including precipitation run-off) is a hazardous waste. (However, materials that are reclaimed from solid wastes and that are used beneficially are not solid wastes and hence are not hazardous wastes under this provision unless the reclaimed material is burned for energy recovery or used in a manner constituting disposal.)

(ii) The following solid wastes are not hazardous even though they are generated from the treatment, storage, or disposal of a hazardous waste, unless they exhibit one or more of the characteristics of hazardous waste:

(A) Waste pickle liquor sludge generated by lime stabilization of spent pickle liquor from the iron and steel industry (SIC Codes 331 and 332).

(B) Waste from burning any of the materials exempted from regulation by §261.6(a)(3)(v) through (viii).

(C) Nonwastewater residues, such as slag, resulting from high temperature metals recovery (HTMR) processing of K061 waste, in units identified as rotary kilns, flame reactors, electric furnaces, plasma arc furnaces, slag reactors, rotary hearth furnace/electric furnace combinations or industrial furnaces (as defined in 40 CFR 260.10 (6), (7), and (12)), that are disposed in subtitle D units, provided that these residues meet the generic exclusion levels identified below for all constituents, and exhibit no characteristics of hazardous waste. Testing requirements must be incorporated in a facility's waste analysis plan or a generator's self-implementing waste analysis plan; at a minimum, composite samples of residues must be collected and analyzed quarterly and/or when the process or operation generating the waste changes. The generic exclusion levels are:

Constituent	Maximum for any single composite sample (mg/l)
Antimony	0.063
Arsenic	0.055
Barium	6.3
Beryllium	0.0063
Cadmium	0.032
Chromium (total)	0.33
Lead	0.095
Mercury	0.009
Nickel	0.63
Selenium	0.16
Silver	0.30
Thallium	0.013
Vanadium	1.26

For each shipment of K061 HTMR residues sent to a subtitle D unit that meets the generic exclusion levels for all constituents, and does not exhibit any characteristic, a notification and certification must be sent to the appropriate EPA Regional Administrator (or delegated representative) or State authorized to implement part 268 requirements. The notification must include the following information: (1) The name and address of the Subtitle D unit receiving the waste shipment; (2) the EPA hazardous waste number and treatability group at the initial point of generation; (3) the treatment standards applicable to the waste at the initial point of generation. The certification must be signed by an authorized representative and must state as follows: "I certify under penalty of law that the generic exclusion levels for all constituents have been met without impermissible dilution and that no characteristic of hazardous waste is exhibited. I am aware that there are significant penalties for submitting a false certification, including the possibility of fine and imprisonment."

(d) Any solid waste described in paragraph (c) of this section is not a hazardous waste if it meets the following criteria:

(1) In the case of any solid waste, it does not exhibit any of the characteristics of hazardous waste identified in Subpart C.

(2) In the case of a waste which is a listed waste under Subpart D, contains a waste listed under Subpart D or is derived from a waste listed in Subpart D, it also has been excluded from paragraph (c) under §§260.20 and 260.22 of this chapter.

§ 261.4 Exclusions.

(a) *Materials which are not solid wastes.* The following materials are not solid wastes for the purpose of this part:

(1)(i) Domestic sewage; and

(ii) Any mixture of domestic sewage and other wastes that passes through a sewer system to a publicly-owned treatment works for treatment. "Domestic sewage" means untreated sanitary wastes that pass through a sewer system.

(2) Industrial wastewater discharges that are point source discharges subject to regulation under section 402 of the Clean Water Act, as amended.

(3) Irrigation return flows.

(4) Source, special nuclear or by-product material as defined by the Atomic Energy Act of 1954, as amended, 42 U.S.C. 2011 *et seq.*

(5) Materials subjected to in-situ mining techniques which are not removed from the ground as part of the extraction process.

(6) Pulping liquors (i.e., black liquor) that are reclaimed in a pulping liquor recovery furnace and then reused in the pulping process, unless it is accumulated speculatively as defined in §261.1(c) of this chapter.

(7) Spent sulfuric acid used to produce virgin sulfuric acid, unless it is accumulated speculatively as defined in §261.1(c) of this chapter.

(8) Secondary materials that are reclaimed and returned to the original process or processes in which they were generated where they are reused in the production process provided:

(i) Only tank storage is involved, and the entire process through completion of reclamation is closed by being entirely connected with pipes or other comparable enclosed means of conveyance;

(ii) Reclamation does not involve controlled flame combustion (such as occurs in boilers, industrial furnaces, or incinerators);

(iii) The secondary materials are never accumulated in such tanks for over twelve months without being reclaimed; and

(iv) The reclaimed material is not used to produce a fuel, or used to produce products that are used in a manner constituting disposal.

(9)(i) Spent wood preserving solutions that have been reclaimed and are reused for their original intended purpose; and

(ii) Wastewaters from the wood preserving process that have been reclaimed and are reused to treat wood.

(10) When used as a fuel, coke and coal tar from the iron and steel industry that contains or is produced from decanter tank tar sludge, EPA Hazardous Waste K087. The process of producing coke and coal tar from such decanter tank tar sludge in a coke oven is likewise excluded from regulation.

(11) Nonwastewater splash condenser dross residue from the treatment of K061 in high temperature metals recovery units, provided it is shipped in drums (if shipped) and not land disposed before recovery.

(b) *Solid wastes which are not hazardous wastes.* The following solid wastes are not hazardous wastes:

(1) Household waste, including household waste that has been collected, transported, stored, treated, disposed, recovered (e.g., refuse-derived fuel) or reused. "Household waste" means any material (including garbage, trash and sanitary wastes in septic tanks) derived from households (including single and multiple residences, hotels and motels, bunkhouses, ranger stations, crew quarters, campgrounds, picnic grounds and day-use recreation areas). Are source recovery facility managing municipal solid waste shall not be deemed to be treating, storing, disposing of, or otherwise managing hazardous wastes for the purposes of regulation under this subtitle, if such facility:

(i) Receives and burns only

(A) Household waste (from single and multiple dwellings, hotels, motels, and other residential sources) and

(B) Solid waste from commercial or industrial sources that does not contain hazardous waste; and

(ii) Such facility does not accept hazardous wastes and the owner or operator of such facility has established contractual requirements or other appropriate notification or inspection procedures to assure that hazardous wastes are not received at or burned in such facility.

(2) Solid wastes generated by any of the following and which are returned to the soils as fertilizers:

(i) The growing and harvesting of agricultural crops.

(ii) The raising of animals, including animal manures.

(3) Mining overburden returned to the mine site.

(4) Fly ash waste, bottom ash waste, slag waste, and flue gas emission control waste, generated primarily from the combustion of coal or other fossil fuels, except as provided by §266.112 of this chapter for facilities that burn or process hazardous waste.

(5) Drilling fluids, produced waters, and other wastes associated with the exploration, development, or production of crude oil, natural gas or geothermal energy.

(6)(i) Wastes which fail the test for the Toxicity Characteristic because chromium is present or are listed in subpart D due to the presence of chromium, which do not fail the test for the Toxicity Characteristic for any other constituent or are not listed due to the presence of any other constituent, and which do not fail the test for any other characteristic, if it is shown by a waste generator or by waste generators that:

(A) The chromium in the waste is exclusively (or nearly exclusively) trivalent chromium; and

(B) The waste is generated from an industrial process which uses trivalent chromium exclusively (or nearly exclusively) and the process does not generate hexavalent chromium; and

(C) The waste is typically and frequently managed in non-oxidizing environments.

(ii) Specific wastes which meet the standard in paragraphs (b)(6)(i)(A), (B) and (C) (so long as they do not fail the test for the characteristic of EP toxicity, and do not fail the test for any other characteristic) are:

(A) Chrome (blue) trimmings generated by the following subcategories of the leather tanning and finishing industry; hair pulp/chrome tan/retan/wetfinish; hair save/chrome tan/retan/wet finish; retan/wet finish; no beamhouse; through-the-blue; and shearling.

(B) Chrome (blue) shavings generated by the following subcategories of the leather tanning and finishing industry: Hair pulp/chrome tan/retan/wetfinish; hair save/chrome tan/retan/

wet finish; retan/wet finish; no beamhouse; through-the-blue; and shearling.

(C) Buffing dust generated by the following subcategories of the leather tanning and finishing industry; hair pulp/chrome tan/retan/wet finish;hair save/chrome tan/retan/wet finish; retan/wet finish; no beamhouse; through-the-blue.

(D) Sewer screenings generated by the following subcategories of the leather tanning and finishing industry: Hair pulp/crome tan/retan/wet finish;hair save/chrome tan/retan/wet finish; retan/wet finish; no beamhouse; through-the-blue; and shearling.

(E) Wastewater treatment sludges generated by the following subcategories of the leather tanning and finishing industry: Hair pulp/chrome tan/retan/wet finish; hair save/chrome tan/retan/wet finish; retan/wet finish; no beamhouse; through-the-blue; and shearling.

(F) Wastewater treatment sludges generated by the following subcategories of the leather tanning and finishing industry: Hair pulp/chrome tan/retan/wet finish; hair save/chrome tan/retan/wet finish; and through-the-blue.

(G) Waste scrap leather from the leather tanning industry, the shoe manufacturing industry, and other leather product manufacturing industries.

(H) Wastewater treatment sludges from the production of TiO$_2$ pigment using chromium-bearing ores by the chloride process.

(7) Solid waste from the extraction, beneficiation, and processing of ores and minerals (including coal, phosphate rock and overburden from the mining of uranium ore), except as provided by §266.112 of this chapter for facilities that burn or process hazardous waste. For purposes of §261.4(b)(7), beneficiation of ores and minerals is restricted to the following activities: Crushing; grinding; washing; dissolution; crystallization; filtration; sorting; sizing; drying; sintering; pelletizing; briquetting; calcining to remove water and/or carbon dioxide; roasting, autoclaving, and/or chlorination in preparation for leaching (except where the roasting (and/or autoclaving and/or chlorination)/leaching sequence produces a final or intermediate product that does not undergo further beneficiation or processing); gravity concentration; magnetic separation; electrostatic separation; flotation; ion exchange; solvent extraction; electrowinning; precipitation; amalgamation; and heap, dump, vat, tank, and

in situ leaching. For the purpose of §261.4(b)(7), solid waste from the processing of ore sand minerals will include only the following wastes:

(i) Slag from primary copper processing;

(ii) Slag from primary lead processing;

(iii) Red and brown muds from bauxite refining;

(iv) Phosphogypsum from phosphoric acid production;

(v) Slag from elemental phosphorus production;

(vi) Gasifier ash from coal gasification;

(vii) Process wastewater from coal gasification;

(viii) Calcium sulfate wastewater treatment plant sludge from primary copper processing;

(ix) Slag tailings from primary copper processing;

(x) Fluorogypsum from hydrofluoric acid production;

(xi) Process wastewater from hydrofluoric acid production;

(xii) Air pollution control dust/sludge from iron blast furnaces;

(xiii) Iron blast furnace slag;

(xiv) Treated residue from roasting/leaching of chrome ore;

(xv) Process wastewater from primary magnesium processing by the anhydrous process;

(xvi) Process wastewater from phosphoric acid production;

(xvii) Basic oxygen furnace and open hearth furnace air pollution control dust/sludge from carbon steel production;

(xviii) Basic oxygen furnace and open hearth furnace slag from carbon steel production;

(xix) Chloride process waste solids from titanium tetrachloride production;

(xx) Slag from primary zinc processing.

(8) Cement kiln dust waste, except as provided by §266.112 of this chapter for facilities that burn or process hazardous waste.

(9) Solid waste which consists of discarded wood or wood products which fails the test for the Toxicity Characteristic solely for arsenic and which is not a hazardous waste for any other reason or reasons, if the waste is generated by persons who utilize the arsenical-treated wood and wood prod-

ucts for these materials' intended end use.

(10) Petroleum-contaminated media and debris that fail the test for the Toxicity Characteristic of §261.24 (Hazardous Waste Codes D018 through D043 only) and are subject to the corrective action regulations under part 280 of this chapter.

(11) Injected groundwater that is hazardous only because it exhibits the Toxicity Characteristic (Hazardous Waste Codes D018 through D043 only) in §261.24 of this part that is reinjected through an underground injection well pursuant to free phase hydrocarbon recovery operations undertaken at petroleum refineries, petroleum marketing terminals, petroleum bulk plants, petroleum pipelines, and petroleum transportation spill sites until January 25, 1993. This extension applies to recovery operations in existence, or for which contracts have been issued, on or before March 25, 1991. For groundwater returned through infiltration galleries from such operations at petroleum refineries, marketing terminals, and bulk plants, until October 2, 1991. New operations involving injection wells (beginning after March 25, 1991) will qualify for this compliance date extension (until January 25, 1993) only if: (i) Operations are performed pursuant to a written state agreement that includes a provision to assess the groundwater and the need for further remediation once the free phase recovery is completed; and

(ii) A copy of the written agreement has been submitted to: Characteristics Section (OS-333), U.S. Environmental Protection Agency, 401 M Street, SW., Washington, DC 20460.

(12) Used chlorofluorocarbon refrigerants from totally enclosed heat transfer equipment, including mobile air conditioning systems, mobile refrigeration, and commercial and industrial air conditioning and refrigeration systems that use chlorofluorocarbons as the heat transfer fluid in a refrigeration cycle, provided the refrigerant is reclaimed for further use.

(c) Hazardous wastes which are exempted from certain regulations. A hazardous waste which is generated in a product or raw material storage tank, a productor raw material transport vehicle or vessel, a product or raw material pipeline, or in a manufacturing process unit or an associated non-waste-treatment-manufacturing unit, is not subject to regulation under Parts 262 through 265, 268, 270, 271 and 124 of this chapter or to the notification requirements of section 3010 of RCRA until it exits the unit in which it was generated, unless the unit is a surface impoundment, or unless the hazardous waste remains in the unit more than 90 days after the unit ceases to be operated for manufacturing, or for storage or transportation of product or raw materials.

(d) *Samples.* (1) Except as provided in paragraph (d)(2) of this section, a sample of solid waste or a sample of water, soil, or air, which is collected for the sole purpose of testing to determine its characteristics or composition, is not subject to any requirements of this part or Parts 262 through 268 or Part 270 or Part 124 of this chapter or to the notification requirements of section 3010 of RCRA, when:

(i) The sample is being transported to a laboratory for the purpose of testing; or

(ii) The sample is being transported back to the sample collector after testing; or

(iii) The sample is being stored by the sample collector before transport to a laboratory for testing; or

(iv) The sample is being stored in a laboratory before testing; or

(v) The sample is being stored in a laboratory after testing but before it is returned to the sample collector; or

(vi) The sample is being stored temporarily in the laboratory after testing for a specific purpose (for example, until conclusion of a court case or enforcement action where further testing of the sample may be necessary).

(2) In order to qualify for the exemption in paragraphs (d)(1)(i) and (ii) of this section, a sample collector shipping samples to a laboratory and al aboratory returning samples to a sample collector must:

(i) Comply with U.S. Department of Transportation (DOT), U.S. Postal Service (USPS), or any other applicable shipping requirements; or

(ii) Comply with the following requirements if the sample collector determines that DOT, USPS, or other shipping requirements d o not apply to the shipment of the sample:

(A) Assure that the following information accompanies the sample:

(1) The sample collector's name, mailing address, and telephone number;

(2) The laboratory's name, mailing address, and telephone number;

(3) The quantity of the sample;

(4) The date of shipment; and

(5) A description of the sample.

(B) Package the sample so that it does not leak, spill, or vaporize from its packaging.

(3) This exemption does not apply if the laboratory determines that the waste is hazardous but the laboratory is no longer meeting any of the conditions stated in paragraph (d)(1) of this section.

(e) *Treatability Study Samples.* (1) Except as provided in paragraph (e)(2) of this section, persons who generate or collect samples for the purpose of conducting treatability studies as defined in section §260.10, are not subject to any requirement of Parts 261 through 263 of this chapter or to the notification requirements of Section 3010 of RCRA, nor are such samples included in the quantity determinations of §§261.5 and 262.34(d) when:

(i) The sample is being collected and prepared for transportation by the generator or sample collector; or

(ii) The sample is being accumulated or stored by the generator or sample collector prior to transportation to a laboratory or testing facility; or

(iii) The sample is being transported to the laboratory or testing facility for the purpose of conducting a treatability study.

(2) The exemption in paragraph (e)(1) of this section is applicable to samples of hazardous waste being collected and shipped for the purpose of conducting treatability studies provided that:

(i) The generator or sample collector uses (in "treatability studies") no more than 1000 kg of any non-acute hazardous waste, 1 kg of acute hazardous waste, or 250 kg of soils, water, or debris contaminated with acute hazardous waste for each process being evaluated for each generated waste stream; and

(ii) The mass of each sample shipment does not exceed 1000 kg of non-acute hazardous waste, 1 kg of acute hazardous waste, or 250 kg of soils, water, or debris contaminated with acute hazardous waste; and

(iii) The sample must be packaged so that it will not leak, spill, orvaporize from its packaging during shipment and the requirements of paragraph A or B of this subparagraph are met.

(A) The transportation of each sample shipment complies with U.S. Department of Transportation (DOT), U.S. Postal Service (USPS), or any other applicable shipping requirements; or

(B) If the DOT, USPS, or other shipping requirements do not apply to the shipment of the sample, the following information must accompany the sample:

(1) The name, mailing address, and telephone number of the originator of the sample;

(2) The name, address, and telephone number of the facility that will perform the treatability study;

(3) The quantity of the sample;

(4) The date of shipment; and

(5) A description of the sample, including its EPA Hazardous Waste Number.

(iv) The sample is shipped to a laboratory or testing facility which is exempt under §261.4(f) or has an appropriate RCRA permit or interim status.

(v) The generator or sample collector maintains the following records for a period ending 3 years after completion of the treatability study:

(A) Copies of the shipping documents;

(B) A copy of the contract with the facility conducting the treatability study;

(C) Documentation showing:

(1) The amount of waste shipped under this exemption;

(2) The name, address, and EPA identification number of the laboratory or testing facility that received the waste;

(3) The date the shipment was made; and

(4) Whether or not unused samples and residues were returned to the generator.

(vi) The generator reports the information required under paragraph (e)(v)(C) of this section in its biennial report.

(3) The Regional Administrator, or State Director (if located in an authorized State), may grant request, on a case-by-case basis, for quantity limits in excess of those specified in paragraph (e)(2)(i) of this section, for up to an additional 500 kg of non-acute hazardous waste, 1 kg of acute hazardous waste, and 250 kg of soils, water, or debris contaminated with acute hazardous waste, to conduct further treatability

study evaluation when: There has been an equipment or mechanical failure during the conduct of a treatability study; there is a need to verify the results of a previously conducted treatability study; there is a need to study and analyze alternativet echniques within a previously evaluated treatment process; or there is a needto do further evaluation of an ongoing treatability study to determine final specifications for treatment. The additional quantities allowed are subject to all the provisions in paragraphs (e)(1) and (e)(2)(ii)(vi) of this section. The generator or sample collector must apply to the Regional Administrator in the Region where the sample is collected and provide in writing the following information:

(i) The reason why the generator or sample collector requires additional quantity of sample for the treatability study evaluation and the additional quantity needed;

(ii) Documentation accounting for all samples of hazardous waste from the waste stream which have been sent for or undergone treatability studies including the data each previous sample from the waste stream was shipped, the quantity of each previous shipment, the laboratory or testing facility to which it was shipped, what treatability study processes were conducted on each sample shipped, and the available results of each treatabiltiy study;

(iii) A description of the technical modifications or change in specifications which will be evaluated and the expected results;

(iv) If such further study is being required due to equipment or mechanical failure, the applicant must include information regarding the reason for the failure or breakdown and also include what procedures or equipment improvements have been made to protect against further breakdowns; and

(v) Such other information that the Regional Administrator considers necessary.

(f) *Samples Undergoing Treatability Studies at Laboratories and TestingFacilities.* Samples undergoing treatability studies and the laboratory or testing facility conducting such treatability studies (to the extent such facilities are not otherwise subject to RCRA requirements) are not subject to any requirement of this Part, Part 124, Parts 262-266, 268, and 270, or to the notification requirements of Section 3010 of RCRA provided that the conditions of paragraphs (f)(1) through

(11) of this section are met. A mobile treatment unit (MTU) may qualify as a testing facility subject to paragraphs (f)(1) through (11) of this section. Where a group of MTUs are located at the same site, the limitations specified in (f)(1) through (11) of this section apply to the entire group of MTUs collectively as if the group were one MTU.

(1) No less than 45 days before conducting treatability studies, the facility notifies the Regional Administrator, or State Direct or (if located in an authorized State), in writing that it intends to conduct treatability studies under this paragraph.

(2) The laboratory or testing facility conducting the treatability study has an EPA identification number.

(3) No more than a total of 250 kg of "as received" hazardous waste is subjected to initiation of treatment in all treatability studies in any single day. "As received" waste refers to the waste as received in the shipment from the generator or sample collector.

(4) The quantity of "as received" hazardous waste stored at the facility for the purpose of evaluation in treatability studies does not exceed 1000 kg, the total of which can include 500 kg of soils, water, or debris contaminated with acute hazardous waste or 1 kg of acute hazardous waste. This quantity limitation does not include:

(i) Treatability study residues; and

(ii) Treatment materials (including nonhazardous solid waste) added to "as received" hazardous waste.

(5) No more than 90 days have elapsed since the treatability study for the sample was completed, or no more than one year has elapsed since the generatoror sample collector shipped the sample to the laboratory or testing facility,whichever date first occurs.

(6) The treatability study does not involve the placement of hazardouswaste on the land or open burning of hazardous waste.

(7) The facility maintains records for 3 years following completion of each study that show compliance with the treatment rate limits and the storage time and quantity limits. The following specific information must be included for each treatability study conducted:

(i) The name, address, and EPA identification number of the generator or sample collector of each waste sample;

(ii) The date the shipment was received;

(iii) The quantity of waste accepted;

(iv) The quantity of "as received" waste in storage each day;

(v) The date the treatment study was initiated and the amount of "as received" waste introduced to treatment each day;

(vi) The date the treatability study was concluded;

(vii) The date any unused sample or residues generated from the treatability study were returned to the generator or sample collector or, if sent to a designated facility, the name of the facility and the EPA identification number.

(8) The facility keeps, on-site, a copy of the treatability study contract and all shipping papers associated with the transport of treatability study samples to and from the facility for a period ending 3 years from the completion date of each treatability study.

(9) The facility prepares and submits a report to the Regional Administrator, or State Director (if located in an authorized State), by March 15 of each year that estimates the number of studies and the amount of wasteexpected to be used in treatability studies during the current year, andincludes the following information for the previous calendar year:

(i) The name, address, and EPA identification number of the facility conducting the treatability studies;

(ii) The types (by process) of treatability studies conducted;

(iii) The names and addresses of persons for whom studies have been conducted (including their EPA identification numbers);

(iv) The total quantity of waste in storage each day;

(v) The quantity and type of waste subjected to treatability studies;

(vi) When each treatability study was conducted;

(vii) The final disposition of residues and unused sample from each treatability study.

(10) The facility determines whether any unused sample or residues generated by the treatability study are hazardous waste under §261.3 and, if so, are subject to Parts 261 through 268, and Part 270 of this Chapter, unless the residues and unused samples are returned to the sample originator underthe §261.4(e) exemption.

(11) The facility notifies the Regional Administrator, or State Director(if located in an authorized State), by letter when the facility is no longer planning to conduct any treatability studies at the site.

(Approved by the Office of Management and Budget under control number2050-0088)

261.5 Special requirements for hazardous waste generated by conditionally exempt small quantity generators.

(a) A generator is a conditionally exempt small quantity generator in a calendar month if he generates no more than 100 kilograms of hazardous waste in that month.

(b) Except for those wastes identified in paragraphs (e), (f), (g), and (j) of this section, a conditionally exempt small quantity generator's hazardous wastes are not subject to regulation under Parts 262 through 266, 268, and Parts 270 and 124 of this chapter, and the notification requirements of section 3010 of RCRA, provided the generator complies with the requirements of paragraphs (f), (g), and (j) of this section.

(c) Hazardous waste that is not subject to regulation or that is subject only to §262.11, §262.12, §262.40(c), and §262.41 is not included in the quantity determinations of this part and Parts 262 through 266, 268, and 270 and is not subject to any of the requirements of those parts. Hazardous waste that is subject to the requirements of §261.6(b) and (c) and Subparts C, D, and F of Part 266 is included in the quantity determination of this part and is subject to the requirements of Parts 262 through 266 and 270.

(d) In determining the quantity of hazardous waste generated, a generator need not include:

(1) Hazardous waste when it is removed from on-site storage; or

(2) Hazardous waste produced by on-site treatment (including reclamation) of his hazardous waste, so long as the hazardous waste that is treated was counted once; or

(3) Spent materials that are generated, reclaimed, and subsequently reused on-site, so long as such spent materials have been counted once.

(e) If a generator generates acute hazardous waste in a calendar month in quantities greater than set forth below, all quantities of that acute hazardous waste are subject to full regulation under Parts 262 through 266, 268, and Parts 270 and 124 of this chapter, and the notification requirements of section 3010 of RCRA:

(1) A total of one kilogram of acute hazardous wastes listed in §§261.31, 261.32, or 261.33(e).

(2) A total of 100 kilograms of any residue or contaminated soil, waste, or other debris resulting from the clean-up of a spill, into or on any land or water, of any acute hazardous wastes listed in §261.31, §261.32, or §261.33(e).

(f) In order for acute hazardous wastes generated by a generator of acute hazardous wastes in quantities equal to or less than those set forth in paragraph (e)(1) or (2) of this section to be excluded from full regulation under this section, the generator must comply with the following requirements:

(1) Section §262.11 of this chapter;

(2) The generator may accumulate acute hazardous waste on-site. If he accumulates at any time acute hazardous wastes in quantities greater than those set forth in paragraph (e)(1) or (2) of this section, all of those accumulated wastes are subject to regulation under Parts 262 through 266, 268, and Parts 270 and 124 of this chapter, and the applicable notification requirements of section 3010 of RCRA. The time period of §262.34(a) of this chapter, for accumulation of wastes on-site, begins when the accumulated wastes exceed the applicable exclusion limit;

(3) A conditionally exempt small quantity generator may either treat or dispose of his acute hazardous waste in an on-site facility or ensure delivery to an off-site treatment, storage or disposal facility, either of which, if located in the U.S., is:

(i) Permitted under Part 270 of this chapter;

(ii) In interim status under Parts 270 and 265 of this chapter;

(iii) Authorized to manage hazardous waste by a State with a hazardous waste management program approved under Part 271 of this chapter;

(iv) Permitted, licensed, or registered by a State to manage municipal or industrial solid waste; or

(v) A facility which:

(A) Beneficially uses or reuses, or legitimately recycles or reclaim its wastes; or

(B) Treats its waste prior to beneficial use or reuse, or legitimate recycling or reclamation.

(g) In order for hazardous waste generated by a conditionally exempt small quantity generator in quantities of less than 100 kilograms of hazardous waste during a calendar month to be excluded from full regulation under this section, the generator must comply with the following requirements:

(1) Section 262.11 of this chapter;

(2) The conditionally exempt small quantity generator may accumulate hazardous waste on-site. If he accumulates at any time more than a total of 1000 kilograms of his hazardous wastes, all of those accumulated wastes are subject to regulation under the special provisions of Part 262 applicable to generators of between 100 kg and 1000 kg of hazardous waste in a calendar month as well as the requirements of Parts 263 through 266, 268, and Parts 270 and 124 of this chapter, and the applicable notification requirements of section 3010 of RCRA. The time period of §262.34(d) for accumulation of wastes on-site begins for a conditionally exempt small quantity generator when the accumulated wastes exceed 1000 kilograms;

(3) A conditionally exempt small quantity generator may either treat or dispose of his hazardous waste in an on-site facility or ensure delivery to an off-site treatment, storage or disposal facility, either of which, if located in the U.S., is:

(i) Permitted under Part 270 of this chapter;

(ii) In interim status under Parts 270 and 265 of this chapter;

(iii) Authorized to manage hazardous waste by a State with a hazardous waste management program approved under Part 271 of this chapter;

(iv) Permitted, licensed, or registered by a State to manage municipal or industrial solid waste; or

(v) A facility which:

(A) Beneficially uses or reuses, or legitimately recycles or reclaims its waste; or

(B) Treats its waste prior to beneficial use or reuse, or legitmate recycling or reclamation.

(h) Hazardous waste subject to the reduced requirements of this section may be mixed with non-hazardous waste and remain subject to these reduced requirements even though the resultant mixture exceeds the quantity limita-tions identified in this section, unless the mixture meets any of the characteristics of hazardous waste identified in Subpart C.

(i) If any person mixes a solid waste with a hazardous waste that exceeds a quantity exclusion level of this section, the mixture is subject to full regulation.

(j) If a conditionally exempt small quantity generator's wastes are mixed with used oil, the mixture is subject to Subpart E of Part 266 of this chapter if it is destined to be burned for energy recovery. Any material produced from such a mixture by processing, blending, or other treatment is also so regulated if it is destined to be burned for energy recovery.

§ 261.6 Requirements for recyclable materials.

(a)(1) Hazardous wastes that are recycled are subject to the requirements for generators, transporters, and storage facilities of paragraphs (b) and (c) of this section, except for the materials listed in paragraphs (a)(2) and (a)(3) of this section. Hazardous waste that are recycled will be known as "recyclable materials."

(2) The following recyclable materials are not subject to the requirements of this section but are regulated under Subparts C through H of Part 266 of this chapter and all applicable provisions in Parts 270 and 124 of this chapter:

(i) Recyclable materials used in a manner constituting disposal (Subpart C);

(ii) Hazardous wastes burned for energy recovery in boilers and industrial furnaces that are not regulated under Subpart O of Part 264 or 265 of this chapter (Subpart H);

(iii) Used oil that exhibits one or more of the characteristics of hazardous waste and is burned for energy recovery in boilers and industrial furnaces that are not regulated under Subpart O of Part 264 or 265 of this chapter (Subpart E);

(iv) Recyclable materials from which precious metals are reclaimed (Subpart F);

(v) Spent lead-acid batteries that are being reclaimed (Subpart G).

(3) The following recyclable materials are not subject to regulation under Parts 262 through Parts 266 or Parts 268, 270 or 124 of this chapter, and are not subject to the notification requirements of section 3010 of RCRA:

(i) Industrial ethyl alcohol that is reclaimed except that, unless provided otherwise in an international agreement as specified in §262.58:

(A) A person initiating a shipment for reclamation in a foreign country, and any intermediary arranging for the shipment, must comply with the requirements applicable to a primary exporter in §§262.53, 262.56(a)(1)-(4),(6), and (b), and 262.57, export such materials only upon consent of the receiving country and in conformance with the EPA Acknowledgment of Consent as defined in Subpart E of Part 262, and provide a copy of the EPA Acknowledgment of Consent to the shipment to the transporter transporting the shipment for export;

(B) Transporters transporting a shipment for export may not accept a shipment if he knows the shipment does not conform to the EPA Acknowledgment of Consent, must ensure that a copy of the EPA Acknowledgment of Consent accompanies the shipment and must ensure that it is delivered to the facility designated by the person initiating the shipment.

(ii) Used batteries (or used battery cells) returned to a battery manufacturer for regeneration;

(iii) Used oil that exhibits one or more of the characteristics of hazardous waste but is recycled in some other manner than being burned for energy recovery;

(iv) Scrap metal;

(v) Fuels produced from the refining of oil-bearing hazardous wastes along with normal process streams at a petroleum refining facility if such wastes result from normal petroleum refining, production, and transportation practices;

(vi) Oil reclaimed from hazardous waste resulting from normal petroleum refining, production, and transportation practices, which oil is to be refined along with normal process streams at a petroleum refining facility;

(vii)(A) Hazardous waste fuel produced from oil-bearing hazardous wastes from petroleum refining, production, or transportation practices, or produced from oil reclaimed from such hazardous wastes, where such hazardous wastes are reintroduced into a process that does not use distillation or does not produce products from crude oil so long as the resulting fuel meets the used oil specification under §266.40(e) of this chapter and so long as no other hazardous wastes are used to produce the hazardous waste fuel;

(B) Hazardous waste fuel produced from oil-bearing hazardous waste from petroleum refining production, and transportation practices, where such hazardous wastes are reintroduced into a refining process after a point at which contaminants are removed, so long as the fuel meets the used oil fuel specification under §266.40(e) of this chapter; and

(C) Oil reclaimed from oil-bearing hazardous wastes from petroleum refining, production, and transportation practices, which reclaimed oil is burned as a fuel without reintroduction to a refining process, so long as there claimed oil meets the used oil fuel specification under §266.40(e) of this chapter; and

(viii) Petroleum coke produced from petroleum refinery hazardous wastes containing oil at the same facility at which such wastes were generated, unless the resulting coke product exceeds one or more of the characteristics of hazardous waste in Part 261, Subpart C .

(b) Generators and transporters of recyclable materials are subject to the applicable requirements of Parts 262 and 263 of this chapter and the notification requirements under section 3010 of RCRA, except as provided in paragraph (a) of this section.

(c)(1) Owners or operators of facilities that store recyclable materials before they are recycled are regulated under all applicable provisions of subparts A through L, AA, and BB of parts 264 and 265, and under parts 124, 266, 268, and 270 of this chapter and the notification requirements under section 3010 of RCRA, except as provided in paragraph (a) of this section. (The recycling process itself is exempt from regulation except as provided in §261.6(d).)

(2) Owners or operators of facilities that recycle recyclable materials without storing them before they are recycled are subject to the following requirements, except as provided in paragraph (a) of this section:

(i) Notification requirements under section 3010 of RCRA;

(ii) Sections 265.71 and 265.72 (dealing with the use of the manifest and manifest discrepancies) of this chapter.

(iii) Section 261.6(d) of this chapter.

(d) Owners or operators of facilities subject to RCRA permitting requirements with hazardous waste management units that recycle hazard-ous wastes are subject to the requirements of subparts AA and BB of part 264 or 265 of this chapter.

§ 261.7 Residues of hazardous waste in empty containers.

(a)(1) Any hazardous waste remaining in either (i) an empty container or (ii) an inner liner removed from an empty container, as defined in paragraph (b) of this section, is not subject to regulation under Parts 261 through 265, or Part 268, 270 or 124 of this chapter or to the notification requirements of section 3010 of RCRA.

(2) Any hazardous waste in either (i) a container that is not empty or (ii)an inner liner removed from a container that is not empty, as defined in paragraph (b) of this section, is subject to regulation under Parts 261 through 265, and Parts 268, 270 and 124 of this chapter and to the notification requirements of section 3010 of RCRA.

(b)(1) A container or an inner liner removed from a container that has held any hazardous waste, except a waste that is a compressed gas or that is identified as an acute hazardous waste listed in §§261.31, 261.32, or 261.33(e) of this chapter is empty if:

(i) All wastes have been removed that can be removed using the practices commonly employed to remove materials from that type of container, e.g., pouring, pumping, and aspirating, and

(ii) No more than 2.5 centimeters (one inch) of residue remain on the bottom of the container or inner liner, or

(iii)(A) No more than 3 percent by weight of the total capacity of the container remains in the container or inner liner if the container is less than or equal to 110 gallons in size, or

(B) No more than 0.3 percent by weight of the total capacity of the container remains in the container or inner liner if the container is greater than 110 gallons in size.

(2) A container that has held a hazardous waste that is a compressed gas is empty when the pressure in the container approaches atmospheric.

(3) A container or an inner liner removed from a container that has held an acute hazardous waste listed in §§261.31, 261.32, or 261.33(e) is empty if:

(i) The container or inner liner has been triple rinsed using a solvent capable of removing the commercial chemical product or manu-facturing chemical intermediate;

(ii) The container or inner liner has been cleaned by another method that has been shown in the scientific literature, or by tests conducted by the generator, to achieve equivalent removal; or

(iii) In the case of a container, the inner liner that prevented contact of the commercial chemical product or manufacturing chemical intermediate with the container, has been removed.

§ 261.8 PCB wastes regulated under Toxic Substance Control Act.

The disposal of PCB-containing dielectric fluid and electric equipment containing such fluid authorized for use and regulated under part 761 of this chapter and that are hazardous only because they fail the test for the Toxicity Characteristic (Hazardous Waste Codes D018 through D043 only) are exempt from regulation under parts 261 through 265, and parts 268, 270, and 124 of this chapter, and the notification requirements of section 3010 of RCRA.

Subpart B -- Criteria for Identifying the Characteristics of Hazardous Waste and for Listing Hazardous Waste

§ 261.10 Criteria for identifying the characteristics of hazardous waste.

(a) The Administrator shall identify and define a characteristic of hazardous waste in Subpart C only upon determining that:

(1) A solid waste that exhibits the characteristic may:

(i) Cause, or significantly contribute to, an increase in mortality or an increase in serious irreversible, or incapacitating reversible, illness; or

(ii) Pose a substantial present or potential hazard to human health or the environment when it is improperly treated, stored, transported, disposed of or otherwise managed; and

(2) The characteristic can be:

(i) Measured by an available standardized test method which is reasonably within the capability of generators of solid waste or private sector laboratories that are available to serve generators of solid waste; or

(ii) Reasonably detected by generators of solid waste through their knowledge of their waste.

§ 261.11 Criteria for listing hazardous waste.

(a) The Administrator shall list a solid waste as a hazardous waste only upon determining that the solid waste meets one of the following criteria:

(1) It exhibits any of the characteristics of hazardous waste identified in Subpart C.

(2) It has been found to be fatal to humans in low doses or, in the absence of data on human toxicity, it has been shown in studies to have an oral LD 50 toxicity (rat) of less than 50 milligrams per kilogram, an inhalation LC 50 toxicity (rat) of less than 2 milligrams per liter, or a dermal LD 50 toxicity (rabbit) of less than 200 milligrams per kilogram or is otherwise capable of causing or significantly contributing to an increase in serious irreversible,or incapacitating reversible, illness. (Waste listed in accordance with these criteria will be designated Acute Hazardous Waste.)

(3) It contains any of the toxic constituents listed in Appendix VIII and, after considering the following factors, the Administrator concludes that the waste is capable of posing a substantial present or potential hazard to human health or the environment when improperly treated, stored, transported or disposed of, or otherwise managed:

(i) The nature of the toxicity presented by the constituent.

(ii) The concentration of the constituent in the waste.

(iii) The potential of the constituent or any toxic degradation product of the constituent to migrate from the waste into the environment under the types of improper management considered in paragraph (a)(3)(vii) of this section.

(iv) The persistence of the constituent or any toxic degradation product of the constituent.

(v) The potential for the constituent or any toxic degradation product of the constituent to degrade into non-harmful constituents and the rate of degradation.

(vi) The degree to which the constituent or any degradation product of the constituent bioaccumulates in ecosystems.

(vii) The plausible types of improper management to which the waste could be subjected.

(viii) The quantities of the waste generated at individual generation sites or on a regional or national basis.

(ix) The nature and severity of the human health and environmental damage that has occurred as a result of the improper management of wastes containing the constituent.

(x) Action taken by other governmental agencies or regulatory programs based on the health or environmental hazard posed by thewaste or waste constituent.

(xi) Such other factors as may be appropriate.

Substances will be listed on Appendix VIII only if they have been shown in scientific studies to have toxic, carcinogenic, mutagenic or teratogenic effects on humans or other life forms.

(Wastes listed in accordance with these criteria will be designated Toxic wastes.)

(b) The Administrator may list classes or types of solid waste as hazardous waste if he has reason to believe that individual wastes, within the class or type of waste, typically or frequently are hazardous under the definition of hazardous waste found in section 1004(5) of the Act.

(c) The Administrator will use the criteria for listing specified in this section to establish the exclusion limits referred to in §261.5(c).

Subpart C -- Characteristics of Hazardous Waste

§ 261.20 General.

(a) A solid waste, as defined in §261.2, which is not excluded from regulation as a hazardous waste under §261.4(b), is a hazardous waste if it exhibits any of the characteristics identified in this subpart.

(b) A hazardous waste which is identified by a characteristic in this Subpart is assigned every EPA Hazardous Waste Number that is applicable as set forth in this Subpart. This number must be used in complying with the notification requirements of section 3010 of the Act and all applicable recordkeeping and reporting requirements under Parts 262 through 265, 268, and 270 of this chapter.

(c) For purposes of this subpart, the Administrator will consider a sample obtained using any of the applicable sampling methods specified in Appendix I to be a representative sample within the meaning of Part 260 of this chapter.

§ 261.21 Characteristic of ignitability.

(a) A solid waste exhibits the characteristic of ignitability if a representative sample of the waste has any of the following properties:

(1) It is a liquid, other than an aqueous solution containing less than 24 percent alcohol by volume and has flash point less than 60°C (140°F), as determined by a Pensky-Martens Closed Cup Tester, using the test method specified in ASTM Standard D-93-79 or D-93-80 (incorporated by reference, see §260.11), or a Setaflash Closed Cup Tester, using the test method specified in ASTM Standard D-3278-7 8 (incorporated by reference, see 260.11), or as determined by an equivalent test method approved by the Administrator under procedures set forth in §§260.20 and 260.21.

(2) It is not a liquid and is capable, under standard temperature and pressure, of causing fire through friction, absorption of moisture or spontaneous chemical changes and, when ignited, burns so vigorously and persistently that it creates a hazard.

(3) It is an ignitable compressed gas as defined in 49 CFR 173.300 and as determined by the test methods described in that regulation or equivalent test methods approved by the Administrator under §§260.20 and 260.21.

(4) It is an oxidizer as defined in 49 CFR 173.151.

(b) A solid waste that exhibits the characteristic of ignitability has the EPA Hazardous Waste Number of D001.

§ 261.22 Characteristic of corrosivity

(a) A solid waste exhibits the characteristic of corrosivity if a representative sample of the waste has either of the following properties:

(1) It is aqueous and has a pH less than or equal to 2 or greater than or equal to 12.5, as determined by a pH meter using either an EPA test method or an equivalent test method approved by the Administrator under the procedures set forth in §§260.20 and 260.21. The EPA test method for pH is specified as Method 5.2 in "Test Methods for the Evaluation of Solid Waste, Physical/Chemical Methods" (incorporated by reference, see §260.11).

(2) It is a liquid and corrodes steel (SAE 1020) at a rate greater than 6.35 mm (0.250 inch) per year at a test temperature of 55° C (130°F) as determined by the test method specified in NACE (National Association of Corrosion Engineers) Standard TM-01-69 as standardized in "Test Methods for the Evaluation of Solid Waste, Physical/Chemical Methods" (incorporated by reference, see §260.11) or an equivalent test method approved by the Administrator under the procedures set forth in §§260.20 and 260.21.

(b) A solid waste that exhibits the characteristic of corrosivity, but is not listed as a hazardous waste in Subpart D, has the EPA Hazardous Waste Number of D002.

§ 261.23 Characteristic of reactivity

(a) A solid waste exhibits the characteristic of reactivity if a representative sample of the waste has any of the following properties:

(1) It is normally unstable and readily undergoes violent change without detonating.

(2) It reacts violently with water.

(3) It forms potentially explosive mixtures with water.

(4) When mixed with water, it generates toxic gases, vapors or fumes in a quantity sufficient to present a danger to human health or the environment.

(5) It is a cyanide or sulfide bearing waste which, when exposed to pH conditions between 2 and 12.5, can generate toxic gases, vapors or fumes in a quantity sufficient to present a danger to human health or the environment.

(6) It is capable of detonation or explosive reaction if it is subjected to a strong initiating source or if heated under confinement.

(7) It is readily capable of detonation or explosive decomposition or reaction at standard temperature and pressure.

(8) It is a forbidden explosive as defined in 49 CFR 173.51, or a Class A explosive as defined in 49 CFR 173.53 or a Class B explosive as defined in 49 CFR 173.88.

(b) A solid waste that exhibits the characteristic of reactivity has the EPA Hazardous Waste Number of D003.

§ 261.24 Toxicity characteristic.

(a) A solid waste exhibits the characteristic of toxicity if, using the test methods described in Appendix II or equivalent methods approved by the Administrator under the procedures set forth in §§260.20 and 260.21, the extract from a representative sample of the waste contains any of the contaminants listed in Table 1 at the concentration equal to or greater than the respective value given in that Table. Where the waste contains less than 0.5 percent filterable solids, the waste itself, after filtering using the methodology outlined in Appendix II, is considered to be the extract for the purpose of this section.

(b) A solid waste that exhibits the characteristic of toxicity has the EPA Hazardous Waste Number specified in Table 1 which corresponds to the toxic contaminant causing it to be hazardous.

Table 1 -- Maximum Concentration of Contaminants for the Toxicity Characteristic

EPA H W No.[1]	Contaminant	CAS No.[2]	Regulatory Level (mg/L)
D004	Arsenic	7440-38-2	5.0
D005	Barium	7440-39-3	100.0
D018	Benzene	71-43-2	0.5
D006	Cadmium	7440-43-9	1.0
D019	Carbon tetrachloride	56-23-5	0.5
D020	Chlordane	57-74-9	0.03
D021	Chlorobenzene	108-90-7	100.0
D022	Chloroform	67-66-3	6.0
D007	Chromium	7440-47-3	5.0
D023	o-Cresol	95-48-7	[4]200.0
D024	m-Cresol	108-39-4	[4]200.0
D025	p-Cresol	106-44-5	[4]200.0
D026	Cresol	....	[4]200.0
D016	2,4-D	94-75-7	10.0
D027	1,4-Dichlorobenzene	106-46-7	7.5
D028	1,2-Dichloroethane	107-06-2	0.5
D029	1,1-Dichloroethylene	75-35-4	0.7
D030	2,4-Dinitrotoluene	121-14-2	[3]0.13
D012	Endrin	72-20-8	0.02
D031	Heptachlor (and its epoxide)	76-44-8	0.008
D032	Hexachlorobenzene	118-74-1	[3]0.13
D033	Hexachlorobutadiene	87-68-3	0.5
D034	Hexachloroethane	67-72-1	3.0
D008	Lead	7439-92-1	5.0
D013	Lindane	58-89-9	0.4
D009	Mercury	7439-97-6	0.2
D014	Methoxychlor	72-43-5	10.0
D035	Methyl ethyl ketone	78-93-3	200.0
D036	Nitrobenzene	98-95-3	2.0
D037	Pentrachlorophenol	87-86-5	100.0
D038	Pyridine	110-86-1	[3]5.0
D010	Selenium	7782-49-2	1.0
D011	Silver	7440-22-4	5.0
D039	Tetrachloroethylene	127-18-4	0.7
D015	Toxaphene	8001-35-2	0.5
D040	Trichloroethylene	79-01-6	0.5
D041	2,4,5-Trichlorophenol	95-95-4	400.0
D042	2,4,6-Trichlorophenol	88-06-2	2.0
D017	2,4,5-TP (Silvex)	93-72-1	1.0
D043	Vinyl chloride	75-01-4	0.2

1 Hazardous waste number.
2 Chemical abstracts service number.
3 Quantitation limit is greater than the calculated regulatory level. The quantitation limit therefore becomes the regulatory level.
4 If o-, m-, and p-Cresol concentrations cannot be differentiated, the total cresol (D026) concentration is used. The regulatory level of total cresol is 200 mg/l.

Subpart D -- Lists of Hazardous Wastes [Interim Final]

§ 261.30 General

(a) A solid waste is a hazardous waste if it is listed in this Subpart, unless it has been excluded from this list under §§260.20 and 260.22.

(b) The Administrator will indicate his basis for listing the classes or types of wastes listed in this subpart by employing one or more of the following Hazard Codes:

Ignitable Waste..(I)
Corrosive Waste...(C)
Reactive Waste..(R)
Toxicity Characteristic Waste...................(E)
Acute Hazardous Waste...........................(H)
Toxic Waste...(T)

Appendix VII identifies the constituent which caused the Administrator to list the waste as a Toxicity Characteristic Waste (E) or Toxic Waste (T) in §§261.31 and 261.32.

(c) Each hazardous waste listed in this Subpart is assigned an EPA Hazardous Waste Number which precedes the name of the waste. This number must be used in complying with the notification requirements of Section 3010 of the Act and certain recordkeeping and reporting requirements under Parts 262 through 265, 268 and Part 270 of this Chapter.

(d) The following hazardous wastes listed in §261.31 or §261.32 are subject to the exclusion limits for acutely hazardous wastes established in §261.5: EPA Hazardous Wastes Nos. F020, FO21, FO22, FO23, FO26, and FO27.

§ 261.31 Hazardous wastes from non-specific sources.

(a) The following solid wastes are listed hazardous wastes from non-specfic sources unless they are excluded under §§260.20 and 260.22 and listed in Appendix IX.

Industry and EPA hazardous waste No.	Hazardous waste	Hazard code
Generic:		
F001	The following spent halogenated solvents used in degreasing: Tetrachloroethylene, tri-chloroethylene, methylene chloride, 1,1,1-trichloroethane, carbon tetrachloride, and chlorinated fluorocarbons; all spent solvent mixtures/blends used in degreasing containing, before use, a total of ten percent or more (by volume) of one or more of the above halogenated solvents or those solvents listed in F002, F004, and F005; and still bottoms from the recovery of these spent solvents and spent solvent mixtures.	(T)
F002	The following spent halogenated solvents: tetrachloroethylene, methylene chloride, tri-chloroethylene, 1,1,1-trichloroethane, chlorobenzene, 1,1,2-trichloro-1,2,2-trifluoroethane, ortho-dichlorobenzene, trichloro-fluoromethane, and 1,1,2-trichloroethane; all spent solvent mixtures/blends containing, before use, a total of ten percent or more (by volume) of one or more of the above halogenated solvents or those listed in F001, F004, or F005; and still bottoms from the recovery of these spent solvents and spent solvent mixtures.	(T)
F003	The following spent non-halogenated solvents: xylene, acetone, ethyl acetate, ethyl benzene, ethyl ether, methyl isobutyl ketone, n-butyl alcohol, cyclohexanone, and methanol; all spent solvent mixtures/blends containing, before use, only the above spent non-halogenated solvents; and all spent solvent mixtures blends containing, before use, one or more of the above non-halogenated solvents, and, a total of ten percent or more (by volume) of one or more of those solvents listed in F001, F002, F004, and F005; and still bottoms from the recovery of these spent solvents and spent solvent mixtures.	
F004	The following spent non-halogenated solvents: cresols and cresylic acid, and nitrobenzene; all spent solvent mixtures/blends containing before use, a total of ten percent or more (by volume) of one or more of the above non-halogenated solvents or those solvents listed in F001, F002, and F005; and still bottoms from the recovery of these spent solvents and spent solvent mixtures.	(T)
F005	The following spent non-halogenated solvents: Toluene, methyl ethyl ketone, carbon disulfide, isobutanol, pyridine, benzene, 2-ethoxyethanol, and 2-nitropropane; all spent solvent mixtures/blends containing, before use, a total of ten percent or more (by volume) of one or more of the above non-halogenated solvents or those solvents listed in F001, F002, or F004; and still bottoms from the recovery of these spent solvents and spent solvent mixtures.	(I, T)
F006	Wastewater treatment sludges from electroplating operations except from the following processes: #(1) Sulfuric acid anodizing of aluminum; (2) tin plating on carbon steel; (3) zinc plating (segregated basis) on carbon steel; (4) aluminum or zinc-aluminum plating on carbon steel; (5) cleaning/stripping associated with tin, zinc and aluminum plating carbon steel; and (6) chemical etching and milling of aluminum.	(T)
F019	Wastewater treatment sludges from the chemical conversion coating of aluminum except from zirconium phosphating in aluminum can washing when such phosphating is an exclusive conversion coating process.	(T)
F007	Spent cyanide plating bath solutions from electroplating operations.	(R, T)
F008	Plating slludges from the bottom of plating baths from electroplating operations where cyanides are used in the process.	(R, T)
F009	Spent stripping and cleaning bath solutions from electroplating operations where cyanides are used in the process.	(R, T)
F010	Quenching bath residues from oil baths from metal heat treating operations where cyanides are used in the process.	(R, T)
F011	Spent cyanide solutions from salt bath pot cleaning from metal heat treating operations.	(R, T)
F012	Quenching wastewater treatment sludges from metal heat treating operations where cyanides are used in the process.	(T)
F024	Process wastes, including but not limited to, distillation residues, heavy ends, tars, and reactor clean-out wastes, from the production of certain chlorinated aliphatic hydrocarbons by free radical catalyzed processes. These chlorinated aliphatic hydrocarbons are those having carbon chain lengths ranging from one to and including five, with varying amounts and positions of chlorine substitution. (This listing does not include wastewaters, waste- water treatment sludges, spent catalysts, and wastes listed in §261.31 or 261.32.).	(T)
F020	Wastes (except wastewater and spent carbon from hydrogen chloride purification) from the production or manufacturing use (as a reactant, chemical intermediate, or component in a formulating process) of tri- or tetrachlorophenol, or of intermediates used to produce their pesticide derivatives. (This listing does not include wastes from the production of Hexachlorophene from a highly purified 2,4,5-trichlorophenol.).	(H)
F021	Wastes (except wastewater and spent carbon from hydrogen chloride purification) from the production or manufacturing use (as a reactant, chemical intermediate, or component in a formulating process) of pentachlorophenol, or of intermediates used to produce its derivatives.	(H)
F022	Wastes (except wastewater and spent carbon from hydrogen chloride purification) from the manufacturing use (as a reactant, chemical intermediate, or component in a formulating process) of tetra-, penta-, or hexachlorobenzenes under alkaline conditions.	(H)
F023	Wastes (except wastewater and spent carbon from hydrogen chloride purification) from the production of materials on equipment previously used for the production or manufacturing use (as a reactant, chemical intermediate, or component in a formulating process) of tri- and tetrachlorophenols. (This listing does not include wastes from equipment used only for the production or use of Hexachlorophene from highly purified 2,4,5-trichlorophenol.).	(H)

F026......Wastes (except wastewater and spent carbon from hydrogen chloride purification) from the production of materials on equipment previously used for the manufacturing use (as a reactant chemical intermediate, or component in a formulating process) of tetra-, penta-, or hexachlorobenzene under alkaline conditions. (H)

F027......Discarded unused formulations containing tri-, tetra-, or pentachlorophenol or discarded unused formulations containing compounds derived from these chlorophenols. (This listing does not include formulations containing Hexachlorophene synthesized from pre-purified 2,4,5-trichlorophenol as the sole component.). (H)

F028......Residues resulting from the incineration or thermal treatment of soil contaminated with EPA Hazardous Waste Nos. F020, F021, F022, F023, F026, and F027. (T)

F025......Condensed light ends, spent filter and filter aids, and spent desiccant wastes from the production of certain chlorinated aliphatic hydrocarbons, by free radical catalyzed processes. These chlorinated aliphatic hydrocarbons are those having carbon chain lengths ranging from one to and including five, with varying amounts and positions of chlorine substitution.

F032[1]....Wastewaters, process residuals, preservative drippage, and spent formulations from wood preserving processes generated at plants that currently use or have previously used chlorophenolic formulations (except potentially cross-contaminated wastes that have had the F032 waste code deleted in accordance with §261.35 of this chapter and where the generator does not resume or initiate use of chlorophenolic formulations). This listing does not include K001 bottom sediment sludge from the treatment of wastewater from wood preserving processes that use creosote and/or pentachlorophenol. (T)

F034[1]....Wastewaters, process residuals, preservative drippage, and spent formulations from wood preserving process es generated at plants that use creosote formulations. This listing does not include K001 bottom sediment sludge from the treatment of wastewater from wood preserving processes that use creosote and/or pentachlorophenol. (NOTE: The listing of wastewaters that have not come into contact with process contaminants is stayed administratively. The stay will remain in effect until futher administrative action is taken.)

F035[1]....Wastewaters, process residuals, preservative drippage, and spent formulations from wood preserving processes generated at plants that use inorganic preservatives containing arsenic or chromium. This listing does not include K001 bottom sediment sludge from the treatment of wastewater from wood preserving processes that use creosote and/or pentachlorophenol. (NOTE: The listing of wastewaters that have not come into contact with process contaminants is stayed administratively. The stay will remain in effect until further administrative action is taken.).

F039.......Leachate (liquids that have percolated through land disposed wastes) resulting from the treatment, storage, or disposal of wastes classified as hazardous under Subpart D or from a mixture of wastes classified under Subparts C and D of this part. (Leachate resulting from the management of one or more of the following EPA Hazardous Wastes and no other Hazardous Wastes retains its EPA Hazardous Waste Number(s): F020, F021, F022, F026, F027, and/or F028.) (T)

---

[1] The F032, F034, and F305 listings are administratively stayed with respect to the process area receiving drippage of these wastes provided persons desiring to continue operating notify EPA by August 6, 1991 of their intent to upgrade or install drip pads, and by November 6, 1991 provide evidence to EPA that they have adequate financing to pay for drip pad upgrades or installation, as provided in the administrative stay. The stay of the listings will remain in effect until February 6, 1992 for existing drip pads and until May 6, 1992 for new drip pads.

*(I,T) should be used to specify mixtures containing ignitable and toxic constituents.

(b) Listing Specific Definitions: (1) For the purposes of the F037 and F038 listings, oil/water/solids is defined as oil and/or water and/or solids.

(2)(i) For the purposes of the F037 and F038 listings, aggressive biological treatment units are defined as units which employ one of the following four treatment methods: activated sludge; trickling filter; rotating biological contactor for the continuous accelerated biological oxidation of wastewaters; or high-rate aeration. High-rate aeration is a system of surface impoundments or tanks, in which intense mechanical aeration is used to completely mix the wastes, enhance biological activity, and (A) the units employs a minimum of 6 hp per million gallons of treatment volume; and either (B) the hydraulic retention time of the unit is no longer than 5 days; or (C) the hydraulic retention time is no longer than 30 days and the unit does not generate a sludge that is a hazardous waste by the Toxicity Characteristic.

(ii) Generators and treatment, storage and disposal facilities have the burden of proving that their sludges are exempt from listing as F037 and F038 wastes under this definition. Generators and treatment, storage and disposal facilities must maintain, in their operating or other onsite records, documents and data sufficient to prove that: (A) the unit is an aggressive biological treatment unit as defined in this subsection; and (B) the sludges sought to be exempted from the definitions of F037 and/or F038 were actually generated in the aggressive biological treatment unit.

(3)(i) For the purposes of the F037 listing, sludges are considered to be generated at the moment of deposition in the unit, where deposition is defined as at least a temporary cessation of lateral particle movement. (ii) For the purposes of the F038 lisitng, (A) sludges are considered to be generated at the moment of deposition in the unit, where deposition is defined as at least a temporary cessation of lateral particle movement and (B) floats are considered to be generated at the moment they are formed in the top of the unit.

§ 261.32 Hazardous wastes from specific sources.

The following solid wastes are listed hazardous wastes from specific sources unless they are excluded under §§ 260.20 and 260.22 and listed in Appendix IX.

Industry and EPA hazardous waste No.	Hazardous waste	Hazard code
Wood preservation:		
K001	Bottom sediment sludge from the treatment of wastewaters from wood preserving processes that use creosote and/or pentachlorophenol.	(T)
Inorganic pigments:		
K002	Wastewater treatment sludge from the production of chrome yellow and orange pigments.	(T)
K003	Wastewater treatment sludge from the production of molybdate orange pigments.	(T)
K004	Wastewater treatment sludge from the production of zinc yellow pigments.	(T)
K005	Wastewater treatment sludge from the production of chrome green pigments.	(T)
K006	Wastewater treatment sludge from the production of chrome oxide green pigments (anhydrous and hydrated).	(T)
K007	Wastewater treatment sludge from the production of iron blue pigments.	(T)
K008	Oven residue from the production of chrome oxide green pigments.	(T)
Organic chemicals:		
K009	Distillation bottoms from the production of acetaldehyde from ethylene.	(T)
K010	Distillation side cuts from the production of acetaldehyde from ethylene.	(T)
K011	Bottom stream from the wastewater stripper in the production of acrylonitrile.	(R,T)
K013	Bottom stream from the acetonitrile column in the production of acrylonitrile.	(R,T)
K014	Bottoms from the acetonitrile purification column in the production of acrylonitrile.	(T)
K015	Still bottoms from the distillation of benzyl chloride.	
K016	Heavy ends or distillation residues from the production of carbon tetrachloride.	(T)
K017	Heavy ends (still bottoms) from the purification column in the production of epichlorohydrin.	(T)
K018	Heavy ends from the fractionation column in ethyl chloride production.	(T)
K019	Heavy ends from the distillation of ethylene dichloride in ethylene dichloride production.	(T)
K020	Heavy ends from the distillation of vinyl chloriden vinyl chloride monomer production.	(T)
K021	Aqueous spent antimony catalyst waste from fluoromethanes production.	(T)
K022	Distillation bottom tars from the production of phenol/acetone from cumene.	(T)
K023	Distillation light ends from the production of hthalic anhydride from naphthalene.	(T)
K024	Distillation bottoms from the production of phthalic anhydride from naphthalene.	(T)
K093	Distillation light ends from the production of phthalic anhydride from ortho-xylene.	(T)
K094	Distillation bottoms from the production of phthalic anhydride from ortho-xylene.	(T)
K025	Distillation bottoms from the production of nitrobenzene by the nitration of benzene.	(T)
K026	Stripping still tails from the production of methy ethyl pyridines. ethyl pyridines.	(T)
K027	Centrifuge and distillation residues from toluene diisocyanate production.	(R,T)
K028	Spent catalyst from the hydrochlorinator reactor in the production of 1,1,1-trichloroethane.	(T)
K029	Waste from the product steam stripper in the production of 1,1,1-trichloroethane.	(T)
K095	Distillation bottoms from the production of 1,1,1-trichloroethane.	(T)
K096	Heavy ends from the heavy ends column from the production of 1,1,1-trichloroethane.	(T)
K030	Column bottoms or heavy ends from the combined production of trichloroethylene and production of trichloroethylene and perchloroethylene.	(T)
K083	Distillation bottoms from aniline production.	(T)
K103	Process residues from aniline extraction from the production of aniline.	(T)
K104	Combined wastewater streams generated from nitrobenzene/aniline production.	(T)
K085	Distillation or fractionation column bottoms from the production of chlorobenzenes.	(T)
K105	Separated aqueous stream from the reactor product washing step in the production of chlorobenzenes.	(T)
K107	Column bottoms from product separation from the production of 1,1-dimethyl-hydrazine (UDMH) from carboxylic acid hydrazines.	(C,T)
K108	Condensed column overheads from product separation and condensed reactor vent gases from he production of 1,1-dimethylhydrazine (UDMH) from carboxylic acid hydrazides.	(I,T)
K109	Spent filter cartridges from product purification from the production of 1,1-dimethylhydrazine (UDMH) from carboxylic acid hydrazides.	(T)
K110	Condensed column overheads from intermediate separation from the production of 1,1-dimethylhydrazine (UDMH) from carboxylic acid hydrazides	(T)
K111	Product washwaters from the production of dinitrotoluene via nitration of toluene.	(C,T)
K112	Reaction by-product water from the drying column in the production of toluenediamine via hydrogenation of dinitrotoluene.	(T)
K113	Condensed liquid light ends from the purification of toluenediamine in the production of toluenediamine via hydrogenation of dinitrotoluene.	(T)
K114	Vicinals from the purification of toluenediamine in the production of toluenediamine via hydrogenation of dinitrotoluene.	(T)
K115	Heavy ends from the purification of toluenediamine in the production of toluenediamine via hydrogenation of dinitrotoluene.	(T)
K116	Organic condensate from the solvent recovery column in the production of toluene diisocyanate via phosgenation of toluenediamine.	(T)
K117	Wastewater from the reactor vent gas scrubber in the production of ethylene dibromide via bromination of ethene.	(T)
K118	Spent adsorbent solids from purification of ethylene dibromide in the production of ethylene-dibromide via bromination of ethene.	(T)
K136	Still bottoms from the purification of ethylene dibromide in the production of ethylene dibromide via bromination of ethene.	(T)
Inorganic chemicals:		
K071	Brine purification muds from the mercury cell process in chlorine production, where separately prepurified brine is not used.	(T)
K073	Chlorinated hydrocarbon waste from the purification step of the diaphragm cell process using graphite anodes in chlorine production.	(T)
K106	Wastewater treatment sludge from the mercury cell rocess in chlorine production.	(T)

Industry and EPA hazardous waste No.	Hazardous waste	Hazard code
Pesticides: K031	By-product salts generated in the production of MSMA and cacodylic acid.	(T)
K032	Wastewater treatment sludge from the production of chlordane.	(T)
K033	Wastewater and scrub water from the chlorination of cyclopentadiene in the production of chlordane.	(T)
K034	Filter solids from the filtration of hexachloroycyclopentadiene in the production of chlordane.	(T)
K097	Vacuum stripper discharge from the chlordane chlorinator in the production of chlordane.	(T)
K035	Wastewater treatment sludges generated in the production of creosote.	(T)
K036	Still bottoms from toluene reclamation distillation in the production of disulfoton.	(T)
K037	Wastewater treatment sludges from the production of disulfoton.	(T)
K038	Wastewater from the washing and stripping of phorate production.	(T)
K039	Filter cake from the filtration of diethylphos-horodithioic acid in the production of phorate	(T)
K040	Wastewater treatment sludge from the production of phorate.	(T)
K041	Wastewater treatment sludge from the production of toxaphene.	(T)
K098	Untreated process wastewater from the production of toxaphene	(T)
K042	Heavy ends or distillation residues from the distillation of tetrachlorobenzene in the production of 2,4,5-T.	(T)
K043	2,6-Dichlorophenol waste from the production of 2,4-D.	(T)
K099	Untreated wastewater from the production of 2,4-D.	(T)
K123	Process wastewater (including supernates, filtrates, and washwaters) from the production of ethylenebisdithiocarbamic acid and its salt.	(T)
K124	Reactor vent scrubber water from the production of ethylenebisdithiocarbamic acid and its salts.	(C,T)
K125	Filtration, evaporation, and centrifugation solids room the production of ethylenebisdithiocarbamic (acid and its salts).	(T)
K126	Baghouse dust and floor sweepings in milling and packaging operations from the production or formulation of ethylenebisdithiocarbamic acid and its salts.	(T)
K131	Wastewater from the reactor and spent sulfuric acid from the acid dryer from the production of methyl bromide.	(C,T)
K132	Spent absorbent and wastewater separator solids from the production of methyl bromide.	(T)
Explosives:		
K044	Wastewater treatment sludges from the manufacturing and processing of explosives.	(R)
K045	Spent carbon from the treatment of wastewater containing explosives.	(R)
K046	Wastewater treatment sludges from the manufacturing, formulation and loading of lead-based initiating compounds.	(T)
K047	Pink/red water from TNT operations.	(R)
Petroleum refining:		
K048	Dissolved air flotation (DAF) float from thepetroleum refining industry.	(T)
K049	Slop oil emulsion solids from the petroleum refining industry.	(T)
K050	Heat exchanger bundle cleaning sludge from the petroleum refining industry.	(T)
K051	API separator sludge from the petroleum refining industry.	(T)
K052	Tank bottoms (leaded) from the petroleum refining industry.	(T)
Iron and steel:		
K061	Emission control dust/sludge from the primary production of steel in electric furnaces.	(T)
K062	Spent pickle liquor generated by steel finishing operations of facilities within the iron and steel industry (SIC Codes 331 and 332).	(C,T)
Primary copper:		
K064	Acid plant blowdown slurry/sludge resulting from the thickening of blowdown slurry from primary copper production.	(T)
Primary lead:		
K065	Surface impoundment solids contained in and dredged from surface impoundments at primary lead smelting facilities.	(T)
Primary zinc:		
K066	Sludge from treatment of process wastewater and/or acid plant blowdown from primary zinc production.	(T)
Primary aluminum:		
K088	Spent potliners from primary aluminum reduction.	(T)
Ferroalloys:		
K090	Emission control dust or sludge from ferrochromiumsilicon production.	(T)
K091	Emission control dust or sludge from ferrochromium production.	(T)
Secondary lead:		
K069	Emission control dust/sludge from secondary lead smelting.	(T)
K100	Waste leaching solution from acid leaching of mission control dust/sludge from secondary lead smelting.	(T)
Veterinary Pharmaceuticals:		
K084	Wastewater treatment sludges generated during the production of veterinary pharmaceuticals from arsenic or organo-arsenic compounds.	(T)
K101	Distillation tar residues from the distillation of aniline-based compounds in the production of veterinary pharmaceuticals from arsenic or organo-arsenic compounds.	(T)
K102	Residue from the use of activated carbon for decolorization in the production of veterinary pharmaceuticals from arsenic or organo-arsenic compounds.	(T)
Ink formulation: KO86	Solvent washes and sludges, caustic washes and sludges, or water washes and sludges from cleaning tubs and equipment used in the formultion of ink from pigments, driers, soaps, and stabilizers containing chromium and lead.	(T)
Coking:		
K060	Ammonia still lime sludge from coking operations.	(T)
K087	Decanter tank tar sludge from coking operations.	(T)

§ 261.33 Discarded commercial chemical products, off-specification species, container residues, and spill residues thereof.

The following materials or items are hazardous wastes if and when they are discarded or intended to be discarded as described in §261.2(a)(2)(i), when they are mixed with waste oil or used oil or other material and applied to the land for dust suppression or road treatment, when they are otherwise applied to the land in lieu of their original intended use or when they are contained in products that are applied to the land in lieu of their original intended use, or when, in lieu of their original intended use, they are produced for use as (or as a component of) a fuel, distributed for use as a fuel, or burned as a fuel.

(a) Any commercial chemical product, or manufacturing chemical intermediate having the generic name listed in paragraph (e) or (f) of this section.

(b) Any off-specification commercial chemical product or manufacturing chemical intermediate which, if it met specifications, would have the generic name listed in paragraph (e) or (f) of this section.

(c) Any residue remaining in a container or in an inner liner removed from a container that has held any commercial chemical product or manufacturing chemical intermediate having the generic name listed in paragraphs (e) or (f) of this section, unless the container is empty as defined in §261.7(b) of this chapter.

(d) Any residue or contaminated soil, water or other debris resulting from the cleanup of a spill into or on any land or water of any commercial chemical product or manufacturing chemical intermediate having the generic name listed in paragraph (e) or (f) of this section, or any residue or contaminated soil, water or other debris resulting from the cleanup of a spill, into or on any land or water, of any off-specification chemical product and manufacturing chemical intermediate which, if it met specifications, would have the generic name listed in paragraph (e) or (f) of this section.

(e) The commercial chemical products, manufacturing chemical intermediates or off-specification commercial chemical products or manufacturing chemical intermediates referred to in paragraphs (a) through (d) of this section, are identified as acute hazardous wastes (H) and are subject to be the small quantity exclusion defined in §261.5(e).

These wastes and their corresponding EPA Hazardous Waste Numbers are:

Haz-ardous waste No.	Chemical abstracts No.	Substance
P023	107-20-0	Acetaldehyde, chloro-
P002	591-08-2	Acetamide, N-(aminothioxo-methyl)-
P057	640-19-7	Acetamide, 2-fluoro-
P058	62-74-8	Acetic acid, fluorosodium salt
P002	591-08-2	Acetyl-2-thiourea
P003	107-02-8	Acrolein
P070	116-06-3	Aldicarb
P004	309-00-2	Aldrin
P005	107-18-6	Allyl alcohol
P006	20859-73-8	Aluminum phosphide (R,T)
P007	2763-96-4	5-(Aminomethyl)-3-isoxazolol
P008	504-24-5	Aminopyridine
P009	31-74-8	Ammonium picrate (R)
P119	7803-55-6	Ammonium vanadate
P099	506-61-6	Argentate(1-), bis(cyano-C) potassium
P010	7778-39-4	Arsenic acid $H_3A_5O_4$
P012	1327-53-3	Arsenic oxide As_2O_3
P011	1303-28-2	Arsenic oxide As_2O_5
P011	1303-28-2	Arsenic pentoxide
P012	1327-53-3	Arsenic trioxide
P038	692-42-2	Arsine, diethyl-
P036	696-28-6	Arsonous dichloride, phenyl-
P054	151-56-4	Aziridine
P067	75-55-8	Aziridine, 2-methyl-
P013	542-62-1	Barium cyanide
P024	106-47-8	Benzenamine, 4-chloro-
P077	100-01-6	Benzenamine, 4-nitro-
P028	100-44-7	Benzene, (chloromethyl)-
P042	51-43-4	1,2-Benzenediol, 4-[1-hydroxy- 2(methylamino) ethyl]-, (R)-
P046	122-09-8	Benzeneethanamine, alpha,alpha-dimethyl-
P014	108-98-5	Benzenethiol
P001	[1] 81-81-2	2H-1-Benzopyran- 2 one, 4-hydroxy-3-(3 oxo-1-phenylbutyl),& salts, when present at concentrations greater than 0.3%
P028	100-44-7	Benzyl chloride
P015	7440-41-7	Beryllium
P017	598-31-2	Bromoacetone
P018	357-57-3	Brucine
P045	39196-18-4	2-Butanone, 3,3-dimethyl-1-(methylthio)-, O-[methylamino) carbonyl] oxime
P021	592-01-8	Calcium cyanide
P021	592-01-8	Calcium cyanide $Ca(CN)_2$
P022	75-15-0	Carbon disulfide
P095	75-44-5	Carbonic dichloride
P023	107-20-0	Chloroacetaldehyde
P024	106-47-8	p-Chloroaniline
P026	5344-82-1	1-(o-Chlorophenyl)thiourea
P027	542-76-7	3-Chloropropionitrile
P029	544-92-3	Copper cyanide
P029	544-92-3	Copper cyanide Cu(CN)
P030	- - - - - - - -	Cyanides (soluble cyanide salts), not otherwise specified
P031	460-19-5	Cyanogen
P033	506-77-4	Cyanogen chloride
P033	506-77-4	Cyanogen chloride (CN)Cl
P034	131-89-5	2-Cyclohexyl-4,6-dinitrophenol
P016	542-88-1	Dichloromethyl ether
P036	696-28-6	Dichlorophenylarsine
P037	60-57-1	Dieldrin
P038	692-42-2	Diethylarsine
P041	311-45-5	Diethyl-p-nitrophenyl phosphate
P040	297-97-2	O,O-Diethyl O-pyrazinyl phosphorothioates
P043	55-91-4	Diisopropylfluorophosphate (DFP)
P004	309-00-2	1,4,5,8 Dimethanonaphthalene, 1,2,3,4,- 10,10-hexachloro-1,4,4a,5,8,8a,-hexa-hydro (1alpha,4alpha,4abeta,5alpha,8alpha, 8abeta)-
P060	465-73-6	1,4,5,8- Dimethanonaphthalene, 1,2,3,4,10,10-hexachlorol,4,4a,5,8,8a-hexa-hydro-, (1alpha,-4alpha,4abeta,5beta,-8beta, 8abeta)-
P037	60-57-1	2,7:3,6- Dimethanonaphth[2,3-b]oxirene, 3,4,5,6,9,9-hexachlorol,a,2,2a,3,6,6a,- 7,7a-octahydro-, (1aalpha,2beta,2aalpha,-3beta,6beta,6aalpha,-7beta,7aalpha)-
P051	[1] 72-20-8	2,7:3,6-Dimethanonaphth [2,3-b]oxirene,3,4,5,6,9,9-hexachloro-1a,2,2a,3,6,6a,7,7a octahydro(1aalpha,2beta,2abeta,3alpha,6alpha,-6abeta,7beta, 7aalpha)-& metabolites

Haz-ardous waste No.	Chemical abstracts No.	Substance
P044	60-51-5	Dimethoate
P046	122-09-8	alpha,alpha- Dimethylphenethylamine
P047	[1] 534-52-1	4,6-Dinitro-o-cresol, & salts
P048	51-28-5	2,4-Dinitrophenol
P020	88-85-7	Dinoseb
P085	152-16-9	Diphosphoramide, octamethyl-
P111	107-49-3	Diphosphoric acid, tetraethyl ester
P039	298-04-4	Disulfoton
P049	541-53-7	Dithiobiuret
P050	115-29-7	Endosulfan
P088	145-73-3	Endothall
P051	72-20-8	Endrin
P051	72-20-8	Endrin, & metabolites
P042	51-43-4	Epinephrine
P031	460-19-5	Ethanedinitrile
P066	16752-77-5	Ethanimidothioic acid, N-[[(methylamino) carbonyl]oxy]-, methyl ester
P101	107-12-0	Ethyl cyanide
P054	151-56-4	Ethyleneimine
P097	52-85-7	Famphur
P056	7782-41-4	Fluorine
P057	640-19-7	Fluoroacetamide
P058	62-74-8	Fluoroacetic acid, sodium salt
P065	628-86-4	Fulminic acid, mercury(2+) salt (R,T)
P059	76-44-8	Heptachlor
P062	757-58-4	Hexaethyl tetraphosphate
P116	79-19-6	Hydrazinecarbothioamide
P068	60-34-4	Hydrazine, methyl-
P063	74-90-8	Hydrocyanic acid
P063	74-90-8	Hydrogen cyanide
P096	7803-51-2	Hydrogen phosphide
P060	465-73-6	Isodrin
P007	2763-96-4	3(2H)-Isoxazolone, 5-(aminomethyl)-
P092	62-38-4	Mercury, (acetato-O)phenyl-
P065	628-86-4	Mercury fulminate (R,T)
P082	62-75-9	Methanamine, N-methyl-N-nitroso-
P064	624-83-9	Methane, isocyanato-
P016	542-88-1	Methane, oxybis[chloro-
P112	509-14-8	Methane, tetranitro- (R)
P118	75-70-7	Methanethiol, trichloro-
P050	115-29-7	6,9-Methano-2,4,3-benzodioxathiepin, 6,7,8,9,10, 10-hexachlorol,5,5a,6,9,9ahexa-hydro-, 3-oxide
P059	76-44-8	4,7-Methano-1H-indene, 1,4,5,6,7,8,8-heptachloro-3a,4,7,7a-tetrahydro-
P066	16752-77-5	Methomyl
P068	60-34-4	Methyl hydrazine
P064	624-83-9	Methyl isocyanate
P069	75-86-5	2-Methyllactonitrile
P071	298-00-0	Methyl parathion
P072	86-88-4	alpha-Napthylthiourea
P073	13463-39-3	Nickel carbonyl
P073	13463-39-3	Nickel carbonyl $Ni(CO)_4$, (T-4)-
P074	557-19-7	Nickel cyanide
P074	557-19-7	Nickel cynaide $Ni(CN)_2$
P075	[1] 54-11-5	Nicotine, & salts
P076	10102-43-9	Nitric oxide
P077	100-01-6	p-Nitroaniline
P078	10102-44-0	Nitrogen dioxide
P076	10102-43-9	Nitrogen oxide NO
P078	10102-44-0	Nitrogen oxide NO2
P081	55-63-0	Nitroglycerine (R)
P082	62-75-9	N-Nitrosodimethyl-amine
P084	4549-40-0	N-Nitrosomethylvinylamine
P085	152-16-9	Octamethylpyrophosphoramide
P087	20816-12-0	Osmium oxide OsO_4, (T-4)-
P087	20816-12-0	Osmium tetroxide
P088	145-73-3	7-Oxabicyclo[2.2.1]heptane-2,3-dicarboxylic acid
P089	56-38-2	Parathion
P034	131-89-5	Phenol, 2-cyclohexyl-4,6-dinitro-
P048	51-28-5	Phenol, 2,4-dinitro-
P047	[1] 534-52-1	Phenol, 2-methyl-4,6-dinitro-, & salts
P020	88-85-7	Phenol, 2-(1-methylpropyl)-4,6-dinitro-
P009	131-74-8	Phenol, 2,4,6-trinitro-, ammonium salt (R)
P092	62-38-4	Phenylmercury acetate
P093	103-85-5	Phenylthiourea
P094	298-02-2	Phorate
P095	75-44-5	Phosgene
P096	7803-51-2	Phosphine
P041	311-45-5	Phosphoric acid, diethyl 4-nitrophenyl ester

Haz-ardous waste No.	Chemical abstracts No.	Substance
P039	298-04-4	Phosphorodithioic acid, O,O-diethyl S-[2-(ethylthio)ethyl] ester
P094	298-02-2	Phosphorodithioic acid, O,O-diethyl S-[(ethylthio)methyl] ester
P044	60-51-5	Phosphorodithioic acid, O,O-dimethyl S-[2-(methylamino)-2-oxoethyl] ester
P043	55-91-4	Phosphorofluoridic acid, bis(1-methylethyl ester
P089	56-38-2	Phosphorothioic acid, O,O-diethyl O-(4-nitrophenyl) ester
P040	297-97-2	Phosphorothioic acid, O,O-diethyl O-pyrazinyl ester
P097	52-85-7	Phosphorothioic acid, O-[4 [(dimethyl-amino)sulfonyl]phenyl] O,O-dimethyl ester
P071	298-00-0	Phosphorothioic acid, O,O,-dimethyl O-(4-ni rophenyl) ester
P110	78-00-2	Plumbane, tetraethyl-
P098	151-50-8	Potassium cyanide
P098	151-50-8	Potassium cyanide K(CN)
P099	506-61-6	Potassium silver cyanide
P070	116-06-3	Propanal, 2-methyl-2-(methylthio)-, O-[(methylamino)-carbonyl]oxime
P101	107-12-0	Propanenitrile
P027	542-76-7	Propanenitrile, 3-chloro-
P069	75-86-5	Propanenitrile, 2-hydroxy-2-methyl-
P081	55-63-0	1,2,3-Propanetriol, trinitrate (R)
P017	598-31-2	2-Propanone, 1-bromo-
P102	107-19-7	Propargyl alcohol
P003	107-02-8	2-Propenal
P005	107-18-6	2-Propen-1-ol
P067	75-55-8	1,2-Propylenimine
P102	107-19-7	2-Propyn-1-ol
P008	504-24-5	4-Pyridinamine
P075	[1] 54-11-5	Pyridine, 3-(1-methyl-2-pyrrolidinyl)-, (S)-, & salts
P114	12039-52-0	Selenious acid, dithallium(1+) salt
P103	630-10-4	Selenourea
P104	506-64-9	Silver cyanide
P104	506-64-9	Silver cyanide Ag(CN)
P105	26628-22-8	Sodium azide
P106	143-33-9	Sodium cyanide
P106	143-33-9	Sodium cyanide Na(CN)
P108	1 57-24-9	Strychnidin-10-one, & salts
P018	357-57-3	Strychnidin-10-one, 2,3-dimethoxy-
P108	[1] 57-24-9	Strychnine, & salts
P115	7446-18-6	Sulfuric acid, dithallium(1+) salt
P109	3689-24-5	Tetraethyldithiopyrophosphate
P110	78-00-2	Tetraethyl lead
P111	107-49-3	Tetraethyl pyrophosphate
P112	509-14-8	Tetranitromethane (R)
P062	757-58-4	Tetraphosphoric acid, hexaethyl ester
P113	1314-32-5	Thallic oxide
P113	1314-32-5	Thallium oxide Tl_2O_3
P114	12039-52-0	Thallium(I) selenite
P115	7446-18-6	Thallium(I) sulfate
P109	3689-24-5	Thiodiphosphoric acid, tetraethyl ester
P045	39196-18-4	Thiofanox
P049	541-53-7	Thioimidodicarbonic diamide $[(H_2N)C(S)]_2NH$
P014	108-98-5	Thiophenol
P116	79-19-6	Thiosemicarbazide
P026	5344-82-1	Thiourea, (2-chlorophenyl)-
P072	86-88-4	Thiourea, 1-naphthalenyl-
P093	103-85-5	Thiourea, phenyl-
P123	8001-35-2	Toxaphene
P118	75-70-7	Trichloromethanethiol
P119	7803-55-6	Vanadic acid, ammonium salt
P120	1314-62-1	Vanadium oxide V_2O_5
P120	1314-62-1	Vanadium pentoxide
P084	4549-40-0	Vinylamine, N-methyl-N-nitroso-
P001	[1] 81-81-2	Warfarin, & salts, when present at concentrations greater than 0.3 %
P121	557-21-1	Zinc cyanide
P121	557-21-1	Zinc cyanide $Zn(CN)_2$
P122	1314-84-7	Zinc phosphide Zn_3P_2, when present at concentrations greater than 10 % (R,T)

[1] CAS Number given for parent compound only.

(f) The commercial chemical products, manufacturing chemical intermediates, or off-specification commercial chemical (a) through (d) of this section, are identified as toxic wastes (T), unless otherwise designated and are subject to the small quantity generator exclusion defined in §261.5(a) and (g).

Haz-ardous waste No.	Chemical abstracts No.	Substance
U001	75-07-0	Acetaldehyde (I)
U034	75-87-6	Acetaldehyde, trichloro-
U187	62-44-2	Acetamide, N-(4-ethoxyphenyl)-
U005	53-96-3	Acetamide, N-9H-fluoren-2-yl-
U240	[1] 94-75-7	Acetic acid, (2,4-dichlorophenoxy)-, salts & esters
U112	141-78-6	Acetic acid ethyl ester (I)
U144	301-04-2	Acetic acid, lead(2 +) salt
U214	563-68-8	Acetic acid, thallium(1 +) salt
see F027	93-76-5	Acetic acid, (2,4,5-trichlorophenoxy)-
U002	67-64-1	Acetone (I)
U003	75-05-8	Acetonitrile (I,T)
U004	98-86-2	Acetophenone
U005	53-96-3	2-Acetylaminofluorene
U006	75-36-5	Acetyl chloride (C,R,T)
U007	79-06-1	Acrylamide
U008	79-10-7	Acrylic acid (I)
U009	107-13-1	Acrylonitrile
U011	61-82-5	Amitrole
U012	62-53-3	Aniline (I,T)
U136	75-60-5	Arsinic acid, dimethyl-
U014	492-80-8	Auramine
U015	115-02-6	Azaserine
U010	50-07-7	Azirino[2',3':3,4]pyrrolo[1,2-a]indole-4,7- dione, 6-amino-8- [[(aminocarbonyl)oxy] methyl]-1,1a,2,8,8a,8b-hexahydro-8a-methoxy-5-methyl-, [1aS-(1aalpha,8beta, 8aalpha,8balpha)]-
U157	56-49-5	Benz[j]aceanthrylene, 1,2-dihydro-3-methyl-
U016	225-51-4	Benz[c]acridine
U017	8-87-3	Benzal chloride
U192	23950-58-5	Benzamide, 3,5-dichloro-N-(1,1-dimethyl-2-propynyl)-
U018	56-55-3	Benz[a]anthracene
U094	57-97-6	Benz[a]anthracene, 7,12-dimethyl-
U012	62-53-3	Benzenamine (I,T)
U014	492-80-8	Benzenamine, 4,4'-carbonimidoylbis[N,N-dimethyl-
U049	3165-93-3	Benzenamine, 4-chloro-2-methyl-,hydrochloride
U093	60-11-7	Benzenamine, N,N-dimethyl-4-(phenylazo)-
U328	95-53-4	Benzenamine, 2-methyl-
U353	106-49-0	Benzenamine, 4-methyl-
U158	101-14-4	Benzenamine,4,4'-methylenebis[2-chloro-

Haz-ardous waste No.	Chemical abstracts No.	Substance
U222	636-21-5	Benzenamine, 2-methyl-, hydrochloride
U181	99-55-8	Benzenamine, 2-methyl-5-nitro-
U019	71-43-2	Benzene (I,T)
U038	510-15-6	Benzeneacetic acid, 4-chloro- alpha-(4-chlorophenyl)-alpha-hydroxy-, ethyl ester
U030	101-55-3	Benzene, 1-bromo-4-phenoxy-
U035	305-03-3	Benzenebutanoic acid, 4-[bis(2-chloroethyl)amino]-
U037	108-90-7	Benzene, chloro-
U221	25376-45-8	Benzenediamine, ar-methyl-
U028	117-81-7	1,2-Benzenedicarboxylic acid, bis(2-ethylhexyl) ester
U069	84-74-2	1,2-Benzenedicarboxylic acid, dibutyl ester
U088	84-66-2	1,2-Benzenedicarboxylic acid, diethyl ester
U102	131-11-3	1,2-Benzenedicarboxylic acid, dimethyl ester
U107	117-84-0	1,2-Benzenedicarboxylic acid, dioctyl ester
U070	95-50-1	Benzene, 1,2-dichloro-
U071	541-73-1	Benzene, 1,3-dichloro-
U072	106-46-7	Benzene, 1,4-dichloro-
U060	72-54-8	Benzene, 1,1'-(2,2-dichloroethylidene)bis [4-chloro-
U017	98-87-3	Benzene, (dichloromethyl)-
U223	26471-62-5	Benzene, 1,3diisocyanatomethyl-(R,T)
U239	1330-20-7	Benzene, dimethyl- (I,T)
U201	108-46-3	1,3-Benzenediol
U127	118-74-1	Benzene, hexachloro-
U056	110-82-7	Benzene, hexahydro- (I)
U220	108-88-3	Benzene, methyl-
U105	121-14-2	Benzene, 1-methyl-2,4-dinitro-
U106	606-20-2	Benzene, 2-methyl-1,3-dinitro-
U055	98-82-8	Benzene, (1-methylethyl)- (I)
U169	98-95-3	Benzene, nitro-
U183	608-93-5	Benzene, pentachloro-
U185	82-68-8	Benzene, pentachloronitro-
U020	98-09-9	Benzenesulfonic acid chloride (C,R)
U020	98-09-9	Benzenesulfonyl chloride (C,R)
U207	95-94-3	Benzene, 1,2,4,5-tetrachloro-
U061	50-29-3	Benzene, 1,1'-(2,2,2-trichloroethylidene) bis[4-chloro-
U247	72-43-5	Benzene, 1,1'-(2,2,2-trichloroethylidene) bis[4-methoxy-
U023	98-07-7	Benzene, (trichloromethyl)-
U234	99-35-4	Benzene, 1,3,5-trinitro-

Hazardous waste No.	Chemical abstracts No.	Substance
U021	92-87-5	Benzidine
U202	[1] 81-07-2	1,2-Benzisothiazol-3(2H)-one, 1,1-dioxide,& salts
U203	94-59-7	1,3-Benzodioxole, 5-(2-ropenyl)-
U141	120-58-1	1,3-Benzodioxole, 5-(1 propenyl)-
U090	94-58-6	1,3-Benzodioxole, 5-propyl-
U064	189-55-9	Benzo[rst]pentaphene
U248	[1] 81-81-2	2H-1-Benzopyran-2-one, 4-hydroxy-3-(3-oxo-1-phenylbutyl)-, & salts, when present at concentrations of 0.3 % or less
U022	50-32-8	Benzo[a]pyrene
U197	106-51-4	p-Benzoquinone
U023	98-07-7	Benzotrichloride (C,R,T)
U085	1464-53-5	2,2'-Bioxirane
U021	92-87-5	1,1'-Biphenyl]-4,4'-diamine
U073	91-94-1	[1,1'-Biphenyl]-4,4'-diamine, 3,3'-dichloro-
U091	119-90-4	[1,1'-Biphenyl]-4,4'-diamine,3,3'-dimethoxy-
U095	119-93-7	[1,1'-Biphenyl]-4,4'-diamine, 3,3'-dimethyl-
U225	75-25-2	Bromoform
U030	101-55-3	4-Bromophenyl phenyl ether
U128	87-68-3	1,3-Butadiene, 1,1,2,3,4,4-hexachloro-
U172	924-16-3	1-Butanamine, N-butyl-N-nitroso-
U031	71-36-3	1-Butanol (I)
U159	78-93-3	2-Butanone (I,T)
U160	1338-23-4	2-Butanone, peroxide (R,T)
U053	4170-30-3	2-Butenal
U074	764-41-0	2-Butene, 1,4-dichloro- (I,T)
U143	303-34-4	2-Butenoic acid, 2-methyl-, 7-[[2,3-dihydroxy-2-(1-methoxyethyl)-3-methyl-1 oxobutoxy]methyl]-2,3,5,7a-tetrahydro-1 H-pyrrolizin-1-yl ester, [1S-[1 alpha(Z),7 (2S*,3R*),7aalpha]]-
U031	71-36-3	n-Butyl alcohol (I)
U136	75-60-5	Cacodylic acid
U032	13765-19-0	Calcium chromate
U238	51-79-6	Carbamic acid, ethyl ester
U178	615-53-2	Carbamic acid, methylnitroso-, ethyl ester
U097	79-44-7	Carbamic chloride, dimethyl-
U114	[1] 111-54-6	Carbamodithioic acid, 1,2-ethanediylbis-, salts & esters
U062	2303-16-4	Carbamothioic acid, bis(1-methylethyl)-, 2,3-dichloro-2-propenyl) ester
U215	6533-73-9	Carbonic acid, dithallium(1+) salt
U033	353-50-4	Carbonic difluoride
U156	79-22-1	Carbonochloridic acid, methyl ester (I,T)
U033	353-50-4	Carbon oxyfluoride (R,T)
U211	56-23-5	Carbon tetrachloride
U034	75-87-6	Chloral
U035	305-03-3	Chlorambucil
U036	57-74-9	Chlordane, alpha & gamma isomers
U026	494-03-1	Chlornaphazin
U037	108-90-7	Chlorobenzene
U038	510-15-6	Chlorobenzilate
U039	59-50-7	p-Chloro-m-cresol
U042	110-75-8	2-Chloroethyl vinyl ether
U044	67-66-3	Chloroform
U046	107-30-2	Chloromethyl methyl ether
U047	91-58-7	beta-Chloronaphthalene
U048	95-57-8	O-Chlorophenol
U049	3165-93-3	4-Chloro-o-toluidine, hydrochloride
U032	13765-19-0	Chromic acid H_2CrO_4, calcium salt
U050	218-01-9	Chrysene
U051	-------	Creosote
U052	1319-77-3	Cresol (Cresylic acid)
U053	4170-30-3	Crotonaldehyde
U055	98-82-8	Cumene (I)
U246	506-68-3	Cyanogen bromide (CN)Br
U197	106-51-4	2,5-Cyclohexadiene-1,4-dione
U056	110-82-7	Cyclohexane
U129	58-89-9	Cyclohexane, 1,2,3,4,5,6-hexachloro-,(1alpha,-2alpha,3beta,4alpha,-5alpha,-6beta)-
U057	108-94-1	Cyclohexanone (I)
U130	77-47-4	1,3-Cyclopentadiene, 1,2,3,4,5,5-hexachloro-
U058	50-18-0	Cyclophosphamide
U240	[1] 94-75-7	2,4-D, salts & esters
U059	20830-81-3	Daunomycin
U060	72-54-8	DDD
U061	50-29-3	DDT
U062	2303-16-4	Diallate
U063	53-70-3	Dibenz[a,h]anthracene
U064	89-55-9	Dibenzo[a,i]pyrene

Hazardous waste No.	Chemical abstracts No.	Substance
U066	96-12-8	1,2-Dibromo-3-chloropropane
U069	84-74-2	Dibutyl phthalate
U070	95-50-1	-Dichlorobenzene
U071	541-73-1	m-Dichlorobenzene
U072	106-46-7	p-Dichlorobenzene
U073	91-94-1	3,3'-Dichlorobenzidine
U074	764-41-0	1,4-Dichloro-2-butene (I,T)
U075	75-71-8	Dichlorodifluoromethane
U078	75-35-4	1,1-Dichloroethylene
U079	156-60-5	1,2-Dichloroethylene
U025	111-44-4	Dichloroethyl ether
U027	108-60-1	Dichloroisopropyl ether
U024	111-91-1	Dichloromethoxy ethane
U081	120-83-2	2,4-Dichlorophenol
U082	87-65-0	2,6-Dichlorophenol
U084	542-75-6	1,3-Dichloropropene
U085	1464-53-5	1,2:3,4-Diepoxybutane (I,T)
U108	123-91-1	1,4-Diethyleneoxide
U028	117-81-7	Diethylhexyl phthalate
U086	1615-80-1	N,N'-Diethylhydrazine
U087	3288-58-2	O,O-Diethyl S-methydithiophosphate
U088	84-66-2	Diethyl phthalate
U089	56-53-1	Diethylstilbesterol
U090	94-58-6	Dihydrosafrole
U091	119-90-4	3,3'-Dimethoxybenzidine
U092	124-40-3	Dimethylamine (I)
U093	60-11-7	p-Dimethylaminoazobenzene
U094	57-97-6	7,12-Dimethylbenz- [a]anthracene
U095	119-93-7	3,3'-Dimethylbenzidine
U096	80-15-9	alpha,alpha-Dimethylbenzylhydroperoxide (R)
U097	79-44-7	Dimethylcarbamoyl chloride
U098	57-14-7	1,1-Dimethylhydrazine
U099	540-73-8	1,2-Dimethylhydrazine
U101	105-67-9	2,4-Dimethylphenol
U102	131-11-3	Dimethyl phthalate
U103	77-78-1	Dimethyl sulfate
U105	121-14-2	2,4-Dinitrotoluene
U106	606-20-2	2,6-Dinitrotoluene
U107	117-84-0	Di-n-octyl phthalate
U108	123-91-1	1,4-Dioxane
U109	122-66-7	1,2-Diphenylhydrazine
U110	142-84-7	Dipropylamine (I)
U111	621-64-7	Di-n-propylnitrosamine
U041	106-89-8	Epichlorohydrin
U001	75-07-0	Ethanal (l)
U174	55-18-5	Ethanamine, N-ethyl-N-nitroso-
U155	91-80-5	1,2-Ethanediamine, N,N-dimethyl-N-2pyridinyl-N-(2-thienyimethyl)-
U067	106-93-4	Ethane, 1,2-dibromo-
U076	75-34-3	Ethane, 1,1-dichloro-
U077	107-06-2	Ethane, 1,2-dichloro-
U131	67-72-1	Ethane, hexachloro-
U024	111-91-1	Ethane, 1,1'-(methylenebisl(oxy) bis(2-chloro-
U117	60-29-7	Ethane, 1,1'-oxybis-(l)
U025	111-44-4	Ethane, 1,1'oxybis(2-chloro-
U184	76-01-7	Ehtane, pentachloro-
U208	630-20-6	Ehtane, 1,1,1,2-tetrachloro-
U209	79-34-5	Ethane, 1,1,2,2-tetrachloro-
U218	62-55-5	Ethanethioamide
U226	71-55-6	Ehtane, 1,1,1-trichloro-
U227	79-00-5	Ethane, 1,1,2-trichloro-
U359	110-80-5	Ethanol, e-ethoxy-
U173	1116-54-7	Ethanol, 2,2'-(nitrosoimino)bis-
U004	98-86-2	Ethanone, 1-phenyl-
U043	75-01-4	Ethene, chloro-
U042	110-75-8	Ethene, (2-chloroethoxy)-
U078	75-35-4	Ehtene, 1,1-dichloro-
U079	156-60-5	Ethene, 1,2-dichloro-, (E)-
U210	127-18-4	Ehtene, tetrachloro-
U228	79-01-6	Ehtene, trichloro-
U112	141-78-6	Ethyl acetate (l)
U113	140-88-5	Ehtyl acrylate (l)
U238	51-79-6	Ethyl carbamate (urethane)
U117	60-29-7	Ethyl ether (l)
U114	111-54-6	Ethylenebisdithiocarbamic acid, salts & esters
U067	106-93-4	Ethylene dibromide
U077	107-06-2	Ethylene dicloride
U0359	110-80-5	Ethylene glycol monoethyl ether
U115	75-21-8	Ethylene oxide (l, T)

Haz-ardous waste No.	Chemical abstracts No.	Substance
U116	96-45-7	Ethylenethiourea
U076	75-34-3	Ethylidene dichloride
U118	97-63-2	Ethyl methacrylate
U119	62-50-0	Ethyl methanesulfonate
U120	206-44-0	Fluornathene
U122	50-00-0	Formaldehyde
U123	64-18-6	Formic acid (C, T)
U124	110-00-9	Furan (I)
U125	98-01-1	2-Furancarboxaldehyde (I)
U147	108-31-6	2,5-Furandione
U213	109-99-9	Furan, tetrahydro-(I)
U125	98-01-1	Furfural (I)
U124	110-00-9	Furfuran (I)
U206	18883-66-4	Flucopyransoe, 2-deoxy-2(3-methyl-3-nitro-soureido)-,D-
U206	18883-66-4	D-Glucose, 2-deoxy-2{(methylnitrosoamino)-caronyl}amino}
U126	765-34-4	Glycidyladehyde
U163	70-25-7	Duanidine, N-methyl-N'-nitro-N-nitroso-
U127	118-74-1	Hexachorobenzene
U128	87-68-3	Hexachorocyclpentadiene
U130	77-47-4	Hexachlorocyclopentadiene
U131	67-72-1	Hexachoroethane
U132	70-30-4	Hexachorophene
U243	1888-71-7	Hexachloropropene
U133	302-01-2	Hydrazine (R, T)
U086	1615-80-1	Hydrazine, 1,2-diethyl-
U098	57-14-7	Hydrazine, 1,1-dimethyl-
U099	540-73-8	Hydrazine, 1,2-dimethyl-
U109	122-66-7	Hydrazine, 1,2-diphenyl-
U134	7664-39-3	Hydrofluoricc acid (D, T0
U134	7664-39-3	Hydrogen fluoride (C, T)
U135	7783-06-4	Hydrogen sulfide
U135	7783-06-4	Hydrogen sulfide H2S
U096	80-15-9	Hydroperoxide, 1-methyl-1-phenylethyl- (R)
U116	96-45-7	2-Imidazolidinethione
U137	193-39-5	Indeno{1,2,3-cd}pyrene
U190	85-44-9	1,3-isobenzofurandione
U140	78-83-1	Isobutyl alcohol (I,T)
U141	120-58-1	Isosafrole
U142	143-50-0	Kepone
U143	303-34-4	Lasiocarpine
U144	301-04-2	Lead acetate
U146	1335-32-6	Lead, bis(acetato-O)tetrahydroxytri-
U145	7446-27-7	Lead phosphate
U146	1335-32-6	Lead subacetate
U129	58-89-9	Lindane
U163	70-25-7	MNNG
U147	108-31-6	Maleic anydride
U148	123-33-1	Maleic hydrazide
U149	109-77-3	Mapnonitrile
U150	148-82-3	Melphalan
U151	7439-97-6	Mercury
U152	126-98-7	Methzcrylonitrile (I, T)
U092	124-40-3	Methanamine, N-methyl- (I)
U029	74-83-9	Methane, bromo-
U045	74-87-3	Methane, chloro- (I, T)
U046	107-30-2	Methane,chloromethoxy-
U068	74-95-3	Methane, dibromo-
U080	75-09-2	Methane, dichloro-
U075	75-71-8	Methane, dichlorodifluoro-

Hazardous waste No.	Chemical abstracts No.	Substance
U138	74-88-4	Methane, iodo-
U119	62-50-0	Methanesulfonic acid, ehtyl esteer
U211	26-23-5	Methane, tetrachloro-
U153	74-93-1	Methanethiol (I, T)
U225	75-25-2	Methane, tribromo-
U044	67-66-3	Methane, trichloro-
U121	75-69-4	Methane trichlorofluoro-
U036	57-74-9	4,7-Methano-1H-indene, 12,3,4,5,6,7,8,8-octcloro-2,3,3a,4,7,7a-hexahydro-
U154	67-56-1	Methanol (I)
U155	91-80-5	Methapyrilene
U142	143-50-0	1,3,4-Metheno-2H-cyclobuta{cd}pentalen-2-one, 1,1a,3,3a,4,5,5,5a,5b,6-decachlorooctahydro-
U247	72-43-5	Methoxychlor
U154	67-56-1	Methyl alcohol (I)
U029	74-83-9	Methyl bromide
U186	504-60-9	1-"Methylbutadiene (I)
U045	74-87-3	Methyl chloride (I, T)
U156	79-22-1	Methyl chlorocarbonate (I, T)
U226	71-55-6	Methyl chloroform
U157	56-49-5	3-Methylcholanthrene
U158	101-14-4	4,4'-Methylenebis(2-chloroaniline)
U068	74-95-3	Methylene bromide
U080	75-09-2	Methylene chloride
U159	78-93-3	Methyl ethyl ketone (MEK) (I, T)
U160	1338-23-4	Methyl iodide
U138	74-2884	Methyl isobutyl ketone (I)
U161	108-10-1	Methyl methacrylate (I, T)
U162	80-62-5	4-Methyl-2-pentanone (I)
U161	108-10-1	Methylthiouracil
U164	108-10-1	Mitomycin C
U010	50-07-7	5,12-Naphthacenedione, 8-acetyl-10-{(3-amino-2,3,6-trideoxy)-alpha-L-lyxo-hyxopyransoy 1)oxy}-78,8,9,10-tetrahydro-6,8,11,-trihydroxy-1-methoxy-, (8S-cis)-
U059	20830-81-3	1-Naphthalenamine
U167	134-32-7	2-Naphthalenamine
U168	91-59-8	Naphthalenamine, N,N'-bis(2-chloroethyl)-
U026	494-03-1	Naphthalene
U165	91-20-3	Naphthalene
U047	91-58-7	Naphthalene, 2-chloro-
U166	130-15-4	1,4-Naphthalenedione
U236	72-57-1	2,7-Naphthalenedisulfonic acid, 3,3'-{(3,3'-dimethyl{1,1'-biphenyl}-4,4'-diyl)bis(azo)bis{5-amino-4-hydroxy}-, tetrasodium salt
U166	130-15-4	1,4-Naphthoquinone
U167	134-32-7	alpha-Naphthylamine
U168	91-59-8	beta-Naphthylamine
U217	10102-45-1	Nitric acid, thalium(1+) salt
U169	98-95-3	Nitrobenxene (I, T)
U170	100-02-71	p-Nitrophenol
U171	79-46-9	2-Nitropropane (I, T)
U172	924-16-3	N-Nitrosodi-n-butylamine
U173	1116-54-7	N-Nitrosodiethanolamine
U174	55-18-5	N-Nitrosodiethylamine
U176	759-73-9	N-Nitroso-N-ethylurea
U177	684-93-5	N-Nitroso-N-methylurea
U178	615-53-2	N-Nitroso-N-methylurethane
U179	100-75-4	N-Nitrosopiperidene

Haz-ardous waste No.	Chemical abstracts No.	Substance
U180	930-55-2	N-Nitrosopyrrolidine
U181	99-55-8	5-Nitro-o-toluidine
U193	1120-71-4	1,2-Oxathiolane, 2,2-dioxide
U058	50-18-0	2H-1,3,2-Oxazaphosphorin-2-amine, N,N-bis(2-chloroethyl)tetrahydro-, 2-oxide
U115	75-21-8	Oxirane (I,T)
U126	765-34-4	Oxiranecarboxyaldehyde
U041	106-89-8	Oxirane, (chloromethyl)-
U182	123-63-7	Paraldehyde
U183	608-93-5	Pentachloroebenzene
U184	76-01-7	Pentachloronethane
U185	82-68-8	Pentachloronitrobenzene (PCNB)
See F027	87-86-5	Pentachlorophenol
U161	108-10-1	Pentanol, 4-methyl-
U186	504-60-9	1,3-Pentadiene (I)
U187	62-44-2	Phenacetin
U188	108-95-2	Phenol
U048	95-57-8	Phenol, 2-chloro-
U039	59-50-7	Phenol, 4-chloro-3-methyl-
U081	120-83-2	Phenol, 2,4-dichloro-
U082	87-65-0	Phenol, 2,6-dichloro-
U089	56-53-1	Phenol, 4,4'-(1,2-diethyl-1,2-ethenediyl)bis- (E)-
U101	105-67-9	Phenol, 2,4-dimethyl-
U052	1319-77-3	Phenol, methyl-
U132	70-30-4	Phenol, 2,2-methylenebis{3,4,6-trichloro-
U170	100-02-7	Phenol, ,4-nitro-
See F027	87-86-5	Phenol, pentachloro-
See F027	58-90-2	Phenol, 2,3,4,6-tetrachloro-
See F027	95-95-4	Phenol, 2,4,5-trichloro-
See F027	88-06-2	Phenol, 2,4,6-trichloro-
U150	148-82-3	L-Phenylalanine, 4-{bis(2-chloroethyl)amino}-
U145	7446-27-7	Phosphoric acid, lead(2+) salt(2:3)
U087	3288-58-2	Phosphorodithioic acid, O,O-diethyl S-methyl ester
U180	1314-80-3	Phosphorus sulfide (R)
U190	85-44-9	Phthalic anhydride
U191	109-06-8	2-Picoline
U179	100-75-4	Piperiddine, 1-nitroso-
U192	23950-58-5	Pronamide
U194	107-10-8	1-Propanamine (I, T)
U111	621-64-7	1-Propanamine, N-nitroso-N-propyl-
U110	142-84-7	1-Propanamine, N-propyl-(I)
U066	96-12-8	Propane, 1,2-dibromo-3-chloro-
U083	78-87-5	Propane, 1,2-dichloro-
U149	109-77-3	Propanedinitrile
U171	79-46-9	Propane, 2-ntiro- (I,T)
U027	108-60-1	Propane, 2,2-oxybis{2-chloro-
U193	1120-71-4	1,3-Porpane sultone
See F027	93-72-1	Propanoic acid, 2-(2,4,5-trichlorophenoxy)-
U235	126-72-7	1-Propanol, 2,3-dibromo-, phosphate (3:1)
U140	78-83-1	1-Propanol, 2-methyl- (O,T)
U002	67-64-1	2-Propanone (I)
U007	79-06-1	2-Propenamide
U084	542-75-6	1-Propene, 1,3-dichloro-
U243	1888-71-7	1-Propene, 1,1,2,3,3,3-hexachloro-
U009	107-13-1	2-Propenenitrile
U152	126-98-7	2-Propenenitrile, 2-methyl- (I,T)
U008	79-10-7	2-Propenoic acid (I)
U113	140-88-5	2-Propenoic acid, ethyl ester (I)

Hazardous waste No.	Chemical abstracts No.	Substance
U118	97-63-2	2-Propenoic acid, 2-methyl, ethyl ester
U162	80-62-6	2-Propenoic acid, 2-methyl, methyl ester (I,T)
U194	107-10-8	N-Propylamine (I,T)
U083	78-87-5	Propylene dichloride
U148	123-33-1	3,6-Pyridazinedione, 1,2-dihydro-
U196	110-86-1	Pyridine
U191	109-06-8	Pyridine, 2-methyl-
U237	66-75-1	2,4-(1H,/H)-Pyrimidinedione, 5-{bis(2-chloroethyl)amino}-
U164	56-04-2	4(1H)-Pyrimidinone, 2,3-dihdro-6-methyl-2-thioxo-
U180	930-55-2	Pyrrolidine, 1-nitroso-
U200	50-55-5	Reserpine
U201	108-46-3	Resorcinol
U202	87-07-2	Saccharin, & salts
U203	94-59-7	Safrole
U204	7783-00-8	Selnious acid
U204	7783-00-8	Selenium dioxide
U205	7488-56-4	Selenium sulfide
U205	7488-56-4	Selenium slulfide SeS$_2$ (R,T)
U015	115-02-6	L-Serine, diazoacetate (ester)
See F027	93-72-1	Silvex (2,4,5-TP)
U206	18883-66-4	Streptozotocin
U103	77-78-1	Sulfuric acid, dimethyl ester
U189	1314-80-3	Sulfur phosphide (R)
See F027	93-76-5	2,4,5-T
U207	95-94-3	1,2,4,5-Tetrachlorobenzene
U208	630-20-6	1,1,1,2-Tetrachloroethane
U209	79-34-5	1,1,2,2-Tetrachloroethane
U210	127-18-4	Tetrachloroethylene
See F027	58-90-2	2,3,4,6-Tetrachlorophenol
U213	109-99-9	Tetrahydrofuan (I)
U214	563-68-8	Thallium(I) acetate
U215	6533-73-9	Thallium(I) carbonate
U216	7791-12-0	Thallium(I) chloride
U216	7791-12-0	Thallium chloride TlcI
U217	10102-45-1	Thallium(I) nitrate
U218	62-55-5	Thioacetamide
U153	74-93-1	Thiomethanol (I,T)
U244	137-26-8	Thioperoxydicarbonic dimide {(HH$_2$N)C(S)}$_2$S$_2$, tetramethyl-
U219	62-56-6	Thiourea
U244	137-26-8	Thiram
U220	106-88-3	Toluene
U221	25376-45-8	Toluenediamine
U223	26471-62-5	Toluene disocyanate (R, T)
U328	95-53-4	o-Toluidine
U353	106-49-0	p-Toluidine
U222	636-21-5	o-Toluidine hydrochloride
U011	61-82-5	1H-1,2,4-Triaxzol-3-amine
U227	79-00-5	1,1,2-Trichloroethane
U228	79-01-6	Trichloroethylene
U121	75-69-4	Trichloromonofluoromethane
See F027	95-95-4	2,4,5-Trichlorophenol
See F027	88-06-2	2,4,6-Trichophenol
U234	99-35-4	1,3,5-Trinitrobenzene (R,T)
U182	123-63-7	1,3,5-Trioxane, 2,4,6-trimethyl-

Hazardous waste No.	Chemical abstracts No.	Substance
U235	126-72-7	Tris(2,3-dibromopropyl) phosphate
U236	72-57-1	Trypan blue
U237	66-75-1	Uracil mustard
U176	759-73-9	Urea, N-ethyl-N-nitroso-
U177	684-93-5	Urea, N-methyl-N-nitroso-
U043	75-01-4	Vinyl chloride
U248	[1]81-81-2	Warfarin, & salts, when present at concentrations of 0.3% or less
U239	1330-20-7	Xylene (I)
U200	50-55-5	Yohimban-16-carboxylic acid, 11, 17-dimethoxy-18-{(3,4,5-trimethoxybenzoyl)oxy},methyl ester,(3beta,16beta,17alpha, 18beta,20alpha)-
U249	1314-84-7	Zinc phosphide Zn_3P_2 when present concentrations of 10% or less

[1]CAS Number given for parent compound only.

(The reporting and recordkeeping requirements contained in this section were approved by OMB under control number 2050-0047.)

(The reporting and recordkeeping requirements contained in this section were approved by OMB under control number 2050-0047.)

§ 261.35 Deletion of Certain Hazardous Waste Codes Following Equipment Cleaning and Replacement.

(a) Wastes from wood preserving processes at plants that do not resume or initiate use of chlorophenolic preservatives will not meet the listing definition of F032 once the generator has met all of the requirements of paragraphs (b) and (c) of this section. These wastes may, however, continue to meet another hazardous waste listing description or may exhibit one or more of the hazardous waste characteristics.

(b) Generators must either clean or replace all process equipment that may have come into contact with chlorophenolic formulations or constituents thereof, including, but not limited to, treatment cylinders, sumps, tanks, piping systems, drip pads, fork lifts, and trams, in a manner that minimizes or eliminates the escape of hazardous waste or constituents, leachate, contaminated drippage, or hazardous waste decomposition products to the groundwater, surface water, or atmosphere.

(1) Generators shall do one of the following:

(i) Prepare and follow an equipment cleaning plan and clean equipment in accordance with this section;

(ii) Prepare and follow an equipment replacement plan and replace equipment in accordance with this section; or

(iii) Document cleaning and replacement in accordance with this section, carried out after termination of use of chlorophenolic preservations.

(2) Cleaning Requirements.

(i) Prepare and sign a written equipment cleaning plan that describes:

(A) The equipment to be cleaned;

(B) How the equipment will be cleaned;

(C) The solvent to be used in cleaning;

(D) How solvent rinses will be tested; and

(E) How cleaning residues will be disposed.

(ii) Equipment must be cleaned as follows:

(A) Remove all visible residues from process equipment;

(B) Rinse process equipment with an appropriate solvent until dioxins and dibenzofurans are not detected in the final solvent rinse.

(iii) Analytical requirements.

(A) Rinses must be tested in accordance with SW-846, Method 8290.

(B) "Not detected" means at or below the lower method calibration limit (MCL) in Method 8290, Table 1.

(iv) The generator must manage all residues from the cleaning process as F032 waste.

(3) Replacement requirements.

(i) Prepare and sign a written equipment replacement plan that describes:

(A) The equipment to be replaced;

(B) How the equipment will be replaced; and

(C) How the equipment will be disposed.

(ii) The generator must manage the discarded equipment as F032 waste.

(4) Documentation requirements.

(i) Document that previous equipment cleaning and/or replacement was performed in accordance with this section and occurred after cessation of use of chlorophenolic preservatives.

(c) The generator must maintain the following records documenting the cleaning and replacement as part of the facility's operating record:

(1) The name and address of the facility;

(2) Formulations previously used and the date on which their use ceased in each process at the plant;

(3) Formulations currently used in each process at the plant;

(4) The equipment cleaning or replacement plan;

(5) The name and address of any persons who conducted the cleaning and replacement;

(6) The dates on which cleaning and replacement were accomplished;

(7) The dates of sampling and testing;

(8) A description of the sample handling and preparation techniques, including techniques used for extraction, containerization, preservation, and chain-of-custody of the samples;

(9) A description of the tests performed, the date the tests were performed, and the results of the tests;

(10) The name and model numbers of the instrument(s) used in performing the tests;

(11) QA/QC documentation; and

(12) The following statement signed by the generator or his authorized representatives:

I certify under penalty of law that all process equipment required to be cleaned or replaced under 40 CFR 261.35 was cleaned or replaced as represented in the equipment cleaning and replacement plan and accompanying documentation. I am aware that there are significant penalties for providing false information, including the possibility of fine or imprisonment.

ENVIRONMENTAL PROTECTION AGENCY REGULATIONS FOR HAZARDOUS WASTE GENERATORS

40 CFR 262

Subpart A -- General

§ 262.10 Purpose, scope, and applicability.

(a)   These regulations establish standards for generators of hazardous waste.

(b)   A generator who treats, stores, or disposes of hazardous waste on-site must only comply with the following sections of this part with respect to that waste: Section 262.11 for determining whether or not he has a hazardous waste, §262.12 for obtaining an EPA identification number, §262.34 for accumulation of hazardous waste, §262.40 (c) and (d) for recordkeeping, §262.43 for additional reporting, and if applicable, §262.70 for farmers.

(c)   Any person who imports hazardous waste into the United States must comply with the standards applicable to generators established in this part.

(d)   A farmer who generates waste pesticides which are hazardous waste and who complies with all of the requirements of §262.70 is not required to comply with other standards in this part or 40 CFR Parts 270, 264, 265, or 268 with respect to such pesticides.

(e)   A person who generates a hazardous waste as defined by 40 CFR Part 261 is subject to the compliance requirements and penalties prescribed in section 3008 of the Act if he does not comply with the requirements of this part.

(f)   An owner or operator who initiates a shipment of hazardous waste from a treatment, storage, or disposal facility must comply with the generator standards established in this part.

262.11 Hazardous waste determination.

A person who generates a solid waste, as defined in 40 CFR 261.2, must determine if that waste is a hazardous waste using the following method:

(a)   He should first determine if the waste is excluded from regulation under 40 CFR 261.4.

(b)   He must then determine if the waste is listed as a hazardous waste in Subpart D of 40 CFR Part 261.

(c)   For purposes of compliance with 40 CFR part 268, or if the waste is not listed in subpart D of 40 CFR part 261, the generator must then determine whether the waste is identified in subpart C of 40 CFR part 261 by either:

(1)   Testing the waste according to the methods set forth in Subpart C of 40 CFR Part 261, or according to an equivalent method approved by the Administrator under 40 CFR 260.21; or

(2)   Applying knowledge of the hazard characteristic of the waste in light of the materials or the processes used.

(d)   If the waste is determined to be hazardous, the generator must refer to Parts 264, 265, 268 of this chapter for possible exclusions or restrictions pertaining to management of his specific waste.

§ 262.12 EPA identification numbers.

(a)   A generator must not treat, store, dispose of, transport, or offer for transportation, hazardous waste without having received an EPA identification number from the Administrator.

(b)   A generator who has not received an EPA identification number may obtain one by applying to the Administrator using EPA form 8700-12. Upon receiving the request the Administrator will assign an EPA identification number to the generator.

(c)   A generator must not offer his hazardous waste to transporters or to treatment, storage, or disposal facilities that have not received an EPA identification number.

Subpart B -- The Manifest

§ 262.20 General requirements.

(a)   A generator who transports, or offers for transportation, hazardous waste for offsite treatment, storage, or disposal must prepare a Manifest OMB control number 2050-0039 on EPA form 8700-22, and, if necessary, EPA form 8700-22A, according to the instructions included in the Appendix to Part 262.

(b)   A generator must designate on the manifest one facility which is permitted to handle the waste directed on the manifest.

(c) A generator may also designate on the manifest one alternate facility which is permitted to handle his waste in the event an emergency prevents delivery of the waste to the primary designated facility.

(d) If the transporter is unable to deliver the hazardous waste to the designated facility or the alternate facility, the generator must either designate another facility or instruct the transporter to return the waste.

(e) The requirements of this subpart do not apply to hazardous waste produced by generators of greater than 100 kg but less than 1000 kg in a calendar month where:

(1) The waste is reclaimed under a contractual agreement pursuant to which:

(i) The type of waste and frequency of shipments are specified in the agreement;

(ii) The vehicle used to transport the waste to the recycling facility and to deliver regenerated material back to the generator is owned and operated by the reclaimer of the waste; and

(2) The generator maintains a copy of the reclamation agreement in his files for a period of at least three years after termination or expiration of the agreement.

§ 262.21 Acquisition of manifests.

(a) If the State to which the shipment is manifested (consignment State) supplies the manifest and requires its use, then the generator must use that manifest.

(b) If the consignment State does not supply the manifest, but the State in which the generator is located (generator State) supplies the manifest and requires its use, then the generator must use that State's manifest.

(c) If neither the generator State nor the consignment State supplies the manifest, then the generator may obtain the manifest from any source.

§ 262.22 Number of copies.

The manifest consists of at least the number of copies which will provide the generator, each transporter, and the owner or operator of the designated facility with one copy each for their records and another copy to be returned to the generator.

§ 262.23 Use of the manifest.

(a) The generator must:

(1) Sign the manifest certification by hand; and

(2) Obtain the handwritten signature of the initial transporter and date of acceptance on the manifest; and

(3) Retain one copy, in accordance with §262.40(a).

(b) The generator must give the transporter the remaining copies of the manifest.

(c) For shipments of hazardous waste within the United States solely by water (bulk shipments only), the generator must send three copies of the manifest dated and signed in accordance with this section to the owner or operator of the designated facility or the last water (bulk shipment) transporter to handle the waste in the United States if exported by water. Copies of the manifest are not required for each transporter.

(d) For rail shipments of hazardous waste within the United States which originate at the site of generation, the generator must send at least three copies of the manifest dated and signed in accordance with this section to:

(1) The next non-rail transporter, if any; or

(2) The designated facility if transported solely by rail; or

(3) The last rail transporter to handle the waste in the United States if exported by rail.

(e) For shipments of hazardous waste to a designated facility in an authorized State which has not yet obtained authorization to regulate that particular waste as hazardous, the generator must assure that the designated facility agrees to sign and return the manifest to the generator, and that any out-of-state transporter signs and forwards the manifest to the designated facility.

Subpart C -- Pre-Transport Requirements

§ 262.30 Packaging.

Before transporting hazardous waste or offering hazardous waste for transportation off-site, a generator must package the waste in accordance with the applicable Department of Transportation regulations on packaging under 49 CFR Parts 173, 178, and 179.

§ 262.31 Labeling.

Before transporting or offering hazardous waste for transportation off-site, a generator must label each package in accordance with the appli-

cable Department of Transportation regulations on hazardous materials under 49 CFR Part 172.

§ 262.32 Marking.

(a) Before transporting or offering hazardous waste for transportation off-site, a generator must mark each package of hazardous waste in accordance with the applicable Department of Transportation regulations on hazardous materials under 49 CFR Part 172;

(b) Before transporting hazardous waste or offering hazardous waste for transportation off-site, a generator must mark each container of 110 gallons or less used in such transportation with the following words and information displayed in accordance with the requirements of 49 CFR 172.304:

HAZARDOUS WASTE--Federal Law Prohibits Improper Disposal. If found, contact the nearest police or public safety authority or the U.S. Environmental Protection Agency. Generator's Name and Address-------------. Manifest Document Number--------------.

§ 262.33 Placarding.

Before transporting hazardous waste or offering hazardous waste for transportation off-site, a generator must placard or offer the initial transporter the appropriate placards according to Department of Transportation regulations for hazardous materials under 49 CFR Part 172, Subpart F.

§ 262.34 Accumulation time.

(a) Except as provided in paragraphs (d), (e), and (f) of this section, a generator may accumulate hazardous waste on-site for 90 days or less without a permit or without having interim status, provided that:

(1) The waste is placed:

(i) in containers and the generator complies with subpart I of 40 CFR part 265; and/or

(ii) In tanks and the generator complies with subpart J of 40 CFR Part 265., except §§265.197(c) and 265.200; and/or

(iii) On drip pads and the generator complies with subpart W of 40 CFR part 265 and maintains the following records at the facility;

(A) A description of procedures that will be followed to ensure that all wastes are removed from the drip pad and associated collection system at least once every 90 days; and

(B) Documentation of each waste removal, including the quantity of waste removed from the drip pad and the sump or collection system and the date and time of removal.

In addition, such a generator is exempt from all requirements in subparts G and H of 40 CFR part 265, except for §§265.111 and 265.114.

(2) The date upon which each period of accumulation begins is clearly marked and visible for inspection on each container;

(3) While being accumulated on-site, each container and tank is labeled or marked clearly with the words, "Hazardous Waste"; and

(4) The generator complies with the requirements for owners or operators in Subparts C and D in 40 CFR Part 265, with 265.16, and with 40 CFR 268.7(a)(4).

(b) A generator who accumulates hazardous waste for more than 90 days is an operator of a storage facility and is subject to the requirements of 40 CFR Parts 264 and 265 and the permit requirements of 40 CFR Part 270 unless he has been granted an extension to the 90-day period. Such extension may be granted by EPA if hazardous wastes must remain on-site for longer than 90 days due to unforeseen, temporary, and uncontrollable circumstances. An extension of up to 30 days may be granted at the discretion of the Regional Administrator on a case-by-case basis.

(c)(1) A generator may accumulate as much as 55 gallons of hazardous waste or one quart of acutely hazardous waste listed in §261.33(e) in containers at or near any point of generation where wastes initially accumulate, which is under the control of the operator of the process generating the waste, without a permit or interim status and without complying with paragraph (a) of this section provided he:

(i) Complies with §§265.171, 265.172, and 265.173(a) of this chapter; and

(ii) Marks his containers either with the words "Hazardous Waste" or with other words that identify the contents of the containers.

(2) A generator who accumulates either hazardous waste or acutely hazardous waste listed in §261.33(e) in excess of the amounts listed in paragraph (c)(1) of this section at or near any point of generation must, with respect to that amount of excess waste, comply within

three days with paragraph (a) of this section or other applicable provisions of this chapter. During the three day period the generator must continue to comply with paragraphs (c)(1)(i) through (ii) of this section. The generator must mark the container holding the excess accumulation of hazardous waste with the date the excess amount began accumulating.

(d) A generator who generates greater than 100 kilograms but less than 1000 kilograms of hazardous waste in a calendar month may accumulate hazardous waste on-site for 180 days or less without a permit or without having interim status provided that:

(1) The quantity of waste accumulated on-site never exceeds 6000 kilograms;

(2) The generator complies with the requirements of Subpart I of Part 265, except §265.176;

(3) The generator complies with the requirements of §265.201 in Subpart J of Part 265;

(4) The generator complies with the requirements of paragraphs (a)(2) and (a)(3) of this section, the requirements of subpart C of Part 265, the requirements of 40 CFR 268.7(a)(4);

(5) The generator complies with the following requirements:

(i) At all times there must be at least one employee either on the premises or on call (i.e., available to respond to an emergency by reaching the facility within a short period of time) with the responsibility for coordinating all emergency response measures specified in paragraph (d)(5)(iv) of this section. This employee is the emergency coordinator.

(ii) The generator must post the following information next to the telephone:

(A) The name and telephone number of the emergency coordinator;

(B) Location of fire extinguishers and spill control material, and, if present, fire alarm; and

(C) The telephone number of the fire department, unless the facility has a direct alarm.

(iii) The generator must ensure that all employees are thoroughly familiar with proper waste handling and emergency procedures, relevant to their responsibilities during normal facility operations and emergencies:

(iv) The emergency coordinator or his designee must respond to any emergencies that arise. The applicable responses are as follows:

(A) In the event of a fire, call the fire department or attempt to extinguish it using a fire extinguisher;

(B) In the event of a spill, contain the flow of hazardous waste to the extent possible, and as soon as is practicable, clean up the hazardous waste and any contaminated materials or soil;

(C) In the event of a fire, explosion, or other release which could threaten human health outside the facility or when the generator has knowledge that a spill has reached surface water, the generator must immediately notify the National Response Center (using their 24-hour toll free number 800/424-8802). The report must include the following information:

(1) The name, address, and U.S. EPA Identification Number of the generator;

(2) Date, time, and type of incident (e.g., spill or fire);

(3) Quantity and type of hazardous waste involved in the incident;

(4) Extent of injuries, if any; and

(5) Estimated quantity and disposition of recovered materials, if any.

(e) A generator who generates greater than 100 kilograms but less than 1000 kilograms of hazardous waste in a calendar month and who must transport his waste, or offer his waste for transportation, over a distance of 200 miles or more for off-site treatment, storage or disposal may accumulate hazardous waste on-site for 270 days or less without a permit or without having interim status provided that he complies with the requirements of paragraph (d) of this section.

(f) A generator who generates greater than 100 kilograms but less than 1000 kilograms of hazardous waste in a calendar month and who accumulates hazardous waste in quantities exceeding 6000 kg or accumulates hazardous waste for more than 180 days (or for more than 270 days if he must transport his waste, or offer his waste for transportation, over a distance of 200 miles or more) is an operator of a storage facility and is subject to the requirements of 40 CFR Parts 264 and 265 and the permit requirements of 40 CFR Part 270 unless he has been granted an extension to the 180-day (or 270-day if applicable) period. Such extension may be granted by EPA if hazardous wastes must remain on-site for longer than 180 days (or 270 days if applicable) due to unforeseen, temporary, and uncontrollable circumstances. An extension of up to 30 days may be granted at the discretion of the Regional Administrator on a case-by-case basis.

Subpart D -- Recordkeeping and Reporting

§ 262.40 Recordkeeping.

(a) A generator must keep a copy of each manifest signed in accordance with §262.23(a) for three years or until he receives a signed copy from the designated facility which received the waste. This signed copy must be retained as a record for at least three years from the date the waste was accepted by the initial transporter.

(b) A generator must keep a copy of each Biennial Report and Exception Report for a period of at least three years from the due date of the report.

(c) A generator must keep records of any test results, waste analyses, or other determinations made in accordance with §262.11 for at least three years from the date that the waste was last sent to on-site or off-site treatment, storage, or disposal.

(d) The periods or retention referred to in this section are extended automatically during the course of any unresolved enforcement action regarding the regulated activity or as requested by the Administrator.

§ 262.41 Biennial Report.

(a) A generator who ships any hazardous waste off-site to a treatment, storage or disposal facility within the United States must prepare and submit a single copy of a Biennial Report to the Regional Administrator by March 1 of each even numbered year. The Biennial Report must be submitted on EPA Form 8700-13A, must cover generator activities during the previous year, and must include the following information:

(1) The EPA identification number, name, and address of the generator;

(2) The calendar year covered;

(3) The EPA identification number, name, and address for each off-site treatment, storage, or disposal facility in the United States to which waste was shipped during the year;

(4) The name and EPA identification no. of each transporter used during the reporting year for shipments to a treatment, storage or disposal facility within the United States;

(5) A description, EPA hazardous waste number (from 40 CFR Part 261 (Subpart C or D), DOT hazard class, and quantity of each hazardous waste shipped off-site for shipments to a treatment, storage or disposal facility within the United States. This information must be listed by EPA identification number of each such off-site facility to which waste was shipped.

(6) A description of the efforts undertaken during the year to reduce the volume and toxicity of waste generated.

(7) A description of the changes in volume and toxicity of waste actually achieved during the year in comparison to previous years to the extent such information is available for years prior to 1984.

(8) The certification signed by the generator or authorized representative.

(b) Any generator who treats, stores, or disposes of hazardous waste on-site must submit a biennial report covering those wastes in accordance with the provisions of 40 CFR Parts 270, 264, 265, and 266. Reporting for exports of hazardous waste is not required on the Biennial Report form. A separate annual report requirement is set forth at 40 CFR 262.56.

§ 262.42 Exception reporting.

(a)(1) A generator of greater than 1000 kilograms of hazardous waste in a calendar month who does not receive a copy of the manifest with the handwritten signature of the owner or operator of the designated facility within 35 days of the date the waste was accepted by the initial transporter must contact the transporter and/or the owner or operator of the designated facility to determine the status of the hazardous waste.

(2) A generator of greater than 1000 kilograms of hazardous waste in a calendar month must submit an Exception Report to the EPA Regional Administrator for the Region in which the generator is located if he has not received a copy of the manifest with the hand-

written signature of the owner or operator of the designated facility within 45 days of the date the waste was accepted by the initial transporter.

The Exception Report must include:

(i) A legible copy of the manifest for which the generator does not have confirmation of delivery;

(ii) A cover letter signed by the generator or his authorized representative explaining the efforts taken to locate the hazardous waste and the results of those efforts.

(b) A generator of greater than 100 kilograms but less than 1000 kilograms of hazardous waste in a calendar month who does not receive a copy of the manifest with the handwritten signature of the owner or operator of the designated facility within 60 days of the date the waste was accepted by the initial transporter must submit a legible copy of the manifest, with some indication that the generator has not received confirmation of delivery, to the EPA Regional Administrator for the Region in which the generator is located.

§ 262.43 Additional reporting .

The Administrator, as he deems necessary under sections 2002(a) and 3002(6) of the Act, may require generators to furnish additional reports concerning the quantities and disposition of wastes identified or listed in 40 CFR Part 261.

§ 262.44 Special requirements for generators of between 100 and 1000 kg/mo.

A generator of greater than 100 kilograms but less than 1000 kilograms of hazardous waste in a calendar month is subject only to the following requirements in this subpart:

(a) Section 262.40(a), (c), and (d), recordkeeping;

(b) Section 262.42(b), exception reporting; and

(c) Section 262.43, additional reporting.

(Information collection requirements approved by the Office of Management and Budget under control number 2050-0039)

Subpart E -- Exports of Hazardous Waste

§ 262.50 Applicability.

This subpart establishes requirements applicable to exports of hazardous waste. Except to the extent §262.58 provides otherwise, a primary exporter of hazardous waste must comply with the special requirements of this subpart and a transporter transporting hazardous waste for export must comply with applicable requirements of Part 263. Section 262.58 sets forth the requirements of international agreements between the United States and receiving countries which establish different notice, export, and enforcement procedures for the transportation, treatment, storage and disposal of hazardous waste for shipments between the United States and those countries.

§ 262.51 Definitions

In addition to the definitions set forth at 40 CFR 260.10, the following definitions apply to this subpart:

"Consignee" means the ultimate treatment, storage or disposal facility in a receiving country to which the hazardous waste will be sent.

"EPA Acknowledgement of Consent" means the cable sent to EPA from the U.S. Embassy in a receiving country that acknowledges the written consent of the receiving country to accept the hazardous waste and describes the terms and conditions of the receiving country's consent to the shipment.

"Primary Exporter" means any person who is required to originate the manifest for a shipment of hazardous waste in accordance with 40 CFR Part 262, Subpart B, or equivalent State provision, which specifies a treatment, storage, or disposal facility in a receiving country as the facility to which the hazardous waste will be sent and any intermediary arranging for the export.

"Receiving country" means a foreign country to which a hazardous waste is sent for the purpose of treatment, storage or disposal (except short-term storage incidental to transportation).

"Transit country" means any foreign country, other than a receiving country, through which a hazardous waste is transported.

§ 262.52 General requirements.

Exports of hazardous waste are prohibited except in compliance with the applicable requirements of this Subpart and Part 263. Exports of hazardous waste are prohibited unless:

(a) Notification in accordance with §262.53 has been provided;

(b) The receiving country has consented to accept the hazardous waste;

(c) A copy of the EPA Acknowledgment of Consent to the shipment accompanies the hazardous waste shipment and, unless exported by rail, is attached to the manifest (or shipping paper for exports by water (bulk shipment)).

(d) The hazardous waste shipment conforms to the terms of the receiving country's written consent as reflected in the EPA Acknowledgment of Consent.

(Approved by the Office of Management and Budget under control number 2050-0035)

§ 262.53 Notification of intent to export.

(a) A primary exporter of hazardous waste must notify EPA of an intended export before such waste is scheduled to leave the United States. A complete notification should be submitted sixty (60) days before the initial shipment is intended to be shipped off site. This notification may cover export activities extending over a twelve (12) month or lesser period. The notification must be in writing, signed by the primary exporter, and include the following information:

(1) Name, mailing address, telephone number and EPA ID number of the primary exporter;

(2) By consignee, for each hazardous waste type:

(i) A description of the hazardous waste and the EPA hazardous waste number (from 40 CFR Part 261, Subparts C and D), U.S. DOT proper shipping name, hazard class and ID number (UN/NA) for each hazardous waste as identified in 49 CFR Parts 171 through 177;

(ii) The estimated frequency or rate at which such waste is to be exported and the period of time over which such waste is to be exported.

(iii) The estimated total quantity of the hazardous waste in units as specified in the instructions to the Uniform Hazardous Waste Manifest Form (8700-22);

(iv) All points of entry to and departure from each foreign country through which the hazardous waste will pass;

(v) A description of the means by which each shipment of the hazardous waste will be transported (e.g., mode of transportation vehicle (air, highway, rail, water, etc.), type(s) of container (drums, boxes, tanks, etc.));

(vi) A description of the manner in which the hazardous waste will be treated, stored or disposed of in the receiving country (e.g., land or ocean incineration, other land disposal, ocean dumping, recycling);

(vii) The name and site address of the consignee and any alternate consignee; and

(viii) The name of any transit countries through which the hazardous waste will be sent and a description of the approximate length of time the hazardous waste will remain in such country and the nature of its handling while there;

(b) Notification shall be sent to the Office of Waste Programs Enforcement, RCRA Enforcement Division (OS-520), Environmental Protection Agency, 401 M Street SW, Washington, DC 20460 with "Attention: Notification to Export" prominently displayed on the front of the envelope.

(c) Except for changes to the telephone number in paragraph (a)(1) of this section, changes to paragraph (a)(2)(v) of this section and decreases in the quantity indicated pursuant to paragraph (a)(2)(iii) of this section when the conditions specified on the original notification change (including any exceedance of the estimate of the quantity of hazardous waste specified in the original notification), the primary exporter must provide EPA with a written renotification of the change. The shipment cannot take place until consent of the receiving country to the changes (except for changes to paragraph (a)(2)(viii) of this section and in the ports of entry to and departure from transit countries pursuant to paragraph (a)(2)(iv) of this section) has been obtained and the primary exporter receives an EPA Acknowledgment of Consent reflecting the receiving country's consent to the changes.

(d) Upon request by EPA, a primary exporter shall furnish to EPA any additional information which a receiving country requests in order to respond to a notification.

(e) In conjunction with the Department of State, EPA will provide a complete notification to the receiving country and any transit countries. A notification is complete when EPA receives a notification which EPA determines satisfies the requirements of paragraph (a) of this section. Where a claim of confidentiality is asserted with respect to any notification information required by paragraph (a) of this section, EPA may find the notification not complete until any such claim is resolved in accordance with 40 CFR 260.2.

(f) Where the receiving country consents to the receipt of the hazardous waste, EPA will forward an EPA Acknowledgment of Consent to the primary exporter for purposes of §262.54(h). Where the receiving country objects to receipt of the hazardous waste or withdraws a prior consent, EPA will notify the primary exporter in writing. EPA will also notify the primary exporter of any responses from transit countries.

(Approved by the Office of Management and Budget under control number 2050-0035)

§ 262.54 Special manifest requirements.

A primary exporter must comply with the manifest requirements of 40 CFR 262.20 through 262.23 except that:

(a) In lieu of the name, site address and EPA ID number of the designated permitted facility, the primary exporter must enter the name and site address of the consignee;

(b) In lieu of the name, site address and EPA ID number of a permitted alternate facility, the primary exporter may enter the name and site address of any alternate consignee.

(c) In Special Handling Instructions and Additional Information, the primary exporter must identify the point of departure from the United States;

(d) The following statement must be added to the end of the first sentence of the certification set forth in Item 16 of the Uniform Hazardous Waste Manifest Form: "and conforms to the terms of the attached EPA Acknowledgment of Consent";

(e) In lieu of the requirements of §262.21, the primary exporter must obtain the manifest form from the primary exporter's State if that State supplies the manifest form and requires its use. If the primary exporter's State does not supply the manifest form, the primary exporter may obtain a manifest form from any source.

(f) The primary exporter must require the consignee to confirm in writing the delivery of the hazardous waste to that facility and to describe any significant discrepancies (as defined in 40 CFR 264.72(a)) between the manifest and the shipment. A copy of the manifest signed by such facility may be used to confirm delivery of the hazardous waste.

(g) In lieu of the requirements of §262.20(d), where a shipment cannot be delivered for any reason to the designated or alternate consignee, the primary exporter must:

(1) Renotify EPA of a change in the conditions of the original notification to allow shipment to a new consignee in accordance with §262.53(c) and obtain an EPA Acknowledgment of Consent prior to delivery; or

(2) Instruct the transporter to return the waste to the primary exporter in the United States or designate another facility within the United States; and

(3) Instruct the transporter to revise the manifest in accordance with the primary exporter's instructions.

(h) The primary exporter must attach a copy of the EPA Acknowledgment of Consent to the shipment to the manifest which must accompany the hazardous waste shipment. For exports by rail or water (bulk shipment), the primary exporter must provide the transporter with an EPA Acknowledgment of Consent which must accompany the hazardous waste but which need not be attached to the manifest except that for exports by water (bulk shipment) the primary exporter must attach the copy of the EPA Acknowledgment of Consent to the shipping paper

(i) The primary exporter shall provide the transporter with an additional copy of the manifest for delivery to the U.S. Customs official at the point the hazardous waste leaves the United States in accordance with §263.20(g)(4).

(Approved by the Office of Management and Budget under control number 2050-0035)

§ 262.55 Exception reports.

In lieu of the requirements of §262.42, a primary exporter must file an exception report with the Administrator if:

(a) He has not received a copy of the manifest signed by the transporter stating the date and place of departure from the United States within forty-five (45) days from the date it was accepted by the initial transporter;

(b) Within ninety (90) days from the date the waste was accepted by the initial transporter, the primary exporter has not received written confirmation from the consignee that the hazardous waste was received;

(c) The waste is returned to the United States.

(Approved by the Office of Management and Budget and assigned under control number 2050-0035)

§ 262.56 Annual reports.

(a) Primary exporters of hazardous waste shall file with the Administrator no later than March 1 of each year, a report summarizing the types, quantities, frequency, and ultimate destination of all hazardous waste exported during the previous calendar year. Such reports shall include the following:

(1) The EPA identification number, name, and mailing and site address of the exporter;

(2) The calendar year covered by the report;

(3) The name and site address of each consignee;

(4) By consignee, for each hazardous waste exported, a description of the hazardous waste, the EPA hazardous waste number (from 40 CFR Part 261, Subpart C or D), DOT hazard class, the name and US EPA ID number (where applicable) for each transporter used, the total amount of waste shipped and number of shipments pursuant to each notification;

(5) Except for hazardous waste produced by exporters of greater than 100 kg but less than 1000 kg in a calendar month, unless provided pursuant to §262.41, in even numbered years:

(i) A description of the efforts undertaken during the year to reduce the volume and toxicity of waste generated; and

(ii) A description of the changes in volume and toxicity of waste actually achieved during the year in comparison to previous years to the extent such information is available for years prior to 1984.

(6) A certification signed by the primary exporter which states:

I certify under penalty of law that I have personally examined and am familiar with the information submitted in this and all attached documents, and that based on my inquiry of those individuals immediately responsible for obtaining the information, I believe that the submitted information is true, accurate, and complete. I am aware that there are significant penalties for submitting false information including the possibility of fine and imprisonment.

(b) Reports shall be sent to the following address: Office of Waste Programs Enforcement, RCRA Enforcement Division (OS-520), Environmental Protection Agency, 401 M Street SW, Washington, DC 20460.

* (Approved by the Office of Management and Budget under control number 2050-0035)

§ 262.57 Recordkeeping.

(a) For all exports a primary exporter must:

(1) Keep a copy of each notification of intent to export for a period of at least three years from the date the hazardous waste was accepted by the initial transporter;

(2) Keep a copy of each EPA Acknowledgment of Consent for a period of at least three years from the date the hazardous waste was accepted by the initial transporter;

(3) Keep a copy of each confirmation of delivery of the hazardous waste from the consignee for at least three years from the date the hazardous waste was accepted by the initial transporter; and

(4) Keep a copy of each annual report for a period of at least three years from the due date of the report.

(b) The periods of retention referred to in this section are extended automatically during the course of any unresolved enforcement action regarding the regulated activity or as requested by the Administrator.

(Approved by the Office of Management and Budget under control number 2050-0035)

§ 262.58 International agreements.
[(Reserved)]

Subpart F -- Imports of Hazardous Waste

§ 262.60 Imports of hazardous waste.

(a) Any person who imports hazardous waste from a foreign country into the United States must comply with the requirements of this part and the special requirements of this subpart.

(b) When importing hazardous waste, a person must meet all the requirements of §262.20(a) for the manifest except that:

(1) In place of the generator's name, address and EPA identification number, the name and address of the foreign generator and the importer's name, address and EPA identification number must be used.

(2) In place of the generator's signature on the certification statement, the U.S. importer or his agent must sign and date the certification and obtain the signature of the initial transporter.

(c) A person who imports hazardous waste must obtain the manifest form from the consignment State if the State supplies the manifest and requires its use. If the consignment State does not supply the manifest form, then the manifest form may be obtained from any source.

Subpart G -- Farmers

§ 262.70 Farmers.

A farmer disposing of waste pesticides from his own use which are hazardous wastes is not required to comply with the standards in this part or other standards in 40 CFR Parts 264, 265, 268, or 270 for those wastes provided he triple rinses each emptied pesticide container in accordance with §261.7(b)(3) and disposes of the pesticide residues on his own farm in a manner consistent with the disposal instructions on the pesticide label.

APPENDIX - FORM - ANNUAL REPORT (EPA FORM 8700-13)

Generator Annual Report, Part A Instructions (EPA Form 8700-13A)
Generator Annual Report for generators who ship their hazardous waste off-site to facilities which they do not own or operate.
Important: READ ALL INSTRUCTIONS BEFORE COMPLETING THIS REPORT

Enter your EPA identification number.

Example:

| X. GENERATOR'S EPA I.D. NO. |
| G N J D 7 8 4 6 2 1 3 8 | I/A C 1 |

Section XI. Facility's Identification Number

Enter the EPA identification number of the facility to which you sent the waste described below in Section XIV (a separate sheet must be used for each facility to which you sent hazardous waste.)

Section XII. Facility Name

Enter the name of the facility corresponding to the facility's EPA identification number in Section XI.

Please print or type with ELITE type (12 characters/inch).

GSA No. 12345-XX
Form Approved by OMB No. 158-R00XX

EPA U.S. ENVIRONMENTAL PROTECTION AGENCY
GENERATOR ANNUAL REPORT — PART A
(Collected under the authority of Section 3002 of RCRA.)

| FOR OFFICIAL USE ONLY (Items 1 and 2) | 1. DATE RECEIVED | — | — 1 9 | X. GENERATOR'S EPA I.D. NO. |
| | 2. TYPE OF REPORT | | G | I/A C |

XI. FACILITY'S EPA I.D. NO.

XIII. FACILITY ADDRESS *(street or P.O box, city, state & zip code)*

XII. FACILITY NAME (specify)

XIV. WASTE IDENTIFICATION

LINE NUMBER	A. DESCRIPTION OF WASTE	B. DOT HAZARD CLASS	C. EPA HAZARDOUS WASTE NUMBER *(see instructions)*	D. AMOUNT OF WASTE	E. UNIT OF MEASURE *(enter code)*
1					
2					
3					
4					
5					
6					
7					
8					
9					
10					
11					
12					

XV. COMMENTS *(enter information by line number — see instructions)*

EPA FORM 8700-13A (5-80)

PAGE ____ OF ____

399

Section XIII. Facility Address

Enter the address of the facility corresponding to the facility's EPA identification number in Section XI.

Section XIV. Waste Identification

All information in this section must be entered by line number. Each line entry will describe the total annual amount of each waste shipped to the facility identified in Section XI, above.

Section XIV—A. Description of Waste

For hazardous wastes that are listed under 40 CFR Part 261, Subpart D, enter the EPA listed name, abbreviated if necessary. Where mixtures of listed wastes were shipped, enter the description which you believe best describes the waste.

For unlisted hazardous waste identified under 40 CFR Part 261, Subpart C, enter the description which you believe best describes the waste. Include the specific manufacturing or other process generating the waste (e.g., green sludge from widget manufacturing) and, if known, the chemical or generic chemical name of the waste.

Section XIV—B. DOT Hazard Class

Enter the two digit code from Table 1 which corresponds to the DOT hazard class of the waste described. (If the waste described has been shipped under more than one DOT hazard class, use a separate line for each DOT hazard class.)

Table 1

DOT hazard class	Code
Combustible	01
Corrosive	02
Etiologic Agent	03
Explosive A	04
Explosive B	05
Flammable gas	06
Flammable liquid	07
Flammable solid	08
Irritating Agent	09
Nonflammable gas	10
Organic peroxide	11
ORM—E	12
Oxidizer	13
Poison A	14
Poison B	15
Radioactive	16

Section XIV—C. EPA Hazardous Waste Number

For listed wastes, enter the EPA Hazardous Waste number from 40 CFR Part 261, Subpart D, which identifies the waste.

For a mixture of more than one listed waste, enter each of the applicable EPA Hazardous Waste Numbers. Four spaces are provided. If more space is needed, continue on the next line(s) and leave all other information on that line blank.

For unlisted hazardous wastes, enter the EPA Hazardous Waste Numbers from 40 CFR Part 261, Subparts C, applicable to the waste. If more than four spaces are required, follow the procedure described above.

Section XIV—D. Amount of Waste

Enter the amount of this waste you shipped to the facility identified in Section XI and include the weight of containers if left at the treatment, storage, or disposal facility.

Section XIV—E. Units of measure

Enter the unit of measure code for the quantity of waste described on this line. Units of measure which must be used in this report and the appropriate codes are:

Units of measure	Code
Pounds	P
Short tons (2,000 lbs)	T
Kilograms	K
Tonnes (1,000 kg)	M

Units of volume may not be used for reporting but must be converted into one of the above units of weight taking into account the appropriate density or specific gravity of the waste.

Section XV. Comments

This space may be used to explain or clarify any entry. If used, enter a cross reference to the appropriate Section number.

ENVIRONMENTAL PROTECTION AGENCY REGULATIONS FOR HAZARDOUS WASTE TRANSPORTERS

40 CFR 263

PART 263 -- STANDARDS APPLICABLE TO TRANSPORTERS OF HAZARDOUS WASTE

Subpart A -- General

Sec.
263.10 Scope.
263.11 EPA Identification Number.
263.12 Transfer facility requirements.

Subpart B -- Compliance With the Manifest System and Recordkeeping

263.20 The Manifest System.
263.21 Compliance with the Manifest.
263.22 Recordkeeping.

Subpart C -- Hazardous Waste Discharges

263.30 Immediate Action.
263.31 Discharge Clean Up.

Authority: Sec. 2002(a), 3002, 3003, 3004 and 3005 of the Solid Waste Disposal Act as amended by the Resource Conservation and Recovery Act of 1976 and as amended by the Quiet Communities Act of 1978, (42 U.S.C. 6912(a), 6922, 6923, 6924, 6925).

Subpart A -- General

§ 263.10 Scope.

(a) These regulations establish standards which apply to persons transporting hazardous waste within the United States if the transportation requires a manifest under 40 CFR Part 262.

(b) These regulations do not apply to on-site transportation of hazardous waste by generators or by owners or operators of permitted hazardous waste management facilities.

(c) A transporter of hazardous waste must also comply with 40 CFR Part 262, Standards Applicable to Generators of Hazardous Waste, if he:

(1) Transports hazardous waste into the United States from abroad; or

(2) Mixes hazardous wastes of different DOT shipping descriptions by placing them into a single container.

§ 263.11 EPA identification number.

(a) A transporter must not transport hazardous wastes without having received an EPA identification number from the Administrator.

(b) A transporter who has not received an EPA identification number may obtain one by applying to the Administrator using EPA Form 8700-12. Upon receiving the request, the Administrator will assign an EPA identification number to the transporter.

§ 263.12 Transfer facility requirements.

A transporter who stores manifested shipments of hazardous waste in containers meeting the requirements of §262.30 at a transfer facility for a period of ten days or less is not subject to regulation under Parts 270, 264, 265, and 268 of this chapter with respect to the storage of those wastes.

Subpart B -- Compliance With the Manifest System and Recordkeeping

§ 263.20 The manifest system.

(a) A transporter may not accept hazardous waste from a generator unless it is accompanied by a manifest signed in accordance with the provisions of 40 CFR 262.20. In the case of exports, a transporter may not accept such waste from a primary exporter or other person (1) if he knows the shipment does not conform to the EPA Acknowledgment of Consent; and (2) unless, in addition to a manifest signed in accordance with the provisions of 40 CFR 262.20, such waste is also accompanied by an EPA Acknowledgment of Consent which, except for shipment by rail, is attached to the manifest (or shipping paper for exports by water (bulk shipment)).

(b) Before transporting the hazardous waste, the transporter must sign and date the manifest acknowledging acceptance of the hazardous waste from the generator. The transporter must return a signed copy to the generator before leaving the generator's property.

(c) The transporter must ensure that the manifest accompanies the hazardous waste. In the case of exports, the transporter must ensure that a copy of the EPA Acknowledgment of Consent also accompanies the hazardous waste.

(d) A transporter who delivers a hazardous waste to another transporter or to the designated facility must:

(1) Obtain the date of delivery and the handwritten signature of that transporter or of the owner or operator of the designated facility on the manifest; and

(2) Retain one copy of the manifest in accordance with §263.22; and

(3) Give the remaining copies of the manifest to the accepting transporter or designated facility.

(e) The requirements of paragraphs (c), (d) and (f) of this section do not apply to water (bulk shipment) transporters if:

(1) The hazardous waste is delivered by water (bulk shipment) to the designated facility; and

(2) A shipping paper containing all the information required on the manifest (excluding the EPA identification numbers, generator certification, and signatures) and, for exports, an EPA Acknowledgment of Consent accompanies the hazardous waste; and

(3) The delivering transporter obtains the date of delivery and handwritten signature of the owner or operator of the designated facility on either the manifest or the shipping paper; and

(4) The person delivering the hazardous waste to the initial water (bulk shipment) transporter obtains the date of delivery and signature of the water (bulk shipment) transporter on the manifest and forwards it to the designated facility; and

(5) A copy of the shipping paper or manifest is retained by each water (bulk shipment) transporter in accordance with §263.22.

(f) For shipments involving rail transportation, the requirements of paragraphs (c), (d) and (e) do not apply and the following requirements do apply:

(1) When accepting hazardous waste from a non-rail transporter, the initial rail transporter must:

(i) Sign and date the manifest acknowledging acceptance of the hazardous waste;

(ii) Return a signed copy of the manifest to the non-rail transporter;

(iii) Forward at least three copies of the manifest to:

(A) The next non-rail transporter, if any; or,

(B) The designated facility, if the shipment is delivered to that facility by rail; or

(C) The last rail transporter designated to handle the waste in the United States;

(iv) Retain one copy of the manifest and rail shipping paper in accordance with §263.22.

(2) Rail transporters must ensure that a shipping paper containing all the information required on the manifest (excluding the EPA identification numbers, generator certification,

and signatures) and, for exports an EPA Acknowledgment of Consent accompanies the hazardous waste at all times.

(3) When delivering hazardous waste to the designated facility, a rail transporter must:

(i) Obtain the date of delivery and handwritten signature of the owner or operator of the designated facility on the manifest or the shipping paper (if the manifest has not been received by the facility); and

(ii) Retain a copy of the manifest or signed shipping paper in accordance with §263.22.

(4) When delivering hazardous waste to a non-rail transporter a rail transporter must:

(i) Obtain the date of delivery and the handwritten signature of the next non-rail transporter on the manifest; and

(ii) Retain a copy of the manifest in accordance with §263.22.

(5) Before accepting hazardous waste from a rail transporter, a non-rail transporter must sign and date the manifest and provide a copy to the rail transporter.

(g) Transporters who transport hazardous waste out of the United States must:

(1) Indicate on the manifest the date the hazardous waste left the United States; and

(2) Sign the manifest and retain one copy in accordance with §263.22; and

(3) Return a signed copy of the manifest to the generator; and

(4) Give a copy of the manifest to a U.S. Customs official at the point of departure from the United States.

(h) A transporter transporting hazardous waste from a generator who generates greater than 100 kilograms but less than 1000 kilograms of hazardous waste in a calendar month need not comply with the requirements of this section or those of §263.22 provided that:

(1) The waste is being transported pursuant to a reclamation agreement as provided for in §262.20(e);

(2) The transporter records, on a log or shipping paper, the following information for each shipment:

(i) The name, address, and U.S. EPA Identification Number of the generator of the waste;

(ii) The quantity of waste accepted;

(iii) All DOT-required shipping information;

(iv) The date the waste is accepted; and

(3) The transporter carries this record when transporting waste to the reclamation facility; and

(4) The transporter retains these records for a period of at least three years after termination or expiration of the agreement.

§ 263.21 Compliance with the manifest.

(a) The transporter must deliver the entire quantity of hazardous waste which he has accepted from a generator or a transporter to:

(1) The designated facility listed on the manifest; or

(2) The alternate designated facility, if the hazardous waste cannot be delivered to the designated facility because an emergency prevents delivery; or

(3) The next designated transporter; or

(4) The place outside the United States designated by the generator.

(b) If the hazardous waste cannot be delivered in accordance with paragraph (a) of this section, the transporter must contact the generator for further directions and must revise the manifest according to the generator's instructions.

§ 263.22 Recordkeeping.

(a) A transporter of hazardous waste must keep a copy of the manifest signed by the generator, himself, and the next designated transporter or the owner or operator of the designated facility for a period of three years from the date the hazardous waste was accepted by the initial transporter.

(b) For shipments delivered to the designated facility by water (bulk shipment), each water (bulk shipment) transporter must retain a copy of the shipping paper containing all the information required in §263.20(e)(2) for a period of three years from the date the hazardous waste was accepted by the initial transporter.

(c) For shipments of hazardous waste by rail within the United States:

(i) The initial rail transporter must keep a copy of the manifest and shipping paper with all the information required in §263.20(f)(2) for a period of three years from the date the hazardous waste was accepted by the initial transporter; and

(ii) The final rail transporter must keep a copy of the signed manifest (or the shipping paper if signed by the designated facility in lieu of the manifest) for a period of three years from the date the hazardous waste was accepted by the initial transporter.

(d) A transporter who transports hazardous waste out of the United States must keep a copy of the manifest indicating that the hazardous waste left the United States for a period of three years from the date the hazardous waste was accepted by the initial transporter.

(e) The periods of retention referred to in this Section are extended automatically during the course of any unresolved enforcement action regarding the regulated activity or as requested by the Administrator.

Subpart C -- Hazardous Waste Discharges

§ 263.30 Immediate action.

(a) In the event of a discharge of hazardous waste during transportation, the transporter must take appropriate immediate action to protect human health and the environment (e.g., notify local authorities, dike the discharge area).

(b) If a discharge of hazardous waste occurs during transportation and an official (State or local government or a Federal Agency) acting within the scope of his official responsibilities determines that immediate removal of the waste is necessary to protect human health or the environment, that official may authorize the removal of the waste by transporters who do not have EPA identification numbers and without the preparation of a manifest.

(c) An air, rail, highway, or water transporter who has discharged hazardous waste must:

(1) Give notice, if required by 49 CFR 171.15, to the National Response Center (800-424-8802 or 202-426-2675); and

(2) Report in writing as required by 49 CFR 171.16 to the Director, Office of Hazardous Materials Regulations, Materials Transportation Bureau, Department of Transportation, Washington, DC 20590.

(d) A water (bulk shipment) transporter who has discharged hazardous waste must give the same notice as required by 33 CFR 153.203 for oil and hazardous substances.

§ 263.31 Discharge clean up.

A transporter must clean up any hazardous waste discharge that occurs during transportation or take such action as may be required or approved by Federal, State, or local officials so that the hazardous waste discharge no longer presents a hazard to human health or the environment.

ENVIRONMENTAL PROTECTION AGENCY INTERIM STATUS STANDARDS FOR OWNERS AND OPERATORS OF HAZARDOUS WASTE FACILITIES

40 CFR 265

265.16
Personnel Training

Subpart C
Preparedness and Prevention

Subpart D
Contingency Plan and Emergency Procedures

Subpart I
Use and Management of Containers

Subpart J
Tank Systems

40 CFR 265.16 Personnel Training

§ 265.16 Personnel training.

(1) Facility personnel must successfully complete a program of classroom instruction or on-the-job training that teaches them to perform their duties in a way that ensures the facility's compliance with the requirements of this part. The owner or operator must ensure that this program includes all the elements described in the document required under paragraph (d)(3) of this section.

(2) This program must be directed by a person trained in hazardous waste management procedures, and must include instruction which teaches facility personnel hazardous waste management procedures (including contingency plan implementation) relevant to the positions in which they are employed.

(3) At a minimum, the training program must be designed to ensure that facility personnel are able to respond effectively to emergencies by familiarizing them with emergency procedures, emergency equipment, and emergency systems, including where applicable:

(i) Procedures for using, inspecting, repairing, and replacing facility emergency and monitoring equipment;

(ii) Key parameters for automatic waste feed cut-off systems;

(iii) Communications or alarm systems;

(iv) Response to fires or explosions;

(v) Response to ground-water contamination incidents; and

(vi) Shutdown of operations.

(b) Facility personnel must successfully complete the program required in paragraph (a) of this section within six months after the effective date of these regulations or six months after the date of their employment or assignment to a facility, or to a new position at a facility, whichever is later. Employees hired after the effective date of these regulations must not work in unsupervised positions until they have completed the training requirements of paragraph (a) of this section.

(c) Facility personnel must take part in an annual review of the initial training required in paragraph (a) of this section.

(d) The owner or operator must maintain the following documents and records at the facility:

(1) The job title for each position at the facility related to hazardous waste management, and the name of the employee filling each job;

(2) A written job description for each position listed under paragraph (d)(1) of this Section. This description may be consistent in its degree of specificity with descriptions for other similar positions in the same company location or bargaining unit, but must include the requisite skill, education, or other qualifications, and duties of facility personnel assigned to each position;

(3) A written description of the type and amount of both introductory and continuing training that will be given to each person filling a position listed under paragraph (d)(1) of this section;

(4) Records that document that the training or job experience required under paragraphs (a), (b), and (c) of this section has been given to, and completed by, facility personnel.

(e) Training records on current personnel must be kept until closure of the facility. Training records on former employees must be kept for at least three years from the date the employee last worked at the facility. Personnel training records may accompany personnel transferred within the same company.

(Approved by the Office of Management and Budget under control number 2050-0013)

40 CFR 265

Subpart C
Preparedness and Prevention

Subpart D
Contingency Plan and Emergency Response Procedures

Subpart C -- Preparedness and Prevention

§ 265.30 Applicability.

The regulations in this subpart apply to owners and operators of all hazardous waste facilities, except as §265.1 provides otherwise.

§ 265.31 Maintenance and operation of facility.

Facilities must be maintained and operated to minimize the possibility of a fire, explosion, or any unplanned sudden or non-sudden release of hazardous waste or hazardous waste constituents to air, soil, or surface water which could threaten human health or the environment.

§ 265.32 Required Equipment.

All facilities must be equipped with the following, unless none of the hazards posed by waste handled at the facility could require a particular kind of equipment specified below:

(a) An internal communications or alarm system capable of providing immediate emergency instruction (voice or signal) to facility personnel;

(b) A device, such as a telephone (immediately available at the scene of operations) or a hand-held two-way radio, capable of summoning emergency assistance from local police departments, fire departments, or State or local emergency response teams;

(c) Portable fire extinguishers, fire control equipment (including special extinguishing equipment, such as that using foam, inert gas, or dry chemicals), spill control equipment, and decontamination equipment; and

(d) Water at adequate volume and pressure to supply water hose streams, or foam producing equipment, or automatic sprinklers, or water spray systems.

§ 265.33 Testing and maintenance of equipment.

All facility communications or alarm systems, fire protection equipment, spill control equipment, and decontamination equipment, where required, must be tested and maintained as necessary to assure its proper operation in time of emergency.

§ 265.34 Access to communications or alarm system.

(a) Whenever hazardous waste is being poured, mixed, spread, or otherwise handled, all personnel involved in the operation must have immediate access to an internal alarm or emergency communication device, either directly or through visual or voice contact with another employee, *unless* such a device is not required under §265.32.

(b) If there is ever just one employee on the premises while the facility is operating, he must have immediate access to a device, such as a telephone (immediately available at the scene of operation) or a hand-held two-way radio, capable of summoning external emergency assistance, unless such a device is not required under §265.32.

§ 265.35 Required aisle space.

The owner or operator must maintain aisle space to allow the unobstructed movement of personnel, fire protection equipment, spill control equipment, and decontamination equipment to any area of facility operation in an emergency, unless aisle space is not needed for any of these purposes.

§ 265.36 [Reserved]

§ 265.37 Arrangements with local authorities.

(a) The owner or operator must attempt to make the following arrangements, as appropriate for the type of waste handled at his facility and the potential need for the services of these organizations:

(1) Arrangements to familiarize police, fire departments, and emergency response teams with the layout of the facility, properties of hazardous waste handled at the facility and associated hazards, places where facility personnel would normally be working, entrances to roads inside the facility, and possible evacuation routes;

(2) Where more than one police and fire department might respond to an emergency, agreements designating primary emergency authority to a specific police and a specific fire department, and agreements with any others to provide support to the primary emergency authority;

(3) Agreements with State emergency response teams, emergency response contractors, and equipment suppliers; and

(4) Arrangements to familiarize local hospitals with the properties of hazardous waste handled at the facility and the types of injuries or illnesses which could result from fires, explosions, or releases at the facility.

(b) Where State or local authorities decline to enter into such arrangements, the owner or operator must document the refusal in the operating record.

§ 265.38 - 265.49 [Reserved]

Subpart D -- Contingency Plan and Emergency Procedures

§ 265.50 Applicability.

The regulations in this subpart apply to owners and operators of all hazardous waste facilities, except as §265.1 provides otherwise

§ 265.51 Purpose and implementation of contingency plan.

(a) Each owner or operator must have a contingency plan for his facility. The contingency plan must be designed to minimize hazards to human health or the environment from fires, explosions, or any unplanned sudden or non-sudden release of hazardous waste or hazardous waste constituents to air, soil, or surface water.

(b) The provisions of the plan must be carried out immediately whenever there is a fire, explosion, or release of hazardous waste or hazardous waste constituents which could threaten human health or the environment.

(Approved by the Office of Management and Budget under control number 2050-0002)

§ 265.52 Content of contingency plan.

(a) The contingency plan must describe the actions facility personnel must take to comply with §§265.51 and 265.56 in response to fires, explosions, or any unplanned sudden or non-sudden release of hazardous waste or hazardous waste constituents to air, soil, or surface water at the facility.

(b) If the owner or operator has already prepared a Spill Prevention, Control, and Countermeasures (SPCC) Plan in accordance with Part 112 of this chapter, or Part 1510 of Chapter V, or some other emergency or contingency plan, he need only amend that plan to incorporate hazardous waste management provisions that are sufficient to comply with the requirements of this part.

(c) The plan must describe arrangements agreed to by local police departments, fire departments, hospitals, contractors, and State and local emergency response teams to coordinate emergency services, pursuant to §265.37.

(d) The plan must list names, addresses, and phone numbers (office and home) of all persons qualified to act as emergency coordinator (see §265.55), and this list must be kept up to date. Where more than one person is listed, one must be named as primary emergency coordinator and others must be listed in the order in which they will assume responsibility as alternates.

(e) The plan must include a list of all emergency equipment at the facility (such as fire extinguishing systems, spill control equipment, communications and alarm systems (internal and external), and decontamination equipment), where this equipment is required. This list must be kept up to date. In addition, the plan must include the location and a physical description of each item on the list, and a brief outline of its capabilities.

(f) The plan must include an evacuation plan for facility personnel where there is a possibility that evacuation could be necessary.

This plan must describe signal(s) to be used to begin evacuation, evacuation routes, and alternate evacuation routes (in cases where the primary routes could be blocked by releases of hazardous waste or fires).

(Approved by the Office of Management and Budget under control number 2050-0002)

§ 265.53 Copies of contingency plan.

A copy of the contingency plan and all revisions to the plan must be:

(a) Maintained at the facility; and

(b) Submitted to all local police departments, fire departments, hospitals, and State and local emergency response teams that may be called upon to provide emergency services.

(Approved by the Office of Management and Budget under control number 2050-0002)

§ 265.54 Amendment of contingency plan.

The contingency plan must be reviewed, and immediately amended, if necessary, whenever:

(a) Applicable regulations are revised;

(b) The plan fails in an emergency;

(c) The facility changes--in its design, construction, operation, maintenance, or other circumstances--in a way that materially increases the potential for fires, explosions, or releases of hazardous waste or hazardous waste constituents, or changes the response necessary in an emergency;

(d) The list of emergency coordinators changes; or

(e) The list of emergency equipment changes.

(Approved by the Office of Management and Budget under control number 2050-0002)

§ 265.55 Emergency coordinator.

At all times, there must be at least one employee either on the facility premises or on call (i.e., available to respond to an emergency by reaching the facility within a short period of time) with the responsibility for coordinating all

emergency response measures. This emergency coordinator must be thoroughly familiar with all aspects of the facility's contingency plan, all operations and activities at the facility, the location and characteristics of waste handled, the location of all records within the facility, and the facility layout. In addition, this person must have the authority to commit the resources needed to carry out the contingency plan.

§ 265.56 Emergency procedures.

(a) Whenever there is an imminent or actual emergency situation, the emergency coordinator (or his designee when the emergency coordinator is on call) must immediately:

(1) Activate internal facility alarms or communication systems, where applicable, to notify all facility personnel; and

(2) Notify appropriate State or local agencies with designated response roles if their help is needed.

(b) Whenever there is a release, fire, or explosion, the emergency coordinator must immediately identify the character, exact source, amount, and a real extent of any released materials. He may do this by observation or review of facility records or manifests and, if necessary, by chemical analysis.

(c) Concurrently, the emergency coordinator must assess possible hazards to human health or the environment that may result from the release, fire, or explosion. This assessment must consider both direct and indirect effects of the release, fire, or explosion (e.g., the effects of any toxic, irritating, or asphyxiating gases that are generated, or the effects of any hazardous surface water run-offs from water or chemical agents used to control fire and heat-induced explosions).

(d) If the emergency coordinator determines that the facility has had a release, fire, or explosion which could threaten human health, or the environment, outside the facility, he must report his findings as follows:

(1) If his assessment indicates that evacuation of local areas may be advisable, he must immediately notify appropriate local authorities. He must be available to help appropriate officials decide whether local areas should be evacuated; and

(2) He must immediately notify either the government official designated as the on-scene coordinator for that geographical area (in the applicable regional contingency plan under Part 1510 of this title), or the National Response Center (using their 24-hour toll free number 800/424-8802). The report must include:

(i) Name and telephone number of reporter;

(ii) Name and address of facility;

(iii) Time and type of incident (e.g., release, fire);

(iv) Name and quantity of material(s) involved, to the extent known;

(v) The extent of injuries, if any; and

(vi) The possible hazards to human health, or the environment, outside the facility.

(e) During an emergency, the emergency coordinator must take all reasonable measures necessary to ensure that fires, explosions, and releases do not occur, recur, or spread to other hazardous waste at the facility. These measures must include, where applicable, stopping processes and operations, collecting and containing released waste, and removing or isolating containers.

(f) If the facility stops operations in response to a fire, explosion or release, the emergency coordinator must monitor for leaks, pressure buildup, gas generation, or ruptures in valves, pipes, or other equipment, wherever this is appropriate.

(g) Immediately after an emergency, the emergency coordinator must provide for treating, storing, or disposing of recovered waste, contaminated soil or surface water, or any other material that results from a release, fire, or explosion at the facility.

(h) The emergency coordinator must ensure that, in the affected area(s) of the facility:

(1) No waste that may be incompatible with the released material is treated, stored, or disposed of until cleanup procedures are completed; and

(2) All emergency equipment listed in the contingency plan is cleaned and fit for its intended use before operations are resumed.

(i) The owner or operator must notify the Regional Administrator, and appropriate State and local authorities, that the facility is in compliance with paragraph (h) of this section before operations are resumed in the affected area(s) of the facility.

(j) The owner or operator must note in the operating record the time, date, and details of any incident that requires implementing the contingency plan. Within 15 days after the incident, he must submit a written report on the incident to the Regional Administrator. The report must include:

(1) Name, address, and telephone number of the owner or operator;

(2) Name, address, and telephone number of the facility;

(3) Date, time, and type of incident (e.g., fire, explosion);

(4) Name and quantity of material(s) involved;

(5) The extent of injuries, if any;

(6) An assessment of actual or potential hazards to human health or the environment, where this is applicable; and

(7) Estimated quantity and disposition of recovered material that resulted from the incident.

(Approved by the Office of Management and Budget under control number 2050-0002)

40 CFR 265

Subpart I
Use and Management of Containers

Subpart J
Tank Systems

Subpart I -- Use and Management of Containers

§ 265.170 Applicability.

The regulations in this subpart apply to owners and operators of all hazardous waste facilities that store containers of hazardous waste, except as §265.1 provides otherwise.

§ 265.171 Condition of containers.

If a container holding hazardous waste is not in good condition, or if it begins to leak, the owner or operator must transfer the hazardous waste from this container to a container that is in good condition, or manage the waste in some other way that complies with the requirements of this part.

§ 265.172 Compatibility of waste with container.

The owner or operator must use a container made of or lined with materials which will not react with, and are otherwise compatible with, the hazardous waste to be stored, so that the ability of the container to contain the waste is not impaired.

§ 265.173 Management of containers.

(a) A container holding hazardous waste must always be closed during storage, except when it is necessary to add or remove waste.

(b) A container holding hazardous waste must not be opened, handled, or stored in a manner which may rupture the container or cause it to leak.

§ 265.174 Inspections.

The owner or operator must inspect areas where containers are stored, at least weekly, looking for leaks and for deterioration caused by corrosion or other factors.

§ 265.175 [Reserved]

§ 265.176 Special requirements for ignitable or reactive waste.

Containers holding ignitable or reactive waste must be located at least 15 meters (50 feet) from the facility's property line.

§ 265.177 Special Requirements for incompatible wastes.

(a) Incompatible wastes, or incompatible wastes and materials, (see Appendix V for examples) must not be placed in the same container, unless §265.17(b) is complied with.

(b) Hazardous waste must not be placed in an unwashed container that previously held an incompatible waste or material (see Appendix V for examples), unless §265.17(b) is complied with.

(c) A storage container holding a hazardous waste that is incompatible with any waste or other materials stored nearby in other containers, piles, open tanks, or surface impoundments must be separated from the other materials or protected from them by means of a dike, berm, wall, or other device.

§265.178-265.189 [Reserved]

Subpart J -- Tank Systems

§ 265.190 Applicability.

The requirements of this subpart apply to owners and operators of facilities that use tank systems for storing or treating hazardous waste except as otherwise provided in paragraphs (a), (b), and (c) of this section or in §265.1 of this part.

(a) Tank systems that are used to store or treat hazardous waste which contain no free liquids and that are situated inside a building with an impermeable floor are exempted from the requirements of §265.193 of this subpart. To demonstrate the absence or presence of free liquids in the stored/treated waste, EPA Method 9095 (Paint Filter Liquids Test) as described in "Test Methods for Evaluating Solid Wastes, Physical/Chemical Methods" (EPA Publication No. SW-846) must be used.

(b) Tank systems, including sumps, as defined in §260.10, that serve as part of a secondary containment system to collect or contain releases of hazardous wastes are exempted from the requirements in §265.193. (Information collection requirement contained in paragraph (a) was approved by the Office of Management and Budget under control number 2050-0050)

(c) Tanks, sumps, and other collection devices used in conjunction with drip pads, as defined in §260.10 of this chapter and regulated under 40 CFR Part 265 subpart W, must meet the requirements of this subpart.

§ 265.191 Assessment of existing tank system's integrity.

(a) For each existing tank system that does not have secondary containment meeting the requirements of §265.193, the owner or operator must determine that the tank system is not leaking or is unfit for use. Except as provided in paragraph (c) of this section, the owner or operator must obtain and keep on file at the facility a written assessment reviewed and certified by an independent, qualified, registered professional engineer in accordance with §270.11(d), that attests to the tank system's integrity by January 12, 1988.

(b) This assessment must determine that the tank system is adequately designed and has sufficient structural strength and compatibility with the waste(s) to be stored or treated to ensure that it will not collapse, rupture, or fail. At a minimum, this assessment must consider the following:

(1) Design standard(s), if available, according to which the tank and ancillary equipment were constructed;

(2) Hazardous characteristics of the waste(s) that have been or will be handled;

(3) Existing corrosion protection measures;

(4) Documented age of the tank system, if available, (otherwise, an estimate of the age); and

(5) Results of a leak test, internal inspection, or other tank integrity examination such that:

(i) For non-enterable underground tanks, this assessment must consist of a leak test that is capable of taking into account the effects of temperature variations, tank end deflection, vapor pockets, and high water table effects,

(ii) For other than non-enterable underground tanks and for ancillary equipment, this assessment must be either a leak test, as described above, or an internal inspection and/or other tank integrity examination certified by an independent, qualified, registered professional engineer in accordance with §270.11(d) that addresses cracks, leaks, corrosion, and erosion.

(c) Tank systems that store or treat materials that become hazardous wastes subsequent to July 14, 1986 must conduct this assessment within 12 months after the date that the waste becomes a hazardous waste.

(d) If, as a result of the assessment conducted in accordance with paragraph (a) of this section, a tank system is found to be leaking or unfit for use, the owner or operator must comply with the requirements of §265.196.

(Information collection requirements contained in paragraphs (a)-(d) were approved by the Office of Management and Budget under control number 2050-0050)

§ 265.192 Design and installation of new tank systems or components.

(a) Owners or operators of new tank systems or components must ensure that the foundation, structural support, seams, connections, and pressure controls (if applicable) are adequately designed and that the tank system has sufficient structural strength, compatibility with the waste(s) to be stored or treated, and corrosion protection so that it will not collapse, rupture, or fail. The owner or operator must obtain a written assessment reviewed and certified by an independent, qualified, registered professional engineer in accordance with §270.11(d)

attesting that the system has sufficient structural integrity and is acceptable for the storing and treating of hazardous waste. This assessment must include, at a minimum, the following information:

(1) Design standard(s) according to which the tank(s) and ancillary equipment is or will be constructed.

(2) Hazardous characteristics of the waste(s) to be handled.

(3) For new tank systems or components in which the external shell of a metal tank or any external metal component of the tank system is or will be in contact with the soil or with water, a determination by a corrosion expert of:

(i) Factors affecting the potential for corrosion, including but not limited to:

(A) Soil moisture content;

(B) Soil pH;

(C) Soil sulfides level;

(D) Soil resistivity;

(E) Structure to soil potential;

(F) Influence of nearby underground metal structures (e.g., piping);

(G) Stray electric current; and,

(H) Existing corrosion-protection measures (e.g., coating, cathodic protection), and

(ii) The type and degree of external corrosion protection that are needed to ensure the integrity of the tank system during the use of the tank system or component, consisting of one or more of the following:

(A) Corrosion-resistant materials of construction such as special alloys or fiberglass-reinforced plastic;

(B) Corrosion-resistant coating (such as epoxy or fiberglass) with cathodic protection (e.g., impressed current or sacrificial anodes); and

(C) Electrical isolation devices such as insulating joints and flanges.

(4) For underground tank system components that are likely to be affected by vehicular traffic, a determination of design or operational measures that will protect the tank system against potential damage; and

(5) Design considerations to ensure that:

(i) Tank foundations will maintain the load of a full tank;

(ii) Tank systems will be anchored to prevent flotation or dislodgement where the tank system is placed in a saturated zone, or is located within a seismic fault zone; and

(iii) Tank systems will withstand the effects of frost heave.

(b) The owner or operator of a new tank system must ensure that proper handling procedures are adhered to in order to prevent damage to the system during installation. Prior to covering, enclosing, or placing a new tank system or component in use, an independent, qualified installation inspector or an independent, qualified, registered professional engineer, either of whom is trained and experienced in the proper installation of tank systems, must inspect the system or component for the presence of any of the following items:

(1) Weld breaks;

(2) Punctures;

(3) Scrapes of protective coatings;

(4) Cracks;

(5) Corrosion;

(6) Other structural damage or inadequate construction or installation. All discrepancies must be remedied before the tank system is covered, enclosed, or placed in use.

(c) New tank systems or components and piping that are placed underground and that are backfilled must be provided with a backfill material that is a noncorrosive, porous, homogeneous substance and that is carefully installed so that the backfill is placed completely around the tank and compacted to ensure that the tank and piping are fully and uniformly supported.

(d) All new tanks and ancillary equipment must be tested for tightness prior to being covered, enclosed or placed in use. If a tank system is found not to be tight, all repairs

necessary to remedy the leak(s) in the system must be performed prior to the tank system being covered, enclosed, or placed in use.

(e) Ancillary equipment must be supported and protected against physical damage and excessive stress due to settlement, vibration, expansion or contraction.

(f) The owner or operator must provide the type and degree of corrosion protection necessary, based on the information provided under paragraph (a)(3) of this section, to ensure the integrity of the tank system during use of the tank system. The installation of a corrosion protection system that is field fabricated must be supervised by an independent corrosion expert to ensure proper installation .

(g) The owner or operator must obtain and keep on file at the facility written statements by those persons required to certify the design of the tank system and supervise the installation of the tank system in accordance with the requirements of paragraphs (b) through (f) of this section to attest that the tank system was properly designed and installed and that repairs, pursuant to paragraphs (b) and (d) of this section were performed. These written statements must also include the certification statement as required in §270.11(d) of this chapter.

(Information collection requirements contained in paragraphs (a) and (g) were approved by the Office of Management and Budget under control number 2050-0050)

§ 265.193 Containment and detection of releases.

(a) In order to prevent the release of hazardous waste or hazardous constituents to the environment, secondary containment that meets the requirements of this section must be provided (except as provided in paragraphs (f) and (g) of this section):

(1) For all new tank systems or components, prior to their being put into service;

(2) For all existing tanks used to store or treat EPA Hazardous Waste Nos. F020, F021, F022, F023, F026, and F027, within two years after January 12,1987;

(3) For those existing tank systems of known and documentable age, within two years after January 12, 1987, or when the tank systems have reached 15 years of age, whichever comes later;

(4) For those existing tank system for which the age cannot be documented, within eight years of January 12, 1987; but if the age of the facility is greater than seven years, secondary containment must be provided by the time the facility reaches 15 years of age, or within two years of January 12, 1987, whichever comes later; and

(5) For tank systems that store or treat materials that become hazardous wastes subsequent to January 12, 1987, within the time intervals required in paragraphs (a)(1) through (a)(4) of this section, except that the date that a material becomes a hazardous waste must be used in place of January 12, 1987.

(b) Secondary containment systems must be:

(1) Designed, installed, and operated to prevent any migration of wastes or accumulated liquid out of the system to the soil, ground water, or surface water at any time during the use of the tank system; and

(2) Capable of detecting and collecting releases and accumulated liquids until the collected material is removed.

(c) To meet the requirements of paragraph (b) of this section, secondary containment systems must be at a minimum:

(1) Constructed of or lined with materials that are compatible with the waste(s) to be placed in the tank system and must have sufficient strength and thickness to prevent failure due to pressure gradients (including static head and external hydrological forces), physical contact with the waste to which they are exposed, climatic conditions, the stress of installation, and the stress of daily operation (including stresses from nearby vehicular traffic);

(2) Placed on a foundation or base capable of providing support to the secondary containment system and resistance to pressure gradients above and below the system and capable of preventing failure due to settlement, compression, or uplift;

411

(3) Provided with a leak detection system that is designed and operated so that it will detect the failure of either the primary and secondary containment structure or any release of hazardous waste or accumulated liquid in the secondary containment system within 24 hours, or at the earliest practicable time if the existing detection technology or site conditions will not allow detection of a release within 24 hours;

(4) Sloped or otherwise designed or operated to drain and remove liquids resulting from leaks, spills, or precipitation. Spilled or leaked waste and accumulated precipitation must be removed from the secondary containment system within 24 hours, or in as timely a manner as is possible to prevent harm to human health or the environment, if removal of the released waste or accumulated precipitation cannot be accomplished within 24 hours.

(d) Secondary containment for tanks must include one or more of the following devices:

(1) A liner (external to the tank);

(2) A vault;

(3) A double-walled tank; or

(4) An equivalent device as approved by the Regional Administrator.

(e) In addition to the requirements of paragraphs (b), (c), and (d) of this section, secondary containment systems must satisfy the following requirements:

(1) External liner systems must be:

(i) Designed or operated to contain 100 percent of the capacity of the largest tank within its boundary;

(ii) Designed or operated to prevent run-on or infiltration of precipitation into the secondary containment system unless the collection system has sufficient excess capacity to contain run-on or infiltration. Such additional capacity must be sufficient to contain precipitation from a 25-year, 24-hour rainfall event;

(iii) Free of cracks or gaps; and

(iv) Designed and installed to completely surround the tank and to cover all surrounding earth likely to come into contact with the waste if released from the tank(s) (i.e., capable of preventing lateral as well as vertical migration of the waste).

(2) Vault systems must be:

(i) Designed or operated to contain 100 percent of the capacity of the largest tank within its boundary;

(ii) Designed or operated to prevent run-on or infiltration of precipitation into the secondary containment system unless the collection system has sufficient excess capacity to contain run-on or infiltration. Such additional capacity must be sufficient to contain precipitation from a 25-year, 24-hour rainfall event;

(iii) Constructed with chemical-resistant water stops in place at all joints (if any);

(iv) Provided with an impermeable interior coating or lining that is compatible with the stored waste and that will prevent migration of waste into the concrete;

(v) Provided with a means to protect against the formation of and ignition of vapors within the vault, if the waste being stored or treated:

(A) Meets the definition of ignitable waste under §262.21 of this chapter,

(B) Meets the definition of reactive waste under §262.21 of this chapter and may form an ignitable or explosive vapor;

(vi) Provided with an exterior moisture barrier or be otherwise designed or operated to prevent migration of moisture into the vault if the vault is subject to hydraulic pressure.

(3) Double-walled tanks must be:

(i) Designed as an integral structure (i.e., an inner tank within an outer shell) so that any release from the inner tank is contained by the outershell;

(ii) Protected, if constructed of metal, from both corrosion of the primary tank interior and the external surface of the outer shell; and

(iii) Provided with a built-in, continuous leak detection system capable of detecting a release within 24 hours or at the earliest practicable time, if the owner or operator can demonstrate to the Regional Administrator, and the Regional Administrator concurs, that the existing leak detection technology or site conditions will not allow detection of a release within 24 hours.

(f) Ancillary equipment must be provided with full secondary containment (e.g., trench, jacketing, double-walled piping) that meets the requirements of paragraphs (b) and (c) of this section except for:

(1) Aboveground piping (exclusive of flanges, joints, valves, and connections) that are visually inspected for leaks on a daily basis;

(2) Welded flanges, welded joints, and welded connections that are visually inspected for leaks on a daily basis;

(3) Sealless or magnetic coupling pumps and sealless valves, that are visually inspected for leaks on a daily basis; and

(4) Pressurized aboveground piping systems with automatic shut-off devices (e.g., excess flow check valves, flow metering shutdown devices, loss of pressure actuated shut-off devices) that are visually inspected for leaks on a daily basis.

(g) The owner or operator may obtain a variance from the requirements of this Section if the Regional Administrator finds, as a result of a demonstration by the owner or operator, either: that alternative design and operating practices, together with location characteristics, will prevent the migration of hazardous waste or hazardous constituents into the ground water or surface water at least as effectively as secondary containment during the active life of the tank system or that in the event of a release that does migrate to ground water or surface water, no substantial present or potential hazard will be posed to human health or the environment. New underground tank systems may not, per a demonstration in accordance with paragraph (g)(2) of this section, be exempted from the secondary containment requirements of this section. Application for a variance as allowed in paragraph (g) of this section does not waive compliance with the requirements of this subpart for new tank systems.

(1) In deciding whether to grant a variance based on a demonstration of equivalent protection of ground water and surface water, the Regional Administrator will consider:

(i) The nature and quantity of the waste;

(ii) The proposed alternate design and operation;

(iii) The hydrogeologic setting of the facility, including the thickness of soils between the tank system and ground water; and

(iv) All other factors that would influence the quality and mobility of the hazardous constituents and the potential for them to migrate to groundwater or surface water.

(2) In deciding whether to grant a variance, based on a demonstration of no substantial present or potential hazard, the Regional Administrator will consider:

(i) The potential adverse effects on ground water, surface water, and land quality taking into account:

(A) The physical and chemical characteristics of the waste in the tank system, including its potential for migration,

(B) The hydrogeological characteristics of the facility and surrounding land,

(C) The potential for health risks caused by human exposure to waste constituents,

(D) The potential for damage to wildlife, crops, vegetation, and physical structures caused by exposure to waste constituents, and

(E) The persistence and permanence of the potential adverse effects;

(ii) The potential adverse effects of a release on ground-water quality, taking into account:

(A) The quantity and quality of ground water and the direction of groundwater flow,

(B) The proximity and withdrawal rates of water in the area,

(C) The current and future uses of ground-water in the area, and

(D) The existing quality of ground water, including other sources of contamination and their cumulative impact on the ground-water quality;

(iii) The potential adverse effects of a release on surface water quality, taking into account:

(A) The quantity and quality of ground water and the direction of ground-water flow,

(B) The patterns of rainfall in the region,

(C) The proximity of the tank system to surface waters,

(D) The current and future uses of surface waters in the area and any water quality standards established for those surface waters, and

(E) The existing quality of surface water, including other sources of contamination and the cumulative impact on surface water quality; and

(iv) The potential adverse effects of a release on the land surrounding the tank system, taking into account:

(A) The patterns of rainfall in the region, and

(B) The current and future uses of the surrounding land.

(3) The owner or operator of a tank system, for which a variance from secondary containment had been granted in accordance with the requirements of paragraph (g)(1) of this section, at which a release of hazardous waste has occurred from the primary tank system but has not migrated beyond the zone of engineering control (as established in the variance), must:

(i) Comply with the requirements of §265.196, except paragraph (d); and

(ii) Decontaminate or remove contaminated soil to the extent necessary to: (A)Enable the tank system, for which the variance was granted, to resume operation with the capability for the detection of and response to releases at least equivalent to the capability it had prior to the release, and

(B) Prevent the migration of hazardous waste or hazardous constituents to ground water or surface water; and

(iii) If contaminated soil cannot be removed or decontaminated in accordance with paragraph (g)(3)(ii) of this section, comply with the requirements of §265.197(b);

(4) The owner or operator of a tank system, for which a variance from secondary contain-

ment had been granted in accordance with the requirements of paragraph (g)(1) of this section, at which a release of hazardous waste has occurred from the primary tank system and has migrated beyond the zone of engineering control (as established in the variance), must:

(i) Comply with the requirements of §265.196(a), (b), (c), and (d); and

(ii) Prevent the migration of hazardous waste or hazardous constituents to ground water or surface water, if possible, and decontaminate or remove contaminated soil. If contaminated soil cannot be decontaminated or removed, or if ground water has been contaminated, the owner or operator must comply with the requirements of §265.197(b);

(iii) If repairing, replacing, or reinstalling the tank system, provide secondary containment in accordance with the requirements of paragraphs (a) through (f) of this section or reapply for a variance from secondary containment and meet the requirements for new tank systems in §265.192 if the tank system is replaced. The owner or operator must comply with these requirements even if contaminated soil can be decontaminated or removed, and ground water or surface water has not been contaminated.

(h) The following procedures must be followed in order to request a variance from secondary containment:

(1) The Regional Administrator must be notified in writing by the owner or operator that he intends to conduct and submit a demonstration for a variance from secondary containment as allowed in paragraph (g) of this section according to the following schedule:

(i) For existing tank systems, at least 24 months prior to the date that secondary containment must be provided in accordance with paragraph (a) of this section; and

(ii) For new tank systems, at least 30 days prior to entering into a contract for installation of the tank system.

(2) As part of the notification, the owner or operator must also submit to the Regional Administrator a description of

the steps necessary to conduct the demonstration and a timetable for completing each of the steps. The demonstration must address each of the factors listed in paragraph (g)(1) or paragraph (g)(2) of this section.

(3) The demonstration for a variance must be completed and submitted to the Regional Administrator within 180 days after notifying the Regional Administrator of intent to conduct the demonstration.

(4) The Regional Administrator will inform the public, through a newspaper notice, of the availability of the demonstration for a variance. The notice shall be placed in a daily or weekly major local newspaper of general circulation and shall provide at least 30 days from the date of the notice for the public to review and comment on the demonstration for a variance. The Regional Administrator also will hold a public hearing, in response to a request or at his own discretion, whenever such a hearing might clarify one or more issues concerning the demonstration for a variance. Public notice of the hearing will be given at least 30 days prior to the date of the hearing and may be given at the same time as notice of the opportunity for the public to review and comment on the demonstration. These two notices may be combined.

(5) The Regional Administrator will approve or disapprove the request for a variance within 90 days of receipt of the demonstration from the owner or operator and will notify in writing the owner or operator and each person who submitted written comments or requested notice of the variance decision. If the demonstration for a variance is incomplete or does not include sufficient information, the 90-day time period will begin when the Regional Administrator receives a complete demonstration, including all information necessary to make a final determination. If the public comment period in paragraph (h)(4) of this section is extended, the 90-day time period will be similarly extended.

(i) All tank systems, until such time as secondary containment meeting the requirements of this section is provided, must comply with the following:

(1) For non-enterable underground tanks, a leak test that meets the requirements of §265.191(b)(5) must be conducted at least annually;

(2) For other than non-enterable underground tanks and for all ancillary equipment, an annual leak test, as described in paragraph (i)(1) of this section, or an internal inspection or other tank integrity examination by an independent, qualified, registered professional engineer that addresses cracks, leaks, corrosion, and erosion must be conducted at least annually. The owner or operator must remove the stored waste from the tank, if necessary, to allow the condition of all internal tank surfaces to be assessed

(3) The owner or operator must maintain on file at the facility a record of the results of the assessments conducted in accordance with paragraphs (i)(1)through (i)(3) of this section.

(4) If a tank system or component is found to be leaking or unfit-for-use as a result of the leak test or assessment in paragraphs (i)(1) through (i)(3) of this section, the owner or operator must comply with the requirements of §265.196.
(Information collection requirements contained in paragraphs (c)-(e), and (g)-(i) were approved by the Office of Management and Budget under control number 2050-0050)

§ 265.194 General operating requirements.

(a) Hazardous wastes or treatment reagents must not be placed in a tank system if they could cause the tank, its ancillary equipment, or the secondary containment system to rupture, leak, corrode, or otherwise fail.

(b) The owner or operator must use appropriate controls and practices to prevent spills and overflows from tank or secondary containment systems. These include at a minimum:

(1) Spill prevention controls (e.g , check valves, dry discount couplings);

(2) Overfill prevention controls (e.g , level sensing devices, high level alarms, automatic feed cutoff, or bypass to a standby tank); and

(3) Maintenance of sufficient freeboard in uncovered tanks to prevent overtopping by wave or wind action or by precipitation.

(c) The owner or operator must comply with the requirements of §265.196 if a leak or spill occurs in the tank system.
(Information collection requirements contained in paragraphs (c) were approved by the Office of Management and Budget under control number 2050-0050)

§ 265.195 Inspections.

(a) The owner or operator must inspect, where present, at least once each operating day:

(1) Overfill/spill control equipment (e.g., waste-feed cutoff systems, bypass systems, and drainage systems) to ensure that it is in good working order;

(2) The aboveground portions of the tank system, if any, to detect corrosion or releases of waste;

(3) Data gathered from monitoring equipment and leak-detection equipment, (e.g., pressure and temperature gauges, monitoring wells) to ensure that the tank system is being operated according to its design; and

(4) The construction materials and the area immediately surrounding the externally accessible portion of the tank system including secondary containment structures (e.g., dikes) to detect erosion or signs of releases of hazardous waste (e.g., wet spots, dead vegetation);

(b) The owner or operator must inspect cathodic protection systems, if present, according to, at a minimum, the following schedule to ensure that they are functioning properly:

(1) The proper operation of the cathodic protection system must be confirmed within six months after initial installation, and annually thereafter; and

(2) All sources of impressed current must be inspected and/or tested, as appropriate, at least bimonthly (i.e., every other month).

(c) The owner or operator must document in the operating record of the facility an inspection of those items in paragraphs (a) and (b) of this section.

(Information collection requirements contained in paragraphs (a)-(c) were approved by the Office of Management and Budget under control number 2050-0050)

§ 265.196 Response to leaks or spills and disposition of leaking or unfit-for-use tank systems.

A tank system or secondary containment system from which there has been a leak or spill, or which is unfit for use, must be removed from service immediately, and the owner or operator must satisfy the following requirements:

(a) *Cessation of use; prevent flow or addition of wastes.* The owner or operator must immediately stop the flow of hazardous waste into the tank system or secondary containment system and inspect the system to determine the cause of the release.

(b) *Removal of waste from tank system or secondary containment system.* (1) If the release was from the tank system, the owner or operator must, within 24 hours after detection of the leak or, if the owner or operator demonstrates that that is not possible, at the earliest practicable time remove as much of the waste as is necessary to prevent further release of hazardous waste to the environment and to allow inspection and repair of the tank system to be performed.

(2) If the release was to a secondary containment system, all released materials must be removed within 24 hours or in as timely a manner as is possible to prevent harm to human health and the environment.

(c) *Containment of visible releases to the environment.* The owner or operator must immediately conduct a visual inspection of the release and, based upon that inspection:

(1) Prevent further migration of the leak or spill to soils or surface water; and

(2) Remove, and properly dispose of, any visible contamination of the soil or surface water.

(d) *Notifications, reports.* (1) Any release to the environment, except as provided in paragraph (d)(2) of this section, must be reported to the Regional Administrator within 24 hours of detection. If the release has been reported pursuant to 40 CFR Part 302, that report will satisfy this requirement.

(2) A leak or spill of hazardous waste that is:

(i) Less than or equal to a quantity of one (1) pound, and

(ii) Immediately contained and cleaned-up is exempted from the requirements of this paragraph.

(3) Within 30 days of detection of a release to the environment, a report containing the following information must be submitted to the Regional Administrator:

(i) Likely route of migration of the release;

(ii) Characteristics of the surrounding soil (soil composition, geology, hydrogeology, climate);

(iii) Results of any monitoring or sampling conducted in connection with the release, (if available). If sampling or monitoring data relating to the release are not available within 30 days, these data must be submitted to the Regional Administrator as soon as they become available.;

(iv) Proximity to down gradient drinking water, surface water, and population areas; and

(v) Description of response actions taken or planned.

(e) *Provision of secondary containment, repair, or closure.* (1) Unless the owner or operator satisfies the requirements of paragraphs (e)(2) through (4) of this section, the tank system must be closed in accordance with §265.197.

(2) If the cause of the release was a spill that has not damaged the integrity of the system, the owner/operator may return the system to service as soon as the released waste is removed and repairs, if necessary, are made.

(3) If the cause of the release was a leak from the primary tank system into the secondary containment system, the system must be repaired prior to returning the tank system to service.

(4) If the source of the release was a leak to the environment from a component of a tank system without secondary containment, the owner/operator must provide the component of the system from which the leak occurred with secondary containment that satisfies the requirements of §265.193 before it can be returned to service, unless the source of the leak is an aboveground portion of a tank system. If the source is an aboveground component that can be inspected visually, the component must be repaired and may be returned to service without secondary containment as long as the requirements of paragraph (f) of this section are satisfied. If a component is replaced to comply with the requirements of this subparagraph, that component must satisfy the requirements for new tank systems or components in §265.192 and 265.193. Additionally, if a leak has occurred in any portion of a tank system component that is not readily accessible for visual inspection (e.g., the bottom of an inground or onground tank), the entire component must be provided with secondary containment in accordance with §265.193 prior to being returned to use.

(f) *Certification of major repairs.* If the owner or operator has repaired a tank system in accordance with paragraph (e) of this section, and the repair has been extensive (e.g., installation of an internal liner; repair of a ruptured primary containment or secondary containment vessel), the tank system must not be returned to service unless the owner/operator has obtained a certification by an independent, qualified, registered professional engineer in accordance with §270.11(d) that the repaired system is capable of handling hazardous wastes without release for the intended life of the system. This certification must be submitted to the Regional Administrator within seven days after returning the tank system to use.

(Information collection requirements contained in paragraphs (d)-(f) were approved by the Office of Management and Budget under control number 2050-0050)

§ 265.197 Closure and post-closure care.

(a) At closure of a tank system, the owner or operator must remove or decontaminate all waste residues, contaminated containment system components (liners, etc.), contaminated soils, and structures and equipment contaminated with waste, and manage them as hazardous waste, unless §261.3(d) of this Chapter applies. The closure plan, closure activities, cost estimates for closure, and financial responsibility for tank systems must meet all of the requirements specified in Subparts G and H of this Part.

(b) If the owner or operator demonstrates that not all contaminated soils can be practically removed or decontaminated as required in paragraph (a) of this section, then the owner or operator must close the tank system and perform post-closure care in accordance with the closure and post-closure care requirements that apply to landfills (§265.310) In addition, for the purposes of closure, post-closure, and financial responsibility, such a tank system is then considered to be a landfill, and the owner or operator must meet all of the requirements for landfills specified in Subparts G and H of this Part.

(c) If an owner or operator has a tank system which does not have secondary containment that meets the requirements of §265.193(b) through (f) and which is not exempt from the secondary containment requirements in accordance with §265.193(g), then,

(1) The closure plan for the tank system must include both a plan for complying with paragraph (a) of this section and a contingent plan for complying with paragraph (b) of this section.

(2) A contingent post-closure plan for complying with paragraph (b) of this section must be prepared and submitted as part of the permit application.

(3) The cost estimates calculated for closure and post-closure care must reflect the costs of complying with the contingent closure plan and the contingent post-closure plan, if these costs are greater than the costs of complying with the closure plan prepared for the expected closure under paragraph (a) of this section.

(4) Financial assurance must be based on the cost estimates in paragraph (c)(3) of this section.

(5) For the purposes of the contingent closure and post-closure plans, such a tank system is considered to be a landfill, and the contingent plans must meet all of the closure, post-closure, and financial responsibility requirements for landfills under Subparts G and H of this Part.

(Information collection requirements contained in paragraphs (a)-(c) were approved by the Office of Management and Budget under control number 2050-0050)

§ 265.198   Special requirements for ignitable or reactive wastes.

(a) Ignitable or reactive waste must not be placed in a tank system, unless:

(1) The waste is treated, rendered, or mixed before or immediately after placement in the tank system so that:

(i) The resulting waste, mixture, or dissolved material no longer meets the definition of ignitable or reactive waste under §261.21 or §261.23 of this chapter; and

(ii) Section §265.17(b) is complied with; or

(2) The waste is stored or treated in such a way that it is protected from any material or conditions that may cause the waste to ignite or react; or

(3) The tank system is used solely for emergencies.

(b) The owner or operator of a facility where ignitable or reactive waste is stored or treated in tanks must comply with the requirements for the maintenance of protective distances between the waste management area and any public ways, streets, alleys, or an adjoining property line that can be built upon as required in Tables 2-1 through 2-6 of the National Fire Protection Association's "Flammable and Combustible Liquids Code," (1977 or 1981), (incorporated by reference, see §260.11).

§ 265.199   Special requirements for incompatible wastes.

(a) Incompatible wastes, or incompatible waste and materials, must not be placed in the same tank system, unless §265.17(b) is complied with.

(b) Hazardous waste must not be placed in a tank system that has not been decontaminated and that previously held an incompatible waste or material, unless §265.17(b) is complied with.

§ 265.200 Waste analysis and trial tests.

In addition to performing the waste analysis required by §265.13, the owner or operator must, whenever a tank system is to be used to treat chemically or to store a hazardous waste that is substantially different from waste previously treated or stored in that tank system; or treat chemically a hazardous waste with a

substantially different process than any previously used in that tank system:

(a) Conduct waste analyses and trial treatment or storage tests (e.g., bench-scale or pilot-plant scale tests); or

(b) Obtain written, documented information on similar waste under similar operating conditions to show that the proposed treatment or storage will meet the requirements of §265.194(a).

§ 265.201   Special requirements for generators of between 100 and 1,000 kg/mo that accumulate hazardous waste in tanks.

(a) The requirements of this section apply to small quantity generators of more than 100 kg but less than 1,000 kg of hazardous waste in a calendar month, that accumulate hazardous waste in tanks for less than 180 days (or 270 days if the generator must ship the waste greater than 200 miles), and do not accumulate over 6,000 kg on-site at any time.

(b) Generators of between 100 and 1,000 kg/mo hazardous waste must comply with the following general operating requirements:

(1) Treatment or storage of hazardous waste in tanks must comply with §265.17(b).

(2) Hazardous wastes or treatment reagents must not be placed in a tank if they could cause the tank or its inner liner to rupture, leak, corrode, or otherwise fail before the end of its intended life.

(3) Uncovered tanks must be operated to ensure at least 60 centimeters (2 feet) of freeboard, unless the tank is equipped with a containment structure (e.g., dike or trench), a drainage control system, or a diversion structure (e.g., standby tank) with a capacity that equals or exceeds the volume of the top 60 centimeters (2 feet) of the tank.

(4) Where hazardous waste is continuously fed into a tank, the tank must be equipped with a means to stop

this inflow (e.g., waste feed cutoff system or by-pass system to a stand-by tank).

(c)   Generators of between 100 and 1,000 kg/mo accumulating hazardous waste in tanks must inspect, where present:

(1)   Discharge control equipment (e.g., waste feed cutoff systems, by-pass systems, and drainage systems) at least once each operating day, to ensure that it is in good working order;

(2)   Data gathered from monitoring equipment (e.g., pressure and temperature gauges) at least once each operating day to ensure that the tank is being operated according to its design;

(3)   The level of waste in the tank at least once each operating day to ensure compliance with §265.201(b)(3);

(4)   The construction materials of the tank at least weekly to detect corrosion or leaking of fixtures or seams; and

(5)   The construction materials of, and the area immediately surrounding, discharge confinement structures (e.g., dikes) at least weekly to detect erosion or obvious signs of leakage (e.g., wet spots or dead vegetation).

(d)   Generators of between 100 and 1,000 kg/mo accumulating hazardous waste in tanks must, upon closure of the facility, remove all hazardous waste from tanks, discharge control equipment, and discharge confinement structures.

(e)   Generators of between 100 and 1,000 kg/mo must comply with the following special requirements for ignitable or reactive waste:

(1)   Ignitable or reactive waste must not be placed in a tank, unless:

(i)   The waste is treated, rendered, or mixed before or immediately after placement in a tank so that (A) the resulting waste, mixture, or dissolution of material no longer meets the definition of ignitable or reactive waste under §261.21 or §261.23 of this chapter, and (B) §265.17(b) is complied with; or

(ii)   The waste is stored or treated in such a way that it is protected from any material or conditions that may cause the waste to ignite or react;or

(iii)   The tank is used solely for emergencies.

(2)   The owner or operator of a facility which treats or stores ignitable or reactive waste in covered tanks must comply with the buffer zone requirements for tanks contained in Tables 2-1 through 2-6 of the National Fire Protection Association's "Flammable and Combustible Liquids Code," (1977 or 1981) (incorporated by reference, see §260.11).

(f)   Generators of between 100 and 1,000 kg/mo must comply with the following special requirements for incompatible wastes:

(1)   Incompatible wastes, or incompatible wastes and materials, (see Appendix V for examples) must not be placed in the same tank, unless §265.17(b) is complied with.

(2)   Hazardous waste must not be placed in an unwashed tank which previously held an incompatible waste or material, unless §265.17(b) is complied with.

ENVIRONMENTAL PROTECTION AGENCY STANDARDS FOR MANAGEMENT OF SPECIFIC HAZARDOUS WASTES AND FACILITIES

40 CFR 266

PART 266 -- STANDARDS FOR THE MANAGEMENT OF SPECIFIC HAZARDOUS WASTES AND SPECIFIC TYPES OF HAZARDOUS WASTE MANAGEMENT FACILITIES

Subparts A -- B [Reserved]

Subpart C -- Recyclable Materials Used in a Manner Constituting Disposal

Subpart D [Reserved]

Subpart E -- Used Oil Burned for Energy Recovery

Subpart F -- Recyclable Materials Utilized for Precious Metal Recovery

Subpart G -- Spent Lead-Acid Batteries Being Reclaimed

Subpart H -- Hazardous Waste Burned in Boilers and Industrial Furnaces

Subparts A-B -- [Reserved]

Subpart C -- Recyclable Materials Used in a Manner Constituting Disposal

§ 262.20 Applicability.

(a) The regulations of this subpart apply to recyclable materials that are applied to or placed on the land:

(1) Without mixing with any other substance(s); or

(2) After mixing or combination with any other substance(s). These materials will be referred to throughout this subpart as "materials used in a manner that constitutes disposal."

(3) [Removed]

(b) Products produced for the general public's use that are used in a manner that constitutes disposal and that contain recyclable materials are not presently subject to regulation if the recyclable materials have undergone a chemical reaction in the course of producing the products so as to become inseparable by physical means and if such products meet the applicable treatment standards in Subpart D of Part 268 (or applicable prohibition levels in §268.32 or RCRA section 3004(d), where no treatment standards have been established) for each recyclable material (i.e., hazardous waste) that they contain. However, zinc-containing fertilizers using hazardous waste K061 that are produced for the general public's use are not presently subject to regulation.

§ 266.21 Standards applicable to generators and transporters of materials used in a manner that constitute disposal.

Generators and transporters of materials that are used in a manner that constitutes disposal are subject to the applicable requirements of Parts 262 and 263 of this chapter, and the notification requirement under section 3010 of RCRA.

§ 266.22 Standards applicable to storers of materials that are to be used in a manner that constitutes disposal who are not the ultimate users.

Owners or operators of facilities that store recyclable materials that are to be used in a manner that constitutes disposal but who are not the ultimate users of the materials, are regulated under all applicable provisions of Subparts A through L of Parts 264 and 265 and Parts 270 and 124 of this chapter and the notification requirement under section 3010 of RCRA

§ 266.23 Standards applicable to users of materials that are used in a manner that constitutes disposal.

(a) Owners or operators of facilities that use recyclable materials in a manner that constitutes disposal are regulated under all applicable provisions of Subparts A through N of Parts 264 and 265 and Parts 270 and 124 of this

chapter and the notification requirement under section 3010 of RCRA. (These requirements do not apply to products which contain these recyclable materials under the provisions of §266.20(b) of this chapter.)

(b) The use of waste or used oil or other material, which is contaminated with dioxin or any other hazardous waste (other than a waste identified solely on the basis of ignitability), for dust suppression or road treatment is prohibited.

Subpart D [Reserved]

Subpart E -- Used Oil Burned for Energy Recovery

§ 266.40 Applicability.

(a) The regulations of this subpart apply to used oil that is burned for energy recovery in any boiler or industrial furnace that is not regulated under Subpart O of Part 264 or 265 of this chapter, except as provided by paragraphs (c) and (e) of this section. Such used oil is termed "used oil fuel". Used oil fuel includes any fuel produced from used oil by processing, blending, or other treatment.

(b) "Used oil" means any oil that has been refined from crude oil, used, and, as a result of such use, is contaminated by physical or chemical impurities.

(c) Except as provided by paragraph (d) of this section, used oil that is mixed with hazardous waste and burned for energy recovery is subject to regulation as hazardous waste fuel under Subpart H of Part 266. Used oil containing more than 1000 ppm of total halogens is presumed to be a hazardous waste because it has been mixed with halogenated hazardous waste listed in Subpart D of Part 261 of this chapter. Persons may rebut this presumption by demonstrating that the used oil does not contain hazardous waste (for example, by showing that the used oil does not contain significant concentrations of halogenated hazardous constituents listed in Appendix VIII of Part 261 of this chapter).

(d) Used oil burned for energy recovery is subject to regulation under this subpart rather than as hazardous waste fuel under Subpart H of this part if it is a hazardous waste solely because it:

(1) Exhibits a characteristic of hazardous waste identified in Subpart C of Part 261 of this chapter, provided that it is not mixed with a hazardous waste; or

(2) Contains hazardous waste generated only by a person subject to the special requirements for small quantity generators under §261.5 of this chapter.

(e) Except as provided by paragraph (c) of this section, used oil burned for energy recovery, and any fuel produced from used oil by processing, blending, or other treatment, is subject to regulation under this subpart unless it is shown not to exceed any of the allowable levels of the constituents and properties in the specification shown in the following table. Used oil fuel that meets the specification is subject only to the analysis and recordkeeping requirements under §266.43(b)(1) and (6). Used oil fuel that exceeds any specification level is termed "off-specification used oil fuel".

USED OIL EXCEEDING ANY SPECIFICATION LEVEL IS SUBJECT TO THIS SUBPART WHEN BURNED FOR ENERGY RECOVERY[a]

Constituent/ property	Allowable level
Arsenic.............	5 ppm maximum.
Cadmium...........	2 ppm maximum.
Chromium..........	10 ppm maximum.
Lead...................	100 ppm maximum.
Flash Point........	100 °F minimum.
Total Halogens....	4,000 ppm maximum.[b]

a The specification does not apply to used oil fuel mixed with a hazardous waste other than small quantity generator hazardous waste.

b Used oil containing more than 1,000 ppm total halogens is presumed to be a hazardous waste under the rebuttable presumption provided under §266.40(c). Such used oil is subject to Subpart D of this part rather than this subpart when burned for energy recovery unless the presumption of mixing can be successfully rebutted.

§ 266.41 Prohibitions.

(a) A person may market off-specification used oil for energy recovery only:

(1) To burners or other marketers who have notified EPA of their used oil management activities stating the location and general description of such activities, and who have an EPA identification number; and

(2) To burners who burn the used oil in an industrial furnace or boiler identified in paragraph (b) of this section.

(b) Off-specification used oil may be burned for energy recovery in only the following devices:

(1) Industrial furnaces identified in §260.10 of this chapter; or

(2) Boilers, as defined in §260.10 of this chapter, that are identified as follows:

(i) Industrial boilers located on the site of a facility engaged in a manufacturing process where substances are transformed in to new products, including the component parts of products, by mechanical or chemical processes;

(ii) Utility boilers used to produce electric power, steam, or heated or cooled air or other gases or fluids for sale; or

(iii) Used oil-fired space heaters provided that:

(A) The heater burns only used oil that the owner or operator generates or used oil received from do-it-yourself oil changers who generate used oil as household waste;

(B) The heater is designed to have a maximum capacity of not more than 0.5 million Btu per hour; and

(C) The combustion gases from the heater are vented to the ambient air.

§ 266.42 Standards applicable to generators of used oil burned for energy recovery.

(a) Except as provided in paragraphs (b) and (c) of this section, generators of used oil are not subject to this subpart.

(b) Generators who market used oil directly to a burner are subject to §266.43.

(c) Generators who burn used oil are subject to §266.44.

§ 266.43 Standards applicable to marketers of used oil burned for energy recovery.

(a) Persons who market used oil fuel are termed "marketers". Except as provided below, marketers include generators who market used oil fuel directly to a burner, persons who receiv used oil from generators and produce, process, or blend used oil fuel from these used oils (including persons sending blended or processed used oil to brokers or other intermediaries), and persons who distribute but do not process or blend used oil fuel. The following persons are not marketers subject to this subpart:

(1) Used oil generators, and collectors who transport used oil received only from generators, unless the generator or collector markets the used oil directly to a person who burns it for energy recovery. However, persons who burn some used oil fuel for purposes of processing or other treatment to produce used oil fuel for marketing are considered to be burning incidentally to processing. Thus, generators and collectors who market to such incidental burners are not marketers subject to this subpart;

(2) Persons who market only used oil fuel that meets the specification under §266.40(e) and who are not the first person to claim the oil meets the specification (i.e., marketers who do not receive used oil from generators or initial transporters and marketers who neither receive nor market off-specification used oil fuel).

(b) Marketers are subject to the following requirements:

(1) *Analysis of used oil fuel.* Used oil fuel is subject to regulation under this subpart unless the marketer obtains analyses or other information documenting that the used oil fuel meets the specification provided under §266.40(e).

(2) *Prohibitions.* The prohibitions under §266.41(a);

(3) *Notification.* Notification to EPA stating the location and general description of used oil management activities. Even if a marketer has previously notified EPA of his hazardous waste management activities under section 3010 of RCRA and obtained a U.S. EPA Identification Number, he must renotify to identify his used oil management activities.

(4) *Invoice system.* When a marketer initiates a shipment of off-specification used oil, he must prepare and send the receiving facility an invoice containing the following information:

(i) An invoice number;

(ii) His own EPA identification number and the EPA identification number of the receiving facility;

(iii) The names and addresses of the shipping and receiving facilities;

(iv) The quantity of off-specification used oil to be delivered;

(v) The date(s) of shipment or delivery; and

(vi) The following statement: "This used oil is subject to EPA regulation under 40 CFR Part 266";

(5) *Required notices.* (i) Before a marketer initiates the first shipment of off-specification used oil to a burner or other marketer, he must obtain a one-time written and signed notice from the burner or marketer certifying that:

(A) The burner or marketer has notified EPA stating the location and general description of his used oil management activities; and

(B) If the recipient is a burner, the burner will burn the off-specification used oil only in an industrial furnace or boiler identified in §266.41(b); and

(ii) Before a marketer accepts the first shipment of off-specification used oil from another marketer subject to

420

the requirements of this section, he must provide the marketer with a one-time written and signed notice certifying that he has notified EPA of his used oil management activities; and

(6) *Recordkeeping*—(i) Used oil fuel that meets the specification. A marketer who first claims under paragraph (b)(1) of this section that used oil fuel meets the specification must keep copies of analysis (or other information used to make the determination) of used oil for three years. Such marketers must also record in an operating log and keep for three years the following information on each shipment of used oil fuel that meets the specification. Such used oil fuel is not subject to further regulation, unless it is subsequently mixed with hazardous waste or unless it is mixed with used oil so that it no longer meets the specification.

(A) The name and address of the facility receiving the shipment;

(B) The quantity of used oil fuel delivered;

(C) The date of shipment or delivery; and

(D) A cross-reference to the record of used oil analysis (or other information used to make the determination that the oil meets the specification) required under paragraph (b)(6)(i) of this section.

(ii) *Off-specification used oil fuel.* A marketer who receives or initiates an invoice under the requirements of this section must keep a copy of each invoice for three years from the date the invoice is received or prepared. In addition, a marketer must keep a copy of each certification notice that he receives or sends for three years from the date he last engages in an off-specification used oil fuel marketing transaction with the person who sends or receives the certification notice.

(The analysis requirements contained in paragraph (b)(1) of this section were approved by OMB under control number 2050-0047. The notification requirements contained in paragraph (b)(3) of this section were approved by OMB under control number 2050-0028. The invoice requirements contained in paragraph (b)(4) of this section were approved by OMB under control number 2050-0047. The certification requirements contained in paragraph (b)(5) of this section were approved by OMB under control number 2050-0047. The recordkeeping requirements contained in paragraph (b)(6) of this section were approved by OMB under control number 2050-0047.)

§ 266.44 Standards applicable to burners of used oil burned for energy recovery.

Owners and operators of facilities that burn used oil fuel are "burners" and are subject to the following requirements:

(a) *Prohibition.* The prohibition under §266.41(b);

(b) *Notification.* Burners of off-specification used oil fuel, and burners of used oil fuel who are the first to claim that the oil meets the specification provided under §266.40(e), except burners who burn specification oil that they generate, must notify EPA stating the location and general description of used oil management activities. Burners of used oil fuel that meets the specification who receive such oil from a marketer that previously notified EPA are not required to notify. Owners and operators of used oil-fired space heaters that burn used oil fuel under the provisions of §266.41(b)(2) are exempt from this notification requirement. Even if a burner has previously notified EPA of his hazardous waste management activities under section 3010 of RCRA and obtained an identification number, he must renotify to identify his used oil management activities.

(c) *Required notices.* Before a burner accepts the first shipment of off-specification used oil fuel from a marketer, he must provide the marketer a one-time written and signed notice certifying that:

(1) He has notified EPA stating the location and general description of his used oil management activities; and

(2) He will burn the used oil only in an industrial furnace or boiler identified in §266.41(b); and

(d) *Used oil fuel analysis.* (1) Used oil fuel burned by the generator is subject to regulation under this subpart unless the burner obtains analysis(or other information) documenting that the used oil meets the specification provided under §266.40(e).

(2) Burners who treat off-specification used oil fuel by processing, blending, or other treatment to meet the specification provided under §266.40(e) must obtain analyses (or other information) documenting that the used oil meets the specification.

(e) *Recordkeeping.* A burner who receives an invoice under the requirements of this section must keep a copy of each invoice for three years from the date the invoice is received. Burners must also keep for three years copies of analyses of used oil fuel as may be required by paragraph (d) of this section. In addition, he must keep a copy of each certification notice that he sends to a marketer for three years from the date he last receives off-specification used oil from that marketer.

(The notification requirements contained in paragraph (b) of this section were approved by OMB under control number 2050-0028. The certification requirements contained in paragraph (c) of this section were approved by OMB under control number 2050-0047. The analysis requirements contained in paragraph (d) of this section were approved by OMB under control number 2050-0047. The recordkeeping requirements contained in paragraph (e) of this section were approved by OMB under control number 2050-0047.)

Subpart F -- Recyclable Materials Utilized for Precious Metal Recovery

§ 266.70 Applicability and requirements.

(a) The regulations of this subpart apply to recyclable materials that are reclaimed to recover economically significant amounts of gold, silver, platinum, paladium, irridium, osmium, rhodium, ruthenium, or any combination of these.

(b) Persons who generate, transport, or store recyclable materials that are regulated under this subpart are subject to the following requirements:

(1) Notification requirements under section 3010 of RCRA;

(2) Subpart B of Part 262 (for generators), §§263.20 and 263.21 (for transporters), and §§265.71 and 265.72 (for persons who store) of this chapter;

(c) Persons who store recycled materials that are regulated under this subpart must keep the following records to document that they are not accumulating these materials speculatively (as defined in §261.1(c) of this chapter);

(1) Records showing the volume of these materials stored at the beginning of the calendar year;

(2) The amount of these materials generated or received during the calendar year; and

(3) The amount of materials remaining at the end of the calendar year.

(d) Recyclable materials that are regulated under this subpart that are accumulated speculatively (as defined in §261.1(c) of this chapter) are subject to all applicable provisions of Parts 262 through 265, 270 and 124 of this chapter.

Subpart G -- Spent Lead-Acid Batteries Being Reclaimed

§ 266.80 Applicability and requirements.

(a) The regulations of this subpart apply to persons who reclaim spent lead-acid batteries that are recyclable materials ("spent batteries"). Persons who generate, transport, or collect spent batteries, or who store spent batteries but do not reclaim them are not subject to regulation under Parts 262 through 266 or Part 270 or 124 of this chapter, and also are not subject to the requirements of section 3010 of RCRA.

(b) Owners or operators of facilities that store spent batteries before reclaiming them are subject to the following requirements.

(1) Notification requirements under section 3010 of RCRA;

(2) All applicable provisions in Subparts A, B (but not §264.13 (waste analysis)), C, D, E (but not §§264.71 or 264.72 (dealing with the use of the manifest and manifest discrepancies)), and F through L of Part 264 of this chapter;

(3) - (4) [Deleted]

Subpart H -- Hazardous Waste Burned in Boilers and Industrial Furnaces

§ 266.100 Applicability.

(a) The regulations of this subpart apply to hazardous waste burned or processed in a boiler or industrial furnace (as defined in §260.10 of this chapter) irrespective of the purpose of burning or processing, except as provided by paragraphs (b), (c), and (d) of this section. In this subpart, the term "burn" means burning for energy recovery or destruction, or processing for materials recovery or as an ingredient. The emissions standards of §§266.104, 266.105, 266.106, and 266.107 apply to facilities operating under interim status or under a RCRA permit as specified in §§266.102 and 266.103.

(b) The following hazardous wastes and facilities are not subject to regulation under this subpart:

(1) Used oil burned for energy recovery that is also a hazardous waste solely because it exhibits a characteristic of hazardous waste identified in subpart C of part 261 of this chapter. Such used oil is subject to regulation under subpart E of part 266 rather than this subpart;

(2) Gas recovered from hazardous or solid waste landfills when such gas is burned for energy recovery;

(3) Hazardous wastes that are exempt from regulation under §261.4 and §261.6(a)(3)(v-viii) of this chapter, and hazardous wastes that are subject to the special requirements for conditionally exempt small quantity generators under §261.5 of this chapter; and

(4) Coke ovens, if the only hazardous waste burned is EPA Hazardous Waste No. K087, decanter tank tar sludge from coking operations.

(c) Owners and operators of smelting, melting, and refining furnaces (including pyrometallurgical devices such as cupolas, sintering machines, roasters, and foundry furnaces, but not including cement kilns, aggregate kilns, or halogen acid furnaces burning hazardous waste) that process hazardous waste solely for metal recovery are conditionally exempt from regulation under this subpart, except for §§266.101 and 266.112.

(1) To be exempt from §266.102 through 266.111, an owner or operator of a metal recovery furnace must comply with the following requirements, except that an owner or operator of a lead or a nickel-chromium recovery furnace, or a metal recovery furnace that burns baghouse bags used to capture metallic dusts emitted by steel manufacturing, must comply with the requirements of paragraph (c)(3) of this section:

(i) Provide a one-time written notice to the Director indicating the following:

(A) The owner or operator claims exemption under this paragraph;

(B) The hazardous waste is burned solely for metal recovery consistent with the provisions of paragraph (c)(2) of this section;

(C) The hazardous waste contains recoverable levels of metals; and

(D) The owner or operator will comply with the sampling and analysis and recordkeeping requirements of this paragraph;

(ii) Sample and analyze the hazardous waste and other feedstocks as necessary to comply with the requirements of this paragraph under procedures specified by Test Methods for Evaluating Solid Waste, Physical/Chemical Methods, SW-846, incorporated by reference in §260.11 of this chapter or alternative methods that meet or exceed the SW-846 method performance capabilities. If SW-846 does not prescribe a method for a particular determination, the owner or operator shall use the best available method; and

(iii) Maintain at the facility for at least three years records to document compliance with the provisions of this paragraph including limits on levels of toxic organic constituents and Btu value of the waste, and levels of recoverable metals in the hazardous waste compared to normal nonhazardous waste feedstocks.

(2) A hazardous waste meeting either of the following criteria is not processed solely for metal recovery:

(i) The hazardous waste has a total concentration of organic compounds listed in Part 261, appendix VIII, of this chapter exceeding 500 ppm by weight, as-fired, and so is considered to be burned for destruction. The concentration of organic compounds in a waste as-generated may be reduced to the 500 ppm limit by bona fide treatment that removes or destroys organic constituents. Blending for dilution to meet the 500 ppm limit is prohibited and documentation that the waste has not been impermissibly diluted must be retained in the records required by paragraph (c)(1)(iii) of this section; or

(ii) The hazardous waste has a heating value of 5,000 Btu/lb or more, as-fired, and so is considered to be burned as fuel. The heating value of a waste as-generated may be reduced to below the 5,000 Btu/lb limit by bona fide treatment that removes or destroys organic constituents. Blending for dilution to meet the 5,000 Btu/lb limit is prohibited and documentation that the waste has not been impermissibly diluted must be retained in the records required by paragraph (c)(1)(iii) of this section.

(3) To be exempt from §§266.102 through 266.111, an owner or operator of a lead or nickel-chromium recovery furnace, or a metal recovery furnace that burns baghouse bags used to capture metallic dusts emitted by steel manufacturing, must provide a one-time written notice to the Director identifying each hazardous waste burned and specifying whether the owner or operator claims an exemption for each waste under this paragraph or paragraph (c)(1) of this section. The owner or operator must comply with the requirements of paragraph (c)(1) of this section for those wastes claimed to be exempt under that paragraph and must comply with the requirements below for those wastes claimed to be exempt under this paragraph.

(i) The hazardous wastes listed in appendices XI and XII, part 266, and baghouse bags used to capture metallic dusts emitted by steel manufacturing are exempt from the requirements of paragraph (c)(1) of this section, provided that:

(A) A waste listed in appendix XI must contain recoverable levels of lead, a waste listed in appendix XII must contain recoverable levels of nickel or chromium, and baghouse bags used to capture metallic dusts emitted by steel manufacturing must contain recoverable levels of metal; and

(B) The waste does not exhibit the Toxicity Characteristic of §261.24 of this chapter for an organic constituent; and

(C) The waste is not a hazardous waste listed in subpart D of Part 261 of this chapter because it is listed for an organic constituent as identified in appendix VII of Part 261 of this chapter; and

(D) The owner or operator certifies in the one-time notice that hazardous waste is burned under the provisions of paragraph (c)(3) of this section and that sampling and analysis will be conducted or other information will be obtained as necessary to ensure continued compliance with these requirements. Sampling and analysis

shall be conducted according to paragraph (c)(1)(ii) of this section and records to document compliance with paragraph (c)(3) of this section shall be kept for at least three years.

(ii) The Director may decide on a case-by-case basis that the toxic organic constituents in a material listed in appendix XI or XII of this part that contains a total concentration of more than 500 ppm toxic organic compounds listed in appendix VIII, Part 261 of this chapter, may pose a hazard to human health and the environment when burned in a metal recovery furnace exempt from the requirements of this subpart. In that situation, after adequate notice and opportunity for comment, the metal recovery furnace will become subject to the requirements of this subpart when burning that material. In making the hazard determination, the Director will consider the following factors:

(A) The concentration and toxicity of organic constituents in the material;

(B) The level of destruction of toxic organic constituents provided by the furnace; and

(C) Whether the acceptable ambient levels established in appendices IV or V of this part may be exceeded for any toxic organic compound that may be emitted based on dispersion modeling to predict the maximum annual average off-site ground level concentration.

(d) The standards for direct transfer operations under §266.111 apply only to facilities subject to the permit standards of §266.102 or the interim status standards of §266.103.

(e) The management standards for residues under §266.112 apply to any boiler or industrial furnace burning hazardous waste.

(f) Owners and operators of smelting, melting, and refining furnaces (including pyrometallurgical devices such as cupolas, sintering machines, roasters, and foundry furnaces) that process hazardous waste for recovery of economically significant amounts of the precious metals gold, silver, platinum, palladium, irridium, osmium, rhodium, or ruth-

enium, or any combination of these are conditionally exempt from regulation under this subpart, except for §266.112. To be exempt from §§266.101 through 261.111, an owner or operator must:

(1) Provide a one-time written notice to the Director indicating the following:

(i) The owner or operator claims exemption under this paragraph;

(ii) The hazardous waste is burned for legitimate recovery of precious metal; and

(iii) The owner or operator will comply with the sampling and analysis and recordkeeping requirements of this paragraph; and

(2) Sample and analyze the hazardous waste as necessary to document that the waste is burned for recovery of economically significant amounts of precious metal using procedures specified by Test Methods for Evaluating Solid Waste, Physical/Chemical Methods, SW-846, incorporated by reference in §260.11 of this chapter or alternative methods that meet or exceed the SW-846 method performance capabilities. If SW-846 does not prescribe a method for a particular determination, the owner or operator shall use the best available method; and

(3) Maintain at the facility for at least three years records to document that all hazardous wastes burned are burned for recovery of economically significant amounts of precious metal.

(Approved by the Office of Management and Budget under control number 2050-0073)

§ 266.101 Management prior to burning.

(a) Generators. Generators of hazardous waste that is burned in a boiler or industrial furnace are subject to part 262 of this chapter.

(b) Transporters. Transporters of hazardous waste that is burned in a boiler or industrial furnace are subject to part 263 of this chapter.

(c) *Storage facilities.* (1) Owners and operators of facilities that store hazardous waste that is burned in a boiler or industrial furnace are subject to the applicable provisions of subparts A through L of part 264, subparts A through L of part 265, and part 270 of this chapter, except as provided by paragraph (c)(2) of this section. These standards apply to storage by the burner as well as to storage facilities operated by intermediaries (processors, blenders, distributors, etc.) between the generator and the burner.

(2) Owners and operators of facilities that burn, in an on-site boiler or industrial furnace exempt from regulation under the small quantity burner provisions of §266.108, hazardous waste that they generate are exempt from regulation under subparts A through L of part 264, subparts A through L of part 265, and part 270 of this chapter with respect to the storage of mixtures of hazardous waste and the primary fuel to the boiler or industrial furnace in tanks that feed the fuel mixture directly to the burner. Storage of hazardous waste prior to mixing with the primary fuel is subject to regulation as prescribed in paragraph (c)(1) of this section.

§ 266.102 Permit standards for burners.

(a) *Applicability*--(1) General. Owners and operators of boilers and industrial furnaces burning hazardous waste and not operating under interim status must comply with the requirements of this section and §§270.22 and 270.66 of this chapter, unless exempt under the small quantity burner exemption of §266.108.

(2) *Applicability of part 264 standards.* Owners and operators of boilers and industrial furnaces that burn hazardous waste are subject to the following provisions of part 264 of this chapter, except as provided otherwise by this subpart:

(i) In subpart A (General), §264.4;

(ii) In subpart B (General facility standards), §§264.11-264.18;

(iii) In subpart C (Preparedness and prevention), §§264.31-264.37;

(iv) In subpart D (Contingency plan and emergency procedures), §§264.51-264.56;

(v) In subpart E (Manifest system, recordkeeping, and reporting), the applicable provisions of §§284.71-264.77;

(vi) In subpart F (Corrective Action), §§264.90 and 264.101;

(vii) In subpart G (Closure and post-closure), §§264.111-264.115;

(viii) In subpart H (Financial requirements), §§264.141, 264.142, 264.143, and 264.147-264.151, except that States and the Federal government are exempt from the requirements of subpart H; and

(ix) Subpart BB (Air emission standards for equipment leaks), except §264.1050(a).

(b) *Hazardous waste analysis.* (1) The owner or operator must provide an analysis of the hazardous waste that quantifies the concentration of any constituent identified in appendix VIII of part 261 of this chapter that may reasonably be expected to be in the waste. Such constituents must be identified and quantified if present, at levels detectable by analytical procedures prescribed by Test Methods for Evaluating Solid Waste, Physical/Chemical Methods (incorporated by reference, see §260.11 of this chapter). Alternative methods that meet or exceed the method performance capabilities of SW-846 methods may be used. If SW-846 does not prescribe a method for a particular determination, the owner or operator shall use the best available method. The appendix VIII, part 261 constituents excluded from this analysis must be identified and the basis for their exclusion explained. This analysis will be used to provide all information required by this subpart and §§270.22 and 270.66 of this chapter and to enable the permit writer to prescribe such permit conditions as necessary to protect human health and the environment. Such analysis must be included as a portion of the part B permit application, or, for facilities operating under the interim status standards of this subpart, as a portion of the trial burn plan that may be submitted before the part B application under provisions of §270.66(g) of this chapter as well as any other analysis required by the permit authority in preparing the permit. Owners and operators of boilers and industrial furnaces not operating under the interim status standards must provide the information required by §§270.22 or 270.66(c) of this chapter in the part B application to the greatest extent possible.

(2) Throughout normal operation, the owner or operator must conduct sampling and analysis as necessary to ensure that the hazardous waste, other fuels, and industrial furnace feedstocks fired into the boiler or industrial furnace are within the physical and chemical composition limits specified in the permit.

(c) *Emissions standards.* Owners and operators must comply with emissions standards provided by §§266.104 through 266.107.

(d) *Permits.* (1) The owner or operator may burn only hazardous wastes specified in the facility permit and only under the operating conditions specified under paragraph (e) of this section, except in approved trial burns under the conditions specified in §270.66 of this chapter.

(2) Hazardous wastes not specified in the permit may not be burned until operating conditions have been specified under a new permit or permit modification, as applicable. Operating requirements for new wastes may be based on either trial burn results or alternative data included with part B of a permit application under §270.22 of this chapter.

(3) Boilers and industrial furnaces operating under the interim status standards of §266.103 are permitted under procedures provided by §270.66(g) of this chapter.

(4) A permit for a new boiler or industrial furnace (those boilers and industrial furnaces not operating under the interim status standards) must establish appropriate conditions for each of the applicable requirements of this section, including but not limited to allowable hazardous waste firing rates and operating conditions necessary to meet the requirements of paragraph(e) of this section, in order to comply with the following standards:

(i) For the period beginning with initial introduction of hazardous waste and ending with initiation of the trial burn, and only for the minimum time required to bring the device to a point of operational readiness to conduct a trial burn, not to exceed a duration of 720 hours operating time when burning hazardous waste, the operating requirements must be those most likely to ensure compliance with the emission standards of §§266.104 through 266.107, based on the Director's engineering judgment. If the applicant is seeking a waiver from a trial burn to demonstrate conformance with a particular emission standard, the operating requirements during this initial period of operation shall include those specified by the applicable provisions of §§266.104, 266.105, 266.106, or 266.107. The Director may extend the duration of this period for up to 720 additional hours when good cause for the extension is demonstrated by the applicant.

(ii) For the duration of the trial burn, the operating requirements must be sufficient to demonstrate compliance with the emissions standards of §§266.104 through 266.107 and must be in accordance with the approved trial burn plan;

(iii) For the period immediately following completion of the trial burn, and only for the minimum period sufficient to allow sample analysis,data computation, submission of the trial burn results by the applicant, review of the trial burn results and modification of the facility permit by the Director to reflect the trial burn results, the operating requirements must be those most likely to ensure compliance with the emission standards 266.104 through 266.107 based on the Director's engineering judgment.

(iv) For the remaining duration of the permit, the operating requirements must be those demonstrated in a trial burn or by alternative data specified in §270.22 of this chapter, as sufficient to ensure compliance with the emissions standards of §§266.104 through 266.107.

(e) *Operating requirements*--(1) General. A boiler or industrial furnace burning hazardous waste must be operated in accordance with the operating requirements specified in the permit at all times where there is hazardous waste in the unit.

(2) *Requirements to ensure compliance with the organic emissions standards*--(i) DRE standard. Operating conditions will be specified either on a case-by-case basis for each hazardous waste burned as those demonstrated (in a trial burn or by alternative data as specified in §270.22) to be sufficient to comply with the destruction and removal efficiency (DRE) performance standard of §266.104(a) or as those special operating requirements provided by §266.104(a)(4) for the waiver of the DRE trial burn. When the DRE trial burn is not waived under §266.104(a)(4), each set of operating requirements will specify the composition of the hazardous waste (including acceptable variations in the physical and chemical properties of the hazardous waste which will not affect compliance with the DRE performance standard) to which the operating requirements apply. For each such hazardous waste, the permit will specify acceptable operating limits including, but not limited to, the following conditions as appropriate:

(A) Feed rate of hazardous waste and other fuels measured and specified as prescribed in paragraph (e)(6) of this section;

(B) Minimum and maximum device production rate when producing normal product expressed in appropriate units, measured and specified as prescribed in paragraph (e)(6) of this section;

(C) Appropriate controls of the hazardous waste firing system;

(D) Allowable variation in boiler and industrial furnace system design or operating procedures;

(E) Minimum combustion gas temperature measured at a location indicative of combustion chamber temperature, measured and specified as prescribed in paragraph (e)(6) of this section;

(F) An appropriate indicator of combustion gas velocity, measured and specified as prescribed in paragraph (e)(6) of this section, unless documentation is provided under §270.66 of this chapter demonstrating adequate combustion gas residence time; and

(G) Such other operating requirements as are necessary to ensure that the DRE performance standard of §266.104(a) is met.

(ii) *Carbon monoxide and hydrocarbon standards.* The permit must incorporate a carbon monoxide (CO) limit and, as appropriate, a hydrocarbon (HC) limit as provided by paragraphs (b), (c), (d), (e) and (f) of §266.104. The permit limits will be specified as follows:

(A) When complying with the CO standard of §266.104(b)(1), the permit limit is 100 ppmv;

(B) When complying with the alternative CO standard under §266.104(c), the permit limit for CO is based on the trial burn and is established as the average over all valid runs of the highest hourly rolling average CO level of each run, and the permit limit for HC is 20 ppmv (as defined in §266.104(c)(1)), except as provided in §266.104(f).

(C) When complying with the alternative HC limit for industrial furnaces under §266.104(f), the permit limit for HC and CO is the baseline level when hazardous waste is not burned as specified by that paragraph.

(iii) *Start-up and shut-down.* During start-up and shut-down of the boiler or industrial furnace, hazardous waste (except waste fed solely as an ingredient under the Tier I (or adjusted Tier I) feed rate screening limits for metals and chloride/chlorine, and except low risk waste exempt from the trial burn requirements under §§266.104(a)(5), 266.105, 266.106, and 266.107) must not be fed into the device unless the device is operating within the conditions of operation specified in the permit.

(3) *Requirements to ensure conformance with the particulate standard.* (i)Except as provided in paragraphs (e)(3)(ii) and (iii) of this section, the permit shall specify the following operating requirements to ensure conformance with the particulate standard specified in §266.105:

(A) Total ash feed rate to the device from hazardous waste, other fuels, and industrial furnace feedstocks, measured and specified as prescribed in paragraph (e)(6) of this section;

(B) Maximum device production rate when producing normal product expressed in appropriate units, and measured and specified as prescribed in paragraph (e)(6) of this section;

(C) Appropriate controls on operation and maintenance of the hazardous waste firing system and any air pollution control system;

(D) Allowable variation in boiler and industrial furnace system design including any air pollution control system or operating procedures; and

(E) Such other operating requirements as are necessary to ensure that the particulate standard in §266.111(b) is met.

(ii) Permit conditions to ensure conformance with the particulate matter standard shall not be provided for facilities exempt from the particulate matter standard under §266.105(b);

(iii) For cement kilns and light-weight aggregate kilns, permit conditions to ensure compliance with the particulate standard shall not limit the ash content of hazardous waste or other feed materials.

(4) *Requirements to ensure conformance with the metals emissions standard.* (i) For conformance with the Tier I (or adjusted Tier I) metals feed rate screening limits of paragraphs (b) or (e) of §266.106, the permit shall specify the following operating requirements:

(A) Total feed rate of each metal in hazardous waste, other fuels, and industrial furnace feedstocks measured and specified under provisions of paragraph (e)(6) of this section;

(B) Total feed rate of hazardous waste measured and specified as prescribed in paragraph (e)(6) of this section;

(C) A sampling and metals analysis program for the hazardous waste, other fuels, and industrial furnace feedstocks;

(ii) For conformance with the Tier II metals emission rate screening limits under §266.106(c) and the Tier III metals controls under §266.106(d), the permit shall specify the following operating requirements:

(A) Maximum emission rate for each metal specified as the average emission rate during the trial burn;

(B) Feed rate of total hazardous waste and pumpable hazardous waste, each measured and specified as prescribed in paragraph (e)(6)(i) of this section;

(C) Feed rate of each metal in the following feed streams, measured and specified as prescribed in paragraphs (e)(6) of this section:

(1) Total feed streams;

(2) Total hazardous waste feed; and

(3) Total pumpable hazardous waste feed;

(D) Total feed rate of chlorine and chloride in total feedstreams measured and specified as prescribed in paragraph (e) (6) of this section;

(E) Maximum combustion gas temperature measured at a location indicative of combustion chamber temperature, and measured and specified as prescribed in paragraph (e)(6) of this section;

(F) Maximum flue gas temperature at the inlet to the particulate matter air pollution control system measured and specified as prescribed in paragraph (e)(6) of this section;

(G) Maximum device production rate when producing normal product expressed in appropriate units and measured and specified as prescribed in paragraph (e)(6) of this section;

(H) Appropriate controls on operation and maintenance of the hazardous waste firing system and any air pollution control system;

(I) Allowable variation in boiler and industrial furnace system design including any air pollution control system or operating procedures; and

(J) Such other operating requirements as are necessary to ensure that the metals standards under §§266.106(c) or 266.106(d) are met.

(iii) For conformance with an alternative implementation approach approved by the Director under §266.106(f), the permit will specify the following operating requirements:

(A) Maximum emission rate for each metal specified as the average emission rate during the trial burn;

(B) Feed rate of total hazardous waste and pumpable hazardous waste, each measured and specified as prescribed in paragraph (e)(6)(i) of this section;

(C) Feed rate of each metal in the following feedstreams, measured and specified as prescribed in paragraph (e)(6) of this section:

(1) Total **hazardous** waste feed; and

(2) Total pumpable hazardous waste feed;

(D) Total feed rate of chlorine and chloride in total feedstreams measured and specified prescribed in paragraph (e)(6) of this section;

(E) Maximum combustion gas temperature measured at a location indicative of combustion chamber temperature, and measured and specified as prescribed in paragraph (e)(6) of this section;

(F) Maximum flue gas temperature at the inlet to the particulate matter air pollution control system measured and specified as prescribed in paragraph (e)(6) of this section;

(G) Maximum device production rate when producing normal product expressed in appropriate units and measured and specified as prescribed in paragraph (e)(6) of this section;

(H) Appropriate controls on operation and maintenance of the hazardous waste firing system and any air pollution control system;

(I) Allowable variation in boiler and industrial furnace system design including any air pollution control system or operating procedures; and

(J) Such other operating requirements as are necessary to ensure that the metals standards under §§266.106(c) or 266.106(d) are met.

(5) *Requirements to ensure conformance with the hydrogen chloride and chlorine gas standards.* (i) For conformance with the Tier I total chloride and chlorine feed rate screening limits of §266.107(b)(1), the permit will specify the following operating requirements:

(A) Feed rate of total chloride and chlorine in hazardous waste, other fuels, and industrial furnace feedstocks measured and specified as prescribed in paragraph (e)(6) of this section;

(B) Feed rate of total hazardous waste measured and specified as prescribed in paragraph (e)(6) of this section;

(C) A sampling and analysis program for total chloride and chorline for the hazardous waste, other fuels, and industrial furnace feestocks;

(ii) For conformance with the Tier II HCl and Cl2 emission rate screening limits under §266.107(b)(2) and the Tier III HCl and Cl2 controls under §266.107(c), the permit will specify the following operating requirements:

(A) Maximum emission rate for HCl and for Cl2 specified as the average emission rate during the trial burn;

(B) Feed rate of total hazardous waste measured and specified as prescribed in paragraph (e)(6) of this section;

(C) Total feed rate of chlorine and chloride in total feedstreams, measured and specified as prescribed in paragraph (e)(6) of this section;

(D) Maximum device production rate when producing normal product expressed in appropriate units, measured and specified as prescribed in paragraph (e)(6) of this section;

(E) Appropriate controls on operation and maintenance of the hazardous waste firing system and any air pollution control system;

(F) Allowable variation in boiler and industrial furnace system design including any air pollution control system or operating procedures; and

(G) Such other operating requirements as are necessary to ensure that the HCl and Cl2 standards under §266.107(b)(2) or (c) are met.

(6) *Measuring parameters and establishing limits based on trial burn data--*(i) *General requirements.* As specified in paragraphs (e)(2) through (e)(5) of this section, each operating parameter shall be measured, and permit limits on the parameter shall be established, according to either of the following procedures:

(A) *Instantaneous limits.* A parameter may be measured and recorded on an instantaneous basis (i.e., the value that occurs at any time) and the permit limit specified as the time-weighted average during all valid runs of the trial burn; or

(B) *Hourly rolling average.* (1) The limit for a parameter may be established and continuously monitored on an hourly rolling average basis defined as follows:

(i) A continuous monitor is one which continuously samples the regulated parameter without interruption, and evaluates the detector response at least once each 15 seconds, and computes and records the average value at least every 60 seconds.

(ii) An hourly rolling average is the arithmetic mean of the 60 most recent 1-minute average values recorded by the continuous monitoring system.

(2) The permit limit for the parameter shall be established based on trial burn

data as the average over all valid test runs of the highest hourly rolling average value for each run.

(ii) *Rolling average limits for carcinogenic metals and lead.* Feedrate limits for the carcinogenic metals (i.e., arsenic, beryllium, cadmium and chromium) and lead may be established either on an hourly rolling average basis as prescribed by paragraph (e)(6)(i) of this section or on (up to) a 24 hour rolling average basis. If the owner or operator elects to use an average period from 2 to 24 hours:

(A) The feed rate of each metal shall be limited at any time to ten times the feed rate that would be allowed on an hourly rolling average basis;

(B) The continuous monitor shall meet the following specifications:

(1) A continuous monitor is one which continuously samples the regulated parameter without interruption, and evaluates the detector response at least once each 15 seconds, and computes and records the average value at least every 60 seconds.

(2) The rolling average for the selected averaging period is defined as the arithmetic mean of one hour block averages for the averaging period. A one hour block average is the arithmetic mean of the one minute averages recorded during the 60-minute period beginning at one minute after the beginning of preceding clock hour; and

(C) The permit limit for the feed rate of each metal shall be established based on trial burn data as the average over all valid test runs of the highest hourly rolling average feed rate for each run.

(iii) *Feed rate limits for metals, total chloride and chlorine, and ash.* Feed rate limits for metals, total chlorine and chloride, and ash are established and monitored by knowing the concentration of the substance (i.e., metals, chloride/chlorine, and ash) in each feedstream and the flow rate of the feedstream. To monitor the feed rate of these substances, the flow rate of each feedstream must be monitored under the continuous monitoring requirements of paragraphs (e)(6)(i) and (ii) of this section.

(iv) *Conduct of trial burn testing.* (A) If compliance with all applicable emissions standards of §§266.104 through 266.107 is not demonstrated simultaneously during a set of test runs, the operating conditions of additional test runs required to demonstrate compliance with remaining emissions standards must be as close as possible to the original operating conditions.

(B) Prior to obtaining test data for purposes of demonstrating compliance with the emissions standards of §§266.104 through 266.107 or establishing limits on operating parameters under this section, the facility must operate under trial burn conditions for a sufficient period to reach steady-state operations. The Director may determine, however, that industrial furnaces that recycle collected particulate matter back into the furnace and that comply with an alternative implementation approach for metals under §266.106(f) need not reach steady state conditions with respect to the flow of metals in the system prior to beginning compliance testing for metals emissions.

(C) Trial burn data on the level of an operating parameter for which a limit must be established in the permit must be obtained during emissions sampling for the pollutant(s) (i.e., metals, PM, HCl/Cl2, organic compounds) for which the parameter must be established as specified by paragraph (e) of this section.

(7) *General requirements*--(i) Fugitive emissions. Fugitive emissions must be controlled by:

(A) Keeping the combustion zone totally sealed against fugitive emissions; or

(B) Maintaining the combustion zone pressure lower than atmospheric pressure; or

(C) An alternate means of control demonstrated (with part B of the permit application) to provide fugitive emissions control equivalent to maintenance of combustion zone pressure lower than atmospheric pressure.

(ii) *Automatic waste feed cutoff.* A boiler or industrial furnace must be operated with a functioning system that automatically cuts off the hazardous waste feed when operating conditions deviate from those established under this section. The Director may limit the number of cutoffs per an operating period on a case-by-case basis. In addition:

(A) The permit limit for (the indicator of) minimum combustion chamber temperature must be maintained while hazardous waste or hazardous waste residues remain in the combustion chamber,

(B) Exhaust gases must be ducted to the air pollution control system operated in accordance with the permit requirements while hazardous waste or hazardous waste residues remain in the combustion chamber; and

(C) Operating parameters for which permit limits are established must continue to be monitored during the cutoff, and the hazardous waste feed shall not be restarted until the levels of those parameters comply with the permit limits. For parameters that may be monitored on an instantaneous basis, the Director will establish a minimum period of time after a waste feed cutoff during which the parameter must not exceed the permit limit before the hazardous waste feed may be restarted.

(iii) *Changes.* A boiler or industrial furnace must cease burning hazardous waste when changes in combustion properties, or feed rates of the hazardous waste, other fuels, or industrial furnace feedstocks, or changes in the boiler or industrial furnace design or operating conditions deviate from the limits as specified in the permit.

(8) *Monitoring and Inspections.* (i) The owner or operator must monitor and record the following, at a minimum, while burning hazardous waste:

(A) If specified by the permit, feed rates and composition of hazardous waste, other fuels, and industrial furnace feedstocks, and feed rates of ash, metals, and total chloride and chlorine;

(B) If specified by the permit, carbon monoxide(CO), hydrocarbons(HC), and oxygen on a continuous basis at a common point in the boiler or industrial furnace downstream of the combustion zone and prior to release of stack gases to the atmosphere in accordance with operating requirements specified in paragraph (e)(2)(ii) of this section. CO, HC, and oxygen monitors must be installed, operated, and maintained in accordance with methods specified in appendix IX of this part.

(C) Upon the request of the Director, sampling and analysis of the hazardous waste (and other fuels and industrial furnace feedstocks as appropriate), residues, and exhaust emissions must be conducted to verify that the operating requirements established in the permit achieve the applicable standards of §§266.104, 266.105, 266.106, and 266.107.

(ii) All monitors shall record data in

units corresponding to the permit limit unless otherwise specified in the permit.

(iii) The boiler or industrial furnace and associated equipment (pumps, values, pipes, fuel storage tanks, etc.) must be subjected to thorough visual inspection when it contains hazardous waste, at least daily for leaks, spills, fugitive emissions, and signs of tampering.

(iv) The automatic hazardous waste feed cutoff system and associated alarms must be tested at least once every 7 days when hazardous waste is burned to verify operability, unless the applicant demonstrates to the Director that weekly inspections will unduly restrict or upset operations and that less frequent inspections will be adequate. At a minimum, operational testing must be conducted at least once every 30 days.

(v) These monitoring and inspection data must be recorded and the records must be placed in the operating record required by §264.73 of this chapter.

(9) *Direct transfer to the burner.* If hazardous waste is directly transferred from a transport vehicle to a boiler or industrial furnace without the use of a storage unit, the owner and operator must comply with §266.111.

(10) *Recordkeeping.* The owner or operator must keep in the operating record of the facility all information and data required by this section until closure of the facility.

(11) *Closure.* At closure, the owner or operator must remove all hazardous waste and hazardous waste residues (including, but not limited to, ash, scrubber waters, and scrubber sludges) from the boiler or industrial furnace. (Approved by the Office of Management and Budget under control number 2050-0073)

§ 266.103 Interim status standards for burners.

(a) *Purpose, scope, applicability.*--(1) General. (i) The purpose of this section is to establish minimum national standards for owners and operators of "existing" boilers and industrial furnaces that burn hazardous waste where such standards define the acceptable management of hazardous waste during the period of interim status. The standards of this section apply to owners and operators of existing facilities until

either a permit is issued under §266.102(d) or until closure responsibilities identified in this section are fulfilled.

(ii) *Existing or in existence* means a boiler or industrial furnace that on or before August 21, 1991 is either in operation burning or processing hazardous waste or for which construction (including the ancillary facilities to burn or to process the hazardous waste) has commenced. A facility has commenced construction if the owner or operator has obtained the Federal, State, and local approvals or permits necessary to begin physical construction; and either:

(A) A continuous on-site, physical construction program has begun; or

(B) The owner or operator has entered into contractual obligations--which cannot be canceled or modified without substantial loss-- for physical construction of the facility to be completed within a reasonable time.

(iii) If a boiler or industrial furnace is located at a facility that already has a permit or interim status, then the facility must comply with the applicable regulations dealing with permit modifications in §270.42 or changes in interim status in §270.72 of this chapter.

(2) *Exemptions.* The requirements of this section do not apply to hazardous waste and facilities exempt under §§266.100(b), or 266.108.

(3) *Prohibition on burning dioxin-listed wastes.* The following hazardous waste listed for dioxin and hazardous waste derived from any of these wastes may not be burned in a boiler or industrial furnace operating under interim status: F020, F021, F022, F023, F026, and F027.

(4) *Applicability of part 265 standards.* Owners and operators of boilers and industrial furnaces that burn hazardous waste and are operating under interim status are subject to the following provisions of part 265 of this chapter, except as provided otherwise by this section:

(i) In subpart A (General), §265.4;

(ii) In subpart B (General facility standards), §§265.11-265.17;

(iii) In subpart C (Preparedness and prevention), §§265.31-265.37;

(iv) In subpart D (Contingency plan and emergency procedures), §§265.51-265.56;

(v) In subpart E (Manifest system, recordkeeping, and reporting), §§265.71-265.77,

except that §§265.71, 265.72, and 265.76 do not apply to owners and operators of on-site facilities that do not receive any hazardous waste from off-site sources;

(vi) In subpart G (Closure and post-closure), §§265.111-265.115;

(vii) In subpart H (Financial requirements), §§265.141, 265.142, 265.143, and 265.147-265.151, except that States and the Federal government are exempt from the requirements of subpart H; and

(viii) Subpart BB (Air emission standards for equipment leaks),except §265.1050(a).

(5) *Special requirements for furnaces.* The following controls apply during interim status to industrial furnaces (e.g., kilns, cupolas) that feed hazardous waste for a purpose other than solely as an ingredient (see paragraph (a)(5)(ii) of this section) at any location other than the hot end where products are normally discharged or where fuels are normally fired:

(i) *Controls.* (A) The hazardous waste shall be fed at a location where combustion gas temperatures are at least 1800 °F;

(B) The owner or operator must determine that adequate oxygen is present in combustion gases to combust organic constituents in the waste and retain documentation of such determination in the facility record;

(C) For cement kiln systems, hazardous waste shall be fed into the kiln; and

(D) The hydrocarbon controls of §266.104(c) or paragraph (c)(5) of this section apply upon certification of compliance under paragraph (c) of this section irrespective of the CO level achieved during the compliance test.

(ii) *Burning hazardous waste solely as an ingredient.* A hazardous waste is burned for a purpose other than solely as an ingredient if it meets either of these criteria:

(A) The hazardous waste has a total concentration of nonmetal compounds listed in Part 261, appendix VIII, of this chapter exceeding 500 ppm by weight, as-fired, and so is considered to be burned for destruction. The concentration of nonmetal compounds in a waste as-generated may be reduced to the 500 ppm limit by *bona fide* treatment that removes or destroys nonmetal constituents. Blending for dilution to meet the 500 ppm limit is prohibited and documentation that the waste has not been impermissibly diluted must be retained in the facility record; or

(B) The hazardous waste has a heating value of 5,000 Btu/lb or more, as-fired, and so is considered to be burned as fuel . The heating value of a waste as-generated may be reduced to below the 5,000 Btu/lb limit by *bona fide* treatment that removes or destroys organic constituents. Blending to augment the heating value to meet the 5,000 Btu/lb limit is prohibited and documentation that the waste has not been impermissibly blended must be retained in the facility record.

(6) *Restrictions on burning hazardous waste that is not a fuel.* Prior to certification of compliance under paragraph (c) of this section, owners and operators shall not feed hazardous waste that has a heating value less than 5,000 Btu/lb, as-generated, (except that the heating value of a waste as-generated may be increased to above the 5,000 Btu/lb limit by *bona fide* treatment; however, blending to augment the heating value to meet the 5,000 Btu/lb limit is prohibited and records must be kept to document that impermissible blending has not occurred) in a boiler or industrial furnace, except that:

(i) Hazardous waste may be burned solely as an ingredient; or

(ii) Hazardous waste may be burned for purposes of compliance testing (or testing prior to compliance testing) for a total period of time not to exceed 720 hours; or

(iii) Such waste may be burned if the Director has documentation to show that, prior to August 21, 1991:

(A) The boiler or industrial furnace is operating under the interim status standards for incinerators provided by subpart O of Part 265 of this chapter, or the interim status standards for thermal treatment units provided by subpart P of Part 265 of this chapter; and

(B) The boiler or industrial furnace met the interim status eligibility requirements under §270.70 of this chapter for subpart O or subpart P of Part 265 of this chapter; and

(C) Hazardous waste with a heating value less than 5,000 Btu/lb was burned prior to that date; or

(iv) Such waste may be burned in a halogen acid furnace if the waste was burned as an excluded ingredient under §261.2(e) of this chapter prior to February 21, 1991 and documentation is kept on file supporting this claim.

(7) *Direct transfer to the burner.* If hazardous waste is directly transferred from a transport vehicle to a boiler or industrial furnace without the use of a storage unit, the owner and operator must comply with §266.111.

(b) *Certification of precompliance--*(1) *General.* The owner or operator must provide complete and accurate information specified in paragraph (b)(2) of this section to the Director on or before August 21, 1991, and must establish limits for the operating parameters specified in paragraph (b)(3) of this section. Such information is termed a "certification of precompliance" and constitutes a certification that the owner or operator has determined that, when the facility is operated within the limits specified in paragraph (b)(3) of this section, the owner or operator believes that, using best engineering judgment, emissions of particulate matter, metals, and HCl and Cl2 are not likely to exceed the limits provided by §§266.105, 266.106, and 266.107. The facility may burn hazardous waste only under the operating conditions that the owner or operator establishes under paragraph (b)(3) of this section until the owner or operator submits a revised certification of precompliance under paragraph (b)(8) of this section or a certification of compliance under paragraph (c) of this section, or until a permit is issued.

(2) *Information required.* The following information must be submitted with the certification of precompliance to support the determination that the limits established for the operating parameters identified in paragraph (b)(3) of this section are not likely to result in an exceedance of the allowable emission rates for particulate matter, metals, and HCl and Cl2:

(i) General facility information:

(A) EPA facility ID number;

(B) Facility name, contact person, telephone number, and address;

(C) Description of boilers and industrial furnaces burning hazardous waste, including type and capacity of device;

(D) A scaled plot plan showing the entire facility and location of the boilers and industrial furnaces burning hazardous waste; and

(E) A description of the air pollution control system on each device burning hazardous waste, including the temperature of the flue gas at the inlet to the particulate matter control system.

(ii) Except for facilities complying with the Tier I feed rate screening limits for metals or total chlorine and chloride provided by §§266.106(b) or (e) and 266.107(b)(1) or (e) respectively, the estimated uncontrolled (at the inlet to the air pollution control system) emissions of particulate matter, each metal controlled by §266.106, and hydrogen chloride and chlorine, and the following information to support such determinations:

(A) The feed rate (lb/hr) of ash, chlorine, antimony, arsenic, barium, beryllium, cadmium, chromium, lead, mercury, silver, and thallium in each feedstream (hazardous waste, other fuels, industrial furnace feedstocks);

(B) The estimated partitioning factor to the combustion gas for the materials identified in paragraph (b)(2)(ii)(A) of this section and the basis for the estimate and an estimate of the partitioning to HCl and Cl2 of total chloride and chlorine in feed materials. To estimate the partitioning factor, the owner or operator must use either best engineering judgment or the procedures specified in appendix IX of this part.

(C) For industrial furnaces that recycle collected particulate matter (PM) back into the furnace and that will certify compliance with the metals emissions standards under paragraph (c)(3)(ii)(A), the estimated enrichment factor for each metal. To estimate the enrichment factor, the owner or operator must use either best engineering judgment or the procedures specified in "Alternative Methodology for Implementing Metals Controls" in appendix IX of this part.

(D) If best engineering judgment is used to estimate partitioning factors or enrichment factors under paragraphs (b)(2)(ii)(B) or (b)(2)(ii)(C) respectively, the basis for the judgment. When best engineering judgment issued to develop or evaluate data or information and make determinations under this section, the determinations must be made by a qualified, registered professional engineer and a certification of his/her determinations in accordance with §270.11(d) of this chapter must be provided in the certification of precompliance.

(iii) For facilities complying with the Tier I feed rate screening limits for metals or total chlorine and chloride provided by §266.106(b) or(e) and §266.107(b)(1) or (e), the feed rate (lb/hr) of total chloride and chlorine, antimony, arsenic, barium, beryllium, cadmium, chromium, lead, mercury, silver, and thallium in each feedstream (hazardous waste, other fuels, industrial furnace feed stocks).

(iv) For facilities complying with the Tier II or Tier III emission limits for metals or HCl and Cl2 (under §§266.106(c) or (d) or 266.107(b)(2)or (c)), the estimated controlled (outlet of the air pollution control system) emissions rates of particulate matter, each metal controlled by §266.106, and HCl and Cl2, and the following information to support such determinations:

(A) The estimated air pollution control system (APCS) removal efficiency for particulate matter, HCl, Cl2, antimony, arsenic, barium, beryllium, cadmium, chromium, lead, mercury, silver, and thallium.

(B) To estimate APCS removal efficiency, the owner or operator must use either best engineering judgment or the procedures prescribed in appendix IX of this part.

(C) If best engineering judgment is used to estimate APCS removal efficiency, the basis for the judgment. Use of best engineering judgment must be in conformance with provisions of paragraph (b)(2)(ii)(D) of this section.

(v) Determination of allowable emissions rates for HCl, Cl2, antimony, arsenic, barium, beryllium, cadmium, chromium, lead, mercury, silver, and thallium, and the following information to support such determinations:

(A) For all facilities:

(1) Physical stack height;

(2) Good engineering practice stack height as defined by 40 CFR 51.100(ii);

(3) Maximum flue gas flow rate;

(4) Maximum flue gas temperature;

(5) Attach a US Geological Service topographic map (or equivalent) showing the facility location and surrounding land within 5 km of the facility;

(6) Identify terrain type: complex or noncomplex; and

(7) Identify land use: urban or rural.

(B) For owners and operators using Tier III site specific dispersion modeling to determine allowable levels under §§266.106(d) or 266.107(c), or adjusted Tier I feed rate screening limits under §§266.106(e) or 266.107(e):

(1) Dispersion model and version used;

(2) Source of meterological data;

(3) The dilution factor in micrograms per cubic meter per gram per second of emissions for the maximum annual average off-site (unless on-site is required) ground level concentration (MEI location); and

(4) Indicate the MEI location on the map required under paragraph (b)(2)(v)(A)(5);

(vi) For facilities complying with the Tier II or III emissions rate controls for metals or HCl and Cl2, a comparison of the estimated controlled emissions rates determined under paragraph (b)(2)(iv) with the allowable emission rates determined under paragraph (b)(2)(v);

(vii) For facilities complying with the Tier I (or adjusted Tier I) feed rate screening limits for metals or total chloride and chlorine, a comparison of actual feed rates of each metal and total chlorine and chloride determined under paragraph (b)(2)(iii) of this section to the Tier I allowable feed rates; and

(viii) For industrial furnaces that feed hazardous waste for any purpose other than solely as an ingredient (as defined by paragraph (a)(5)(ii) of this section) at any location other than the product discharge end of the device, documentation of compliance with the requirements of paragraphs (a)(5)(i) (A), (B), and (C) of this section.

(ix) For industrial furnaces that recycle collected particulate matter (PM) back into the furnace and that will certify compliance with the metals emissions standards under paragraph (c)(3)(ii)(A) of this section:

(A) The applicable particulate matter standard in lb/hr; and

(B) The precompliance limit on the concentration of each metal in collected PM.

(3) Limits on operating conditions. The owner and operator shall establish limits on the following parameters consistent with the determinations made under paragraph (b)(2) of this section and certify (under provisions of paragraph (b)(9) of this section) to the Director that the facility will operate within the limits during interim status when there is hazardous waste in the unit until revised certification of precompliance under paragraph (b)(8) of this section or certification of compliance under paragraph (c) of this section:

(i) Feed rate of total hazardous waste and (unless complying with the Tier I or adjusted Tier I metals feed rate screening limits under §266.106(b) or (e)) pumpable hazardous waste;

(ii) Feed rate of each metal in the following feed streams:

(A) Total feed streams, except that industrial furnaces that comply with the alternative metals implementation approach under paragraph (b)(4) of this section must specify limits on the concentration of each metal in collected particulate matter in lieu of feed rate limits for total feedstreams;

(B) Total hazardous waste feed; and

(C) Total pumpable hazardous waste feed, unless complying with the Tier I or adjusted Tier I metals feed rate screening limits under §266.106(b) or (e);

(iii) Total feed rate of chlorine and chloride in total feed streams;

(iv) Total feed rate of ash in total feed streams, except that the ash feed rate for cement kilns and light-weight aggregate kilns is not limited; and

(v) Maximum production rate of the device in appropriate units when producing normal product.

(4) Operating requirements for furnaces that recycle PM. Owners and operators of furnaces that recycle collected particulate matter (PM) back into the furnace and that will certify compliance with the metals emissions controls under paragraph (c)(3)(ii)(A) of this section must comply with the special operating requirements provided in "Alternative Methodology for Implementing Metals Controls" in appendix IX of this part.

(5) Measurement of feed rates and production rate--(i) General requirements. Limits on each of the parameters specified in paragraph (b)(3) of this section (except for limits on metals concentrations in collected particulate matter (PM) for industrial furnaces that recycle collected PM) shall be established and continuously monitored under either of the following methods:

(A) Instantaneous limits. A limit for a parameter may be established and continuously monitored and recorded on an instantaneous basis (i.e., the value that occurs at any time) not to be exceeded at any time; or

(B) Hourly rolling average limits. A limit for a parameter may be established and continuously monitored on an hourly rolling average basis defined as follows:

(1) A continuous monitor is one which continuously samples the regulated parameter without interruption, and evaluates the detector response at least once each 15 seconds, and computes and records the average value at least every 60 seconds.

(2) An hourly rolling average is the

arithmetic mean of the 60 most recent 1-minute average values recorded by the continuous monitoring system.

(ii) *Rolling average limits for carcinogenic metals and lead.* Feed rate limits for the carcinogenic metals (arsenic, beryllium, cadmium, and chromium) and lead may be established either on an hourly rolling average basis as prescribed by paragraph (b)(5)(i)(B) or on (up to) a 24 hour rolling average basis. If the owner or operator elects to use an averaging period from 2 to 24 hours:

(A) The feed rate of each metal shall be limited at any time to ten times the feed rate that would be allowed on a hourly rolling average basis;

(B) The continuous monitor shall meet the following specifications:

(1) A continuous monitor is one which continuously samples the regulated parameter without interruption, and evaluates the detector response at least once each 15 seconds, and computes and records the average value at least every 60 seconds.

(2) The rolling average for the selected averaging period is defined as the arithmetic mean of one hour block averages for the averaging period. A one hour block average is the arithmetic mean of the one minute averages recorded during the 60-minute period beginning at one minute after the beginning of preceding clock hour.

(iii) *Feed rate limits for metals, total chloride and chlorine, and ash.* Feed rate limits for metals, total chloride and chlorine, and ash are established and monitored by knowing the concentration of the substance (i.e., metals, chloride/chlorine, and ash) in each feedstream and the flow rate of the feedstream. To monitor the feed rate of these substances, the flow rate of each feedstream must be monitored under the continuous monitoring requirements of paragraphs (b)(5)(i) and (ii) of this section.

(6) *Public notice requirements at precompliance.* On or before August 21, 1991 the owner or operator must submit a notice with the following information for publication in a major local newspaper of general circulation and send a copy of the notice to the appropriate units of State and local government. The owner and operator must provide to the Director with the certification of precompliance evidence of submitting the notice for publication. The notice,

which shall be entitled "Notice of Certification of Precompliance with Hazardous Waste Burning Requirements of 40 CFR 266.103(b)", must include:

(i) Name and address of the owner and operator of the facility as well as the location of the device burning hazardous waste ;

(ii) Date that the certification of precompliance is submitted to the Director;

(iii) Brief description of the regulatory process required to comply with the interim status requirements of this section including required emissions testing to demonstrate conformance with emissions standards for organic compounds, particulate matter, metals, and HCl and Cl2;

(iv) Types and quantities of hazardous waste burned including, but not limited to, source, whether solids or liquids, as well as an appropriate description of the waste;

(v) Type of device(s) in which the hazardous waste is burned including a physical description and maximum production rate of each device;

(vi) Types and quantities of other fuels and industrial furnace feedstocks fed to each unit;

(vii) Brief description of the basis for this certification of precompliance as specified in paragraph (b)(2) of this section;

(viii) Locations where the record for the facility can be viewed and copied by interested parties. These records and locations shall at a minimum include:

(A) The administrative record kept by the Agency office where the supporting documentation was submitted or another location designated by the Director; and

(B) The BIF correspondence file kept at the facility site where the device is located. The correspondence file must include all correspondence between the facility and the Director, state and local regulatory officials, including copies of all certifications and notifications, such as the precompliance certification, precompliance public notice, notice of compliance testing, compliance test report, compliance certification, time extension requests and approvals or denials, enforcement notifications of violations, and copies of EPA and State site visit reports submitted to the owner or operator.

(ix) Notification of the establishment of a facility mailing list whereby interested parties shall notify the Agency that they wish to be pla-

ced on the mailing list to receive future information and notices about this facility; and

(x) Location (mailing address) of the applicable EPA Regional Office, Hazardous Waste Division, where further information can be obtained on EPA regulation of hazardous waste burning.

(7) *Monitoring other operating parameters.* When the monitoring systems for the operating parameters listed in paragraphs (c)(1) (v through xiii) of this section are installed and operating in conformance with vendor specifications or (for CO, HC, and oxygen) specifications provided by appendix IX of this part, as appropriate, the parameters shall be continuously monitored and records shall be maintained in the operating record.

(8) *Revised certification of precompliance.* The owner or operator may revise at any time the information and operating conditions documented under paragraphs (b)(2) and (b)(3) of this section in the certification of precompliance by submitting a revised certification of precompliance under procedures provided by those paragraphs.

(i) The public notice requirements of paragraph (b)(6) of this section do not apply to recertifications.

(ii) The owner and operator must operate the facility within the limits established for the operating parameters under paragraph (b)(3) of this section until a revised certification is submitted under this paragraph or a certification of compliance is submitted under paragraph (c) of this section.

(9) *Certification of precompliance statement.* The owner or operator must include the following signed statement with the certification of precompliance submitted to the Director:

"I certify under penalty of law that this information was prepared under my direction or supervision in accordance with a system designed to ensure that qualified personnel properly gathered and evaluated the information and supporting documentation. Copies of all emissions tests, dispersion modeling results and other information used to determine conformance with the requirements of §266.103(b) are available at the facility and can be obtained from the facility contact person listed above. Based on my inquiry of the person or persons who manages the facility, or those persons directly responsible for gathering the information, the information submitted is, to the best of my knowledge and belief, true, accurate, and complete. I am aware that there are significant penalties for submitting false information, including the possibility of fine and imprisonment for knowing violations.

I also acknowledge that the operating limits established in this certification pursuant to §266.103(b)(3) and (4) are enforceable limits at which the facility can legally operate during interim status until: (1) A revised certification of precompliance is submitted, (2) a certification of compliance is submitted, or (3) an operating permit is issued."

(c) *Certification of compliance.* The owner or operator shall conduct emissions testing to document compliance with the emissions standards of §§266.104(b) through (e), 266.105, 266.106, 266.107, and paragraph (a)(5)(i)(D) of this section, under the procedures prescribed by this paragraph, except under extensions of time provided by paragraph (c)(7). Based on the compliance test, the owner or operator shall submit to the Director on or before August 21, 1992 a complete and accurate "certification of compliance" (under paragraph (c)(4) of this section) with those emission standards establishing limits on the operating parameters specified in paragraph (c)(1).

(1) *Limits on operating conditions.* The owner or operator shall establish limits on the following parameters based on operations during the compliance test (under procedures prescribed in paragraph (c)(4)(iv) of this section) and include these limits with the certification of compliance. The boiler or industrial furnace must be operated in accordance with these operating limits and the applicable emissions standards of §§266.104(b) through(e), 266.105, 266.106, 266.107, and 266.103(a)(5)(i)(D) at all times when there is hazardous waste in the unit.

(i)   Feed rate of total hazardous waste and (unless complying the Tier I or adjusted Tier I metals feed rate screening limits under §266.106(b) or (e)), pumpable hazardous waste;

(ii) Feed rate of each metal in the following feedstreams:

(A) Total feedstreams, except that industrial furnaces that must comply with the alternative metals implementation approach under paragraph (c)(3)(ii) of this section must specify limits on the concentration of each metal in collected particulate matter in lieu of feed rate limits for total feedstreams;

(B) Total hazardous waste feed (unless complying with the Tier I or adjusted Tier I metals feed rate screening limits under §266.106(b) or (e)); and

(C) Total pumpable hazardous waste feed:

(iii) Total feed rate of chlorine and chloride in total feed streams;

(iv) Total feed rate of ash in total feedstreams, except that the ash feed rate for cement kilns and light-weight aggregate kilns is not limited;

(v) Carbon monoxide concentration, and where required, hydrocarbon concentration in stack gas. When complying with the CO controls of §266.104(b), the CO limit is 100 ppmv, and when complying with the HC controls of §266.104(c), the HC limit is 20 ppmv. When complying with the CO controls of §266.104(c), the CO limit Is established based on the compliance test;

(vi) Maximum production rate of the device in appropriate units when producing normal product;

(vii) Maximum combustion chamber temperature where the temperature measurement is as close to the combustion zone as possible and is upstream of any quench water injection, (unless complying with Tier I adjusted Tier I metals feed rate screening limits under §266.106(b) or (e));

(viii) Maximum flue gas temperature entering a particulate matter control device (unless complying with Tier I or adjusted Tier I metals feed rate screening limits under §266.106(b) or (e));

(ix) For systems using wet scrubbers, including wet ionizing scrubbers (unless complying with the Tier I or adjusted Tier I metals feed rate screening limits under §266.106(b) or (e) and the total chlorine and chloride feed rate screening limits under §266.107(b)(1) or (e));

(A) Minimum liquid to flue gas ratio;

(B) Minimum scrubber blowdown from the system or maximum suspended solids content of scrubber water; and

(C) Minimum pH level of the scrubber water;

(x) For systems using venturi scrubbers, the minimum differential gas pressure across the venturi (unless complying the Tier I or adjusted Tier I metals feed rate screening limits under §266.106(b) or (e) and the total chlorine and chloride feed rate screening limits under §266.107(b) (1) or (e));

(xi) For systems using dry scrubbers (unless complying with the Tier I or adjusted Tier I metals feed rate screening limits under §266.106(b) or (e) and the total chlorine and chloride feed rate screening limits under §266.107(b)(1) or (e));

(A) Minimum caustic feed rate; and

(B) Maximum flue gas flow rate;

(xii) For systems using wet ionizing scrubbers or electrostatic precipitators (unless complying with the Tier I or adjusted Tier I metals feed rate screening limits under §266.106(b) or (e) and the total chlorine and chloride feed rate screening limits under §266.107(b)(1) or (e)).

(A) Minimum electrical power in kilovolt amperes [kVA] to the precipitator plates; and

(B) Maximum flue gas flow rate;

(xiii) For systems using fabric filters (baghouses), the minimum pressure drop (unless complying with the Tier I or adjusted Tier I metals feed rate screening limits under §266.106(b) or (e) and the total chlorine and chloride feed rate screening limits under §266.107(b)(1) or (e)).

(2) *Prior notice of compliance testing.* At least 30 days prior to the compliance testing required by paragraph (c)(3) of this section, the owner or operator shall notify the Director and submit the following information:

(i)   General facility information including;

(A) EPA facility ID number;

(B) Facility name, contact person, telephone number, and address;

(C) Person responsible for conducting compliance test, including company name, address, and telephone number, and a statement of qualifications;

(D) Planned date of the compliance test;

(ii) Specific information on each device to be tested including:

(A) Description of boiler or industrial furnace;

(B) A scaled plot plan showing the entire facility and location of the boiler or industrial furnace;

(C) A description of the air pollution control system;

(D) Identification of the continuous emission monitors that are installed, including;

(1) Carbon monoxide monitor;

(2) Oxygen monitor;

(3) Hydrocarbon monitor, specifying the minimum temperature of the system and, if the temperature is less than 150 degrees C, an explanation of why a heated system is not used (see paragraph (c)(5) of this section) and a brief description of the sample gas conditioning system;

(E) Indication of whether the stack is shared with another device that will be in operation during the compliance test;

(F) Other information useful to an understanding of the system design or operation.

(iii) Information on the testing planned, including a complete copy of the test protocol and Quality Assurance/Quality Control (QA/QC) plan, and a summary description for each test providing the following information at a minimum:

(A) Purpose of the test (e.g., demonstrate compliance with emissions of particulate matter); and

(B) Planned operating conditions, including levels for each pertinent parameter specified in paragraph (c)(1) of this section.

(3) *Compliance testing.--*(i) *General.* Compliance testing must be conducted under conditions for which the owner or operator has submitted a certification of precompliance under paragraph (b) of this section and under conditions established in the notification of compliance testing required by paragraph (c)(2) of this section. The owner or operator may seek approval on a case-by-case basis to use compliance test data from one unit in lieu of testing a similar on-site unit. To support the request, the owner or operator must provide a comparison of the hazardous waste burned and other feedstreams, and the design, operation, and maintenance of both the tested unit and the similar unit. The Director shall provide a written approval to use compliance test data in lieu of testing a similar unit if he finds that the hazardous wastes, the devices, and the operating conditions are sufficiently similar, and the data from the other compliance test is adequate to meet the requirements of §266.103(c).

(ii) *Special requirements for industrial furnaces that recycle collected PM.* Owners and operators of industrial furnaces that recycle back into the furnace particulate matter (PM) from the air pollution control system must comply with one of the following procedures for testing to determine compliance with the metal standards of §266.106(c) or (d):

(A) The special testing requirements prescribed in "Alternative Method for Implementing Metals Controls" in appendix IX of this part; or

(B) Stack emissions testing for a minimum of 6 hours each day while hazardous waste is burned during interim status. The testing must be conducted when burning normal hazardouswaste for that day at normal feed rates for that day and when the air pollution control system is operated under normal condi-

tions. During interim status, hazardous waste analysis for metals content must be sufficient for the owner or operator to determine if changes in metals content may affect the ability of the facility to meet the metals emissions standards established under §266.106(c) or (d). Under this option, operating limits (under paragraph (c)(1) of this section) must be established during compliance testing under paragraph (c)(3) of this section only on the following parameters:

(1) Feed rate of total hazardous waste;

(2) Total feed rate of chlorine and chloride in total feed streams;

(3) Total feed rate of ash in total feed streams, except that the ash feed rate for cement kilns and light-weight aggregate kilns is not limited;

(4) Carbon monoxide concentration and where required, hydrocarbon concentration in stick gas;

(5) Maximum production rate of the device in appropriate units when producing normal product; or

(C) Conduct compliance testing to determine compliance with the metals standards to establish limits on the operating parameters of paragraph (c)(1) of this section only after the kiln system has been conditioned to enable it to reach equilibrium with respect to metals fed into the system and metals emissions. During conditioning, hazardous waste and raw materials having the same metals content as will be fed during the compliance test must be fed at the feed rates that will be fed during the compliance test.

(iii) *Conduct of compliance testing.* (A) If compliance with all applicable emissions standards of §§266.104 through 266.107 is not demonstrated simultaneously during a set of test runs, the operating conditions of additional test runs required to demonstrate compliance with remaining emissions standards must be as close as possible to the original operating conditions.

(B) Prior to obtaining test data for purposes of demonstrating compliance with the applicable emissions standards of §§266.104 through 266.107 or establishing limits on operating parameters under this section, the facility must operate under compliance test conditions for a sufficient period to reach steady-state operations. Industrial furnaces that recycle collected particulate matter back into the furnace and that comply with paragraphs (c)(3)(ii)(A) or (B) of this section, however, need not reach steady state conditions with respect to the flow of metals in the system prior to beginning compliance testing for metals.

(C) Compliance test data on the level of an operating parameter for which a limit must be established in the certification of compliance

must be obtained during emissions sampling for the pollutant(s) (i.e., metals, PM< HCl/Cl$_2$, organic compounds) for which the parameter must be established as specified by paragraph (c)(1) of this section.

(4) *Certification of compliance.* Within 90 days of completing compliance testing, the owner or operator must certify to the Director compliance with the emissions standards of §§266.104(b), (c), and (e), 266.105, 266.106, 266.106, and paragraph (a)(5)(i)(D) of this section. The certification of compliance must include the following information:

(i) General facility and testing information including:

(A) EPA facility ID number;

(B) Facility name, contact person, telephone number, and address;

(C) Person responsible for conducting compliance testing including company name, address, and telephone number, and a statement of qualifications;

(D) Date(s) of each compliance test;

(E) Description of boiler or industrial furnace tested;

(F) Person responsible for quality assurance/quality control (QA/QC), title, and telephone number, and statement that procedures prescribed in the QA/QC plan submitted under §266.103(c)(2)(iii) have been followed, or a description of any changes and an explanation of why changes were necessary.

(G) Description of any changes in the unit configuration prior to or during testing that would alter any of the information submitted in the prior notice of compliance testing under paragraph (c)(2) of this section, and an explanation of why the changes were necessary; and

(H) Description of any changes in the planned test conditions prior to or during testing that alter any of the information submitted in the prior notice of compliance testing under paragraph (c)(2) of this section, and an explanation of why the changes were necessary; and

(I) The complete report on results of the emissions testing.

(ii) Specific information on each test including:

(A) Purpose(s) of test (e.g., demonstrate conformance with the emissions limits for that particulate matter, metals, HCl, Cl$_2$, and CO)

(B) Summary of test results for each run and for each test including the following information:

(1) Date of run;

(2) Duration of run;

(3) Time-weighted average and highest hourly rolling average CO level for each run and for the test;

(4) Highest hourly rolling average HC level, if HC monitoring is required for each run and for the test;

(5) If dioxin and furan testing is required under §266.104(e), time-weighted average emissions for each run and for the test of chlorinated dioxin and furan emissions, and the predicted maximum annual average ground level concentration of the toxicity equivalency factor;

(6) Time-weighted average particulate matter emissions for each run and for the test;

(7) Time-weighted average HCl and Cl_2 emissions for each run and for the test;

(8) Time-weighted average emissions for the metal subject to regulation under §266.106 for reach run and for the test; and

(9) QA/QC results.

(iii) Comparison of the actual emissions during each test with the emissions limits prescribed by §§266.104(b), (c), and (e), 266.105, 266.106, and 266.107 and established for the facility in the certification of precompliance under paragraph (b) of this section.

(iv) Determination of operating limits based on all valid runs of the compliance test for each applicable parameter listed in paragraph (c)(1) of this section using either of the following procedures:

(A) *Instantaneous limits.* A parameter may be measured and recorded on an instantaneous basis (i.e., the value that occurs at any time) and the operating limit specified as the time-weighted average during all runs of the compliance test; or

(B) *Hourly rolling average basis.* (1) The limit for a parameter may be established and continuously monitored on an hourly rolling average basis defined as follows:

(i) A continuous monitor is one which continuously samples the regulated parameter without interruption, and evaluates the detector response at least once each 15 seconds, and computes and records the average value at least every 60 seconds.

(ii) An hourly rolling average is the arithmetic mean of the 60 most recent 1-minute average values recorded by the continuous monitoring system.

(2) The operating limit for the parameter shall be established based on compliance test data as the average over all test runs of the highest hourly rolling average value for each run.

(C) *Rolling average limits for carcinogenic metals and lead.* Feed rate limits for the carcinogenic metals (i.e., arsenic, beryllium, cadmium, and chromium) and lead may be established either on an hourly rolling average basis as prescribed by paragraph (c)(4)(iv)(B) of this section or on (up to) a 24 hour rolling average basis. If the owner or operator elects to use an averaging period from 2 to 24 hours:

(1) The feed rate of each metal shall be limited at any time to ten times the fed rate that would be allowed on a hourly rolling average basis;

(2) The continuous monitor shall meet the following specifications:

(i) A continuous monitor is one which continuously samples the regulated parameter without interruption, and evaluates the detector response at least once each 15 seconds, and computes and records the average value at least every 60 seconds.

(ii) The rolling average for the selected averaging period is defined as the arithmetic mean of one hour block averages for the averages for the averaging period. A one hour block average is the arithmetic mean of the one minute averages recorded during the 60-minute period beginning at one minute after the beginning of the preceding clock hour; and

(3) The operating limit for the feed rate of each metal shall be established based on compliance test data as the average over all test runs of the highest hourly rolling feed rate for each run.

(D) *Feed rate limits for metals, total chloride, and chlorine, and ash.* Feed rate limits for metals, total chlorine and chloride, and ash are established and monitored by knowing the concentration of the substance (i.e., metals, chloride/chlorine, and ash) in each feedstream and the flow rate of the feedstream. To monitor the feed rate of these substances, the flow rate of each feedstream must be monitored under the continuous monitoring requirements of paragraphs (c)(4)(iv)(A) through (C) of this section.

(v) *Certification of compliance statement.* The following statement shall accompany the certification of compliance:

"I certify under of penalty of law that this information was prepared under my direction or supervision in accordance with a system designed to ensure that qualified personnel properly gathered and evaluated the information and supporting documentation. Copies of all emission test, dispersion modeling results and other information used to determine conformance with the requirements of §266.103(c) are available at the facility and can be obtained from the facility contact person listed above. Based on my inquiry of the person or persons who manages the facility, or those persons directly responsible for gathering the information, the information submitted is, to the best of my knowledge and belief, true, accurate, and complete. I am aware that there are significant penalties for submitting false information, including the possibility of fine and imprisonment for knowing violations.

I also acknowledge that the operating conditions established in this certification pursuant to §266.103(c)(4)(iv) are enforceable limits at which the facility can legally operate during interim status until a revised certification of compliance is submitted."

(5) *Special requirements for HC monitoring systems.* When an owner or operator is required to comply with the hydrocarbon (HC) controls provided by §§266.104(c) or paragraph (a)(5)(i)(D) of this section, a conditioned gas monitoring system may be used in conformance with specifications provided in appendix IX of this part provided that the owner or operator submits a certification of compliance without using extensions of time provided by paragraph (c)(7) of this section.

(6) *Special operating requirements for industrial furnaces that recycle collected PM.* Owners and operators of industrial furnaces that recycle back into the furnace particulate matter (PM) from the air pollution control system must:

(i) When complying with the requirements of paragraph (c)(3)(ii)(A) of this section, comply with the operating requirements prescribed in "Alternative Method to Implement the Metals Controls" in appendix IX of this part; and

(ii) When complying with the requirements of paragraph (c)(3)(ii)(B) of this section, comply with the operating requirements prescribed by that paragraph.

(7) *Extensions of time.* (i) If the owner or operator does not submit a complete certification of compliance for all of the applicable emissions standards of §§266.104, 266.105, 266.106, and 266.107 by August 21, 1992, he/she must either:

(A) Stop burning hazardous waste and begin closure activities under paragraph (1) of this section for the hazardous waste portion of the facility; or

(B) Limit hazardous waste burning only for purposes of compliance testing (and pretesting to prepare for compliance testing) a total period of 720 hours for the period of time beginning August 21, 1992, submit a notification to the Director by August 21, 1992 stating that the facility is operating under restricted interim status and intends to resume burning hazardous waste, and submit a complete certification of compliance by August 23, 1993; or

(C) Obtain a case-by-case extension of time under paragraph (c)(7)(ii) of this section.

(ii) The owner or operator may request a case-by-case extension of time to extend any time limit provided by paragraph (c) of this section if compliance with the time limit is not practicable for reasons beyond the control of the owner or operator.

(A) In granting an extension, the Director may apply conditions as the facts warrant t ensure timely compliance with the requirements of this section and that the facility operates in a manner that does not pose a hazard to human health and the environment;

(B) When an owner and operator request an extension of time to enable them to obtain a RCRA operating permit because the facility cannot meet the HC limit of §266.104(c) of this chapter:

(1) The Director shall, in considering whether to grant the extension:

(i) Determine whether the owner and operator have submitted in a timely manner a complete Part B permit application that includes information required under §270.22(b) of this chapter; and

(ii) Consider whether the owner and operator have made a good faith effort to certify compliance with all other emission controls, including the controls on dioxins and furans of §266.104(e) and the controls on PM, metals, and HCl/Cl2.

(2) If an extension is granted, the Director shall, as a condition of the extension, require the facility to operate under flue gas concentration limits on CO and HC that, based on available information, including information in the part B permit application, are baseline CO and HC levels as defined by §266.104(f)(1).

(8) *Revised certification of compliance.* The owner or operator may submit at any time a revised certification of compliance (recertification of compliance) under the following procedures:

(i) Prior to submittal of a revised certification of compliance, hazardous waste may not be burned for more than a total of 720 hours under operating conditions that exceed those established under a current certification of compliance, and such burning may be conducted only for purposes of determining whether t he facility can operate under revised conditions and continue to meet the applicable emissions standards of §§266.104, 266.105, and 266.107;

(ii) At least 30 days prior to first burning hazardous waste under operating conditions that exceed those established under a current certification of compliance, the owner or operator shall notify the Director and submit the following information:

(A) EPA facility ID number, and facility name, contact person, telephone number, and address;

(B) Operating conditions that the owner or operator is seeking to revise and description of the changes in facility design or operation that prompted the need to seek to revise the operating conditions;

(C) A determination that when operating under the revised operating conditions, the applicable emissions standards of §§266.104, 266.105, 266.106, and 266.107 are not likely to be exceeded. To document this determination, the owner or operator shall submit the applicable information required under paragraph (b)(2) of this section; and

(D) Complete emissions testing protocol for any pretesting and for a new compliance test to determine compliance with the applicable emissions standards of §§266.104, 266.105, 266.106, and 266.107 when operating under revised operating conditions. The protocol shall include a schedule of pre-testing and compliance testing. If the owner and operator revises the schedule date for the compliance test, he/she shall notify the Director in writing at least 30 days prior to the revised date of the compliance test;

(iii) Conduct a compliance test under the revised operating conditions and the protocol submitted to the Director to determine compliance with the applicable emissions standards of §§266.104, 266.105, 266.106, and 266.107; and

(iv) Submit a revised certification of compliance under paragraph (c)(4) of this section.

(d) *Period Recertifications.* The owner or operator must conduct compliance testing and submit to the Director a recertification of compliance under provisions of paragraph (c) of this section within three years from submitting the previous certification or recertification. If the owner or operator seeks to recertify compliance under new operating conditions, he/she must comply with the requirements of paragraph of (c)(8) of this section.

(e) *Noncompliance with certification schedule.* If the owner or operator does not comply with the interim status compliance schedule provided by paragraphs (b), (c), and (d) of this section, hazardous waste burning must terminate on the date that deadline is missed closure activities must begin under paragraph (1) of this section, and hazardous waste burning may not resume except under an operating permit issued under §270.66 of this chapter. For purposes of compliance with the closure provisions of paragraph (1) of this section and §§265.112(d)(2) and 265.113 of this chapter the boiler or industrial furnace has received "the known final volume of hazardous waste" on the date that the deadline is missed.

(f) *Start-up and shut-down.* Hazardous waste (except waste fed solely as an ingredient under the Tier I (or adjusted Tier 1) feed rate screening limits for metals and chloride/chlorine) must not be fed into the device during start-up and shut-down of the boiler or industrial furnace, unless the device is operating within the conditions of operating specified in the certification of compliance.

(g) *Automatic waste feed cutoff.* During the compliance test required by paragraph (c)(3) of this section, and upon certification of compliance under paragraph (c) of this section, a boiler or industrial furnace must be operated with a functioning system that automatically cuts off the hazardous waste feed when the applicable operating conditions specified in paragraphs (c)(1)(i) and (v through xiii) of this section deviate from those established in the certification of compliance. In addition:

(1) To minimize emissions of organic compounds, the minimum combustion chamber temperature (or the indicator of combustion chamber temperature) that occurred during the compliance test must be maintained while hazardous waste or hazardous waste residues remain in the combustion chamber, with the minimum temperature during the compliance test defined as either:

435

(i) If compliance with the combustion chamber temperature limit is based on a hourly rolling average, the minimum temperature during the compliance test is considered to be the average over all runs of the lowest hourly rolling average for each run; or

(ii) If compliance with the combustion chamber temperature limit is based on an instantaneous temperature measurement, the minimum temperature during the compliance test is considered to be the time-weighted average temperature during all runs of the test; and

(2) Operating parameters limited by the certification of compliance must continue to be monitored during the cutoff, and the hazardous waste feed shall not be restarted until the levels of those parameters comply with the limits established in the certification of compliance.

(h) *Fugitive emissions.* Fugitive emissions must be controlled by:

(1) Keeping the combustion zone totally sealed against fugitive emissions; or

(2) Maintaining the combustion zone pressure lower than atmospheric pressure; or

(3) An alternate means of control that the owner or operator can demonstrate provide fugitive emissions control equivalent to maintenance of combustion zone pressure lower than atmospheric pressure. Support for such demonstration shall be included in the operating record.

(i) *Changes.* A boiler or industrial furnace must cease burning hazardous waste when changes in combustion properties, or feed rates of the hazardous waste, other fuels, or changes in the boiler or industrial furnace design or operating conditions deviate from the limits specified in the certification of compliance.

(j) *Monitoring and Inspections.* (1)The owner or operator must monitor and record the following, at a minimum, while burning hazardous waste:

(i) Feed rates and composition of hazardous waste, other fuels, and industrial furnace feed stocks, and feed rates of ash, metals, and total chloride and chlorine as necessary to ensure conformance with the certification of precompliance or certification of noncompliance;

(ii) Carbon monoxide (CO), oxygen, and if applicable, hydrocarbons (HC), on a continuous basis at a common point in the boiler or industrial furnace downstream of the combustion zone and prior to release of stack

gases to the atmosphere in accordance with the operating limits specified in the certification of compliance. CO, HC, and oxygen monitors must be installed, operated, and maintained in accordance with methods specified in Appendix IX of this part.

(iii) Upon the request of the Director, sampling and analysis of the hazardous waste (and other fuels and industrial furnace feed stocks as appropriate) and the stack gas emissions must be conducted to verify that the operating conditions established in the certification of precompliance or certification of compliance achieve the applicable standards of §§266.104, 266.105, 266.106, and 266.107.

(2) The boiler or industrial furnace and associated equipment (pumps, valves, pipes, fuel storage tanks, etc.) must be subjected to thorough visual inspection when they contain hazardous waste, at least daily for leaks, spills, fugitive emissions, and signs of tampering.

(3) The automatic hazardous waste feed cutoff system and associated alarms must be tested at least once every 7 days when hazardous waste is burned to verify operability, unless the owner or operator can demonstrate that weekly inspections will unduly restrict or upset operations and that less frequent inspections will be adequate. Support for such demonstration shall be included in the operating record. At a minimum, operational testing must be conducted at least once every 30 days.

(4) These monitoring and inspection data must be recorded and the records must be placed in the operating log.

(k) *Recordkeeping.* The owner or operator must keep in the operating record of the facility all information and data required by this section until closure of the boiler or industrial furnace unit.

(l) *Closure.* At closure, the owner or operator must remove all hazardous waste and hazardous waste residues (including, but not limited to, as, scrubber waters, and scrubber sludges) from the boiler or industrial furnace and must comply with §§265.111-265.115 of this chapter.

(Approved by the Office of Management and Budget under control number 2050-0073.)

§ 266.104 Standards to control organic emissions.

(a) *DRE standard*--(1) *General.* Except as provided in paragraph (a)(3) of this section, a boiler or industrial furnace burning hazardous

waste must achieve a destruction and removal efficiency (DRE) of 99.99% for all organic hazardous constituents in the waste feed. To demonstrate conformance with this requirement, 99.99% DRE must be demonstrated during a trial burn for each principal organic hazardous constituent (POHC) designated (under paragraph (a)(2) of this section) in its permit for each waste feed. DRE is determined for each POHC from the following equation:

$$DRE = 1 - \frac{W_{out}}{W_{in}} \times 100$$

where:

W_{in} = Mass feed rate of one principal organic hazardous constituent (POHC) in the hazardous waste fired to the boiler or industrial furnace; and

W_{out} = Mass emission rate of the same POHC present in stack gas prior to release to the atmosphere.

(2) *Designation of POHCs.* Principal organic hazardous constituents (POHCs) are those compounds for which compliance with the DRE requirements of this section shall be demonstrated in a trial burn in conformance with procedures prescribed in §270.86 of this chapter. One or more POHCs shall be designated by the Director for each waste feed to be burned. POHCs shall be designated based on the degree of difficulty of destruction of the organic constituents in the waste and on their concentrations or mass in the waste feed considering the results of waste analyses submitted with part B of the permit application. POHCs are most likely to be selected from among those compounds listed in part 261, appendix VIII of this chapter that are also present in the normal waste feed. However, if the applicant demonstrates to the Regional Administrator's satisfaction that a compound not listed in appendix VIII or not present in the normal waste feed is a suitable indicator of compliance with the DRE requirements of this section, that compound may be designated as a POHC. Such POHCs need not be toxic or organic compounds.

(3) *Dioxin-listed waste.* A boiler or industrial furnace burning hazardous

waste containing (or derived from) EPA Hazardous Wastes Nos. F020, F021, F022, F023, F026, or F027 must achieve a destruction and removal efficiency (DRE) of 99.9999 % for each POHC designated (under paragraph (a)(2) of this section) in its permit. This performance must be demonstrated on POHCs that are more difficult to burn than tetra-, penta-, and hexachlorodibenzo-p-dioxins and dibenzofurans. DRE is determined for each POHC from the equation in paragraph (a)(1) of this section. In addition, the owner or operator of the boiler or industrial furnace must notify the Director of intent to burn EPA Hazardous Waste Nos. F020, F021, F022, F023, F026, or F027.

(4) *Automatic waiver of DRE trial burn.* Owners and operators of boilers operated under the special operating requirements provided by §266.110 are considered to be in compliance with the DRE standard of paragraph (a)(1) of this section and are exempt from the DRE trial burn.

(5) *Low risk waste.* Owners and operators of boilers or industrial furnaces that burn hazardous waste in compliance with the requirements of §266.109(a) are considered to be in compliance with the DRE standard of paragraph (a)(1) of this section and are exempt from the DRE trial burn.

(b) *Carbon monoxide standard.* (1) Except as provided in paragraph (c) of this section, the stack gas concentration of carbon monoxide (CO) from a boiler or industrial furnace burning hazardous waste cannot exceed 100 ppmv on an hourly rolling average basis (i.e., over any 60 minute period), continuously corrected to 7 percent oxygen, dry gas basis.

(2) CO and oxygen shall be continuously monitored in conformance with "Performance Specifications for Continuous Emission Monitoring of Carbon Monoxide and Oxygen for Incinerators, Boilers, and Industrial Furnaces Burning Hazardous Waste" in appendix IX of this part.

(3) Compliance with the 100 ppmv CO limit must be demonstrated during the trial burn (for new facilities or an interim status facility applying for a permit) or the compliance test (for interim status facilities). To demonstrate compliance, the highest hourly rolling average

CO level during any valid run of the trial burn or compliance test must not exceed 100 ppmv.

(c) *Alternative carbon monoxide standard.* (1) The stack gas concentration of carbon monoxide (CO) from a boiler or industrial furnace burning hazardous waste may exceed the 100 ppmv limit provided that stack gas concentrations of hydrocarbons (HC) do not exceed 20 ppmv, except as provided by paragraph (f) of this section for certain industrial furnaces.

(2) HC limits must be established under this section on an hourly rolling average basis (i.e., over any 60 minute period), reported as propane, and continuously corrected to 7 percent oxygen, dry gas basis.

(3) HC shall be continuously monitored in conformance with "Performance Specifications for Continuous Emission Monitoring of Hydrocarbons for Incinerators, Boilers, and Industrial Furnaces Burning Hazardous Waste" in appendix IX of this part. CO and oxygen shall be continuously monitored in conformance with paragraph (b)(2) of this section.

(4) The alternative CO standard is established based on CO data during the trial burn (for a new facility) and the compliance test (for an interim status facility). The alternative CO standard is the average over all valid runs of the highest hourly average CO level for each run. The CO limit is implemented on an hourly rolling average basis, and continuously corrected to 7 percent oxygen, dry gas basis.

(d) *Special requirements for furnaces.* Owners and operators of industrial furnaces (e.g., kilns, cupolas) that feed hazardous waste for a purpose other than solely as an ingredient (see §266.103(a)(5)(ii)) at any location other than the end where products are normally discharged and where fuels are normally fired must comply with the hydrocarbon limits provided by paragraphs (c) or (f) of this section irrespective of whether stack gas CO concentrations meet the 100 ppmv limit of paragraph (b) of this section.

(e) *Controls for dioxins and furans.* Owners and operators of boilers and industrial furnaces that are equipped with a dry particulate matter control device that operates within the tempera-

ture range of 450-750°F, and industrial furnaces operating under an alternative hydrocarbon limit established under paragraph (f) of this section must conduct a site-specific risk assessment as follows to demonstrate that emissions of chlorinated dibenzo-p-dioxins and dibenzofurans do not result in an increased lifetime cancer risk to the hypothetical maximum exposed individual (MEI) exceeding 1 in 100,000:

(1) During the trial burn (for new facilities or an interim status facility applying for a permit) or compliance test (for interim status facilities), determine emission rates of the tetra-octa congeners of chlorinated dibenzo-p-dioxins (PCDDs) and dibenzofurans (CDDs/CDFs) using Method 23, "Determination of Polychlorinated Dibenzo-p-Dioxins and Polychlorinated Dibenzofurans (PCDFs) from Stationary Sources", in appendix IX of this part;

(2) Estimate the 2,3,7,8-TCDD toxicity equivalence of the tetra-octa CDDs/ CDFs congeners using "Procedures for Estimating the Toxicity Equivalence of Chlorinated Dibenzo-p-Dioxin and Dibenzofuran Congeners" in appendix IX of this part. Multiply the emission rates of CDD/CDF congeners with a toxicity equivalence greater than zero (see the procedure) by the calculated toxicity equivalence factor to estimate the equivalent emission rate of 2,3,7,8-TCDD;

(3) Conduct dispersion modeling using methods recommended in Guideline on Air Quality Models (Revised) or the "Hazardous Waste Combustion Air Quality Screening Procedure", which are provided in appendices X and IX, respectively, of this part, or "EPA SCREEN Screening Procedure" as described in Screening Procedures for Estimating Air Quality Impact of Stationary Sources (incorporated by reference in §260.11) to predict the maximum annual average off-site ground level concentration of 2,3,7,8-TCDD equivalents determined under paragraph (e)(2) of this section. The maximum annual average on-site concentration must be used when a person resides on-site; and

(4) The ratio of the predicted maximum annual average ground level concentration of 2,3,7,8-TCDD equivalents to the risk-specific dose for 2,3,7,8-TCDD provided in appendix V of

this part a (2.2 X 10-7) shall not exceed 1.0.

(f) *Alternative HC limit furnaces with organic matter in raw material.* For industrial furnaces that cannot meet the 20 ppmv HC limit because of organic matter in normal raw material, the Director may establish an alternative HC limit on a case-by-case basis (under a part B permit proceeding) at a level that ensures that flue gas HC (and CO) concentrations when burning hazardous waste are not greater than when not burning hazardous waste (the baseline HC level) provided that the owner or operator complies with the following requirements. However, cement kilns equipped with a by-pass duct meeting the requirements of paragraph (g) of this section, are not eligible for an alternative HC limit.

(1) The owner or operator must demonstrate that the facility is designed and operated to minimize hydrocarbon emissions from fuels and raw materials when the baseline HC (and CO) level is determined. The baseline HC (and CO) level is defined as the average over all valid test runs of the highest hourly rolling average value for each run when the facility does not burn hazardous waste, and produces normal products under normal operating conditions feeding normal feedstocks and fuels. More than one baseline level may be determined if the facility operates under different modes that may generate significantly different HC (and CO) levels:

(2) The owner or operator must develop an approach to monitor over time changes in the operation of the facility that could reduce the baseline HC level;

(3) The owner or operator must conduct emissions testing during the trial burn to:

(i) Determine the baseline HC (and CO) level;

(ii) Demonstrate that, when hazardous waste is burned, HC (and CO) levels do not exceed the baseline level; and

(iii) Identify the types and concentrations of organic compounds listed in appendix VIII, part 261 of this chapter, that are emitted and conduct dispersion modeling to predict the maximum annual average ground level concentration of each organic compound. On-site ground level concentrations must be considered for this evaluation if a person resides on site.

(A) Sampling and analysis of organic emissions shall be conducted using procedures prescribed by the Director.

(B) Dispersion modeling shall be conducted according to procedures provided by paragraph (e)(2) of this section; and

(iv) Demonstrate that maximum annual average ground level concentrations of the organic compounds identified in paragraph (f)(3)(iii) of this section do not exceed the following levels:

(A) For the noncarcinogenic compounds listed in appendix IV of this part, the levels established in appendix IV;

(B) For the carcinogenic compounds listed in appendix V of this part, the sum for all compounds of the ratios of the actual ground level concentration to the level established in appendix V cannot exceed 1.0. To estimate the health risk from chlorinated dibenzo-p-dioxins and dibenzofurancongeners, use the procedures prescribed by paragraph (e)(3) of this section to estimate the 2,3,7,8-TCDD toxicity equivalence of the congeners.

(C) For compounds not listed in appendix IV or V, 0.1 micrograms per cubic meter.

(4) All hydrocarbon levels specified under this paragraph are to be monitored and reported as specified in paragraphs (c)(1) and (c)(2) of this section.

(g) Monitoring CO and HC in the by-pass duct of a cement kiln. Cement kilns may comply with the carbon monoxide and hydrocarbon limits provided by paragraphs (b), (c), and (d) of this section by monitoring in the by-pass duct provided that:

(1) Hazardous waste is fired only into the kiln and not at any location downstream from the kiln exit relative to the direction of gas flow; and

(2) The by-pass duct diverts a minimum of 10% of kiln off-gas into the duct.

(h) *Use of emissions test data to demonstrate compliance and establish operating limits.* Compliance with the requirements of this section must be demonstrated simultaneously by emissions testing or during separate runs under identical operating conditions. Further, data to demonstrate compliance with the CO and HC limits of this section or to establish alternative CO or HC limits under this section must be obtained during the time that DRE testing, and

where applicable, CDD/CDF testing under paragraph (e) of this section and comprehensive organic emissions testing under paragraph (f) is conducted.

(i) *Enforcement.* For the purposes of permit enforcement, compliance with the operating requirements specified in the permit (under §266.102) will be regarded as compliance with this section. However, evidence that compliance with those permit conditions is insufficient to ensure compliance with the requirements of this section may be "information" justifying modification or revocation and re-issuance of a permit under §270.41 of this chapter.

§ 266.105 Standards to control particulate matter.

(a) A boiler or industrial furnace burning hazardous waste may not emit particulate matter in excess of 180 milligrams per dry standard cubic meter (0.08 grains per dry standard cubic foot) after correction to a stack gas concentration of 7% oxygen, using procedures prescribed in 40 CFR part 60, appendix A, methods 1 through 5, and appendix IX of this part.

(b) An owner or operator meeting the requirements of §266.109(b) for the low risk waste exemption is exempt from the particulate matter standard.

(c) For the purposes of permit enforcement, compliance with the operating requirements specified in the permit (under §266.102) will be regarded as compliance with this section. However, evidence that compliance with those permit conditions is insufficient to ensure compliance with the requirements of this section may be "information" justifying modification or revocation and re-issuance of a permit under §270.41 of this chapter.

§ 266.106 Standards to control metals emissions.

(a) *General.* The owner or operator must comply with the metals standards provided by paragraphs (b), (c), (d), (e), or (f) of this section for each metal listed in paragraph (b) of this section that is present in the hazardous waste at detectable levels using analytical procedures specified in Test Methods for Evaluating Solid Waste, Physical/Chemical Methods (SW-846), incorporated by reference in §260.11 of this chapter.

(b) *Tier I feed rate screening limits.* Feed rate screening limits for metals are specified in appendix I of this part as a function of terrain-adjusted effective stack height and terrain and land use in the vicinity of the facility. Criteria for facilities that are not eligible to comply with the screening limits are provided in paragraph (b)(7) of this section.

(1) *Noncarcinogenic metals.* The feed rates of antimony, barium, lead, mercury, thallium, and silver in all feed streams, including hazardous waste, fuels, and industrial furnace feed stocks shall not exceed the screening limits specified in appendix I of this part.

(i) The feed rate screening limits for antimony, barium, mercury thallium, and silver are based on either:

(A) An hourly rolling average as defined in §266.102(e)(6)(i)(B); or

(B) An instantaneous limit not to be exceeded at any time.

(ii) The feed rate screening limit for lead is based on one of the following:

(A) An hourly rolling average as defined in §266.102(e)(6)(i)(B);

(B) An averaging period of 2 to 24 hours as defined in §266.102(e)(6)(ii) with an instantaneous feed rate limit not to exceed 10 times the feed rate that would be allowed on an hourly rolling average basis; or

(C) An instantaneous limit not to be exceeded at any time.

(2) *Carcinogenic metals.* (i) The feed rates of arsenic, cadmium, beryllium, and chromium in all feed streams, including hazardous waste, fuels, and industrial furnace feed stocks shall not exceed values derived from the screening limits specified in appendix I of this part. The feed rate of each of these metals is limited to a level such that the sum of the ratios of the actual feed rate to the feed rate screening limit specified in appendix I shall not exceed 1.0, as provided by the following equation:

$$\sum_{i=1}^{n} \frac{AFR_{(i)}}{FRSL_{(i)}} \leq 1.0$$

where:

n = number of carcinogenic metals
AFR = actual feed rate to the device for metal "i"
FRSL = feed rate screening limit provided by appendix I of this part for metal "i".

(ii) The feed rate screening limits for the carcinogenic metals are based on either:

(A) An hourly rolling average; or

(B) An averaging period of 2 to 24 hours as defined in §266.102(e)(6)(ii) with an instantaneous feed rate limit not to exceed 10 times the feed rate that would be allowed on an hourly rolling average basis.

(3) *TESH.* (i) The terrain-adjusted effective stack height is determined according to the following equation:

$$TESH = Ha + H1 - Tr$$

where:

Ha = Actual physical stack height
H1 = Plume rise as determined from appendix VI of this part as a function of stack flow rate and stack gas exhaust temperature.
Tr = Terrain rise within five kilometers of the stack.

(ii) The stack height (Ha) may not exceed good engineering practice as specified in 40 CFR 51.100(ii).

(iii) If the TESH for a particular facility is not listed in the table in the appendices, the nearest lower TESH listed in the table shall be used. If the TESH is four meters or less, a value of four meters shall be used.

(4) *Terrain type.* The screening limits are a function of whether the facility is located in noncomplex or complex terrain. A device located where any part of the surrounding terrain within 5 kilometers of the stack equals or exceeds the elevation of the physical stack height (Ha) is considered to be in complex terrain and the screening limits for complex terrain apply. Terrain measurements are to be made from U.S. Geological Survey 7.5-minute topographic maps of the area surrounding the facility.

(5) *Land use.* The screening limits are a function of whether the facility is located in an area where the land use is urban or rural. To determine whether land use in the vicinity of the facility is urban or rural, procedures provided in appendices IX or X of this part shall be used.

(6) *Multiple stacks.* Owners and operators of facilities with more than one on-site stack from a boiler, industrial furnace, incinerator, or other thermal treatment unit subject to controls of metals emissions under a RCRA operating permit or interim status controls must comply

with the screening limits for all such units assuming all hazardous waste is fed into the device with the worst-case stack based on dispersion characteristics. The worst-case stack is determined from the following equation as applied to each stack:

$$K = HVT$$

Where:

K = a parameter accounting for relative influence of stack height and plume rise;
H = physical stack height (meters);
V = stack gas flow rate (m^3/second); and
T = exhaust temperature (°K).

The stack with the lowest value of K is the worst-case stack.

(7) *Criteria for facilities not eligible for screening limits.* If any criteria below are met, the Tier I (and Tier II) screening limits do not apply. Owners and operators of such facilities must comply with the Tier III standards provided by paragraph (d) of this section.

(i) The device is located in a narrow valley less than one kilometer wide;

(ii) The device has a stack taller than 20 meters and is located such that the terrain rises to the physical height within one kilometer of the facility;

(iii) The device has a stack taller than 20 meters and is located within five kilometers of a shoreline of a large body of water such as an ocean or large lake;

(iv) The physical stack height of any stack is less than 2.5 times the height of any building within five building heights or five projected building widths of the stack and the distance from the stack to the closest boundary is within five building heights or five projected building widths of the associated building; or

(v) The Director determines that standards based on site-specific dispersion modeling are required.

(8) *Implementation.* The feed rate of metals in each feedstream must be monitored to ensure that the feed rate screening limits are not exceeded.

(c) *Tier II emission rate screening limits.* Emission rate screening limits are specified In Appendix I as a function of terrain-adjusted effective stack height and terrain and land use in the vicinity of the facility. Criteria for facilities that are not eligible to comply with the screening limits are provided in paragraph (b)(7) of this section.

(1) *Noncarcinogenic metals.* The emission rates of antimony, barium, lead, mercury, thallium, and silver shall not exceed the screening limits specified in Appendix I of this part.

(2) *Carcinogenic metals.* The emission rates of arsenic, cadmium, beryllium, and chromium shall not exceed values derived from the screening limits specified in Appendix I of this part. The emission rate of each of these metals is limited to a level such that the sum of the ratios of the actual emission rate to the emission rate screening limit specified in Appendix I shall not exceed 1.0, as provided by tile following equation:

$$\sum_{i=1}^{n} \frac{AER_{(i)}}{ERSL_{(i)}} \leq 1.0$$

where:

n = number of carcinogenic metals
AER = actual emission rate for metal "i"
ERSL = emission rate screening limit provided by appendix I of this part for metal "i".

(3) *Implementation.* The emission rate limits must be implemented by limiting feed rates of the individual metals to levels during the trial burn (for new facilities or an interim status facility applying for a permit) or the compliance test (for interim status facilities). The feed rate averaging periods are the same as provided by paragraphs (b)(1)(i) and (ii) and (b)(2)(ii) of this section. The feed rate of metals in each feedstream must be monitored to ensure that the feed rate limits for the feedstreams specified under §§266.102 or 266.103 are not exceeded.

(4) *Definitions and limitations.* The definitions and limitations provided by paragraph (b) of this section for the following terms also apply to the Tier II emission rate screening limits provided by paragraph (c) of this section: terrain-adjusted effective stack height, good engineering practice stack height, terrain type, land use, and criteria for facilities not eligible to use the screening limits.

(5) *Multiple stacks.* (i) Owners and operators of facilities with more than one onsite stack from a boiler, industrial furnace, incinerator, or other thermal treatment unit subject to controls

on metals emissions under a RCRA operating permit or interim status controls must comply with the emissions screening limits for any such stacks assuming all hazardous waste is fed Into the device with the worst-case stack based on dispersion characteristics.

(ii) The worst-case stack is determined by procedures provided in paragraph (b)(6) of this section.

(iii) For each metal, the total emissions of the metal from those stacks shall not exceed the screening limit for the worst- case stack.

(d) *Tier III site-specific risk assessment*--(1) *General.* Conformance with the Tier III metals controls must be demonstrated by emissions testing to determine the emission rate for each metal, air dispersion modeling to predict the maximum annual average off-site ground level concentration for each metal,and a demonstration that acceptable ambient levels are not exceeded.

(2) *Acceptable ambient levels.* Appendices IV and V of this part list the acceptable ambient levels for purposes of this rule. Reference air concentrations (RACs) are listed for the noncarcinogenic metals and 10^{-5} risk- specific doses (RSDs) are listed for the carcinogenic metals. The RSD for a metal is the acceptable ambient level for that metal provided that only one of the four carcinogenic metals is emitted. If more than one carcinogenic metal is emitted, the acceptable ambient level for the carcinogenic metals is a fraction of the RSD as described in paragraph (d)(3) of this section.

(3) *Carcinogenic metals.* For the carcinogenic metals, arsenic, cadmium, beryllium, and chromium, the sum of the ratios of the predicted maximum annual average off-site ground level concentrations (except that on-site concentrations must be considered if a person resides on site) to the risk-specific dose (RSD) for all carcinogenic metals emitted shall not exceed 1.0 as determined by the following equation:

$$\sum_{i=1}^{n} \frac{\text{Predicted Ambient Concentration}_{(i)}}{\text{Risk-Specific Dose}_{(i)}} \leq 1.0$$

where: n = number of carcinogenic metals

(4) *Noncarcinogenic metals.* For the noncarcinogenic metals, the predicted maximum annual average off-site ground level concentration for each metal shall not exceed the reference air concentration (RAC).

(5) *Multiple stacks.* Owners and operators of facilities with more than one on-site stack from a boiler, industrial furnace, incinerator, or other thermal treatment unit subject to controls on metals emissions under a RCRA operating permit or interim status controls must conduct emissions testing and dispersion modeling to demonstrate that the aggregate emissions from all such on-site stacks do not result in an exceedance of the acceptable ambient levels.

(6) *Implementation.* Under Tier III, the metals controls must be implemented by limiting feed rates of the individual metals to levels during the trial burn (for new facilities or an interim status facility applying for a permit) or the compliance test (for interim status facilities). The feed rate averaging periods are the same as provided by paragraphs (b)(1)(i) and (ii) and (b)(2)(ii) of this section. The feed rate of metals in each feedstream must be monitored to ensure that the feed rate limits for the feedstreams specified under §§266.102 or 266.103 are not exceeded.

(e) *Adjusted Tier I feed rate screening limits.* The owner or operator may adjust the feed rate screening limits provided by appendix I of this part to account for site-specific dispersion modeling. Under this approach, the adjusted feed rate screening limit for a metal is determined by back-calculating from the acceptable ambient level provided by appendices IV and V of this part using dispersion modeling to determine the maximum allowable emission rate. This emission rate becomes the adjusted Tier I feed rate screening limit. The feed rate screening limits for carcinogenic metals are implemented as prescribed in paragraph (b)(2) of this section.

(f) *Alternative implementation approaches.* (1) The Director may approve on a case-by-case basis approaches to implement the Tier II or Tier III metals emission limits provided by paragraphs (c) or (d) of this section alternative to monitoring the feed rate of metals in each feedstream.

(2) The emission limits provided by paragraph (d) of this section must be determined as follows:

(i) For each noncarcinogenic metal, by back-calculating from the RAC provided in appendix IV of this part to determine the allowable emission rate for each metal using the dilution factor for the maximum annual average ground level concentration predicted by dispersion modeling in conformance with paragraph (h) of this section; and

(ii) For each carcinogenic metal by:

(A) Back-calculating from the RSD provided in appendix V of this part to determine the allowable emission rate for each metal if that metal were the only carcinogenic metal emitted using the dilution factor for the maximum annual average ground level concentration predicted by dispersion modeling in conformance with paragraph (h) of this section; and

(B) If more than one carcinogenic metal is emitted, selecting an emission limit for each carcinogenic metal not to exceed the emission rate determined by paragraph (f)(2)(ii)(A) of this section such that the sum for all carcinogenic metals of the ratios of the selected emission limit to the emission rate determined by that paragraph does not exceed 1.0.

(g) *Emission testing*--(1) *General.* Emission testing for metals shall be conducted using the Multiple Metals Train as described in appendix IX of this part.

(2) *Hexavalent chromium.* Emissions of chromium are assumed to be hexavalent chromium unless the owner or operator conducts emissions testing to determine hexavalent chromium emissions using procedures prescribed in Appendix IX of this part.

(h) *Dispersion modeling.* Dispersion modeling required under this section shall be conducted according to methods recommended in appendix X of this part, the "Hazardous Waste Combustion Air Quality Screening Procedure" described in appendix IX of this part, or "EPA SCREEN Screening Procedure" as described in Screening Procedures for Estimating Air Quality Impact of Stationary Sources (the latter document is incorporated by reference, see §260.11) to predict the maximum annual aver-age off-site ground level concentration. However, on-site concentrations must be considered when a person resides on-site.

(i) *Enforcement.* For the purposes of permit enforcement, compliance with the operating requirements specified in the permit (under §266.102) will be regarded as compliance with this section. However, evidence that compliance with those permit conditions is insufficient to ensure compliance with the requirements of this section may be "information" justifying modification or revocation and re-issuance of a permit under §270.41 of this chapter.

§ 266.107 Standards to control hydrogen chloride (HCl) and chlorine gas (Cl₂) emissions.

(a) *General.* The owner or operator must comply with the hydrogen chloride (HCl) and chlorine (Cl_2) controls provided by paragraphs (b), or (c) of this section.

(b) *Screening limits*--(1) *Tier I feed rate screening limits.* Feed rate screening limits are specified for total chlorine in Appendix II of this part as a function of terrain-adjusted effective stack height and terrain and land use in the vicinity of the facility. The feed rate of total chlorine and chloride, both organic and inorganic, in all feed streams, including hazardous waste, fuels, and industrial furnace feed stocks shall not exceed the levels specified.

(2) *Tier II emission rate screening limits.* Emission rate screening limits for HCl and Cl_2 are specified in Appendix III of this part as a function of terrain-adjusted effective stack height and land use in the vicinity of the facility. The stack emission rates of HCl and Cl_2 shall not exceed the levels specified.

(3) *Definitions and limitations.* The definitions and limitations provided by §266.106(b) for the following terms also apply to the screening limits provided by this paragraph: terrain-adjusted effective stack height, good engineering practice stack height, terrain type, land use, and criteria for facilities not eligible to use the screening limits.

(4) *Multiple stacks.* Owners and operators of facilities with more than one on-site stack from a boiler, industrial furnace, incinerator, or other thermal treatment unit subject to controls on HCl or Cl_2 emissions under a RCRA operating permit or interim status controls must comply with the Tier 1 and Tier II screening limits for those stacks assuming all hazardous waste is fed into the device with the worst-case stack based on dispersion characteristics.

(i) The worst-case stack is determined by procedures provided in §266.106(b)(6).

(ii) Under Tier I, the total feed rate of chlorine and chloride to all subject devices shall not exceed the screening limit for the worst-case stack.

(iii) Under Tier II, the total emissions of HCl and Cl_2 from all subject stacks shall not exceed the screening limit for the worst-case stack.

(c) *Tier III site-specific risk assessments*--(1) *General.* Conformance with the Tier III controls must be demonstrated by emissions testing to determine the emission rate for HCl and Cl2 air dispersion modeling to predict the maximum annual average off-site ground level concentration for each compound, and a demonstration that acceptable ambient levels are not exceeded.

(2) *Acceptable ambient levels.* Appendix IV of this part lists the reference air concentrations (RACs) for HCl (7 micrograms per cubic meter) and Cl_2 (0.4 micrograms per cubic meter).

(3) *Multiple stacks.* Owners and operators of facilities with more than one on-site stack from a boiler, industrial furnace, incinerator, or other thermal treatment unit subject to controls on HCl or Cl_2 emissions under a RCRA operating permit or interim status controls must conduct emissions testing and dispersion modeling to demonstrate that the aggregate emissions from all such on-site stacks do not result in an exceedance of the acceptable ambient levels for HCl and Cl_2.

(d) *Averaging periods.* The HCl and Cl_2 controls are implemented by limiting the feed rate of total chlorine and chloride in all feedstreams, including hazardous waste, fuels, and industrial furnace feed stocks. Under Tier I, the feed rate of total chloride and chlorine is limited to the Tier I Screening Limits. Under Tier II and Tier III, the feed rate of total chloride and chlorine is limited to the feed rates during the trial burn (for new facilities or an interim status

441

facility applying for a permit) or the compliance test (for interim status facilities). The feed rate limits are based on either:

(1) An hourly rolling average as defined in §266.102(e)(6); or

(2) An instantaneous basis not to be exceeded at any time.

(e) *Adjusted Tier I feed rate screening limits.* The owner or operator may adjust the feed rate screening limit provided by Appendix II of this part to account for site-specific dispersion modeling. Under this approach, the adjusted feed rate screening limit is determined by back-calculating from the acceptable ambient level for Cl_2 provided by Appendix IV of this part using dispersion modeling to determine the maximum allowable emission rate. This emission rate becomes the adjusted Tier I feed rate screening limit.

(f) *Emissions testing.* Emissions testing for HCl and Cl_2 shall be conducted using the procedures described in Appendix IX of this part.

(g) *Dispersion modeling.* Dispersion modeling shall be conducted according to the provisions of §266.106(h).

(h) *Enforcement.* For the purposes of permit enforcement, compliance with the operating requirements specified in the permit (under §266.102) will be regarded as compliance with this section. However, evidence that compliance with those permit conditions is insufficient to ensure compliance with the requirements of this section may be "information" justifying modification or revocation and re-issuance of a permit under §270.41 of this chapter.

§266.108 Small quantity on-site burner exemption.

(a) *Exempt quantities.* Owners and operators of facilities that burn hazardous waste in an on-site boiler or industrial furnace are exempt from the requirements of this subpart provided that:

(1) The quantity of hazardous waste burned in a device for a calendar month does not exceed the limits provided in the following table based on the terrain-adjusted effective stack height as defined in §266.106(b)(3):

EXEMPT QUANTITIES FOR SMALL QUANTITY BURNER EXEMPTION

Terrain-adjusted effective stack height of device (meters)	Allowable hazardous waste burning rate (Gallons/month)	Terrain-adjusted effective stack height of device (meters)	Allowable hazardous waste burning rate (Gallons/month)
0 to 3.9........	0	40.0 to 4.9........	210
4.0 to 5.9.....	13	45.0 to 49.9......	260
6.0 to 7.9.....	18	50.0 to 54.9......	330
8.0 to 9.9.....	27	55.0 to 59.9......	400
10.0 to 11.9.	40	60.0 to 64.9........	490
12.0 to 13.9.	48	65.0 to 69.9......	610
14.0 to 15.9.	59	70.0 to 74.9......	680
16.0 to 17.9.	69	75.0 to 79.9......	760
18.0 to 19.9.	76	80.0 to 84.9.......	850
20.0 to 21.9.	84	85.0 to 89.9.......	960
22.0 to 23.9.	93	90.0 to 94.9.......	1,100
24.0 to 25.9.	100	95.0 to 99.9.....	1,200
26.0 to 27.9.	110	100.0 to 104.9..	1,300
28.0 to 29.9.	130	105.0 to 109.9..	1,500
30.0 to 34.9.	140	110.0 to 114.9...	1,700
35.0 to 39.9.	170	115.0 or greater	1,900

(2) The maximum hazardous waste firing rate does not exceed at any time 1 percent of the total fuel requirements for the device (hazardous waste plus other fuel) on a total heat input or mass input basis, whichever results in the lower mass feed rate of hazardous waste.

(3) The hazardous waste has a minimum heating value of 5,000 Btu/lb, as generated; and

(4) The hazardous waste fuel does not contain (and is not derived from) EPA Hazardous Waste Nos. F020, F021, F022, F023, F026, or F027.

(b) *Mixing with nonhazardous fuels.* If hazardous waste fuel is mixed with a nonhazardous fuel, the quantity of hazardous waste before such mixing is used to comply with paragraph (a).

(c) *Multiple stacks.* If an owner or operator burns hazardous waste in more than one on-site boiler or industrial furnace exempt under this section, the quantity limits provided by paragraph (a)(1) of this section are implemented according to the following equation:

$$\sum_{i=1}^{n} \frac{\text{Actual Quantity Burned}_{(i)}}{\text{Allowable Quantity Burned}_{(i)}} \leq 1.0$$

where:

n means the number of stacks;

Actual Quantity Burned means the waste quantity burned per month in device "i";

Allowable Quantity Burned means the maximum allowable exempt quantity for stack "i" from the table in (a)(1) above.

(d) *Notification requirements.* The owner or operator of facilities qualifying for the small quantity burner exemption under this section must provide a one-time signed, written notice to EPA indicating the following:

(1) The combustion unit is operating as a small quantity burner of hazardous waste;

(2) The owner and operator are in compliance with the requirements of this section; and

(3) The maximum quantity of hazardous waste that the facility may burn per month as provided by §266.108(a)(1).

(e) *Recordkeeping requirements.* The owner or operator must maintain at the facility for at least three years sufficient records documenting compliance with the hazardous waste quantity, firing rate, and heating value limits of this section. At a minimum, these records must indicate the quantity of hazardous waste and other fuel burned in each unit per calendar month, and the heating value of the hazardous waste.

(Approved by the Office of Management and Budget under control number 2050-0073)

§ 266.109 Low risk waste exemption.

(a) *Waiver of DRE standard.* The DRE standard of §266.104(a) does not apply if the boiler or industrial furnace is operated in conformance with (a)(1) of this section and the owner or operator demonstrates by procedures prescribed in (a)(2) of this section that the burning will not result in unacceptable adverse health effects.

(1) The device shall be operated as follows:

(i) A minimum of 50 percent of fuel fired to the device shall be fossil fuel, fuels derived from fossil fuel, tall oil, or, if approved by the Director on a case-by-case basis, other nonhazardous fuel with combustion characteristics comparable to fossil fuel. Such fuels are termed "primary fuel" for purposes of this section. (Tall oil is a fuel derived from vegetable and rosin fatty acids.) The 50 percent primary fuel firing rate shall be determined on a total heat or mass input basis, whichever results in the greater mass feed of primary fuel fired;

(ii) Primary fuels and hazardous waste fuels shall have a minimum as-fired heating value of 8,000 Btu/lb;

(iii) The hazardous waste is fired directly into the primary fuel flame zone of the combustion chamber; and

(iv) The device operates in conformance with the carbon monoxide controls provided by §266.104(b)(1) Devices subject to the exemption provided by this section are not eligible for the alternative carbon monoxide controls provided by §266.104(c).

(2) *Procedures to demonstrate that the hazardous waste burning will not pose unacceptable adverse public health effects are as follows:*

(i) Identify and quantify those nonmetal compounds listed in appendix VIII, part 261 of this chapter that could reasonably be expected to be present in the hazardous waste. The constituents excluded from analysis must be identified and the basis for their exclusion explained;

(ii) Calculate reasonable, worst case emission rates for each constituent identified in paragraph (a)(2)(i) of this section by assuming the device achieves 99.9 percent destruction and removal efficiency. That is, assume that 0.1 percent of the mass weight of each constituent fed to the device is emitted.

(iii) For each constituent identified in paragraph (a)(2)(i) of this section, use emissions dispersion modeling to predict the maximum annual average ground level concentration of the constituent.

(A) Dispersion modeling shall be conducted using methods specified in §266.106(h).

(B) Owners and operators of facilities with more than one on-site stack from a boiler or industrial furnace that is exempt under this section must conduct dispersion modeling of emissions from all stacks exempt under this section to predict ambient levels prescribed by this paragraph.

(iv) Ground level concentrations of constituents predicted under paragraph (a)(2)(iii) of this section must not exceed the following levels:

(A) For the noncarcinogenic compounds listed in appendix IV of this part, the levels established in appendix IV;

(B) For the carcinogenic compounds listed in appendix V of this part, the sum for all constituents of the ratios of the actual ground level concentration to the level established in appendix V cannot exceed 1.0; and

(C) For constituents not listed in appendix IV or V, 0.1 micrograms per cubic meter.

(b) *Waiver of particular matter standard.* The particulate matter standard of §266.105 does not apply if:

(1) The DRE standard is waived under paragraph (a) of this section; and

(2) The owner or operator complies with the Tier I or adjusted Tier I metals feed rate screening limits provided by §266.106(b) or (e).

§ 266.110 Waiver of DRE trial burn for boilers.

Boilers that operate under the special requirements of this section, and that do not burn hazardous waste containing (or derived from) EPA Hazardous Waste Nos. FO20, F021, F022, F023, F026, or F027, are considered to be in conformance with the DRE standard of §266.104(a), and a trial burn to demonstrate DRE is waived. When burning hazardous waste:

(a) A minimum of 50 percent of fuel fired to the device shall be fossil fuel, fuels derived from fossil fuel, tall oil, or, if approved by the Director on a case-by-case basis, other nonhazardous fuel with combustion characteristics comparable to fossil fuel. Such fuels are termed "primary fuel" for purposes of this section. (Tall oil is a fuel derived from vegetable and rosin fatty acids.) The 50 percent primary fuel firing rate shall be determined on a total heat or mass input basis, whichever results in the greater mass feed rate of primary fuel fired;

(b) Boiler load shall not be less than 40 percent. Boiler load is the ratio at any time of the total heat input to the maximum design heat input;

(c) Primary fuels and hazardous waste fuels shall have a minimum as-fired heating value of 8,000 Btu/lb, and each material fired in a burner where hazardous waste is fired must have a heating value of at least 8,000 Btu/lb, as-fired;

(d) The device shall operate in conformance with the carbon monoxide standard provided by §266.104(b)(1). Boilers subject to the waiver of the DRE trial burn provided by this section are not eligible for the alternative carbon monoxide standard provided by §266.104 (c);

(e) The boiler must be a watertube type boiler that does not feed fuel using a stoker or stoker type mechanism; and

(f) The hazardous waste shall be fired directly into the primary fuel flame zone of the combustion chamber with an air or steam atomization firing system, mechanical atomization system, or a rotary cup atomization system under the following conditions:

(1) *Viscosity.* The viscosity of the hazardous waste fuel as-fired shall not exceed 300 SSU;

(2) *Particle size.* When a high pressure air or steam atomizer, low pressure atomizer, or mechanical atomizer is used, 70% of the hazardous waste fuel must pass through a 200 mesh (74 micron) screen, and when a rotary cup atomizer is used, 70% of the hazardous waste must pass through a 100 mesh (150 micron) screen;

(3) *Mechanical atomization systems.* Fuel pressure within a mechanical atomization system and fuel flow rate shall be maintained within the design range taking into account the viscosity and volatility of the fuel;

(4) *Rotary cup atomization systems.* Fuel flow rate through a rotary cup atomization system must be maintained within the design range taking into account the viscosity and volatility of the fuel.

§ 266.111 Standards for direct transfer.

(a) *Applicability.* The regulations in this section apply to owners and operators of boilers and industrial furnaces subject to §§266.102 or 266.103 if hazardous waste is directly transferred from a transport vehicle to a boiler or industrial furnace without the use of a storage unit.

(b) *Definitions.* (1) When used in this section, the following terms have the meanings given below;

Direct transfer equipment means any device (including but not limited to, such devices as piping, fittings, flanges, valves, and pumps) that is used to distribute, meter, or control the flow of hazardous waste between a container (i.e., transport vehicle) and a boiler or industrial furnace.

Container means any portable device in which hazardous waste is transported, stored, treated, or otherwise handled, and includes transport vehicles that are containers themselves (e.g., tank trucks, tanker-trailers, and rail tank cars), and containers placed on or in a transport vehicle.

(2) This section references several requirements provided in subparts I and J of parts 264 and 265. For purposes of this section, the term "tank systems" in those referenced requirements means direct transfer equipment as defined in paragraph (b)(1) of this section.

(c) *General operating requirements.* (1) No direct transfer of a pumpable hazardous waste shall be conducted from an open-top container to a boiler or industrial furnace.

(2) Direct transfer equipment used for pumpable hazardous waste shall always be closed, except when necessary to add or remove the waste, and shall not be opened, handled, or stored in a manner that may cause any rupture or leak.

(3) The direct transfer of hazardous waste to a boiler or industrial furnace shall be conducted so that it does not:

(i) Generate extreme heat or pressure, fire, explosion, or violent reaction;

(ii) Produce uncontrolled toxic mist, fumes, dusts, or gases in sufficient quantities to threaten human health;

(iii) Produce uncontrolled flammable fumes or gases in sufficient quantities to pose a risk of fire or explosions;

(iv) Damage the structural integrity of the container or direct transfer equipment containing the waste;

(v) Adversely affect the capability of the boiler or industrial furnace to meet the standards provided by §§266.104 through 266.107; or

(vi) Threaten human health or the environment.

(4) Hazardous waste shall not be placed in direct transfer equipment, if it could cause the equipment or its secondary containment system to rupture, leak, corrode, or otherwise fail.

(5) The owner or operator of the facility shall use appropriate controls and practices to prevent spills and overflows from the direct transfer equipment or its secondary containment systems. These include at a minimum:

(i) Spill prevention controls (e.g., check valves, dry discount couplings); and

(ii) Automatic waste feed cutoff to use if a leak or spill occurs from the direct transfer equipment.

(d) *Areas where direct transfer vehicles (containers) are located.* Applying the definition of container under this section, owners and operators must comply with the following requirements:

(1) The containment requirements of §264.175 of this chapter;

(2) The use and management requirements of subpart I, part 265 of this chapter, except for §§265.170 and 265.174, and except that in lieu of the special requirements of §265.176 for ignitable or reactive waste, the owner or operator may comply with the requirements for the maintenance of protective distances between the waste management area and any public ways, streets, alleys, or an adjacent property line that can be built upon as required in Tables 2-1 through 2-6 of the National Fire Protection Association's (NFPA) "Flammable and Combustible Liquids Code," (1977 or 1981), (incorporated by reference see §260.11). The owner or operator must obtain and keep on file at the facility a written certification by the local Fire Marshall that the installation meets the subject NFPA codes; and

(3) The closure requirements of §264.178 of this chapter.

(e) *Direct transfer equipment.* Direct transfer equipment must meet the following requirements:

(1) *Secondary containment.* Owners and operators shall comply with the secondary containment requirements of §265.193 of this chapter, except for paragraphs §265.193(a), (d), (e), and (i) as follows:

(i) For all new direct transfer equipment, prior to their being put into service; and

(ii) For existing direct transfer equipment within 2 years after August 21, 1991.

(2) *Requirements prior to meeting secondary containment requirements.* (i) For existing direct transfer equipment that does not have secondary containment, the owner or operator shall determine whether the equipment is leaking or is unfit for use. The owner or operator shall obtain and keep on file at the facility a written assessment reviewed and certified by a qualified, registered professional engineer in accordance with §270.11(d) of this chapter that attests to the equipment's integrity by August 21, 1992.

(ii) This assessment shall determine whether the direct transfer equipment is adequately de-

signed and has sufficient structural strength and compatibility with the waste(s) to be transferred to ensure that it will not collapse, rupture, or fail. At a minimum, this assessment shall consider the following:

(A) Design standard(s), if available, according to which the direct transfer equipment was constructed;

(B) Hazardous characteristics of the waste(s) that have been or will be handled;

(C) Existing corrosion protection measures;

(D) Documented age of the equipment, if available, (otherwise, an estimate of the age); and

(E) Results of a leak test or other integrity examination such that the effects of temperature variations, vapor pockets, cracks, leaks, corrosion, and erosion are accounted for.

(iii) If, as a result of the assessment specified above, the direct transfer equipment is found to be leaking or unfit for use, the owner or operator shall comply with the requirements of §§265.196(a) and (b) of this chapter.

(3) *Inspections and recordkeeping.* (i) The owner or operator must inspect at least once each operating hour when hazardous waste is being transferred from the transport vehicle (container) to the boiler or industrial furnace:

(A) Overfill/spill control equipment (e.g., waste-feed cutoff systems, bypass systems, and drainage systems) to ensure that it is in good working order;

(B) The above ground portions of the direct transfer equipment to detect corrosion, erosion, or releases of waste (e.g., wet spots, dead vegetation); and

(C) Data gathered from monitoring equipment and leak-detection equipment, (e.g., pressure and temperature gauges) to ensure that the direct transfer equipment is being operated according to its design.

(ii) The owner or operator must inspect cathodic protection systems, if used, to ensure that they are functioning properly according to the schedule provided by §265.195(b) of this chapter:

(iii) Records of inspections made under this paragraph shall be maintained in the operating record at the facility, and available for inspection for at least 3 years from the date of the inspection.

(4) *Design and installation of new ancillary equipment.* Owners and operators must comply with the requirements of §265.192 of this chapter.

(5) *Response to leaks or spills.* Owners and operators must comply with

the requirements of §265.196 of this chapter.

(6) *Closure.* Owners and operators must comply with the requirements of §265.197 of this chapter, except for §§265.197(c)(2) through (c)(4).

(Approved by the Office of Management and Budget under control number 2050-0073)

§ 266.112 Regulation of residues.

A residue derived from the burning or processing of hazardous waste in a boiler or industrial furnace is not excluded from the definition of a hazardous waste under §261.4(b)(4), (7), or (8) unless the device and the owner or operator meet the following requirements:

(a) The device meets the following criteria:

(1) *Boilers.* Boilers must burn at least 50 % coal on a total heat input or mass input basis, whichever results in the greater mass feed rate of coal;

(2) *Ore or mineral furnaces.* Industrial furnaces subject to §261.4(b)(7) must process at least 50 % by weight normal, nonhazardous raw materials;

(3) *Cement kilns.* Cement kilns must process at least 50% by weight normal cement-production raw materials;

(b) The owner or operator demonstrates that the hazardous waste does not significantly affect the residue by demonstrating conformance with either of the following criteria:

(1) *Comparison of waste-derived residue with normal residue.* The waste-derived residue must not contain appendix VIII, part 261 constituents (toxic constituents) that could reasonably be attributable to the hazardous waste at concentrations significantly higher than in residue generated without burning or processing of hazardous waste, using the following procedure. Toxic compounds that could reasonably be attributable to burning or processing the hazardous waste (constituents of concern) include toxic constituents in the hazardous waste, and the organic compounds listed in appendix VIII of this part that may be generated as products of incomplete combustion. Sampling and analyses shall be in conformance with procedures prescribed in Test Methods for Evaluating Solid Waste, Physical/Chemical Methods, incorporated by reference in §260.11(a) of this chapter.

(i) *Normal residue.* Concentrations of toxic constituents of concern in normal residue shall be determined based on analyses of a minimum of 10 samples representing a minimum of 10 days of operation. Composite samples maybe used to develop a sample for analysis provided that the compositing period does not exceed 24 hours. The upper tolerance limit (at 95% confidence with a 95 % proportion of the sample distribution) of the concentration in the normal residue shall be considered the statistically-derived concentration in the normal residue. If changes in raw materials or fuels reduce the statistically-derived concentrations of the toxic constituents of concern in the normal residue, the statistically-derived concentrations must be revised or statistically-derived concentrations of toxic constituents in normal residue must be established for a new mode of operation with the new raw material or fuel. To determine the upper tolerance limit in the normal residue, the owner or operator shall use statistical procedures prescribed in "Statistical Methodology for Bevill Residue Determinations" in appendix IX of this part.

(ii) *Waste-derived residue.* Waste-derived residue shall be sampled and analyzed as often as necessary to determine whether the residue generated during each 24-hour period has concentrations of toxic constituents that are higher than the concentrations established for the normal residue under paragraph (b)(1)(i) of this section. If so, hazardous waste burning has significantly affected the residue and the residue shall not be excluded from the definition of a hazardous waste. Concentrations of toxic constituents of concern in the waste-derived residue shall be determined based on analysis of one or more samples obtained over a 24-hour period. Multiple samples may be analyzed, and multiple samples may be taken to form a composite sample for analysis provided that the sampling period does not exceed 24 hours. If more than one sample is analyzed to characterize waste-derived residues generated over a 24-hour period, the concentration of each toxic constituent shall be the arithmetic mean of the concentrations in the samples. No results may be disregarded; or

(2) *Comparison of waste-derived residue concentrations with health-based limits--(i) Nonmetal constituents.* The concentrations of

nonmetal toxic constituents of concern (specified in paragraph (b)(1) of this section) in the waste-derived residue must not exceed the health-based levels specified in appendix VII of this part. If a health-based limit for a constituent of concern is not listed in appendix VII of this part, then a limit of 0.002 micrograms per kilogram or the level of detection (using analytical procedures prescribed in SW-846), whichever is higher, shall be used; and

(ii) *Metal constituents.* The concentration of metals in an extract obtained using the Toxicity Characteristic Leaching Procedure of §261.24 of this chapter must not exceed the levels specified in appendix VII of this part; and

(iii) *Sampling and analysis.* Waste-derived residue shall be sampled and analyzed as often as necessary to determine whether the residue generated during each 24-hour period has concentrations of toxic constituents that are higher than the health-based levels. Concentrations of toxic constituents of concern in the waste-derived residue shall be determined based on analysis of one or more samples obtained over a 24-hour period. Multiple samples may be analyzed, and multiple samples may be taken to form a composite sample for analysis provided that the sampling period does not exceed 24 hours. If more than one sample is analyzed to characterize waste-derived residues generated over a 24-hour period, the concentration of each toxic constituent shall be the arithmetic mean of the concentrations in the samples. No results may be disregarded; and

(c) Records sufficient to document compliance with the provisions of this section shall be retained until closure of the boiler or industrial furnace unit. At a minimum, the following shall be recorded.

(1) Levels of constituents in appendix VIII, part 261, that are present in waste-derived residues;

(2) If the waste-derived residue is compared with normal residue under paragraph (b)(1) of this section:

(i) The levels of constituents in appendix VIII, part 261, that are present in normal residues; and

(ii) Data and information, including analyses of samples as necessary, obtained to determine if changes in raw materials or fuels would reduce the concentration of toxic constituents of concern in the normal residue.

APPENDIX 1. -- Tier 1 and Tier 2 Feed Rate and Emissions Screening Limits for Metals

Appendix F

Discussion Questions and Hazardous Waste Management Quiz

DISCUSSION QUESTIONS

1. What is the generator certifying when he or she signs the manifest?

2. True or False: Under the small-quantity generator exclusion, individuals or organizations that generate between 100 and 1000 kilograms of hazardous waste per month do not need to manifest shipments of hazardous waste.

3. Define "consignment state" and "generator state."

4. A company in South Carolina plans to manifest a shipment of hazardous waste to a disposal facility in New Jersey. From what source (i.e., State or Federal agency) should the manifest be obtained?

5. A waste from a product used as a sizing in the textile industry is identified as containing the following ingredients:

   50% Phenol
   50% 1,1,1-Trichloroethane

   A generator wishes to dispose of three 55-gallon drums, each filled with 50 gallons of the waste mixture. When manifesting the waste, what is the proper U.S. DOT description (i.e., proper shipping name, hazard class, and DOT identification number) that would correctly identify the waste?

6. DAPCO Enterprises uses ERC Formula XY47 as a general cleaning and degreasing solvent. Technical information from the Material Safety Data Sheet revealed the mixture has the following composition:

Xylene	60%
Silver nitrate	30%
Sodium laurel sulfate	8%
Silicon Dioxide	2%

Additionally, the mixture has a flash point of 95°F. The Hazardous Material Table in 49 CFR 172.101 yields the following information:

Component	Hazard Class	ID No.	RQ
Xylene	Flammable liquid	UN 1307	1000/454
Silver nitrate	Oxidizer	UN 1493	1.0/0.454
Sodium laurel sulfate	-	-	-
Silicon dioxide	-	-	-

What is the proper US DOT description for a shipment of one drum of hazardous waste?

MANAGEMENT OF HAZARDOUS WASTE QUIZ

True	False		
(✓)	( )	1.	Because RCRA is the primary Federal hazardous waste statute, it supersedes State hazardous waste regulations in authorized States.
(✓)	( )	2.	Personnel who work at hazardous waste accumulation points or TSD facilities must receive annual hazardous waste management training that covers how these personnel must do their jobs in a manner that complies with the regulations and implementation of the contingency plan.
( )	(✓)	3.	All wastes classified as hazardous wastes by EPA are also classified as solid wastes by EPA.
( )	(✓)	4.	A characteristic hazardous waste is a waste that is ignitable, corrosive, reactive, and toxic.
(✓)	( )	5.	Spent solvents used for degreasing are examples of wastes from a specific source, which are called K-wastes.
( )	(✓)	6.	Small-quantity generators are not required to have written RCRA contingency plans.
( )	( )	7.	Land disposal restriction certifications are sent along with hazardous waste manifests only when hazardous wastes are sent to hazardous waste land disposal facilities.
( )	( )	8.	The difference between the classification of P-wastes and U-wastes is that P-wastes are acutely toxic.
( )	( )	9.	If a material on the P-list is used in a cleaning process that produces a waste that is a mixture of several materials (including some of the material on the P-list), the resulting waste stream is a P-listed waste.
( )	( )	10.	Listed hazardous wastes can be mixed with other non-hazardous solid wastes to make a safe mixture that is not classified by EPA as hazardous waste.
( )	( )	11.	Residues from the treatment of hazardous waste (such as by incineration) remain hazardous wastes unless EPA or the authorized state delists the waste for the facility that treated the waste.
( )	( )	12.	If a generator does not know what his waste is and he wants to ship the waste off-site for disposal, he can describe the waste on the manifest as: HAZARDOUS WASTE, LIQUID OR SOLID, N.O.S., ORM-E.
( )	( )	13.	Not more than 1 kilogram of acute hazardous waste may be accumulated at an accumulation point. If more than 1 kilogram is accumulated, the excess must be removed from the accumulation point within 3 days.
( )	( )	14.	A hazardous waste generator may use his or her knowledge of a waste's components to determine if the waste is hazardous and, therefore, analytical testing is not always necessary.
( )	( )	15.	All hazardous waste accumulation points must be inspected at least weekly for signs of leaks and deterioration.
( )	( )	16.	Before mixing incompatible wastes in a container, a small amount of each waste type should be mixed together to see if any incompatible reactions take place.
( )	( )	17.	Accumulation points that store ignitable or reactive wastes in containers should be located at least 50 feet from the facility's property boundary.
( )	( )	18.	One way you can determine if a container is compatible for the accumulation of hazardous waste is to determine if it meets the DOT specification for the waste to be accumulated.

MANAGEMENT OF HAZARDOUS WASTE QUIZ (continued)

True False

( )   ( )   19.   When accumulating hazardous waste in containers at an accumulation point, each container must at least be marked with the words "HAZARDOUS WASTE" and this mark must always be visible for inspection.

( )   ( )   20.   Drums with severe rust or sharp-edged creases are acceptable for the accumulation and transportation of hazardous waste so long as the drums are in good condition.

( )   ( )   21.   A facility's contingency plan must cover each accumulation point and TSD unit on-site.

( )   ( )   22.   Both routine and non-routine exposure to hazardous waste must be covered in your company's written OSHA Hazard Communication Plan.

( )   ( )   23.   Hazardous waste manifests are required for all off-site shipments of hazardous wastes from facilities classified as either hazardous waste generators, small-quantity generators, or TSD facilities.

( )   ( )   24.   A small-quantity generator may accumulate up to 6,000 kilograms of hazardous waste on-site for up to 180 days without a permit.

( )   ( )   25.   Spent xylene, a spent solvent with a flash point of 81°F, would be classified as both a F003 and a D001 hazardous waste.

( )   ( )   26.   The proper abbreviation for drums on a uniform hazardous waste manifest is "DR".

( )   ( )   27.   Accumulation points must be equipped with immediately available communications equipment such as a telephone or two-way radio that is capable of summoning emergency assistance.

( )   ( )   28.   An aqueous waste with a pH of 12 is considered a corrosive hazardous waste.

Index